Thomas Hakl has given us here the definitive stud
ess, has sharpened and deepened our understand
of religion. A magnum opus fully deserving the n
conversation.   Jeffrey

Any complete history of Eranos must convey a sense of its inner meaning as well as adhere to high standards of scholarly documentation. Thomas Hakl's revised and newly translated study more than meets both of these criteria. In discussing the many personalities, controversies, and themes which have figured in its history he adds immeasurably to the literature about this important incubator for a new global humanism.

Jay Sherry, author of *Carl Gustav Jung, Avant-garde Conservative*

Every year since 1933 many of the world's leading intellectuals have met on Lake Maggiore to discuss the latest developments in philosophy, history, art and science and, in particular, to explore the mystical and symbolic in religion. The Eranos Meetings – named after the Greek word for a banquet where the guests bring the food – constitute one of the most important gatherings of scholars in the twentieth century.

Eranos presents a set of portraits of some of the century's most influential thinkers, all participants at Eranos: Carl Jung, Erich Neumann, Mircea Eliade, Martin Buber, Walter Otto, Paul Tillich, Gershom Scholem, Herbert Read, Joseph Campbell, Erwin Schrödinger, Karl Keréyni, D. T. Suzuki, and Adolph Portmann. The volume presents a critical appraisal of the views of these men and how the exchange of ideas encouraged by Eranos influenced each, and examines the attraction of these esotericists towards authoritarian politics.

ERANOS

Eranos

An Alternative Intellectual History of the Twentieth Century

Hans Thomas Hakl

Translated by Christopher McIntosh
with the collaboration of Hereward Tilton

Published by Equinox Publishing Ltd.

UK: Unit S3, Kelham House, 3 Lancaster Street, Sheffield, South Yorkshire S3 8AF
USA: ISD, 70 Enterprise Drive, Bristol, CT 06010

www.equinoxpub.com

First published 2013

ISBN   978-1-84553-115-7   (hardback)
ISBN   978-1-78179-016-8   (paperback)

British Library Cataloguing-in-Publication Data

A catalogue record for this book is available from the British Library.

Library of Congress Cataloging-in-Publication Data

Hakl, Hans Thomas.
    [Verborgene Geist von Eranos. English]
    Eranos : an alternative intellectual history of the twentieth century / Hans Thomas Hakl ; trans-
lated by Christopher McIntosh with the collaboration of Hereward Tilton. -- English (rev. and
expanded) ed.
       p. cm.
    Includes bibliographical references (p.   ) and index.
    ISBN 978-1-84553-115-7 (hardcover) -- ISBN 978-1-78179-016-8 (pbk.)
    1. Psychology and religion--History--20th century. 2. Occultism--History--20th century. 3.
Eranos Conference--History. I. Title.
    BF51.H2513 2012
    200.1'9--dc23
                          2012027426

Printed and bound in the UK by the MPG Books Group

For my dear wife, Franziska

Contents

❧ Preface and Acknowledgments

Just over two years were needed to complete the first version of this book. Since then a further decade has passed. There have been numerous new publications on the main Eranos protagonists and on more peripheral figures, as well as specialized studies on particular themes addressed at the meetings. All of this has made possible a more accurate picture of Eranos. The unfinished Eranos manuscript of Catherine Ritsema, wife of the long-standing Eranos president, has also come to light, as has Gerhard Wehr's unpublished manuscript on the history of Eranos. And the history of Eranos itself has continued and demands to be told. Furthermore, it has become increasingly clear how significant Eranos was for the history of religion and for the scholarly study of esotericism. If ten years ago Eranos was a largely unknown subject, today there is a whole series of publications bearing its name in their titles, and an Internet search will yield tens of thousands of entries. Thus the need for an expanded and corrected edition of this book had become pressing. This meant that the English translation, which had been on the agenda for several years, had to be delayed, added to which the task proved difficult since many passages and quotations had very subtle undertones and were far from straightforward, presenting a special challenge to the translator. For her great patience, my thanks are due first of all to Janet Joyce of Equinox, and I also thank Kate Williams of Acumen for her accuracy and immediate responses and Tristan Palmer, also of Acumen, in spite of our occasional differences of opinion. Next I wish to thank translator Christopher McIntosh, himself an author, for his friendly cooperation over several years. I have greatly admired his intuitive ability to find the right tone and to evoke in his translation the things that consistently moved me while writing the original. I would also like to thank Hereward Tilton, who assisted with parts of the translation in the final stages.

My friend Professor Allison Coudert, an expert on the history of religion and esotericism, put me into contact with Equinox, for which I am extremely grateful. Thanks are also due to two people who were always willing to keep me informed about new material in the archives of the venerable Eranos Foundation in Moscia-Ascona, namely Riccardo Bernardini and Giovanni Sorge, both of whom have carried out research into Eranos—the former wrote his doctoral dissertation on the subject and has published essays and independent works on Eranos. Another person who most kindly provided me with information about the Eranos Foundation was Gisela Binda, who for many years has been taking care of the administration there. And John van Praag, then president of the foundation, was always willing to receive me when I was in Ascona, despite his limited time. So was Fabio Merlini, who succeeded him.

As always, my friend Giovanni Casadio gave me great help, especially with the task of correction and supplying me with specific information. Warmest thanks are also due to Gerhard Wehr and Augusto Sabbadini Shanteena for enabling me to consult hitherto unpublished manuscripts and fragments on Eranos. Mac Linscott Ricketts generously gave me copies of his English translation of the unpublished diaries of Mircea Eliade.

If I continue with a straight list of names it does not detract from the thanks that I owe to each person individually for the help they have given me. Without putting them in alphabetical order (which would be rather too artificial) I would like to mention the following: Erik Hornung, Elisabeth Staehelin, Petteri Pietikäinen, Mihaela Gligor, Annemarie Aeschbach, Gustavo Benavides, Florin Turcanu, Alfred Ribi, Walter Thys, Angela Stadler, Konstantin Burmistrov, Claudio Bonvecchio, Friedrich Niewöhner, Peter Mulacz, Gerhard Zwieauer, Hans Pichler, Ralf Liedtke, Matthias Korger, Fabrizio Frigerio, Ferdinand Leopold, Willem Hofstee, Hubert Treiber, Wigbert Grabert, Jeff Kripal, Christoph W. Abdelmu'min Clairmont, Olaf Räderer, Michael Kuper, David Williams, Basil Wilby, Bruno Fellinger, Nuccio d'Anna, Deborah Forman, Eugen Ciurtin, Hermann Jung, and Axel Voss. I also want to thank Harvey Shoolman for a decade's long encouragement and the lesson he taught me. Many thanks also go to Chas Clifton, my copy-editor, for his competence and patience with this complicated text and its endless notes. My particular thanks are due to Werner Hausheer and his firm, the Verlagsgemeinschaft für europäische Editionen, for his support—which was not only moral and intellectual but also of a distinctly concrete kind.

Sadly, but unavoidably, I must report the deaths in recent years of Magda Kerényi, Rudolf Ritsema, and William McGuire as well as Annemarie Schimmel, without whom this book would never have become what it is now. May they rest in peace. It is to be wished that the influence of their legacy may continue, and this was one of the main reasons why I undertook the often arduous task of revising the book and helping with the translation.

This book is intended to serve—and why should I not declare this openly?—as a plea for mental and spiritual expansion. This calls for tolerance above all—tolerance and understanding not only towards foreign cultures but also towards other modes of thinking within our own cultural sphere even if they concern past political attitudes. As a trained lawyer I regard the ancient Roman maxim *audiatur et altera pars* (hear the other side also)—especially when we do not really want to hear it—as no outmoded relic but a living principle that is close to my heart. It is also my profound conviction that our culture cannot survive just on reason and technological efficiency. We need to be able to draw strength from the deeper levels of our being too, and these can only be activated through myths, images, and symbols. And that is precisely what this book is about. At Eranos, I believe, the trail was blazed for an "alternative intellectual history of the twentieth century," running counter to the domineering claims of materialism and positivism, those sterile parents of a mathematical, technical, and predominantly economic worldview which is out of touch with humanity and in which the "gods" are finally dead. *UNFORTWATLY NO TAXX*

Acknowledgements for the First Edition

The fact that this work has been accomplished at all is due to the help of many friends, acquaintances, and correspondents. Not all of them wish to be named, and this desire must be respected. Nevertheless they can be assured of my thanks. In listing the following names I have treated their titles as implicit, since most of them are doctors, professors, or holders of honorary titles. The order of names does not imply any judgment on my part as to the value of their contribution.

In expressing thanks it is always difficult to know where to begin, so I shall start by thanking the publishing firm of *Scientia Nova* for their understanding and for the way in which they relieved me of much time-consuming work by organizing long-distance library loans and by visiting on my behalf the German Literature Archive at Marbach. The debt of thanks that I owe to William McGuire can hardly ever be repaid. His support ranged from providing me with copies of his own original material to putting me into contact with important persons connected with Eranos. Magda Kerényi assisted me with many important questions and corrected the sections dealing with her late husband. I thank her also for providing me with many photocopies and for her permission to quote from her reports and reviews. Equally helpful was Ximena de Angulo, who has been involved with Eranos since 1933(!). By virtue of her close contacts with Olga Fröbe, C.G. Jung, and other prominent Eranos figures, she was able to give me much important information. She also gave me access to the correspondence between her mother, Cary Baynes, and Olga Fröbe, and she drew my attention to the only book published (privately) by Fröbe. Furthermore, she allowed me to quote from her lively unpublished report on Eranos as well as from private correspondence. I must also thank her for many heart-warming conversations.

My friend Antoine Faivre played a valued role in paving the way for an objective attempt to penetrate the esotericist thicket. He encouraged me by his positive reaction to my initial outline and cautioned me not to rush into publication too quickly, which meant that I had time to gather additional material and to think more carefully about the main focus of the book. In addition he made available his uncensored diary entries about Eranos as well as much other material, including private photographs of the meetings, and he gave me valuable guidance both orally and in correspondence. He also most willingly read and corrected the manuscript. Erik Hornung, for his part, facilitated my access to the manuscript department at Basel University and thus to the literary estate of Adolf Portmann. He also provided me with articles and tips and granted me many informative discussions. Ultimately he was even prepared to read the entire completed manuscript and drew my attention to various mistakes.

Sonu Shamdasani also most selflessly read the finished manuscript with the eyes of a Jung expert and made a number of important corrections. Tilo Schabert not only provided me with literature but also gave me the benefit of his often highly critical comments. Walter Thys told me, in connection with André Jolles, much about the early life of Olga Fröbe, which would otherwise have escaped me. In particular he found out for me the address of R.A. Beguin, the grandson of Olga Fröbe, who generously allowed me to publish any material from his grandmother's writings that I considered relevant. Without these verbatim quotations this book would have been much less authentic. Mr. Beguin deserves my special thanks for this.

One set of documents that came as a complete surprise to me, as I was previously unaware of their existence, were those given to me by Gertrude von Schoeler on the subject of Eranos and especially concerning Erwin Rousselle. Margaret Dierks has my thanks for her comments and also putting me in touch with Martin Kraatz, who gave me many valuable insights regarding Rudolf Otto and brought to my attention Otto's letters to Olga Fröbe. I thank him also for his detailed corrections to the first draft of my portrayal of Otto and for bringing to my attention the Friedrich Heiler letters that I have quoted. Uwe

Bredehorn of the Marburg University Library then kindly made copies available to me of the correspondence between Heiler and Fröbe. He also provided corrections and pointed me in the direction of further sources. Shaul Baumann deserves thanks for giving me a summary of his dissertation on Jakob Wilhelm Hauer and the transcript of a talk that he had given on the same subject, thereby affording me new insights. James Hillman I thank most warmly for his illuminating corrections to the passages dealing with him personally. I am grateful to David Miller for his positive appraisal of the manuscript and for his permission to quote from it for publicity purposes. To the following people I am grateful for encouraging me to persevere or for giving me important and interesting pointers or actual material: Gerhard Wehr, Nicholas Goodrick-Clarke, Jay Sherry, Martin Erler, Annemarie Schimmel, Aleida Assmann, Ada and Hans Gottfried von Stockhausen, Marianne New, Irmgard Schnetzler, Viviane Hartenberg, Angela Stader, Maria Babwasingh, Yvonne and Fritz Hugelmann, Eveline Hasler, Rudolf Deelmann, Ulrich Linse, Friedrich Niewöhner, Julia Encke, Ron Margolin, Bruno Rhyner, Karlheinz Weißmann, Michael Großmann, Giovanni Filoramo, Piero Fenili, Giovanni Monastra, and Mario Gandini.

Natale Spineto deserves my heartfelt thanks for providing me with an important book as well as two hitherto unpublished manuscripts by him and some photocopies of relevant Italian newspaper articles. I am especially grateful to him for bringing me into contact with Stella Corbin, who allowed me to examine the papers of her late husband, kept in Zurich, and to quote from certain parts of them, even though they did not yield a huge amount of material, unfortunately. I thank the heirs of C.G. Jung most warmly for being allowed to examine certain interesting material from the as-yet-unpublished papers of their illustrious forebear and for permission to quote from them. My thanks go also to Moshe Idel, who was able to tell me much about Mircea Eliade, as both of them came from Romania. My friend Giovanni Casadio was a valuable interview partner, gave me an abundance of documents and tips and made a number of corrections. Yvonne Bölt told me much about the town of Ascona and its environs. Barbara von Reibnitz, for her part, allowed me to see her as yet unpublished work on Eranos. Similarly, I obtained a preview of an essay by Wouter Hanegraaff on the significance of Eranos for the academic treatment of esoteric themes, and for this I thank him sincerely.

Another important contact was with Steven Wasserstrom, who has expressed concern about the danger of losing the proven standards of—originally God-inspired—ethics and objective science in the study of religion (as in the world as a whole?) with the onward march of "esoteric" and therefore more individualistic approaches. I respect his point of view even though I myself believe that we need a carefully considered re-orientation, with all its problems and birth pains. Steven Wasserstrom kindly gave me some pre-publication glimpses of his book *Religion after Religion*, which has meanwhile appeared, and has given me much food for thought and above all confirmation. There were inevitably certain overlaps and parallels between our two books, although I had the undeniable advantage of being able to consult his book—somewhat late but nonetheless in time to benefit from it. For both of us, after studying abundant source material, have identified the essentially esoteric underlying character of Eranos, even though we evaluate it differently.

I must also acknowledge Rudolf Ritsema and Christa Robinson, the latter now president of the Eranos Foundation in Moscia. Although they were not always unreservedly happy with my changing approach to the project, I am grateful to them for the criticisms and improvements that they made (unfortunately only in the early stages). I would have dearly liked to spend more time in the Eranos archive in Moscia, but unfortunately did not at first receive the necessary permission. Only when the book had already been set did the situation change, thanks especially to the new director of Eranos Moscia, Jay Livernois, but also to Christa Robinson. Unfortunately it was only possible at that point to insert a few additions, otherwise the publication would have been excessively delayed. We hope, however, to bring out a supplementary volume with important documents and additions.

The California bookseller Todd Pratum always endeavored promptly to obtain for me any out-of-print and also new books from the English-speaking world that I required. Laszlo Toth performed a similar service for me in France. Gunther Nickel of the German Literature Archive in Marbach, Michele McKnee of the Kristine Mann Library in New York, and Yvonne Voegeli from the Library of the Swiss Federal Institute of Technology in Zurich were always willing to help me in my researches and, where necessary, to grant me permission for quotations. All the letters to or from C.G. Jung that I have quoted are held, unless otherwise stated, in the C.G. Jung archive at the Swiss Federal Technical Institute. Matthias Dalvit from the Central Library in Zurich also supported me and provided me with additional valuable materials. Thanks are also due to my friends and business partners Werner Hausheer and Charles-Pierre Schöbi, for together we created the material basis that has made possible at all the pursuit of such "hobbies" as writing a book about Eranos. Last but definitely not least, I would like to express special thanks to my friend Joscelyn Godwin, who relieved me of a large burden of work that really should have fallen to me, and thus enabled me to continue working on the present book.

There is one important point that I would like to make concerning the documents and letters from public and private archives that I have made use of. In quoting from these I have taken it upon myself to correct obvious orthographic mistakes, without indicating this each time. Leaving such mistakes uncorrected would only have made the language flow less easily for the reader, without adding to the authenticity of the passages concerned.

Here I would like also to express general thanks to all the publishing houses from whose books I have continually quoted—while naturally observing the accepted scholarly rules. One that deserves a special mention is Princeton University Press, publisher of the celebrated Bollingen Series, which played such a key role for Eranos, as this book has made clear. Another that I wish to thank is Hohe Warte (Franz von Bebenburg) Verlag, formerly publisher of a periodical from which I have quoted two extensive passages. Unfortunately it was not always possible for my publisher or myself to locate all copyright owners. This applied not only to textual passages but also to photographs. In many cases I had received the photographs from private individuals who no longer had any idea who had taken them. Several probably were from the Vienna photographer Margaretha Fellerer, whose heirs we have not been able to identify. I and my publisher would like to emphasize that we had no intention of infringing any copyright. If anyone is the holder of such copyright, we invite them to make themselves known to us so that they can be compensated according to the usual practice.

I cannot express high enough praise for the patience of my wife Franziska, especially as she must already assume that after this work I shall of course embark on another one. What is more, the whole house was constantly overflowing with books and periodicals, and notes written on sheets of paper often lay in places where they did not belong (even from my rather tolerant perspective), but my reproachfully questioning glance immediately fell on *her* when there was something *I* was not able to find. My parents too, who are no longer as mobile as they were, have learned that a mania for research can easily fill up days, weeks, months, while everything else gets short shrift. And only dog owners will know how much my dog suffered while his master sat for so long at the computer when the world outside smelt so enticing. To the Swiss Confederation, which constitutes the setting for my story and where I spent so many enriching years, I also partially dedicate this book in the hope that the country will not fall victim to the great simplifications of our age. And perhaps—who knows?—I should also thank the unknown *genius loci* of Eranos. Similarly I must thank the beneficent and demanding spirits of a private library, which already contained the great majority of the books used for this work, so that I only had to reach out when I needed them.

ઈ• Introduction: How This Book Emerged

"Books have their fates," as the old saying has it. The present book is a wonderful example. Originally I planned to write an introduction of some twenty pages to a selection of Eranos lectures with distinctly esoteric themes. I felt such an introduction to be necessary in order to make the reading public familiar with the history and significance of the Eranos meetings, although at that time I myself did not know a great deal about the subject. Not all that many people are in fact aware that, over a period of seventy years, men and women enjoying a high academic reputation met regularly at Ascona on Lake Maggiore in order to give scholarly lectures to a relatively small audience about their latest insights in the fields of religion, philosophy, history, art, and science. But these people were not motivated merely by the desire to transmit detailed knowledge, as is usually the case in universities. Their concern was rather to locate such knowledge within a universal spiritual stream reaching from antiquity to the present day, from East to West and from North to South, stimulating all humanity. This, incidentally, was what sparked off my interest in the subject.

Then came the first surprise: there appeared to be no published reports or historical information about the meetings and how they came into being (I shall say more about this in the next chapter). After some initial research, however, there began to come my way—at first slowly and then ever faster—information that was highly intriguing and evidently important.

When I then tried to squeeze all the facts that I had gathered into the prescribed parameters, I realized how much highly interesting material simply could not be accommodated. Very well, I thought, forty pages will certainly be enough. I informed the publishing house accordingly: there would be a delay. However, as it was the seeking and finding of material that I most enjoyed, more and more stuff accumulated, and gradually it became clear to me that in Eranos I was dealing with something far more important than I had originally assumed. My rather general interest in the meetings began to deepen. Having initially concentrated on printed material, albeit including published primary sources such as diaries and conference reports, I extended the search to unpublished manuscripts, letters, and diary entries. This led to conversations and correspondence with a number of Eranos speakers and participants. The leading figures in the story came more and more clearly into focus, becoming real human beings rather than just world-famous names from diverse academic disciplines. They came to life again in all their feelings and emotions—envy and joy, pride and vanity—but also in their self-sacrifice and their metaphysical longing. Their long-forgotten hopes and disappointments were revived—if only in my mind. Furthermore, what had previously been for me a purely intellectual sympathy for spiritual and cultural strivings in general, now became more and more emotionally tinged and increasingly focused on Eranos in particular.

Equally gradually I began—at first only dimly—to perceive connecting threads. Had the *genius loci*, the daemon of Eranos, which had touched so many of the protagonists of these meetings, also possessed me? I cannot and will not deny that something stirred in me as I stood alone one day in the summer of 1998 in front of the famous stele in the garden of Eranos in Moscia-Ascona—that same stele which had been erected in honour of the "daemon of the place" by the psychologist Carl Gustav Jung, the religion scholar and clergyman Gerardus van der Leeuw, and the founder of Eranos Olga Fröbe-Kapteyn. How many important people had already stood there like me, carrying their dreams, hopes, and disappointments with them?

But let us go on with the story of this book. Forty pages, or so I thought, would be enough for what I wanted to write. Naturally they were not nearly enough. Could it still truthfully be called an "introductory essay"? And the publisher was still waiting patiently. Other tasks, other duties distracted me. The work on Eranos lay fallow for a long time. Then I took it up again, as I had been looking forward to doing. Meanwhile the extensive correspondence with authors and professors who had already written about Eranos, as well as with libraries and booksellers all over the world, had continued unabated. The books had gone on piling up, and heaps of newspapers and above all copies of manuscript material from archives and legacies lay unread in my study. As I wrote on and on, and the pile grew only fractionally smaller, while at the same time new sources of material opened up, it became increasingly clear that, instead of a mere introduction, I would have to write a complete book.

There came another discussion with the publisher, and of course once again the dead-line—already postponed three times—could not be met. As I immersed myself ever more deeply in the minds and lives of the leading Eranos figures, I found that the story's connecting threads, of which I had already become dimly aware, took on the quality of a firm, albeit finely woven web that went far beyond the individual *dramatis personae* and reached out into some far wider realm of collective thought and consciousness.

Olga Fröbe's introductions to the conference yearbooks made it quite clear that the dance was meant to continue, even if individual dancers went away. What was being striven towards was a "new humanism", which tried, within the world of classical antiquity as well as in foreign religions and cultures, to find certain familiar tones constituting the "primal melody" that is common to all humanity. This quest also went far beyond the individual research endeavors for which the Eranos protagonists were already famous.

The search for our spiritual roots, the intuitive knowledge of a common transcendent origin of humankind, and the corresponding longing for a "return" to what in religious language is called the "divine"—all of this seemed to me to constitute the deeper connecting motivation that sustained the Eranos project for so many decades. This longing is expressed in images and thus supra-rationally in the famous *Hymn of the Pearl*,[1] in which a "king's son" falls, as it were, from "heaven" into matter, forgets at first who he is and then, after various wanderings and false turnings, is able to return to the splendid realm from which he came. Arguably (according to the theory of Victor Magnien) the same meaning can be found in the Eleusinian mysteries, based on the myth of Persephone's descent into the underworld and her mother's search for her and struggle to bring her back to the upper world. In this connection, the "psycho-anthropologist" Giuseppe Lampis, in the first volume of his work *Maschere e démoni* (Masks and Demons),[2] develops the scenario of a conflict in ancient times between humans and gods. The defeat of the humans in this struggle means that they now have to make an immense effort in order to return to the gods and therefore to themselves. This long-ing for a (spiritual) "home" that characterizes so many of the "Eranians" is not just my projection but is also backed up by the official writings cited in this book as well as by the personal observations of Eranos participants.

This book did not therefore arise out of a long-prepared and well thought out "master plan." On the contrary, a series of small fragments of information and insight gradually came together, until finally an increasingly clear picture began to emerge, as in a mosaic where the pattern emerges slowly out of a mass of tesserae laid out on the ground.[3]

Despite the ample size that this study finally reached, it still cannot be described as an even moderately comprehensive history of Eranos. For that it would be necessary to include many more biographical sketches of the participants, and furthermore it would be essential to deal at least with the salient lectures given at the meetings. However, considering the sheer bulk of important material contained in the Eranos yearbooks, this would have necessitated a work of several volumes. Consequently, although the lectures are the most important aspect of Eranos, I decided from the start to leave them almost entirely aside.[4] Only individual, in-depth studies by specialists in different fields can really throw a clear light on the great influence of Eranos in intellectual history. My study therefore is intended primarily to offer an initial historical overview, encompassing numerous original documents and dealing especially thoroughly with the prehistory and early years of the Eranos meetings.

Although occasionally the flow of this narrative is interrupted by digressions on matters of intellectual history or philosophy, I do not feel called to embark on a real analysis of Eranos in its entirety because of the great complexity of the material involved. Hence my analyses do not go beyond certain obvious elements such as anti-historicism, anti-positivism, interdisciplinarity, and the emphasis on spiritual perspectives. However, I have intentionally emphasized the "esoteric" and "political" dimensions of Eranos (and also of the speakers, especially those of the first, "critical" years). Some people will prob-ably, and with some justification, say that I have been too one-sided and that certain countervailing aspects should have been emphasized. But, taking into account how dif-ficult it is to give a balanced portrait of even one single prominent person (and there were enough of those at Eranos), I hope readers will tolerate my leaning more to one side in the balancing act. It is for this reason that the role of artists, philosophers, and scientists—with the exception of Adolf Portmann—appears in the framework of this study to be less significant than it probably was. At the same time it must be said that certain famous people, such as the physicist Erwin Schrödinger, the philosopher Karl Löwith, the sociologist Helmuth Plessner and others, attended only once. The reason for this probably lay in the particular spiritual climate of Eranos, by which one felt either attracted or put off, even excluded.

Undoubtedly it was this particular mental climate that gave rise to the frequent criti-cal comments about Eranos. What were and what are these criticisms? First of all there is the accusation of irrationalism (because of too pronounced a sympathy for esoteri-cism of whatever hue), and second there are the alleged links to authoritarian and fas-cist currents of thought. This might, incidentally, be one of the reasons why Eranos has been given such an unfairly small amount of space in academic literature. In giving at least a provisional answer to these accusations, and in trying to elucidate the true facts of the matter, it was necessary to carry out as exact a stocktaking as possible, nei-ther ignoring unwelcome facts nor taking these as indicative of a whole way of life or thought. Hence the many quotations from documents of the time that are not always easily accessible.

In the perspective of that period and on the basis of more precise information, it will become easier to understand certain facts, such as the participation of National Socialists like Jakob Wilhelm Hauer and Gustav Heyer at the Eranos meetings. Nevertheless, some readers will feel impelled to deliver a verdict of more or less gross carelessness in dealing with tyranny. Such a verdict, of course, cannot be applied to Eranos as a whole but only to certain speakers. However, a thorough treatment of this question would demand an entire book on its own and therefore, in my expositions on this theme, I have concentrated on the less well known participants. On the well known entanglements of C.G. Jung and Mircea Eliade there is already enough informative literature that is relatively easily accessible. In this whole debate one should, however, never forget the following passage from Nietzsche's *On the Genealogy of Morals*:

> My opinion is that it's certainly best to separate an artist far enough from his work, so that one does not take him with the same seriousness as one does his work. In the final analysis, he is only the precondition for his work, its maternal womb, the soil or, in some cases, the dung and manure, on and out of which it grows—and thus, in most cases, something that we must forget about, if we want to enjoy the work itself.[5]

And when one looks more closely at the "esoteric" aspect of Eranos one must ask oneself the question what is in fact meant by the word "esoteric" and whether the accusation is an accusation at all.[6] To anticipate this question right away: the term "esoteric"[7] is defined here— in contrast to the scholarly definition of Antoine Faivre—as simply the conscious pursuit of a religiously motivated path "inwards", a path towards a Know-thyself (that is, one's "divine" self). In other words the "esotericism" of Eranos is concerned with "individuation", with a "*descensus ad inferos = ascensus ad superos*", which takes place in the spiritual and symbolic realm and not in the world of the rational intellect, but can nevertheless be recognized by the intellect. Hence the skepticism that one finds again and again at Eranos towards a purely and exclusively rational attitude, and hence the deliberate incorporation of analogical, "mythical" thinking. Only those who make themselves open to the "inner" world are capable of bridging the boundaries between cultures, epochs, and disciplines, as Eranos aims to do. For in the "inner" dimension we find something which deeply connects all human beings and which, although manifesting itself in countless different outward forms, is always one and the same—the "archetypal", to use Jung's term. The way to that place requires myths, symbols, that is to say "pictures" that work on the psyche. Esoteric disciplines such as astrology, tarot or the Chinese *I Ching* offer particularly suitable images for this purpose. In this sense Eranos is a place where one "experiments in touching the boundaries of one's own being" and also where one "puts one's ear to the secret *stream* of time"[8] and does not become lost in the fleeting fashions of the moment. This is what is "anachronistic" or, more accurately, "timeless" about Eranos. Only thus is it possible to span the boundaries between cultures and epochs with their different conceptions of time.

Another reason why the "esoteric" component of Eranos has moved into the foreground is that I did not want an undue emphasis on the "masculine" academic approach to push aside the "feminine" perspective, so sensitively represented by Olga Fröbe-Kapteyn (and which she herself characterized as "irrational"), since both elements were important for the continuing vitality of Eranos.[9] Rather, I wanted to place the central role of Olga Fröbe—with all her anguished efforts on behalf of Eranos and her own personal struggles—clearly in the foreground. Apart from the unquestionable legitimacy of Olga Fröbe's "esoteric" viewpoint, which will be described in due course, there was certainly also enough support from the male side for her course. For one reason or another, the "feminine" side of Eranos has up to now stood too much in the shadow. Without the personal efforts of Fröbe and the financial support of Mary Mellon, perhaps also the services of Cary Baynes as an intermediary, all those participants—however distinguished— would never have been able to come together to even engage in discussion. In this sense, one can undoubtedly see Eranos as a modern continuation of the "salon" tradition, which was so widespread in the two preceding centuries and in which women also played the central role. It seems that the female sex simply has more social skills than the male.

At any rate, my wish was to gather as much basic material as possible, so as to stimulate further sound research—perhaps focusing on other aspects of the topic. This may arouse in the reader the regrettable—but hopefully not permanent—impression of a heap of papers spilt from an overturned filing cabinet. And this touches on the biggest problem that I faced when writing this book. According to which criteria was I to decide what information to include and what to leave out, when I had such an abundance of useable material?[10] Further difficulties becomes apparent when, for example, I use long notes to deal with questions that may not directly concern the history of Eranos but are of great importance for understanding the intellectual background of the meetings and the lecturers.

Such questions are, for instance, how precisely to assess the phenomenon that is designated here as "esoteric" or "gnostic": how to address its transmission as a current of thought from the Renaissance, through the Romantic era to the present day; its interaction with (as well as opposition to) the scientific tradition; the fascination exerted by myths as well as the links between mythology and politics; the equally politically relevant debate about the nature of "modernity"; the great abundance in the first half of the twentieth century (in comparison to the present day) of widely varied—indeed contrasting—publications in the field of intellectual history and works addressing the fundamental ethical questions of humankind; the way in which writers and teachers are embedded in their age and the responsibilities which result from that situation; and so forth. I would like in advance to apologize for any questionable conclusions or factual errors that specialist readers find in this work as a result of the volume of material that I drew upon. Despite the help of good friends I was not able to check the accuracy of every printed source and every piece of orally transmitted information.

A further point requires clarification. The fact that I deal only summarily with speakers from the late 1970s, in contrast to those of earlier years, has nothing to do with the magnitude of their achievement and does not reflect any lack of interest on my part or fear that I might bore the reader. The reason lies rather in my reticence in expressing judgments about people who are still in the midst of their work. My concern was that they would inevitably have been given short shrift. Some of the present-day Eranos speakers are people that I know and value personally. I simply do not want to touch living matter unnecessarily. It winces and gets tense. It was difficult enough to attempt to do justice to the various Eranos meetings since 1988 and those responsible for them. I am naïve enough to hold to my belief in the Socratic doctrine that the human will is, by its very nature, geared to strive for moral goodness (who has the right to define it?), and that consequently evil can only come about through ignorance.[11] Therefore I have ventured to follow Socrates and believe in the "goodwill" of the protagonists. It is only regrettable that people—despite their striving for the "good"—have so little ability to forget their own "I." When this is placed in the foreground it all too easily obscures the "good."

All in all I did not want to conceal my sympathy for Eranos and its goals. Certainly I feel such sympathy to be justified, as Eranos is undoubtedly one of the most significant intellectual adventures of the twentieth century. At any rate, the "cast list" of this adventure is unique. I accept that such sympathy is not consistent with the standards of pure scholarship, but this I did not aim for. I sometimes, for example, also quote (albeit rarely) from letters that are not publicly accessible and therefore cannot be checked as sources. And one other thing kept my ambitions within bounds, namely the realization of my own limitations, which became increasingly clear to me, the deeper I went into this material.

🐝 1. The Significance of Eranos

For more than seven decades the Eranos meetings have played a unique role in the cultural and intellectual history of our age, taking place each year with amazing regularity (with the single exception of 1989). The deaths of the founder and the key early participants have altered nothing except for the outer form. On 30 March 1957, C.G. Jung wrote, "May the light of the European spirit, which has radiated out from Eranos for so many years during this time of darkness, enjoy a further lease of life so that it can fulfill its role as a beacon lighting the way towards the unification of Europe."[1] As he had already remarked in 1951, Eranos was "the only place in Europe where scholars and interested lay participants could come together and exchange ideas, unrestricted by academic boundaries."[2]

Jung's follower, the well-known psychologist Erich Neumann, went even further when he described Eranos as "inconspicuous and off the beaten track, and yet a navel of the world, a small link in the Golden Chain,"[3] by which he meant the Golden Chain of wisdom teachers, beginning with Hermes Trismegistus. And Mircea Eliade, probably the best-known religious scholar of the twentieth century, wrote in his autobiography: "Ascona and the Eranos group fascinated me from the start."[4] No wonder, for there he met intellectual giants like Jung, Gershom Scholem—the most influential Kabbalistic scholar of our age—and Karl Kerényi, the mythologist and expert on ancient Greece. In the foreword to the second volume of his diaries he described the "spirit of Eranos," the theme that we shall examine in detail in this volume, as "one of the most creative cultural experiences in the modern Western world."[5] In an issue of the Swiss journal *Du*, dedicated to the Eranos meetings, he even compared these to "certain 'circles' during the Italian Renaissance or the German Romantic period, that is to say [with] groups that, at a certain moment in history, represent the most fruitful and advanced intellectual tendencies."[6] The significance of this remark will be apparent to anyone who knows the central role that these Renaissance groups played in the history of ideas and the importance that Eliade attached to them.

Art historian, writer, publisher, and critic Sir Herbert Read for his part saw in Eranos the upsurge of a "new humanism,"[7] and the biologist Adolf Portmann went so far as to say that his "encounter with the circle that met during the Eranos meetings at Moscia-Ascona was like a stroke of destiny"[8] and that Eranos came to be a center of his "innermost life."[9] Another commentator, Michel Cazenave, responsible for the French translation of Jung's works and himself a much-respected author, called Eranos "one of the richest centres of intellectual and spiritual interchange known to our century" and a place of central importance in the life of Jung.[10]

This provisional selection of quotations should for the time being suffice to make clear that Eranos was no commonplace phenomenon. The list of contributors contains one prominent name after another. Besides those already mentioned, the participants included the physicist and Nobel prize-winner Erwin Schrödinger; the theologians Paul Tillich, Ernst Benz, and Hugo Rahner; the Japanese scholar Daisetz Taitaro Suzuki, who brought Zen Buddhism to the West; the ethnologist Paul Radin; the expert on Gnosticism Gilles Quispel; the philosopher and sociologist Helmuth Plessner, who described Eranos as the "Bayreuth of depth psychology"; the classical scholar Walter F. Otto; the philosophers Karl Löwith and Hans Leisegang; the scholars of religion R.C. Zaehner and Robert Eisler; the philosopher and humanist Martin Buber; the prominent rabbi Leo Baeck; and the orientalists Giuseppe Tucci, Hellmut Wilhelm, Henry Corbin, and Heinrich Zimmer. Later the names include the "archetypal" psychologist James Hillman, the mythologist Joseph Campbell, the expert on Western esotericism Antoine Faivre, and the "alternative" physicist Herbert Pietschmann. In addition, the cultural philosopher Jean Gebser took part in the sessions between 1942 and 1948 and established fruitful contacts with Jung, Kerényi, and Portmann, although he did not actually give any lectures.[11]

From the most recent times one could mention, *inter alia*: Annemarie Schimmel, Moshe Idel, Reinhold Merkelbach, Ilya Prigogine, Erik Hornung, Zwi Werblowsky, Jan Assmann, Moshe Barash, David Carrasco, Remo Bodei, and Elémire Zolla. The smaller-scale Eranos meetings, which have taken place in Moscia since 1990 with an emphasis on the *I Ching*, have included such names as Stephen Karcher, Michiyoshi Hayashi, Bruno Rhyner, Claudio Risé, and Claudio Bonvecchio. And we shall encounter other important participants as we explore the history of these meetings. The Swiss psychological journal *Zeitschrift für Psychologie* has commented, "Eranos is among the most important manifestations of the present age."[12] Perhaps I will succeed, within the scope of the present investigation, to show that this description is not merely rhetorical exaggeration.

Consequently, I could not understand why there was hardly any information to be found about such an important and long-standing intellectual forum. There is no reference to Eranos in any of the relevant reference books on the history of religion (including the sixteen-volume *Encyclopedia of Religions*, edited by Mircea Eliade, nor in the second edition edited by Lindsay Jones), nor in standard works on anthropology, psychology, and philosophy (not even in the index to the truly comprehensive *Encyclopédie Philosophique Universelle*, published by the Presses Universitaires Françaises, with its 11,000 large-format pages and its countless cross-references), nor in numerous dictionaries of esotericism, symbolism, and mythology. I was able to find only two entries on the subject. The first one, in the third volume of the *Lexikon für Theologie und Kirche* (Dictionary of theology and the Church), although very brief, does at least mention Rudolf Otto's description of Eranos as "a place of encounter between East and West."[13] The second, somewhat longer, entry was written by Magda Kerényi and appears in the six-volume *Schweizer Lexikon* (Swiss lexicon).[14] One might argue that the thematic range of Eranos is too wide for a specialized dictionary, but even the twenty-five-volume *Meyers Enzyklopädisches Wörterbuch* (Meyer's encyclopedic dictionary) and the twenty-four-volume *Brockhaus* mention only the ancient Greek word *eranos*, meaning a banquet, without saying a single word about the meetings.[15]

The world-famous *Encyclopedia Britannica*—at least in the Internet version, which one would assume to be complete—also contains not a single entry. However, under the entry "religion, study of" one finds a passage referring to Eranos in the context of an article about C.G. Jung, stating that the Eranos circle has made a considerable contribution to the history of religion and that this movement was one of the main factors in the modern resurgence of interest in the analysis of myths. Giovanni Filoramo, a religious historian at the University of Turin, in a chapter on Eranos in his interesting work *Il risveglio della gnosi ovvero diventare dio* (The revival of gnosis or how to become God),[16] which I shall return to later, also laments the lack of a proper history of these meetings. It is true that Olga Fröbe had in 1958 conceived a plan to collect contributions from the Eranos speakers themselves and work these into a history of the project, but this plan was never realized.[17]

Nevertheless, after some searching I did find a book that, although primarily not a history of the Eranos meetings, nevertheless yields the largest amount of information that has hitherto been available on the subject.[18] Its author, William McGuire, was for many years the editor of the valuable Bollingen book series that also included Jung's collected works translated into English. Through his work with and for Jung, McGuire went to Switzerland regularly from 1951 for almost twenty years and visited Ascona, where he got to know many of the key participants at Eranos. This series was financed by the American Bollingen Foundation, created by Paul and Mary Mellon, who undertook, at enormous expense, to have works (largely European ones) in the history of ideas and similar fields translated into English and made available in the United States. A large number of authors and researchers were by this means enabled, free of economic worries, to occupy themselves with specialized themes that would never have interested a purely commercial publisher. As the founder of Eranos as well as many of the speakers were also supported by the Bollingen Foundation, there were close connections between the two institutions. Thus, in his history of Bollingen, William McGuire also provides much interesting information about Eranos.

Looking further, we find that the Austrian "intellectual" radio network ORF 1 broadcast on 18 September 1998, as part of the series TAO, an informative forty-minute program on the Eranos meetings, which I have made use of in this work. There was also a report on Eranos broadcast by the Swiss radio network DRS in its first program on 22 April 1999 as part of the series Az.B. ("For Example").

At the end of 1999 Princeton University Press published a book by the religious scholar Steven Wasserstrom that partly deals with a particular but very important episode in the history of Eranos. The book is entitled *Religion after Religion: Gershom Scholem, Mircea Eliade and Henry Corbin at Eranos*. However, it contains no historical overview of the conferences or their participants. Instead the focus is on the "mystical" approach of the three scholars of religion, which Wasserstrom attributes to the "esoteric" atmosphere of Eranos and which he in part sharply criticizes. The fact that this atmosphere existed is not to be denied, but the question is whether one should judge it as negatively as Wasserstrom does. One of the main reasons for Wasserstrom's critical attitude lay in the real or imagined political implications of these esoterically tinged attitudes, which he associated with fascist or fascistoid worldviews.[19]

Thus, up to the appearance of the German first edition of this book in 2001 there was no historical treatment of the conferences and their emergence—a fact that still surprises me. Even essays on the subject of Eranos in specialized journals were rare.[20] Besides the articles already mentioned and the journal *Du*,[21] which I shall come to later, it was only the Spanish periodical *Anthropos* that covered Eranos to any extent.[22] *Anthropos* contained several substantial essays and even a complete list of the speakers and lectures up to 1988. In addition, the journal published a review, averaging two pages, of each Eranos yearbook up to the 1988 volume. Furthermore, in that year there appeared a comprehensive supplement, containing a whole series of mainly philosophical essays about Eranos. This added up to a large amount of material but no historical facts.

Even the Internet offered practically nothing on Eranos in 2001. In the meantime this has changed. Awareness of the significance of Eranos has been significantly raised, probably first by Steven Wasserstrom's work and the discussion that followed it, and later by my own rather more historically focused book. Gradually more and more scholars, especially younger ones, have begun to delve into the subject.

In 2004 a further book came on to the market thanks to the initiative of the Amici di Eranos (since dissolved) under the leadership of Tilo Schabert.[23] The subtitle of this book, mentioning Eranos, aroused certain expectations, but for me at least it is somewhat disappointing, as I had hoped for more investigation and new insights. Too many of the contributions deal only peripherally with Eranos.

However, since the first German edition of this book, research on Eranos has taken a further step forward thanks to Riccardo Bernardini whose dissertation *Da Monte Verità a Eranos* (From Monte Verità to Eranos) includes a mass of documentation containing previously unknown information. Much of it is from the archive of Eranos-Moscia, which was at that time closed to me. The dissertation also contains important information that adds new detail to the picture, especially concerning Oscar R. Schlag. But what is particularly striking about this documentation are the numerous photographs of Olga Fröbe and the leading participants at the meetings. Also included is a complete list of participants up to 1953.

I know of no dissertations on Eranos apart from that by Riccardo Bernardini already mentioned, although the conference organizer at the Amici de Eranos, Tilo Schabert, had plans to encourage scholarly work on certain aspects of Eranos. These plans were evidently abandoned when the Amici di Eranos were dissolved in 2007.

However, in the meantime a number of very interesting partial studies have appeared, the most important of which I would like to draw attention to, especially the report of the proceedings of the 2004 conference of the International Association for Analytical Psychology, held in Barcelona.[24] These contain the lectures given on 1 September 2004, which are grouped together under the title "Walking in the Footsteps of Eranos" and include contributions from Eranos speakers David Miller and Gilles Quispel as well as from the director of the Daimon publishing firm, Robert Hinshaw, who has close connections to Eranos. Particularly noteworthy is a "photographic journey" presented by Paul Kugler, who showed previously unknown photographs of the Eranos conferences. As these pictures appeared regrettably small in the proceedings, the "photographic journey" was also published in the *Festschrift* commemorating the seventieth birthday of David L. Miller, this time in considerably larger format.[25] I shall return later to this source of information on Eranos.

A particular gem of a book on Eranos appeared in 2007, again involving Riccardo Bernardini, the general theme of which is C.G. Jung at Eranos.[26] Apart from the scholarly articles, two things about the book stand out: first and most conspicuously, the numerous wonderful photographs, printed on art paper, most of which had never been seen by the general public before; second, a document, previously thought to have been lost, relating to a 1943 seminar given by Jung on the medieval author and miniature painter Opicino de Canistris, on which no report had been published.

Two further valuable documents have come to light since the death of the long-standing President Rudolf Ritsema. One is the manuscript of a book on the history of the conferences by Gerhard Wehr, Jung expert and specialist on mysticism. The book had been commissioned by the Eranos Foundation in Moscia, but evidently had not been to their liking. The work had been paid for but never printed and subsequently kept more or less under lock and key. The second document is an unfinished history of Eranos by Catherine Ritsema, the wife of Rudolf.[27]

Meanwhile the name Eranos crops up more and more in scholarly publications, and often particular aspects of the subject are addressed. This is a further hopeful sign of an increasing recognition of the important role that the conferences have played in the intellectual history of the twentieth century. While at first the outer history of Eranos consisted largely of gaps, the inner and intellectual content of the meetings has always been openly accessible and is, in every sense of the word, weighty. It has been assembled in almost ninety yearbooks (if one includes the three different Eranos factions), which contain all the lectures (although not the discussions) in an extended form. These fill some 30,000 printed pages, and a whole series of important lectures are recorded on cassette. As F.C. Kunz writes in *Main Currents in Modern Thought* (published in 1954, since when over forty more volumes have appeared): "The value of these [Eranos] yearbooks is truly incalculable. A fabulously rich store of learning."[28] And the University of Jerusalem affirms that the Eranos volumes constitute one of the most valuable acquisitions that have enriched its library during the past few years.[29] The opinion of North German Radio on the volumes is also perhaps of interest: "As can be seen, there is hardly anything comparable to them; the Corpus Eranos will remain as one of the few encyclopedias of our time."[30]

Originally Eranos was conceived by its founder, Olga Fröbe-Kapteyn, as a forum for interchange between Eastern and Western religion and spirituality. Over time, however, the scope widened to include not only subjects such as psychology, art history, music, and natural science but also "hermetic" and "esoteric" themes.[31] Eranos was thus not exclusively concerned with learned scholarship but equally (although not in the case of all participants) with the spiritual transformation of humanity. Both the rational and the "mythical" sections of humanity were to be given their due. As a justification for why I want to examine the mythical/esoteric aspect in greater detail later on—besides dealing in a regrettably fragmentary and partly anecdotal way with the history of Eranos (unfortunately it was not possible to deal with all the speakers in equal measure)—for the time being a quotation from the biologist and long-time head of Eranos, Adolf Portmann, will have to suffice:

> The Eranos meetings have always aimed to serve the life that exists within the mesocosm [i.e. the intermediary spiritual world between the macrocosm and the microcosm].[32] Their exploration of archaic traditions of thought has not been for the sake of irrationality per se nor because of any fundamental opposition to the existence of rational attitudes. The reason for cultivating this archaic world view was because it offered a domain where a richer and purer form of harmony exists between rational and irrational experience, and because here the creative powers can bear forceful witness to the vastness of the inner, spiritual realms and to things that have the power to make us whole, things which we are in danger of losing— indeed which many people in the West have already lost sight of to an alarming extent … Eranos is a grand, earnest game, which is played repeatedly. Each time the game resembles that of the previous year, yet every year the old form is filled with new content, giving us a glimpse of what a re-sanctification of life and the cosmos can bestow on us and how it can bring us a sense of comforting shelter and vital well-being.[33]

🐾 2. An Esoteric Prelude to Eranos

Olga Fröbe: An Extraordinary Woman

The story of Eranos—at least over the first twenty years—is unthinkable without its founder, Olga Fröbe. Even someone with as skeptical a mind as Gershom Scholem could write in 1979, after three decades of participation at Eranos,[1]

> When we, Adolf Portmann, Erich Neumann, Henry Corbin, Ernst Benz, Mircea Eliade, Karl Kerényi and many others—scholars of religion, psychologists, philosophers, physicists and biologists—were trying to play our part in Eranos, the figure of Olga Fröbe was crucial—she whom we always referred to among ourselves as "the Great Mother."[2] Olga Fröbe was an unforgettable figure for anyone who came here regularly or for any length of time. I have never been a great Jungian … but I have to say that Olga Fröbe was the living image of what in Jungian psychology is called the Anima and the Animus.

Henry Corbin, the great expert on esoteric Islam, dedicated to her a very hieratic poem, full of alchemical and mystical allusions, in which he called her "The one who let the call go out from the *centre*, who worked the miracle and who caused a divine gift to flow into our souls."[3] Heinrich Zimmer, for his part, addressed her in his letters as "Liebe, verehrte Urmutter (dear adored Ur-mother)"[4] and Rudolf Otto once gave her the title "Honorable Mother."[5] Mircea Eliade, in one of his diary entries,[6] described a waking dream in which he had seen her in the manner of a "high priestess of a new religion."[7] The only dissenting voice was Julius Evola, the Italian cultural philosopher and esotericist, who was well known for his provocative way of putting things. In a hitherto unpublished letter of 8 June 1952, addressed to Mircea Eliade, who must have told him about Olga Fröbe, he wrote:[8]

> So you are now in Ascona. That is a place which has certainly attained a special renown, but which I found to be dull. Apart from her fanatical devotion to Mr. Jung, she [Olga Fröbe] belongs to the category of those elderly women who present themselves as being highly spiritual and whom I wholeheartedly detest. I once went to her house when I was staying with a female friend whose villa is almost opposite that of Olga Fröbe. At any rate, I wish you an entertaining time[9] at Eranos.[10]

Olga Fröbe had Dutch parents, but was born in London in 1881 and grew up in Bloomsbury.[11] Her mother, Truus Muysken, was an anarchist by philosophy and a friend of George Bernard Shaw and the famous anarchist Prince Kropotkin. By contrast, her father, Albertus Kapteyn (alternatively written Kapteijn), was an engineer and inventor, who worked as director of the British Westinghouse Brake and Signal Company. He was also an enthusiastic photographer. Later on, Olga Fröbe often said that her deep interest in archetypal images could be traced back to the fascinating hours that she had spent as a child in her father's darkroom, watching films being developed and seeing the pictures gradually taking shape.

In 1900 the family moved to Zurich, since Albertus Kapteyn's business obliged him to travel a great deal and he wanted to live in a more central location in Europe. From 1906 to 1909, Olga was a student at the School of Applied Arts and then attended lectures in the history of art at Zurich University. There she learned German, French, and Italian. Dutch and English she already knew.

In 1909 she married Iwan Fröbe, a Croatian orchestra conductor of Austrian parentage, but her married life was short, as her husband was killed in an air crash in 1915 while testing an aerial camera for the army behind the Russian lines. As Deirdre Bair writes, there was also a rumor that he had been executed as an enemy spy.[12] During her married years Olga Fröbe lived first in Munich and then in the Berlin suburb of Wannsee. Also living at that time in Wannsee with his family was the philologist and expert on classical but also modern literature André Jolles, who was already a friend of Olga's parents. As the Jolles expert Walter Thys informed me in a letter, Olga developed a deep friendship with André.[13]

Jolles, a Dutchman by birth, had originally come to Germany as a student and loved the country. He had married the daughter of the mayor of Hamburg, Johann Georg Mönckeberg, and in due course had adopted German citizenship. Shortly after the outbreak of the First World War he even enlisted in the German army. What is more, in the spring of 1933 he joined the National Socialist Party. By profession he was a university professor of Germanic studies. Later, on account of his special knowledge of symbolism, he worked for the Reich Security Office, Section VII (for research into hostile *Weltanschauungen*), and also served as an expert on Freemasonry for the SD (the security service of the SS), which he joined in 1937. In 1944 he won the Goethe Prize and received the medallion that went with it, the last one to be handed over by Hitler in person. According to Walter Thys, this award was for Jolles' totally non-political book *Einfache Formen* (Simple forms),[14] although Gerd Simon believes that it was for his masonic researches.[15]

But let us return to the period before the First World War. An evocative account of these years has been left by Annemarie Pallat, who also lived in the Berlin suburb of Wannsee at that time with her husband, the archaeologist and educator Ludwig Pallat. Annemarie Pallat recounts that Jolles had built up a lively and many-faceted circle of friends, which included painters, musicians, and writers. They would meet once a week for readings or musical performances. "What I enjoyed especially," she writes:

> were the musical evenings hosted by the Fröbes in the small wooden house opposite the Jolles. Olga Fröbe was a quiet Dutch woman with an air of refined reserve, who kept modestly behind her husband, but who created an agreeable atmosphere through her style of home-making. Iwan Fröbe, a fiery Hungarian, was an orchestra conductor and played every instrument that exists, especially the flute. We enjoyed wonderful chamber music there.[16]

In 1911 Jolles also founded a sewing club called The Needle, to which Annemarie Pallat and Olga Fröbe also belonged. Jolles was especially keen to develop a new style of women's clothing based on ancient Greek motifs, in which cutting was kept to a minimum, and the material was shown off to best advantage by using its natural folds. Olga Fröbe ornamented the clothes with "wonderful embroidery" and beads. Her fondness for such clothing was something that she was also known for in later years.

After the death of her husband Iwan in 1915, Olga sold the house in Wannsee and returned to Zurich, where she had studied. Interestingly, she did not go back to her parents in Scheveningen, Holland. To the great regret of Annemarie Pallat, the artistic circle of friends in Berlin came to an end (Jolles had also gone to the front), as did the small school for local families, which Jolles had also founded and where Olga had taught English.

It was only after the death of her husband that Olga Fröbe gave birth to twin daughters, on whom André Jolles later kept a very kindly eye. One of them, Ingeborg, was mentally handicapped owing to a birth complication: twins had not been expected, and medical help arrived too late. Placed in a nursing home in Germany, Ingeborg died under mysterious circumstances during the National Socialist regime, possibly under the so-called euthanasia program. This is of significance because there were repeated rumors, which I shall go into later, that Fröbe had National Socialist sympathies. Deirdre Bair in her Jung biography mentions a collection of letters in an unnamed private archive, according to which Olga Fröbe went to the home to visit her daughter and found her missing.[17] Only then was she informed of her death. According to the same source, this tragic event led to a strong "anti-Nazi activism" on her part, which only ceased with the German invasion of Holland, when she was threatened with the arrest of her second daughter, Bettina, who lived there. Allegedly C.G. Jung himself knew about all these events. Unfortunately there are no further details about the above-mentioned report.

Quite apart from this, one can say that Olga Fröbe evinced a decidedly anti-Nazi attitude from at least 1934. This is clear, for example, from the following quotation from her letter of 24 June 1934 to the theologian and scholar of religion Friedrich Heiler, who was going to be transferred away from his position because of his political standpoint: "It is also difficult for us living abroad to look on and know that nearly all our friends are facing inner as well as outer conflicts." Evidence that she even feared National Socialism, at least from 1937 onwards, is contained in a diary entry by Ludwig Pallat of 28 July 1937.[18] Pallat mentions how Olga Fröbe, evidently through his mediation, had gone to see an official of the Nazi Party. The official had apparently been "very amused at her astonishment that he, as a Party member, had not immediately eaten her alive or raped her."[19] In earlier years she is said to have had a fondness for Germany, doubtless influenced by her father, who was reputed to be strongly pro-German, as well as by the equally pro-German André Jolles, who undoubtedly exerted a strong influence on her in all matters. However, such an outlook should not be confused with National Socialist sympathies.

From 1915 to 1920, that is to say during and immediately after the First World War, Olga Fröbe lived in Zurich (although she did not become a Swiss citizen until 1934).[20] There she applied her artistic talents and became known for her remarkable embroidery and jewelry work. She was also a daring equestrian and a successful skier, as well as being one of the first women to undergo the risks and exertions involved in climbing Mont Blanc, which she did by a particularly difficult route.

One person who knew her at this time was the writer and professor of German literature Robert Faesi, who stemmed from a patrician Swiss family and knew all the prominent poets of his age from Rilke to Hesse. In his memoirs he recounts that in the post-war period in Zurich she already had a salon, where readings took place and which was evidently intended as a continuation of the meetings run by Jolles in the

Berlin years.[21] Faesi reports that on one occasion there was a reading from the *Epic of Gilgamesh*, which by then had become well known. Another of Fröbe's guests at that time was André Germain, a restless, wandering art enthusiast whose father was the founder of the French bank Crédit Lyonnais. At the same time, his interest in literature prompted him to acquire certain literary rights, for example the French rights to Maxim Gorky's works. Being a person of considerable wealth, he was at that time patron of Alastair, an esoterically minded illustrator as well as an imaginative dancer, singer, and poet, who had a good knowledge of ancient cults and medieval fraternities. Alastair had met Germain in 1914 through Gabriele d'Annunzio. The latter, after he had seen Alastair dance in Paris, had drawn him into his large circle of aquaintances.[22] Thus Fröbe also came into contact with Alastair (the name means "fallen star") who is said to have claimed, shortly before his death in Munich in 1969, that he was the illegitimate son of King Edward VII.

She must have known Alastair well since at least 1920, for there exists a copy of his book of verse, *Das flammende Tal*,[23] presented to her with the inscription: "To dear and true Olga in friendship and trust. Munich 1920. Your epistolary friend Alastair." And, in a letter of 1 February 1928, she wrote to Ludwig Derleth's sister, Anna, that Alastair wanted to come and visit her at the Casa Gabriella, but that she could "not have him at the moment." Robert Faesi also knew Alastair and described him as an extremely attractive personality. Alastair, whose real name was Hanns Henning Otto Harry Baron von Voigt, was born in Karlsruhe in 1889. After graduating from school, he studied philosophy for a time, traveled widely and taught himself to draw. He became best known as a *Jugendstil* book illustrator, strongly influenced by Aubrey Beardsley.[24] In addition he designed posters and many costumes. Accordingly he traveled with numerous pieces of luggage containing his magnificent garments.[25] He could rarely pay the hotel bills, but he gave the staff handsome tips, commensurate with his reputation for extravagance and largesse.[26] As a dancer he was a partner of Isadora Duncan, who revolutionized choreography. Many international friendships—for example with Gabriele d'Annunzio as already mentioned and Count Kessler—also contributed to his mysterious and esoteric aura. He lived mainly in London, Paris, and Munich, where he gained access to the circle of Stefan George. At the *Jours*, the regular meetings hosted by the poet Karl Wolfskehl, who also belonged to the George circle, Alastair would appear with his hair dyed a flaming red color, accompanied by some dark-skinned beauty.

Within this milieu he also formed a friendship with the poet Ludwig Derleth.[27] After the latter's death he wrote: "Ludwig Derleth liberated me to myself; I found myself through him." Here are a few selective quotations from the two hundred or so letters to his friend: "You are the only pure spring at which I can kneel down" (28 February 1912). "Your image is for me painted in the clearest colors on the gold background of love" (22 February 1918). "There are certain people who, in a special sense, cannot do ill (and also those who cannot do good)—even when they wish to—you belong to the first of these groups" (15 February 1922). And finally: "How many hearts have been stirred up by the heavenly, turbulent glow of your authenticity" (29 August 1933). Ludwig Derleth, to whom we shall return in some detail, was undoubtedly among the strongest influences on Olga Fröbe. Besides Derleth, Alastair also knew Rainer Maria Rilke and apparently counted Elke Lasker-Schüler among his admirers. He was also in contact with politicians such as Walter Rathenau and scientists like Werner Heisenberg and Werner von Braun, with whom he even lodged for a time.

Hans Blüher, who was acquainted with Sigmund Freud and the sexologist Magnus Hirschfeld and who chronicled the *Wandervogel* movement and its erotic aspects, described Alastair as:

> an old soul … which must have had a previous and very passionate life in the early Middle Ages and which did not really fit into its present incarnation. He could only think in old-fashioned Catholic-ecclesiastical categories, and the modern world was so alien to him that he constantly needed to seek orientation. As a lover of women, however, he was not at all suited.[28]

A few lines from a poem by Alastair, dealing with the symbolic death and resurrection of the mythical figure of Adonis, will perhaps serve to give a small insight into the kind of creative milieu in which Olga Fröbe moved at that time.

> Here lies the sacrifice
> Hyacinths lifting a maimed perfume
> From his blood
> Violets binding his mortal wounds
> With a soothing, faded intimacy.
> This still repose seems merely slumber
> Yet already through the matted hair
> Shimmers the message of decay
> The maw of the grave yawns wide, the wailing of the sisters
> Fades away and silent there they stand
> With singed hair and deathly pale cheeks
> Fingernails clawing at the breast
> Already is revealed to the gaze
> New devotedness
> New wonders
> New raptures.[29]

Even before 1920, Olga and her father had taken a health cure at the Monte Verità Sanatorium above Ascona, which specialized in natural treatment. As Olga never wanted to leave this beautiful place again, she lived for a time in the Casa Monte Tabor in Porto Ronco, where she received a number of visits from Ludwig Derleth. Albert Kapteyn then decided to buy the Villa Gabriella, lying directly on the shore of Lake Maggiore at Moscia-Ascona, which had previously been the home of André Germain.[30] Olga Fröbe finally moved in there permanently in April 1920. Only in 1927, after the death of her father, who left a princely legacy, did she learn that he had already made the house over to her seven years earlier. Until receiving this inheritance she had been obliged to live from his rather meager donations.[31] With the inherited wealth she could now enter fully into the role to which she had long felt called, namely to invite artists, poets, and people of esoteric interests to her home. She was free to pursue her religio-philosophical interests and her theosophical inclinations. Above all, she was able to build on her property the lecture room that was to play such a leading role at Eranos. She was altogether not well disposed towards the artists' colony at Monte Verità. In a letter to Annemarie Pallat of 20 July 1920 she wrote, "The Ascona Bohemian crowd is of a kind that I do not like, all of them parasitical, half-talented types who consider themselves geniuses."[32]

A little-known fact about this period is that in the early 1930s Olga Fröbe burned all her old photographs, letters, and other memorabilia in order to forget the past and concentrate on her future activity as organizer of Eranos, as Catherine Ritsema has recorded.[33]

She appears to have traveled around a great deal and to have frequented various literary, artistic, and philosophical study circles. In 1926 she visited the cultural Semaine Européenne in Lausanne, organized by her friend André Germain. There she met Aadrian Roland Holst, probably the Netherlands' most significant modern poet.[34] Holst, with his unquestionable poetic gifts, possessed, like Fröbe, artistic dreams and mythical leanings, and they quickly discovered many things in common. He was also a great charmer and ladies' man, who was supported by his banker father and never needed to work. Nevertheless he was constantly short of money. Olga Fröbe soon invited him to visit her at Moscia. However, it was not until 1929, when Holst was suffering from a creative block, that he actually accepted her invitation, for on Lake Maggiore he could find exactly the peaceful conditions that he wanted. There she introduced him to various interesting people and helped him with the English translation of his prose autobiography *De Afspraak* (The agreement). The two of them, as Holst's biographer van der Vegt recounts, spent much time together at the translation work and at mealtimes, "but did not share the same bed."[35] Holst did not leave Moscia until 23 June the following year.

In April 1933 Holst paid another visit. Some time had elapsed since Fröbe had written to him saying that although she could only express her feelings with difficulty, he was welcome to come back whenever he wanted. In the middle of July he departed again, and therefore did not take part in the first of the Eranos meetings. Despite his penchant for the transcendental, he had no scholarly interest in the subject, and C.G. Jung's researches left him cold. He was equally uninterested in taking part in the "simple ceremonies that Fröbe, clad in a white robe, performed in the garden house."[36] Her "occult activities," which had been ironically described to him in a letter from a friend in Ascona, could have been the reason why he did not make a further visit in 1936, as his biographer believed.[37]

It was not until 1938 that Roland Holst visited Olga Fröbe again. Then he had to leave in the summer because the villa was needed for other guests. Fröbe, who was now short of money, rented out individual rooms, and the summer was the most profitable time for this. Holst stayed in Ascona and moved in with a Russian Jewish woman friend named Elena Frank. Nevertheless Olga Fröbe, who saw him subsequently in Amsterdam, invited him to stay with her again in 1939. Holst, however, preferred to stay with Elena Frank, with whom he was having a love affair. Unfortunately Elena "could not keep her mouth shut for an instant," as Holst's biographer relates, and this made it impossible for him to work. On the other hand, Fröbe was becoming more and more "immersed in the occult." Holst's friend the lawyer Wladimir Rosenbaum, of whom we shall have more to say later, wrote him a long letter and advised him to go to Olga, who was admittedly "somewhat meschugge, but at the same time tolerant, honest and no preacher."[38] But, as men will be men, Roland Holst naturally opted for Elena Frank. In 1947 Holst came again to Ascona, this time accompanied by a woman thirty years his junior, and Olga invited them both to stay with her. On this occasion he made the acquaintance of the mythologist Karl Kerényi.

However, of all her friends and all the artists and writers with whom she mingled, Ludwig Derleth was probably the one who influenced her most strongly and who laid the foundation for her later course.

The Munich "Cosmics" and Eranos

Ludwig Joseph Moritz Derleth (1870–1948), after a many-faceted course of studies in Munich (ancient philology, literature, chemistry, theology, philosophy, and later on even psychology), had become a grammar school teacher, a career during which he was transferred many times.[39] During school holidays he traveled a great deal. In 1897 he was drawn to Rome, entering a monastery but leaving soon afterwards. Further important experiences in his life took place in Paris, where he mingled with the most famous French estericists of the time, such as Papus (Gérard Encausse), the Catholic Rosicrucian Sâr Péladan, and the very prolific writer Sédir (pseudonym of Yvon Leloup). In the late 1890s he came into contact with the circle of Stefan George, a group that will be mentioned frequently in this book. In 1906 he finally gave up his teaching profession. Later stages in his life took him back to Rome, then to Basel, to Perchtoldsdorf near Vienna, and finally to the Tessin district of Switzerland, where he died in 1948.[40] His late marriage to Christine finally freed him of all financial worries, so that in the Tessin he was able to live in style in a palazzo in Stabio.

Derleth professed an ascetic and militant Christianity, strict and medieval, not to say ancient, in character,[41] in which Christ and Caesar were merged into the figure of Christus Imperator. Besides striving for a radical reform of the Church, he advocated a new theocracy as a counter-reaction to the mass democracy that he found so repulsive. In order to bring this about, he wanted to found a rigorously hierarchical, exclusively male order[42] composed of lay members, a "golden beehive, a close band of warm hearts in a world grown cold for lack of love."[43] Only an elite, he believed, was capable of bringing about a decisive change in the world. However, his efforts over some decades in this direction proved to be in vain, probably because his authoritative behavior alienated prospective members. Male sodalities such as the Templars, the Assassins, and the Jesuits were for him both exemplary models and objects of research. At the same time some of his concepts borrowed elements from the French socialist Charles Fourier, whose writings were required reading for Derleth's followers. Fourier's principle that "paradisical man is the beginning and end of creation" was also Derleth's motto. His aim was to create an ideal community, which he called Rosenburg. Politically, he was vehemently opposed to democracy, which he saw as an ethos of the masses. He was equally resistant to progress and science in the usual modern sense of the word. Contemporary Christianity was also anathema to him.

Consequently, for a time Derleth even took it into his head to become pope, since according to Catholic doctrine it is basically possible for any baptized Catholic to take that position. Derleth, who always dressed in black, was anything but a straightforward figure. His wife wrote about him, "Everyone thinks they know the poet, but this poet had so many faces, was so full of contrasts and so difficult to reduce to any common denominator that any statement about him would bring denials from his friends, because they claimed to have experienced him otherwise."[44]

As a poet, Derleth was discovered by Harry Kessler, a man who busied himself with many political and artistic activities and who published a number of Derleth's poems in the famous journal *Pan*.[45] For decades Derleth worked on his conceptually monumental magnum opus, *Der fränkische Koran* (The Franconian Koran), which he did not live to see printed in its entirety.[46] In this work, written in a highly contrived language, Derleth sought to bring together the two powerful themes that drove him: that of his native

Franconia and that of the Islamic Orient, which he interpreted in a strict Catholic sense. *Der fränkische Koran* was intended—like the Koran itself—to be to a work of poetry as well as a prayer book, a set of laws and a book of general guidance for both East and West and for this life and beyond. The Catholicism expressed in it is so exaggeratedly grandiose, so seamless, and all-encompassing that even the Middle Ages could not have matched it. The language of the work is often perceived today as overloaded, turgid, and hard to understand. Whoever reads it, however, should realize that its poetic side is only one aspect. The prophetic, apodictic, and profoundly pious nature of the work places it also in the category of religious writing.[47] In terms of content, the work deals with the pilgrimage of the human soul—away from the dense matter of the earth and towards God.

Lothar Helbig, the alter ego of the Stefan George-follower Wolfgang Frommel, in his essay *Ludwig und Anna Derleth*, reports having been told by the poet himself that it was he, Derleth, who had first made Olga Fröbe "acquainted with Creuzer, Bachofen and with various of the mysteries such as those of Baalbek, Eleusis and Samothrace."[48] Furthermore, there were "hidden threads leading from the Munich Cosmics (*Kosmiker*) to the foundation of Eranos in Ascona." In other words Derleth—who at the turn of the century had been close to Stefan George's circle of aesthetes, poets, and esotericists[49]—was the one who first introduced Fröbe to the mythology and mystery teachings of classical antiquity that were later to play such an important role at Eranos. He also encouraged her to study symbols and images, an interest that later resulted in the Archive for Research in Archetypal Symbolism, which I shall speak about later. Apparently Olga Fröbe also wanted to involve Ludwig Derleth in the foundation of Eranos, but for unknown reasons this did not happen.[50]

The Derleth scholar Dominik Jost, in his book on the poet, adds that Olga Fröbe-Kapteyn had written "a series of letters that provide valuable documentation for research on the prehistory of Eranos."[51] And the mythologist Karl Kerényi mentions in his *Tage- und Wanderbüchern 1953–1960* that, after taking into his care the literary estate of Walter F. Otto, he had been invited to visit Christine Derleth "just at the moment when there were certain gaps to be filled in the pre-history of Eranos."[52] Unfortunately he remains silent about this prehistory "because it was at that moment not ripe for publication."[53] And even Mircea Eliade mentions "meetings and surprising discoveries, that preceded the founding and first phase of the Eranos circle." He also adds, however, that "unfortunately I was unable to set down in the *Journal* everything."[54]

It is not clear what Eliade and Kerényi meant by these hints. And as Olga Fröbe herself also drew a veil over her own history in the period preceding Eranos, it has not yet been possible for me to find out what events are here being alluded to.[55] I was, however, able to see the letters, mentioned by Dominik Jost, from Fröbe to Anna Derleth and, more importantly, those that she wrote to the poet himself. Altogether there are about a hundred of these missives. It is not possible, however, to say whether this collection is complete. At any rate, Christine Derleth and her friend Angela Stader, who for many years shared a household, handed over all surviving letters to the German Literature Archive in Marbach on the Neckar, where the entire literary estate of Ludwig Derleth is preserved in eighty-five filing boxes. I have not, however, been able to discover the "valuable documentation for research on the prehistory of Eranos" that Dominik Jost mentions. The content of the letters is, as we shall see, of a rather different nature. And unfortunately Dominik Jost, who was professor at the Cantonal School in St. Gallen and *Privatdozent* for German literature at St. Gallen University, died many years ago, taking with him whatever further information he might have been able to provide on the subject.

It is clear from the correspondence between Fröbe and Derleth, which stretches into the 1940s but is particularly extensive during the 1920s, that Fröbe not only regarded Derleth as a spiritual master but also had feelings of love towards him. In all probability Derleth, as in the case of other women, did not return this love (at least in the usual mundane sense).[56] Anna Derleth, writing on 2 May 1962 to Dominik Jost on the occasion of Olga Fröbe's death, says that Ludwig was not capable of this kind of love, for "his love was so strong that it transcended the earthly kind." And she added another reason: "During his lifetime everything flowed into his writing."

Olga Fröbe was not alone in her veneration of Derleth. A whole circle of artistic and, in some cases, aristocratic women swarmed around him. Even Katia Pringsheim, who later married Thomas Mann, is said to have been a devotee of the poet, as was the undoubtedly free and emancipated writer Franziska zu Reventlow.[57] In a succession that went on in subsequent years, female devotees came repeatedly to visit him, and he favored them with long, individual conversations. For Derleth himself, however, it appears to have been his sister Anna who played the central role in his female cosmos. Even the marriage to his wife Christine, a woman with inherited family wealth, only came about after she had been in effect his secretary for ten years. Derleth, not the easiest person to live with on account of his moodiness and dictatorial behavior, had a basically negative attitude toward the thought of marriage.[58] Stefan George had early on put his finger on it in his poem *An Derleth* (To Derleth):[59]

> In our circle, one thing makes us twins:
> Free of all ties of house and goods,
> Only we, whenever the first rush comes,
> Can go forth from where we stand to follow the fanfare.

The letters from Olga Fröbe are mostly without any salutation, sometimes undated and frequently unsigned. They are partly in German and partly in English (when she wants to express difficult thoughts precisely and yet with lyrical feeling). Sometimes she addresses Ludwig Derleth with the familiar pronoun *du* only to revert a little later to the formal *Sie*. These are deeply felt writings, revealing someone of great sensitivity, who often torments herself in the search for meaning. They all revolve around a single point: Ludwig Derleth, from whom she expects physical, mental, and spiritual redemption. She suffers so intensely from this longing for love and redemption that she even believes herself to have taken a powerful love potion in a previous life: "The fire that consumes me is perhaps age-old, older than the world."

The rather rare salutations include "Dear Ludwig," "Beloved Maître fabuleux," and "Dear Master of my heart" and are followed by fervent pleas for a visit, a meeting or the answer to some question that has been weighing on her. The letters themselves are highly intimate, revealing a person trembling like a volcano about to erupt, at the same time modest and yet unbounded. When one reads these letters, with their intelligence and reflective depth, their delicate and yet always vigorous language, strewn with lyrical turns of phrase, one realizes the profound well of energy, intuition, and unwavering determination that this woman possessed. Her endurance and strength of will were intense, even perhaps measureless, commensurate with the intensity of her self-doubt and her inner anguished struggle. She sought the "Master" in order to find direction, orientation, and tranquility. On 27 August 1921 she wrote to Derleth: "In seeking a fixed point in the midst of the chaos, an unchanging star or a fiery cloud, I was always seeking someone infinitely superior to myself—a soul so strong and wise that my understanding could be burned and renewed in his flame." And in another letter to the poet she says, "You are the great unbroken string, a strange and unfathomable harmony with apparently a great dissonance at its origin—an extraordinary mixture of the Marseillaise and the Te Deum laudamus."

She believed that Derleth had implanted something eternally abiding in her heart, something that would require a lifetime—her lifetime—to come to maturity. But at the same time she also perceived it as a "seed of madness," from which she hoped the angels would protect her. In her earliest letters to Derleth she writes how much she owes to him in terms of knowledge of symbolism, and says that more and more she recognizes the symbolic-mythological background of everything that surrounds her. Thus, in a letter of 23 August 1921, she says: "It was really you who first brought me into contact with classical antiquity, and for this I am deeply grateful to you." In the same letter she reports that her friend from earlier times, André Jolles, while spending a holiday at her house, had recounted the myth of Ariadne and the labyrinth and had spoken of a Romanesque church as the "highest form of magic."[60] She also writes about the Kabbalists, about the hermaphrodite as secret goal, and about the *arcanum* of sexuality: "the awesome, blood-red mystery." She also sometimes describes her dreams and her artistic activities.

On 23 February 1922 she wrote a long letter in English under the title "The Quest." As Derleth was still in financial difficulties at that time, she tried to persuade him to spend at least part of the year in her house. Her daughter Bettina had also taken warmly to Derleth, whom she addressed as the "magician" and to whom she wrote a child-like and highly moving letter, accompanied by one of her own drawings. On 3 September 1940, writing on notepaper with the heading "Eranos Meetings," Fröbe speaks about her coming trip to the United States and says that the meeting with Derleth and his wife had once again created an oasis of peace for her. She also mentions the "symbolic" Eranos meeting of 1940 and says that, despite the adverse circumstances, forty people had attended.

In this context an Italian professor of German literature, Furio Jesi, who died tragically at a relatively young age,[61] makes the serious accusation that Ludwig Derleth had devised pseudo-magical and darkly anti-Semitic rites.By way of background, he explains that Stefan George had idolized the Austrian Empress Elisabeth (Sisi), murdered in Geneva by the anarchist Luccheni, as well as her sister Sophie, who died in a fire in Paris. George had seen them as almost heavenly figures. Derleth had allegedly gone even further and regarded these blows of fate against the houses of Habsburg and Wittelsbach as the work of an "esoteric and exoteric Jewish international, working in secret."

According to Jesi, Derleth believed that through magical means he could restore a sacred protection to both royal houses. And Jesi further maintains that "there are indications that a not entirely coincidental connection exists between Derleth's disciples and the esoteric circle [i.e. Eranos] which emerged in Switzerland around C.G. Jung and which was supported through the financial resources and dedication of Olga Fröbe-Kapteyn." Fröbe herself was allegedly an "extremely willing disciple" in precisely these "anti-Semitic rituals."[62]

Unfortunately Jesi gives no sources for his accusations. In the reference section relating to the passages in question he mentions Edith Landmann's *Gespräche mit Stefan*

George,[63] Ludwig Thormaehlen's *Erinnerungen an Stefan George,*[64] and Kurt Hildebrandt's *Erinnerungen an Stefan George und seinen Kreis,*[65] but only in a general way, without giving page numbers and quoting the title of Hildebrandt's book in a incomplete form. Having searched through these writings, however, I have found no reference to any such rites having been carried out by Derleth. Hildebrandt mentions Derleth only three times and merely *en passant,* Thormaehlen only twice and in an equally unimportant connection. Only Edith Landmann, besides three short references, has a passage in which she expands on Derleth a little more. She says of him: "Derleth, like Ignatius [Loyola], drew people to him and assigned prayer exercises to them."[66]

Jesi repeats his accusations against Derleth, albeit without mentioning Fröbe, in *Cultura di Destra,* his perhaps best-known work.[67] In this case, however, he gives no sources whatever. Turning to another book by Jesi, *Germania Segreta,*[68] one might expect from the promising title, which he took from Stefan George, that the book would yield rather more detailed information on this question, yet interestingly the name of Derleth is totally absent. As we are dealing here with serious accusations that could significantly compromise the early history of Eranos, and as Jesi's bibliographical evidence is deficient or blatantly inaccurate, I found it necessary to carry out my own researches into Derleth in order to examine the truthfulness of Jesi's charges.

In the above-mentioned letters from Fröbe to Derleth there is absolutely nothing remotely connected with anti-Semitism, magical rituals, and the like. Apart from a few references to symbolism, the letters deal with her relationship to Ludwig Derleth and nothing else. If there had really been any anti-Semitic rituals stemming from Derleth, then one would have expected to find at least some allusions to Judaism in the more than one hundred letters, especially as she wanted to make Derleth positively disposed towards her and was continually asking him for a meeting. In Christine Derleth's memoirs of her husband, to which I have already alluded, one would not necessarily expect to find such events reported,[69] and the same would apply to Dominik Jost's above-mentioned biography.

Jost also gives some additional information concerning the friendship between the poet and Fröbe, and he describes a journey that she made with him to Rome in October 1922. He also makes it clear that she continued to visit Derleth, who later also lived in Tessin, right up to the end of his life.[70] He furthermore quotes the following passage from a letter that she wrote to the poet: "My meeting with you belongs to the eternally beautiful things of my life. I have not forgotten. That experience lies within my rich present-day life like a concealed treasure, a 'rose garden of the blood.'"[71] In his second book on Derleth,[72] which Jost calls an "introduction to the work," he deals with the way in which Derleth demanded strict obedience.[73] At the same time Jost recognizes that for Derleth— who doubtless did behave in an authoritarian manner—obedience was important "for the inner process of spiritual unfolding." Jost also makes clear that Derleth's work is full of "many and various *topoi* from traditional mysticism" and that the poet is rooted in a "world of archaic, pre-civilized values."

The philosopher of religion Alfons Rosenberg, who stayed for weeks with Fröbe and in whom she confided closely during their many conversations, recounts, in one of his *Flugblätter* (circular letters)[74] to his friends, that Derleth had once invited Fröbe to Munich and arranged to meet her at midnight on the Marienplatz.[75] He had then walked with her through the streets of Munich until daybreak. In this way, as Rosenberg relates, Derleth made her familiar with the symbolism of Munich, indeed he "turned the city into a carpet woven out of symbols." Thus Derleth acted as her mystagogue, introducing her to a symbolic way of thinking and giving her access to her own inner, un-manifest life. "This," according to Rosenberg, "was the beginning of a road that would lead to the foundation of Eranos." The importance of this event is also pointed out by Tilo Schabert, then head of the Friends of Eranos association, in his introduction to the 1998 meeting.

Rather less personal consideration for Derleth was to be expected from Stefan Breuer's work *Ästhetischer Fundamentalismus*.[76] Breuer does, it is true, give a very clear survey of Derleth's life, describing his attempt to "reactivate a militant and heroic Christianity" and characterizing him as "a missionary prophet demanding from the world a form of active asceticism." But of magical rituals Breuer apparently knows nothing. However, what must surely be the most searchingly critical view of Derleth is provided by Richard Faber, an expert on the "Cosmics."[77] Faber's ironic quotations from other people's remarks about Derleth speak for themselves; one gave him the sobriquet "Jesus Bonaparte," while the theologian Hans Urs von Balthasar, who was essentially well disposed towards Derleth, described his ideas as "Genghis Khan Catholicism." One can therefore assume that Faber, who is also an expert on the extreme right, would hardly have omitted to mention the anti-Semitic magical rituals if they had indeed been carried out. But there is not a single line about them.

Another book dealing with the anti-Semitism of that era is *Dichter, Denker, Fememörder*, by Hermann Wilhelm, who is described on the book jacket as a chronicler of the history of Munich.[78] Here also there is no trace of such accusations, although Derleth is not exactly dealt with in a friendly manner. Even in a dissertation on Ludwig Derleth,[79] submitted to the University of Vienna in 1943 while National Socialism still held sway, there is not a single mention of anti-Semitic rituals to be found, and this despite the fact that the author Friedrich von Dauber felt obliged to explain why a preoccupation with Derleth was relevant at that time. He characterized the poet as a man who had pointed to the signs of decline that marked his era and thus had become "the builder of a bridge to a new Germany." Derleth had discovered "the light of our ethnicity" and ultimately he was without doubt "a German poet" both "by blood" and "in his innermost being." It is apparent from the several pages of explanation given by von Dauber that he felt under pressure to justify himself. Thus, if Derleth had really been responsible for anti-Semitic activities or written statements, these would have been gladly mentioned by the author of the dissertation, although he was really more concerned with Derleth's poetic work.

After looking through numerous writings and studies from the extensive literature relating to Stefan George,[80] I can only assume—until documentary evidence proves otherwise—that Furio Jesi's accusations are totally groundless and probably based on hearsay. Being a Marxist, devoted to pure rationalism and the spirit of the Enlightenment, Jesi would surely have seen the Eranos meetings as imbued with the irrationalism which he so feared and which he saw as leading inexorably to racism and fascism. This is what he wanted to react demonstrably against.

Nevertheless, it is undeniable that a virulent anti-Semitism did exist among the circle surrounding Stefan George and especially among the Munich "Cosmics."[81] This, however, has more to do with figures such as Alfred Schuler[82] and Ludwig Klages[83] and very little to do with Derleth.[84] As Alfred Schuler did indeed venerate the Empress Elisabeth (Sisi), I must conclude—sad though it is for Furio Jesi's reputation—that Jesi simply confused Ludwig Derleth with Alfred Schuler, as both of them were to be counted among the "Cosmics." Schuler believed that he discerned in the Empress Elisabeth "nothing less than the living vessel of undiluted cosmic fire."[85] He perceived her as being, like himself, lonely and "overshadowed by baleful experiences." However, as she had power at her disposal which she could have used to change the conditions of the age that he so lamented, he wished to be granted an audience with her. After several rather inept attempts, he spent one and half years and the remainder of his fortune making a precious work of art as a gift for her, containing a parchment scroll with his petition written in magnificent calligraphy.

Just when he was close to achieving his goal of meeting the Empress, there came the news of her assassination by Luigi Luccheni in Geneva. As his friend Klages observed, "The effect on him was terrible. He saw Luccheni's shameful act as a piece of contract work; in the background, behind the curtains, he saw Jesuit conspirators and secret societies working as instigators." In his seventh lecture *Die Entscheidung im Zentrum* (The decision at the center), in which he also counts Ludwig II of Bavaria among the victims of history, Schuler says: "They fell as the last line of resistance under the turning black wheel that now reigns over much of the earth." This sentence also points more to the notion of a Jesuit rather than a Jewish hegemony.

As Schuler was interested in ancient cult practices such as "blood brotherhood, blood vengeance, atonement through blood, and the use of blood in healing and protective magic," the Cosmics Schuler and Klages contemplated literally "forging the desired connection with the past through a magical blood sacrifice."[86] Their master Stefan George, however, rejected the idea. When they nevertheless came to the point of wishing to perform the sacrificial ceremony, "they did not dare to make a real blood sacrifice, nor did they know the correct moment at which to carry it out." All that was left to them was "their fruitless attempts at the nocturnal meeting place to experience the 'primal cosmic shiver,'" and "they soon felt, like Schuler in the autumn of 1903, the unutterable horror of being thrown again and again back into the old inactivity."[87] Derleth himself wrote scornfully about them: "They are practicing magic? I would say they know everything and yet they couldn't move a straw from here to there."[88] So here again we find no real rituals and certainly not anti-Jewish ones. While Schuler may appear as a somewhat peculiar figure, he must also have had a fascinating side, otherwise Rainer Maria Rilke would not have sent him a letter of admiration and thanks on 30 November 1917, in which he wrote: "You know that I consider what you have to give to be of incalculable value."[89]

Nevertheless, we have adduced a few points that could help to explain the background to Jesi's most probably groundless accusations against Eranos, although this in no way excuses his carelessness in confusing Derleth with Schuler. While both men can be counted among the Cosmics and although they shared many points of view and undoubtedly influenced each other, nevertheless there existed a surprising enmity between them, which led to a final break in 1901. Already in 1896, Derleth had spoken unflatteringly about Schuler to Count Harry Kessler during a visit from the latter. Derleth had described Schuler as an "intense swamp, lacking any noble side but with a fine understanding of all manifestations of culture."[90] Schuler's fanatical brand of matriarchal Neopaganism and Derleth's equally fanatical ascetic-Catholic Caesarism could presumably not be reconciled with each other. And when George broke with Schuler and Klages because of their anti-Semitism, George's friendship with Derleth remained intact. Indeed, as soon as Derleth heard about the rupture he went straight to George and handed him his first poems for publication in George's *Blätter für die Kunst*.[91]

One of the reasons for Jesi's negative attitude towards Derleth could have to do with Thomas Mann, a writer with whom Jesi was intensely preoccupied. Because of the close connection between aestheticism and violence in Derleth's work, Mann regarded him—at least for a time—as a precursor of National Socialism and took him as the model for two of his fictional characters. Derleth first crops up in *The Magic Mountain* and then again, in a parodied form, as Daniel zur Höhe, both in the short story *At the Prophet's*[92] and in *Doctor Faustus*. Later on, however, Mann largely abandoned this rather sombre assessment.[93]

Theosophy and the Arcane School

After pursuing this lengthy—but necessary for the sake of a more accurate understanding of Eranos—digression, we can now return to Olga Fröbe during the 1920s and 1930s. Maggy Anthony, in the context of a work on Jung, also discusses her and maintains that in the pre-Eranos period she lived an extremely reclusive life, even to the extent that for seven years she had contact with no one save her domestic servant. During this time she is said to have been mainly preoccupied with the study of Vedanta and other Indian spiritual paths until the onset of a neurosis forced her to seek medical help and she was treated by Jung. Allegedly Jung concluded that such a withdrawn life was harmful for someone of her rather extraverted nature, and he advised her to seek friendships with people who shared her interest in oriental forms of spirituality. It was then (1928) that she built the large conference room in which the Eranos meetings later took place.[94]

In her Eranos manuscript, Catherine Ritsema quotes a document, the original of which has unfortunately never come my way. It concerns a talk about Eranos which Olga Fröbe is supposed to have held in several European cities in 1939 and in which she said:

> Eranos first emerged in 1927, at a time when I was very much preoccupied with a geometrical drawing—one of a series of about two hundred … While in this frame of mind (that is, the frame of mind in which one makes such drawings),[95] the idea came to me to build an auditorium in the garden, and to hold conferences there related to the studies that I have been pursuing for many years.

Thus in building this room Fröbe appears to have followed an inner impulse, without having any clear idea in mind as to what she wanted to do with it. As Magda Kerényi reported to me, she even asked Jung how she should use the room. Evidently Jung then suggested that it should serve as a lecture room that would be a "meeting place between East and West."[96] Commenting on the matter in 1959, Fröbe recalled that at that time she was only vaguely contemplating founding a sort of summer school with lectures, intended for people with spiritual interests, although she admitted that she had no contacts of that kind.[97] She therefore experimented, as she wrote, "for some years with smaller groups such as the circle around Rudolf Maria Holzapfel, creator of a doctrine that he called 'pan-idealism.'"[98]

Rudolf Maria Holzapfel belonged to those "prophets of a new and better world," who were much talked about at the beginning of the twentieth century, but later fell into total obscurity. His admirers included such famous intellectual figures as Ernst Mach, Thomas Mann, Hermann Bahr, Arthur Schnitzler, Hermann Graf Keyserling, and Romain Rolland. The last-named, who had also been active in spreading the ideas of Ramakrishna and Gandhi, contributed a foreword to Vladimir Astrov's adulatory book on Holzapfel, *Das Leben Rudolf Maria Holzapfels*,[99] in which Rolland describes visiting Holzapfel near

Lausanne. Even the *New York Herald Tribune*, reviewing Holzapfel's book *Panideal*, said that it presented an almost religious ideal of a new age and described it as a guide to perfection in every sphere of life and a foundation upon which the kingdom of the spirit will be built.[100] Other newspapers that commented on the book included *De Telegraaf* of Amsterdam and *Der Bund* of Bern. The Berlin *Tageblatt* positively overflowed, describing the book as "incomparable and unparalleled by any other creative work," although it then went on to draw a comparison with the work of Leonardo da Vinci.

There were, however, those who voiced rather different opinions. One of them was Heinrich Berl, who was excluded in 1939 from the *Reichsschrifttumskammer* (the German writers' guild) because of his opposition to National Socialism and who was also a contributor (e.g. in 1923 and 1924) to Martin Buber's journal *Der Jude* (The Jew). Berl summed up Holzapfel as follows: "Rudolf Maria Holzapfel was a noble and mighty spirit. He was much too clever to have compared himself with Christ. What is Christ when compared with a Holzapfel? A partial ideal and nothing more."[101]

Holzapfel, the son of an Austrian doctor, was born in Krakow and led an eventful life that took him to South Africa, England, and Switzerland. The doctrine that he propounded was most notably presented in his magnum opus *Panideal: Das Seelenleben und seine soziale Neugestaltung* (Panidealism: the life of the soul and its social reform),[102] which the author dedicated to "the pilgrims who are seeking a new world."[103] Perceiving a general sense of loneliness and universal longing,[104] Holzapfel tried to give human beings a new kind of conscience, which would oppose any form of individual or collective egoism, whether of a national or a racist character. The goal was the perfection of humankind, which was to be achieved by educating people towards a new "panidealistic" culture. To this end he devised a plan for an "academy," whose task would be to develop and promote creative minds. In these ideas we already find some of the basic elements that were to characterize the subsequent endeavors of Olga Fröbe. Holzapfel later developed his thinking along religious lines, as expressed in his two-volume work *Welterlebnis* (Experience of the world),[105] which is dedicated to "the pilgrims who are seeking a new heaven" and covers a wide spectrum of topics ranging from the stages of consciousness to the erotic dimension of life.

Sybille Rosenbaum-Kroeber gives a somewhat different version from Maggy Anthony of Fröbe's early spiritual history. As Rosenbaum-Kroeber was in close personal contact with the subsequent founder of Eranos she can perhaps be credited with a better knowledge of the immediate circumstances. At any rate, she reports that in 1924 Fröbe had taken part in a course at Monte Verità given by Martin Buber about Lao-Tse (Laozi),[106] and that she had first met Jung in 1930 in Darmstadt at a meeting of Count Hermann Keyserling's School of Wisdom.[107] This version is also confirmed by a certain H.A.W., who published an article in *Die Tat* of 16 September 1950, entitled "Begegnungen in Eranos" (Encounters at Eranos), based on an interview with Fröbe. H.A.W. writes that she first met Jung "in the circle connected with Keyserling and the School of Wisdom."

Fröbe also had early contacts with members of the Ramakrishna movement as well as with the Theosophical Society, and she is said to have even been close to the then-president of the Theosophical Society, Annie Besant (successor to the founder, Helena Petrovna Blavatsky), and to her "foster son" Krishnamurti.[108] When Krishnamurti then withdrew from the role of "World Teacher," which had been assigned to him without his consent, a scandal blew up and many people turned away from Theosophy.

Thus one can certainly discern a Theosophical influence on Fröbe, and the question arises to what extent Theosophical ideas co-influenced the original concept of Eranos. Such an influence seems to me highly probable, and this can be supported by quoting the three objectives of the Theosophical Society, as stated in its constitution:

- To form a nucleus of the Universal Brotherhood of Humanity, without distinction of race, creed, sex, caste or color.
- To encourage the study of Comparative Religion, Philosophy and Science.
- To investigate unexplained laws of Nature and the powers latent in man.[109]

The statutes of the Austrian Theosophical Society in my hand, which are in line with those of the main Society, state furthermore that:

> The Theosophical Society pursues no political goals. It is not a religious sect and has no dogmas. It recognizes no authority in spiritual matters and does not represent a form of religion. It is an association of seekers after truth, who wish to collaborate in the spiritual development of humankind and seek to promote the ideal way forward for the human spirit.[110]

One could of course argue that these aims and principles are expressed in such a general way that they could be applied to any group that was preoccupied with spiritual and esoteric matters in the broadest sense. At the same time one should not forget that the tenets of the Theosophical Society were formulated in the second half of the nineteenth century, when colonialism in Africa and Asia was still generally accepted policy in world affairs. However skeptical one may be towards some of the Theosophical Society's esoteric teachings, one has to admit that it was responsible for conveying the notion of a spiritual community of all peoples (including the "primitive" ones) to a widespread audience in Europe and the United States—and this despite its doctrine about the various "root races," which seems quite odd to us today.

After the seven years of "disciplined concentration" Fröbe finally established contact with another esoteric teacher, namely Alice Bailey.[111] Bailey came from a prosperous English family and by her fifteenth year had made three suicide attempts. According to her own account, at the age of fifteen she came into contact for the first time with a "Master of Wisdom," who appeared to her dressed in European clothes but with a turban on his head. He informed her that she would later serve the same spiritual hierarchy to which he belonged and which worked in secret for the benefit of humanity. Her first marriage ended in divorce owing to the violent tendencies of her husband, by which time she was living in the United States, where in 1915 she came into contact with the Theosophical Society. In 1919 she married again, and she and her husband, Foster Bailey, soon attained high standing in this society.

In 1920 came a quarrel over leadership issues with Annie Besant, whose position as president had been shaken by the debacle over the "World Teacher" Krishnamurti. This, together with the independently channeled messages that Alice Bailey began to receive in 1919, led to a break with the Theosophical Society.[112] Finally in 1923 she founded the so-called Arcane School on the basis of her channelings. Her husband remained at her side and always supported her fully. Even in the books that later appeared under his own name he explained that the teachings contained in them stemmed from his wife and from the secret Master.[113] Mircea Eliade, who met him and Alice Bailey in London in 1940, described him as a "nonentity" and found her books to be "unreadable and absolutely worthless."[114]

The Alice Bailey writings teach a comprehensive plan of spiritual evolution for human-kind, which around the year 2025 will supposedly culminate in a world federation of nations and universal brotherhood. At the same time human beings will move beyond crass materialism and live in harmony with divine principles. The Arcane School empha-sized especially the belief that humankind is entering a New Age, namely the much her-alded "Age of Aquarius," a concept that was first popularized by Alice Bailey. Furthermore, the messiah of this age, namely Christ, who is identical with the Buddha Maitreya, is just about to return.[115] These prophecies allegedly came from a "Master" whom Bailey called Djwahl Khul, the "Tibetan." The Arcane School saw its task as being to train its pupils to enter into contact with the finer-plane Masters, who were believed to direct the destiny of the world.[116] To this end Bailey founded a whole range of esoteric organizations. In addition to the Arcane School, these included the Lucis Trust, the New Group of World Servers, and the so-called Triangles (followers working in groups of three), all of which were intended to further the evolution of humankind towards the goals described.

In her autobiography[117] Alice Bailey gives a detailed account of her acquaintance with Olga Fröbe. She writes that, at the time when they became acquainted through corre-spondence, Fröbe already had a good foundation of knowledge. Evidently Fröbe was also interested in the teachings of the Arcane School (Frank McLynn even describes her as having mediumistic gifts[118]) and intended to contribute to its dissemination in the world. Alice Bailey recounts that in 1930 Fröbe turned up in Stamford, Connecticut, where the Baileys lived, and told them of her plan to form in Ascona a non-sectarian, spiritual center that would be unrestrictedly "open to esoteric thinkers and occult students of all groups in Europe and elsewhere."[119]

The Summer School before Eranos

The first course in Fröbe's auditorium was organized for the summer of 1930 under the spiritual leadership of the Baileys. A prospectus about the summer school was issued in English, designating Fröbe as "Organizing Secretary" and inviting the reader to a "School of Spiritual Research," encompassing "the study of Theosophy, Mysticism, eso-teric Sciences and Philosophies, and all forms of spiritual research."[120] In the prospectus Olga Fröbe guarantees that the gathering will be free of dogma and sectarianism and that a multiplicity of spiritual paths will be represented. She especially emphasizes that the acquired knowledge "will be of very actual help to students." The meeting began at 5 p.m. on 3 August 1930 with an opening speech by Fröbe, describing the aims of the teaching. A short extract from this speech should suffice to make clear Fröbe's idealistic thinking, which also probably lay behind the Eranos initiative:

> We represent no society, order or fraternity, no special creed or faith. Our pur-pose is to create a meeting point where those of every group and faith may gather for discussion and synthetic work along spiritual lines. We hope that the most broadminded in the many various groups may make use of this centre, and that gradually a nucleus may grow up around it, a Tree with many branches, rooted in the Supreme One, Who enfolds all beings. We are profoundly conscious that the source and the goal of humanity are one and the same for every unit, and that here lies the fundamental truth of Brotherhood. The paths of men diverge, according to race, temperament, mentality and tradition, but the goal is the same for all.[121]

She went on to speak of the aim to create "a meeting place for East and West, where the spiritual ideals and methods of both may be discussed and ways of synthesis suggested." Western psychology had already begun to recognize the importance of the soul, and the West was also beginning to sense the potency of Eastern art, just as the East had come to value Western science. "If a spirit of synthesis could replace the spirit of competition, the world culture would be greatly heightened, wars would cease, and all problems of a political and social nature would be greatly simplified."

The course lasted three weeks and the teaching took place every day except Sunday. A fourth week was given over to private conversations with the lecturers. At midday those who wished could attend a general meditation session led by Sri Vishwanath Keskar. The lecture topics ranged from meditation to "Man and Superman" and from mystery schools to "Thought Forms and Telepathy." Grand Duke Alexander of Russia spoke about "The Spiritual Nature of the Human Being." Other speakers included Prof. Vittorio Vezzani of Turin on yoga, and the esoteric writer Violet Tweedale, who featured the subject of her book *The Cosmic Christ*. Fröbe herself contributed to a lecture on symbolism, illustrated by the already mentioned paintings of occult geometrical symbols, which can still be seen today at the Casa Anatta on Monte Verità.[122]

Interestingly, another person who attended in 1930 was Alexandra David-Neel, famous to this day for her accounts of her travels in Asia. She signed her name in the guest book, but evidently gave no lecture. Instead of entering her place of residence like the other guests, she simply wrote beside her name the words "*de partout*" (from everywhere).

One sentence that is given special emphasis in the *Report of First Session* will serve to make clear Fröbe's main intention at that time and most probably also subsequently. "Above all we are seeking to make this centre one in which the quality of the speakers will be so high, and the message so spiritual, yet so full of practical purport, that it will serve as a focal point on the physical plane for those subjective forces and spiritual leaders of the race, who are working strenuously at the uplift of humanity." She stated furthermore that it was important to keep the summer school free of self-promotion, sectarianism, and dogmatism. This was the only way that people could "find their way onto the path of discipleship." Through harmony and solidarity the liberation of humankind could be brought about.

In the first year it was a rather small group that came in the mornings and afternoons to the lectures, albeit an international one including people from fifteen different nations. However, as the Baileys, who always traveled with their three daughters, loved Lake Maggiore and kept coming back every year, the audience increased steadily, drawing people from many parts of the world. At any rate, Bailey described these meetings as a "great success."

In Ascona Alice Bailey met for the first time the psychologist Roberto Assagioli, who had already been acting as her representative in Italy. Assagioli had worked with Sigmund Freud and, after 1915, above all with C.G. Jung. Freud in particular had placed great hopes in his gifted Italian pupil. Assagioli was Jewish, but even as a child had already come into contact with Theosophy through his mother. According to his own account, he was strongly influenced by the mystical tradition of Venetian Judaism.[123] He was also the editor of an anthology of the writings of the so-called "Magus of the North," Johann Georg Hamann.[124] After working as deputy director of the Theosophical journal *Ultra*, whose contributors included Julius Evola and the Tibetologist Giuseppe Tucci, he founded in 1926 his Institute for Psychosynthesis. Here he propounded a teaching that combined Theosophical ideas with humanistic psychology.[125] Prompted by the Italian racial laws of 1938 and the need to keep a low profile after a one-month imprisonment for pacifist activities, Assagioli withdrew to his country estate near Arezzo. After the war he became increasingly active in the United States, and a number of his books were written directly in English. His influence can also be detected in the famous American Esalen Institute, whose one founder, Michael Murphy, traveled to Florence in 1970 to meet him.[126] Assagioli was also in friendly contact with Martin Buber and was distinguished by his tolerant character. He died in Florence in 1974.

At the first meeting most of the lectures were given by Assagioli and Alice Bailey. The former had a superb command of English and French as well as Italian and apparently could hold his audience spellbound. Fröbe had evidently already known Assagioli for some time, for she mentioned his name in a postcard which she sent to Ludwig Derleth from Turin in 1928 and which is preserved in the Eranos Archive in Moscia.[127]

In a letter from Fröbe to Jung, dated 30 January 1931, repeating her invitation to him to lecture in August at the Summer School, she already announced the provisional program for the event. Besides Alice Bailey and Roberto Assagioli, it included Count Kuno von Hardenberg and Rabbi Leo Baeck, who later became one of the Eranos lecturers.[128] Both had also been speakers at Count Hermann Keyserling's School of Wisdom, which I shall deal with later.[129] There was also a plan to mount an exhibition of paintings by the Russian artist and expert on Tibet, Nicolas Roerich. The theme of meditation and Indian ceremonies was to be covered by Sri Vishwanath Keskar, who had already participated in the 1930 meeting.

There were also unsuccessful attempts to invite the translator of the so-called *Tibetan Book of the Dead,* W.Y. Evans-Wentz, as well as the former Theosophist and expert on India and Gnosticism, G.R.S.Mead, and the cultural philosopher Salvador de Madariaga. Even Einstein received a letter, but he was just about to depart for Princeton. Another person who was considered, as is mentioned in a letter from Fröbe to Alice Bailey, was the poet Paul Claudel, who combined a classical and philosophical education with an understanding of the symbolic worldview of the Orient and who was much preoccupied with the tension between spirit and matter.

The Summer School attracted a considerable number of people from the nearby colony of Monte Verità, a community devoted to the free exploration of alternative life-styles and modes of thought, despite the fact that Alice Bailey disapproved of their bohemian way of living and warned her daughters emphatically against their "impure" notions. She was equally disapproving of the lakeside residents, predominantly German and French people, whom she described as being "peculiarly decadent and objectionable." Furthermore, Alice Bailey believed that the area around Ascona was afflicted by a curse, due to the fact that in ancient times it had been the "centre of Black Mass in Central Europe."[130] Nevertheless it was precisely in Ascona in 1932 that she received a particularly important communication from her Master. In her autobiography she calls it positively "epoch-making." This communication resulted in the creation of the "New Group of World Servers," which was intended to serve as a nucleus of the coming world civilization.[131]

Alice Bailey finally left Ascona in 1932, when "German professors" overran Ascona, which altered "the whole tone and quality of the place," and "the teaching given shifted from a relatively high spiritual plane to that of academic philosophy and a spurious esotericism," as she puts it in her autobiography.[132] Olga Fröbe was apparently not unduly sad about Alice Bailey's departure. According to Rudolf Ritsema, who succeeded her as the person in sole charge of the Eranos meetings, Fröbe had found the activities of the School for Spiritual Research, and especially the people who attended it, too lightweight for her taste. However, William McGuire attributes the end of the relationship to a quarrel between these two very strong-willed women, leading to the closure of the School for Spiritual Research.

The behavior of Bailey's three daughters probably also played a role in the rupture. They were apparently all too happy with the "decadent" and "impure" atmosphere of Monte Verità, and there were rumors of various erotic escapades. At any rate, a strongly reproachful letter of 22 March 1933 from Fröbe to Alice Bailey survives. Already Foster Bailey, Alice's husband, had aroused Fröbe's disapproval by bathing in the nude, and now the behavior of the daughters was altogether too much for her to tolerate. She accused Alice Bailey of acting hypocritically in this rather unclear affair. On the one hand Bailey would sharply reproach other people for their behavior, but when it came to her daughters, she apparently set entirely different standards:

> As head of this place, everything falls back on me, and consequently this whole affair does interest *me* [underlined in original]. This matter of the girls has so utterly disgusted me … that I believe it would be better for all of us and for the work of both of us, if we did not meet for at least a year. I therefore propose that you do not come to Ascona this year.

What is also interesting about this missive is the letterhead, which bears the name Eranos and the description "a meeting place between East and West."

A further detail on this episode is contributed by the philosopher of religion Alfons Rosenberg.[133] As already mentioned, he was well acquainted with Olga Fröbe, as he had researched for weeks in her picture archive. What she told Rosenberg was that Jung had induced her to turn away from the group surrounding Alice Bailey. At one point Fröbe, whose artistic talents have earlier been alluded to, had designed the large tableaux showing geometrical forms (as already twice mentioned), following Bailey's instructions. These were effective, but "radiated a horrifyingly cold atmosphere." When Jung saw these pictures exhibited in the lecture room he criticized them so vehemently that Fröbe was distinctly shaken and underwent a change of direction. From the way the images were presented, Jung told her, one could see that she "was dealing with the devil."[134] She continued painting, but restricted herself to small, representational pictures, which she showed only to a few friends.

For Alfons Rosenberg, to whose regular newsletters I owe many of the interesting details of my story, Eranos was of paramount importance. It is particularly moving to read his account of how, in 1934 or 1935, he was visiting the shop of a bookseller he knew and there saw the name Eranos on the cover of the 1933 yearbook, entitled *Yoga and Meditation in East and West*, which was undoubtedly not a common item in the Germany of that era. The importance of this first encounter for him is clear from his words: "And as I leafed through the book I was possessed by the certainty that I was no longer alone in my quest, but now belonged secretly, as the youngest and least experienced member, to a globally dispersed group of researchers into the deeper and wider dimensions of life."[135] At the time he did not think he would ever be able to take part in the meetings, since they were held in Tessin. He did not imagine that events would later force him to emigrate to Switzerland and thus lead him to Eranos.

The fact that Alice Bailey belongs to the prehistory of Eranos was apparently seen by James Webb as being important enough to mention in his classic work *The Occult Establishment*,[136] which warns its readers of an upsurge of "irrational" thinking in the modern world. However, in the section where he refers to Bailey, Webb is primarily concerned with the role of Jung and his occult and political interests. His book probably served as the antecedent for Richard Noll's "scandal-mongering" books about the psychologist.[137]

✎ 3. Yearning for the East:
Monte Verità and the School of Wisdom

In order to understand Olga Fröbe's endeavors and the emergence of Eranos fully we must also take into consideration the general intellectual climate of the 1920s—especially in Germany and the German-speaking lands. With its widespread skepticism towards the notion of progress, this epoch was very open towards oriental and esoteric modes of thought.[1] Many people were searching hopefully for the "true meaning" of life at a time when the outcome of the First World War had made high economic and political goals impossible for the defeated nations, that is to say primarily Germany and Austria.[2] In the German-speaking realm there were several Buddhist journals of high quality (e.g. *Der Buddhist, Buddhistischer Weltspiegel, Buddhistische Welt, Der Pfad, Zeitschrift für Buddhismus*), which continually brought out new translations of Far Eastern texts.[3] There were similar publications on China such as the journal *Sinica*, edited by Richard Wilhelm and Erwin Rousselle, both of whom were important figures for Eranos.

Thus it was not only India that held a fascination for intellectuals, as is well known, but also China, and especially Taoism.[4] Ulrich Linse even maintains that the Jewish philosopher of religion Martin Buber attained more influence in Germany through his translation of the parables of Chuang Tse (1910) than through all his work on Hasidism.[5] Taoism was enthusiastically received in Germany and its influence was felt in surprisingly diverse circles. Thus, for example, Gustav Wyneken, leader of the Free School movement and friend of the *Wandervogel* historian Hans Blüher, published Lao Tsu's *Tao Te Ching* in his journal. Even Kaiser Wilhelm II, in exile at Doorn in Holland, gave a lecture on the subject of "The Chinese Monad," in which he spoke in detail about *yin* and *yang* and explored the connections between Chinese images and symbolic motifs in general, including the swastika.[6]

This general pro-oriental mood is described in rather drastic terms in C.G. Jung's speech *Zum Gedächtnis Richard Wilhelms* (In memory of Richard Wilhelm), given in May 1930. After lamenting that "England and Holland, the two oldest colonial powers in the East, are also the most infected by Indian Theosophy," he went on to say that:

> the spirit of the East is indeed *ante portas*. Thus it really seems to me that the realization of meaning, the search for the Tao, has already become a stronger collective phenomenon than is generally thought. For example, I consider it a decidedly significant sign of the times that Wilhelm and the Indologist Hauer have been invited to lecture on yoga at this year's German Psychotherapy Congress[7] … Thus the spirit of the East is penetrating through all pores and reaching the most vulnerable parts of Europe. It could be a dangerous infection, but perhaps also a remedy.[8]

The almost desperate search for meaning led people not only towards Buddhism and Taoism but also towards an exploration of their own ethnic roots in the Germanic past or—in the case of German Jews—towards Hasidism or the Kabbalah, and it often led more secular-minded people towards nationalism or Zionism. This is a phenomenon that has been too little researched, and it could contribute much to an understanding of the deeper causes of the lamentable National Socialist era.[9]

The tendency among a certain section of the intellectual elite to turn to the Orient in search of meaning is also reflected in literature. Here we might mention briefly Hermann Hesse ("Europe's longing for the spiritual culture of the ancient East" and "The entire East breathes religion as the West breathes reason and technology"), Max Dauthendey, Stefan Zweig, and Rudolf Kassner.[10] The paradoxical statement of the Surrealists, "L'Orient est partout" (the Orient is everywhere), could also be included here. From a more critical standpoint, Max Scheler, in a lecture shortly before his death, spoke of the "strange penchant of our age for dark mysticism."[11] A similar view was voiced by Thomas Mann, writing from Berlin, in his *Appell an die Vernunft* (Appeal to reason), in which he spoke of the "sense of a turning point in history" and a "turning away from belief in reason."[12] The theologian Paul Tillich, later to be a speaker at Eranos, included in his 1926 monograph *Die religiöse Lage der Gegenwart*, as though as a matter of course, a chapter on mystical movements outside of the Church, dealing especially with the "occult mysticism" of Rudolf Steiner.[13]

Already in 1890 Hermann Bahr had called for an "overcoming of naturalism" in art, and the following year Heinrich Mann had published an essay about the *Neue Romantik* (new Romanticism) and how it was characterized by an atmosphere of "mystical uncanniness." Another person who addressed this topic was Max Weber in a series of lectures delivered in 1918 and subsequently published under the title *Wissenschaft als Beruf*, in which he spoke of a "modern intellectual romanticism," which he regarded, however, as having no future.[14] A Würzburg professor of Germanic philology, Franz Rolf Schröder, on the other hand, defends this "romantic" attitude in his pamphlet *Die Parzivalfrage* (The Parsifal question), in which he writes,

> The philosophical outlook of the present day [the 1920s] has many points of contact with the universal-historical outlook of romanticism. Our age also "feels the pull towards holistic thinking." Certainly there are not a few who feel obliged to raise their voices to prevent the critical consciousness of others from falling asleep.

"It is certainly true that there is no progress without specialized research," writes C.H. Becker in his deeply thoughtful lecture *On the Nature of the German University*, "but does that mean that science should now be devoid of that which was seen as the essence of science in earlier times, namely the endeavour to synthesize knowledge into a coherent whole?"[15] And the philosopher Ferdinand Jakob Schmidt went on the offensive in his collected works, which appeared a few years earlier under the title *Die Wiedergeburt des Idealismus* (The rebirth of idealism), where he stated in the foreword that all the studies collected in the volume "have entirely and solely emerged out of the struggle for idealism against the idols of this age: psychologism, historicism and positivism."[16]

Jung, who sought clarity even in the midst of this tidal wave of esotericism, is worth quoting here for his clear and concise analysis. In his 1930 speech in memory of Richard Wilhelm, above, he argues:

> Occultism has experienced an unparalleled renaissance in our era. It is almost eclipsing the light of the occidental intellect, by which I do not mean academe and its

representatives … I know that the universities have ceased to function as bringers of light. People have become weary of scientific specialization and rational intellectualism. They want to hear of a truth that does not restrict but expands, that does not obscure but illuminates, that does not flow over us and off us like water but rather penetrates into the very marrow of our bones. There is an anonymous but broad section of the population that is in danger of being led astray by this type of longing.[17]

The famous sociologist Karl Mannheim, in his *Heidelberger Briefe* (Heidelberg letters), composed in 1921, expressed the prevailing mood in Germany at that time as follows:

Everywhere people are waiting for prophets, the air is full of prophets, small and large. One person swears by Steiner, another by Spengler. There is Blüher and there is Kayserling [*sic*], there are centres to reform entire cultures, there are the apostles of Wyneken and George. There is an enormous openness—mental but not psychological—to any form of salvation at hand, there is a certain emptiness, a sense of need that one never succeeds in filling.[18]

And Siegfried Kracauer, in the face of the overflowing wave of esotericism, wrote of the "deep sadness" of the "academics, business people … and intellectuals of all types" and of the "metaphysical *malaise* due to the lack of any higher meaning in the world."[19] This wave of esotericism in the 1920s in the German-speaking realm, with its links to fringe political currents as well as to generally alternative modes of thought and practice, ranging from agriculture to town planning and from medicine to alternative theories of science, can be seen again today in an almost mirror-image form. The old dogmas of science, economic progress, belief, and morals are once again shaking, and the future is looking for figures who can shape it.

This quest for meaning and the resulting tendency to turn towards the East, in all its apparent otherness, is embedded in a longing that is much older and must be conceived in a much broader way, namely the search for the so-called "new man," who can, it is hoped, be "created" given the right circumstances. This longing probably underlies most of the movements of spiritual renewal, from the Pythagoreans through Christianity and Gnosticism up to modern times, as well as revolutionary political impulses (the French Revolution, Socialism, Marxism,[20] and National Socialism) right up to the so-called "generation of '68."[21] Its influence was also deeply felt in the 1920s.

In this connection we should briefly mention the circle of Stefan George, with his conception of "re-embodiment," as well as Richard Wilhelm and Count Hermann Keyserling, as all of these men had a decisive influence in the early history of Eranos. Richard Wilhelm spoke of this "new man" as one who "returns" to us after a contemplation of the deepest cosmic interconnections, in order to give back to the West the long-lost insight that metaphysics, ethics, and the study of the human being form an indivisible whole. Indeed Wilhelm's thinking even extended to the "overcoming of death" through the conquest of the ego and an integration of the self into the cosmic order.[22] On the subject of Keyserling it should be mentioned that the opening article in the first issue of the journal *Der Leuchter* (The light source), which documented the meetings of Keyserling's School of Wisdom in Darmstadt, bore the title "Vom Kommenden Menschen" (On the coming man).[23]

Especially important in this context is Keyserling's friend, psychotherapist, and colleague Oskar A.H. Schmitz, who as Jung's pupil attended some of the latter's seminars.

Schmitz came to the conclusion that with Jung psychoanalysis had for the first time reached the point where it could contribute to the "higher development" of human beings. In 1922 or 1923 he succeeded in getting Keyserling interested in Jung, and at the same time he began to treat him psychoanalytically. Subsequently Jung was invited to the Darmstadt meetings and became personally acquainted with the count himself as well as with Richard Wilhelm.[24] In his book *Psychoanalyse und Yoga* (Psychoanalysis and yoga)[25] Schmitz, who must also have been a remarkably gifted astrologer,[26] devotes the entire third part to the theme *Der neue Mensch im Werden* (The emerging new man). Another book that should not be forgotten is *Neues Menschentum* (New humanity) by the successful esoteric writer Manfred Kyber, which was re-published in 1949 after the Second World War.[27]

The concept of the new man seems to have arisen as a necessity in response to the ever-widening gap between human beings and the modern culture which they themselves had created.[28] This left essentially two possible solutions: either humans could "free" themselves by casting loose from their traditional emotional and religious ties and giving central importance to scientific achievements, or they could turn towards their "true" emotional/spiritual needs, letting go of the innovations of science and in this way making themselves "free." One way was seen as "progressive," the other as "reactionary."

Among those in search of the "new man" were the inhabitants of Monte Verità in Ascona, who settled there at the turn of the last century. I would therefore like to insert here a brief overview of the history of Monte Verità, that "Mountain of Truth" which attracted so many remarkable people.[29] As the Monte Verità "biographer" Robert Landmann reports, there were contacts, albeit not close ones, between Olga Fröbe and the inhabitants of this health-conscious, spiritual, and artistic colony, with their "spiritually advanced thinking." If one compares her conservative and morally strict outlook with the mores of most of the Monte Verità residents, it is clear that such contacts could only have been of a loose nature, despite many shared theosophical perspectives.[30] Another factor was her decidedly anti-Communist attitude, which would have militated against any intimate contact with the anarchistic and socially revolutionary atmosphere of Monte Verità. She was even on a hostile footing with her sister in Holland, who had very different political views and whom she dismissed as a "Communist."[31]

This sister was a friend of the poet Else Lasker-Schüler, who visited Monte Verità in 1933. Her visit coincided with Eranos and she wanted to meet Heinrich Zimmer, who was taking part in the conference. However, on 13 August 1933 she wrote to him from Locarno: "Mrs. Fröbe or Fröbel was so rude to me on the telephone. So I cannot come tomorrow. It seems to me that she is angry with her sister, and I am a friend of her sister."[32]

As early as 1889 the Locarno philosopher Alfredo Pioda, along with the well-known Theosophists Countess Constance Wachtmeister and Franz Hartmann, planned a sort of international lay monastery on the hill above Ascona, which was later named Monte Verità. However, it was only in the second decade of the twentieth century that anything resembling an actual reformist colony was founded on the initiative of the feminist Ida Hoffmann, along with Henri Oedenkoven, son of a rich industrialist, and the brothers Karl and "Gusto" Gräser[33] (the so-called "guru" of Hermann Hesse).[34] The world-famous dancer Rudolf von Laban, who also corresponded with Jung, founded there his many-faceted "School for the Arts." A sanatorium was also built, with vegetarian food and arrangements for air- and sun-bathing. The guests included Theosophists, political revolutionaries, and people simply interested in spiritual renewal. However, the practice of nudism and a liberal approach to love relationships soon caused offence.

An early arrival in 1903 was Franziska zu Reventlow, whose book *Herrn Dames Aufzeichnungen*, was a *roman à clef* set in the milieu of the Munich Cosmics, constituting a certain connection between Monte Verità and the Cosmics. Further important visitors included Prince Kropotkin, Erich Mühsam, Otto Gross, Karl Kautsky, August Bebel, the *völkisch* painter Fidus, the leading Theosophist Dr. Franz Hartmann, and Countess Constance Wachtmeister. In 1916 Theodor Reuss, leader of the occult group Ordo Templi Orientis (OTO) came to Monte Verità at the invitation of Ida Hofmann. There he immediately founded the lodge Verità Mistica of which Oedenkoven, von Laban, and Ida Hofmann became members. In 1917 Reuss convened a conference at Monte Verità on the position of women, modern education, and cooperative societal forms. From then until Reuss' death Monte Verità was the international headquarters of his magical order.[35]

The founders of this "colony" emigrated to Brazil in 1920, and a trio of artists took over the leadership. In 1926 the banker, art collector, and philanthropist Baron Eduard von der Heydt, who was later the object of certain serious accusations, bought up the whole property. In view of the baron's importance for Eranos and for Olga Fröbe personally, it is relevant to go into this story in some detail.[36]

The son of a banker, he had, after sojourns in New York and London, founded his own very successful bank in Holland with a branch in Berlin.[37] As someone who supported the return of the monarchy in Germany, he was on friendly terms with the exiled German Kaiser Wilhelm II, whom he assisted in financial matters.[38] The kaiser, during his exile in Holland, even lived for a time in his house in Zandvoort. While on holiday in Locarno in 1926 he was telephoned by his friend André Germain (whom we have already encountered), art lover and son of the founder of Crédit Lyonnais, who invited him to have dinner with Olga Fröbe. Also present was the theosophically inclined Russian painter Baroness Marianne von Werefkin, who was influenced by the "Caucasian magus G.I. Gurdjieff"[39] and who was enthused about the beauties of Monte Verità.[40] In due course von der Heydt went there himself and was also impressed. Three years later he was offered a very favorable opportunity to buy the entire complex. At first he was uninterested because of the distance from Holland and his chronically heavy work load. However, as Monte Verità had made such an exceptional impression on him, he decided—half in fun and half out of business intuition—simply to offer half the asking price. To his surprise, he found himself the owner. Once in possession, he commissioned two architects, Emil Fahrenkamp of Düsseldorf and Willy Roelli of Ascona, to build a hotel, which is still standing today. This also gave him a place in which to display his impressive art collection.[41] His intention had been to use this hotel as a venue for artists, but in fact some very distinguished guests stayed there. These included King Leopold of Belgium; the president of Israel, Chaim Weizmann; the composer Richard Strauss; the actor Emil Jannings; the writers Thomas Mann and Gerhart Hauptmann; as well as "Russian grand dukes, Parisian coquettes, and many members of the English aristocracy."[42] Kaiser Wilhelm II, however, was not among the visitors.

Apart from his wealth, Baron von der Heydt was an interesting personality. As a young man he had read Schopenhauer and thereby come into contact with Indian philosophy and especially Buddhism. Hence it was natural for him to collect Buddhist and Far Eastern art. He had also been a vegetarian for many years and was very much taken by the reformist ideas of Henri Oedenkoven. He disdained elegant clothes, as did the guests of the hotel. He himself wore white shorts, sandals, a small red parasol, and an open shirt, the so-called *Lufthemd* (air shirt), which he also enjoined the hotel guests to wear.[43] He claimed that by discarding formal clothes they would also put aside all their major worries. The guests were very willing to go along with him. It was only in the matter of vegetarianism that most of them demurred. Baron von der Heydt did not insist however, but his menus always included vegetarian food.[44]

An amusing description of him is given by the historian of magic[45] Elizabeth M. Butler in her autobiography *Paper Boats*.[46] Von der Heydt had contacted her after reading with unreserved admiration her book *The Tyranny of Greece over Germany*. The baron found the art of Greece to be rather lifeless and much too sober. As already mentioned, his passion was for the fulsome, imaginative, and luxuriant art of the Far East. Von der Heydt had visited Elizabeth Butler in England, arriving in a Rolls Royce and shocking everyone present by eating only vegetables and drinking nothing but water. Apart from his knowledge of art, he showed himself to be "terrifyingly well read" and "cosmopolitanism incarnate." Elizabeth Butler was so intimidated that it was only after some hesitation that she accepted his invitation to Ascona.

Her visit there, however, proved "extremely exciting." Of von der Heydt she wrote that "munificence was his middle name and benevolence his general attitude" as he always pretended not to notice what delicacies the guests were eating or drinking. She also reported that the well-patronized hotel was the scene of "orgiastic rites" of the Ordo Templi Orientis, which had turned into sexual Saturnalias that could have competed with the events organized by the permissive Otto Gross. Of the Eranos conference (1937), which was taking place at the same time, she had a low opinion. She felt she owed it to the baron to attend a few of the lectures, but she found "each more boring than the last, Mrs. Baynes on Gnosticism being the worst of all." She departed before Jung's arrival, having become weary of listening to one of his female followers holding forth on the subject of the unconscious. She records having been struck by the somewhat weird contrast between the valuable paintings and Buddha statues in the Baron's hotel and the man in the "white underwear" and red sunshade as well as the slightly crazy guests.[47]

Extending our list to include some of the illustrious residents in the immediate vicinity of Monte Verità, one name that should be mentioned is that of Eugen Grosche (Gregor A. Gregorius), founder of the Fraternitas Saturni, probably the most important magical order in Germany. During the Nazi period Grosche lived nearby in Versico. His secretary and mistress, Hanne Wildt, even took part in the 1950 and 1951 Eranos meetings.[48] Thus, although there is no direct thread of influence linking Monte Verità with Eranos, nevertheless our story points to the existence of something that Harald Szeemann, in the subtitle to his book *Monte Verità*, calls a "sacred topography."

On the death of Baron von der Heydt in 1956 the Monte Verità complex passed, under the terms of his will, to the Canton of Tessin. Finally, in 1989 a foundation to administer the property was set up, consisting of the Canton of Tessin, the town of Ascona, and the Swiss Federal Institute of Technology (ETH) in Zurich, who jointly assumed financial responsibility. The aim of the foundation, which was obliged to assume the outstanding debts, is to run the place as an international venue for meetings and seminars.

Looking at the various spiritual and intellectual influences that fed into Eranos, it is clear that Monte Verità, while geographically closer, was less important than Keyserling's School of Wisdom.[49] It was there that Jung and Fröbe met, whether for the first time (which seems most likely) or not, and it was there that she probably first came to appreciate this kind of discussion forum, with its elevated and yet private and intimate atmosphere, which was later to become typical of Eranos. It was not without reason that some of the lecturers at the School of Wisdom also spoke at Eranos a decade later.

Count Hermann Keyserling, scion of a Baltic noble family who had lost his entire fortune during the Russian Revolution, was known by the 1920s as a philosopher and was recognized by Hermann Hesse, C.G. Jung, Thomas Mann, Paul Valéry, Ortega y Gasset, and others.[50] As he now had to earn a living for himself, he finally, despite initial skepticism, agreed to the plan of his publisher Otto Reichl, who wanted to develop a "colony of philosophers" in Darmstadt. In his pamphlets *Deutschlands wahre Mission* (Germany's true mission)[51] and *Was uns Not tut: Was ich will* (What is needful for us: What I wish to do)[52] Keyserling had, probably following Goethe,[53] already argued that Germany should apply itself solely to exerting a spiritual and philosophical influence in the world. The Germans, so it was argued, are by their nature a non-political people and therefore cannot successfully pursue an international political mission. Instead Keyserling envisioned a synthesis of mind and soul, which could bring human beings back into a state of balance. Philosophy, he believed, must once again become a way of synthesizing wisdom and must overcome its fragmentation and excessively scientific approach. He even contemplated a "rebirth of Plato's Academy."[54]

The plan to form a group of sponsors, made up of distinguished university professors, never came to fruition, as the professors did not share Keyserling's conception of philosophy as both art and wisdom. However, through a donation from the Grand Duke of Hesse, the School of Wisdom was finally able to open its doors in Darmstadt on 23 November 1920.[55] At the opening ceremony Keyserling gave two lectures, one on the Indian and Chinese legacy, the other on the wisdom of the classical and the modern world—themes that were later to play a central role at Eranos. By 1930 there had been ten meetings or seminars. Lecturers included Leo Baeck, C.G. Jung, Gerardus van der Leeuw, and Erwin Rousselle who were also to reappear at Eranos. Also among the participants were names as prominent as Thomas Mann, Alfred Adler, Paul Dahlke, Leo Frobenius, Leopold Ziegler, Max Scheler, Ernst Troeltsch, Rabindranath Tagore, and, from the Stefan George circle, Rudolf Kassner and Oskar A.H. Schmitz.

The biologist and influential parapsychologist Hans Driesch gives a good impression of the meetings in his autobiography:

> The Darmstadt meetings have been described a "snobbish," and certainly there were a number of people who only attended because it was considered good form and because, despite the Republic, they liked to bask in the aura of the Grand Duke of Hesse, who attended all the lectures … But, snobbish or not, the meetings were *richly stimulating* for many people, and nearly everything offered was of *high quality*. Discussion was not permitted. One was supposed to absorb the lectures in a pure form and "meditate" on their content—a very good practice, since discussions almost never bring forth anything of value and can too easily dissipate the impression that a good, self-contained lecture can make. There is also a tendency for discussions to be dominated by those who can only provide tolerable criticism (and sometimes not even this) but no really positive contribution.[56]

The last few sentences could easily have been voiced by Olga Fröbe herself, for it was exactly these arguments that she used, rightly or wrongly, to forbid all discussion at Eranos.

The lectures, as already mentioned, were subsequently published in *Der Leuchter*. In 1931 an exceptional meeting was held in Formentor, Mallorca.[57] In 1932 Keyserling had to devote the entire year to his book *Südamerikanische Meditationen* (South American meditations), and in 1933 he did not wish to hold a meeting.[58] On this matter Hans Driesch makes the following remarks, which are worth taking to heart:

> The Darmstadt meetings were later discontinued by the count himself, and that was all to the good. Such institutions cannot maintain themselves continuously at the highest level, yet they are only worthwhile in so far as they do just that. As soon as one discerns the slightest decline it is best to close down immediately. That was always Keyserling's intention, and he acted accordingly. Thus he pre-empted the inevitable passive break-up of his creation; for after 1933, like everything else of spiritual value, it would undoubtedly have been forcibly closed down.[59]

Eranos, which began in a similar spirit in 1933 in neutral Switzerland, thus came at a highly appropriate time, even if one cannot exactly speak of an actual transmission of the same spiritual "torch." Nevertheless, I believe that I have pointed here to certain parallels. In this context it may be relevant to quote the following sentence by Keyserling, the message of which Fröbe saw as positively fundamental to Eranos:

> The lectures held at these [meetings] have a common basic theme, which is adapted by the various speakers according to their personality and world view, but always from a certain accepted outlook. Thus the different lectures act spontaneously as coordinates, pointing to a deeper focal point of meaning than would be possible with a single lecture.[60]

On the other hand, Keyserling, in contrast to Fröbe, thought it important to distance himself somewhat from oriental thought and to seek the roots of wisdom in classical antiquity, even though he made use of certain themes and methods from the East.[61] Thus from 1921 to 1924 courses involving meditation exercises were given by Erwin Rousselle to a smaller circle. These took place three times a year, lasted for a week and were taken by thirty-five people at the most. The symbolism of the Grail knight was an important theme at these sessions.[62]

In Darmstadt Jung met the sinologist Richard Wilhelm, who had been responsible for bringing the *I Ching*, later to be so important for Eranos, to the attention of a wide public.[63] Keyserling had met Richard Wilhelm, a former evangelical missionary in China, on his voyage around the world.[64] The special qualities of Richard Wilhelm's *I Ching* translation, which the sinologist Wolfgang Bauer described as "unsurpassable," included not only the brilliant choice of words and the illuminating commentary but also the fact that it rested on a genuine understanding of the Chinese esoteric tradition behind the text, something that was only possible through Wilhelm's collaboration with the Chinese scholar Lao Naixuan (or Nai-Hsüan).[65]

According to Erwin Rousselle, Richard Wilhelm was probably the first European to be initiated into a Taoist secret order.[66] On the subject of the spiritual relationship between East and West it is relevant to quote here another observation of Wilhelm's, which not only applies to that era but is also meaningful in today's context. According to Wilhelm, the West is intent on "developing the autonomous individual self to its utmost intensity, until it gains the strength to withstand the pressures of the external world," whereas the Eastern tradition is concerned with "penetrating deeply into one's own sub-conscious until a vista opens on to all of life, experienced intuitively in a mystical vision of unity."[67] Jung incidentally wrote the following sentence referring to himself and Wilhelm: "Fate seems to have assigned to us the role of two pillars supporting a bridge between East and West."[68]

Wilhelm's well-known influence on Jung can also be traced back to the occasion— before the publication of Wilhelm's *I Ching* translation—when Jung was shown the book during a visit of the sinologist to Zurich. He immediately consulted it and was immeasurably impressed by the apparently illuminating message that he received.[69] He already knew the James Legge version of the *I Ching*, but owing to the inadequate translation, it had not aroused his enthusiasm. Jung, in his obituary of Richard Wilhelm, went so far as to describe the *I Ching* as the fulcrum "by which our western world view could be prised out of its hinges."[70]

Richard Wilhelm unfortunately never spoke at Eranos, as he died before the first conference. His son Hellmut Wilhelm, however, spoke several times at Ascona on the subject of the *I Ching*. These lectures were published first by Rhein-Verlag in Zurich and later by Eugen Diederichs in Düsseldorf.[71] Even the first sentence from the publisher's foreword by Diederichs shows why the *I Ching* was of such key importance not only for Jung[72] but for Eranos in general, where it continued to play a key role: "The 'Book of Changes' raises the question of continuity within change and the order of things in the midst of a transient world." This was also the profound question which Eranos, consciously or unconsciously, was posing—for after all it is the eternal question about the meaning of human life and about its place in the cosmos as a whole.

The mutually enriching interchange between Jung, Wilhelm, and Keyserling must have been important to all three men, as the surviving correspondence between them shows. Jung, who analyzed Keyserling's dreams, even described the count as the mouthpiece of the *Zeitgeist* or, more precisely, the *Zeitgeist* of the spiritual human being.[73] Keyserling, however, gradually came to the conclusion that Jung's advice was too abstract or simply wrong.[74] Finally he stopped replying to Jung and held the conviction that Jung's efforts to decipher a universal language of symbols were basically misdirected.[75] He also wrote that no real human relationship had ever developed between himself and Jung.

At the same time Jung's impression of Keyserling was not unreservedly positive, as is evident from his unpublished autobiographical notes.[76] Above all he was put off by Keyserling's habit of speaking nonstop like a fast-flowing stream, which made any real conversation impossible, however many wise remarks were thrown up. For this reason Jung could not remember any of the actual content of Keyserling's gushing monologues. In Jung's view Keyserling, while certainly an important man and an impressive phenomenon, was someone with a disturbing and compulsive (although not vain) tendency to strive for prestige. To Jung, with his "earthbound" character, Keyserling, the "spiritual high-flier" might have seemed "somehow unsympathetic, not to say sinister."[77]

It was not only Jung who took exception to the count's penchant for continuous monologues. The historian and diplomat Carl J. Burckhardt described this as "a flood, an endless succession of words, spoken in a strong Baltic accent, which fluttered around ostensibly weighty themes."[78] Burckhardt's exquisite description of Keyserling, covering several pages, gives a totally unexpected picture, which is hard to reconcile with the count's philosophical works. Apparently a tendency to drink unbelievably large quantities of alcohol, frequent night spots, and pinch the bottoms of chambermaids alternated with spontaneous and inspired lectures on every conceivable subject.

By contrast, Hans Driesch writes, "He often visited us, once staying for several days. He was a very pleasant, quiet guest, who demanded neither champagne nor the company of young ladies to inspire him, but only very strong coffee before giving a lecture." Perhaps the truth is that Keyserling was simply being flexible, adapting himself to whichever host he was with. Driesch also characterizes him as a typical representative of the Baltic German aristocracy: "extremely intelligent, highly educated, very lively," radiating the aura of the *grand seigneur* with people who were not of his level, "despotic, but basically good-natured, more 'Russian' than German." Driesch appreciated him more as an aphorist than as a systematic thinker.[79]

Among other well-known contemporaries he was also not rated particularly highly as a philosopher. Thus Gottfried Benn, in a letter of 16 May 1936 to F.W. Ölze, writes:

Regarding Keyserling, I would like to add right away, between ourselves, that the book [Keyserling's *Buch vom persönlichen Leben* (Book of the personal life)] reads on the whole like a brochure issued by a concert agency. There's a lot of unction going on here, with affirmation oil and all sorts of cosmetics. Nevertheless, such a book must be welcomed at the present time. It comes from the heart and does not address itself to the rabble.[80]

An even more provocative assessment of Keyserling came from Franz Blei, writer, *feuilletoniste*, and generally a key literary figure in the early part of the twentieth century:

More musical than mathematical (he played Bach vividly), more artistically than logically gifted, Hermann's work is not very highly regarded by academic philosophers, but it appeals to women like nothing else. In philosophy too there is something like chamber music, which does not imply bad philosophy but rather a philosophy that has been concocted with cleverness and taste. Keyserling speaks of the "impudence, which remains to this day the key to the puzzle of my rapid success" … A charming, very clever man, because a man who has understood that nowadays one can set philosophy up as a limited company.[81]

Finally a quote from Julius Evola, who met Keyserling in Rome. Evola's characteristically harsh observation was, "When I met him it was clear to me that I had before me a mere 'salon philosopher,' vain, narcissistic and arrogant beyond measure."[82]

🐚 4. Toward Eranos

Olga Fröbe and C.G. Jung: A Difficult Couple

Let us return to Olga Fröbe. By now she had been subject to many different influences, and still she could not say what would really satisfy her innermost yearnings. Her soul, pulled this way and that by conflicting impulses, did not permit a simple "yes." She suffered, she sketched and painted pictures, probably hundreds of them, and she also wrote. In the years 1932–33 she even penned a book of stories for her friends, most of them written in moments of inner crisis, as she mentioned in an undated letter to Cary Baynes.[1] In the same letter she added that these stories were her way of empathizing with the psychological situations of other people. Only later, she explained, did she realize that they also expressed her own set of psychological problems. The book was in fact a large-format manuscript, which she had mimeographed and bound. She entitled it *Gleichnisse* (Similes). In the foreword she said that the stories had been written for individual people, often in relation to some question or questions they had raised. They were "similes" because "the deepest things in human life … can only be expressed in images." Her aim was to "penetrate the depths of the soul and very quietly indicate ways to reality."

These similes are "fairy tales" for adults and reveal the writer's deep psychological sensitivity. They are fairy tales in the sense that they deal with a realm that concerns us all, one that is not reality (material reality: Latin *res* = thing) in the literal sense, yet is undeniably real (i.e. realizes something). Here it is not the author who stands in the foreground, with all his or her "complexes" and "inner concerns," as in so much modern literature. Rather it is that which is universal and time-transcending that constitutes the essential content. But even the form in which the tales are written is appealing—despite some stylistic and grammatical flaws, which are understandable considering that German was not the author's mother tongue. She does not drive home the moral with a flail, but rather conveys an unobtrusive message through images. The people to whom the stories are addressed are usually indicated by their initials. One is dedicated to "A.R.H." (undoubtedly Adriaan Roland Holst), another to "J. v. S." (probably Jay von Seldeneck), and another to "K.F." (unidentified). Certain stories, however, are clearly assigned. These include *Die Drei Könige: ein Märchen für mich* (The three kings: a story for me) and *Die Geschenke des Zauberers—Für Bettina* (The gifts of the magician—for Bettina). Bettina was Olga Fröbe's daughter, already mentioned as having written a moving letter to the "Magician," who can be identified as Ludwig Derleth. In the story this is confirmed by certain details that point unambiguously to Derleth and clearly reflect the poet's aura. In order to appreciate the reaction that Derleth could evoke in Fröbe it will suffice to quote one sentence from the story: "And today,[2] when I contemplate these seven gifts [given by the 'Magician' during the course of the story],[3] I know that the Magician spoke the truth and that, through these gifts, I have found the path and the gate, beyond which I now stand, living in the real world, which is timeless and everlasting and as bright as the stars."[4] Derleth is also said to have been one of the "twelve knights" of a "Round Table" which was probably imaginary but which must have played an important role for Fröbe, as accounts by her friends confirm.

Perhaps in Olga's mind this Round Table turned later into the Eranos Round Table, which she mentions in a letter to Jung of 11 March 1960: "You once talked about the Eranos Round Table, as you came down the path to my house, and you spoke of a Grail, suspended between heaven and earth. The festive table resembled a picture that one might see in some old manuscript. That was right at the beginning of Eranos, and I have not forgotten your words."[5] One contribution to *Gleichnisse*, headed *Der Durchgang: ein Symbol* (The way through: a symbol), is not a story in the traditional sense but rather a meditation on the position of humankind in relation to the timeless, the divine. The theme is the "permeability of the heart—the human heart as a focus of everything spiritual, sacred and transcendent." Her elevated goals—which were undoubtedly also reflected in Eranos—are clearly expressed in the following sentence: "It is only through human beings that the divine—the transcendent reality—can become visible and tangible. Each person must fulfil his destiny, sooner or later, by becoming a transmitter; not for his own sake but for others." I am convinced that this book is a key to Olga Fröbe's psychology. Without it any attempt at a real evaluation of her personality (which would go far beyond the present work) can only be fragmentary.

As she had already shown with her summer school project, Olga Fröbe was determined to put her lecture room to good use by bringing together people engaged in some form of spiritual endeavor. After the initial failure to include esoteric themes, the decision was taken in 1933 to give the meetings an academic character. Nevertheless, the theme of the first conference was "Yoga and Meditation in East and West." The first scholar whom she contacted was Heinrich Zimmer from the University of Heidelberg. Zimmer quickly and enthusiastically accepted, even offering to help with the organization of Eranos.[6] She had found Zimmer's name in the journal *Yoga: Internationale Zeitschrift für wissenschaftliche Yoga-Forschung* (Yoga: International journal for the scientific study of yoga).[7] The editorial board of the journal comprised an impressive list of names including Walter Y. Evans-Wentz, Helmuth von Glasenapp, Jakob Wilhelm Hauer, Caroline A.F. Rhys-Davids, Erwin Rousselle, Johannes H. Schultz, Sir John Woodroffe (Arthur Avalon), and Heinrich Zimmer. Among these were several people who were later to appear as speakers at Eranos. This periodical, combining high-quality academic articles with book notices and relevant reviews, was planned as a multilingual publication. However, owing to the general economic crisis, it was forced to close after the first issue.

The foreword by the publisher, Helmut Palmié, reflects the same ideas and visions as those that inspired Fröbe. Palmié writes, "Despite the present world-wide cultural and economic crisis, an imposing array of outstanding scholars from this country and abroad are prepared … by drawing consciously from the age-old wisdom of all countries and periods, to find new spiritual ways to the inner concentration of man and to a renewal of our whole way of living." The journal, he explains, is entitled *Yoga* because, in the words of J.W. Hauer, yoga has attempted "since time immemorial to penetrate to a reality that is hidden to normal consciousness." It is true, he says, that psychoanalysis has recognized the critical situation of humankind, but has interpreted it in a one-sided perspective.[8] "Yoga eludes any such one-sided interpretation of its essential approach. It addresses itself to the whole human being and is therefore best adapted to bring harmony and inner enlightenment to the individual as well as to humanity as a whole." The publisher then appeals to "all philosophers, anthropologists, orientalists, scholars of religion, psychologists and doctors of all countries and races" to support these endeavors.

J.W. Hauer's introductory essay "Yoga und Zeitenwende" (Yoga and the turning point of the age) elaborated further on these aims and was undoubtedly one of the decisive influences on the way Fröbe later developed the Eranos project. Hauer spoke of a "guided journey of the soul" (printed letterspaced for emphasis in the original), a choice of words that probably influenced the titles of the 1934 and 1935 Eranos conferences. Furthermore, he emphasized that "deep down and in its essential structure, human nature is uniform [letterspaced in the original]."[9] Hauer pointed to Jung as the only psychologist who clearly addressed these decisive questions. Jung's work, he said, incorporated certain important forces that were poised for a break-through. Other figures given a special mention by Hauer included Gandhi and D.T. Suzuki, who was later to be a speaker at Eranos. There was an English introduction to the journal by Rhys-Davids and another in French by Paul Masson-Oursel, both of them subsequently speakers at Eranos. Looking at this brief selection from the journal, one can understand the influence that it had on Eranos and why the first meeting was devoted to the theme of yoga.

Fröbe also sent a letter of invitation to C.G. Jung, but initially Jung declined, ostensibly because of her close connection to the Theosophical movement[10] and to Roberto Assagioli,[11] who was himself associated with Alice Bailey. However, when Fröbe later told him that she had received acceptances from various of his acquaintances and colleagues, he apparently immediately agreed to attend and also to give a lecture.[12] Eliade records in his diary[13] that Jung's own circle "sabotaged" Fröbe, since the Psychology Club in Zurich perceived Eranos as competition. And Jung himself is reported to have been rather hard on her in the early years. She, however—and Eliade gives one to understand that he had heard this from Fröbe herself—always felt a deep connection to him. One day, when the two of them were invited to the house of some friends in Ascona, Jung had drunk rather more than usual and induced her to drink quite a bit as well. Then Jung carried out a ritual. Taking his ring, inscribed with the word *Abraxa*, from his finger, he placed it in a glass filled with wine, uttered some mysterious formulae, and then slipped the ring on to her finger. The next day Fröbe said to him that he, as a psychologist, had done something grave with this gesture, and she told him: "You have bound me to you!" Jung, however, is said to have answered: "It was not I that did it, but the Self."

In contrast to Fröbe, however, Jung appears not to have taken this episode seriously. Her close friend, the analytical psychologist and doctor Cary Baynes,[14] tried to convince her of the insignificance of the event, but did not succeed, as it was always difficult to exert a moderating influence on her.[15] In the early years of Eranos a great deal of drinking went on. Ximena de Angulo, the daughter of Cary Baynes, remembers being there as a young girl and helping along with a friend of her own age to serve the food and drinks. Finally, after one tipsy guest fell into the garden pond, these evenings of jovial lubrication were brought to an end by Fröbe, who was basically a teetotaler and regarded the drinking sessions as a desecration of the lecture forum. Alfons Rosenberg also speaks in his pamphlet on Eranos about the "rather merry character" of the meetings up to the Second World War.

In view of the importance of Carl Gustav Jung for Eranos it would be appropriate here to mention some of the significant stages of his life.[16] Born the son of a pastor in eastern

Switzerland, he studied medicine at Basel University, where he soon came into the sphere of influence of certain important figures who lectured or had lectured there. Especially worth mentioning are the influential cultural historian Jakob Burkhardt, the expert on matriarchy Johann Jakob Bachofen (who influenced him in developing a sensitive approach to the interpretation of symbols), and the (by then already mentally deranged) "philosopher with the hammer," Friedrich Nietzsche.[17] However, in an interview he gave to Ximena de Angulo in 1952, he described these people (in contradiction to what has usually been reported) as "peripheral influences."[18] The most important influences, he said, were Kant, Schopenhauer,[19] Carl Gustav Carus,[20] and Eduard von Hartmann.[21] With regard to the contextualization of Jung in the spiritual life prevailing in Switzerland and Germany at that time, reference should also be made to Jay Sherry's painstakingly researched work *Carl Gustav Jung*, which fills a gap that until now has been too little illumined.[22]

Jung's unusual interests are further indicated by his doctoral dissertation, which was on the subject of mediumistic phenomena.[23] After the completion of his studies he took up a position at the psychiatric hospital of Burghölzli in Zurich. In the same year appeared the epoch-making work *Traumdeutung* (The interpretation of dreams) by Sigmund Freud, whose ideas were immediately supported by Jung. In 1907 he met Freud for the first time, and the collaboration between them became so close that Freud believed he had found in Jung his intellectual heir and successor. Five years later, however, there came a rift in the friendship, the reason (among others) being that Jung found the primarily sexual interpretation of neuroses to be too limiting.[24] As a result Jung also experienced something of an excommunication amongst Freudians and was not taken seriously. Such was the fate of Freudian "apostates." It appears that a secret committee under the leadership of the highly influential English psychoanalyst Ernest Jones ensured that Jung was unanimously rejected as a charlatan.[25]

Soon afterwards Jung began his studies of Gnosticism and the Gnostics, which found their expression in the strange, prophetic-gnostic work *Septem Sermones ad Mortuos* (Seven sermons to the dead).[26] In the early 1920s he bought a piece of land at Bollingen on the south bank of Lake Zürich, not far from his home at Küsnacht on the so-called Gold Coast. Here he would build the famous tower that became his retreat.

His encounters with the Pueblo Indians in New Mexico and with the indigenous tribes of Uganda and Kenya brought him into direct contact with archaic forms of thought. His open, receptive manner made it possible for him to engage in intensive discussions and even to develop friendships with African medicine men and a Taos Pueblo chief.[27] Even in India, which he visited somewhat later in his life, he was treated as an equal by a Tibetan lama in the north and a Brahmin in the south. Regarding him as a wise teacher, they felt able to speak freely with him about their religious mysteries. This openness expressed itself also in his loud laugh. The South African explorer and writer Laurens Van der Post remarked that, apart from Jung, he had never met anyone who could "laugh like a bushman."[28] Jung, in his overpowering manner and his choice of words, did not always conform to the conventional academic image. He was famous for his voracious appetite and, as Fröbe's gastronomy was not exactly renowned, he had nightly sessions devouring delicacies that he had bought secretly, as Eliade reports.[29]

Although Jung was a man of undoubted charisma, especially (and certainly not to his regret) where women were concerned, he was not the cult figure that certain people have recently accused him of being. If one reads, for example, the observations about him by the psychoanalyst Mary Esther Harding, who knew him for forty years, one is struck particularly by his simplicity and directness.[30] It was this simplicity that so positively impressed the sponsor of the Bollingen Foundation, Paul Mellon.[31] Jung always emphasized that he saw himself only as a doctor and that he only reported facts and had no desire to appear as a philosopher or spiritual guide.[32] For this he was undoubtedly much too self-critical. Petteri Pietikäinen, a lecturer at the University of Helsinki who has dealt with Jung in a number of books, addresses this question with what seems to me a very plausible opinion that Jung was a modern creator of myths who aimed to develop a therapeutic cure for the symbolic impoverishment of Western culture.[33]

In support of this thesis one could adduce the publication of the *Red Book* in 2009, which can only be described as sensational.[34] The "book that is not a book,"[35] which Jung began in 1913 and worked upon for sixteen years, was kept secret from the public for fifty years until it recently appeared in a facsimile edition (with translation) in all its splendor and glory. We are dealing here with a superbly illuminated calligraphic manuscript whose content derives from Jung's unconscious and came to light through "active imagination." The book is so impressive that it has already been compared with the Irish Book of Kells and must undoubtedly be regarded as a work of art. The editor, Sonu Shamdasani, speaks of it unequivocally as "nothing less than the central book in [Jung's] oeuvre" and "the single most important documentary source." Jung's scientific achievements also have their foundation in the insights wrested from the unconscious that were set down in this book, which constitute the mission of the psychologist. The language is hieratic, prophetic, contradictory—hence Jung's lifelong reluctance to submit it to the criticism of the broader public. Nevertheless, Jung apparently believed that he was close to discovering a key—perhaps the most important one of all—to understanding the world. He wanted to proclaim this message to humanity and if necessary to fight for it, even if this sometimes meant treating others with a lack of consideration or making strategic alliances with influential people.

However, he was probably not interested in being a cult leader. At the same time one can clearly detect a touch of the messianic in the way he perceived himself. This would explain why, towards the end of his life, he repeatedly regarded himself as having failed. But he failed only in relation to the high goals and ambitions that he set himself. Naturally, in real life one can never live up to the self-image of a messiah with a "healing" mission in the world. "I am the most damned dilettante who ever lived. I live by borrowing. Again and again I borrow knowledge from others."[36] These were bitter words from his own mouth.

The view that Jung had a "messiah complex" is argued by the analytical psychologist Michael Fordham, who had been prompted to visit Jung because the latter had written to one of Fordham's colleagues, lamenting bitterly over his inability to open people's eyes to the essence of his teaching, namely that the human being has a soul. The letter concluded with the words: "Why indeed should I continue to exist?"[37] Perhaps Jung's suffering stemmed from a failure to reach his great goal of creating out of psychology—conceived as an all-embracing doctrine of the soul—a type of meta-science comprising within itself all the humanities, in order to counteract their increasing fragmentation and specialization.[38] As his reputation grew, Jung received honorary doctorates from several universities, became president of various medical and psychotherapeutic associations, and was named a professor at the Swiss Technical University in Zurich. On account of his lively interest in parapsychology he also became an honorary member of the Society for Psychical Research in London.[39]

In 1937 he undertook a journey to India, a nation which impressed him deeply but at the same time made him realize that his way was a Western one.[40] His study of alchemy became increasingly intensive, and he came to see the Great Work of the alchemists, the *opus magnum*, as an individuation process of inner development towards wholeness, similar to what he had already seen reflected in the images produced by the ancient Gnostics.[41] In his opinion the Gnostics were the first thinkers to concern themselves "naturally in their own particular way" with the content of what Jung called the collective unconscious.

Here it is necessary to cite the words on this subject of Sanford L. Drob, a clinical psychologist and philosopher as well as a writer on theology and editor of the *New York Jewish Review*: "Jung has frequently been called a 'Gnostic,' but for reasons which I will detail in this chapter, it is my view that Jung is far more Kabbalistic than he is Gnostic, and he is 'alchemical' largely to the extent that the alchemists borrowed from and relied upon Kabbalistic ideas."[42] Ten years later Drob developed this astounding passage into a complete book which reaches some very interesting conclusions.[43] The author has no doubt that Jung delved into Kabbalistic themes and used the insights he gained there in his psychological theories as well. Drob even thinks that these studies triggered an exceedingly creative period for Jung, during which unmistakable parallels between Kabbalistic and Jungian theories (e.g. in relation to dream theory) emerged. Drob also dedicates a long chapter to the consonance of Kabbalistic doctrine with the Jungian view of the development of the psyche, in the course of which he delivers a completely archetypal interpretation of the Lurianic system of the Kabbala.[44] Likewise, he alludes to analogies concerning the *coincidentia oppositorum* in both worldviews. An entire chapter is also devoted by Drob to what he calls the "Kabbalistic visions" experienced by Jung after his heart attack in 1944, which amongst other things comprise the divine wedding between the *sephirot* Tipheret and Malkut.[45]

Given these circumstances it is almost self-evident that Drob changed his attitude towards the anti-Semitic accusations repeatedly directed at Jung, arriving at a very differentiated assessment of the matter.

After leaving his professorship at the Swiss Technical University, Jung later took up the chair of psychology at the University of Basel, but immediately had to give it up for medical reasons. Serious health problems, whose "spiritual" nature he refers to in his *Memories, Dreams, Reflections*, caused him to concentrate on writing down his ideas. He died in 1961.

The influence of Jung's *oeuvre* has been immense, and Eranos is only one example. Here of course it would be impossible and unnecessary to go into all the dimensions of his work, but in relation to Eranos two aspects are important: the doctrine of the archetypes and the concept of the individuation process.[46] The archetype is an invisible but powerful structure present in the psyche, around which one's inner experiences arrange themselves. It is to be distinguished from the concept of the archetypal image, which comes from the depths of the soul, in other words from the so-called collective unconscious. Such images are imbued with the incredible psycho-dynamic force of the archetype, and this explains the numinous fascination that they exert on the observer. The archetype itself, in Jung's view, is *psychoid*, that is to say it extends far beyond the boundaries of the individual personality. What is especially interesting is that, according to Jung, these archetypal structures are common to all human beings, regardless of race, religion, or culture. Hence, for example, the primal images of the Wise Old Man, the Great Mother, and the Hero, which crop up all over the world.

All myths, therefore, have a common basis, even though they may vary in form from one culture to another, and this provides a firm foundation for a real unity of humankind. This notion is central to the Eranos project with its aim of creating a common platform, bringing together themes from East and West, from antiquity and modernity, from the arts and from religion, so as to uncover their innermost commonality and thus blaze the way to a new humanism and an integrated view of humankind.[47] At the same time it is important to realize that the unconscious and the archetypal structures are believed to have a creative life of their own, steering human beings in a direction that is to some extent "preconceived." And this touches on Jung's second important doctrine, namely that of individuation, meaning a process by which the archetypes automatically lead each person towards his or her innermost fulfillment. In order for this to happen, however, it is necessary to put aside one's everyday mask, the persona, in order to become that which one truly is in one's most essential being. Jung saw the archetypal images as being all facets of the so-called self, that is to say of the archetype itself, which represents the ultimate goal. At the end of the process all these images would come together to form a wonder-fully harmonious *mandala*, in which the individual's contradictions would be incorpo-rated without being disruptive (*coincidentia* or *complexio oppositorum*). In the course of this book we shall see how strongly Fröbe was influenced by this way of thinking.

In this connection one more important point should be mentioned. The well-known Jungian psychologist Marie-Louise von Franz has emphasized that Jung, especially in his later works, allowed his unconscious to participate in the writing and thus work in accordance with the archetypes. In this way, his writings have the capacity not only to convince the reader logically but also to evoke a resonance within the soul. Jung himself remarked, "I have written everything on two levels"[48] And this perhaps makes it easier to understand the far-reaching and emotional impact of his work.

Rudolf Otto: Academic and Mystic

The name Eranos, as Fröbe herself acknowledged, was suggested by the scholar of reli-gion Rudolf Otto, whom she had visited in November 1932 at Marburg an der Lahn in order to discuss her intention of organizing a less esoteric and more academic type of summer school. It is true that the date of the founding of Eranos was 1933, but from the extant documentation it can be gathered that Fröbe was at that point not thinking in terms of a fresh inauguration but rather of a modified version of the summer school that she had been running since 1930.

Only a month after Fröbe's visit to Marburg, Otto went for several weeks to Ascona. Fröbe was keen to work out plans for the project that was later to become Eranos, and for this she urgently needed expert advice. For him, however, the visit apparently had just as much to do with the beneficial climate of Ascona, which he hoped would relieve the bronchial and lung complaints from which he suffered.[49] According to Magda Kerényi, Jung himself had advised Fröbe to contact Rudolf Otto, although the actual meeting did not take place until a year later.[50]

What appears to be the first letter from Otto to Fröbe is dated 17 September 1931 and contains the surprising remark that he already "knows" her "work."[51] This could mean that the summer academy had achieved a wider resonance than has hitherto been assumed and that, after all, Fröbe's reputation did not rest entirely on Eranos. Furthermore, Otto speaks of Fröbe's "circle." He greatly welcomes the prospect of ties between Fröbe's "circle" and the *Religiöser Menschheitsbund* (Interreligious league of mankind), which had been founded by him in 1921.[52] The league, after a promising start to its activities, had not developed to the extent that he had hoped for. Nevertheless Otto, in his letter, declines to give lectures himself in Ascona and instead suggests Herbert Grabert, who was at that time serving as de facto secretary of the league,[53] emphasizing that Grabert had "occupied himself particularly with the question of religious mutual understanding and the encounter between different religions, both historically and as a principle to be applied."[54]

Later Fröbe, with her tendency to a certain credulous enthusiasm, saw this first meeting with Otto as having been brought about by higher powers, and she described the visit as "an experience of timelessness" and as a "pre-determined moment."[55] In the already mentioned report by her on the occasion of the 1952 Eranos conference, she elaborates on the meeting as follows: "Hardly had we been talking together for five minutes when he [Rudolf Otto] handed me a box with hundreds of names and said, I am handing over to you the card index of my project, the League of Mankind, which I am not able to bring to fruition. Perhaps you will now do with Eranos what I wanted to do and could not."[56] As it turned out, Otto was unfortunately too ill to be able to take part himself in the Eranos meetings. Otto, however, appears not to have been drawn to Eranos in the way that Fröbe wished. On 9 September 1934 he wrote a postcard to her with the following words: "It was to be expected that Heiler would not in the long run fit into your circle. The same applies to me. My dry researches cannot compete with the soaring flights of your prophets."[57] According to Martin Kraatz, in all of Otto's nine hundred or so letters and postcards that have been preserved, there are very few references to Eranos.

The name suggested by Otto for Fröbe's meetings could have been borrowed from the earlier Eranos circle in Heidelberg, although he himself was not a member of it. This circle, conceived as an interdisciplinary discussion group for scholars of religion, was founded in 1904 by the distinguished theologian Gustav Adolf Deissmann[58] and the philologist Albrecht Dieterich.[59] The latter is noted for his work *Eine Mithrasliturgie* (A Mithraic liturgy), a book that exerted considerable influence, especially on Jung. The sociologist Max Weber was also a member of this circle, as Marianne Weber reports in her biography of her husband.[60] Other members included the theologian and philosopher of history Ernst Troeltsch as well as the philosopher Wilhelm Windelband. This was a purely academic circle working within a strict set of rules. It met once a month on a Sunday, rotating between the homes of the ten or so members. Wives, however, were excluded.[61] The host had to give a talk on a religious theme, and an orderly discussion ensued. This was followed by a meal, after which the discussion was continued more freely. To quote clause "g" of the regulations, "The members regard attendance at the meetings as a duty from which exemption is allowed only for the most compelling reasons."[62] Minutes of some twenty-nine sessions have been preserved, covering the years 1904–9. Any similarity to the later Eranos meetings consists at most in the interdisciplinary nature of the gatherings and in the sociability of the shared meals. In its approach to religious studies, the circle was rather philosophically oriented.

The word *Eranos* means a festive meal, to which each guest had to bring a gift.[63] In the case of the meetings at Ascona, the gifts were the prepared lectures. Karl Kerényi points out that in antiquity an *eranos* was an established social practice and that such festive meals were also sacrificial feasts. As the most famous example, he cites the Symposium of Plato, at which the speeches were expressly declared to be gifts in honor of the god of love: from Eranos to Eros. But that does not mean that the two words have a common etymological root.[64] And certainly it would not have been seen by the participants as a negative omen that Pallas Athene, the goddess of wisdom, was the first in Greek literature to use the word Eranos.

Rudolf Otto was born in Peine, Hanover, the son of a factory owner. He held a special professorship in Göttingen and then became professor of systematic theology in Breslau and subsequently in Marburg. In 1929 he retired earlier from his professorship for health reasons.[65] His influence in the area of the history of religion, and in particular on the scholars of religion who spoke at Eranos, was considerable.[66] Friedrich Heiler, Gerardus van der Leeuw, Gershom Scholem, Mircea Eliade,[67] Henry Corbin, Karl Kerényi, Ernst Benz—these and many others held him in high regard and recognized how much they had learned from him.[68] Rudolf Otto had taken the concept of religion beyond the purely theological realm and had coined the term "the numinous" to describe the ineffable emotional and spiritual energy that is special to the religious domain.[69] His aim was to counterbalance the rationalistic approach to theology, as this approach on its own, he believed, could never come close to the real essence of the divine.[70] That essence, he held, only becomes "truly" accessible in those deeply stirring moments when we experience the "holy" as something emotionally compelling, as a *mysterium tremendum*. Such an experience can never be comprehended rationally, and consequently the most appropriate reaction to it is to remain silent. It is therefore not the intellectual but the feeling part of us that is the organ for religious perception.

The historian of religion Hans G. Kippenberg sees Otto as "a genuine representative of German mysticism."[71] In person, Otto must also have been an imposing figure. The scholar of religion and Protestant theologian Heinz Röhr, who was himself from Marburg, reports having been told by various of Otto's contemporaries that the great man did not simply walk through the streets but rather "*strode* like the embodiment of 'The Holy.'"[72] The theologian Karl Barth, who met him at Marburg in 1922, described him as "the very image of an Indian Raja."[73] A similar impression was gained by Joachim Wach, who taught religious studies in Chicago and also paved the way for Mircea Eliade there. Wach wrote of Otto, "Neither before nor since my meeting Otto have I known a person who impressed one more genuinely as a true mystic. There was something about him of the solitude into which an intimate communion with the Divine has frequently led those who were favoured in this way."[74]

This "mystical" disposition of his appears to be be what allowed him to so fully understand foreign spirituality "from within," as it were. Furthermore, his religious perceptions and observations were derived from actual experiences on his travels far more than they were from the study of holy scriptures.

At any rate, the influence of Otto must have been considerable, judging by the fact that 1929 saw the twenty-second printing of his book *Das Heilige* (The holy) since its first publication in 1917.[75] Nor should one forget to mention Otto's 1899 re-edition of *Reden über die Religion* (Talks on religion) by Friedrich Schleiermacher (the "Christian Plato"), a work that had long been forgotten, despite its great significance (for Novalis among others).[76] Schleiermacher's book, which will feature several more times in this study, is important in so far as it was written as a weapon against the so-called *Gebildeten* (roughly translatable as "intellectuals") of the time. The latter, feeling themselves committed to the abstract rationality of the Enlightenment, rejected religion as something antiquated. Schleiermacher in contrast saw religion as a matter of the heart and attempted to foster a more deeply felt relationship to religious phenomena. Religion meant for him the act of "gazing at the universe" and "beholding the eternal with astonishment." At the same time he wanted, by awakening religious feeling, to heal the divisions of the age caused by its intellectual and political upheavals. Thus it was precisely the Enlightenment itself that would have need of religion. Only religion could lead to true human completeness. The re-publication of Schleiermacher's work could not have been more timely or more necessary, coming as it did after the triumphal rise of positivism in the nineteenth century. Around 1900 Protestant thinking in Germany was dominated by the school of Albrecht Benjamin Ritschl, who rejected all mystical leanings and especially Schleiermacher, whom he saw as a relic of romanticism.

In addition to all these achievements, it is worth mentioning Otto's preoccupation with India,[77] especially as evinced in his work *West-Östliche Mystik*, which first appeared in 1926.[78] This book primarily compares the Indian philosopher Shankara with the German mystic Meister Eckhart, but it also deals in detail with the nature of mysticism itself. Furthermore, something that is scarcely known about Rudolf Otto is that he was the first scholar of religion to acquaint himself directly with Zen Buddhism in Japan. There he not only met various Zen masters, but he also studied the practices taught in the Zen monasteries. This experience was reflected in his book *Aufsätze das Numinose betreffend* (Essays concerning the numinous).[79] Included in this book is the essay "Über Zazen als Extrem des numinosen Irrationalen" (On zazen as an extreme form of numinous irrationality), about which the Eranos lecturer Ernst Benz wrote, "This essay is at the present time [1962] the best that has been written about Zen."[80] Also of great significance is Otto's short preface to an early anthology of Zen Buddhist texts, where he dares to write sentences such as: "There matter disappears and the movement of the spirit becomes all. There duality disappears and multiplicity merges into the indefinable unity in an almost sensually perceptible manner. There 'mountain and water' flow together … There *samsara* itself becomes *nirvana*."[81] From the 1920s, Otto was in contact with the Japanese Zen scholar D.T. Suzuki, also later to be a lecturer at Eranos.

However, although Otto occupied himself intensively with foreign religions, translated Sanskrit texts, and even founded the Interreligious League of Mankind, he was never in favor of a syncretic religion with interchangeable parts from different traditions. Quite the contrary, his aim was to sift out the differences between religions, including the fine nuances. In his essay *"Universalreligion?"* Otto writes, "What is desirable is neither a mixing and mingling nor a smoothing, neutralizing and artificial equalizing. What is called for in our present situation is not a process of 'universalizing' but rather of individualizing and concretizing."[82] Something to which he attached particular importance, and which he regarded as essential in Christian missionary work, was precise knowledge of the religious beliefs one was dealing with, so that one could be clear about where both sides, Christian and non-Christian, stood doctrinally.

Another thing to which Otto attached central importance, and which we find again at Eranos, was the significance of "salvation." Understanding and existential awareness were not to be pursued for purely intellectual reasons but because they made possible salvation in this world and from this world. Otto himself saw this as being something decidedly irrational, although the reduction of his teaching to a form of "irrationalism" is far too simplistic. This accusation is also likely to be the main reason for the silence that has long surrounded him. Although Paul Tillich, Joachim Wach, and also Mircea Eliade held his banner high, that does not seem to have sufficed. The times are not favorable for his phenomenology. However, Gregory Alles has recently translated important essays and autobiographical sketches of his into English, and thereby renewed a certain interest.[83]

A point that is relevant here, although it has hitherto received insufficient attention in the biographies of Otto, is his contact with the Theosophical Society of Helena P. Blavatsky. As we have already seen, Fröbe was also in touch with various representatives of this organization. Rudolf Otto, for his part, mingled fairly regularly with the circle of people around Wilhelm Hübbe-Schleiden, who was a central figure in German Theosophy and editor of the long-standing occult periodical *Sphinx*, a showpiece of its kind.[84] Otto "diligently" borrowed books from Hübbe-Schleiden's library, as the two men were almost next-door neighbors in Göttingen.[85] His brother-in-law Ernst Ottmer must also have played a role in mediating Otto's contacts with Theosophy. Furthermore, there exists a photograph, taken on Otto's trip to India, in which he is seen together with the second president of the Theosophical Society, Annie Besant. He even appears to have known Krishnamurti.

The question of how far this contact with Theosophy really went has not yet been researched. Another movement with which Otto was more closely preoccupied was the so-called Oxford Group, founded in 1921 by Frank Buchman, out of which the world-wide organization Moral Re-Armament emerged in 1938. He speaks of it in a letter to Fröbe dated 19 June 1933. Otto also read literature on parapsychology and spiritualism, which she lent to him. For example, in some of his communications with her he mentions the names of Podmore and Myers, that is to say Frank Podmore, author of historic works on mesmerism and spiritualism, and Frederic W.H. Myers, whose colossal work *Human Personality and its Survival of Bodily Death* had appeared in 1903 and achieved wide renown. Otto also knew the English mystical writer Evelyn Stuart Moore, for in a letter of 12 January 1935, he recommends that Fröbe visit her in London.

⁊ 5. The First Eranos Meeting: An Idea Comes to Life

The first Eranos meeting to be named as such took place in August 1933 with more than two hundred participants.[1] However, there was at this point no clear break with Olga Fröbe's earlier meetings, for she herself did not regard the "Eranos period" as having begun precisely in 1933. It was only over the next few years that the meetings took on a more clearly academic character, a development that I would ascribe to the influence of Jung, to whom everything "theosophical" was suspect.[2] Altogether the meeting lasted about two weeks. Originally it was planned that three extra days at the end would be reserved for concluding discussions among the speakers.[3] The month of August was kept for all the subsequent meetings.

Usually a speaker talked, with intermissions, for the whole morning. In the breaks a glass of champagne was given to the lecturers, while the members of the audience strolled about in front of the house, hoping to speak with one or other of the celebrities. A gong signaled the end of the intermission. Questions from the audience were strictly forbidden.[4] There were lectures in three different languages—English, French, and German—and the audience was expected to understand the speaker without any interpretation.[5] Usually the lecturers spoke in their mother tongue. The official program ended for the audience at about midday, and most of them walked or drove back into Ascona. The lecturers and a few of Fröbe's special guests then sat down to lunch at the celebrated round table.

I have already explained how the theme of "Yoga and Meditation in East and West" was chosen for the first conference. Heinrich Zimmer opened the round of talks with an address on "The Meaning of Indian Tantric Yoga," a theme that was still very exotic at that time. Despite his initial enthusiasm, Zimmer's assessment of the Eranos atmosphere must have been ambivalent, although he came again repeatedly as a lecturer. As Maggy Anthony reports,[6] he wrote to his colleague F.M. Cornford of Oxford University, advising him not to attend Eranos: "Don't go to Ascona. The föhn [a warm, dry alpine wind] blows all the time and the place is full of women with transferences."[7] On the other hand, Eranos must have been intellectually of great significance for Heinrich Zimmer, if only because he always met C.G. Jung there. As he writes in his autobiography "Notizen zu einem Lebenslauf":

> The fact that this unique human being, with his towering strength, entered my world was [as I see it] one of the greatest blessings in my spiritual life, indeed for my whole existence on earth—one of those gifts which life brings us and which we cannot contrive or petition for, but which flow down to us like a mysterious recompense from a benign providence.[8]

Jung's "mere presence stimulates discussion and causes one's thoughts to soar." At breakfast time, when Zimmer always sat close to Jung, the whole room was said to have echoed with Jung's loud, resounding laughter.[9]

Heinrich Zimmer was the son of a university professor, also called Heinrich, who was an expert on the Celts and the Indo-European heritage. In particular, the culture of ancient India was a subject that he had studied intensively.[10] Thus, from his early childhood onwards the young Heinrich grew up in an atmosphere of great learning.[11]

On the other hand, it was to his mother and grandmother that he attributed his predilection for mysticism, myth, and symbol. Tragically, when Heinrich Zimmer was twenty, his father committed suicide.[12] Zimmer's studies in Berlin embraced art history, Germanic philology, and Sanskrit. However, "German studies lost all appeal for me at that time because they were geared to the mass-production of future schoolteachers and because of the over-emphasis on problems of secondary importance."[13] After immersing himself in the study of Nietzsche and the Chinese language, he entered the army in 1914, receiving the rank of lieutenant. He experienced the war at the front and returned with the Iron Cross. Part of his service may have involved secret intelligence work, possibly connected with India on account of his special linguistic knowledge. The collapse of the German Empire and the subsequent Communist agitations made no deep impression on Zimmer, who described himself as a "decidedly non-political, not to say anti-social, type." For years he worked away at "boring manuscripts" of Buddhist provenance, until the moment when he came across John Woodroffe, alias Arthur Avalon, and his massive works of translation and commentary,[14] opening up the treasure house of the Tantric tradition.[15] Zimmer was immediately captivated. Avalon represented for him the opposite of what his teachers were doing, bound as they were "to the logic of scientific positivism" without having "any inner connection to the real content of the material." Zimmer, however, wanted to re-formulate the Eastern wisdom "so that it could be understood in terms of our own experience and way of thinking."[16] For him this meant "a process of mutual transmutation and adaptation," since "spiritual nourishment, when it is assimilated, also assimilates the person who has received it. It forms and changes his substance."[17]

For Zimmer this was "the only possible approach to the heritage of esoteric wisdom and philosophy, contrasting with the critical, skeptical attitude of modern thought, as represented by Descartes, Hume, or Kant, which begins with total doubt, proceeds by careful criticism and remains confined to the realm of the intellect." The real task, as he saw it, was to find "a legitimate way of connecting the esoteric message from afar with our own nature and tradition. At the same time one must be careful to avoid … the sterile dissecting and embalming methods of scientific philosophy with its purely intellectual approach."[18] Zimmer acknowledged that, in developing this approach, he owed much to the work of Johann Jakob Bachofen and his theory of "mother right." Bachofen had given Zimmer a valuable key to the understanding of symbols and myths.

This attitude was also what lay behind Zimmer's interest in Tantrism and in Jung's depth psychology, both of which stimulate us to self-transformation through the creative imagination and demand that we seek the "gods" within ourselves and not outside.[19] In his first Eranos lecture, "Zur Bedeutung des indischen Tantra Yoga"[20] (On the meaning of Indian Tantra yoga), Zimmer said:

> Whoever worships the gods no longer in winds and rocks, in springs and stars, but in the only place where he can experience them directly, namely in his own body, will find that, as with the yogi, the reality of his body will become reality pure and simple. He will discover that this reality contains everything and that all external phenomena are only a reflection of his own being.

In the same lecture he speaks in a similar vein about depth psychology: "The achieve-ment of modern depth psychology is to reveal, in a form that is appropriate for our own age, that which is timeless within us, so that we can grasp it and live by it."[21] And, in a tone of skepticism towards the Judeo-Christian tradition, he says, "In contrast to Job, who cried out to Jehovah, 'What is a man, that you consider him great?', the Indian, through the annihilation of his ego, makes himself equal to God, transcends God and finds peace in the recognition of his own self as Brahman."[22]

His inner standpoint evinced a certain similarity to the integral tradition of René Guénon. It is therefore not surprising that he entered into contact with Guénon's fol-lower, the art historian and scholar of religion Ananda Coomaraswamy, whose profound and sympathetic interpretation of Indian spirituality was a constant inspiration to him. Thus, in an undated letter to Coomaraswamy, preserved in the Princeton collection, he wrote, "I need not say how much it means to me to have met you personally. Your inspir-ing way of dealing with Hindu art and religion has, since I became a student, been one of the main elements of my initiation into this revelation of truth."[23] Coomaraswamy also helped Zimmer during the latter's exile in the United States.

Zimmer's attitude to more clearly esoteric questions was also anything but negative.[24] It was not only that he later preoccupied himself with the Tarot cards and the myth of King Arthur, but in the 1920s and 1930s he enjoyed a close friendship with Alexander von Bernus. Both a poet and a practicing alchemist, von Bernus kept a well-equipped laboratory in his castle of Donaumünster. His two books on alchemy are still considered classics and are highly regarded even by specialists.[25]

After Zimmer's marriage the friendship continued, and the Zimmers often visited Bernus together.[26] After Zimmer's early death, Bernus wrote a moving obituary to him in verse form.[27] Another of Bernus' friends was Rudolf Steiner, who often came with his wife to lunch with Bernus when the latter was living in the Munich district of Schwabing. Steiner also wrote articles for the journal *Das Reich*, edited by von Bernus, which appeared between 1916 and 1920 and to which Emil Preetorius and Max Pulver also contributed—both of them later to be speakers at Eranos.[28] Bernus had the aim—enthu-siastically applauded by Steiner—of using the periodical to bring anthroposophical and alchemical ideas (e.g. the work of Jollivet-Castelot) into the world of literature. Bernus, who was later to describe the universities as bastions of materialistic thinking and teach-ing, had already begun as a young man to gather around him a group of artists, esoteri-cists, and literati at his residence, Stift Neuburg near Heidelberg.[29] His milieu included Rainer Maria Rilke, Thomas Mann, Elke Lasker-Schüler (who also published articles in *Das Reich*), and members of the Stefan George circle.[30] At Stift Neuburg, Bernus also dedicated himself to the production of medicines, using spagyric alchemy and astrology. Here he also organized lectures and readings. In general he was rather skeptical towards academics, with certain exceptions such as Heinrich Zimmer and Edgar Dacqué, a critic of the Darwinist theory of evolution, who was influential at the time but is now almost totally forgotten.[31] Zimmer was also in contact, if only by correspondence, with one of the greatest poets of the twentieth century, namely Gottfried Benn, who greatly valued Zimmer's studies on India.[32] Referring to his essay "Goethe und die Naturwissenschaften" (Goethe and the natural sciences),[33] Benn even says in a letter to Zimmer of 29 March 1932, "In spirit it was a sort of dedication to you and by way of thanks for your great understanding of certain things that are accessible only to a few."[34] On the other hand, in a letter of 1 September 1935 to F.W. Oelze,[35] Benn writes rather dismissively about

Zimmer, "Is always sending things, writes and talks a lot[36] and, despite good work, he gives the impression of being a small man. However, he does perceive and understand connections. A connecting type." Heinrich Zimmer mentions Gottfried Benn only once, comparing him to T.S. Eliot (whom he mistakenly calls G.T. Elliott).[37]

It is also interesting to look at the list of the other speakers at this first meeting. Besides C.G. Jung, these included Caroline Rhys Davids, president of the Pali Text Society, and Erwin Rousselle, who had already taken part the previous year in the so-called summer school. Erwin Rousselle's son-in-law Walter Haug, a professor of medieval history and himself an Eranos speaker in later years, wrote that Rousselle "was able to a greater extent than anyone else to satisfy Olga Fröbe-Kapteyn's demand that academic research should be united with personal experience in the sense of mental and spiritual renewal." After all, Rousselle was both an academic and an esotericist.[38] At any rate, in 1933 Rousselle gave a rich lecture on "Seelische Führung im lebendigen Taoismus" (Soul guidance in living Taoism). Rousselle had completed dissertations in the fields of Hebrew studies[39] and law and had studied a vast range of languages (Arabic, Turkish, Hebrew, Chinese, Syrian, Persian, Tibetan, Manchurian). Then, influenced by his work at Hermann Keyserling's School of Wisdom and by a lengthy stay in China, he had devoted himself fully to the study of the Chinese mind. At the University of Beijing he became professor of German philosophy. Through Richard Wilhelm's mediation he was then initiated into a Taoist esoteric society and went through all the grades.[40] In 1930 Rousselle succeeded Richard Wilhelm as director of the China Institute in Frankfurt. In 1940 he lost his university teaching post because of political unreliability, and in 1942 his position at the China Institute was also taken away.[41] In January 1943 he was permanently forbidden by the Nazi Gauleiter to speak in public.

Equally anti-Nazi in his outlook was the theologian and scholar of religion Friedrich Heiler, who also spoke at Eranos in 1933.[42] As he was closely involved in a declaration by the Marburg theologians against the so-called *Arierparagraph* (Nazi racial regulation against Jewish people), he was threatened with removal from the Marburg theological faculty. This was, however, avoided through the intervention of Marburg colleagues who spoke in his favor, and instead he was merely transferred to another faculty within the Philips University.[43] Nevertheless, he was badly affected mentally and physically.[44] Thus, his wife Anne Marie writes, in a letter of 22 February 1934,[45] of her husband's "increasingly weak heart" and declares, "These nervous complaints are not due to the pressures of lecturing and university work but have their cause in a 'wider sphere.'" Later she added, "More could be said, but one prefers to remain silent. Our newspapers do the same." When Olga Fröbe asked if Heiler would object to staying in her house with the pro-Nazi Jakob Hauer, Anne Marie Heiler replied that this would not present a problem: "Despite their differences of opinion the two have always understood each other quite well and will continue to do so, even though the gap between their points of view is perhaps now even wider."

As already mentioned, during her visit to Marburg, where she met Rudolf Otto, Olga Fröbe also visited Friedrich Heiler, whom Erwin Rousselle had recommended as a practical expert on Christian mysticism. The direct contact was arranged by Privy Councillor Pallat of the Central Institute for Education and Teaching in Berlin, whom she had known since her Berlin days. In a letter to Heiler of 3 November 1932, Pallat speaks of his high regard for Fröbe "as spiritually developed person and a genteel and friendly personality" who had actively helped his Institute during difficult times. It is striking that he uses the expression "spiritually developed" (*geistig hochstehend*), which is used in Theosophical

and esoteric circles to this day to denote someone who is strongly preoccupied with esoteric philosophy and who had reached a somewhat "higher level of human development."

After Heiler had basically agreed to participate in Eranos, Fröbe asked him whether
he would be willing to take over the lectures on contemplation in Christian mysticism,
which were originally supposed to be given by Jean Baruzi. In her letter she then adds
another request, which clearly shows the continuity from the earlier meetings before the
name Eranos was adopted:

> Then I have a further request: if you would agree, it would be very nice if you could
> organize some spiritual exercises for a small group from the audience. As the whole
> conference only deals with the subject of contemplation on a theoretical level, this
> would be very enriching for those who wish to engage in some real practices. And
> ultimately that is the point of the whole thing … I personally would be very pleased
> if you were to do this, as I have been engaged in meditational practices for many
> years. This is the source from which all my drawings have sprung.

Heiler wrote back by return of post on 30 May 1933, giving his consent to both requests.
Regarding the "spiritual exercises" he wrote: "The exercises would be based on the mystical path of salvation in its entirety (via purgativa, illuminativa, unitiva, activa)."

Confirmation of these exercises, which have hitherto not been publicly known about,
is found in a letter of 26 September 1933 from Rudolf Otto to his colleague in religious
studies, Birger Forell, which is preserved in the Marburg University Library.[46] Otto writes,
"The conference in Ascona is said to have been brilliant. Heiler carried out his spiritual
exercises there, whether in bishop's regalia I don't know, but I hope so. Rousselle assisted
as officiant. It must have been inspiring, and my hairs stand on end. But they usually do
that anyway." Otto had already written on 15 June 1933 to his colleague Jakob Wilhelm
Hauer, announcing, "Heiler intends to come, hold 3 lectures about Christian mysticism
and add some spiritual exercises for a somewhat smaller circle."

Annemarie Schimmel, undoubtedly the most important German scholar of the esoteric parts of Islam and later to be a speaker at Eranos, described Heiler as a "really deeply
pious person" in his personal life, who every Sunday celebrated Martin Luther's German
Mass in the small chapel in his house.[47] Annemarie Schimmel had worked closely with
Heiler, under whose supervision she gained her doctorate in theology—the first ever to
be awarded to a woman in this faculty.

Olga Fröbe seems to have got on particularly well with Friedrich Heiler. During the
conferences she invited him into the house as her personal guest and in one letter to him
used the salutation "Dear Professor Krishna," an allusion to Heiler's interest in oriental spirituality. For his *Habilitation* (a German post-doctoral degree without which it is
impossible to teach at universities), Heiler had written a text entitled *Die buddhistische
Versenkung* (Buddhist meditation) as a supplementary work to his extensive doctoral
dissertation.[48] The *Habilitation* amounted to a comparison between Christianity and
Buddhism which, however, came down clearly on the side of Christianity.

Heiler provoked some controversy by standing up for an Indian sadhu who had converted to Christianity in his youth but later attracted some adverse talk on account of
his garrulous and inventive stories about his life.[49] In the same context belongs Heiler's
interest—indeed probably belief—in an allegedly three-hundred-year-old maharishi
from the Kailash mountain.[50] What must have particularly impressed Heiler was that
this maharishi was also said to have been a Christian.

Heiler was also in contact with the influential occultist Arnoldo Krumm-Heller, who spent the last years of his life in Heiler's home town of Marburg. Krumm-Heller was the founder of the Fraternitas Rosicruciana Antiqua, belonged to the Ordo Templi Orientis (OTO), famous for its sexual magic practices, and knew its leader Theodor Reuss as well as Aleister Crowley and others. He was also patriarch of the Gnostic Catholic Church, which is connected with the OTO.[51]

Heiler also wrote for the journal *Zeitschrift für Buddhismus*, and he was a leading exponent of religious phenomenology, which strongly informed the Eranos meetings. This approach gave particular emphasis to empathy, that is to say one's felt perception of what religion is, and attached less importance to its historical or sociological dimensions. Heiler was someone who worked to promote an ecumenical approach to the world's religions.[52]

Another speaker at the first meeting who had set himself against the prevailing *Zeitgeist* was Ernesto Buonaiuti. A friend of Rudolf Otto and Friedrich Heiler, he exerted a fascination on his audience through his lively and personal way of lecturing. The philosopher and theologian Ernst Benz, who was himself to lecture several times at Eranos, even said that Buonaiuti was "the first real Christian I have met in my life."[53] Buonaiuti had been excommunicated by the Vatican because of "modernistic" aberrations. He was suspected of being the author of a theologically radical manifesto entitled *Programma dei modernisti* (Program of the modernists) and of an even bolder document called *Lettere di un prete modernista* (Letters from a modernist priest). These suspicions were not unjustified because much later Buonaiuti acknowledged the authorship, although it appears that others had collaborated in writing the *Programma dei modernisti*.

It is debatable whether the term "modernist" is appropriate here, because Buonaiuti's reformist ideas were based on a return to the original roots of Christianity.[54] Thus Buonaiuti called himself more of an "archaist" than a "modernist," although he fought in the modernist ranks and found recognition there. He was not a modernist in the sense of promoting a rationalistic, de-mythologizing approach, as many others did, but rather in the sense of Joachim of Fiore and the Franciscan spiritual reformers,[55] who demanded a spiritual and charismatic renewal of the Church, an *ecclesia spiritualis*.[56] Buonaiuti argued that according to Joachim of Fiore "contemplation and joy" held "a more effective power of salvation" than did "discipline and clerical profession."[57] Buonaiuti's ideal was a charismatic living together of the Christian community, the so-called "vita associata," resting on a brotherly love that would demolish all barriers, with the Catholic Eucharist manifesting the actual presence of Christ. In his spiritual testament, composed shortly before his death, Buonaiuti wrote, "One single ideal has ruled my life from beginning to end: to re-validate the original values of Christianity."[58]

In 1933 Julius Evola, the Italian cultural philosopher and crusader against the "decadence of modernity," wrote an essay in which he attacked Buonaiuti's endeavors, seeing in them "Communist" tendencies directed against the Roman Church's strictly hierarchical system, which had always given the Church order and stability.[59] Evola argued that, instead of perceiving religion as a spiritual striving for transcendence, Buonaiuti saw it as a primarily "social" phenomenon. Evola also accused Buonaiuti of posing as a martyr in order to attract young people as well as elderly women.

One of the works that clearly influenced Buonaiuti was Rudolf Otto's *The Holy*, which he translated into Italian and published in 1926. The Fascist minister of education, under ties of obligation to the Vatican through the Lateran Treaty, advised Buonaiuti to give up his state teaching post, although it was not in fact under ecclesiastical jurisdiction.

Buonaiuti thus became a kind of football between the church and the government. The church did not want to accept his teaching position, even though it was a purely secular one, while the Fascist regime was always bringing the case up when it wished to bring pressure on the church. Buonaiuti finally solved the dilemma himself in 1931 by refusing to take the oath of loyalty to the Fascist state that was required of all university professors. After that he could only teach from his private residence.[60] There, however, he gathered around him a community of students, including Ernst Benz, who had a "deeply felt veneration for their master."

Even the journal *Religio*, which he ran, was no longer allowed to appear, and when he was offered a professorship in the *Protestant* theological faculty at Lausanne, his passport was taken away in July 1939. Interestingly, Mussolini himself ordered that the passport be returned so that Buonaiuti could give lectures and other presentations abroad.[61]

A few words still need to be said about the obvious question of why Buonaiuti, as a Catholic, should have been appointed to a Protestant faculty. Already at an earlier date Pastor Franco Panza, head of the Italian Protestant community in Lausanne, had invited him to lecture to the faculty. Buonaiuti received altogether a more sympathetic hearing among Protestants—such as Heiler, Otto, or Benz—than among Catholics. It was even suggested to him that he should convert to Protestantism, but this he vehemently rejected, as he continued to regard himself as a Catholic priest, despite the interdict of the Church. At that time there appears to have existed an "unofficial" collaboration between Catholic "modernists," Protestants, and Masonic circles. Pastor Franco Panza, for example, was a Freemason, as was the skeptical philosopher Giuseppe Rensi, one of Buonaiuti's closest friends.[62]

The Vatican's interdict survived the end of Fascism, and Buonaiuti did not live to see the belated recognition that came to him with the pontificate of John XXIII who, in his *aggiornamento* (bringing up to date) saw eye to eye with Buonaiuti on many issues. It is an interesting fact that Angelo Roncalli—later John XXIII—and Buonaiuti were fellow students at the theological seminary in Rome, where they were destined not only to be table companions but also to share walks together. Buonaiuti even assisted Roncalli at the latter's ordination as priest.[63]

There exists a highly interesting account of this interaction, written by Giulio Andreotti, who was seven times prime minister of Italy, participated in thirty-three different governments, and was undoubtedly the most prominent symbol of the alleged collaboration between the Mafia, the Catholic Church, and successive Italian governments. In his book *I quattro del Gesu* (Four for Jesus),[64] he tells the story of four young seminarians in Rome who, as close friends, share a wish to shape a new future for the Catholic Church. The four in question were Angelo Roncalli, the future Pope John XXIII, who did in fact steer the church in a new direction through the Second Vatican Council; Ernesto Buonaiuti; Giulio Belvedere, uncle of Andreotti's wife; and finally Alfonso Manaresi, later a teacher of church history, who got into difficulties with the church because of his modernist views and decided against taking holy orders.

As a curiosity I want to point out that probably the fiercest of Italian anti-Semites during the Fascist period, namely Giovanni Preziosi, originally also belonged to those "modernist" priests and was even defrocked because of his association with Buonaiuti. It also seems that it was Preziosi who greatly influenced Julius Evola's ideas of a world-wide "Jewish and Masonic" conspiracy. They happened to be associated on several important occasions.[65]

Buonaiuti was also interested in Gnosis and the ancient mystery cults. He was convinced that one could only understand the original Christianity if one had some conception of the Gnostic teaching.[66]

It was not only Ernst Benz who was captivated by Buonaiuti but also Mircea Eliade. In an article in the Romanian journal *Cuvântul* of 29 May 1928, Eliade wrote enthusiastically, "I have never before experienced such a Christian atmosphere and with such a feeling of joy. Nor have I ever felt the Christian belief so close at hand, so vital, so authentic and so fruitful."[67] And in his *Italian Diary* (1927–28), he goes so far as to describe Buonaiuti as "the religious mind in Italy most glowing with enthusiasm."[68]

Buonaiuti had come to Eranos on Olga Fröbe's invitation, probably prompted originally by Friedrich Heiler or Rudolf Otto. As Buonaiuti was at that time forbidden to lecture and had hardly any possibility to present his ideas to the public, he was overjoyed to receive the invitation. Nevertheless in his autobiography—from which Ernst Benz translated selected passages referring to Eranos[69]—he writes, "I did not, however, feel any particular sense of spiritual kinship in the Eranos milieu. From all quarters it brought together experts on psychoanalysis and on esoteric philosophies as well as adherents of the boldest forms of free religious criticism. Furthermore it was marked by the unrestricted dominance of C.G. Jung, the famous psychoanalyst of Zurich." Buonaiuti then continues, "Thus I was lecturing in an entirely secular milieu, to an audience in which there was perhaps a certain undercurrent of distrust and antipathy towards anything that smacked of normal Christianity." Ernst Benz, however, believed that this complaint was a "literary overstatement," since Buonaiuti after all spoke every year at Eranos from 1933 to 1940 and undoubtedly had a circle of friends there.

Remembering that 1933 was the year in which Hitler came to power in Germany, it is noteworthy that a large majority of the speakers had no sympathy at all for the Nazi movement. On the other hand it is difficult to judge how much justification there was in Olga Fröbe's repeated declarations that Eranos was gradually becoming a countervailing force against National Socialism. Here it is worth quoting the philosopher of religion Alfons Rosenberg, who lived in exile in Switzerland during the Nazi period and who, as already mentioned, always maintained the closest contacts to Fröbe and Eranos, as for many years he lived a reclusive existence close by at Monte Brè sopra Locarno. Rosenberg wrote, "It is a measure of Olga Fröbe's courage … that she … came forward with the Eranos project precisely in the fateful year 1933. For, intentionally or unintentionally, Eranos was an answer to the polluters of the spirit."[70]

This statement needs to be qualified somewhat, as we shall see later on, as Fröbe had to make compromises with the National Socialist regime in order to secure the participation of German professors at Eranos.

However, in view of the already mentioned accusations that Fröbe and Eranos in general were in some sort of rapport with National Socialism, I shall try, as far as possible, to always probe more deeply into any such instances of suspicion. Basically it was her wish that the meetings should be kept free from the political issues of the day.

There was, however, one speaker at this first meeting who belonged, at least *prima facie*, to a milieu sympathetic to Nazism, namely the doctor and psychologist Gustav-Richard Heyer.[71] Stemming from an old Prussian family of foresters and civil servants, Heyer was born in Bad Kreuznach on the Rhine in 1890. His maternal grandfather was a deputy in the German Reichstag. Edgar Salin describes the home in Potsdam, where the family later settled, as "little different from those of other members of the Potsdam civil servant class, with their stifling atmosphere of comfortable respectability and dismal boredom."[72] After completing his schooling at a humanistic *Gymnasium*, Heyer studied first forestry and then medicine, qualifying as a doctor in 1918. Despite interruptions for military service, he was able to accelerate the completion of his studies, using periods of injury leave. For his war service he was awarded the Iron Cross, Second Class.

Heyer, together with his younger brother Wolfgang, soon came into contact with Stefan George and Friedrich Gundolf. In particular, he often frequented the circle in Heidelberg where Gundolf held his impressive readings from works of the Romantic period[73] and where the two brothers "highlighted the detrimental and anti-life nature of modern science ... coming up repeatedly with new examples from the natural sciences."[74] Salin gives an interesting description of Heyer from this period:

> Despite his genuinely passionate mind and his unbridled and often excessive dis-
> plays of temperament, Heyer remained, in the words of the Master [Stefan George],
> rooted in the soil from which he came; having been first a forester and then a doc-
> tor, he never entirely lost the somewhat abrasive manner, arrogant tone and false
> 'patriotism' characteristic of the type that George found so irritating, namely the
> Prussian official.[75]

Heyer was always "visibly outraged" when Gundolf's pupils met the famous sociologist Max Weber, and the latter, in a totally prosaic fashion, was unable or unwilling to interpret any art form in other than purely rational terms. During a visit together to Rome, for example, there was a discussion of the "spirit of the Gothic," which Gundolf explained beautifully. Max Weber, who was himself of a highly excitable nature and who did not appreciate the aristocratic attitude of George and his followers, replied that the emergence of the Gothic had nothing to do with a particular spirit, but "was nothing more than the result of a technical solution to the technical problem of building a vaulted structure." This drew loud cries of protest from Heyer.[76]

Gustav Heyer began his medical career as assistant doctor in the Second University Medical Clinic in Munich, where he began—unusually for that era—to treat patients suffering from functional circulatory disorders, digestive problems, and so on, not with drugs but with psychological methods, at first using hypnosis.[77] Although the results were good they could not be published in the reports of the clinic on account of their "unscientific" character. For the same reason he was unable to proceed to his *Habilitation* degree.[78] However, soon afterwards Heyer abandoned hypnotic treatment and began to preoccupy himself with the depth psychology methods of Freud, Adler, and Jung.[79] From 1925 he ran a private practice in Munich, especially for nervous disorders, but he also brought out editions of various books that had influenced him significantly.[80] Thus, for example, in 1927 his edition of Oskar Kohnstamm's *Erscheinungsformen der Seele* appeared, with a contribution by Karl Wolfskehl, a leading member of the George circle, about his memories of Kohnstamm. Wolfskehl and Heyer knew each other well.[81]

In Munich around 1930 Heyer gathered around him a psychological study circle. The lectures for doctors and students took place at first in his private apartment and then in the university, thanks to the help of, among others, the famous surgeon Ferdinand Sauerbruch, who allowed Heyer the use of his auditorium between 8 and 10 p.m. after the end of the day's lectures, as Heyer's teachings were officially frowned upon.[82] He jokingly dubbed this group the "Amazon Circle," as women were in the majority. Heyer, like Jung, was undoubtedly a man who, by virtue of his preoccupation with "the soul," had the propensity to attract the female sex. Women were grateful for his understanding of psychological processes, however deficient it may have been in practical terms.[83] By the standards of that time, the classes were carried out in a very informal way. His medical colleague Ernst Speer, who also underlined Heyer's talents as a speaker and presenter, was convinced, after his first experience of this circle, that "I had found my way into a group of Bohemians" and he went on to cite the chairman of a local association who characterized Heyer as "a real Gypsy."[84] In his concluding sentence, however, he says, "My gratitude is also the gratitude of the medical psychotherapeutic profession in Germany, which owes a limitless amount to Heyer's life work."[85] The psychoanalyst Werner Kemper makes the comment that Heyer's opponents "wanted to dismiss him as an emotionally uncontrolled and muddle-headed individual, an illusionist, a 'Pied Piper of Hamlyn' ... someone who, into his old age, remained a lively and hectic person."[86]

Part of the work from Heyer's Munich years was published in the two-volume work *Reich der Seele*.[87] Besides essays by Heyer and his wife Lucy, whom he married in 1918, this work contains an essay by Heinrich Zimmer and another by Sigrid Strauß-Klöbe, who later also spoke at Eranos. The spectrum of themes ranges from philosophy and Greek mythology to the Indian doctrine of the "guiding of souls." This study group was eventually dissolved as part of the centralizing policy of National Socialism and was absorbed into the German Institute for Psychological Research and Psychotherapy in Berlin, where Heyer worked as a head of department from 1939 to 1944.[88] This was an important position, which demanded Party membership, as his daughter recalls. She also emphasizes that her father was anything but subservient to the regime. Heyer had already joined the National Socialist German Workers' Party (NSDAP) in 1937 but only, according to his second wife, Zoe, after long deliberation.[89] Nevertheless, he spoke at Eranos again in 1938. There is unfortunately no original documentary evidence on these matters, as all of Gustav Heyer's papers were destroyed in a bombardment of Berlin. Cocks, who certainly has investigated these questions most thoroughly, describes Heyer's decision to join the Nazi Party as "a mixture of opportunism, a certain degree of ideological approval and an altruistic desire to apply the values embedded in psychotherapy."[90] The professor of history Geoffrey Cocks, however, also cites several of Heyer's colleagues who describe him as a constant supporter of the regime. He is said to have worn his Party badge with pride, although this is denied by his second wife, who was known for her anti-Nazi attitude. He is also reported to have worn a uniform frequently. His daughter Viviane, however, interprets this observation in a totally different way.[91] Heyer explained to her that he was able to establish better contact with the soldiers in the military hospital if he appeared as one of them and not as a civilian. The fact that he appeared in uniform in the morning after a night shift was of course natural.

Both of his wives rejected the accusation that Heyer was a racist.[92] However, the fact is that with the further duration of the regime he increasingly deleted positive references to Jewish authors such as Freud and Adler.[93] This may in fact have been a prerequisite for publication. In this connection, Cocks underlines particularly the relative changes and progressively tighter wording in the successive editions of Heyer's book *Der Organismus der Seele* between 1932 and 1937.[94]

In his 1944 memoir, Heyer wrote that his path had led him "over the years—and long before the turning point [the Nazi revolution] to reject the old system of the Jewish analysts. I left no doubt about this in my work and often defended my position at the congresses, which at that time were pervaded by the Jewish influence."[95] On the other hand, the head of the Charité in Berlin, Max de Crinis, in writing about the Reichsinstitut für Psychologische Forschung (Reich Institute for Psychological Research), where Heyer worked, said that it had "unfortunately not abandoned the Jewish approach of Freudian psychoanalysis, and German psychiatry will soon find it necessary to act against these symptoms of decadence, which are cloaked in a national garb."[96] Today it is no longer possible to determine the truth of the matter, but it is not unlikely that Heyer pretended to be more anti-Jewish than he was, for what was at stake was his career path and his hoped-for appointment as professor.

In this connection it is worth relating one incident which, while not proving anything conclusive, is nevertheless emotionally revealing. The already mentioned *Festschrift* for the Eranos speaker David Miller includes a charming snapshot in which Jung's Jewish colleague Jolande Jacobi is leaning out of a window towards Gustav Heyer, and both have very happy and expectant expressions.[97]

Regine Lockot, probably the best-informed German expert on the history of depth psychology and psychotherapy at that time, takes the view that Heyer in the early years was "a convinced opponent of the National Socialists" and had even contemplated leaving Germany because of the Nazi regime, but had remained on the urging of C.G. Jung to improve the situation from within. Only later, she says, did he become more and more convinced by National Socialism.[98]

Jung's biographer Deirdre Bair even describes Heyer as a "double agent."[99] She maintains that this can be proved by archival material from Eranos that she had received from its then director, Jay Livernois. On the one hand, Bair says, Heyer had ostensibly supported National Socialist policy, but on the other hand he had helped Jung and others to smuggle money into Germany to assist Jewish doctors. This was apparently why he was invited to Eranos in 1938, although Olga Fröbe, as Bair writes, was "rabidly anti-Nazi." It is, of course, possible that Heyer thought and acted differently at various points in time.

At any rate, Heyer's colleague Käthe Bügler, who, being half-Jewish, "must have suffered quite badly under National Socialism,"[100] remained loyal to her former chief after the war and wrote a contribution entitled "Dem Freunde G.R. Heyer" (To my friend G.R. Heyer) for the *Festschrift* published to celebrate his sixty-fifth birthday. She had met him originally in 1923. Speaking of Heyer's work at the University Clinic in Munich, which was marked by struggles against resistance from scientific orthodoxy, she describes it as "pioneer work on the body of medicine." "As students in his ward we had the unique opportunity to really experience that the human being has to be seen and treated as a whole entity and not on the principle: here the illness, there the patient."[101] His colleague Wilhelm Bitter went even further and claimed that Heyer was even the true founder of the psychosomatic approach.[102]

In the foreword to the second edition of his work *Praktische Seelenheilkunde*, Heyer happily welcomed the above-mentioned integration of his Munich study group into the all-German Institute for Psychological Research and Psychotherapy. His words make clear the prevailing political and intellectual climate which surrounded him at that time (i.e. 1941):

> We need no better or more gratifying proof that the goals represented in this book are coming closer to realization. Just as we old soldiers of the World War are deeply moved by observing, how our armies are today reaping the harvest that we sowed, so we old campaigners for a spiritually and holistically based therapy can also still cooperate in achieving the victory of our ideas.[103]

From 1942 to 1944 Heyer practiced internal medicine as a volunteer in a Berlin military hospital.

After the war, because of his Nazi associations, Heyer was obliged to earn his living as an independent therapist and writer at Nussdorf am Inn, Bavaria, which at first proved very difficult. Fortunately, however, his works found a large readership, and when an opinion survey was carried out among medical specialists in the field, Heyer's significance for the practice of psychotherapy was rated higher than that of Jung and in third place after J.H. Schultz, the founder of autogenic training, and Sigmund Freud.[104] However, any real form of public recognition, such as a professorship, remained denied to him, even though various prominent people, above suspicion of Nazi sympathies, like Jean Gebser and Emil Preetorius, stood by him.[105]

In 1933 the political situation, seen from the Swiss perspective, was significantly different from the way it looked by, say, 1939. Quite apart from that, it cannot have been easy for Olga Fröbe to obtain interesting lecturers—after all, they were not paid—and she must often have been glad when well-wishing speakers invited their colleagues to come. Furthermore her main concern to begin with was less with the political attitudes of the lecturers than with the spiritual content of their teachings and researches. And in this respect Heyer fitted her concept very well. First of all, he had known her idol, C.G. Jung, for a long time and—probably during the course of the Eranos meetings—had come to be on intimate terms with him,[106] to the extent of using the familiar pronoun *Du*, something that happened rarely with Jung.[107] Second, his declared aim was to develop the purely rational form of psychotherapy into one informed by the living images of mythology.[108] Hence he writes in the foreword to his textbook *Praktische Seelenheilkunde*, "One cannot become a doctor who understands the mind if one cold-heartedly memorizes facts and data; rather it is the other way round—the initial work that such a doctor must carry out, is not on the object but rather on himself."[109]

As Heyer emphasized, what he was trying to do was to emulate "the old—for example, the pre-Socratic—philosophers, precisely because they wanted to integrate the irrational mysteries and powers of the world and humanity into their work."[110] Such a "synthesis of artistic vision and philosophical understanding … such as Carus possessed and Novalis sensed, attempted and promoted" is what we should again be striving for in the future.[111] However, "the eerie feeling of the magical world view" is not in itself enough. "In addition to belief and love we also need the insights of the rational mind." One could almost be inclined to take these sentences as a description of the goals of Eranos as a whole. After all, the purpose that Eranos had originally set itself was to be a mediator between antiquity and modernity as well as between science and spiritual knowledge. Subsequently Heyer continued to see himself as a mediator, as evidenced by his book *Vom Kraftfeld der Seele* (On the force field of the soul), published in 1949, in which he ventured to adopt a view embracing both depth psychology and modern physics in order to arrive at a unified whole.[112] Heyer was also the one who borrowed from physics the concept of the force field and incorporated it into psychology.

Heyer was also interested in problems that went beyond physics. For example, he frequented the home of the parapsychologist Albert von Schrenk-Notzing and was also acquainted with the equally well-known parapsychologist Traugott Konstantin Österreich.[113] In his work *Seelen-Räume* Heyer even speaks of how he improved the health of his bull terrier through magnetic hand strokes. He also writes of his conviction "that the human soul can occasionally be open to those worlds that are commonly called 'daemonic.'"[114] Again, in a letter to his medical colleague Lennemann of 6 May 1953, he writes, "There exist many credible reports (only they are withheld from the world of the universities) that testify to such clairvoyant experiences, sometimes occurring in dreams or daydreams, sometimes in spontaneous or artificially induced meditational states." And in another letter to the same colleague of 9 May 1951, he says, " You know of course that I am an old friend of homoeopathy."[115] Another person with whom he was well acquainted was Dr. Herbert Fritsche, the "magus," patriarch of the Crowleyan Gnostic-Catholic Church, and editor of the important esoteric journal *Merlin*.[116]

Jung undoubtedly had a high regard for Heyer up to 1941, as evidenced by his alleged remark: "If I were not Jung I would like to be Heyer."[117] Furthermore, Jung considered appointing Heyer as editor of his projected periodical *Weltanschauung* (to which we shall return later) on account of Heyer's "intuition" and his "aggressive temperament."[118] Reviewing Heyer's book *Der Organismus der Seele*, Jung became exceedingly positive in his praise: "I know of no book that, in such an informed, unprejudiced and unbiased way, has grasped the essential issues concerning the various therapeutic approaches of today."[119]

The opinions of the two men did not always coincide, and Jung was not sparing in his criticism (nor was he with other people) when Heyer behaved in some way that was not acceptable to him. This, however, did not lead to any breach in their basic mutual under-standing. As one example of such a controversy, I would like to quote a three-page letter from Jung of 4 December 1931, because it highlights a theme that is important both for Jung and for Eranos and constitutes a counterbalance to the simplistic criticism voiced by Richard Noll concerning Jung's alleged promotion of a mystic-pagan cult. At the time in question, Heyer had for the second time written a report on one of Jung's seminars.

Now Jung took Heyer to task for the fact that his report could easily give rise to a false picture among the "generally unprepared medical readership," and he continued:

Furthermore people will find in your report confirmation of the accusation of mysticism, which I know you wanted to avoid. However, you did not succeed in presenting the mystical aspect in such a way as to highlight the psychological side, which is for us of primary importance. At the same time the demonology of which I have also been accused is underlined by you through your allusion to [my] para-psychological experience ... Nowadays we must be very strict in guarding against a mingling of the parapsychological with the psychological aspect. While I certainly recognize the fact, I would never want my conception of the unconscious to be even remotely associated with parapsychology, for then the unconscious would take on a concretized form, making impossible the psychological approach that is so necessary for us. The same goes for so-called mysticism. I consider it much more important that we exercise psychological criticism towards this area of experi-ence—even if we have to put up with the accusation of being skeptics—rather than emphasizing mysticism and parapsychology in their concrete manifestations and thereby hampering the psychological approach. We must continue for quite a long time to stick to the territory of critical psychology if we want to avoid the danger of conjuring up a new Theosophy. One cannot be too careful to guard against the temptation to regard the manifestations of mysticism and parapsychology from the outside, which was the fallacy up to now. The whole thrust of analytical psychology is to open up the territory from inside, that is from within the soul, and it is only this method that can really reveal the meaning and value of this area of experience.

The familiarity between the two psychotherapists received its first dent when Heyer was obliged, apparently for political reasons connected with the Nazi regime, to speak out publicly against Jung. In a letter to Olga Fröbe of 19 September 1941, Jung wrote:

Heyer must have a bad conscience. H. has apparently had to disavow me. The article appeared recently in the *Journal for Psychiatric Neurology*. H. has not yet sent it to me; I heard about it through Prof. Staehelin in Basel. However, he seems to have treated me as mildly as possible. I am portrayed as an anglicized liberal, who naturally understands nothing about the new order.

The reason why Heyer did not send the article emerges from his letter to Jung of 24 September 1941, in which he writes:

As it is not permitted at present to do this privately, I have requested the publisher of the *Journal for Psychiatric Neurology*, at Marhold-Halle, to send you an off-print of my essay, in which, speaking from my German viewpoint and soul, I take issue with certain points in your book about religion and psychology. I would not like to think of this small essay being in your hands without the message that I would otherwise have added by hand: "This too in friendship, gratitude and admiration."

The letter is signed *Dein getreulicher* (your very true friend). Evidently Jung was right in supposing that Heyer was under political pressure. The fact that Heyer continued to have a positive attitude toward Jung is indirectly confirmed by a review of Heyer's book *Der Organismus der Seele* in the journal *Die Ärztin* (issue not mentioned), which the publisher, Lehmann, quoted when advertising the book in 1942. The reviewer writes, "Closely involved with C.G. Jung's typology and investigations of symbolism, Heyer has found the locus of his work at the point where the treatment of psychosomatic disorders merges with a psychology grounded in religion and ethics."[120] Jung only started to become seriously negative towards Heyer when he wrote to Fröbe on 27 May 1946, after the collapse of National Socialism. He mentioned in the letter that Heyer had been expelled from the Psychology Club and that he was no longer replying to Heyer's letters.[121] In addition he describes him as a "Nazi" and accuses him of gross opportunism.

Jung was replying to a letter that Fröbe had written to him on 19 May 1946, in which she said, "Also I have had a letter from Heyer, who is seeking contact once again as a friend and an Eranos friend. Here I have great doubts. How should one behave to a person who collaborated as opportunistically as he did? ... Of all my German friends only Lucy Heyer was quite unambiguous in her attitude towards Nazism." Lucy Heyer was the first wife of Gustav Heyer, by whom she had a son, Anselm. Viviane, the daughter of Gustav Heyer and his second wife Zoe, told me in a letter that it was Jung personally who had "very strongly advised" her mother to marry Heyer.[122] Lucy Heyer wanted to write the very first biography of Jung. She obtained Jung's agreement, and Paul Mellon wanted to finance the book. She started work in 1953 and inteviewed Jung once a week. Jung, however, was dissatisfied with the results and broke off the project.[123]

It is not altogether clear to what extent Jung wanted to cover himself by this negative attitude towards Heyer in order to avoid attracting further political gossip. That would certainly have been understandable, as his reputation would undoubtedly have suffered if he had continued to have a *Du* friendship with a known ex-Nazi. Gustav Heyer's daughter recalls that, in answer to the frequently asked question why the break with Jung had taken place, her father repeatedly replied that their views had diverged too widely. He, Heyer, was primarily concerned with the future, that is, the goal, of the patient, whereas Jung concentrated on the past.[124] Jung furthermore had little interest in art, whereas Heyer was deeply preoccupied with literature (Rilke, Mallarmé, Ernst Jünger) as well as with music and painting (Franz Marc, Paul Klee) and tried to create an interaction between depth psychology and art.[125] At any rate, Jung and Heyer did not meet any more after the Second World War.

Barbara Hannah reports having been told by a certain Dr. Gerda Bertram of Bremen that this rupture had become very painful for Heyer towards the end of his life.[126] Nevertheless, it was Heyer who wrote the extensive entry on complex psychology (i.e. on Jung) in the five-volume *Handbuch der Neurosenlehre und Psychotherapie*, edited by Viktor Frankl *et al.*

Despite their different political attitudes, Heyer always felt himself bound to Jung by ties of friendship. This was apparently less true of his feelings towards Eranos. Writing to Jung on 2 February 1936, he said:

> Are you going to speak this year in Ascona? I have had to turn Fröbe down—because of an inner feeling that the place is, for me at least, no longer wholesome. I have always reacted to my visits there with certain acute symptoms, which used to have a positive, loosening-up effect, but are gradually taking on a purely negative character.[127] I do not know whether the cause lies with me or has to do with Fröbe's propensity for floating in the clouds. But whenever I thought about the next meeting there came to my mind the fine word "*Aetherhurerei*."[128]

Unfortunately no direct reply from Jung has been preserved. Only on 13 January 1937 did he write to Heyer, "I missed you at the last Eranos, as I would have liked to receive some news of you again."

Finally a few words about the people who attended the first Eranos conference. The names entered in the guest book included the following: the astrologer Heinz Arthur Strauß; Myrrha Holzapfel; Herta Jay von Seldeneck, of whom more will be said in the next chapter; the Asia expert and author Hans Hasso von Veltheim; Rudolf Bernoulli, who was to give his first lecture in 1934; Max Pulver, who was to speak there for the first time in 1941; Olga Fröbe's friend and lawyer Vladimir Rosenbaum, whose name will come up again several times; and Alice Sprengel, a collaborator of Rudolf Steiner and Theodor Reuss, who had already taken part in the summer academy in earlier years, and of whom we shall have more to say later.

✿ 6. Eranos and National Socialism

Carl Gustav Jung

The second conference, in 1934, on the subject of "The Psychopomp in Eastern and Western Symbolism" (*Ostwestliche Symbolik und Seelenführung*), was for several reasons an important and successful event.[1] In her welcoming speech, reproduced in the foreword to the Eranos yearbook, Olga Fröbe emphasized that there had always been not only an Eastern but also a Western "tradition of yoga": "One only needs to think of the Hermetic and Pythagorean schools or, later on, the alchemical and Rosicrucian traditions." Equally, in the analytical psychology of C.G. Jung she detected "the beginnings of a modern and Western yoga … a method of spiritual orientation, guidance and discipline."[2] By comparing East and West one could bring about a much-needed balance as well as "the beginnings of a path to salvation for our age, which today, in the midst of our general disorientation … would be particularly beneficial." And she continued, "Thereby, at the same time, the work of the Eranos meetings would be justified by virtue of their contributing something essential, on the inner and outer levels, to the formation of this Western path of salvation."[3] The program included a number of lecturers who had already spoken at the first conference, namely C.G. Jung, Erwin Rousselle, Heinrich Zimmer, C.A.F. Rhys-Davids, Friedrich Heiler, Gustav Heyer, and Ernesto Buonaiuti. The fact that so many speakers appeared again shows, I believe, that a certain community feeling had been established and that Eranos from the beginning answered to a spiritual and, perhaps equally, to an emotional need.

One important speaker, whose appearance was to have repercussions for the reputation of both Jung and Eranos, has already been mentioned, namely the Tübingen religious scholar and later Nazi Party member Jakob Wilhelm Hauer, who spoke on the subject of *Symbole and Erfahrung des Selbstes in der indo-arabischen Mystik* (Symbolism and experience of the self in Indo-Arab mysticism). What makes Hauer's lecture particularly significant is that it laid special emphasis on fourfold patterns and thus, as Jung himself stated, became one of his sources for the theoretical formulation of the archetype of the Self.[4] Here we should also not forget that Hauer's religious-historical presentation of the self must have been for Jung a highly welcome confirmation of his own psychological theories. Attunement to the Self rather than to the ego was for Jung the goal of individuation and therefore of the inner life as a whole. This was exactly what Hauer conveyed in his lectures, even if the Jungian concept of the Self was rather different from the Indian. Hauer emphasized particularly that one cannot rely on the vacillating little ego, but only on the Self, which constitutes the innermost essence of one's whole being. Hauer had translated a number of sacred Indian texts from the Sanskrit, such as Patanjali's classic *Yoga Sutras*, and had been deeply influenced by their content. He was fully convinced of the possibility of a direct experience of God, that is to say without an external mediator. He must have had a general "inner sympathy" towards Jung's teachings[5] and perhaps also towards the esoteric aspects of Eranos.[6]

Olga Fröbe had already wanted to recruit Hauer for the first Eranos conference and had visited him in November 1932 in Tübingen. However, as Hauer's legacy reveals, the contact was established not through Jung but through the Zentralinstitut für Erziehung und Unterricht (Central institute for pedagogy and education) in Berlin. There she knew Privy Councillor Pallat, whose wife Annemarie had written the report, quoted earlier, on Fröbe's early years in Berlin. It was Pallat who had helped her to make the initial contact with Friedrich Heiler. Hauer had to turn down the invitation, as he was heavily preoccupied with building up his Germanic Faith Movement (*Deutsche Glaubensbewegung*). Rudolf Otto, who himself was unable to come to Ascona on account of illness, and who was a friend of Jakob Wilhelm Hauer, enjoined him several times, at Fröbe's request, to try after all to come and speak at Eranos. If he did not come, Otto said, it would be "a great shame, because without your lecture the core of the meeting would be missing."[7] Otto wrote an equally pressing letter to Hauer on 7 August 1933, that is to say just before the meeting:

> Olga Fröbe conveyed to me on the telephone her despair over the fact that you are not coming ... If you can somehow manage it you should do so, even if it is only for a few days. It is a rare opportunity for you, and your presence there would actually be to your own advantage. But certainly the fate of the whole conference depends essentially on your participation.[8]

In a letter to Jung of 16 August 1933 Hauer explained to Jung that he had not been able to travel "owing to the political change of course in Germany" and he continued:

> It has not been easy for me to miss Ascona, especially because of you and your circle ... However, I must confess that Zimmer did not draw me. I did not hold against him the tirade that he gave at the end of my seminar in Zurich. You remember it ... as a demoted professor he had to find a way of getting his revenge. But it remains doubtful whether I can ever work with him fruitfully on yoga. What would you say if, for example, Adler were to be invited to a professional gathering as an opponent? Furthermore he reviewed my book in some neurological journal in a manner that I found untoward. If you want me to come again, I will gladly do so. But alone! It is not because I shy away from criticism—I value it highly—but because I believe that, if there is to be a fruitful collaboration with the aim of grasping the real essence of yoga, then there must be a certain amount of substance in common.

Jung replied on 31 August 1933 and said that he had already agreed with Rousselle and Zimmer that they would meet again in Ascona the following year, and he hoped that Hauer would also come. Then he went on:

> I believe you take Zimmer too seriously. He belongs to the clan of the so-called Kosharee, the delight-makers among the Pueblo Indians. While the other religious clans occupy themselves earnestly with carrying out important magical rites, the Kosharee are there to make fun of the proceedings and monkey around while the serious ritual is going on. They are veritable clowns. Zimmer seems to me to be

rather like one of those delight makers. I would not regard him as your opponent but rather as an opponent of solemnity … Incidentally, I had no idea that
Zimmer was in such a high degree lacking in tact,[9] otherwise I would have kept
him away from our Zurich meeting … By the way, I must say that he has considerably improved in the past few months. Lately he has been not nearly so superficial
and subconscious, and he is beginning to understand the deeper aspects of things
to a certain degree. When we have you to speak again in Zurich I will keep Zimmer
away, but in Ascona the cacophony cannot be avoided.

However, what is controversial about Hauer is not his personal animosities but rather
the question of whether Jung[10] and Eranos itself were tainted with a National Socialist
influence through contact with Hauer.[11] In this connection, regardless of whether or not
I have any expertise in the matter, it is not possible for me to provide any conclusive
analysis, since the theme of this book is wider. Nevertheless, in the next few pages I can at
least bring up some of the points that support a negative answer to the question. So much
has already been written on the subject of Jung in relation to National Socialism and anti-
Semitism,[12] and with such different conclusions, that, not wishing to do an injustice to
the manifold arguments involved, I must largely refrain from dealing in detail with this
specific question even though Jung was undoubtedly one of the driving forces of Eranos
during its first twenty years. Certainly Jung made several utterances that point to racist
and anti-Jewish prejudices. On the other hand, this does not alter the fact that he gave
a generous helping hand to several individual Jews. In my view, what Jung essentially
attempted to do, with varying degrees of skill, was to reconcile his own lofty and ambitious aims with the realities of the time. Thus on the one hand, when visiting Germany,
he gave interviews that (from today's perspective) appear tame if not approving.[13] On
the other hand, at a seminar in Switzerland in 1933, at which four Jewish analysts were
present, he was already speaking of the gloomy outlook for the "new" Germany, as
Barbara Hannah reports. Perhaps we should also not overlook the fascination that he
may have felt when seeing the emergence of archetypal symbols in National Socialism,
for these seemed to provide another welcome confirmation of his theories.[14] We should
also not underestimate the deep longing for a mystical rebirth of the individual within
the bosom of his *Volk*, a longing which National Socialism as well as fascist movements
throughout Europe promised to satisfy. Petteri Pietikäinen introduces a further and
most interesting perspective.[15] He believes that Jung and the National Socialists shared a
spiritual connection, in that they longed to experience a "sacred time" and strove to promote an order that would transcend historical time with its subservience to chance. The
Germans, Pietikäinen maintains, were searching for a mythical primal era of the Aryan
peoples, whereas Jung saw this as having been realized in the collective unconscious.

One finds at least a fleeting fascination with the archetypal images of that era in the
case of a number of other prominent minds, such as Martin Heidegger, Ernst Jünger,
Gottfried Benn, Knut Hamsun, Ezra Pound, Fernando Pessoa, and Louis-Ferdinand
Céline. All of these figures were, over varying periods of time, impressed by the sudden
revival of old myths in a modern, progressive, and technologically successful society, and
believed that they were struggling against a world of decadence, degenerate materialism,
and crass individualism. Furthermore, it was certainly not always easy for people of that
time—even for the most educated of them—to foresee at an early stage to what deadly
consequences a dictatorial regime could lead. A relatively well-known example is that

of Sigmund Freud, who in 1933 wrote a dedication to Mussolini in a copy of the book *Warum Krieg?* (Why war?), which he had written together with Albert Einstein. The dedication read, "To Benito Mussolini with the devoted greeting of an old man who sees in the ruler a cultural hero."[16]

Allen W. Dulles, then head of the American intelligence organization, the Office of Strategic Services (a precursor to the CIA), who met Jung for the first time in 1936, exonerated him from all accusations of this kind and said, "I do not recall the slightest trace of anything Jung said which indicated other than a deep anti-Nazi and anti-Fascist sentiment."[17] In Dulles' war dispatches to the OSS bureaus in Washington and London, Jung was even referred to as "Agent 888."[18] In the meantime, however, doubts have arisen about Allen Dulles himself, who is alleged to have been excessively pro-German, whether out of commercial motives or because he saw the advantage of collaborating with former Nazis in the struggle against Communism. Evidently he felt that any actions to help the United States in the last phase of the war deserved to be rewarded.[19] This would explain Dulles' intervention in the Nuremberg trials on behalf of the high-ranking SS officer Karl Wolff.[20] It should also be mentioned that Dulles, with his book *Germany's Underground*, was the first prominent United States citizen to express sympathy for the Germans and especially for those who were part of the struggle against the Nazi regime. However, to claim that there had also been "good Germans" aroused astonished incredulity among the public, and the book was a commercial flop.[21] Stereotypes always require to be confirmed, as every marketing man knows.

Jung probably had an influence on Dulles' wife Clover, who, like Dulles himself, had met Jung through Mary Bancroft.[22] The latter, who belonged to the family of the publisher of the *Wall Street Journal*, was an attractive, intelligent, and emancipated woman, who had been in constant contact with Jung since the 1930s. On the other hand one should not overestimate Clover's influence on her husband. Apart from the fact that he was continually absent on official missions, Dulles was anything but communicative, and the couple had totally different interests. From 1947 they lived in *de facto* separation.[23] While Dulles did not at first like Jung, he eventually realized the latter's usefulness for intelligence-gathering purposes. Thus he informed Jung in advance, via Mary Bancroft, of the famous plot of 20 July 1944 against Hitler. This was at a time when the group around Stauffenberg was still being formed. The risk that Dulles took in so doing would itself appear to be clear proof that he was fully convinced of Jung's anti-Nazism.

Essentially what Dulles wanted was Jung's psychological assessment of certain political factors. Thus he invited Jung several times to discussion sessions so that he could find out what the perceptive psychologist thought about the leading Allied politicians. In this connection Dulles later said, "Jung's judgment was of real help to me in gauging the political situation. His deep antipathy to what Nazism and Fascism stood for was clearly evidenced in these conversations." After the war Dulles continued to correspond with Jung in order to obtain his advice as to how the German people could be freed from Nazi indoctrination and led towards a democratic social order.[24]

Thomas Mann's rejection of National Socialism is well known. Therefore it seems to me that his verdict on Jung's work is particularly worth quoting in this context. In a letter of 18 February 1941 to Karl Kerényi, he remarks that the mythological researches developed by Kerényi and Jung had taken mythology out of the hands of the "dark men of fascism" and given it a "humanistic function." A mythology based on archetypes could not be exploited so badly for the purposes of a racial ideology.[25]

A more balanced view of Jung might also be served by a quotation from his 1934 Eranos lecture, at which Hauer was also present and which must certainly have run counter to the latter's Germanic and *völkisch* outlook. The relevant passage reads as follows:

> If the so-called ethnically alien Christianity had really been profoundly unsuited to the Germanic peoples, they could easily have repelled it when the prestige of the Roman legions had faded. The American Negroes do not allow themselves to be parted from their Voodoo, and the Pueblo Indians celebrate their buffalo and snake dances happily in the church.[26]

Magda Kerényi and Ximena de Angulo, both of whom knew Jung closely over many decades, denied emphatically that he could have been an anti-Semite. On the other hand, they were able to concede that there might have been a certain political näiveté in his attitude towards National Socialism.[27] Furthermore, Magda Kerényi, who proclaimed her own Jewish ancestry, emphasized that Jung was foremost among those who enabled Leopold Szondi to emigrate to Switzerland, thus saving him from threatened deportation to a concentration camp.[28]

There are, however, statements that weigh against him. The following, admittedly taken out of context, is a serious example, especially when one takes into account the heated mood of the time: "The Jew, as a relative nomad, has never and will never in the foreseeable future develop his own form of culture, since all his instincts and talents presuppose a more or less civilized host nation if they are to develop."[29] It is not exactly a sign of sensitivity and responsibility, at a time of growing anti-Jewish agitation, to argue publicly that there is a specifically Jewish psychology, as Jung did. This criticism holds even if he was convinced of the correctness of his thesis.[30] Even Sigmund Freud said in a letter to his student and colleague Karl Abraham, "Be tolerant and don't forget that it is easier for you than for Jung to understand my thinking, since, first of all, you are completely independent, and furthermore you are closer to my intellectual constitution through racial kinship."[31]

There is, however, another way of interpreting Jung's conception of "Jewish psychology," if one reads his letter of 9 September 1934 to the Jewish analytical psychologist Gerhard Adler. Jay Sherry has called this "the most precise formulation, Jung ever made of what he meant by 'Jewish psychology.'"[32] The relevant passage in the letter reads:

> It is typically Jewish that Freud can forget his roots to such an extent. It is typically Jewish that the Jews can utterly forget that they are Jews despite the fact that they know they are Jews … So when I criticize Freud's Jewishness I am not criticizing the Jews but rather the damnable capacity of the Jew, as exemplified by Freud, to deny his own nature … I speak in the interests of all Jews who want to find their way back to their own nature.[33]

Judging by this passage, Jung may have wished to lead the Jews back to their own collective soul as a people by pointing out specific traits in "their" psychology. This could partly explain the attraction that many Jewish analysts felt towards him. According to this interpretation, his remarks could also have been intended to support the Zionists and criticize the assimilated Jews.

After the war Jung appears to have clearly re-oriented himself and adapted to the new power structure. At the same time I do not wish to deny that he was genuinely shaken by the extent of the Nazi extermination operations, which were coming increasingly to light. As proof of Jung's "re-orientation" I quote the well-known German esoteric writer and poet Herbert Fritsche, whose admirers included Hermann Hesse and Else Laske-Schüler.[34] Fritsche had been arrested by the Gestapo in 1941 and placed in protective custody.[35] In a letter of December 1948 to the poet and alchemist Alexander von Bernus, Fritsche wrote, in his famously caustic style:

> What pleased me particularly in your alchemy book was your *contretemps* with C.G. Jung[36] ... Frankly, even though you cut him down to size, you deal too politely with him when you treat him as the great, unique psychologist. We saw what kind of a psychologist he is when, in 1945, he proclaimed to the world that all Germans are fascists, even when they are anti-fascists—and that any German who came to him with psychological problems would have to collapse with remorse and deliver a confession of collective guilt, otherwise he would be untreatable.[37]

This very emotional statement is supported in a letter of 12 September 1945 to Erwin Rousselle from Baroness Hertha Jay von Seldeneck, a friend of Olga Fröbe who lived at that time at the Villa Sogno in Ascona:[38]

> The [Eranos] meeting took place without me. The theme was the spirit. You will understand what kind of spirit reigned when I tell you that I did not go. The utterances of the wise old man [Jung] on the psychological inferiority of the Germans have naturally been a great success and have done incalculable damage. He made them in an interview, but this went through the entire press. Such things make one sick. Up to now I have not been able to bring myself to visit him.[39]

And she goes on, "It is high time that members of the intelligentsia gather together once more so that they can discover that in the [German] Reich there are still many free minds—martyrs for their convictions." In a letter to her friend Lilly von Schnitzler, of 30 September 1945, Hertha von Seldeneck gives a clearer explanation as to why she did not take part in that year's Eranos meeting.

> I do not know whether I will have the opportunity to speak with Jung. His various judgments have done endless damage and have become a slogan among people who were already stirred up. He, who has the ear of the world, should have had more sense of responsibility. I could not take part in the meeting, as Olga F. had it conveyed to me that there would be a certain antipathy towards everything coming from the Reich.[40] This shows you the situation clearly. Anyone who has not at least suffered in a concentration camp does not count here.

Erwin Rousselle, who knew Jung well and had himself lost his teaching post during the Nazi period, also wrote to Jung in this connection on 15 March 1947, sending him a twenty-page letter.[41] On the subject of Jung's much-touted statements, Rousselle concedes that he knows "only the interview printed in the *Weltwoche* headed 'Will the Souls Find Peace?', which you have rejected as being inauthentic." In this interview Jung expressed the view that it was naïve to distinguish between respectable and unrespectable Germans.[42]

> *All* of them, consciously or unconsciously, actively or passively, are involved in the brutalities; one knew nothing of these things and yet one did know, as it were in a sort of *contrat génial*. The question of *collective guilt* ... is for the psychologists a

plain fact, and it will be one of the most important therapeutic tasks to bring the Germans to an acknowledgement of this guilt.

On this subject, it may be worth quoting a sentence from Jung's 1945 article "Nach der Katastrophe" (After the catastrophe) in the newspaper *Neue Schweizer Rundschau*, although it should be said that the article as a whole takes a more balanced view of the question of collective guilt:

> If a German recognizes his moral inferiority as being a collective guilt before the world and does not attempt to explain away this guilt or to mitigate it through inadequate arguments, then he has a reasonable chance, after a certain time, to be accepted as a possibly decent human being and thus be exculpated, at least by a few, from the collective guilt.[43]

Brigitte Spillmann and Robert Strubel offer an interesting explanation for this abrupt U-turn after the war:

> His cold, indeed brutal, change of course after the catastrophe [of Germany] indicates an inner counter-reaction, intended to avoid the loss of self-identity and self-regard entailed by an abandonment of those values that he had previously upheld with such personal conviction. Here he was in the same boat as all those Germans on to whom after the war he so vociferously projected his own failure, speaking of their collective guilt and psychopathic condition. And his experience was similar to theirs when he hastily dropped his former ideals in order to avoid a partial loss of self.[44]

If these authors are right, then Jung's change of direction was for narcissistic rather than objective reasons. Altogether, they bring out Jung's fundamentally divided nature, as revealed in his behavior, his writings, and even in his own retrospective self-evaluation.[45] They argue that this tension between the fragmented parts of his personality had its effect on those with whom he came into contact and who could not tell with whom they were really dealing. This would also explain why judgments about him were usually expressed "not with calm, scientific objectivity, but frequently with one-sided vehemence."[46]

During the war Jung had still behaved in a more nuanced way towards the Germans, as is proved by a short exchange of letters between him and Olga Fröbe, which also throws a different light on other things. On 22 June 1942 she wrote to him with the following question:

> Mrs. Dr. Supan in Munich has written to me saying that she and Mrs. Lucy Heyer would like to come to the meeting and that she needs a statement from me, for the Propaganda Ministry, that her presence at the meeting is desired. I have the feeling that it is not advisable for Eranos to have direct contact with Germany at this time, and I am unwilling to send an invitation of an official nature as she requests. What would you advise me to do?

She adds that she is asking the question out of anxiety that after the war it might be held against Eranos that there had been a collaboration with Germans. Jung immediately answered on 24 June 1942:

> I would advise you to go along with the request of Mrs. Supan and Mrs. Lucy Heyer. Mrs. Heyer is a person of very respectable attitude, and I would not like to

make life more difficult for these people. Ultimately we in Switzerland are neutral, and moreover in such official matters we cannot afford to pursue a one-sided policy. If two German ladies take part in our meetings, no one can make that into a reason for accusing Eranos of having, so to speak, collaborated with the Germans. We represent no political or social interests, only spiritual ones.

Regarding Jung's views on the Germans—as with his attitude towards the Jews a few years earlier—it is not my intention to make any moral accusations. We know from the Bible who has the right to cast the first stone—or indeed subsequent ones. Furthermore, we must always be as well informed as possible about the precise circumstances, for only through a discriminating analysis is it possible to come close to the truth. And only from the truth is it possible (sometimes) to draw moral conclusions. As already indicated, I personally would rather incline to the view that, where these statements of Jung are concerned, it was not a matter of the Germans or Jews *per se*, but primarily a matter of himself and his teaching. He was so fully convinced of the importance of his researches that he was prepared to bring them to the broad public under (almost) any circumstances. We should not forget that for decades he had felt ignored by the scientific world.[47] When one wants to "sell" something, and this something moreover is one's own teaching, there is unfortunately a great temptation to sing the tune of anyone who can help. Then it can also happen that one throws off moral "ballast" that is threatening to hinder one's upward flight. Even the most eminent members of our species are not immune to human weakness.

His former friend Gustav Heyer commented very trenchantly on this matter in a letter of 13 September 1956 to a recipient identified only as Michaelis:

> In our personal relations I came into uncomfortable contact with Jung's "shadow" … for example the way in which he, the former passionate fellow traveler of National Socialism, carefully distanced himself from us when the regime went wrong, and after 45 not only propagated the horrible doctrine of collective guilt but, without a qualm, threw his old German friends and pupils as fodder to the denazification authorities according to the well-tried motto "stop thief," a strategy that brought him complete success. This and other things gave me cause to speak of a miserable character: and in fact I am convinced that Jung would not contradict this.[48]

In the many discussions about Jung's negative traits—including his love affairs with female patients—there is always the great danger of thereby overlooking his enormous achievements as a pioneer of psychology. The Jungian Verena Kast even suspects that there is "a tendency to point to his 'Nazi past' in order to avoid having to come to grips with his ideas."[49] One finds it hard to avoid the impression that often enough this is indeed the case, whether it happens consciously or unconsciously. Of course one should not turn a blind eye to the negative aspects of eminent people, but by the same token one should not forget the positive ones. Can we not accept that no human being is either good or evil but a mixture of both? Every person is the sum total of many contradictions that can never be logically resolved in a fully satisfactory way. Oddly enough we tend to accept this more readily in the case of artists, but we also need to accept it in the case of scientists, politicians, and, indeed, every individual. "Only the paradoxical can come anywhere near capturing the fullness of life; that which is uncontradictory and uniform in meaning is inevitably one-sided and therefore not capable of expressing the ineffable."[50]

Jakob Wilhelm Hauer

I would now like to mention a few essential facts regarding the life of Jakob Wilhelm Hauer, which I owe largely to Margarete Dierks' biography *Jakob Wilhelm Hauer 1881–1962*,[51] a valuable work despite having been criticized for lack of objectivity.[52] Jakob Hauer came from a Swabian Pietist background. His family owned a plastering firm. He initially trained as a mason, then became a missionary in India—where he apparently failed to convert a single soul—and returned to Europe full of enthusiasm for yoga. With the support of the Basel Missionary Society he matriculated at Oxford University and took a first in Greats (the study of classical languages, ancient history, and philosophy). In 1915, the year after the outbreak of the First World War, he was repatriated to Germany as a citizen of an enemy nation. He then worked as a pastor for the Provincial Church of Württemberg and, in parallel, took courses in religious studies, Sanskrit, philosophy, and ancient history at Tübingen. In 1918 he took a doctorate with a thesis on "Die Anfänge der Yogapraxis" (The origins of the practice of yoga).

He distanced himself more and more from the institutional church and left the pastorate. Like so many of his era, he was enthused by the youth movement and joined the Köngener Group, of which he soon became chancellor.[53] This was also his decisive step away from Christianity. In 1922 he married for the first time, and in 1925 he was appointed to an extraordinary professorship at the University of Tübingen. In 1927 he received a regular professorship for general religious history and Indology at the same university. His various travels included a trip to the Middle East in 1928. He attended an orientalists' conference in Oxford and participated in a religious world peace conference in Geneva. By the beginning of the 1930s his *völkisch* views and especially his religious ideas had already become very concrete. Hauer's aim was not to reinterpret Christianity in an "Aryan" perspective, as a number of others did, but rather to develop an Indo-Germanic religion, which would be in keeping with the "German essence." As the basis for this religion he envisaged "the Nordic literature, the sacred scriptures of ancient India, the writings of the Greek world including Neoplatonism, German mysticism as exemplified by Meister Eckhart, German idealism and the works of our great poets."[54]

Hitler's first policy statement after taking power, in which he showed a surprisingly friendly attitude towards the Christian churches, came as a shock to the advocates of a *völkisch* religion, who had renounced the Church.[55] Thus, as early as July 1933, a number of groups professing a Germanic or Nordic religion, along with some members of the independent religious communities, came together to form the *Arbeitsgemeinschaft Deutsche Glaubensbewegung* (Working group for the German Faith Movement). The main motivation for this union was that National Socialism, while evincing certain anti-Christian traits, did not wish to have anything to do with the "New Heathens,"[56] who hoped, through this union, to secure their own position more effectively. Hauer took over the leadership of this "working group"[57] and succeeded, as Hubert Cancik relates,[58] in "winning the trust of all concerned, including some radical SA [Storm Troopers] members."[59] The common basis for this was the way in which the new faith was anchored in racial thinking.[60]

Cancik quotes a further very significant sentence written by Hauer at that time and contained in a communication to his Working Group. I should like to repeat this statement, as it shows Hauer's position very clearly:

It is *obvious* that, in a Working Group of the German Faith Movement … or in a German Faith Movement, no Jew can be present. This must be observed by every group and every individual entering the Working Group. Here there can be no compromise. This does not, however, alter my continuing conviction that every *truly religious person*, of whatever race or nationality, is ultimately my brother in the same way as any individual who *stands up bravely for his own people*.

He expressed similar sentiments in his essay "Eine religiöse Bruderschaft der Erde" (A religious brotherhood of the earth):[61]

When we refer to the idea and experience of a religious brotherhood of humanity we are not speaking of a syncretic religion embodied in this brotherhood. Rather, what is meant is *that people who are strongly rooted in their own religious history and who live and develop their faith closely connected to it, without surrendering any of their ancestral ground, will in turn be able to recognize others as brethren in their own distinctness and specialness.*[62]

Undoubtedly this nuanced approach did not meet with great acceptance at that time. Herbert Grabert, a trusted friend and former student of Hauer and himself a long-standing member of the German Faith Movement, whom we have already encountered as secretary of Rudolf Otto's Religious League of Mankind, wrote the following in 1936: "Judgments about Hauer are generally split into two camps. One side perceives him as a crypto-Christian; the others—his real enemies and the public at large—see him as an anti-Christian. Both judgments are false."[63]

Hauer's ability to take a nuanced view, his capacity to perceive different aspects of a situation, and his talent for bringing people together—these traits are confirmed by Karl O. Paetel, the "Don Quixote in Miniature,"[64] in his autobiography.[65] As a young man in the years after the First World War, Paetel had been an ardent nationalist, but he soon adopted socialist and Communist ideas and can be regarded as one of the leading "National Bolsheviks." In 1935 he had to flee from Germany, going first to Sweden and then to Belgium and France, where he collaborated with Willi Münzenberg, the representative of the German Communist Party, and also became acquainted with Heinrich Mann and Manés Sperber. In 1939 he was condemned to death *in absentia* in Germany. In 1940 he had to flee from France and managed to travel via Portugal to the United States, where he remained until 1949. Karl Paetel, who knew Hauer well, wrote as follows about the latter's reconciliatory style and his way of making connections between different people:

The essential thing about the "Chancellor" [as Hauer was generally called in his capacity as leader of the Köngener youth movement] was his ability to understand others. Later on, at the meetings of the Working Group on the Comburg, there were Communists and National Socialists, Jews and anti-Semites, Christians and non-Christians gathered side by side.[66] He had the capacity to build bridges and to bring about a dialogue free of rancor. At these meetings I made the acquaintance, even though somewhat fleetingly, of the great Jewish philosopher Martin Buber and—if I remember rightly—the well-known Catholic theologian Romano Guardini.

After initial doubts about Hitler, Hauer began, from the second half of 1933, to evince more and more enthusiasm for the Führer and rapidly became fully convinced of the rightness of the latter's National Socialist mission. Thus he characterized the "German

Faith," which he himself had developed and shaped, as a "deeper-level interpretation of National Socialism."[67] Already in 1933 he joined both the Hitler Youth and Alfred Rosenberg's *Kampfbund für deutsche Kultur* (Militant alliance for German culture). Subsequently he was inducted by Heinrich Himmler and Reinhard Heydrich personally into the SS and the SD (Sicherheitsdienst, the National Socialist security service).

On the other hand he realized that in the "new order" many shameful things were happening. Perhaps he was describing his own inner disquiet when he spoke of the "others" who found it difficult at that time to find the "right attitude." In the same text—written *after* the Nazis had already seized power—he continues:

> We are thinking in particular of those who ardently long to throw their glowing hearts into the movement, but who cannot, for reasons of conscience, accept certain things that have happened and are still happening … These people include many of the most worthy members of our folk … They feel a heavy burden of conscience when Jews whom they simply had to value as human beings are severely affected by the new order of things, even if they are in favor of "purifying" our national life by freeing it from excessive alien influences. And many of the best German men and women are unable, on account of these matters of conscience, to achieve the liberating break-through that they long for.[68]

Hauer goes on to write the following gravely disturbing statement, which—expressed again and again in similar terms throughout history—has been used to justify the most heinous crimes:

> Do these people not perhaps live too much according to the view that history is a moral calculation that must always produce clean results? When great revolutionary changes happen, when centuries-old institutions and attitudes have to be shattered so that something new can emerge, then events cannot proceed without injustice and guilt. Yes, ultimately the man who wishes to lead a people to new goals must be willing to shoulder a burden of guilt for the sake of those goals. And no true leader will shy away from accepting responsibility for this before the ultimate tribunal. This implies that all who lead must be prepared to ask themselves with deadly earnestness whether guilt has to be incurred. For guilt avenges itself. No one can relieve the leader of this decision, nor can any moral code do so.

He then adds, in a somewhat more nuanced manner:

> However, the question facing us is whether the same rules apply to the philosophical and religious break-through in the German revolution as to the political break-through.[69] For the political break-through it is absolutely necessary for the masses to be ranged in unity with their leader in pursuit of the immediate goal. This requires uniformity and a certain primitive single-mindedness of purpose, since otherwise the people would not have grasped the goal and would not have followed. The spiritual and religious break-through happens however in a different way. A person only attains the fulfillment of their true being when their whole inner world awakes to a strong, highly tuned vitality, and the person forces it, through long and hard struggle, to form itself. Any attempt to enforce a uniformity of mind will cripple this development, as every schoolteacher knows. This is a matter of unbreakable inner laws.

In a speech published in the same volume, Hauer therefore insists that "what features in liberalism as the ultimate demand, namely the right to freedom in ultimate decisions" must also be incorporated into the code of the new National Socialist Reich. Quoting the New Testament, he adds, "What does it profit a man that he should gain the world and yet suffer damage to his own soul?" Certainly Hauer posed the right questions to the new regime. Whether he answered them correctly is another matter.

What is significant is the way in which Hauer's political utterances—such as his recognition that political action is often accompanied by guilt—conform to his interpretation of the Hindu *Bhagavad Gita*, which, as he saw it, upheld the duty to act for a greater good, even if such action conflicts with the individual will and conscience.[70]

Hauer also spoke out publicly against the proposal of the philosophy faculty of his university (Tübingen) to confer an honorary doctorate on Adolf Hitler. In a letter to Gustav Bebermeyer, the National Socialist "official with special powers" attached to the university, Hauer wrote, "It is my opinion that it will not contribute to the reputation of the faculty and university to which I belong, if this honorary doctorate will be conferred … In order to take the burden away from my faculty, I am prepared personally to assume the sole blame for the failure of the initiative regarding the doctorate."[71] In fact Hitler decided on his own volition to decline the honorary doctorate. This certainly spared Hauer some potential difficulties, but it also must have strengthened his belief in the "upright" character of Hitler and his leadership.

Hauer also made statements about the "decadent Jewish intellect" and argued (like Jung) strongly that there is a distinct Jewish psychology and conception of religion.[72] Under other circumstances, such utterances might have been much more harmless, but in the overheated fanaticism of that period they must have added further poisonous grist to the mill of the Nazis and strengthened them in their anti-Semitic sentiments and deeds. Hauer also advocated a hierarchy of human races but was not so blindly fanatical as to acknowledge only the "Aryans." He gave particular attention, in keeping with his profession, to individual religions, which, as we have seen, he regarded as being racially determined. "What is important here," he writes, "is to realize that only a few races are able to advance to the highest stages," which "have been reached only by the Indo-Germans, the Near Eastern/Semitic peoples and, among the Mongolian races, the Chinese."[73]

In this connection Horst Junginger[74] speaks of "a striking discrepancy between his [Hauer's] public and private actions."[75] Publicly, he held back from making anti-Semitic statements. But away from the public eye, Junginger maintains, Hauer acted against the employment of Jewish professors[76] and even spied for the SD, the security service of the SS. Junginger adduces evidence for his accusations and surmises that Hauer did not wish to admit publicly how much he had changed under the influence of National Socialism. In this way he allegedly deceived many old acquaintances, including Martin Buber. Hauer's anti-Semitism, Junginger maintains, was not religiously but rather politically motivated.[77] There was no question of any hatred of Jews. His enemy was not Judaism but rather the Christian churches, for it was they who were foremost in combating the German Faith movement.[78]

For Junginger this ambivalence "can hardly be described as anything other than hypocritical." I am certainly not entitled to make a judgment on this matter, but it seems to me more likely that Hauer was under illusions about himself, about his own power, and about National Socialism in general, believing that he could change everything according to his own agenda. Otherwise he would not have been able to make the following state-ment, totally misrepresenting the real situation at a time when there were at most ten thousand members of his movement, who were, moreover, very diverse in their motiva-tions: "Today the German Faith movement has grown into a force that is now impossible for anyone to overlook. We have erected a sign around which all who stand for a free German faith are rallying. This sign stands today over all of Germany, visible to millions. No one will dare to pull it down."[79]

In 1936 Hauer finally resigned from the leadership of the German Faith Movement. During the period when National Socialism was consolidating its political power, it had no official interest in this or that experiment in religious belief. Rather, its primary concern was to reach an understanding with the Christian churches with their mass following. According to Hans Buchheim, who was the first after 1945 to begin studying the history of the German Faith Movement, Hauer had since 1934 been experiencing various difficulties in his dealings with Reinhard Heydrich, at that time leader of the Gestapo in Berlin and later head of the Reich Security Service. It was Heydrich who encouraged the young National Socialists within the German Faith Movement. Their aim was to transform what was initially a religious organization of unorthodox minds into an active anti-clerical force.[80] Furthermore, Hauer's belief in the separation of religion and politics was not acceptable.[81] Thus Hauer appears finally to have been forced to resign. This account of the matter is confirmed by Wolfgang Dierker.[82] Apparently Hauer had refused to direct his efforts in the German Faith Movement solely to the struggle against the Church and Christianity. In the opinion of the SD he was too inclined to perceive himself "as a prophet and religious leader, who stands beside or above our Führer."

Here it is relevant to quote a letter from the Hitler Youth leader Baldur von Schirach, written to Hauer on 6 July 1935:

> The Hitler Youth has already freed millions of young people from the plague of confessional religion. I do not wish these young people to be plunged into new doubts and new struggles ... The faith movement of these young people is called the National Socialist German Workers' Party ... The withdrawal of the Hitler Youth leaders from the German Faith Movement is in full conformity with my educational work."[83]

Accordingly, already in August 1935 the German Faith Movement was forbidden from engaging in public meetings and propaganda. And the organ of the SS, *Das Schwarze Corps* (The black corps), could not refrain from criticizing the movement's "mixture of pseudo-scientific Germanizing and ill-conceived enthusiasm for the world of Germanic mysticism."[84] Even Joseph Goebbels noted in his diary on 25 April 1936: "And Graf Reventlow told me about the founders of new religions, Hauer etc. A conglomeration of chatterboxes, intriguers, malicious time-servers. No, this is not the way for a new religion to emerge. Nor is it the way to overthrow Christianity."[85] Nevertheless Hauer joined the Nazi Party in 1937 and as a member of the SS he was also entered as volunteer worker relating to matters of ideology into Section VII of the Reich Head Office for Security.[86] In 1941 he received the rank of Hauptsturmführer, although he never commanded a unit.

How this promotion came about is described by Uwe Werner in his already men-tioned book *Anthroposophen in der Zeit des Nationalsozialismus* (Anthroposophists in the National Socialist period). Hauer had a long-standing interest in Anthroposophy (but also in Theosophy) and had written a book entitled *Werden und Wesen der*

Anthroposophie (Anthroposophy: its becoming and its being)[87], based on four lectures that he had given. His attitude towards both movements is basically open but in the last analysis very critical.[88] Thus he writes, "We must reject Anthroposophy's claim to be the science of the super-sensory, since the Anthroposophical method is incapable of offering any proof, and proof is essentially what constitutes all science."[89] What he took exception to was originally not so much Anthroposophy *per se*, but rather its failed endeavor to unite science and religion. Steiner, he felt, could in this way only abuse the honorable name of science. On the positive side, however, he wrote that Anthroposophy dealt with "deep human issues not from the standpoint of a particular set of dogmas." And it was to Anthroposophy's credit that it stimulated people to study such areas at all. At the same time he felt that the movement was increasingly losing its openness. Hauer took a decidedly negative view of the "occult" teachings which he felt Anthroposophy was propagating.

During the Nazi period Hauer's critical attitude to Steiner's ideas became increasingly sharp. Thus, for example, he described the Waldorf schools, which operated according to Steiner's principles, as a "serious danger for German education."[90] Uwe Werner believes that Hauer's severity towards the Anthroposophists was intended to bring him an appointment to Himmler's staff, although certainly Hauer was genuinely convinced that Steiner's teachings were damaging. The outcome was that Hauer was indeed "rewarded" with the promotion to Hauptsturmführer. A year earlier, in response to a request from the Nazi Party for documentation on Anthroposophy, Hauer had written: "So please do what you can to eliminate the influence of Anthroposophy in the spot that you mention. The Anthroposophists are the worst enemies of our Reich."[91] A further danger that Hauer perceived, according to Werner, lay in the fact that "the Jewish element in Anthroposophy had always been very strong."[92]

It may be of interest here to quote Martin Buber, reviver of Hasidic mysticism and an enthusiastic student of Taoism, who also spoke at Eranos in 1934, where he eagerly engaged in discussion with Hauer. In 1949, when he was asked for his opinion on Hauer, he said, "Hauer is someone who lives according to an earnest and deeply religious worldview. This has led him to a passionate longing for a renewal of the German nationhood from its essential roots." On the subject of Hauer's involvement with the National Socialism, Buber added with admirable tolerance, "When someone falls into such an error he is not thereby disgraced as long as he distinguishes, within the movement that he joins, between truth and lies, between sincerity and falseness of spirit. To my knowledge, Hauer has done this."[93] Buber also said it had come to his knowledge that Hauer had "repeatedly helped endangered Jews."[94] This is backed up, albeit indirectly, in a statement of Gershom Scholem, reported by Mircea Eliade, to the effect that Hauer was among the very few National Socialists against whom Scholem had no objection. Hauer had, according to Scholem, "adopted two or three Jewish children, or a Jewish girl."[95]

After the war, as the Hauer expert Schaul Baumann has said in a lecture, Buber even visited Hauer twice in Tübingen and after the latter's death dedicated an essay to his widow.[96] At any rate, the relationship between Hauer and Buber was certainly an unusual one, as one can see from the correspondence between them. Even the forms of address are revealing: "Most revered, dear Martin Buber" or "Dear and revered Jakob Wilhelm Hauer."[97] One exchange, dating from 1932 or thereabouts,[98] deals with a project for a "German Faith Movement Week," at which Hauer wanted both National Socialists and Jews to speak and discuss solutions to the political problems of the day.[99] This bears witness not only to his profound *völkisch* beliefs but also to his respect for people of other worldviews. Evidently he believed that the only solution for a peaceful cohabitation lay in a separate development of peoples of different origin. Unfortunately, however, in a nation this fails to solve the problem of a just sharing of political and economic power, and the result is usually a system in which violence prevails over tolerance and envy over *Geist*.[100] Schaul Baumann, in the already mentioned lecture at Tübingen University in October 1999, said that Hauer perceived similarities "between Meister Eckhart, Jakob Boehme (the subject of Buber's dissertation), even Angelus Silesius—all of them heretics who set themselves against dogmatism—and Buber, who also set himself against conventional orthodox Judaism." Buber was furthermore "a heretic of a nationalist cast, who even perhaps had an unspoken leaning towards a racially oriented mystical piety."

By contrast, Tadeus Reichstein, who was present at the Kundalini seminars given by Hauer and Jung, saw Hauer as a "fanatic," with whom any real discussion was impossible, as he was "so totally self-convinced" and "only gave validity to what he himself said."[101] Jung's seminar, on the other hand, had been open and "very impressive" for him. Heinrich Zimmer, who had been obliged to flee from the Nazis, was even harsher in his opinion of Hauer, whom he described as "an indologist, who was unreliable both as a researcher and in character," but who "was endowed with a demonic, shimmering vitality consisting of primitive antipathies and ambitions."[102] A different view again was expressed by the Swiss analytical psychologist C.A. Meier, Jung's successor as professor at the Swiss Federal Institute of Technology in Zurich and a close friend of the Kerényi family. Meier described Hauer as a "typically dry German scientist, an excellent Sanskritist" and furthermore "a very nice chap."[103]

Another positive assessment came from Georg Feuerstein, who knew about Hauer's dedication to the German Faith Movement and who valued him as someone "to whom we owe a great deal in the study of Yoga and Samkhya" and who "not only possessed a rich knowledge of Indian thought, but was also well acquainted with Western culture."[104] The following statement by Feuerstein is somewhat surprising: "The central theme of all his work is man as a religious being, and Hauer himself was a sincere god-seeker and mystic." The theologian Fritz Heinrich of the University of Göttingen, who had also studied at Hauer's home university in Tübingen, confirms this when saying, "Hauer's religiosity appears as a pietistic search for truth, which lost its biblical foundation and strives therefore in the world of religions after an experience of the same emotional intensity as in a mystical Christian awakening."[105] The scholars of religion Gustav Mensching and Helmuth von Glasenapp also gave positive assessments of Hauer in 1948, although it is hard to say to what extent such assessments, delivered in a court of law, may have involved an element of self-protection. Hauer had been interned by the Allies in 1945 and even kept for part of the time in solitary confinement. In 1949 the Tübingen University *Spruchkammer* (a body charged with making judgments in university matters) classified him as a fellow traveler under the Nazi regime but not as a perpetrator of misdeeds, which was probably thanks to an exonerating letter from Martin Buber.[106]

In the same year Hauer founded a "working group for Free Research on Religion and Philosophy" with the goal of making it into a "Free Academy." The earliest members, it must be said, were mainly former avowed National Socialists such as the Jakob Boehme expert Hans Grunsky, the Germanist and mythologist Bernhard Kummer, and the ideologist of racism Hans F.K. Günther, but Hauer's intention was to accept also dedicated opponents of National Socialism. At the same time Hauer took an active part in the pacifist movement and in the campaign against the reintroduction of military service in Germany.[107] Thus it came about that he undertook certain publications together with the Catholic poet Reinhold Schneider and with Martin Niemöller who, as representative of the "Confessional Church" and as Hitler's "personal prisoner," had been an inmate of Sachsenhausen concentration camp.[108] Religious tolerance remained the core of his thinking, and he maintained that the "prophetic," monotheistic religions were generally intolerant, whereas the mystical ones were tolerant.[109]

In his later years Hauer developed the concept of a "holistically oriented study of religion." It should be remembered that in the 1920s he had been active alongside Rudolf Otto in the Religious League of Mankind, which had campaigned for inter-religious cooperation (in 1924 he even became its president). Hence Margaret Dierks emphasizes Hauer's fundamental affinity with liberal theology and the ecumenical movement[110] and with figures such as Rudolf Otto[111] and Friedrich Heiler[112]. She does not include him in the ranks of the "Germanic nationalist" thinkers such as Herder, Fichte, and Lagarde. Ulrich Nanko, normally rather neutral in his opinions, tends towards a similar judgment.

In 1960 Hauer even had the opportunity to speak at the Tenth International Congress for the History of Religion at Marburg an der Lahn, where he delivered a lecture on the "Ursprung und Anfänge der Religion in der Sicht einer ganzheitlichen Religionsforschung" (The origin and inceptions of religion in the perspective of a holistic study of religion). Speakers at the same congress included the Eranos lecturers Gershom Scholem, Erwin Goodenough, Erik Hornung, and Zwi Werblowsky as well as other prominent scholars of religion such as Hans-Joachim Schoeps, Geo Widengren, and C.J. Bleeker.[113] The meeting was organized by two other Eranos people: Friedrich Heiler and Annemarie Schimmel, the renowned expert on Sufism.[114] The latter described Hauer as "very nice and quite gentle" in his latter years.[115]

However, the Israeli scholar of religion Schaul Baumann disputes the view that Hauer was mainly a victim of the circumstances of his time. In his doctoral dissertation on the German Faith Movement, he emphasizes Hauer's identification with the Nazi regime.[116] Baumann detects a pronounced anti-Christian and anti-Jewish attitude, a belief in the racial superiority of the Aryans and a belittling of democratic values.[117] Above all, according to Baumann, Hauer had succeeded in mobilizing a large number of respected scholars for the Nazi *Weltanschauung* and thus contributing support for the regime from within the academic world. Baumann also thinks that the German Faith Movement gave the Nazi regime an ideological basis for all-out war. In order to document his dissertation he made several visits to Tübingen to consult Hauer's papers. In particular Baumann draws attention to Hauer's close association with his student Paul Zapp, later secretary of the German Faith Movement. In a trial for war crimes Zapp was found guilty of personal and possibly even active responsibility for the murder of thirteen thousand people in the Ukraine and the Crimea and was sentenced to life imprisonment. During the trial, Zapp declared that his actions were the direct result of Hauer's teachings. According to Baumann, Zapp had "single-handedly achieved the synthesis of Hauer's German Faith and Hitler's *Weltanschauung*."[118]

Jung first met Hauer in 1930 at the already mentioned psychotherapy congress in Baden-Baden. Already on 20 November 1931 Hauer wrote a letter asking if he could dedicate his yoga book to Jung.[119] The latter replied almost by return of post on 30 November 1931, that this was a "delightful surprise and a cause for lively expression of thanks."[120]

The following dedication duly appeared at the beginning of Hauer's book *Der Yoga als Heilweg*: "C.G. Jung, dem Erforscher neuer Wege zum Menschen [To C.G. Jung, the discoverer of new paths into man's being]."[121] Subsequently Hauer gave a number of lectures at Jung's Psychology Club in Zurich.[122]

One of the most important of these lecture series was on Tantric yoga and took place on 3–8 October 1932. Those who spoke included Jung himself as well as Heinrich Zimmer and Gustav Heyer. Zimmer had asked Jung, whom he already knew,[123] whether he could attend the seminar given by Hauer. It was there that arose the controversy between Hauer and Zimmer, which I have already mentioned. The transcripts of this lecture series of 1932 are, incidentally, free of political partisanship.[124] However, Barbara Hannah writes that the audience at the Tantra seminar were perplexed by the sheer amount of relevant new material, much of it in an unfamiliar terminology, that was heaped upon them. Consequently Jung felt himself obliged, in three of his lectures, to translate the essential points into a language comprehensible to psychologists.[125]

Jung invited Hauer, and also Heinrich Zimmer,[126] to collaborate with him on an international journal that he intended to create on the encouragement of the publisher Daniel Brody, who later published the Eranos volumes. The intended goal was "a synthesis of the different disciplines" and the title was to be simply *Weltanschauung*. In a letter of 23 December 1932 to his collaborator Jolande Jacobi he wrote that "Prof. Hauer, Prof. Zimmer [and] Prof. Pauli [for modern physics]" had already agreed to take part. Further names that he mentioned included Leopold Ziegler,[127] Hermann Keyserling, and Hermann Broch.[128] Although the project never came to fruition it can be seen as another of the antecedents that foreshadowed the interdisciplinarity of Eranos. A close contact also developed between Hauer and Jung's long-standing "muse," mistress, and empathic assistant Toni Wolff, who even hosted Hauer and his wife and daughter for a few days' vacation in Switzerland.

At the second Eranos meeting in 1934 Hauer was one of the main speakers and was even called upon to give the closing address. Outside of the main sessions there was some discussion of current political events, as is revealed in the files of Section III/2 of the SD (the German security service). These contain a two-page summary of the conversations between Hauer and Buber.[129] According to Junginger, this summary was probably composed by Hauer's secretary Paul Zapp, whose later sentence for war crimes has already been mentioned. The SD report begins by saying that Hauer's talk in front of about two hundred people had been received with great interest and sympathy. Jung had shown "a degree of understanding for Germany and the National Socialist movement" that was rare for a Swiss. The conversation with Buber had been about a possible agreement between the Third Reich and the leaders of the Zionist movement, according to which the Jewish influence in Germany would be voluntarily restricted. Buber had reportedly been largely in agreement with the suggestions. However, at this point in time it is hard to say whether this report was intended merely to satisfy the German authorities and cover Hauer against any difficulties with them, or whether it really corresponded to the facts. Another report describes the heated discussion that ensued when Hauer defended the political developments in Germany. Buber apparently defused the embarrassing situation by steering the discussion towards the subject of Meister Eckhart.[130] Olga Fröbe invited Hauer to come again in 1935, but he was obliged to refuse. Apart from the fact that the German government would probably not have granted him permission to travel, there were other reasons for his refusal, which he spoke about very openly.[131] A section of the German press had been attacking the Eranos circle not only for being under Jewish influence but also for its penchant towards occultism, something that the National Socialists considered highly suspect. "A visit to Ascona," Hauer wrote, "would be exploited by my enemies to malign me crudely."[132] His contacts with Martin Buber at Eranos had already led to attacks against him. Furthermore, he said, he no longer fitted in there. Although he supported the principle of brotherhood in religious matters, he felt it necessary to make clear that there were "great differences at the level of race and the racial soul." Furthermore he found in Ascona too much "spiritual and philosophical epicurianism" and not enough "metaphysical and religious profundity." In an undated letter to Cary Baynes, Olga Fröbe wrote that Hauer had caused much difficulty for her and the Rhein-Verlag publishing house as "apparently he has been scared by certain people in his circle and has written that he cannot possibly allow his lectures to be published in the same volume along with those of Martin Buber. And he gives other reasons as well." In the same letter Fröbe added that "Heyer[133] and Brody have written very serious messages to him, as I myself have also done, and I still hope that the matter can be cleared up."[134]

In November 1935 Hauer was forced to issue a press communiqué declaring that he had once merely delivered an academic lecture before the Eranos circle, but did not belong to it. Defending both himself and therefore also Eranos, he said that he had not been aware of any "Judaeo-Masonic machinations or occult exercises." In a letter of March 1936 Olga Fröbe expressed understanding for Hauer's refusal. We can obtain a clear idea of the mood of hostility against Eranos in general and Hauer in particular from the following somewhat longer quotation from a polemical writing by H. Rehwaldt, a member of the Ludendorff coterie:

> The other gateway through which Europe is being invaded by Far Eastern occultism is Switzerland ... It is there that the Eranos Society, which has already been mentioned several times, is busy concocting a "synthesis of all spiritual cultures," and the "free democracy" of the liberalistic Swiss constitution offers the best breeding ground for such divisive growths and poisonous infestations. This is an association of intellectuals from all over the world, who are dissatisfied with ecclesiastical Christianity and with the moral and ethical standard of "humanity" and who are "seeking the truth" ... The price and size [of the Eranos yearbooks], besides the impenetrability of their "high spiritual" content, ensure that these yearbooks are accessible only to a certain well off and educated readership ... Actually what happens is that the assembled company are first allowed to show off their intellectuality hour after hour in highly learned lectures, then they are given objective and authoritative instructions from a true initiate.[135]

The writer goes on to mention the whole cast of speakers at the 1934 meeting, along with their titles. Finally comes a direct attack on Hauer:

> It is a mystery to us how Professor Hauer, a German of *völkisch* persuasion, who has claimed a lease on the cause of ancestral heritage and wisdom, can find it consistent to take part in such a motley conference. But this must remain his affair. We have known Herr Hauer for a long time. He has denied his membership of the Eranos Society in a letter that reminds us of certain declarations at the time of the anti-Freemasonry struggle. In this letter he claims not to be a member of the "Eranos

movement" or "Eranos circle" (as we know, it is called the "'Eranos Society") and not to have noticed any "Jewish-Masonic machinations." It seems, therefore, that he has overlooked a colleague of the ilk of Professor Dr. Martin Buber!

After accusing Hauer of giving lectures "side by side with a Jew," Rehwaldt mentions Olga Fröbe's opening speech (which I have quoted earlier), locating it within the hermetic, Gnostic, Pythagorean, alchemical, and Rosicrucian traditions. The text then goes on:

> So it is these occult teachings that are the basis of the learned Eranos Society, which perpetuates the venerable tradition of a "Count" of Saint-Germain, a Cagliostro— or whatever the names of these Rosicrucian and occultist swindlers may be—in the shape of Freudian psychoanalysis and the form given to it by C.G. Jung. To this end they [the society] investigate "western" and "eastern" symbolism and are paralyzed by admiration when they find an equivalence or similarity between these two variants of induced madness.[136] The fact that Judaism is not excluded can be judged from the international character of the meeting and from the fact that the "galloping religion" or the "synthesis of all spiritual cultures" also has a warm place in its heart for the religion of Jehovah in its Mosaic and Talmudic form.[137]

This passage from Rehwaldt's text is based on two reports that appeared in the Ludendorffs' fortnightly journal *Am Heiligen Quell Deutscher Kraft* (At the sacred spring of German strength), which had the not inconsiderable circulation of forty-five thousand copies. The first of these reports appeared under the title "Glaubensbewegung: Symbol und Yoga" (Faith movement: symbolism and yoga), written by "L." It focused mainly on Jung and Eranos and only indirectly attacked Hauer. The following introductory sentences are significant: "One society that has assumed the task of bestowing on us the symbolism and yoga of the Indian religions, and further entangling us in mind-addling occultism, is the Eranos Society." Symbols were studied:

> in pursuit of the Western path of salvation (that is the modern expression for the occult teachings of the Eranos Society and others). This includes the practice of staring at the symbols to the point of self-hypnosis, in other words a similar state to that produced by meditation or yoga. The methods are different, but the induced madness is the same, as is the damage to the soul of the persons concerned.[138]

The second and longer report from the same periodical, with the more drastic title "Glaubensbewegung: Hinein ins Irrenhaus" (Faith movement: into the madhouse) was also written by L., who was, if nothing else, well informed. This time he or she directly targets Hauer, the intention being to show that "the effect of this society [Eranos] flows deeply and unmistakably into the world of so-called scholarship." The author quotes extensive passages both from Hauer's Eranos talks and from his Tantric yoga seminar under the auspices of the Psychology Club in Zurich. He or she explains:

> We must deal with his presentations, because they claim to be transmitting sup- posedly Indo-Aryan traditions of thought. Here we must object. What we have seen reflected in his speech is not Aryan. It was not known to our ancestors in our homeland. It is a product of the sultry air of India, from the time of Indo-Aryan decline, and has nothing to do with our thought.

Towards the end of the piece comes another frontal attack on Eranos:

What the Eranos Society brings is the murky occultism of the East, combined with the danger of mental disorder of the most serious kind … Eranos means a love-feast or a communal meal … The word is also used in the sense of something contributed, a service of love. In the case of Eranos this service of love is for the benefit of the Jew, who seeks to devour all peoples through his occult teachings. The Hasidic-*völkisch* Jew Martin Buber will certainly have been satisfied with the results of the meeting.

Gustav Heyer is also attacked in this article because of his participation at Eranos and his method of psychotherapy allegedly stemming from there.[139]

In Switzerland also Hauer's participation did not meet with universal approval. There was, for example, a plan—in which even the famous painter Max Ernst was involved—to tar and feather Hauer on his arrival in Ascona. The plan was, however, not carried out.[140] On the other hand, the cultural philosopher Walter Robert Corti, to whom we shall return in detail later, felt compelled to come to Hauer's defense in his already mentioned essay in the *Schweizer Annalen*, published in 1935.[141] In this essay he writes, "The figure of Hauer has been the cause of much confusion in the way people have judged the conference. Today there are more people than ever who are so fixed in their views that merely a name or a word is enough to make them blind and deaf. Even the best Swiss newspapers have presented a distorted image of Hauer." In exoneration he then mentions the attacks on Hauer by German racists.

Despite the accusations and difficulties that have already been mentioned, even in the Germany of 1935 there were those who spoke out in favor of Eranos. This can be illustrated by a quotation from an article by H. Werner entitled "Zur modernen Psychologie" (On modern psychology) in the *Kölnische Zeitung* of 28 July 1935.

The Eranos movement, which meets every year at Ascona in Switzerland, is one of the many channels through which oriental and especially Indian thought penetrate into our European mental universe. This is no closed movement of sect-like nature. Its members include some of the most independent and original minds of the age, especially from the world of German scholarship.

Then he goes on to mention Rousselle, Hauer, Heiler, Rhys-Davids, and Buber. "Common to all of them is simply an interest in the world of symbols and in the religions and philosophies of the East, in the hope that this source of knowledge can lead to a revitalization of the cramped world of the Western mind."

I do not wish to go in greater detail into the subsequent relationship between Jung and Hauer, as this hardly has any further relevance for Eranos. In his famous essay "Wotan," written in 1936 and dealing with the way in which the Germans were "possessed" by the archetypes of their gods, Jung does expressly mention Hauer, but is less than flattering when he describes Hauer's book *Deutsche Gottschau* (The German contemplation of deity) as a "tragic and truly heroic attempt by a conscientious scholar."[142]

Even as late as 1938 Hauer again held a series of lectures at the Psychological Club in Zurich. These, however, were marked by tense arguments about the political situation. From then on there is no evidence of any further contact between Hauer and Jung.[143] In his book *Der Yoga: ein indischer Weg zum Selbst* (Yoga, an Indian path to the self), Hauer devotes a chapter to the relationship between yoga and psychotherapy in which he takes issue with the "too hasty identification" of the Tantric mythical images with the archetypes as understood "in Jungian circles." He was also skeptical about Jung's conception of the "innate archetypes." He felt that the empirical evidence for it from the history of religion was extremely weak, and the theory was for him "not convincing." On the other hand, the archetypes were "hypostasized into mystical and transcendental, indeed metaphysical phenomena." At the same time they were not seen as "true metaphysical realities" and were relegated to the psychological sphere." This led, in Hauer's view, "to a spiritual anti-realism (irrealism), in which everything is relativized."[144]

On the subject of his relationship with Jung, there is an interesting letter from Hauer to Emma von Pelet, dated 10 February 1941, saying that Jung had at first aroused certain hopes in him and that he had tried to make clear to Jung and his circle:

> that the developments in Germany, in terms of *Weltanschauung* and political direction, come from a burgeoning spring of life's reality, and that new and creatively vital powers are revealing themselves ... I have had and still have the greatest admiration, indeed love, for Jung. But, as this circle is holding itself at a distance from the lived reality of the German people and from that which we are struggling for, I have to recognize a deeply regrettable fact: the deep insights that have been attained by this circle remain infertile in the context of the totality of the German people and will have to remain so, failing the recognition that we have a destiny and that this destiny is determined by land and blood.[145]

I hope that my detailed investigation of this topic will help to provide a more nuanced view of the situation at the time. Ultimately there seems to me to be no justification for attaching any blame to Eranos or indeed to Jung in connection with Hauer, especially as the authors who have dealt with this topic in less or more detail—particularly Shamdasani and, more superficially, Webb and Noll—describe the situation in similar ways, even if not all of the above details were known to them. It should be no surprise, however unpalatable it might seem to us today, that in those days many intellectuals throughout Europe thought in *völkisch* terms in varying ways according to whatever "folk" they belonged to.[146] Every thinker is a product of his *Zeitgeist*, and we today are no exception. It is always easier in retrospect to recognize mistakes and blinkered attitudes, but to recognize them with the benefit of hindsight is better than not at all. Jakob Wilhelm Hauer formulated it in this way: "Man is not just a wheel rolling according to his own volition. He is also a link in the chain of history, and his fate is shaped accordingly."[147]

✿ 7. The Years 1934–37

Eranos 1934

Martin Buber
Martin Buber had spoken at Eranos in 1934. He also intended to come in 1935 and even traveled as far as Zurich, but withdrew at the last minute. Although an order forbidding him to speak in public was only valid in Germany, nevertheless he decided not to appear even at "such a neutral event" as Eranos.[1]

Buber was born in Vienna in 1878.[2] At the age of three he lost his mother, who disappeared without trace. His real connection with Judaism was first awakened when he began his university studies, which took him to Berlin, Leipzig, and Zurich.[3] He became editor of the official Zionist periodical *Die Welt*, then quarreled with Theodor Herzl, the founder of Zionism, who set greater store by political activities than cultural ones. After this break Buber and a group of friends founded the Jüdischer Verlag (Jewish publishing company) and launched their own monthly journal entitled *Der Jude* (The Jew).[4] From 1925 onwards he held a professorship at the University of Frankfurt until forced to resign with the advent of National Socialism in 1933. Thereafter he organized the "Jewish Centers for Adult Education," which for a time were permitted to continue in Germany. When this activity also became impossible, he settled in Palestine. On the occasion of the Eichmann trial in Jerusalem in 1961, he pleaded that the charges be dropped and the death penalty not carried out. What is less well known is that Buber never entered a synagogue after the age of thirteen and described himself as "ritually abstinent."[5] A certain disdain for Talmudic Judaism was also evident in him. It was not that he wished to abolish the Talmud, but rather that he regarded it as partially outdated. His mission was to supply it with new life and new interpretations.[6]

His wide influence in Europe and especially in the German-speaking world at that time is today largely forgotten, although the available literature by and about him remains extensive. We have already mentioned his successful work in the field of Taoism. Also strikingly successful were his books on Hasidism. As Klaus Samuel Davidowicz points out in his study *Gershom Scholem und Martin Buber*, even today—especially in the German-speaking realm—"people all too often think in terms of Buber's concepts when talking about Hasidism."[7] Only a few people are aware that Buber presented a rather idiosyncratic interpretation of Hasidism, which corresponded to his own somewhat mystical and emotional temperament.[8] In Buber's later years this interpretation led to the well-known dispute with another distinguished Eranos speaker, Gershom Scholem. The debate turned on the question of whether Buber's interpretations conformed to scholarly standards. In a fairly abrasive manner Scholem set about de-mythologizing Buber, as he felt that the enthusiasm for Buber, especially in the German-speaking realm, was based on a misunderstanding of Judaism and Hasidism.[9]

The tenor of the attacks can be judged from two remarks taken from Scholem's letters. In one he says that "Buber is a religious anarchist and his teaching is religious anarchism," and in the other he complains that "Buber misuses Hasidism and, what is more, in an academically irresponsible way, since he goes against the theoretical literature on Hasidism and one-sidedly emphasizes certain aspects of the Hasidic legend in order to promote his own philosophy."[10] Scholem, having studied linguistic philosophy in his youth under Walter Benjamin and Fritz Mautner, wanted to correct Buber's intuitive approach. On the other hand he probably knew that Buber was not aiming at historical and philosophical precision. Klaus Davidowicz therefore speaks of a "deliberate misunderstanding" on Scholem's part and fittingly describes Buber's Hasidic works as "a thought-provoking and deeply moving literary work."[11] For Scholem, it was rational understanding that would form the true basis for a cultural renewal, not personal experience, which was what Buber placed in the foreground.[12]

This controversy was, however, confined to academic circles and in no way curtailed Buber's fame. On the contrary, in his latter years Buber was not only given many honors (such as the Hanseatic Goethe Prize, the Peace Prize of the German Book Trade,[13] the Munich Cultural Award of Honor,[14] and the Erasmus Prize), but again and again he received genuine veneration. No one put it more clearly than Davidowicz:

> For many people—especially in Europe—he represented the embodiment of "true Judaism"—a "Jewish theologian for non-Jews," as Leibowitz once said. In Germany and Austria many people saw in him the classic image of a "Jewish scholar" and they perceived in his writings a form of Judaism that could easily be combined with the idealized pre-war notion of a "German-Jewish symbiosis."[15]

However, while seeing in Buber the figure of the "Jewish scholar," we should not forget the Jewish "wise man," a role that, in my opinion, he embodied even more clearly, with his tolerance and human understanding.

It was not only towards the Germans that Buber showed a wise and heartfelt understanding but also towards the Arabs. Already at the twelfth Zionist Congress in Karlsbad in 1921 Buber appeared as a strong advocate of an understanding with the Arabs.[16] Against the position of the *Realpolitiker*, he wanted to take Arab interests into consideration and to build the future state of Israel on a strongly ethical foundation. Later, however, Buber developed a philosophy of ethical action, in which he recognized that high ethical ideals had to be subject to compromise when it came to applying them in this corrosive world. In the process one was bound to get one's hands dirty, and the guiding principle should be, "Our hands willing to knead must be plunged deep into the clay."[17] This philosophy of ethical action was probably a reaction to a letter from his friend and biographer Hans Kohn, in which the latter wrote, "I fear that we are promoting something that we cannot vouch for. Something which, out of a false sense of solidarity, is pushing us ever deeper into the swamp. Zionism must either be peaceful or do without me. *Zionism* is *not* Judaism."[18]

Mention should also be made of the fact that in 1953 Martin Buber wrote a letter together with two fellow campaigners to the leader of the Israeli Knesset, in which they protested vehemently against the expropriation of Arabic land in the absence of clear-cut security concerns.[19] Shortly before his death he published an article in which he advocated a federation between the Arabic peoples and Israel, stating,

In order that so immense a work, an unprecedented work in fact, may succeed, it is indeed necessary that *spiritual*[20] representatives of the two peoples enter into a true dialogue with one another, a dialogue based on shared sincerity and mutual recognition alike. Only such a dialogue can lead to a purification of the atmosphere, and without such a purification even the first steps on the new way are bound to fail. These spiritual representatives must be independent in the full sense of this word; they must be individuals whom no consideration of any kind hinders from serving without reservation the cause that they have recognized as true and just.[21]

What makes Buber particularly interesting within philosophical history is his endeavor to shift the forms of philosophy away from the subject–object relationship and on to an I–Thou level, and thus to open up a new human (and theological) perspective.[22] All in all, in light of his broad knowledge from Taoism to Judaism, from art and politics to philosophy, Martin Buber must be seen as a polymath in the classical sense of a Goethe, whose ideals were still upheld by many German-speaking Jews at a time when the Germans themselves had already given up these educational objectives.[23]

Oskar R. Schlag and Sigrid Strauß-Klöbe: Spiritism and Astrology

Another person who was invited to speak in 1934 was Rudolf Bernoulli, a member of a famous Basel family of scholars, who lectured on the symbolism of the Tarot. Bernoulli had studied art history, philosophy, and psychology in Basel, Berne, and Berlin, and had been employed at the Museum of Applied Arts in Berlin. After working at the Swiss National Graphic Collection in Zurich, he became an associate lecturer in art history and then a professor at the Swiss Technical School in Zurich. Bernoulli was well acquainted with Albert Freiherr von Schrenck-Notzing, the "leader of parapsychology in Germany," as he is often called in biographical dictionaries. After Schrenck-Notzing's death in 1929, Bernoulli became co-editor of the *Zeitschrift für Parapsychologie* (Journal for parapsychology).[24] Bernoulli also admired the writer of occult fiction Gustav Meyrink, as is clear from his afterword to one of Meyrink's works.[25]

Bernoulli co-founded the so-called *Hermetische Gesellschaft* (Hermetic society), which, even before its official inauguration, is said to have had an important influence on the direction in which Eranos was to develop.[26] Allegedly—these assertions come from brothers of the order—the building of the Eranos lecture hall and possibly even the founding of the Eranos meetings themselves can be traced back to an initiative that came from this society. There are said to be documentary proofs of this, but they are not accessible to the public.[27] All that could be proved up to now is that Fritz Allemann, the most important co-founder and probably the real external spiritual head of the Hermetic Society, repeatedly gave Olga Fröbe great financial and moral support.[28] We shall return to this theme later. This part of the Eranos story is still unresearched for lack of documentation. It also includes the support that the Eranos meetings later received from a number of women from rich families, for example, Marie Amélie de Robilant[29] and Adriana Scopinich, the divorced Baroness of Mörl.

Allemann, who was born in Alexandria, Egypt, in 1884, belonged to the third generation of a Swiss cotton dynasty. After his education in Switzerland he returned to Egypt, where he became a partner in the family business. He returned repeatedly, however, to Switzerland, sometimes for prolonged visits. There he soon made the acquaintance of Jung, joining the latter's Psychology Club in 1930 and giving him considerable financial support.[30] Allemann was also present at Jung's October 1932 series of lectures on Tantric yoga in Zurich.[31] Before the Second World War, Allemann left Egypt, taking with him his entire fortune, and returned to Switzerland. There he participated in various business enterprises, but did not play a publicly conspicuous role.

For many years he was vice-president of the Swiss Banking Corporation (today UBS). He was also involved in various social causes. For example, in 1937 he contributed a large sum of money to the creation, together with Dr. Max Bircher, of the Bircher People's Sanatorium, which later became the Foundation for the Susenberg Clinic. A practitioner of complementary medicine, Bircher used natural means to cure Allemann of severe sciatica. Allemann could be one of the great unknown figures in the esoteric history of the twentieth century. According to the accounts of several people who knew him, he was an important, albeit reticent, mystic.

Since 1998 there has existed in Zurich the Institute for Philosophy and Ethics/Fritz Allemann Foundation. It was founded by his daughter, Dr. Rosa Schild-Allemann, in honor of her father. Its purpose is to promote philosophy and ethics by organizing lectures, seminars, and conferences as well as issuing related publications. The foundation is under the supervision of the Swiss Ministry of Internal Affairs. Fritz Allemann had always emphasized that ethics are of great importance in economic matters, and he repeatedly expressed the wish to create an institution that would reflect these concerns. There have also been courses of an esoteric nature, including some given by the Tarot expert Hans-Dieter Leuenberger and others by the complementary therapist Rüdiger Dahlke. Its president is Bruno Fellinger, private banker and philosopher and one of Allemann's few pupils.[32] He is also president of the advisory board of the Susenberg Clinic. Fellinger made the acquaintance of Fritz Allemann in 1951 after his entry into the Hermetic Society, of which Allemann was "Wise Master" (to use the title he held in the group), and soon became part of the latter's inner circle. After the death of his mentor in 1968 he took over the leadership of the Hermetic Society and remained there for eight years.

Allemann was also in friendly contact with the German psychotherapist and Zen master Count Karlfried Dürckheim. He had several meetings with the Dalai Lama and in the last years of his life, which he spent in Montagnola, he was a neighbor of Hermann Hesse, whom he also assisted financially, as is allegedly proved by still unpublished correspondence.

Apparently it was through Jung that Allemann made the acquaintance of Oskar Rudolf Schlag (ORS), one of the most gifted mediums of the twentieth century, who features with ever-increasing prominence in the specialist literature of this field.[33] It was in Lucerne that Fritz Allemann, Rudolf Bernoulli, and Oskar Schlag met to prepare the foundation of the Hermetic Society, which was formally launched in Zurich at the end of the 1940s.[34] This group emphasized the symbolism of the Tarot, with which ORS was closely preoccupied. On Schlag's instructions, the Swiss artist Max Hunziker finally created his own version of the twenty-two major Arcana.[35] Even Jung is said to have been a member of the Hermetic Society until—as Oskar Schlag informed me—the psychologist's expulsion was made necessary by the rivalry between "Atma," the guiding spirit of the Hermetic Society, and "Philemon," Jung's spiritual guide, whom he claimed had accompanied him since the age of three.

Schlag, born in 1907, grew up in Landshut, Bavaria, in rather poor circumstances. Already in his puberty he experienced psycho-energetic manifestations, which soon attracted the attention of Albert von Schrenk-Notzing, who set up a laboratory for Schlag in Landshut, when the latter was only sixteen.[36] From the future Eranos speaker Max Pulver ORS learned the art of graphology, which he mastered to a high degree, as this author knows from experience.[37] Although he had no formal academic qualification, he was appointed lecturer for graphology at the University of Zurich. He underwent a training analysis with Oskar Pfister in order to be able to practice as a psychotherapist. From 1938 he was also a lecturer at the Zurich Institute for Applied Psychology, a position he retained for over twenty years. There he held a series of lectures on *Grenzgebiete der Psychologie* (border areas of psychology), thereby coining this phrase. In the 1940s he was already lecturing on the psychology of yoga, Tantra, alchemy, and magic. Some twenty-five volumes of notes remain from these lectures, although "they have not been checked by the lecturer," as Schlag somewhat ironically remarks.[38] In addition he was co-founder of the Swiss Parapsychological Association. In 1948 he joined the Masonic lodge Sapere Aude in Zurich and in 1949 the lodge Uhland in New York. In the Swiss Alpina Lodge he even held the office of Worshipful Master. Here many of his "building elements" (*Baustücke*, the lodge term for lectures) must surely be preserved, in addition to which there are the numerous lectures that he gave to the Hermetic Society.

In addition, Schlag was a keen philatelist and a great collector of books and works of art, especially Tibetan thangkas.[39] Exactly how ORS came by his riches has been the subject of much speculation, and the matter has never been explained. Over the years I have heard varying accounts from the man himself, and they seem to me to possess little credibility. Due to his esoteric and psychological activities, Oskar Schlag was much admired in female circles· and because there were many members of affluent families among his female admirers, he was repeatedly given valuable gifts.[40] This explains, though only in part, how he amassed such costly collections. The greater part of his book collection appears to be derived from the effects of the parapsychologist Gerda Walther, which she in turn received as executor of the estate of Baron Albert Schrenck-Notzing. In this connection it also appears Walther's apartment in Ticino was robbed. It seems that the collection then came into the hands of Schlag via an antiquarian bookseller in Zurich.[41] In 1986 the Zurich Central Library held an exhibition entitled "Wissende, Eingeweihte und Verschwiegene. Esoterik im Abendland" (Knowers, initiates, and those sworn to silence: esotericism in the West), the lion's share of which consisted of the finest works from Schlag's collection.

In an interview in the parapsychological journal *Neue Wissenschaft* Jung describes how he conceived and successfully carried out, together with Oskar Schlag, an experiment in telekinesis.[42] And on the occasion of a joint visit to Baroness Gabriele von Schrenk-Notzing, he explained to the psychoanalyst Gustav R. Heyer (whom we encountered earlier) that he was convinced of the genuineness of Oskar Schlag's mediumistic phenomena, despite Schlag's controversial reputation. Jung related how he once held Schlag firmly in his arms yet was unable to prevent the latter's jacket from being removed in a way that ruled out any trickery.[43]

These parapsychological activities were, however, only one of Oskar Schlag's many facets. What he himself regarded as much more important was his activity as an intermediary to the hereafter with the aim of spreading certain esoteric teachings. The results of this work are embodied in the *Lehren des A* (The teachings of A) which, from Schlag's death to the time of writing (2011), have appeared in fourteen volumes, edited and with a commentary by Antoine Faivre[44] and Erhart Kahle with the assistance of Annelis Bergmaier.[45] The well-known Swiss esotericist Hans-Dieter Leuenberger even regards

Oskar Schlag as "one of the greatest spiritual masters of this [i.e. the twentieth] century."[46] And Thorwald Dethlefsen, probably the esotericist with the widest influence in the German-speaking realm after the War, is reported to have had long-standing contacts with ORS.[47]

Apart from the channeled messages there are only some newspaper articles and a few volumes of poetry from the pen of ORS.[48] More texts by him are sure to exist in the archives of the Hermetische Gesellschaft. Apparently he attended the Eranos meetings only in 1939 and 1941.

Another person who gave a lecture was the Viennese art historian Carl Moritz von Cammerloher, who also had studied medicine and from 1938 worked as an analytical psychologist. At the same time he was much preoccupied with oriental cultures and religions and even made translations from the Sanskrit.[49] Someone who came directly from India was Swami Yatiswarananda, who spoke on Hindu symbolism in relation to various meditational exercises for spiritual development. The swami was head of the Ramakrishna Ashram in Bangalore, south India. The Indian mystic Ramakrishna enjoyed enormous fame in the Western world during the 1920s, as his visions and mystical experiences embraced not only Indian deities but also the Virgin Mary. The literature about him is very extensive and includes positive assessments from such people as Aldous Huxley and Arnold Toynbee.[50] The person who contributed most to spreading the teachings of Ramakrishna was his favorite disciple, Swami Vivekananda, who made numerous journeys to the West and wrote many books, making yoga and Vedanta accessible to a wider readership.[51] One of the people who contributed most to the fame of the Indian holy man in the early 1930s was the writer Romain Rolland with his work *The Life of Ramakrishna*.[52] Rolland has been mentioned earlier because of his veneration for Rudolf Maria Holzapfel. On the other hand, Walter Robert Corti—mentioned earlier as a commentator on Eranos—was not particularly impressed by Swami Yatiswarananda's debut. "The lecture by the one real representative of the orient, however warmly delivered, was noticeably deficient in terms of content."[53]

At this point, before dealing with the next speaker, the psychotherapist and astrologer Sigrid Strauß-Klöbe, I would like to fill out the psychological profile of Olga Fröbe by briefly examining her relationship to the other women at Eranos. William McGuire, who knew her very well, writes in his book on Bollingen that she had great difficulty in working together with other women on her own level.[54] During the 1938 meeting she came into conflict for unknown reasons with the British archaeologist V.C.C. Collum, and thereafter up to the time of her death women were implicitly excluded as lecturers.

She was apparently equally unenthusiastic when speakers brought their wives with them. In this connection Antoine Faivre recounts in his diary an anecdote about Mrs. Scholem. The latter was immersed in a conversation with the lecturers when Olga Fröbe abruptly ended the discussion and demanded that she leave the room, since women had "nothing to discuss with the professors."[55]

On this issue she even risked a quarrel with her supremely treasured mentor Jung. On 7 May 1942 she wrote to him that the role of his "Catholic advisor" Jolande Jacobi would be "superfluous" at Eranos. Jung took her to task over this matter in a letter of 9 April 1942, but the issue continued to be a problem until shortly before her death. As late as January 1960, Jung analyzed in a letter one of her dreams as follows: "In your case we are dealing with a father complex involving an over-valuing of the masculine, and for this reason you should be initiated by *a woman into a women's order*.[56] That would also be most favorable for the future of Eranos. The male sex lacks for you the necessary maternal element."

Sigrid Strauß-Klöbe, meanwhile, in her youth had come into contact with the work of the parapsychological writer Carl du Prel and his observation, "We need the brain for perceiving the world as revealed through the senses but not for perceiving all things."[57] This had convinced her of the existence of something that went beyond normal consciousness. Later, when she encountered Jung's concept of the unconscious, it seemed to point in exactly the same direction. After taking a degree in Germanic studies and then a course in dramatic arts, she wrote a play about Hypatia, the ancient Greek female philosopher, and Pagan, who was stoned to death by a Christian mob.

One book that deeply influenced Strauß-Klöbe (and undoubtedly many other people as well) was *Paideuma*, by the anthropologist Leo Frobenius.[58] In this work Frobenius made the case for an intuitive mode of research. He named his key concepts *Ergriffenheit* (an untranslatable word meaning something between "inspiration" and "ecstatic possession")[59] and *Tiefenschau* (seeing in depth). These terms were used by at least two other Eranos speakers, namely Walter F. Otto and Karl Kerényi. Sigrid Strauß-Klöbe and her husband, Heinz Arthur Strauß, also a noted astrologer and historian of astrology, produced their first astrology book in 1927 with the publisher Kurt Wolff.[60] In 1928 and 1929 there appeared, under the editorship of Heinz Arthur Strauß and with a different publisher, the *Jahrbuch für kosmobiologische Forschung* (Yearbook for cosmobiological research),[61] to which Richard Wilhelm also contributed an essay.[62] When Wilhelm produced a translation of the Chinese alchemical work (devoted to the aim of immortality), *The Secret of the Golden Flower*,[63] with a commentary by Jung from the point of view of depth psychology, it was Strauß-Klöbe who checked the manuscript and her husband who oversaw the publication.

She met Jung and Wilhelm at the home of Count Hermann Keyserling, with whom she also carried on a correspondence. The couple also enjoyed a friendship with Edgar Dacqué, whose heterodox views on zoology have already been mentioned and who was famous for his mythological and anti-Darwinist views on evolution. Between 1931 and 1934 she was also in close contact with Heinrich Zimmer. In 1933 Strauß-Klöbe wrote an essay, which elicited a letter from the psychoanalyst Alexander Mitscherlich, who was later to play an important role for the 1968 generation.[64] Mitscherlich declared that he found the essay "outstanding" and that he read her work with the greatest interest. He was convinced that psychology and astrology could fruitfully complement each other.

Through her work as a depth psychologist Strauß-Klöbe was preoccupied on a daily basis with the symbolic language of the unconscious, and she soon began to link these symbols with the planets of astrology, which she regarded ultimately as "gods in us." Out of these preoccupations emerged her Eranos lecture on "The Psychological Significance of the Symbol in Astrology." Jung reacted by saying that she was, to his knowledge, the first person to think deeply about the astrological symbols in terms of psychology. Jung himself had already been experimenting with astrology since 1909 and later he cast horoscopes for many of his patients, seeing in the horoscope the archetypes of the collective unconscious at work. And Strauß-Klöbe's pronouncements even inspired Heinrich Zimmer to exclaim, "This is pure gold."

At the same time Strauß-Klöbe worked on some astonishing analogies between astrology and the *I Ching*. Her work "Tierkreis-Symbolik und Bilderwelt des I Ging" (Zodiac symbolism and the images of the *I Ching*) was published with introduction by Edgar

Dacqué in the *Europäische Revue* and subsequently included in the compendium *Reich der Seele*, edited by G. Heyer and F. Seifert, who found the piece enormously insightful.[65]

Although astrology was officially scorned during the years of the National Socialist regime, Strauß-Klöbe collected a great deal of material for comparative study, which is still available to research today. Further books followed, including *Das kosmopsychische Phänomen*, which attempted to "translate" the astrological birth chart into the terms of analytical psychology and was aimed primarily at depth psychologists and psychothera-pists.[66] Helmut Barz, president of the governing board of the C.G. Jung Institut in Zurich, wrote to her, "The Jungian psychologists should note that your book has now done for astrology what Jung did for alchemy, namely uncovered its significance in terms of depth psychology."[67] In 1938 and 1939 she came again to Eranos, but did not lecture.

From the Eranos guest book we learn that the 1934 meeting was also attended by the psychoanalyst Toni Sussmann, "muse" of the poet Theodor Däubler, as well as Olga Fröbe's friends Cary Baynes, Marianne Pallat, and Hertha Jay von Seldeneck. Also present were the esoterically inclined writer G.H. Mees from The Hague, Baron von Veltheim-Ostrau, and graphologist Max Pulver.

The 1934 meeting was reported in the journal *Die Tat* by a certain Dr. A.E. After a detailed survey of the individual lectures, the author sums up by saying:

> Why all the effort? The answer must be: We human beings need symbols, we can-not live without them. Symbols are the form in which our awareness of ultimate things is manifest. On our wandering journey through the forest of symbols we come to the self and [here he paraphrases the author Jakob Wilhelm Hauer] when the energies flow into the depths of our being we experience a liberation.[68]

Eranos 1935

Dangerous Encounters with National Socialism

Concerning the political issues that had already cropped up in 1934, Olga Fröbe declared quite openly in her foreword to the 1935 meeting, "Hence there are no barriers here between different faiths and different races. Eranos is therefore a real meeting place, it is a 'tent of encounter.'" And yet this could have been the very last Eranos meeting, for Jung had declared that he would be unable to attend, as he was going to be in Harvard.[69] She visited him shortly afterwards at Küsnacht and gave him an ultimatum: If he did not come, that would mean the end of Eranos altogether. To her surprise, Jung suddenly accepted after all. She wrote in her records that she had thereby "won a victory, and one that would hold for many years." To this report (which may have been embroidered with her wishful fantasies) Aniela Jaffé added that it was not Fröbe but rather the *Eranos* archetype that had won the victory. Later we shall look more closely into the matter of this archetype and its "personification" in the form of the *genius loci* of Eranos.

In 1935 the financial difficulties that would follow Fröbe throughout her life were becoming acute. Writing to her friend Roland Holst, she said that at any moment the bank could foreclose on the mortgage on the Eranos building and that she therefore urgently needed to find money in order to avoid jeopardizing the whole property.[70] And there was another problem that began to be virulent: Nazi Germany was no longer will-ing to permit speakers to travel to Ascona and simply confiscated their passports. From then on, before the meeting she made a point of going to the Ministry of Education in Berlin to convince them that it would be a loss for Germany if the speakers were not able to take part. Evidently she succeeded often enough, because many German speakers came.

As Geoffrey Cocks relates, between 1935 and 1938 various organs of the German state tried to obtain detailed information about Eranos.[71] On 29 July 1936 Fröbe wrote to Jung informing him that the German government had forbidden German speakers to take part in Eranos and that this would apply basically to all German university lecturers. As she later explained in a 1944 statement to the American Embassy in Bern, Martin Buber's participation in the 1934 Eranos conference had led to difficulties with the German Ministry of Education, which in 1936 took the precaution of forbidding German speakers to travel abroad.[72] However, she was able, through the mediation of Professor M.H. Göring, *Reichsführer* for Psychotherapy, to plead her case at the ministry and gain permission for Germans to continue participating at Eranos. But in 1938 the eyes and ears of the National Socialist regime outside Germany reported that Jews had been present at the meetings, that the content of some of the lectures had been politically dangerous, and that the whole Eranos organization was altogether mysterious. Thereafter the National Socialist authorities demanded a report on the 1938 meeting, which was provided by Gustav Heyer's pupil Olga von König-Fachsenfeld. She indicated that she had heard nothing political at Eranos. Some Jews had been present in the audience, but none had delivered a lecture. She added that especially the Swiss contingent had been careful not to criticize Germany. Following this report, in 1939 Germans were again permitted to participate in Eranos. In December 1939 a further report was submitted by the German Consulate in Locarno, indicating that, while the meetings were unusual, they did not serve the interests of Jews, Freemasons, or foreign powers. The only restriction, which seems extraordinary from today's perspective, was that Germans should not lecture to an audience in which Jews were present.

At the sixth congress of the European Association for the Study of Religion, held in Bucharest in September 2006, the scholar of religion Horst Junginger of the University of Tübingen threw additional light on these matters in his paper on the Eranos meetings during the 1930s, based on new research. In this lecture, which was published in the Romanian journal *Archaeus*, Junginger drew attention to an anonymous handwritten memorandum of June 1936 in the archives of the Reich Ministry for Science, Teaching and People's Education, suggesting that "all applications to attend the Eranos conferences in Ascona should be rejected in view of the totally unacceptable goals of the Eranos movement."[73] The writer went on to say that Eranos wished to "infiltrate our 'Western' Christendom with Oriental occult elements." The archive also contains a further document, dated January 1937, stemming from the SD, the Security Service of the SS, and describing Eranos as an endeavor with Freemasonry-like traits and hidden goals as well as a high proportion of Jewish participants. There is also mention of Jakob Wilhelm Hauer and his (for that time) courageous positive assessment of Martin Buber and C.G. Jung.

Junginger also confirms Olga Fröbe's meeting with the Ministry of Education in Berlin through the mediation of Professor Göring on 8 September 1936. The main topic was the participation of the ethnologist Theodor Wilhelm Danzel, one of whose grandparents was not of Aryan descent. Fröbe must indeed have convinced the officials to allow Danzel to take part. At the beginning of 1938 she returned to Berlin, once again to plead for travel permission for German speakers. She argued that this would prove that there was no restriction of academic freedom under the National Socialist regime. Nevertheless, Erwin Rousselle's attendance was not approved. Surprisingly, however, Heinrich Zimmer's was, even though his wife counted as Jewish under the Nuremberg Laws.

In 1939 Fröbe intervened again, and this time various other organs of the National Socialist government were involved, so puzzling did Eranos appear. After a process of investigation the authorities showed themselves inclined to grant the requested permission on condition that no Jews and emigrants were admitted to the conference and that the invited professors were loyal. The Berlin ethnologist Richard Thurnwald, who was one of the invited participants, confirmed in a letter to the rector of his university that Fröbe had expressly assured him that no Jews would be invited.[74] Another participant was the orientalist Hans Heinrich Schaeder, who claimed he had only agreed to take part on the express guarantee that neither Jews nor emigrants would be invited. After the conference he wrote a detailed report, confirming in tones of praise that the organizers of Eranos had indeed fulfilled this undertaking.

Evidently, therefore, we have to admit that Olga Fröbe made a pact with the National Socialist regime at the expense of certain innocent individuals. As we have no testimonies on the matter, we have no means of knowing whether or to what extent her conscience troubled her on this account. Nor have any opponents of the National Socialist regime subsequently come forward with statements about her behavior during that period. Was this because she was able to keep quiet about her actions? Or were such compromises seen at that time as unavoidable? Psychologically we can understand why she acted as she did, for Eranos was her priority over everything else, even her daughter Bettina, as we know. Eranos was the archetype with which she fully identified herself and without which she did not wish to live.

She admired Germany, and her preference for German speakers might also have had to do with this admiration and not only with their individual achievements as scholars. In her private notes on her meditation images (inspired by Alice Bailey among others) she speaks of her identification with Germany. One of these images shows a swastika and is captioned "The Beginning of Creation." After having described the golden and the black OM-Mantra it was perhaps to this image that she was referring when she wrote the following English text, preserved in the Eranos archive and quoted by Riccardo Bernardini in his dissertation:

> The Golden Swastika is a Sun symbol = a symbol of sun-energy and power. The black swastika or the lefthand swastika, as it is in Germany = a symbol of dark power = destruction. With both these symbols I was identified!!![75] Here lies the root, the deepest root of my identification with Germany!!! Both these black symbols of highest but destructive power mean possession by the Devil. Just as Germany is possessed by him, the dark aspect of the Self. Or by Kali the Destroyer.[76]

It is not known when she wrote this text, but various things indicate a probable date of around 1945, even though the meditational images stem from before 1933.[77] This, at any rate, is the opinion of Riccardo Bernardini, who discovered these notes. However, the intensity of the above quotation shows without a doubt that she could not have written these words as a follower of the National Socialist regime. Probably, as with so many other people, she was pulled back and forth between fear and fascination.

A small but significant episode involving Alice Sprengel shows Fröbe in a less pro-German light. Alice Sprengel had been a close collaborator of Rudolf Steiner, and when

Steiner had married in 1914, she had transferred her allegiance to Theodor Reuss, founder of the OTO, who even authorized her to establish new OTO lodges.[78] In the archive of the Swiss Psychosophic Society, which encompasses the Swiss OTO, there is a long letter to Fröbe from Margarethe Hardegger, a close friend of Gustav Landauer and a prominent socialist and women's rights activist, who became the first workers' secretary of the Swiss Federation of Labor.[79]

In her letter of 15 August 1935 Margarethe Hardegger spoke vehemently in favor of Alice Sprengel, declaring that she had "acted as a spiritual mother for me" and had "opened up [in me] a sense of the correspondences." It was only thanks to Alice Sprengel that she, Margarethe Hardegger, was able to understand the teachings from Eranos. Apparently, on account of pressure from the German authorities, Olga Fröbe had originally wanted to bar Alice Sprengel from Eranos and had denied her an entrance ticket. There had even been threats of "political surveillance" of Eranos unless the emigrant Alice Sprengel were kept away. In the letter Margarethe Hardegger expressed her thanks to Fröbe for finally issuing a ticket for Alice Sprengel, and she also thanked God for "giving a courageous heart to the Keeper of the Garden." Here we see an example of how Fröbe did indeed also stand up against National Socialism in so far as she was able to do so, although she must have had some anxiety on account of the many German lecturers. This is another indication that no sympathy for National Socialism can be attributed either to her or to Eranos.

Most of the speakers at the 1935 meeting were returning from previous years, but a new face was that of Robert Eisler.[80] Born in Vienna, the son of a millionaire, Eisler studied there and in Leipzig where he graduated *summa cum laude*. He took doctorates both in political economy and in art history. Having fallen in love with the daughter of an Austrian painter, he accepted to be baptized as a Christian. His attempts to take his *Habilitation* failed repeatedly for reasons which Scholem describes as follows: "He was equally unwelcome to Christians because of his decidedly Jewish appearance and to Jews because of his conversion."[81]

As a member of the Austrian Historical Institute, his travels included visits to the excavations at Ephesus and Knossos. In 1910, he published what I regard as his main work, *Weltenmantel und Himmelszelt* (The cloak of the world and the tent of heaven),[82] fascinating for its linguistic style and wide intellectual breadth. In this work he attempted to show that Greek philosophy developed out of the cosmology of the "Orphic" cult of Chronos-Aion, which in turn he connected with the Iranian religion of Zervanism. In the foreword he expressed a view that most of the other Eranos speakers would have agreed with:

> The time in which we live needs first to look back and remember the past before we can even grasp what a *world picture* or a *world view* is in the literal sense. The ultimate dream of the modern age … was a gigantic, all-embracing *mathematical formula* that would capture the world. It was emphatically not a *world view*, and even less was it a tangible *symbol* or *image* for the way in which the All-and-Everything manifests itself, extending into the endless reaches of space and time, into the infinitely large and the infinitely small.

Between 1910 and 1914, Eisler wrote many articles for the journal *The Quest*, to which he remained loyal, with some interruptions, into the 1930s.[83] Perhaps one of the most interesting scholarly esoteric journals of the first half of the twentieth century, *The Quest*, then a quarterly, was edited by G.R.S. Mead, former private secretary to H.P. Blavatsky. Mead had a reputation extending beyond esoteric circles on account of his many books, especially on Gnosticism.[84] Mead had founded this journal in 1909, following his resignation from the Theosophical Society after twenty-five years on account of a (still unclear) pedophilia scandal involving the prominent Theosophist C.W. Leadbeater.

Eisler's first article, on Orpheus, was based on a lecture that he had given at a conference in Oxford on the history of religion. The lecture must have aroused interest, for John M. Watkins, probably England's most famous esoteric bookseller, who also published *The Quest*, then brought out a book presenting Eisler's theses.[85] From an article by Eisler on the October 1914 issue of *The Quest* it is clear that the author, even in his younger years, was interested in " Recent Experiments in Clairvoyance," as his article was entitled. During the First World War, Eisler fought for the Austrian monarchy and was seriously wounded. After the end of the war he resumed his lecture trips. Thus, for example, he spoke at the Warburg Institute in Hamburg, for which he also carried out research.[86] His skill as a lecturer must have been phenomenal. Scholem writes on his subject as follows: "Eisler's eloquence was as amazing as his education. It was impressive, but not quite serious. I, at any rate, had never seen such a display of learning—brilliantly riveting, sparkling and at the same time suspect."[87]

Through support from England, Eisler was chosen as head of the Section for Intellectual Cooperation at the League of Nations in Paris. However, the Austrian government (Eisler was an Austrian) had not been consulted in advance and protested at the appointment for political reasons, with the result that Eisler's ambition tragically came to nothing.[88]

During this period Eisler also lectured at the Sorbonne. Then followed several years of research in his own country. In 1938 he was called to the University of Oxford, but was prevented from taking up his post owing to the annexation of Austria by Nazi Germany. In his homeland Eisler was arrested as a Jew and spent fifteen months in Buchenwald and Dachau concentration camps. Fortunately he was released and went to England, where he was able to teach at Oxford after all. Nevertheless, his wife Lily von Pausinger "literally had to take care of his nourishment by working as a house maid."[89] The after-effects of the concentration camps became more and more evident, and he died in 1949.

His specialty was the early Christian era, but his interests extended much further. They included parapsychology, as already mentioned, as well as the ancient mystery cults and also astrology, although he was never a "believer" but decidedly the contrary.[90] His concern was rather to delve meticulously into historic roots and parallel phenomena.[91]

Ernst Robert Curtius calls Robert Eisler a "real *Aufklärer*" (literally "enlightener," i.e. working in the spirit of the Enlightenment), and he adds reflectively, "But, as C.G. Jung says, the Enlightenment, while removing the godly from nature and from human institutions, 'overlooked' a god of terror that inhabits the soul." Eisler was, according to Curtius, "one of the most personally engaging of speakers" and one who "showed with uncanny clarity, where the cold dialectic of the white man's intellect leads—to a petrifaction, a *rigor mortis* of the world perceived as concept. What remains is the melancholic inner malaise of Solomonic world-weariness." And, perhaps suspecting worse times to come, Curtius adds, "But the god of terror avenges himself in the terrible revolt of the masses against the de-mystification of that which is sacred to him."[92]

Eisler's book on lycanthropy (the supposed metamorphosis of man into wolf) remains the standard work on the subject, although its scope is much wider than one would suppose from the title, since it also covers crimes of violence from prehistory. Here he invokes Jung's concept of the collective unconscious, and in the foreword he thanks the psychologist for his part in the organization of Eranos, where he, Eisler, had been able to learn so much from Jung. Olga Fröbe at first regarded Eisler highly. In a letter to Jung of 1 September 1935 she described how one of her cats, whom Eisler was fond of petting, had shown him great trust by giving birth to a litter of kittens in his presence. Later on, however, her opinion of Eisler deteriorated. She suspected that he sometimes used his outstanding intellectual abilities to prove something that he knew to be untrue, simply for the sake of intellectual amusement.

The year 1935 saw what was probably the first attempt by someone from the outside to categorize Eranos in terms of its philosophical and spiritual orientation. I am referring to the essay by Walter Robert Corti, "Die Eranos-Begegnungsstätte für Ost und West in Moscia-Ascona" in the *Schweizer Annalen*, from which I have already quoted several times. Although Corti wrote his report after only two visits to the Eranos conferences, his tone is quite unhesitant.

> The real focus of these efforts [i.e. of Eranos] is occidental man in all his uncer-
> tainty; what is being attempted here is to use the particular methodology of
> East-West comparison to probe his [Western's man's] apparently fragmented rela-
> tionship to himself and to the essence of being ... Nor is [Eranos] a "School of
> Wisdom" where a Socratic figure sits there like an electric ray, sending out flashes
> of uplifting wisdom or autocratically directing a series of lectures. At the same time
> it would also be wrong to compare the whole affair to some market of late antiq-
> uity, full of Gnostics and philosophers peddling their worldviews. For, as soon as
> the speakers gather around a common theme, it becomes apparent that—with the
> notable exception of Martin Buber[93]—they are kindred spirits in many important
> ways. And ultimately the whole gathering is under the spell of this remarkable
> woman with her unerring energy, who knows exactly how to balance opposite
> poles in a life-enhancing way. If Lao-Tse warns us against the sole rulership of the
> white man's intellect to prevent the *yang* pole from becoming unduly strong—a
> danger that constantly threatens the male sex—Mrs. Fröbe is there as a reminder,
> standing out as a rare *yin* figure in a forest of male preoccupations.[94]

Corti emphasizes that the aim is not just the accumulation of knowledge "but rather to bring about a transformation and create greater self-integration in the participants." Yet there was always "a sharp, analytical spirit at work" and "however much the whole endeavor was informed by Eastern traditions of thought, it preserved a decidedly Western face: Promethean, Caesarian, Wotan-like." And, "despite the lecturers' penchant for images and the morbus symbolicus that was occasionally evident, there was an unmistak-able desire to work in an academically rigorous way."

Despite the great fascination that Eranos held for Corti, by 1935 he was still not con-vinced that the whole undertaking could really produce anything fruitful. "But out of the passionate ferment of these seekers no Western ethos is likely to make itself felt in the near future." Indeed Corti becomes more explicit still: "This writer is full of inner doubt as to whether anything good can ever come out of Ascona. Ascona is in fact a curious repository of all the bizarre and also often dangerous aberrations of humankind." Then, qualifying his statement, he goes on, "The Ascona atmosphere, although it may occasion-ally spill over to Moscia, is *not* the same ground on which Eranos flourishes."

It is interesting to note that Corti is careful to distance himself from anything that is clearly and solely esoteric, although it is unfortunately not clear whether he came to this position through conversations with Olga Fröbe. Thus Corti writes, "It is abundantly evident that there is neither an Eranos movement, nor a real Eranos circle, and that the leading speakers are clearly determined to have nothing to do with Theosophy, with Rudolf Steiner or with people such as René Guénon." At the same time Corti poses the question "whether the Eranos level of discourse does not imply an absolute renunciation of the exclusive validity of Christ's word."[95] However, all these pronouncements bear witness to a deeper involvement with the subject than is normal in journalistic writings. It is clear that Corti was personally preoccupied with the questions addressed by Eranos and was looking for answers. What is unclear is whether at that time there already existed the close mental rapport between Corti and Fröbe, which would later burn brightly only to end in a clash. At any rate, Corti was one of the people who visited Eranos regularly over decades and who repeatedly wrote about it in the press with critical sympathy.

One of the guests at the 1935 meeting who should be mentioned is Mia, the first wife of Hermann Hesse, who had already been present at the 1932 meeting during the Alice Bailey phase.

Eranos 1936

The theme of the 1936 Eranos meeting was "The Development of the Idea of Salvation in East and West."[96] The meeting is mentioned in a letter by Jung of 16 June 1936, addressed to the president of the Analytical Psychology Club in London, in which Jung suggests that the conference would be a good opportunity for the various analytical psychology clubs to get to know each other; he mentions specifically those of Basel, Berlin, Paris, London, and New York. Probably he aimed both to assist Fröbe in her efforts to attract enough educated people willing to pay the attendance fee, and to further his own ambitions, which he undoubtedly had not lost sight of.[97]

Olga Fröbe's introduction to the lecture program for 1936 contains some interesting revelations about herself, which do not necessarily apply to Eranos itself. In the foreword to the collected proceedings she writes, "We stand between two eras, at the transition between one *Weltanschauung* and another, and we are experiencing the re-formation of religious concepts." Later in the foreword she refers again to "two ages" and "two zodiacal signs," no doubt having in mind the so-called Age of Aquarius. After speaking of the "inner world" she goes on:

> That is where our path of salvation is leading us. And only by way of this gate of immanence, it seems to me, can we experience the reality of the first and last things. We carry the kernel of salvation within us as a hidden treasure, a sealed fountain that holds the water of life … Thanks to analytical psychology we have a method or a system of signposts, which enables us bring our inner experiences into our conscious awareness. This is the same path of initiation that human beings have trod since time immemorial, led by psychotherapists, who have existed in all eras.

If we were to believe that Olga Fröbe was acting here as merely the "mouthpiece" of Jung, then we might be tempted to go along with the central thesis of Richard Noll, who sees Jung as the founder of a new religion or cult, characterized by a direct experience of the divine in the individual person (Christ, sun, self).[98] The only trouble is that the relationship between Olga Fröbe and Jung was of a quite different nature and was certainly not one of harmonious agreement.[99] She later even wrote that one could more accurately call it a struggle than a relationship.

From the beginning they carried on a lively correspondence, which primarily, however, concerned the planning of the Eranos program. The academic level of Eranos certainly made it appealing to Jung, who was at that time not widely acclaimed as a psychologist, as it offered him for the first time an opportunity to bring his ideas to the attention of a wider scholarly public.[100] There was also the attraction of having his work published along with the other lectures.[101] And yet he did not want to stand in the foreground, as he was anxious to avoid giving the impression of any exclusive "patronage" on his part. Thus, in a letter to Fröbe of 27 March 1942, he strongly resists being identified with Eranos, stating that "as a matter of principle I am only a collaborator." This sentiment is confirmed in a further quotation from another letter to her: "I most definitely do not wish it to seem as though the independent and voluntary work of the others had been diverted into a psychological groove and thus pressed into my service." Clearly, therefore, some misgivings of this kind did exist.

As this question of Jung's relationship to Eranos seems to me very important, I would like to quote here some further observations by various long-standing and therefore well-informed participants. For example, Mircea Eliade writes, "Jung was the *spiritus rector* of Eranos, yet one cannot say that the lecturers were exclusively Jungians. Most of them were only superficially familiar with the problems of modern psychology."[102] Gershom Scholem, in a letter to the historian Morton Smith, refers to "Ascona (where the influence of C.G. Jung is very tangible, since he is the moving spirit behind the series of conferences known as 'Eranos')."[103] And Walter Robert Corti describes him as the "inner regent of the Eranos undertaking."[104] Olga Fröbe herself, in the special edition for Jung's seventy-fifth birthday,[105] remarks, "Through his collaboration as a lecturer and his advice in the development of the work, he played a distinct and fundamental role in furthering Eranos."

At any rate, Jung was a piece of luck for Fröbe in two ways. First, he had a wide circle of acquaintances, extending into many foreign countries, especially the United States, and these contacts would soon prove essential for the viability of Eranos. Second, Jung's theory of archetypes gave her the necessary basis and structure to deal with her own stubborn intuitions and psychological problems. And, as we shall see, her personal psychological development and her intuitive decisions were of decisive importance for Eranos.

Fröbe's ideas on psychology, however, did not conform to those of Jung—at least not in the early years. Thus, on 10 February 1936 she wrote to Friedrich Heiler, whom she considered more receptive to esoteric ideas, "And it seems to me that we can already see the beginnings of a transcendental psychology that strives towards a synthesis between mental conflicts and true mystical experience." Then comes a direct attack on Jung:

> I believe that Jung, for example, reduces mystical experiences too much to the primitive, phallic element, so that actually nothing remains except the feeling that one has merely imagined something … His "collective unconscious" is one single chaotic realm, whereas it seems to me necessary to distinguish between the different layers or departments of this collective domain. There exists undoubtedly something like a "super-consciousness," and it seems to me that Jung does not take this into account. There are also ways of expanding consciousness beyond all forms

and symbols (direct spiritual perception) and of experiencing unity, an experience that cannot be reduced to the usual primal symbols known to analysis.

Aniela Jaffé characterizes the connection between Jung and Fröbe as an "impersonal" one, based on the fact that both of them were "possessed by one and the same archetype (namely Eranos)."[106] For a "strong and forceful personality" like Olga Fröbe it was certainly not easy, as Jaffé writes, "to confront the force and creative superiority of Jung." Fröbe herself reported that for a long time she projected on to Jung the image of a powerful, evil, and unjust demon.[107] Nevertheless, in 1960, after a serious operation, she wrote to Jung, "and thus I have realized what a blessing your collaboration in Eranos was for the work and for me personally. Despite the many personal difficulties I have always heeded your words." Although they saw each other seldom in later years, they went on corresponding, and right to the end Jung continued to interpret her dreams in his letters.

Mary Bancroft, mentioned in connection with Allen Dulles and who lived in Switzerland during the Second World War, once described the relationship between the two as follows:[108]

> Mrs. Fröbe was walking along the road to Ascona with Jung—walking, talking, talking—and Jung was clumping along beside her, smoking his pipe and *listening*.[109] She was dressed as always—large hat, loose garment that was too long to be fashionable, and around her neck chains of beads or "things" of esoteric significance. I got the impression that she was in possession of some mysterious talisman—and Jung in a way was *it*. It always seemed to me so odd that she could *do* anything— organize anything. She struck me as one of those people who float through life an inch or two off the ground. And yet I realized she had to be enormously efficient to organize those conferences.

In 1936 the speakers included a small French delegation. From the Ecole Pratique des Hautes Etudes in Paris, which would send further generations of its staff to Ascona, came the indologist Paul Masson-Oursel[110] and the expert on Gnosticism Henri-Charles Puech. Henri-Charles Puech, who also taught at the Collège de France, had been appointed at the early age of twenty-seven to a chair for the History of the Early Church.[111] His special area of interest was the development of Christian theology within the surrounding philosophical and mystical milieu, focusing particularly on the earliest Church Fathers such as Clement of Alexandria and Origen. In 1946, when the famous Nag Hammadi texts were discovered, he began to translate these Gnostic manuscripts and to write a commentary on them. In due course he brought out, together with G. Quispel and M. Malinine, the so-called *Jung Codex*[112] (*Evangelium Veritatis*[113] and *De Resurrectione*[114]). His expertise in the areas of Gnosticism, Hermeticism, and Manichaeism brought him world-wide recognition.

Puech brought two insights to Gnostic scholarship. First, he maintained that there was a phenomenological and historical kinship between Manichaeism and Gnosticism. Second, Gnosticism was for him primarily a process of uncovering the true self, which is not identical with the empirical, everyday self. In his interpretation there is no trace of the profoundly negative view of the world that many other scholars (such as Hans Jonas or Eric Voegelin) have perceived in Gnosticism. One quotation will suffice to show his understanding of Gnosis and his enthusiasm for the subject: "What is a 'gnosis' if not a realization ... but a realization that is not solely and completely devoted to the search for salvation, but rather brings salvation to the individual human being or—better still—is itself salvation, in that it reveals to the individual his or her own essential being and opens up the knowledge of God and of all things."[115] As Barbara Hannah reports, at Eranos his fame preceded him, and consequently his lecture was awaited with the greatest interest.[116] He also became well known as editor of *Histoire des Religions*, a work of world-wide scope in several volumes, which was translated into a number of other languages and is considered a standard work.[117]

Friedrich Spiegelberg reports on the 1936 meeting in the *Europäische Revue*,[118] edited by Prince Karl Anton Rohan. Spiegelberg had studied theology, philosophy, history of religions, and indology. His teachers had included such great names as Rudolf Otto, Heiler, Bultmann, Heidegger, and Nicolai Hartmann, and in 1933 he took over the professorship previously occupied by Paul Tillich at the Technical University in Dresden. Spiegelberg was one of the participants at the seminars on yoga given by Jung and Hauer at the Psychological Club in Zurich. Fleeing from National Socialism, he emigrated to the United States and finally became a professor in the Department of Asiatic and Slavic Studies at Stanford University, where he became famous for his lectures, which were always full to capacity. In India he had visited Sri Aurobindo and Sri Ramana Maharshi. From 1956 he also taught at the C.G. Jung Institute in Zurich.[119] He wrote a considerable number of books including one on the spiritual practices of India, to which his friend the "hippy philosopher" Alan Watts contributed a foreword. He also wrote a book, strongly influenced by D.T. Suzuki, on the art of Zen, with a foreword by the Eranos lecturer Herbert Read.[120] In addition, he was the author of a book on alchemy, which he illustrated with magical sigils from the sixteenth-century Kabbalistic-magical text *Liber (Sefer) Raziel*.[121]

In his article Spiegelberg attaches particular importance to the effort made at Eranos to "consider the Eastern and Western views of the soul's journey and the path to salvation not simply as contrasting approaches, but rather as based on the common goal of attaining a higher stage in the development of human consciousness." The Eranos circle had, he said, turned away from the "errors" of a one-sided viewpoint, which could only lead to narrowness and the "usual flight from the valuable possibilities of self-development." Instead, Eranos was inclined to the view that one should learn as much as possible from the East and in so doing "at the same time rediscover our own eternal spiritual heritage and raise up that which had been concealed and rejected." Spiegelberg considered it important that there was an interaction between psychotherapists, on the one hand, and mythologists and scholars of religion on the other, giving rise to the realization that their researches would unearth the same humanity-wide symbols.

Friedrich Spiegelberg is also important as a link between Eranos and the spiritual center of Esalen in California. Esalen also seeks, if perhaps in a more "alternative-practical" way (e.g. in their courses on Tantra), to create a spiritual synthesis between East and West of the kind that inspired Eranos. Spiegelberg not only lectured at Esalen, as also did the Eranos speaker Paul Tillich, the historian Arnold Toynbee or the parapsychologist J.B. Rhine, but he also steered Esalen's founder, Michael Murphy, on to the spiritual path that would lead him to Esalen.[122] As Michael Murphy told me personally in April 2005, Eranos was for him one of the models for the development of Esalen.

Also in 1936 a local newspaper, the *Tessiner Illustrierte*, published an interview with Olga Fröbe on the subject of Eranos, which can undoubtedly be considered an "official" statement of the founder's position. She explained that her intention was to create "a meeting place and focal point for spiritually minded people who would be able, through the annual lecture programme, to receive stimuli from different areas of study." She emphasized particularly "the need for collaboration, unity and synthesis on all levels of human thinking and action," since "the fragmentation of our time, the individualism and the generally materialistic outlook, stemming from need—all of these constituted a global syndrome that can only be healed through an inner readjustment, a change of consciousness." Here the Swiss location had decisive advantages. "Switzerland, an island of synthesis in a chaotic Europe, offers a starting point for these idealistic and international endeavours. It deserves the thanks of everyone working for a future in which greater harmony and a more profound togetherness of all human beings will be possible."

Fröbe was careful to emphasize that "the centre in Moscia does not belong to any school, organization or group." Furthermore, "It has neither a membership nor any definite leader, but is a meeting place for followers of many existing groups." In contrast to the Anthroposophists, Theosophists, and other groups, who set much tighter boundaries, her intention was to create a place "that opens its doors to all who are working towards a deepening, an inner enrichment and a synthesis of human existence." Yoga, for instance, was approached in relation to Western psychoanalysis, not forgetting the value of meditation. She also talked about the prospects for the future and how she wanted to expand the basic scope of the meetings. For example, in the future she wanted the lectures "not to be restricted only to religious, mystical and psychological themes but to extend also to issues in the field of art, philosophy, natural science and sociology." Thus even at this early date there were far-reaching plans which, however, were not to be fully realized until much later.

Meanwhile, her financial problems were becoming more and more urgent, and a solution had to found without further delay. Consequently she decided to sell the Casa Shanti, which stood on the lakeside plot next to the lecture room. By a great stroke of luck, she found the ideal buyer in Emma von Pelet, already mentioned as the translator of Vivekananda. Emma von Pelet wanted the place as her actual home and brought in as her co-resident the psychologist Alwine von Keller, who from then on worked as a Jungian analyst in Moscia-Ascona. Alfons Rosenberg described her in his *Eranos-Flugblatt* as "a worthy, white-haired and wise sybil." For Rudolf Ritsema, who later became president of the Eranos Foundation, Von Keller played a very important role.

She herself underwent her first analysis in Berlin with Jung's pupil Ernst Bernhard. After Bernhard was forced for racial reasons to move to Rome, she continued the analysis with Jung himself. On the occasion of Olga Fröbe's seventieth birthday in 1951 she wrote the following about Eranos:

> I have come to the conviction that both the lecturers and the audience have been actively working together in the formation of a new "science of humanity," which rests on the basis of the psychological concept of "becoming conscious." This problem, which has existed continuously since antiquity, has become an urgent one for our age. What is man? And what is he in relation to the forces within and outside of himself? This question has become the theme addressed at all Eranos conferences in endless permutations.[123]

Alwine von Keller's warm-heartedness and intuition often helped Olga Fröbe over her psychological difficulties. Furthermore, both she and Emma von Pelet were very interested in Eranos, always attended the conferences and offered active support—sometimes of a finacial nature.[124]

A letter from Fröbe to Jung of 16 July 1936, preserved in the C.G. Jung archive at the Swiss Federal Institute of Technology, indicates that, even at that time, she was interested in putting the meetings on a firmer organizational footing.[125] That is to say, she planned the foundation of a "Society of the Friends of Eranos." The main reason for this move was discrepancy between the predictable expenses and the unpredictable income. While she wished to keep under her own wing the management and organization as well as the secretariat, there would be an expert committee of lecturers, "representing various countries," who would confer during each meeting to plan the next one. The business organization would be taken over by a financial committee whose task would consist primarily in "seeking honorary members or benefactors, who could gradually build up a fund." Her wish was that this fund would then acquire part of her property including the lecture room. She also wanted to have a solid membership who would enjoy the right to attend the meetings in return for an annual fee of thirty Swiss francs, thus ensuring a certain regular income. This plan, however, came to nothing, probably for lack of interest among the leading speakers. Fröbe therefore continued to carry the financial worries alone.

Eranos 1937

The theme for 1937 was the same as for 1936, namely the idea of salvation in East and West. Olga Fröbe even went so far as to say that actually the theme of all five Eranos meetings up to that date had been "the idea of the path of salvation, the way of individuation, the way of the centre, of enlightenment or salvation." And she remarked further, "Connecting with ancient times, with the tradition of our ancestors, corresponds to the notion of the Catena Aurea [The golden chain], of which we are now becoming part."

One new speaker at this meeting was the ethnologist and member of the Academia Sinica (with a guest professorship in Nanking), Theodor-Wilhelm Danzel. Like many of his German Eranos colleagues, he ceased teaching in Germany in 1933 and resumed only after 1945. Danzel saw himself as an ethnological psychologist, who studied the cultic practices and mythical teachings of communities living close to nature. To describe their beliefs he often used the term "magic," although he always maintained that the distinction between magic and religion was untenable, at least within the discourse of ethnological psychology.[126] His intellectual mentors were Lucien Levy-Bruhl, Wilhelm Wundt, and the holistically minded psychologist Felix Krüger. During an era when it was still strongly doubted that "primitive" peoples were capable of complex structures of thought and belief, his work came as an important counterbalance.[127]

✿ 8. Eranos 1938: The United States Shows Interest

Mary and Paul Mellon

The year 1938 was a particularly important one for Eranos, for it was then that a firm decision to continue the meetings became possible. Olga Fröbe had used up almost her entire fortune for the organization of Eranos and for her own travels in connection with it. While she paid no fees to the speakers, she still had to cover their travel expenses. Accommodation, at least in the period 1933–39, was usually in the Hotel Monte Verità, belonging to Baron von der Heydt, who regarded the lecturers as his personal guests and charged them nothing.[1] In the spring of 1938 she applied for support to the Rockefeller Foundation in New York, but was turned down. Then came the decisive meeting with Mary and Paul Mellon,[2] which came about thanks to her "talis-man," C.G. Jung.

Mary Mellon (Mima) had begun in 1934 to occupy herself seriously with Jung's teaching, although up to that point she had led a life more oriented to pleasure and social events than to intellectual matters. In 1935 she married Paul Mellon, who stemmed from a wealthy family and was prominent in the banking world as well as being an active art collector. His father was at that time United States ambassador in London. The young couple's home was Pittsburgh, but New York was more to their taste, and they went there frequently. In New York they underwent a Jungian analysis with Ann Moyer and her husband, Erlo van Waveren. The latter had been the "business manager" of Alice Bailey who, together with Olga Fröbe, had organized the School for Spiritual Research in Ascona.[3] Thus there was already a link to the Ascona milieu. Through the van Waverens, the Mellons were brought into contact with Jung's teaching and came to value it highly.

In 1937 Jung was invited to lecture at Yale University, after which he came to New York to hold a seminar in which Mary and Paul Mellon also participated. He quickly won them over through his easy, nonchalant manner.[4] Thus it came about that in December 1937 Paul Mellon wrote to Jung and asked to take part in Jung's next seminar, to be held in Zurich in the spring of 1938. The Mellons reached Zurich in early May 1938 and spent eight weeks there, during which they attended the (later famous) Zarathustra Seminar at the Psychology Club.[5] There they came for the first time into contact with the *I Ching*, for one of the participants, the psychologist Cary Baynes (a friend of Olga Fröbe), had begun with Jung's encouragement to translate Richard Wilhelm's German version of the Chinese oracle into English. Mary Mellon's first consultation of the oracle was so successful that she immediately said she was prepared to finance the publication and its translation.

After the seminar, Cary Baynes and the van Waverens suggested a visit to Ascona so that the Mellons could meet Olga Fröbe. The couple readily agreed, especially as Jung intended to take a holiday in Ascona and was ready to have a meeting with them alone, which had not been possible in Zurich. Here we see again how important Cary Baynes was for Fröbe, not only as her good friend and psychological advisor but because she was in equally friendly contact with the Mellons and with Jung.[6] Her efforts as an intermediary on behalf of Eranos, between Jung and Olga Fröbe and between her and the Mellons, can probably not be valued highly enough. It was she who, by making a guest room in her home available, made it possible for Olga Fröbe to come to Zurich at any time to talk to Jung about Eranos. She repeatedly made financial contributions to Eranos and encouraged her friends to do so. She also maintained contact with the Mellons when Fröbe was traveling. Her daughter, Ximena de Angulo, thus knew Fröbe (and also Jung) from the time when she was a small girl.

In this way the decisive step for Eranos was taken. The Mellons talked with Olga Fröbe about Jung, visited her collection of paintings, and looked through the already published *Eranos* volumes and, as Erlo van Waveren later said, "Olga cast her spell on Paul and Mima. They clicked right away. Olga had magic, but so had Mima, and she caught fire immediately."[7] Paul Mellon also remembered that "Olga was a very powerful, mysterious sort of woman, brimful of all kinds of mystical learning."[8] Some years later Mary Mellon wrote to Olga Fröbe, "The first thought that went through my mind when I stepped onto the terrace at Casa Gabriella was 'This is where I belong.'"[9] Even before they left Ascona the Mellons had committed themselves to making a financial contribution to publishing the proceedings of the forthcoming conference on the "The Great Mother."[10] Furthermore, they were ready to pay for Fröbe to visit Italy and Greece, where she wished to seek pictures with archetypal motifs for her archive.[11]

In Crete Fröbe had what she described in a letter to Mary Mellon as "the greatest psychological experience of my life." In two letters, each covering several pages, written to her friend and analyst Cary Baynes on November 1938, she writes about this experience in detail. She describes the panic and the psychosomatic fever that afflicted her during her stay and which she attributed to an identification with the "Great Mother." While looking for archaeological traces of the "Great Mother," she had fallen into the danger of being completely taken over by her. In Crete, where a snake goddess was worshipped in the palace of Knossos, she recognized herself as an "island" with ancient traditions, and she realized why the little island in Lake Maggiore, opposite the Casa Gabriella, on which an Aphrodite temple was supposed to have stood, had occupied such an important place in her visions ever since 1934 when she had begun her work with Jung. From there she had once "seen" a procession of priests and mystics flowing directly into her lecture hall. The vision was so strong that she even made a drawing of it.[12] And in her own analysis she equated the concept of an island with the lotus, the Grail, the mandala, and the palace of the self as the center of individual consciousness in the midst of the unconscious. In her visions she also saw herself confronted by the Minotaur and realized that behind him was the *deus absconditus*, the dark side of the self. She now understood why she had gone to Crete and spent some time there although the journey hardly provided any picture material for her archive.

Nothing, however, came of the planned American volume on the "Great Mother," even though Jung wrote a foreword to make it appealing to the American public. In this foreword, the draft of which is in the library of the Swiss Federal Technical University in Zurich,[13] Jung addresses a theme of central importance for Eranos, namely the need for interdisciplinarity as a prerequisite for any real understanding of the world. By the same token he draws attention to the negative effects of ever-increasing specialization.

However, since even the greatest genius with the most phenomenal memory must remain a dilettante in many fields, it is necessary, he says, to find other ways to achieve a complete picture of the world. Eranos would now provide just such a platform for many different disciplines. This was also the aim of his projected journal *Weltanschauung*, which was intended to cover an even wider spectrum.

At the time Fröbe was hoping to publish other Eranos lectures in English. Jung, however, had to be left out of her calculations, as he did not wish to make his lectures available. He was at that point convinced that he would be able to bring out all his essays and lectures together with an English-language publisher, and naturally he would not have certain lectures appearing simultaneously with two different publishers. In a letter to Fröbe of 18 March 1938 he wrote, "Incidentally, I believe that, if you put together a good collection of other contributions and my name is lacking, this would be no great misfortune. It would do no harm to reassure the world that Eranos has not been monopolized by me. You know how my enemies maintain that I grab everything for myself and bring it under my influence."

As planned, the theme of the 1938 meeting was *The Figure and Cult of the "Great Mother."*[14] The program included lectures on the Mother Goddess in antiquity, in Shiite Islam, in India, among the Celts, in Christianity, and in psychology. Looking back in 1955, Jolande Jacobi described this as "corrective magic,"[15] alluding to the fact that up to this point there had only been three women among the approximately seventy speakers. One of these was Vera Christina Chute Collum, who has already been briefly mentioned and whose difficulties with Fröbe led to the virtual exclusion of female speakers at Eranos. Collum, who had been born in India, had carried out archaeological investigations in India, Japan, and Brittany. Her main intention was, like many modern feminists, to seek proof of a cosmic Mother Goddess cult, present throughout the world. In doing so she expressly included insights taken from esoteric worldviews. She quoted knowledgably from Tantric and Kabbalistic writings and was not averse to Pythagorean numerology.[16] She credited the Gnostics and Druids (e.g. in Brittany) with the transmission of esoteric traditions from antiquity (interestingly, she expressly uses the term "esoteric"). With her extensive academic and esoteric knowledge, she was, on the one hand, undoubtedly an ideal lecturer for Fröbe, but on the other hand, perhaps also a serious competitor.

This year for the first time the participants were shown, as an accompaniment to the lectures, a series of enlarged photographs of the pictures collected by Fröbe showing archetypal symbols. A pair of lengthy reports on the 1938 conference have been preserved. These were written by two members of the New York Analytical Psychology Club, who had taken part and subsequently lectured on Eranos in the United States. One of them, by Hildegard Nagel, summarizes the contents of all the lectures.[17] She must have been very impressed by Eranos, for she writes, "I feel like someone who has gone to see the ocean and come back with nothing to show but a few broken shells and a tin cup half-full of salt water, not knowing anymore how to explain what one has experienced." In addition she gives thumbnail portraits of the individual speakers.

She describes Heinrich Zimmer as an excellent speaker who, over a glass of wine "spouts vocabulary like a geyser, or like James Joyce." To hear him was like listening to music or experiencing a skillful dance performance. It was simply "mythology orchestrated."[18] Zimmer, incidentally, sent a copy of his lecture on "Die indische Weltmutter" (The Indian world-mother) to Thomas Mann, who was grateful to receive the lecture and used the material in it for his own story "Die vertauschten Köpfe" (The transposed heads).[19] She was less satisfied by Gustav Heyer's talk, despite his light and relaxed style of speaking. She found that he spoke from too masculine a standpoint. In his opinion, the Great Mother was so eternally powerful that her impact, both positive and negative, could not be overestimated. Hildegard Nagel went so far as to describe the lecture as "disturbing" and was comforted by the fact that Jung was to speak on the following day. Erwin Rousselle she described as an aristocrat from the age of Goethe as portrayed by a Chinaman, a cross between a Prussian officer and a Chinese holy man. She described his lecture as curiously "silky" and "Chinese." Ernesto Buonaiuti won her over through his great liveliness and warmth, which she compared to the glow of a mature red wine. She also quoted an observation of his, which he had already made at the 1935 meeting: "From the beginning it has always been the heretics who have saved the Church."

The other extant report on this meeting is an unpublished typewritten manuscript, written by Ellen Thayer and now preserved in the Kristine Mann Library in New York, which specializes in Jungian material.[20] Thayer's report complements that of Nagel in that she does not write about the lectures, but rather presents a sort of prospectus, giving potential American visitors to Eranos an impression of the participants and the social atmosphere and providing some practical information. Here also Jung's pre-eminent position is made evident. It was not just that he was able, by his jovial manner and good command of English, to loosen up the rather stiff atmosphere (especially for Americans) at the lectures, but a large proportion of the one hundred fifty participants had come expressly because of him. Jungian groups from numerous different countries were present, as were many people who had been through a Jungian analysis. Most of the participants, however, were Swiss Germans. The fact that questions were not permitted in the lecture sessions is once again pointed out in Ellen Thayer's report, but she mentions that one Sunday morning was kept free for a so-called colloquium. However, the questions to the lecturers had to be submitted in writing in advance. This experiment came to nothing, because the questions were written in such a way as merely to demonstrate the impressive knowledge of the questioners. It was therefore decided that only the speakers would have the right to comment on and criticize each other's lectures. Unfortunately, Ellen Thayer reported, there had been no formal occasion, apart from one afternoon tea, when lecturers and guests came together, even though Fröbe often invited smaller groups to tea. Despite this lack, the conference had made a strong impression on her.

In 1938 an Egyptologist spoke for the first time: Alexandre Moret, author of numerous works on Egyptian religion. As the equally renowned Egyptologist Erik Hornung told me, Moret was also very open-minded about esoteric matters. As he died soon afterwards there was no manuscript of his lecture, and therefore it did not appear in the Eranos yearbook.

Before the War: Walter F. Otto, Hans Leisegang, and Louis Massignon

Nineteen thirty-nine was the year the Second World War began. In these troubled times Olga Fröbe was deeply concerned about the fate of Eranos and twice asked the *I Ching* what the outlook was for her conferences in the general world situation. To her relief, the answer was very positive on both occasions.[21] The psychologist Barbara Hannah writes of an almost unbearable political tension that summer, which even appeared to affect the weather.[22] Never before or since had she experienced such heavy rainstorms. On the drive to Ascona with Jung and his wife (Barbara Hannah often acted as their chauffeuse) they were going over the St. Gotthard Pass when an avalanche of earth and rock fell just behind them, blocking the road for several days. Fortunately Jung, seized by a premonition, had spurred the convoy of cars to travel faster than usual (several friends always drove in a group to Ascona). Lake Maggiore had overflowed its banks, and the water reached almost to the level of the lecture room. Jung even spoke of a "feeling that the Last Judgment was in the air." It was also the first time, as Barbara Hannah reports, that a definite tension was felt between the Germans and the other nationalities, although, as far as she was aware, there was hardly anyone among the Germans who was a Nazi sympathizer. Nevertheless, it was possible to detect in them a certain "abaissement du niveau mental" on account of the Nazi propaganda. Jung attributed this to the fact that the Germans had, in his opinion, a low threshold between the conscious and unconscious realms.

The theme of the meeting itself was the symbolism of rebirth as a religious concept. Speakers included such renowned scholars as Walter F. Otto, who spoke at Eranos in 1939 and 1955,[23] hailed from Hohenzollern, and early on came into contact with the Munich Cosmics, attending courses given by Ludwig Klages.[24] He also knew Alfred Schuler, Karl Wolfskehl, and the Derleths, brother and sister.[25] Having taken his *Habilitation* in classical philology, he held professorships in Vienna, Basel, Frankfurt am Main, and Königsberg, from which he fled in 1944 on account of the war, leaving behind his books and manuscripts for ever. After the war he held appointments in Munich, Göttingen, and Tübingen.[26] Reaching out far beyond the narrow academic confines of his subject, he appealed to Europe to find its way back to its true self by re-experiencing the ancient deities. Martin P. Nilsson went so far as to write of Otto's *Dionysos*, "This book is not scholarship as I am obliged to understand it, but rather a work of prophecy," only to add that prophecy, too, has a mission to fulfill.[27] Walter F. Otto can therefore be seen to a certain extent as the "rediscoverer" of the world of the Greek gods. Undoubtedly he felt a profound sympathy for them.[28] Furthermore, he does not conceive of any "evolution" of these gods from primitive origins. Rather, in his view the gods had revealed themselves all at once in a moment of mystical revelation.[29] Otto's belief in Goethe's concept of *Schauen* (beholding) as a way of cognition earned him criticism from purely rationally minded scholars, although his expert knowledge was never questioned. Myths were for him not mere "fables" but something that had as much claim to truth as the "cult," which stemmed from the "manifestation of the divine," that is to say from a divine revelation. Thus myth was for him (as for Schelling) a primal phenomenon of religion that cannot be traced back any further and cannot be explained in terms of any other phenomenon. Indeed, he even speaks of an "elevation of man to the verity of myth."[30] He also says that "the human mind cannot be truly creative through its own resources, but requires the contact and stimulus of a marvellous other." This "other" is for him a "higher state of being."[31] Consequently Otto opposes the mechanistic and purely rationalistic thinking of modern man.

His books were read beyond the confines of academe, and some of them even appeared in pocket book form.[32] He enjoyed a long-standing friendship with the influential scholar Leo Frobenius and with Karl Kerényi, who credited him with "reverence and sensitivity towards every primal form of religious phenomenon" as well as with "the incisiveness of a passionately independent thinker." Kerényi, who was not one for indiscriminate praise, even sees these contrasting characteristics of Otto's mind as being "perhaps for the first time … united in a single individual."[33] Even during the Second World

War, Otto attempted, together with the Italian Ernesto Grassi, to keep alive the ethos and spirit of antiquity through the publication of the yearbook series *Geistige Überlieferung* (Spiritual tradition).[34] In his introduction, headed "Erwägungen aus der italienischen Überlieferung" (Thoughts from the Italian tradition) to the second yearbook (1942), Grassi outlined the three groups of problems that the two editors had set themselves: "to elucidate the classical world view and mode of thinking, to illuminate the essence of humanism and the Renaissance [and] finally to examine the relationship of classical antiquity to the 19th and 20th centuries." Contributors to these yearbooks included Martin Heidegger, Karl Reinhardt, and Wilhelm Furtwängler.

The SD (Security Service of the SS) and Alfred Rosenberg's watchdog office for ideological and cultural matters classified Otto as "hostile." According to an SD assessment,[35] "By actively building a coterie in a spirit of cultural propaganda, Otto has been able to spread his old-style humanism. Thus he was the real moving spirit behind the liberal humanistic circle which, before and for some time after the seizure of power, played a large role at Frankfurt University and in the cultural life of Frankfurt." The same report accuses him of having consorted "with men such as the emigré to New York, Paul Tillich, and the Jewish professor of history, Kantorowicz." Walter F. Otto was also one of the founders, in 1949, of the still successful Wissenschaftliche Buchgesellschaft (Academic book society) in Darmstadt, of which he was the first president.[36]

One person who would certainly have been an asset to Eranos was the philosopher Hans Leisegang, who was a specialist in Greek thought but had also studied science. Unfortunately, however, for political reasons the German government did not permit him to travel to Ascona. Nevertheless, his lecture on the "Mystique of the Snake," which greatly impressed Olga Fröbe, was included in the volume of the conference proceedings.

Leisegang had made intensive studies of Plato and Philo of Alexandria and had also written a standard work on Gnosticism, which went through numerous editions.[37] He also published in 1922 a work entitled *Die Grundlagen der Anthroposophie* (The foundations of Anthroposophy) in which he berated the Anthroposophical Society for the fact that they kept certain of their writings secret and thus withheld them from discussion. He criticized Rudolf Steiner as a "credulous occultist" due to his "inner lack of groundedness" and "a susceptible temperament that was attracted to everything mysterious as though by a magical force." This led to "an astonishingly uncritical outlook and a stubborn tendency to hold on to that which he had accepted as truth." Once Steiner had adopted such a position, nothing could shake him from it, "not even revelations of the worst cheating and deception." Furthermore, Leisegang accused Steiner of demanding from his disciples an attitude of veneration, devotion, unconditional faith, and suppression of all criticism.[38] In 1924 there followed a short work on *Die Geheimwissenschaften* (The occult sciences). Besides his general writings on philosophical history and his introductory works on philosophy, it is worth mentioning his *Religionsphilosophie der Gegenwart* (Religious philosophy of today) and his edition of Friedrich Schleiermacher's *Reden über die Religion* (Talks on religion), a seminal work for the phenomenology of religion, as we know. The 1950 special *Eranos* volume, published for C.G. Jung's seventyfifth birthday, contains Leisegang's essay *Der Gottmensch als Archetypus* (The god-man as archetype), a theme of central importance for Eranos and for Jung. Leisegang's particular suitability as an Eranos speaker can also be seen from his book *Denkformen* (Thought forms), published in 1928 by Walter de Gruyter in Berlin, which can unhesitatingly be described as one of his magna opera.[39]

Leisegang was primarily concerned with "the elucidation of meaning." Thus, in his foreword to *Denkformen*, he writes:

> Any document that we have to deal with in the humanities consists of several lay-
> ers of meaning. The full depth of meaning that can be extracted is not just a mat-
> ter of the document itself but depends more on the researcher ... thus any work
> in the humanities will be commensurately more fruitful according how deeply
> the searcher has descended into his own self and what wider possibilities have
> unfolded within him.

Leisegang dedicated the book "To the task of understanding the mind of another and to question the possibility of such understanding." By the same token he opposed the increasing dominance of logical thinking in all areas including biology and religion. Taking the plant kingdom as an example, he said that a plant has its own immanent logic, and if modern man is to understand this logic, "he must abandon the mathematical-mechanical thinking that he is used to applying in the case of his own creations." "Compasses and ruler" are inadequate instruments for this purpose, since a plant is an organism of which one part (the seed) can give rise to the whole—something that is not possible in the case of mechanical things.[40]

He was deeply preoccupied with the idea of "the whole," as is evident in his book *Dante und das christliche Weltbild*[41] (Dante and the Christian worldview), in which he describes Dante's world as one "that is always and everywhere present as a world entity, in such a way that humanity and the world, macrocosm and microcosm mirror each other and cannot be separated." Leisegang's specific interest in such esoteric perspectives is also apparent in an earlier work with the rather misleading title *Der heilige Geist* (The Holy Ghost) and the more informative subtitle *Das Wesen und Werden der mystisch-intuitiven Erkenntnis in der Philosophie und Religion der Griechen* (The essence and emergence of mystical-intuitive understanding in the philosophy and religion of the Greeks).[42] Altogether one could say that Leisegang was concerned with a "sacralization of exist-ence," which demanded something more than mechanistic thinking.

Politically Leisegang could be described as a German nationalist.[43] During the First World War he was assigned to a machine gun company and was awarded the Iron Cross First Class for extraordinary bravery. In 1918 he was wounded but in 1920 returned to military service in Upper Silesia as a volunteer with the Free Corps, whose aim was to combat Socialist and Communist agitation in Germany. He was also a member of the conservative Stahlhelm, an organization of former front-line soldiers who wanted to exert a conservative influence in politics. However, despite his folkish worldview, he was against National Socialism. In 1930 he was appointed to the chair in philosophy at Jena. After Hitler's seizure of power in 1933, he refused to comply with the Nazis' demand that the University Senate dissolve itself and consequently he was struck from the list of sena-tors. The Nazis had wanted to replace the Senate with a directorate of four party members to run the university.[44]

In 1934 Leisegang found himself in even greater political trouble. At the burial of President Field Marshall Hindenburg the funeral oration was given by Adolf Hitler, and someone denounced Leisegang for having made "a disparaging and contemptuous remark about a corporal holding an oration for a Field Marshall."[45] Although Leisegang attempted to play down the importance of this occurrence, he was brought to court, sentenced to six months in prison, and immediately incarcerated.[46] It also weighed against him that several of his students were not happy with his lectures on Nietzsche at the University, as he drew attention to Nietzsche's critical remarks about the Germans.[47] It is interesting to read the State Prosecutor's reasons for imposing the sentence: While there was no doubt that Leisegang had a nationalist outlook, he was opposed to the "Socialism" that was "inseparable from National Socialism, the person of the Fuehrer and the new Reich." Consequently the accused was "one of the people who must be classified as reactionary."[48]

In his prison diary Leisegang deplores the "people of our time who have made their human weaknesses into an evil delusion, an *idée fixe* and a dark fanaticism, and who … with unimaginable cold-bloodedness, torment and destroy others."[49] A number of students and professors, however, came to Leisegang's support and drew up a petition. Particularly surprising was the "fabulous" (to quote Leisegang's wife) support from the well-known racial theorist H.F.K. Günther. This is all the more remarkable in view of the fact that Leisegang's chair had originally been earmarked for Günther by the Nazi minister Frick, but because of vigorous protests of the professors Günther had not been chosen. Günther even arranged to meet various high-ranking Nazi Party officials in order to help Leisegang more effectively.[50] After four months Leisegang was released on probation.

On 3 December 1935, a few months after his release, Leisegang wrote a letter to his fellow philosopher and colleague Theodor Litt, who was also forbidden to give conferences, containing the following words, which apply not only to National Socialism but to all overtly or covertly unjust regimes of whatever era:

> People know all about the evil and malicious misdeeds, the base and contemptible things that are being done around us and with us. Yet, despite their knowledge, they go along with it. Not only that, but they proclaim it all to be great and good in such a loud voice and with such a tone of conviction that the voice of bad conscience is drowned out.[51]

After the end of the Second World War Jena came under Soviet occupation. Leisegang remained, however, at "his" university and his lectures attracted huge audiences. As he pointed out the one-sidedness of Marxism he soon got into difficulties and in 1948 was dismissed from the university because of "anti-democratic" behavior. As the situation became progressively more difficult for him he fled to West Berlin, a free enclave within the Soviet zone, although even here he was not completely safe, as blacklisted people were often kidnapped and taken from there to the East. Nevertheless, he turned down an invitation to teach at Darmstadt in West Germany, as he felt that he had more important tasks to fulfill in Berlin. In 1951, a few weeks after his sixty-first birthday, he died of a sudden heart attack, probably because of the continual stress that he had been under.

Olga Fröbe originally intended also to invite Jakob Wilhelm Hauer in 1938, as she was convinced that "he might give us a very wonderful study of the rebirth symbolism in the Germanic and Indo-Germanic myths. I am afraid Jung will be against having him, but will propose it."[52]

The proceedings of the Eranos meeting of 1939 appeared in 1940, that is to say, after the beginning of the war. In her foreword Fröbe wrote, "The appearance of this book at a dark time in history points to the constancy of a principle that has operated unbroken in all the great transitions in the history of culture and to whose direction we are subordinate."[53] Apparently she was especially happy with this meeting, as this was the first time that she succeeded in balancing the German speakers, hitherto in the majority, with a large French contingent. Furthermore, despite the looming war, she sensed a much warmer atmosphere among the various nationalities, as she emphasized later during a lecture tour in the United States. Perhaps encouraged by the two positive *I Ching* consultations, she was feeling very optimistic about Eranos. She believed that 1939 marked the end of a seven-year period of preparation for a "Christian cycle which was now dawning," and that "Eranos is only now starting to address its real task."[54]

In 1939 Mary and Paul Mellon came for the first time to take part in an Eranos conference. As Olga Fröbe nearly always invited them to join the lecturers at mealtimes, they had the opportunity to come into close contact not only with Jung but also with Heinrich Zimmer. By then Zimmer had left Germany and was teaching at Oxford University. His reason for leaving Germany was that he was married to a daughter of the Austrian writer Hugo von Hofmannsthal, and the Hofmannsthals were of partly Jewish extraction. For this reason Zimmer was dismissed from his teaching post in the winter semester of 1937–38. The fact that he had been able to withstand for so long the "growing pressure and peril from the Nazi regime as well as the increasingly debilitating, deadening atmosphere that made itself felt in the concentration camp that Germany had become" he attributed to the "good fortune" that he was able to count Jung "among the people who showed interest in the things that I had to offer."[55]

The Mellons also befriended the Islamicist Louis Massignon[56] who, like Zimmer, possessed great talent as a speaker, and plans were made to publish various of his works in the United States, notably his study of the Islamic mystic and martyr al-Hallāj. Massignon led a very eventful, not to say adventurous life. His father was a well-known painter and sculptor, and in his youth Louis Massignon fell wholly under the influence of the famed French novelist Joris-Karl Huysmans, who had turned his back on literary decadence and become an ardent Catholic.[57] Huysmans also introduced Massignon to the followers of Mélanie Calvat, who had experienced an apparition of the Virgin Mary as a weeping woman in La Salette, France in 1846.[58] The revelation of the Mother of God was akin to an act of flagellation, promising stern punishments and catastrophes for disbelievers and those who ignored the hardships of the poor. Alongside this revelation, the visions of the famous mystic and stigmatic Anna Katharina Emmerich were also significant for Massignon's journey through life.

Another major influence upon Massignon was the French mystic Charles de Foucauld, who experienced a profound turn to Christianity in the Islamic environment of North Africa, and who was beatified by Pope Benedict XVI in 2005. In 1907 Massignon was imprisoned by the Turks during an archaeological expedition to Mesopotamia (today's Iraq) that may also have been a secret service mission.[59] He too sensed the "actual presence of God" through the experience of great danger, fear of death, and close contact with an intense Islamic spirituality. Like de Foucauld, this deeply moving experience led him to convert to Catholicism. Here Massignon was also convinced of the intercession of his friend on the divine level.

In the First World War Massignon had not only been awarded the Croix de Guerre for bravery at the front, but had also played an important military role in French North Africa. It is also said he worked for the French secret service. There he came into contact with T.E. Lawrence ("Lawrence of Arabia") and learned much from his contact with the Arabian mentality.[60]

According to Hildegard Nagel's report, mentioned above, much of Massignon's knowledge was acquired during long conversations "sitting cross-legged over black coffee" with his Arab friends. Through these conversations he came within the orbit of Shiite

Islam, which recognizes Ali, the cousin and son-in-law of Mohammed, as the legitimate successor of the Prophet; he drew particularly close to those groups which revere Ali not only as a victim of the Sunnis (who do not accord Ali this high position) but also as a divine incarnation and teacher of Islamic esotericism.

Amongst these groups one deserves special mention, namely the Alawis, who are to be equated with the Nusayri, a group famed in the world of occultism.[61] In Syria, where France held dominion from 1920 to 1945 following the downfall of the Ottoman Empire, the Alawis, with their alleged friendly disposition towards the French, came to be the ruling group, and reportedly it was Massignon who helped them to power. Indeed, the Alawis remain rulers to this day. With its power base residing primarily in the armed forces, the leading Ba'ath Party is a predominantly Alawi movement. After many years of struggle, its leader Hafez al-Assad came to power in 1970 via the military, and the office of president was assumed after his death by his son Bashar al-Assad, who still governs today.[62] The future outcome of the unrest that broke out in Syria in 2011 remains unclear.

Massignon's circle of acquaintances encompassed virtually the whole intellectual elite of France at the time and included Gabriel Marcel, Léon Bloy, Paul Claudel, Jacques Maritain, Louis Aragon, Jean Cocteau, Gaston Bachelard, and the Eranos speaker Cardinal Jean Daniélou. Massignon, who was a professor at both the Collège de France and the Ecole Pratique des Hautes Etudes, was even honored on his centenary for his outstanding academic work by a commemorative session and exhibition at UNESCO, which also issued a booklet in his honor.[63] He belonged to a dozen or so of the most prestigious academic societies world-wide and was the editor of the *Revue des Études Islamiques* and the *Annuaire du Monde Musulman*.

Massignon first spoke at Eranos in 1937 and for eighteen years he was one of the most faithful of the regular speakers. When he gave his last lecture there in 1955 he infringed one of the cardinal rules of Eranos, for which Olga Fröbe never forgave him and he was not invited again. His offence was to include in his lecture a political appeal for the independence of Algeria from France. This advocacy, which resulted from his love of the Arab world, had also brought him many difficulties in his homeland. The French philosopher and expert on Christian mysticism, Marie-Madelaine Davy, who also taught at the École Pratique des Hautes Études, reports that Massignon's Eranos lecture went even further.[64] In it he spoke, as he often did, in harsh, almost violent, language, drawing attention to the fact that certain French bishops even ran brothels in Algeria, earning themselves a substantial profit.[65] His strongly anti-Zionist and pro-Palestinian views may also have played a role in Massignon's dismissal from Eranos.

At the same time Massignon can be described as a genuine mystic who, judging by the accounts of his friends and colleagues, was marked by an incredibly intense yearning for God. His restless quest had led him to convert from Catholicism to Islam and then back to Catholicism. Yvonne Chauffin calls him "a man devoured by love of God. He went like a blazing torch along paths where no one dared to follow him."[66] A similar opinion was expressed by Massignon's former student Henry Corbin, another Eranos speaker.[67] Corbin also spoke of the "passion that blazed in Massignon," adding that "his influence was inescapable. His fiery soul, his intrepid penetration into the secrets of Islamic mystical life in a way that no one had achieved before, his noble indignation at the oppression of that world—all of this must inevitably have left deep traces in his young listeners." Corbin went so far as to say that "Massignon gave us the courage to take a stand even against the certainties and positivistic laws of mundane history."[68]

Another person who left an eye-witness account of Massignon was the celebrated German orientalist and later Eranos speaker Annemarie Schimmel. When Friedrich Heiler introduced her to him in 1950 she felt, like many others, intoxicated by his presence. "Never before or since have I met a man who was so suffused with light. It was as though one saw in his narrow, beautifully chiseled face a distillation of all of Hallaj's love of God, combined with his own passion for divine love and compassion but also with the knowledge of the necessity to accept suffering." She relates how, at their last meeting in the crowded elevator of a Tokyo hotel, he spoke of the *rosa mystica*, the rose as a symbol of divine beauty and glory. And she adds: "We were unaware of the crowdedness of the elevator—he took me into a higher world of consciousness. And that is how he remains in my memory: a man of saintly ilk, yes a true saint."[69]

Marie-Madelaine Davy, who first met Massignon at Eranos, mentions twice in the already quoted interview with her the impression he made when he talked. Although one saw Massignon before one's eyes, it was not he who spoke but rather "the eternal that flowed through him" and of which he was only the instrument.[70] The existential philosopher Gabriel Marcel must have sensed something similar, for he wrote in a letter to the already deceased Massignon: "No one was less of a prisoner of the present age than you. Undoubtedly you are the only person I have ever known who could transport me directly into the presence of the eternal."[71] As for Massignon, he saw himself as "a man of prayer and consuming passion (for God)."[72]

In terms of scholarly methodology, Massignon evinced a "lively aversion to Aristotelian reasoning." He saw himself as an "interiorist" for whom inspiration and an attitude of belief and sympathy were necessary in order to reveal the "pure divine transcendence" in the sacred writings.[73] Thus he knew and regularly practiced the prayer rituals of all three Abrahamic religions. According to one story, he was once the only passenger on a Turkish ship who knew the correct ritual prayers for a deceased Muslim. Every year he visited Jerusalem in order to pray at the Wailing Wall, reciting the Psalms, which he knew by heart. In Jerusalem he would also carry out Christian obeisance, lying prostrate in the Holy Sepulchre.[74]

Following in the footsteps of Charles de Foucauld, Massignon was also a tertiary in the Franciscan order and in 1954 was ordained priest in the Melchite Greek Catholic Church, which follows the Byzantine Rite.[75] At the same time he worked actively to promote an intensive dialogue between the religions, especially between Christianity and Islam. In Italy he inspired in particular the Catholic priest Giulio Bassetti-Sani to devote his life to this dialogue.[76] The two men had often met each other at the Eranos conferences. Bassetti-Sani even wrote a book about Massignon which expresses his deep reverence for the mystical orientalist, whom he describes as an untiring advocate of inter-religious dialogue, justice, and peace in the world.[77]

Nor should one forget the social causes in which he was engaged. As Annemarie Schimmel confirms, "Massignon always stood up for the oppressed (for example the Algerians and Palestinians), even if it was dangerous for him."[78] With equal vehemence he opposed Zionism because it was leading to the expulsion of the Arabs from their homelands. From Gandhi, whom he ardently revered, he took to heart the principle of non-violence. He stood equally firmly for unshakeable honour of one's word and for the sacred principle of hospitality, which included for him the right to asylum.[79]

An overpowering tendency towards strict asceticism was another of his striking characteristics. As the aforementioned Gnosis expert and Eranos speaker Henri-Charles

Puech reports, he sometimes insisted that his family and even his domestic pets take part in his periods of fasting.[80]

The American scholar of religion Jeffrey Kripal has studied Louis Massignon and interprets his excessive self-mortification as a form of purification and a penance for the homoerotic leanings that he acknowledged to himself.[81] Kripal does not deal with this topic in the crude, accusatory manner of so-called investigative journalism but rather in a careful and thoughtful way, searching Massignon's life and writings for concealed hints. Sufism especially, with its devotion to the "Loved One" (Allah) would be attractive to someone with homoerotic leanings. But, as Kripal points out, basically any creed possessing a God with male attributes, as in the case of Christianity, Judaism, and Islam, evinces a latent homoerotic structure when it comes into contact with a male believer who is full of emotional zeal and divine longing. The already mentioned "saintliness" and asceticism of Massignon could be interpreted as a sublimation of his homosexual leanings, which were not compatible with his Catholic faith.[82]

Massignon himself, in an unpublished letter to his wife, dated 20 October 1934, writes of his fundamental aversion to sexual experience:[83]

> Since 1908 certain things have become entangled in my mind—the memory of a liaison with a woman of the Paris music halls of 1904–1906, and then the sensual aberrations that come from unnatural lust, into which I was (indirectly) initiated by my friend the apostate Spaniard L. de Cuadra, as these aberrations were (according to him) the only possibility to really understand Arab Islam (1906–1908)—with the result that, since my conversion, I have been filled with horror and an instinctive aversion at the thought of the carnal act.[84]

This letter may astound the general reader. But for a man so dedicated to a wholly spiritual life as well as to honor and truthfulness, it was a necessary act of purification.

Massignon and Jung were close friends, although Massignon never became a Jungian. It was to Massignon that Jung owed much of his knowledge of Islam. One figure who especially aroused Jung's interest was the legendary saint El Khidr (Al Chadir) who, it was said, had drunk from the "fountain of life" and would not die until the Day of Judgment. Massignon also felt a close rapport with Martin Buber, as to him Buber was "the last one to keep alive the sense of the sacred in Israel."[85]

Massignon's major work was published in English as *The Passion of al-Hallāj* in 1982, long after his death, appearing in four volumes in the Bollingen Series. Mary Mellon had taken the project under her wing in 1939. The first French edition had appeared in 1922, but had quickly sold out.[86] A sentence from the divan (collection of poetry) of Hallāj, which Massignon translated, may serve to give a taste of this great mystic's work: "I saw my Lord with the eye of the heart and I asked him, 'Who art Thou?' And he said to me, "Thine own self!'"[87]

At this point it is frankly difficult to move on from this account of Massignon, so fascinating is he as a person, thinker, politician, scholar and mystic, fighter, and deep sufferer.

After the end of the conference C.G. Jung, Toni Wolff, the Mellons, and various others met in order to find a solution to the urgent problem of Olga Fröbe's ever-increasing financial difficulties. Her fortune was almost exhausted, and she was talking of selling her home, the Casa Gabriella. Jung, who set great store by symbol-laden traditions, could not accept this, as it would have meant the end of the "Round Table," around which the speakers had conducted so many illuminating discussions. Erlo von Waveren had made efforts to bring some clarity into Fröbe's financial affairs and had calculated how much money would be needed to continue the project. As a solution he proposed that everyone present should make contributions in accordance with their fortunes. The Mellons and Fritz Allemann (who also, as already mentioned, possessed a considerable fortune) declared themselves prepared to donate enough to overcome the immediate crisis, but they also undertook to come to the rescue in the future if necessary. On 30 June 1939, before that year's meeting, Fröbe wrote to Jung that she had found seven people—starting with Fritz Allemann—who were willing to donate a regular fixed sum to Eranos.

While the Mellons remained in Switzerland, Olga Fröbe travelled to the United States in order to give a series of lectures about Eranos. She took with her about three hundred enlarged photographs from her picture collection on the theme of the "Great Mother," which she intended to display in the New York Analytical Psychology Club. There she held on 27 October a lecture on "The Psychological Background of Eranos," which I shall come back to later. At the same time she mooted the idea of continuing the meetings in the United States[88] if Switzerland were to be occupied by Germany.[89] She also made a further attempt to obtain funds from the Rockefeller Foundation for Eranos, but again without success although the director, Dr. Stevens, had at first seemed positive. At the end of 1939 she returned to Switzerland.

The Mellons were so taken by Jung that in April 1940 they took a holiday in Locarno at the same time as he did. After they had got to know each other better, Jung invited them to his famous tower at Bollingen on Lake Zürich, which he had built himself and where he withdrew again and again for contemplation. This place made such a strong impression on Mary Mellon that she chose the name Bollingen as the imprint for her book-publishing project. From then on her interest in mysticism, religion, symbolism, and especially alchemy became ever deeper. From Jung's secretary she obtained a list of the books in his library and soon set about reconstructing the library in the United States—which proved relatively easy given the financial resources at her disposal—so that, in the event of a German occupation of Switzerland, Jung could continue his researches at the Mellons' home.[90] In May 1940, as the war took on ever worse dimensions, Mary Mellon left Switzerland. On 19 June of that year Jung sent a hurried letter to her, assuming that postal service to the United States would not be possible for much longer. He wrote, "Night has descended over Europe. Heaven only knows when and under what circumstances we shall meet each other again. Only one thing is certain: nothing can cause the inner light to be extinguished."[91]

✍ 9. The War Years

The "Symbolic Meeting": Max Pulver and Karl Kerényi

During the Second World War the meetings became smaller, but "these were the years in which the participants felt most closely connected with each other." Only lecturers resident in Switzerland were able to come. "What was lost in terms of breadth and variety was gained in terms of depth and through reduction to essentials."[1]

Aniela Jaffé writes that one of the most impressive meetings took place in 1940. Only one single—as it were symbolic—lecture was announced, to be given by the mathematician Andreas Speiser, who was to speak about Plato and the Trinity. Speiser had already spoken at the 1937 Eranos meeting. He aimed to bridge the gap between the realm of mathematics and science and that of philosophical contemplation. Being a great expert on Plato and a thinker who combined both of these realms, Speiser was largely successful in this aim. He was equally deeply preoccupied with Goethe's theory of color and Dante's philosophy of nature.[2]

Olga Fröbe had asked him whether he would be prepared to hold a lecture for her alone, so that he would stand symbolically for all the lecturers and she for the audience. Afterwards they would have a meal in the garden and drink a bottle of Chianti. Thus a valid meeting would have taken place. Surprisingly, in spite of everything, Jung came to the meeting along with his wife. According to William McGuire there was an audience of only about forty people.[3] Jung had apparently even advised his own students not to attend the meeting, as his long-standing pupil and subsequent collaborator Barbara Hannah reported.[4] Nevertheless, at the Swiss Federal Institute of Technology in Zurich (ETH) a speech of Jung is preserved, which he then held at the table. He expressly thanked Olga Fröbe for the organization of Eranos, ending with the cheer "*Frau Fröbe lebe hoch, hoch, hoch!*" (Three cheers for Mrs. Fröbe!).

In her introductory speech Fröbe explained "with the seriousness characteristic of her" that, even if no one had come, she would still have held the Eranos meeting. After being greatly impressed by Speiser's lecture, Jung was also prepared to give an improvised lecture the next day on the psychology of the concept of the Trinity.[5] These two lectures were then reproduced in a large-format, mimeographed volume, prepared by Liliane von Frey-Rohn and with an introduction by Fröbe.[6] Later these lectures were re-published almost unaltered in vol. 8 (1940–41) of the regular Eranos series, published by Rhein Verlag.

In the autumn of 1940 Olga Fröbe flew to the United States, once again at the invitation of Paul and Mary Mellon, to give a series of lectures. The return flight to Zurich proved unfortunate, as she had to go via Stuttgart and her passport was stamped with a German visa. This visa proved to be a problem during her next stay in the United States. When she flew back again to Europe in March 1941, this visa attracted the attention of the

British secret service when she went through passport control in Bermuda. Furthermore, the collection of archetypal images in her luggage also aroused their suspicion. The full consequences came only later, but were all the more unpleasant when they came.

The 1941 meeting was again very small, with only three lectures. C.G. Jung spoke about the symbolism of transformation in the Mass, the graphologist and writer Max Pulver lectured on Gnosticism, and Karl Kerényi, to whom we shall return in greater detail on account of his great importance, gave a talk on mythology and Gnosis.[7] But first Max Pulver deserves a few words, and not just because he was a gifted graphologist, indeed president of the Swiss Graphological Society. He was also deeply preoccupied with mankind's integration into the cosmos, and his thinking had a strongly esoteric and Gnostic bent, as is shown by the following words from one of his essays:

> Within the soul it is only the lower part, the secondary soul as Iamblichus calls it (*On the Egyptian Mysteries*, VII, 6), that is subject to the rule of fate, not the higher or divine soul. The recognition of this divine portion of the soul is what constitutes Gnosis; and it is the task of the mystery orders to transmit this initiation to the worthy. The person who advances in initiatic knowledge and esoteric insight progresses beyond the domain of *heimarmene*, for this has power only over the sub-planetary spheres … Once we are on the path of insight and rebirth we are free to choose whether we direct our actions according to the corporeal and sensual part of ourselves or towards the divine and spiritual in us.[8]

Max Pulver had a large circle of friends and acquaintances, which included Gustav Meyrink, Paul Klee, Franz Kafka, Rainer Maria Rilke, Walter Benjamin, and Alexander von Bernus, the poet and alchemist.[9] He was also for many years the graphological mentor of Oskar R. Schlag and often took part in the latter's mediumistic sessions.[10] In addition he edited the writings of the philosopher and mystic Franz von Baader, considered as one of the successors to Jakob Boehme. Despite their shared esoteric outlook, Olga Fröbe did not always agree with what Pulver said in his lectures and did not hold back her criticisms. Mircea Eliade even reports in his diary that she had an "aversion" to Pulver.[11]

A correspondence between Rainer Maria Rilke and the publisher Kurt Wolff (to whom we shall return in greater detail) reveals that Pulver was always trying to put himself in the foreground, a trait that did not exactly make him a sympathetic figure.[12] A similar opinion was expressed by Ninon Hesse, the partner of Hermann Hesse during the last thirty-five years of his life. Writing about the 1943 Eranos meeting, she says, "Today Pulver spoke, unfortunately very well—unfortunately because he is so terribly unsympathetic."[13]

Another person who appeared for the first time in 1941 was Karl Kerényi, who subsequently became a central figure in the Eranos program. Kerényi was born in Temesvar (now Romania, then part of the Austro-Hungarian Empire), the son of a Swabian whose heart beat for Hungary.[14] In Hungary he taught classical philology and religious studies and was a student (and friend) of Walter F. Otto, through whom he came into contact with another of Otto's students, namely the influential expert on ancient history Franz Altheim. This contact developed into a close friendship, and the two men undertook many journeys together. The friendship later suffered damage on account of the political events in Germany.[15] Kerényi's daughter Grazia was arrested and deported to a concentration camp following the German occupation of Hungary, and Altheim's cold reaction to the event surely cut far deeper than any political differences. However, it seems that Altheim's intervention ultimately secured the daughter's release.[16]

Kerényi was also in close contact with the "wise astrologer" and philologist Franz Boll.[17] From his youth he was familiar with the poetry of Friedrich Hölderlin.

Early on, Kerényi received a lectureship at the University of Budapest. His student Angelo Brelich, who went to the university in 1933 and heard Kerényi's weekly lectures on Greek religion, described him as very successful with the students. "He was an enthusiast in the best sense of the word and he communicated this enthusiasm to his audience," which was also the case at Eranos.[18] In 1934, Kerényi journeyed to Dalmatia together with Bela Hamvas, a budding author of the same age. Hamvas wanted to bring about a cultural renewal of the Hungarian people. To this end he sought a hard core of followers with whom he could collaborate. He later spoke of this as "the heroic (pagan Greek) attempt to create a new Magyar community."[19] This was supposed to occur through "sacred means," "thus halting an entire people on the path to decline."[20] Hamvas convinced Kerényi to create a small circle named "Stemma" (Crown) with him. However, according to Hamvas, Kerényi misunderstood the sacred endeavor and his "enormous vanity" took central stage instead, whereupon the literary-cultural circle— "which evinced a certain similarity to the George circle"—disintegrated. Nevertheless, in 1935 there appeared in Budapest the first of a series of annual volumes named *Sziget* (Island), which pressed ahead with these ideas.[21] *Sziget* was only short-lived, however. Only three volumes were published between 1935 and 1939. Interestingly, Béla Hamvas was the first Hungarian to engage seriously and sympathetically with the work of the Traditionalist authors Julius Evola, René Guénon, and Leopold Ziegler.[22] Towards the end of the 1930s Kerényi also came into personal contact with Julius Evola, as indicated by a letter written to him by Evola in 19 October 1957, deposited in the Deutsches Literaturarchiv in Marbach, reminding him of their meeting "in Budapest on the occasion of my lecture to the cultural circle of Countess Zichy" and suggesting that they meet again in Rome.[23] This meeting did in fact take place, as Magda Kerényi reported,[24] although apparently the two men no longer had much to say to each other, as their life journeys had gone in very different directions.

In the 1930s, however, there could well have been a kinship of a partly spiritual nature between Kerényi and Evola.[25] This would also partly explain the strong aversion of the Marxist literary scholar Georg Lukács towards both Kerényi and Béla Hamvas. In 1947, when Kerényi wished to return to Hungary from his Swiss exile, he was refused the chair of classical philology at the University of Budapest. Lukács, as a member of the Hungarian Parliament and a respected professor of aesthetics in the post-war years, exerted a powerful influence on the intellectual climate of his now Communist country. And it was Lukács who, in a newspaper article, "decisively destroyed [Kerényi's] expectations of a possible reintegration into the academic life of the country."[26]

Already in the early 1930s Kerényi came into contact with Thomas Mann, with whom he had a long correspondence.[27] Equally important was his friendship with C.G. Jung,[28] who brought him to Fröbe's attention. William McGuire[29] even reports that she chartered a private airplane in order to fly to Rome and meet Kerényi so that she could invite him to Eranos.[30] Magda Kerényi remembered how her husband had spoken of the long walks with Fröbe through the Eternal City. In 1942 Kerényi became Hungarian cultural attaché for Switzerland, with residence in Ascona.[31] When Germany finally occupied Hungary during the war, Kerényi remained with his family in permanent exile in Switzerland, as his wife was a Jew. It was Fröbe who found the Kerényis' first home in Ascona, the so-called Villa Sogno.[32] Living in the Tessin, Kerényi also had the opportunity to visit

Ludwig Derleth, who was so important to Fröbe and who lived in nearby Stabio. He also twice visited the Swiss diplomat and historian Carl J. Burckhardt in Vinzel, in the canton of Waadt.[33]

However, Kerényi's situation in his new homeland was not exactly easy, as he now had to live by his writings and lectures. While his wife worked as a translator and freelance journalist, Kerényi lectured and conducted study tours to Greece with paying guests.[34] He also taught Hungarian language and literature at the University of Basel,[35] although he never obtained a chair. His dream was a professorship in Italy, but for administrative reasons this was not possible. Professorships in Italy were reserved for native Italians.

Jung regarded Kerényi highly and saw him as the successor to Richard Wilhelm and Heinrich Zimmer. Jung also owed him many interconnections between his own theory of archetypes and the ancient Greek myths.[36] Although Kerényi was one of the founders of the Jungian Psychological Institute in Zurich and lectured there for many years, he was ultimately not convinced by Jung's teaching.[37]

What distinguished Kerényi from other experts on antiquity was that he looked in the past not for what was historically unusual but rather for what was of timeless validity. His role model here was Johann Jakob Bachofen, and undoubtedly Walter F. Otto as well.[38] Mythology was for him, as for Bachofen, not the history of various ancient gods and goddesses. Rather, he saw therein a teaching that is still of relevance to all of us today. Our interpretation of the ancient gods should therefore start from the present world situation.[39] Thus he intentionally wrote not only for specialists but for his contemporaries in general, of whom he said: "It is precisely the human being of today who needs something that he cannot make use of."[40] Victor Faessel puts it in the following way: "Insofar as each manifestation of a divine image … intends meaning, it is a record of a human 'solution' to a 'problem' of human existence."[41]

For Kerényi the old gods were no mere projections of the ancient Greeks. Rather, as he believed, the Greeks had actually perceived and "recognized" the gods in all their special qualities.[42] A purely historical and positivist approach to religion and mythology was for him insufficient.[43] He regarded the psychology of religion not as a science of the "illusions of the soul" but rather of the "realities of the soul."[44] He saw these realities as manifesting themselves in art, especially in painting, and here a cross-connection arises with Jungian psychology and the theory of the archetypes.

A term used by Frobenius held special significance for Kerényi, namely *Ergriffenheit* (meaning something between "emotion" and "possession," or being deeply moved). "The capacity and the tendency to experience *Ergriffenheit* signify in a double sense the drawing together of science and religion."[45] In an essay of 1936 with the title "Ergriffenheit und Weisheit" Kerényi goes even further and writes: "Ergriffenheit is the sense that the truth has chosen me and not the other way round … In this basic feeling the experience of the religious person and the scientist are identical."[46] And he emphasizes "that the truths of science also operate as realities of the soul, that is to say they take hold of us." Finally he makes a statement that strikes the modern reader as surprising: "The life of the researcher, which is characterized by a continuous trait of possession (*Ergriffensein*), is anyway already a religious life."[47]

Similarly, he applied Frobenius' concept of culture as an organism specifically also to mythology. Kerényi and Frobenius had first met each other in 1934, and further meetings followed. They were both, along with Thomas Mann, united in their rejection of the National Socialist regime. In 1936, on the occasion of a lecture in Rome about Hölderlin, he met the existentialist philosopher Martin Heidegger,[48] who in his major work *Sein und Zeit* (Being and time) had also dealt with the concept of *Ergriffenheit*.

Kerényi was famous at Eranos for his theatrical talent, which turned his lectures into almost "shamanistic" performances, as McGuire observes.[49] Mircea Eliade—perhaps in a spirit of rivalry—even speaks of a "dubious attentiveness" on the part of the audience at his lectures, which he delivered "without notes, slowly, with emphasis, theatrically, intelligently."[50]

Eliade's autobiography is not lacking in occasional sideswipes at his then much more famous colleague. For example, he describes a seminar on the history of religion, which he and Kerényi held in the 1950s in the Austrian resort of Alpbach. Eliade comments on the meeting as follows: "Methodologically we found ourselves in different positions, and often our discussions threatened to turn into polemics. But, since I admired his work, I didn't lose my temper."[51] Eliade speaks rather more clearly in a letter from Alpbach on 27 September 1952 to his Swedish colleague Stig Wikander:[52] "I was fairly happy with the result. Kerényi less so; it is very difficult to work with him (Mrs. Fröbe said to me that he suffers from a 'primadonna complex').[53] But I like him and put up with all his swings of mood."[54] Eliade had also told Fröbe about the tense situation in Alpbach, for she wrote to him on 1 January 1953 about Kerényi: "He is rather obsessive where his own success is concerned." Eliade is just as frank in his comments to his friend Philipp Wolff-Windegg, the real publisher of the highly interesting mythological and literary-esoteric journal ANTAIOS, which for reasons of publicity was nominally run by Mircea Eliade and Ernst Jünger. Eliade states:

> He [Kerényi] is a great scholar, indeed he possesses genius. But alas!—human relations with him are always unpredictable … If only you knew the origins of his antipathy for me! Because I admire him so much, in 1950 I recommended that Payot [a French publisher] translate his *Mythologie*. Since then he has been against me. I have learnt my lesson. I still admire him—but only from a distance![55]

Up to 1950 Kerényi was undoubtedly one of the stars of Eranos. Then came a change in the situation. McGuire writes that he had simply become "too charismatic for Mrs. Fröbe."[56] She even seems to have feared that he might take over the leading role in Eranos and push her into the background. Only in 1963, after her death, did he return as a speaker, thanks to the pleading of the musicologist Viktor Zuckerkandl, who was able to convince the then director Adolf Portmann, although the latter was also somewhat skeptical about Kerényi.[57]

As Kerényi's departure coincided with the first appearance of Eliade at Eranos, one might be tempted to assume that Fröbe had simply changed favorites and that Eliade had won the "competition" against Kerényi. One should not forget that Eliade, like Kerényi, lived in exile in straitened circumstances and also felt compelled to contend for any assignments that might bring him profit or enhance his reputation. By that time Kerényi was already a recognized scholar, whereas Eliade was still struggling to establish his reputation. Thus Eliade suspected Kerényi of being primarily concerned with his own publicity and believed that Kerényi saw his rival's influence over Fröbe as the reason why he was no longer invited to the Eranos meetings.[58] Kerényi, for his part, judged Eliade's work to be "trivial," because it was insufficiently analytical.[59]

However, the Eliade specialist Natale Spinato of the University of Turin, who has edited the correspondence between the two men, has been able to show convincingly that Fröbe's decision was probably due to unbridgeable differences of character, disagreements about the conduct of Eranos, and so forth. The heartfelt tone of the letters between Kerényi and Eliade remained unaffected by the departure of Kerényi from Eranos. Furthermore, Kerényi continued to say very positive things about Eliade even after the former's departure from Eranos.[60]

However, there is no doubt that the two men differed in their conceptions of what myth exactly is. Kerényi preferred not to speak of myth but rather of mythology, fearing that he might be confused with the school of thought which sees myth as something independent, lying outside of humanity—something capable of taking us over and carrying us away.[61] Eliade, by contrast, saw theophanies everywhere, "manifestations of the divine." In this respect he saw more eye to eye with Frau Fröbe than Kerényi did. In addition, his "esoteric" flair,[62] combined with his experience in an Indian ashram and his knowledge of yoga, must have made him more interesting in her eyes. Furthermore, there was a rumor that Eliade had taken part in Tantric rites, which gave him an additional aura of mystery. Kerényi, by contrast, tended to be rather antipathetic towards the esoteric.

In a personal conversation, Magda Kerényi gave me another version of the break between her husband and Fröbe. As Fröbe saw it, Kerényi had in some way acted against the "spirit of Eranos" and for this reason had no longer been invited. In this matter Adolf Portmann, later the co-leader of Eranos, had apparently played a decisive role. Can one perhaps detect a connection here with what Anna Ruchat wrote in her introduction to an Italian translation of some of Kerényi's essays?[63] She indicates that Kerényi had perhaps wanted to accuse the official organizers of Eranos of having betrayed the original spirit of Eranos. In his essay on Eranos in the magazine *Du* he had chosen a decidedly gruesome example of an *eranos* (i.e. a meal for invited guests) rather than a joyful and festive one. Furthermore, he expressly pointed out the potential for unpredictable disaster to which an *eranos* is subject, but added, "Any development, however, is unforeseen when it involves a spiritual unfolding." And Anna Ruchat adds her belief that Kerényi did remain faithful to the authentic spirit of Eranos, even if he did not always agree with the changes and development.

Although Anna Ruchat's remarks are written with question marks, they arouse the suspicion that she knows more than she says and has access to information that is not generally known. Kerényi's widow Magda, however, considers such suppositions to be insubstantial. The contrast between Kerényi's well-known anti-Fascist position and Eliade's sympathy, then already half-known, for the Romanian Iron Guard, was not a significant factor according to Moshe Idel.[64] Kerényi could see on a daily basis how well Eliade got on with Gershom Scholem.

In the light of this knowledge it is easier to make sense of Kerényi's diary entries about Eranos in later years. Thus, in an entry for 21 August 1957 he gives his reactions to one of the lectures. After speaking of the "tired out" and "stony" impression that Olga Fröbe gave, he continues:

The speaker helplessly lost in terminology instead of experienced reality. It is positively tragic how the dimension of spiritual experience, of expansion, for which this auditorium was intended by its owner, has been perceptibly barred off by a dense grid of terminology. Total dependence on what is fought against or what is to be replaced. I no longer even feel the urge to protest."[65]

The fact that this negative judgment was not an isolated case is proved by an entry a year later, of 22 August 1958:

> Among the many unnatural things about the Eranos situation—and this is one of a number of reasons why I have avoided it in recent years—is that one finds oneself being glad that time is passing: another 20 minutes and then another hour is over. The large audience seizes the slightest excuse to laugh and thereby reveal their suppressed, self-righteous rebellion against what they see as unnatural … The meeting ends with a display of completely inappropriate behavior, the audience flapping uncontrollably like birds around the ghostly seeming presence of Mrs. Fröbe. A sad ending.

This is all very far from the atmosphere of "magic and mystery" that is often attributed to these meetings. It is clear, however, from the words of the 1957 commemorative brochure by Olga Fröbe, *25 Jahre Eranos*, how closely Kerényi felt himself linked to Eranos. There he writes: "Eranos certainly has a biographical significance for the speakers who took part in it. But it is also a theme within intellectual history, to which I hope one day to give my attention again according to its true history." Unfortunately—very unfortunately—he never carried out this wish.

The 1941 meeting was reviewed by Armin Kessler in the *Neue Zürcher Zeitung* of 24 August of that year.[66] In a very positive manner he honored the efforts of Eranos and gives special praise to Jung's contribution on "Symbols of Transformation in the Mass" as "a great and serious attempt to elucidate the psychological content of a centuries-old mystery, using a highly developed technique of exposition." There were also detailed summaries of the lectures by Max Pulver and Karl Kerényi. Kessler was particularly taken with Kerényi's interpretation of mythology and commented that mythology "is not a mere form of expression that is as valid as any other, but is a phenomenon sui generis, which we can never adequately 'translate' and explain. The sole task of the mythologist is to let the myth speak for itself, for myths continue to sing even in death, like the severed head of Orpheus, and even from a remote distance."[67]

Problems in the United States

In January 1942, Mary Mellon's plans to publish a special Bollingen Series in the United States began to take more concrete shape. The prerequisite was to secure funding for the books, and this was to come from the Bollingen Foundation, which had been expressly created for the purpose. Soon, however, the events of the war forced the closure of the first Bollingen Foundation;[68] only in 1945 was it resurrected as an independent legal entity. It was unclear which book should appear first. A translation of the *I Ching*, originally intended for the debut, was seen as being too specialized, and a collected volume of Eranos papers was not considered advisable in the midst of the war, even if J.W. Hauer's lectures were left out. Heinrich Zimmer was engaged as an adviser. He voted that something related to America should mark the beginning of the series, and this suggestion was then implemented.[69]

Via Oxford, where he was able to teach but was not paid, Zimmer had finally moved to the United States, where he supported his family by giving lectures at various universities (especially Columbia) and at the New York Analytical Psychology Club.[70] Thanks to his skill as a speaker, these lectures were a great success. Myths were for him not mere curiosities for academics but rather models that could help one to understand one's own life.[71] And he gave forceful expression to this view. Among his earliest students was Joseph Campbell, who himself later became famous as a mythologist and was to edit the English-language version of a series of Eranos lectures. Campbell reports that in the first semester, Zimmer had an audience of only four, but in the second semester there were fifty. Fortunately Zimmer had made the acquaintance of the Mellon family during the 1939 Eranos conference, and the Mellons were now willing to help him by involving him in the Bollingen project.

Mary and Paul Mellon also continued to help their friends in Switzerland, sending them regular food packages. They also corresponded with various people in Switzerland about possible publications in the United States. In the midst of the war, however, this could be very dangerous, since the so-called Trading with the Enemy Act forbade, on pain of imprisonment or heavy fines, any trade with hostile foreigners, regardless of whether this happened directly or indirectly. And theoretically the Mellons' contacts in Switzerland could have been agents for the German enemy. The family's lawyers therefore urgently advised them to cease all postal contact or financial interchange with everyone apart from those living in the United States or perhaps England, especially in view of the fact that the extensive postal contact with Switzerland had already attracted the attention of the authorities.[72] The risk was further exacerbated by the fact that the FBI had already opened a file on Olga Fröbe[73] because, as already mentioned, her return flight from America via Germany and the mysterious picture collection in her luggage had attracted the attention of the British intelligence service. Foundations were the most popular route for Germans and Japanese to conduct business with the United States, and this fact alone would have been enough to make the Bollingen Foundation a target of suspicion.

This menacing turn of events had the result that, suddenly and without forewarning, the Mellons had to cancel all financial support for Eranos. Jung was informed of these developments in a long and carefully phrased letter from Mary Mellon. Jung conveyed the contents to Olga Fröbe, who was profoundly shaken by it, although this "Job's message was not entirely unexpected."[74] Already, on 20 March 1942, she had written to Jung that Eranos, and therefore she herself, was fully dependent on Mary Mellon. She was trying to sell some of her land, but she found it "not right that it's always I alone who have to sacrifice all that I have." In the same letter she entreats Jung to write to Mary Mellon and draw attention to the memorandum that she (Fröbe) had written, looking back over ten years of Eranos, "since everything that she [Mary Mellon] does for Eranos is largely on your account [Jung]." After the termination of the American payments, Fröbe now considered looking for paid work for the winter. Earlier on Fritz Allemann and Tadeus Reichstein had agreed to give her financial support, but they did not want to be the only ones to contribute.

The Mellons also closed their bank account in Switzerland and handed over the entire Swiss correspondence to the FBI. This action had the support of Heinrich Zimmer, who told them that the I Ching was fully behind the decision. Then in the early summer of 1942 the Bollingen Foundation was completely dissolved, as the decision had been taken to suspend all "foreign" activities for the duration of the war.[75] The already existing translations of Eranos lectures and also the English version of the I Ching were given to Yale University Press but disappeared for the time being into the archives.

A further interesting episode occurred, although it is not clear whether it had any influence on the actions described. During the war Paul Mellon worked in London for the Office of Special Investigations (OSS), the forerunner of the CIA.[76] As Paul Mellon had a delicate job demanding the utmost confidence of his superiors, it was necessary for him to exercise great caution. On the other hand, his boss in London, David Bruce, was married to Mellon's sister Ailsa (once dubbed the richest woman in the world),[77] which must certainly have made explanations easier. Here I should like to mention one particular anecdote without, however, wishing to imply any connection with Eranos. When Paul Mellon once lamented to the essayist and poet Allen Tate that so many writers were left-wing, Tate replied that writers were always in financial need and that Mellon should award scholarships and prizes, which would dampen the revolutionary ardor of the writers. Thereupon Mellon, as the story goes, founded the Bollingen-Mellon prizes of twenty thousand dollars each.[78]

The Eranos meeting of 1942 took place despite all the adverse circumstances and financial difficulties.[79] Five lecturers turned up to speak on the theme of the "Hermetic Principle." As Fröbe reported in a letter to the Analytical Psychology Club of New York, "Of course Jung's lecture … was the most gripping," although Kerényi spoke too and was given two whole mornings and an evening for his presentation.[80] There was also a celebration marking the tenth anniversary of Eranos. Her letter goes on, "We all had the feeling that it was the most united, the most peaceful, and the most human Eranos meeting we ever had." A report in the newspaper *Die Weltwoche* was equally positive and spoke of a rather large number of participants that year. However, because of the withdrawal of help from the United States, Eranos was in difficult straits. Shortly after the meeting Jung appealed to the foundation Pro Helvetia for support, explaining that the meetings "are at present the only European platform where representatives of the European world of learning can still meet on a level beyond political misunderstandings and tensions … I therefore consider this endeavor to be of the highest importance for the defense of the intellectual life in our country." He went on to speak of the important cultural role of Eranos, its value for international relations, and its implications for Switzerland. Pro Helvetia did in fact respond by providing assistance, as did the Swiss Federal Technical Institute, where Jung taught,[81] so that at least the most pressing needs could be relieved.

Despite the dissolution of the Bollingen Foundation, Mary Mellon did not want to give up her publishing activities. Foreign religions, mythology, and the ideas of Jung had become the most important subjects in her life, and she was not to be deterred from publishing books on these areas.[82] However, Yale University Press, which had taken over all the Bollingen documents, was not in any way the right publishing house for her to work with. So Heinrich Zimmer suggested a new publisher, who had only recently taken refuge in America but was eminently qualified. This was Kurt Wolff, whose publishing house in Leipzig and later in Munich had specialized in contemporary literature and had enjoyed great success.[83]

Already in Munich Wolff had moved in the influential circle of Frobenius and Edgar Dacqué, where he met, among others, Oswald Spengler. The latter's best-selling work *Der Untergang des Abendlandes* (Decline of the West), which has remained influential to this day, had been offered to Wolff for publication, but he had turned it down, feeling that it was not suitable for his publishing house.[84] As Wolff's mother was Jewish he had to cease his business activities in Germany during the 1930s. After sojourns in Italy, Switzerland, and France, he emigrated to the United States, where he founded Pantheon Books. His aim was to publish in America editions of European authors such as Jakob Burckhardt, Stefan George, J.W. von Goethe, Dante Alighieri, Jan Comenius, Nikolai Gogol, Leo Tolstoy, Paul Claudel, Charles Péguy, and many others.[85] This agenda, together with his enormous knowledge of European culture, were exactly what Mary Mellon was looking for, and they proceeded quickly to draw up a contract for their collaboration.[86] Finally, in May 1943, a budget was set up for a publishing project called the Bollingen Series. Thus, finally the necessary capital was available. Even the logo of the series, the Gnostic wheel, had already been chosen by the Mellons themselves. However, the man who had played such a central role as an advisor in building up the series, namely Heinrich Zimmer, had recently died. He had held private lectures on the symbolism of the Tarot[87] and on one occasion, despite a terrible cold, he had not wanted to cancel his lecture. A few days later he died from an undiagnosed lung inflammation in the fifty-second year of his life.

At this time, early 1943, Olga Fröbe once again came under political attack. This time the accusations of pro-Nazism came from within Switzerland. On Jung's advice she turned to Allen Dulles, head of the OSS in Bern. Dulles investigated the case and found no evidence, thus putting an end to the accusations once and for all. The already mentioned chic "spy" and friend of Allen Dulles, Mary Bancroft, is also said to have spoken out in Olga Fröbe's favor.[88]

Fröbe had been in the sights of the FBI since March 1941, when her name had come to their attention as a result of her return flight via Stuttgart and the "cryptic" pictures in her luggage. It had also been noticed that all her travel expenses for the trip had been paid by Paul Mellon and that she had given his residence as her address during the visit. Furthermore, when her money was running out as a result of her numerous purchases of paintings, she had written several times to Eleanor Roosevelt, wife of the president, asking for support for Eranos and herself. In reply she had received only a non-committal letter from the president's secretariat.[89]

In response to the accusation of having been pro-Nazi, she made a written declaration to the American embassy in Bern, which has been preserved. In this document she mentions two people whom she suspects of having denounced her. The first was the owner of Monte Verità, Baron von der Heydt. In her opinion he wanted to be regarded as the real founder of Eranos, and in 1942 he had engineered or at least tolerated certain newspaper articles to that effect. She believed that her article in the *Neue Zürcher Zeitung*, explaining the true situation, had stirred him up against her. However, in view of Fröbe's well-known sensitivity where competition was concerned, one might justifiably doubt whether her proof was well founded.

Baron von der Heydt was a hotel proprietor and art collector, but certain suspicious indications point to his sympathy for Nazi Germany. In the magazine section of the Zurich newspaper, the *Tagesanzeiger*, of 20 December 1980, there appeared an article headed "opportunism," accusing Baron von der Heydt of having exploited the neutrality of Switzerland during the war for financial transactions and of having misused his Swiss citizenship (which, as a German, he had acquired) to the advantage of German military espionage.[90]

Further details are given by Peter Kamber in a chapter added, by way of amplification, to the new edition of his book *Geschichte zweier Leben*.[91] Kamber claims that von der Heydt joined the National Socialist Party soon after it seized power in 1933, having allegedly saved it from financial collapse in 1929 by bringing Hitler and Göring into contact with foreign donors.

After taking Swiss citizenship in 1937 he then became a member of the *Bund treuer Eidgenossen nationalsozialistischer Weltanschauung* (Association of loyal Swiss citizens of National Socialist worldview) and sent out birthday congratulations to a number of prominent Nazis, which led to his receiving a police warning on account of Switzerland's neutrality. Via a bank in Locarno he is said to have paid the wages of German spies abroad and to have made transactions on behalf of the SS when they blackmailed Jews to pay money in return for their freedom.

However, it is reported that at least one of these payments saved a small group of Jews. It was for this reason that Switzerland reversed a decision to revoke his citizenship. The already mentioned lawyer Wladimir Rosenbaum (who also worked for Fröbe), in a 1979 radio interview, said about von der Heydt, "He was not even a Nazi. He merely worked for the Nazis."[92] There was, however, another factor that was decisive in enabling him to keep his citizenship: already in 1946 he had donated a large part of his extensive art collection to the city of Zurich. Thanks to this donation, the Rietbergmuseum in particular was able to establish its world-famous Asiatic collection.[93]

We must leave unanswered the question as to what extent Baron von der Heydt followed the Nazi Party line. An affinity with "Nordic" ideas is indicated by his conference report on the Second Nordic Thing (assembly) in Bremen, in which Julius Evola also took part.[94] And in the periodical *Nordische Welt—Zeitschrift der Gesellschaft für germanische Ur- und Vorgeschichte*[95] there is a report of a lecture given by the Baron on "Nordic Man and the Art of East Asia," in which he said that commonalities exist between Nordic and East Asian art, whereas the "Mediterranean artistic ideals are basically foreign to our way of being." He lamented furthermore that Europe had been "overrun by three semitic religions coming from the Mediterranean region."

On the other hand, there was the case of the poet René Schickele, who had already left Germany in 1932 because of pre-Nazi agitations and gone to the south of France and then finally to Switzerland.[96] Schickele visited Baron von der Heydt at Monté Verità, intending to spend eight days there, but instead he stayed for eight weeks and even dedicated a poem to the baron.[97] There is also the case of Heinrich Zimmer, who had been persecuted by the Nazis because of his Jewish wife. Baron von der Heydt enabled Zimmer to study valuable Indian works of art in Switzerland without having to undertake long and expensive journeys. Joseph Campbell even refers expressly to Baron Heydt as a "friend" of Zimmer.[98] We see here another example of how human beings can have many contradictory facets.

The second person suspected by Fröbe of having denounced her was Gérard Heym, who remains well known today as a historian of alchemy and who had been very helpful to her in London when she was collecting pictures for the Eranos archive. In his case she suspected that his aversion to Germany was the motive for denouncing Eranos as a "German center." Furthermore, she believed that Heym had worked in collaboration with Scotland Yard. She never, however, produced any proof of these suspicions. Even before her declaration to Allen Dulles, she had written to Jung on 13 January 1944:

> Through my chance discovery at the last meeting that Hauer's participation at Eranos in 1934 had been the subject of negative comment in the USA, it occurred to me who it is that must have been denouncing me and Eranos from London over the past ten years! ... Mr. Gérard Heym. I have a good memory and I have been able to reconstruct everything since 1934. Heym was also at the meeting where

Hauer spoke. And already in the winter of 1934 he had said to me: "Now remember, don't you have any more damn Germans!"

Gérard Heym was born in 1888 in Leipzig, the son of a doctor, and was still a child when he emigrated to the United States with his parents. In due course he studied at Harvard and then at various European universities.[99] His father had evidently been a great nationalist, and the boy had been bombarded with German nationalistic sentiments from an early age. It was probably this upbringing—and of course, later on, the advent of National Socialism—that turned him against Germany[100] and caused him in the end to become a germanophobe.[101] In the early 1920s he finally settled in England. By the 1930s he owned a rich alchemical library, which he kept in his flat in Chelsea, London. In 1936 he co-founded the Society for the Study of Alchemy and Early Chemistry, which has published since 1937 the journal *Ambix*, for which he wrote a few articles and many book reviews.[102] He also wrote for the journal *Quest*.[103]

Fortunately his books survived the German air bombardment of London undamaged, but most of his notes were lost, which is probably the reason why, despite his enormous knowledge, he left so little written work of his own. As his obituary in the scientific journal *Ambix* mentioned in a mildly critical tone, he favored the "traditional" interpretation of alchemy, propounded by such figures as Fulcanelli, Eugène Canséliet, Claude d'Ygé, and others.[104] For him alchemy was a process of spiritual ennoblement. He had particularly good contacts with the French alchemists and alchemical experts, and articles by him appeared in French esoteric magazines such as *Initiation et Science* and *La Tour Saint-Jacques*. He also wrote a very informative introduction to the French edition of Gustav Meyrink's esoteric novel *The White Dominican*.[105]

But Heym had an equally high regard for the works of Mircca Eliade and C.G. Jung. Thus, in a letter of 23 September 1958 to Philipp Wolff-Windegg, the real editor of the journal *Antaios*, Heym said, "Believe me … Eliade is the only one who understands alchemy, and in other directions as well he is, as you know, a deep thinker."[106]

Jean-Pascal Ruggiu, imperator of the French Ahathoor Temple No. 7 of the Hermetic Order of the Golden Dawn (Ordre Hermétique de l'Aube Dorée) and active in various other magical groups, remarks in his essay "Rosicrucian Alchemy and the Hermetic Order of the Golden Dawn" that Heym—apart from being a friend of S.L. MacGregor Mathers, who headed the Golden Dawn for many years, and Mathers' wife Moina Bergson—was also a member of the society known as Les Amants de la Licorne (The Unicorn Lovers), which was preoccupied with alchemy and alchemical symbolism.[107] Ruggiu even conjectures that Heym was also a member of the French Rosicrucian group called F.A.R.+C., which was supposedly the only European group to practice the Chinese form of alchemy. Heym also appears to have been in contact with the practicing alchemist Archibald Cockren, and declared that he himself was a practicing alchemist.[108]

After the war Heym, in keeping with the role of the practicing alchemist, was constantly in financial difficulties. Most antiquarian bookshops refused to sell him books any longer, as the Antiquarian Booksellers' Association had placed him on their list of "incorrigible rogues."[109] Both the esotericist Oskar Schlag, already mentioned as possessor of one of the most important libraries, and the antiquarian bookseller Nicholas Schors never let Heym browse unsupervised among their books for fear that afterwards they would be several books short. Schlag had an altogether negative opinion of Heym and linked him with the secret services. He believed, for example, that Heym had enjoyed direct contact with Winston Churchill and that the latter had on occasions helped Heym when he was in a tight spot because of book pilfering.[110]

In the spring of 1943, probably acting on the advice of friends, Olga Fröbe separated herself legally from Eranos and created a Swiss foundation. The endowment given over to the foundation included the Casa Eranos, the lecture hall together with the studio flat above it, half of the garden, a piece of land in the mountains, her library, and the picture archive. Thus the way was opened for donations from private benefactors or public institutions.

The 1943 Eranos meeting focused on solar cults in antiquity and the symbolism of light in Gnosticism and early Christianity. For the first time Jung was not an official speaker, much to her regret, as he was busy writing his book *Mysterium Coniunctionis* and did not want to interrupt his research. Nevertheless, he gave an improvised talk on a fourteenth-century mystic and miniaturist named Opicinus de Canistris, although it was delivered on the terrace rather than in the seminar room. For a long time nothing was known about the content of the talk, until the notes of Alwine von Keller were eventually found in the Eranos archive in 2006. The content can be reconstructed very well from the nine typewritten pages. In the meantime a detailed analysis has appeared.[111] The fact that eight official speakers were announced, including Kerény, Massignon, and Pulver, suggests that this was an almost normal and no longer truncated Eranos programme. Louis Massignon and Charles Virolleaud (a French assyriologist who had already lectured in 1938 and 1939) were not able to attend in person, as by that time France was under German occupation, but their lectures were read out.

Someone who spoke for the first time at this meeting was the Catholic theologian and Jesuit Hugo Rahner, who was to be invited back repeatedly in subsequent years until 1948, and who was particularly interested in the study of early Christianity in the midst of the tensions of antiquity. He was extremely impressed by Eranos; the conferences offered him the opportunity to get out of the Swiss town of Sion and breathe a somewhat freer air. He had not always felt understood in Sion: "A lot of things there seemed narrow and petty to him."[112]

As late as 1966 Hugo Rahner wrote the following words on Eranos:

> What we see here is a living Round Table, a veritable gift to those who believe that our western civilization collapsed in order to be reborn, those who belong to the Eranos of the far-sighted, who, like Plato in his immortal seventh letter, are able to look beyond the political ruins to the realm of the eternal; those who are aware of the reassuring spiritual law that the demon in us is permitted to demolish only so that the angel in us can shyly uncover the springs of life anew … There are many people involved in this effort to bring us back home, and whoever feels called to this task is assured of our admiration and thanks. It is not out of any academic whim but strictly out of a sense of commitment when learned minds gather at the Eranos meetings, in this country where Erasmus felt so at home, in order to reopen the buried springs of true humanism.[113]

It seems rather surprising for a theologian to quote, as Rahner does at the beginning of his book, the following rather esoteric sounding statement of Pythagoras, transmitted by Porphyry: "And every word, to quote Pythagoras, is directed only to the few who are capable of learning, not to the many who only listen. 'Little is said, all else remains concealed.'" And the title of the second part of the book, *Seelenheilung* (Healing of the soul), speaks for itself. Rahner is seen as a rediscoverer of the symbol-oriented theology of the early Church Fathers, which integrated the symbolic, mythical, and poetic dimensions into the interpretation of the Christian faith. His fellow Jesuits had little sympathy for this "un-theological" form of interpretation, so that Rahner spoke regretfully of an "intellectualization of the creed." Alfons Rosenberg, in his *Flugblätter für Freunde* (circular letters to friends),[114] writes not only about his own first visit to Eranos but also about Hugo Rahner's first encounter with Eranos. The latter had also come across the first Eranos yearbook and had found that it struck a deep resonance with him. As he lived and worked at that time at the Jesuit College in Innsbruck, Austria, he had no more possibility than Rosenberg to attend the Eranos meetings. However, after the annexation of Austria by the German Reich in 1938 the whole college moved to Sion in French-speaking Switzerland, and from there he was invited by Olga Fröbe to come to Ascona.

In 1943 Fröbe suggested to Jung that he invite Rahner to give a lecture in Zurich, but Jung declined, saying that the idea was tempting:

> but I must ask you to bear in mind that, in Zurich especially, as a *Jesuit*, he could attract unwelcome attention for *political reasons* [Jung's emphasis]. The Jesuits as such are forbidden here and even the Catholic clergy do not look upon them favorably, they are afraid of the confessional peace being disturbed, perhaps rightly so, as they are a militant order.[115]

Jung added that at Eranos this would be no problem, as other speakers would also be present.

The last Eranos meeting during the war, that of 1944, was dedicated to "the Mysteries." The names of the ten lecturers, including Kerényi, Pulver, and Rahner, testify to the drawing power of these meetings, which by now had become an institution. The discussions covered the Orphic, Egyptian, Persian, and Gnostic as well as the Islamic and Christian mysteries. One newcomer among the speakers demands special attention, namely the islamicist Fritz Meier, of whom Annemarie Schimmel, herself a renowned Islamic scholar, said, "For me he was the greatest of us in Islamic scholarship."[116] And elsewhere she commented: "Meier was a perfectionist, a man of infinitely wide and thorough knowledge, a philologist of the first rank, but equally well versed in philosophy and history."[117]

Born in Basel in 1912 he studied at the university there, beginning with Assyriology and Semitic and Greek philology but soon switching to Islamic studies.[118] In 1935 he was sent by his teacher Rudolf Tschudi to the famous orientalist Helmut Ritter in Istanbul, and two years later he traveled to Persia, mainly to study old manuscripts. In 1941, when he was still under thirty, he took his *Habilitation*. The title of his *Habilitation* lecture, "Vom Wesen der islamischen Mystik" (On the essence of Islamic mysticism), indicates the special direction of his interests.[119] In the foreword he writes that what makes his work new is that he does not look for a historical source, but rather seeks to "discover the human origins of Islamic mysticism" and "to reveal the primal experience underlying it." The following quotation shows how his conception of mysticism went far beyond the realm of Islamic scholarship:

> The mystic differs from the ordinary individual in so far as ... what is unconscious becomes to him conscious, and the two poles of consciousness and unconsciousness come together as the central point of a new total consciousness. Thus, when

it is said that the selfhood of the mystic is replaced by the selfhood of God, what is meant by God (whichever deity it may be) is in fact the higher self of the mystic, which, in the way that I have indicated, emerges from the super-consciousness and invades the conscious mind of the mystic, to the point where the latter becomes one with that entity that he had previously worshipped as God and whose intentions he had seen as being fulfilled in his own fate. That is to say he merges with his own cosmic self, the transcendental "I," whose will he henceforth assumes and fulfils in his worldly actions.[120]

After an assignment in Alexandria, Meier was appointed in 1949 to the professorship of oriental philology at the University of Basel, where he remained until his retirement in 1982. Apart from Arabic and Persian philology, he dedicated himself above all to the history of Islam and in particular to Islamic mysticism, producing outstanding biographies of the great mystics of Central Asia. He derived great satisfaction from the many international honors that he received and especially from the translation of some of his books and articles into Persian. In his latter years he preoccupied himself increasingly with Gnostic literature. On the way home from celebrating his eighty-sixth birthday, he died of a heart attack, still holding a bouquet of roses in his hand.

***

In terms of subject matter, the conference of 1944 was the last one with a somewhat "esoteric" tone. Jung, on account of a heart attack, was unable to attend, and his absence, as Barbara Hannah wrote, changed the whole atmosphere of the meeting, since the center of the group was lacking.[121]

The war years showed how important Swiss neutrality was for Eranos. As Fröbe recounted to the Eranos speaker Laurens van der Post, Jung regarded the Swiss mountains as a kind of protective rampart, a magic circle that shielded Eranos and at the same time resembled an earth-mandala, in whose center—that is, Eranos—the quest had to continue throughout the war.[122] It was not only the neutrality of Switzerland that made it ideal for Eranos but also the fact that it was a meeting point of the German, French, and Italian linguistic and cultural realms. It was thus a fruitful and open setting for wide-ranging intellectual interchange. Hence, out of the original concept of an encounter between East and West, Eranos also emerged as a meeting place between North and South. Furthermore, in true *yin–yang* fashion, it was also a meeting of modernity and antiquity, of the natural sciences and the humanities, of science in general and religion, of the outer and inner worlds, of matter and spirit, of rationality and intuition, of word and image, of definition and myth, of extraversion and introversion, of multiplicity and unity. Thus we have here a "mandala" in whose center the proverbial *coincidenta oppositorum*, the coming together of opposites, took place.[123] On this theme, Jan Hondius, who translated some of Jung's works into Dutch, wrote in 1947, "The nations of the world are striving towards political union; over the past decade and a half the Eranos meetings have constituted a unique and successful effort to straddle intellectual and spiritual frontiers and to overcome the barriers of nationality, language and race, and the divide between East and West."[124]

Hondius himself, a great authority on Far Eastern philosophy, was the husband of Ada Hondius, a particularly close friend of Olga Fröbe (who lived in Holland, however).[125] In 1935 the two went to an Eranos conference for the first time and were very enthusiastic.

In her Eranos manuscript Catherine Ritsema published a whole series of letters from Olga Fröbe to Ada Hondius, some of which were very personal.[126] Hence in a letter dated 3 April 1937 she spoke of her stay in Berlin, the purpose of which, aside from visiting museums, was to secure travel permits for lecturers. On this subject she remarked that Fröbe told her she had to summon a great deal of courage at that time in order to stand up to the German authorities.

Ritsema also mentions that Jan Hondius led a "School voor Wysbegeerte," that is to say, a type of philosophical-esoteric study center, in the Dutch town of Amersfoort and that an exchange not only of experiences but also of speakers took place with Eranos.[127] Such is confirmed in a book by E. van Everdingen, which traces the history of this study center.[128] Founded in 1915, the institution had invited Martin Buber as a speaker by as early as 1925, and he returned there in the 1930s. Paul Tillich, too, was a guest there in the pre-war years, as well as in 1961 and 1964. In 1935 even C.G. Jung and Heinrich Zimmer attended. In 1947 Martin Buber appeared again, and in 1948 and 1955 Jung's colleague Jolande Jacobi was present. In 1949, 1955, 1959, and 1964, Karl Kerényi attended, and Erich Neumann was there in 1952, 1954, and 1956.

The Danish philosopher of religion, director, and successful author J. Anker Larsen (author of *Der Stein der Weisen*, 1923), who also spoke there, said of the school: "One gains the impression that here one aspires to knowledge and insight in the old classical sense, in which right knowledge and right living were indivisible and mutually dependent."[129] A resonance with Eranos can clearly be detected here. Further speakers who were not present at Eranos range from Ernst Bloch to Albert Schweizer. J.M. Hondius first became director of the school in 1961.

Today it is no longer possible to gauge whether there were any further links between the School voor Wysbegeerte and Eranos in terms of ideas. In my estimation the connection was not of great importance, otherwise the Amersfoort group would have appeared in the documents and literature more often. On the other hand it is necessary to bear in mind that the friendship between Fröbe and the Hondius family stretched back to as early as 1935, and an exchange of experience is likely to have taken place primarily in a purely private context.

In conclusion, an appropriate passage from the *I Ching*, the *Book of Changes* was quoted by Olga Fröbe in the foreword to the report of the 1940 and 1941 meetings and was taken by her as a motto for the period of "ordeal by fire": "While externally total disorder reigns, internally order is already pre-formed." Similarly, she declared, in times of destruction one must preoccupy oneself with things of an indestructible nature, which thus paradoxically become not only timeless but highly up to date.

In 1945 appeared the twelfth Eranos volume, under the title *Studien zu C.G. Jung* (Studies for C.G. Jung), in honor of his seventieth birthday. Unusually, the contributions had not previously been delivered as lectures. A further volume was therefore published (although not until 1946) containing the talks actually given at the 1945 meeting under the overall heading of *Der Geist* (The spirit). In the foreword to this volume Fröbe once again described how Eranos perceived its mission, or perhaps how she perceived it: "We have a tendency … in our technical age to forget … that in the age of the mysteries the sciences were guarded by the priests. Here lies the living root of what we are doing here and hope to continue doing in the future."

🐾 10. New Prospects after the World Conflict

Adolf Portmann, the Great Innovator

After the end of the war, Olga Fröbe considered inviting to Ascona certain leading political figures who were interested in cultural renewal in Europe, including the American Secretary of State John Foster Dulles, who himself had been active in various peace initiatives. But when she asked for Jung's opinion he was strongly against the idea, telling her that "the Eranos audience does not come to hear about politics." For such a project she would have to establish a special conference with its own audience.[1] Nevertheless, the year 1946 saw a real innovation. The meeting, under the general theme of "Spirit and Nature," included for the first time a number of established scientists, and these were by no means of insignificant rank. The most notable were the Nobel prize-winner Erwin Schrödinger, who spoke on the "Spirit of Science,"[2] the biophysicist Friedrich Dessauer, and the biologist Adolf Portmann, a key figure in the history of Eranos, who was to hold altogether thirty lectures there: more than any other speaker.

Portmann had come to Fröbe's attention through his radio broadcasts. and she had already approached him during the war, but he had been unable to accept on account of his military duties. The reason for her interest was undoubtedly his opposition to a scientific approach "that regarded the only true aim of research as being to reduce all biological phenomena to chemical and physical processes."[3] He was equally opposed throughout his life to a purely mechanistic conception of evolution, driven purely by "chance mutation" and "selection." Evolution, he believed, was much too complex for such simplistic explanations.[4] What Portmann wanted was rather to develop "a science of living forms," a program of "research into life" itself. To describe what was common to all living things at a profound level, he used the term *Innerlichkeit* (indwelling spirit).[5] His aim was to bridge the gap between science and the humanities, and he saw in Eranos the best opportunity for doing this.

His particular conception of nature also explains why Eranos became so central to his life and why so few other scientists felt at home there. Nevertheless, with the advent of Portmann, Eranos appears to have undergone a change, moving away from a somewhat esoteric approach to philosophy and religion towards a *Weltanschauung* that was more modern and scientific, but still spiritually oriented. One woman, who had attended almost all meetings since the 1940s and had experienced the change at first hand, remarked to me that "after Portmann came, Eranos became something different." The lady did not wish to be named, and by now she has probably died. It is likely that Karl Kerényi's reservations about Eranos had partly to do with Adolf Portmann. The broadening of the circle to other thematic areas brought with it a different way of thinking, and the old "intimacy" suffered somewhat. This different way of thinking, however, appears to have corresponded entirely to Fröbe's intentions. According to Jay Livernois, who was for a short time director of Eranos Moscia in the late 1990s, Olga Fröbe wanted to move away from the esoteric beginnings of the project in the hope that it would gain greater scholarly recognition. Hence any scientist, even an idiosyncratic one, was highly welcome to her. It was probably this fact, in addition to Adolf Portmann's great personal commitment, that motivated her later on to name Portmann as president of the Eranos Foundation after her death. Similar reasons probably lay behind the supposed destruction of old documents pointing to the esoteric origins of Eranos.

Portmann was born in Basel, where he studied zoology and took a doctorate with the highest possible mark. After further studies in Paris, Berlin, and elsewhere, he worked for many years in various marine laboratories. In 1931 he became professor of zoology at Basel, and from 1947 held the post of rector. There he dedicated himself increasingly to the comparative morphology of vertebrates, working in a spirit inspired by Goethe's striving for wholeness. In addition he had strong artistic impulses, which he expressed in painting. What was important for him was the "form" of living things, especially animals: that is to say, something that goes beyond the purely material. In the form, Portmann perceived what might be called the symbol of a hidden reality, a "signature." Other traits of his were a strong sense of responsibility and social commitment. He came from a socialist and working-class background, but also possessed a deep Christian faith and therefore always endeavored to make his knowledge available to less privileged groups. Hence he delivered more than two hundred radio lectures, which were designed to be comprehensible to a general audience.[6] He also regarded it as his duty, after every Eranos meeting, to drive to Basel and give a broadcast about what had been discussed in Ascona.[7]

Portmann always linked his knowledge of nature with philosophical, cultural, and religious issues, in order to bring about a true inner renewal for human beings and to deepen our religious experience.[8] A few sentences from his writings should serve to illustrate this. Portmann distinguished two different ways of studying biological phenomena: "The researcher into nature can approach living beings from two different perspectives. Taking a purely materialistic approach, he can regard the manifold forms of nature in the same way as he would look at a piece of rock, a crystal or a magnetic field, that is to say as though these things were lifeless forms." This is the way of the chemist and the physicist. The second way is totally different and "starts from an acceptance of the very things that the physical/chemical approach to biology consciously ignores, namely the quality of indwelling spirit. This is a domain which we can understand best from our own experience and which must be charted by the compass of our deepest inner perceptions."[9]

Portmann goes even further and speaks of "alchemical thinking." This type of thinking, he writes, is "para-scientific, not pre-scientific, for what is aimed at here is a human goal which science does not strive towards and which today appears more urgent and necessary than ever—namely the goal to come back into contact with ourselves and into harmony with the world in its totality."[10] Understandably, he was deeply interested in mythology and was strongly influenced by Jung's analytical psychology. He saw a connection with biology in the doctrine of the archetypes.[11] At the same time he criticized some aspects of Jung's concept, thereby arousing the latter's annoyance. Ximena de Angula, writing to her mother, Cary Baynes,[12] said that Jung "was building up an animosity against Portmann"; he was saying that scientists would do better to ask him before entering a territory of which they knew nothing. Jung's sharp reaction is not surprising in view of the fact that his unproven (and perhaps not provable) theory of the archetypes was at stake, and with it the whole theory of the collective unconscious.

Portmann also made frequent reference to Daoism, which attaches crucial importance to the integration of human beings into the totality of the world. And it is interesting to observe that Portmann even had a certain influence on philosophy and sociology. Helmuth Plessner, later also an Eranos speaker, who continued Max Scheler's work in founding "philosophical anthropology," took up many of Portmann's pronouncements and incorporated them into his own thinking. Even world-famous philosophers such as Karl Jaspers and Martin Heidegger were in contact with Portmann[13] and Arnold Gehlen had in his latter years repeatedly made reference to him.[14]

In 1946 Mary Mellon wanted to go to Switzerland to work with Jung and visit Eranos, but shortly before her departure she was obliged to cancel the trip for health reasons. As she had already arranged to hold discussions with Jung about the publication of his works in English, she sent John Barrett as her representative. Barrett, a long-standing friend of hers, was co-publisher and, as McGuire reports, after 1946 the main moving spirit behind the Bollingen book series. Having lived for many years in Europe, he was considered an ideal mediator between the two continents. With both Jung and Fröbe he immediately established very warm personal contact.

Immediately after the 1946 meeting a long-awaited discussion session was held in the Casa Gabriella to decide upon the future of Eranos. Barrett, Jung, and Herbert Read were among the participants. Read already knew Jung, as he had been commissioned by an English publishing house to plan a collected edition of Jung's works, and later he was to play an important role in the Bollingen Series. The issue at this meeting was how to secure the future financial survival of Eranos and of Olga Fröbe herself. A certain amount of sponsorship money had already been provided. Now Mary Mellon had proposed, in a letter to Fröbe, that she sell part of her property in Moscia-Ascona to her in order to raise cash. The arrangement would allow Fröbe to continue living in the house for the remainder of her life, acting as curator of Eranos and drawing a commensurate salary. In this letter Mary Mellon said that she herself had not come to the negotiations, as she had received a negative message to that effect from the *I Ching*. In the end nothing came of the property sale. Three Swiss lawyers who were present saw too many legal obstacles. Mary Mellon was quite disappointed about this outcome and, furthermore, was no longer convinced that the Eranos lectures should be published in English. In October of the same year she died unexpectedly at the age of only forty-two after heavy attacks of asthma, which she had suffered from since her youth. On the day following her death, her husband, Paul Mellon, told John Barrett that he strongly wished to continue the publication plans that had meant so much to his wife.

Leo Baeck, Judaic Scholar and Humanitarian

The 1947 meeting was attended by the "old regular" Kerényi as well as by Jung, Massignon, Rahner, and a number of new lecturers such as the Catholic priest Victor White, the rabbi Leo Baeck and the expert on Gnosticism Gilles Quispel. Leo Baeck, founder of the institute that was later to play such an important role for Judaic studies (also in the German context), was born in the former German province of Posen.[15] His home town of Lissa was characterized by particularly good relations between Germans and Jews, a fact which must have contributed greatly to Leo Baeck's well-known tolerance and capacity for mediation. Thus, for example, the Baeck family (the father was also a rabbi) lived in the house of a Calvinist pastor. The *Gymnasium* (grammar school) that Leo Baeck attended had been founded by Amos Comenius, the well-known pedagogue and founder of the pansophical movement, whose outlook was tinged with a Rosicrucian type of spirituality. This school was also characterized by a spirit of openness. Hans I. Bach describes Baeck as having grown up in an atmosphere of religious tolerance that did not, however, gloss over religious differences, but rather integrated them within a higher sense of community. Even more importantly, Bach remarks, he recognized early on that religious tolerance between two sides can only really exist when both are securely rooted in their respective faiths.[16]

However, this tolerance did not prevent Baeck from later on sharply and even polemically criticizing Christianity, for one thing because it had sprung from Judaism and he saw in the Christian religion a betrayal of something valuable inherited from Judaism. Baeck's pupil Albert H. Friedländer expresses it as follows:

> Baeck does not criticize Christianity because of its belief, but rather because it believes blindly; not because it creates feelings of dependence, but because this dependence leads to a surrender of the individual's autonomy of action; not because it has a vision of the future, but because this vision has become detached from reality and transferred to a beyond that cannot be attained by work but only by grace.[17]

After his studies and a period as a military rabbi, Baeck became in 1922 president of the German Rabbinical Association and then grand president of the Bnai-Brith lodges until their dissolution by the Nazis in 1937. In 1933, when the Nazis seized power, he was unanimously elected president of the *Reichsvertretung der Juden in Deutschland* (the Jewish representative body). In this role he represented the entire Jewish population of the country.[18] This task meant negotiating daily to mitigate excessively harsh treatment, keeping up morale, organizing emigration as far as it was possible, and creating a comprehensive system of support in the form of Jewish schools, charitable institutions, and cultural organizations.[19] In the course of this work, although he was not a Zionist, he became co-founder of the Jewish Agency for Palestine, and from 1939 he was president of the World Union for Progressive Judaism. Despite the increasingly dangerous situation, he did not leave Germany, and even after the outbreak of war in 1939 he succeeded in printing and publishing the final volume of the periodical *Monatsschrift für die Geschichte und Wissenschaft des Judentums*. He also taught at the Berlin Academy for the Study of Judaism until it was forced to close its doors at the surprisingly late date of 1942.

He was arrested five times before finally being sent in 1943 at the age of nearly seventy to Theresienstadt concentration camp, where he became seriously ill on account of the harsh conditions and physical strain. The liberation of the camp by the Russians came just in time. However, Baeck refused to be flown to safety and remained in the camp until it had been dissolved. By virtue of his authority he was able to prevent the inmates from lynching any German in the vicinity they could get hold of. He is even reported to have placed himself in front of the concentration camp guards in order to shield them. He then flew to London to join his family. Leo Baeck was by then known world-wide on account of his life story, and he received one honor after another. In 1954 a *Festschrift* was published in commemoration of his eightieth birthday containing contributions by such famous names as Martin Buber, Albert Einstein, Karl Jaspers, Jacques Maritain, and Gershom Scholem.[20] The following remark by him is characteristic of his outlook on life:

"True honour is something that each person confers on himself—he confers it through a life that is inviolable and pure, simple and upright, a life marked by the self-containment that is the sign of inner strength."[21]

In addition to his work in the public sphere, Leo Baeck also carried out valuable work in the field of scholarship. Thus, for example, between 1933 and 1939 he made three translations of the New Testament from Greek into Hebrew in order to distinguish its Jewish substance from the Greek interpolations and additions (in terms of both language and thought content). In the 1920s he had also taken part in Count Keyserling's meetings, which have been mentioned earlier.[22] As late as 1949 there appeared in *Mensch und Kosmos*, yearbook of the Keyserling Society, an article by him entitled *Geist und Blut*.[23] Besides his essays for the Keyserling publications he also wrote on Jewish mysticism for publications with a wider audience such as the *Süddeutsche Monatshefte* and *Die Tat*, published by Eugen Diederichs and one of the most important German organs of *völkisch* romanticism.[24] In his early years, Baeck, like most of his Jewish academic colleagues, was totally hostile towards mystical currents in Judaism[25] and had, for example, several times attacked Friedrich Schleiermacher.[26]

Later, however, he came to realize the importance of the mystical element in Judaism—and indeed some time before Scholem, as Alexander Altmann underlines.[27] His change of view came in 1911 with the recognition that Jewish mysticism possessed a unique character, which he maintained had nothing in common with other mystical traditions, whose ultimate goal is a "dissolving in non-being," that is to say a merging with the divine. According to Baeck, Jewish mysticism, on account of its particular conception of God, is immune against such notions of union with the divine[28] and remains firmly in the ethical realm, which he always saw as the Jewish domain *par excellence*.[29] In his detailed studies of the Kabbalistic writings such as the *Sepher Bahir* and the *Sepher Yetzirah* he repeatedly emphasizes this element and speaks of the cosmic ethical system contained in these texts, which he sees as the distinguishing feature of Jewish mysticism.[30]

Baeck's conception of Judaism was summarized as follows by Rabbi Georg Sulzberger in a memorial speech after Baeck's death:[31]

> According to Baeck, the Jewish religion is neither a religion of mysticism nor merely a religion of laws. Furthermore, it is not so much a religion of salvation—and all salvation is a release from the I and therefore from the will—but rather a religion of reconciliation, that is to say reconciliation between God and humanity. Its mysticism is a mysticism of the will, an active mysticism, and its watchword is not belief but action, ethical action.

Here we touch upon an issue of fundamental importance, namely the question of the place of ethics within Gnostic/esoteric thinking. Especially on the ethical level there are certain objections that could be made towards this mode of thought. To identify oneself with the divine is to stand in one's own eyes above the usual categories of good and evil, opening the door to delusions of superiority, titanic hubris and superhuman posturing. Such a tendency cannot be held in check by purely human laws but only by a "God," who alone can credibly be seen as "pure" and transcendent. However, when someone identifies with God and starts to relativize good and evil, what generally seems to happen is that it is the evil that primarily becomes relativized. This applies, for example, to the Jungian notion of "integrating evil" (the "shadow") in pursuit of wholeness (the "self"), a notion vehemently criticized by Martin Buber.[32] Unfortunately it is not possible to deal here with this enormous subject, even superficially, but already we can discern one of the main lines of argument raised by the three great monotheistic religions against the Gnostic-esoteric worldview.[33]

Gilles Quispel and Gnosticism

We now turn to another important figure at Eranos during the post-war years. Gilles Quispel came to Eranos through his contact with Jung, to whom he had sent an article about Gnosticism.[34] Born in Rotterdam, Quispel had, unusually for the time, come into contact with the Greek mysteries and Christian mysticism even in his school days. He studied classical philology and became a teacher. At the same time he began a study of theology. During the Second World War he laid the firm foundations of his research into Gnostic systems of thought, devoting himself especially to the study of Valentinus. He regularly visited and lectured at Eranos,[35] where Jung and Scholem became formative influences on him. Jung convinced him that the Gnostic thinkers had derived their ideas from the deeper levels of the unconscious, while Scholem opened his eyes to the importance of Jewish mysticism within the Gnostic systems of the ancient world.

In 1950 he spent a year in Rome with the help of a subsidy from the Bollingen Foundation, and then became professor of early church history at Utrecht. He is also known in connection with a Coptic codex from Nag Hammadi, the only one to have left Egypt, which he acquired for the Jung Institute; hence the manuscript became known as the Jung Codex. Jung was very interested in the Nag Hammadi texts, as he found in them certain parallels to his own discoveries in psychology. In 1951 he invited Quispel to lecture at the C.G. Jung Institute in Zurich.[36] Subsequently Quispel devoted a large part of his research career to the Nag Hammadi finds. Nevertheless, his interests were not merely focused on antiquity. On the contrary, he studied many varieties of gnostically oriented thought up to the modern age. On occasion he characterized himself as a *homo religiosissimus*, for whom religion was immensely important. Thus as a lecturer he had an ability to transmit his own enthusiasm for Gnosis to his audience.[37] I recall being present at a seminar given by him at the Summer University in Amsterdam in 1994, where he expressed his firm conviction that Gnosis would be the key religion of the twenty-first century. Again, the author of an article in the journal *Janus*[38] quotes Quispel as saying, "I assume that the religion of the 20th century will be Gnostic", an opinion that is perhaps not so extraordinary. Gnosis is above all a religion of the individual who looks inwards. In an age in which the individual seems to be written larger than the community, Gnosis as a religion can only experience an upswing.

Gnosis, as Quispel understands it, is a religious tradition that depends on inner experience and expresses itself not in discourse but in pictures. For him Gnosis is a "mythical expression of self-experience."[39] As examples, he cites Hermeticism, the teachings of the Cathars, and the Christian mystics, but also Goethe, William Blake, and Jung. Thus Gnosis is distinct from two other strands within European culture, which he characterizes as "belief" (the recognized church) and "reason" (the tradition of rationalism).[40]

At the Eranos meeting of 1947 an important foundation stone was laid for Jung's success in the English-speaking world when in the Casa Gabriella he signed the contracts for the publication of his collected works in England and the United States.[41] Paul Mellon himself came for the event. After Mary Mellon's death Fröbe had virtually given up all hope that the Bollingen Foundation or Paul Mellon would continue to support her. Still she was determined to continue. When she and Mellon went through the budget, Mellon realized that a continuation of Eranos would be practically impossible without his help. He therefore declared himself ready to enter into an arrangement whereby Mrs. Fröbe would receive an annual salary of $3,000 from the Bollingen Foundation plus a one-off donation of the same amount from Mellon himself. In addition, Eranos received a further $3,000 from him. As Barbara von Reibnitz has calculated, $3,000 at that time was the equivalent of about 55,000 Swiss francs in the year 2000, and she adds that "what the Bollingen foundation provided was not just a contribution, but covered, over at least 15 years, the basic financing of Eranos as well as a substantial proportion of Mrs. Fröbe's personal needs."[42] And that was not all. Bollingen also paid the travel costs of the speakers who came from far away, such as Erich Neumann. In addition, a long succession of Eranos speakers were given so-called fellowships, which meant that their living costs were covered while they were carrying out their researches, the results of which were then published by Bollingen.

Olga Fröbe had, however, further debts that she had overlooked during the discussion with Paul Mellon. Consequently she turned to him again in 1948 and suggested that he should buy not only the piece of land by the lake but also the hill behind the house, which would have brought her about $50,000. In this way she hoped to merge Eranos with Bollingen and thus be rid of financial worries once and for all. This idea was, however, rejected by Mellon, who wrote to her lawyer, "It has always seemed to me that the Eranos Foundation, well established as it is in Switzerland, should be able to obtain more substantial financial support among the Swiss people themselves."[43] She then became panic-stricken and thought she was going to lose Mellon's support entirely, but in fact it continued until her death. In 1950 Mellon even brought his second wife, a friend of his first since their youth, to Ascona and introduced her to Fröbe. Still, as William McGuire describes,[44] Olga Fröbe brooded through the long winters, alone in her stone house, asking herself what the sense of Eranos was. Sometimes she felt herself surrounded by disembodied persons. Richard Wilhelm, for example, appeared several times to her in this way, although she had never met him, as she herself confirmed.

Joseph Campbell, Charismatic Mythologist, and Eranos' Secret Inner Life According to Olga Fröbe

Meanwhile the plan to publish the Eranos lectures in English had been taken up again by the president of the Bollingen Foundation, John "Jack" Barrett, whom Olga Fröbe had always seen as the good angel of Eranos and who, together with his long-standing colleague Vaun Gillmor, had always seen to it that Eranos received generous subsidies. As editor for the publication project, she had in mind Joseph Campbell,[45] who later became a celebrity[46] through his lively and captivating television broadcasts and radio interviews as well as his highly successful books, tapes, and video recordings.[47] Of Irish origin, Campbell was born in New York. After studying medieval literature, he went to Paris where he discovered James Joyce's magnum opus *Ulysses*, which, as he said, opened up the modern world for him. He learned German,[48] Sanskrit, and Russian, read Oswald Spengler, Thomas Mann, Leo Frobenius, and C.G. Jung. He also occupied himself intensively with the works of Johann Jakob Bachofen,[49] whose importance in the renaissance of an empathetic approach to mythology cannot be overestimated.

Campbell's interest in oriental thought was awakened by a meeting with Jiddu Krishnamurti, the former protégé of the Theosophical Society President Annie Besant, who had seen him as the future World Teacher.[50] From 1934 he taught history of literature at Sarah Lawrence College near New York. He also helped Swami Nikhilananda with the translation of the Upanishads and a book about Ramakrishna, and at the Ramakrishna-Vivekananda center in New York he came to know Heinrich Zimmer. Through Zimmer's private lectures Campbell came into contact for the first time with the esoteric world of the Tarot cards, and much later he produced an article on the symbolism of the so-called Marseilles Tarot.[51] Campbell's interest in esoteric studies also manifested itself in his preoccupation with the Grail mythos[52] and later in his numerous seminars at the Esalen Institute at Big Sur, California.[53] After Heinrich Zimmer's death he took care of Zimmer's literary estate, which he expertly organized, often adding new information and ultimately seeing the material through to publication.[54] In this task he had recourse to valuable advice from Ananda K. Coomaraswamy, the great art scholar of mixed Ceylonese and English parentage, who had aligned himself with the so-called Integral Tradition of René Guénon and his school. Heinrich Zimmer is also known to have been one of Coomaraswamy's admirers.

Campbell not only concerned himself with Zimmer's writings but also wrote many books of his own. The best known of these is *The Hero with a Thousand Faces* which, after the *I Ching*, became the best-selling book in the Bollingen Series.[55] What makes Campbell so important is his ability to convey the fundamental significance of religious and mythological studies to a widely dispersed modern public and to bring out their relevance to contemporary culture. His main concern was to compare similar mythical motifs and legends in East and West.

At the same time Campbell had plenty of critics among scholars of religion.[56] One of the accusations against him was that his real area of study had been literature and therefore he was equally concerned about the literary impact of his works. Thus Florence Sandler and Derrell Reeck call him the "most artful of storytellers,"[57] thinking primarily of his bestseller *The Hero with a Thousand Faces*. This truly thrilling book sets out to uncover universal patterns in myths, folk tales, and legends world-wide, ranging from Hindu traditions through Maori folklore to the Arthurian cycle. The reader is struck by the way in which, again and again, the same type of hero crops up in varying forms in many different cultures. Not surprisingly, Campbell's work chimed in with the endeavors of Fröbe and Jung. At the same time, Campbell was intent on promoting mutual understanding between different peoples by showing that "truth is one." This is of course a misleading exaggeration, and the task of comparative religion is rather to identify differences.

In recent years, however, there have been an increasing number of public utterances accusing Campbell of evincing not only anti-monotheistic views but also racist sentiments in his writings. Anti-Semitic observations and remarks against blacks are mentioned in this context. I have mentioned this question but will not enlarge upon it, as it has no connection with the accusations of National Socialist links in the case of Eranos. However, one might raise the important question as to why so many people who are inspired by the mythical domain are also drawn to such political positions that are no longer tenable. This is the theme of Robert Ellwood's book *The Politics of Myth*, which contains a long section on Joseph Campbell. I recommend this book highly, if only for its balanced approach.

As already mentioned, Campbell's work on Zimmer's literary legacy had aroused the attention of Olga Fröbe, and finally the Bollingen Foundation commissioned him to read through all the Eranos yearbooks from 1933 to 1948 and make a proposal for a publication. Meanwhile the publisher Kurt Wolff had put forward Ralph Manheim as a competent translator. In the end only sixty-seven of the lectures were published, and the others were put on ice. The assiduous and efficient Manheim later also translated for Bollingen such authors as Erich Neumann, Jolande Jacobi, Karl Kerényi, Henry Corbin, and Johann Jakob Bachofen.

At the end of 1949 Campbell duly made his proposal for the publication of the Eranos lectures, summarizing each one. John Barrett agreed, but Olga Fröbe was totally opposed to the proposal. In a letter to Campbell of 24 April 1950, she wrote,

> But I think I must tell you that I was very much upset about your method of tak-
> ing apart all the volumes, and then, for the greater part, rearranging them under
> headings of your own … The group of speakers at every meeting are a unit, bound
> in close relationship by their own relationship to the central theme and to that
> dynamic force that we call Eranos … My own upset was not personal. I am not
> Eranos, I serve it.

And in a further letter of 6 May 1950 she elaborated:

> The central theme of every volume is an archetypal idea, and the group of speak-
> ers formulate [sic] their lectures within that frame … And the valuation of these
> lectures must therefore never be undertaken from a merely intellectual or per-
> fectionist point of view. The material being what it is (to use a much discredited
> word)—esoteric, a very different standard has to be held. That is why we don't
> appreciate academic lectures of the old style … And anyone who has come into con-
> tact with archetypal energy will know that he is up against something immensely
> powerful, immensely alive and creative, in fact the creative forces themselves …
> All the lectures given here seem to move around a centre, not represented by any
> personality, but by an idea, which we call Eranos. It stands for the Quest, or for the
> Self as defined by Jung, or the Way of the Soul … but au fond it escapes definition
> being a paradox and irrational thing.

Particularly interesting is her summing-up sentence: You see how very un-intellectual the roots of Eranos are.

This quotation perhaps gives the best rational insight into what Eranos really meant to her and why she was so deeply moved by it. Through these letters, combined with what we know of the "genius" of the place (or perhaps one could say "daemon" in the Aristotelian sense), that is to say the "transcendent" or "esoteric" side of Eranos, of which we shall have more to say later, we can begin to obtain a more complete picture of "the Eranos" as the founder and presumably also the "inner" circle and even some of the inheritors of the project conceived it. What we are dealing with, therefore, is a "whole entity," existing within its own center, in the circle of speakers, in the commu-nity of participants, but also as a "being" inhabiting the "mesocosmos," the realm of the imagination or the world between human beings and the absolute. It was perceived as something eternal and timeless, yet "fallen into time" since, although it was in itself formless, it required worldly form and expression in order to function in the world. Hence, those who carried forward the Eranos concept (or "insight" as Fröbe would probably have called it) always had the sense of being merely humble servants of this "entity."[58]

Campbell's essentially rational approach to the compilation of the Eranos lectures was not acceptable to her, as what was important to her was not the intellectual content but rather the spirit of Eranos as a whole. Furthermore, certain lectures, for example, one by Paul Radin that Campbell found brilliant, were totally rejected by Fröbe. Inevitably there ensued a hefty discussion between them. She urged Campbell to come to Ascona so that he could sense the true spirit of Eranos. She also mentioned that the deceased Heinrich Zimmer would certainly have shared her position, as he had understood very well what Eranos really was.

Despite the overall coherence of the lectures on account of their shared archetypal character, she was willing to leave out many that did not lend themselves to publication in the English version. These included, in particular, the talks by Hauer, Heyer, Mrs. Strauß-Klöbe, Eisler, Mrs. Rhys-Davids, Rudolf Bernoulli, and Swami Yatiswarananda. Even some contributions by Kerényi she was willing to sacrifice at this point in time (1950). Unfortunately she gives no detailed reasons for these decisions. In the case of Hauer and Heyer the reason is fairly obvious and, as far as the two female speakers are concerned, one can have suspicions. It is interesting that a number of lectures that were decidedly esoteric were also omitted, including those of Bernoulli.

At any rate it seemed impossible to reach an agreement with Campbell, and Fröbe had at this point given up all hope that these English volumes would ever appear. In a letter to the "intermediary" John Barrett of 13 January 1953 (that is, three years later) she said Campbell was of the opinion that her selection was not worthy to appear in the Bollingen Series. The reason for this is not given in the correspondence. Perhaps her selection was not "scholarly" enough. But her final sentence in this letter is unequivocal: "I have the responsibility towards Eranos concerning this publication, and I cannot accept anything that will be fundamentally detrimental to the inner significance of the whole. Much better not to publish at all, than to illegitimately break the inner continuity."

Writing to Jung, she said that Campbell's "standard of values" was:

> literary, formalistic and perfectionist … Of Eranos there was nothing left to be seen. The main difficulty is that neither Campbell nor Barrett know what an archetype is. Must I make compromises that I cannot make with a good conscience? On the other hand Campbell and Barrett must think I am a "trouble-maker" because they do not understand my reasons at all. This is an impasse out of which I can only escape with the help of the Holy Spirit. My own responsibility has unmistakable limits. It is not I alone who carries the responsibility for Eranos. Essentially the responsibility lies in a totally impersonal sphere. My task is, first and foremost, to grasp and bring to realization something that has neither form nor name.[59]

On 6 March of the same year she resumed, after a long interruption, her attempt to reach an agreement and wrote to Campbell:

> ERANOS has a definite basic pattern. (To me it is a pre-existent pattern such as exists for any creative and cultural work, issuing from an archetypal source, which we cannot name, but which is responsible for all great changes in the history of culture.)
> Of this pattern of ERANOS only fragments at a time become visible and tangible as the work develops and according to our awareness or sensing of the subterranean

outline. Each Eranos meeting with its central theme represents an essential unit within the complete pattern. It is of utmost importance, year by year, to sense the next bit of the unseen mosaic, which it is our task to reproduce in reality ... The volumes of the Jahrbücher, as originally published have given a correct picture of the lectures, which have not aimed at literary perfection or form, nor at completeness or even coherence. Their value is *evocative* [underlined by Fröbe]. They touch upon unusual themes and facts and analogies, each speaker, as it were, carrying a lantern which lights up points here and there in the landscape he has chosen for his lecture. Not more than that.

But in evoking the great archetypal images of the depths, he touches the unconscious psyche of the listeners and this creates the extraordinary dynamic atmosphere of the conference.[60]

I considered it important to include these long quotations to clearly illustrate her way of thinking, which is not only totally legitimate but is part and parcel of the whole ethos and self-image of Eranos, which is what we are investigating here. It must certainly have been very difficult for Campbell to continue debating with her when uppermost in his mind were the scholarly criteria and perhaps "marketing" considerations. After all, who can fight against archetypes? Only a *Hero with a Thousand Faces* (to recall the title of Campbell's most widely sold book). So things took their inevitable course and a compromise was reached.[61] Six volumes were finally published between 1954 and 1968. Some of these were more in line with the yearbooks, others less so.[62] In 1953 Campbell attended Eranos as a member of the audience, and in 1957 and 1959 he came as a lecturer. As Campbell's biographers Stephen and Robin Larsen write, "If the Campbells were entranced by Eranos, so was Mrs. Fröbe by the voluble and gracious Joseph and the graceful and aristocratic Jean [Campbell's wife]."[63] Despite all their differences of opinion it was Olga Fröbe's wish that Campbell and his wife should organize an Eranos-like project in the United States. Financing was to be provided by the Bollingen Foundation. On 21 January 1954 she wrote to Paul Mellon as follows: "The Daimon that rules and energizes Eranos, the Genius loci ignotus to whom Jung told me to erect a stone ... has been the guiding and impelling force in the whole work. Mary felt this the first time she came here and it was this influence that also gripped her when she planned an Eranos in America." The idea of an Eranos in the United States has never materialized, even though similar plans have been repeatedly mooted up to the present day, always failing because of the financing issue. But let us return to the history of the meetings.

The Final Upturn for Eranos: Erich Neumann and Gerardus Van Der Leeuw

In 1948 there were a number of newcomers among the lecturers. Two of these deserve special mention, namely Gerardus van der Leeuw and the psychologist and Jung disciple Erich Neumann from Tel Aviv. The latter, writing in 1950 to Olga Fröbe, said:

When I came back to Europe in 1947 for the first time after the World War and having being away for eleven years, I was sure that, after all that had happened to me, Europe would seem alien and disturbing. There was one place, however, where I found my initial foothold—a ground for myself, my way of life, my work— and that was in the Eranos archive ... For some years now I have been coming to

Switzerland and to Europe, but strangely enough—or is it in fact so strange?—in truth it is always to Ascona and to Eranos that I come.[64]

Here it should not be forgotten that Neumann was a much sought-after speaker, not only in Switzerland but also in Holland, Spain, and latterly even in Germany again.

It is worth quoting from another of his letters to the Eranos hostess, voicing sentiments that were later echoed clearly by Fröbe herself.[65]

> You know that it is not by coincidence that I am living in Israel, and to a large extent I belong there ... But another—unconditional and differently conditioned—part of me, which is essentially without a homeland ... was joyfully surprised to find a piece of home ground within Eranos, whose spirit lives in your heart, in the talks at the big round table on the terrace by the lake, and in the wide-reaching efforts of many speakers to grasp the real essence of the Western spirit. Believe me that this joy goes together with a deep sense of gratitude for being blessed again and again in every conceivable way with new gifts from that mandala.

Neumann was born in Berlin in 1905, studied psychology and philosophy after the First World War, and took his doctorate in 1927.[66] Already in his doctoral dissertation his affinity with the ideas of the Kabbalah and the Hasidim is evident. He also completed a medical degree. In 1933 he went to Zurich to be trained by Jung. Soon afterwards he was forced by the Nazi seizure of power to leave his homeland and emigrate to Tel Aviv, where he practiced as an analytical psychologist. Nevertheless, his writings evince no trace of any kind of hatred towards Germany. On the contrary, he retained a strong connection with German culture. In 1936 he again studied under Jung and later returned repeatedly to Zurich to lecture at the C.G. Jung Institute. Furthermore, he developed a lasting friendship with Jung, who had a great regard for him,[67] and the two men carried on a wide-ranging correspondence. In the foreword to Neumann's book *Ursprungsgeschichte des Bewusstseins*,[68] Jung wrote that a work had "seldom been so welcome to him as this one" and went on to praise it even more highly by saying that Neumann in this book "reaches some of the most important conclusions and insights that have ever been attained in this area." It was also Neumann who recommended Gershom to read Jung.[69] His wife was also an analyst. Interestingly, she practiced palm reading and possessed a large collection of palm prints for purposes of comparison.[70]

Neumann, who was regarded by many as the most gifted of Jung's pupils, was also president of the Israel Association for Analytical Psychology.[71] He died in Tel Aviv in 1960. He originally came to Eranos when he spent a vacation at Ascona in 1947. During this visit his friend from youth, the psychologist Gerhard Adler, introduced him to Olga Fröbe and John Barrett.[72] His first lecture at Eranos, "*Der mystische Mensch*" (Mystical man), was a great success and earned him effusive praise from Jung.[73] Neumann spoke regularly at Eranos from 1948 and had a large circle of followers there, as he always touched on points of central interest. Furthermore, he cast his net very wide and could speak with as much eloquence about ethical questions[74] as he could about Mozart, Leonardo da Vinci, Marc Chagall, or Franz Kafka.

Fröbe especially was impressed by Neumann from his very first talk, as is clear from her letters. The encounter with the numinous, of which Neumann spoke on that occasion, was very familiar to her. His sudden death was therefore a great shock to her, for apparently no one had known how ill he was. In a letter of 12 November 1960 to John

Barrett she wrote of Neumann, "Looking back it has become clear to me that in the last twelve years Eranos has developed against the background of Neumann's vision of the inner man. His creative work in those years was all for Eranos and when one looks at his creation it seems to be a finished and round whole."

What made Neumann's lectures so interesting was that he always made a connection to our spiritual problems in the present day and did not simply hold forth in an abstract way about distant cultures. He was convinced "that the peril of present-day mankind springs in large part from the one-sidedly patriarchal development of the male intellectual consciousness, which is no longer kept in balance by the matriarchal role of the psyche."[75] Only a synthesis of the male/rational and female/spiritual modes can bring about a wholeness of the human psyche.

Neumann's 1950 lecture on "The Psychological Significance of Ritual" was, as Ximena de Angulo wrote, one of the high points of that year's meeting. She regretted that not more young people were there to benefit from the talk. Fröbe, who saw herself as guided by higher powers, must have been gripped by statements such as the following:

> Because of our dependence and reliance on the transpersonal we are forced to remain in contact or repeatedly to make contact with this higher, numinous and very real level, for it is on this level that life, in its real sense, takes place, and it is from this level that earthly and human life is directed … Without this communication with the transpersonal powers human life cannot be viable, let alone unfold its creative potential. The life of mere facts, without a connection to the transpersonal forces working in the background, is unreal and powerless.

Fröbe, as we know from her later remarks, was particularly impressed by the final words of the lecture: "The creative world of the numinous reveals itself in the inner, psychic realm, and its sacred executor is the individual 'I' to which this numinosity appears. This means, however, that the person's life loses its individual character and becomes a symbolic life."[76] Like his mentor Jung, Neumann saw the psychological development of a person as being a dialectical process between the individual and the mythical world of the collective unconscious. In order to reach the central symbol of the self, which is analogous to the Sun, to Christ, and to the alchemical stone of the philosophers, the "I" has to gain the necessary degree of freedom from the unconscious. At the same time, however, it receives from the unconscious and the archetypes the energy that it needs in order to carry through this arduous, spiral process.

An area with which Neumann was much preoccupied was that of ethics. Here he developed a "new ethics," which was strongly influenced by C.G. Jung and sought to solve the problem of "evil." Here I would like to quote a few sentences by Neumann which, in my opinion, are among the most important insights that analytical psychology has ever offered as regards the nature of human beings and how they can best coexist.

> The need to come to terms with evil in a self-directed way leads us to postulate the ethical duty to bring it into consciousness. This imperative takes on a central importance when one realizes what disastrous results are produced by the unconscious through suppression at the individual and the collective level. By accepting evil, modern man accepts his own self and the world in all their perilous double-sided nature. This self-affirmation is to be understood in its deepest sense as an affirmation of human totality, a totality which encompasses both the unconscious

and the conscious and whose centre lies not in the "I" that is the focus of consciousness nor in the so-called "super-ego," but rather in the self.[77]

However, Neumann goes on to say that the implications of this deep insight are for many (perhaps most?) people not easy to accept, although they follow quite logically from the preceding thoughts:

> It is good to acknowledge one's own evil. It is bad to wish to be too good, that is to say to strive to leap beyond the limits of the good that is achievable and within reach. It is ethically good when someone does evil consciously—that is to say, always in the awareness of the attendant responsibility—and without distancing himself from it. The suppression of evil is always accompanied by an inflated self-evaluation and is therefore itself evil, even when it stems from a "good conscience" or "good will."[78]

Unfortunately Neumann is not talked about very much these days, even if someone as well known as the New Age philosopher Ken Wilber is fond of referring to him.[79]

Gerardus van der Leeuw

The second important newcomer in 1948 was Gerardus van der Leeuw. Born in the Hague, he had studied theology, then worked as a pastor of the Dutch Reformed Church and at the early age of twenty-eight had been appointed to the theological faculty at the University of Groningen.[80] Already in his inaugural lecture he argued that the study of the history of religions is important for understanding theology. In 1945–46, affected by the experience of the Second World War, he held office for the Workers' Party as Minister for Education, Art and Science. His behavior before and during the Nazi occupation of the Netherlands shows how difficult it is in such exceptional situations to act in the politically "right" way (as seen by posterity).

Willem Hofstee, a scholar of religion at Leiden, dealt with this subject in some detail in the context of a conference on "The Study of Religion under the Impact of National Socialist and Fascist Ideologies in Europe," held at Tübingen in 2004.[81] Already in the 1930s van der Leeuw had become concerned about the loss of moral and ethical values. In particular he lamented the lack of belief, community spirit, and respect for authority, as this must lead to nihilism and despair. Consequently he found himself in the company of other intellectuals who shared a critical attitude towards such modern developments. In the political sphere he urged neutrality, as he rejected both National Socialism and Communism. In 1940, when Nazi Germany occupied the Netherlands after a short struggle, van de Leeuw wrote a newspaper article arguing that the country should remain neutral and not hope for a victory of the Allies, "which would only differ marginally from a victory of the totalitarian forces." Indeed, van der Leeuw even became a member of a political movement that argued for a "critical collaboration" with the German occupiers, even though he had many times spoken and written against National Socialism and Fascism. This movement fell apart, however, after a year, as a critical collaboration with the German authorities turned out to be impossible.

At the same time, van de Leeuw had consistently declined to join a protest group of Dutch intellectuals against National Socialism and anti-Semitism, which had been founded in 1936, some time before the occupation. In his commendably balanced discussion, Willem Hofstee makes the reasons for this clear. Van der Leeuw was, as already mentioned, against both National Socialism and Communism. The latter, however, he feared more, as it was atheistic and opposed to Christian belief, whereas Hitler and Mussolini had at least concluded concordats with the Church. In the protest group in question there was a strong Communist faction.

When requested by the German scholar of religion Gustav Mensching to delete references to Jewish authors in the German translation of one of his major works, he agreed to remove an acknowledgement to Levy-Bruhl, to whose concept of the *mentalité primitive* he owed much. On the other hand, as early as 1933 he and some of his colleagues had made efforts to help endangered German Jews. In 1943 van der Leeuw was even arrested by the German authorities, probably because his two sons had refused to take the oath of loyalty to National Socialism that was required of students. As there was no evidence against him, he was soon released. From then on up to the end of the occupation van der Leeuw kept a low profile, writing some essays about ancient Egypt and a book on the poetry of Novalis, none of which could cause any annoyance.

One point made in Hofstee's lecture deserves to be emphasized. While clearly spotlighting van der Leeuw's behavior at that time, he asks, by way of counterbalance, how critical we ourselves are in the case of hidden power struggles in present-day political life. Here too it behooves us to take a position.

A key influence on van der Leeuw's ideas about religion was his teacher W.B. Kristensen, who lived fully immersed in the religious world of antiquity and was always contrasting it with "modernity." He had an equally high regard for romanticism.[82] What interested him in the religions of antiquity was their underlying meaning and symbolic content. For van der Leeuw, too, what was important was the inner "understanding" of religion, and this was later to become the main thrust of his work. Within the humanities in general the quest for genuine and emotional-intuitive "understanding" enjoyed an upsurge after the turn of the century, as exemplified by the philosopher Wilhelm Dilthey, who saw the value of "inner experience" as being equal to that of empirical experience in the sciences. In arguing for his conception of "understanding," through which he wanted to fathom the essence of religion, van der Leeuw constantly invoked relevant German works that took a stance against the one-sided and positivistic approach to knowledge (he had incidentally spent the period 1913–14 in Germany). In his faculty of religious studies he had recourse especially to Rudolf Otto, Friedrich Heiler, and Walter F. Otto, all of whom were connected with Eranos. In his 1950 Eranos lecture (which unfortunately did not appear in the yearbook, because his death intervened before he could prepare it for publication) he began with a polemic against attempts to "de-mythologize" religion, as Ximena de Angulo-Roelli informs us in her unpublished manuscript account of the meeting. In this talk—which he perhaps conceived as his farewell address, since he knew of his illness—he praised Eranos as a place of openness to the spirit, a place where the really important things could be discussed, away from narrow factions and dogmas. As Mircea Eliade has said, van der Leeuw was also strongly concerned to tear down the disciplinary boundaries within the humanities, which chimed in well with Eranos' well-known striving for interdisciplinarity.[83] This was not surprising, considering van de Leeuw's threefold academic background as scholar of religion, theologian, and historian. Fröbe had invited him to Eranos without knowing his address, using Gilles Quispel as the intermediary.[84]

At any rate, van der Leeuw seems to have enjoyed his visits to Eranos. This is evident from his diaries, which are preserved in an archive at the University of Groningen.

Willem Hofstee has published the relevant extracts.[85] Van der Leeuw particularly appreciated the eating and drinking as well as the respect that he enjoyed among the participants. Jung also made a strong impression on him. Eliade adds that van der Leeuw was an avid reader and, like himself, succumbed to the danger of getting captivated by the occult novels of Talbot Mundy, which Olga Fröbe always put into their rooms.[86] She was convinced that van der Leeuw had felt such a powerful bond with her that after his death he had caused her to stumble and fall on her face. As in the case of Max Pulver, she therefore carried out a ritual separation as described in Dion Fortune's book *Psychic Self Defence*.[87]

Van der Leeuw's main work, *Phänomenologie der Religion*,[88] which exerts a positive fascination for many of its readers, begins as early as the first paragraph by addressing the central concept of "power" that pervades the entire book. Religion for van de Leeuw is essentially a matter of "experiencing, encountering and dealing with power," although the word "power" here also encompasses the notion of *mana*, that is to say "magic." It is the "holy" of Rudolf Otto, the "numinous," something strikingly "other,"[89] which one has to experience through systematic introspection. This "power" pervades our life and finds its particular expression in eros and in death. But "power" does not only come from "above." We seek it because we want to have a share of it. And connected with this search is also the search for meaning, which is why human beings create culture. Phenomenology for van der Leeuw means understanding human experience by perceiving it on two levels, but in an ordered way, so that the underlying structures and meaning can be recognized. This form of research thus becomes a "science of experience."[90]

Although van der Leeuw was a pastor, he by no means restricted himself to Christianity. On the contrary, he was interested in everything that religions had in common in terms of structural characteristics. In van der Leeuw we find again that transcendent, mediating, and interdisciplinary quality that characterizes many of the Eranos speakers. Van der Leeuw is especially important in the context of Eranos because Mircea Eliade, with his phenomenological approach to religions (even though markedly independent), can be considered the Dutch scholar's pupil.[91] Both of them were dissatisfied with positivism and with the purely historical approach (as was the case with Eranos as a whole), and both favored phenomenology.[92] And herein lies what I see as the strongest "German" influence on Eranos, for the phenomenological approach, which was already seen in Schleiermacher and was sharpened by Wilhelm Dilthey, Rudolf Otto, and Friedrich Heiler, and philosophically developed by Edmund Husserl,[93] then arguably reached its peak in Eliade,[94] at least as far as the Eranos milieu goes. It is indisputable that the modern origins of this approach lie in German idealism.[95] It is also well documented that the German romantic movement had "occult" roots.[96] This is perhaps what has given rise to the accusation of irrationality against Eranos. But it would be wrong to label this influence as "fascistic" merely because it was predominantly "German."[97]

The invited speakers for 1948 included for the first time someone from over the Atlantic, namely the mathematician Hermann Weyl from Princeton. He was, however, too ill to come, and his lecture was read out by someone else. Thus the Eranos circle was, at least symbolically, widened still further.

11. The Heyday Begins

Gershom Scholem and the Kabbalah

In 1949 the first-time lecturers at Eranos were Paul Radin, ethnologist, anthropologist, and specialist on Native Americans; Henry Corbin, expert on Persia and Shiite Islam; and the Kabbalistic scholar Gershom Scholem. Scholem's name and his historical and philological work on the Kabbalah are so renowned that I will give only a few basic facts about his life and turn instead to less-known aspects of his work instead.

He was born and brought up in Berlin, and what is less well known about him is that he studied mathematics and physics before turning to Judaic studies, a fact that would explain the rationalistic streak in his work. He grew up in an assimilated family which even professed German nationalism and in which no one spoke Hebrew.[1] Nevertheless, he came into contact early on with the Zionist movement. Joseph Dan, holder of the Gershom Scholem Chair of Kabbalah at Hebrew University in Jerusalem, believes in fact that Scholem turned to Zionism in a spirit of rebellion against the German nationalism of his parental home. This early attraction towards Judaism led to a deeper preoccupation with Jewish culture, out of which his later interest in the Kabbalah grew.[2] In Dan's view Scholem was first and foremost a Jewish nationalist and no mystic, who satisfied his leaning towards the "mystical" Kabbalah by studying it as a scholar. There are, however, divergent views on this point, which is an important one in this context and to which I shall return later.

Gershom (or Gerhard, as he was then called) Scholem came into contact with the Zionist movement through his brother Werner, who was two years older. Werner's sympathy for Zionism was, however, short-lived, and he soon threw in his lot with the youth section of the Social Democratic Workers' movement. Although a pacifist, Werner Scholem was called up for military service in 1915 and a year later was seriously wounded. In 1917 he took part in an anti-war demonstration wearing his uniform and was prosecuted for treason (the country was after all at war). This caused the final breach with his father, who, as a good German patriot, had expected that his son would even volunteer for the military. In his early memoirs Gershom Scholem describes a "terrible scene at the lunch table" in which his father was seized by an attack of fury and ordered both him and his brother out of the house. "He had had enough of both of us. Social Democracy and Zionism, it was all the same—just a lot of pacifistic and anti-German machinations, which he no longer wanted in his house."[3] Werner Scholem then joined the Communist Party of Germany and became the youngest member of the Prussian Parliament. In 1926, however, he was expelled from the party for speaking out against the Stalinist abuses in Russia.

Werner's subsequent fate was a tragic one.[4] During the night of the Reichstag fire he was arrested. After two years' investigative detention he was released but arrested again immediately afterwards. A promise of a further release was never fulfilled, and in 1937 he was transferred to Dachau concentration camp and then in 1938 to Buchenwald, where he was murdered in 1940. In Buchenwald he was spokesman for all groups of prisoners including criminals, Jews, and Communists: a precarious position, and not only *vis-à-vis* the Nazi bosses. Because of his atheism and his marriage to a non-Jewish woman, he was not even fully accepted by the Jewish prisoners. Worse still, because of his opposition to the Stalinist regime, he was totally ostracized by the Communist inmates, who were the strongest faction in the camp. The official cause of his death in the camp was by "shooting while trying to escape," but it is decidedly possible, if not probable, that his former Communist Party comrades seized on some (perhaps fabricated) offence to denounce him to the SS, who then simply shot him.[5]

Gershom Scholem, on the other hand, emigrated as early as 1923 to Palestine. For one thing, he believed that only there could he find the intellectual freedom to pursue studies which were at that time not well regarded by German Jewish academics.[6] But undoubtedly a further reason was that in Germany he could see no basis for his future life. In 1915 he had already met Walter Benjamin,[7] which led to a mutually fruitful friendship.[8] In Jerusalem, after initially working as a librarian at the University of Jerusalem, he eventually became professor of Jewish mysticism in 1933. On account of his groundbreaking works, he achieved high recognition and became a member of many scholarly associations. Moshe Idel, professor of Judaica at the University of Jerusalem and himself later an Eranos speaker, said:

> Gershom Scholem's contribution to the modern understanding of Judaism in general and Jewish mysticism in particular can hardly be over-estimated. His work not only laid the foundation for the modern systematic study of Judaism but brought a new and clearer light to the whole research field of Judaic studies, as is shown, directly or indirectly, by any study in this field.[9]

Scholem was among those authors subsidized by the Bollingen Foundation after the publisher Karl Wolff drew his attention to this possibility. Without this support, his thousand-page opus on the Kabbalistic and heretical rabbi Sabbatai Sevi, which Scholem himself counted among his most important scholarly achievements, would probably never have seen the light of day.[10] It was another Eranos lecturer, Paul Radin, who convinced John Barrett, director of the Bollingen Foundation, of the importance of this work.[11]

Certainly Scholem did not have a mystic-Kabbalistic mind in the classical sense of being *primarily* interested in direct experience of God and drawn to Kabbalistic studies *exclusively* out of his own search for transcendence—if only because of his scientific precision. In a letter to Arnold Gottschalk, he himself revealed his own clear position on this matter: "I am certainly *no* mystic, because I believe that science demands a distanced attitude."[12] And yet, in the wider context of Scholem's work, this statement takes on some deeper shades of meaning. Steven Wasserstrom, who has preoccupied himself intensely with this question, quotes a tribute from Joseph Weiss, one of Scholem's closest pupils, published in the German-language Tel Aviv daily newspaper *Yedioth Hayom* on 5 December 1947, on the occasion of Scholem's fiftieth birthday:[13]

> The balance of power between his personal and scholarly sides is very complex. This is not by coincidence nor from any lack of ability but rather out of a consciously

cultivated private esotericism. Scholem does not want anyone really to get to the bottom of him, either in his dialectical negations or his paradoxical affirmations. It is impossible to try to paint a portrait of his mind without revealing the decidedly mystical tone of his esotericism … His esotericism is not in the nature of an absolute reticence, it is a kind of camouflage. On the public level, by means of weighty volumes crammed with texts and philological researches, he reduces the figure of the metaphysician to that of the scholar. But his metaphysics reveals itself in a hidden way, in the form of half sentences, camouflaged beyond recognition and inserted in between "purely" academic analyses … thus the crypto-metaphysician disguises himself as the exact scholar.

This accords with what the American rabbi Herbert Weiner writes in his book 9½ Mystics,[14] reporting a conversation with Scholem in Jerusalem, in which the latter was asked about his personal attitude to the Kabbalah. Scholem, adopting a cryptic manner which he obviously enjoyed, replied as follows: "It is all written down, but only in the form of incidental remarks—hints, scattered through my writings."[15]

Wasserstrom, in his study of Eranos, attempts to adduce further evidence that Scholem, Mircea Eliade, and Henry Corbin formed a natural trio of mythically inclined scholars, even though Scholem did not go as far in this direction as the other two, and his strongly dialectic way of thinking should not be forgotten.[16] Wasserstrom shows that Scholem continued to "champion" mythical thinking[17] despite the way in which the National Socialists had glorified violence while appealing to the sense of mythical longing in human beings. Here Scholem stood in contrast to his fellow émigré scholars Cassirer, Bloch, Horkeimer, and Adorno. Furthermore, Scholem also affirmed the mythological side of the Jewish religion, whereas the "Jewish leadership, intellectual and political, Zionist and non-Zionist" saw Judaism as the religion of reason and "therefore as the original and final enemy of myth," as Wasserstrom writes.[18] But here also one must take note of how Scholem, true to his dialectical way of thinking, affirmed mythology as a basic principle of religion but also cautioned against a regression into the archaic.

Moshe Idel, later an Eranos speaker and today perhaps the best-known expert on the Kabbalah, has also thrown some light on the question of Scholem's mystical side. Idel takes the view that Scholem, while exceptionally successful as a historian of mystical texts and ideas, was nevertheless "in his own eyes, rather a failure qua mystic, yet one who longed for mystical experience." He therefore calls Scholem a "theoretical mystic." He also reports that Scholem in his youth had carried out practical exercises based on Abraham Abulafia's mystical techniques.[19] In contrast to Scholem, Idel's work[20] emphasizes mystical practice and the importance of ecstasy in the Kabbalah.[21] Even Theodor A. Adorno, famous philosopher and member of the Frankfurt School of Sociology, offers an opinion in this context: "The mystical spark [must] have been ignited in himself" (Der mystische Funke [müsse] in ihm selbst gezündet haben).[22]

David Biale is of the opinion that Scholem tried to find "a third way between the rationalism of Judaic scholarship and the irrationalism of Buber."[23] In contrast to Buber, however, he never wished to "blur the historical division between the mystic and the historian" but rather to make use of the "vital energies" that he believed to exist in "the irrational." The mystical and irrational semed to offer the most promising answer to the feeble rationalism of German bourgeois and German Jewish culture. Wouter Hanegraaff, incumbent of the Chair for the History of Hermeticism and Related Currents at the

University of Amsterdam, also sees Scholem as having followed a "third" way, lying between an anti-esoteric position and a mystical universalism.[24]

Steven Wasserstrom has posed the question how much Scholem had in common with his Eranos colleagues Eliade and Corbin in terms of methodology. Here I find the words of Andreas Kilcher enlightening:

> Important though the Eranos forum was for Scholem, his methodology remained distinct from that of Jung or Eliade. It is true that he became open to a phenomenological approach to the Kabbalah, yet he resisted any form of ahistorical essentialism. If Scholem spoke of Kabbalistic "symbols" he did not mean timeless and universal archetypes but rather particular semanticized hermeneutic categories, historically determined and Jewish in terms of cultural specificity. Already in his first Eranos lecture on *Kabbalah and Myth*, he made this unmistakably clear: "For us the symbols of the Kabbalists can only be accessed, if at all, with considerable effort. Their hour has come and gone." That was a clear rejection of the speculative theory of archetypes as upheld by comparative religion.[25]

At the same time, Kilcher is convinced that Scholem's preoccupation with the Kabbalah "was through Romanticism, his 'Romanticism.'" Novalis appears to have been the main source. Kilcher even quotes a passage from the philosopher Jürgen Habermas, who had come to the same conclusion.[26] Of great importance for Scholem, as he himself did not deny,[27] was Franz Joseph Molitor, the most important Christian Kabbalist of the nineteenth century and, in Scholem's words, a "Christian scholar with mystical leanings."[28]

It is worth mentioning another small piece of evidence indicating Scholem's personal interest in mystical-occult currents. In 1928 he published an essay (later to be expanded) entitled "Alchemie und Kabbala"[29] in the journal *Alchemistische Blätter*, a publication of unambiguously occult orientation.[30] This periodical was published by Otto Wilhelm Barth, probably the most important occult publisher and bookseller in Germany at the time, along with the Pansophist Heinrich Tränker, with whom Barth collaborated. His publishing house, O.W. Barth Verlag, still exists today although no longer independent.[31] In terms of content, the periodical *Alchemistische Blätter* kept up an impressively high level, and its contributors also included the French alchemist Jollivet-Castelot and the German alchemist and Rosicrucian Ferdinand Maack. Interestingly, none of the Scholem bibliographies available to me contained any reference to the publication of Scholem's essay in this journal.[32]

The point was taken up by the Scholem specialist Friedrich Niewöhner in reviewing the first edition of the present book in *Gnostika*. Niewöhner believes that Scholem's essay was pirated by the publisher O.W. Barth, as a whole series of Latin and Hebrew quotations were missing or inaccurately reproduced, and Scholem would never have permitted this. Unfortunately, owing to lack of documentation, this accusation can be neither proved nor disproved. However, Konstantin Burmistrov, who had several times carried out research in Gershom Scholem's extensive library,[33] informed me, in an email message of 14 August 2003, that Scholem could very well have been in contact with O.W. Barth, as his library contained a number of books published by Barth, which Scholem had ordered direct from the publisher.

Subsequently the question of Scholem's mystical-occult interests has been further investigated by Konstantin Burmistrov, who has written the most informative essay to date on this subject.[34] Burmistrov comes to certain surprising conclusions. Not only did Scholem possess many classics of occultism (Eliphas Lévi, Papus, Francis Barrett, McGregor Mathers, A.E. Waite, Israel Regardie, etc.), but his handwritten marginal notes prove that he had studied these works intensively. According to Burmistrov the essay on "Alchemie und Kabbala" even reveals the strong influence of A.E. Waite, and, astonishingly, certain parts conform 100 percent to an essay by Waite, although Scholem elsewhere speaks rather negatively of him.

Burmistrov's findings also make it more likely that Scholem was in fact acquainted with the publisher O.W. Barth, as the latter had in 1928 planned the publication of a journal with the title *Kabbalistische Blätter*, which would undoubtedly have interested Scholem. Furthermore, the remaining stock of Scholem's first edition of *Geheimnisse der Schöpfung* was taken over by O.W. Barth in 1936.[35] From Scholem's letters we also know that he went to visit the occult novelist Gustav Meyrink (of whom he did not form a particularly high opinion) and that he expressed a rather positive opinion about the parapsychological investigations of Emil Matthiesen into life after death.[36]

Perhaps more astounding is Scholem's apparent interest in chiromancy, an account of which is given by Lorenz Jäger, an editor of the *Frankfurter Allgemeine Zeitung* (*FAZ*).[37] Three women—called the three "witches" by Scholem—were his interlocutors on this matter, all of whom were associated with Eranos: the graphologist and student of Jung Anna Teillard-Mendelsohn;[38] Hilde Unseld, first wife of Siegfried Unseld, the all-powerful Suhrkamp publisher; and Ursula von Mangold, a niece of Walther Rathenau and later director of the above-mentioned O.W. Barth publishing house. During an Eranos meeting Scholem proudly showed them how long his life line was. In the *Jewish Encyclopedia* he had already written on chiromancy and physiognomy, as medieval and Renaissance masters of the Kabbalah apparently selected their students according to such criteria.

Naturally none of this constitutes proof that Scholem's interest in the occult and the mystical extended beyond the purely academic, but all in all it is somewhat thought-provoking.

The writer and Nobel prize-winner Isaac Bashevis Singer, on the other hand, was one person who must have been unconvinced that Scholem was really animated by the living spirit of the Kabbalah. During a car journey Singer is reported to have remarked to the writer Edward Hoffman, "It takes real genius for someone like Scholem to turn the Kabbalah into something so dry that one doesn't want to read about it anymore."[39]

George Steiner, often referred to as the last cosmopolitan intellectual of our time, believes that the key to the question of whether Scholem was a mystic or not lies in his early interest in mathematics. Although on the one hand Steiner refers to Scholem as an ironic agnostic, on the other hand he says that for Scholem, as for the Neoplatonists, the divine principle, in its highest and most arcane emanations, is analogous to pure mathematics.[40]

Yet another point of view is voiced by Brigitte Hamacher in her book *Gershom Scholem und die Allgemeine Religionsgeschichte*, a masterly study of Scholem's influence, making use of probably the entire body of the then available relevant literature. In this work she convincingly seeks to show that certain of Scholem's central ideas are based on the phenomenological approach of the so-called Marburg school of religious studies and particularly on the work of Rudolf Otto and Friedrich Heiler. This would further support my contention that German currents of thought were of great importance for Eranos. Hamacher refers several times to Eranos, but rejects the view that Scholem's "phenomenological" perspective was first acquired through his contact with other Eranos participants.[41]

In 2003 there appeared a further detailed and informative book on Scholem by Daniel Weidner, dealing in particular with the interplay between Scholem's political writings and those on religion.[42] This book also deals briefly with Eranos.

It seems appropriate at this point to talk more extensively about how Scholem came to Eranos, not only because of Scholem's own importance but also because we will touch here on the already mentioned controversy concerning Jung's attitude to National Socialism. Fortunately Scholem's testimony on this subject has been preserved.[43] In a letter to Aniela Jaffé he relates how Leo Baeck visited him in Jerusalem. Scholem had just received an invitation to Ascona and asked Baeck what he thought of the idea. Baeck said that he must "definitely" go there, even though Jung's reputation had suffered considerably over the past few years owing to his not always emotionally neutral attitude to Judaism.

Baeck, who knew Jung well through Keyserling's School of Wisdom, had also been taken aback, as he had not in any way expected an anti-Semitic attitude on Jung's part. Thus, on a trip to Zurich for the first time after his release from the concentration camp, he had not wanted to visit Jung. The latter, however, having heard of Baeck's visit, looked him up in his hotel and "a very lively two-hour discussion ensued." When Baeck raised the matter of the accusations, Jung defended himself but admitted, "Yes, I slipped."[44] After this had been cleared up, the two men were reconciled. "Because of this explanation from Baeck," Scholem later wrote, "when a second invitation to Eranos came in 1949 I decided to accept."

Scholem's postscript to this letter is worth quoting, although it does not bear directly on the theme that we have been discussing.

> The intention of this short exposition was not to idealize the image of C.G. Jung, nor to diminish it. Rather the aim was to free it from the two extremes of hate and hero worship. It is usually difficult for human beings to be in the presence of greatness and at the same time to maintain their own dignity. They tend either to uncritical admiration on the one hand or to equally uncritical exaggeration of actually existing defects on the other hand … Even more difficult than accepting and putting up with greatness in others is to bear the destiny of greatness oneself. Greatness is like an in-flowing of the transcendent. It is a life task that sets extreme demands. Hence the kind of personality that makes the strongest impression on us is one that combines greatness with humanity, the individual with the collective dimension and inner light with wandering in the dark. It is through having to endure this tension that great artists and scientists or simply great human beings develop their deep involvement with the world, marked by a spirit of enquiry, understanding or love.[45]

Gershom Scholem had also given courses at the C.G. Jung Institute in Zurich.[46] His recollection of Eranos, looking back in 1979 after thirty years of participation there, is something that we shall return to later as valuable evidence in assessing the quality of "magic" that characterized Eranos.

It is also worthwhile to glance briefly at Scholem's relationship to Germany. It is obvious that this relationship, already difficult in his youth, could not have improved after the Second World War. Here it is relevant to quote two passages from a letter written by Scholem to Manfred Schlösser on 18 December 1962.

> I dispute that there has ever been such a German-Jewish dialogue in any true sense *as a historical phenomenon*. For a dialogue it is necessary to have two

parties who listen to each other, each side being prepared to acknowledge the other, what he is and represents, and to respond. Nothing can be more misleading than to apply such a concept to the interaction between Germans and Jews over the past 200 years. This dialogue died in its earliest inceptions and has never come about.

And then again, later in the same letter he wrote: "The allegedly indestructible spiritual commonality between Germans and Jews in their essential nature, consisted, as long as the two lived together, solely of a chorus of Jewish voices. On the level of historical reality it was never more than a fiction and, if you will permit me to say so, one that was paid for too dearly."[47]

If Scholem's assertions were rather cutting, they were also honest. His identity was unambiguously Jewish rather than a German-Jewish "hyphenated identity," as Lorenz Jäger aptly expresses it.[48] On this matter he cites a draft paper written by Scholem at the tender age of seventeen to his co-religionists: "You are not Europeans, you are from the Middle East. You are Jews and human beings, not Germans and decadents."

His position *vis-à-vis* Christianity was just as clear-cut: in connection with the Jewish-born Catholic convert and mystic Simone Weil, he writes of the "abhorrent odour of inwardness" which explains "why I find Christianity so completely insufferable." He goes on to speak of the "lie of pure inwardness," about which he can "only say," "Happy the Jews who resolutely refused to yield to it in the course of world history."[49] Elettra Stimili offers these words of explanation: "The Messianic turn toward inwardness was considered by Scholem to be a type of 'flight,' an attempt to withdraw 'the legitimacy of the Messianic claim' from the theatre of history." Judaism is bound to a conception of salvation that plays itself out in public, in history and in the community, rather than in the spiritual realm and in the unseen, as is the case in Christianity.[50]

Despite his acerbic manner of speaking Scholem appears to have been a man of peace. Thus Steven Wasserstrom states that as an Israeli citizen he belonged to the unpopular peace movement Brit Schalom, and that he "counted among the first seven professors of the Hebrew University who signed a declaration condemning the annexation of the West Bank in August 1967."[51] Toward the end of his life he even became convinced that for the sake of peace the state of Israel must give back all its land gains except for Jerusalem and the Golan Heights.

Paul Radin

Paul Radin was also one of the group of Bollingen fellows, that is the group of scholars whose living costs were covered by the foundation to enable them to carry out extensive research and produce a book. In the case of Radin,[52] a rabbi's son born in Poland who had gone to the United States as a child, this financial support would continue to the end of his life.[53] Initially he studied zoology, then came a two-year sojourn in Germany (his mother was German), where he turned to anthropology. After returning to the United States he studied with the famous anthropologist Franz Boas, then focused on ethnology and carried out studies of the Winnebago Indians. After the end of the First World War he spent five years in Cambridge, where he obtained a series of teaching assignments, giving German lessons to supplement his income. In the 1920s he took part in Jung's seminars in Zurich, although he was never a Jungian. In fact his skeptical and rationalistic outlook was perhaps even strengthened by his contact with Jung. Nevertheless, Jung and Radin always remained in friendly contact, although Radin was very critical of Jung's literary "excursions" into anthropology.

Already in the 1920s Paul Radin had earned high praise from recognized experts such as Marcel Mauss and John Dewey. In the context of Eranos, what made Radin stand out from his more "esoteric" Eranos colleagues was his skepticism and his thorough rationalism.[54] This must naturally have brought him into conflict with Olga Fröbe, whose hyper-energetic "mystic-obsessive" character was not at all to his taste.[55] But all of this was outweighed by his jovial personality. Eliade described Radin as always laughing and endowed with an enormous belly. He reported that the previous year his wife had one night seen a "likeable" dragon in the garden of the Casa Gabriella, but that he had not returned.[56] Stanley Diamond, editor of the *Festschrift* for Radin's seventieth birthday, even wrote: "[Radin] has a sorcerer's charm, undimmed by age; he bewitches."[57] It was not without reason that he contributed to the volume entitled *Der Göttliche Schelm* (The divine rascal).[58] His life's journey also took him to the universities of Michigan, Berkeley, and Brandeis. Always his goal was to remain independent. In addition to his other activities he acted as an adviser to Mary Mellon and later to the Bollingen Foundation. From 1952 to 1956 he lived in Lugano.

Henry Corbin and Sufism

I must now speak in greater detail about Henry Corbin,[59] who attended Eranos every year between 1949 and 1978.[60] His influence on Eranos can hardly be overestimated and involved many of the participants, including Mircea Eliade, whom he first brought to Eranos as a speaker, Gilbert Durand, Antoine Faivre, David Miller, and the archetypal psychologist and Jung pupil James Hillman. His unusual personal aura has been vividly described by Marie-Madeleine Davy, an expert on medieval theology and a long-standing friend and neighbour of Corbin.[61] He was, she wrote, "someone who had re-awakened before reaching the far shore. In his face and eyes something shone forth that reflected the world to which he belonged. In his written works and lectures he knew how to reveal the sphere of the angels. Reading him one could almost hear the sound of their wings as they passed by."

Corbin was born in Paris, where he later studied philosophy, especially the works of the scholastics. Early on he developed an interest in the German mystics Meister Eckhart, Valentin Weigel, and Jakob Boehme. While researching in the Bibliothèque Nationale he had a "fateful" encounter with Louis Massignon, leading immediately to a collaboration. When Massignon gave him a text of the Iranian mystic and philosopher Suhrawardi, Corbin saw this symbolically as a transmission from master to pupil, as Charles J. Adams has emphasized.[62]

In 1930 came Corbin's first journey to Germany, which was to prove no less fateful. His destination was the University of Marburg on the Lahn, a place of great importance in the study of religion and intellectual history, and the first visit he paid to Rudolf Otto. In his *Post-Scriptum biographique à un Entretien philosophique* he mentions two "coincidences" that occurred during this visit.[63] The first was that the Indian poet and philosopher Rabindranath Tagore was in Marburg for a meeting with Rudolf Otto. The second was that Olga Fröbe was also there at the time to discuss her plans with Otto. Another person who taught at Marburg was Friedrich Heiler, who was much preoccupied with contesting the (at that time) provocative ideas of Rudolf Bultmann about the de-mythologizing of Christianity. As Bultmann saw it, there was something in the modern view of the world and humanity that could not longer accept miracles in the ecclesiastical sense and could not tolerate the idea of divine or demonic interventions. Bultmann thus started a massive attack on the notion of the "numinous" experience, which Rudolf Otto saw as being central to religion.[64]

It was in Marburg that Corbin began his lifelong preoccupation with the Swedish mystic Emanuel Swedenborg. Between 1931 and 1936 Corbin made frequent visits to Germany, where he met Karl Barth, Karl Löwith (later to be an Eranos speaker), Ernst Cassirer, and, most notably, Martin Heidegger. He also visited the Warburg Institute in Hamburg with its wonderful library (now in London).[65] Corbin's excellent knowledge of German led to his translating Heidegger's work *Was ist Metaphysik?* (What is metaphysics?) into French.[66] From October 1935 to July 1936 he worked at the French Institute in Berlin. Corbin is a further example of someone who was influenced by the German phenomenological school, which sought to revitalize the sacred Hermetic texts and thereby strengthen their inner "esoteric" meaning.[67] Another current of thought, emanating from Germany, was to have a decisive influence on his life and work, namely the Romantic thinkers such as Johann Georg Hamann, Friedrich von Schelling, and Franz von Baader.[68] Steven Wasserstrom even quotes a remark to the effect that "Corbin was in many ways the last of the German Romantics."[69]

In 1937 Corbin obtained his first academic post at the Ecole Pratique des Hautes Etudes in Paris. The breadth of his interests is shown by his friendship with figures as diverse as the specialist on Indo-European mythology Georges Dumézil, the literary scholar Georges Bataille, the mythologist Roger Caillois, the playwright Eugène Ionesco, the painter René Magritte, and the philosopher Nikolai Berdyayev. In his short biography of Corbin, the Islamicist and prominent representative of the so-called Traditionalist school (Perennialism), S.H. Nasr, describes how at that time the writings of René Guénon and soon after of Frithjof Schuon, who were both his own teachers, were widely discussed in French intellectual circles.[70] Their doctrine, based on the idea of a primal tradition that manifests itself in varying forms in all religions, was especially critical of the modern world and its philosophical and religious conceptions. Thus they had certain points in common with the phenomenological school with its stance against a purely positivistic approach to scholarship, although the latter was of course much less radical. Corbin, however, did not feel attracted by traditionalism in the narrow sense propounded by Guénon.[71]

In 1940 Corbin went to the French Archaeological Institute in Istanbul in order to study some unpublished texts of the Islamic tradition. Because of the German occupation of France during the war he was obliged to stay in Turkey until 1945. Before moving fully back to France he paid his first visit to Teheran, a city to which he would return for three months every year between 1955 and 1973 under the auspices of the Franco-Iranian Institute.[72] There he founded the Bibliothèque Iranienne, a book series in which numerous important writings on Iranian spirituality appeared. The Islamic specialist Seyyed Hossein Nasr, himself an Iranian, has even said the Corbin's work is altogether the most impressive achievement of orientalist scholarship in the domain of Islamic philosophy.

In 1974 Corbin, together with his colleagues Gilbert Durand, Antoine Faivre, and others, founded the University of Saint John of Jerusalem, to which we shall return later. There he attempted to move away from strictly legalistic forms of monotheism by emphasizing the living world of the soul and direct personal religious experience in all its variety. As Pastor Richard Stauffer emphasized in his speech at Corbin's funeral, Corbin was not only a scholar but also "a believer, an unconditional believer … that is, a man who is calmly attuned to the word of God."[73] In the same speech Corbin was described as a "master," who was "not content just to transmit knowledge. In the true sense of the word, he 'prophesied.'"

Corbin characterized his own philosophical position as "phenomenological" and aiming at "understanding"[74] But he went even further and described his method as "a drawing away of the veil," which in Sufi terminology signifies the way to the ultimate truth and to a truly spiritual world. Thus his conception of philosophy includes what one might call "traditional wisdom" or "sophia" in the classical sense. Consequently his interest in Islam is primarily focused on the esoteric side. At the same time his philosophical works are not merely descriptive; they call for a spiritual rebirth. This is clear from the following passage in the foreword to his translation of a collection of writings by Sohrawardi under the title *L'Archange Empourpré*:[75] "Any philosophy that does not lead to spiritual experience is an empty waste of time. And, in reverse, any mystical experience that is not preceded by serious philosophical training is a prey to illusions, aberrations and other maladies of the soul."

Under the rubric of the University of Saint John of Jerusalem, Corbin championed the idea of a spiritual "knighthood" which would have the task of preserving the spiritual and religious heritage of humanity and defending it against modernism,[76] secularization, and historicist worldview. For Corbin, modernity, which found its ultimate expression in Descartes' separation of matter and spirit, had already begun in the West in the twelfth century, when Avicenna's worldview, linked with the Orphic and Platonic traditions, had been displaced by the Aristotelian and purely rational philosophy of Averroes. The former was concerned with self-recognition and the path to transcendence.[77] Corbin saw this as being linked with the concepts of "active intelligence" or "imagination" which will be discussed later on.

Corbin's central concept is the so-called *mundus imaginalis*, the "imaginal" world, a concept whose importance for an understanding of the spiritual realm in general cannot, in my opinion, be overestimated.[78] This realm, according to Corbin, mediates between the absolutely unknowable God and the earthly world in which we live. It therefore forms the "intermediate realm" which, in classical antiquity and in other highly developed cultures, is given central importance because it is the medium through which the divine powers operate on earth.[79] The imaginal world is also the abode of our "soul," the sphere of the "angels" as mediators, and the place where sacred events happen. In its own way it is as real as the world of sensory perception "below" and that of universal divinity "above."[80] At the same time the *mundus imaginalis* can be seen as the *mundus archetypalis*, that is to say the world of "souls,"[81] in which the archetypes as "imaginal" beings have their domain. These archetypes appear as images accessible by means of a particular method of perception that has been termed "active" or "true imagination,"[82] in order to distinguish it from pure fantasy. For Corbin this true imagination possesses a noetic value on account of the comprehensive (in the highest sense) insights that it yields. The content involved is of a spiritual nature, which in no way should be confused with the merely pictorial.[83]

In order to set this active imagination going we need "images." These can be mandalas, symbols, Tarot cards, and so on. They can also be mental images that are called forth within us through appropriate poetic or meditative texts. Only through this mediating function of the "active imagination," which is in fact a function of the "heart,"[84] is it possible for us to come into contact with the pure but essentially unknowable world of the supreme spirit, or indeed to have any true religious experience. Thus Corbin was convinced that "with the loss of the *imaginatio vera* and the *mundus imaginalis* came the beginning of nihilism and agnosticism."[85]

The *mundus imaginalis* is the world of symbols in the deepest sense, where "the spirits take on a body and the body takes on a spirit." Hence it is the connecting link between the realm of the here and now and the world of transcendence. In no way can it be compared with a world of allegories or arbitrary mathematical symbols. According to this view, it is only through this "true" imaginal world that we can find the "way back to God." Thus it is also a world of the "eternally present." Access to it, as we have said, is through the so-called *imaginatio vera*, the "true imagination," a spiritual faculty that is basically inherent, but must nevertheless be developed and cultivated.[86] This faculty is based on the old law of analogy, which says that only like can recognize like. This is most clearly expressed by Plotinus:[87]

> But if your eye is yet infected with any sordid concern, and not thoroughly refined, while it is on the stretch to behold this most shining spectacle, it will be immediately darkened and incapable of intuition, though some one should declare the spectacle present, which it might be otherwise able to discern. For, it is here necessary, that the perceiver and the thing perceived, should be similar to each other, before true vision can exist. Thus the sensitive eye can never be able to survey the orb of the sun, unless strongly endued with solar fire, and participating largely of the vivid ray. Every one, therefore, must become divine, and of godlike beauty, before he can gaze upon a god, and the beautiful itself.

For this type of "hermeneutics" Corbin uses the Arabic term *ta'wil*, meaning "to lead something back to its origin, to its authentic reality." *Ta'wil* is, freely translated, a symbolic form of understanding, the transformation of everything visible into symbols and the transformation of the intuitively perceived innermost essence of something into an image.[88] Or, in other words, *ta'wil* is concerned with the esoteric interpretation of sacred writings.

In Islam the imaginal world is the "eighth sphere," which lies beyond the seven spheres perceptible to the senses. When one treads this path of understanding from the outer to the inner, from the macrocosmos to the microcosmos, one ultimately learns that the microcosmos is a reflection of the macrocosmos and *vice versa*. Thus physical things are reflected images of the imaginal realm belonging to the universal soul, in which there is even an "imaginal geography," which is equally real, that is, common to all "souls," albeit pictorial.[89] In this way one moves from a quantitative to a qualitative perception. In fact, when we look at the world around us and simultaneously contemplate the "soul," we experience a hierophany, a manifestation of the "holy." However, these "images" or archetypes should in no way be confused with Plato's ideal forms, which are completely disconnected from anything material. The archetypal images, on the other hand, while distinct from matter itself, are not separate from all its material envelopments. Thus, although they are not perceptible to the senses, they can be perceived by the active imagination.[90]

Naturally Corbin's work also sometimes met with lack of understanding. Annemarie Schimmel, herself a highly renowned Islamicist and also an Eranos speaker, to whom we owe the only translation to date of a Corbin work into German,[91] repeats the following anecdote of Corbin's in her informative introduction to the book:

I remember an international colloquium held about twenty years ago, where a colleague from a distant country, hearing me speak about Shiism in the manner to which I am accustomed, whispered to his neighbour: how can someone talk in such language about a religion when it is not his own? Unfortunately there are certain people who can only think in terms of "conversion," for this enables them to pin a collective label to one's person. No. To speak of "conversion" means understanding nothing about what esotericism is ... The community, the *umma* of the esotericists of all places and times is that "Inner Church," which requires no act of joining to make one belong to it.

This accords well with the rallying call "heretics of all religions, unite," which Corbin is said to have let forth on the way to an Eranos meeting. The anecdote is related by his friend Denis de Rougemont, author of the brilliant study *L'amour en occident*, with whom the young Corbin had founded a journal, and who was later to receive a Bollingen scholarship.[92] The same remark is quoted by Steven Wasserstrom,[93] who has a rather critical attitude to Corbin, as well as by Corbin's friend Michael Waldberg.[94] Unfortunately, however, neither mentions that Corbin himself later had no recollection of the incident. Rather, he assumed that he must have said "esotericists" instead of "heretics," as Denis de Rougemont mentions in a postscript to his article. Corbin's work is, of course, not easily comprehensible—if only because of its uniqueness and the often opaque words that he coined—and his lectures were renowned for being difficult to understand.[95] John Barrett called them "pure Mozart." And even Annemarie Schimmel, a professor of Islamic studies at Islamic universities (as well as at Harvard and Bonn), said that she would not dare to translate all of Corbin's works, as not even she could be sure to have understood everything properly.[96]

Both Hossein Nasr and Charles J. Adams emphasize, in their essays on Corbin, that Eranos occupied an important place for him. In 1949 he attended Eranos for the first time; Olga Fröbe had been trying to invite him since 1946, but he had been unable to schedule a visit. In his previously mentioned "Post-Scriptum biographique à un Entretien philosophique"[97] Corbin himself describes this invitation as "a call" that was to have clearly discernible consequences "for the programme and rhythm of my researches." He also emphasizes the "decisive role" that Eranos played, in that it led to a "holistic spiritual freedom" from every form of "ecclesiastical or academic orthodoxy," which subsequently one would never lose. He also emphasized the inexplicable harmony that existed between the individual talks, although nothing had been agreed in advance apart from the common theme. Elsewhere[98] he calls this phenomenon a "homophonie" and describes how it completely surprised the speakers each time that it happened. In the same piece of writing he even expresses the conviction that Eranos contributed to the *traditio lampadis* (transmission of the spiritual light).

Fröbe recognized Henry Corbin as a special confidant. This is evident from a number of letters excerpted in Catherine Ritsema's Eranos manuscript. At the request of Catherine Ritsema, it was Corbin's wife, Stella, who passed on these numerous letters written by Fröbe to Corbin. In a letter dated 30 November 1951, only two years after their first acquaintance, she writes,

> We are both possessed by an archetypal idea [she by Eranos, he by Iran], and it seems to me that you have expressed your vision for the first time. And thus we are no longer alone. Speaking personally, I was cast into a terrible loneliness during my

work for Eranos. However, nobody realized that I had no other choice. Even Jung, who actually did know, often worked against Eranos. And that was hard. You are the first person to whom I have spoken about this matter.[99]

Or two years later: "It is good to know that you have such a deep understanding of Eranos in its mysterious aspects."[100]

Fröbe was totally enthused when Corbin authored the foreword to the third volume of translated Eranos essays edited by Joseph Campbell.[101] She wrote, "I am absolutely delighted about it. You have said things which nobody associated with Eranos realized, and I am very grateful for this profound article."[102] On 26 February 1957 she broached the subject again:

> There is nobody else who understands Eranos as fundamentally as you do. When I answer questions on the subject of Eranos, people always have the impression I am somewhat crazy. Even Jung, I believe … Precisely because it is so seldom that I meet someone who brings to bear such an understanding as you do, however fragmentary, I say to you: Thank you. Your foreword was such a great affirmation for me.[103]

The reason for her joy may well have been Corbin's statement that a historian with his critical methods alone would never be able to grasp the essence of Eranos, and without fail would completely misunderstand the "Eranos phenomenon," which did not concern schools, influences or themes, but rather the inner "meaning." As in the case of the other speakers—such as Jung, Kerényi, and, later on, Hillman—many of Corbin's most important essays were originally conceived as Eranos lectures. Eranos was also important to him on account of the friendships that he made or consolidated there, for example with Gershom Scholem and Ernst Benz, to name only two. In a letter of 5 April 1973 Scholem wrote to Corbin,

> We have known each other now for almost 25 years, and I am glad that it was granted to me to know, in you, one of the few scholars whose scholarship is of a truly spiritual level and is illuminated by deep penetration into the nature of things. You are, dear Corbin, one of the few scholars of religion of whom one can say that you know what you know. Furthermore you have always impressed me with your great humanity and nobility of character, and you and Stella Corbin are among the people with whom I have the certainty of experiencing a truly human relationship beyond any purely outward form of contact.[104]

And when Corbin died in 1978,[105] Scholem wrote the following in his letter of condolence to Corbin's widow Stella:

> We [Scholem and his wife Fania] can tell you that he was loved and honoured by us from the first time we met him nearly thirty years ago at the first Eranos meeting of 1949. For me he was not only a friend and comrade but a man who had devoted his life to understanding and researching a world that was as close as I could imagine to the one to which I have devoted my own life. We were, in the truest sense, honest, and possibly we were the first academics to excavate the world of the esoteric imagination, as manifested in Islamic and Jewish Gnosticism. Of all the Eranos speakers, it was he to whom I felt the closest kinship. He alone had that sort of inner empathy which enabled him to illuminate the dark and difficult paths of the

mystical world, and which I consider to be absolutely necessary if one is to carry out genuinely significant and at the same time academically sound work in these areas. His death meant for me the loss of a spiritual brother.[106]

Thus Scholem and Corbin appear to have been genuine soul-mates which is surprising in the light of Scholem's reluctance to esoteric thinking. Corbin, for his part, in a letter of thanks to Scholem, speaks with emotion about their "old friendship."[107] After mentioning Eranos, he then goes on, in the second part of the letter, to make the following surprising remark: "It is largely thanks to you that I have the feeling of our common base in the Abrahamic tradition as well as the conviction that the deep roots of this commonality lie in the esoteric sphere."

It seems appropriate to end this all too brief portrait of such an outstanding Eranos lecturer with a quotation from Gilbert Durand's article on Henry Corbin in the *Dictionnaire critique de l'ésoterisme*:

By virtue of his monumental opus (20 original works, 200 articles and introductions, many translations and the editorship of the 33 volumes of the Bibliothèque Iranienne) this famous Islamicist, together with the group of friends with whom he founded the University of Saint John of Jerusalem, acted as the "reawakener" of the western esoteric tradition in the light of the ever-present "oriental" esotericism, as preserved in the Islamic tradition … [Corbin] had come to the conclusion that Christianity and its Reformation, over the past two or three centuries, had lost the heritage of the Johannite tradition, which still appeared here and there in the works of mystical Protestants (Böhme, Oetinger), in Swedenborg and in the Romanticism of Schleiermacher and Schlegel. The Word lost in the occident had been preserved intact only among Islamic thinkers and above all among the Schiites.[108]

A more critical voice is that of Steven Wasserstrom, not that he throws doubt on Corbin's enormous achievements as a translator and commentator. However, he disputes, understandably from his viewpoint, that Corbin can be described as an Islamicist, since he is concerned only peripherally with the things that the great majority of Muslims consider central to their faith, namely the Koran, the Sharia, and the Prophet Mohammed. What was important for Corbin was rather his Gnostic belief, which he found reflected in the Shiite and Sufi writings. Hence Wasserstrom calls Corbin a "prophetic philosopher"[109] and moreover a dangerous one, since he uses his academic platform to recruit students for his form of esotericism, leaving out in the cold the "true" religious scholarship, based on historical facts and a rational approach.[110] Furthermore, Wasserstrom is alarmed when he sees in Corbin's teaching a further example of a spiritual version of an "all-too- familiar assault on democracy and science." According to Wasserstrom esotericism as a teaching for an exclusive elite is based on secret knowledge and leadership by a master. Elsewhere Wasserstrom says about Corbin: "It is my conviction that he may have been the most sophisticated and learned esotericist of the century."[111] Wasserstrom's view of Corbin is vehemently challenged by Pierre Lory, professor of Islamic studies at the Ecole Pratique des Hautes Etudes of the Sorbonne in Paris.[112] Lory accuses Wasserstrom of often confusing Corbin's own ideas with those of the Muslim authors whom he writes about and characterizes Wasserstrom's interpretation of Corbin as "superficial, full of prejudices and above all badly documented." He calls Wasserstrom's book a pamphlet which partly resembles a novel of the political fiction genre. Lory, who himself had attended many of Corbin's lectures, emphasizes that Corbin always refused to be categorized as an Islamicist, but rather had always seen himself as a philosopher with a particular interest in Islamic authors. This would invalidate Wasserstrom's charge that Corbin had led Islamic studies into false directions. As for Wasserstrom's accusation that Corbin was a prophet and apostle of his own esoteric teaching and no scholar, Lory says that this would have been laughable to anyone who had heard Corbin lecture. His lectures were always strictly academic, the audience was always small, and the French Islamicists had deliberately ignored him.[113] Corbin had most definitely never seen himself as a "guru," being of the conviction that every man and woman must pursue his or her own search for the "truth."

The conference of 1949, at which the well-known Austrian esoteric novelist Hans Sterneder was also present as a member of the audience, has been described in a detailed report by the analytical psychologist Violet de Laszlo. Particularly interesting is what she writes about the astonishingly contrasting lecturing styles of Kerényi and E.O. James, who spoke at that meeting on "Myth and Ritual," as her remarks clearly reflect the prevailing atmosphere of Eranos. Kerényi, who belonged to the preferred speakers, "seemed to penetrate his material in a manner analogous to the adept-hunter entering into the very skin of the animal quarry, expressing it through an intuitive-feeling process." James, however, "approached his material in the manner of an observer remaining wholly outside the observed phenomena, defining myth and ritual in the traditional positivist way as symbolic tale."[114] James, by the way, spoke only once at Eranos.

✿ 12. The Early 1950s

Mircea Eliade and Raffaele Pettazzoni: Fresh Influences and Old Shadows

The subsequent year, 1950, saw the seventy-fifth birthday of C.G. Jung, and for this reason the eighteenth Eranos volume is dedicated to him. It was edited by Olga Fröbe herself. The next volume, number 19, then reverted to the usual collection of Ascona papers. In the foreword, written as always by Fröbe, she gives a résumé of the previous meetings. Here she characterizes Eranos as a "game" in the sense that the word is used by Johan Huizinga, Hermann Hesse, and Hugo Rahner.[1] "The game," she says, "is, as it were, the natural counterweight to the purely intellectual … The Eranos circle derives its integral character from the centre and the central idea … The idea is both master and ruler of the game." Hence the idea demands flexibility and selflessness on the part of the speakers. In an earlier passage she explains that the lectures invariably revolved around "a single, if complex, idea, namely the idea of the Inner Man." Or, to quote another source, "the dancers move on, but the dance remains."[2]

In 1950 Mircea Eliade participated for the first time and was very taken by Eranos, even though he spoke of the atmosphere being "semimundane, semitheosophical."[3] He had already studied the Eranos volumes in Romania and felt flattered to have been invited to speak at Ascona. Not long before this he had become convinced that myths, symbols, and god forms represented fundamental and existential human situations and were not merely products of fantasy.[4] Here the cool "objectivity" of the natural scientist was not the right approach for understanding these spiritual realities. Rather, one needed the "intelligent sympathy of the hermeneutist."[5] Again and again in his diaries and in his autobiography he stresses how important the conversations with Corbin, Scholem, Jung, Benz, and Kerényi in Ascona had been for him.

And yet he felt a certain loneliness—first because the conversations at the Round Table were often in German and he was not able to understand everything, and second because all other colleagues were financially secure, with university positions or supported by stipends, and could therefore live "free from worries, free from fear." When, he asked himself, would he finally be able to enjoy a similar position—he who, in terms of scholarship, was "at least a generation ahead" of most of his colleagues? Thus he expressed his discontent in his diary entry for 22 August 1950 (unpublished extract from the English translation by Mac Linscott Ricketts, also unpublished).

Furthermore, his relationship to the other participants was not as smooth as it might have seemed. We have already spoken about Kerényi. In the case of Scholem, Eliade also felt the need to be cautious or even evasive after serious rumors began to be voiced concerning his earlier sympathy for the anti-Semitic Iron Guard. I will go into this in greater detail later on.

Even the relationship with Jung was not all joy and harmony. On the one hand, there are letters like one (preserved in the Jung archive) that Eliade wrote to Jung on 4 September 1950, addressing him as "Cher maître" (although this was a form of address that he also used with others such as Raffaele Pettazzoni). After thanking Jung for their conversations in Ascona, he went on to say that the meeting was one that "counted among the most decisive intellectual encounters of my life."[6] And, in a letter to Jung of 22 January 1955, he called Jung's work "the greatest discovery of my spiritual maturity."[7] On the other hand the two men had very different views on such central and fundamental themes as the archetypes, the sacred and the symbolic.[8] Natale Spineto, in his very instructive biography of Eliade, *Mircea Eliade, storico delle religioni*, even speaks of a "fundamental incapacity to find common ground for a dialogue."[9] On one occasion Eliade felt compelled to beat a hasty retreat and retract a statement on the unconscious, as Jung was so incensed.[10] In the unpublished part of his diary, under the date 21 August 1951, he remarks that Jung's "spiritual universe suffocates me sometimes" and further "Jung's archetypes horrify me" because he, Eliade, needed the transcendental dimension. However, despite their differences of opinion, there is no doubt that Eliade valued the psychologist's wisdom and learned much from him.[11]

On the other hand, Harry Oldmeadow stresses that, as well as the undeniable differences (e.g. Jung focused primarily on Europe, whereas Eliade had a world-wide perspective) there were distinct parallels between them. Most notably they shared "a unified view of reality in which physical and psychical energy are two aspects, or dimensions, of a single reality (hence the possibility of para-normal powers and the like)." This, according to Oldmeadow, meant that both of them could more willingly accept the spiritual messages that they found in the documents that they studied. A further parallel that Oldmeadow identifies is that both men experienced hostility from certain circles (Jung from the Freudians and Eliade from the anthropologists).[12]

Eliade was a *confidant* of Fröbe, to whom she spoke in a very open way.[13] Thus Eliade reports that she regaled him with stories about the English Theosophist G.R.S. Mead, the occultist A.E. Waite,[14] and the university teachers Eisler, Hauer, and Zimmer.[15] She also told him that she had invited the Russian philosopher of religion N. Berdyayev to Ascona, but that he had been unable to come, as he had found no one to look after his dog. Eliade also became somewhat worked up at the quantity of "mediocre books," including the occult novels of Talbot Mundy, that Fröbe left on his table for him to read, which he sometimes did and enjoyed.[16] During the meetings Eliade and his second wife, Christine, were allowed to stay in the room in her house that had been used by Alice Bailey in the early 1930s. On one occasion Alice Bailey had performed a ritual there to exorcise definitively the astral form of a Tibetan monk who had regularly been visiting the room at night.

Up to 1963 Eliade spoke almost every year at Eranos and thus counted among the apparently most faithful of the participants. However, after his last lecture on 3 September 1963 he noted in his diary, "I gave my Eranos lecture. No better and no worse than usual. The feeling that I was speaking, if not for the last time, at least for the last time in this series … I think I can take a rest now for a couple of years … Never will I forget what I owe to Eranos and Olga Fröbe. But I feel that, for the time being, I must detach myself from the past."[17]

After the death of Fröbe, to whom he had felt an obligation, he was less and less inclined to come to Eranos, although he still liked to visit Europe in the summer, especially as his growing fame now gave him ample opportunity to exert his influence culturally on a world-wide scale. In any case, his enthusiasm for Eranos had already begun to wane some years earlier. Thus, in an unpublished part of his diary, under the date 13 August 1959, he wrote, "I dream of a summer vacation without this Eranos, which is beginning to feel like a dead weight on my shoulders." On 25 August of the same year he confessed to a feeling (in fact wishful thinking) that this would be the last year in which he would participate in an Eranos conference. However, the next year he went again and expressed his dissatisfaction even more strongly in a diary entry of 15 August 1960, saying that "this year's Eranos seems to me to be quite unnecessary. It no longer interests me; I'm forcing myself to work, but I won't produce anything interesting."

Nevertheless, Eliade's lectures at Ascona were always very successful, even though they were usually prepared hastily and at the last minute out of his own writings. The audience, however, did not seem to notice this.[18] In 1962 he prepared nothing in advance. Instead he recounted an old dream and for the rest of the time read excerpts from one of his essays for the *Revue de l'Histoire des Religions*.[19]

Looking at Eliade's general attitude towards Eranos, one has the impression that he was little captivated by the "magic" of the conferences. He did too little advance preparation, was often unwilling to take part at all, and, at least in the early years, did not really feel at ease there. All that he could really appreciate were the contacts which he made there and which proved immensely useful to him. Can we therefore say that he did as much for Eranos and exerted as great an influence there as some people believe? Probably not. Rather, I would argue that it was his writings outside the context of Eranos, and not his lectures there, that accounted for his special nimbus and his influence at Eranos.

As Eliade's life and achievements have been well publicized,[20] I shall not dwell at too much length on his biographical details, except for the particular phase of his youth in Romania, which had political implications. He was born in Bucharest in 1907 and already at the age of fourteen began publishing articles ranging in subject matter from entomology to alchemy.[21] Early in his life he began having mystical experiences.[22] Soon after beginning his studies in the Faculty of Philosophy at the University of Bucharest, he founded the *Revista Universitara* and came increasingly under the influence of Nae Ionescu, the so-called master of Romania's "young generation," of whom we shall have more to say later in view of his importance.[23]

There followed sojourns in Italy, where he came into contact with famous names such as the writer Giovanni Papini, the philosopher Giovanni Gentile, the modernist theologian Ernesto Buonaiuti, and the historian of religion Raffaele Pettazzoni, one of his mentors in the field of religious studies. On his visit to Italy he collected above all material for his dissertation on Renaissance philosophy, for which he was awarded a doctorate summa cum laude.[24] What is striking is the attention that Eliade gave to the hermetic and occult aspects of the Renaissance. He was equally fascinated by the incipient interest in the Orient that was present in the Renaissance, and in Italy he was already searching for material on India and especially on Tantrism. However, he was not able to meet the orientalist Giuseppe Tucci, who was in Bengal at the time.[25] Thanks to a grant from an Indian maharaja, Eliade was then able to spend four years in India intensively studying yoga.

After returning to his homeland Eliade became assistant to Nae Ionescu at the University of Bucharest. Ionescu, although a devout Orthodox Christian, gave Eliade his first opportunity to teach comparative religion. Furthermore, he sacrificed part of his professor's salary to provide Eliade with a modest income, which further increased

Eliade's admiration for Ionescu.[26] This influence was not, however, confined to Eliade but extended over the entire young intelligentsia of Romania,[27] including subsequently well-known names such as the philosopher and aphoristic writer Emil Cioran and Eliade's Jewish friend Mihail Sebastian, of whom more will be said later.[28] In 1970, thirty years after Ionescu's death, Eliade wrote a late and probably carefully worded essay in honor of Ionescu's memory, in which he remarked, "How can one explain the admiration, devotion and love that his students showed towards him from 1925 until his death?"[29]

As Ionescu's assistant, Eliade had produced in 1937 a volume of his mentor's collected essays,[30] containing an afterword in which Eliade wrote: "Wherever Nae is spoken about one senses the presence of a legend or of hate; both testify equally to the extraordinary power of this man, who has for fifteen years been changing and rebuilding a whole country. There are few people who are honoured by so much hate."[31] Mihail Sebastian wrote with equal enthusiasm:

> Nae Ionescu was the leader of our consciousness … His writings made clear to us certain essential things that without him would have remained confused. His presence helped us to keep our inner control. It provided a standard that we would otherwise have lacked. He was a man who spoke in simple words about love, life and death as one speaks about decisive things and not about opinions.[32]

On the other hand Ionescu was also described as a "good second-rate actor," a political opportunist and an "agile Balkan sophist."[33]

Eliade's lifelong devotion to this man later caused him considerable difficulties, for Ionescu was not without reason considered to be an important precursor of the Romanian version of fascism.[34]

Ionescu had taken his doctorate in Munich in 1919 and spent altogether six years in Germany before being called to an academic position in Bucharest. He was strongly influenced by German philosophy, especially by Edmund Husserl and Friedrich Nietzsche; and through Ionescu Eliade was also exposed to the influence of German intellectual life.[35] Thus Eliade's acquaintance with the work of Rudolf Otto as well as with that of Edmund Husserl can be traced back to Nae Ionescu. There is even a correspondence between Eliade and Otto that has been preserved.

However, what created even greater difficulties for Eliade were his close contacts—by now proven beyond doubt—with the so-called Iron Guard (the Legion of the Archangel Michael),[36] led by the charismatic figure of Corneliu Z. Codreanu, an organization of strongly nationalistic and anti-Semitic character.[37] The charge most often leveled against Eliade is that he never explicitly distanced himself from this group.[38]

Furthermore, in his Romanian years Eliade not only sympathized with the Iron Guard but was also active in campaigning and carrying out propaganda for the ideas of Codreanu. The Iron Guard is widely known not only as an anti-Semitic but also as a terrorist organization.[39] Already in 1924 (i.e. before the founding of the Iron Guard) Codreanu assassinated the police prefect of Iași. The latter had previously ordered Codreanu's arrest (unjustly, as Codreanu maintained) and, when a re-arrest seemed likely, Codreanu shot the prefect with his own hand. Similarly, two prime ministers and several former ministers were killed by the Iron Guard. Furthermore, there were numerous well-attested acts of vandalism and plundering of Jewish businesses. One must, however, add that the greatest excesses of the Iron Guard, including terrible anti-Jewish pogroms, were committed after the period of Eliade's involvement and following the murder of Codreanu in 1938 on the order of King Carol II. The most horrifying was the three-day uprising in Bucharest in January 1941, when Eliade was already in England. Hundreds of Jews were killed and many hung up on meat hooks. Influential Jews were accused of being behind governmental repression of the legion. But also within the Iron Guard itself deserters or traitors were dealt with unmercifully.

At the same time, one should also remember that, apart from the anti-Semitic component, there were other sides to the Iron Guard movement, such as an ascetic, Christian mystical tendency, an interest in Romanian folklore,[40] and a preoccupation with the already mentioned quest for the "New Man." The amount of written material on this subject has grown enormously during the past few years, and here we can look at only part of this literature more closely. The sheer volume of this material indicates not only the importance of Eliade but also the intense controversy concerning the connections between religion and myth on the one hand and politics on the other: an issue that goes far beyond Eliade. Besides the scholarly literature (which can unfortunately also be marked by one-sidedness when such polarizing themes are concerned), there is also a large amount of partisan writing, stemming from the followers of the Iron Guard and available in several languages, making the written works of Codreanu and those of his most important followers widely accessible.

Corneliu Zelea Codreanu possessed enormous charisma, like Nae Ionescu but probably to an even greater degree than the latter.[41] There can be no doubt of this charisma, for Codreanu could even cast a spell over a man like N.M. Nagy-Talavera, who himself had suffered under the anti-Jewish pogroms of the Iron Guard, survived both Auschwitz and a Siberian labor camp, and finally emigrated to the United States, where he became professor of history at California State University, Chico.[42] In his book *The Green Shirts and Others*, he recalls a meeting with Codreanu when he, Nagy-Talavera, was eight years old:

> There was suddenly a hush in the crowd. A tall, darkly handsome man dressed in the white costume of a Romanian peasant rode into the yard on a white horse. He halted close to me, and I could see nothing monstrous or evil in him. On the contrary. His childlike, sincere smile radiated over the miserable crowd, and he seemed to be with it yet mysteriously apart from it. Charisma is an inadequate word to define the strange force that emanated from this man. He was more aptly simply part of the forests, of the mountains, of the storms on the snow-covered peaks of the Carpathians, and of the lakes and rivers. And so he stood amid the crowd, silently. He had no need to speak. His silence was eloquent; it seemed to be stronger than we, stronger than the order of the prefect who denied him speech. An old, white-haired peasant woman made the sign of the cross on her breast and whispered to us, "The emissary of the Archangel Michael!" Then the sad little church bell began to toll, and the service which invariably preceded Legionary meetings began. Deep impressions created in the soul of a child die hard. In more than a half of a century I have never forgotten my meeting with Cornelius Zelea Codreanu.[43]

A similar reaction was recorded by the prominent Jewish writer and essayist Felix Aderca, friend of the already mentioned Mihail Sebastian. The latter records how Aderca "told me that he regretted the death of Codreanu, who had been a great man, a genius, a moral force of nature, whose 'saint's death' had represented an irreparable loss."[44]

In this connection I would also like to mention a report of a memorable meeting between Corneliu Codreanu and Rabbi David Safran that allegedly took place in January 1937 in the Casa Verde, headquarters of the Iron Guard in Bucharest. This report is mentioned in an article published in the *Gazeta de Vest* in January 1991, written by a student from Timisoara who sympathized with the Iron Guard.[45] The article claims that this meeting is described in a book by the rabbi entitled *Karl Marx, Antisemite*. Some years later Michael Shafir, writing in *Radio Free Europe/Radio Liberty East European Perspectives* of 18 December 2002, said that the report was a forgery, since Rabbi David Safran had written a quite different account of Codreanu in his memoirs.

As a counter-reaction, the Romanian newspaper *Romania Libera* of 6 May 2005 published a Romanian translation of the relevant chapter from the book, which had appeared in Jerusalem in 1979. A picture of the book cover was included as proof. Evidently Michael Shafir had been talking about a different Rabbi David Safran and a different book from *Karl Marx, Antisemite*. As I do not have access to *Romania Libera* nor to Rabbi Safran's book, but have taken my information from the Internet, I must leave open the question of the veracity of the story.[46] Nevertheless, on account of the unusual content I would like to quote Rabbi Safran's alleged account of his meeting with Codreanu from the version published in *Romania Libera*:

> We had been speaking for two hours. But it had not been the usual official type of discussion; the pains and sufferings of the world were present … His truths and mine blazed up, tormenting brain and soul, as we desperately looked for answers and arguments, finally parting as friends. I can still see him standing up, his hand outstretched as he said to me, "This conversation has given me great joy. I do not know whether we have solved our problems, but we have certainly touched on some fragments of the great mystery of creation. I am not here to preach hatred and revenge. My soul is pure. I cannot say, however, if all legionnaires think this way. When a Jew is attacked or morally injured I ask you to forgive the guilty ones. They are only human beings and perhaps even good Christians. It is not the superior human beings that we try to educate, but rather the simple ones.

On the other hand, Codreanu explicitly talks of the "dirtiest tyranny, namely the talmudic, Jewish tyranny" and the "criminal Jewish hand of Moscow."[47] The starting point of Codreanu's anti-Judaism was his conviction that Bolshevism and Judaism were identical. He has been quoted as saying: "When I say Communist, I mean Jew."[48] Furthermore, he published a sort of catechism containing a collection of anti-Semitic quotations from Romanian nationalist intellectuals and politicians. The Eliade specialist Mihaela Gligor of the Romanian Academy in Cluj-Napoca believes that Codreanu perceived the Jews as mere "exploiters," who produced nothing.[49] Their primary victims, as he and the Iron Guard saw it, were the farmers, whose products were bought by the Jews for a pittance and then sold for exorbitant prices. Moreover, they had allegedly strewn the villages with taverns, turning the Romanians into drunkards. Michaela Gligor mentions a catalogue of other accusations by the Iron Guard that all belong to the familiar anti-Semitic repertoire, whether in France, Germany, or Russia. Jews' alleged misdeeds included taking control of the universities, banks, and large enterprises and gaining a monopoly of the press, leading to a corruption of the political class.[50] Evidently Codreanu and the entire Iron Guard felt their country, its agrarian culture, and its Christian belief to be profoundly threatened by the Jewish presence and were therefore intent on pushing it back or even eliminating it.

Alternatively, Gligor emphasizes that the Iron Guard, as a "Romanian form of Fascism," was a highly religious organization, which nearly always introduced religious themes into its propaganda. Communal praying, hymn-singing, and processions, often accompanied by spontaneous "miracles": these were things that appealed to the rural population and were supported by most of the clergy. But the Iron Guard also attracted many "idealistic urban intellectuals," who were disenchanted by the weak and scandal-ridden government. As Gligor writes, "many of the most highly educated of the 'younger generation,' who believed in the 'primacy of the spiritual' became followers."

As already mentioned, it is necessary to take into account not only the nationalistic and decidedly anti-Semitic aspects of the Iron Guard, but also the side that was marked by asceticism, Christian mysticism, and Romanian folklore—after all, the Guard had taken the Archangel Michael as its symbol. In Eliade's case there is much evidence that this spiritual aspect was foremost, as indicated by a newspaper article that he wrote at that time:

> The significance of the revolution for which Corneliu Codreanu is fighting is so deeply mystical that its success would mean a further victory for the Christian spirit in Europe, that great Europe in which Christ has not always been victorious although millions of people have believed in him … What is important is not the seizure of power at any price but rather, indeed above all, a new human being, one for whom the spiritual life really *exists*.[51]

And in another article[52] signed by Eliade[53] he shows himself equally clearly to be convinced by Codreanu's Christian belief: "I believe in this victory because I believe above all in the victory of the Christian spirit. A movement that arises from and is nourished by the Christian spirit is a spiritual revolution which above all fights against sinfulness and unworthiness—such a movement is no political movement. It is a Christian revolution."

The historian N.M. Nagy-Talavera explains this as follows:

> The Legionaries were always aware of their great differences with the Nazis and Fascists on that account. One of their leading intellectuals, Mihai Polihroniade, explained, "Fascism worships the state, Nazism the race and the nation. Our movement strives not merely to fulfill the destiny of the Romanian people—we want to fulfill it along the road of salvation." Another Legionary intellectual, Gârcineanu, called the Legion "the only political movement with a religious structure." Even "the ultimate goal of the nation [must be] Resurrection in Christ." The Legionaries perceived the whole history of mankind, and particularly that of Romania, as an uninterrupted Passion, a mystical Easter story, in which every step, every motivation, consequently every goal, was a struggle between light and darkness. The road of the Legion must be a road of suffering, sacrifice, crucifixion, and resurrection. Moța declared: "As God resurrected Christ in order to help the good to victory, so will the Legion triumph, too—even if only by miracle."[54]

Besides the Christian-mystical element, what was important for Eliade was the striving to make Romania into a spiritual superpower. Thus Marta Petreu writes that initially the obsession of the younger generation was to pull Romanian culture out of its provincialism and raise it up to something of universal validity.[55] They worked, she says, as though possessed and their creative activity proceeded in a frantic rhythm. "It was not by coincidence that its (contested) leader, Mircea Eliade, required in 1928 that the young Romanian intellectuals live and create as if the present year were the last year of their lives." At the same time, Petreu maintains that the intellectuals had a purely cultural and not a political goal. As proof of this she mentions the autumn of 1932, when these strivings gave rise to the so-called Criterion Group, where discussions were held about such diverse figures as Lenin, Mussolini, Greta Garbo, André Gide, Charlie Chaplin, Gandhi, and Bergson, and where representatives of both the extreme right and the left were present. Hannelore Müller likewise confirms that Eliade's published work from 1927 was primarily focused on the striving "to build up Romanian culture" and that his studies in the field of religion only came to the fore after 1936–37.[56]

The conservative Berlin publicist Wolfgang Saur also detects in Eliade the strong influence of the Indian struggle for independence, which the latter had experienced close at hand in his earlier years. In Saur's view this influence then colored his political engagement in Romania. Saur believes Eliade had been surprised to discover that politics and spirituality have identical roots. "They share the principle of liberation and the message that salvation is not given away but has to be fought for."[57]

These three elements taken together—the nationalist, the Christian-mystical, and the cultural-activist—were probably what prompted Eliade to give his active support to the Iron Guard. Presumably he believed that only by joining forces with this radical organization would he have a chance of realizing his ideals.

Eliade's Early Political Views

Now we should turn to the question of whether Eliade personally incurred any guilt on account of his association with the Iron Guard and to what extent he himself was tainted with the anti-Semitism of the Guard. Here opinions are widely divided, as might be expected. Leon Volovici detects no anti-Semitism in Eliade before 1930, but finds that after that Eliade changed rapidly: "At the time of his enthusiastic adoption of the ideology and mystical spirit of the Iron Guard ... Anti-Semitism became ideologically (and patriotically) justified."[58]

A similar view is taken by Emanuela Costantini: "His full involvement in the Iron Guard brought with it the adoption of thoroughly antisemitic positions."[59] She also writes: "The article in which [Eliade's] antisemitic convictions appear in an unquestionable way was published in the autumn of 1937" and she quotes the following passage as proof: "It would be absurd to suppose that the Jews would be content to remain a minority with certain rights and many responsibilities after they have tasted the nectar of power and have attained so many positions of power. The Jews struggle for their positions of power in anticipation of a future attack."[60]

A rather more differentiated view is taken by Hannelore Müller, who sees Eliade more as a religious philosopher than as a scholar of religion. In her dissertation on Eliade,[61] Müller, in exemplary fashion, brings together and comments on a very comprehensive range of basic material[62] on Eliade's early years.[63] Müller grew up in Romania and then studied Protestant theology and comparative religion in Germany. Given her origin, linguistic competence, academic background, and knowledge of the country concerned, she is particularly well qualified to write about Eliade. Concerning the just mentioned essay ("Blind Pilots"), which she reproduces in full translation in her book,[64] she writes:

> This newspaper article, one of the sharpest and most polemical written by Mircea Eliade, is quoted in the secondary literature as the ultimate proof of Eliade's anti-Judaism. However, what is usually overlooked is that Eliade attacks not only the

Jewish population but also the Hungarian and Slavic minorities in Romania. The central theme of the article are the members of the Romanian government, whom Eliade calls "blind pilots," as their domestic and foreign policy had brought the Romanian people to national and economic ruin.

Müller therefore speaks of Eliade's "decidedly chauvinistic characteristics" but not of any pure anti-Semitism. As early as 1933, he also took an opposing attitude towards the Siebenbürger Saxons, an ethnic German community in Romania.[65]

It is also interesting to hear the voice of Bryan Rennie,[66] whose book *Reconstructing Eliade: Making Sense of Religion*[67] is perhaps one of the most effective empathetic stud-ies on the theoretical underpinnings of Eliade's ideas on religion. Rennie also includes, in his collection *Mircea Eliade: A Critical Reader*,[68] a full translation of the article in question, along with a further and similarly incriminating article.[69] Rennie's comment on these texts is the reverse of the usual view: "That these were the most extreme expres-sions that have ever been ascribed to his hand appears itself to be evidence of his *lack* of antisemitism." Rennie adds that, as head of press relations and propaganda in London and Lisbon, Eliade had ample opportunity to write much worse things.

Rennie sums up as follows: "Eliade's own writings express no clear anti-Semitism. Only three of his 'Legionary' articles mention Jews, and it is clear that his rhetoric proceeded from a sentiment of general xenophobia commonly associated with nationalism."[70] Rennie also mentions that Eliade publicly intervened on behalf of certain individual Jews, as he feared that their expulsion could weaken the cultural potential of his country. It is also unclear, according to Rennie, whether Eliade actually joined the Iron Guard as a full member, as up to now no definite proof on this point has been found.[71] On the other hand it cannot be denied that he publicly and in writing supported a clearly anti-Semitic movement, whose leader affirmed a belief in theories of a Jewish conspiracy.

The first concrete accusations of a political nature against Eliade to come to the atten-tion of a broader public[72] appeared in 1972 in *Toladot*, a Romanian-language periodical published in Israel.[73] In the aftermath there were accusations against Gershom Scholem because he had participated in a *Festschrift* in honor of Eliade. However, Scholem had apparently known nothing of the past history of his Eranos colleague. Finally, on 6 June 1972, Scholem wrote an enquiring letter, in which his tone remained extremely friendly: "In all the long years that I have known you I have had no reason whatever to believe you to be an antisemite or even a fomenter of antisemitism. I regard you as an honest and upright man, whom I hold in great respect."[74] In his reply of 10 March 1973 Eliade emphasized that he had never been an anti-Semite and during the war had even been harassed by the Romanian secret police.[75] On 29 March Scholem wrote back, keeping his fair and friendly tone but asking for a more precise explanation in view of a forthcoming visit by Eliade to Jerusalem, which apparently never in fact took place.[76] Eliade appears simply to have avoided him.

What proved particularly damaging to Eliade were the articles and conference state-ments of Adriana Berger. She had worked as a research consultant for Eliade during his lifetime and thereby had gained access to and analyzed many unknown and compromis-ing documents.[77] Bryan Rennie, however, relativizes Berger's statements by off-setting them with other and more recent documents.[78]

Among Eliade's well-known accusers is Alexandra Laignel-Lavastine, even though she herself says that she wishes to avoid "the logic of a trial and a historical tribunal" and claims that she would reject such an approach. "Our intention," she says "to clarify it once again, is not that of the Inquisition."[79] At the same time, she maintains without differentiating that in the 1930s Eliade constantly evinced xenophobia and anti-Semitism.[80] She sets particular store by her researches in hitherto unknown archives, citing documents from the English Secret Service milieu, in which Eliade is described as "the biggest Nazi in the [Romanian] legation."[81] She links him with known Nazis and Fascists and shows herself to be convinced that Eliade was thoroughly steeped in pro-Fascist and anti-Semitic attitudes. So she sees the Iron Guard episode as no coincidence and certainly no mere youthful folly.

Mac Linscott Ricketts, a student of Eliade, has analyzed this book in minute detail over one hundred and forty pages and concluded that the book resembles a "Stalinist show trial."[82] The quotations, instead of being drawn from unknown archives as claimed, are in fact often taken from other books without acknowledgement of the source. The book, Ricketts says, is not a work of scientific precision but is swarming with errors such as incorrect page numbers, wrong historical dates, and confusion of names. The work is also dishonest, as the author shortens quotations and removes them from their context.[83] He also mentions other reviewers such as Edgar Reichmann of *Le Monde* who, although not renowned as a friend of Eliade, confirms Ricketts' sharp criticisms. Reichmann speaks of a "tangle of contradictions" resting on "a false *a priori* assumption."[84]

Another person who must be counted among Eliade's fiercest opponents is Daniel Dubuisson, who sees in Eliade a "militant Fascist" and confirmed anti-Semite, whose pernicious views also pervade his work in the field of religious studies.[85] Consequently, he says, one should reject this work wholesale. In a book with the decidedly polemical title *Impostures et pseudo-science: L'Oeuvre de Mircea Eliade*, he lists multiple incidents where Eliade has allegedly distorted the facts in order to exculpate himself.[86] These facts, Dubuisson writes, "show above all that Eliade never hesitated to lie in order to cast a veil over his opinions and his past guilt."

Rennie, on the other hand, criticizes Dubuisson for making accusations that are not supported by proof.[87] He also finds fault with the "disturbingly unscholarly style"[88] and accuses Dubuisson of applying a "totalitarian methodology"[89] because of the way in which he simply assumes an anti-Semitic attitude on Eliade's part and concludes that his non-political writings must also be infected, without providing any real proof of this.

A particularly negative attitude towards Eliade is evinced by the celebrated playwright Eugène Ionesco, a friend from the days of their youth. In a letter of 19 September 1945 to Tudor Vianu, Ionesco wrote:

> In the next few days Eliade will arrive, perhaps he is already here. For him everything is lost, as "Communism has won."[90] He is one of the biggest culprits. Yet even he and Cioran … are victims of the late and hateful Nae Ionescu. If it had not been for him we would now have a worthy generation of leaders between 35 and 40 years of age. Because of him all of them have become Fascists. He created a stupid, alarming and reactionary Romania. The other guilty one is Eliade … Eliade too influenced a group of fellow members of his generation as well as the whole intellectual posterity.[91]

Ionesco, as a left-oriented intellectual, appears to have remained uninfluenced by the propaganda of the Iron Guard, leaving aside a few unclear patches in his biography.

Steven Wasserstrom has produced further compromising material in the form of a series of passages from Eliade's writings on religion, which indeed indicate at least a strongly critical attitude towards the Jewish religion.[92] Here Wasserstrom has an ally (albeit from a rather different camp) in Claudio Mutti, who states clearly that "apart from the significance that antisemitism had for the Iron Guard, we find nothing positive in Eliade's attitude towards Judaism."[93] This, he maintains, is also true, incidentally, of other "Eliadian" scholars such as Culianu. Mutti is a professing Muslim and no judaeophile, but as a multilingual researcher with a mastery of Romanian he had already indicated Eliade's closeness to the Iron Guard while Culianu was apparently still upholding the "innocence" of his old mentor. The question now arises whether Eliade's criticisms were directed specifically at Judaism or at monotheism as a whole.

Here I would like to mention a book that sets itself the admirable task of letting the voices on both sides of the debate speak for themselves, so that readers can form their own judgment.[94] As it is not possible to discuss every contribution, I would like to mention just one essay that goes far beyond the alleged "fascism" of Eliade and deals with a wider problem, namely the unwarranted tendency to equate fascism with the irrational and hence frequently with esotericism, mysticism, and even religious experience.[95] The author, Elaine Fischer, emphasizes the danger of what she calls the *argumentum ad nazium* or *reductio ad Hitlerum*, following Leo Strauss. She warns us to avoid the kind of false conclusion that she illustrates with the following example: Hitler liked painting watercolors, therefore the painting of watercolors must be fascist.[96]

Rather than continuing to quote a series of accusations and counter-accusations, it seems to me more profitable to consider the recollections and appraisals of his friend Mihail Sebastian, which are contemporaneous with Eliade's involvement with the Iron Guard and therefore not influenced by the knowledge of a later generation and by the better informed political hindsight of today, based on what has since come to light.[97]

It has to be said that a reading of Sebastian's diaries leaves one profoundly shaken. In their oppressively honest way they show not only the mortal dangers facing a Jewish writer in ever more perilous times, but also the self-doubt, the constant humiliations, and the sense of appalled astonishment that a deeply humane thinker feels when suddenly abandoned by his former friends, colleagues, and idols.[98]

On 18 March 1941 Sebastian writes, "I was sad the whole day long. My heart is heavy, not just because I have to pay an unaffordable rent or to give up my one-room apartment … my heart is heavy because of this ridiculous, gratuitous cruelty, whose sole purpose is to do harm to us [the Jews] and to mock us. This pure desire to be evil and spiteful."[99]

Sebastian's clearest verdict on Eliade seems to me to be the entry for 2 March 1937,[100] which I would like to quote at greater length, especially because Sebastian emphasizes that he is only reproducing Eliade's words:

Long political discussion with Mircea at his home. Impossible to summarize everything. He was lyrical, nebulous, full of exclamations, interjections, rhetorical turns of phrase … Out of all this I shall record only his final profession of loyalty, stating that he loves the "Iron Guard," places his hope in them and looks forward to their victory.

When asked why Gogu Rădulescu, a Communist sympathizer, had been beaten with wet ropes in the headquarters of the Guard, Eliade replied: traitors deserved nothing else. He, Mircea Eliade, would not have stopped there but would have gouged Mr. Gogu's eyes out. All those who were not Guardists and all who represented a policy other than that of the Guardists were traitors to the people and deserved the same fate.

I shall also not forget the explanation he gave for his passionate devotion to the "Iron Guard": "I have always believed in the primacy of the spirit." He is neither a liar nor a madman. He is simply just naïve. But naivety can take on catastrophic forms.

It is also appropriate to quote here the judgment of one person who is certainly unusually well informed on this subject, Andrei Oişteanu of the Center for Jewish Studies at the University of Bucharest, president of the Romanian Association for the History of Religions (RAHR), and an expert on the Romanian holocaust. In his article "Mircea Eliade between Political Journalism and Scholarly Work" he argues unambiguously for a distinction to be made between Eliade's journalistic writing for the Iron Guard and his work in the area of literature and religious studies:

> My conclusions, inevitably partial and therefore risky, differ to a large extent from those of Daniel Dubuisson, in whose footsteps walked Alexandra Laignel-Lavastine in her recent book (*Cioran, Eliade, Ionesco*) ... As for myself I think Mircea Eliade's scholarly work was relatively little infested by the microbe of far right ideology (sometimes punctually, sometimes implicitly: most often not at all). The issue is very complicated and can bear infinite nuances ... Nevertheless, nuanced or categorical, I think that an opinion must be formulated ... In general, I don't think that could be found ultra-nationalistic or fascizing perspectives in Eliade's scholarly work, nor an "anti-Semitic ontology" (Dubuisson's formula) in his books on the history of religions. This conclusion also refers to his scholarly works elaborated during the critical period of Mr. Eliade's political engagement ... We rightfully hold against his pro-legionary option of the '30–'40s as well as his anti-Semitic slip in his journalism of the time ... But I think we should also note that in general, with few exceptions, he had the strength not to make political compromises in the most important part of his work, that dealing with the history of religions.[101]

Finally I quote the statement of Eliade's Jewish university colleague Douglas Allen: "What is remarkable about my encounters with Eliade is that his warm, generous and supportive relations with me, as with many of his other individual Jewish colleagues and friends, never exhibited the usual manifestations of anti-Semitism or personal hostility."[102]

Some of the older relevant literature, despite its importance, has remained practically unmentioned. In view of the results of recent research and improved access to sources, this literature has today understandably receded into the background. Nevertheless, it remains the foundation for all research on this subject. One book worth mentioning is Russel T. McCutcheon, *Manufacturing Religion: The Discourse on sui generis Religion and the Politics of Nostalgia*,[103] a book that is not exactly friendly to Eliade. Much informative material has also been worked through by Ivan Strenski in the Eliade chapter of his book *Four Theories of Myth in Twentieth-Century History: Cassirer, Eliade, Lévi-Strauss and Malinowski*.[104] Strenski attempts to place the mythological theories of these scholars in their wider political, human, and temporal settings. In Eliade's case he argues that the experiences of Eliade's Romanian years are the key to his theory of myth. Consequently Strenski analyzes these years very thoroughly, leaving Eliade's work as a scholar of religion somewhat diminished.

A very balanced piece of work is the section on Eliade in Robert Ellwood's *The Politics of Myth*.[105] Of particular significance for the German-speaking realm was Norman Manea's essay "Felix Culpa: Erinnerung und Schweigen: Mysterien bei Mircea Eliade" (Felix culpa: memory and silence: mysteries in the case of Mircea Eliade) and Edward Kanterian's reply "Wie glücklich war Eliades Schuld?" (How happy was Eliade's guilt?).[106] It is also worth mentioning that the national-Bolshevist Italian periodical *Orion* was probably the first central European magazine to translate and publish Eliade's "Guardist" essays in their entirety.[107]

The political issues are of course also discussed very thoroughly by Eliade's biographers Florin Țurcanu, Natale Spineto, and Alessandro Mariotti.[108] All deal with this topic in a very differentiated way, primarily because they treat Eliade within his broader context as a scholar of religion and do not single out his undeniable political zeal of earlier years.

The obvious question arises: why did Eliade later on never publicly go into the subject of his youthful political ambitions? Was it that he lacked the courage to admit to his mistakes and culpability? I don't think so. Rather it seems to me that he simply did not recognize any guilt on his part. Admittedly he must have blamed himself for certain errors of judgment and he probably regretted the worst excesses of the Iron Guard.[109] But he undoubtedly felt no personal responsibility for what had happened. Eliade was, in my opinion, aware, however, that he would never be able to explain to his contemporaries why he had so unconditionally supported Codreanu's agenda. How, after the catastrophe of the Second War, after the deportation and mass extermination of the Jews, could he possibly have explained that the openly anti-Semitic pronouncements of the Guard had not disturbed him in the way that we today would assume? And how could he have explained to today's "anti-Fascist" intellectuals the convictions that he had held during an age that tended towards "pro-Fascist" attitudes.[110]

He was convinced, probably rightly, that he would stand no chance in any deep, honest discussion, that is to say one without hypocrisy and without opportunistic statements. Anything other than a complete, unconditional, and honest confession of guilt would not have been accepted, and even then the outcome would have been uncertain. But he did not see himself as being in a position to make such a confession. He had different convictions, which he could not or would not throw overboard. For, *by the standards of those earlier times of his youth and considering what was then known,* they seemed to him, or so I believe, to be justified and coherent.

In the case of a limited "confession," which he might conceivably have considered, everything, literally everything—his researches, his respected position at the university, his secure existence—would have been at stake. Often enough in his life he had experienced insecurity and uncertainty, and he undoubtedly did not want to face them again. Given the strict American penalties for immigrants who concealed a Communist or Fascist background, it could well have come to an expulsion from the United States. It would not even have been possible for him to return to his homeland of Romania, which stood until 1989 under Communist rule and where his Iron Guard background was known. What alternatives did he have other than to keep silent? He must simply have been intent on stirring up the minimum amount of political attention and on keeping a low profile for as long as possible in order to remain unscathed. But fear must have been his constant companion.

This is also the gist of the letter which has now come to light, written by Eliade on 17 January 1978 to his friend and later successor, Ioan Coulianu:[111]

> As for C.Z.C., I don't know what to think; he was, assuredly, an *honest* man and managed to awaken a whole generation; but since he lacked political discernment, he also made possible the avalanche of repression (Carol II, Antonescu, the Communists) which decapitated the whole generation he had "brought to life" … I do not think anyone can write an objective history of the Iron Guard movement or draw a portrait of C.Z.C. Available documents are rare and insufficient. What's more, an "objective" attitude may be fatal to the author who would undertake it. Today, the only thing that is accepted is either the apology (for a small number of fanatics of all nations) or the execution (for the majority of European and American readers). After Buchenwald and Auschwitz, even honest people can no longer afford to be "objective."

As Eliade saw it, there was only one possible solution, and even that could not help him. He described this last option in 1945 just after he had arrived in Paris, when he submitted his personal thoughts on the Iron Guard to his friend of earlier years, Eugène Ionesco:

> Psychiatry treats listlessness and nervous problems by helping the patient to integrate into his personality certain conflicts, traumas, obsessions etc., which are damaging his life. This is exactly what we must do, by integrating the traumas, the insults, the mistakes, the crimes and the fury of the Guard—in order to overcome them. It is not a question of bringing the process to an end but rather of making a creative act of will and understanding.[112]

To sum up, after considering so many utterances on the subject of Eliade, one is inevitably left with the by-no-means-novel realization that man is a complex and contradictory being. Praiseworthy, even brilliant traits are not necessarily incompatible with anxiety, insecurity, vanity, and careerism. Concealment, covering up, excuses, and fear are the unpleasant consequences. However, in making any judgment about others, we also judge ourselves and our own consciences. Therefore we should not primarily be concerned with condemnation or acquittal but rather with what we can learn for our own future. From Eliade we can certainly learn how perilous it is to transfer spiritual, religious, or mythical ideas directly into the political realm. This leads to the unleashing of unsuspected and dangerously powerful forces. It would be equally wrong, however, to think that we have to go to the opposite extreme and seek salvation in a purely materialistic and rational system of thought. Human beings have always sought both earthly connectedness and a sense of meaning in life that reaches beyond themselves. Only a finely tuned system of force and counter-force can help to achieve this.[113]

After this detailed but necessary excursus I shall return to Eliade's life. In 1940 Eliade became Romanian cultural attaché in London, then in 1941 moved to Lisbon, where he became press officer and then again cultural attaché. In the latter function he wrote a short history of Romania in French at the request of Portuguese officials, presenting the Romanians as a "people of the earth," with the farmers forming a strong social group.[114] At the same time they were, like the Romans, ready to bravely take up weapons if need be. It was these qualities, he maintained, that had enabled the Romanian people to survive.[115]

Portugal was ruled at that time by the Catholic autocrat Antonio Oliveira Salazar, whom Eliade admired and to whom he even dedicated a book.[116] In the foreword he wrote:

> This book on political history is written by someone who is concerned neither with history in the narrower sense nor with politics. It arose out of an inner restlessness and was written in order to answer a question which the author has been tirelessly pondering for the past ten years: "Is a spiritual revolution possible? Can one, in the framework of history, bring about a revolution with people who believe in giving precedence to things of the spirit?" The Portugal of today, the Portugal of Salazar is perhaps the only country in the world that has sought an answer to this question.

He then went on to say: "The moral and material revolution of Salazar has succeeded."[117]

Apart from the fact that Eliade probably wrote this text with the aim of strengthening relations between Portugal and Romania, one can undoubtedly draw certain conclusions from these words about his own political outlook. Emanuela Costantini puts it clearly: "Eliade ... nourished the same hopes that he had nourished in Romania: he still believed in the 'Christian Revolution.' Even if the revolution of the Legionnaires had failed, he saw in Portugal an example of how his views could be successfully applied. Salazar had succeeded in creating a totalitarian Christian state."[118]

During his years in Portugal Eliade kept a diary, which at first appeared only in Spanish.[119] In contrast to his other diaries, the published version was taken unabridged from the original manuscript.[120] In this sense this diary is the most honest of all, since it still breathes the spirit of the time in which it was written and was not edited by the author before publication. This can be seen from the entry for 13 June 1941, where Eliade writes, "Never before have I had such a clear feeling of being a great writer."[121] And on the December he even remarks: "My ability to understand and relate to culture in all its forms is limitless ... I do not believe that I have ever encountered a genius of comparable complexity. In any event, my mental horizons are much wider than those of Goethe."[122]

The other side of the coin, which is also revealed in his diary, took the form of continual nervous crises and depressions: "The nervous crises are returning, in an almost hysterical form. The rest of the time I am struggling with weak nerves. Always the same story: the lost youth, the superficial life that weighs upon me, the yearning for stormy and tragic adventures such as I experienced in 1928, 1930 and 1932."[123] And, in another entry: "Each time my nerves are more exhausted. Hardly a day goes by without a crisis."[124]

He speaks out equally clearly about his basic outlook on religion: "In reality the tragedy of my life can be reduced to the following formulation: 'I am a Pagan, a perfect classical Pagan who has the intention to become a Christian.'"[125]

The diary also throws some light on his past in the Iron Guard. Under "July, Bucharest, 1942" he reports on a weighty discussion with his former friends about the recent political history of his homeland: "Now and then I spoke up in the discussion and pointed out that, *although a legionnaire*, I left my views on internal politics open as long as the war with Russian continued" (emphasis added).

Eliade's diary is also very frank with regard to his sexual life. The Eliade expert Giovanni Casadio discusses this theme in an article in *Rinascata*, the "national daily newspaper of the Left."[126] His conclusion is that Eliade was obsessed by the "antithesis between the libido copulandi and the libido scribendi," both of which Eliade saw as forms of creative potency. "To think what I might have created," Eliade lamented "had I been less of a slave to my flesh." The honesty of his diary is emphasized by Casadio, who repeatedly highlights the importance of Eliade and is often among his promoters at conferences of scholars of religion. Eliade is, as he points out, "an author who even well-disposed critics like N. Spineto and B. Rennie regard as a big liar, who reconstructed and manipulated his personal image for posterity."

In 1945, on account of the Communist occupation of Romania, Eliade finally fled from Portugal into exile in Paris. Having arrived there without any financial reserves, he was obliged to get by through occasional paid lectures and articles. One person who helped him obtain such work was the Eranos lecturer and expert on Manichaeism, Henri-Charles Puech. In 1950, at the suggestion of Henry Corbin, Eliade came to Eranos, and at this point his life took a decisive turn for the better. In the same year, through the mediation of John Barrett, Eliade became a Bollingen fellow, bringing to an end at least his most acute financial hardship. Henry Corbin had interceded with Barrett on his behalf.

The high point of his career came in 1956, when he was hired by the University of Chicago and, after a period as a visiting professor, was appointed Sewell Avery Distinguished Service Professor of the History of Religions. For this he also had Eranos to thank, for in his first year as a participant he had met the scholar of religion Joachim Wach, who had fled from National Socialism and was at that time visiting his sister, who lived in Ascona. Wach immediately wanted to invite Eliade as a guest lecturer to Chicago. There Wach held the chair that Eliade was later to take over and occupy until his retirement in 1983.

Here I am concentrating on Eliade's career as a scholar of religion as well as on his political activities. However, and this is worth a special mention, I do not wish to forget his great literary achievement, which took the form of numerous successful novels and a number of less successful plays.[127] This bears witness to an almost unbelievable creative capacity.

Eliade and the Study of Religion

It was not only because of his earlier political involvement that Eliade attracted criticism but also because of his essentialist phenomenological methods, which he applied to the study of religion.[128] This meant playing down the cultural and historical differences between religions and emphasizing their common essence.[129] What was important for Eliade was the ahistorical core within shared religious experience. In the opinion of Sorin Alexandrescu of the University of Amsterdam, these criticisms apply more to Edmund Husserl, the founder of phenomenology and the one who attempted to provide a philosophical basis for this methodology.[130] Husserl ascribed an ahistorical essence to every historical fact and insisted that, in order to understand any phenomenon fully, both aspects—the historical and the ahistorical—must be taken into account. Alexandrescu believes that Eliade, especially in the years of exile in Paris, came strongly under the influence of Husserl.

Because Eliade gives insufficient weight to cultural and political factors, he has also been accused of supporting the prevailing political power structure. He insists, his critics say, on seeing religion as something irreducible to anything else. Consequently he treats the study of religion as a discipline *sui generis*, which only has to obey its own rules, and this makes religion appear to be independent of the social and political context. This, his attackers argue, is "naïve" and leads in practice to making religion unassailable and "sacrosanct" to the point of becoming a "fetish" that does not tolerate any external influence and at the same time does not concern itself with political and social conditions.[131]

This issue acquires a particular significance by virtue of the fact that the study of religion meant much more to Eliade than the mere description of religious practices and beliefs. He saw the discipline as a pre-eminent source of strength for a general cultural renewal. In his essay "Krisis und Erneuerung der Religionswissenschaft" (Crisis and renewal of the study of religion), published in the journal *Antaios*, to which he and Ernst Jünger gave their names as editors without doing the work, Eliade wrote:

> The study of religion is not just a historical discipline like, for example, archaeol-ogy or numismatics. It is a *Gesamthermeneutik* [roughly, a total or all-embracing hermeneutic approach; original emphasis]. Its mission is to decipher and interpret every form of human encounter with the holy, from prehistory to the present day. Out of modesty, or perhaps out of excessive anxiety, scholars of religion shy away from placing the results of their researches in their proper cultural light.

Thus, since the beginning of the twentieth century up to the present day, there has been "an increasing loss of creative energy and a concomitant loss of interpretative cultural synthesis in favour of a fragmentary, analytical type of research."[132]

A few pages later in the same essay he writes:

> Last but not least, this creative type of hermeneutic *changes* [original emphasis] the person; it is more than a way of explaining things, it is a technique of the mind which makes it possible to change one's very being. This applies especially to the historical-religious type of hermeneutic.[133] A good book on the study of religion should stir the reader up—as for example "Das Heilige" or "Die Götter Griechenlands" does. Thereby the basis for a "new humanism" will be created.[134]

Thus what Eliade wanted was a total hermeneutic approach, which could offer a compre-hensive interpretation of the existential situation of modern man. The foundation for this approach was to be provided by the discipline of the study of religion, since every human being was essentially a *Homo religiosus*. In the modern world, where sacredness was so absent, the "holy" had to be given once again a central position.[135]

Hence the extreme importance that Eliade attached to myth and in particular to its specific religious function, namely to "guarantee the experience of the holy and thus to preserve the continuity and identity of a particular religion."[136] And hence also the way in which Eliade repeatedly contrasted archaic man, anchored in a traditional culture, with modern man. While the former feels himself to be one with the cosmos and its rhythms and thus sees his life as being filled with intense meaning, the latter is in danger of perceiving his life as absurd and of falling into nihilism.[137] Similarly, for the tradition-oriented person, history is embedded in a higher, metaphysical reality, which imbues historical events with meaning, whereas for modern man history, with all its horrors, is merely an arbitrary process, to which human beings are subject and in which they are unable to perceive any higher goal.[138]

In this connection it may be appropriate to mention Eliade's attitude to what is loosely termed esotericism. This is expressed particularly clearly in his book *Occultism, Witchcraft and Cult Fashions*, in which he evinces a rather dismissive attitude to this domain. It is also well known that Eliade had close ties to the so-called Integral Tradition or Perennialist movement, as represented by figures such as Julius Evola, René Guénon, and Ananda Coomaraswamy. However, we cannot go into this theme here, as there is already an abundance of literature on this subject.[139]

In 2008 there appeared a book by the Italian language expert Marcello de Martino, which addresses the question of the "esoteric" Eliade. This work was presented in Rome by two Eliade experts, Florin Țurcanu and Roberto Scagno, which says something about the authority of the book.[140] Interestingly, the author does not focus on Eliade's scholarly work but rather primarily on his novels. De Martino presents an abundance of details and skillfully connects extracts from Eliade's novels and diaries with motifs from the history of esotericism. Eliade is convincingly presented as someone who was indeed influenced by esotericism and in sympathy with its aims.

When de Martino uses the terms "esotericism" or "shamanism" he does not of course mean that Eliade performed magical rituals, practiced mystical techniques or carried out shamanic healing, but rather that he affirmed the "Holy," in Rudolf Otto's sense, as the *fascinosum et tremendum* that has the power to stir us in our innermost depths. This, de Martino argues, was something that Eliade regarded as a foundation stone and essential guiding principle in his life. His basic *Weltanschauung*, according to de Martino, was therefore "spiritual" rather than "scientific": something that is mostly scorned as unacceptable by the academic world of today. Consequently, Eliade did everything he could to conceal his personal convictions. De Martino even maintains that Eliade adopted the same strategy with regard to these convictions as he did with his former close association with the Iron Guard: he simply avoided mentioning them. De Martino cannot support his thesis with hard evidence that would stand up in court, but he can make a good case based on circumstantial evidence.

De Martino of course also deals with Eliade's contacts with people such as Julius Evola and Ananda Coomaraswamy, as well as the deep impression made on Eliade by René Guénon's works, but it is the quotations from Eliade's own works that carry the most conviction. These are presented in the context of the history of esotericism, and de Martino repeatedly finds esoteric parallels, whether in the teachings of the so-called Fedeli d'Amore or the doctrines of Madame Blavatsky and the Theosophists.

A different opinion is held by the esotericism scholar Antoine Faivre, who characterizes the esoteric influence on Eliade as rather minimal, possibly because Faivre has a somewhat different conception of esotericism from de Martino.[141] Faivre, who knew Eliade well, does not deny that the Romanian was personally interested in esotericism, but believes that it did not fit into Eliade's "programme of transhistorical anthropology." Mac Linscott Ricketts, on the other hand, argues that Faivre underestimates Eliade's interest in esotericism, although Ricketts does not perceive Eliade as a dedicated believer.[142] He mentions, however, Eliade's contacts with Gurdjieffians in Paris, especially Philippe Levastine, grandfather of Eliade's fierce critic, Alexandra Laignel-Levastine.

Possibly the liveliest and most personal description of an Eranos meeting that I know has been provided by Ximena de Angulo, who even as a young girl had accompanied her mother to Zurich when the latter had gone there to see C.G. Jung. In this account, which exists only in manuscript form, she describes Mircea Eliade as someone full of youthful enthusiasm, with a habit of gesticulating forcefully as he spoke, his mane of hair waving about. She was amused to see how eager he was, when attending other people's lectures, not to miss a single word. And in the evenings, when he sometimes frequented the cafés of Ascona, there was no mistaking his rapid flow of talk, punctuated by laughter and wild gestures.

Raffaele Pettazzoni

In 1950 the scholar of religion Raffaele Pettazzoni came to Ascona to speak about the Babylonian festival of Akitu, with which he had been intensively preoccupied and therefore probably needed little time to prepare the lecture. Pettazzoni, who occupied the chair for the study of religion at the University of Rome, has to be seen as Italy's leading protagonist in the field of objective religious studies during the inter-war period.[143] Without doubt he must also be counted in the global context among the most important architects of religious studies as a university discipline.[144] As early as 1925 he founded the important Italian journal in this field, *Studi e materiali di storia delle religioni*, which still exists today. The Italian Society for the History of Religion was also his creation. In 1950 he was unanimously elected president of the International Association for the History of Religions (IAHR),[145] at a moment when it was in a precarious phase. As a sign of the stabilization of the Association, he founded, as its organ, the much respected periodical *Numen*, which is also still published.

Pettazzoni's aim was to find a synthesis between the historical and phenomenological school of religious studies, a synthesis that he hoped to be "general religious studies."[146] He was among the first of the Italian scholars who supported Eliade in the 1920s, and Eliade himself repeatedly described himself as a pupil of Pettazzoni.[147] In a letter of 23 June 1936 Eliade wrote to Pettazzoni, "You are really my first and most valued master in the study of religion."[148] Pettazzoni's important work *I misteri* on the ancient mysteries was apparently a decisive influence for Eliade to enter the religious field.[149] The contact between the two men was continuous, and their exchange of letters is the most protracted correspondence of Eliade that has been preserved.

Although Raffaele Pettazzoni had been a Freemason since 1907 and had even proceeded to higher-degree Masonry in 1913, receiving the fourth grade of the Ancient and Accepted Scottish Rite,[150] there is evidence that he had certain leanings towards the Fascist regime (probably more for career reasons than ideological ones). Following the advent of the Fascist government there is no further evidence of masonic activity on Pettazzoni's part. After a time the Fascists prohibited Freemasonry, partly under pressure from the Catholic Church and partly also for reasons of internal power politics, even though Freemasonry had been a significant influence within the early Fascist party.[151]

Pettazzoni's contacts with the Fascist regime were linked with his efforts to obtain a regular chair of religious studies.[152] However, such a chair did not yet exist in Italy. The first one was founded in Rome with the support of Giovanni Gentile in 1922. Gentile, a philosopher and professor of philosophy, had been made minister of education in the Mussolini regime. This enabled him to realize his aim of getting the study of religion established in Italy, although at the same time he had made some critical remarks about Pettazzoni's scholarly work. Gentile was also the author of the famous *Manifesto degli intellettuali fascisti* (1925), in which he described Fascism as a potential force for the moral and religious rebirth of Italy.

From that moment the study of religion in Italy quickly took a dramatic upturn. Within fifteen years a number of additional chairs were established in the country, and the subject was at least being taught at several more universities. It must of course remain pure speculation whether this rapid development would not have happened without the Fascist regime.

While Pettazzoni may not have felt any inward kinship with Fascism, on the other hand, as Michael Stausberg says in his study (see note 152), there is no evidence of any anti-Fascist resistance on Pettazzoni's part. He swore, as demanded, the oath of loyalty to government, king, and country (it will be recalled that Ernesto Buonaiuti refused, but he was only one of twelve professors to do so). In 1933 he even joined the PNF (Partito Fascista Nazionale), and he did not protest at the removal of Jewish colleagues from the universities.[153] On the other hand, he does not appear to have participated in party events, nor to have worn the black shirt, the equivalent of the Nazi brown shirt. He did, however, sign the (in)famous Manifesto sulla Razza (Manifesto of racism) as did many other intellectuals, a fact which Michael Stausberg interestingly does not mention.[154] On the question of whether Pettazzoni signed voluntarily, judgment must remain suspended.[155]

Pettazzoni came to Eranos in 1950 after receiving in February a letter of invitation from Mrs. Fröbe, which he immediately accepted, partly because at the back of his mind he liked the idea of a few days' rest in Switzerland.[156] It remains on open question why Pettazzoni lectured there only once. Was it because of differences in outlook between him and the other participants, or were there deeper reasons? Ximena de Angulo says in her diary that he spoke a wonderful Italian, but at the same time was very deaf, which made conversation with him at the Round Table extremely difficult. When he was introduced to the gathering and some amusing stories were related, which were translated for his benefit, he hardly reacted at all, giving rise to the question whether it was his hearing or his humor that was lacking.[157]

When Lucy Heyer later on asked him, as she asked all the conference participants, what he had thought of Eranos, Pettazzoni replied that he had "preserved a lasting memory of it," which had partly to do with the beauty of the landscape but more to do with the "light of the mind" and the "stream of sympathy" that flowed back and forth between the speakers and the audience.[158]

Jung's Departure from Eranos

The year 1950 saw the return to Ascona, after a long absence, of Ximena de Angulo, who had held an editorial position at the Bollingen Foundation during its early period in the United States. Together with her husband, Willy Roelli, she even produced a silent film about Eranos.[159] Unfortunately a collaboration with Fröbe proved impossible. Evidently the founder of Eranos invariably clashed with people, and especially women, who, even with the best intentions, wished to act independently in the interests of Eranos. She was fully aware of this and had an explanation for it. In her very clear letter to Ximena de Angulo of 7 September 1951 she wrote,

> Eranos is my way of individuation. It was so in its beginnings, in its entire develop-
> ment and it is so today in its greatest intensity. It happens to be my destiny to have
> had to work out my way of individuation in this way. And I have had to do it alone.
> Everyone is alone on his or her inner way. There is no alternative. That is why I
> have never worked together with anyone, why I just had to do everything con-
> nected with Eranos alone ... That is the reason that I get "worked up" when anyone

interferes with any part of those activities. If anyone touches the psychic process of anyone else, there must be trouble. Because no one can stand that.

This insight into her own psychological make-up, whether one accepts it or not, explains to a large extent her often irrational attitude when decisions had to be made about Eranos. It was never just Eranos itself that was at issue but also her own inner being, her psychological and physical health. This caused Fröbe to be convinced that Eranos would not be continued after her death, for the simple reason that Eranos was, as she saw it, her own path to individuation and no one else's. In later years, however, she changed her position on this matter.

At any rate, de Angulo did not enter into a conflict with the founder of Eranos and did what was most sensible in such a case: she avoided discussion and only consulted with Fröbe when the latter expressly wished it, which was often enough. Even Alfons Rosenberg, who was very well disposed towards Fröbe, confirms that she could react very strongly when Eranos was involved. "However," he adds:

generally she was very reserved and withdrawn. Her face, and especially her mouth, gave the impression of a dam holding back an inner flood that she wanted at all costs to prevent from gushing forth uncontrollably. It was obvious that behind the cool, deadpan, often mask-like face there lay turbulent passions, a multitude of thoughts, feelings, different faces, but also vulnerabilities and renunciations.[160]

Jung held his last Eranos lecture in 1951. The theme was "synchronicity," the occurrence of non-causal but meaningful coincidences, in which parallel phenomena manifest themselves both within the psyche and in the outer world.[161] This was the first time that he presented this scientifically hazardous idea to a wider public. I have already mentioned how Jung used the Eranos meetings very often (in fact the psychologist Ira Progoff would have said "invariably") as a platform for new ideas. For Jung Eranos may even have been a sort of incarnation of his conception of an archetype: a unifying entity, embracing peoples and individuals.[162] "I look back with pleasure and gratitude," he wrote to Olga Fröbe on her seventieth birthday, "on countless evenings which were richly stimulating and instructive and which brought me the very thing that I needed so much, namely personal contact with other areas of knowledge." However, the most important discussions at meals took place at the so-called Round Table, at which the speakers, much to the regret of the audience, were alone amongst themselves.

There must have been something special about this Round Table. Olga Fröbe related in a letter[163] that Jung once arrived alone at the Casa Gabriella, pointed to the table and said: "That is the real Eranos."[164] And Henry Corbin tells of a photograph showing the table with empty seats. When Jung saw it he exclaimed spontaneously: "The picture is complete. They are all there." In the same vein, Michel Cazenave eloquently described Eranos as a circle of people who were always present even if they did not show themselves, or were *still* present even if they had passed on.[165] Fröbe herself saw the Round Table as a mandala, the most profound symbol of the self, with all its numinous qualities, and the concrete embodiment of Eranos *par excellence*. In an unpublished memoir, which she wrote towards the end of her life, she mentioned that, in the earliest days of the meetings, this table did not yet have any special role. At that time Jung and the other speakers were accommodated at Monte Verità or elsewhere.[166] It was only after the outbreak of the Second World War that the situation changed and the big, green table attracted the most important speakers as if by magic, taking on its role as a creative circle. The former president of the Eranos Foundation in Moscia-Ascona, Mrs. Robinson, said in a communication to me that the real essence of the meetings took place at the Round Table, adding that, "In this sense Eranos is esoteric, otherwise not."

It is interesting that Jung was particularly fond of inviting members of the Catholic clergy to Eranos.[167] These included Hugo Rahner, Henri-Charles Puech, Victor White, Martin d'Arcy, and Ernesto Buonaiuti. Their recognition of his work (though of course only partial) pleased him greatly and was something that he could not expect to come so readily from the Protestant side.[168] He also maintained close contact with one particular Catholic priest outside the Eranos context, namely Gebhard Frei, who was professor of comparative religion at Zurich and whose interest in yoga, magic, and the paranormal closely corresponded to Jung's own interest in these areas. The great significance attributed to symbolism by both analytical psychology and Catholicism could be one of the reasons for this affinity and might also account for the relative lack of interest in Jung's work from the Protestant side.[169]

Another Eranos focal point in the earlier times were the so-called *Mäuerchen-Sitzungen* (wall sessions) with Jung, who would sit on the low wall of the terrace and deliver answers to various questions. As Maggy Anthony writes, it was predominantly women who gathered around him. Where else would they have had the opportunity to speak to Jung in person? She reports that these female admirers acquired the name "Jung-Frauen" (a German pun on the word *Jungfrau*, meaning "virgin"). One of them described the scene as follows: "When the lecture was over, Jung used to sit on this wall, and in a flash we were clustering around him like bees around a honey pot, much to the annoyance of the other participants."[170] As Ellen Thayer remarked in her lecture "Eranos and Ascona," "It seemed to me I had never conceived that so many beautiful, elegant, and graceful ladies could be interested in analysis." And Stella Corbin described an occasion when a group of young women went for a swim in Lake Maggiore after a lecture. When they came back one of them said: "Now we have bathed in the Collective Unconscious," which caused Jung to have one of his famous laughing fits.[171]

Jung's success with women is legendary and has been extensively written about in the literature on him.[172] Particularly revealing is the testimony of Margaret Flinters, who had been a regular patient of Jung in the 1920s: "Bringing me down to earth was literally the problem. I don't know how he did it quite. First of all I think it was his own peasant solidity which gave me the feeling I was in touch with a real man for the first time in my life."[173] It was only when Erich Neumann joined the wall sessions that they took on a rather different character. After that Jung always spoke to Neumann, and the "Jung-Frauen" sat around and listened.

As Aniela Jaffé reports, Jung apparently took pleasure in these sessions, for increasingly he invited his female admirers into the house afterwards.[174] Some of these discussions were recorded by Margret Ostrowski-Sachs, who lived next to Hermann Hesse[175] in Montagnola near Ascona. In this connection, Gerhard Wehr reports[176] how Jung confessed that he longed to converse with adequate partners, but that in his local [female] circle he seldom had the opportunity to do so. In Eranos, however, it was different.

Even in this circle, however, Jung could not always count on unanimous agreement. On one occasion, for example, Alfons Rosenberg held a lecture in a small reception room in a friend's nearby villa, where he sometimes stayed. In the lecture he defended the notion of the divine Trinity against the well-known Jungian theory of the quaternary, on which Jung had just lectured at Eranos. The only trouble was that half the Eranos audience were present at Rosenberg's lecture, which led to a split in the "community," much to Jung's displeasure. Rosenberg pointed out that the issue of the Trinity versus the quaternary had already been the subject of heated debate in the Middle Ages, reaching a climax at the Milan architects' congress of 1366, which debated whether the Milan Cathedral should be built according to the law of the square or the triangle. Finally it was decided to use both the square and the triangle, merging the two. Therefore, Rosenberg argued, one must reject Jung's notion that the Trinity, being incomplete, should be submerged in the quaternary.

In 1951 the technical physicist Max Knoll came to give a lecture at Ascona and subsequently came twice more. Knoll, whose wife was a Jungian analyst, was a personal friend of Jung, with whom he always held long conversations. Jung was always at pains to create a bridge between his theories and the world of natural sciences, especially physics. It is evident from a letter written by Fröbe to Ximena de Angulo on 30 December 1951, that Knoll's lecture was somehow a failure because of the way in which he had been put under pressure beforehand, especially by Jung.[177] One thing that made Knoll's presence important was that he was in contact with D.T. Suzuki, the Zen master *par excellence*. Through Knoll's mediation and that of Christmas Humphreys, president of the British Buddhist Society, an invitation was conveyed to Suzuki to come to Eranos. The visit planned for 1952 fell through, but in 1953 Suzuki came.

In the Eranos yearbook for 1951 the name of Erwin R. Goodenough crops up for the first time. However, his talk had to be read aloud by someone else, as Goodenough was so ill that he could not speak from the lectern. He had already been invited in 1938, but had declined. In 1939 he accepted but had to withdraw because of his wife's illness. In 1947 he had a meeting with Olga Fröbe, and in 1951 he came but in a sick condition, as mentioned. In 1956 and 1957 he went again to Eranos but only as a member of the audience. Nevertheless, I should like to mention him briefly here, simply because he dedicated his life in a very interdisciplinary and inter-religious way to the study of mystical symbols and currents in antiquity and thus acted very much in the spirit of Eranos. Jacob Neusner, in his foreword to Goodenough's thirteen-volume magnum opus *Jewish Symbols in the Greco-Roman Period*,[178] calls Goodenough "the greatest historian of religion America ever produced." His special area was Hellenistic Judaism, from which he showed that many elements of early Christianity are derived. Hence his strong interest in Philo Judaeus, the Hellenized Jewish philosopher, who was so enthusiastically greeted by the early Christians because they believed him to be a secret Christian.

Goodenough was born in Brooklyn into a family of fundamentalist Methodists. His studies in theology and history of religion took him via Harvard to Oxford, where he took a doctorate. Thereafter he immediately took up a teaching position at Yale, where he was to remain for the rest of his academic career, gaining additional doctorates in theology and Hebrew literature. He played an essential role in the founding of the American Society for the Study of Religion of which he was the first president.[179]

In his monumental magnum opus he analyzed Pagan symbolism in Jewish synagogues and graveyards of the early centuries AD. In this way he sought—despite lack of explicit written evidence—to show that the Jewish religion was at that time much more complex and varied than one would suppose from the extant Talmudic literature. He believed that there existed at that time a Hellenistic-Jewish mystical theology, which was closer to the Kabbalah than to the rabbinic form of Judaism that is thought to have been dominant at that time. Goodenough was much influenced by Jung's theory of archetypes and Jung himself mentions Goodenough several times in his writings. It was Jung who prompted Fröbe to invite Goodenough in 1938.[180]

Helmut Wilhelm, the son of Richard Wilhelm, also spoke at Eranos in 1951 for the first time and was to come a further six times. The significance of the *I Ching* has been mentioned several times already, and Helmut Wilhelm's lectures, which were all on this subject, were enthusiastically received. Helmut Wilhelm, who was known as one of the world's leading experts on the *I Ching*, had spent his youth in China, completed his studies in Germany, and then returned to China where he was a professor at the University of Peking from 1933 to 1944. During the Japanese occupation of China he lived a withdrawn life, dedicating himself to his studies. From 1948 he taught sinology at the University of Washington at Seattle.[181] His relationship to Eranos is expressed in the saying of Confucius that he quoted in the booklet *25 Jahre Eranos* (25 years of Eranos): "To gather friends in a civilized place and, through friends, to pave the way for humanity."

In 1951 Fröbe finally gained recognition from her (at least ancestral) homeland of the Netherlands, which must have given her great satisfaction. The Dutch Queen Juliana invited her to a two-hour conversation, which took place in the queen's study where the bookshelves were full of Eranos yearbooks. Queen Juliana had herself pursued religious studies and had retained her interest in religious phenomenology. As Fröbe reported in a letter of 4 November 1951 to the Bollingen representative Vaun Gillmor, the queen was much better informed in the area of religious studies than she was, and therefore she had kept the conversation focused on the legend of Eranos with all its irrational happenings. Subsequently a close *confidante* of Queen Juliana visited the Eranos meetings regularly and gave the queen reports on them.[182] After this conversation Gilles Quispel was also invited to an audience with the queen and asked to give her his impressions.

In 1952 Jung came to Ascona again but did not lecture. Although his visit was purely private, he was besieged by the other guests and bombarded with questions. According to his wish, Olga Fröbe made sure that he was introduced to all the new speakers and that he could question them at leisure. For Jung it was important to be able, for once, to ask questions himself and compare research findings, for in Zurich he was himself usually the target of questions, which nearly always concerned specific aspects of his psychological work.[183] However, during the conference he did find time to give a detailed interview to Mircea Eliade, taking Jung's "notorious" book *Answer to Job* as the starting point. The interview was published in the journal *Combat: de la Résistance à la Révolution*.[184]

After 1952 Jung had to bow to the effects of old age and ceased coming to the meetings. Nevertheless, he remained in contact with Eranos. Writing to Fröbe on 2 June 1956, he said:

> The Eranos meetings have always offered me abundant stimuli for the mind; the exchange of thoughts with people of similar interests as well as the resonance from an educated audience were for me a wonderful and important experience. Unfortunately my age now forbids me to take part in the meetings. The unavoidable crowd of people besieging me would be too much for my strength. More than ever I need peace and must carefully avoid all organized gatherings. So the Yearbooks are all the more valuable to me, as they bring me the spirit and essence of the meetings, even if the sunlight, the lake and the company of old friends have to be conjured up in my mind.

The 1952 meeting was the first and only one to include a lecture by the Heidelberg philosopher Karl Löwith, who spoke about historicism and his criticisms of it—in tune with the generally anti-historicist tenor of Eranos. His standard work (and almost a best-seller) *Weltgeschichte und Heilsgeschehen*, first published in English in the United States in 1949 under the title *Meaning in History*, was hailed as a "farewell to the historicist view of history."[185] On the other hand, he recognized that we have a very limited capacity to judge and evaluate history and historical phenomena.[186] Nevertheless, in the memorial volume *25 Jahre Eranos* (25 years of Eranos), he expressed "gratitude for the encounter between nature and spirit in East and West during the Eranos gatherings."

Another who gave his "inaugural" lecture in 1952 was Herbert Read. Olga Fröbe had already invited him earlier, but a certain timidity had caused him to decline. Read has already been mentioned in connection with his work for the English edition of Jung's writings. Together with John "Jack" Barrett, he had met Jung every year in August to talk about how the edition was progressing and to discuss further works for the English-speaking public.[187] Read's lecture was marked by a particular incident. He had chosen to speak about Picasso and was giving various examples of the latter's approach to art when Jung stood up and left the room, signaling his opposition to what Read was saying. Previously Jung had sat next to Read at dinner, and had been displeased when Read had announced that he was going to speak about Picasso. Then, during the lecture, Read began to quote Jung without clearly distinguishing between his own opinions and what Jung had actually meant. It was at this point that Jung angrily left the room. Read was considerably upset by the incident.[188]

An interesting interpretation of Read's views on art is given by Philip Sherrard, friend of the poet Kathleen Raine, who herself later became an Eranos speaker.[189] He treats Read as a prototype of the modern aesthete, whose conception of art he vehemently opposes.[190] He even describes Read as the leading figure in the artistic and literary avant-garde between 1930 and 1960. Furthermore, Sherrard maintains that Read had worked out the fundamental principles for the understanding of modern art: principles that are still applied today. In doing so he had also made possible the success of modern art. Central to Read's approach was, as Sherrard maintained, the former's positive attitude to modern science, especially as it was manifested in the theory of evolution and in modern physics. Read saw art as an organic, evolutionary process, which originates in the formlessness of the unconscious and eventually takes visible shape. Thus art is above all an unconscious process. Hence Read's interest in C.G. Jung.

However, Sherrard argues, if art is understood primarily as an unconscious process, then everything that emerges from the unconscious falls under the heading of art, and there can be no criteria for judging what is "true" art and what is mere "aberration". Read himself was evidently unhappy about this situation and had been repeatedly outraged by the so-called art that was exhibited at the Institute of Contemporary Arts in London, which had been founded with Read's dedicated support.[191]

Sherrard believes that the deeper reason for this view of art—which remains the dominant orthodoxy today—lay in Read's atheism. A believer of whatever faith always has certain firmly based guiding images. Sherrard sees these images as ancient "archetypes" implanted in creation, to which the believing artist will always subordinate himself. The atheist, on the other hand, knows no such guiding images. To him art is only creative when it is new in style or content—in other words when it has been "invented" by him or someone else. Thus newness becomes the essential, if not the only, criterion for what is to be considered authentic creative art. That which is eternally valid, however, is denigrated and dismissed as imitation.

After the controversy with Jung, Read took a break from lecturing at Eranos, but then returned as one of the regular speakers from 1956 to 1964. He also played a highly important role in sustaining the external continuity of Eranos by repeatedly acting as a contact person between Ascona and the Bollingen Foundation, as he came regularly to the meetings and knew the key people on both sides. Read, too, expressed his gratitude to Eranos, if only because of the many interesting contacts that he made there.[192] He said, for example, that he had not really been able to understand oriental art until meeting D.T. Suzuki at Ascona in 1935. With Suzuki he retained a lifelong friendship.[193] Herbert Read was also very interested in the Russian-Georgian "magus" and teacher of wisdom George Ivanovich Gurdjieff, and for a time he attended lectures by Gurdjieff's leading disciple P.D. Ouspensky.[194] His study of the Gurdjieff teaching is perhaps less surprising when one remembers that a whole series of intellectuals, including Katherine Mansfield, T.S. Eliot, and Frank Lloyd Wright, were also attracted by Gurdjieff's message.

Read is another of the considerable number of speakers who would hardly have been able to travel to Ascona without the support of the Bollingen Foundation. These also included Paul Radin, Joseph Campbell, Hellmut Wilhelm, Erwin Goodenough, and the musicologist Victor Zuckerkandl, who spoke at Eranos from 1960 to 1964 and finally took up residence in the Casa Gabriella until his death in 1965.[195] The Bollingen Foundation not only provided these people with scholarships but also paid their travel costs to Europe so that they could give lectures at Eranos. I have already mentioned that many of the most important figures connected with Eranos—including Olga Fröbe, Henry Corbin, Louis Massignon, Mircea Eliade, Heinrich Zimmer, Gilles Quispel, and Gershom Scholem—were able to carry out much of their important work thanks to the fellowships awarded by the Bollingen Foundation. But a number of other Eranos speakers still to be mentioned, such as D.T. Suzuki, the orientalist Fritz Meier, the psychotherapist Ira Progoff, the theologian Ernst Benz, and the writer Kathleen Raine, also benefited from the generosity of Bollingen.[196] It will by now be apparent that, without the support of Bollingen, Eranos would already have run aground in the late 1930s, despite all good intentions and Mrs. Fröbe's intuitive leadership.

It should therefore be clearly pointed out that Eranos, although widely perceived as a European institution, was only able to survive because of American generosity (albeit because of the special features of the American tax system and perhaps also a hidden political agenda). Without this nonetheless admirably generous patronage, many important works of cultural history would never have been written, and the interdisciplinary Eranos meetings, which have had such a decisive influence, at least on analytical psychology and religious studies, would not have taken place. There had always been little prospect of finding rich patrons in Switzerland. The Swiss businessman Fritz Allemann had warned Fröbe of this from the start, as she reported in a letter to Paul Mellon of 6 December 1948. The reason that Allemann had given was that "as Eranos is an international project it means nothing to them." As for the people who attended the meetings, they were mainly hard-working but modestly paid psychologists, writers, and artists, from whom one could expect little by way of financial contributions. One option that Olga Fröbe had always wanted to pursue was the sale of part of her land, but the portion overlooking the lake was needed for the conferences and the part on the hillside was not attractive to buyers.[197] In any case, such a sale would only have relieved the situation for a few years. It was only in 1943, during the time when support from the Bollingen Foundation was suspended, that she succeeded in selling a piece of land, but the proceeds only sufficed for the organization of two small conferences.

Before I go on to the next Eranos meeting I should mention some of the more important members of the audience at the 1952 meeting, as listed in the Eranos guest book. Among these, I would give first place to the great Dadaist Hans Richter, who came with his wife. Further well-known names included the influential psychoanalyst and writer Alexander Mitscherlich, the analytical psychologist James Kirsch, and Gustav Heyer's first wife, Lucy.

The Lure of the Far East: Deisetz T. Suzuki and Giuseppe Tucci

In 1953 there were again several new and well-known speakers, namely Giuseppe Tucci, probably Italy's most prominent orientalist and one of the most famous in the field worldwide; the theologian and scholar of religion Ernst Benz; the theologian and later cardinal Jean Daniélou, who had been invited through Mircea Eliade; and the Japanese Zen expert Daisetz Teitaro Suzuki. Joseph Campbell relates a nice anecdote about Suzuki's first appearance at Ascona.[198] Suzuki, then ninety-one years old, stood up in front of his audience, surveyed them, and then said: "Nature against God. God against nature. Nature against man. Man against nature. Man against God. God against man. Very curious religion." Another anecdote is related by Ernst Benz in a memorial essay on Suzuki. Benz reports that Suzuki postponed his departure from Ascona by one day so that he would be there for the full moon.[199] What European, asks Benz, would postpone his departure just so that he could sit quietly on a terrace and contemplate the moon and its reflection in a lake?

Suzuki came from an old but impecunious samurai family. When he was six years old, his father died, plunging the family into even greater hardship. At the age of seventeen or eighteen Suzuki began to reflect on his difficult fate and turned to Zen through family connections.[200] At that time there was a growing interest in world-wide cultural and religious exchange, and the Zen master of Suzuki's temple, Shaku Sōen,[201] therefore wanted to give an address at the World Parliament of Religions, set to take place in the framework of the Chicago World Exhibition of 1893. Suzuki translated the address into English, as he had studied the language at Tokyo University and also taught it.

The World Parliament of Religions, which brought together over two hundred delegates from forty-five different religions and religious groupings, cannot be overestimated for its importance in spreading Buddhism in the West.[202] It triggered off the American interest in the Buddhist religion, an interest that continues to increase to this day.[203]

In 1897, four years after the World Parliament of Religions, Suzuki was chosen by his Zen master to travel to the United States as a representative of his monastery in order to create a wider awareness of Zen Buddhism in the wake of the Chicago meeting. In the end Suzuki remained for fifteen years in the United States, where he worked in publishing, staying in the house of the German-American publisher, writer, and philosopher Paul Carus, who supported him. Together they translated the *Tao Te Ching* and other works of oriental wisdom. During the course of their collaboration he came strongly under the influence of Carus' monistic philosophical outlook.

After his return to his homeland Suzuki resumed the teaching of English, this time in some of the great universities of Japan. Soon he began to translate Zen texts into English and, as often happens with translators, this prompted him to begin writing on his own account. His important work *Introduction to Zen Buddhism* was translated into German by Heinrich Zimmer, and appeared in 1939 with a foreword by C.G. Jung. This helped to spread his reputation to the German-speaking realm.

In his later years Suzuki again resided mainly in the United States, teaching at Columbia University but continuing to travel frequently. Thanks to a subsidy from the Bollingen Foundation, he was able to afford the trip to Ascona for himself and his female assistant, despite initial difficulties in obtaining a visa from the Swiss consulate. As a special guest of honor, Suzuki was allowed to stay in the quarters above the lecture room, where the Jung family had also stayed. As William McGuire reports, the local Zen enthusiasts in Ascona repeatedly tried to gain access to him, to present him with flowers or even to request some of his bathwater.

Suzuki is without doubt the most famous and influential Zen expert known to the West. His books have been translated into many languages and are still in print today. Nevertheless there have been some legitimate criticisms of him, which are not generally known about except among scholars of religion. The Buddhist scholar Masao Abe, who is basically pro-Suzuki, sums up these criticisms as follows:[204]

> First of all, what Suzuki publicized in the west was Rinzai Zen, to which he himself belonged, whereas the Soto form of Zen is mentioned by him only *en passant*. Furthermore it was Suzuki who conveyed the impression that Japan and Japanese culture are based entirely on Zen. The importance of Shinto and other religious traditions is almost entirely ignored. He also over-emphasizes the technique of the *koan*, that is to say the experience of sudden enlightenment through the contemplation of a paradoxical question, whereas he neglects the practice of *zazen*, which involves sitting in meditation.

This raises the question of whether Suzuki wished to be seen as a scholar or as a "missionary" for his own conception of Zen. Masao Abe, who knew him personally, tends towards the latter view. Abe maintains that Suzuki believed the West to be in dire need of the Eastern spiritual heritage. Hence he saw himself compelled to speak primarily from his own religious experience and not to talk about other traditions. The consequence of this one-sided approach, according to Abe, was that important people such as C.G. Jung, who after the war had no other access to authentic sources, were also led to make one-sided statements.

A much stronger critical stance is taken by Robert H. Sharf in his essay "The Zen of Japanese Nationalism."[205] Sharf teaches East Asian languages and cultures at the University of California, Berkeley, and thus doubtless a proven expert. First of all, he describes Zen Buddhism as something completely different from the way it is generally perceived in the West. Among Western Zen followers, at least among those of average education, Zen Buddhism is seen as a direct way to enlightenment, which stands over and above religious divisions and can therefore be practiced by adherents of any religion. Sharf, on the other hand, drawing on Japanese written sources, points out that Zen is actually one of the most ritualized forms of Buddhist meditation that exist. He also maintains that there is a misunderstanding regarding the *koans*, that is, the riddles spoken by the master, which, according to common belief, cannot be understood rationally but only by means of a direct break-through to the super-rational (*satori*). These riddles, Sharf says, are in no way a method of direct liberation. On the contrary, their solution involves a highly demanding exegesis of classical Buddhist and Zen Buddhist scriptures, which would only be possible for someone of great knowledge and learning. Furthermore, the experience of *satori* (enlightenment) is basically not an inner experience but consists rather of a public procedure that is deliberately contrived and choreographed.

Sharf is not the only one to hold this view about Zen Buddhism. Others who see it in a similar light include Bernard Faure, Kao Professor in Japanese Religion at Columbia University, New York, whose specialities include Zen as well as Tantric and so-called esoteric Buddhism. Faure maintains that the originally highly complex nature of Zen is reduced in Suzuki's description to an over-simplified, mythical picture of what Zen was in the past. Precisely, in the Zen monasteries a rigidly hierarchical order prevailed, and it is really paradoxical, Faure says, that, in the modern approach to the practice, which is here in question, the Zen masters claim that there is no hierarchy, while at the same time they do not permit their teaching authority to be questioned.[206] Another authority who should be mentioned here is the Italian scholar Paolo Vicentini, who is a philosopher by discipline but has written numerous articles on the relations between philosophy and Buddhism and is the co-founder of a Buddhist center in Venice. Vicentini describes Suzuki as having "an image of Zen and of his masters that was not only idealized and stereotypical but also biased."[207]

Such comments from experts in the field must of course be disappointing for those who have encountered Zen Buddhism via such authors as Philippe Kapleau, Karlfried Graf Dürckheim, Alan Watts, or D.T. Suzuki himself. The students will surely have to ask themselves what it really is or was that they have been taught and are still being taught by the "Zen masters" who are famous in the West. Is it perhaps only a more or less effective spiritual technique which, however, has precious little to do with classical and traditional Zen Buddhism?

It should furthermore be mentioned that Suzuki himself was never a recognized Zen teacher and always remained a lay practitioner.[208] His study of classical Zen Buddhism was restricted to weekends and holidays during his student years. As Robert Sharf emphasizes, ten years earlier this type of study would not even have been possible for a layman.[209] In Suzuki's case it was only possible because his teacher Shaku Sōen (author of the first book on Zen in English) was very interested in and strongly influenced by Western culture, and because he had a university education.

Jørn Borup, an expert on Japanese religious history at Aarhus University in Denmark, takes a middle course between Suzuki's critics and apologists.[210] He maintains that Suzuki must primarily be seen as an "apologetic voice of tradition, he interpreted and revealed." From this point of view, he was a Zen theologian with many illuminating insights and had an emic approach, that is to say one informed by a perspective from within Buddhism. Borup perceives Suzuki as someone influenced by both East and West, a "translator of cultures" who transmitted Zen to the West and then, to some extent, re-transmitted it back to Japan, thus helping the country to rediscover its own sense of identity, which had been eroded by the increasingly Western influence. Instead of de-mystifying the Orient, as called for by Edward Said in *Orientalism* (1978), Suzuki had re-mystified and re-orientalized the Orient.

Yet, if one is to understand fully why Suzuki's conception of Zen Buddhism was so idealized in a distinctly Western way and probably therefore so well received in the West, one must realize how strongly he was influenced by Western mystical thinking. The Western influences on Suzuki included the monism of Paul Carus and especially the teachings of the Swedish mystic Emmanuel Swedenborg and those of the Theosophical Society. Suzuki in his early years was one of the key people responsible for the dissemination of Swedenborg's teachings in Japan. He traveled twice, in 1908 and 1911, to Europe as a guest of the Swedenborg Society and even translated some of the seer's work into Japanese.[211]

On the other hand, the influence of the Theosophical Movement on Suzuki remained for a long time unresearched. Recently, however, Adele S. Alego has thrown much light on this subject in her article "Beatrice Lane Suzuki and Theosophy in Japan."[212] In 1911 Suzuki married an American woman, Beatrice Erskine Hahn, in Yokohama, and the two of them subsequently spent many years in Japan. Beatrice's mother, Dr. Emma Hahn, was among the earliest followers of the Baha'i movement on the American East Coast. This fact is probably also significant, as she lived with the Suzuki family. In 1920 all three of them joined the Tokyo International Lodge of the Theosophical Society. In the same year the lodge was reorganized and D.T. Suzuki was elected president, as revealed in a letter of 25 September 1920 to the International Secretary of the Theosophical Society in Adyar, India. In 1921 his wife Beatrice was made acting secretary of the lodge, and the couple continued to be involved in the lodge until the 1930s. Suzuki is also reported to have been involved in the Theosophical Order of the Star, which wished to elevate Krishnamurti to the role of a world teacher.[213]

Suzuki's concept of Zen Buddhism was surely shaped by these various groups, all of which strove to promote mutual respect between religions and nations, with the ultimate goal of world brotherhood. Just as the teachings of these groups, being non-country-specific, could be disseminated world-wide, so Suzuki wanted to make Zen Buddhism internationally known and acceptable. Consequently he had to present it as a *Weltanschauung* and path of salvation that transcended religious and national boundaries, playing down those aspects of the religion that were specific to Japan and the Japanese historical context.

In doing so he presented his own personal and idealized view of Zen and Japanese culture, as though they embodied a universal truth. The same criticism, however, can be levelled at many other people who write about political and philosophical issues. The tendency to overestimate one's own perceptiveness and to be over-enthusiastic in the pursuit of one's ideals is not one that can be ascribed to Suzuki alone.

However, the debate about Suzuki's understanding of Zen was not the only controversy involving the Japanese scholar. There was also the matter of his political stance. The Buddhist expert Brian Daizen Victoria has accused Suzuki of having supported Japan's militaristic system during the Second World War through his writings, especially through his interpretation of *bushido*, the traditional ethic of the samurai, with its glorification of heroic death. This, Victoria argues, was fully in line with the aims of the imperial army leadership.[214]

However, this accusation also requires a few words of clarification, and once again I would like to refer to the work of Robert H. Sharf. The Meiji era (1868–1912) was characterized by great upheaval and rapid Westernization of the country. This led to certain ideologists of the regime criticizing Japanese Buddhism as being not only backward, but also corrupt, parasitical, superstitious, and detrimental to modernization and technical progress in the country. Buddhism was even accused of being "foreign" (Indian) and contrary to the true culture and spiritual essence of Japan. However, there soon came a counter-reaction. A few university-educated Buddhists of a decidedly modern turn of mind vehemently rejected these threatening criticisms. While admitting a certain amount of corruption and degradation, they pointed out all the more emphatically to the original, pure, spiritual sources of Buddhism, from which the current religious leaders had deviated.

At that time Japanese universities in general were strongly under Western influence. Thus the defenders of Buddhism were also familiar with the criticisms leveled at institutional Christianity by European philosophers such as Schleiermacher, Dilthey, and Nietzsche. Inspired by these writers, they set about trying to free Japanese Buddhism also from its institutional encrustation. The result was the so-called "new Buddhism." Suzuki's teacher Shaku Sōen was a member of this movement.

In their eagerness to present Buddhism as something no longer backward but rather rational, modern, socially relevant, and of practical value to the country, they compliantly followed the nationalistic ideological tenets of the regime. This inevitably influenced the character of the "new Buddhism." With Japan's rise to the status of a modern colonial power to be reckoned with throughout Asia, the previously negative connotation of Buddhism as something "foreign" actually became an advantage, since Buddhism could now serve as a cultural bridge to all parts of Asia. Then, with the increasing success of Japan's armed forces (the defeat of China in 1895 and of Russia in 1905), military circles in Japan increasingly attributed these victories to the "original Japanese" *bushido*, the so-called "way of the warrior" as practiced by the samurai caste, with its virtues of fearlessness in the face of death, self-discipline, and unreserved devotion to one's superiors, which evinces certain parallels with Zen.

These notions were reinforced by numerous legends drawn from Japanese history. From here it was only a short step to regarding *bushido* as the essence of the Japanese way of life altogether, although the term *bushido* hardly ever appeared in Japanese writings before the modern period.[215] This perception not only took hold in Japan but also became widely held in the West. At the same time there appeared the first writings in English on Zen Buddhism, completing the Western picture of Japan as a land of high spirituality, great selflessness, and aesthetic refinement.

The spirit of Zen and that of *bushido* go well together. Suzuki himself gives several reasons for this, including the following:

> The military mind, being ... comparatively simple and straightforward and not at all addicted to [intellectual] philosophizing, finds a congenial spirit in Zen. This is probably one of the main reasons for the close relationship between Zen and the Samurai. Secondly Zen discipline is simple, direct, self-reliant, self-denying; its ascetic tendency goes well with the fighting spirit.[216]

The third reason he gives is that since the Middle Ages there has been a close connection between Zen and the Japanese ruling strata.

It is therefore not surprising that during the Second World War Suzuki, with his "new Buddhist" patriotism and his conception of *bushido* and Zen, did in fact follow the political and ideological line of the Emperor and his military leaders. However, according to Brian Victoria, after the war and his sojourn in the United States, Suzuki underwent a distinct change of outlook and subsequently blamed Shinto primarily for Japan's military excesses. Nevertheless, he later conceded what he described as a lack of Buddhist spirituality on the part of the Zen masters of that period, and hence admitted a certain degree of guilt, albeit of a collective nature. In this connection, Victoria is equally critical of

Suzuki's influence on Western orientalists, notably Giuseppe Tucci, who wrote an enthusiastic foreword to a work by Suzuki dealing in detail with *bushido*.[217]

Another person who evinces a very negative view of Suzuki is the brilliant, multilingual writer, scholar, ex-Communist, ex-Zionist, and parapsychologist Arthur Koestler. In his book *The Lotus and the Robot* he takes to task the Western understanding of Buddhism. Further, in an article in the literary magazine *Encounter*, he accuses the Suzuki variety of Buddhism of "intellectual and moral nihilism."[218] Instead of promoting a fruitful collaboration between intuition and reason, it attempts to "castrate reason." For Koestler, although he was certainly no apologist for absolute rationalism, the anti-rational component of Suzuki's Zen Buddhism went much too far, evincing a "flexibility" that could equally well adapt itself to "anarchism, Communism or democracy," and even to the gas chambers.

The general picture of Suzuki that emerges here is hardly consistent with the myth of the wise old Zen master that is still current in the West. However, it would be equally wrong to conclude that Suzuki deliberately misled people through his writings. Like others—in fact like all of us—he was a child of his times and most probably he was filled with the best intentions. It is just that Suzuki's personal charisma and his contacts with "New Age" circles and spiritual movements such as Esalen have also contributed to making a legend out of him.

The widely acclaimed "Zen philosopher" Alan Watts even called Suzuki "about the most gentle and enlightened person I have ever known." Thomas Merton, the Christian Zen monk and mystic, compared him with Einstein and Gandhi. The psychologist Erich Fromm described him as "an authority purely by his being." For Christmas Humphreys, a judge and co-founder of the Buddhist Society in England, Suzuki was quite simply "the greatest Buddhist mind of [the] century." Harry Oldmeadow of LaTrobe University in Bendigo, Australia, who collected these and other tributes to Suzuki, adds that one thing about Suzuki stands out again and again, namely his "saintly qualifications as a person—simplicity, humour, generosity, humility, his freedom from egoism, from selfish desires and ambitions."[219]

Harry Oldmeadow, however, also accepts Sharf's criticisms of Suzuki up to a point, but what he finds upsetting is the generally derogatory and disparaging impression conveyed by Sharf's essay.[220] In his opinion this is mainly because Sharf sees D.T. Suzuki as being primarily a religious teacher and does not accept him as "rightful" scholar of religion, since Suzuki breaks one of the iron rules of modern comparative religion, namely that the discipline must remain totally neutral. The scholar of religion must not see religion as something *sui generis* with a core of common religious experience, independent of time and place and transcending what can be grasped by the human intellect. And heaven forbid that religion in this sense should touch the scholar of religion in his essential self, as was manifestly the case with Suzuki. Here again we see the basic problem of religious phenomenology raising its head, the problem associated with Eliade and with Eranos in general, as dealt with by Steven Wasserstrom in his book *Religion after Religion*, which also vehemently attacks the "essentialist" concept of religion.

In this section on Suzuki I may have drawn too much attention to critical comments about him. I have done so mainly because such comments are much less well known than the admiring testimonies about him, and they therefore call for a more detailed explanation. I would not, however, wish my readers to form a false and one-sided view. Deisetz Teitaro Suzuki was undoubtedly, as even his critic Robert Sharf emphasizes, an exceptional person who inspired generations of philosophers, theologians, artists, and scholars, including such prominent names as Martin Heidegger, Karl Jaspers, Arnold Toynbee, and Aldous Huxley.[221] Sharf also underlines the fact that Suzuki, besides his more popular works, was also a talented philologist who made a considerable contribution to the scholarly study of early Zen manuscripts. This becomes evident when one considers his complete works in Japanese, which comprise some thirty-two volumes.

Giuseppe Tucci

Another newcomer, Giuseppe Tucci, deserves a few additional words, although he spoke only once at Eranos. This was because, as he explained, "the tyranny of research" forced him "to spend many months of the year in Asia." He much regretted not being able to come regularly to the annual meetings, "for it is difficult to find a more appropriate, learned and at the same time relaxed setting, where problems of direct relevance to life can be discussed in an atmosphere of intellectual freedom and scholarly depth." Especially in an era when the emphasis was placed on the natural sciences, he considered it a "noble undertaking" to concern ourselves with the "high hopes and great fears" that accompany us "on this short journey between the two mysteries that we call life."[222]

Giuseppe Tucci can undoubtedly be considered the greatest Italian orientalist of the twentieth century. His most eminent but very fair critic Gustavo Benavides, of Villanova University in America, has recognized that "Tucci's accomplishments are such that only a fraction of them would be enough to satisfy most scholars."[223] As Mircea Eliade reports in his *Indian Diary*, Tucci is said to have slept only two or three hours a night or not at all.[224] He received countless honors and decorations from learned societies, universities (including eight honorary doctorates), and state institutions in many different countries.[225]

Giuseppe Tucci was born in 1894 in Macerata in the Marche region of central Italy. At the age of eleven he was already studying ancient Hebrew, at twelve Sanskrit and at thirteen ancient Persian. Tibetan only followed when he was twenty, by which time he had already published his first scholarly work in Latin.[226] He took part in the First World War, finishing with the rank of lieutenant, and only a year after the end of the war he took a doctorate at the University of Rome. Despite his early academic success he was no friend of the average university curriculum, which seemed to him dry, monotonous, and designed to teach peripheral things. Thus, throughout his life he saw himself rather as an autodidact. From 1925 to 1930 he lived in India, where he taught Chinese, Tibetan, and Italian at the universities of Calcutta and Shantiniketan.

There, via the Sanskrit professor Carlo Formichi, he also made friends with the poet and winner of the Nobel Prize for Literature, Rabindranath Tagore. In 1926 Formichi arranged for Tagore to be invited to Italy, where he was received with great fanfare and twice met Benito Mussolini. Despite a certain degree of skepticism, Tagore was impressed with Mussolini and spoke well of him.[227] In India he also met Mohandas "Mahatma" Gandhi, whom he came to admire,[228] as well as the philosopher and subsequent President of India, Sarvepalli Radhakrishna, and the poet and "spiritual father of Pakistan," Mohammad Iqbal.

His adventurous expeditions to Tibet, Nepal, Pakistan, Afghanistan, and Iran have become legendary. Like Sven Hedin, he was a great explorer, crossing deserts, climbing mountains, and even fighting off brigands with a gun.[229] As an archaeologist he discovered priceless remains from the past, analyzed them, and, in the case of written documents, translated them. His bibliography runs to three hundred sixty titles, including dozens of books, many of which were written for a wider public. He was also a great bibliophile, and Mircea Eliade describes his "gigantic library" for which he had to construct a special building.[230]

Tucci was distinguished by his deep sympathy for spiritual values other than his own, a trait that indicates his genuinely comprehensive religious perspective and his profound humanism. His specialty was Buddhism in its various forms. The scholar of religion Edward Conze, with whom he worked, maintained furthermore that Tucci was "also a believing and to some extent even practising Buddhist." Moreover, Tucci believed that he had been a Tibetan in a previous life. Only this could account for his exceedingly friendly reception by the Tibetans.[231] Not only was he able to travel, with the support of the local authorities, unhindered throughout the country between 1927 and 1949, but he was also allowed to buy enormous quantities of art objects and texts and to take them out of the country. Tucci used his own money for these purchases. However, during the Fascist period the regime also provided very generous support.

In 1930 he assumed the chair for Chinese at the University of Naples, a year after being made a member of the Italian Academy. Finally, in 1932 he was given the chair for Indian Religion and Philosophy at the University of Rome, which he held until his retirement in 1969.

In 1933 Tucci played a leading role in the foundation of the Italian Institute for the Middle and Far East (IsMEO) together with his friend and university colleague Giovanni Gentile, who was minister of education in the first Fascist cabinet and was murdered by Communist partisans in 1944. At that time the Fascist state had a strong interest in political and cultural collaboration with the Far East, which was undoubtedly one of the motives behind the founding of the Institute, of which Gentile was the first president. Tucci became president only in 1947 and kept the position until 1978.

Here some discussion is called for regarding Tucci's involvement with the Fascist regime, bearing in mind that the already mentioned author Brian Victoria, himself a Zen expert and Zen priest, has accused Tucci of having openly supported Fascism.[232] Victoria provides no proof of this, but rather refers to the findings of Gustavo Benavides, who has already been mentioned. The latter, however, is considerably more cautious in his statements and merely points out that Tucci had succumbed to the *Zeitgeist*, which (at least in its rhetoric) valued heroism and willingness to risk death higher than material well-being. This comes across less in Tucci's scholarly work than in his more journalistic writings (as Benavides calls them) about Japan, Zen Buddhism, *bushido*, and the samurai—writings that evince the strong influence of D.T. Suzuki. These pieces were written between 1937 and 1943, in other words, to put it crudely, in wartime, when Tucci, like so many others, was more nationalistic and bellicose in attitude than he was later on in peacetime. But to equate such an attitude automatically with the political system of Fascism seems to me rather too reductionist.

However, what Benavides does correctly point out is that Tucci nurtured certain attitudes, such as belief in the mystical identity of life and death or the need to sacrifice the ego—attitudes that lent themselves to exploitation by a regime that did not shy away from violence. Benavides calls these attitudes "mystical clichés." The fact that Tucci shared this "mystical" outlook, however, cannot be denied. Nor can his fascination with death, which his critics have ascribed to him.[233] There is a distinct affinity between mystical ecstasy and death (the death of the individual ego and its replacement by transcendental concepts or higher states of being). This, however, as Benavides points out, can be derived not only from the Samurai and the notion of the mystical death of the ego, but also from the well-known story in the *Bhagavadgītā* where the god Krishna tells the warrior Arjuna that death and warfare belong to his task in life, that is, to his *dharma*.

However, Benavides shows that this was only one side of Tucci. The other side was equally fixated on logic, and Tucci saw it as one of his most important tasks to translate old Indian treatises on logic.[234] He stressed that nothing could be more erroneous than to see India only as a land of mystics and ascetics, willing to renounce the pleasures and power games of life. Accordingly, one of Tucci's first significant works was a history of materialistic philosophy in India.[235] One can judge the extent of his enthusiasm and the magnitude of his achievements in this area when one knows that he translated some of the oldest and most important treatises of Buddhist logic, such as the *Tarkaśāstra* and the *Upāyahçdaya*, from Tibetan and Chinese, not into any Western language but back into Sanskrit, that is to say, into the language of the original texts, which had become lost over the course of the centuries.[236] Thus he not only gave back to India a part of its ancient spiritual heritage but also, by translating back into the original language, he facilitated a clearer understanding of these texts, as they were based on the thought and speech patterns of Sanskrit. His love of clarity and logical thinking could be traced back to his repeated reading of the *Summa theologiae* of Saint Thomas Aquinas, to which he returned continually throughout the whole period from his school days up to his death.[237]

The realistic, down-to-earth side of Tucci also accounts for his often sobering descriptions of Tibet, which have surprised many of his readers. Although Tucci traveled through Tibet at a time when it was still almost untouched, he observed to his own surprise that, apart from a few exceptions, there was a conspicuous lack of spirituality and wisdom. He attributed this partly to the very number of monasteries ("elephantiasis" was the word Tucci used). In such a vast multitude, he said, any creative belief had expired. Everywhere he saw only the observance of time-honored norms and rules, which had extinguished the living spirit. And the ancient texts were only considered sacred because there was no longer anyone who understood their true meaning.[238] He also condemned the poverty of the indigenous population and the autocratic and indifferent behavior of the local monks and abbots.

However, in contrast to this rather severe analysis, he occasionally fell back into the typical Western habit of romanticizing the Orient that he himself had warned against.[239] On these occasions he enthused about the general connectedness with the cosmos, how time stands still, how the essential relationship is not between human beings but rather between them and God, and how there is a general atmosphere of contemplation and continuous inner peace. Because of these two contrasting sides of Tucci it would be wrong, as Benavides emphasizes, to "regard him merely as one of the exponents of a clearly anti-modern, authoritarian, and irrationalist version of the *philosophia perennis*."[240] Similarly, he could not be called a political opportunist.

Rather, Benavides sees Tucci's attitude towards the Fascist regime "as the result of a deep antagonism toward a fragmented modern world: like many others, he seems to have believed for a time that in the exaltation of violence, in the dissolution of the individual in the will of the nation … one surpasses … the limits of time, and the illusory limits of individuality."[241] Similarly, his romantic view of the Orient stemmed from "a deep dissatisfaction with modernity" which "led him to imagine an Orient in which he could always find the wholeness no longer available in the West."[242] Here it is appropriate to quote an observation of Tucci's recorded by Raniero Gnoli: "The uniformity of customs and traditions, the monotony that enchains us, the levelling process that crushes everything in its path … these things make our days cheerless … Nowhere is there any solitude, everywhere someone is watching us, poking his nose into our lives and even into the secrets of our minds and hearts."[243]

In theory Tucci wanted nothing to do with politics. "If there is anything," he wrote "that I detest, it is politics in all countries and all territories."[244] In practice, however, Tucci maintained good relations with certain sections of the Fascist elite, which is understandable given the position that he held and the honors that he received. Giovanni Gentile, the philosopher and theoretician of the Fascist state, has already been mentioned. Tucci also knew the German major general and university professor Karl Haushofer, who was military attaché in Tokyo from 1908 to 1910 and, after the failed Munich putsch of 1923, several times visited Rudolf Hess in Landsberg prison, where Hitler was also detained. For somewhat obscure reasons Haushofer has over time become a legendary figure, who is credited with having had an important although more or less occult influence on National Socialism. He is said, for example, to have made a mysterious visit to Tibet, for which there is in fact no historical evidence. Any significant political influence can also be ruled out. After all, Hitler knew that Haushofer's wife, Martha, was Jewish.[245]

In 1937 and 1941 Haushofer gave two lectures on Japan at IsMEO, of which Tucci was a co-founder, and on the second occasion Tucci himself made some introductory remarks.[246] Tucci definitely had a high regard for Haushofer, who was described by the renowned historian Hans-Adolf Jacobsen as a "universally educated, cosmopolitan, artistically gifted and spirited scholar with an almost encyclopaedic knowledge and an astonishing memory."[247] And it is most likely that Tucci took from Haushofer certain important insights for his theory of Eurasia, especially as Tibet was central to this theory. Eurasia as a geographical, spiritual, and, probably, also political unity was one of Tucci's favorite ideas.[248]

In connection with Tucci's political involvement during the Fascist period, another matter should be mentioned, which the Italian psychologist Aldo Carotenuto has recorded, namely the fact that Giuseppe Tucci was responsible for freeing Ernst Bernhard, founder of the analytical psychology movement in Italy, from an internment camp. After the enactment of the Italian race laws in 1940, Bernhard, as a Jew, was arrested and eventually placed in a camp at Ferramonti near Cosenza. Tucci, who knew the psychologist through their discussions about mandalas, intervened successfully through friends, leading finally to Bernhard's release after less than a year of confinement.[249]

On the other hand, it should also be mentioned that Tucci belonged to the group of people—not exactly small in number—who openly supported the Italian racial laws.[250] As already mentioned, these included also Raffaele Pettazzoni, who was otherwise regarded as more or less a socialist. Probably Tucci was another example of the many people who generally welcomed racial laws, but wished to exempt personal acquaintances who were affected.

In recent years Tucci has been the object of hefty discussion on account of his rapport with Fascism—as in the case of Jung, Eliade, and others. This subject has been addressed by Enrica Garzilli, an indologist, expert on Tucci, founder of the online magazine *International Journal of Tantric Studies* and the *Journal of South-East Asian Women Studies*, and author of a forthcoming thousand-page study of Italian foreign policy in Asia from Mussolini to Andreotti, containing countless previously unpublished documents as well as hitherto unknown material about Tucci. On her blog, she published a letter from Gilda Tucci, granddaughter of Giuseppe, defending her grandfather.[251] Gilda Tucci points out that his literary work alone proves how much he valued foreign cultures (which is also confirmed by the brief *curriculum vitae* given above). It would therefore be absurd, she says, to call him a racist. She maintains also that his truly immense collection of thangkas, oriental objects, and original manuscripts would never have come to Europe and would probably have been lost irretrievably had Tucci not cooperated with the Fascist regime. Although it was worth millions, Tucci never sold this collection, but left it to the Italian state with the result that students from all over the world can now work on its unique contents.

In another of her blog entries Enrica Garzilli also mentions Tucci's sexual hyperactivity—a trait found in many creative researchers and artists. Tucci was not only married three times but, according to his photographer and fellow ethnologist Fosco Maraini, who accompanied him on many journeys, he was "a great lover of beauty in all its forms" and especially "appreciated Indian women at close quarters."[252]

Giuseppe Tucci's penchant for "mystical clichés," as Benavides calls them, has already been touched upon. But Tucci's involvement went deeper than that, as Raniero Gnoli clearly points out in an essay written for the hundredth anniversary of Tucci's birth.[253] Tucci actually wanted to partake of those "mystical" experiences that he so often wrote about. Thus he was initiated into various Tantric schools in India and Tibet and took part in their complex rituals. During the expedition to Tibet in 1935 Tucci even went so far as to participate in the "subtle liturgies" that ultimately shake the foundations of the ego which determines our perceptions, triggering off totally different ways of seeing the world.[254] Furthermore, although he always had an Italian doctor with him on his expeditions, he in no way scorned the help of local magicians. Once in the More Desert in Tibet he suddenly fell seriously ill and had a magician called from a nearby tribe. The magician spoke some prayers, drew a mandala, and fell into a trance. After waking up, he told Tucci that a local deity of the land was angry with him because he had pitched his tent on sacred ground. In order to cure himself, all that would be necessary would be to move his tent, speak some magical formulae, and offer the angry god something to eat. Tucci did as he was bidden, and the next day his fever had gone.

Tucci stated openly:

> No, I am not proud of my rational side, which can prove anything: with the most impeccable logic it can prove both the existence and non-existence of God. What remains certain, however, is the mystery, not as a limit but as a possession, as the sun of our divine loneliness … I have tried to travel not only on the earth but also into our own inner depths with their frightening and lavish treasures. But of these one should not speak. They are treasures that one keeps in the depths of one's soul, and the more one speaks about them the dimmer they become.[255]

John Snelling, general secretary of the Buddhist Society in London and himself a great traveler around Asia, writes about Tucci in his book on pilgrimages to the sacred mountain of Kailash. He emphasizes Tucci's Buddhist outlook and believes that the Italian undertook his expeditions to Kailash more as a pilgrim than as a researcher and consequently was able to gather priceless knowledge. Because of his deep personal empathy, he enjoyed a high degree of trust on the part of the sādhus, the holy men of the region. As an example, Snelling mentions Sādhu Bhumānānda, with whom Tucci felt a deep spiritual kinship and with whom he undertook various journeys.

The Italian Buddhist journal *Pāramitā* devoted an entire article to Tucci's religious and spiritual worldview.[256] The author, Corrado Pensa, credits him with a special kind of "religious intelligence" in understanding spiritual interconnections. Thus the explorer of the Himalayas became also an explorer of the inner realms. In this connection Pensa quotes various passages in Tucci's work emphasizing the importance of a "genuine inner empathy" for the understanding of Asiatic traditions, even for the scholar, since the Buddhist scriptures are not just abstract doctrinal writings that can be interpreted through purely philological tools. Rather they provide the means to spiritual self-realization. However, Tucci was in no way an uncritical advocate for the spiritual orientalization of Europe. On the contrary, like Jung, whom he much admired,[257] he warned of the possible spiritual disruptions that not infrequently occur when Westerners engage in oriental meditational practices.

Giuseppe Tucci's liking for mystically or esoterically minded people also evinced itself in Europe, for example in the choice of his colleagues. Thus in 1950, when he founded the religious studies journal *East and West*, he installed as editor Massimo Scaligero (pseudonym for Antonio Massimo Sgabelloni, 1906–80) and in 1955 promoted him to the position of overall director.

It was probably thanks to Scaligero that a much more famous and controversial esotericist and philosopher, Julius Evola, contributed to *East and West* from the very first issue[258] and altogether wrote fifteen articles and three book reviews.[259] Here it should be mentioned, however, that Evola and Tucci had already known each other since at least 1925 via the Lega Teosofica Independente Ultra (Independent Theosophical League Ultra) in Rome, where they were both lecturers.

Olga Fröbe was given Tucci's address by Rudolf Otto as early as 1933, and already there was talk of inviting him to Eranos. In 1936 Tucci declared his willingness to attend, but was prevented from doing so by illness. She finally visited him in Rome in 1938 with the intention of inviting him again, but this time he was in the midst of preparations for an expedition to Tibet. However, he gave her a number of his publications to take away with her, and she strongly hoped that he would at least write a contribution to the yearbook, even if he could not attend the meeting itself.[260]

After his retirement from his professorship Tucci withdrew to a country estate near Tivoli, where he died in the spring of 1984. His pupil and friend Raniero Gnoli has preserved his last statement:

> When the Law that governs the worlds—whether it be the Dharma of the Hindus or Buddhists or the Tao of the Chinese—begins to weaken, then the saviours will descend to what remains of the extinguished universe, in order to revive and reawaken it in its primal worth. I am not ashamed to confess that I too believe this. The fact that science does not support me has no meaning for me, for I am more inclined to believe my masters, with whom I have often spoken in their solitary abodes on the peaks of the Tibetan mountains—those masters, walled in or locked away in their cells, who did not know who I was, but had known that one day a pilgrim from the west would come to seek them out in their voluntary seclusion, where they awaited the final dissolution in the supreme light. I have always placed more trust in what they revealed to me than in our science. If we insist on continuing to live as we do now then we shall become standard-bearers of the Apocalypse, whose imminence is foretold by all religions—that moment at the end of the aeons,

when human folly has exceeded all measure and everything will be destroyed in a great conflagration.[261]

Ernst Benz

One of the very few German scholars who carried out and published serious work on esotericism, even after the Second World War, was Ernst Benz, who also spoke at Eranos for the first time in 1953. Rudolf Otto had recommended him as early as 1934 to Mrs. Fröbe and described him as a "brilliant mind."[262] Ernst Benz was born in 1907 at Friedrichshafen on Lake Constance.[263] Initially he studied classical philology and archaeology and, in addition, immersed himself in the study of a whole range of modern European languages and later several oriental ones. In 1927 he met Ernesto Buonaiuti and was deeply impressed by the latter's actively lived Christianity. Prompted by Buonaiuti, he eventually decided to study theology. Under the influence of his teacher Erich Seeberg, who had made an intensive study of Gottfried Arnold and the mysticism of his age, Benz also began to study the history of mysticism. In particular, his great books on Emanuel Swedenborg and Jacob Boehme deserve to be highlighted.

It was thanks to a seminar on the mysticism of the Apostle Paul, given by Gustav Adolf Deissmann, that Benz came to the firm view that one cannot talk about such higher realities unless one has experienced them oneself, for that would be like having "almost drunk champagne."[264] To "almost drink" champagne is the same as not drinking and does not enable one to measure the effects of drinking. Benz therefore practiced meditation exercises and saw mysticism as a life's task. From 1935 he worked as an auxiliary professor and from 1937 as a regular professor in the theological faculty at the University of Marburg.

At this time Benz came into contact with National Socialism, which was exerting an increasingly strong influence on university life. In 1936 he planned a protest letter to the London *Times* against what he saw as one-sided reporting by foreign journalists on the German *Kirchenkampf* (the conflict within the churches regarding their stance towards the NS regime). The Evangelical Church was divided between the so-called "German Christians" and the *Bekennende Kirche* (roughly, the "professing church"). The latter rejected any interference by the state in church affairs. However, this did not necessarily imply opposition to the National Socialist regime, as many members of the *Bekennende Kirche* were also members of the Nazi Party. Benz belonged to the German Christian faction and acted as spokesman for the circle founded by his teacher Erich Seeberg.[265]

In 1937 Benz successfully applied for membership of the Nazi Party.[266] Like many other professors he probably thought that, as a party member, he would be able to use his influence in the interests of the theological profession. Soon afterwards, however, the Party decided that it no longer wanted any clergymen in its ranks and pressed them to opt for an "honorable resignation." Evidently the party feared that its absolute claim to authority would not be respected by the clergy. On the other hand, Benz protested against the measures taken by the *Reichsschrifttumskammer* (the state office concerned with books and publications) against the distribution of books on theology and religious subjects through general bookshops.[267] The party wanted to restrict their sale to "confessional" bookshops and thus prevent them from having a wider influence.

Benz's writings are unusually extensive, encompassing hundreds of articles as well as some fifty books and monographs, on subjects ranging from Christianity to New Age movements in the United States, and from the philosopher Schelling to the founder of animal magnetism therapy, Franz Anton Mesmer.[268] The many-faceted writer Gerhard Wehr, who knew Benz well, has commented, "Even parapsychology, Brazilian spiritualism and the development of the modern belief in UFOs came within the reach of his almost boundless interests."[269]

As a pupil and companion of the Marburg scholar Rudolf Otto, Benz obviously could not sympathize with the de-mythologizing agenda of Rudolf Bultmann, who also taught at Marburg. Neither was he interested in the then fashionable dialectical theology of Karl Barth, who wanted to rid Protestant theology of anything mystical. Altogether Benz struggled against the growing secularization of the world and lamented the loss of modern man's faculty for perceiving transcendental realities.

The traditionalist philosopher and René Guenon follower *sui generis* Leopold Ziegler was, like the well-known theologian Teilhard de Chardin, among the people to whom Benz felt particularly indebted.[270] Towards the end of the 1940s Benz launched the respected journal *Zeitschrift für Religions- und Geistesgeschichte* together with Hans-Joachim Schoeps, a pugnacious and at the same time highly erudite person, well versed in the fields of politics, history, and many other areas. The journal continues to be published today under the co-editorship of Joachim Schoeps' son, Julius H. Schoeps. On his numerous journeys throughout the world, often as a visiting professor, Benz was always at pains to understand other forms of piety, even though for him Christianity always came first. In particular, his encounters with Hinduism, Buddhism, and Shinto challenged him to seek new interpretations, but always looking for links and parallels with Christianity. Given such a background, it is not surprising that Ernst Benz was invited so often to speak at Eranos. He also lectured at the University of Saint John of Jerusalem,[271] inspired by Henry Corbin, and also at the conference of the Keyserling-Gesellschaft für freie Philosophie (Keyserling society for free philosophy) of 22–5 June 1963.[272] As Benz spoke out clearly and distinctly for a spiritualization of the world, he came under attack within his home university in the neo-Marxist late 1960s.[273]

Jean Daniélou

One further newcomer to Eranos in 1953 needs to be spoken about, namely Jean Daniélou, who was the only Eranos speaker ever to be made a cardinal in the Roman Catholic hierarchy—and will probably remain the only one, as members of the Catholic clergy have long since ceased to give lectures there. The career of this heterodox priest is at the same time an indication that Catholicism is much more open than its reputation would suggest. This is confirmed by a remark of Daniélou's. In his book *L'Oraison*, dealing with "prayer as a political problem," published in 1965, he wrote: "There is one religion in the West. This religion is ancient Greek, Roman, Celtic or Germanic Paganism … this Paganism is as good as all others and is not so remote from us. In fact we will never be anything other than converted Pagans … The Pagan is one who recognizes the divine through its manifestation in the visible world."[274]

In 1929 Daniélou entered the Jesuit order, was ordained a priest in 1938, and then taught at a Jesuit school and at the Catholic Institute in Paris. In 1962 he was called by Pope John XXIII to take part in the upcoming Vatican Council, and in 1969 he was made a member of the College of Cardinals. In 1972 he received a special honor for his wide-ranging writings, when he was elected to the French Academy.

In his books Daniélou aims to convey a Christianity that goes deeper than mere moral recipes. He looks with sympathy on myth as a manifestation of our search for God, who reveals himself in the *mysterium*, whereas he looks upon dry intellectualism as a betrayal of culture.[275] His strong opposition to existentialist philosophy, then so much in vogue, brought his name to the attention of a wider audience. At a time when it was fashionable to be a Marxist worker priest, Daniélou stood for a living and transcendent God, upheld an objective, church-based moral order, and condemned the notion of an individual, arbitrarily chosen set of ethical values.

A close friend of Daniélou was Louis Massignon, whom he revered as a mystic *par excellence*. In 1943 Massignon asked his friend to say a mass once a month for homosexuals. Daniélou agreed and kept his promise up to Massignon's death in 1962. Because of the aversion to homosexuality within the Church, these masses took place very discreetly.

Daniélou also devoted himself to giving spiritual care and practical help to prostitutes, and it was at the door of a prostitute's apartment (not her workplace in a bar) that he died of heart failure. This gave rise to much wry comment, although probably unfairly. The prostitute stated that Daniélou had been bringing money for a lawyer to defend her husband, who had been arrested a short time earlier. The police, after examining the evidence and questioning various parties, came to the conclusion that there was no reason to doubt the prostitute's version.

Jean Daniélou's brother, Alain Daniélou, commented on this episode as follows: "He [Jean] died like a saint. Saints are not people whom one decks with honours, but rather those on whom one spits with scorn." And in his own autobiography Alain emphasized that his brother had always supported criminals, prisoners, and women of the street. He added that he [Alain] would have been pleased if his brother Jean had indeed, at the end of his life, known the "pleasures of the flesh," as many people insinuated.[276]

The last remark is understandable, as Alain went as a professing homosexual to India, converted to the Shaivite tradition,[277] became an expert on Tantra, wrote among many others a book on the phallus, and translated the famous *Kama Sutra*. He also spoke out sharply against Gandhi, criticizing the Western public which adulates the "hypocritical" Mahatma (his real first name was Mohandas) Gandhi purely out of modern humanitarian considerations and not for traditional religious reasons.[278] As a leading world expert on Indian music, Daniélou enjoyed friendly contact over the course of his life with Rabindranath Tagore, Jawaharlal Nehru, Yehudi Menuhin, André Gide, Jean Cocteau, and Igor Stravinsky.[279]

Alain Daniélou was invited to Eranos by Henry Corbin, but came only once, as he found the conference "boring and pretentious, with psycho-mystical tendencies that were far removed from human reality."[280] In this connection it is worth mentioning that he described Corbin as a true Sufi, although Corbin himself never spoke of this. Mircea Eliade, on the other hand, he saw as a man of external knowledge without any real spiritual experience.

In conclusion to this account of the 1953 meeting, again I would like to list the distinguished members of the audience, as entered in the Eranos guest book for that year, namely Lucy Heyer, the first but thwarted biographer of C.G. Jung; the scholar of religion Joachim Wach; the sculptor Paul Speck; the Maecenas and esotericist Fritz Allemann; the mythologist Joseph Campbell; the psychoanalyst and developmental psychologist René Spitz (perhaps a surprise participant for many); the yoga expert Jacques Masui; Eduard von der Heydt; and (perhaps another surprise) Erich Maria Remarque, author of *All Quiet on the Western Front*.

Walter Robert Corti and the Platonic Academy

In 1953 the celebrated journal *Psyche*, co-edited by Alexander Mitscherlich, devoted several pages to an article in praise of Eranos by Walter Robert Corti, whom we have already encountered as a long-standing participant.[281] He later also spoke at Eranos, and nearly became a business partner of Olga Fröbe. Corti saw Eranos as being in the tradition of the Platonic Academy, which he deemed to be the "highest form and eternal model of all sodalities, whether educational or involving a shared way of life."[282] He placed Fröbe deservedly at the center of Eranos, which, he affirmed, owed its existence entirely to the "resolute effectiveness" of this "intuitive woman." Corti emphasized Mrs. Fröbe's great talents and strong ability to "endow her spiritual experiences and intuitions with graphic and forceful expressions," a quality which was "especially precious" in building up Eranos. The aim of the meetings, he said, was to play an educative role for humanity, whereby "the speakers and the audience formed a community of searchers and knowers" in which "all that was expected of them was honesty and openness of mind." At the same time Corti emphasized the importance of Western methodology in the study of the religious symbolism of different peoples and epochs. Thus he saw the Eranos meetings, since their inception, as "a reflection of the struggle of the rational western mind to interpret the mythical, gnostic symbols as manifestations springing from the soul's deepest reality." He saw it as unavoidable that, as one worked with these archetypes, they would begin to act of their own accord, which would account for the unity and group dynamics of the meetings.

Corti's analysis is particularly significant, coming from a long-standing participant who had written several times about Eranos and moreover was close to Olga Fröbe. Corti, born in Zurich in 1910, intended to follow a medical career, but broke off his studies. While still a young man he came into contact with C.G. Jung. In his early years he also met Richard Coudenhove-Kalergi, head of the Pan-European Movement, and subsequently became leader of its Youth section.[283] In 1942 the city of Zurich awarded him the Conrad Ferdinand Meyer Prize for cultural promotion, and in the same year he became co-editor of the Swiss cultural magazine *Du*, in which role he remained until 1958. He founded an Archive for Genetic Philosophy to pursue a special form of *Naturphilosophie* and the idea of what he called the *werdender Gott* (God in the process of becoming). The archive was later absorbed into the Academy for Ethical Research.[284] As founder of the children's village for orphans in the Swiss town of Trogen, he gained a certain degree of fame, which took him as far as the United States. He also organized philosophical conferences in Winterthur, especially on American philosophers such as Charles Peirce, John Dewey, and George Herbert Mead.[285] In 1975 he received the Albert Schweizer Prize in Brussels.

Despite the pragmatic tenor of this kind of philosophy, Corti saw the human being as an organ of God. And in other ways too he had an unmistakeably mystical strain, which comes across clearly in his essay "Vom kleinen und vom großen Ich" (On the lesser and the greater Self),[286] arguing that the greater self is part of the Being and embedded in the "totality" whereas the lesser self is characterized by the way in which it acts out of a restricted and egoistic consciousness. His cast of mind is also revealed by the foreword that he wrote for Bruno Goetz, the poet and translator, for whom poetry is of sacred origin.[287]

In his capacity as editor of the journal *Du*, he devoted a large part of the issue of April 1955 to Eranos. The issue was illustrated with pictures from mystical books and large-format photographs of prominent Eranos lecturers. Contributors included Jolande

Jacobi, Mircea Eliade, Adolf Portmann, Gershom Scholem, Karl Kerényi, Henry Corbin, and Aniela Jaffé. The opening piece was a letter from Fröbe to Walter Robert Corti on the question: "What is Eranos?" As she felt unable to give a rational answer, she simply described a walk around her garden, ending with the words: "So all of this is the garden of Eranos, a place of simplicity and blossom, serving as a venue where kindred spirits can meet. How the garden came to bear such a mighty cargo of the human spirit will for ever remain its own secret."

Walter Robert Corti contributed a lengthy programmatic introduction to this issue, written in his typically graphic and florid style:

> A cold, counting, calculating spirit has long since become the uncertain master of the world … a spirit of power-hungry megalomania that seeks to make everything fit its mould, a self-righteous tyrant and schoolmaster seized by noxious moods of zeal to enlighten the world, an iconoclast and *Kinderausbader*,[288] a murderous adversary of the soul. Wherever this spirit is at work it destroys the ground on which it lives. *Frau Seele*,[289] however, perishes in the standardized neon-lit rooms and hygienic nurseries … where chemically purified milk and psychologically purified education hold sway and where dreams are treated like an inner rash that must be eliminated … It's all a question of how the clarity of the mind comes to an understanding with the dark depths of the soul … The forces of the soul, when impelled by blind violence, are capable of destroying the works of the mind, while the forces of the mind can throttle and strangle the vitality of the soul—only through their loving marriage, the marriage of brain and heart, knowledge and life, perception and feeling, insight and belief, mind and soul, can wholeness and completeness be achieved.

We can assume that, with this appreciation of Eranos in a respected journal, a deeply held wish of Olga Fröbe's was fulfilled.

Up to now I have discussed the meetings individually, as each one brought new speakers who influenced the "inner form" of Eranos to varying degrees. Now we have reached the mid-1950s, and such a meticulous description of each Eranos meeting no longer serves our purpose. From this point I will therefore mainly concentrate on particular events. This does not mean, of course, that after this date no more important figures came to Eranos. However, their influence could no longer change the overall nature of Eranos in any fundamental way. Nevertheless, I shall discuss a number of further participants in some detail, especially those who contributed to the inner or outer continuity of the meetings or who extended and deepened the subject area of Eranos. Naturally I shall also consider the essential changes to the organization, which inevitably occurred when some influential participant withdrew or died.

By 1961 several noteworthy speakers had joined the Eranos community, including the Protestant theologian Paul Tillich and the president of the Bavarian Academy of Fine Arts, Emil Praetorius. With the latter's advent the artistic voices gained a stronger role in the choir. These were years in which the word *Mensch* (human being) featured repeatedly in the titles of the conferences, further underlining the way in which Eranos, the "meeting place between East and West," became increasingly a forum oriented to Western thinking.

Before appearing at Eranos in 1954, Paul Tillich had already received and taken up an invitation from Fröbe to deliver a lecture in 1936.[290] However, this is not recorded in either the corresponding yearbook or the meticulous Eranos indices compiled by Mrs. Magda Kerényi, for which reason I have not mentioned Tillich until now. The reason for the omission was the fact that Tillich's contribution—as well as that of a second speaker, the Jewish Jungian Max Westman—could not be included because the book would have been banned in its biggest market, Nazi Germany. Nevertheless, through the initiative and active financial assistance of Heinz Westman[291] the omission was rectified in 1986, and the two lectures were printed as a separate booklet.[292]

In a diary entry Tillich himself mentions his visit to Eranos in 1936.[293] Under the date 12 August 1936 he writes, "I speak for one and a half hours with a pause in the middle. Mrs Fröbe is on tenterhooks in case of political derailments. But none occur, even though my words are politically very radical."

Although Paul Tillich spoke only twice at Eranos he deserves more than a brief mention for two reasons: first, because, along with Karl Barth, he was probably the most important Protestant theologian of the twentieth century and second because his influence extended far beyond the field of theology.[294] Born in the province of Brandenburg,[295] where his father was a Protestant pastor, Paul Tillich was, from his youth, marked by religious leanings. At university he studied first philosophy, choosing to write his dissertation on a theme from Schelling related to religion. He then studied theology, returning to the subject of Schelling for his licentiate examination, writing on mysticism and consciousness of guilt in Schelling's philosophical development. After being ordained as a pastor he volunteered for service as a military chaplain at the start of the First World War in 1914. In 1924 he became Extraordinary Professor of Systematic Theology at the University of Marburg, an institution whose seminal influence I have already mentioned. In his very last lecture there, on *Die Bedeutung der Religionsgeschichte für den systematischen Theologen* (The significance of the study of religious history for the systematic theologian), he recalled holding a seminar on Schleiermacher which had aroused great unease on account of its approach based on comparative religion. (Schleiermacher and the German Romantic movement repeatedly acted as important footholds for the Eranos participants in their inner development.) There followed regular professorships in Dresden (for religious studies), Leipzig (for systematic theology), and Frankfurt am Main (for philosophy and sociology).

But Tillich was more than a theologian. According to Bernd Wikus, "Tillich saw himself as a bridge builder and mediator between philosophy, sociology and theology. The frontier was, for him, a place of decisive insight."[296] The influence of his thinking was felt by thinkers as diverse as Max Horkheimer and Theodor Adorno.

With the advent of the National Socialist regime in 1933 Paul Tillich was one of the first non-Jewish professors to lose a teaching position for political reasons. As advocate of a symbiosis of Christianity and socialism, he had edited a periodical entitled *Neue Blätter für den Sozialismus* and had even become a member of the Social Democratic Party.[297] Soon after his dismissal from the university he was prompted by warnings from good friends to emigrate to the United States, where he was able to continue his university career. In 1940 he took American citizenship. From the spring of 1942 to May 1944, probably as part of the American psychological warfare campaign, he gave a series of weekly speeches to the German people, which were broadcast over the Voice of America network.[298]

His professorships at Harvard and Chicago and his winning of the prestigious Peace Prize of the German Book Trade: these distinctions bear witness to the wide recognition accorded to this many-faceted German scholar. In Chicago he held a two-year series of joint seminars with Mircea Eliade which, as he acknowledged, had provided him with some important insights into the Christian rite.[299] As Tillich himself wrote, he considered himself as belonging to the "old, almost forgotten tradition, running from Duns Scotus and the nature philosophy of the Renaissance through Luther and Jacob Boehme to Oetinger and Schelling."[300] For him the experience of the holy in the here and now was the universal foundation of religion. And he believed that this holiness could be "seen, heard and grasped … despite its ecstatic-mystical character."[301] His particular concern was to balance the potentially destructive effects of ecstasy (possession by the divine spirit) with the rational structures of the human mind, which was also essentially the basic aim of Eranos. This preoccupation with the "ecstatic" element also led Tillich to promote a new appreciation of both Christian and non-Christian mysticism and even to suggest commensurate liturgical reforms.

Tillich attached particular importance to the concept of the "demonic," which he saw as an independent spiritual element in the world. He even counted his treatise on this subject as one of his most important writings.[302] Explaining why he believes the demonic element to be so dangerous to humanity, he writes: "The demonic principle manifests itself as an invasion of the center of the personality, as an attack on the synthesizing and unifying function of the mind, as an overarching and yet not unspiritual nature-like power. The inner locus from which it bursts forth is the *unconscious*" (original emphasis).[303] Thus the unconscious—whose products are so important for both modern psychology and art—was perceived by Tillich as the prime entry point for the demonic in man.[304] Unusually for that era, Tillich and his wife were both interested in modern art and psychoanalysis and had decorated their Dresden flat with modern paintings.

Hence also their friendship with the expressionist dancer Mary Wigman, who had a reputation for being "possessed" and who had moved from Monte Verità to Dresden in 1919. The Tillich family regularly attended the rehearsals of her dance group, and Tillich himself took courses in modern dance. Most probably it was partly the expression of the demonic in dance that interested him.[305]

Another speaker at Eranos who only spoke once (in 1956) was Laurens van der Post, into whom I can only go briefly, although his life would fill several volumes.[306] Van der Post was a South African who left his country because of its racial policies, a world traveler, a soldier for Great Britain, which awarded him a knighthood in 1980 for his services during the Second World War, an expert on Japan and on the Kalahari Desert. He made a series of expeditions into the Kalahari and left an immortal record of the desert and its bushmen in his books and reports as well as in his documentary film *The Lost World of the Kalahari*. He was also a gifted writer, whose works included novels, a long-standing friend of C.G. Jung, about whom he wrote a book,[307] and an advisor to Prince Charles and Margaret Thatcher. These are only some of the highlights of his life.

However, in 2002 a book appeared, claiming to expose many essential details of his life as mere "stories."[308] According to the author, van der Post's knowledge of Japan was minimal, he had done little of military consequence during the war, and his friendship with C.G. Jung had been rather superficial. Countless other colorfully recounted details of his life were allegedly either invented or borrowed from the lives of other people. The author of the book, the journalist and writer J.D.F. Jones, had access to family documents, carried out detailed archival research, and interviewed friends of van der Post, who had died in 1996 at the age of ninety. Interestingly, he still received the family's permission to publish. It therefore seems probable that his account is basically accurate.[309]

Nevertheless, Laurens van der Post was one of those rare people with the ability, through the spoken and written word (and, in his case, also through film), to speak directly to another's soul and to the deepest levels of the imagination. Anyone can confirm this by simply opening one of his books. Many people have drawn strength from them and gained a new perception of the Dark Continent. Equally indubitable are his efforts on behalf of the nonwhite population and his environmental work.

In his Eranos lecture he spoke about the culture of his native Africa, which until then had been treated somewhat as a poor relation at Eranos. In things to do with Africa, the really big name would actually have been Leo Frobenius, who had influenced many of the earlier Eranos speakers, but who had turned down an invitation to speak there himself. Laurens van der Post had, incidentally, also contributed to the journal *Antaios*, nominally edited by Mircea Eliade and Ernst Jünger.

The 1955, 1956, and 1958 meetings of Eranos featured lectures by Chang Chung-yuan, who followed Suzuki's lead in forging a link with oriental traditions of thought, especially Taoism, the belief system underlying the *I Ching* oracle, which was so important for Eranos. Chang was in close personal contact with Suzuki and it was through the mediation of the latter that he received a Bollingen scholarship to translate a Chinese Zen classic of the fifteenth century. Chang held professorships at several Chinese and American universities and thus was familiar with both Chinese and Western culture. He even lectured at Oxford and at the Royal Institute of Philosophy. In 1956 and 1957 he lectured at the C.G. Jung Institute in Zurich. His expanded Eranos lectures appeared as a book, which was highly praised and several times re-published and which made the elusive concept of the Tao accessible to Western readers.[310]

Before I continue with the outer history of Eranos and especially with the events surrounding Walter Robert Corti, I would like to speak briefly about Hans Kayser's involvement in Eranos, although he too only spoke there once, in 1958.[311] Kayser was a private scholar who, working completely on his own, set out to revive the forgotten science of harmonics in the tradition of Pythagoras. According to this teaching, the entire structure of the universe is based on certain mathematical-musical laws. In terms of ideas, Kayser was a successor to Albert von Thimus and Johannes Kepler, although their work had been carried out much earlier. He was born in Württemberg and studied briefly composition in Berlin, but left because of a quarrel with the university and completed his studies in Erlangen. He took private lessons with Arnold Schoenberg and, despite financial difficulties, devoted himself almost exclusively to his researches.[312] He approached the publisher Insel Verlag with a proposal for a book series on mysticism, which was accepted and Hans Kayser was put in overall charge of the project. The result was the beautiful thirteen-volume series *Der Dom: Bücher deutscher Mystik* (The cathedral: books of German mysticism), which is still much sought after. The volumes on Jakob Boehme and Paracelsus in the series were edited by Kayser himself, which ensured him financial independence for a few years.

This assignment, which included a volume on Johannes Kepler, probably gave Kayser his first impulse in the direction of his later studies in musical harmony. Kayser came into possession of a printing press, which became a financial liability but which at least enabled him to produce his first two books on harmony. In 1933, when Hitler came to power, Kayser followed the advice of friends and left Germany with his Jewish wife and family, moving to Bern where he found employment with the businessman Gustav Fueter, an admirer of his work. It was in Bern that he wrote his greatest works, in which he sought to demonstrate that harmonic laws exist not only in music[313] but also in the plant world[314] and in architecture.[315] He consistently declined offers of a university professorship or a position at the musical conservatory, preferring to concentrate on his researches. However, from 1957 to 1958 he was able to live on a subsidy from the Bollingen Foundation.

In his work *Orphikon—eine harmonische Symbolik*,[316] written late in life and brought out posthumously by Julius Schwabe, he even attempted to extend the validity of the harmonic laws to the metaphysical and religious realms. Interestingly, although Kayser was also a composer, his harmonical works have hardly influenced other composers. The only exception is Paul Hindemith, who was interested only in the practical side of Kayser's work rather than the philosophical.[317] Nevertheless, Kayser's researches have created new impulses, and there are even medical studies indicating the presence of harmonic laws in the human body and its functions.[318]

At the 1957 Eranos meeting Walter Robert Corti spoke at Olga Fröbe's invitation on "Die platonische Akademie im Wandel der Geschichte und als Aufgabe unserer Zeit" (the Platonic Academy over the changing course of history and as a task for our age).[319] Already he had published an essay entitled "Plan der Akademie" (Plan for the Academy), first in the newspaper *Neue Zürcher Zeitung* and then as a separate booklet.[320] Corti's plan was for an academy of the spirit, arising "out of a sense of consternation over the tragic confusion of our epoch and out of a search for ways of remedying the age and bringing clarity to it."[321] The goal was "to create a supra-national forum for conceptualizing the ethical integration of all sciences." For Corti it was particularly significant that Plato had known the Pythagorean brotherhood at first hand and had gathered important experience there. In that brotherhood scientific pursuits had been set within the context of a religious cult, which provided their orientation. Similarly, the place where Plato later founded his own school was a grove consecrated to the hero Akademos, from which the term "academy" is derived.

The Platonic Academy was intent on seeking the truth, and the method it used was *symphilosophein*, collective philosophizing. For this purpose, teachers and pupils lived together. As already mentioned, the Platonic Academy lasted for over eight hundred years and was finally dissolved by the Emperor Justinian on the grounds that the Neoplatonic approach contradicted Christian belief. In his Eranos lecture Corti spoke of several spiritual successors to the original academy, such as the Accademia Platonica in Renaissance Florence and Cambridge University in the Middle Ages. He also mentioned the pedagogue and pansophic philosopher John Amos Comenius, who was called to England to develop such an academy. At the same time, Corti believed that the notion of this kind of academy touched on "archetypal impulses in the soul, on a primal human dream." Hence he also alluded to Rabelais' Abbey of Thelema, Hermann Hesse's *Glass Bead Game*, and Nietzsche's projected school of "free spirits."

While Corti's academy bore Plato's name, he did not intend it to work "in the spirit of simply any form of Platonism," for one had to separate that which was ephemeral and time-bound from that which was timelessly valid. His essential agenda was to strengthen philosophy as a love of wisdom against an excessive scientism. In this connection Corti cited Nietzsche's *Beyond Good and Evil*, §204. Because of its topicality I would also like to quote from this work at some length:

It is especially the sight of those hotch-potch philosophers, who call themselves "realists," or "positivists," which is capable of implanting a dangerous distrust in the soul of a young and ambitious scholar … All of them are persons who have been vanquished and brought back again under the dominion of science and who at one time or another claimed more from themselves … After all, how could it be otherwise? Science flourishes nowadays and has the good conscience clearly visible on its countenance, while that to which the entire modern philosophy has gradually sunk, the remnant of philosophy of the present day, excites distrust and displeasure, if not scorn and pity. Philosophy reduced to a "theory of knowledge," no more in fact than a diffident science of epochs and doctrine of forbearance: a philosophy that never even gets beyond the threshold, and rigorously denies itself the right to enter—that is philosophy in its last throes, an end, an agony, something that awakens pity. How could such a philosophy—rule![322]

According to Corti, philosophy was not intended to rule, but should at least strengthen its voice and be a mentor to the rulers. Its task consisted in "grasping the totality of being" without thereby impairing what was individual and particular. No finished teaching should be expected from it. Its task was simply "to educate the whole human being, in all his moral substance, to be a carrier of the community, but in such a way that this circle of people surrounding him does not infringe and submerge his true freedom."

The plan to create a Platonic Academy in his homeland of Switzerland had already been publicly announced by Corti in the magazine *Du* in 1954, and he gave a detailed report on the reactions to the plan in the famous Eranos issue of *Du* of 1955. Among the responses to the proposal, one stands out in particular, namely a letter from Karl Jaspers dated 27 October 1954 and published in the December 1954 issue of the magazine *Neue Schweizer Rundschau*. In the letter Jaspers lists five objections to the Platonic Academy, but then refutes all of them. The main problem, as he sees it, is that such an intellectual/spiritual undertaking is not something that can be planned and organized. Nevertheless, he states, "It is the task of the free world to find a free structure to serve as a meeting place for people who have proved themselves to be of steadfast earnestness and adequate talent, people who are steered not by an individual but by an idea which unfolds in an undefined way and which belongs to all and none."

Finally, on 27 February 1955 the first step was taken towards the realization of Corti's plan when the *Bauhütte* (literally "building site hut") of the academy was founded in Zurich. The word *Bauhütte* was used as an allusion to the medieval cathedral builders and also because the exact form of the academy was still nebulous. A number of Swiss university professors and other prominent people signed the document and thereby declared themselves willing to collaborate. The Swiss Philosophical Society assumed the patronage, and a certain amount of money had already been collected. Clearly such an undertaking was bound to arouse the interest of Fröbe, especially when combined with the enthusiasm and persuasive charm of Robert Corti, whom she had already known for a long time. Having thought that Eranos would not survive her death, she now saw more and more clearly the possibility of a collaboration with the academy and finally a fusion, which would guarantee the continuation of the Eranos conferences under Walter Robert Corti. Another factor in favor of this development was that the Academy had decided to operate from Ascona.

In a letter of 15 August 1959 Mrs. Fröbe wrote full of enthusiasm to John Barrett, "Eranos and the Academy spring from the same root, and he [Corti] sensed that fact much earlier than I did." She said that Corti's academy had her full sympathy and that the time had come when firm legal arrangements could be made for a collaboration. Eranos would remain unchanged, and she would continue to be in charge of the meetings as long as she was able. Then Corti would take over the leadership. Eranos and the academy would then be in fact united. In this way she would have solved the question of succession and the academy would have a lecture room that it could already use in the immediate future for smaller meetings. In order to carry this through successfully an institution or private person would have to buy the Casa Gabriella and the Casa Eranos and then donate them to the Academy as its headquarters. The proceeds of the sale would have to pass to her daughter Bettina. Not wishing to make the purchase too unrealistic from the outset, she had in mind a sum of 500,000 Swiss francs. The ideal partner for this transaction would naturally be the Bollingen Foundation or Paul Mellon himself. In this quarter, however, the interest was unfortunately very slight.

During the 1959 Eranos meeting the merging of Eranos and the Academy was decided upon. Then towards the end of 1959 a circular letter of explanation was sent out to all the "Friends of Eranos." A year earlier Fröbe had made approaches to the Bollingen Foundation to grant a fellowship to Walter Robert Corti as her partner. He was duly given the award for five years in order to carry out research on the development and influence of the Platonic Academy from antiquity to the present day.

The problems began to arise shortly after the official signing of the merger agreement, when the academy held its first few meetings in the Eranos lecture room.[323] This emerges from handwritten documents left by Adolf Portmann, who strongly supported Fröbe during this difficult period. It became apparent to her that there were serious differences of view, and she soon deeply regretted the overly hasty step that she had taken.[324] She was now convinced that the academy would never be in a position to continue Eranos in her spirit. Hence she felt herself compelled to dissolve the agreement without delay, whatever the cost. The problem was that the contract granted the right to buy the Casa Gabriella for the Academy at a specially favorable price. The academy therefore argued that it would suffer a financial set-back if the agreement were cancelled. It would only agree to a cancellation in return for an adequate compensation. As the academy saw it, Fröbe's change of mind was incomprehensible and her accusations were unfounded. After much legal wrangling Fröbe was finally obliged to donate to the academy two plots of land on the other side of the road after clearing them of all debts and obligations. She also had to renounce any objections to possible future building plans on these sites.[325]

According to the lawyers entrusted to negotiate on behalf of the *Bauhütte*, the main reason for insisting on the enforcement of the contract was that Corti and his associates had committed themselves to continuing the Eranos meetings and did not want to lose the necessary resources to do so. The ill feeling between Fröbe and Corti's side was further exacerbated by the fact that Mrs. Fröbe had agreed to sell part of her land to a German property firm, which planned to erect luxury villas on the site, a plan to which Corti was strongly opposed. There is, however, an alternative version of the situation, namely that concealed behind Corti were Swiss commercial interests that allegedly wanted to acquire Fröbe's beautiful property with the intention of demolishing the existing buildings to clear the way for construction and then erecting as many dwellings as possible directly adjoining the lake. For real estate agents this would certainly have been a more than tempting proposition.

The continuation of the Eranos meetings had been a serious issue since the beginning of the quarrel with the academy, and now Fröbe and Adolf Portmann had to address this problem earnestly. Since 1958 each Eranos conference had included a lecturers' meeting at which she and the speakers decided the contents of the next conference. Now in addition it was decided to form an "inner circle" of Friends of Eranos, which would secure the full continuity of the conferences. A letter to this effect, written by Adolf Portmann, was sent to Henry Corbin, Mircea Eliade, Sir Herbert Read, Gershom Scholem, Hellmut Wilhelm, and Viktor Zuckerkandl. However, the letter also explained that it had not yet been decided what was to happen to Eranos after Fröbe's death. The purpose of the letter was to seek help for the period in which Fröbe, whose health was already precarious, would continue to "determine the content" of the meetings.[326] All the addressees responded very positively. Valuable help came also from Rudolf Ritsema, who in his youth had studied biology and psychology in Geneva, but had been obliged to break off his studies because of the war. Fröbe lamented the fact that for career reasons he was never able to devote more than a few days at a time to Eranos.[327] The outcome of these efforts was that the continued existence of Eranos was secured for the time being despite all the problems and financial losses.

In 1961 it was no longer Fröbe but Portmann who wrote the foreword to the conference proceedings, choosing the title "Vom Sinn und Auftrag der Eranostagungen" (The meaning and task of the Eranos meetings). He perceived the rapid pace of development as "a fearful danger threatening to cause the wasting away of all that is more fully human" and he demanded "a massive turn-around." Eranos, he said, was "attempting to contribute its part to this change of consciousness. He emphasized the importance of "das Übergeschichtliche" (that which transcends history) and of "hierophanies," to use a term that Eliade had employed to describe "those multifarious expressions of the 'wholly other.'"

The Death of Olga Fröbe and its Immediate Aftermath

In March 1962 Olga Fröbe evidently suffered a slight stroke, which made her realize that she would have to give up her Eranos activities. She therefore placed overall authority in the hands of Rudolf Ritsema so that the administration of the meetings would not break down. Adolf Portmann was in agreement with this step. On 25 April 1962 Olga Fröbe died in her eighty-first year.[328] On the next day a simple farewell ceremony was held at the Casa Gabriella. Rudolf Ritsema, who had hurried there from Holland, read out a few lines from the *I Ching* that spoke of the continually changing nature of things. The ashes of the founder of Eranos were placed in her garden. In her will she laid down that an Eranos Foundation should be established under the leadership of Adolf Portmann and that the Casa Eranos and the garden should pass to the foundation.[329] The Casa Gabriella was to go to her daughter in Holland, Bettina Beguin-Fröbe, but on condition that she sell it to the Eranos Foundation at a price well below the market value.[330] The *Bulletin of the Analytical Psychology Club of New York* published an obituary by Hildegard Nagel, who dealt briefly with the history of Eranos.[331] She gave special prominence to Adolf Portmann's foreword to the 1961 Eranos yearbook and the essential question of the deeper meaning of the human condition in the modern world. As "coincidence" would have it, the article that came after the obituary in the *Bulletin* was a short piece on the *I Ching*.

Fröbe had never seen herself as the moving force behind Eranos, but was convinced that her work was serving a higher principle. She always maintained that Eranos was without plan or program[332] and was guided by an archetypal spirit to which she had intuitive access.[333] Thus in her foreword to the 1942 yearbook she said "Eranos is not my property." Rudolf Ritsema reported in his 1987 lecture "Eranos: Ursprünge und Werk" (Eranos: origins and work)[334] that in 1935, that is after only three meetings, Olga Fröbe wanted to give up the whole project, as Eranos had already fulfilled its purpose. Only the protests of speakers and members of the audience had proved to her that Eranos had developed a surprisingly strong life of its own. The various turns of fate that came with the war years further strengthened her in this belief. It is clear from her forewords to the yearbooks that, as she saw it, her task lay not in consciously directing Eranos but rather in putting herself intuitively in touch with its spirit, which would find its own way to express and manifest itself. In the foreword to the 1951 yearbook she even speaks of "demands from the timeless," and she makes clear her conviction that Eranos could only have emerged in a time of hardship and misery, for it is only then that such help from the "timeless" is forthcoming.

At the 1955 meeting, which had the theme "Sympathy of all Things," Olga Fröbe declared this "sympathy" to be a central concept for Eranos and described it as "a cohesive force, which is stronger and more meaningful than any outward bond, and which possesses its own life." Only if all the parts were completely free could the essential work of Eranos be accomplished. Non-organization was therefore an advantage. "It is our experience that each one of them [i.e., the speakers], when he speaks from his own centre, can be sure of being supported by the flow of energy from the central source and can therefore touch us at the most profound level." Writing to Jung on 30 October 1951, Fröbe said that she could not thank him enough for suggesting the policy of non-organization.

The same view was taken by Dr. Daniel Brody, head of the publishing firm of Rhein-Verlag, which produced the Eranos yearbooks. He wrote about Fröbe as follows:[335]

> And she began to "bring about" the Eranos meetings. She did not organize them, rather one should say that she conjured them together. Her work grew like an organic formation or an artistic creation, without intention, without "programme," in the service of the as yet Unknown, which was ready to manifest itself. She created an "enabling" space, a force field for fruitful encounters.

Thus the spirit of Eranos cannot be understood only in a purely abstract way but also in a "concrete" sense. In 1949 C.G. Jung and the Dutch theologian and phenomenologist of religion Gerardus van der Leeuw came to the shared conclusion that behind the Eranos phenomenon there must lie more than just a habitual process. This "more" seemed to them to be an unknown "spirit," a personification of an archetype that animated the setting of the meetings. Thus it was that the sculptor Paul Speck created a stele, which was installed in the garden of the Casa Gabriella and bore the inscription *Genio loci ignoto* (to the unknown spirit of the place).[336]

If one looks more closely at this stele[337] one discerns in the middle, between the upper and lower parts of the inscription, a pair of triangles pointing towards each other, one from above (heaven) and the other from below (earth), without their points actually touching (yet). Assuming that they continue in the same direction they will converge and then finally cross over each other, thus forming the six-pointed "star of David," which expresses the unity of "God" and the "world." What is shown on the stele, however, is only the first tentative approach. A true "meeting" has not yet taken place. Another striking feature is that the sculptor—consciously or unconsciously—has made the upper, "heavenly" triangle bigger than the lower, "earthly" one. Thus the force from above is depicted as being the more powerful. The stele is in any case "top-heavy," as the stone has been carved in such a way that the upper part is more massive. The mysterious quality of the stele is accentuated vividly by the fact that its position is half hidden by shrubbery (which perhaps grew up around it only later). If you stand for a while alone in front of it, knowing of its meaning, you will sense the magic emanating from it.[338]

Olga Fröbe's own struggle with this "genius" is clearly described in a letter that Jung wrote to her in 1945, addressing the conflict between her duties as the mother of a daughter and as leader of Eranos. He writes, "One of these is imperative, but the other also. There can be no deciding between them but only a patient enduring of the contrasting sides ... Accept your daughter's claim that you are a bad mother and defend your duty as a mother against Eranos."[339]

In her unpublished 1952 report on Eranos, which has already been quoted a number of times, she writes as follows about this internal tug-of-war:

> My daughter hated Eranos, which was understandable, but this was also the reason why I never let her take part in the meetings. I was so surrounded by difficulties, so burdened by technical and other problems, that I could not afford to be dealing in addition with the boundless problem of my relationship to Bettina during the meetings. My situation between family and Eranos was always so difficult that it was hardly bearable. People may tell me endlessly that it was my own fault, which is not true because I had no choice. The inner compulsion was a hundred times greater than any outward solution. It had to do with an idea, an idea which claimed me totally and which prohibited and prevented everything else. One might think it would not be difficult to live with an idea. But I have the experience of thirty years behind me, and my experience is unique.

A few years later this conflict with the *genius loci* led to severe psychosomatic problems, and, as Fröbe recorded in a handwritten note towards the end of the 1950s, she came to the conclusion that there was only one solution: to let go and keep letting go. The ego had to give way to the self (the genius) and to find a new equilibrium with it.

At the fiftieth-anniversary meeting the speakers included Gilbert Durand, who spoke explicitly about the *genius loci*. Rudolf Ritsema and his wife, Catherine, also felt an obligation towards this genius, as they themselves have affirmed. Catherine Ritsema's determined involvement in matters connected with Eranos should not be underestimated. For example, she attempted to write a history of Eranos. As has already been mentioned, during the last few years before Fröbe's death Rudolf Ritsema acted as her executive secretary and had already begun to participate in the organization of Eranos. With her unexpectedly sudden death, he was faced by totally new tasks that required rapid decisions. As Ritsema himself has recounted, he and his wife had only four hours in which to decide whether they were willing for their lives to take a completely new direction.[340] A consultation with the *I Ching* provided the decisive impetus.

After consulting with John Barrett, president of the Bollingen Foundation, who was as always vehemently committed to Eranos, Ritsema gave up both his newly built house and his secure position in Leiden with the oriental department of the renowned academic publishing firm of Brill. Likewise his wife interrupted her career as a pianist and the couple moved to Ascona, initially for three years and then permanently, in order to continue Fröbe's work according to her vision. In addition Ritsema contributed a considerable sum of money in order to buy out Bettina Fröbe. James Hillman, later to be an Eranos speaker, also contributed generously for the same purpose, as Jay Livernois informed me. Livernois, as former editor of the journal *Spring*, with which Hillman was closely connected, and as director of Eranos-Moscia, can be considered particularly well informed about these matters.

Already in 1961 Ritsema, with Fröbe's support, had sought and received a grant from the Bollingen Foundation for research into the *I Ching*. Now the foundation gave Eranos an assurance of financial support for the next few years. One can say with certainty that, without this generous help, the meetings would have come to an end.[341] John Barrett was also present at the Eranos meeting of August 1962, the first to take place without Fröbe. In addition, Portmann organized a meeting of the "inner circle," at which the continuation of Eranos in the old spirit was re-affirmed. This time Ernst Benz was also involved in the work of the inner circle.

There exists an English text of 1962, written under the heading of the Eranos Foundation and presumably connected with this meeting. This text expresses the view that only the immutable "archaic" or "archetypical" human structures can be the foundation for an evolution of our social life. The document goes on to say that Eranos under Fröbe's leadership has set itself the task of placing this prerequisite for future development at the center of its research endeavors, with the aim of combating the danger of our lives being restricted to material goals and rationalistic values. "The central group of the Eranos speakers is decided to do its best not only to maintain the spirit of these meetings but to extend their influence." More weight was to be given to English and French lectures. Furthermore, the audience should be enlivened, and there should be a more intensive collaboration with people of an appropriate educational level. The document continues:

> This archaic aspect of our mental development is never a primitive period destined to be replaced by the better ways of modern rational thinking. The archetypal structure is perennial and fundamental. The results of the secondary world of science have to be organically incorporated in the basic structure of our first imaginative outlook.

The existential conflicts faced by many millions of people of other cultures, now being confronted unprepared with the technical outlook of Western civilization, constituted a tragic proof of the urgent need to investigate ways of integrating both modes of existence. Eranos, it was stated, had from the beginning been committed to a creative synthesis of this kind.

In 1962 the new speakers once again included a physicist, Gerald Holton, whom Fröbe had invited personally while she was still alive. Holton, who had been educated in Vienna and Oxford, was one of the rather rare (except at Eranos) scientists who are equally at home in history, philosophy, and other areas of the humanities. In his numerous books he presents, often in case studies, the development of physics in a humanistic and cultural context. Even the university-level introductory course on physics, which he wrote together with Duane Roller, shows that he also wishes his work to be understood by a broader public.[342] His aim is to respond to the ecologically oriented attacks on science and technology, which are becoming increasingly strident in the present age, and to provide unadorned clarification, pointing out both the advantages and disadvantages. At the same time he gives a clear warning against the pitfalls of the pseudo-sciences.[343]

Besides his professorship at Harvard, Gerald Holton is still active in several international scientific associations and has received numerous honorary titles.

In 1963 Ira Progoff stood for the first time at the speakers' lectern, to which he was to return frequently. Progoff must have been the first social scientist to examine the Jungian theories in the perspective of that discipline, as he did in his doctoral thesis, which he subsequently sent to the Bollingen Foundation at a time when the foundation was just beginning the project of publishing the collected works of Jung in English. Cary Baynes saw the work, considered it important and sent it to Jung. At the same time she asked her daughter, Ximena de Angulo, who was living in Switzerland by that time, to note down Jung's comments. As Jung gave it his approval, subject to a few small corrections, Progoff was given a grant which enabled him to study with Jung in Zurich in 1953. In that year he also visited the Eranos conference, where he came under the influence of D.T. Suzuki.[344] From 1959 to 1971 he was head of a university institute for depth psychology in the United States. In addition he was active as a practicing psychotherapist. His special focus was the application of the methods of depth psychology to the social and spiritual problems of the modern age. Ira Progoff was also one of the founders of the Association for Humanistic Psychology.

Progoff's interests are evident from a glance at the titles of some of his books, such as *Jung's Psychology and its Social Meaning*; *Jung, Synchronicity and Human Destiny*; *The Image of an Oracle*;[345] and *The Symbolic and the Real*. Also important is his edition with commentary of the English classic of mysticism *The Cloud of Unknowing*. In his psycho-therapeutic practice he developed a method that he called process meditation, which was intended to enable people, even in today's world, to have genuine spiritual experiences and thus come into contact with the universal spiritual foundations of humanity.[346] His books have reached a wide readership and some are also used as study materials in American universities. Progoff's overall agenda was to create a new conception of the totality and greatness of the human being. To this end he combined data gathered from biology, existential philosophy, and the study of religion. His idea was that human beings should in this way develop the capacity and stature to react adequately to the problems of the modern world. From these few words it will be clear how close Progoff's efforts were to the interdisciplinary approach of Eranos. Consequently Progoff strove repeatedly to propagate the importance of Eranos.

A year later, in 1964, Gilbert Durand came for the first time to speak at Eranos and was to become a long-standing and enthusiastic lecturer there. He was introduced by his friend Henry Corbin; as already mentioned, Durand was a devoted spiritual fellow traveler of Corbin, for a total of sixteen years. He was a pupil of the philosopher Gaston Bachelard, strongly influenced by psychoanalysis, who had a special interest in sym-bolism and had early on begun to probe into the realm of the imaginal. Durand was active in the resistance during the war, and in 1962 he took over the chair for sociology and cultural anthropology in Grenoble. In 1966 he became co-creator of a university research center for the study of the imaginal, which in the 1990s had forty-three branches scattered over the entire world.[347] In addition he was one of the founders of the journal *Cahiers internationaux du symbolisme*. In addition to his efforts for Eranos and for the Université Saint-Jean de Jérusalem, he also took part in other important anti-positivist colloquia such as the one held at Cordoba in 1979, where the other speakers included his Eranos acquaintances David Miller, James Hillman, Toshihiko Izutsu, Kathleen Raine, and Jung's friend and successor at the Swiss Federal Institute of Technology, C.A.

Meier.[348] The cause to which Durand was especially strongly and clearly committed was to bring about a spiritual but scientifically well-founded mode of thought which would act as a counter-weight to the positivistic currents within the modern humanities.[349] His so-called *nouvel esprit anthropologique* (new anthopological spirit) is an attempt, on the hermeneutic, symbolic, and epistemological level, to investigate the forms in which the transcendental and imaginal sphere manifests itself.[350] Here he employs an innovative structural method.[351] In describing this method he uses various artificial terms incorporating the word "myth," such as *mythanalyse*, *mythodologie* and *mythocritique*. As an antidote to reductionist historicism, he is intent on introducing myth into anthropology as a way of obtaining deeper insight. Hermetic gnosis also plays a role here on account of its non-separation of subject and object. At Eranos he spoke, *inter alia*, about the principle of hermetic similarity, dealing first with the historical manifestations of Hermeticism up to the Romantic period and then going on to argue that modern-day anthropology, if it wished to make any real progress, would also, willingly or unwillingly, have to have recourse to the principle of similarity.

Some sentences from Mircea Eliade's diaries must have impressed him particularly, for he took them as the opening motto of his book on the interconnection between art and the sacred.[352] The passage reads, "We must therefore bring about a de-mystification with the opposite prefix. Freud and Marx have taught us to discover the 'profane' in the 'sacred.' In the approach that I am talking about the critics will discover the 'sacred,' implicit and concealed in the 'profane.'" In answer to the accusation of irrationality, Durand said that it was a question of recognizing new categories of cognition, like those which were manifesting themselves in the sciences (synchronicity for example) and which were equally inexplicable in terms of purely causal criteria.[353] In mentioning three French philosophers who are still widely admired today, namely Roland Barthes, Jacques Lacan, and Louis Althusser, he goes so far as to speak of the three "brakes" of Freudianism, structuralism, and Marxism, which he sees as deriving from the Promethianism of the nineteenth century.[354] Durand was also interested in purely occult subjects and wrote a foreword to a large encyclopedia of divination.[355]

Durand has published a summary of a portion of his Eranos lectures and added a beautiful foreword on Eranos.[356] Here he makes the interesting remark that Eranos exercised a sort of internal quality control. Because 85 percent of the audience were professorial colleagues, they were able to give immediate critical feedback to the lecturers. Only 15 percent of the audience were lay people. At the same time, the lecturers could freely articulate truths that one otherwise dared not express at the universities. Durand goes on to say that at Eranos "a voluntary alliance of about 200 scholars created the third millennium 'from the sidelines.'"[357]

Durand is also clearly influenced by certain currents from German intellectual history. Thus, for example, he repeatedly refers to Johann Wolfgang von Goethe, Oswald Spengler, Wilhelm Dilthey, Ernst Cassirer, and Max Scheler. In his works of literary criticism he is particularly concerned with the writings of Hermann Hesse, but also shows a profound interest in the occult fiction writer Gustav Meyrink.[358] Although Durand's extensive *oeuvre* (his bibliography has two hundred seventy separate entries[359]) is by no means easy to read, it has already had a considerable influence within the humanities.

The classical philologist and ancient historian Reinhold Merkelbach, who specialized in the ancient mysteries (Mithras and Dionysos) came to Eranos in 1965 and then repeatedly, at irregular intervals, until 1990. Also making their appearance in 1965 were a historian of science from Jerusalem, Schmuel Sambursky, and the Jung scholar James Hillman. Sambursky, born in Königsberg, had emigrated to Jerusalem in 1924, where he worked as an experimental physicist on atomic and molecular spectra. However, his interest in philosophy and history then prompted an investigation into the beginnings of the science of physics in ancient Greece, which led to a comprehensive study of the whole history of physics. His anthology *Der Weg der Physik: 2500 Jahre physikalischen Denkens* brought together texts ranging from Anaximander to Wolfgang Pauli.[360] Each epoch had an introduction by Sambursky explaining the general cultural context. I am told that Sambursky was very popular at Eranos and represented a sort of ideal model of the polymath Eranos lecturer. Thus, he could talk about Plato during the first half of a lecture and then about the latest discoveries in physics in the second half. For many years Sambursky featured regularly on the Eranos program and was one of the few natural scientists, along with Portmann, who had a long-term foothold there. He was also known for his humorous and sometimes sarcastic verses about colleagues and friends.[361]

❧ 13. Polytheism Versus Monotheism

James Hillman

James Hillman deserves a more detailed treatment in view of the fact that, despite being a late-comer, he must certainly be considered a key figure in the history of Eranos. For one thing, he spoke very frequently there: fifteen times between 1965 and 1990, albeit at irregular intervals. Furthermore, his "archetypal psychology" (sometimes also called "imaginative psychology"), the system he developed from the Jungian teaching, is one of the schools of thought which most strongly influenced Eranos over the decades.[1] Several representatives of this school came to speak at Eranos, including David Miller, Alfred Ziegler, and Wolfgang Giegerich. I would not go so far as to claim that Hillman, through his exceptional personality, had assumed the role of royal successor to Jung, but there might be a grain of truth in this.[2] Women apparently also flocked around Hillman,[3] although his name did not lend itself to the pun "Jung-Frauen." One of the places where this happened, at least on one occasion, was the Hotel Tamaro in Ascona, as eye-witnesses have reported. Usually, however, he stayed at smaller hotels. For twelve years he rented a room in the Casa Gabriella, where he wrote a number of important essays.[4]

Just how important Eranos was for Hillman is clear from his insistence that the "biographical origins" of archetypal psychology can be traced back to the Eranos conferences.[5] And in his book *The Myth of Analysis*, containing expanded versions of three of his most influential Eranos lectures, Hillman writes: "The congeniality and stimulation of the Eranos circle have contributed beyond measure to this work."[6]

Born in New Jersey in 1926, Hillman enlisted in the Marines Corps in 1944, serving as a medical corpsman.[7] In 1946 he came to Europe to write news reports for a radio station in the bombed-out city of Frankfurt am Main. There followed periods of study in Paris and Dublin. Then came a year in India, where he began to suffer from increasing bouts of neurosis and consulted a famous guru, Gopi Krishna, who advised him to go as high as possible into the mountains, for there one could "meet God." After experiencing a nightmare among the peaks, he made a hasty descent and, after a period of indecision, decided in 1953 to go to Zurich to study with Jung. He had already encountered Jung's writings, which had appealed to him, although he had not become a "fanatical fan."[8]

However, in the same year he matriculated at the University of Zurich in the faculty of psychology and also began to study at the Jung Institute. Despite initial language difficulties he completed his studies with a doctorate *summa cum laude* from the university and a diploma in analytical psychology from the Jung Institute, where he eventually became director of studies and remained in that position for ten years. In 1978 he returned to the United States, where he co-founded the Dallas Institute of Humanities and Culture and in addition worked as a psychotherapist and counselor and wrote his influential books.

An important step for Hillman's international reputation was his assumption in 1970 of the editorial direction of the publishing firm Spring, which published, among other things, the journal *Spring*, devoted to Jungian psychology and later also archetypal psychology. Names that appeared in it included not only various "polytheistic" speakers but also other Eranos lecturers such as Erik Hornung, Adolf Portmann, Gilbert Durand, Henry Corbin, and Rudolf Ritsema. In 1973 Hillman delivered the famous Terry lectures at Yale University, which he subsequently turned into his book *Re-Visioning Psychology*. In 1937 the Terry lectures had been given by Jung. In 1974 Hillman was a visiting professor at Yale, and in 1976 he became a faculty member in the department of religious studies at Syracuse University in New York.

Hillman's highly successful book on dreams, *The Dream and the Underworld*, was published in 1979.[9] The German edition was appropriately entitled *Am Anfang war das Bild* (In the beginning was the image), as images are the starting point for archetypal psychology.[10] The image is regarded as an irreducible fact that cannot be explained in terms of anything other than itself. The source of all images is the soul, which simply creates images and itself consists of images.[11] Dreams are a direct outflow from the soul's activity and have a central role in archetypal psychology, which is concerned primarily with "soul-making," that is, the free development of the soul. The soul constitutes an intermediary between body and mind. It is the *third* organ of perception, the one *between* the other two.[12] Rafael Lopez-Pedraza calls this level of perception "Hermetic consciousness,"[13] as it mediates between the worlds like Hermes, messenger of the gods.

The soul, as conceived by archetypal psychology, should not be confused with what is understood by the term in literature, Christianity, or psychology in general. For Hillman the soul is something that reaches far beyond the individual human being, even extending to the Neoplatonic world soul. Consequently it can never be precisely defined. In this perspective the soul is not enclosed in the individual body. Rather it is the individual who moves about within the sphere of the soul. Similarly, dreams are not located within the individual, but rather the individual is embedded in the world of dreams. Fantasy and reality are for Hillman not in contrast to each other, but rather can changes places with each other. A fantasy image can easily become embodied in "real" life and thus itself become real. And the world of "hard facts" is at the same time always the bodily expression of a certain fantasy image. The image is not confined to the individual but is in resonance with a collective image. Thus a personal experience can take on a universal significance. That which is true for the realm of the soul, and manifests itself in the individual, is in this sense also true for the world soul. As above, so below. As within, so without.

It is self-evident that myth occupies a central position within this school of thought. Thus, whereas conventional psychology concentrates on the individual, archetypal psychology has a much wider reach, extending to the world of culture, literature, art, politics, and society. Hillman sees his task as being to re-"ensoul" and re-"animate" the world. Hence Hillman's involvement in ecology and politics. In common with oriental philosophies such as Advaita-Vedanta or Zen, archetypal psychology aims to achieve a blurring of the boundary between subject and object, to dissolve the ego and the illusion of "substancem" and to reveal the emptiness of Western positivism. At the same time archetypal psychology sees itself as the only psychological school of thought which dispenses with a dogmatic, that is to say permanently unchanging, content. Instead of propagating a definite psychological "ideology" it is characterized by a continual process of re-envisioning, of repeatedly observing and imagining anew.[14]

Human existence is undoubtedly manifold and many-leveled, and the same is true of the soul. Consequently, for Hillman it is logical that religion should also reflect this manifold nature of the soul. "This means polytheism. For the soul's inherent multiplicity demands a theological fantasy of equal differentiation."[15] But in archetypal psychology the point is not to believe in or worship a set of deities. Rather, the gods are metaphors for modes of experience and living. "They are cosmic perspectives in which the soul participates. In archetypal psychology Gods are *imagined*."[16] Within this multiplicity of gods we find those that best express the manifold nature of our own soul, or discover those places where we feel "at home" and protected and where we can turn to the particular deities that we need most. Thus there is no need for us to regard our own special mode of life as being abnormal or pathological merely because it may not fit into a prescribed monotheistic framework.

If the independent self has to adapt to the narrowness of monotheism it is faced with a very difficult task, which in Hillman's view can lead to schizophrenia. In polytheism one can live out this multiplicity within oneself and therefore one has no need to project it outwards. It is precisely the outward projection of this inner disunity, according to Hillman, that is in danger of causing the fragmentation and destruction of our world.[17] By analogically relating something that we experience inwardly to some comparable event in the annals of the gods we can find a degree of inner peace, and in a polytheistic world there is always some such analogy to be found. Hillman points out that this type of psychological approach was used for thousands of years in astrology, alchemy, and nature philosophy, where microcosm and macrocosm were kept in balance, as the soul requires. Here Hillman quotes a statement of Rafael Lopez-Pedraza, who also belongs to the archetypal school of thought: "The many contains the unity of the one, without losing the possibilities of the many."[18] Hillman also maintains that, with the increasing secularization of monotheism and its transference into monomaniac ideologies, the danger of human beings tearing each other apart had become even greater.

Understandably, the polytheistic approach has aroused a certain amount of protest within Eranos and the monotheistic context of the West,[19] if only, as Hillman says, because the monotheistic heritage makes it very difficult for us even to understand what a polytheistic soul is. One only needs to look at the (unintended) consequences of this heritage. Before the advent of a monotheistic worldview, every town, every people, and every kingdom had its own patron deities. Likewise the mountains, rivers, trees, and plants were populated by gods, demons, nymphs, or elves. When everything became concentrated on a single, all-transcending, *other-worldly* deity, suddenly all these gods and divine beings had to disappear, and *this* world became a barren and "godless" place, where phenomena were explained only in terms of mechanistic natural laws. Thus the world was reduced to mere physical matter, and "godlessness" was compounded by "spiritlessness." And, as we human beings are undoubtedly part of nature, we too were regarded as ultimately nothing more than matter and therefore explicable according to the same natural laws. The human being became as "spiritless" as nature and, as a consequence, psychology degenerated into a mechanistic science. "Certainly idolatrous worship of multiple gods was thereby abolished, but at the same time 'all good spirits' were also driven out of nature."[20] In addition one had to recognize the danger that a secularized monotheism tends towards dictatorship.

This controversy between polytheism[21] and monotheism[22] is also connected with the age-old conflict between the "unambiguous" word and the polymorphous image, which was bound to intensify in the modern age because words, in comparison to those used in ancient times, were becoming more and more one-dimensional in meaning. What they had gained in terms of precision and clarity they had lost in terms of depth and symbolic power, and the gap between word and image had become ever larger.[23]

For some time there had been a concern that Eranos was undermining the monotheistic position. Jung's teachings, widely perceived as gnostic, had already aroused the suspicion that they were aimed against the monotheistic religions. This was what lay behind the written controversy between Jung and Martin Buber.[24] Indeed, one could regard depth psychology in itself as an attack on monotheism, since it works on the basis of an image-laden and therefore "polytheistic" soul.[25]

Henry Corbin took a middle position on this question. While declaring himself unambiguously as a follower of a monotheistic religion, he saw in the practice of the official monotheistic religions the consequences of a metaphysical error. This consisted in confusing the unrecognizable, ultimate divinity with *one* specific god, that is to say *being in itself* was confused with a *particular being*. The difficulty, as Corbin argued, is that the ultimate mystery of being can only be approached by means of the "negative path" in theology, and this path has never been very popular in monotheism, with its structure of officialdom. This ultimate divinity, Corbin said, can of course only be a unity, but its theophanies (divine manifestations) are multifarious. It is this multiplicity of theophanies that enables the one divinity to manifest itself within us in its profundity. In addition there is Corbin's wide-reaching doctrine of the angels, who, as already mentioned, have their being in the imaginal realm. They are necessary for human beings because they represent the level at which the body becomes spiritualized and the spirit becomes embodied.[26] Thus the angels are the helpers who show us the way to transcend the state of merely being human.[27]

Charles Upton, the American writer and leader of a traditionalist Frithjof Schuon study circle, raises the objection that Hillman commits a metaphysical error because, in emphasizing the manifold nature of the soul, he overlooks the transcendental unity of divinity, which stands over all and constitutes the transpersonal unity of the individual. Upton argues that the human personality always needs this transcendental unity. It cannot be attained simply by one's own efforts to "hold together" one's inner multiplicity, as Hillman himself says. The only way to this higher unity, Upton maintains, is for the personality to transcend itself. But Hillman, he says, is not interested in this unity, as is shown by the fact that he completely leaves out of account the Jungian doctrine of the self as archetype of this unity and does not even concern himself with the process of individuation, which leads to the complete self. Hillman, according to Upton, remains stuck in the manifold nature of the soul.[28] On the other hand, for Hillman the Jungian self is a sort of attempt to fit a monotheistic hat on to the doctrine of the manifold archetypes.[29] Jung's emphasis on individuation and the myth of the hero is absent in Hillman, if only because he was convinced that this approach was based on the (erroneous) Western belief in progress.

The insistence on emphasizing the image and placing it on a par with the soul, which in turn constitutes an intermediate level, bears witness to the fact that archetypal psychology stems from Jung, Corbin, and Durand. Hillman, however, goes even further back and finds his ideas already present in Plato and Neoplatonism. Equally important for him was the inspiration that he found in Italian Renaissance figures such as Marsilio Ficino and Giambattista Vico.[30] Hillman, therefore, basically locates himself within a "southern" tradition, in contrast to Jung, who belongs rather to a northern tradition with a German background. Hillman feels himself closer to the polytheistic paganism of the

Mediterranean region, the study of which has been so worthily promoted by the Warburg Institute in London, rather than to the Protestant morality and monotheistic climate of the north. And in fact archetypal psychology has found more adherents in Italy than anywhere else in Europe. All Hillman's books have been translated into Italian and are continually reprinted. One expression of this veneration is a book entitled *Caro James*, in which Hillman responds to questions of an admiring or critical nature from twenty-five Italian authors.[31] On account of Hillman's vividly graphic and rhetorical style his books have reached a wider public in countries such as Japan or Brazil than in Germany or France.

In the past few years the question of monotheism and polytheism has again come to the fore thanks to another Eranos speaker. I speak here of Jan Assmann, Egyptologist and theorist of "cultural memory." His book *The Price of Monotheism*[32] caused something of a stir due to its contention that the introduction of monotheism in ancient Egypt and in Judaism led to intolerance, hatred, and persecution. However, anyone who reads this book will immediately recognize that the author in no way wishes to insinuate accusations or promote a return to polytheistic beliefs, which would surely be impossible in any case. For it is not "the distinction between the One God and many gods" that appears crucial to Assmann here, but rather "the distinction between truth and falsehood in religion, between the true God and false gods, true doctrine and false doctrine, knowledge and ignorance, belief and unbelief."[33]

It was therefore not due to the question of the One God or the many gods that hatred emerged, but rather because the followers of the One God necessarily regarded the adherents of polytheism as servants of false gods, as heretics and more or less conscious deviants from the true path. Assmann also stresses that monotheism requires this pronounced enmity towards polytheists for its own internal cohesion. The hatred is essentially directed against its own ranks, in order that they do not stray from the "true" faith. Thus polytheism is first and foremost a polemical term, employed to eradicate that which is false in one's own religion rather than the surrounding paganism.

To censure monotheism because of this intolerance would be just as foolish as condemning the ancient Greek philosophers for destroying the "cosmic unity" by separating subject and object from one another. For scientific thought is just as intolerant as monotheism. And Assmann further contends, "Polytheism is cosmotheism. The divine cannot be divorced from the world. Monotheism, however, sets out to do just that."[34] Only a God divorced from the world allows as its corollary a human divorced from the world in the sense of a fully autonomous individual.

In 1967 Toshihiko Izutsu spoke at Eranos for the first time. The conference of that year had the philosophical-esoteric theme of "Polarity of Life." Subsequently Izutsu came repeatedly to Ascona, as his knowledge and interests fitted perfectly into the milieu that had become so recognizably typical of Eranos. He had grown up in Tokyo in the world of Zen Buddhism, which he repeatedly placed at the center of his Eranos lectures.[35] He had also studied many languages (including Hebrew) and many philosophical and mystical systems. His areas of expertise ranged from Taoism to Sufism (he was a corresponding member of the Academy of Arabic Language), and he even edited a scholarly edition of the Koran.

Western philosophy was also no foreign territory to him. Hence it is understandable that his efforts were directed towards what he called a "world philosophy," which would bring together the various branches of the world's wisdom and combine them into a new and unified pattern. After teaching at Keio University in Tokyo and as a visiting professor at McGill University in Montreal, he was called to the Imperial Iranian Academy of Philosophy in Teheran, which, until the fall of the Shah, was a Mecca of (mainly but not exclusively) Islamic wisdom, and also of the so-called Integral Tradition. If one browses through the journal founded by this academy, whose title *Sophia Perennis* has in itself become a watchword, one finds contributions by Eranos speakers such as Henry Corbin, Elémire Zolla, and Toshihiko Izutsu, a bibliography of Antoine Faivre, and articles by classic "traditionalists" such as Frithjof Schuon, Seyyed Hossein Nasr, and Leo Schaya. In Teheran he was as likely to speak about, say, the *I Ching* as about Ibn Arabi. Izutsu's wife and colleague was a recognized expert on Japanese aesthetics.

In Ascona he was always eagerly awaited by James Hillman, who was not only excited by Izutsu's new scientific findings and his authoritative treatment of themes. He was interested above all in the psychological insights which he gained through the Japanese man, which came from "seemingly non-psychological topics and texts." In the *Festschrift* in honour of Izutsu Hillman mentioned as an example the Japanese art of garden design, which lent him the realization that "in the garden I was in the psyche."[36]

Changes

Unnoticed by most of the audience, the year 1967 brought a marked caesura for Eranos. Paul Mellon had decided to let the Bollingen Foundation come to an end. John Barrett, president of the foundation and editor of its book series, retired, and Paul Mellon did not wish to continue. Since the creation of the foundation in 1945 he alone had provided the necessary financial support. In the intervening years almost $17 million had been spent on the Bollingen fellows and their books. Although the books often sold well, the foundation remained dependent on fresh subsidies from Paul Mellon.[37] From 1966 to 1968 support for Eranos still amounted to $6,000 per year, but now the conferences had to be self-supporting, which did not prove easy. While contributions continued to come from various foundations and benefactors, the buildings and lecture hall in Moscia were rented out whenever possible to outsiders for congresses and the like. Attendance fees also brought some income.

The title of the 1968 conference was *"Tradition und Gegenwart"* (Tradition and the present day). This was the first since 1938(!) to include a woman speaker, namely Kathleen Raine, who was so enthused by the notion of the imaginal world and related ideas, which were typical of Eranos, that she herself later organized conferences and founded the journal *Temenos* in the same spirit. Kathleen Raine had studied natural sciences at Cambridge and, following the trend of the time, had at first adopted a decidedly agnostic position. While at Cambridge she had established contact with Graham Greene and T.S. Eliot. It was through her pioneering works on William Blake and W.B. Yeats that she became well known: works that she wrote after a complete change of spiritual outlook. Her big two-volume study *Blake and Tradition*[38] could only be completed and published thanks to the support she received from the Bollingen Foundation,[39] against opposition from positivistic literary scholars who objected to her theses and methods. Damaging to her reputation was her frankness about her adherence to the so-called *philosophia perennis*, that is to say humankind's timeless heritage of wisdom. However, the fact that she was one of the most renowned poets in Britain[40] is thought to have been the final deciding factor in the publication of the book.[41]

Through the Greek Orthodox traditionalist and poet Philip Sherrard,[42] who was one of the early readers of her works on Blake, she was introduced to the works of René Guénon, founder of the "Integral Tradition" movement, and his pupil Ananda K. Coomaraswamy, art historian and supporter of Mircea Eliade. It was Guénon and Coomaraswamy who turned her whole worldview upside down.[43] Nevertheless, the Integral Tradition does not appear to have played any major role in her work. Marsilio Ficino was more important for her.

Through her visits to Watkins Bookshop in London, a leading and time-honored outlet for esoteric literature, she also came into contact with the works of Thomas Taylor the Platonist as well as with Hermes Trismegistos, Paracelsus, Fludd, Agrippa, Swedenborg, and Dante, all of whom were among the sources used by William Blake.[44] Her investigations into Gnosticism, Hermeticism, and alchemy stood her in good stead for her searching studies on the Irish poet William Butler Yeats,[45] who is known to have been strongly influenced by esoteric thought and was even a member of the Hermetic Order of the Golden Dawn, the most important magical order in Britain in the late nineteenth and early twentieth centuries.

She was also interested in Jung, although she never became a Jungian. "My master is William Blake, who spoke for the imagination," she declared in an interview in 1992.[46] Nevertheless, she gave many lectures at the Jungian Analytical Psychology Club of London.[47] Although she converted to Catholicism, she believed that this entailed no conflict with "pagan" polytheism, since the angelic hierarchies in Christianity and the Tree of Life in Judaism provided a polytheistic counterbalance.[48]

Especially gratifying to her was the recognition that she received from Charles, Prince of Wales, who sent her many personal letters and generously supported the Temenos Academy that she co-founded. She had been introduced to Prince Charles by the Eranos speaker Laurens van der Post, who, as already mentioned, was one of the prince's mentors. Kathleeen Raine died in 2003 at the age of 95. As a last word on her, let me quote a remark of hers that succinctly illustrates her worldview: "Of what use are the arts, if not to reflect our vision of heaven in the beautiful forms of music, painting, poetry, architecture, and the other arts?"[49]

Another remarkable woman should be mentioned in connection with the 1971 Eranos meeting, namely Aniela Jaffé, Jung's secretary and colleague from 1955 until his death. She performed a great service as the true author of Jung's "autobiography" *Memories, Dreams, Reflections* and as such has earned the sobriquet of "Jung's Eckermann" (referring to Johann Peter Eckermann, Goethe's friend and recorder of his conversations).[50] She was born in Berlin and studied in Hamburg. Being Jewish by birth, she had to flee to Switzerland during the National Socialist era. In 1937 she embarked on an analysis with Jung. However, she was not only interested in psychology but also in literature, fairy tales, and parapsychology. One of the books she wrote was a study of the English occultist and founder of the Hermetic Society, Anna Kingsford.[51] Much of what we know about Jung's last years is thanks to her observations. Encouraged by Laurens van der Post, she wrote a much-quoted essay on Jung and National Socialism, in which she exonerated him from accusations of anti-Semitism.[52] In 1975 she spoke again at Eranos, on the subject of "C.G. Jung and the Eranos Conferences."

Another who spoke for the first time at Eranos in 1971 was the ethnologist and sociologist Jean Servier. Although Servier was essentially a specialist on the Berber culture of North Africa, his book *L'homme et l'invisible*[53] had brought him recognition beyond the boundaries of his speciality. In this book, drawing on his ethnological studies and using highly poetic language, he upholds the unity of human thought, in contrast to most other ethnologists, who insist on the diverse ways of thinking of indigenous peoples.[54] Servier emphasizes his view of traditional societies as having the same basic conceptions world-wide. The mere crass materialism of the West had led to an abandonment of this timeless core of basic beliefs, centered on the soul, God, and the sacred. As a result, the West had destroyed not only its own world but also the inner core of many other cultures, filling the resulting void with its own industrial products. Here there is an obvious connection with the socially critical thinking of Gilbert Durand and Henry Corbin. Servier followed up *L'homme et l'invisible* with a companion volume in which he pursues these lines of thought further, exploring myths and symbols of traditional peoples and of the ancient world that give human beings pointers to the spiritual realm.[55] Here he gives a central place to divinatory methods such as geomancy and the *I Ching*. Significantly, the book begins with a sentence from Agrippa of Nettesheim. Referring to these various "marvellous operations" that lift human beings up to higher levels, Agrippa says that their effective cause lies neither in the underworld nor in the stars but solely in ourselves. In the present context, it is particularly interesting that the book carries the dedication "Eranos, Genio Loci Ignoto."

Jean Servier also collaborated in the University of Saint John of Jerusalem. A further subject that preoccupied him was that of utopias, which he saw as containing the patterns of certain traditional ideas such as that of the "perfect city." His book on the history of utopias is dedicated to Martin Buber, who originally stimulated his interest in the subject.[56] Subsequently Jean Servier devoted himself more and more to the academic treatment of esoteric themes. Thus he produced, for example, a small explanatory book on magic.[57] He also translated the first great classic work on magic, Agrippa von Nettesheim's *De occulta philosophia*, into French and added an introduction and footnotes.[58] His final project was to edit an almost 1500-page *Dictionnaire critique de l'ésotérisme*,[59] which encompasses practically all periods of history and all peoples. In the preface Servier makes no bones about his own pro-esoteric attitude. To Jean Servier as holder of a "ring of Eranos" I will return later.

The year 1972 saw the liquidation of the publishing firm of Rhein-Verlag, which had brought out the Eranos conference volumes right from the beginning. It would be no exaggeration to say that Dr. Daniel Brody, the owner of the firm, contributed as much to the world-wide reputation of Eranos as Olga Fröbe or C.G. Jung.[60] Published regularly and with considerable sacrifice, often under difficult circumstances, including the war years, these books always ensured the prompt dissemination of the lectures.[61] Without them, many of the speakers would have had much less incentive to come to Ascona. Thanks to these books it was possible for the lecturers to reach not merely the modest hundred or so who made up the early audiences, but a whole world of people with the relevant cultural interests. Access to the yearbooks is greatly facilitated by the two indexes published by Rhein-Verlag for the periods 1933–56 and 1957–61, both of them compiled by Magda Kerényi with enormous dedication over a period of six years. They contain a continuous index of 13,000 key words as well as details about each author and lecture.[62] Already, at the end of the first conference, Brody had declared himself willing, at his own risk, to print and market the conference volumes. This was, both economically and idealistically, a very noble gesture, which spared Fröbe the laborious task of finding a publisher and convincing them of the importance of the project.

The Catholic theologian Karl Rahner spoke as follows in his address on the occasion of Brody's seventy-fifth birthday:

> When we speak of a book, we say—unconscious of the deeper meanings inherent in language—that it has "appeared," just as we speak reverently of the "appearance" of a spirit. Only angels and books can "appear." Hence, everything that a person can do to bring about the appearance of books is a sacred act and a holy task, dedicated to the divine.[63]

And in 1953 Jung wrote to Brody:

> Farsightedly and undaunted by the unfavourable conditions of the time, you have done something decisive for a cultural enterprise which, through its dissemination world-wide, has been of enormous benefit to me personally. Your work as a publisher has for me opened up paths to the world, for which a pioneer can only be grateful. In this way you have extended a helping hand not only to me but also to many others.[64]

A particularly personal and heartfelt letter, five pages long, was sent by Fröbe to Brody when the twentieth Eranos volume appeared:

> When I think back over those years, with all their joys and difficulties, with their hopes, insecurity and risk, when I remember the war years, which you spent in Mexico[65] but nonetheless made provision for the Eranos yearbooks, when I consider this Eranos road that I have had to travel—but which you traveled continuously with me—then I know how profoundly this was intended by fate. I was already "possessed" by Eranos long before 1933. But in 1933 you were also possessed by it, and you will certainly know how much this kind of possession demands of one. Should we have refused it? I believe not … Your faithfulness to Eranos, to me personally, to all the speakers, to the whole circle, is so far removed from being merely a publishing undertaking that it is hard for me to find words to express our thanks. You engage fully in everything, your heart always has a say, and all of this has worked greatly to the benefit of Eranos … The Eranos yearbooks are in fact your "OPUS" … Just as I found my own personal opus in Eranos and never abandoned it (just as it never abandoned me), so it happened in a different way with many speakers and audience members and also with yourself. All of us are working our way forward within something that is larger and deeper than ourselves, something to which we have given the name Eranos.

Daniel Brody's high regard for Eranos is clearly expressed in the introductory words that he wrote to the booklet *25 Jahre Eranos*: "Eranos is for all of us a signpost to a better and more real understanding of ourselves. Here, each of us comes in his or her own way, without slogans and important-sounding words, to experience—as with the Tao—the unity within the multiplicity of all that is." Earlier in the same text he remarked on something that other visitors had also observed:

> Probably many came for the first time with an attitude of skepticism, whether they were speakers or audience members, but within a few days, struck by the aura of the meeting, the intellectual substance of the lectures, the harmony between people from all parts of the world and between the atmosphere of the place and the surrounding nature, they had become enthusiastic adherents of Eranos.

Brody, a native of Budapest, had been the editor-in-chief of a major newspaper and then had joined the publishing firm of Kurt Wolff at the time when it was still based in Germany. In 1929 he took over the Rhein-Verlag. Two great literary names in particular lent prestige to the firm: James Joyce and Hermann Broch. And here I cannot refrain from quoting two sentences of Broch that show the affinity of his thought to Eranos:

> I am convinced that the mythic way of thinking constitutes an integrating part of the Logos, in other words that all our logical forms—which are commonly regarded as autonomous—have a second, mythical, structure; indeed I believe that this is how the unity is created between the rational and irrational, which is so fundamental to our life and being.[66]

Similarly, in a letter Broch writes that "the esoteric, the religious, the mystical lives and moves and is felt in the soul of each individual."[67]

After the closure of the Rhein-Verlag, the publication and distribution of the Eranos proceedings was taken over by the renowned Dutch publisher E.J. Brill, probably at the instigation of Rudolf Ritsema. The books now took on a somewhat more international flair, with the titles given in three languages. The lectures appeared not only in the form of the original text but also accompanied by résumés in two other languages. However, the cooperation with Brill did not last long, as the firm was not satisfied with the sales figures. In 1977 the task of publication was taken over by Insel Verlag in Germany, but the delays in production became ever longer, and years went by before the lectures appeared in print.

In 1973 Antoine Faivre, at that time a professor of German studies, spoke at Eranos for the first time, having attended the conferences regularly since 1967. To the audience he was already well known, as in earlier years he had volunteered to write and deliver German résumés of Henry Corbin's often difficult lectures. Faivre had written his dissertation on the eighteenth-century Christian theosophist Karl von Eckartshausen and had already made a name for himself as an expert in this by no means simple domain.[68] The following year he lectured again, in a tone of personal engagement, comparing the modern secularization of the cosmos with the Christian-theosophical approach, in which God is perceived as being manifest in the cosmos. However, in his Eranos diaries, which he kindly let me read, Antoine Faivre reports that the lecture did not meet with an entirely warm response from the organizers and from the academics present.

Indeed, Antoine Faivre was altogether not always of one mind with the organizers, despite his undoubted suitability for Eranos in view of his multilingualism and the way in which he had followed both an academic and a spiritual path. Apart from the inevitable but ultimately peripheral "market of vanities" that one finds (as one still does today) at such conferences, what disturbed Antoine Faivre particularly was the sharp division between the lecturers, in all their authority, and the rest of the participants.[69] He complained that there was practically no opportunity to speak with or question the speakers. When Faivre came again in 1975, albeit not as a speaker, he even brought a written petition calling for a change in this policy, signed by many people including long-standing and respected lecturers.

However, this attempt fell on stony ground, as had earlier approaches to Olga Fröbe, who had refused to allow question periods on the grounds that most questioners only wanted to assert themselves and hear their own voices. This was the main reason, as Antoine Faivre wrote to me in a letter, why he withdrew from Eranos, despite his agreement with its fundamental aims.[70] This kind of elitism, which today is hardly applicable any longer, has changed fundamentally since the 1990s. When the conferences were resumed, first by the Amici di Eranos, there was a two-hour "round table" every afternoon, at which the lecturers were available to have a dialogue with the audience and answer their questions. And in the conferences that still take place today in the Casa Serodine and in Moscia-Ascona the audience members also have the opportunity to express themselves.

Antoine Faivre's diary also reveals that Gerhard Wehr was present in Ascona in 1974. Wehr is an expert on Jung and Rudolf Steiner as well as the author of numerous books on Christian Theosophy and, as we now know, the author of an as-yet-unpublished book on Eranos.[71] It was Ernst Benz who had prompted him to go to Eranos and had introduced him to Faivre and Corbin. Under the date 21 August 1974 is the following interesting entry by Faivre:

> Quite a lively discussion between Corbin and Durand about the word "mythos" and about the next conference of the U.S.J.J. [Université de Saint-Jean de Jérusalem]. Corbin is annoyed when we use the word "mythos," which to his ears always has a reductionist flavour. But what else can one say? He suggests *histoire transsubtile* … Surely rather cumbersome … Stella Corbin took our side against her husband.

This argument continued for several days, until Gilbert Durand, to please Corbin, suggested the word "hierogony." It seems that even great minds find it difficult to achieve a distanced view of their own, admittedly deep, studies. Despite his winning outward personality and charm, Corbin was evidently not always an easy person to get along with, as he was all too fond of upholding his own position. As Corbin was always totally identified with what he said, he had difficulties with differing positions. This could easily lead to outbreaks of anger on his part, although these quickly turned into sentiments of close friendship.

Faivre's diary entries for 1975 clearly express his concern that there were hardly any younger people in the audience. Various ideas occurred to him for reaching a wider public, such as publicizing Eranos in the universities and extending the lecture hall as far as technically possible. The dismissive attitude of the conference management to these suggestions remained incomprehensible to him. It was a matter of regret to him that Scholem was absent from the 1975 meeting, as were Eliade and Aniela Jaffé.[72] However, this was compensated for by highly interesting conversations with the elegant and many-faceted James Hillman and his "polytheistic" colleague David Miller. Another person whom the diary mentions as having been present was the celebrated soprano Rita Streich. The musicologist Hildemarie Streich had already in 1973 spoken at Eranos about the musical correspondences of Michael Maier's *Atalanta Fugiens*.[73] Subsequently she gave several more lectures, for which her husband provided the musical accompaniment.[74] Thus the world of music was once again represented at Eranos, as it had been earlier by Viktor Zuckerkandl.

In 1979 Faivre was appointed to what was for a long time the only university chair in the world for the history of esotericism, namely at the Ecole Pratique des Hautes Etudes within the Sorbonne, where many earlier Eranos lecturers, such as Puech, Massignon, and Corbin had taught.[75] His continual striving to find a unified terminology and his insistence on a clear scholarly distinction between the various esoteric currents have contributed to lending this area of research an academic reputation.[76] Among the many books written by Antoine Faivre, his two-volume work *Accès de l'Ésotérisme occidental* is regarded as the best introduction to Western esotericism and its development.[77] Faivre is also responsible for two prestigious book series, namely the *Bibliothèque de l'Hermétisme*, comprising works by important individual authors, and the *Cahiers de l'Hermétisme*, where the volumes consist of collections of contributions by various authors on themes connected with esotericism.[78] Looking at the original editorial team of the *Cahiers*, which included Eranos speakers such as Ernst Benz,[79] Gilbert Durand, Mircea Eliade, and Henri-Charles Puech, one sees, despite the overall scholarly level, the nature of their common interests. In the meantime these series already comprise fifty volumes.

There have always been speculations and even accusations that Faivre's academic activity is esoterically rather than academically motivated. This is the allegation leveled above all by Steven Wasserstrom.[80] Across many pages in his volume *Esotericism and the Academy* Faivre's one-time pupil Wouter Hanegraaff analyzes the scholarly activity and development of his teacher.[81] His conclusion: until circa 1990 Faivre was indeed bound to an "essentialist" viewpoint influenced by Eranos. Then via his submission of esoteric thought to academic analysis there nevertheless occurred a distinct about-face in the direction of empiricism and methodological agnosticism. Hence it is an extreme over-simplification when Steven Wasserstrom in his book simply characterizes Faivre as an "esoterist" and member of an "esoterist community." The academically impeccable historical, definitional, and analytical works that have since appeared from Faivre have assured his place in the world of scholarship. If it is true that Faivre, as a private individual, evinces certain "esoteric" attitudes,[82] these are not discernible in his academic works. Sympathy and empathy do not necessarily lead to a shifting of one's horizons.

In 1975 a French speaker once again came to the rostrum, namely the philosopher Jean Brun, a member of the circle that included Henry Corbin, Antoine Faivre,[83] Jean Servier, and Gilbert Durand, who were all active in the University of Saint John of Jerusalem. This involvement alone is enough to show that Jean Brun also counted among those philosophers who did not go along with the elimination of any form of transcendence in our age, an age in which it was said that "God (but which one?) is dead." Brun even poses the question whether we are today seeing a return of "Dionysos," in the form of either Eros or knowledge, both of which are expressions of our longing as humans to raise ourselves above our existence as separate and isolated beings. This direction of thought is already evident in the title of his first book, *Les conquêtes de l'homme et la séparation ontologique*.[84] Similarly, he is critical of an exaggerated technocracy.[85] Thus he perceives machines not only as tools but also as a playground for irrational fantasies in which mankind seeks by mechanical means to rise above the limitations of time and space and, in so doing, drives the world into an inextricable turmoil. The compulsive swing to the machine is, however, not ideologically neutral, for, as Jean Brun writes, "machines are only 'tricks' by means of which a conjurer, disguised as a scholar, engineer or politician, seeks to present himself as a saviour."[86] Brun's further achievements include his works on Plato and the Platonic Academy, Neoplatonism, and the history of European philosophy.

It is striking how after 1945 the "sceptre" of Eranos passed away from the German-speaking professors, who had been dominant in the pre-war years, and into the hands of French scholars of a spiritual turn of mind. This observation is in no way negatively meant. On the contrary, interests of this kind had practically no aficionados in Germany after the baleful experiences of National Socialism, with its mythically (but not esoterically) tinged ideology. In Germany there was a desire to get away from anything that smacked of myth, romanticism, gnosis, and the world of the gods. The pendulum had swung in the opposite direction, and now logic, positivism, and the Enlightenment spirit were the order of the day—or rather of the decades.[87] The French "Eranians," as we have seen, had originally often taken their intellectual and spiritual raw material from the German world of learning, and now they carefully cultivated this material, developing it further and even bringing it into prestigious academic institutions. English-speaking scholars, such as Hillman and Miller, added further facets and brought this heritage of thought, transmitted to us from "southern" antiquity via the Renaissance, into a safe haven across the Atlantic. It was only through Jakob Boehme, Romanticism, and the "romantic" conception of antiquity (Winkelmann, etc.) that this heritage became German.

David Miller

I have already mentioned David Miller as a polytheist, but his academic training was in fact theological. He gained a bachelor of divinity degree from Bethany Theological Seminary and a doctorate from Drew University in the field of theology and culture. In 1975, on the hundredth anniversary of Jung's birth, he came for the first time to speak at Eranos. Altogether, between 1975 and 1988, he would speak there nine times, which clearly shows the influence of archetypal psychology at Eranos. But his success there was also due to his great rhetorical talent, which turned his lectures into veritable sermons.

However, Miller's interests encompass not only depth psychology but also religion and literature, as was already apparent in his doctoral dissertation on the relationship of Aristophanes' comedies to Greek religion and culture. As a further proof of his interdisciplinary studies, he spent fifteen years researching the use of ancient Greek mythological and literary images in Christianity (the good shepherd, the holy fool, the descent into the underworld, etc.). He has a special knack for being constructively provocative, which comes across in book titles such as *Christs: Archetypal Images in Christian Theology* and in a lecture he once gave entitled "Nothing to Teach, No Way to Teach It, Together with the Obligation to Teach." His reputation as a teacher can only be described as exceptional. Thus in 1996–99 he became the first recipient of the William P. Tolley Distinguished Teaching Professorship in the Humanities. He also received the Outstanding Teacher Award of the Alumni Society of University College, Syracuse University, and at least two other similar awards for special teaching achievements.[88]

The various academic associations to which David Miller belongs include the International Society for Humor Studies. His main career was as professor of religion at Syracuse University, but he has also given seminars at the C.G. Jung Institute in Zurich. David Miller has played a particularly central role at the Pacifica Graduate Institute in Santa Barbara, California, a highly interdisciplinary institution with a world-wide reputation. Its study program, while centered on depth psychology, embraces also world literature, religion, art, and mythology. It was not without reason that Joseph Campbell was one of the most prominent teachers there. Recently the Pacifica Graduate Institute has entered into a close collaboration with the Eranos Foundation in Moscia.

For Miller polytheism corresponds to the manifold nature of our inner life, and the "God who is dead" is only the God of monotheism. The gods and the goddesses, on the other hand, live on in the stories, tragedies, and comedies that feature them. Even modern technology, Miller argues, is not free of these stories of the gods, being no less than the fulfillment of the myths of Prometheus or Hephaistos. And it is "Pan" whom one must hold responsible for explosions of irrationality in the form of wars. But what is the conclusion in the afterword to his book *The New Polytheism*—that the gods are laughing?[89] It is the liberating and redeeming effect of laughter in the midst of tragedy that Miller sees as one of the main goals of his work.

The Struggle Between Monotheists and Polytheists

The title of the 1976 meeting, "Oneness and Variety," reflects the stronger polytheistic emphasis, although the only classical polytheist who spoke was James Hillman. An account of the meeting is given in the form of an article by the poet and playwright Margaret Barker, who was generally rather disappointed, as she had expected more from the event.[90] In particular she had two complaints: first, that most of the lecturers spoke in German, which she did not understand; and second, that there was no possibility and, as she wrote, no inclination to allow a discussion with the speakers. Margaret Barker goes so far as to say that she "felt a heaviness, a foreboding, a kind of intellectual death." The only part of the meeting that she really enjoyed was a flute and guitar concert. Furthermore, she found that the fabric of the lectures was woven too much out of mere erudition. For her, at any rate, it was not an atmosphere that breathed creativity, although most of the audience seemed to be attuned to the prevailing spirit. Her report also reveals that the audience included the Jungian Charles Poncé, an expert on alchemy, Kabbalah, and esotericism in general.[91]

In 1977 the Egyptologist Erik Hornung, who was later to play a key role in the revival of the classical Eranos meetings in 1989, came to speak at Eranos through the good offices of Adolf Portmann. At that time, as Hornung kindly informed me in a letter, he found the "struggle" between the "monotheists" and the "polytheists" in full swing, with each side uttering warnings about the other. Born in Riga, Erik Hornung taught in the early 1960s at the University of Münster and from 1967 to 1998 was professor of Egyptology in Basel. A central preoccupation of his life was the study and translation of the Egyptian literature relating to the underworld, which only a few had previously investigated. He was responsible for the first complete German translation of the so-called *Egyptian Book of the Dead* and also for much of the archaeological work in the famous Valley of the Kings. His numerous books, written in a clear and brilliant style and accessible to non-specialists,[92] have greatly contributed to making knowledge about ancient Egypt available to a wider public and promoting a less narrow and one-sided view of its history.

For the philosophers of classical antiquity the wisdom of Ancient Egypt still had a clear and central position. In modern times, however, Egypt came increasingly to be seen as the fount of a primal esoteric knowledge, and other aspects of the culture were pushed into the background. Hornung, especially in his book *Geist der Pharaonenzeit*, attempted to create an awareness of these original aspects of Egyptian thought.[93] He is of the firm conviction that "one-sidedness leads nowhere."[94] In the same spirit, he produced a further work in 1999, dealing in a scholarly but sympathetic way with the image of "esoteric Egypt" over the course of history.[95] This book was enormously successful and was translated into several languages.

Another speaker at Eranos in 1977 was the political scientist Eric Voegelin. The fact that he spoke there only once might have been on account of his age or because he did not fully conform to the basic "Eranian consensus."[96] On the other hand, in his favor were his holistic conception of politics, which also encompassed the transcendental dimension, as well as his belief in a metaphysical "Platonic" order of things. By the same token, he believed that there are higher, supra-human forces that play a decisive role in politics and history. Furthermore, he was firmly convinced that man is part of a hierarchy of being, reaching up to the transcendental realm.[97] On the other hand, his extremely negative view of Gnosticism as a "revolt against God" must, I would suppose, have gone against one of the—at least unconsciously held—tenets of Eranos.[98]

I feel it is appropriate to say a bit more about Eric Voegelin, not only because of his involvement in Eranos, but because his conception of Gnosticism became very influential and was (and is) indirectly responsible for the negative assessment of Eranos in certain philosophical and political circles.

Voegelin was born in Cologne but studied in Vienna, where he was strongly influenced by two men: Hans Kelsen, legal expert and author of the Austrian constitution, and the "holistic" thinker Othmar Spann. Both men acted as his doctoral supervisors.[99] Kelsen's categories and his doctrine of "pure law" were closer to Voegelin's way of thinking,[100] but Othmar Spann brought him into contact with Plato and Aristotle as well as with German idealism.[101] Among the other strong influences on him, Voegelin includes Max Weber, Karl Kraus, and the Stefan George circle; it is often overlooked that the George milieu also brought forth important achievements in the world of learning, such as those of Kantorowicz in history, Gundolf in the field of literature, and Bertram in philosophy. A two-year sojourn in America led to an intellectual break-through and a discovery of the value of *common sense*, something that he felt to be lacking in Germany. After a further year in France, he returned to Vienna as an extraordinary professor.

In 1938, with the annexation of Austria by National Socialist Germany, he felt compelled to emigrate to America, where he taught at various universities including Harvard. In 1958 he accepted a professorship in Munich, where he co-founded the Geschwister-Scholl Institute for Political Science in order to convey his political ideas and fears to a Germany that was still prostrate from the war. After his retirement from the Munich chair he retired to the United States, where his influence, especially in neo-conservative circles, became much stronger than in the German-speaking realm. He even acted as advisor to the United States government at the Hoover Institution on War, Revolution and Peace at Stanford University.

Voegelin is also well known in Italy, and many of his works have been translated into Italian. His leading supporter there was Gian Franco Lami, formerly a student of Augusto del Noce. Lami taught political science for a time at the University of Terramo near Rome and moved later to the Sapienza University of Rome. Among other things, he wrote an extensive introduction to a dialogue between Voegelin and Hannah Arendt, in which he included a review by Arendt and a counter-reply from Voegelin.[102] In this text he attempts to elucidate the political philosophy of Voegelin. He also edited a collection of papers on Voegelin, contributed by a dozen or so internationally known experts, including Tilo Schabert, the Erlangen philosopher and conference organizer of the Amici di Eranos.[103]

Here I would like to concentrate on Voegelin's conception of gnosis, as this is especially important in relation to Eranos.[104] It began in 1938 with his work *Die politischen Religionen* (later published in English as *The Political Religions*), in which he described National Socialism and Communism as religious movements. Later, to characterize these "political religions," he used the term "gnosis," by which he meant the human attempt—vain, as he saw it—to transfer an ideal of transcendental perfection into the earthly realm of historical reality. As he considered such attempts at self-redemption to be logically impossible, he categorized them as "pathological." More specifically, adapting Schelling's terminology, he used the word "pneumopathological" (*pneumopathologisch*), meaning a more profound and radical form of mental disorder than is normally implied by the term "psychopathology." Gnosis is for him not only an unacceptable outlook but a "diseased growth," a "cancer-like tumor in the body of reality," which must be cured and, if necessary, forcibly removed.[105] Gnosis, if not suppressed, would lead to the "death of a civilization." The obvious comparison with the methods of the Inquisition arises—a comparison that was not rejected by Voegelin.[106]

Through a more intensive consideration of gnosis and Gnosticism—a process in which the Eranos speakers Henri-Charles Puech, Karl Löwith, and Gilles Quispel played a role—Voegelin came to the realization that he had in fact been using the term gnosis incorrectly and had meant rather the ideas of the millenarian revolutionary movements. Thus increasingly (e.g. in his Eranos lecture) he spoke of "activism" and the "magic of the extreme." He never, however, abandoned the negative connotation of the word "gnosis," which had taken hold in his mind. Altogether one is struck by Voegelin's frequent use of "esoteric" concepts such as magic (in his consideration of Hegel), gnosis, and witchcraft. In this way he shows his hostility towards certain tendencies of thought which, in his opinion, characterize the process of decline inherent in modernity: a decline which he sees as having begun in the early Middle Ages.[107] At the same time, he saw himself as a pure champion of the "light" and the "truth." Wouter Hanegraaff, in the essay mentioned earlier, quotes a letter that Voegelin sent to his old friend Gregor Sebba, in which he said: "It will shock you, but I *am* a mystical philosopher."

Despite the intensive research and publishing activities of the Eric Voegelin Archive, founded in the early 1990s at the Maximilian University in Munich,[108] Voegelin's efforts to bring about a complete reform of political science according to his vision appear to have so far not borne fruit. Nevertheless, the literature on him continues to grow steadily. Thus Stephen A. McNight, in his essay "Voegelin's New Science of History," compares Voegelin's historical writings with those of Oswald Spengler, Arnold Toynbee, and Ernst Cassirer.[109] A wide range of other appellations has been applied to Voegelin. Marion Montgomery has called him a "prophetic philosopher," Lewis P. Simpson, on account of his "sense of dramatic structure" and the "sweep of his imagination," has described him as a "poet, the author of an epic summation of the spiritual history of modernity."[110] His theses against the madness of modernization and on the prospect of a secure human order under strong divine leadership clearly hit a nerve amongst a certain group of our apprehensive fellow men.

On the conference of 1977 we have the report of a prominent eye-witness, namely the scholar of religion, Ioan P. Culianu, who, like his associate Mircea Eliade, had fled from his native Romania. In 1991 he was murdered in Chicago. At the beginning of his report Culianu describes the Eranos yearbooks as perhaps the most important regular series of publications in the field of religious studies in the twentieth century.[111] After a brief statement on the history and importance of Eranos, he focuses in particular on the lectures of James Hillman, Jean Servier, and Hermann Landoldt (a student of Corbin). Servier spoke about geomancy in North Africa and described how, as a child, he had learned the practical basics of this form of prediction from Moroccans. Thus he was able to give concrete illustrations in his talk.

Culianu was particularly impressed by the rhetoric of the trickster-like figure, David Miller, who held forth about the "good shepherd" and his "flocks," referring to the history of political mass movements. That summer the lake rose to an abnormal level, and even the Casa Eranos was flooded, which meant that the lecture by Jean Brun had to be cancelled. Nevertheless, Culianu came away with pleasant memories of the concerts and the singing recitals of Rita Streich. However, his report ends with the observation that nothing could make up for the absence of the master and founder, C.G. Jung.

The *grande dame* of analytical psychology, Marie-Louise von Franz, who died in 1998, spoke for the first time at Eranos in 1978. An interesting report on this conference by Max Schoch appeared in the *Neue Zürcher Zeitung* of 27 September 1978. The author observed a change from earlier meetings, namely that the proceedings were much more clearly oriented to certain overall principles, rather than being merely a series of individual presentations. These principles and the general ethos of the conferences took precedence over purely individual perspectives. Max Schoch gave particular praise to Adolf Portmann, whose concluding presentation highlighted this fundamental commonality.

At the 1979 meeting it was the sinologist and expert on Chinese medicine Manfred Porkert and the Tibetologist Detlef I. Lauf who spoke for the first time at Eranos. Lauf's talk included photographs illustrating Tibetan religion. Another who spoke was the specialist on Christian Kabbalah, François Secret, whose chair at the Ecole Pratique des Hautes Etudes was, after being re-named, taken over by Antoine Faivre.[112] Adolf Portmann's scheduled lecture, entitled "*Persönliches zu den drei Jahrzehnten Eranos*" (Personal reflections on three decades of Eranos), had to be cancelled, as Portmann became ill and had to stop speaking after only a few minutes. Unfortunately he was also unable to commit the lecture to writing. However, notes for the planned lecture were included in his literary estate, which is now preserved in the Basel University Library. At the previous year's meeting Portmann had also had to forgo making a written version of his summing-up lecture.

In 1980 Adolf Portmann was unable to attend Eranos at all, and he died in 1982, the same year as Gershom Scholem.[113] The regular summing-up talk at the end of each meeting, which for many years had been delivered by Portmann, then fell to Erik Hornung: proof of his position as primus *inter pares*. Portmann's departure also meant that Rudolf Ritsema became the sole official organizer of the meetings—a task which was not easy for an individual and undoubtedly weighed heavily on him.[114] In that year the cultural anthropologist Gilbert Durand gave a grand speech looking back over more than fifty years of Eranos under the title "Le Génie du Lieu et les heures propices" (The spirit of place and propitious moments), in which he again surveyed all the important speakers.[115] The goal of Eranos, he said, was to rediscover the civilizing ethos of the West, which had become lost in a "morass of secularized ethnocentrism."

From subsequent years I could list the names of many newcomers or of speakers who have not yet been mentioned. These include Ulrich Mann, Roger A. Stamm, Hayao Kawai, Victor Weisskopf, Hans-Joachim Klimkeit, Morton Smith, Yves A. Dauge, Walter Burkert, Dominique Zahan, Jean Hulin, Shizuteru Ueda, Herbert Pietschmann—all well known in the world of learning, authors of numerous books, and above all people capable of looking beyond the boundaries of their disciplines. This rather unfairly curtailed and incomplete list must unfortunately suffice, for by then the essential pillars of Eranos had already been put in place.

🦋 14. An End, Some New Beginnings, and Repeated Turbulence

We now come to the trickiest part of this book, for nothing is harder than to pin down and interpret historical events that are still in the process of unfolding. The protagonists are all, in one way or another, still actively involved in Eranos. Unfortunately, however, they no longer work together, but pursue—as I hope—the same noble goals in different ways. As they do not see eye to eye with each other there are also conflicting interpretations of the recent history of Eranos. Therefore I have tried—without guarantee—to rely as far as possible only on published sources and to quote oral testimonies only if they agree. Hence it is inevitable that there are certain gaps in this account. At any rate, my version of the story has met with very contrasting reactions from various long-standing Eranos participants. Some have judged it to be objective and balanced, while others have said that it diverges from the facts "to the point of caricature." What is striking is the zeal—not to say quasi-religious fanaticism—with which individual positions are defended. Is the *genius loci* really so powerful?[1] At any rate, I regret that, through my account, I have lost some valued friendships.

In 1986 Tilo Schabert spoke for the first time at Eranos, although he had been attending meetings since 1970. Later, together with Erik Hornung, he was to lead the conferences of the Amici di Eranos until 1999. He had studied in Munich at the Institute for Political Studies, founded by Eric Voegelin, as mentioned earlier.[2] It was through Voeglin's connection with Adolf Portmann that Schabert finally came to Eranos. In addition to his political studies, Schabert had also concerned himself with ideas for architecture and town planning, producing several articles and an outstanding book on the subject.[3] Taking his lead from Plato, he sees worldly architecture as an image of "divine" ideas, which are reflected particularly in the forms of the circle and the square. A classic example of this notion is the "heavenly Jerusalem."

In 1987 a serious hiatus arose. Rudolf Ritsema, who was in sole charge, announced in his closing speech that Eranos was "about to complete a span of time corresponding to a whole life cycle." In 1988 Ritsema then caused astonishment and no doubt much dismay among his audience with a lecture entitled "Allumfassende Wendigkeit: Schlußstein des Eranos-Projekts" (All-encompassing flexibility: capstone of the Eranos project) in which he explained what he meant by "completion of the life cycle." He referred to a statement by Olga Fröbe that made Eranos subject to an astrological scheme of seven-year cycles. As this was the fifty-sixth meeting, completing eight cycles of seven, it meant that Eranos was about to enter a new stage of its existence, ruled by the "outer" planets: Uranus, Neptune, and Pluto. The time had come when the complex of images with which Eranos had been working should be integrated into the individual's life pattern. Just as a caterpillar shuts itself away in a chrysalis before turning into a butterfly and reawakening, so the Eranos conferences, with their general lectures, should come to an end and the participants should concern themselves with their own individuation.

Furthermore, in a circular communication of January 1989 entitled *Neues von ERANOS: zurück zu den Quellen* (News from Eranos: back to the sources), Rudolf Ritsema declared that this new orientation was "both a return to and a reminder of the original purpose of Eranos as a meeting place between East and West." The interdisciplinary form hitherto taken by the Eranos conferences had been conceived only "as a preparation for such a meeting in the true sense of the word as a psychological encounter and experience such as is granted to a person on the path to individuation." An exceptionally important aid on this path, he said, is the *I Ching*, the *Book of Changes*. And here Ritsema referred back to the beginnings of Eranos and to C.G. Jung and Richard Wilhelm, who had already pointed the way.

Ritsema expressed himself in even greater detail in the already mentioned article "Images of the Unknown: The Eranos *I Ching* Project 1989–1997," written in collaboration with Shantena Sabbadini.[4] Here he argued that it had been Olga Fröbe's lifelong wish to integrate both the study and practice of the *I Ching* into the Eranos meetings, as she had always consulted it about private matters as well as about current problems related to Eranos. Already in 1934 she had told Jung that she wished to use it in connection with the conferences. Jung, however, felt that the time was not ripe and rejected the idea, finding it more fruitful to first explore the archetypal forms that constituted a foundation common to all human beings. This Jungian approach, Ritsema said, had prevailed for more than fifty years, but Fröbe herself had never given up the hope that one day a personal and experiential focus on the *I Ching* would find its rightful place at Eranos. As Ritsema emphasized, this common interest, which they had shared since 1948, had formed the basis for the friendship between Fröbe and himself.

He himself had come into contact with the *I Ching* in 1944 through his analyst, Alwine von Keller, who also belonged to Fröbe's circle of friends and with whom he had studied Jungian psychology. This had led to his study of classical Chinese and subsequently to his new translation of the *I Ching*,[5] carried out in collaboration with Stephen Karcher.[6] For all these reasons Ritsema now wished the work of Eranos to be devoted exclusively to the *I Ching*. In a lengthy newspaper article in the *Neue Zürcher Zeitung* of 17 August 1990, entitled "Streit um Eranos—Debatten und Fronten in Ascona" (Conflict over Eranos: debates and opposing fronts in Ascona), the author Max Schoch, who was familiar with the conferences, gave further reasons for Rudolf Ritsema's decision. The first of these was "lack of money to continue the conferences." In addition there was the realization "that the traditional lecture event no longer appealed to the younger generation." Ritsema wanted to get away from the "holiday event" and put the emphasis on "soul guidance" of the participants, as Olga Fröbe had in fact originally intended.

Ritsema evidently had deeply felt further "esoteric" reasons for ending the Eranos conferences, as is indicated by a then unpublished text by him entitled "Il periplo dell'archetipo di Eranos" (A journey around the Eranos archetype), which had originally been delivered privately as a lecture at the Round Table and although due to be published in the Eranos yearbook volume 69 (2000), did not, however, appear until a decade later.[7] Ritsema's text is informed by Buddhism and the Buddhist idea of the dissolution of all attachments in Nirvana. Ritsema advances twenty-one theses, which consistently emphasize the dissolving of all dense material forms in a great universal river. The final thesis then talks explicitly of the dissolution of the legal entity—the foundation—in the river of the *esoteric* archetype of Eranos.

Further reasons were communicated to me in conversations with various people who had been familiar with Eranos over the years. According to them, Ritsema had become unhappy with the development of Eranos and would in any case have desired a change, being no longer satisfied with the level of particular lectures. Consequently the yearbooks often contained totally different, or at least heavily reworked, versions of the original texts. Another factor was increasing pressure on the Ritsemas (and the strong influence of his wife Catherine should not be forgotten) from a number of professors who wished to be invited again the following year. These direct and indirect pressures, for example in the form of presents, evidently placed great strain on them. The reason why these speakers were so eager to come to Eranos was because they profited from the international reputation of the meetings. In some cases, especially in the United States, they could even obtain financial support from their home universities as a result of the Eranos connection.

Ritsema's strict formality—especially toward young people—was a further aggravating factor. Evidently he was so identified with Eranos that he was even prepared to see it come to an end with his own death.

It is of course not possible to provide documentary evidence to judge whether and to what extent these accusations are true, but because of the importance of the 1988 hiatus, I decided to include these personal communications.

As Tilo Schabert emphasized in an interview,[8] the announcement that Eranos would end in 1988 came totally unexpected, without any legal basis or prior consultation with lecturers and helpers, and was the work of Ritsema alone. Schabert, like many others, was evidently not able to accept this and stood against Ritsema. Erik Hornung, who traditionally gave the final speech at each conference, made a last-minute decision to change his lecture in view of the new situation.[9] He had planned to talk about the Pharaoh Akhenaten, who banished all the Egyptian gods except for Aten, god of light, whom he wished to establish as the sole ruler of heaven. Hornung's address finally included the following words:

> The fundamentalism that is everywhere raising its head, has no future. For Akhenaten teaches us, and history—that most infallible of oracles—also teaches us that what is important for human beings is the totality of things and that any kind of one-sidedness leads nowhere and must inevitably fail. Eranos has lived for 55 years in affirmation of the wholeness and multiplicity of human life and will live on wherever this wholeness is perceived and realized.

The following day Tilo Schabert, Erik Hornung, and Gilbert Durand voiced their opinions, and other conference participants were asked for their views. David Miller, James Hillman, and Jean Servier were especially strongly in favor of a continuation of the conferences, but did not feel able to undertake the organization themselves. Shortly before the speakers departed, Ritsema called them once more to a meeting and declared unequivocally that this was the last conference. This happened so close to the departure that no further discussion was possible, which embittered many of the participants.[10] Thus this final attempt failed to reverse Ritsema's decision and avoid a breach with him.

The end result was the foundation of the "Associazione Amici di Eranos" (Association of the friends of Eranos), which took over responsibility for the continued running of the conferences in a modernized form. Fourteen people were present at the inaugural meeting on 11 February 1989 in the restaurant Al Porto in Ascona. Erik Hornung and Tilo Schabert were chosen as president and vice-president respectively with the understanding that they would change places at intervals. The idea was to create a joint leadership,[11] which was also reflected in the joint editorship of the new series of Eranos volumes.[12] An important role in sustaining the project was played by the women involved, especially Ingeborg Schnetzler, who was able to exploit her local connections. Thus, for example, she was able to seek the support of Fritz Hugelmann, who, through his political influence, was able to secure financial support from the municipality of Ascona. The creation of the new association was also enthusiastically welcomed by Magda Kerényi as well as by Hellmut Wilhelm's widow and by Marianne New, the former companion of Adolf Portmann.[13] They also helped the rebuilding process by supplying address lists and suchlike. The Swiss Department of the Interior also authorized these developments, so that the name "Eranos" could be legally used.

Schabert and Hornung see their Eranos activities in no way as a secession, but rather as a necessary and legitimate continuation of Eranos. Schabert emphasizes that his central role fell to him unexpectedly and that he felt supported by the "overwhelming sentiment of all speakers and attendees," who desired a continuation of the conferences in the accustomed style. Schabert emphasized that he saw himself as having been pushed into taking on the leadership role. Furthermore, many participants had the feeling that they had been circumvented by the decision to end the traditional meetings, in the way that a spouse feels when finding out, after many years together, that the other partner no longer sees any future in the marriage. Despite the creation of the Amici di Eranos, no conference took place in 1989, as there was not yet an adequate organizational basis, because nobody had expected such a development and nothing had been planned. However, the first conference, in 1990, was a complete success with almost two hundred participants.

In October of the same year Rudolf Ritsema also resumed public conferences, albeit on a much smaller scale.[14] This was required by the statutes of the Eranos foundation.[15] Thereby fears were allayed that the Eranos Foundation in Moscia might develop in the direction of a mere life-enhancement group.

Max Schoch reported furthermore, in his already mentioned article in the *Neue Zürcher Zeitung* of 17 August 1990, that the Amici di Eranos would gladly have assumed legal succession to the Eranos Foundation in order to gain tenure of the library and the real estate. In their opinion, the transformation of the conferences into *I Ching* sessions did not reflect the aims of the Eranos Foundation as conceived by its founder Olga Fröbe. They had therefore appealed to the Swiss Ministry of the Interior and "met with understanding and sympathy." However, as Schoch pointed out, this did not imply anything regarding their prospects in any potential legal conflict, as the juridical situation was not as clear as it seemed. At the same time Schoch said, in Ritsema's favor, that the *I Ching* offered "a comprehensive way of seeking a path" and was applicable consequentially to "current problems relevant to the generality of humanity."

The analytical psychologist Christa Robinson, as the then president of the "old" Eranos Foundation in Moscia, who had been taking part in the conferences since 1977, naturally perceived the situation according to her own perspective.[16] She emphasized that Olga Fröbe had in her will established the Eranos Foundation and appointed Adolf Portmann as her successor.[17] Portmann, in turn, had appointed Rudolf Ritsema as the sole legitimate president. Thus, Christa Robinson argued, Ritsema was the only person who had the right (and, as she believed, the duty) to change what she saw as an obsolete way of conducting the meetings in order to remain true to the spirit and task of the Eranos Foundation as conceived by the founder. Nor could she see in the new *I Ching* approach any infringement of the legal statutes. She regarded the Assoziazione Amici di Eranos as merely a cultural initiative under the umbrella of the Ascona Tourist Office. The name "Eranos" was not legally protected. Hence the Associazione Amici di Eranos and the Eranos Foundation had nothing in common apart from the name.

In the period 1990–2002 Rudolf Ritsema's Eranos Foundation regularly organized up to three or sometimes four working conferences per year.[18] Apart from Ritsema and his co-translator Stephen Karcher, the better-known participants included Claudio Risé, Eiji Uehiro, Pio Filippani-Ronconi, Benjamin Sells, Claudio Bonvecchio, Robert Bosnak, and Lorenz Bichler. Evidently, at these meetings all participants were actively involved. There were five or six speakers and all of them invited discussion following their talks. In contrast to the earlier Eranos meetings, all participants sat at the Round Table, so that there was no hierarchical division between the speakers and the audience. In conformity with the structure of the *I Ching*, there were always eighteen people at the table (five or six lecturers, nine or ten participants, and three hosts). The participants were chosen from a group of applicants. The resulting reduction in numbers was intended to bring about a more intensive group dynamic with a greater emphasis on felt experience and meaningful interaction between the members. Thus more delicate and personal issues could be dealt with. Through the work with the *I Ching* it was intended to place the emphasis no longer on academic discourse but on themes that would speak to the heart.

The sessions lasted three days, and greater importance was now attached to the collective meals—that is to the Eranos in the sense of a convivial feast. Other guests could also participate in informal discussions during the breaks. Bruno Rhyner, an analytical analyst and expert on Japan and Zen Buddhism, who was one of the speakers at the new-style conferences, told me in a letter that he agreed with Ritsema's decision. He argued that a purely academic series of lectures, however brilliant they might be, could appeal only to the intellect and could not give the participants what they needed in terms of tangible inspiration and orientation for life. Rather, what was desirable was "a combination of the two or a balance between them." It would be perfectly legitimate to regard the Eranos conferences as a "therapeutic working community of limited duration." For the same reasons he himself did not work only at the university but had, in parallel, built up a private practice as a psychotherapist.

The first meeting of 1992 took the form of an international conference on the *I Ching* under the leadership of Rudolf Ritsema as director of the Eranos Foundation and sponsored by the Japanese Uehiro Foundation for Practical Ethics and Education. The focus of the conference on ethical questions was justified by the fact that the visible institutions which had previously been ethical standard-bearers were now becoming increasingly weak, and people were consequently looking for orientation within their own inner world of images.[19] As the *I Ching* constituted a systematic expression of this inner world, it offered a way of "translating" the archetypal images into the language of our practical world.

The Associazione Amici de Eranos,[20] under the leadership of Erik Hornung and Tilo Schabert,[21] now of course no longer had the use of the Casa Eranos in Moscia-Ascona. After various temporary solutions they decided to return to the old Monte Verità tradition. It was there that the conferences took place until 1999 and under the joint leadership of Tilo Schabert and Erik Hornung. Thereafter up to 2006 (except for the year 2002 when there was no conference) the participants met under the sole leadership of Tilo Schabert either in the Hotel Monte Verità at the top of the mountain or in the Collegio Papio in Ascona itself. Elisabetta Barone detected in this "new" series of meetings a more "philosophical" spirit, basing her judgment also on Tilo Schabert's works. However, what she meant was not philosophy in the dry, hair-splitting sense, but rather a return to a searching dialogue and the deeply rooted concept of a "festive encounter"[22]—a philosophy that stood under the sign of Eros, the god who creates a sense of community and at the same time transcends the world as the One from which everything emerges. Appropriately, the 1997 conference theme was "Cultures of Eros."

There continued to be no lack of qualified speakers. At the beginning of this book I have already mentioned names like Annemarie Schimmel, Ilya Prigogine, Erik Hornung, Moshe Idel, and Jan and Aleida Assmann. It is remarkable that the conferences could be continued basically in the accustomed form—with all the expense involved in bringing speakers from many parts of the world—and even expanded. This was due not least to the financial support of the Ascona municipality and the canton of Tessin, who together contributed 80,000 francs per year.[23] The initiator of this public support was Fritz Hugelmann, Ascona councillor and owner of a gallery specializing in Greek and Etruscan artifacts. His wife, Yvonne Hugelmann-Tièche, acted as business manager for the Amici until 1998 and thereby shouldered a large part of the administrative work. Fritz Hugelmann had learnt his trade under Wladimir Rosenbaum, the previous owner of the gallery and an important figure in the Eranos story, as he had for decades assisted Eranos in legal and administrative matters. Yvonne Hugelmann had also worked in the gallery under Rosenbaum and had at that time already been entrusted with the tasks relating to Eranos.

Rosenbaum had for decades taken part in all the Eranos meetings, had sat at the Round Table and had known Jung since the 1930s. For some time he had conducted a flourishing practice as a lawyer in Zurich and through his first wife, the writer Aline Valangin,[24] had known prominent writers such as Kurt Tucholsky, Ignazio Silone, Thomas Mann, James Joyce, Elias Canetti, and Robert Musil, as well as artists like Max Ernst, Hans (Jean) Arp, and Meret Oppenheim.[25] One of the regular guests at the Rosenbaum home, La Barca, in Comologno,[26] was the Eranos speaker Max Pulver, who "stood out most of all."[27] Pulver even claimed that Himmler had once requested him to make a graphological analysis of the handwriting of Goering and Goebbels.[28] Another person who visited Rosenbaum's house was the émigré indologist Heinrich Zimmer, who talked ceaselessly without noticing how wearisome his academic monologues were for his listeners.[29]

Rosenbaum was known for having in the 1930s defended Jews against the anti-Semitic attacks that occurred even in Switzerland. This and his legal expertise led to his becoming a trusted contact person for the Republican side in the Spanish Civil War, and he even became "an intermediary in the internationalist effort to procure weapons for Republican Spain."[30] However, an indiscretion caused this activity to be exposed, resulting in legal measures against him and ultimately leading (albeit for different reasons) to the loss of his license to practise as a lawyer. Being practically ruined financially, he moved to the Tessin district and made a living by buying and repairing antique objects, which he sold to local dealers.[31] Eventually he moved to Ascona and rented the Casa Serodine, where he opened the antique business that Fritz Hugelmann took over. There he met the Eranos speaker and excommunicated priest Ernesto Buonaiuti, with whom he developed a particularly close relationship.

Wladimir Rosenbaum did not speak well of C.G. Jung, although originally he had greatly admired him, indeed he had even been analyzed by Jung and had taken part in the Psychology Club. As a result of Jung's harsh words and actions towards him, which greatly offended him and which he interpreted as anti-Semitic,[32] Rosenbaum had changed his opinion about Jung completely and during the Eranos meetings had "seen through him."[33] Earlier Rosenbaum had already become incensed by the way in which Jung had characterized the works of James Joyce and Pablo Picasso as the expression of "schizophrenic" minds. Rosenbaum was always on good terms with Olga Fröbe. She often drew on his legal expertise and, from the early days of Eranos, she asked him to draft and write important letters. He also advised her during the unpleasant conflict with Walter Corti. Several people with a long-standing familiarity with Eranos agree that Rosenbaum's efforts on behalf of the conferences can hardly be valued highly enough. One person even described him to me as the undisputed number two in the "eternal hierarchy" of Eranos.

By 1999 the Amici di Eranos were beset by quarrels. Because of differences of opinion over issues such as modernization, simultaneous translation, video recordings, overseas branches,[34] and the choosing of speakers and subjects, there had been no governing board meeting for a year and a half, and the Hugelmann family had resigned from the board. During the Eranos meeting the general assembly came together and held a turbulent session, which had to be adjourned at midnight. After two further sessions, arranged *ad hoc*, a new management was finally elected, but this was only possible because Erik Hornung had withdrawn his further candidature.[35] After a number of interventions from the audience, some of them quite embarrassing, Tilo Schabert provisionally took over the running of the Amici di Eranos. There was to be no meeting in 2000, as the new board, which was not free of opposing voices, wanted to agree on a new *modus operandi*. In February 2000 the new council, minus Erik Hornung, held a session and elected Giuseppe Zarone of the University of Salerno as president.[36] Tilo Schabert, however, remained responsible for the Eranos conferences.

There was no "proper" Eranos meeting in 2000. However, in September of that year a semi-public colloquium was organized by Elisabetta Barone, Matthias Riedl, and Alexandra Tischel, with the purpose of encouraging up-and-coming academics to engage with the history of Eranos, an aim that was expressly supported by the town of Ascona. There were eighteen "research projects," the themes of which ranged from Monte Verità to Thomas Mann and from Martin Buber to Adolf Portmann. A resulting volume was published in 2004,[37] but unfortunately yielded less in terms of new research than one might have expected.[38] In the summer of 2001, however, another full conference took place under the title "Prophets and Prophecies." These conferences then continued until 2006 (with the exception of 2002 as already mentioned). The proceedings are documented in a series of volumes, published in Würzburg by Königshausen & Neumann.

At this point the subsidies from the Ascona municipality, the Canton of Tessin, and the Tourist Bureau of Lake Maggiore were apparently withdrawn, and unfortunately no further conferences could be held. On 12 November 2007 the Assoziazione Amici di Eranos was even deleted from the business register—a severe blow for Tilo Schabert, who had made great efforts for "his" conferences.[39] At the present time it is not yet clear to what extent the Eranos Conference Group, planned by him and his supporters, can be viable.

The subsidies (of 80,000 francs per year, as mentioned) were granted because the region had expressed a clear commitment to uphold the old tradition of Monte Verità.

Despite other attractions that drew larger numbers of tourists (such as the Locarno film festival) the world-wide reputation of the mysterious "Mountain of Truth" was of special importance, with its artistic and alternative life-style and its esoteric aura. This was apparent at the 1999 conference, where both the *Neue Zürcher Zeitung (NZZ)* and the *Frankfurter Allgemeine Zeitung (FAZ)* sent well-informed correspondents and subsequently published informative reports covering several columns.[40]

The Eranos Foundation in Moscia also received its share of media attention in 1999. On 22 April the Swiss radio station DRS 1 broadcast an almost one-hour program including long interviews with Rudolf Ritsema and Christa Robinson. But, as the NZZ reported in its column *Am Radio gehört* (Radio programs listened to), the broadcast evidently left the listeners unsatisfied. What really went on at the famous Round Table had not been made clear. And to anyone interested in the subject of Eranos it was no secret that the foundation was in a precarious financial situation and hoping for a "miracle," as had often happened in the past.

Meanwhile a new group had formed around Erik Hornung (who had, as reported, disassociated himself from Schabert's initiatives), Annemarie Schimmel, and Andreas Schweizer, a Jungian analyst from Zurich, with the aim of continuing the Eranos tradition. Through the mediation of Schweizer it even seemed that a reconciliation with Eranos-Moscia was possible.[41] Thus on 20–22 April 2001 and 12–14 April 2002 two meetings of the new group were indeed held in Moscia. The subjects were "Menschenbilder" (Images of man) and "Fra Diavolo" (Fra Diavolo, literally Brother Devil, but also the nickname of an Italian brigand).[42] Meanwhile in Eranos-Moscia Christa Robinson had been succeeded by Wanda Luban, a psychologist from Locarno, as president of the foundation.

Although outwardly these two conferences went to the full satisfaction of everyone, they were to be the last joint ones. There were fears that, because of the precarious financial position of the Eranos Foundation, the use of the traditional lecture hall would no longer be possible the following year. Thus, henceforth, the Eranos-Moscia Foundation and the group around Erik Hornung and Andreas Schweizer went their separate ways (Annemarie Schimmel had withdrawn for health reasons and died on 26 January 2003). The 2003 meeting of the latter group was held in the beautiful Casa Serodine in the center of Ascona, which has remained the venue up to the time of writing (2011). These conferences too were significant events, as can be seen from the list of speakers. Apart from the organizers, the names included Annemarie Schimmel, Jan Assmann, Herbert Pietschmann, Hubert Herkommer, Roger Alfred Stamm, Alois M. Haas, Josef van Ess, and Gudrun Schubert, to name only a few.

The group, which now calls itself the Verein zur Förderung der wissenschaftlichen Tagungen von Eranos (Association for furthering the scholarly conferences of Eranos), sees itself as having a special obligation to continue the original Eranos as faithfully as possible.[43] One fact supporting this is that Erik Hornung had originally been introduced to Eranos by the long-standing president, Adolf Portmann, whose memory is particularly respected.

The Verein, which is legally based in Zurich, tries to ensure that if possible an entire day is devoted to each speaker. In the morning the lecture is delivered in two parts (as it was done in Olga Fröbe's time and was greatly appreciated by the speakers). A detailed discussion then takes place in the afternoon.[44] This is intended to favor the unhurried and contemplative atmosphere considered appropriate to the spirit of Eranos, in contrast to the usual hectic style of university conferences with their dozens of lectures every day. The meetings are always held towards the end of August (Olga Fröbe's conferences were also held in that month).

As the Verein receives no subsidies from the municipality or the canton, it is financed solely from conference fees and minor contributions from a few sponsors. This means that it enjoys great independence. The presence of a core group of regular attendees guarantees the continuity of the events, bearing in mind that the Casa Serodine has no more than sixty places. Larger expense items, such as for guests from Asia or the United States, are not affordable under these circumstances. This, however, has not detracted from the lasting success of the meetings. Thus, happily the Eranos conferences of the Verein have become a regular part of the calendar of events in Ascona.

Meanwhile, what had become of the Eranos-Moscia Foundation? Here the main problem was the ever-growing financial deficit that hung over the foundation like a Damoclean sword. In the late 1990s the Volkart Foundation of Winterthur, Switzerland, which had financed the activities of the Eranos Foundation for decades, had already begun to speak of demanding a repayment, in whole or in part. At the beginning of the new millennium it was therefore no longer certain whether the Eranos Foundation could be continued or not. By 2004 the debt, including the accumulated interest, had risen to four million Swiss francs. There was talk of declaring insolvency and selling off the assets. Something needed to be done urgently.

How such a vast debt had arisen nobody can explain in detail, but the burden of debt had begun with Fröbe's will, in which she had *de facto* left 250,000 francs to her daughter Bettina. To begin with, this sum was apparently advanced fifty-fifty by Rudolf Ritsema and James Hillman and was then covered by a loan from the Volkart Foundation. The Volkart Foundation was founded in 1951 to mark the one hundred-and-fiftieth anniversary of the Volkart world-wide trading group. Its purpose is to support in particular institutions in the area of art and culture. As the Eranos conferences usually lost money, and as there were urgent repairs to the buildings to be paid for, the debt grew constantly as long as the Volkart Foundation was willing to keep extending the credit.[45] Ritsema and his wife also had living expenses, and they continually bought large quantities of books and periodicals. The translation work on the *I Ching*, which Ritsema had commissioned, was also very expensive.[46]

As neither Ritsema nor the Eranos Foundation had any money, the danger grew more real that the beautiful lakeside plot would have to be sacrificed. It would be necessary to find a bank that was prepared to take over from Volkart in providing long-term credit. Soon various initiatives from Tessin began to take shape. Daniele Bonetti of Locarno was particularly active in his efforts not only to save Eranos financially but also to preserve its spiritual and intellectual heritage. A public appeal was also issued. Finally the canton of Tessin and the town of Ascona agreed under certain conditions (such as the drawing up of new statutes) to provide a bank guarantee of two million francs in order to prevent an insolvency.[47] But clearly this could not be a long-term solution.

Suddenly a real prospect of help arose when John van Praag, a successful Dutch businessman and former chairman of the InterContinental Hotels Group, began to take an interest in the Eranos project. The contact was brought about by Claudio Metzger, a local gallery owner, numismatist, and director of the Ascona Art Center.[48] The two men, together with van Praag's wife, Laiping Fok, and a German expert on Chinese art, Jürgen Fischer, created an East West Foundation in Ascona. According to a document that I was able to examine, entitled "A Fresh Start for Eranos" and dated London, 4 July 2005, the aim of this foundation was to bring about a revival of the Eranos conferences.

At this point opinions became divided. One view is that John van Praag promised several millions in order to bring the Eranos Foundation under his leadership. Allegedly it was largely on the basis of such promises that the municipality, the canton, and the foundation's new president, Maria Danioth, were persuaded to give up control of the foundation. However, the then elected new board of the foundation, chaired by John van Praag himself, issued a press communiqué in February 2007, expressly rejecting this version of events. It stated that John van Praag had never mentioned bringing in his own private fortune. However, what he did intend to do, and meanwhile had actually done, was to hold talks with rich American foundations and private individuals with a potential interest in the spiritual and intellectual agenda of Eranos. The communiqué went on to say that opposition and disruptive tactics by local politicians had unfortunately ruined the prospect of immediate help.

Here I must insert a few words about another side to John van Praag. He was not only a businessman, but had studied ancient philology at the University of Utrecht and was deeply knowledgeable about classical antiquity. He had also published poems of an esoteric tenor.[49] One of these I would like to quote, as it reveals much about his outlook. As with all the poems in the booklet *Empty Sea* the focus is on the encounter with oneself.

I lit candles in the sunlight,
Searched and struggled in the night,
And rushed to find
I was already here.

It was thanks to his "esoteric" interests that John van Praag enjoyed good contacts with American benefactors, especially the Fetzer Institute and the Pacifica Graduate Institute. The Fetzer Institute in Kalamazoo, Michigan, is a foundation which, according to the Internet, has the aim of promoting peaceful and harmonious coexistence in the world.[50] "Love, forgiveness and compassion" are the three concepts that together form the *Leitmotiv* of the Institute.

The Pacifica Graduate Institute, on the other hand, is an accredited institute of higher education, located near Santa Barbara, California, offering courses in the humanities with a special focus on depth psychology.[51]

The two institutes have committed themselves to a close cooperation with the Eranos Foundation, whereby all major decisions are taken by mutual agreement and all related costs (including the continuing interest burden) are carried jointly. This arrangement is served by the so-called Eranos Coordinating Council, which comprises the three organizations and meets regularly. The aim of these meetings is to coordinate their respective activities in relation to Eranos. At the same time each organization remains independent from the others and fully responsible for its own events. The role of moderator of the council revolves between the heads of the three organizations.[52]

All three organizations are concerned to take recent holistic insights from medicine, psychology, and philosophy and make them available within a broader social context. Other important themes are contemporary spirituality and the dialogue between different spiritual traditions.

Naturally this new development, which also includes an openness to New Age thought, has not been welcomed by everyone. There has been talk of a "betrayal" of the old ideals of Olga Fröbe, who—at least in the later years—was committed to a scholarly approach. And some people have spoken of a takeover of Eranos by American business interests. Particularly aggressive in tone was Joseph Hanimann's article entitled "Geistlos" (Spiritless) in the *Frankfurter Allgemeine Zeitung*.[53] Hanimann writes, "It looks as though the new Eranos is moving towards the kind of mediocrity of content and persons that already prevails in dozens of elegantly restored conference centres." He goes on to warn that Eranos, with its "far-reaching themes," must be prevented from sinking into a spirit of "as you like it" by eminent podium speakers. Under the new leadership this could not be guaranteed. The article also contains an *ad hominem* attack on the Italian political scientist Claudio Bonvecchio for having taken part in one of the disdained "new" conferences. This is, to say the least, surprising when one considers that Bonvecchio is professor of the philosophy of social science at the University of Insubria (Varese), having taught previously in Palermo and Trieste, and has an impressive publications list to his name.

This article also mentions Tilo Schabert, who is understandably disappointed that he no longer receives support from the canton and the municipality for his Eranos meetings, which he has led with so much idealism. Schabert poses the provocative question: "What is more important for a legacy like that of Eranos: the spirit or the real estate?" He proposes that the plot should be sold so that all debts could be paid off and a new cycle of conferences could begin. However, whether the sale of the family silver would be a good basis for a new start is open to doubt. Arguably it would lead sooner or later to a new financial disaster, especially in view of Schabert's—in principle praiseworthy—plans for new initiatives such as providing assistance to impecunious students wishing to attend. Such help is apparently no longer available from public sources.

One can, of course, understand why critics were skeptical about the new plans of the Eranos Foundation. But, unfortunately, high ideals alone are not sufficient. This had already become clear when the Eranos Foundation had been faced with the prospect of bankruptcy. So who was prepared to finance the necessary renovation of the three houses on the property? Who was willing to take over the debt of four million francs and pay the annual interest? Certainly the municipality and the canton could not come up with these sums. In order to keep the foundation above water it was unavoidably necessary to draw up—*horribile dictu*—a "business plan" and to install a realistically minded management. And if income has to be derived from conferences and other events in order to cover the high running costs, then that means catering for the needs of a wider public. As long as additional meetings of academic calibre are held, as has happened up to now, the critics must hold back or else put forward better suggestions.

More grist to the mill of the skeptics was provided when John van Praag and his wife purchased the Casa Shanti on the Eranos property.[54] On the face of it, this looked bad—the president of the Eranos Foundation buys from the foundation a house with 916 square meters of lakeshore (one fifth of the entire plot) and uses it for private purposes. On closer consideration, however, one can see the arguments in favor of the sale. A news release issued by the foundation in February 2007 explained that the sale of the house was "unavoidable" in order to "reduce the foundation's debt." The document also mentions that the house had been sold once before, when Olga Fröbe had been facing financial difficulties, and only in 1980 had it come back to the foundation. The argument for selling the house to John van Praag rather than to an outside party was that collaboration with him would be easier than with a total stranger.[55]

This point of view was supported by Fausto Castiglione, the cantonal representative on the board of the Eranos Foundation,[56] who stated emphatically:

> Ceding part of the property to the President of the Foundation was the only practicable way to achieve various aims at the same time, namely halving the accumulated debt and restoring this part of the property at the cost of the new owner. At the same time this move also opened up the possibility to obtain a loan in order to restore the rest of the property (two houses and over three quarters of the entire plot).

Furthermore Fausto Castiglione announced that the Volkart Foundation had already set in motion all necessary legal steps to recover the debt as quickly as possible, which would inevitably have led to the property being auctioned off.

At that point van Praag had stepped in and suggested that he take over the Casa Shanti for two million francs, which would have halved the debt immediately. A consequence of this, Castiglione explained, was that the Banca dello Stato del Cantone Ticino (BancaStato) had been prepared to finance the remaining debts on condition that they received a guarantee that the interest would be paid, and provided that a three-year plan was submitted for the resumption of the Eranos programme. Furthermore, Van Praag had been willing to continue letting rooms in his house to participants at future conferences, as foreseen in the conference document. Castiglione also emphasized that "two million francs had been the maximum possible asking price for the Casa Shanti." Two assessments from local architects would confirm this. In this connection it should also not be forgotten that John van Praag had played a leading role in other charitable organizations. For eleven years he was chairman of the respected Dartington Hall Trust, and he was also actively involved in the Royal Society for the Encouragement of Arts, Manufactures and Commerce.

I have dealt in some detail with these public disputes, as they were also widely reported in the press and therefore had caused much insecurity. However, what is more important is the question of what had been happening at the Eranos Foundation in the meantime (I am writing in the spring of 2010), for "by their fruits ye shall know them."

One of the first steps was to make a preliminary scientific assessment of Eranos in all its parts. This included the library, which is to be made accessible to the public. The collection contains numerous documents on the history of Eranos, which up to now have been hidden away and only very selectively shown (on this topic I could write volumes). The assessment was carried out mainly by Riccardo Bernardini from the University of Turin and Giovanni Sorge from the Swiss Federal Institute of Technology in Zurich. Together they also wrote the script of a DVD entitled *Eranos Reborn*, which was made into a film.[57] This included extracts from the documentary film of the 1951 Eranos meeting, made by Ximena de Angulo and Willy Roelly. At this point a complete reorganization of the archive and library is called for, but for this it would be necessary to make conversions to the Casa Gabriella, for which at present the funds are lacking. Further scholarly work on Eranos is planned, but again would have to be financed in advance.[58]

On the more practical side, the Casa Eranos has meanwhile been fully renovated, after Rudolf Ritsema, probably owing to a shortage of money, had carried out hardly any repairs, not even repainting. His flat has now been made into four beautiful rooms with a shower.[59] The lecture hall remains as it was, but central heating has been installed throughout the house. Thus the building, including the lecture hall, is usable also in the autumn and winter, enabling the organized events to take place throughout the year.

The most important cause of criticism, however, was the concern that had been voiced regarding the academic level of the talks.[60] To give a brief overview: during the years 2006–2008 (but not 2009) there were regular conferences, and the first two included speakers of an "esoteric" bent, such as Werner Erhardt and Ervin Laszlo. At the same time Luigi Zoja, president of the International Association for Analytical Psychology, was also among the speakers. In 2008 the lecturers included William Gispen, rector of the University of Utrecht, and Lawrence Sullivan from the University of Notre Dame in Indiana. In the same year a particularly noteworthy speaker was Stanislaw Grof, president of the International Transpersonal Association and well known world-wide for his books and research work.

Fetzer also presented conferences with decidedly academic participants. These included an interesting series called the Eranos Dialogues, one of which, entitled "On the Transformative Power of Love," I find particularly noteworthy. The speakers included university professors such as Antoine Faivre, Moshe Idel, William Chittick, Ursula King, and Giovanni Casadio. The Pacifica Graduate Institute also organized a number of memorable events in the field of depth psychology. Altogether the conferences can indeed be seen as scholarly, even if the "esoteric" aspect is more prominent than in the earlier years (with no negative consequences as far as I can see).

In 2010 there appeared the Eranos volume number 69, covering the years 2006, 2007, and 2008, under the presidency of John van Praag.[61] It contains the lectures, plans, and presentations for those years, in which John's son Alexander van Praag collaborated. Unintentionally this volume contains a sort of summing-up of this era, which could be grist to the mill of both critics and supporters, for in October 2009 the leadership of the foundation changed hands again. John van Praag, who deserves credit for having put the Eranos Foundation back on a sound financial footing, resigned, evidently on account of disagreements with local decision-makers. He was succeeded by Fabio Merlini, director of the Italian-Swiss branch of the Swiss Federal Institute for Vocational Education and Training and Professor of Ethics at the Italian University of Insubria in Varese. Merlini's special area is the philosophy of history. Already in earlier years he was in contact with Rudolf Ritsema and took part in some of the conferences. He was also involved with the rescue initiatives when Eranos was in financial difficulties.

Fabio Merlini's aim is to connect Eranos more strongly with the present cultural life of Tessin and thereby strengthen the Italian-speaking element in Switzerland. Equally, his intention is that the canton "Tessin itself should participate in the spirit of Eranos."[62] Initial successes show clearly that the local population and press are very willing to support Eranos. "In Tessin too one senses the need to rediscover dimensions that go beyond those dictated by the present hegemony of economic ontology."[63]

The new president plans, in the medium term, to create additional, multi-functional space to accommodate the library as well as offices and reading rooms, and thus be in a better position to serve the numerous visitors from home and abroad. In this undertaking, Merlini is strongly supported by the entire foundation board as well as by scholarly advisors Riccardo Bernardini and Giovanni Sorge.

A promising start to this collaboration was the series of events continuing through 2011 under the title *Eranos Jung Lectures*, which were intended to mark the fiftieth anniversary of Jung's death. In addition there is the 2011 conference, organized with the collaboration of, *inter alia*, Michel Maffesoli, Jean-Jacques Wunenberger, and Adriano Fabris. There is therefore no lack of distinguished speakers.

If I were asked to sum up the prospects for Eranos in the light of everything that has been described, I would say that, despite the many turbulences, there seems enough reason to feel positive about the way the Eranos idea has so far been carried forward in the third millennium. And the enthusiasm of both the Verein, under Andreas Schweizer and Erik Hornung, and the Eranos Foundation of Moscia-Ascona, under Fabio Merlini, gives cause for optimism—at least for the near future.

By way of a (provisional) conclusion to the history of Eranos, I would like to mention a hitherto unpublicized "mysterious" tradition, which is connected with Eranos (I do not know to what extent). The story concerns a superb Gnostic medallion made of amber and set in silver, which was owned by Olga Fröbe and which she is said to have left to her good friend, the Eranos speaker Jean Servier, who was also an esotericist and Freemason. The medallion is a variation of the classical Abraxas type of emblem from the early Christian era. Jean Servier then left it to the former Eranos president Christa Robinson with the request that she in turn should give it to someone whom she considered to be of similar character to Servier. Robinson duly gave it to Claudio Bonvecchio, who is still in possession of it today. He also sees himself as having the obligation to entrust the medallion before his death to another worthy individual. Claudio Bonvecchio, to whom I am indebted for this information, was unwilling to reveal further details. Such traditions should be respected and not profaned by being trumpeted too loudly.

Before dealing with various critical and hostile attitudes towards the "spirit" of Eranos, I must say a little more about the Eranos picture archive. Enough has been said already about the importance of images for the soul. At the outset, therefore, Olga Fröbe had begun to illuminate the conference themes through pictures and symbols. The collecting of these illustrations, which she pursued with particular intensity from 1935 to 1938, was driven by her conviction that phenomena in the visible world are the expression of images or ideas in the invisible world. Fröbe was by nature visionary and image-oriented.

To begin with she kept the collection of pictures in her bedroom, but this led to insomnia and a kind of possession by the archetypes represented by the images. C.G. Jung even felt that this was "threatening her personal existence and that of Eranos."[64] He urged her to give up her identification with Eranos and return to her identity as Olga Fröbe. Over time the collection became ever larger and soon comprised several thousand items. Erich Neumann, as already mentioned, was one person who made use of the library. Another was Mircea Eliade, who wrote in his book *The Forge and the Crucible*, "I am also indebted to my friend Mrs. Froebe-Kapteyn, who was kind enough to put at my disposal the collections of the Archiv für Symbol-Forschung which she has established at Ascona."[65] In general, however, much to her chagrin, the collection received very little attention.[66] It was especially disappointing that the Jung circle showed hardly any interest in it. Consequently Olga Fröbe decided to donate the pictures to the Warburg Institute in London and to give only duplicate copies to the C.G. Jung Institute in Zurich and the Bollingen Foundation in New York.

The new owners considerably extended the collection and re-classified it. In the end, however, the C.G. Jung Foundation in New York acquired the entire collection, which at that time was already called the Archive for Archetypal Symbolism (ARAS) and was divided into nine main sections. Besides Fröbe, Jung himself, Jolande Jacobi, and Jesse E. Fraser contributed to enlarging the collection.[67] By now the archive encompasses religious and symbolic images from all cultural epochs. By 1990 it contained thirteen thousand items, and at the time of writing this has risen to seventeen thousand. The archive is now being made available to a wider public through a book series entitled *An Encyclopedia of Archetypal Symbolism*. The first volume, under that title, was published in 1991.[68] A second volume, devoted to the body and its symbolism, appeared in 1996.[69] A third volume is entitled *The Book of Symbols*.[70] Since 2009 there is also the *ARAS/Art and Psyche Online Journal*.[71]

🐾 15. Delicate Questions and Attempts to Answer Them

Critical Comments

Hans Heinz Holz,[1] who attended at least one Eranos meeting, in 1997,[2] came out with a strongly critical analysis of the Eranos phenomenon in his essay "Eranos: eine moderne Pseudo-Gnosis."[3] This greatly displeased the Eranos sympathizers. However, it perhaps deserves to be looked at again in a somewhat more dispassionate spirit.[4] For, although Holz often overshoots the mark, his observations are nevertheless worth considering, in keeping with the Eranos spirit of self-reflection. Essentially Holz sees in Eranos a late bourgeois flight from the world, an egocentric obsession with self-realization that distracts people from engaging in political efforts towards a better world. In this connection he uses somewhat harsh expressions such as "sectarian impression" (250) and "secularized mystery sect" (251).[5] Holz does, however, make a clear distinction between the conferences, with their predominant ethos of expectation, and the yearbooks, which he recognizes as a goldmine for research in the history of ideas. Although it is not possible here to enter into a detailed questioning of his analysis, which would involve examining his basic premises and clarifying his terms, nevertheless some discussion of his main points of criticism is called for.

His main accusation (whose political implications I shall discuss later) is that Eranos, at least according to the intentions of its founder, is geared to the participants' craving for inner salvation. In this restricted formulation the accusation might appear justified. However, it must be said that in fact during the Eranos conferences the "craving for inner salvation" was and is not fulfilled. Otherwise how is one to interpret the following observations by Jung's colleague Jolande Jacobi? "One is basically alone, alone to a degree that can only be endured by someone of maturity. At Eranos one must leave behind all childlike longing for affirmation or loving concern … Someone who confuses community with social conviviality … will be disappointed."[6] Here it must be added, however, that Jolande Jacobi was a very extroverted woman.[7] Before her association with Jung she had spent time in Vienna (although she hailed from Budapest), organizing the so-called Kulturbund (Cultural league),[8] at which Jung lectured in 1931 and 1932.[9]

On the other hand, Olga Fröbe often made remarks (many of which I have quoted) pointing in the direction of a guided process towards "salvation." This is made clear in the second Eranos yearbook, which explicitly refers to the "Gnostic, Hermetic and Pythagorean schools" as well as the "alchemical and Rosicrucian traditions."[10] Here, however, the endlessly debatable question arises whether a "spiritually therapeutic" aim should be treated as something morally reprehensible. Here we come to the fundamental question: Do we believe that human beings are in need of "spiritual healing" or not? If they need at least the promise of healing in order to experience "happiness" and a fulfilling sense of meaning, then they must be grateful for anything that helps to show them the way. If, on the other hand, we do *not* believe that human beings are impelled by their essence to seek this "healing," then the accusation must be seen as such, for all such striving would then be an illusion that deserved to be destroyed, as it would have the effect of leading people away from more important activities—such as building a more just world—and keeping them trapped in egocentric and illusory pursuits. The question boils down to a truly fundamental issue: is *Homo sapiens* in fact a *Homo religiosus* (in Eliade's sense), in other words is religion—in the sense of a guided progress towards "salvation"—something fundamental to the human condition, or is the human being merely a *zoon politikon*, a social being who should preferably be steered by reason and thereby strive towards ever "better" and "higher" things.[11]

I am inclined to suspect that Eranos had its sights on another solution to this problem, namely to regard *Homo sapiens* as a being of "both ... and ..." and not the irreconcilable "either ... or ..." which is eternally torn between mythos and logos. There is much evidence that Eranos upheld the possibility of a *tertium datur* that could encompass both the intellect and, shall we say, the expectation of "salvation" (in the sense used above). Donna and Charles Scott of Vanderbilt University call this a "rationality that does not reduce or fragment what it sees, but which enriches, synthesizes, and evokes response."[12]

This approach remains unaltered in the "new" Eranos under the Amici di Eranos. In the programmatic statement issued by Erik Hornung and Tilo Schabert, *Eranos—Einige Erläuterungen*, appears the following:

> The life of Eranos is derived from the inspired learnedness of its speakers. Olga Fröbe chose them according to clear criteria. Anyone who speaks at Eranos "looks into the fullness of his inner visions and attempts to order them in a scientific way." This connection between the imaginative/creative faculty and the ability to think scientifically remains a valid principle for Eranos.

It would be an over-simplification to attribute the so-called "esoteric" part of this third solution to Fröbe alone. This is clear from the many quotations I have cited from the writings and lectures of the speakers. And plenty of material, at least on C.G. Jung's "esoteric" side, has come to the attention of a broader public. The individuation process simply amounts to a process of self-salvation and is dependent on the premise that human beings are eminently in need of "spiritual healing."

Eliade too confirms that, in addition to the interdisciplinarity of Eranos, one of its typical characteristics from the beginning was its interest in spiritual disciplines and mystical techniques.[13] At the same time he emphasizes that this did not mean a mere fascination with the occult or with a cheap spirituality, but rather involved an attempt to identify certain existential documents that are today largely forgotten.[14] These are, he said, "of immeasurable worth, since they represent the peak achievements of the human spirit". They are important for two reasons: first, we cannot go on living indefinitely cut off from an essential part of our being; second, it is only through an understanding of this form of spirituality that we can conduct a true dialogue with Asia and with traditional peoples (i.e. those that used to be called "primitive").

The psychologist Ira Progoff, writing in the same publication, goes even further and says that the atmosphere of Eranos brought an experience that went far beyond intellectual cognition. The aim of the meetings was "indeed to bring about more than an understanding but rather a *knowing through direct experience*," and he goes on to repeat the closing words of his 1963 Eranos lecture:

> In our time the particular need is for a doorway of initiation, a way of entry to a larger dimension of experience ... and living symbols, places that stand for the no-place of the soul, and can be present and available for us as [the symbol of] Jerusalem was for Meister Eckhart ... And I think you will agree with me that one such living symbol ... is unfolding here at Eranos in the midst of us.

For Henry Corbin too Eranos meant one essential goal. In his memorial speech[15] on the deaths of Fröbe and Jung in 1962 he formulated it as follows: "To press on into the innermost part of ourselves, pursuing that truth until we reach its farthest limit." And in his essay "Eranos-Zeit" (Eranos time)[16] he said that it would be impossible for a future historian of Eranos to understand its prevailing spirit unless he is prepared to go beyond a purely scholarly approach. Inevitably, a historian who only paid attention to the historical circumstances, currents, and influences would overlook the "primal creative source of Eranos." Instead of the "pseudo-dialectic of facts" what was called for was a "hermeneutic of the human individual," for every fact was inseparably connected with a person. There was always something unique involved. Eranos was a "sign," but with "signs," "hierophanies," and "theophanies" one could not make history.

Even a natural scientist like Adolf Portmann said in October 1961 on Olga Fröbe's eightieth birthday, "Our reflections go to the hidden sources from which greatness springs. All the origins are in darkness ... To absorb ... the secret of the living spirit, with an alert mind to express what is expressible while being aware that the inexpressible is always present—it is in this spirit that the work of Eranos is carried out."[17] In this connection Portmann even spoke of "danger zones of thought."

Gilbert Durand, in a lengthy speech of homage to Eranos, delivered there in 1982, went even further in the direction of regarding Eranos as something timeless. Thus he emphasized that Eranos had created a space and time that were better adapted to the human universe than the Kantian *a priori* concepts. He particularly underlined the importance of "correspondences and analogies," which explained the attraction felt by Eranian thinkers towards "Hermeticism, alchemy and Gnosis," and he regretted that astrology had hardly featured as a lecture topic. At the same time he called for a struggle "against the awful cultural and ethical collapse" of the age. He believed that "the most secret or at least most hidden" aspect of the Eranian project could be seen in a preparation for the "return of the gods," and here he referred explicitly to the polytheistic leanings of James Hillman, Karl Kerényi, and David L. Miller.

Monotheists like Corbin had, as a compensation, their predilection for the multitudinous hierarchies of angels. Towards the end, Durand asked, since he had mentioned so many things that bore witness to the existence of special presences at Eranos, whether he could be permitted to ask "the question, the ultimate question," namely, "Is Eranos 'divine'?" Here he referred to the stele, dedicated to the spirit of the place. Paraphrasing his friend Henry Corbin, he added, "For half a century we will have been the mouthpiece of a world which, since the descent of the Fravartis[18] to earth, has never yielded to the demonic powers, and we will have contributed to the *traditio lampadis* (the transmission of the light) because this intransient world has been our passion." In his afterword to the lecture, Rudolf Ritsema expressly emphasized that this was precisely "the self-image of Eranos that should guide it on the threshold of its sixth decade."

Elsewhere Durand also emphasizes the great importance of Eranos as a force in the background.[19] After writing about the many encounters between Eliade and Jung in the context of Eranos, he writes:

> Here is not the place to stress the vital and discreet—not to say secret!—role that this scholarly institution has played in the working out of concepts fundamental to our time and to the science and ethics of the near future ... One can say that it was at these Eranos meetings that the premises of the true "New Philosophy" were forged and the pillars of the *philosophia perennis*, long concealed by the demented imagery of our age, were unveiled.[20]

Giovanni Filoramo summarizes the "esoteric programme, the hidden face of Eranos" as follows: "To reawaken one's own individual self as well as that of others and thereby to win back the self of a forgotten tradition." However, by "tradition" he did not mean the "integral" variety of a Guénon or a Schuon, but rather a Christian tradition, especially as expressed in *Naturphilosophie* in Goethe's sense of the word. Its essential characteristic was an attempt to return to unity. "A science of the living, a universe of qualities, colours and forms" should be set against the mechanistic concept of science. And the lifeless world of modern technology should give way to an *"unus mundus* of universal sympathies, correspondences and hidden harmonies."[21]

All of these statements point to a special kind of Eranos climate, which Wouter Hanegraaff, in one of his essays, calls a "cultic milieu," an expression that I find highly appropriate.[22] In using it, Hanegraaff follows the lead of Colin Campbell, who makes a distinction between a "sect" and a "cult" as well as between a "cult" and a "cultic milieu."[23] A cult is for him something that is individualistic, loosely structured, tolerant, short-lived, with a changing belief content, without rigid boundaries, and which makes hardly any demands on its "adherents." A sect, on the other hand, is collectivist, tightly structured, intolerant, long-lived, with a dogmatic belief content, and makes many demands on its adherents. By the term "cultic milieu" Campbell means not a diluted form of individual cult (which, incidentally, does not have to have a religious content), but rather a particular type of environment within a society, one that does not directly further any individual cult, but rather creates a general climate which facilitates the emergence of such cults.

Although such cultic milieux differ widely, what they have in common is a tendency to see themselves as heterodox and something "other" than the dominant cultural norm. They are marked by great tolerance and openness towards other forms of thought and belief, because they know from experience what it means to be in the minority. A loose cohesion is created through periodicals, lectures, and informal meetings, where different ideas and worldviews are discussed. Another factor that contributes to the group identity is that the members of a cultic milieu define themselves above all as a "community of seekers," who regard the traditional solutions of the majority as inadequate for the problems of their own lives. We see, therefore, that a cultic milieu is not strictly organized, exerts no tutelage over its (in any case informal) membership, and in no way attempts to propagate any special idea, worldview, or problem-solving approach as the sole "truth." On the contrary, there are seen to be many ways that lead to "salvation." Therefore to describe the generally esoteric climate of Eranos as a cultic milieu, as Wouter Hanegraaff suggests, seems to me not only legitimate but also illuminating. It goes without saying that this assessment is very different to the one of Hans Heinz Holz.

Furthermore, Hanegraaff points out clearly in his essay that the Eranos conferences, which he sees as "religionist and counter-cultural," have played a central role in facilitating the incorporation of esoteric themes into academic discourse. The fact that over many decades such themes were discussed at Ascona by prominent scholars from the point of view of various academic disciplines (history, comparative religion, philosophy, etc.) has, Hanegraaff argues, paved the way for the existence today of university chairs for the history of esotericism[24] and of special study groups on the historical influence of esotericism, which operate within associations of scholars of religion. In this context I would also like to draw attention to Steven Wasserstrom's observation on Eranos, namely that Scholem, Eliade, and Corbin "institutionalized, in the academic study of religion, an original esotericism."[25]

The word "esoteric"—so suspect (often rightly so) in politics and academe—crops up repeatedly in the present context as a way of getting to the essence of Eranos. Once again I emphasize that the word is used here in its wider sense and, as I made clear in the Introduction, has nothing to do with Antoine Faivre's scholarly definition of esotericism.[26] Eranos was and is "esoteric" in so far as one understands it as a listening-in to the unknown and potentially dangerous depths of the human consciousness, a process that goes beyond the limits of rationality. It may also be relevant to quote more extensively a remark by Henry Corbin that I quoted earlier. Corbin emphasized that "we in Eranos never had the intention of adapting ourselves to some given model, we never paid heed to any orthodoxy, and we were concerned with only one thing, namely to press on into the innermost part of ourselves, pursuing that truth until we reach its farthest limit."

But, as Henry Corbin also said, Eranos is closely bound up with the people who are active in it, and some of these may place more emphasis on inner experience, others on the scientific side. Therefore there is no contradiction to the "third way," which is the one that I favor, embracing both of the other two. Tilo Schabert also talks about this middle position in the interview with him in the journal *LiLit*, which I mentioned earlier, stressing that neither a "guru esotericism" nor a "tedious, positivistic academicism" should dominate Eranos.

Obviously such a feat of tightrope walking cannot always be accomplished. Not every participant is able to live up to this noble ideal. And some may simply have lacked sympathy with it. This would explain why there was so much bandying about of the "scandalous" statement by Gershom Scholem, which he made when reminiscing about his thirty-year association with Eranos.[27] He began by praising the things about Eranos that had been particularly important for him, especially the fact that he had not been confined to the usual fifty-minute lecture time and therefore had been able to develop his thoughts freely rather than in aphoristically condensed form. He then proceeded to pay tribute to Adolf Portmann, to whom he attributed the generally high speaking quality of the lecturers. They nearly always stayed to the end of each conference, because they did not want to miss Portmann's always brilliant concluding talk. Portmann, he said, had been "the pillar on which the conferences had rested for thirty years."

Finally Scholem picked up on the title of his lecture "Identifizierung und Distanz" (Identification and distance) and spoke about the difficulties of maintaining an attitude of scholarly distance to the subject in question while at the same time speaking with lively identification. Olga Fröbe had always wanted identification, that is to say speakers who were "inspired" (Jung had once said that only the inspired speaker can inspire) "and no professors, even though they are all called professors." Then came the "scandalous" sentence: "There was [at Eranos], so to speak, a bit of swindle involved."[28] Scholem emphasized that he himself had lectured from this tense position between distance and identification. "A scholar," he said, "is not a priest; it is a mistake to try to make a priest out of a scholar." He also mentioned Henry Corbin, who had lectured "out of an extraordinary feeling of immersion, of almost-identification," but who at the same time had preserved the distance of a profoundly scholarly mind. Finally he asked himself whether it was at all possible to study the natural sciences and the humanities with the same methods. The answer was yet to be provided, but "the effort to find an answer … is one of the great central factors of our lives at Eranos."

Here we should not forget what Scholem had said a few years earlier in his essay "Betrachtungen eines Kabbala-Forschers" (Reflections of a Kabbalah Researcher) in the Eranos issue of *Du* (66):

> Symbols too have grown over time and are saturated with historical experience. To understand them requires both a "phenomenological" willingness to perceive things holistically and a capacity for historical analysis. These two things complement and permeate each other and, when combined, they promise infinitely fruitful results. Among the circle of researchers who came together at the Eranos conferences, a great deal has been done by way of bringing together and working with these two approaches. And here Kabbala research has also, in a good sense, "come home."

It is true that Scholem expressly did not wish to be associated with Jung's thought.[29] Nevertheless, he shared Jung's view that human beings carry within them two poles, that is, of rationality and myth, which continually strive to find a balance.[30] Indeed, he was of the opinion that the vitality of Judaism lay precisely in this conflict between mythos (i.e. the Kabbalistic strain) and anti-mythos (its strictly legalistic character). In an interview he said on this topic:

> I have been much preoccupied with the question of whether a purely halachistic, a purely legalistic conception of Judaism would have been able on its own to yield sufficient vitality for this group, this people, this community of the Jews through all the storms of history and all the persecution … I believe that the Kabbala has played a significant role here, and indeed precisely for those who were most receptive in a religious sense. To them the Kabbala provided an answer, a very impressive and partly successful answer, which brought some sense of meaning for the existence of the Jews in the historical world; that is to say, it yielded a symbolic interpretation of this existence as the manifestation of some deeper reality.[31]

At the same time it should be emphasized that Scholem considered Kabbalistic ways of thinking to be of absolutely no relevance any longer in the present age. This, according to Hyam Maccoby, contributed to his dispute with Martin Buber.[32]

Maccoby adds that Scholem never belonged to the inner circle of Eranos and was only an "interested onlooker"—a somewhat surprising assertion, considering Scholem's thirty-year involvement with Eranos and his close contacts with Olga Fröbe, Henry Corbin, Adolf Portmann, and even—despite ideological differences—with Eliade and Jung.[33] Maccoby's view is supported by Joseph Dan, who writes, "He [Scholem] was the most prominent non-participating participant (a member but not a follower)."[34] Dan seeks to substantiate this statement by analyzing Scholem's lectures, which reveal "his implacable rejection of Jung's approach to the investigation of cultural phenomena." Here it should also be remembered that Scholem did not stay in Moscia like other prominent Eranos speakers but rather in the tradition-laden Hotel Tamaro in Ascona, which enabled him, at least outwardly, to preserve a certain distance. On the other hand it should be noted that it was the "atmosphere" of the Eranos meetings that prompted Scholem, as he once declared, to return after 1949 to writing part of his scholarly work in German, a language that must have held painful memories for him.[35]

At this point the question arises: why did Scholem become involved with the Eranos movement and why did he remain faithful to it? Joseph Dan sees this question as one of the most difficult in Scholem's biography, since his participation in Eranos must have given the impression that he had some sympathy with Jung and his thinking, which would have been very much contrary to his intentions. Dan supposes that in post-war Europe there was probably no other significant "German-speaking" group with which Scholem could have associated himself.[36] And, as Dan points out, "at that time much was perceived differently from today." Probably, he thinks, Scholem could not resist the need to remain in contact with the German-speaking culture that had shaped his childhood and youth, despite all the painful things that he had experienced.

This supposition is to some extent confirmed by a touching observation made by Carl Burckhardt in a letter written on 19 November 1962 after a visit to Israel:

> There in the prized library of Scholem, that witty and profoundly experienced man, a dozen professors and writers are gathered, and all of them speak German, and all of them talk of Germany, of German memories, German literature … It is exactly as it was 50 years ago, they know just as much as they knew then, they talk brilliantly and compellingly, but there is now something new that they do not want to acknowledge: a homesickness, a profound homesickness, that transfigures even their most critical utterances … Among the members of this circle there is no trace of vindictiveness.[37]

As also mentioned, Steven Wasserstrom has his own view on Scholem's involvement with Eranos.[38] For him Scholem's work and thought are decidedly in line with those of Eranos. Indeed, he "*did* identify with the Eranos enterprise."[39] This thesis pervades Wasserstrom's entire book and may even have been a major reason for writing it. Wasserstrom maintains that Scholem, like the other participants, was concerned to privilege the spiritual element in religion rather than the ethical and legalistic considerations that are so central to the monotheistic religions. What was important to him was the visionary and even ecstatic dimension that has no place in traditional religious institutions. He was equally opposed to the "reductionism" of the social scientists and the positivistic historians. Wasserstrom even speaks of a "soteriologically vibrant conversation of like-minded intellectuals" and "a transcultural circle of intensely learned but entirely non-practising believers."[40] We should also not forget Scholem's own assessment, which he gave on the occasion of a prize-giving in Munich,[41] namely that Eranos had given him the possibility to achieve a synthesis which he had worked towards for thirty years without thereby sacrificing historical criticism or philosophical thinking.

According to Wasserstrom's analysis, Scholem consciously went to Eranos and remained there because he had decided to be a scholar of religion with a world-wide audience and wished to make his knowledge available not merely to Jews. And in fact non-Jews probably still form the majority of his readers today. Furthermore, his Eranos colleagues evidently not only gave him moral support for his particular religious position but also provided excellent opportunities to spread his message. These included not only the Eranos yearbooks but also invitations to conferences, frequent reviews of his books by prominent experts, and last but not least the Bollingen scholarship.

To return to the main issue that we are addressing here, Hans Heinz Holz sees Scholem's "bit of swindle" as "positively central to Eranos." According to Holz, the scholarly content conveyed by the lecturers was only a veil concealing an underlying message of salvation. This may be true for certain members of the audience. To what extent, however, this was also intended by the majority of the lecturers is much more difficult to determine. But to write off the whole of Eranos (apart from the yearbooks) as a "swindle" is surely going too far. Apart from anything else, one must consider the two diverging versions of Eranos after 1988. Holz himself refers to this in the special issue of *Du* devoted to C.G. Jung, in which he says, "The scholars have separated themselves from the gurus, and since then there have been two parallel Eranos meetings held each year at the foot of the Mountain of Truth." The statement is in fact also inaccurate, as Eranos-Moscia organized more than one meeting per year, in addition to the yearly meetings of the Amici di Eranos, and the latter took place on the *summit* (not at the foot) of the "Mountain of Truth." Furthermore, it would have been better to place the quoted sentence at the beginning of the article, since, apart from this sentence, Holz is writing in 1995 entirely about an Eranos that, in this form, had not existed for years.[42]

Political Implications

Gnosis: The Ultimate Evil?

In his analysis Holz also maintains that Eranos was pervaded by a strict dualism between the self and the world, according to which the world represents the principle of evil, from which the pure, spiritual self must withdraw completely if it desires salvation. In fact, the soul teachings of Corbin, Hillman, Miller, and even Jung represented rather the opposite view. And, furthermore, Holz is merely repeating here the conception of Gnosticism laid out in Hans Jonas' fundamental work *Gnosis und Spätantiker Geist* (Gnosis and the spirit of late antiquity), a conception that was subsequently applied almost automatically to any system allegedly Gnostic.[43] This view remained unchallenged until a few years ago.

Here we have one of the central points from which the rejection (not to say damnation) of "esoteric" thinking in the twentieth century sprang. In order to understand the implications of this accusation of dualism it will be necessary to look briefly at the thinking of Hans Jonas.[44]

Jonas' influential attempt to interpret the Gnostic phenomenon had its antecedents in Heidegger's work *Sein und Zeit* (Being and time), which features such concepts as *Geworfenheit in die Nichtigkeit der Welt* (the state of having been thrown into the nullity of the world), *Verlorensein* (the state of being lost), and *Angst als Grundbefindlichkeit* (fear as a basic mental state). Jonas was Heidegger's pupil and believed that he had found in Heidegger's existential categories the key to understanding the manifold fantastic and unfathomable myths contained in the Gnostic teachings. If the Greeks saw the cosmos as a rational, harmonic, and orderly whole, which gave human beings a sense of security as part of the universe, for Jonas the Gnostics held exactly the opposite view. They saw the cosmos as a place of alienation, darkness, and abandonment, into which they had been "thrown." This led inevitably to a *Weltangst* (fundamental inner fear of the world), and consequently the god who had created the universe could only be an evil demiurge. The only hope for human beings was to leave this dreadful world fully behind and withdraw to a completely extra-mundane realm of light, by virtue of their *pneuma*, their soul of light. Here we see the radical dualism that Jonas talks about, between the indescribable misery of this world and the bliss of the world beyond: two poles that were always contrary and never complementary. This dualism existed "between man and the world as well as, in parallel, between the world and God."[45] Liberation could only come about through "gnosis," that is, through the revelation of a secret knowledge. The prerequisite for this was a conscious "alienation from the world."

If one follows the development of Jonas' own thinking, one sees that in the 1970s he was strongly opposed to any tendency towards "alienation from the world," which he saw as an incalculable danger for our common life and for the *Weiterwohnlichkeit der Welt* (the continuing habitability of the world). In his widely known book *Das Prinzip Verantwortung* (The principle of responsibility),[46] Jonas proposed a new ethic involving a personal and collective responsibility for everyone in view of the technical, ecological and political disasters that threaten us. For him, alienation from the world came close to nihilism. What was called for was rather an active involvement based on ethical commitment.[47]

Jonas' anti-Gnostic attitude was also nourished by other factors. Despite the possible Jewish roots of ancient Gnosticism, Jonas was convinced that Gnostic systems were characterized by an underlying anti-Jewish sentiment, which had its roots in the identification of the hated Gnostic demiurge Ialdabaoth with the God of the Hebrews. Ialdabaoth was considered an "evil" god, as he had created this "evil" world. In Judaism, by contrast, the created universe was and is good, as God made it in his own image. For Jonas a further aspect of Gnostic anti-Judaism was the fundamental rejection of laws and ethical rules, which stood unavoidably in sharp contradiction to the profoundly ethical and law-abiding religion of Judaism.[48] Jonas also rejects modern Gnostic currents of thought, which he sees as one-sided, other-world-oriented doctrines of salvation and "religious spells of magic under the heading of post-modern neo-mythologizing"[49] and which he condemns *in toto*.[50]

Gnosticism speaks repeatedly of gods and demons, spiritual beings that are held in thrall by the powers of the lower world. However, since the groundbreaking Gnosis congress of 1966 in Messina, we can probably no longer regard these beings literally. It was at this congress that the famous scholar of Gnosticism Carsten Colpe argued convincingly that the names of these beings denoted not gods but rather different aspects of the "soul" (in psychological language, various aspects of consciousness or of the "self").[51] The scholar of religion Hans Kippenberg considered this discovery to be one of Colpe's greatest achievements in his academic life and was convinced that the linguistically well-versed Colpe had been able to prove his point philologically as well.[52]

Thus the goal of the gnosis lies not in the freeing of a divine "redeemer" but rather in the release of a divine part of us enclosed in bodily matter, that is to say the "soul" or the "self" to use the language of psychology. In other words, what is meant here is a divine "illumination" of the individual and an activation of the higher consciousness. This in turn leads to an abandonment of the old collective ethic and its replacement by a new, individual one. Institutionalized religious communities (such as Judaism and Christianity), which are concerned to preserve group cohesion, must naturally reject such a development.

The scholar of religion Ioan Culianu has discussed this so-called existential interpreta-tion of Gnosticism thoroughly in his book *Hans Jonas: Gnosticismo e pensiero moderno.*[53] As to the world-denial, world-weariness, and pessimism that Jonas postulates, Culianu sees these as being rooted in the German *Zeitgeist* of the 1930s, when Jonas wrote his influential book, rather than in the era of ancient Gnosticism. In other words, Jonas' theory could well be a (thoroughly understandable) projection of his own feelings rather than an accurate representation of the ancient Gnostics' worldview.

Culianu refers to earlier work by Ugo Bianchi[54] and especially Barbara Aland, posing the question whether for the ancient Gnostics the sense of joy at being redeemed might have been much more intense than the pain of being trapped bodily in this world.[55] Aland, who prefers to restrict her analysis initially to Christian gnosis, even argues that, while there is much in the Gnostic texts about the grimness of the world, "there is much more about the indescribable joy of those who have received from the Father of Truth the grace of being able to recognize him through the power of the Logos (*Evangelium Veritas 16*, 31–4)."[56]

Unfortunately it is not possible to give an accurate answer to the question of how the ancient Gnostics really perceived their position, as they have left behind no authentic descriptions of their lives.[57] However, Kurt Rudolph has researched into the external "social context of the Gnostics in late antiquity—as far as is possible—and has tried to reconstruct at least some of the circumstances of their lives, although of course it is ques-tionable whether one can legitimately draw any conclusions about inner attitudes from such outward circumstances."[58] Rudolph begins by discussing the thesis of Gerd Theissen, who argues that Gnosticism was primarily rooted in the upper strata. Rudolph himself makes a distinction between the Gnostic elites, who were unquestionably well educated and of high standing, and the community rank-and-file, who were drawn from almost all social classes. However, he maintained that members of the middle and lower strata predominated: tradespeople, hand workers, scribes are attested. For him, Gnosticism has no interest in the reform of worldly conditions but only in their complete dissolution and the re-establishment of the "primal ideal world of the *spirit*." This of course entailed a critical attitude towards the rulers. Rudolph even goes as far as to interpret an extant Gnostic document as calling for the "abolition of social differences and of private prop-erty," which "one could characterize as communist."[59]

The philosopher Peter Koslowski takes a clear position here:

> Gnosis as a theory about the totality of reality cannot be described in terms of dualism or world-rejection … Gnosis as a general concept is an attitude of mind and a way for the spirit to create a dynamic theory about the genesis and totality of things, weaving together a consciousness of the total reality, of the absolute and of the nature of man. The genesis of the totality is recognized as a process which proceeds through creation/manifestation/formation of the self, fall/disintegration and then redemption/reintegration/return. These stages are both integral to the process and constitute steps in the development of the self.

Koslowski goes even further and sees the (Christian) gnosis as involving the notion of co-responsibility for the creation and therefore as the opposite of a flight from the world. Through this co-responsibility, "the other-worldly and divine part of the human *pneuma*, the center of the human persona, is represented in the creation process."[60] Koslowski goes on to say, "In the medieval world-view man was seen as merely an imitator of God and was therefore *under*estimated; modernity saw man as a demiurge and therefore *over*estimated him. Postmodernity, in accordance with true Christian gnosis and Theosophy, will see man as God's collaborator." This task will fall to man as an intermediary being between God and nature. And Koslowski elaborates further: "From the point of view of Christian gnosis and Theosophy there exists a basic and compelling interaction between, on the one hand, mystical self-understanding and, on the other hand, co-creation and effective practical action in the world."

Since Ralf Liedtke's wide-ranging study *Die Hermetik* the extreme dualism of Gnosticism, whether ancient or modern, can no longer be taken for granted.[61] Liedtke discerns in the Hermetic writings—which Jonas unhesitatingly categorizes as Gnostic[62] –not so much a strict dualism as an "inner difference." In other words, the Hermetic position is not unequivocal but rather ambivalent. On the one hand there are world-denying tendencies, but there are also statements of a very different kind, that speak of worldly love and passion. According to Liedtke, Hermeticism is characterized by precisely such differences and internal tensions. One can arrive at very different conclusions depending on which point of view one takes. Hence the purely pessimistic, dualistic, and world-denying interpretation of Gnosticism adopted by Jonas (and Holz) is seen to be invalid. Anyone who has looked into Gnosticism and esotericism will have discerned the strong impulse to overcome all dualism and strive towards an over-arching unity, even if this turns out to be a *coincidentia oppositorum*.

Holz claims—as the title of his essay indicates—to have detected in Eranos a form of pseudo-gnosis. To assign Eranos to the Gnostic tradition of thought might be understandable, but—as Filoramo says—to dismiss it with the term "pseudo-gnosis" is questionable.[63] Filoramo also characterizes Holz's whole essay as "polemical." Furthermore, in categorizing Eranos as Gnostic, Holz—following Jonas—thereby stamps it with the well-worn charge of duality (higher self and evil world), without bothering to check whether this really corresponds to the truth. Only in our Western system of thought, with its dislike of contradictions, does a preoccupation with the self lead automatically to a rejection of the world. Anyone who—like many Eranos speakers—has examined Indian systems of thought, knows that in that tradition the self (not in the Jungian sense)—the *atman*—is ultimately identical with the all-encompassing *brahman*. In other words, it is precisely through a preoccupation with the most fundamental of all spiritual questions that our perception becomes free to take in the great connections in the outer world—although not in the scientific nor in the political sense.

The emphasis on "inner" gnosis—in contrast to the political variety as interpreted by Voegelin— could have been the reason why certain key Eranos people—despite some attraction—were not carried away by Fascism and National Socialism, or at least learned a lesson from them later on. Robert Ellwood believes that Jung, Eliade, and Campbell, through "bitter experience," came to the conclusion that gnostic wisdom is intended for the soul and not for the state, and (consequently?) they presented no models that could also have been applied in the political realm.[64] He argues that the longing for transformation, which necessarily grows out of the gnostic revelation, must remain confined to the individual and cannot be realized in the political sphere. Inward contemplation rather than outward action is called for.

Along with the charge of dualism goes the accusation of anti-modernism and opposition to progress, for world-rejecting people cannot by definition be interested in worldly reforms. Eranos, however, cannot be accused of such a generalized opposition to modernity, since it is just as much rooted in "enlightenment" as in antiquity, as shown by the consistently scholarly and scientific approach of nearly all the Eranos speakers. What Eranos is indeed opposed to (and here it is not alone) is modernity in the sense of something materialistic and technology-obsessed, which denies the archetypal dimension and sees the new as being automatically superior to the old.[65] What is opposed here is above all the, as Alain Finkielkraut once put it, modern obsession that the real is to be equated with the rational.

As has already been emphasized, Eranos always tried to give equal value to the old and the new, to reason and to myth. Hence Robert Ellwood characterizes the Eranos protagonists not as "reactionary" but rather as "integrationist."[66] They wanted simply to integrate myth fully into modern life. Myth was for them a "timeless truth," which could still find its place in the continually changing flux of the modern world. At the same time they were probably not conscious of the fact that their (and the Eranos) conception of myth was itself thoroughly modern. The question of whether myth ever really had the "whole-making" function of salvation by bringing together man and the cosmos, religion and politics—this question must remain in abeyance. It was only through the modern separation of these domains that such "romantic" notions could arise. For someone living in a unified tradition of myth such a division would be unimaginable. Hence Steven Wasserstrom describes Scholem, Eliade, and Corbin as "antimodernist moderns."[67]

Academics, and especially sociologists, are fond of leveling the charge of anti-modernism against anything that one might call "esoteric." But here it is necessary to differentiate, for there are not only anti-modern but also hyper-modern forms of esotericism, such as cyber-magic or the use of cutting-edge technical apparatus in spiritualism. The anti-modernist accusation also ignores the fact that esoteric currents of thought contributed significantly to the development of modern science, as has been shown by scholars such as Frances Yates (who sometimes exaggerates) and Allen Debus, to name only two.[68] Scholars vie with each other for the right to define what is modern and "progressive" and what is not, and where exactly the dividing line is to be drawn, but in fact such arguments are fundamentally about vested interests and jockeying for power.

This brings me to the central focus of Holz's accusations—the kind of accusations that we have already seen clearly in our discussion of Hans Jonas' conception of Gnosticism. As we know, the accusation of flight from the world follows from the charge of dualism. Holz, in considerably more elegant words, makes the same complaint that Hans A. Pestalozzi makes in his book *Die sanfte Verblödung* (The gentle dumming-down),[69] namely that spirituality is merely a diversion from the much more important task of participating in effective public, political action.

In addition, Holz perceives in Eranos a strict division between the *savants* (the lecturers) and the passively led audience. He argues that this entails the danger of subservience to authority, so it is not surprising that he claims to discern, in the first ten years of Eranos, "a closeness if not an affinity" to elements of National Socialist ideology. He falsely, as it seems to me, interprets the pronouncements made by Olga Fröbe in 1933 and 1934 concerning an imminent turning point in history. Holz automatically relates this to Hitler in a way that is only possible in the context of our present-day fixation on and knowledge of the National Socialist atrocities. In fact, Mrs. Fröbe does not speak of a political turning point but rather of an esoteric and astrological one, namely the Age of Aquarius, which is so much trumpeted today and even then was beginning to be talked about.[70] In her foreword to the 1936 Eranos volume (9) she expresses this very clearly:

"We are in a process of regeneration between two world periods, between two signs of the Zodiac."[71]

Most probably the political earthquake of that time and its possible consequences were much less evident to her and the others than we tend to assume today. Furthermore, there is no evidence that she connected the Age of Aquarius with Hitler: rather the opposite. When Fröbe traveled to America in 1940 she was struck by the Great Seal of the United States printed on the dollar notes and bearing the motto *Novus ordo seclorum* (A new order of the ages), which she immediately connected with the hoped-for New Age. The connection seemed so important and full of promise that she even wrote a letter to Eleanor Roosevelt, asking her to draw the president's attention to the significance of the seal. It may or may not be a coincidence that Roosevelt actually spoke of a new order of the centuries in his first formal talk after his re-election.

Ideally one would have to deal in greater detail with the issues raised by Holz, and undeniably much of what he says would apply to many of the participants.[72] What is disturbing, however, is the apodictic tone of his analysis, as though there were no other possible point of view. However, as already pointed out, esoteric thinking (as an ideal type) does not deal in mutually exclusive opposites and eternally irreconcilable contrasts, but rather builds on complementarities. It is not free of contradictions, but swings back and forth from one pole to another, finally culminating in a *coincidentia oppositorum*. Although one could discourse for much longer over issues of freedom, irrationalism, politics, and the search for salvation, at some point one must close the discussion. Perhaps someone else will come forward to discuss the matter in a much broader and less one-sided way, for the issues that Holz addresses concern not just Eranos but all spiritually oriented groups. This is amply demonstrated, on the one hand, by the persistently virulent problem of guru-ism and, on the other hand, by the revolt against institutional religious communities, combined with political initiatives based on "gnostic" spirituality.[73]

Here I would like to quote some words from a well-informed source on the topic of mysticism, gnosis, and irrationalism. The philosopher Peter Koslowski, in his foreword to the book edited by him entitled *Gnosis und Mystik in der Geschichte der Philosophie*, writes:

> Philosophical mysticism and gnosis are not a form of irrationalism but rather attempts to employ reason and feeling to reach the limits of cognition. What distinguishes them from the objectivism of the positivistic sciences is the conviction that true knowledge cannot be something external to the human self, but is something that touches and changes us in the innermost centre of ourselves. The prerequisite for this insight is the recognition that the human and the divine soul are not fully distinct and separate and that there exists a common soul-substance.[74]

Surely there can be no clearer statement of the controversial esoteric foundations of Eranos—whether one chooses to use the term gnosis or esotericism. And here one should not omit to mention the passage in the *Corpus Hermeticum*, X, 9, which describes gnosis as a "particular capacity (*areté*) of the soul."[75] Hence Elaine Pagels translates the word gnosis as "insight" and not merely as "knowledge," for gnosis involves "an intuitive process of knowing oneself."[76] I would like to quote another, somewhat polemical, remark by the philosopher Peter Sloterdijk, who has repeatedly made headlines on account of his sharp way of expressing himself. Sloterdijk has fanned the debate over Gnosticism by his uninhibited attempt to highlight what he sees as the most important background factor in the debate. "A person who is attracted to Gnosticism," he writes "is one who wishes to be clever rather than pious where issues of truth are concerned."[77]

As this chapter has made frequent reference to gnosis and the original Gnosticism, it is now appropriate to address the fundamental question whether "Gnosticism" can still legitimately be used as an overall term for various quite diverse spiritual and religious currents of the early centuries AD. This question has already aroused debate among scholars such as Michael Allen Williams, author of *Rethinking "Gnosticism": An Argument for Dismantling a Dubious Category*.[78] The title of the book already makes clear the thrust of the argument. Williams hopes that the abolition of the term "Gnosticism" will help to combat the false impression of a unified religious movement or even a monolithic system of thought. Williams maintains that the term is used today in such a broad and contradictory sense that it no longer conveys any clear message. Williams' book is also notable for the way in which it deals in a differentiated way with such familiar "Gnostic" stereotypes as flight from the world, denial of the body, asceticism, sexual license, and elitism.

Similar arguments are advanced by Karen L. King.[79] In her view there is no such thing as Gnosticism in the sense of an ancient religious belief with a unified origin and a clearly distinguishable set of characteristics. She writes: "Gnosticism is, rather, a term invented in the early modern period to aid in defining the boundaries of normative Christianity."[80] For her Gnosticism is only a rhetorical term that has been mistaken for an actual historical phenomenon.

Barbara Aland, in her comprehensive book *Was ist Gnosis?*, does not go so far as to say that the term should be abolished, but she is certainly against delineating gnosis precisely by attributing definite characteristics to it.[81] This she considers impossible and refers to the "typological model" of the noted scholar of gnosis Christoph Markschies.[82] The latter argues that a mode of thought can be termed gnostic if eight characteristics or ideas are present. These include the "notorious" dualism, the so-called demiurge and the notion that the creation of the world is evil. Barbara Aland's view is that gnosis is too multifarious a phenomenon to be given a consistent and precise set of features.

It appears, therefore, that the essential definition of gnosis—and even the concept itself—stand on shaky ground, perhaps because the term has been loaded with political or ideological baggage that does not belong to it. By the same token, certain important accusations against the Gnosticism of Eranos, such as dualism and flight from the world, also lose their force—at least in the crudely simplistic form in which they are often presented. Modern attacks on the gnostic way of thinking are usually abrasive and—psychologically speaking—emotionally overloaded (precisely because the attackers seem to be unsure of themselves). Unfortunately one has the impression that these opponents are not aware of the research of recent decades or have consciously ignored it.

"Das Völkische": Not Just a German Phenomenon

Having considered some general political issues with regard to Eranos, it may be appropriate to devote a few pages to an aspect that I shall describe with the German word "*völkisch*," for which—like the word "*Volk*"—there is no exact English equivalent ("folkish" and "folk" are imperfect translations).[83] The word "*völkisch*," in its original meaning of "belonging to the *Volk*," came to be used increasingly after 1875 for reasons of linguistic purity as a substitute for the French "national."[84] However, from about 1930 and especially after 1933, it lost its neutral character. Even the so-called "Young Conservatives," like Moeller van den Bruck and Max Hildebert Boehm, who saw themselves as "*völkisch*," disapproved of the term because under National Socialist propaganda it had come to be used in a narrowly racist sense to mean simply a decidedly anti-Semitic form of nationalism. This mean that *"völkisch"* should not automatically be equated with "National Socialist," but the fact is that in twentieth-century Germany *völkisch* thinking ended in National Socialism.

It is well known that *völkisch* attitudes were in no way confined to Germany. We have already spoken about Mircea Eliade's Romanian *völkisch* activities. In the same spirit one spoke of an "Italian race"[85] and a "French race."[86] I have also touched on the connection between Zionism and the *völkisch* worldview.[87] At the same time there have been *völkisch* currents that were not at all aggressive, let alone racist, such as those represented by Martin Buber and by the socialist and non-violent anarchist Gustav Landauer. "Why," Landauer once asked, "should one call for an end to all specific ties and therefore an end to all differences between human beings?"[88]

One should also distinguish *völkisch* thinking from that which is simply chauvinistic and nationalistic. The essence of the *völkisch* worldview is that every people is coupled with a metaphysical entity, a "soul," which is formed by the nature of the homeland and is, as it were, God-given.[89] Hence also the significance of an agrarian "rootedness," spanning many generations and giving the individual a sense of connection with his own "soil,"[90] although on the other hand this can easily lead, as it almost always has done, to a persecution of "rootless" and "nomadic" people. Usually *völkisch* thinking goes hand in hand with a strong opposition to modernity, liberalism, industrialization, and free trade, as these are held to be to blame for "internationalism" and thus for the dissolution of *völkisch* values.[91] As the Hauer expert Shaul Baumann wrote to me on 28 July 2000, "The moral of the story is that, despite the necessity to preserve one's national cultural heritage, one should think of humanity first and foremost."

The origins of the *völkisch* worldview are to be found (once more) in the (German) Romantic era, which sought to promote an organic conception of nature and therefore of the state, in opposition to mechanistic rationalism. The key notion here was the sense of alienation that we experience in the face of modernity. Basically Romanticism is centered on the individual, and one would therefore expect it to be non-political. However, opposition to the French Revolution, which was seen as a mass movement, soon caused a political Romanticism to emerge. The emphasis switched from the individual person to the individual *Volk*, with all its emotions, traditions, and peculiarities. A further antimodern characteristic of the Romantic view is the belief that our salient problems cannot primarily be solved by external rational and technical means, but rather by looking into and from within ourselves.

Earlier I have spoken of the esotericism of Eranos as a sensitive listening-in to the unknown and potentially dangerous depths of the human consciousness. Here one can clearly discern the bridge between the esoteric-religious and the *völkisch* worldview.[92] In one case one listens in to one's inner self. In the other one listens in to the potentially equally dangerous depths of one's own *Volk*, or to both at the same time.[93] Here we see perhaps *one* explanation for the fascination exerted by the *völkisch* persuasion, an explanation that in my opinion has hitherto not received the attention it deserves. A clear example of what I mean can be seen in the output of the publisher Eugen Diederichs, who was directly and indirectly connected with Eranos via people such as Rudolf Maria Holzapfel, Richard Wilhelm, and Heinrich Zimmer. At the same time he can be considered one of the most important trailblazers of the *völkisch* movement.[94] Consciously or unconsciously, the twofold "listening-in" that I have mentioned is clearly reflected in his publishing program.[95] In one of the volumes of the series *Der deutsche Buchhandel in Selbstdarstellungen* (The German book trade as portrayed by itself),[96] Diederichs presents a résumé of his life as a publisher, emphasizing that "the main emphasis currently [i.e. in the firm's later period] is on religion." One name that stands out here is Richard Wilhelm. Between 1910 and 1930, Wilhelm published nine volumes of translations from ancient Chinese literature and philosophy (including the *I Ching*, which was to be so important for Eranos) under the Diederichs imprint, a task that was of crucial financial importance for him.[97] Eugen Diederichs himself was deeply interested in the work of the sinologist and on certain occasions wore the Chinese sage's robe that Wilhelm had given him as a present.[98] Equally important was the series *Die religiösen Stimmen der Völker* (Religious voices of the nations), coordinated by Walter F. Otto from 1912, which made great organizational demands on the publisher, because this series mostly published first translations of basic religious texts of other cultures. Diederichs was concerned to make the series independent of confessional affiliation and accessible to a broader public. His volumes on mysticism were informed by the same spirit. He also published the writings of Giordano Bruno and Pico della Mirandola, possibly the two most important esoteric thinkers of the Renaissance. His list also included Masonic literature. On the other hand he avoided practical occultism, despite its salability. Diederichs was also in contact with the reformers at Monte Verità through his friendship with the poet Gusto Gräser and through his publication of the writings of the dancers Rudolf Laban and Mary Wigman.

A further, and somewhat unexpected, side of Diederichs was his commitment to publishing the works of leading feminists of the time. These included the esoterically inclined socialist and pacifist Rosa Mayreder as well as Lou Andreas Salomé, known for her friendship with Nietzsche and Rilke and for her own writings on psychoanalysis. Diederichs even wrote an essay entitled "Der Aufstieg der Frau" (The ascent of woman) for a *Festschrift* in honor of Rosa Mayreder, who largely agreed with his conclusions.[99] She in turn contributed to a *Festschrift* in honor of his sixtieth birthday, emphasizing that the upsurge of her literary career really began with Diederichs.[100]

Max Weber somewhat disrespectfully described Diederichs' publishing house as a "warehouse of *Weltanschauungen*."[101] Marino Pullio puts it rather less disparagingly in his assiduous and circumspect work on the early years of the monthly journal *Die Tat*, taken over by Diederichs in 1912. He writes, "Diederichs was the patron saint of those who embraced the counter-culture, the *Lebensreform* movement, the avant-garde and all forms of alternative ferment, ranging from the nationalist right to the non-Marxist left—all of them sharing the common denominator of a radical criticism of modernity."[102]

How can we explain the convergence of conservative-*völkisch* currents with the *Lebensreform* faction, the ecology movement,[103] early women's liberation and the opening to alternative forms of religion—a convergence that seems so surprising from today's perspective? A deep emotional chord is struck by the themes of one's own *Volk*, of peace-giving religion, of the local soil that demands such careful nurturing, of one's own mother, indeed of the "feminine" in general. This chord vibrates again and again in the same register, which can best be characterized by the German word *Geborgenheit*, implying a reassuring sense of security against that which is new and strange. Admittedly the notion of the "feminine," as it was then talked about, does not exactly correspond to today's equivalent. Nevertheless, one can understand the sentiments behind it. In another work, it would certainly be worthwhile to investigate the connections between the domain of the feminine and that which can be characterized as "*völkisch*." After all, one should not overlook the fact that many women of that era identified themselves with *völkisch* currents of thought.

The coexistence of *völkisch*-political and religious writing was not confined to the firm of Eugen Diederichs. When Heinrich Zimmer, who can in no way be suspected of *völkisch* sympathies, came to publish his book *Karman: Ein buddhistischer Legendenkranz* in 1925, he placed it with the Munich firm of F. Bruckmann, which had also published *the* classic work of the *völkisch* movement, namely *Die Grundlagen des 19. Jahrhunderts* (Foundations of the nineteenth century) by Houston Stewart Chamberlain, which by then was in its fourteenth printing. Such facts may appear stranger to us today than they would have done at that time, and we would do well to bear this in mind when we are tempted to make judgments about the people of that era, who were no doubt just as repeatedly fallible as we are today.

It is a characteristic of "myth" that it leaves room for contradictions—indeed by its nature it is ambivalent. The fascination exerted by "myth" is what unites those of a *völkisch* and of a religious turn of mind (including of course the esotericists). And here we are confronted again with fundamental ethical issues. The ambivalence of myth has the effect of suspending ethical concerns, as myth knows no "clear" boundaries between good and evil. This quality makes myth not only fascinating but also dangerous. Disconcertingly, it seems that in the political realm the most fascinating myths are those that unleash suffering and tragedy through their seductive glitter—whether the theme is blood and soil, the classless society, or the terrifying prospect of the end of the world. And yet I heartily agree with the following words of Jeanne Hersch:

> Political truth is not attained by extinguishing myth but rather by accepting in the present the tension between contrasting myths. In doing so one shoulders the resulting contradictions as well as the irreconcilable demands of different values. This does not mean that the values are false and that everything is permitted, but rather, on the contrary, that all are valid and that everything must be attempted without the promise of a perfect outcome.[104]

🏶 16. Eranos as a Prototype

After what has probably been a necessary digression, let us return to the connection between scholarship and esotericism (not their conflation), which is in fact one of the central points of this investigation. Eranos is by no means alone in its quest to illuminate "esoteric," "gnostic" or "mystical" matters with academic methods, and to filter out the "best" from both sides. There were and still are many such associations, study groups, and conferences. Releasing their results for the most part only in booklet form, they have not received attention from the mainstream media, and as a consequence have remained largely unknown to the public. A few of these at least deserve some mention in the following pages. One might ask why they are going to be dealt with here, in some cases in considerable detail. First, I believe these groupings and organizations have, by and large, played a very important role in promoting a reappraisal of esoteric thought within the universities. Second, up to this point they have received no overview to speak of in the literature. In addition there are substantial difficulties in accessing the original documents of these organizations, which mostly appeared in relatively small print runs and were only very occasionally acquired by big libraries.

On purely geographical grounds I would like to begin with an initiative from Lugano, situated about an hour's travel from Ascona. Hardly anything has ever been published on the Istituto Ticinese di Alti Studi or ITAS (Ticinian Institute for High Studies), which held summer seminars in Lugano between 1970 and 1973.[1] Here too the attempt to harmonize mythos with logos lay to the fore, as academics and professors voiced unorthodox views on the connections between science and a spiritual way of life, in the process unequivocally postulating the supremacy of a sacral dimension in human beings. Counting a few Eranos speakers among their number, the lecturers included personages as well known as Jean Servier, Hans Sedlmayr, Karl Kerényi, Margarethe Riemschneider, Elémire Zolla, Pio Filippani Ronconi, Marius Schneider, and Seyyed Hossein Nasr, as well as Armando Plebe.[2]

The idea for these conferences came from Elémire Zolla, a literary expert, philosopher, Eranos speaker, and mystic;[3] Pio Filippani-Ronconi, an orientalist who was also an esotericist (a student of Evola); and the son-in-law of Ezra Pound, Prince Boris de Rachewiltz, an Egyptologist and esotericist (from the milieu of Giuliano Kremmerz). Boris de Rachewiltz, whose ancestral castle Brunnenberg lies near Meran in the South Tyrol, was the director of the Ludwig Keimer Foundation in Basel, which conducted a new form of archaeological research. Testimony was to be derived not only from "dead" artifacts; the living culture still existing *in situ* at the time of the excavations was also to be considered conjointly with ethnological research.[4] The Ludwig Keimer Foundation sought after localities rich in history where it might convene its courses, and in Lugano it was met with welcome arms as well as financing from local banking institutions. In

Ticino an independent university was already being considered, and it was supposed that initial experiences could be gained with such post-university courses. What is more, a suitable organizer was available locally in the person of Romano Amerio, a traditionalist Catholic philosopher (the "most learned," in Zolla's opinion).[5]

The first conference in 1970 also witnessed the official presentation of *Conoscenza Religiosa*. Zolla had established this journal in 1969, and it must surely be counted among the most important European publications to deal in a scholarly way with religious and above all esoteric themes.[6] The subject matter of its articles ranged from shamanism to Satanism and included mysticism, number symbolism, Sufism, yoga, and the Kabbalah. Among the contributing authors were Henry Corbin, Antoine Faivre, Jean Servier, Gershom Scholem, and Seyyed Hossein Nasr.[7] The journal was continued until 1983. In the first years printed lectures from the ITAS conferences were also to be found in its pages. The keen anti-modern and spiritual tendencies of the journal are already evident in the preamble to the first volume of *Conoscenza Religiosa*, where mention is made of the dissemination of *un lembo di quella sapienza che tutto nella civiltà moderna cospira a reprimere* (a little piece of that wisdom which everything in modern civilization colludes to suppress).[8] However, according to Zolla's words in an interview with Radio Montenceneri (Ticino) on 17 September 1970, ITAS was equally concerned with the evocation of that which helps us to understand other peoples. A great deal of support for these post-university courses came from the canton. Hence there were scholarships, and from 1971 onwards the courses were even convened in the magnificent Villa Heleneum in Castagnola, which belonged to the municipalities of Lugano and Castagnola.

A "pause" in the courses was planned for 1974.[9] Unfortunately the conferences did not get under way again. Political disagreements (there was talk of "reactionary" meetings) apparently played an important role in their cessation. But practical considerations seem to have been equally important. The activities of ITAS—which were orientated purely towards the humanities and, what is more, proceeded within a rather "traditionalist" context[10]—were surely regarded by the canton as less lucrative than the studies oriented towards commerce and banking that became the focal point thereafter.

The enthusiasm for these conferences was exceptional, as my sources confirm. Cristina Campo, recognized *littérateuse* (and one-time "muse" of Elémire Zolla), writes on the first conference in a letter from Lugano dated 26 August 1970, "The congress, which like all things El. [Elémire Zolla] planned for a long time, is absolutely beautiful. Humble and generous sages, who reveal a world to us every day."[11]

I have already mentioned the Université Saint-Jean de Jérusalem several times, and as a number of important Eranos speakers were united precisely in this institution, I would like to deal with it in more detail. Defined as an "international center for comparative spiritual research," it was founded by Henry Corbin, Gilbert Durand, Antoine Faivre,[12] Richard Stauffer, and Robert de Chateaubriant.[13] Mircea Eliade made himself available as an intellectual advisor.[14] Ernst Benz, Kathleen Raine, and Jean Brun were further Eranos participants who actively collaborated there.

The Université Saint-Jean de Jérusalem stood under the aegis of the Order of St. John (The Chivalric Order of Saint John of the Hospital at Jerusalem) and had its seat at the abbey of Vaucelles, where the French priory of the order was also domiciled.[15]

In this connection it is significant that the Order of St. John inherited the spiritual legacy of the Knights Templar, as an undated leaflet of the Université formulates the matter. Other points of reference are the so-called "Friends of God,"[16] German mysticism, and also the Grail cycle.[17]

Despite the predominantly Christian impression conveyed by these motifs, the work of the university centered upon the commonalities between the three "religions of the book"—that is to say, Judaism, Christianity, and Islam.[18] The stated goal is to establish a "spiritual knighthood" that opposes "the utter confusion in the spirit, in the souls and in the hearts" of the people—"precisely the confusion that has resulted from the debacle of secular institutions in the West."[19] However, the objective of the university goes "deeper than simply replacing the old institutions with new ones." The "God is dead" theology cannot be accepted and is comparable to the "destruction of the Temple."[20] As combatants "against historicism and agnosticism" and other "bulwarks" that hinder the conferral of meaning beyond the purely temporal, members are aware of their anachronistic task; indeed, a "new birth" is expected of them.[21]

In a far more detailed and presumably unpublished draft of this leaflet entitled *Pour le concept de l'université Saint Jean De Jérusalem*, Henry Corbin adds that he envisions an "inner church" of the kind that has emerged "from Joachim of Fiore through Schelling to Berdyaev." The mystics of Shi'ite Islam were also inspired by the same endeavor. The aim is the rebuilding of the "destroyed Temple" in accordance with the ideal of the "heavenly Jerusalem." The first task entailed by this concept is "the reform of the humanities," which in French are known simply as "sciences humaines," and which are now no longer "the handmaiden of theology" but might rather be named "the handmaiden of sociology." However, dogmatic squabbles have no place at the Université, as the point is not to replace one dogma with another, but rather "to penetrate into the forest of symbols together, so that we may together understand where we find ourselves." Of central concern thereby are the spiritual orientation and academic basis for comparative studies. According to a plan annexed to the draft leaflet, the organizational structure is divided into members who are simply spectators and those who wish to be comrades-in-arms. Above these stand a scientific council of twelve, an administrative council, and the inner order of the Knights of the Temple of Saint John.[22]

On the occasion of the inauguration of the Université de Saint-Jean de Jérusalem the political dignitaries of Cambrai, where the Abbey of Vaucelles is situated, also held an official reception. As photographs published at the time reveal, this inauguration was a very colorful affair.[23] The journal *Combat* from 12 July 1974 describes it in the following way: "Jews dedicated to the tradition of the Kabbalah sat next to Muslims from Iran and Mali; the Archbishop of Cambrai and theologians of all obediences shared the same uncomfortable benches with Freemasons and other Masonic members."

Between 1974 and 1987 a total of fourteen colloquia were held at the Université de Saint-Jean de Jérusalem. After the death of Henry Corbin the presidency was taken up by his wife, Stella Corbin. The Université met its demise because she was of the opinion that the goal once set by her husband had been attained.[24] However, many participants did not agree: a parallel with Eranos. But in her capacity as president Stella Corbin deregistered the organization with the responsible authorities, and thus the deed was done. The lectures were published in Paris by Berg International in fourteen so-called *Cahiers de l'Université Saint-Jean de Jérusalem*.

To some extent the Université de Saint-Jean de Jérusalem continued in the form of the Groupe d'Etudes Spirituelles Comparées, in which a very similar goal prevailed.[25] It was founded in its turn by Gilbert Durand and Antoine Faivre, as well as Robert Salmon and others. Its president was Durand,[26] who in his inaugural address expressed the explicit hope that there might once again arise "the spirit which we brought to the knightly brotherhood twenty years ago and which accompanied our master Corbin to the Abbey of Vaucelle."[27] Here too the themes of a comparative study of religion addressing the three biblical faiths were taken up yearly in a colloquium and then published in the form of a *cahier*.[28]

Larger in scope are the colloquia of Cerisy, which have taken place since 1952 and also encompass artistic, philosophical, and political issues. Within these broader parameters there are also meetings on the themes of mythology, esotericism, and religious studies, which are then conveyed to the interested reading public through the *Cahiers de l'Hermétisme*, whose pages cover an even wider range of topics.[29] The directors are Antoine Faivre and Fréderick Tristan. As briefly aforementioned, the original editorial committee again comprised many names that we already know from Eranos: Ernst Benz, Henry Corbin, Gilbert Durand, Mircea Eliade, Henri-Charles Puech, and Jean Servier.

The proceedings of the Loge nationale de recherches Villard de Honnecourt are well established in the domain of Freemasonic research. However, general themes relating to Hermeticism and esotericism are also dealt with in a scholarly manner in this extensive body of material. Connections with the Université de Saint-Jean de Jérusalem can hardly be overlooked. Henry Corbin himself was an honorary member of Villard de Honnecourt[30] and the names of the leading members of the Université de Saint-Jean de Jérusalem, Antoine Faivre, and Gilbert Durand, appear again here.[31] Other names common to both bodies (for example the Eranos lecturer Jean Servier) are also to be found among the list of participants.[32] Likewise, a detailed report on the 1981 session of the Université de Saint-Jean de Jérusalem appeared in the journal of the lodge.[33]

The lodge itself belongs to the Régime Ecossais Rectifié (Scottish rectified rite; RER), which emerged from the National Convention of the French Templars in Lyon in 1778. At that time the Order of the Chevaliers bienfaisants de la Cité Sainte was founded under the leadership of the decidedly esoterically inclined Jean-Baptiste Willermoz, and the supposedly direct derivation of this group from the Order of the Templars was rejected. Besides the cultivation of charity, its goal was the perfection of man, conceived as a return to his original purity. The path thither was via an esoteric Christianity or Christian gnosis. The influence of Martinès de Pasqually and his Order of the Elus Coens was and remains today of particular importance in this regard. Pasqually's chief work deals precisely with this Christian process of perfection, which is spoken of as "the reintegration of each being with its original individuality, virtue and divine spiritual power."[34] Similarly we find significant links with the so-called Christian Kabbalah (Johannes Reuchlin) here.[35]

Within the aforementioned Chevaliers bienfaisants de la Cité Sainte there was even a higher degree with the title Chevalier de la Cabale. Another degree, the Chevalier du soleil, was also characterized as "Cabaliste."[36] The instructional materials further included the mystical writings of Louis Claude de Saint-Martin, who also belonged to the Elus Coens and was influenced by Jakob Boehme. The above-mentioned plan of the Order that emerged from the National Convention of Lyon in 1778 was officially accepted at the 1782 Convention of Wilhelmsbad, which was a landmark in the development of Freemasonry. It had been planned as a general masonic congress but primarily assembled Templar Knights. Rather than proclaiming a historically unverifiable link directly from the Templars to the Freemasons, one now spoke only of an analogy between the two, above all in relation to their spirituality.[37]

Here, then, are the principal features of the genesis of the Régime Ecossais Rectifié, whose significance for the serious contemporary study of esotericism in France should not be underestimated. Particular note should be made of this system's fundamentally Christian basis, to which great importance is attached within the Loge Villard de Honnecourt. The symbolism of the Grail is also prominent.[38] There can be just as little doubt that the temple symbolism of Henry Corbin is related to Freemasonry and the Régime Ecossais Rectifié in particular. In a homage to Corbin[39] published in the *Travaux de la loge de recherches Villard de Honnecourt* and focusing on the spiritual path of his master and friend,[40] Gilbert Durand describes Corbin's intense preoccupation with the Templar legend, the Grail, and the rituals of Martinès de Pasqually's order. He also describes the way in which Corbin's striving for a community of kindred spirits resulted in the founding of the Université de Saint-Jean de Jérusalem, whose first vice-president was Durand himself. He goes on to recount that Corbin had already told him of such plans at Eranos in 1964.[41]

In conclusion, another point that may be surprising: the first article of the first volume of the lodge publications was written by Mircea Eliade and is entitled "Initiation et monde moderne."[42] It reproduces an address delivered by Eliade on the occasion of an evening organized by the lodge in the salons of the Eiffel Tower on 29 September 1979.[43] What is more, Frédérick Tristan delivered a memorial address in the name of the Grand Lodge of France on the occasion of the death of Eliade.[44]

Here I cannot go into the numerous regular publications of the Freemasonic research lodges as a whole, although they undoubtedly form a connecting link between "inner" wisdom and "outer" scholarship. The yearbooks of the Quatuor Coronati research lodge in Bayreuth or the *Ars Quatuor Coronatorum* of the Quatuor Coronati Lodge in London, which has been publishing its transactions since the nineteenth century, are evidence enough. As it regularly takes up themes that are also dealt with by the Loge Villard de Honnecourt, I do not wish to leave unmentioned the French masonic journal *Renaissance Traditionnelle—Revue d'Etudes Maçonniques et Symboliques*, which possesses similar aims to those of the said research lodges. Indeed, an overlapping of authors (Antoine Faivre, for example) is evident. Numerous detailed articles may be found therein on the Régime Ecossais Rectifié (e.g. in issue 3, then in issues 31, 80, 96, etc.), on and by Louis-Claude de Saint-Martin and Jean-Baptiste Willermoz, on the Elus Coens and the Templars. The journal was founded in 1969 by René Désaguliers. Today it is run by Roger Dachez and Pierre Mollier, who are also known as book authors and who are associated with other journals in the field as well.

The colloquia of the Association pour la Recherche et l'Information de l'Esotérisme (ARIES) also stood under the direction of professors Roland Edighoffer and Antoine Faivre. Pierre Deghaye counted among the editors of the journal *Aries* which has existed since 1985 and which publishes articles of the highest academic quality on Western esotericism since the Renaissance. The original scholarly committee included the Eranos participants Mircea Eliade, Moshe Idel, Gilbert Durand, and Elémire Zolla, among others. Since 2001 *Aries* has been published by the renowned Dutch publisher E.J. Brill in Leiden, which had already published some of the Eranos volumes. The editorship of the new series was originally shared by the Chair for the History of Hermetic Philosophy and Related Currents at the University of Amsterdam and the Chair for Esoteric and Mystical Currents in Modern and Contemporary Europe at the Ecole Pratique des Hautes Etudes (Sorbonne). The Association pour la Recherche et l'Information de l'Esotérisme no longer organizes conferences. Since 2005 this task has been taken up in its stead by

ESSWE (the European Society for the Study of Western Esotericism), which organizes a congress every two years and which has also taken over publication of the journal *Aries*.

Special mention should be made of the annual conferences of Politica Hermetica, led by Jean-Pierre Laurant, a lecturer at the Ecole Supérieure des Hautes Etudes, and Jean-Pierre Brach, the latter having been chosen as the successor to Antoine Faivre at the same university. As its name suggests, Politica Hermetica deals with the relationship between politics, history, and esotericism. Here, too, Antoine Faivre is on the advisory board. The conference proceedings are regularly published.

At this point perhaps one might also recall the interesting volumes of the *Etudes Carmelitaines*, which were published from the end of the 1930s until the beginning of the 1970s by the Belgian publishing house Desclée de Brouwer. The topics addressed therein ranged from mysticism and mythology to C.G. Jung. Louis Massignon counted among regular contributors who were also Eranos speakers, and Henri-Charles Puech also made contributions.

Hence it is apparent that France has been a particularly fruitful country for such initiatives. In the German-speaking lands the situation is not quite so good, although not nearly so bad as one might imagine. Admittedly, "explicit" societies of academics or indeed university lecturers with clear esoteric goals, like the University of St. John of Jerusalem, are scarcely imaginable there. "Esotericism" runs, or used to run, rather more covertly as an undercurrent within academic organizations, and often opposing camps would form: one friendly to esotericism and the other hostile.

As an example of this phenomenon I would like to mention an association known since 2009 as Symbolon: Gesellschaft für wissenschaftliche Symbolforschung (Symbolon: society for the scientific study of symbolism). Based originally in Basel but now in Heidelberg, this society still holds annual conferences whose lectures are then published in a yearbook. However, in recent years its "esoteric" component has all but ceased to exist.

The stimulus for this society's creation came from a Geneva physician, M. Engelson, who established the Société pour l'ètude scientifique du Symbolisme in 1953 and held the first congress in that same year.[45] At the second congress the following year the Basel author and translator Julius Schwabe was invited to present a paper; he was subsequently asked by Engelson to organize a similar society for German-speaking Switzerland and southern Germany.[46] Engelson believed he could discern concepts in modern physics that were similar to those underlying ancient religious and mythical traditions; he wished to study this "traditional symbolism and mythology" scientifically and then impart an understanding of the matter to modern natural scientists.[47]

As Schwabe writes in his preface to the first yearbook, "While positivist science is essentially content to establish and order relevant facts, the study of symbolism now has the task of unlocking the meaning of these facts, of demonstrating that meaning and of locating it within ever wider contexts of meaning."[48] Thus Schwabe's wish, as expressed in the preface, was "to recover a holistic world view and philosophy of life, without which culture will cease to exist in the long run." Through "the astonishing progress ... not only the spiritual harmony of humankind but its very existence, indeed the existence of all life on our planet, is threatened." In addition the society wished to maintain its distance from psychology, which believed it held a virtual monopoly on the understanding of symbols: "Without excluding psychology, from which we all have learnt, we *as trustees of the traditions* must nevertheless approach matters from another perspective and from different premises."[49]

Schwabe goes on to praise the "classical methods of the comparative study of myth and symbol" and looks upon men such as Bachofen, Usener, Jeremias, Frobenius, and so on as paragons. Then come two sentences that are exceedingly surprising given the scholarly posture of the first conference volume:

> Because in most religions esotericists have been and still remain the actual bearers and spiritual guardians of traditional symbolism—wherever cultures with old traditions survive—so naturally we desire the collaboration of real initiates and true sages. Consequently I have also striven from the beginning to secure individual representatives of religious esotericism as congress speakers.

Accordingly, the Traditionalist philosopher and Sufi initiate Titus Burckhardt spoke at the first conference, which was held at the University of Basel. On the cover of the conference volume the Traditionalist philosopher Leopold Ziegler is cited as follows: "The spiritual characters of all peoples are nourished and fed by the same underground stream of the same tradition, and that is what all real 'initiates' undisputedly experience time and again as the unity of all traditions." The cover text also proclaims that, although the studies published in *Symbolon* are not intentionally coordinated, they nevertheless "radiate out from a common centre like the spokes of a wheel" because of this shared tradition. This is a claim that Olga Fröbe always made in regard to Eranos too.

On the other hand, someone who was by no means an "aficionado" of the esoteric sciences—a fact he had already proven as a participant at the Eranos conferences—also spoke at the first conference, namely the ethnologist Paul Radin, whose lecture was entitled "The Earth and the Cosmos in the Conception of the Winnebago Indians."[50] In any case, the first conference had a classic esoteric theme: "Microcosm-Macrocosm." At the first two conferences two further Eranos speakers took part, Hans Kayser and Marie-Louise von Franz. The renowned sinologist Carl Hentze and the Indo-Iranist Hermann Lommel also spoke there.

In later years the erstwhile Eranos participants Erik Hornung, Andreas Speiser, Ernst Benz, and Hildemarie Streich were also to be found at the conferences of the society. There was certainly no shortage at the conferences of other recognized scholars as well. As examples we might mention Karl Narr, Herbert Kühn, Margarete Riemschneider, Cyrill von Corvin-Krasinsky, and Brigitte Luchesi. Amongst the esotericists speaking at the conferences I would like to point to Alfons Rosenberg, who also played a certain role at Eranos, to the Kabbalist Friedrich Weinreb and to the Traditionalist Matthias Vereno. Noteworthy too is the fact that lectures were also held here by Philipp Wolff-Windegg, the principal editor of *Antaios* (a bimonthly journal published in Basel and inspired by similar interests) as well as by the philosopher Franz Vonessen from the University of Freiburg, who also played an important role in *Antaios*.[51]

However, the current president of the society, the music historian Hermann Jung, who kindly supplied me with information, suggests that Julius Schwabe "probably didn't have in mind as a 'prototype' the Eranos conferences with their orientation towards *Mentalitätsgeschichte* [the history of world views and spiritual perspectives],"[52] but rather wished to place the study of symbolism in all its diverse currents "on a scientifically reliable foundation within a firmly based institution."[53]

Due to his advancing years, Julius Schwabe's Society for the Scientific Study of Symbols was converted from a "loose community" into a registered association in 1970, and the sculptor and lawyer Ernst Thomas Reimbold was appointed its president.[54] The conference site had already been moved to neighboring Germany. Likewise, the publisher of the conference volumes was changed. Because of the new management the numbering of the volumes began once again with Volume 1 and the appended words "new series." Although the foreword to the first volume states that "the goals of the society have not changed," the emphasis has nevertheless shifted somewhat. The esoteric aspect has receded further and further into the background. The talk is still of taking up "diverse points of view," but it is made abundantly clear that one is striving for a "hermeneutic that seeks to fathom deeper connections without leaving the firm ground of critical scholarship and losing oneself in speculations."[55]

The turn away from the original concept is already very clear in the third volume of the "new series." In a positive commentary on the society, the scholar of religion and Paracelsus researcher Kurt Goldammer asks "what exactly could have been meant" by the "collaboration of real initiates and true sages" wished for by Julius Schwabe.[56] In the same volume Reimbold replies that the "true sages" are the "true lovers … who in the coalescence of perceiver and the object of perception are lovingly wed." This, he says, contrasts with a purely scientific theory of knowledge "which understands perception as comprehension (a taking hold of), and far from allowing the symbol an intrinsic value, wishes to define the symbol through concepts and reduce it to concepts."[57] In order to shore up his position Reimbold alludes in this contribution to the difficulty of finding a scientific definition of the concept of symbols; the talk now is of Wittgenstein rather than Guénon, Evola, or Ziegler.

Regarding this question Hermann Jung has emphasized "that the so-called 'esoteric' component of symbolism, understood as 'secret knowledge' for 'initiates,' does not count among the society's research areas, or if so then only very peripherally." The same view, he points out, had been held by his predecessors Thomas Ernst Reimbold, the art historian Joachim Gaus, and the theologian Botho Hermann. Nevertheless, he maintains, there has been an opening towards serious research in areas such as psychology, psychotherapy, and medicine, among others.[58]

The fact that the society is still organizing conferences today (2011) is testimony to a great commitment by the board, for, like all groups occupied with questions at the boundaries of mythology, symbolism, science, and esotericism, this one too suffers from aging and dwindling of membership due to a lack of attraction for younger people. Clear evidence for this fact is supplied by the minutes of the general meeting of 18 April 1998, in which the treasurer bemoans the great arrears in membership payments and even declares her inability to produce a current list of members. This is because members rarely cancel their membership, but rather simply cease paying, and "some memberships end without appropriate cancellation due to advancing age or sickness." Since the creation of a website the situation has nevertheless clearly improved, as Hermann Jung writes, and queries to the society are happily on the rise.[59] As far as I could ascertain the current membership already numbers more than fifty people.

I am grateful to Hermann Jung for also drawing my attention to the Gesellschaft für Symbolforschung (Society for the study of symbolism), based in Zurich, a group led by the Germanist Paul Michel, which likewise organizes annual conferences whose results are subsequently published.

The conferences at Filzmoos near Salzburg organized by the Gesellschaft für Ganzheitsforschung (Society for holistic research) also linked scientific themes with spiritual content, albeit often with very different emphases (especially economic issues).

These conferences were established by the Viennese economist Walter Heinrich.[60] Heinrich was a student and successor of Othmar Spann, an Austrian sociologist, economist, philosopher of religion, and founder of the doctrine of Universalism, who had immersed himself deeply in the study of Meister Eckhart, German Idealism, and Franz von Baader. Similarly, Walter Heinrich, alongside his scholarly activities as a professor of economics, also demonstrated a lifelong interest in the Vedanta, Schelling, Leopold Ziegler, René Guénon, and Julius Evola.

After the death in 1950 of Othmar Spann, Heinrich attempted to further cultivate the so-called Universalist doctrine, which opposes individualism, pure empiricism, and materialism, based on Plato and German Idealism. To this end he established in 1957 a newsletter, which was initially produced in mimeographed form. With the development of the Gesellschaft für Ganzhzeitsforschung the newsletter was transformed into a printed quarterly entitled *Zeitschrift für Ganzheitsforschung*. The foreword to the first volume contains the following words:

> For more than 600 years, since the victory of nominalism in philosophy, the West, and with it humanity, has been threatened with the dissolution of all spiritual meaning. Spiritual unity was lost, the individual sciences established their own separate methods, pursuing them in isolation, turning them into absolutes without paying any heed to other branches of learning ...
>
> Following the example of science, the various other domains of life also adopted an absolutist attitude. Without a will to unity, without a spiritual centre and without a common legal authority, the individual domains of life entered ... into a hostile competition.

In order to halt this progressive destruction, Heinrich argued, it is necessary to develop a "spiritual overview," which "is, however, impossible without a general theory of wholeness, without a holistic logic and a unity of scientific method."

In 1974 Hanns J. Pichler, professor at the Vienna University of Economics and Business, took over management of the *Zeitschrift für Ganzheitsforschung* from Walter Heinrich. The content of the issues is fundamentally interdisciplinary (indeed, holistic) in orientation, although particular emphasis is naturally placed on Othmar Spann, Walter Heinrich, and other representatives of the "Universalist doctrine." Nevertheless, among the contributors to the journal are also to be found "integral Traditionalists" such as Julius Evola, Matthias Vereno, Hans Küry, Frithjof Schuon, Silvano Panunzio, and Jean Borella and philosophical esotericists such as Alfons Rosenberg and Robert Müller-Sternberg. Between 1957 and 1959 the Eranos speaker Ernst Benz also published work in the *Zeitschrift für Ganzheitsforschung*. Another who did so was Rudolf Haase, who attempted to continue the legacy of his harmonic master Hans Kayser, also an Eranos speaker. Herbert Pietschmann may also be mentioned as a later Eranos speaker among the authors. Further contributors included the art historian Hans Sedlmayr, the philosopher Franz Vonessen, G.K. Kaltenbrunner—who died in 2011 and in the later decades of his life increasingly developed into a mystic—and the Leopold Ziegler specialist Sophie Latour.

The year 1949 saw the first few gatherings of a circle of friends around Othmar Spann, which then developed into regular conferences at which numerous renowned lecturers from outside the circle also spoke. From the early 1950s the conferences took place at Filzmoos in the province of Salzburg, with only brief relocations elsewhere. In addition, a scientific advisory committee under the direction of Geiserich E. Tichy—who was also a professor of economics and a publicly certified auditor—organized evening meetings with selected individual lectures. As a rule these took place three times per year.

In 1999 the fiftieth jubilee year of these conferences was celebrated. These meetings came to an end with the very last held in 2006, the fifty-fifth meeting, held in Filzmoos itself. The *Zeitschrift für Ganzheitsforschung* also ceased publication after fifty years of regular quarterly appearances, as finances were no longer sufficient to guarantee the quality of its content and presentation. However, the sessions of the scientific advisory committee still continue. All volumes of the journal as well as the accompanying literature reviews have meanwhile been digitized at the instigation of Geiserich E. Tichy as president of the society's board of trustees. Thus they are documented and accessible on the Internet.[61]

The journal *Gnostika*, published from Sinzheim in Germany, was founded in 1996 by Wolfram Frietsch and me specifically in order to address the tension between esotericism and science. Here too the already well-known names of Antoine Faivre, Wouter Hanegraaff, Erik Hornung, Annemarie Schimmel, Moshe Idel, and Elemire Zolla crop up again. In addition there are regular interviews with important representatives of the academic study of esotericism, such as Antoine Faivre,[62] Joscelyn Godwin,[63] Wouter Hanegraaff, Nicholas Goodrick-Clarke, Marco Pasi, and so forth. Although plans for annual conferences have repeatedly been made, thus far they have unfortunately failed to materialize.

Pride of place in this gallery must be taken by a journal which has already been mentioned several times, namely *Antaios*, which existed from 1959 to 1971 and was outstanding in the way that it achieved an interplay of science and spirituality.[64] Indeed, *Antaios* can rightly be portrayed as a particularly important link for those interested in esoteric matters from a scholarly point of view in a post-war Germany that has been fundamentally hostile towards esotericism and other streams of thought depicted as "irrational." However, even if the journal brought together many excellent minds, it offered no conferences and meetings in order to deepen the individual perspectives with personal encounters. But there is a link with the Eranos conferences, as the chief editor Philipp Wolff-Windegg was present at many of these meetings and was able to hold detailed conversations with Mircea Eliade, Ernst Benz, and Gershom Scholem.

Antaios was published by Ernst Jünger and Mircea Eliade, though only in name. The selection of the contributions to appear, contact with authors, indeed the entire management lay solely in the hands of Philipp Wolff-Windegg. At most there came letters of approval from Jünger and Eliade, often months after the appearance of *Antaios*. Besides Eranos speakers such as Henry Corbin, Karl Kerényi, Joseph Campbell, Mircea Eliade, Adolf Portmann, Jean Daniélou, Ernst Benz, Elémire Zolla, and Laurens van der Post, in the journal one also frequently finds representatives of the integral tradition. Of these the best known are Leopold Ziegler, Julius Evola, Titus Burckhardt, and Frithjof Schuon. One is also struck by the numerous contributions on famous "esotericists" such as Jakob Boehme, Carl von Eckartshausen, William Blake, Agrippa von Nettesheim and so on.

In the foreword to the first issue Ernst Jünger writes, "The journal … wishes to serve freedom in the world. A free world can only be a world of the mind and spirit [*eine geistige Welt*]. Freedom increases with spiritual perspective, with the securing of a firmer, more elevated vantage point."[65]

Italy is also an interesting region for the academic reappraisal of spiritual themes. Giuseppe Tucci, for example, organized meetings of the Istituto Italiano per il Medio ed

Estremo Oriente (IsMEO) similar to Eranos.[66] In the second volume of his autobiography Mircea Eliade also describes how he was invited by Tucci to Rome in 1950 to talk on Tantrism and shamanism in the *aula prima* of the university.[67] He was particularly pleased that the scholars of religion Angelo Brelich and Karl Kerényi were also present there—that was a sign of the beginnings of his international recognition.[68]

Brief mention should also be made of the Istituto Mythos and its journal *átopon*, dealing with "symbolic psychoanthropology and religious traditions." Gilbert Durand is a member of its scientific committee. Here the relationship with Eranos is referred to explicitly in an account on the website of the institute, in which it is stated that Eranos "possessed the transformative power of a rite" (*aveva la forza trasformante di un rito*).[69] The contact with Eranos was sustained above all by Marie Amélie de Robilant, a student of Corbin, who regularly invited a group of Eranos attenders to meet in her magnificent residence at Bougy St. Martin on Lake Geneva.[70] From this the Istituto Mythos emerged in Italy in 1981.

In the English-speaking world it is above all the Temenos Academy that is worthy of mention. Stella Corbin, widow of Henry Corbin, was also among its founders. Nevertheless, the leading role was played by Kathleen Raine. Sadly both have passed away in the meantime. This academy, which has been offering regular lectures since 1990,[71] is derived from the journal *Temenos* (Greek: sacred place), which was instigated by Kathleen Raine, Keith Critchlow, Brian Keeble, and Philip Sherrard and appeared in thirteen issues between 1981 and 1992. Contributions from Eranos participants such as Henry Corbin, Gilbert Durand, Annemarie Schimmel, Elemire Zolla, and Kathleen Raine herself are to be found there, among others. There are also contributions from a more "traditional" slant, such as those of Philip Sherrard and Seyyed Hossein Nasr. Charles, HRH The Prince of Wales, is also associated with the journal through the late Laurens van der Post, Eranos participant and friend of Jung.

Out of these publishing activities there increasingly developed a "teaching organization," which since 1998 has once again been publishing a journal in the old style but under the new name of *Temenos Academy Review*. The lectures themselves were originally held in the Prince of Wales' Institute of Architecture, but the academy now holds its meetings in a variety of venues in London. Prince Charles, who has taken up the patronage of Temenos, speaks in the foreword to the third volume of the *Review* of an "arrogant technology that seeks not to work with but to subdue Nature," as well as of the "common and disheartening inability to understand both the continuing centrality of that which is sacred, and the timeless importance of the traditional forms of understanding of our place in the world." Therefore the work of Temenos is so exceedingly important to him, as Temenos has taken up the commitment of "fostering a wider awareness of the great spiritual traditions we have inherited from the past."[72]

Brief mention should also be made of the London Convivium for Archetypal Studies with the journal *Sphinx*, founded by Noel Cobb and Eva Loewe, who died much too young. David Miller and other "polytheists" have collaborated there alongside Kathleen Raine.

For sure one must not forget here the Warburg Institute. Even if Eranos played no central role here, Kathleen Raine and Raffaele Pettazzoni from Eranos have nevertheless participated. But the work of Edgar Wind, Fritz Saxl, Jean Seznec, and Frances A. Yates was so groundbreaking with regard to the re-acquaintance of the European academic world with the "pagan" antique and "esoteric" spiritual heritage that one must in any case recall their institute. From 1937 until the present day it has published what was known until 1939 as the *Journal of the Warburg Institute*, and since that time as the *Journal of the Warburg and Courtauld Institutes*.

Here must without doubt also be introduced a group of friends who originally met only as a round table discussion group for esoteric themes, without initially having any particular academic ambitions, even though almost all participants were academics. Nevertheless, from their conversations there emerged what is perhaps the most important official association for the scholarly investigation of esotericism, namely the European Society for the Study of Western Esotericism (ESSWE). I am speaking of the, somewhat ironically named, Academia Palladiana (Palladian academy). In January of 1997 the Anglo-American music professor Joscelyn Godwin, who counts among the most important researchers of esotericism, issued an invitation for a week-long meeting in the Villa Saraceno near Vicenza which he described as a "winter house party." The magnificent Villa Saraceno was designed by Andrea Palladio and belongs to the Landmark Trust, an English foundation that maintains and reactivates historical buildings. As it was available to rent at a very reasonable price, the villa formed the perfect surrounding for conversations among friends from six nations.

Besides Antoine Faivre, who at that point held the only chair for "academic esotericism," five other people were invited who years later would also teach this subject at diverse universities, namely Wouter Hanegraaff, Jean-Pierre Brach, Nicholas Goodrick-Clarke, Marco Pasi, and Christopher McIntosh. Unfortunately Goodrick-Clarke was not able to take up this invitation, although he did come to the second meeting. Also present were Mark Stavish, an author in the field; Deborah Belle Forman, who would later take up a leading position in the Swedenborg Foundation; and publisher David Fideler.[73] (I was fortunate to participate also.) In 1999 I myself organized the second meeting in southern Styria, Austria. Here there were already numerous discussions on how one might further promulgate the scholarly study of esotericism and bring it to a university setting. This time the René Guénon specialist Jean-Pierre Laurant from the Ecole Pratique des Hautes Etudes also came to the meeting, as well as the late Nicholas Goodrick-Clarke and his wife Clare, who taught at the University of Exeter.

In 2001 Rosalie Basten—as the spiritual and material founder of the endowment supporting the Amsterdam Chair for Hermetic Philosophy and Related Currents[74]—announced her willingness to make her château, the Domaine de Taurenne in Provence, available for further meetings, also with changing participants. At the first meeting there in June 2002, as well as at subsequent gatherings, plans for ESSWE ripened, and eventually it was officially founded in 2005. In the meantime ESSWE has become a recognized organization, which presides over its own scholarly organ of publication in the form of *Aries* as well as its own book series under the name of *Gnostica*. In 2007 it was already able to celebrate a great success with its first big conference in Tübingen. This conference was organized by Andreas Kilcher of the University of Tübingen. In 2009 the second conference was held in Strasbourg, and in 2011 the third took place at Szeged in southern Hungary.

ESSWE describes itself as a society whose aim is "to advance the academic study of the various manifestations of Western esotericism from late antiquity to the present, and to secure the future development of the field."[75] This is to be achieved through the organization of academic conferences, the encouragement of contacts between researchers in the field, the publication of journals and books, as well as the general support of interdisciplinary and critical perspectives on the theme. ESSWE also strives for the recognition by other academic associations of the importance of Western esotericism for intellectual life as a whole. In the United States an organization closely related to ESSWE with exactly the same goals has emerged: the ASE (Association for the Study of Esotericism). It was established in 2002 by Arthur Versluis, a professor at Michigan State University who is also president of the association. The organization has an associated online journal named *Esoterica* which has top-class articles in this field. It also publishes a book series: Studies in Esotericism. ASE holds academic conferences every two years, thereby alternating with those of ESSWE.

Without doubt reference must also be made to a world-famous organization most commonly classified as purely "esoteric" and "New Age": the Esalen Institute in California, because here (perhaps surprisingly for some) direct contacts with Eranos can be demonstrated. Thus I have already mentioned that one of the founders of the Institute, Michael Murphy, told me in April 2005 that the Eranos conferences were in fact a prototype for him during the construction of Esalen.[76] It should not be forgotten either that Friedrich (Frederic) Spiegelberg was an important mentor of Murphy. Spiegelberg knew C.G. Jung and experienced Eranos conferences himself before the war.[77] The role of Joseph Campbell in the construction of Esalen should also not be forgotten. He held seminars there for twenty years, beginning with his first participation in 1966.[78] Paul Tillich and James Hillman are other Eranos speakers who were also active at Esalen.

Jeffrey J. Kripal even sees clear parallels to the Eranos meetings on the grounds of the conferences which have "consistently attracted both world-class scientists and humanist scholars" since the inception of Esalen in 1962.[79] The first meeting took place on 6–7 October of that year. However, the first conference—in the sense of a gathering where several speakers addressed a common theme over more than two days—took place from 29 to 31 January 1965. In the 1970s the conferences were already running from Sunday until Friday and the number of speakers was growing. Indeed, in their heyday during the later years of that decade up to twenty such conferences were being held per year. The Center for Theory and Research (CTR) was subsequently formed as the organizational instrument for the meetings. Six to seven symposia are still held every year, and in some cases the proceedings are published.[80] Thereby "Esalen's relationship to the university has always been a very intimate one," as Kripal emphasizes.[81] Naturally the focal point of Esalen was not always the purely intellectual, but rather the body. Thus somatic therapies and Tantrism were frequently discussed and practiced topics.

Esalen can also be seen as the cradle of the human potential movement. Here, *par excellence*, the human being was seen as the bearer of enormous potential, which only has to be conjured forth in order to enable us to live happy and fulfilled lives.[82] Fritz Perls, Abraham Maslow, and Alan Watts are among the key representatives of this tradition. The number of celebrities who have taught at Esalen is truly legion. They include, to name only a few, Aldous Huxley, Linus Pauling, Arnold Toynbee, B.F. Skinner, Alexander Lowen, Stanislav Grof, Paul Tillich (Eranos lecturer), Albert Hofmann, Carlos Castaneda, and the singer Joan Baez.

Esalen is best known as one of the centers of the American "counterculture." In the 1960s and 1970s it was associated with the hippy culture, the anti-war movement, environmental protection, drug consumption (although officially it was against drugs), free sexuality, racial and sexual equality, and so on.[83] Thus it helped to release a "consciousness shift" in a largely puritanical America.[84]

As one can see, many groups and organizations have taken an impulse from Eranos and gone on to develop it in their own way. The role of Eranos as a model has therefore been considerable.

In addition to the numerous organizations already mentioned, I would like to list a few other initiatives which are only remotely connected with Eranos but which are also involved in esoteric themes as an object of serious study. I greatly value such initiatives, as I know from abundant personal experience what valuable work they do in acting as a corrective to one-sidedness in the modern world.

A particularly outstanding example is the Bibliotheca Philosophica Hermetica in Amsterdam, which was founded in 1984 by the Dutch businessman Joost R. Ritman and made accessible to the public. In the meantime the library, focusing on Hermeticism, Christian mysticism, Rosicrucianism, and alchemy, has been recognized as a national treasure enjoying the protection of the state. It has approximately twenty thousand volumes, including numerous unique and irreplaceable treasures. More recently it has begun to collect modern works as well. It holds regular exhibitions and has its own publishing imprint. However, in 2010, to the dismay of many people, serious financial and legal problems arose, the final outcome of which is still not foreseeable at the time of writing.

Another initiative that should certainly be mentioned is the Center for the Study of New Religions (CESNUR, based on its Italian acronym) based in Turin and led by Massimo Introvigne under the auspices of the Catholic Church. The Center possesses an extensive library focusing on the so-called new religions (unfortunately usually labeled with the negative word "sects"). Every year it holds a big conference, largely attended by academics, at which the development of esotericism (especially in modern times) is discussed in a generally objective way. Massimo Introvigne, who heads the research center in his capacity as a sociologist, has also made a name for himself as a highly prolific author of immensely informative works on the history of esotericism.

In the United States as well there are a number of important initiatives that have existed for some time within the framework of the American Academy of Religion (AAR). One of these, the Hermetic Academy, operated within the framework of the AAR from 1980, and from 1986 to 1990 various members of it organized special sessions at the AAR conferences under the title Esotericism and Perennialism Group.[85] After 1993 this became the Theosophy and Theosophic Thought Seminar. Then in 1995, at the 17th International Congress of the International Association for the History of Religion (IAHR) in Mexico City, there appeared a new special section entitled "Western Esotericism and the Science of Religion."[86]

I should also mention the superbly produced magazine *Parabola*, published since 1976, which now bears the subtitle "Where Spiritual Traditions Meet." Interestingly, the first article of the first issue was Mircea Eliade's essay "Nostalgia for Paradise." In the pages of *Parabola* are to be found a whole array of Eranos lecturers from Joseph Campbell through Annemarie Schimmel to Kathleen Raine. The magazine also organizes regular lectures and meetings. Unfortunately I do not have space here to go into such educational institutions as the California Institute for Integral Studies, the Esalen Institute or the Pacifica Graduate Institute, which have actually entered into collaboration with Esalen.

I have already mentioned the conferences and the journal *Sophia Perennis* of the Imperial Iranian Academy of Philosophy and the various speakers connected therewith. Since the fall of the shah the academy of course no longer exists. Moving to Argentina, one should mention the Centro de Investigaciones de Filosofia e Historia de las Religiones

(CIFHIRE), which published until very recently the journal *Epiméleia—Revista de Estudios sobre la Tradición*. The first issue (1992) contained the previously mentioned article on Eranos "Approximaciones a Eranos." The first article in the first issue was "Los usos de la imaginacion" by the Eranos speaker Elemire Zolla. The academic advisory board includes, *inter alia*, the scholars of religion Giovanni Filoramo and Kurt Rudolph, and the expert on René Guénon and Traditionalism Jean-Pierre Laurant. CIFHIRE is based in the philosophy faculty of John F. Kennedy University in Buenos Aires and is led by F. García Bazán.

If I have listed here a considerable number of scholarly institutions and journals that are attempting to integrate the—purely descriptive—study of "esoteric" currents of thought into academe, it has not of course been my intention to arouse a sort of paranoia in the academic world in the face of overflowing "irrational" currents of thought. I am just as impatient with Georg Lukàcs' widely echoing battle cry against "The Destruction of Reason"[87] or James Webb's anxiety-ridden vision in *The Flight from Reason*[88] and *The Occult Establishment* as I am with the conspiracy theorists who see the world as writhing inescapably in the jaws of plutocratic powers. I simply see these academic initiatives in the area of esotericism as nothing other than the perfectly natural expression of a need, present in many thinking people, for some foundation to their lives that is not purely rational. There is probably an inborn urge in human beings to ask not only "How does that work?"—to which science can no doubt supply highly interesting answers—but also "Why does it exist at all?" Causal thinking is here no longer sufficient, and the search begins for a wider and deeper pattern of meaning. If there were no such initiatives and if esotericism were completely banished from the academic realm, then one would have cause to suspect that censorship was beng exerted.

ɣ. 17. The End of a Cycle …
or Perhaps Not

The overall picture of Eranos turns out to be essentially more consistent than one might expect of such a long-lasting and far-reaching project. This basic consistency, hopefully by now apparent to the reader, has to do with a readiness to extend scientific enquiry beyond the boundaries set by reason and into areas where myth, imagination, and religious experience play their roles. At the same time it is a consistency that is subject to change. The history of Eranos can be divided into three phases.[1] The first was undoubtedly the most esoterically tinged phase, as is apparent from the titles of the conferences. Equally characteristic of this phase was the search for a balance between East and West.[2] It was during this period that the influence of Olga Fröbe and C.G. Jung was strongest, although, as I see it, Fröbe was the one who pushed the esoteric agenda, whereas Jung attempted to restrain her.[3] From the beginning of the 1940s the focus of the conferences was increasingly on the Occident with the emphasis on classical antiquity.

In the mid-1940s Adolf Portmann joined the group and increasingly took the helm; like Jung, he was good at pressing his own intellectual/spiritual interests with Fröbe. From then on esotericism, gnosis, and the mysteries receded into the background and man as a biological and cultural being became the central focus. This again can be seen from the conference titles, which always had the human being as the main reference point. However, the faction surrounding Eliade, Corbin, and to some extent Scholem held its own effectively and helped to pave the way for the prominent role that the "polytheist" group around Hillman and Miller would later play. Their "archetypal psychology," although it perceived itself to be a science, left plenty of room for "esoteric" thinking in the sense used here, if only by virtue of its philosophical forebears from antiquity up to the Middle Ages. The debate between the "polytheists" and "monotheists" is therefore not just a matter of religion or confession but also of the choice between the sharp, narrow logic of the word and the fluidity and open-endedness of the image. Ultimately the question is which should take precedence: a clear-cut, one-dimensional rationalism based on words and concepts or a more inward-looking, more multi-dimensional approach, involving images and multivalent insights.[4]

Evidently this tension within Eranos was one of the decisive reasons for the success of the meetings, a tension that I can only regard as positive, since tension goes together with vitality and dynamism and encourages the search for an over-arching perspective. At the same time it could have been this tension—or rather the perceived tendency to lean more strongly towards the rational side—that was one of the reasons for Rudolf Ritsema's decision in 1988 to discontinue the meetings in their accustomed form. He said clearly enough that he wished to go back to the original intentions of Olga Fröbe and these were certainly more esoteric than the lectures given in the late 1980s. Furthermore, the more "intimate" style of meeting introduced by Ritsema, with only eighteen people and involving *I Ching* consultations using the traditional yarrow stalks, was, for all its outward facets, primarily focused on the inward gaze.

The Amici di Eranos, under Erik Hornung and Tilo Schabert, chose from the outset to follow a more academic and interdisciplinary path.[5] At the period around the turn of the millennium, when I myself attended the conferences, I was struck how the academically open-minded and well-educated audience—indeed what other kind of audience could have followed lectures in four languages—quite frequently came up with "esoteric" references. They, however, were nearly always handled (I could almost have said "circumvented") in a purely scholarly way by the lecturers; after all, academic reputations are easily ruined. This is not necessarily a criticism but rather simply an observation, shared by many of those who attended. Nevertheless, one former leading member of the Amici confided to me that a true Eranos lecture should always contain a pinch (no more) of esotericism. Otherwise it would be simply a conventional academic lecture of the kind that can be heard in similar form at many other conferences.

Up to now at any rate the programs offered by the two surviving Eranos groups in Ascona and Moscia appear to have been well attended, so that in the short to medium term the end of the cycle is not on the agenda. But it is less easy to predict whether Eranos can survive in the long term as a purely intellectual and cultural-historical project. I believe that the individual seeker (not only the kind who comes to Eranos) desires affirmation on the level of the inner self, as well as a feeling of inclusion and I daresay even some degree of guidance. Only thus do such people have the possibility to change, and change is what they wish to attain, otherwise they would not be seeking—even if in the end no change takes place.

Information is ubiquitous, but the intellect on its own is not enough. The soul also demands its due. Here, as always, a balance between the inner and the outer is called for. A predominance of one side alone is never beneficial. This has been recognized by the scientific world itself, as can be seen in the following clear observation by Hartmut and Gernot Böhme:

> Freud brought a reflexive approach into European thinking, which makes a lot of so-called philosophy appear naïve. Since then no philosophy of consciousness makes sense unless it is also a philosophy of the unconscious; no use of reason can any longer be accepted as adequate if reason is seen purely as immanent—that is, resting on logical structures and fixed principles of argumentation—rather than in relation also to the "irrational."[6]

A further possible and logical step, which has already been partly implemented by the Eranos Foundation in Moscia, would be the practical application of the study material. As will be recalled, something of the kind took place at the very early meetings under Fröbe, where the programs included group meditations and the celebration of masses. In this way the unity of mythos and logos, of the inner and the outer, could partly become integrated with and finally become one with everyday life. However, this would involve the danger that the project would come closer to the activities of a religious group. There would be less place for scholarly and distanced objectivity. On the other hand, it would make for a feeling of closer connection with Eranos.

All of this relates to the "feminine" aspect of Eranos that I mentioned in the preface, an aspect which, in the public perception of Eranos, was overshadowed by the "masculine" scientific side.[7] However, as we all know, without the full personal and financial commitment of Olga Fröbe, Eranos would, in the first place, never have come into being, second would not have continued, and third would have collapsed as soon as major difficulties arose. It was her total identification with Eranos that made the apparently unattainable possible, albeit at the cost of great mental and physical distress, especially in later years, as is clear from her unpublished written material. Here a profoundly important factor was her unshakeable "irrational" belief in the "daemonic" basis of Eranos, which gave her the necessary "irresistible" strength. Olga Fröbe "knew" with profound certainty that she, and she alone, was the living channel of this "spiritual force" here on earth.

This fact might also give us a clue as to what would have to be done if the foundations of Eranos should ever begin to crack and the institution be threatened with final collapse. In that case, if one wished to continue Eranos in her spirit and be guided by her "knowledge," then only a renewed contact with the daemon, the *genius loci*, would offer any real help. This, however, would demand a new "sacrifice," as in her case. That would mean the completion of the cycle and a return to the beginning. However, it would be well to remember the theologian Paul Tillich's caution against dealing with "daemons" and his warning that such "sources of energy" are more likely than people realize to develop a "vampiristic" life of their own.

In this sense, Fröbe can correctly be seen as the inner "life" of Eranos, for which she sacrificed her own outer life. However brilliantly the men may have basked in the limelight and demonstrated their intellects, without *her life* they would have been mere dry leaves on a dying branch.

Tribute should also be paid to another woman, without whom Eranos would have come to an end in the 1940s, namely Mary Mellon. After all, it was she who was behind the initiative of the Bollingen Foundation to support the research of various important Eranos lecturers and enable them to survive as scholars. Despite her early death, it was thanks to her impetus that financial support for Eranos continued for more than two decades. These contributions from the United States also constituted a feminine "stream of life." They formed the *mater*-ial foundation of Eranos, without which the intellect would very soon have died from hunger and thirst. Nor should I forget to mention Cary Baynes, whose close friendship with the leading figures in the early phase of Eranos—Fröbe, Jung, and the Mellons—was a key stimulating factor in the ensuing collaboration.

Another woman who should not be forgotten is Magda Kerényi. Her work over some decades, compiling reports on the Eranos meetings and writing reviews of them for *Die Tat* and the *Neue Zürcher Zeitung*, contributed significantly to publicizing Eranos and thus attracting both lecturers and audience members to Ascona.[8] My highlighting of this "life-giving" impulse does not of course mean that I wish to diminish in any way the intellectual inspiration that has emanated from the female speakers who have appeared in increasing numbers at Eranos in recent years.

As regards the feminine aspect, Eranos has certain parallels in the French and German salons of the seventeenth century and later. One could name, as a few examples, those of the Marquise de Sevigné, Ninon de Lenclos, Princess Mathilde, Karoline Schlegel, Henriette Herz, and Rahel Varnhagen, which also acted as incubators for political, scientific, and literary developments.[9] Always it was the women who created a lively space where the guests felt at home and where especially the men were induced to wield the sharp intellectual rapier, not daring to brandish the crude club in such a setting. This was belligerence and competitiveness of a refined sort. And the women, in their own way, knew how to show their thanks.

Just how important the feminine element has been in the success of Eranos is emphasized by Erik Hornung, when he writes, "Eranos, founded by a woman, does not live from the mind alone. It has a soul, which must be preserved and tended, and without which it is not viable."[10] It is true that he does not mention the daemon, and yet for many Eranos aficionados that was precisely what it was all about.

The fact that Eranos has been able to survive up to the present day—after so many eminent people and so many difficulties have come and gone—is for many people sufficient proof that something deeper or higher has had the strength to hold this complex structure together. It is of secondary importance whether one calls this a "daemon" or speaks of a "hierophany," as Eliade does.

But, even thinking purely pragmatically, I believe that nothing can achieve long life unless it can make room for contradictions and perceive them as complementarities and opportunities. Eranos has done precisely this, always correcting one-sidedness with balance.

On the same pragmatic level the question arises whether Eranos possesses something enriching and perhaps necessary for the future, something that can fulfill human beings on an inner level. Here too I believe the answer is more affirmative. In view of the ever-advancing globalization of the world, which primarily has to do with business and consumerism, some spiritual counterbalance is called for, *yin-yang*-wise. Eranos could be part of this. Eranos too strives to dismantle mental and spiritual barriers—between East and West, between antiquity and modernity, between academic disciplines, and between science and the humanities. However, if such an undertaking is to succeed then the "inner human being," in Erich Neumann's sense, must, in all his "timelessness," be the central focus. Belief, hope, and trust are urgently needed. If we find them, then we can look forward to a future in which there is a fine balance of both continuity and change.

 Notes

Introduction: How This Book Emerged

1. Gilles Quispel spoke about this text in his 1965 Eranos lecture. Interestingly, he sees it not as a Gnostic text but simply as an "amplification" of a passage in the Bible. See also Alfred Adam, *Die Psalmen des Thomas und das Perlenlied als Zeugnisse vorchristlicher Gnosis* (Berlin: Alfred Töpelmann, 1959), 49ff.

2. Giuseppe Lampis, *Trasformazioni di uomini e dei nella Grecia antica*, vol. 1 (Rome: Mythos edizioni, 1999).

3. I intentionally use a simile that Olga Fröbe used repeatedly in describing the Eranos project.

4. I believe that, if the lectures were included, this would reinforce my claim about the importance of esotericism in the history of Eranos.

5. Friedrich Nietzsche, *On the Genealogy of Morals: A Polemical Tract by Friedrich Nietzsche*, Ian Johnston (trans.) (http://records.viu.ca/~johnstoi/nietzsche/genealogy3.htm).

6. When it comes to the concept of esotericism, the works of Antoine Faivre are particularly authoritative. See, for example, his introduction to his book *Accès de l'ésotérisme occidentale*, vol. I, 13–49 (Paris: Gallimard, 1986; vol. I rev. ed. and vol. II, 1996) and his introduction to his *L'ésotérisme* in the series *Que sais-je?* (Paris: Presses Universitaires Françaises, 1992), 3–32. See also his Introduction to Antoine Faivre and Jacob Needleman (eds), *Modern Esoteric Spirituality* (New York: Crossroad, 1992), xi–xxii, as well as his essay "Renaissance Hermetism and the Concept of Western Esotericism," in *Gnosis and Hermeticism from Antiquity to Modern Times*, Roelof van den Broek and Wouter Hanegraaf (eds) (Albany, NY: SUNY Press, 1998), 109–23, and esp. 117ff. Unfortunately, definitions in this kind of area can only be provisional constructs, necessarily subject to changes. I should not omit to mention the criticisms of Faivre's approach that have been raised by, among others, Wouter Hanegraaff, Kocku von Stuckrad, and Arthur Versluis. I am unable to discuss these here.

7. Instead of "esoteric" one could in our context, with equal imprecision, say "gnostic," "hermetic," "mythological," or "spiritual." The term "gnostic," however, usually has (unjustly in my opinion) somewhat negative connotations, and "hermetic" is often taken to refer only to alchemy or to the tradition of thought stemming from the *Corpus hermeticum*. Again, the terms "mythological" and "spiritual" are used in a wide variety of other contexts. So unfortunately one has to live with the imprecision of the word "esoteric," but at the same time it is worth pointing out that imprecision or "uncertainty" (as in Heisenberg's principle) is itself precisely one of the characteristics of esoteric thinking. On the other hand, I would reject the term "occult," which tends to imply rather a secularized form of esotericism that arose from the collision of modern *practical* experimentation with the spiritual legacy of the Renaissance. For the specialist on esotericism, Antoine Faivre, however, occultism is basically the *practical* side of the mainly theoretical esoteric superstructure. See his entry on "Occultism," in Mircea Eliade (ed.), *Encyclopedia of Religion* (New York: Macmillan, 1987), vol. 11, 36–40. For Wouter Hanegraaff, holder of a chair for the history of esotericism (like Antoine Faivre in earlier years), the terms "esoteric," "gnostic," and "mystical" are expressions connoting a whole complex of religious thought, and it is hard to draw boundaries between them. As all these terms are charged with historically conditioned associations, no general consensus has emerged as to how they should be defined, and everyone uses them as they think fit. Hanegraaff therefore suggests that all of these terms be retained—see his groundbreaking article "Empirical Method in the Study of Esotericism," in *Method and Theory in the Study of Religion* 7(2) (1995), 121–4. However, it would be desirable to determine ideal-typical distinctions between them. Without extending this discussion too far, I would like also to mention Julia Iwersen's essay "Was ist New Age? Was ist Esoterik?," *Zeitschrift für Religions- und Geistesgeschichte* 52(1) (2000). In contrast to Faivre and Hanegraaff, Iwersen sees no insuperable contrast between science and esotericism. Esotericism, she argues, should be seen as a special type of religion, which, by virtue of its underlying monism, seeks to integrate not only "religious traditions of whatever origin" but also holistic approaches in science. Thus her concept of esotericism comes close to that which I consider to be characteristic of many aspects of Eranos. Elsewhere I described esoteric thinking as follows: "Very vaguely formulated, we are talking about a more subjective, emblematic, analogical, inwardly transformative way of thinking, which involves the imagination and is credited by its followers with a kind of therapeutic power, in contrast to logical and concept-oriented forms of thought, which are outward-looking and directed towards communication with others" ("Kaleidoskop," *Gnostika* 14 [2000], 4). One could also add that it prefers a circular to a linear modality, that is to say it moves in a circle or

a spiral, returning to the point of departure or to an analogically "higher" point. As Antoine Faivre has said, it is an independent form of thought that obeys its own premises.

8. As expressed by unidentified Eranos representatives recorded for the program on Eranos broadcast by Austrian Radio ORF I on 18 September 1998.

9. It is not without intention that "feminine" is more or less equated with "esoteric" here. Although such an equation is of course absurd, I would like to let it stand, since there is at least a mutual sympathy between these two things. It is hardly in dispute that the emergence of the New Age was accompanied by a heightened regard for the feminine perspective. This incidentally can also be seen in the nineteenth century in the case of the early spiritualist movement and especially in the Theosophical Society. These esoteric groups were the first organizations in which women not only were regarded as equals but also had no problem in occupying the very top positions. Can one perhaps see the scientific community's war against the so-called irrationalism of esotericism as a concealed "power instrument of the patriarchy"?

10. The best proof of this is the over-abundance of notes, for which there are two main reasons. First, they permit an independent scrutiny of interesting connections; second, they enable me to substantiate more precisely certain facts that are not widely known. Furthermore, the notes could be seen as a compensatory feature for the author, who does not have an academic background in the disciplines featured in this book, such as religious studies, philosophy, or psychology, but rather works out of love and pleasure in the spirit of a dilettante—from *diletto* (delight).

11. However, I doubt whether such a benevolent pre-judgment is compatible with Sir Karl Popper's assessment of Socrates as a shining example of a critical rationalist, nor with Bertolt Brecht's view of him as a pre-Marxist thinker.

1. The Significance of Eranos

1. Facsimile in Aniela Jaffé, *C.G.Jung, Bild und Wort* (Olten: Walter Verlag, 1977), 187. These words also appear at the beginning of the volume edited by Olga Fröbe, *25 Jahre Eranos* (Zurich: Rhein-Verlag, 1957).

2. Quoted from Aniela Jaffé, "C.G. Jung und die Eranos-Tagungen: zum 100. Geburtstag von C.G. Jung," *Eranos Jahrbuch* 44 (1975), 5.

3. *Ibid.*, 5.

4. Mircea Eliade, *Autobiography: Exile's Odyssey*, vol. 2 (1937–60) (Chicago, IL: University of Chicago Press, 1988), 146.

5. Mircea Eliade, *Journal II, 1957–1969* (Chicago, IL: University of Chicago Press, 1989), xiii. Originally published under the title *No Souvenirs* (New York, Harper & Row, 1977).

6. Mircea Eliade, "Les Danseurs Passent, La Danse Reste," *Du* 15(4) (April 1955), 60.

7. Herbert Read, "The Creative Nature of Humanism," *Eranos Jahrbuch* 26 (1957), 315–50.

8. Adolf Portmann, *An den Grenzen des Wissens* (Vienna: Econ, 1974), 223.

9. Rudolf Ritsema, "Adolf Portmann 1897–1982," *Eranos Jahrbuch* 51 (1982), 2.

10. Michel Cazenave, *Jung: L'Expérience intérieure* (Monaco: Editions du Rocher, 1997), 122.

11. Jean Gebser, *Gesamtausgabe* (Schaffhausen: Novalis Verlag, 1980), vol. 7, 440. Gebser's contributions to cultural philosophy are discussed in Bremer Volkshochschule (ed.), *Wege zum integralen Bewußtsein: Eine Festgabe für Jean Gebser zum 20. August 1965* (Bremen: Bremer Volkshochschule, 1965).

12. Quoted from the dust-jacket of the 1951 Eranos yearbook.

13. Josef Höfer and Karl Rahner (eds), *Lexikon für Theologie und Kirche* (Freiburg: Herder, 1959), vol. 3, 954ff.

14. Magda Kerényi, "Eranos," in *Schweizer Lexikon* (Lucerne: Verlag Schweizer Lexikon, 1992).

15. The *Festschrift* for Hugo von Hofmannsthal on his fiftieth birthday (published in a large-format edition of 1050 copies by the Bremer Presse, Munich, with three original prints), which also bore the title *Eranos*, should be mentioned here for the sake of completeness. I could not find even the remotest connection here with the prehistory of the meetings, even though Hofmannsthal had direct contact with Stefan George, "whose attempts intellectually to embrace Hofmannsthal were avoided by the latter in order to avoid the danger of being suffocated" (Hans-Albrecht Koch, *Hugo von Hofmannsthal*, Erträge der Forschung, vol. 265 [Darmstadt: Wissenschaftliche Buchgesellschaft, 1989], 15). See also the correspondence betwen George and Hofmannsthal (S. George, *Briefwechsel zwischen George und Hofmannsthal* [Berlin: Georg Bondi, 1938]) as well as Kurt Singer, "Der Streit der Dichter: Gedanken zum Briefwechsel zwischen George und Hofmannsthal," *Castrum Peregrini* 60 (1963), 5–28. The George circle in fact exerted, through Ludwig Derleth, a decisive influence on Olga Fröbe. A further contact to the Stefan George entourage came about through Hofmannsthal's friend the poet Rudolf Borchardt whose fulsome so-called "Eranos" letter, which he wrote for the *Festschrift*, evoked a stormy reaction from the sensitive Hofmannsthal, who even demanded that the *Festschrift* be pulped (on this subject see Cornelius Borchardt [son of Rudolf Borchardt], "Borchardt–Hofmannsthal," *Criticón* 16 [1999]: 20–24). It is also worth remarking that Christiane von Hofmannsthal, daughter of the poet, was married to one of the first Eranos lecturers, the indologist Heinrich Zimmer.

16. Giovanni Filoramo, *Il risveglio della gnosi ovvero diventare dio* (Bari: Laterza, 1990), 22.

17. See the negative answer from Jung to Fröbe of 5 June 1958, in which he writes that at his age he can no longer allow himself such tasks. Their correspondence is kept in the C.G. Jung archive at the Eidgenossische Technische Hochschule in Zurich.

18. William McGuire, *Bollingen: An Adventure in Collecting the Past* (Princeton, NJ: Princeton University Press, 1982). This book provided me with so many details that it was not always possible in each instance to be as scrupulous in

quoting the source as would normally be customary. As the present book is in any case overloaded with endnotes it is only in the case of verbatim quotations that I have mentioned McGuire's fundamental work by name. I hope that the author, whom I also have to thank for much original material, will pardon me for this shortcoming.

19. Wasserstrom's book has received numerous (partly vehemently negative) reactions and has alsoe led to a symposium during the annual conference of the American Academy of Religions in 1999. See the following extensive reviews: Tomoko Masuzawa, "Reflections on the Charmed Circle," Hugh B. Urban, "Syndrome of the Secret: 'Esotericism' and the Work of Steven M. Wasserstrom," and Gustavo Benavides, "Afterreligion after Religion," all in the *Journal of the American Academy of Religion* 69(2) (2001), 429–36, 437–47, and 449–58, respectively; Pierre Lory, "Note sur l'ouvrage *Religion after Religion: Gershom Scholem, Mircea Eliade and Henry Corbin at Eranos*," *Archaeus* 9 (2005), 1–4, 107–113.

20. The most historically comprehensive is undoubtedly the paper by Barbara von Reibnitz, "Der Eranos-Kreis—Religionswissenschaft und Weltanschauung oder der Gelehrte als Laien-Priester," which the author kindly sent me before publication. The paper appeared in *Kreise, Gruppen, Bünde: Zur Soziologie moderner Intellektuellenassoziationen*, Richard Faber and Christine Holste (eds) (Würzburg: Königshausen & Neumann, 2000). This volume also contains two contributions on the subject of the Stefan George circle. An introductory overview is also provided by two essays by Erik Hornung. The first, entitled "Wo sich grosse Geister finden," appeared in *Turicum* (June–July 1993), 24–8. The second is an unpublished manuscript entitled *Abenteuer Eranos*. A text by Alfons Rosenberg is also worth mentioning, although it is in the form of a circular communication addressed only to a small number of friends, namely "Eranos, der Geist am Wasser," to which I shall return later.

21. See *Du* 4 (April 1955).

22. See *Anthropos* 153 (February 1994), "El Circulo de Eranos: Una Hermeneutica Simbolica del Sentido."

23. Elisabetta Barone, Matthias Riedl, and Alexandra Tischel (eds), *Pioniere, Poeten, Professoren: Eranos und der Monte Verità in der Zivilisationsgeschichte des 20. Jahrhunderts* [Pioneers, poets, professors: Eranos and Monte Verità in the history of civilization of the twentieth century] (Würzburg: Königshausen & Neumann, 2004). An Italian version of this book has also appeared: E. Barone, A. Fabris, and F. Monceri (eds), *Eranos, Monte Verità, Ascona* (Pisa: ETS, 2003).

24. Lyn Cowan (ed.), *Barcelona 04: Edges of Experience: Memory and Emergence. Proceedings of the 16th International IAAP Congress for Analytical Psychology* (Einsiedeln: Daimon, 2006).

25. Christine Downing (ed.), *Disturbances in the Field: Essays in Honor of David L. Miller* (New Orleans, LA: Spring Journal Books, 2006).

26. Gian Piero Quaglino, Augusto Romano, and Riccardo Bernardini (eds), *Carl Gustav Jung a Eranos 1933–1952* (Turin: Antigone Edizione, 2007).

27. Catherine Ritsema, *L'Oeuvre d'Eranos et vie d'Olga Froebe-Kapteyn*. Unpublished manuscript.

28. Quoted on the jacket of *Eranos Jahrbuch* 23 (1954).

29. Quoted on the jacket of the *Eranos Jahrbuch* 20 (1951).

30. Quoted on the jacket of the *Eranos Jahrbuch* 27 (1958).

31. As Giovanni Filoramo, whom I have already mentioned, correctly remarks (*Il risveglio della gnosi ovvero diventare dio*, 23 *inter alia*), there are also certain disciplines whose absence can be considered significant. These include, in particular, history, philosophy of the purely academic kind, and sociology (despite the presence of Helmuth Plessner and possibly also Ira Progoff). There must be only very few scholars who are capable of combining these disciplines with a "mythical" and archetypal worldview.

32. On other occasions Portmann repeatedly emphasized the importance of the mesocosm, which he even equated with the "real" world of human beings.

33. *Eranos Jahrbuch* 30 (1961), 25–7.

2. An Esoteric Prelude to Eranos

1. Gershom Scholem, "Identifizierung und Distanz: Ein Rückblick," *Eranos Jahrbuch* 48 (1979), 463.

2. This fits entirely with Fröbe's own image of herself. Thus, on 11 March 1960 she wrote to Jung, "I am aware that my relationship to the speakers is always that of a mother to her son, as all the speakers are continually telling me, whether they understand anything of psychology or not."

3. Christian Jambet (ed.), *Henry Corbin* (Paris: L'Herne, 1981), 264.

4. See Margaret H. Case (ed.), *Heinrich Zimmer: Coming into His Own* (Princeton, NJ: Princeton University Press, 1994), 32.

5. See his letter of 16 December 1933. In other letters (to Birger Forell and Ernst Benz) he calls her, with similar touch of irony, "Mother Fröbe" and "Domina Fröbe." Otto was also ironic about himself. Writing on 19 June 1933, evidently in reply to her question as to whether he was able to organize spiritual exercises of yoga, he said that "only a true mahatma can do that. I am only a stuffed one."

6. Mircea Eliade, *Journal I, 1945–1955* (Chicago, IL: University of Chicago Press, 1990), 137.

7. For example, when deaths occurred she advised the bereaved relatives how they could release themselves from the deceased through the power of the imagination. See Gerhard Wehr, *Jean Gebser* (Petersberg: Via Nova, 1996), 90.

8. For information on the long-standing and little-known connection between Eliade and Evola, see H.T. Hansen (ps. H.T. Hakl), "Mircea Eliade, Julius Evola und die Integrale Tradition," in J. Evola, *Über das Initiatische: Aufsatzsammlung*, 9–50 (Sinzheim: Archiv für Altes Gedankengut und Wissen, 1998), and also the richly documented essay by Paola Pisi, "I tradizionalisti e la formazione del pensiero di Eliade," in Luciano Arcella, Paola

Pisi, and Roberto Scagno, *Confronto con Mircea Eliade* (Milan: Jaca Book, 1998). See also the essay by the Eliade specialist Natale Spineto, "Mircea Eliade and Traditionalism," in *Aries: Journal for the Study of Western Esotericism* 1(1) (2001), 62–87. Spineto considers the influence of the traditionalist school on Eliade's view of the history of religion to have been not very significant.

9. In the letter, written in French, the German words *gute Unterhaltung* have been inserted.

10. Evola writes even more drastically about Eranos in an unpublished letter, now in a private collection, written to Franz Altheim on 27 May 1955. Here, while referring to Mircea Eliade, whom he much valued, Evola says, "The milieu of Fröbe in Ascona is a dreadful nest of old women, most of them devotees of the demi-god C.G. Jung. Unfortunately a participation in this group is not without practical advantages" (original in German).

11. In her manuscript, *L'Oeuvre d'Eranos et Vie d'Olga Froebe-Kapteyn* (Ascona, n.d.), Catherine Ritsema, as a long-standing confidante of Fröbe and fellow resident at Moscia-Ascona, provides an abundance of details about her parents.

12. Deirdre Bair, *Jung: A Biography* (Boston, MA: Little Brown, 2003), 412, 782.

13. Olga's sister May later married one of André Jolles' best friends. Walther Thys, who drew my attention to these connections, has edited an annotated collection of letters from and about André Jolles, which appeared in 2000 under the title *André Jolles (1874–1946). "Gebildeter Vagant": Brieven en documenten* (Amsterdam: Amsterdam University Press and Universitätsverlag Leipzig, 2000).

14. André Jolles, *Einfache Formen: Legende, Sagen, Mythe, Rätsel, Spruch, Kasus, Memorabile, Märchen, Witz* (Halle: Max Niemeyer, 1929). The Jolles expert Walter Thys, in an email to me of 30 November 2006, posed the question of what this award signified. There are rumors that Jolles belonged to the legendary Thule Society and that he taught the use of the runes to the notorious anti-Semitic Nazi ideologist Johannes von Leers, although there is absolutely no proof of this. The writer on esotericism Michael Kuper believes that details about this matter are to be found in a memorandum in the possession of the electric appliances manufacturer Frits Philips, who died in 2005. The memorandum was allegedly written by the Dutch historian Johan Huizinga (author of *The Waning of the Middle Ages*), who had a long friendship with Jolles (private communication, 2005).

15. Gerd Simon, "Germanistik und Sicherheitsdienst," in *Nachrichtendienst, politische Elite und Mordeinheit: Der Sicherheitsdienst des Reichsführers SS*, Michael Wildt (ed.) (Hamburg: Hamburger Edition, 2003), 199ff.

16. Annemarie Pallat, "Uit de 'Autobiographie' en het 'Tagebuch'," in *André Jolles (1874–1946)*, W. Thys (ed.), 994–1002 (Leipzig: Leipziger Universitätsverlag, 2000).

17. Bair, *Jung*, 799 n.146.

18. Ludwig Pallat, "Uit het Dagboek van Ludwig Pallat," in Thys (ed.), *André Jolles (1874–1946)*, 1009.

19. Unfortunately it is not known what this conversation was about. It might have been about the repeated attempts by the Nazi authorities to influence Eranos or perhaps it concerned her daughter Ingeborg.

20. On Olga Fröbe's life story, see McGuire, *Bollingen*, 21ff.; Christine Derleth, *Das Fleischlich-Geistige: Meine Erinnerungen an Ludwig Derleth* (Bellnhausen über Gladbach: Hinder & Deelmann, 1973), 96 (although this contains a few small contradictions to McGuire's account); Harald Szeemann (ed.), *Monte Verità: Die Brüste der Wahrheit* (Milan: Electa, 1978), 117; and especially a summary of her life, written in 1944 by Olga Fröbe herself.

21. Robert Faesi, *Erlebnisse, Ergebnisse, Erinnerungen* (Zurich: Atlantis Verlag, 1963), 224ff.

22. See the comprehensive documentation provided in the catalogue, edited by Ines Janet Engelmann, to the exhibition *Alastair: Kunst als Schicksal* (Halle: Stiftung Moritzburg, 2004), 121. Especially impressive are the numerous photographs there showing Alastair during his artistic appearances.

23. Alastair, *Das flammende Tal: Gedichte* (Munich: Hyperionverlag, 1920). It was printed in an edition of 680 copies.

24. Thus, for example, he illustrated books by Oscar Wilde, Abbé Prévost, Georges Bernanos, and Barbey D'Aurevilly. See also the work edited by Robert Ross in a limited edition of 500 copies: *Forty-Three Drawings by Alastair with a Note of Exclamation* (London: John Lane, 1914). Ross describes (xxviii) many of Alastair's drawings as dances on paper. Alastair also translated into German and edited a collection of letters from Mary Queen of Scots. See Maria Stuart, *Ich flehe, ich fordere, ich bekenne! Der Königin Briefe*, H.H. von Voigt-Alastair (trans.) (Leipzig: Verlagsanstalt Hüthing, 1940).

25. Derleth, *Das Fleischlich-Geistige*, 98, has a photograph of him wearing such a costume.

26. Most of the following information, including the quotations, comes from Dominik Jost, *Ludwig Derleth, Gestalt und Leistung* (Stuttgart: W. Kohlhammer, 1965), 78ff.

27. See also Carl Friedrich von Weizsäcker, *Zeit und Wissen* (Munich: Carl Hanser Verlag, 1992), 992. The author, a physicist of world renown, also makes the surprising statement on page 995 of the book: "And later I was seized upon by someone who could neither fully bind me nor let me go: Alastair."

28. Hans Blüher, *Werke und Tage: Geschichte eines Denkers* (Munich: Paul List, 1953), 447. With the observation that Alastair was not suited to being a lover of women, Blüher, who among other things specialised in homoerotic researches, is probably alluding to his homosexual tendencies.

29. Translated from the poem *Grablegung des Adonis*, in Alastair, *Das flammende Tal*.

30. Riccardo Bernardini, *Da Monte Verità a Eranos: Elementi di una rete culturale per lo studio della psiche e della complessità umana* (doctoral thesis presented in the Faculty of Psychology at the Università degli Studi, Turin, 2002–3), 124.

31. Report by Olga Fröbe concerning the case of W.R. Corti, unpublished and undated but written around 1959, in the literary estate of Adolf Portmann, University Library, Basel.

32. Quoted from an unpublished manuscript of Gerhard Wehr on the history of Eranos, 22.

33. Catherine Ritsema, *L'Oeuvre d'Eranos*, 16ff.

34. See Jan van der Vegt, *A. Roland Holst: Biografie* (Baarn: de Prom, 2000).
35. *Ibid.*, 284.
36. *Ibid.*, 313.
37. *Ibid.*, 329.
38. *Ibid.*, 360.
39. An informative analysis of Derleth and his work is to be found in Georg Dörr, *Muttermythos und Herrschaftsmythos: Zur Dialektik der Aufklärung um die Jahrhundertwende bei den Kosmikern, Stefan George und in der Frankfurter Schule* (Würzburg: Königshausen & Neumann, 2007), 223–33. See also the concise overview by Georg Dörr, *Ludwig Derleth: Prophet und Mystiker* (Ascona, 2001), which I consider more important than the essay by the same author "Archetyp und Geschichte oder München—Ascona: Typologische und menschliche Nähe (Mit einigen Briefen Olga Fröbes an L. Derleth)," in Barone *et al.*, *Pioniere, Propheten, Professoren*, 155–69, as the former work incorporates new research findings. In particular I would like to quote the concluding remark by Dörr. After describing Derleth as one of the "losers of history," Dörr says: "Do only the victors count, or can we also learn something from those who are almost forgotten and, if so, what?"
40. Where Derleth and Hugo von Hofmannsthal were practically neighbors. Derleth lived in a former hunting lodge of the Empress Maria Theresa. Both of them were also present in Basel as visitors at the home of the diplomat Carl J. Burckhardt. The differences in their characters, however, probably explain why there is a lack of evidence regarding contact between them. See the instructive study by Christoph W. Abdelmu'min Clairmont, *Ludwig Derleth (1870–1948): Das literarische Werk. Eine kritische Würdigung* (Ernen, n.d. [probably 2002]). Clairmont, as a convert to Islam, was understandably interested in Derleth's work. However, he criticized (p. 21) Derleth's book title *Der fränkische Koran*, on the grounds that there could only be *one* Koran. It was equally impossible to imagine a Franconian Bible.
41. Friedrich Wolters, a fellow member of the George circle, said on this point, "His Catholicism was something neither oriental and fantastic nor Germanically mystical, but rather was nourished by the world of antiquity." See Friedrich Wolters, *Stefan George und die Blätter für die Kunst: Deutsche Geistesgeschichte seit 1890* (Berlin: Georg Bondi, 1930).
42. It is his opinion (in common with other men of many different eras and regions) that it is the feminine (the *apate*) that holds the male back from conquering heaven.
43. Jost, *Ludwig Derleth*, 96.
44. From an unpublished letter from Christine Derleth to the author F.A. Schmid-Noerr, now in a private collection. Schmid-Noerr had visited Derleth in Munich in 1932 and had published a very positive article on Derleth's work.
45. Like Derleth, Count Harry Kessler is also listed in Bernd-Ulrich Hergemöller's dictionary of homoeroticism, *Mann für Mann* (Hamburg: MännerschwarmSkript Verlag, 1998), 417ff. However, Rolf Hinder, in his introduction to Christine Derleth's book *Das Fleischlich-Geistige*, writes in this connection about Derleth, "The boy-loving Hellenophile, who subjects his earthly existence to strict self-discipline and the renunciation of ego-centred erotic fulfilment, will, in his failure, be free for his work" (p. 16).
46. The publication was a joint venture of Dominik Jost, Christine Derleth, and Rolf Hinder. See Ludwig Derleth, *Das Werk*, 6 vols. (Gladenbach: Hinder & Deelmann, 1971–72).
47. André Germain, who has already been mentioned, said of him: "He wanted to be a prophet against the will of the Holy Spirit, which refused to breathe on him; and with his foot he pushed away another profession—that of poet—as though it were unworthy of him." Quoted in Jost, *Ludwig Derleth*, 110. The sensitive writer and translator Ursula von Mangoldt, head of the Otto Wilhelm Barth publishing house (to which we shall return as an important theme later on) writes about Derleth in her memoirs as follows: "Derleth was a Titan and reminded one of Napoleon, but through vanity and power lust he overreached himself and his own abilities" (*Auf der Schwelle zwischen Gestern und Morgen: Begegnungen und Erlebnisse* [Weilheim: O.W. Barth, 1963], 111).
48. Lothar Helbig [Wolfgang Frommel], "Ludwig und Anna Derlich," in *Ludwig Derleth Gedenkenbuch* (Amsterdam: Castrum Peregrini, 1958), 70.
49. Because of his aesthetic anti-modernism, George came under suspicion of being a forerunner of National Socialism, although in 1933 he refused the leadership of the Nazi-sponsored German Academy of Poets, and it was probably because of the regime that he emigrated to Switzerland. As an interesting red herring, it may be mentioned that while the first Eranos meeting was taking place, George died at Munisio, very close to Ascona.
50. He received at least one volume of the *Eranos Jahrbuch* from Olga Fröbe as a present, as indicated in a dedication preserved in an *Eranos Jahrbuch* volume in his possession.
51. Jost, *Ludwig Derleth*, 99ff.
52. Karl Kerényi, *Tage- und Wandrbücher 1953–1960* (Munich: Langen-Müller, 1969), 260.
53. According to his widow, Magda Kerényi, this prehistory consisted merely of things that Olga Fröbe had told him about her relationship to Derleth.
54. Mircea Eliade, *Autobiography* II, 161.
55. I assume, like Magda Kerényi, that it "merely" involved Olga Fröbe's close connection to Ludwig Derleth, to which, in her own individual way, she gave an esoteric interpretation. Therefore I do not believe that I have overlooked any essential aspects of the prehistory of Eranos.

56. Unfortunately Olga Fröbe appears to have almost invariably encountered difficulties with the men to whom she was drawn. This may have partly been the reason for her well-known aversion to other women who were "competitors."

57. Derleth, however, rejected "tender feelings." See Derleth, *Das Fleischlich-Geistige*, 183. She attributes Thomas Mann's "abrasive criticism" of Derleth to jealousy over the situation. Christoph W. Abdelmu'min Clairmont, however, in his study *Ludwig Derleth* considers this illogical (p. 59). Clairmont characterizes the two writers as "to the highest degree polar opposites of one another" (p. 57). In Inge Jens and Walter Jens, *Frau Thomas Mann: Das Leben der Katharina Pringsheim* (Reinbek: Rowohlt, 2004), Derleth is not mentioned at all.

58. I do not know to what extent it was mere malice which led some people to maintain that it was all a matter of the expected inheritance from his wife, i.e. of ensuring security for his "work." Christine Derleth cites, as the "motto" of her (probably platonic) marriage, a sentence by Ludwig Derleth: "Look towards me, even when I do not look at you, and be mine." See Christine Derleth, *Das Fleischlich-Geistige*, 82. His ideal was the chaste "androgyne," 152ff.

59. Stefan George, *Der siebente Ring* (Berlin: Georg Bondi, 1909), 106.

60. André Jolles, who was an enthusiastic traveler to Italy and a great art lover, visited Olga Fröbe almost every year on his way there or back. Usually he appeared with his second wife, Grittli Boecklen, a teacher of drawing. She and Olga, who was a gifted craftswoman, would make marionettes and other objects together (Walter Thys, personal communication, 23 July 1999).

61. Furio Jesi is an interesting figure, who had a lifelong interest in myth and religion and especially their attendant political dangers. At the age of sixteen he left his *Gymnasium* and educated himself independently through reading, travel, and contact with various intellectuals. German intellectual and literary history became his special area. At the age of thirty-five he was even appointed as professor of German Studies at the University of Palermo, even though he did not even possess a school-leaving certificate. On the side he painted and wrote a short novel about vampires, of which the German edition, *Die letzte Nacht* (Freiburg: Beck & Glückler, 1991), contains an interesting afterword by Barbara Kleiner, from which I have drawn for the information given here.

62. See his foreword to the Italian translation of Oswald Spengler's *Decline of the West* (*Il Tramonto dell' Occidente*) (Milan: Longanesi, 1981), esp. xvii.

63. Edith Landmann, *Gespräche mit Stefan George* (Dusseldorf: Helmut Küpper, 1963).

64. Ludwig Thormaehlen, *Erinnerungen an Stefan George* (Hamburg: Dr. Ernst Hauswedell, 1962).

65. Kurt Hildebrandt, *Erinnerungen an Stefan George und seinen Kreis* (Bonn: H. Bouvier, 1965).

66. Landmann, *Gespräche mit Stefan George*, 77.

67. Furio Jesi, *Cultura di Destra* (Milan: Garzanti, 1979), 58. This book attempts to offer evidence of a "conspiracy from the right," although it deals mainly with the areas of mythology, religion, and spiritual worldviews in general. In these areas Jesi postulates the existence of a language based on "wordless ideas." These ideas, being wordless, impel people in a not explicit, yet efficient way to violence, even to mass murder, such as that of the Jews. One of his main targets of attack was Mircea Eliade. Julius Evola was another.

68. Furio Jesi, *Germania Segreta: Miti nella cultura tedesca del 900* (Milan: Feltrinelli, [1967] 1995).

69. Even to her long-standing and close friend Angela Stader, Christine Derleth never mentioned anything pertaining to such rituals. Derleth did, however, possess a portrait of the Empress Elisabeth, which was sold after his death.

70. Derleth had even for a time considered setting up his utopian monastic community in Ascona. This, however, had nothing to do with Olga Fröbe's wish to involve Derleth in Eranos.

71. Jost, *Ludwig Derleth*, 103, 147, esp. 136. The date is 24 July 1937. Derleth's visitors, incidentally, also included Karl Kerényi.

72. Dominik Jost, *Die Dichtung Ludwig Derleths* (Bellnhausen über Gladenbach: Hinder & Deelmann, 1975), 67, 73.

73. See especially Derleth's early work *Proklamationen* (dating originally from 1904), included in Derleth, *Das Werk*, vol. 1, esp. 54, where the influence of Nietzsche is predominant in terms of both style and content. These proclamations are said to have deeply impressed the writer and artist Alfred Kubin, as Georg Dörr mentions in his book *Muttermythos und Herrschaftsmythos*, 227.

74. It is mimeographed, undated, and bears the title *Eranos, der Geist am WASSER*.

75. According to Magda Kerenyi, Olga Fröbe was asked on these occasions to bring Derleth some of her completed drawings.

76. With the subtitle *Stefan George und der deutsche Antimodernismus* (Darmstadt: Wissenschaftliche Buchgemeinschaft, 1995), 118–22.

77. See his book *Männerbünde mit Gräfin: Die "Kosmiker" Derleth, George, Klages, Wolfskehl und Franziska zu Reventlow* (Frankfurt: Peter Lang, 1994), 104–25. See also his essay "Genii locorum. Schwabings neureligiöse "Kosmiker" zwischen Wilhelmismus und Faschismus," in Moritz Baßler and Hildegard Châtelier, *Mystique, mysticisme et modernité en Allemagne autour de 1900/Mystik, Mystizismus und Moderne in Deutschland um 1900* (Strasbourg: Presses Universitaires de Strasbourg, 1998), 149–64.

78. With the subtitle *Rechtsradikalismus und Antisemitismus in München von der Jahrhundertwende bis 1921* (Berlin: Transit, 1989), 28–31. This book contains two photographs of Derleth as well one of his garret apartment.

79. Friedrich von Dauber, *Ludwig Derleth: Der Dichter und sein Werk* (PhD thesis, Department of Philosophy, University of Vienna, 1943), 5ff.
80. The standard literature includes especially Thomas Karlauf, *Stefan George: Die Entdeckung des Charisma* (Munich: Karl Blessing, 2007) and Robert E. Norton, *Secret Germany: Stefan George and His Circle* (Ithaca, NY: Cornell University Press, 2002).
81. As a counterbalance to the works of modern literary criticism mentioned here, which are not exactly sympathetic in attitude, I would like to cite a work that is very widely informed and strives to arrive at an inner understanding of the subject, namely *Kosmik: Prozessontologie und temporale Poetik bei Ludwig Klages und Alfred Schuler: Zur Philosophie und Dichtung der Schwabinger Kosmischen Runde* (Munich: Telesma, 2007), by the literary scholar Baal Müller.
82. As far as Schuler is concerned, the fundamental work is his collected writings, with commentaries and introduction by Baal Müller: Alfred Schuler, *Gesammelte Werke* (Munich: Telesma Verlag, 2007).
83. Ludwig Klages' reputation too has suffered on account of his anti-Semitism. For example, his previously much lauded "philosophy of life" (the "soul" must take precedence over the "rational mind") was condemned by Marxist literary critics such as Georg Lukács. A more understanding position is taken by Reinhard Falter in *Ludwig Klages: Lebensphilosophie als Zivilisationskritik* (Munich: Telesma, 2003). He draws attention especially to Klages' subsequent influence on scientists and philosophers such as Hans Prinzhorn, Theodor Lessing, Max Scheler, Walter Benjamin, C.G. Jung, and the Eranos speaker Walter F. Otto.
84. On this theme see Stefan Breuer, *Ästhetischer Fundamentalismus*, 95-113, as well as the editorial comments in Roderich Huch, *Alfred Schuler, Ludwig Klages, Stefan George: Erinnerungen an Kreise und Kriesen der Jahrhundertwende in München-Schwabing* (Amsterdam: Castrum Peregrini, 1973), 56, where it is pointed out, however, that the "Gnostic" anti-Semitism of Schuler was not to be equated with the racism of the National Socialists. Thus, for example, Schuler's anti-Judaic matriarchal theories were directed against the "patriarchy" of Jehovah and not against Judaism as such. Interestingly, even Karl Wolfskehl, a Jewish member of the George circle who was a victim of this anti-Semitism, described Schuler as "honourable, marvellous and full of profound weight." See Karl Wolfskehl, *Zehn Jahre Exil, Briefe aus Neuseeland 1938-1948*, Margot Ruben (ed.), Veröffentlichungen der Deutschen Akademie für Sprache und Dichtung Darmstadt series, no. 13 (Heidelberg: Lambert Schneider, 1959), 264. On the subject of Schuler see also Franz Wegener, *Alfred Schuler, der letzte deutsche Katharer: Gnosis, Nationalsozialmus und mystische Blutleuchte* (Gladbeck: Kulturförderverein Ruhrgebiet, 2003). As the title and subtitle imply, Wegener concocts an unholy chain leading from the Gnosis of ancient times up to National Socialism, which I for one am not able to follow. Wegener does mention, however, that in 1902 Schuler, along with Magnus Hirschfeld, was among the Munich forerunners of the Scientific-Humanitarian Committee of Berlin, which aimed, among other things, to make homosexuality no longer a punishable offence. Schuler also has an entry in Bernd-Ulrich Hergemöller's dictionary on alleged homosexuals *Mann für Mann*, 646-8.
85. See the introduction by Ludwig Klages to Alfred Schuler, *Fragmente und Vorträge aus dem Nachlaß* (Leipzig: J.A. Barth, 1940), 61ff. and 268. See also Alfred Schuler, *Cosmogonische Augen: Gesammelte Schriften* (Paderborn: Igel Verlag, 1997). On 307ff. is reproduced the entire text of Schuler's letter to the Empress Elisabeth, written in his strangely idiosyncratic and turgid prose. The comments of the editor, Baal Müller, are on 31 and 453.
86. See Stefan Breuer, *Ästhetischer Fundamentalismus*, 96ff.
87. See Friedrich Wolters (their contemporary and also a member of the George circle), *Stefan George und die Blätter für die Kunst*, 279.
88. *Ibid.*
89. Gerd-Klaus Kaltenbrunner, "Zwischen Rilke und Hitler: Alfred Schuler," in *Zeitschrift für Religions- und Geistesgeschichte* 19 (1967), 333-47. Kaltenbrunner was one of the first essayists to present the lesser-known side of Schuler. See, for example, Gerd-Klaus Kaltenbrunner, "'Ans Herz des Lebens schlich der Marder Juda': Alfred Schulers pagane Gnosis," in *Wort und Wahrheit*, 23(6) (1968), 531-45.
90. See the catalogue to the 1968 exhibition mounted by the German Literature Archive at the National Schiller Museum in Marbach am Neckar, *Stefan George 1868-1968: Der Dichter und sein Kreis*. Then again, Carl Friedrich von Weizsäcker reports Schuler himself as having said: "I am the mother sow. They all drink from me and then leave me lying there." See Carl Friedrich von Weizsäcker, *Zeit und Wissen*, 993.
91. See Derleth, *Ludwig Derleth Gedenkbuch*, 7.
92. *Beim Propheten*, in Thomas Mann, *Erzählungen* (Frankfurt: Fischer Taschenbuch, 2005), 401-20.
93. Concerning *Doctor Faustus*, see Thomas Mann's letter in Jost, *Ludwig Derleth*, 53. And regarding *At the Prophet's* (*Beim Propheten*) see Dirk Heißerer, *Wo die Geister wandern: Eine Topographie der Schwabinger Bohème um 1900* (Munich: Diederichs, 1993), 163. On the subject of the story *At the Prophet's*, Mann himself, in a letter of 2 April 1904 to his friend Kurt Martens, writes: "For the Easter issue of the *Neue Freie Presse*, as they would not give me any peace, I have thrown together an incredible concoction in one and a half days and henceforth regard my literary self as no longer unblemished." See also his letter of 1 April 1950 to the lawyer Otto Reeb, in which he declares that he had not wanted to offend anyone. Reeb, as a former *Gymnasium* pupil of Derleth, had praised the latter highly. In the letter, Mann writes, among other things: "In Munich I often met him and his sister, the 'evil nun,' as

George called her, and was always fascinated and amused by the strict and proud playfulness of the brother and sister." See Christine Derleth, *Das Fleischlich-Geistige*, 179–84.

94. As reported by Maggy Anthony in *The Valkyries: The Women around Jung* (Longmead: Element Books, 1990), 70ff. Olga Fröbe herself, in an unpublished report on Eranos written in 1952, mentions a seven-year period of concentrated discipline without giving further details. However, according to Christa Robinson, a former president of the Eranos Foundation, Rudolf Ritsema (whose important role in the history of Eranos will be described later), in his conversations with contemporaries, had never found any confirmation of the alleged seven-year period of isolation and neurosis. According to his account, although Fröbe had been very introverted, she had never been a patient of C.G. Jung. Fröbe herself, in a letter to Jung dated 11 March 1960, wrote, "I have never been through an analysis but have just followed all your seminars (as the books were mostly too difficult for me), and I found the vividness of the seminars more meaningful to me." This is confirmed by information given by Kerényi and Ximena de Angulo-Roelli: yes, Olga Fröbe had addressed her personal problems to Jung (as she did later to other analysts such as Erich Neumann and Leopold Szondi), but he had only advised her to record her dreams and try to interpret them herself. She should only come to him from time to time when she was really at a loss for advice. Olga Fröbe is incidentally said to have been punctilious in devoting four hours every day, 10–12 a.m. and 4–6 p.m., to reflection on her psychological development or the study of relevant writings.

95. Olga Fröbe undoubtedly meant by this a state of semi-trance.

96. Olga Fröbe adopted exactly this description, word for word, for her Eranos project in its early years. Mrs. Ritsema maintains in her manuscript (p. 21) that Olga Fröbe's use of the description was prompted by Rudolf Otto's book *West-östliche Mystik* [Mysticism East and West].

97. Unpublished and undated addendum to the case of W.R. Corti.

98. Holzapfel even came in 1933 and 1934 to the Eranos meetings, although not as a speaker. See Riccardo Bernardini, *Da Monte Verità a Eranos*, 139.

99. Vladimir Astrov, *Das Leben Rudolf Maria Holzapfels* (Jena: Eugen Diederichs, 1928), ix–xxiii.

100. Quoted from the publisher's promotional material appended to Holzapfel's two-volume work *Welterlebnis: Das religiöse Leben und seine Neugestaltung* (Jena: Eugen Diederichs, 1928). The other press comments that I have quoted are taken from the same place.

101. Heinrich Berl, *Gespräche mit berühmten Zeitgenossen* (Baden-Baden: Hans Bühler, 1946), 135. The quotation is from the chapter entitled "Der Schöpfer einer neuen Religion," 135–40.

102. The revised edition, in two finely bound large volumes, was published at Jena in 1923 by Eugen Diederichs.

103. On the subject of the doctrine, see also Hans Zbinden (ed.), *Ein Künder neuer Lebenswege: Einzelbilder zur Seelenforschung Rudolf Maria Holzapfels* (Jena: Eugen Diederichs, 1923).

104. One of Holzapfel's poems contains the passage: "und unsre Seele ist wie ein schwarzes sturmgepeitschtes Schiff riesenhafter, alldurstiger Sehnsucht" (and our soul is like a black, storm-tossed ship of gigantic, insatiably thirsty longing). Quoted in Waldimir Astrow, *Das Leben Rudolf Maria Holzapfels*.

105. Other publications that should be mentioned in this connection are Bettina Holzapfel (ed.), *Rudolf Maria Holzapfel: Nachgelassene Schriften: Zur Psychologie des sozialen Verkehrs, des Kultus, des Schaffens und der Erkenntnis* (Zurich and Leipzig: Max Niehans, 1939), and Rudolf Herwin, *Vom Kunstschaffen und seinen neuen Zielen. Einblicke in Rudolf Maria Holzapfels Erforschung des Schaffens* (Leipzig: Psychokosmos-Verlag, 1928).

106. See Szeemann, *Monte Verità*, 117. Apparently Olga Fröbe stood out as being the only one who demanded a chair, while all the other participants sat on the grass.

107. The first letter from C.G. Jung to Olga Fröbe of which I am aware is dated 13 October 1930 (C.G. Jung archive at the Eidgenossische Technische Hochschule in Zurich). In this letter Jung replied somewhat evasively to Fröbe's question whether he would be willing to give a lecture on *The Secret of the Golden Flower* at the August 1931 meeting of the "Summer School," which we shall have much to say about in due course. Jung finally declined in a letter of 3 February 1931.

108. Annie Besant and Krishnamurti are also said to have visited Monte Verità, but no proof of this is available. Olga Fröbe is said to have even expected them on her own property: Robert Landmann, *Monte Verità, Ascona: Die Geschichte eines Berges* (Ascona: Pancaldi, 1934), 223.

109. Quoted from the homepage of Theosophical Society International Headquarters, Adyar, India: www.ts-adyar.org

110. "Adyar," (Vienna, 1946), 1.

111. See the article on Alice Bailey by James A. Santucci in the *Dictionary of Gnosis and Western Esotericism*, vol. 1, Wouter J. Hanegraaff *et al.* (eds) (Leiden: Brill, 2005), 158–60, an indispensable work for anyone researching into esotericism. A sample of her numerous works is to be found in *Ponder on This: From the Writings of Alice A. Bailey and the Tibetan Master Djwhal Khul* (London: Lucis Press, 1971). For a more detailed study, see the massive *Master Index of the Books of Alice Bailey* (London: Lucis Press, 1997).

112. See also the counter-version given by Alice Leighton Cleather and Basil Crump, writing from a point of orthodox Blavatsky Theosophy, in their brochure *The Pseudo-Occultism of Mrs. A. Bailey* (Manila, 1929). The brochure analyzes certain individual books of Bailey, suggesting that the doctrines contained in them stem from "shadow brethren." As an example the authors cite the teachings about the erotic life, which diverge from the Blavatsky view. See also Victor Endersby (ed.), *A Study of the Arcane School of Alice A. Bailey, Theosophical Notes Special*

Paper (1963). On the other hand, the Theosophist J. Miller, in his article "In Defence of Alice A. Bailey," in *Theosophical History* 2(6) (1988), 190–207, exonerates her from the charges leveled at her by Theosophists.

113. See the foreword to Foster Bailey, *Changing Esoteric Values* (Tunbridge Wells: Lucis Press, 1955), 7ff., and to his *The Spirit of Masonry* (Tunbridge Wells: Lucis Press, 1957), 9.

114. Eliade, *Journal I, 1945–1955*.

115. In 1982 the imminent arrival of the "Maitreya Christ" was announced by Benjamin Creme, an English follower of Alice Bailey, who even proclaimed the message on television. According to Creme, the Maitreya had been living in London since 1977. See H.-J. Ruppert, "Esoterik zwischen Endzeitfieber und Erlösungshoffnung," *Materialdienst* 62 (1999), 298. *Materialdienst* is the bulletin published by the Evangelische Zentrale für Weltanschauungsfragen (the German Evangelical Church body dealing with alternative belief systems; www.ekd.de/ezw/).

116. See Bruce F. Campbell, *Ancient Wisdom Revived: A History of the Theosophical Movement* (Berkeley, CA: University of California Press, 1980), 150–53.

117. Alice A. Bailey, *The Unfinished Autobiography* (New York: Lucis Press, 1973), 217ff.

118. Frank McLynn, *Carl Gustav Jung* (New York: St. Martin's Press, 1997). Ronald Hayman, in *A Life of Jung* (New York: W.W. Norton, 2001), confirms this and even claims that Jung made use of her mediumistic gifts and sent patients to her. She only needed to sit passively in a room with the patients, and they began to see images in their minds. Even Liliane Frey, a close collaborator of Jung, experienced the same thing.

119. Bailey, *The Unfinished Autobiography*, 217. However, as William McGuire writes in an essay on the Arcane School in Ascona, certain documents preserved in Ascona contain clear evidence that Olga Fröbe first went to the United States in 1928, when she visited her brother on Long Island. See William McGuire, "The Arcane Summer School," in *Spring* 40 (1980), 146–56, which has yielded much important information for this section. See also his "Report of First Session, August 1930," International Center of Spiritual Research, C.G. Jung Archiv, ETH, Zurich, Archivnr. As 1016. 29 949.

120. See Landmann, *Monte Verità, Ascona*, 226, where the letter is reproduced in full.

121. McGuire, "The Arcane Summer School," 150.

122. These pictures can probably be seen as a further step, following Derleth's original stimulus, towards the creation of what later became the Archive for Archetypal Symbolism.

123. Massimo Introvigne, *Storia del New Age 1962–1992* (Piacenza: Christianità, 1994), 64.

124. See the informative article by Marco Rossi, "Roberto Assagioli, dalla Teosofia Alla Psicosintesi," in *Esoterismo e Fascismo*, G. De Turris (ed.), 63–6 (Rome: Edizioni Mediterranee, 2006).

125. Concerning the relationship between Assagioli and Bailey, see Paola Giovetti, *Roberto Assagioli: La vita e l'opera del fondatore della Psicosintesi* (Rome: Edizione Mediterranee, 1995), 44ff. Assagioli's connection with the ideas of Alice Bailey appears to have lasted until his death. See Roberto Assaglioli, *Le vie dello spirito* (reprint, n.p., n.d.), a collection of Assagioli's contributions to the esoteric journal *Verso la Luce* from 1963 to 1974. Here Bailey's teachings are repeatedly mentioned in a positive way (e.g. see 143, 264). The editor of the journal, Giuseppe Filipponio, in his foreword describes Assagioli as "one of the best interpreters of the whole corpus of esoteric and exoteric teachings and communications which are contained in the writings of the Tibetan Master D.K. and which were received telepathically by Alice Bailey." Through the Bailey network, psychosynthesis achieved a wide dissemination in the United States, which it still enjoys. Conversely, Alice Bailey took over certain ideas from Assagioli.

126. See Eugene Taylor, *Shadow Culture: Psychology and Spirituality in America* (Washington, DC: Counterpoint, 1999), 249.

127. Riccardo Bernardini, *Da Monte Verità a Eranos*, 131. In this work Bernardini also mentions that in 1963, Rudolf Ritsema, who was then in charge of Eranos, invited Roberto Assagioli to give a lecture at Eranos but received a negative reply.

128. Leo Baeck was intended as one of the speakers for the first Eranos meeting in 1933, but did not attend.

129. A communication of 29 October 1932 from Olga Fröbe to the Marburg theologian and scholar of religion Friedrich Heiler reveals that the sinologist Erwin Rousselle, also a prominent lecturer at the School of Wisdom and later at Eranos, was a speaker at the third Summer School in 1932.

130. As late as the 1970s rumors were circulating that the Eranos speakers were given to performing black magic rites, in which chickens were slaughtered and animal blood was drunk. And Eugen Grosche, grand master of the Fraternitas Saturni, Germany's most important magical order, wrote in a letter of 13 June 1963 to his fellow member Orpheus (Horst Kropp): "There are places and locations on earth that are strongly laden with magic, for example the mal-canton [*sic*.] on Lake Maggiore—the cursed canton—where the light of the full moon and the astral vibrations are particularly strong" (quoted from Alexander Popiol and Rainer Schrader, *Gregor A. Gregorius: Mystiker des dunklen Lichts* [Bürstadt: Esoterischer Verlag: 2009], 81).

131. Bailey, *The Unfinished Autobiography*, 230.

132. *Ibid.*, 225. Christa Robinson wrote to me that Bailey visited from 1929 to 1931, although this does not tally with the other documents quoted here. Bailey herself was also undoubtedly inaccurate in giving 1933 as her last year at Ascona.

133. Rosenberg, *Eranos*, 2. Gerhard Wehr also mentions the episode in his Jung biography, *Carl Gustav Jung: Leben, Werk, Wirkung* (Munich: Kösel, 1985), 239.

134. Not everyone, however, shared Jung's opinion. The philosopher of religion Friedrich Heiler, for example, wrote to Olga Fröbe on 30 October 1933, after she had sent him photographs of the meditation tableaux: "I also thank you warmly for the photographs, which are most valuable to me, both for myself and for introducing others to meditational symbology. From the original example that I saw at Professor Otto's house I received a strong impression of the effect of the colours. My wife also derived great joy from the meditation tableaux."

135. Rosenberg, *Flügblätter für Freunde* 80 (1977), 7.

136. James Webb, *The Occult Establishment* (La Salle, IL: Open Court, 1976), 7.

137. Richard Noll, *The Jung Cult* (Princeton, NJ: Princeton University Press, 1994) and *The Aryan Christ* (New York: Random House, 1997). I shall later return briefly to the former book.

3. Yearning for the East: Monte Verità and the School of Wisdom

1. See, for example, Thomas Krämer, *Eine andere Moderne? Zivilisationskritik, Natur und Technik in Deutschland 1880–1933* (Paderborn: Ferdinand Schöningh, 1999). Also Corinna Treitel, in her interesting book *A Science for the Soul: Occultism and the Genesis of the German Modern* (Baltimore, MD: Johns Hopkins University Press, 2004), points out that for Germany the transition to modernity was altogether painful, since towards the end of the nineteenth century the Germans, while appreciating their new material power, perceived at the same time that the country was thereby becoming spiritually poorer. Esotericism, she argues, had come at just the right moment to re-enchant their world.

2. When people are unable to find any tangible meaning within themselves, they do seek for it in the realm of "otherness"; in the case of Nietzsche this was ancient Greece, and later in Germany it was the Far East. Two great dangers can be observed here. One may over-idealize the "other" and later experience a disillusionment to the point of rage. Or, if the over-idealizing is accompanied by an unacknowledged weakness in oneself, one may end up hating and wishing to destroy the "other." In both cases a potentially dangerous outward projection is involved.

3. See especially Volker Zotz, *Auf den glücklichen Inseln: Buddhismus in der deutschen Kultur* (Berlin: Theseus, 2000). On the reception of Eastern bodily and breathing exercises, as in yoga, Mazdaznan and New Thought, see Bernd Wedemeyer-Kolwe, *"Der neue Mensch"—Körperkultur im Kaiserreich und in der Weimarer Republik* (Würzburg: Königshausen & Neumann, 2004), 129ff.

4. See especially Ulrich Linse's essay "Asien als Alternative?," in Hans G. Kippenberg and Brigitte Luchesi (eds), *Religionswissenschaft und Kulturkritik* (Marburg: Diagonal-Verlag, 1991), 325–64. Linse is an expert on the spirit-ualistic and esoteric underground currents in Germany around the late nineteenth and early twentieth centuries.

5. Martin Buber had also given his attention to the teachings of the Upanishads. See, for example, his essay "Dem Gemeinschaftlichen folgen," in *Die Neue Rundschau* 67(4) (1956), 582ff., in which he compares the sayings of Heraclitus and the Taoist masters with the early Upanishads. The "magical" national epic of Finland, the *Kalevala*, also impressed him deeply, as shown by his preface "Das Epos des Zauberers" to Schiefner's new 1914 edition of the *Kalevala*. See the reprint in Martin Buber's *Die Rede, die Lehre, das Land: Drei Beispiele* (Leipzig: Insel Verlag, 1917), 97–126, as well as the foreword to the volume itself.

6. See Kaiser Wilhelm II, *Die chinesische Monade: Ihre Geschichte und Deutung* (Leipzig: K.F. Köhler, 1934). The kaiser, who had actively supported the research expeditions of Leo Frobenius to Africa during his reign, headed the so-called Doorner Arbeits-Gemeinschaft (Doorn study group), where learned people regularly gathered. Furthermore, under his editorship there appeared, with the same publisher in 1936, a work entitled *Vergleichende Zeittafeln der Vor- und Frühgeschichte Vorderasiens, Ägyptens und Mittelmeerländer*.

7. In the foreword to his book *Der Yoga: ein indischer Weg zum Selbst* (Stuttgart: W. Kohlhammer, 1958), a greatly expanded edition of his earlier work *Der Yoga als Heilweg*, Jakob Wilhelm Hauer recalls this lecture, which he had "delivered with a certain enthusiasm that also animated C.G. Jung, who was in the audience." Also present was the founder of Autogenic Training, J.H. Schultz, who then invited Hauer to participate with him in a colloquium on the subject.

8. C.G. Jung, *Gesammelte Werke*, vol. 15 (Olten: Walter Verlag, 1971), 70. For Jung it appears obvious that the fas-cination exerted by the Orient involves a strong projection of elements from within the unconscious mind of the "West." It was precisely in order to understand such pressures from our own unconscious, and thus to avoid the "irrational" element from getting out of hand, that Jung preoccupied himself so intensively with alchemy and gno-sis, for it was there that the dark side was clearly discernible. Thus I do not see Jung as a pioneer of "irrationalism," as he is often regarded today, but rather as someone who tried to deal with the undeniable irrational elements in human beings in such a way that they did not give rise to dangerous outbursts.

9. George Mosse has already made an important contribution here. See especially his book *Ein Volk, ein Reich, ein Führer: Die völkischen Ursprünge des Nationalsozialismus* (Königstein: Athenäum, 1979). On the political implications of this search for meaning, see also Norbert Bolz, *Auszug aus der entzauberten Welt: Philosophischer Extremismus zwischen den Kriegen* (Munich: Wilhelm Fink Verlag, 1989).

10. On this subject see the study by Christiane C. Günther, *Aufbruch nach Asien* (Munich: Judicum, 1988), which also speaks about the significance of Count Hermann Keyserling, who will also feature in this chapter. Equally important—especially in connection with Keyserling and C.G. Jung—is Michael Hulin and Christine Maillard

(eds), *L'Inde inspiratrice: Réception de l'Inde en France et en Allemagne (XIXe & XXe siècles)* (Strasbourg: Presses Universitaires de Strasbourg, 1996).

11. On this viewpoint see the second chapter of the fundamental work by Kurt Sontheimer, *Antidemokratisches Denken in der Weimarer Republik* (Munich: Nymphenburger, 1962).

12. *Ibid.*, 46. Mann spoke of an almost unbearable nervous tension, a notion which is also reflected in the title of Joachim Radkau's book *Das Zeitalter der Nervosität* [The age of nervousness] (Munich: Carl Hanser, 1998), dealing with the era "between Bismarck and Hitler." There was an expectation that authoritarian ideologues of will and power would help to overcome this nervousness, which was felt as an affliction. Jung, in a lecture in 1932, expressed the opinion that "we unquestionably live in an age of enormous restlessness, nervousness, confusion and philosophical disorientation." See Jung, *Gesammelte Werke*, vol. 11, 363.

13. Paul Tillich, *Die religiöse Lage der Gegenwart* (Berlin: Ullstein, 1926), 103, 110.

14. Max Weber, *Wissenschaft als Beruf* (Munich: Duncker & Humblodt, 1919); published in English as *Science as a Vocation*, Peter Lassman, Irving Velody, and Herminio Martins (eds) (London: Unwin Hyman, 1989). See also the interesting essay by Jean Séguy, "Moderne, Rationalisierung, 'Entzauberung der Welt' bei Max Weber," in *Verabschiedung der (Post-) Moderne*, Jacques le Rider and Gérard Raulet (eds), 23–38 (Tübingen: Gunter Narr, 1987). Contrary to the widely held view that a "disenchantment" of the world took place around 1900, Ulrich Linse, who has already been mentioned (note 4, above), asks whether an attentive observer of that era would not rather have been struck by "an extraordinary multiplicity of 'new religions,' proving that one cannot speak of 'secularization' in the sense of a loss of individuals' need for religious 'orientation.'" See his essay "Säkularisierung oder neue Religiosität? Zur religiösen Situation in Deutschland um 1900," *Recherches Germaniques* 27 (1997), 117–41. Linse even proposes, on the basis of his historical researches, to abandon the "secularization hypothesis" altogether as a historiographical category (p. 122). As the question of secularization is now raised repeatedly, it may be appropriate to quote a remark by the Catholic theologian Johann Baptist Metz, which was repeated in an interview given by Joseph Ratzinger, then Prefect of the Sacred Congregation for the Doctrine of the Faith and now Pope Benedict XVI. According to Ratzinger, following Metz, the motto of today is "God no, religion yes. People want to have some kind of religion, whether it be esoteric or whatever. What they don't want is a personal God who speaks to us, knows us, has given a specific message, turns to us with definite expectations and is ready to direct us. It is true that people don't want completely to do without this feeling of distinct otherness, which is what is special about the religious domain, and they want to have it in many different forms. But this is essentially noncommittal, if God is not there. To this extent we are not in a crisis of religion—for religions are positively proliferating—but rather in a crisis of God." See "Ganze Größe von Gottes Wort," *Focus* 37 (2000), 48–9.

15. Franz Rolf Schröder, *Die Parzivalfrage* (Munich: C.H. Beck, 1928), 1ff.

16. F. J. Schmidt, *Die Wiedergeburt des Idealismus* (Leipzig: Verlag der Dürr'schen Buchhandlung, 1908). As we shall see, the struggle against historicism and positivism would also be a *Leitmotiv* at Eranos.

17. Jung, *Gesammelte Werke*, vol. 15, 68.

18. Eva Karàdi and Erzsébet Vezér (eds), *Georg Lukács, Karl Mannheim und der Sonntagskreis* (Frankfurt: Sendler, 1985), 81.

19. Linse, *Asien als Alternative?*, 333ff.

20. Thus the Austrian Marxist Max Adler, a leading figure in both the theoretical and the political sphere, edited a series of writings under the title *Neue Menschen* (New men), published by the Laubsche Verlagsbuchhandlung, Berlin.

21. Gottfried Küenzlen, in his book *Der Neue Mensch: Zur säkulären Geschichte der Moderne* (Munich: Wilhelm Fink, 1994), deals especially with Christianity, Marxism, the German youth movement, the student movement of 1968, and psychoanalysis. As founding fathers of the modern search for the new man, he cites above all Condorcet, Marx, and Nietzsche. In 1999 this theme was the subject of an informative exhibition in Dresden. See the detailed exhibition catalogue by Nicola Lepp, Martin Roth, and Klaus Vogel, *Der Neue Mensch: Obsessionen des 20. Jahrhunderts* (Ostfildern-Ruit, Cantz-Verlag, 1999). In my opinion it is impossible fully to understand the intellectual and spiritual history of the twentieth century with all its disturbing political developments, without recourse to the primarily *spiritual* idea of the "new man." The purely materialistic approach to historiography, despite some important analyses, seems to me over-simplistic.

22. On this theme see his lecture "Kosmische Fügung," in Richard Wilhelm, *Der Mensch und das Sein* (Jena: Eugen Diederichs, [1931] 1939), 8–27, as well as the other essays in the volume. Stephan Kuttner in his introduction gives a very good overview of Wilhelm's basic thinking, in which the term "new human being" crops up again and again.

23. Alexander Gleichen-Russwurm, "Von Kommenden Menschen," *Der Leuchter: Weltanschauung und Lebensgestaltung* (Darmstadt, Otto Reichl Verlag, 1919), 13–26.

24. Karl Baier, *Yoga auf dem Wege nach Westen: Beiträge zur Rezeptionsgeschichte* (Würzburg: Königshausen & Neumann, 1998), 194ff. See also Hayman, *A Life of Jung*, 245.

25. Oskar A.H. Schmitz, *Psychoanalyse und Yoga* (Darmstadt: Otto Reichl, 1923).

26. Von Mangoldt, *Auf der Schwelle zwischen Gestern und Morgen*, 148.

27. Subtitled *Betrachtungen in zwölfter Stunde* (Leipzig: Hesse & Becker Verlag, 1931).
28. The sociologist Georg Simmel calls this the "tragedy of culture." And Günther Anders spoke of the "antiquated nature of human beings," in comparison to their technical creations.
29. On this subject see: Szeemann, *Monte Verità*; Eduard von der Heydt and Werner von Rheinbaben, *Auf dem Monte Verità: Erinnerungen und Gedanken über Menschen, Kunst und Politik* (Zurich: Atlantis-Verlag, 1958); Robert Landmann, *Ascona, Monte Verità: Auf der Suche nach dem Paradies* (Zurich: Benziger, 1973); Emil Szittya, *Das Kuriositäten-Kabinett* (Konstanz: See-Verlag, 1923), 89–105; Günther Mahal (ed.), *Gusto Gräser: Aus Leben und Werk* (Knittlingen: Melchior, 1987); A. Grohmann, *Die Vegetarier-Ansiedlung in Ascona und die sogenannten Naturmenschen im Tessin* (Halle: Carl Marhold, 1904); Elisabeth Ries, "Monte Verità, Ascona, Oberfläche und Unterströmungen—Am Berg der Wahrheit," in Barone *et al.*, *Pioniere, Poeten, Professoren*, 21–32; Martin Green, *The Mountain of Truth: The Counterculture Begins, Ascona, 1900–1920* (Hanover, NH: University Press of New England, 1986); Riccardo Bernardini, *Da Monte Verità a Eranos*, 5–117; Giò Rezzonico, *Antologia di cronaca di Monte Verità* (Locarno: Rezzonico editore, 2008); Mara Folini, *Il Monte Verità di Ascona* (Berne: Società di Storia dell'Arte in Svizzera, 1998); Philippe Baillet, "Monte Verità (1900–1920) ou la complexité du 'romantisme anticapitaliste'—Une première approche historique et bibliographique," *Politica Hermetica* 14 (2000), 199–218, and his essay "Monte Verità: Une 'communité alternative' entre mouvance völkisch et avant-garde artistique," *Nouvelle Ecole* 52 (2001), 109–35. A jubilee conference entitled "100 Jahre Monte Verità" [One hundred years of Monte Veritá] was held in 2000. The lectures were published in Andreas Schwab and Claudia Lanfranchi (eds), *Sinnsuche und Sonnenbad: Experimente in Kunst und Leben auf dem Monte Verità* (Zurich: Limmat Verlag, 2001). The contents include contributions from experts whom we have already mentioned, such as Bernd Wedemeyer, Ulrich Linse, and Martin Green and also contemporary photographs. One of the editors has also analyzed the economic and touristic aspects of Monte Verità: Andreas Schwab, *Monte Verità: Sanatorium der Sehnsucht* (Zurich: Orell Füssli, 2003).
30. On the links between Theosophy and Monte Verità, see the comprehensive study by Walter Schönberger, "Monte Verità und die theosophischen Ideen," in Szeemann (ed.), *Monte Verità*, 65–79.
31. Bernardini, *Da Monte Verità a Eranos*, 34.
32. I am grateful to Andreas Kilcher for informing me about this incident.
33. Hermann M. Urspring, "Gusto Gräser: Der deutsche Laotse," appendix to Arthur Gusto Gräser, *Tao: Das heilende Geheimnis* (Wetzlar: Büchse der Pandora, 1979). In 1916 Gräser, while on a lecture tour in Switzerland, was apprehended and deported back to Germany. Only through a donation collected by Hermann Hesse was Gräser's family able to survive the winter without suffering. Hesse's novel *Demian* is a monument to their friendship. See also Ulrich Linse, *Barfüssige Propheten: Erlöser der zwanziger Jahre* (Berlin: Siedler, 1983), 68–75. Linse, in his book *Ökopax und Anarchie* (Munich: DTV, 1986), 61, describes Gräser as "one of the first alternative drop-outs." There is also a chapter about Gräser in Hermann Wilhelm's book *Die Münchener Bohème: Von der Jahrhundertwende bis zum ersten Weltkrieg* (Munich: Büchendorfer Verlag, 1993), 181–8. This book includes some rare pictures. A chapter is also devoted to the Monte Verità resident Franziska von Reventlow.
34. However, in his essay "Das Terrain ist besetzt. Mythos Monte Verità," in *Monte Verità—Landschaft, Kunst, Geschichte*, Hans-Caspar Bodmer, Ottmar Holdenrieder, and Klaus Seeland (eds), 27–52 (Frauenfeld: Verlag Huber, 2000), Andreas Schwab makes clear that Oedeken and Hoffmann soon pushed the "gurus" and "alternative" people into the sidelines in order not to jeopardize the financial prospects of the sanatorium.
35. For a detailed treatment of this subject see Peter R. König, *Der OTO, Phänomen Remix* (Munich: ARW, 2001), 70–76. See also Marco Pasi, *Aleister Crowley e la tentazione della politica* (Milan: Franco Angeli, 1999), 38 n.4.
36. Eduard von der Heydt, "Beglückender Monte Verità," in Eduard von der Heydt, Erich Mühsam, *et al.*, *Ascona und sein Berg Monte Verità* (Zurich: Verlag der Arche, 1979).
37. Much of the information given here is taken from von der Heydt and von Rheinbaben, *Auf dem Monte Verità*.
38. Curt Reiss, *Ascona: Geschichte des seltsamsten Dorfes der Welt* (Stuttgart: Deutscher Bücherbund, 1964), 93. Here one finds further details on Eduard von der Heydt's life.
39. Email from Riccardo Bernardini of 2 September 2003.
40. On Marianne Werefkin, who died in Ascona in 1938, see Bernd Fäthke, *Marianne Werefkin: Leben und Werk 1860–1938* (Munich: Prestel Verlag, 1988) and Konrad Federer (ed.), *Marianne von Werefkin: Zeugnis und Bild* (Zurich: Verlag der Arche, 1975), a collection of pieces by her friends, notably Else Lasker-Schüler and Friedrich Glauser.
41. Among the collection were paintings by van Gogh, Cézanne, Degas, Ingres, and Picasso. However, especially close to von der Heydt's heart were Asiatic, especially Buddhist works of art.
42. Carl Riess, *Ascona* (Zurich: Europa Verlag, 1964), 94.
43. Bair (*Jung*, 413), describes him as a "flamboyant transvestite" who only married his wife, Verena, in order to give the appearance of bourgeois respectability.
44. Landmann, *Monte Verità, Ascona*, 212ff.
45. With works such as *The Fortunes of Faust, Ritual Magic* and *The Myth of the Magus*.
46. E.M. Butler, *Paper Boats: An Autobiography* (London: Collins, 1959), 136ff. This book is also interesting for its

description, several pages long (166ff.), of the English magus Aleister Crowley ("Old Crow"). Her reaction to him oscillated between boredom and revulsion.

47. The book by Eduard von der Heydt and Werner von Rheinbaben, *Auf dem Monte Verità*, includes opposite page 160 a photograph of the German ex-chancellor Konrad Adenauer, who had also visited Monte Verità. On the same page is a photograph showing Baron von der Heydt in his characteristic outfit.

48. Bernardini, *Da Monte Verità a Eranos*, 136.

49. For Keyserling himself the title "School of Wisdom" was an intentional paradox. As he said: "First, the thing that we are creating is anything but a school! And second, wisdom is not teachable." Quoted from F. Sch. "Zehn Jahre Schule der Weisheit," *Europäische Revue* 7 (1931), 158–9. Also James Webb, in his section on the prehistory of Eranos (*The Occult Establishment*, 395ff.) points out the significance of Keyserling's school.

50. I rely here mainly on a well-researched book by Thomas Seng, *Weltanschauung als verlegerische Aufgabe: Der Otto Reichl Verlag 1909–1954* (St. Goar: Otto Reichl, 1994), 161–230. A book that can be highly recommended is Ute Gahlings' comprehensive biography *Hermann Graf Keyserling: Ein Lebensbild* (Darmstadt: Justus von Liebig Verlag, 1996).

51. Hermann Keyserling, *Deutschlands wahre Mission* (Darmstadt: Otto Reichl, 1919).

52. Hermann Keyserling, *Was uns Not tut: Was ich will* (Darmstadt: Otto Reichl, 1919).

53. In the aftermath of the so-called wars of liberation against France, Goethe feared an upsurge of exaggerated German nationalism which, in view of the geographically enclosed position of the country, could turn into an urge for military conquest. Hence the often (intentionally or unintentionally) misunderstood remark taken from Goethe's conversations: "I have often felt a bitter anguish when thinking about the German people, so admirable as individuals and so lamentable as a whole." See Johann Wolfgang Goethe, "Conversation with Heinrich Luden" of 13 December 1813, in Johann Wolfgang von Goethe, *Artemis- Gedenkausgabe* (Zurich: Artemis Verlag, 1948–54), vol. XXII, 713.

54. Eliade reports in his already mentioned *Journal I, 1945–1955*, 164, that Olga Fröbe saw Eranos as being in the lineage of Plato's Academy.

55. See Werner Killian von Tryller, "Die Eröffnung der Schule der Weisheit," in *Der Weg zur Vollendung: Mitteilungen der Gesellschaft für Freie Philosophie, Schule der Weisheit*, Hermann Keyserling (ed.), vol. 1, 49–54 (Darmstadt: Otto Reichl, 1920). In the same volume (pp. 5–23) Keyserling summarized his basic conception of his project under the title "Die Schule der Weisheit." On the subject of the school in general, see the post-doctoral thesis by Anne-Marie Buisson-Maas: *Hermann Keyserling et l'Inde* (Université de Lille, 1978), 527–611.

56. Hans Driesch, *Lebenserinnerungen: Aufzeichnungen eines Forschers und Denkers in entscheidender Zeit* (Basel: Ernst Reinhardt, 1951), 20ff.

57. In the post-war years similar meetings were held in Wiesbaden, and some of the proceedings were published under the title *Terra Nova: Veröffentlichungen der Keyserling-Gesellschaft für freie Philosophie*. See, for example, the series of lectures on the theme of *Das große Gespräch der Religionen* [The great dialogue of religions], held on 22–3 June 1963 and published under the editorship of Eleonore von Dungern (Munich: Ernst Reinhardt Verlag, 1964). The participants included the Eranos speakers Ernst Benz and Annemarie Schimmel.

58. A precise list of meetings, lecturers, and themes is to be found in the book *Sinnsuche oder Psychoanalyse: Briefwechsel Graf Hermann Keyserling—Oskar A.H. Schmitz aus den Tagen der Schule der Weisheit* (Darmstadt: Hessische Literaturfreunde, 1970), 42ff. Jung also corresponded with Oskar A.H. Schmitz. See C.G. Jung, *Briefe I (1906–1945)* (Olten: Walter Verlag, 1972). The correspondence between Keyserling and Schmitz affords many insights into the intellectual and spiritual life of that era. Names that crop up repeatedly include those of Wilhelm Ostwald and Ernst Haeckel, whom Richard Noll in his book *The Jung Cult* describes as having been key influences for Jung. The influence of Haeckel naturally went far beyond the Jung circle and reached a large contingent of the intellectuals of the time, ranging from Rudolf Steiner to those involved in the early social democratic movement, for whom Darwinism and Socialism were almost synonymous. See Fritz Bolle, "Darwinismus und Zeitgeist," *Zeitschrift für Religions- und Geistesgeschichte* 14 (1962), 143–78, and Johannes Hemleben, *Ernst Haeckel, der Idealist des Materialismus* (Hamburg: Anthroposophische Buchhandlung, 1974) and, by the same author, *Rudolf Steiner und Ernst Haeckel* (Stuttgart: Freies Geistesleben, 1968). In a letter to me, the Jung specialist Sonu Shamdasani expresses doubt that Haeckel had a special influence on Jung and his circle, except from the then widely recognized biogenetic law.

59. Driesch, *Lebenserinnerungen*, 208ff.

60. Hermann Keyserling, *Schöpferische Erkenntnis* (Darmstadt: Otto Reichl-, 1932), 513. This book brings together his lectures in the framework of the School of Wisdom.

61. Buisson-Maas, *Hermann Keyserling et l'Inde*, 589ff.

62. Gahlings, *Hermann Graf Keyserling*, 151ff. In 1923, in the context of these exercises, Rousselle gave a lecture about the mystic and occultist Bô Yin Râ.

63. See Richard Wilhelm, *Wandlung und Dauer: Die Weisheit des I Ging* (Düsseldorf: Eugen Diederichs, 1956), containing four essays on the *I Ching* that had already been published in 1931 in the anthology *Der Mensch und das Sein*.

64. Salome Wilhelm (ed.), *Richard Wilhelm: Der geistige Mittler zwischen China und Europa* (Düsseldorf: Eugen

Diederichs, 1956), 215. This book has a foreword by Walter F. Otto, one of the Eranos speakers. Keyserling was impressed by the "serene clarity" of the Chinese scholars, but considered the West to be basically superior on account of its greater "vitality" and "nervous energy." In Shanghai, Keyserling issued a *Message to the Peoples of the East*, written in English, which was then published in translation in the Chinese and Japanese press. In the German version of this speech, published in 1913 as a pamphlet under the title *Über die innere Beziehung zwischen den Kulturproblemen des Orients und Okzidents* (Jena: Eugen Diederichs, 1913), Keyserling points out that it is not curiosity this time that causes the Westerner to look eastwards, but rather it is "because the things that we are still seeking and striving for we find there already achieved and realised" (18).

65. Lao Naixuan was, up to the end of the Chinese Empire, head of the Imperial University of Peking and the last link in a chain of traditional oral interpreters of the *I Ching*. See Ulf Diederichs (ed.), *Erfahrungen mit dem I Ging: vom kreativen Umgang mit dem Buch der Wandlungen* (Cologne: Eugen Diederichs, 1987).

66. See his review "Innen ein Heiliger, nach aussen ein Souverän," in *Geheimnis der Goldenen Blüte*, Richard Wilhelm and C.G. Jung (eds) (Munich: Eugen Diederichs, 1998), 188. In the appendix to this book are two further documents relating to the collaboration between Jung and Wilhelm.

67. Quoted from Linse, *Asien als Alternative?*, 345. On Wilhelm's position within the Jungian movement, see "Chinesische Kontemplationen: Zu Richard Wilhelms Gedächtnis," in *Die kulturelle Bedeutung der Komplexen Psychologie*, Psychologischer Club Zurich (ed.) (Berlin: Julius Springer Verlag, 1935), 195-208. Here the difference between European and Chinese thought is explored in a series of quotations from Wilhelm.

68. S. Wilhelm (ed.), *Richard Wilhelm*, 375.

69. See the essay by Wolfgang Bauer, "Zeugen aus der Ferne: Der Eugen Diederichs Verlag und das deutsche China-Bild," in *Versammlungsort moderner Geister: Der Eugen Diederichs Verlag: Aufbruch ins Jahrhundert der Extreme*, Gangolf Hübinger (ed.) (Munich: Diederichs, 1996), 462ff. On Wilhelm see also the essay by the Eranos speaker Walter F. Otto, "Richard Wilhelm," in W.F. Otto and E. Schmalzriedt, *Mythos und Welt* (Darmstadt: Wissenschaftliche Buchgesellschaft, 1963), 221-9.

70. Jung, *Gesammelte Werke*, vol. 15, 65.

71. Hellmut Wilhelm, *Die Wandlung: Acht Essays zum I-Ging* (Zurich: Rhein-Verlag, 1958). Reprinted under the title *Sinn des I Ging* (Düsseldorf: Eugen Diederichs, 1972). There is also an English version: *Heaven, Earth, Man and the Book of Changes* (Seattle: University of Washington, 1977). Hellmut Wilhelm was, incidentally, one of the scholars who were supported by the Bollingen Foundation.

72. Jung was drawn not only to the *I Ching* but to Taoism in general. The analytical psychologist David Rosen, who holds the only full professorship of Jungian psychology in the United States, shows in his book *The Tao of Jung: The Way of Integrity* (New York: Viking Penguin, 1996) that there are astonishing parallels between Taoism and the Jungian doctrine of the soul.

73. See Noll, *The Jung Cult*, 95, and Jung, *Briefe I*, index.

74. Keyserling had, however, studied Jung carefully. This is clear from the numerous works by Jung with marginal notes by Keyserling, which have been preserved. The Eranos volume for 1941, incidentally, also contains annotations by the count. On this subject see the two extensive interviews that Gene F. Nameche carried out in 1970 with Keyserling's wife, Countess Gödela, and his son, Count Manfred, on the subject of Keyserling's relations with Jung. These are preserved in the Jung Oral Archive in the Countway Medical Library in Boston (I am grateful to Sonu Shamdasani for drawing my attention to these documents).

75. McLynn, *Carl Gustav Jung*, 322ff.

76. I am grateful to Sonu Shamdasani for providing me with the excerpts relating to Keyserling.

77. Gahlings, *Hermann Graf Keyserling*, 187.

78. See his work *Memorabilien: Erinnerungen und Begegnungen* (Munich: Georg Callwey, 1977), 321.

79. Driesch, *Lebenserinnerungen*, 206.

80. Gottfried Benn, *Briefe—Briefe an F.W. Oelze 1932–1945* (Frankfurt: Fischer Taschenbuch, 1986), letter 78, 120.

81. Franz Blei, *Erzählungen eines Lebens* (Vienna: Paul Zsolnay, 2004), 335.

82. Julius Evola, *Il cammino del cinabro* (Rome: All'insegna del pesce d'oro, 1972), 37.

3. Toward Eranos

1. These included physical symptoms.

2. That is to say 1932–33, when Fröbe had already known Derleth for about fifteen years.

3. Derleth collected all kinds of objects, valuable and worthless, which he regarded as relics and to which he attached enormous symbolic significance.

4. Olga Fröbe, *Gleichnisse* [Similes] (unpublished), 9.

5. Incidentally, Emma Jung thanked Fröbe, in a letter of 1 January 1947, for sending the "lovely picture of the Round Table."

6. See Case, *Heinrich Zimmer*, 32.

7. *Yoga: Internationale Zeitschrift für wissenschaftliche Yoga-Forschung* 1(1) (1931).

8. The new edition of C.G. Jung's Kundalini seminar of 1932 (*The Psychology of Kundalini Yoga* [Princeton, NJ: Princeton University Press, 1996]) contains an introduction by the historian of psychology Sonu Shamdasani.

Here Shamdasani surveys the history of the interchange between psychoanalysis and yoga, drawing attention to what is probably the earliest treatment of this theme, by F.I. Winter in his articles "The Yoga System and Psychoanalysis" and "Psychoanalysis and the Yoga Aphorisms," *The Quest* 10 (1919), 182–96, 315–35. *The Quest* was perhaps the foremost esoteric journal of the early years of the twentieth century. Its contributors included, besides esotericists, also poets and scholars (such as Karl Joel, Ezra Pound, W.B. Yeats, and Ananda Coomaraswamy). It was edited by H.P. Blavatsky's former secretary, G.R.S. Mead. As Shamdasani reports, Jung possessed the above-mentioned volume and others. In fact, as the published catalogue of his library reveals, Jung owned in total seventeen volumes of the journal. What strikes one when reading Winter's articles is that, apart from giving a good overview of the current state of knowledge about the subject, they already contain the basis for the doctrine of the archetypes, later developed by Jung. Winter begins by dealing with the contrasting methodological approaches in East and West, noting, "But behind the difference lies *the unity of human nature* … The fact that this internal struggle [of human beings towards self-understanding] is the same in east and west is proved by *the similarity in the symbolic representation of these striving forces within*" (emphasis added). On the relationship between depth psychology and yoga, see also Baier, *Yoga auf dem Wege nach Westen*, 193–255.

9. An interesting statement, considering that it came from someone who was often considered an apologist for *völkisch* and Nazi ideas. As we will see, Hauer's thinking is more complex than this. It seems to me unlikely, however, that Hauer was influenced here by Jung. In later years he even explicitly rejected Jung's doctrine of the archetypes, with its claim to universality. For a detailed discussion of these questions, see J.W. Hauer, *Der Yoga: ein indischer Weg zum Selbst* (Stuttgart: W. Kohlhammer, 1958), 419ff.

10. On the other hand, Gilles Quispel (another subsequent Eranos speaker) reports having been told by Fröbe of a trip to England that she had made together with Jung in 1930. There, she said, they had met G.R.S. Mead (already mentioned as a leading Theosophist, but by then no longer actively involved), whose *Fragments of a Faith Forgotten* was very highly valued by Jung. See John Cooper, "Professor Gilles Quispel," *Theosophical History* 6 (1995), 202.

11. There were certain differences of opinion between the two, including the fact that Assagioli considered Jung's theoretical approach to be scientifically too narrow. See Roberto Assagioli, *Jung and Psychosynthesis* (New York: Psychosynthesis Research Foundation, 1967). On the other hand, Paola Giovetti's (admittedly rather uncritical) biography, *Roberto Assagioli*, 29ff., describes the relationship between the two men as being extremely friendly. The book quotes a letter from Assagioli to Jung, dated 18 January 1946, which appears to confirm this. Furthermore, in the early days Jung also used the term psychosynthesis in contrast to psychoanalysis to describe his work—the very name later adopted by Assagioli for his method of therapy.

12. This is evident from a document concerning Eranos, written by Fröbe in 1952, in which she mentions the acceptances of Heinrich Zimmer, Jakob Hauer, Erwin Rousselle, Friedrich Heiler, and Rudolf Otto. On the other hand, in the already mentioned unpublished document of Fröbe regarding the case of W.R. Corti, she writes that she approached Jung with the program drawn up by her and Otto, and that Jung "immediately promised his cooperation."

13. Eliade, *Journal I, 1945–1955*, 165ff.

14. On the subject of Cary Baynes, see William McGuire, "Jelliffe: His Correspondence with Sigmund Freud and C.G. Jung, in John C. Burnham, *Jelliffe: American Psychoanalyst and Physician* (Chicago, IL: University of Chicago Press, 1983), 269 n.2. Details about her life are to be found in William McGuire's *Bollingen* and in the essay by Paul Bishop, "The Members of Jung's Seminar on Zarathustra," *Spring* 56 (1994), 103. In an unpublished letter of 3 March 1954, Fröbe wrote to Cary Baynes: "You backed me up in all my difficulties with Jung, with my psychological work, which I have had to do alone, with matters in Eranos … You sent me the first $250 that you received for the *I Ching*. And so on. My memory is good and I have forgotten nothing. You have been the only woman friend I had in my life before I met Frau von Keller in 1937. She is the second."

15. This episode led to the so-called "Jung conflict," in which Fröbe tried to avoid her mentor Jung for a long time. In a letter of 7 September 1951 to Ximena Roelli, she even wrote that it was not until 1951 that she again had a conversation with Jung after he had behaved so "intolerably," in 1948. In connection with the ring affair she sought the psychological help of Erich Neumann, Leopold Szondi, and Alwine von Keller (information given to the author by Roelli).

16. Among the numerous biographies, the following provide a suitable introduction: A. Jaffé (ed.), *Memories, Dreams, Reflections*, Richard Winston and Clara Winston (trans.) (New York: Vintage Books, 1989). This is not, as often assumed, an autobiography but was processed by Aniela Jaffé. Also Sonu Shamdasani, *Jung and the Making of Modern Psychology: The Dream of a Science* (Cambridge: Cambridge University Press, 2003), 23ff. On the other hand, the Zurich analytical psychologist Alfred Ribi, in a letter to me of 13 December 2001, expresses the opinion that *Memories, Dreams, Reflections* is an "objective representation" of Jung's life. This was confirmed to him by Marie Luise von Franz, probably Jung's closest pupil. See also Gerhard Wehr, *Jung: A Biography*, D.M. Weeks (trans.) (Boston, MA: Shambhala, 2001).

17. See Philipp Wolff-Windegg, "C.G. Jung: Bachofen, Burckhardt and Basel," *Spring* (1976), 146. Patricia Dixon shows in her study, *Nietzsche and Jung: Sailing a Deeper Night* (New York: Peter Lang, 1999), what astonishingly

close parallels there are between the thought of Jung and Nietzsche. This is seen particularly in the theme, which was so important for Jung, of the search for wholeness in the modern world. For Nietzsche as well the decadence of modernity can be attributed to its one-sidedly rational perspective.

18. See her essay "Comments on a Doctoral Thesis," in *C.G.Jung Speaking. Interviews and Encounters*, William McGuire and J.F.C. Hull (eds) (Princeton, NJ: Princeton University Press, 1977), 205ff. In the same book is a report (pp. 273ff) about his meeting with the pianist Margaret Tilly, which sharply contradicts the widespread misconception that Jung had no interest in music.

19. Schopenhauer, he said, had showed him that man possesses a force (the "will"), which is not the same as the ego. The will is the libido, which is the dynamic force behind the psyche.

20. Jung expressly assigned the beginning of psychoanalysis to a German scientist and philosopher of the Romantic period, Carl Gustav Carus. It was he and not Freud who first coined the term "the unconscious."

21. The German philosophical tradition is of utmost importance in the case of Jung. Jack Herbert, "C.G. Jung and the German Tradition," in *Inward Lies the Way: German Thought and the Nature of Mind*, Stephen Cross and Jack Herbert (eds), 111–36 (London: Temenos Academy, 2008) is particularly insightful in this regard.

22. Jay Sherry, *Carl Gustav Jung: Avant-Garde Conservative* (New York: Palgrave Macmillan, 2010). Interestingly, its cover shows a portrait of Jung drawn by the famous Maronite Christian mystic Khalil Gibran, with whom Jung became acquainted through Beatrice Hinkle, ostensibly the first analytical psychologist in the United States.

23. See Stefanie Zumstein-Preiswerk, *C.G.Jungs Medium. Die Geschichte der Helly Preiswerk* (Munich: Kindler Verlag, 1975). F.X. Charet even claims, in his work *Spiritualism and the Foundations of C.G. Jung's Psychology* (Albany, NY: SUNY Press, 1993) that only in the light of these spiritualistic researches can Jung's psychological approach really be understood, and that these investigations contributed an important influence on his central concepts. Charet may well have been mistaken here, as Sonu Shamdasani emphasizes in his letter to me of 8 December 2000. At any rate, Jung was not only preoccupied with spiritualism and occult matters in general; his esoteric interests were much wider. Early on, as is recorded in Jaffé, *Memories, Dreams, Reflections*, he read Justinus Kerner, Joseph von Goerres, and seven volumes of Emmanuel Swedenborg's work. Swedenborg probably exercised even further influence on him, as James Webb plausibly argues in his book *The Occult Establishment*, 389ff.. His astrological interests are dealt with in detail in Bair, *Jung*. There are also links between Jung and the occult teacher G.I. Gurdjieff. For instance, Maurice Nicoll, one of Gurdjieff's leading followers, underwent a training with Jung (see Beryl Pogson, *Maurice Nicoll: A Portrait* [New York: Fourth Way Books, 1987]). Even after Nicoll's departure from Zurich they remained in contact—see the letter of condolence from Emma Jung to Nicoll's widow dated 7 December 1953, reproduced in *A Wakeful Wife* (Utrecht: Eureka Editions, 1999; limited edition of 50 copies), 88ff., in which Emma Jung speaks of several meetings having taken place. Jung's interests must also have extended to magic, as one can assume from a glance at the catalogue of his library. He possessed, for example, four volumes of the important periodical *The Occult Review* and, surprisingly, all five volumes of *Saturngnosis*, a rare and more or less internal publication of the Fraternitas Saturni, the most important group in the German-speaking realm for ritual and sexual magic. Furthermore, in a letter of 13 October 1953 to John Symonds, literary executor of Aleister Crowley, probably the most famous "black magician" of the twentieth century, Jung indicated that he knew Symonds' biography of Crowley, *The Great Beast*. See C.G. Jung, *Briefe II (1946–1955)* (Olten: Walter Verlag, 1972), 350.

24. A good summary of the differences between Freud's and Jung's views is to be found in the essay by Jacques Cazenave, "De la psychologie freudienne aux théories de Jung," *Le Disque Vert* (1955), 302–16.

25. Andrew Samuels, *Jung und seine Nachfolger* (Stuttgart: Klett, 1989), 466.

26. The question of how strongly Jung was influenced by gnosis is dealt with by the analytical psychologist Alfred Ribi in the book that he wrote under the inspiration of Gilles Quispel, *Die Suche nach den eigenen Wurzeln: Die Bedeutung von Gnosis, Hermetik und Alchemie für C.G. Jung und Marie-Louise von Franz und deren Einfluss auf das moderne Verständnis dieser Disziplin* (Bern: Peter Lang, 1999). Whether Jung was in fact a "Gnostic" is a matter of controversy. Various arguments for and against are cited in detail by Robert A. Segal in the foreword to his anthology *The Gnostic Jung* (Princeton, NJ: Princeton University Press, 1992). An unambiguously positive answer to this question is given by Stephan A. Hoeller, who describes himself as a Gnostic and esotericist, in his book *The Gnostic Jung and the Seven Sermons to the Dead* (Wheaton, IL: Theosophical Publishing House, 1985). Equally affirmative is Gilles Quispel in his review essay "How Jung became a Gnostic," *San Francisco Jung Institute Library Journal* 13(2) (1994), 47–50. Quispel is of the opinion, however, that this characterization is only accurate from 1951, when Jung came into contact with the Russian Orthodox priest Zacharias. At the same time the entire Jung circle was deeply influenced by a series of articles entitled "Der werdende Gott" [The God becoming], written by Walter Robert Corti, whom we encounter repeatedly in the history of Eranos.

27. His name was Ochwiay Biano and he belonged to the council of elders of Taos Pueblo. In his book *C.G. Jung and the Sioux Tradition: Dreams, Visions, Nature and the Primitive* (New Orleans, LA: Spring Journal Books, 2009) the Native American scholar Vine Deloria Jr. expresses the opinion that the chief led C.G. Jung in his unconscious (this can be read in Jung's own description of the visit in Jaffé (ed.), *Memories, Dreams, Reflections*) and thereby triggered a series of insights and emotions that supposedly influenced Jung throughout his life.

Accordingly the book consistently points out the parallels that exist between the psychology of Jung and Native American wisdom.

28. Laurens van der Post, *Jung and the Story of Our Time* (London: Hogarth Press, 1976), 48. As Van der Post recounts, Olga Fröbe also told him of this marvellous natural talent Jung possessed. At Eranos it often came about that people from the street above the lecture hall came down to ask who had laughed so wonderfully. And Heinrich Berl writes of Jung in *Gespräche mit berühmten Zeitgenossen*, 94: "A short conversation—and a single laugh. Jung is the psychoanalyst without complexes. For me the single psychoanalytic riddle."

29. Eliade, *Journal I, 1945–1955*, 113. Other people also knew of Jung's predilection for good food. Stella Corbin, wife of the long-standing Eranos lecturer Henry Corbin, once presented him with some caviar.

30. New York Association for Analytical Psychology and Analytical Psychology Club of New York, *Carl Gustav Jung (1875–1961): A Memorial Meeting, New York, 1 December 1961* (New York: Analytical Psychology Club of New York, 1962), 4ff.

31. *Ibid.*, 26.

32. On this theme, see the already mentioned interview with Ximena Roelli de Angulo in McGuire and Hull (eds), *Jung Speaking*, 206.

33. See Petteri Pietikäinen, *C.G. Jung and the Psychology of Symbolic Forms* (Helsinki: Annales Academiae Scientiarium Fennicae, 1999).

34. Carl Gustav Jung, *The Red Book. Liber Novus*, Sonu Shamdasani (ed.) (New York: W.W. Norton, 2009).

35. Wolfgang Giegerich, "*Liber Novus*, That is, The New Bible. A First Analysis of C.G. Jung's *Red Book*," *Spring* 83 (2010), 361–411, esp. 362.

36. Shamdasani, *Jung and the Making of Modern Psychology*, 22. This book must be regarded as one of the best-researched works on the emergence of Jungian psychology.

37. *Ibid.*, 351.

38. *Ibid.*, 22.

39. In 1935 he asked Fröbe, who was visiting London, to bring back a lecturer from the Society for Psychical Research to give a report on the latest developments in parapsychology. Parapsychological phenomena continued to interest him to a high degree even later in his life. See, for example, his foreword to Fanny Moser, *Spuk: Irrglaube oder Wahrglaube? Eine Frage an die Menschheit*, vol. 1 (Baden bei Zürich: Gyr-Verlag, 1950).

40. Jung is often falsely regarded as a trailblazer for oriental thinking in the West. His attitude was, in fact, much more complex, and he rejected the unquestioning adoption of "foreign" ideas. Possibly this can be attributed to an attitude which one might in a certain sense call *völkisch* and which values the rootedness of culture and beliefs in a particular territory. For example, in his essay "Yoga und der Westen" (in *Gesammelte Werke*, vol. 11, 576), he wrote: "I say to anyone I can: Study yoga. You will learn an infinite amount from it, but do not apply it." On the question of Jung and oriental spirituality, see the outstanding introduction by J.J. Clarke in his edited collection of those writings of Jung that deal with this issue, published under the title *Jung and Eastern Thought* (London: Routledge, 1994). Perhaps the most thorough treatment by an orientalist of everything that Jung said on this subject is Luis O. Gómez' critical yet empathic essay, "Oriental Wisdom and the Cure of Souls: Jung and the Indian East," in *Curators of the Buddha: The Study of Buddhism under Colonialism*, Donald R. Lopez, Jr. (ed.) (Chicago, IL: University of Chicago Press, 1995), 197–250. As regards Jung and Zen Buddhism, it is worth mentioning a book by the Eranos lecturer Ernst Benz, *Zen in westlicher Sicht: Zen-Buddhismus—Zen Snobbismus* (Weilheim: O.W. Barth, 1962). This work also deals with the ideas of Rudolf Otto and Friedrich Heiler on the subject of Zen. On the subject of Jung and India, see also Christine Maillard, "L'Apport de l'Inde à la pensée de Carl Gustav Jung," in *L'Inde inspiratrice*, Michel Hulin and Christine Maillard (eds) (Strasbourg: Presses universitaires de Strasbourg, 1996), 155–68.

41. A particularly interesting critique of Jung's alchemical conceptions by two American historians of chemistry is to be found in Lawrence M. Principe and William R. Newman, "Some Problems with the Historiography of Alchemy," in *Secrets of Nature: Astrology and Alchemy in Early Modern Europe*, William R. Newman and Anthony Grafton (eds) (Cambridge, MA: MIT Press, 2001), 401–12. In his book *The Quest for the Phoenix: Spiritual Alchemy and Rosicrucianism in the Work of Count Michael Maier (1569–1622)* (Berlin: Walter de Gruyter, 2003), 9–34, Hereward Tilton vehemently rejects this critique in turn.

42. Sanford L. Drob, *Kabbalistic Metaphors: Jewish Mystical Themes in Ancient and Modern Thought* (Northvale, NJ: Jason Aronson, 2000), 290.

43. Sanford L. Drob, *Kabbalistic Visions: C.G. Jung and Jewish Mysticism* (New Orleans, LA: Spring Journal Books, 2010).

44. *Ibid.*, 123–60.

45. *Ibid.*, 207–27.

46. A comprehensive analysis of the impact of Jung at Eranos is to be found in Gian Piero Quaglino, Augusto Romano, and Riccardo Bernardini, eds. *Carl Gustav Jung a Eranos: 1933–1952*.

47. In a letter of 2 August 1956 to her benefactor Paul Mellon, Olga Fröbe, in attempting to define Eranos, speaks unambiguously of "the conception of a rebirth of humanism."

48. Marie-Louise von Franz, *C.G. Jung: Sein Mythos in unserer Zeit* (Frauenfeld: Verlag Huber, 1972), 8.

49. Alluding playfully to this in a letter of 23 January 1933, he calls Fröbe "ehrwürdige Pflegemutter" [revered mother

nurse]. On 23 January 1935 he asks her again whether the March weather in Ascona promises to be good, as he has to go south because of his catarrh.

50. However, according to handwritten notes by the subsequent director of Eranos, Adolf Portmann, Fröbe had been in contact with Rudolf Otto since about 1928. Nevertheless, a certain amount of unclarity on this issue remains. In the Eranos archive at Moscia there is a guest book, beginning in 1930, in which speakers and participants at the meetings could enter their names. This book, which is reproduced as an appendix to Riccardo Bernardini's dissertation, *Da Monte Verità a Eranos*, already bears the name Eranos, which, as I have said, Fröbe claimed to have first heard from Otto in 1932—a claim that up to now has been generally accepted. Was the book perhaps later re-bound and the name Eranos inserted? To a layman's eye, this is not apparent from the binding. Or was the title of the guest book perhaps initially left blank? Alternatively, had Fröbe already spoken with Otto before 1930, which seems to me improbable, this guest book could also provide a further indication that Fröbe launched Eranos in 1930 and not 1933.

51. All of the correspondence mentioned here between Rudolf Otto and Fröbe is preserved in the University Library, Marburg.

52. Here it should not be forgotten that Rudolf Otto served from 1913 as a delegate of the National Liberal Party in the Prussian Parliament. He founded the Interreligious League of Mankind in response to the nationalistic catastrophe of the First World War. See his essay "Religiöser Menschheitsbund" [Interreligious league] in *Deutsche Politik* 9(6) (1921), 234–8, in which he calls for an "awakening of a common world conscience" and a "struggle against any form of historical materialism," since the latter postulates an "allegedly inflexible mechanism of blind social laws" that leaves no room for freedom of belief. Originally Otto wanted his friend Richard Wilhelm to be secretary general of the organization, but the latter declined. Another member was D.T. Suzuki, later a speaker at Eranos. See Gregory D. Alles, "Rudolf Otto and the Politics of Utopia," in *Religion* 21 (1991), 235–56. Besides the Interreligious League of Mankind, Otto also created an important collection of works on religion at Marburg.

53. Later there arose tension between Otto and Grabert. In a letter of 10 April 1936 to Carola Barth, Otto writes of Grabert: "What a piece of luck that Hauer has parted company with satellites like him." Grabert, rightly or wrongly, evidently felt he had been stalled or obstructed for too long by Hauer in his chosen academic career. For Hauer, however, the separation was a great disappointment. See Horst Junginger, *Von der philosophischen zur völkischen Religionswissenschaft: Das Fach Religionswissenschaft an der Universität Tübingen von der Mitte des 19. Jahrhunderts bis zum Ende des Dritten Reiches* (Stuttgart: Franz Steiner Verlag, 1999), 119ff.

54. See especially the pamphlet by Herbert Grabert, *Religiöse Verständigung: Wege zur Begegnung der Religionen bei Nicolaus Cusanus, Schleiermacher, Rudolf Otto und J.W. Hauer* (Leipzig: C.F. Hirschfeld, 1932). Herbert Grabert, who for "inner reasons" had shied away from service in the Church, was at first anti-Nazi in his attitude; he even pilloried Rosenberg's racial dogmas and the idea of the Aryan race as self-glorification. Then, however, from 1933 to 1936 he was actively involved with Jakob Wilhelm Hauer and his "Deutsche Glaubensbewegung" [German belief-movement] as well as playing a leading role in the journal *Deutscher Glaube* [German belief]. In 1936 he had already clearly made the transition from "religious to national socialism" and founded with Hans Kurth the so-called *Deutschgläubige Bewegung* (with a similar meaning to Hauer's movement but differently worded) in order to steer a more emphatically German-nationalistic course than Hauer. After working with the *Ahnenerbe* [Ancestral heritage], founded by Heinrich Himmler as a research organization of the SS, he took a doctorate at the University of Würzburg in 1941. In 1945, after a long de-nazification procedure, he was classified as a "*Mitläufer ohne Maßnahmen*" [fellow traveller exempt from disciplinary measures], but could not any longer teach at a German university. After being obliged to take several provisional jobs in order to support his large family, he founded the Grabert-Verlag in Tübingen, specializing in historical revisionist and New Right literature, which is run today by his son Wigbert Grabert. See the account of his life in the chapter "Herbert Grabert (1901–1978) und Traugott Konstantin Österreich (1880–1949)," in Horst Junginger, *Von der philosophischen zur völkischen Religionswissenschaft*, 114–23ff., as well as the more uniformly critical essay by Martin Finkenberger, "Herbert Grabert: Vom völkischen Religionswissenschaftler zum Geschichtsrevisionisten," *Spirita* 1 (1997), 26–7. Lastly, an entire book on Grabert stretching to the present day has appeared under the editorship of Martin Finkenberger and Horst Junginger. Its title, which is too partisan and polemical for my taste, is *Im Dienste der Lügen: Herbert Grabert (1901–1978) und seine Verlage* (Aschaffenburg: Alibri Verlag, 2004) [In the service of lies. Herbert Grabert (1901–1978) and his publishing houses]. Of note therein are the contributions by Horst Junginger, which deal with Grabert as a *völkisch* scholar of religion and the Tübingen school of "*völkisch* religious studies."

55. McGuire, *Bollingen*, 146.

56. Otto's Marburg colleague and friend Friedrich Heiler wrote to Fröbe on 30 July 1933, that is just before the meeting, "I had already feared that Professor Otto would decline. His physical and mental state of health is very changeable. I spoke to him recently, and he said it is quite impossible for him to travel."

57. At the same time Fröbe visited Friedrich Heiler in Marburg and invited him to Eranos. More on this subject in the section on Heiler.

58. His distinction is indicated by the book that was issued in his honour: Karl Ludwig Schmidt (ed.), *Festgabe für Adolf Diessmann zum 60. Geburtstag, 7. November 1926* (Tübingen: J.C.B. Mohr, 1927).

59. The standard treatment of this subject is Hubert Treiber, "Der 'Eranos': Das Glanzstück im Heidelberger Mythenkranz?," in *Asketischer Protestantismus und der "Geist" des modernen Kapitalismus: Max Weber und Ernst Troeltsch*, Wolfgang Schluchter and Friedrich Wilhelm Graf (eds) (Tübingen: Mohr Siebeck, 2005), 75–153.

60. Marianne Weber, *Max Weber: Ein Lebensbild* (Heidelberg: Lambert Schneider, 1950), 456.

61. See also Gesa von Essen, "Max Weber und die Kunst der Geselligkeit," in *Heidelberg im Schnittpunkt intellektueller Kreise*, Hubert Treiber and Karol Sauerland (eds) (Opladen: Westdeutscher Verlag, 1995), 464ff.

62. Hubert Treiber, "Der 'Eranos': Das Glanzstück im Heidelberger Mythenkranz?"

63. See also Karl Kerényi, "Was bedeutet der Name Eranos?," in *Du* (April 1955), 39ff.

64. I wish to thank Riccardo Bernardini for precise scholarly evidence on this matter.

65. See the essay by Gregory D. Alles, "Rudolf Otto (1869–1937)," in *Klassiker der Religionswissenschaft: Von Friedrich Schleiermacher bis Mircea Eliade*, Axel Michaels (ed.) (Munich: C.H. Beck, 1997), 198–210, which gives an admirable summary of Otto's life and the history of his influence. A very empathic study of Rudolf Otto has also emerged from the philosopher of religion Harry Oldmeadow, who dedicates a long chapter to him in his book *Mediations: Essays on Religious Pluralism & the Perennial Philosophy* (San Rafael, CA: Sophia Perennis, 2008), 44–63, emphasizing above all Otto's deep understanding of Eastern wisdom.

66. See the fundamental study by Todd A. Gooch about Otto's achievement and the genesis of his thinking, *The Numinous and Modernity: An Interpretation of Rudolf Otto's Philosophy of Religion* (Berlin: Walter de Gruyter, 2000).

67. In his obituary "A la mort de Rudolf Otto," in Mircea Eliade, *Une nouvelle philosophie de la lune* (Paris: L'Herne, 2001), 123, Eliade elevated him to "the most popular philosopher of religion of the twentieth century" and praised him above all as a great mediator between East and West.

68. On the particular style of religious scholarship in Marburg, which was so markedly influenced by Rudolf Otto and Friedrich Heiler, see the third part, "Allgemeine Religionsgeschichte in der Weimarer Republik," in Elisabeth Hamacher, *Gershom Scholem und die Allgemeine Religionsgeschichte* (Berlin: Walter de Gruyter, 1999), 73–104. The hallmark of this school is a process of listening inwardly in a spirit of empathy and intuition, with the help of which one aims to understand the *a priori*, "irrational" core of religion as a holistic entity. With this method, also applicable in other disciplines, Otto exerted an influence that went beyond his own departmental colleagues and reached much wider circles, including some that were to a certain extent esoteric. See, for example, Frater Harold Hudson II, "Rudolf Otto and the Concept of the Numinous," in the *Transactions 1983 and 1984 of the Metropolitan College of the Societas Rosicruciana in Anglia*, 1–15.

69. On this subject, see also Ansgar Paus, *Religiöser Erkenntnisgrund: Herkunft und Wesen der Aprioritheorie Rudolf Ottos* (Leiden: Brill, 1966).

70. But only after he had worked through the rational side of religion in his work *Kantisch-Fries'sche Religionsphilosophie und ihre Anwendung auf die Theologie*. On the relationship between Otto and Fries, see Alles, "Rudolf Otto (1869–1937)," 201ff.

71. See Hans G. Kippenberg, *Die Entdeckung der Religionsgeschichte: Religionswissenschaft und Moderne* (Munich: C.H. Beck, 1997), 252.

72. Heinz Röhr, "Rudolf Otto: ein Jahrhundertphänomen," *Spirita* 2 (1988), 23–7.

73. *Ibid.*

74. J. Wach, *Types of Religious Experience* (Chicago, IL: University of Chicago Press, 1951), 211.

75. Todd A. Gooch describes *The Holy* as "probably the most widely read German theological work of the twentieth century," *The Numinous and Modernity*, 1. Mircea Eliade says in his obituary of Otto: "Only he who has read this extraordinary book *The Holy* knows the incredibly masterly way in which Otto has analysed and explained many of the dark aspects of the religious experience." Mircea Eliade, "La moarte, lui Rudolf Otto", *Revista Fundatiilor Regal* 4 (1937), 676–9. However, the history of the reception of this work has continued much further. See, for example, Hubert Siewert, "Zurück zum Heiligen?," *Spirita: Zeitschrift für Religionswissenschaft* 2 (April 1988), 27–30. See also Carsten Colpe (ed.), *Die Diskussion um das "Heilige"* (Darmstadt: Wissenschaftliche Buchgesellschaft, 1977), and his *Über das Heilige: Versuch, seiner Verkennung kritisch vorzubeugen* (Frankfurt: Anton Hain Meisenheim, 1990). Otto's book is, incidentally, still in print. It has been translated into many languages.

76. With the subtitle *Reden an die Gebildeten unter ihren Verächtern*. See also the edition of *Reden über die Religion* with a commentary by A. Messer (Stuttgart: Stecker und Schröder, 1923). Messer also perceived that his era (not long before Eranos) was characterized by a longing for religion and at the same time a prejudice that religion was not compatible with modern science and education—a prejudice for which Schleiermacher could provide the best remedy.

77. Otto was equally interested in China and visited Richard Wilhelm in 1912 at the latter's missionary post in Tsingtau. There soon developed a heartfelt friendship between the two men.

78. Subtitled *Vergleich und Unterscheidung zur Wesensdeutung*, Gustav Mensching (ed.) (Munich: C.H. Beck, 1971).

79. Rudolf Otto, *Aufsätze das Numinose betreffend* (Gotha: Leopold Klotz Verlag, 1923).

80. Benz, *Zen in westlicher Sicht*, 7.

81. Schuej Ohasama and August Faust (eds), *Zen: Der lebendige Buddhismus in Japan. Ausgewählte Stücke des Zen-Textes* (Gotha-Stuttgart: Friedrich Andreas Perthes, 1925).
82. In Herbert Grabert, *Religiöse Verständigung*, 67.
83. Rudolf Otto and Gregory Alles, *Autobiographical and Social Essays* (Berlin: Walter de Gruyter, 1996).
84. It was in this publication that the young Max Dessoir coined the term "parapsychology," as Peter Mulacz has kindly informed me.
85. See Norbert Klatt, *Theosophie und Anthroposophie: Neue Aspekte zu ihrer Geschichte aus dem Nachlaß von Wilhelm Hübbe-Schleiden (1846–1916) mit einer Auswahl von 81 Briefen* (Göttingen: Eigenverlag, 1993), 47ff.

5. The First Eranos Meeting: An Idea Comes to Life

1. See the guest book in the appendix to Riccardo Bernardini, *Da Monte Verità a Eranos*. This means that there was a further sharp increase in the number of participants, which had already been increasing constantly since 1930.
2. In a letter to Jakob Wilhelm Hauer of 31 August 1933 (now in the Jung archive at the Swiss Technical University, Zurich) Jung described the audience at the first meeting as "very mixed, with an unmistakeably Theosophical undercurrent." He added that these people are accustomed "to living on spiritual credit."
3. See the letter from Olga Fröbe to Friedrich Heiler dated 28 May 1933.
4. Ample opportunity to question the lecturers is now allowed at the meetings that still continue under the auspices of the Eranos Foundation in Moscia-Ascona, as well as those of the Verein zur Förderung der wissenschaftlichen Tagungen von Eranos led by Erik Hornung and Andreas Schweizer, both of which organizations see themselves as carrying on the work of Olga Fröbe. The same practice was followed at the conferences of the Amici di Eranos, which have in the meantime unfortunately been discontinued.
5. Italian only became a regular medium in the 1990s, although before that Raffaele Pettazzoni for one had used Italian. There were no interpreters present.
6. Anthony, *The Valkyries*, 70.
7. In the psychological sense of feelings such as love, attraction, hate or fear, which are "projected" on to another person, even though that person is not the cause of such feelings.
8. Heinrich Zimmer's "Notizen zu einem Lebenslauf" was first published posthumously in the journal *Merkur* 7(1) (1953) and incorporated into his collection of essays, *Die indische Weltmutter* (Frankfurt: Insel Verlag, 1980), 233–54, which also contains his Eranos lectures. See also Zimmer's essay "Dr. Jung's Impress on my Profession," in *Spring* 1 (1941): 104–5.
9. Jung, for his part, also wrote about his meetings with Zimmer, whom he described as a "puer aeternus." See Jaffé (ed.), *Memories, Dreams, Reflections*, appendix.
10. See the biographical foreword by Friedrich Wilhelm in Heinrich Zimmer, *Kunstform und Yoga im indischen Kultbild* (Frankfurt: Suhrkamp, 1987). The manuscripts left behind by Zimmer also included some biographical notes with further details about his life,. published by his wife Christiane in Henry R. Zimmer, *Two Papers* (New York: n.p., 1944).
11. On this subject the mythologist Joseph Campbell, an important figure for Eranos, during an interview with Michael McKnight, made the following comments in his usual effusive way: "Zimmer was brought up in a world of major scholarship—I mean that late nineteenth-century German scholarship that has not been equaled. It's basic to the whole thing—I don't care what subject you're interested in—those are the men who *did* it! They were the first professional scholars in the world. The Germans looked the field over and asked: what's to be done? and went in and did it." See Michael McKnight, "Elders and Guides: A Conversation with Joseph Campbell," *Parabola* 5(1) (1980), 57–65. This conversation was mainly about Heinrich Zimmer and therefore also contributed to the information given here.
12. *Ibid.*, 64.
13. Zimmer, "Notizen zu einem Lebenslauf," in *Die indische Weltmutter*, 237. Subsequent quotations from Zimmer are also taken from this document.
14. In fact he did not make the translations himself, as we know from Kathleen Taylor, *Sir John Woodroffe, Tantra and Bengal: "An Indian Soul in a European Body?"* (Richmond: Curzon Press, 2001).
15. He told Joseph Campbell: "I drank those in as a baby drinks in milk." See McKnight, "Elders and Guides," 60.
16. A nice example of this is Heinrich Zimmer's book *Der Weg zum Selbst* (Düsseldorf: Diederichs, [1944] 1976), which deals with the life of the Indian sage and holy man Sri Ramana Maharshi. C.G. Jung even contributed a foreword to the first edition of 1944, discussing the psychological problems of mysticism. In this foreword he shows his high regard for Zimmer, of whom he says: "In the process of our collaboration he afforded me invaluable insights into the eastern soul, not only through his rich expert knowledge but above all through the brilliant way in which he grasped the meaning of the Indian mythology." See C.G. Jung, *Gesammelte Werke*, vol. 11, 622.
17. "All his work was part of his life and his life was part of his work. The answers he found in dealing with religion were valid for himself." Thus writes his daughter Maya Rauch in her contribution "Heinrich Zimmer from a Daughter's Perspective," in *Heinrich Zimmer: Coming into His Own*, Case (ed.), 15–20. This book is a collection of

lectures given at a conference marking the hundredth anniversary of Zimmer's birth. The papers touch on many other aspects of his life and work.

18. Zimmer, "Notizen zu einem Lebenslauf," in *Die indische Weltmutter*, 250ff.

19. The Tantra expert Hugh Urban, who teaches at Ohio State University, calls Zimmer "an irrepressible romantic and dreamy idealist" who, although not always totally reliable, has had a formative influence on modern Indology. See Urban's *Tantra: Sex, Secrecy, Politics and Power in the Study of Religion* (Berkeley, CA: University of California Press, 2003), 169.

20. Heinrich Zimmer, "Zur Bedeutung des indischen Tantra Yoga," *Eranos Jahrbuch* 1 (1933), 9–94, esp. 54.

21. *Ibid.*, 50.

22. Heinrich Zimmer, *Philosophies of India* (Princeton, NJ: Princeton University Press, [1969] 1989).

23. Roger Lipsey, *Coomaraswamy: His Life and Work*, Bollingen Series LXXXIX (Princeton, NJ: Princeton University Press, 1977).

24. The two scholars of religion Florence Sandler and Darrell Reeck have even written: "He is a seeker after wisdom, an adept in his own scholarly way of Shiva ... or a reader of runes or symbols. He may be called, indeed, a comparative esotericist" (*The Masks of Joseph Campbell*, 3; quoted in Harry Oldmeadow, *Journeys East: 20th Century Western Encounters with Eastern Religious Traditions* [Bloomington, IN: World Wisdom, 2004], 105).

25. *Alchymie und Heilkunst* (Nuremberg: Hans Carl, [1936] 1948) and *Das Geheimnis der Adepten: Aufschlüsse über das Magisterium der Alchymie, die Bereitung der großen Arkana und den Weg zum Lapis Philosophorum* (Sersheim: Osirirs Verlag, 1956).

26. See Mirko Sladek and Maria Schütze, *Alexander von Bernus* (Nürnberg: Hans Carl, 1981), 131.

27. *Ibid.*, 131.

28. See Götz Diemann (ed.), *Die anthroposophischen Zeitschriften von 1903 bis 1985* (Stuttgart: Verlag Freies Geistesleben, 1987), 205–9. Alexandr von Bernus also published several political articles in *Das Reich* on the state of Germany, including one entitled "Gleichheit, Freiheit, Brüderlichkeit" (*Das Reich* [January 1919], 469–83). This essay was a reaction to the Munich Republic, which did not in his view represent the desired revolution for Germany.

29. As the adopted son of Alexander Friedrich Freiherr von Bernus, he became proprietor of the residence in 1908. See the unpaginated historical appendix to *Stift Neuburg: Eine Gedichtfolge von Alexander von Bernus mit zehn Holzschnitten von Joachim Lutz* (Mannheim: Gengenbach & Hahn, 1926).

30. See Rainer Maria Rilke, Hermann Hesse, and Friedrich Schnack, *Worte der Freundschaft für Alexander von Bernus: Zum siebzigsten Geburtstag* (Nuremberg: Hans Carl, 1949).

31. Jung described Dacqué as a kind of martyr of the dominant *Zeitgeist*. See the lecture he gave in 1931 at the Kulturbund in Vienna, "Die Entschleierung der Seele," now included in C.G. Jung, *Gesammelte Werke*, vol. 8, 389. I am grateful to Jay Sherry for pointing out this reference.

32. See Friedrich Wilhelm, "Gottfried Benns Briefe an den Indologen Heinrich Zimmer," in *Benn Jahrbuch 2*, Joachim Dyck, Holger Hof and Peter D. Krause (eds) (Stuttgart: Klett-Cotta, 2004), 15–34. Unfortunately only Benn's letters are extant. Those of Zimmer cannot be found.

33. Gottfried Benn, "Goethe und die Naturwissenschaften," *Die neue Rundschau* 43(4) (1932).

34. Wilhelm, "Gottfried Benns Briefe an den Indologen Heinrich Zimmer," 19.

35. Gottfried Benn, *Briefe an F.W. Oelze 1932–1945* (Frankfurt: Fischer Taschenbuch, 1986), 64.

36. At Heidelberg University Zimmer was known as "Sprech-Zimmer," a pun on his surname (meaning "room") and on the German word *Sprechzimmer* (literally "speaking room," meaning a "consulting room"). See Wilhelm, "Gottfried Benns Briefe an den Indologen Heinrich Zimmer."

37. Heinrich Zimmer, *Ewiges Indien: Leitmotive indischen Daseins* (Postdam: Müller & Kiepenhauer, 1930), 159 n.16.

38. See Barone *et al.* (eds), *Pioniere, Poeten, Professoren*, 211.

39. He was given a doctorate *summa cum laude* for his translation of and commentary on the *Tosepha-Traktat Pesachim*. My information on Rousselle's life has been taken from Harmut Walravens, "Erwin Rousselle: Notizen zum Leben und Werk," in *Monumenta Serica 41* (1993), 283–98. See also Gahlings, *Hermann Graf Keyserling*, 150ff., esp. 187.

40. In a letter of 15 March 1947 to Jung, Rousselle writes, "I will never forget how the Taoists in China, who were no Christians, but were mystics, made me vow, at the initiation marking the start of my meditation training, that I would hold fast until death to the Christianity into which I had been born."

41. Rousselle was a Freemason, although it is not clear when he was initiated. See the commentary by Br. Otto Wolfskehl in *II. Fragebuch* of the Große Landesloge von Deutschland (Grand National Lodge of Freemasons in Germany) (p. 1). Rousselle also wrote a commentary to this *Fragebuch*, which is printed in *Zirkelkorrespondenz* 107(10) (1979), 359–80.

42. Heiler was in fact not a theologian by academic background, but after intensive private studies and following his conversion to Protestantism in 1920 he was given a post in the theological faculty of the Philipps University, obtaining also the right to hold services and give sermons. Later he was even ordained priest and subsequently bishop within the so-called *Hochkirchliche Vereinigung* (High Church Union). His aim throughout his life was to promote "Protestant Catholicism" (communication from Uwe Bredehorn, 4 October 2000).

43. See Hans Hartog, *Evangelische Katholizität: Weg und Vision Friedrich Heilers* (Mainz: Matthias-Grünewald-Verlag, 1995), 90.

44. See Michael Pye, "Friedrich Heiler (1892–1967), in Michaels (ed.), *Klassiker der Religionswissenschaft*, 280.

45. All the Heiler correspondence quoted here is to be found in his papers (Ms 999) in the University Library, Marburg.

46. On the friendship between Rudolf Otto and the Swedish pastor and religious scholar Birger Forell, as well as the latter's efforts in helping Germans who had suffered damage in the war, see Martin Kraatz, "Birger Forell 1893–1993," *Alma Mater Philippina* (Summer 1994), 4–8.

47. Annemarie Schimmel, *Auf den Spuren der Muslime: Mein Leben zwischen den Kulturen* (Freiburg: Herder, 2002), 33.

48. *Das Gebet in der Mystik: Eine religionspsychologische Untersuchung* (Munich: Ernst Reinhardt, 1918). The work appeared as a regular book publication in the same year and with the same publisher under the title *Das Gebet: Eine religionspsychologische Untersuchung*.

49. See Friedrich Heiler, *Sâdhu Sundar Singh: Ein Apostel des Ostens und Westens* (Munich: Ernst Reinhardt, [1924] 1925) and Heiler's defence of Sundar Singh, *Apostel oder Betrüger: Dokumente zum Sadhu-Streit* (Basel: Friedrich Reinhardt, 1925). See also Oskar Pfister, *Die Legende Sundar Singhs: Eine auf Enthüllungen protestantischer Augenzeugen in Indien gegründete religionspsychologische Untersuchung* (Bern: Paul Haupt, 1926). Sundar Singh must have been a decidedly charismatic personality, who gave the impression of being in daily contact with God. This emerges very vividly in the work by the woman missionary A. Parker, *Le Sâdhu Sundar Singh* (Toulouse: Société d'Edition de Toulouse, 1926); unfortunately I have only been able to obtain the French version. See also the entry in Kurt Galling (ed.), *Die Religion in Geschichte und Gegenwart: Handwörterbuch für Theologie und Religionswissenschaft*, 3rd rev. edn (Tübingen: J.C.B Mohr [Paul Siebeck], 1986), vol. 6, 562ff. The article points out that, in discussing the controversy about Sundar Singh's credibility, one should not forget that, in the simple Indian village from which he came, myths, visions, and "real" life were easily intermingled. See also Sâdhu Sundar Singh, *Gesammelte Schriften*, translated with commentary by Friso Melzer, 3rd edition (Stuttgart: Evangelischer Missionsverlag, 1953).

50. Alber Goetz (ed.), *Der 300jährige Maharishi vom Kailas als Prophet biblischer Wahrheiten: Nach authentischen Dokumenten des Professor Heilers und glaubwürdigen Augenzeugenberichten von Sadhu Sundar Singh* (Hamburg: "Mehr Licht" Verlag, n.d. [probably late 1930s]); see esp. 12, 17.

51. Olaf Räderer, "Dr. Herbert Frietsche: Konstitutioneller Grenzgänger und Grenzüberschreiter (1911–1960)," Part 2, in *Gnostika* 37 (2007), 57.

52. See his essay "Die Religionsgeschichte als Wegbereiterin für die Zusammenarbeit der Religionen: Acht Studien," in *Grundfragen der Religionswissenschaft*, Mircea Eliade and Joseph M. Kitagawa (eds), 40–74 (Salzburg: Otto Müller Verlag, 1963). Most of the contributions in this volume are from Eranos speakers.

53. Ernst Benz, "Einige Erinnerungen an Ernesto Buonaiuti (1881–1946)," in *Zeitschrift für Religions- und Geistesgeschichte* 28 (1976), 167.

54. See Giorgio Levi della Vida, *Fantasmi ritrovati* (Venice: Neri Pozza Editore, 1966), 129. In these memoirs the orientalist Levi della Vida gives a remarkably vivid and detailed description of his friendship with Buonaiuti and of the latter's difficult life (pp. 127–54). On Buonaiuti's life see also the sympathetic introduction by Ernst Benz to Ernesto Buonaiuti, *Die exkommunizierte Kirche*, edited and introduced by Ernst Benz (Zurich: Rhein Verlag, 1966), 9–55. This volume contains all Buonaiuti's Eranos lectures in a new translation, as those published in the Eranos volumes were in parts unintelligible.

55. In this connection, see his influential book *Gioacchino da Fiore—I tempi—la vita—il messaggio* (Cosenza: Lionello Giordano, [1931] 1984). However, in his extensively documented introduction, Antonio Crocco of the University of Salerno points out that Buonaiuti, in his enthusiasm and reforming zeal, repeatedly reads his own ideas and wishes into the words of Joachim of Fiore.

56. See Bernardino Greco's detailed work *Ketzer oder Prophet?: Evangelium und Kirche bei dem Modernisten Ernesto Buonaiuti (1881–1946)* (Zurich: Benziger Verlag, 1979). Significantly, the foreword to the German edition was written by Hans Küng, who himself lost his teaching position on account of "modernistic" aberrations in later years. See also Ernesto Buonaiuti, "Die Botschaft Joachim von Floris und die franziskanische 'Religio,'" in *Deo omnia unum. Eine Sammlung von Aufsätzen Friedrich Heiler zum 50. Geburtstage dargebracht*, Christel Matthias Schröder (ed.) (Munich: Ernst Reinhardt, 1942), 200–211.

57. *Ibid.*, 196.

58. Ernst Benz, introduction to Ernesto Buonaiuti: *Die exkommunizierte Kirche*, 21.

59. Julius Evola, "L' 'apostolo' Buonaiuti e la chiesa romana," in *La Nobiltà della Stirpe*, April 1933. Reprinted in Julius Evola, *La Nobiltà della Stirpe, La Difesa della Razza*, edited by Gian Franco Lami (Rome: Fondazione Julius Evola, 2002), 104–9.

60. This situation also had important repercussions for Eranos. Writing to Jung on 18 April 1939, Olga Fröbe mentioned a series of Vatican professors (including the subsequent Eranos speaker Raffaele Pettazzoni), who had a strong interest in Eranos but would not come because they were afraid that Buonaiuti would be present.

61. See the facsimiles of the relevant written documents in Tullio Gregory, Marta Fattori, and Nicola Siciliana de Cumis (eds), *Filosofi Università Regime: La Scuola di Filosofia di Roma negli anni trenta. Mostra storico-documentaria* (Rome: Istituto di Filosofia della Sapienza, 1985), 115–21.

62. See Anna Maria Isastia, *Uomini e idee della Massoneria nella storia d'Italia* (Rome: Atanor, 2001), 158ff. This book also says that a Masonic group stands behind Eranos. Stated in such a bald form, this cannot be substantiated, but it is undeniable that individual benefactors and important speakers at Eranos were active Freemasons, albeit belonging to distinctly different Masonic obediences. Anna Maria Isastia's book is in no way tinged with anti-Masonic conspiracy theories. The author is Professor of Contemporary History at La Sapienza University, Rome, and a specialist on left-wing democratic movements as well as on Masonic history. The book appeared with an avowedly pro-Masonic publisher.

63. Greco, *Ketzer oder Prophet?*, 71ff.

64. Giulio Andreotti, *I quattro del Gesù: Storia di un'eresia* (Milan: Rizzoli, 1999). In the foreword, Andreotti emphasizes that he wrote the book in order to enable readers to understand the Second Vatican Council better. In writing it, he used very confidential sources. Andreotti did not know Buonaiuti personally, as the latter was under an ecclesiastical ban and any contact with him was frowned on by the Catholic Church at that time. However, Andreotti made no secret of his admiration for Buonaiuti.

65. Dana Lloyd Thomas, *Julius Evola e la tentazione razzista: L'inganno del pangermanesimo in Italia* (Mesagne: Giordano Editore, 2006), 111ff.

66. See Ernesto Buonaiuti, *Lo Gnosticismo: Storie di antiche lotte religiose* (Genoa: [1907] 1987), 9, and also his joyfully optimistic book *La Gnosi cristiana* (Rome: Atanòr, 1987), in which he points out the importance attached to social justice—a cause close to his heart—within certain Gnostic currents.

67. Quoted here from Marin Mincu and Roberto Scagno (eds), *Mircea Eliade e l'Italia* (Milan: Jaca Book, 1987), 64ff.

68. *Ibid.*, 68.

69. In Ernesto Buonaiuti, *Die exkommunizierte Kirche*, 45–7.

70. Rosenberg, *Eranos*, 2.

71. For information on his life, see especially Regine Lockot, *Erinnern und Durcharbeiten: Zur Geschichte der Psychoanalyse and Psychotherapie im Nationalsozialismus* (Frankurt: Fischer, 1985), 161ff. See pages 167–72 for a biography written by Heyer himself. See also the book by Geoffrey Cocks, *Psychotherapy in the Third Reich: The Göring Institute* (2nd, exp.edition, New Brunswick, NJ: Transaction Publishers, 1997), 36ff.

72. Edgar Salin, *Um Stefan George: Erinnerungen und Zeugnis* (Munich: Helmut Kopper, 1954), 95.

73. See Friedrich Gundolf, *Romantiker* (Berlin-Wilmersdorf: Heinrich Keller Verlag, 1930), in which the longest contribution (pp. 141–275) is devoted to Friedrich Schleiermacher, who is such an important figure in the context of the present work. Among those who studied under Friedrich Gundolf, who was of Jewish ancestry, were Joseph Goebbels and the famous scholar of religion Joachim Wach. The latter, according to a letter of 26 January 1933 from Rudolf Otto to Ernst Benz, had been invited to take part in the first Eranos meeting in 1933. See Eric J. Ziolkowsky, "Wach, Religion, and 'The Emancipation of Art,'" *Numen* 46(4) (1999), 347ff. Joseph Goebbels was evidently an enthusiastic listener and even wanted to write his dissertation under Gundolf. The latter, however, directed him to his colleague Max Baron von Waldberg, who was also Jewish. See the biography by David Irving, *Goebbels: Mastermind of the Third Reich* (London: Focal Point, 1996). Irving is often remarkably well documented, despite his controversial reputation. In the 1920s Gundolf was revered as a "saint of the city," and when he died people wept in the streets. See Michael Landmann, *Figuren um Stefan George*, vol. 2 (Amsterdam: Castrum Peregrini Press, 1988), 40.

74. Salin, *Um Stefan George*, 130.

75. *Ibid.*, 95.

76. *Ibid.*, 109. Heyer was certainly of a belligerent nature, which had political repercussions and brought him into danger. Thus Lockot, in her book *Erinnern und Durcharbeiten*, 134, quotes letters from medical colleagues mentioning that Heyer had, in medical matters, "attracted the enmity of the important leaders of the regime including Hess" and that this had harmed him professionally. In the early 1930s Rudolf Hess, the so-called "deputy of the Führer," had even been one of Heyer's patients. See *ibid.*, 226, and also Cocks, *Psychotherapy in the Third Reich*, 84.

77. In 1913–14 he had published an account of his work on the neurotic causes of intestinal ulcers. See Lockot, *Erinnern und Durcharbeiten*, 162.

78. Nevertheless, the accounts of his work in this area were translated by him into English. See Ernst Jolowicz and Gustav Heyer, *Hypnosis and Hypnotherapy* (London: C.W. Daniel, 1931).

79. See the editor's introduction to Lucy Heyer-Grote (ed.), *Atemschulung als Element der Psychotherapie* (Darmstadt: Wissenschaftliche Buchgesellschaft, 1970). This book contains two contributions by Gustav Heyer on the subject of breath, illustrating his psychosomatic healing methods.

80. See Traugott Konstantin Österreich's introduction to G.R. Heyer, *Seelen-Räume: Psychotherapeutische Beobachtungen zum Kollektiv-Seelischen*, vol. 10 of the *Beiträge zur Philosophie und Psychologie* (Stuttgart: W. Kohlhammer, 1931), v–vii.

81. See Gerda Walther, *Zum anderen Ufer: Vom Marxismus und Atheismus zum Christentum* (Remagen: Der Leuchter, Otto Reichl Verlag, 1960), 365ff.

82. *Ibid.*, 308.

83. Erika Hantel also uses the term in her essay "Die 'Amazonen' um Heyer," in *Das Kraftfeld des Menschen und Forschers Gustav Richard Heyer: Eine Festschrift zu seinem 65. Geburtstag*, K. Bügler and G. R. Heyer (eds) (Munich: Kindler Verlag, 1955), 12–15.

84. Ernst Speer, "Begegnungen mit G.R. Heyer," in *Das Kraftfeld des Menschen und Forschers Gustav Richard Heyer: Eine Festschrift zu seinem 65. Geburtstag* (Munich, Kindler Verlag, 1955), 7.

85. Unfortunately it is not possible here to go in greater detail into Heyer's psychotherapeutic approaches. His involvement with National Socialism, whatever form it may have taken, sadly appears to have dissuaded people in the field from more intensive research and publication on his work.

86. Ludwig J. Pongratz, *Psychiatrie in Selbstdarstellungen* (Bern: Hans Huber, 1973), 284ff. However, in the revised 1977 edition of this book Kemper's contribution is not included.

87. Gustav Richard Heyer and Friedrich Seifert (eds), *Reich der Seele: Arbeiten aus dem Münchener psychologischen Arbeitskreis* (Munich: J.F. Lehmann, 1937).

88. These biographical details are taken from Maria Hippius (ed.), *Durchbruch in die Transzendenz: Beitrag und Widerhall, Festschrift zum 70. Geburtstag von Graf Dürckheim* (Weilheim: O.W. Barth, 1966), 499.

89. Cocks, *Psychotherapy in the Third Reich*, 37ff.

90. *Ibid.*, 77ff.

91. Undated letter to the author, April 2006.

92. Geoffrey Cocks, *Psychotherapy in the Third Reich*, 84.

93. In his Eranos lecture of 1933—three months after the Nazis had publicly burned the works of Freud—Heyer nevertheless spoke of Freud's "genius" which, however, would "continually misunderstand" itself. See G.R. Heyer, "Sinn und Bedeutung östlicher Weisheit für die abendländische Seelenführung," in *Eranos Jahrbuch* 1 (1933), 215.

94. Gustav Richard Heyer, *Der Organismus der Seele: Eine Einführung in die analytische Seelenheilkunde* (Munich: J.F. Lehmann, 1932); published in English as *The Organism of the Mind: An Introduction to Analytical Psychotherapy* (London: Kegan Paul, 1933).

95. Quoted from Michael Philipp, *Vom Schicksal des deutschen Geistes: Wolfgang Frommels Rundfunkarbeit an den Sendern Frankfurt und Berlin 1933-1935 und ihre oppositionelle Tendenz* (Potsdam: Verlag für Berlin-Brandenburg, 1995), 109.

96. *Ibid.*, 109.

97. Paul Kugler, "Eranos and Jungian Psychology: A Photographic History," in *Disturbances in the Field*, C. Downing (ed.), 77.

98. Lockot, *Erinnern und Durcharbeiten*, 10-11.

99. Bair, *Jung*, 793.

100. Regine Lockot, *Die Reinigung der Psychoanalyse: Die Deutsche Psychoanalytische Gesellschaft im Spiegel von Dokumenten und Zeitzeugen (1933-1951)* (Tübingen: Edition Diskord, 1994), 120.

101. *Das Kraftfeld des Menschen und Forschers Gustav Richard* yet published on Heyer's achievements in psychology and psychotherapy.

102. Nina Kindler, "G.R. Heyer in Deutschland," *Psychologie des 20. Jahrhunderts* 3(2) (1977), 820-40, esp. 821. This essay is without doubt the most significant monograph on him. Lockot, *Erinnern und Durcharbeiten*, 162.

103. Gustav Heyer, *Praktische Seelenheilkunde: Eine Einführung in die Psychotherapie für Ärzte und Studierende* (Munich: J.F. Lehmanns Verlag, 1942), 8.

104. Kindler, "G.R. Heyer in Deutschland," 825.

105. Thus Jean Gebser wrote a contribution to Heyer's *Festschrift* and gave him the opportunity to participate in the Munich lecture series *Die Welt in neuer Sicht* (The world in a new perspective), which was incidentally somewhat reminiscent of Eranos in its goals. See G.R. Heyer, "Vom neuen Denken in der Tiefenpsychologie," in *Die Welt in neuer Sicht: Sechs Vorträge* (Munich-Planegg: Wilhelm Barth Verlag, 1957), 47-65. Adolf Portmann, later president of Eranos, also gave a lecture there. Unfortunately this initiative by Jean Gebser appears not to have been continued after 1958. Heyer's *Seelenkunde im Umbruch der Zeit* (Bern: Hans Huber, 1964) even contained an accompanying text by Gebser. Heyer in turn contributed to the *Festschrift* for Gebser on his sixtieth birthday. See G.R. Heyer, "Einige Fragen der Psychosomatik im Licht der Erkenntnisse Jean Gebsers," in *Transparente Welt*, Günter Schulz (ed.) (Bern: Hans Huber, 1965), 131-51. In Fritz Hollwich (ed.), *Im Umkreis der Kunst: Eine Festschrift für Emil Preetorius* (Frankfurt: Insel Verlag, 1953), there is a contribution by Heyer on "Die Tiefenpsychologie im Ringen um das neue Weltbild." This must have been very gratifying for him, as the other contributors to the *Festschrift* included such prominent names as Gottfried Benn, Martin Heidegger, Romano Guardini, Werner Heisenberg, Herbert von Karajan, and Thomas Mann.

106. Heyer had met Jung for the first time in May 1928 on the occasion of a lecture that Jung gave in Munich, as Zoe Heyer reports (see Kindler, "G.R. Heyer in Deutschland"). Before that, however, he had preoccupied himself intensively with Jung's ideas and had founded an informal Jungian discussion group. In 1930, according to Regine Lockot (*Erinnern und Durcharbeiten*, 162), he began a training analysis with Jung. In a letter to Jung of 9 November 1931, Heyer writes, "I often dream about you. The inner self turns to the guru." Jung's answers are always addressed "Mein lieber Heyer"(My dear Heyer).

107. The first letter using the "Du" form that I have been able to examine is dated 20 December 1933. Concerning the close relationship between the two men, see also Jung's letter to Heyer dated 20 April 1934, in C.G. Jung, *Briefe I*, 205ff., in which Jung confidentially asks Heyer to come with him to a congress in Germany where he had been invited to speak. He says that, on account of the political climate, he does not know how he should conduct

himself in such a way as to avoid his appearance being politically exploited. In several letters to Heyer, Jung writes negatively about M.G. Göring, *Reichsführer* (national leader) of the German psychotherapists and cousin of Reich Marshall Hermann Göring, with whom he had co-published the *Zentralblatt für Psychotherapie* since 1936. This bears witness to the trust that Jung had towards Heyer, but it also shows that Heyer as well must have had a skeptical attitude towards the supremo of psychotherapy, Göring.

108. In this connection, see Maria Hippius-Dürckheim, "Am Faden von Zeit und Ewigkeit," in *Transzendenz als Erfahrung: Beitrag und Widerhall Festschrift zum 70. Geburtstag von Graf Dürckheim*, K. Dürckheim and M. Hippius (Weilheim: O.W. Barth, 1966), 25. Maria Hippius, the wife of the famous Zen teacher and psychotherapist Karlfried Graf Dürckheim, had carried out her training analysis first under Heyer and then under Erich Neumann (also an Eranos lecturer). See Maria Hippius-Dürckheim, *Geheimnis und Wagnis der Menschwerdung: Schriften zur Initiatischen Therapie* (Schaffhausen: Novalis, 1996), title page. Heyer's influence, however, extended not only to representatives of Germany's war generation, but also to the widely read Anglo-American "hippy philosopher" Alan Watts. In his autobiography, *In My Own Way* (New York: Pantheon Books, 1972), he counts Heyer among those researchers who had freed him from the sexual confusions and guilt feelings of his youth. In November 1933 Olga Fröbe herself consulted Heyer in Munich to seek help for her digestive problems.

109. Heyer, *Praktische Seelenheilkunde*, quoted from the 2nd edition (1942), 6.

110. In his fundamental work *Der Organismus der Seele*, 6.

111. Here it is also worth mentioning that Heyer contributed a long foreword to a new edition of Gotthilf Heinrich Schubert's work *Die Symbolik des Traumes* (Stuttgart: Belser Presse, 1958), illustrated with nine original engravings by Ernst Fuchs. Schubert belonged to exactly the same current of romantic thought as Novalis and Carus.

112. Subtitled *Zwei Abhandlungen zur Tiefenpsychologie* (Stuttgart: Ernst Klett, 1949).

113. See Gerda Walther, "Erinnerungen an Freud und Jung," *Grenzgebiete der Wissenschaft* 47(4) (1998), 362.

114. Heyer, *Seelen-Räume*, ix.

115. Both letters are in a private collection.

116. See the letter written to Heyer on 21 June 1960 by Fritsch's personal doctor and friend, W.R. Schürmeister, who devotes four pages to a description of the last hours of Fritsche's life. The letter is in the Thelemic archive at Stein, Appenzell, Switzerland.

117. Kindler, "G.R. Heyer in Deutschland," 822.

118. Jung, *Briefe I*, 151. The letter was addressed to Jolande Jacobi and dated 23 December 1932.

119. C.G. Jung, Review of Heyer, *Der Organismus der Seele*, *Europäische Revue* 9(2) (1933), 639.

120. The relevant words were also printed in bold in the original. The advertisement is to be found as an appendix in Heyer's book *Praktische Seelenheilkunde*.

121. Barbara Hannah, in her biography, *Jung: His Life and Work: A Biographical Memoir* (Wilmette, IL: Chiron, 1997), 289, describes this expulsion as "a distasteful task, for it seemed like kicking a man when he was already down." Nevertheless she justifies the expulsion—which only affected Heyer and one other member, the psychotherapist Otto Curtius—on the grounds that both of these people had a total lack of understanding of Jungian psychology—a rather strange statement considering Jung's high regard for Heyer.

122. Heyer's daughter came twice to Eranos and was able to hear Jung's lecture on synchronicity, which deeply impressed her.

123. A detailed account of this undertaking, in which Cary Baynes was also meant to collaborate, is found in Sonu Shamdasani, *Jung Stripped Bare by His Biographers, Even* (London: Karnac, 2005), 13ff. This is a highly readable exposition of the difficulties and pitfalls inherent in writing a biography of Jung. Shamdasani comes to the conclusion that the "most reliable and important" biography is the one by Barbarah Hannah, which I have also made use of. See also Sonu Shamdasani, "Misunderstanding Jung: The Afterlife of Legends," *Journal of Analytical Psychology* 45 (2000), 459–72. This essay is concerned with the continually proliferating biographies of Jung, which Shamdasani calls "history light," as the authors indiscriminately resurrect old legends without bothering much about the original sources, simply in order to attract a wide public. Shamdasani also includes two authors whom I have already mentioned, namely Frank McLynn and F.X. Charet.

124. Heyer had already emphasized this in his autobiography, written during the Nazi period: "There are various differences between us. For example, he is more of a researcher than a doctor. Also, he does not accept my inclusion of the bodily dimension in psychotherapy." See Lockot, *Erinnern und Durcharbeiten*, 170.

125. Kindler, "G.R. Heyer in Deutschland," 826.

126. Hannah, *Jung*, 826.

127. Heyer suffered from a stomach ulcer.

128. As the letter is in longhand the word is not very legible, but this is the most likely rendering, in which case it would mean something like "whoring around in the ether." Theoretically it could also be "*Aetherhörerei*" (listening to the ether) or less probably "*Hellhörerei*" (clairaudience).

6. Eranos and National Socialism

1. Olga Fröbe wrote to Friedrich Heiler on 10 June 1934, "I have many more applications than places available."

2. This last observation expressed exactly what J.W. Hauer had said in his introductory essay to the journal *Yoga*, mentioned earlier.

3. *Eranos Jahrbuch* 2 (1934), 8–9.

4. Not only Jung was impressed by this lecture series. Fröbe, in a document about Eranos that she wrote in 1952, commented that these lectures suddenly made clear to her "that all the lectures held at Eranos revolved around this great symbol." Hence the idea of the Eranos Mandala, which became the symbol for the whole spiritual and intellectual energy behind Eranos and the vital focal point of her endeavors.

5. In the *Festschrift* for Jung's sixtieth birthday, *Die kulturelle Bedeutung der komplexen Psychologie*, Psychologischer Club Zürich (eds), Hauer contributed a more specific study on "Die indo-arische Lehre vom Selbst im Vergleich mit KANTs Lehre vom intellegiblen Subjekt." Other contributors to this *Festschrift* included the Eranos friends H. Zimmer, E. Rousselle, and G. Heyer.

6. A letter from Hauer to Jung, dated 24 December 1936 and preserved in the Jung archive, indicates that Hauer too was not averse to the *I Ching* oracle and made use of it from time to time.

7. Message to Hauer dated 15 June 1933. Otto was deeply convinced of Hauer's value for Eranos. Thus, in a postcard to Olga Fröbe, dated 16 December 1933, he wrote, "In the summer you should have Hauer talk about his new German religion, and you should include it in your program. That would bring a *Völkerwanderung* to Ascona."

8. In subsequent years Otto and Hauer became increasingly alienated from each other.

9. On this somewhat sensitive matter, compare the opinion of the historian Carl Burckhardt, who also knew Zimmer: "Zimmer is a clever Berliner, rich in ideas, quick on the uptake, somewhat crude, able to formulate things in a succinct way—a German of the new type … He administers the legacy with philological discipline, but whether with tact I don't know." Burckhardt is referring to Hugo von Hofmannsthal's legacy. Carl J. Burckhardt and Max Rychner, *Briefe 1926–1965* (Frankfurt: S. Fischer, 1970), 25, letter of 13 September 1929. At one point in these letters Burckhardt speaks of the "shamanic lower depths of Eranos-Ascona" (209). By contrast, it may be worth quoting the remark by Karl Wolfskehl, follower of Stefan George, who had been forced during the Nazi period to take refuge in New Zealand, much to his distress. Referring in a letter to the early death of Heinrich Zimmer, with whom he had always maintained contact, he said simply, "I always liked him." See Karl Wolfskehl, *Zehn Jahre Exil*, 182.

10. The relations between Jung and Hauer are dealt with in detail in the article by Petteri Piettikainen, "The Volk and its Unconscious: Jung, Hauer and the 'German Revolution,'" *Journal of Contemporary History* 35(4) (2000), 523–39.

11. Olga Fröbe at any rate seems to have had (not necessarily political) reservations about Hauer, for in a letter to Friedrich Heiler dated 10 June 1934, she wrote, "Prof. Hauer will stay here in the house; otherwise, he would not come at all. I believe he is only tempted by the lake and the proximity to nature. As I must have him at all cost, as the only yoga expert, I must adjust myself to him." Mircea Eliade was also in correspondence with Hauer in the late 1920s and early 1930s. See Steven Wasserstrom, *Religion after Religion: Gershom Scholem, Mircea Eliade, and Henry Corbin at Eranos* (Princeton, NJ: Princeton University Press, 1999), 102.

12. See, for example, Aniela Jaffé, "Aus Leben und Werkstatt von C.G. Jung," Zurich 1968, 85–104 (a reworked version of this essay, under the title "C.G. Jung und der Nationalsozialismus," is to be found in Aniela Jaffé, *Parapsychologie, Individuation, Nationalsozialismus: Themen bei C.G. Jung* [Zurich: Daimon, 1968], 141–64). Another work dealing with this theme is Aryeh Maidenbaum and Stephen A. Martin (eds), *Lingering Shadows* (Boston, MA: Shambhala, 1991), containing contributions by a number of controversial voices. In 2002 a new and extended edition of this book, edited by Aryeh Maidenbaum, was published under the title *Jung and the Shadow of Anti-Semitism: Collected Essays* (Berwick, ME: Nicolas-Hays, 2002). This stands out as containing a number of very objective contributions. A comparable collection on this theme has also appeared in Italy, namely Patrizia Puccioni Marasco (ed.), *Jung e l'Ebraismo* (Florence: Guintina, 2001). A striving for objectivity also marks the essay by Jay Sherry, "Jung, the Jews and Hitler," *Spring* 46 (1986), 163–76; and the article by Brigitte Spillmann, "Die Wirklichkeit des Schattens," in *Analytische Psychologie* 29(4) (1998) 272–95. Equally well documented is Deirdre Bair's *Jung*, 431–63. By contrast, a work that is strongly against Jung is Heinz Gess, *Vom Faschismus zum Neuen Denken: C.G. Jungs Theorie im Wandel der Zeit* (Lüneburg: zu Klampen, 1994), which contains a chapter of almost fifty pages dealing with "Jungs Antisemitismus." Also generally critical is the article by Beat Mazenauer and Severin Perrig entitled "C.G. Jung und der Nationalsozialismus," *Du* 8 (August 1995), an issue devoted to Jung. A different view is expressed by the analytical psychologist Thomas B. Kirsch in his book *The Jungians: A Comparative and Historical Perspective* (London: Routledge, 2000), 132: "My parents, both Jewish, were in analysis with Jung all through the 1930s … Neither of them felt a trace of anti-Semitism in their work with Jung in the 1930s. A number of other Jewish people saw Jung during that period, and they all have stated that they could not find any anti-Semitism in the work." At the same time Kirsch believes that, with the rise of National Socialism and the exodus of so many Freudians, Jung saw an opportunity to promote his own theories. A very balanced view of the issue is provided by the American scholar of religion Robert Ellwood in his book *The Politics of Myth: A Study of C.G. Jung, Mircea Eliade, and Joseph Campbell* (Albany, NY: SUNY Press, 1999), 37–77. This book is particularly relevant to our topic, as all three of the men discussed by Ellwood were connected with Eranos, and all of them were exposed to similar accusations of fascist—or at least authoritarian—thinking and anti-Semitism. See also Robert W. Brockway, *Young Carl Jung* (Wilmette, IL: Chiron Publications, 1986), 41ff., 50ff., in which Brockway

also discusses the *völkisch* element in the context of that era. Finally, a valuable summary of Jung's theories in connection with war, politics, and National Socialism is provided by the political scientist and analytical psychologist Nicholas Lewin in his book *Jung on War, Politics and Nazi Germany: Exploring the Archetypes and the Collective Unconscious* (London: Karnac Books, 2009). Lewin argues for a more differentiated view of the matter, taking into account the historical context, rather than a simple black-and-white judgment.

On the other hand, Richard Noll's works on Jung, which are intent on proving the existence of a *völkisch* sun cult under his leadership, strike me as being too one-sided. In this connection, see the statements by Sheila Grimaldi-Craig in *Spring*, esp. *Spring* 57 (1995), 143ff. See especially the detailed work by the Jung expert Sonu Shamdasani, *Cult Fictions: C.G. Jung and the Founding of Analytical Psychology* (London: Routledge, 1998), which brings forward new documentation, and also Shamdasani's letter published in *Spring* 62 (1987), 144ff., in which he characterizes Noll's works as "fiction." Noll also emphasizes Jung's connection with the Theosophical Society, although Noll's statements reveal his poor knowledge of this organization. In this connection see Robert Ellwood's expert review of Shamdasani's *Cult Fictions* in "Cult Fictions," *Theosophical History* 7(4) (2000), 148–9. Noll seems to be unaware of Jung's repeated swipes at the Theosophical Society, which are also mentioned in these pages. Furthermore Noll's writings suffer from faulty translations from the German, which in some cases even turn the original meaning upside down and yet are still adduced as proof of Noll's thesis. It is equally astonishing that even reputable American university presses seem unable to reproduce quotations and names of people or places in German or other non-English languages correctly (this also applies incidentally to Brockway's book). Such deficient linguistic knowledge can lead to the understandable, if often unjust, impression that the writer has an inadequate knowledge of the sources.

13. On the subject of his well-known links to psychotherapeutic initiatives in Nazi Germany, and in particular his editorship of the Leipzig journal, *Zentralblatt für Psychotherapie*, see the balanced article by Geoffrey Cocks, "C.G. Jung and German Psychotherapy 1933–1940: A Research Note," *Spring* 10 (1979), 221–7, and the subsequent "Postscript to Cocks" by Wolfgang Giegerich in the same issue. The question is discussed in great detail in the already mentioned book by Geoffrey Cocks, *Psychotherapy in the Third Reich*, and in Regine Lockot's *Erinnern und Durcharbeiten*, also mentioned earlier. These two works are the most comprehensive and reliable studies on psychotherapy under the Nazi regime.

14. According to the former Chilean diplomat and mystical admirer of Hitler Miguel Serrano, who died in 2009, Jung allegedly made the remark: "I am not of this world. I am a Hyperborean." However, this can hardly be substantiated as a historical fact; nor can the rest of the book from which the quotation stems and which deals with UFOs and gods. See Miguel Serrano, *Nos: The Book of Resurrection* (London: Routledge & Kegan Paul, 1984), 64ff.

15. Petteri Pietikäinen, "Dynamic Psychology, Utopia and Escape from History: The Case of C.G. Jung," in *Utopian Studies* 12(1) (2001), 50.

16. The original copy of the book is in the "Inventario Beni ex Mussolini" under the number 170 in the Italian State Archive in Rome. The information comes from the essay by Aniela Jaffé, "C.G. Jung und der Nationalsozialismus," in Jaffé, *Parapsychologie, Individuation, Nationalsozialismus*, 156.

17. McGuire, *Bollingen*, 26.

18. Bair, *Jung*, 492.

19. See Peter Grose, *Gentleman Spy: The Life of Allen Dulles* (Amherst, MA: University of Massachusetts Press, 1996).

20. Michael Salter, *Nazi War Crimes, US Intelligence and Selective Prosecution at Nuremberg: Controversies regarding the Role of the Office of Strategic Services* (Oxford: Routledge-Cavendish, 2007), 94.

21. *Ibid.*, 262.

22. On Mary Bancroft see her book *Autobiography of a Spy* (New York: William Morrow, 1983); Bair, *Jung*, 482ff.; and Anthony, *The Valkyries*, 87, 88. According to Anthony, on Jung's eightieth birthday Mary Bancroft asked him: "Have you ever seen a helpless woman, for I never have?" Jung replied that only the helplessness of a man can be real, but "a woman's was one of her best stunts. As she is by birth and sex on better terms with nature, she is never quite helpless as long as there is no man in her vicinity."

23. See Grose, *Gentleman Spy*, 262ff.

24. *Ibid.*, 254.

25. See Thomas Mann and Karl Kerényi, *Thomas Mann–Karl Kerényi: Gespräche in Briefen* (Zurich: Rhein Verlag, 1960), 98. In the quoted letter he praises Jung and Kerényi as two "initiates" whose collaboration could only bring forth something of significance. In his letter of 7 September 1941 to Jung he repeats the same sentences almost word for word: "The way in which mythology and psychology are working hand in hand is a very pleasing development. It is necessary to remove mythology from intellectual fascism and re-adapt it so that it serves a human function." Mann's positive assessment is also confirmed in a letter of 19 October 1945 from Olga Fröbe to Jung, in which it emerges that Mann had told the Institute for Advanced Studies in Princeton (evidently in positive terms) about Eranos.

26. *Eranos Jahrbuch* 2 (1934), 190.

27. The expressionist dancer Jean Erdman, wife of the Eranos lecturer Joseph Campbell, who was invited with her husband to visit Jung at Bollingen, said that Jung was brilliant in conversation as long as the topic was psychology or mythology, but that in social or political questions he gave the impression of being rather limited, like a Swiss

petit bourgeois. See also Ellwood, *The Politics of Myth*, 142. I personally sympathize rather more with the analysis of the Jung expert Jay Sherry in his article "Turning a Blind Eye: Misreading Jung," *Spring* 64 (1998), 121–6. He writes as follows, "He [Jung] can best be seen as adhering to a nineteenth-century liberalism that emphasised individual freedom and was suspicious of excesses of state power and collectivism." This is confirmed by Jung's colleague Marie Louise von Franz in her foreword to Volodymyr Walter Odajnik's *Jung and Politics. The Political and Social Ideas of C.G. Jung* (New York: New York University Press, 1976), ix. What she says here is noteworthy in a wider context: "Though he was a convinced supporter of the Swiss democracy, I never heard him recommend its constitution as a panacea for all other countries. What he was passionate about were *les droits de l'homme*, the security of man's basic rights and the freedom of the individual, which are guaranteed not only by a 'just' state, but far more by the maturity, wisdom, and consciousness of all the members of a community. The individual matters more than the system. Though Jung naturally rejected all forms of dictatorship and tyranny, he did not much believe in forcibly changing a social system before man himself had changed." One must also take into account Jung's rejection of Marxism, which caused him to overlook much that was negative in National Socialism.

28. Page 8 of Karl Bürgi-Meyer's (unpublished?) interview with Magda Kerényi on 17 September 1991 in Ascona: "Jung enjoyed meeting Szondi in Ascona's old Hotel Tamaro, where they would grumble against academic psychology." See Karl Kerényi, *Tage- und Wanderbücher*, vol. 3, entries for 1 and 3 January 1955. "I listened to the two psychologists as they swapped platitudinous criticisms of the modern medical profession. They were right."

29. From the 1934 essay "Zur gegenwärtigen Lage der Psychotherapie," in *Zentralblatt für Psychotherapie und ihre Grenzgebiete.* Now available in Jung, *Gesammelte Werke*, vol. 10, 190.

30. Wolfgang Martynkewicz, in his essay, "Ludwig Klages und Sigmund Freud" (www.literaturkritik.de [no. 1, January 2006]), draws attention to a letter written by Alphonse Maeder, a close associate of Jung and president of the Zurich branch of the Psychological Association under the influence of Ludwig Klages. In the letter, addressed to the psychoanalyst Sándor Ferenczi, Maeder attributes the quarrel between Freud and Jung to the racial factor. Freud was against this interpretation, as he feared that it could lead to psychology being perceived as a purely "Jewish" form of therapy. He therefore preferred to interpret the quarrel as a father–son conflict. The analyst Karl Abraham was also not averse to a "racist" interpretation. It is also not unlikely that Jung himself attributed the quarrel at least partly to racial factors.

31. Sigmund Freud, *Sigmund Freud–Karl Abraham, Briefe 1907–1926* (Frankfurt: S. Fischer Verlag, 1965), 47 (letter of 3 May 1908).

32. Sherry, *Carl Gustav Jung*, 125ff.

33. C.G. Jung, *Letters* (Princeton, NJ: Princeton University Press, 1975), vol. 1, 164–5. See also the critical essay by Hans Krieger "'Bei den abgehauenen Naturdämonen.' Hinunter ins Dunkel. Die Tiefenpsychologie Carl Gustav Jungs in seinen Briefen," *Die Zeit* 7 (9 February 1973).

34. Fritsche also had a certain kinship with the work of Georg Grosz. He felt a connection with the Hasidism of Martin Buber, acted as a reader for the renowned publishing firm of Ernst Klett, was invited to Ernst Jünger's sixtieth birthday celebration, was patriarch of the Crowleyan Gnostic-Catholic Church and publisher of the prestigious esoteric journal *Merlin*. See Herbert Fritsche, *Baum der Käuze* (Berlin: Corvinus Presse, 1991), 104ff.

35. On Fritsche see the informative essays by Olaf Räderer, "Herbert Fritsche: Konstitutioneller Grenzgänger und Grenzüberschreiter (1911–1960)" and "Herbert Fritsche (1911–1960): Grenzgänger im Niemandsland," in *Nova Acta Paracelsica*, new series, 17 (2003), 63–94. Quotation here from 64.

36. Bernus, as a practicing alchemist, could naturally not accept Jung's mainly psychological interpretation of alchemy. Interestingly, historians of alchemy are coming more and more to the view that so-called spiritual alchemy, as Jung primarily conceived it, can hardly have existed before the sixteenth century—a conclusion that could shake the whole foundation of Jung's analyses. See the chapters "Jung, Silberer, and Active Imagination" and "Theories of Spiritual Alchemy," in Dan Merkur, *Gnosis: An Esoteric Tradition of Mystical Visions and Unions* (Albany, NY: SUNY Press, 1993), 37ff., 65ff., and 75. According to Merkur, it was Paracelsus who first wove together spiritual elements and chemical processes. Here Merkur was relying on the researches of the well-known historian of chemistry John Read.

37. Sladek and Schütze, *Alexander von Bernus*, 109ff.

38. The two women must have known each other well, as Fröbe complained in a letter to Jung of 29 July 1936 that several women, such as Jay von Seldeneck and the Eranos photographer Margarethe Fellerer, always came to her for advice about their psychological problems. Jay von Seldeneck was a friend of the German poet Ina Seidel, whom she even invited to Eranos. Her close friend the poet and alchemist Alexander von Bernus had planned to appoint her as the "Swiss" contact point for his projected journal *Die Mitte*, in which Max Pulver and Erwin Rousselle were also to be included among the collaborators.

39. During the Eranos meetings Jung had several times been a guest in her house and had immortalized himself in her guest book in some rather curious poems. On 10 August 1937, however, he wrote in a sympathetically self-ironic way: "This time sober." Some letters from Jung to Jay von Seldeneck have also been preserved, including an invitation to Bollingen. She also tried, like Olga Fröbe, to gather interesting people around her to form a regular discussion circle, but was not so successful.

40. Olga Fröbe, probably also feeling the strain of this difficult period, wrote to Jung on 27 October 1946 in connection with a suggested lecture by Karl Jaspers, who had been proposed by Leo Baeck, himself later a speaker at Eranos. In the letter she wrote, "I believe it would be good if Eranos, without too much delay, were to seek contact with German scholars who are not burdened."

41. Rousselle had, among other things, spoken at the Psychological Club in Zurich.

42. This also appeared in the periodical *Ausblick. Zeitfragen im Lichte der Weltmeinung* (August 1945), 53–7.

43. Now included in Jung, *Gesammelte Werke*, vol. 10, 223. Originally spaced for emphasis.

44. Brigitte Spillmann and Robert Strubel, *C.G. Jung. Zerrissen zwischen Mythos und Wirklichkeit. Über die Folgen persönlicher und kollektiver Spaltung im tiefenpsychologischen Erbe* (Giessen: Psychosozial-Verlag, 2010), 95ff.

45. *Ibid.*, 126.

46. *Ibid.*, 127.

47. As late as 1953 he wrote to Henry Corbin: "I am used to living in a more or less complete intellectual vacuum." See Jung, *Briefe II*, 332.

48. Quoted from Regine Lockot, *Die Reinigung der Psychoanalyse*, 119.

49. Verena Kast, *Der Schatten in Uns: Die subversive Lebenskraft* (Zurich: Walter Verlag, 2000), 70.

50. Jung, *Gesammelte Werke* (*Psychologie und Alchemie*), vol. 12, 30.

51. Margarete Dierks, *Jakob Wilhelm Hauer 1881–1962* (Heidelberg: Lambert Schneider, 1986). This book, which relies heavily on largely unknown primary sources, was published by the firm of Lambert Schneider, which also published the complete edition of Martin Buber's works.

52. In his book *Von der philosophischen zur völkischen Religionswissenschaft*, which contains a wealth of new documentation about Hauer, Horst Junginger describes Margarete Dierks' work as "to a considerable extent overly uncritical" (190). Junginger's study can certainly be seen as a necessary complement to Dierk's book. There is an enormous number of papers in Hauer's legacy that have not yet been worked on. Junginger estimates more than fifty thousand pages of text. A much more severe judgment is given by Karla Poewe in her *New Religions and the Nazis* (Abingdon and New York: Routledge, 2006), 19. Poewe alludes to the *völkisch* and National Socialist background shared by Margarete Dierks and Hauer and points out that this ruled out any critical distance between the two. Despite its title, her work is mainly about Jakob Wilhelm Hauer and his German Faith Movement. As a study of Hauer and his work in the spirit of National Socialism, it stands out as being the most thorough of its kind in terms of its searching use of primary and secondary sources. However, she shows no understanding of Hauer's particular life situation nor of the pressures that he was subject to in his efforts to attain what he saw as the religious liberation of his people. Her role is that of a prosecuting lawyer in a trial in which Hauer stands accused on account of his deep involvement with National Socialism. To this end she certainly makes good use of her assembled documents. However, she shows the tendency that one often finds in such cases where, out of eagerness to expose the "all-pervasiveness of evil," the writer does not address the thought processes of the person they are so vehemently attacking. Why bother to do so, as they are all Nazis? Here again one has the feeling that the author is intent on giving a sharp warning: any involvement with Pagan currents of thought will inevitably lead to National Socialism and mass murder. However, the fact that Karla Poewe draws support from the forged *Gespräche* of Hermann Rauschning, former president of the Danzig Senate, does not speak for a very profound knowledge of the historical literature of the period.

It is also worth mentioning a work written in the National Socialist period but from a Christian and critical point of view, namely Helmut Lother's *Neugermanische Religion und Christentum* (Gütersloh: C. Bertelsmann, 1934). This informative book also deals with other forms of Neo-Germanic religion.

53. On the subject of this group, see Hans-Christian Brandenburg and Rudolf Dauer, *Die Brücke zu Köngen: Fünfzig Jahre Bund der Kongener 1919–1969* (Stuttgart: J.F. Steinkopf Verlag, 1969), which contains abundant visual and written documentation on Hauer's involvement with the group. Certain sections of this association were influenced by esoteric and life-reforming ideas. One example was the Leipzig section, which was, in its early years, strongly influenced by the Swiss esoteric writer Werner Zimmermann (still read today) and his journal *TAO*. See Hauer's journal *Kommende Gemeinde* 5(1) (1933), 78.

54. J.W. Hauer, *Unser Kampf um einen freien Deutschen Glauben, Flugschriften zum geistigen und religiösen Durchbruch der Deutschen Revolution*, vol. 3 (Stuttgart: C.L. Hirschfeld, 1933).

55. Steps were even taken to make it obligatory by law for all children to receive a Christian education.

56. *Völkisch* occultists, such as the "rune gymnast" Friedrich-Wilhelm Marby and the "Kristus" mystic H.A. Weishaar (Kurt Paehlke), were even thrown into concentration camps.

57. In 1934 it became simply the German Faith Movement (Deutsche Glaubensbewegung). Hauer remained leader and Count Reventlow became his deputy. The latter had forged a contact with Rudolf Hess and thus secured a certain semi-official recognition for the movement.

58. See Hubert Cancik, "'Neuheiden' und totaler Staat: Völkische Religion am Ende der Weimarer Republik," in *Antik, Modern: Beiträge zur römischen und deutschen Kulturgeschichte*, Richard Faber, Barbara von Reibnitz, and Jörg Rüpke (eds), 187–227 (Stuttgart: J.B. Metzler, 1998).

59. *Ibid.*, 188. In his already mentioned letter to Jung, of 16 August 1933, Hauer wrote, "Through the political turn of events in Germany I have been forced to place myself at the service of the movements that have renounced

Christianity—I had no other choice, as there was no one else who would have had the trust of the various groups." Hauer's organizational abilities even attracted attention in Italy. See Mario Bendiscioli, *Neopaganesimo razzista* (Brescia: Morcelliana, 1937), 36ff. The author mentions that evidently Hauer succeeded in this way in opening up various closed groups and getting them to appear together in public places, with music, banners, processions, flyers, ceremonial gatherings, radio broadcasts, and newspaper reports. Thus public opinion had to deal with Hauer, and neither friend nor foe could bypass him. Even the authorities could not ignore him.

60. As Hauer writes in *Deutsche Gottschau: Grundzüge eines Deutschen Glaubens* (Stuttgart: Karl Gutbrod Verlag, 1935), "The German Faith Movement of today is *one phase* in the struggle that has been going on for thousands of years between the Near Eastern Semitic world and the Indo-Germanic world." (On the same page, however, Hauer specifies, "Indo-germanic is not a racial concept but rather a linguistic and cultural one.") At the same time he emphasizes that the struggle is on three levels: first, biological and racial; second, political and economic; third, philosophical and religious. "The *geo-biological basis* for the contrast between these two worlds lies in *racial* and *territorial* differences" (p. 4). On page 161 of the same book Hauer surprisingly highlights a clear polarity within Nordic-Germanic man, without which he cannot be understood: namely the polarity between reason and myth, enlightenment and romanticism, strict clarity and ecstatic enthusiasm. Hauer argues that this leads inevitably to tensions within the Germanic soul, which have to be integrated into a higher totality. Here one sees the influence of Indian thought on Hauer as well as possibly the ideas of Jung.

61. In Grabert, *Religiöse Verständigung*, 82ff.

62. This and subsequent italicized passages are also emphasized in the original text.

63. Herbert Grabert, *Der protestantische Auftrag des deutschen Volkes: Grundzüge der deutschen Glaubensgeschichte von Luther bis Hauer* (Stuttgart: Karl Gutbrod Verlag, 1936), 253. Grabert, who devotes thirty pages to describing "Hauer's path from Christianity to Nordic-Germanic religion," emphasizes Hauer's anti-dogmatism. Particularly interesting is Grabert's comment that "Hauer now honors Jesus purely as a 'great Jew.'"

64. *Don Quichotte en miniature* was the title of the *Festschrift* published for Paetel's sixty-fifth birthday (private edition, 1971).

65. Karl O. Paetel, *Reise ohne Unrzeit: Autobiographie*, Wolfgang D. Elfe and John M. Spalek (eds) (Worms: Georg Heintz, 1982), 29ff.

66. For example, at the 1931 meeting, a Communist member of the Reichstag, Schneller, spoke on the "Weg und Ziel der kommunistischen Bewegung" (Path and goal of the Communist movement). Other speakers included the Social Democrat professor Eduard Heimann from Hamburg and the economist Georg Schmitt, who spoke about economic democracy. In 1929 Hauer even gave a platform to a Jewish Communist, Friedrich Wolf, author of the contemporary drama *Cyankali*, who argued for the revoking of paragraph 218 of the German legal code (relating to homosexuality). For this Hauer was criticized by Wilhelm Stapel, a journalist of National Socialist sympathies, in his article "Zum Streit um Hauer" [On the Hauer controversy], published in Stapel's journal *Deutsches Volkstum* (October 1935), 795.

67. Hauer was of the opinion that only the (i.e. his) German Faith or the movement towards it could "bring about the inner foundation of the Third Reich." See the foreword to his book *Deutsche Gottschau*. In a letter of 4 June 1941 to Fritz Gericke, Hauer goes even further and says that he has committed himself to National Socialism "come what may." Quoted from Uwe Werner, *Anthroposophen in der Zeit des Nationalsozialismus (1933–1945)* (Munich: R. Oldenbourg, 1999), 309.

68. Quoted from Hauer's essay "Vom totalen Sinn der Deutschen Revolution," *Kommende Gemeinde* 5(2–3) (1933), 7.

69. In the original this sentence is printed spaced out for emphasis.

70. J.W. Hauer, *Eine indo-arische Metaphysik dea Kampfes und der Tat: Die Bhagavad-Gita in neuer Sicht mit Übersetzungen* (Stuttgart: Kohlhammer, 1934). This connection is made clear by the American scholar of religion Gregory Alles in his essay "The Science of Religion in a Fascist State: Rudolf Otto and Jakob Wilhelm Hauer during the Third Reich," *Religion* 32 (2002), 177–204, which I would rate as one of the most balanced statements yet written about Hauer's activities, *Weltanschauung*, and personal accountability. Equally fascinating is the comparison that Alles draws with Rudolf Otto, who, in a very different and less spectacular way, also "swam" with the National Socialist current. While Hauer basically supported National Socialism, he found himself *de facto* opposed to it on the issue of the Christian religion, which he wished to combat, whereas Hitler saw Christianity as a necessary partner in order to win over the people. Otto, on the other hand, who was decidedly on the side of Christianity, found himself *de facto* in agreement with the National Socialists on this issue, even though that was not his intention. One wishes that there were more such well-informed analyses dealing with this perilous area.

71. Dierks, *Jakob Wilhelm Hauer*, 277ff., and in greater detail in Junginger, *Von der philologischen zur völkischen Religionswissenschaft*, 127ff. Karla Poewe, on the other hand, does not mention this incident in her *New Religions and the Nazis*.

72. In *Religion und Rasse* (Tübengen: J.C.B. Mohr, 1941), 2ff., he expressed this as follows: "The dominant idea of the present epoch is that of race. This is also the leading scientific concept of our time … Anyone who does not align themselves with this idea is out of touch with the age. It is clear that this is not a matter of some passing fashion but rather of a necessity of Life that demands obedience." On page 42 of the pamphlet he speaks of an "often insoluble

problem" arising from the fact "that we do not possess a single cultural and religious sphere within which a pure race is in force. All peoples are racially mixed. Therefore one must rely on the racially dominant element."

73. In Jakob Wilhelm Hauer, *Das religiöse Artbild der Indogermanen und die Grundtypen der indo-arischen Religion* (Stuttgart: W. Kohlhammer, 1937), 7–10, quoted here from Richard Flasche, *Gab es Versuche einer Ideologisierung der Religionswissenschaft während des Dritten Reiches?*," in *Gnosisforschung und Religionsgeschichte*, Holger Prießler and Hubert Seiwert (eds)(Marburg: Diagonal-Verlag, 1994), 418.

74. Junginger, *Von der philologischen zur völkischen Religionswissenschaft*, 182–92.

75. Karla Poewe supports Junginger's judgment on this matter, e.g. in her *New Religions and the Nazis*, 32ff.

76. Hauer himself admitted this in a letter of 9 September 1934 to the high-ranking National Socialist Werner Best, quoted by Karla Poewe in *New Religions and the Nazis*, 181.

77. As the sociologist and historian Stefan Breuer writes in his book *Die Völkischen in Deutschland* (Darmstadt: WBG, 2008), 262: "Hauer … was no 'racist' working towards a re-structuring of the population according to racist criteria."

78. See, for example, the work by Pastor J. Lorentzen of Kiel, *Das christliche Bekenntnis und die deutsche Glaubensbewegung: eine Auseinandersetzung mit Graf Reventlow und Professor Hauer*, vol. 1 of a series published by the Evangelical-Lutheran Church in Schleswig-Holstein (1935). See also Hans Pfeil, *Die Grundlehren des deutschen Glaubens: Eine Bewertung und Ablehnung* (Paderborn: Verlag der Bonifacius-Druckerei, 1936).

79. From his speech in 1934 to the Scharzfeld meeting of the German Faith Movement, quoted here from Wilhelm Hauer, *Was will die deutsche Glaubensbewegung?*, H. Grabert (ed.) (Stuttgart: Karl Gutbrod Verlag, 1935), 31.

80. The following words, spoken by Martin Buber, were expressly endorsed by Hauer: "A true community is composed of religious people … emerges in such a way that the group has a common centre. Through these rays from the centre arises the circle … Religious reality is not handed down by the spirit from above, but rather emerges through our behaving in a human way to each other. This is how the name of God dwells amongst us" (Dierks, *Hauer*, 198).

81. The main source of all this information was Hauer himself. Here I can only pass on what Ulrich Nanko writes in his indispensable book on this subject, *Die Deutsche Glaubensbewegung: Eine historische und soziologische Untersuchung* (Marburg: Diagonal-Verlag, 1993), 14ff.

82. Wolfgang Dierker, *Himmlers Glaubenskrieger: Der Sicherheitsdienst der SS und seine Religionspolitik 1933–1941*. (Paderborn: Ferdinand Schöningh, 2003), 207.

83. Quoted here from Manfred Müller, "'Selbst eine Kirche werden': Christentum und Politik im III. Reich," *Neue Ordnung* 2(5) (2005), 22.

84. From the article "Wie steht es um den deutschen Glauben?," in the issue of 23 April 1936. Quoted here from Cancik, '*Neuheiden' und totaler Staat*," 217.

85. Joseph Goebbels, *Tagebücher Band 3: 1935–1939*, Ralf Georg Reuth (ed.) (Munich: R. Piper, 1992), 953.

86. It was only three years after his entry into the SS that Hauer was able to join the Nazi Party. According to Junginger, this was mainly due to the mistrust the Nazis had against him on account of his leadership of the German Faith Movement. However, Hauer was apparently very fond of putting on his SS uniform. Junginger even speaks of Hauer's "almost childish-seeming pleasure," when he wore it (*Von der philologischen zur völkischen Religionswissenschaft*, 129).

87. With the subtitle *Eine Wertung und eine Kritik* (Stuttgart: W. Kohlhammer, [1921] 1923).

88. Werner, *Anthroposophen in der Zeit des Nationalsozialismus*, 108.

89. Thus Hauer repeatedly challenged Rudolf Steiner to consult the akashic records with the help of his alleged clairvoyant faculties in order to solve the historic riddle of the Aegean culture and to decipher its preserved inscriptions. Steiner did not reply, but his close associate Friedrich Rittelmeyer said that one cannot simply switch on the clairvoyant faculty on command in order to investigate this or that area of reality (Hauer, *Werden und Wesen der Anthroposophie*, 93).

90. Werner, *Anthroposophen in der Zeit des Nationalsozialismus*, 122.

91. Letter from Hauer to Stengel von Rutkowski, dated 29 September 1940. Quoted here from Werner, *Anthroposophen in der Zeit des Nationalsozialismus*, 301.

92. Quoted here from Junginger, *Von der philologischen zur völkischen Religionswissenschaft*, 201.

93. At that time, however, Buber could have known little or nothing of Hauer's unpublicized activities. In particular, as Junginger emphasizes, Hauer's collaboration with the SD was unknown to him. This collaboration included Hauer's leadership of a unit for the *Erforschung und Abwehr des Okkultismus* (Research into and combating of occultism), which was integrated into the Aryan Institute, also led by Hauer. According to Junginger, the archival record points unavoidably to the conclusion that in this way Hauer "collaborated at the highest level in the persecution of domestic political enemies." See Junginger, *Von der philologischen zur völkischen Religionswissenschaft*, 301ff.

94. Dierks, *Hauer*, 345.

95. Interview published in the Jung Oral History Archive, 11, quoted in Sonu Shamdasani's introduction to C.G. Jung, *The Psychology of Kundalini Yoga: Notes of the Seminar Given in 1932 by C.G. Jung*, Sonu Shamdasani (ed.) (Princeton, NJ: Princeton University Press, 1999), xlii.

96. Mentioned in Baumann's lecture "Völkische Religionen und Antisemitismus," delivered in October 1999 at Tübingen University.

97. W.R. Corti goes even further and even sees a deep inner rapport between Buber and Hauer. In his essay "Die Eranos-Begegnungsstätte für Ost und West in Moscia-Ascona," *Schweizer Annalen* 1(1935), 52–9, Corti writes, "The Hasidic pansacramentalism [i.e. the belief that man, through his deeds, participates in God's work of redemption] is profoundly present in that 'godly brotherhood of all things' of which Hauer speaks in his work *Deutsche Gottschau*."

98. Dierks, *Hauer*, 201ff.

99. Hauer writes on this topic in *Kommende Gemeinde* 5 (July 1933): 115: "Some of our friends have not been able to understand why we would even allow a Jew to speak on folkish matters at our German Faith Movement Weeks. These weeks, however, have long been guided by the principle that we always allow those holding the most convinced positions to voice their views on the issues preoccupying us. This is based on the realization, gained through long experience, that when someone makes a pronouncement that is not based on personal involvement, however well presented it may be, it does not go to the core of the matter and will remain fruitless."

100. In his journal *Kommende Gemeinde* 5(4–5) (December 1933), Hauer writes in the introduction, "We have never and can never abandon this ultimate goal of mutual religious understanding. This is more than mere tolerance; it is a struggle for genuine community in the highest reality and without any desire to blur the fateful differences between religions. Such an abandonment would mean denying our belief in the God who appears to human beings in a thousand different ways and yet remains the eternal reality in whom we all have our beginning and end."

101. Reichstein, who was professor of organic chemistry at Basel, later supported Olga Fröbe financially in building up her picture archive (letter from Fröbe of 22 June 1942).

102. Here, to be fair, one must take into account the already mentioned antipathy that apparently existed between the two men.

103. Quoted in Shamdasani's introduction to Jung, *The Psychology of Kundalini Yoga*, xxxiii.

104. A comprehensive and informed account of Hauer's contribution to the reception of yoga in Europe is to be found in Baier, *Yoga auf dem Weg nach Westen*, 257–80.

105. Fritz Heinrich, *Die deutsche Religionswissenschaft und der Nationalsozialismus: Eine ideologiekritische und wissenschaftsgeschichtliche Untersuchung* (Petersberg: Michael Imhof Verlag, 2002), 157.

106. On this theme see also the entry on Hauer by the historian Hermann Weiss in Hermann Weiss (ed.), *Biographisches Lexikon zum Dritten Reich* (Frankfurt: S. Fischer, 1998), 184ff.

107. On the other hand Gustavo Benavides, in his essay "Jakob Wilhelm Hauer, or Karmayoga as a Cold War Weapon," in *The Academic Study of Religion during the Cold War: East and West*, Iva Doležlová, Luther H. Martin, and Dalibor Papoušek (eds) (New York: Peter Lang, 2001), 228, complains that "barely thirteen years after the end of the war" Hauer's commentary to the *Bhagavad-Gita* contained remarks such as "death is only an attack on empirically manifest form" or "The warrior who has to kill does not thereby become a destroyer of human beings, he is only carrying out what the way of the world has ordained." See Hauer, *Der Yoga: Ein indischer Weg zum Selbst*, 381. Here, however, one could argue that Hauer is merely interpreting the god Krishna's injunction to his military leader Arjuna, not necessarily expressing his own opinion.

108. Ulrich Nanko, "Religiöse Gruppenbildungen vormaliger 'Deutschgläubiger' nach 1945," in *Antisemitismus, Paganismus, Völkische Religion*, Hubert Cancik and Uwe Puschner (eds) (Munich: K.G. Sauer, 2004), 123.

109. See the report by Lothar Stengel von Rutkowski "Toleranz und Freiheit. Bericht über die erste Jahrestagung der 'Freien Akademie' auf dem Ludwigstein 24.–31. Juli 1957," *Wirklichkeit und Freiheit. Blätter für die "Freunde der Freien Akademie e.V.,"* Jahresrundbrief 3 and 4 (December 1957), 77. See also J.W. Hauer, *Toleranz und Intoleranz in den nichtchristlichen Religionen: Beitrag zu einer weltgeschichtlichen Betrachtung der Religion* (Stuttgart: Kohlhammer, 1961). In this connection, I would most strongly recommend Jan Assmann's masterly study *Die Mosaische Unterscheidung oder der Preis des Monotheismus* (Munich: Carl Hanser, 2003), to which I shall return later on.

110. Hence the accusation made by Wilhelm Stapel, whom we have already mentioned, that Hauer did admittedly "reject vulgar pacifism but taught a religious pacifism." See Stapel, "Zum Streit um Hauer," 795.

111. Hubert Cancik in his essay "'Neuheiden' und totaler Staat," 190, also confirms that the German Faith Movement stemmed from the ecological movement, which cultivated tolerance and pacific ideals.

112. On his own admission Heiler had, in 1925, helped to secure for Hauer the chair of Indology at Marburg.

113. See Organisationsausschuss (ed.), *X. Internationaler Kongress für Religionsgeschichte. 11–17. September 1960 in Marburg/Lahn* (Marburg: N.G. Elwert, 1961).

114. Annemarie Schimmel, *Morgenland und Abendland. Mein west-östliches Leben* (Munich: C.H. Beck, 2002), 159ff.

115. Personal communication, 29 July 2001.

116. *Die Deutsche Glaubensbewegung und ihr Begründer Jakob Wilhelm Hauer (1881–1962)*. This dissertation, written in Hebrew, has subsequently been published in German (Marburg: Diagonal, 2005).

117. Baumann argues that theologically the German Faith Movement gave prominence to anything that distinguished it from Christianity. It attacked the central Christian notions of redemption, forgiveness of sins, and a transcendental God, and replaced them with a glorification of death.

118. See also Horst Junginger, *Von der philosophischen zur völkischen Religionswissenschaft*, 140.

119. It is not very well known that Jung himself practiced yoga for a time during the acute psychotic crisis that he suffered between 1914 and 1918. "I was often so churned up that I had to switch off my emotions through yoga exercises" (Jaffé (ed.), *Memories, Dreams, Reflections*, 180ff.).

120. Both letters are in the Jung archive at the Eidgenössische Technische Hochschule, Zurich.

121. This is, incidentally, the very first comprehensive and scholarly work on yoga to be published in German.

122. The relationship between Jung and Hauer is dealt with thoroughly by Dierks in *Jakob Wilhelm Hauer*, 283–99.

123. Jung's attention had been drawn to Zimmer by the latter's book *Kunstform und Yoga im indischen Kultbild*, which appeared in Berlin in 1926. Here, for the first time, appeared a study of mandalas and similar diagrams. Jung was struck by the similarity of these to the drawings of his patients.

124. See the German-language documents prepared by Linda Fierz and Toni Wolff in December 1932 for distribution to the participants. These also included the last four days of Jung's winter seminars on yoga. Mary Foote edited the manuscripts of the English-language seminars given by Hauer and Jung (Zurich, autumn 1932). See also Jung, *The Psychology of Kundalini Yoga*.

125. Barbara Hannah, *Jung*, 206. However, the introduction by Sonu Shamdasani to Jung's *The Psychology of Kundalini Yoga*, 34, quotes another participant, C.A. Meier, as saying that the presentations were very clear and that he had no recollection of any general sense of confusion.

126. See Jung's letter of 21 November 1931 in Jung, *Briefe I*, 142ff.

127. Leopold Ziegler is known today chiefly as an (independent) German apologist for the Traditionalist René Guénon. Jung even visited him and his house in Überlingen on Lake Constance. See the interview (p. 18), which Jolande Jacobi gave to the American psychoanalyst Gene F. Nameche and which is preserved in the Jung Oral Archive in the Countway Medical Library in Boston (my attention was drawn to this by Jay Sherry).

128. This journal was supposed to appear monthly and it was intended that it should also include artistic contributions. Jung considered making the poet Hermann Broch responsible for the literary part. This was what led to a meeting between the two men. See Hermann Broch, *Briefe I: 1913–1938* (Frankfurt: Suhrkamp, 1986), 225ff. To begin with Broch was very impressed with Jung's work, but later he spoke only of a "very limited acceptance" of it (letter of 3 November 1944 to Wolfgang Sauerländer). Broch was also a reader of the Eranos volumes, as indicated in a letter of 19 April 1935 and by one to Karl Kerényi of 25 September 1947. On the subject of Broch's gnostic background, see the essay "Der Gnostiker Hermann Broch" by the eminent literary scholar Joseph Strelka in *Gnostika* 35 (2007), 42–54.

129. My source here is Junginger, *Von der philosophischen zur völkischen Religionswissenschaft*, 137ff.

130. In 2006 the bestselling author Robert Temple (*The Sirius Mystery*) gave a talk in the context of the reconstitution of the Eranos Foundation in Moscia, in which he maintained that Hauer had been thrown out following this dispute. However, I have not been able to find any confirmation of this. See Robert Temple, "Eranos: Past and Future," in *Eranos Jahrbuch* 69 (2006, 2007, 2008), 85.

131. As we know, at that time obtaining an exit visa was also a problem for other participants. On 1 August 1935 Erwin Rousselle wrote to his friend Hertha Jay von Seldeneck, who lived in Ascona, that he had still not received official travel permission and did not know whether he would be able to speak at the Eranos meeting, due to begin a few days later, or even whether he would be allowed officially to attend. In the same letter he surmised that this was also the reason why Hauer and Zimmer had declined to take part.

132. Hauer was in any case exposed to many attacks, political and otherwise, including the accusation that he was trying to propagate yoga in Germany. On 25 July 1935 he defended himself in detail with an article in the *Reichswart* under the title *Wider das undeutsche Wesen der Lüge und Verleumdung* [Against the un-German practice of lies and slander], in which he emphasized that he had "adopted a positive stance towards National Socialism long before the revolution." Quoted from Stapel, "Zum Streit um Hauer," 794.

133. This certainly proves Heyer's sincerity and courage. His contribution was also included in this volume.

134. In the event, when *Eranos Jahrbuch* 2 (1934) was published, the lectures of Buber, Hauer, Heyer, and also Zimmer appeared quite harmoniously together. As we shall see, it was only with the 1936 yearbook that difficulties of this kind arose and two contributions were excluded.

135. *Vom Dach der Welt: Über die "Synthese aller Geisteskultur," in Ost und West* (Munich: Ludendorffs Verlag, 1938), 33–5. The movement surrounding General Erich von Ludendorff and his wife Mathilde was one of the most vociferous of the groups that were warning against Masonic, occult, and oriental teachings. Eranos was regarded by them as a focal point for all these tendencies. See also *Asekha: Der Kreuzzug der Bettelmönche* (Düsseldorf: Verlag Deutsche Revolution, 1937), written by another Ludendorffian, Fritz Wilhelmy, who mentions Eranos on pages 18 and 24, citing newspaper articles to support his case. Hauer is mentioned by name but with the additional remark that he had "in the meantime withdrawn." In 1964 Dietrich Bonder used these statements in his scantily referenced but well-known book *Bevor Hitler kam* (Geneva: Marva, 1975), 224. Bonder spoke of Hauer's "considerable occult-mystical leanings" and added that he "possessed close ties to the occult Eranos movement in Ascona (Switzerland), where he collaborated with the well-known Jewish scholar Professor Dr. Martin Buber."

136. The term "induced madness" (*induziertes Irresein*) was used by Mathilde von Kemnitz-Ludendorff (the wife of General Erich von Ludendorff) to apply to all "occult" and esoteric teachings.

137. The mocking tone of these accusations, leaving aside the anti-Judaic remarks, may strike readers as being surprisingly similar to rationalist attacks on Eranos that are heard today.

138. L., "Glaubensbewegung: Symbol und Yoga" [Faith movement: symbolism and yoga], *Am Heiligen Quell Deutscher Kraft* 6(14) (20 Gilbhardts 1935), 562–66.

139. L., "Glaubensbewegung: Hinein ins Irrenhaus" [Faith movement: into the madhouse], *Am Heiligen Quell Deutscher Kraft* 6(15) (5 Nibelungs 1935), 599–607.

140. Peter Kamber, *Geschichte zweier Leben: Wladimir Rosenbaum & Aline Valangin* (Zurich: Limmat Verlag, 1990), 176ff.

141. Corti, "Die Eranos-Begegnungstätte für Ost und West in Moscia-Ascona."

142. Now included in Jung, *Gesammelte Werke*, vol. 10, 215ff.

143. Deirdre Bair is therefore wrong when she writes, in *Jung*, that Jung had already broken off all relations with Hauer in 1934. Equally untrue is her claim that Hauer was excluded from Eranos in 1934.

144. Hauer, *Der Yoga: Ein indischer Weg zum Selbst*, 407–39.

145. Quoted from Dierks, *Jakob Wilhelm Hauer*, 289.

146. This was also called *Kulturbiologie* (cultural biology). See, for example, Walter Scheidt, *Kulturbiologie: Vorlesungen für Studierende aller Wissensgebiete* (Jena: Gustav Fischer, 1930). Although not exactly equivalent, there was in the Anglo-Saxon world at that time the concept of "geographical determination" which, at least in its general approach, leaned in a similar direction. Even today it is possible to find comparable studies. See, for example, Tetsuro Watsuji, *Fudo: Wind und Erde. Der Zusammenhang von Klima und Kultur* (Darmstadt: Wissenschaftliche Buchgesellschaft, 1997). On the question of the *völkisch* movement, see the penultimate chapter of this book.

147. Here I can only agree with what Steven Beller says in his essay "Herzl, Wagner and the Ironies of 'True Emancipation," in *Tainted Greatness: Antisemitism and Cultural Heroes*, Nancy A. Harrowitz (ed.) (Philadelphia, PA: Temple University Press, 1994), 152: "And that Herzl [the founder of Zionism] thought along lines similar to those of the anti-Semitic Wagner does not make Wagner 'good' or Herzl 'bad.' It simply shows us how complex and difficult the task is of reconstructing the constellations of thought of a past era and how treacherous the exercise is of applying too simplistically our own moral categories to that past."

7. The Years 1934–37

1. Martin Buber, *Briefwechsel aus sieben Jahrzehnten, vol. II: 1918–1938*, Grete Schaeder (ed.) (Heidelberg, Lambert Schneider, 1972), 567–8.

2. The biographical details are taken from Elinor Slater and Robert Slater, *Great Jewish Men* (Middle Village, NY: Jonathan David, 1998), 76ff. The best biography remains Maurice Friedmann, *Martin Buber's Life and Work* (New York: E.P. Dutton, 1981–83). For a concise account of Buber's life see Gerhard Wehr, *Martin Buber* (Reinbek: Rowohlt, 1986). Wehr's earlier book *Der deutsche Jude Martin Buber* (Munich: Kindler, 1977) focuses more on Buber's mental and spiritual universe.

3. In Berlin he attended lectures by Wilhelm Dilthey, a significant figure in the field of phenomenology of religion, an important theme at Eranos.

4. At the time this was a provocative title. See also Eleonore Lappin, *Der Jude 1916–1928. Jüdische Moderne zwischen Universalismus und Partikularismus* (Tübingen: Mohr Siebeck, 2000). In the introduction to the book, Buber is described as the *spiritus rector* of the so-called Jewish Renaissance, "which blossomed in Germany from the beginning of the 20th century."

5. Pinchas Lapide, *Heinrich Heine und Martin Buber: Streitbare Gottsucher des Judentums* (Vienna: Pincus Verlag, 1991), 10.

6. Asher D. Biemann (ed.), Introduction, *The Martin Buber Reader: Essential Readings* (New York: Palgrave Macmillan, 2002), 6. Although this introduction may be short, it nevertheless offers the reader essential insights.

7. Subtitled *Die Geschichte eines Mißverständnisses* (Neukirchen: Neukircher Verlag, 1995), 104ff.

8. Buber dealt with Jakob Boehme in his doctoral dissertation. See Grete Schaeder, *Martin Buber: Hebräischer Humanismus* (Göttingen: Vandenhoek & Ruprecht, 1966), 37. This book contains an observation that, in my opinion, throws an important light on the mood of the time around the turn of the century and seems to me to be of great significance for the early period of Eranos: "Buber's generation … whose belief in creative man was influenced by Nietzsche, leaned unreservedly towards mysticism without the discrimination of a historically distanced view; in mysticism they recognized their own vital sense of meaning." Buber, however, later turned against mysticism and especially against its rejection of the ego, as is shown in his *Ich und Du* [I and Thou], first published in 1923. Today Buber's "mystical phase" is generally limited to the earlier years, 1904–12.

9. As an eighteen-year-old, Scholem had already turned to Martin Buber as editor of *Der Jude*, offering him an article. Contact between the two was never really broken off, and it was Scholem who pushed for Buber's appointment at Jerusalem. Nevertheless, Buber was hurt by Scholem's critique of his conception of Hasidism. See Grete Schaeder, "Martin Buber: Ein biographischer Abriß," in Martin Buber, *Briefwechsel aus sieben Jahrzehnten, vol. I: 1897–1918*, Grete Schaeder (ed.) (Heidelberg, Lambert Schneider, 1972), 19–141.

10. Quoted from Gershom Scholem, *Briefe II, 1948–1970*, T. Sparr (ed.) (Munich: C.H. Beck, 1995), 27. On this

question see also Scholem's Eranos lecture "Martin Bubers Auffassung des Judentums" in *Eranos Jahrbuch* 35 (1966), 9–55, as well as his article *Martin Bubers Deutung des Chassidismus*, originally published in the *Neue Züricher Zeitung* of 20–21 May 1962, and now included in Gershom Scholem, *Judaica 1* (Frankfurt: Suhrkamp, 1981), 165–206.

11. In a letter to the author dated 16 October 2008, Swami Matthias Vereno—Christian-Hindu mystic, priest, university professor, and Mircea Eliade's onetime colleague—made an idiosyncratic remark concerning Buber and Scholem which stemmed from the Hasidic author and interpreter of the Kabbalah Friedrich Weinreb. Weinreb confided to Swami Matthias, "Buber—I don't know how one can live like that. Scholem—I know one can't live the way he lives."

12. It was precisely this failure to adopt a purely rational attitude that also led Theodor W. Adorno to deride the mystically inclined Martin Buber, calling him a *Religionstiroler* (Tyrolean of religion) and reproaching him for secretly bringing the plague of "irrationalism" back to life. To this day the struggle against "irrationalism" (who defines the term?) remains one of the main objectives of the Frankfurt School to which Adorno belonged. See Micha Brumlik, "Theology without Thorns: Adorno's Critique of Buber," in *New Perspectives on Martin Buber*, Michael Zank (ed.) (Tübingen: Mohr Siebeck, 2006), 247.

13. His willingness to adopt a reconciliatory attitude to Germany (despite strong opposition in Israel) led him as early as 1953 to say, "My heart, which knows the weakness of human beings, refuses to condemn my fellow man because he could not bring himself to be a martyr." Quoted in Lapide, *Heinrich Heine und Martin Buber*, 11. This sentence is all the more commendable in light of another fact that is worthy of consideration yet not as pervasive in the popular consciousness as it should be. The well-known Zionist and publicist Robert Weltsch describes it thus: "National Socialist theory, which sequestered the Jews from the German national community, pertained not only to race but to the entirety of cultural existence in which the German Jews had felt secure after a hundred years of emancipation. With one fell blow the German Jews were thrust into a vacuum: they were threatened by a spiritual breakdown that was even more calamitous than the material damage inflicted upon them by the regime." See Robert Weltsch, "Einleitung," in Martin Buber, *Politische Schriften*, Abraham Melzer (ed.) (Frankfurt: Zweitausendeins, 2010), 29.

14. On this subject, see the booklet *München ehrt Martin Buber* (Munich: Ner-Tamid-Verlag, 1961) which includes the accolades delivered on that occasion as well as the recollections of Schalom Ben-Chorin, *Martin Buber in München*.

15. His winning effect on non-Jews was already apparent in 1928 in the *Festschrift* edited by Franz Rosenzweig for Buber's fiftieth birthday, in which only just over half of the congratulatory messages were from Jews. One of the non-Jewish contributors, Wilhelm Michel, had already said of Buber two years earlier, "He is one of us; he is ours. There lives in him the sense of *Germany's* destiny in the world, however much he may appear to be exclusively concerned with the special issues of Judaism … No one speaks the German language as he does unless he has been deeply and seriously captivated by the spirit of the people from whom this language arose." Quoted in Ernst Simon, "Martin Buber und das deutsche Judentum," in *Deutsches Judentum: Aufstieg und Krise: Gestalten, Ideen, Werke*, Robert Weltsch (ed.) (Stuttgart: Deutsche Verlagsanstalt, 1963), 36.

16. Martin Buber, "Nationalismus," in *Martin Buber, Ein Land und zwei Völker: Zur jüdisch-arabischen Frage*, Paul R. Mendes-Flohr (ed.), 70–83 (Frankfurt: Insel Verlag, 1983).

17. Wolfgang Raupach-Rudnik, "Die Notwendigkeit des Friedens—Martin Buber," in Michael Buckmiller, Dietrich Heimann and Joachim Perels (eds), *Judentum und politische Existenz. Siebzehn Porträts deutsch-jüdischer Intellektueller* (Hannover: Offizin, 2000), 111–34.

18. *Ibid.*, 131.

19. Martin Buber, *Ein Land und zwei Völker*, 334–7.

20. Emphasis added.

21. *Ibid.*, 381ff.

22. Two original lectures on these themes delivered by Buber in 1962 and 1963—"Elemente des Zwischenmenschlichen" (Elements of the interpersonal) and "Das Wort, das gesprochen wird" (The word that is spoken)—are available on CD from Auditorium-Netzwerk, Müllheim/Baden, 2007.

23. Asher D. Biemann (ed.), Introduction, *The Martin Buber Reader*, 1.

24. Data from Oskar R. Schlag, *Von alten und neuen Mysterien. Die Lehren des A.* (Würzburg: Ergon, 1998), xxix–xxx.

25. See Gustav Meyrink, *Der Golem* (Zurich: Rascher Verlag, 1946), 301–2.

26. *Hermetische Gesellschaft* is only the name for the outer organizational structure. The inner "esoteric" society bears a name that even the members themselves never speak aloud. Founding member Oskar R. Schlag believed that the spiritual leaders—the "unknown superiors"—of this Hermetic Society were identical with those of the Hermetic Society of Anna Bonus Kingsford as well as those of the Hermetic Order of the Golden Dawn.

27. The possible proofs relate mainly to Fritz Allemann. But it was Allemann's abiding wish that no personal publicity should be attached to him. His family understandably respected this position, but in all probability there is much material on Eranos worthy of attention that remains hidden away in the legacy.

28. Fritz Allemann should not be confused with Fritz René Allemann, the editor of *Der Monat* and author of numerous books including a biography of the Egyptian leader Gamal Abdel Nasser.

29. De Robilant is also one of the central personalities of the Centro Studi Mythos and the journal *Àtopon*. She is a fellow of the Temenos Academy as well. Both are associations which hold Eranos-like seminars, and we will briefly touch upon them later. For this information I would like to thank Matthias Korger, who knew these women and was himself present at an Eranos conference in 1982.

30. Paul Bishop, "The Members of Jung's Seminar on Zarathustra," *Spring* 56 (1994), 101.

31. See, for example, pages 123 and 137 of the transcript.

32. See his collection of aphorisms, *Sanduhr* (Zurich: IPE, 2003).

33. See especially Peter R. König, *Das OTO-Phänomen* (Munich: ARW, 1994), *passim*, and also the expanded edition *Der OTO-Phänomen Remix* (Munich: ARW, 2001), *passim*, in which many voices are quoted on the subject of ORS. See also Riccardo Bernardini, *Da Monte Verità a Eranos*, 188–223.

34. Lucerne was chosen because Schlag's mediumistically manifested spirit guide Atma, who previously called himself the "Tibetan" and the "Wanderer," had spoken of "a shining city on the Lake of the Four": the German name for the Lake of Lucerne is the Vierwaldstättersee ("Lake of the four wooded places), and the name Lucerne is from the Latin *lux* (light). This information is derived from personal communications from Oskar Schlag to the author dating from the late 1980s.

35. Oskar Schlag himself gave a number of introductory lectures entitled "On the Origin and Symbolism of the Tarot." However, these were held exclusively within Freemasonic and quasi-Masonic lodges. Nevertheless, an excellent introduction to Max Hunziker's Tarot cards—and thus also into this aspect of Oskar Schlag's inner world—is the small book by Olaf Räderer, *Tarot. Säulen der Einweihung* (St. Gallen: Verlag RGS, 2003). It contains colored reproductions of the cards, elucidated by corresponding quotations from the *Lehren des A* (The teachings of A, Schlag's spirit guide).

36. See the article "Oscar R. Schlag" by Peter Mulacz, president of the Austrian Parapsychological Society, *Journal of the Society for Psychical Research* 60 (1995), 263–76.

37. It was Oskar Schlag who made a graphological analysis of the "Anna Sprengel" letters for Ellic Howe—letters which played such an important part in the founding of the Hermetic Order of the Golden Dawn—and revealed the letters to be a forgery.

38. See his letter of 27 August 1987 to Bernhard Kilga, to whom I offer my heartfelt thanks for supplying a copy of this correspondence.

39. Through the sale of a Salvador Dali painting, which he had bought after the war for a few thousand Swiss francs, he was able to finance his Oskar R. Schlag Foundation and to see that his book collection was organized under the auspices of the Zurich Central Library, while the books themselves would remain in his former dwelling house.

40. For references on Schlag's homosexuality, see also www.pararelion.ch/schlag.htm (accessed December 2012).

41. Adalbert Schmid, email message to the author, 16 February 2011.

42. C.G. Jung, "C.G. Jung über Parapsychologie: Ein Interview," *Neue Wissenschaft* 2(9) (1952), 297.

43. Walther. "Erinnerungen an Freud und Jung," 82. ORS is also mentioned in Walther's autobiography *Zum anderen Ufer* (428, 431, 440–42), where he is merely identified as "O." Even the highly critical parapsychologist Fanny Moser writes positively about ORS in her book *Der Okkultismus: Täuschungen und Tatsachen*, which was reissued under the title *Das Große Buch vom Okkultismus* (Olten: Walter Verlag, 1974), 893ff.

44. How Antoine Faivre, former holder of the first chair of Esoteric and Mystical Currents in Modern and Contemporary Europe at the Sorbonne, came to know Oskar Schlag is described in his article "Meine Begegnungen mit Oskar R. Schlag," *Gnostika* 28 (October 2004), 50–55.

45. See also Albert Anderes, *Reflexionen zu den "Atma"-Durchsagen des Mediums Oskar Schlag* (Uster: Ratio Humana, 2005). Some further references can be found in my review of the first volume *Von alten und neuen Mysterien*, in *Aries* 20 (1966), 94–7. See also the review by Inge Franz in *Zeitschrift für Ganzheitsforschung* 45(4) (2001), 191–6.

46. Hans-Dieter Leuenberger, "Oskar R. Schlag: Der große Unbekannte," *Esotera* 6 (1996), 28–32.

47. Angelika Koller, *Thorwald Dethlefsen: Die Reinkarnationstherapie und Kawwana: Ein Beitrag zur Psychotherapie- und Religionsgeschichte* (Norderstedt: Books on Demand, 2004), 241ff. and Martin Frischknecht, "Kampf der Finsternis," *Spuren* 56 (Summer 2000), available at www.spuren.ch/archiv/archiv/56/.

48. For example, Oskar R. Schlag, *Frühe Gedichte* (Zurich: Origo Verlag, 1955) and *Das Büchlein von der Volleingedenkheit* (Zurich: Verlag des Schwanes, n.d.). In terms of style these are all reminiscent of the channeled messages from A.

49. See Magda Kerényi (ed.), *Eranos-Index für die Jahrbücher I–XXV, 1933–1956* (Zurich: Rhein-Verlag, 1961), 325.

50. Carl A. Keller's book *Ramakrishna et la voie de l'amour* (Paris: Bayard, 1997) is regarded as the most reliable study.

51. Emma von Pelet, translator of numerous works by Vivekananda into German, will occupy our attention a little later.

52. Romain Rolland, *The Life of Ramakrishna*, E.F. Malcolm-Smith (trans.) (Calcutta: Advaita Ashrama, 2003).

53. Corti, "Die Eranos-Begegnungsstätte für Ost und West in Moscia-Ascona."

54. William McGuire, *Bollingen*, 27.

55. Antoine Faivre in his unpublished diary, 29 August 1974.

56. Jung's underlining.

57. The following data are taken almost exclusively from the essay by Irmgard Gottmann, "Zum Leben und Werk von Sigrid Strauß-Klöbe," in *Symbole der inneren Welt: ein Mosaik gewidmet Sigrid Strauß-Klöbe zum 85. Geburtstag*, V. von Brasch (ed.) (Bad Soden: Viktor von Brasch, 1981).

58. Subtitled *Umrisse einer Kultur- und Seelenlehre* (Jena: Eugen Diederichs, 1921). Fröbe had tried to bring Leo Frobenius to Ascona but without success. See McGuire, *Bollingen*, 146. Frobenius was one of a long list of people whom she invited to Eranos but who never came. They included Salvador de Madariaga, André Malraux, Robert Oppenheimer, Erwin Panofsky, John Woodroffe, Arthur Waite, Arnold Toynbee, Alexis Carrell, Arthur S. Eddington, Walter Y. Evans-Wentz, and T.S. Eliot.

59. Fröbe also used this word in order to describe the passionate eagerness of the Eranos circle, as Henry Corbin reported. See "De l'Iran à Eranos," in *Henry Corbin*, Christian Jambet (ed.) (Paris: L'Herne, 1981), 262.

60. Heinz Arthur Strauß, *Astrologie: Grundsätzliche Betrachtungen* (Leipzig: Kurt Wolff, 1927).

61. Heinz Arthur Strauß (ed.), *Jahrbuch für kosmobiologische Forschung* (Augsburg: Dom-Verlag, 1928–1929).

62. Richard Wilhelm, "Die Einordnung des Menschenlebens in den kosmischen Verlauf im chinesischen Kulturgebiet", in Strauß (ed.), *Jahrbuch für kosmobiologische Forschung*, 11–20. Further essays were contributed by the harmonic musicologist and subsequent Eranos lecturer Hans Kayser, as well as Edgar Dacqué and the astrologer Thomas Ring.

63. Richard Wilhelm and C.G. Jung, *Das Geheimnis der Goldenen Blüte* (Munich: Dorn-Verlag, 1929).

64. Sigrid Strauß-Klöbe, "Kosmos und Seelenwelt: Von Wahrheit und Wahn astrologischen Glaubens," *Deutsche Rundschau* (January 1933).

65. Sigrid Straus-Klöbe, "Tierkreis-Symbolik und Bilderwelt des I Ging," *Europäische Revue* 10(2) (July–December 1934), 589–603.

66. Sigrid Strauß-Klöbe, *Das kosmopsychische Phänomen: Geburtskonstellation und Psychodynamik* (Olten: Walter-Verlag, 1977).

67. Gottmann, "Zum Leben und Werk von Sigrid Strauß-Klöbe," 11.

68. A.E., "Glossen zur Zeit," *Die Tat* 26(10) (1935), 790–92.

69. Aniela Jaffé, "C.G. Jung und die Eranostagungen," *Eranos Jahrbuch* 44 (1975), 10.

70. Van der Vegt, *A. Roland Holst*, 318.

71. Cocks, *Psychotherapy in the Third Reich*, 138.

72. Jung also mentioned this in a letter of 1 August 1936 to Gustav Heyer, in which he wrote, "As I hear from Mrs. Fröbe, the Germans have been excluded one and all from the Eranos meetings by an internal ban. This is much regretted abroad. So we shall have to use French and English as our preferred languages of communication. O quam mirabiles sunt viae vestrae! [Oh, how strange are your ways]." Travel difficulties were not the only problems that the Eranos speakers had with the National Socialist regime. For example, correspondence with Friedrich Heiler and Rudolf Otto was opened and inspected.

73. Horst Junginger, "Harmless or Dangerous? The Eranos Conferences in the 1930s from the Perspective of National Socialist Germany," *Archaeus* 14 (2010), 41–55.

74. Thurnwald was from Vienna and an expert on constitutional law. Initially employed in government service, he then moved to Berlin and began to work for the Museum of Ethnology. He also co-founded the German Association for Racial Hygiene. He traveled to the South Pacific with his wife, also an ethnologist, and sojourned in the United States, where he taught at the University of California, Berkeley, from 1915 until America entered the First World War in 1917. He then returned to Germany, where he took his *Habilitation* degree. Further research trips even brought him a guest professorship at Harvard. In 1937 he returned to Germany and was given an extraordinary professorship in Berlin. See Marion Melk-Koch, *Auf der Suche nach der menschlichen Gesellschaft, Richard Thurnwald* (Berlin: Staatliche Museen Preußischer Kulturbesitz, 1989).

75. The notes stem from Olga Fröbe herself.

76. Bernardini, *Da Monte Verità a Eranos*, documentary appendix preceding page 188.

77. Riccardo Bernardini, email message to author, 18 March 2011.

78. A facsimile of her handwritten account of her life, "Lebenslauf und Horoskop von Fräulein Spengel," appeared in *Gnostika* 31 (2005), 78–9. See also König, *Das OTO Phänomen*, 43.

79. This remarkable woman is the subject of Regula Bochsler's book *Ich folgte meinem Stern. Das kämpferische Leben der Margarete Hardegger* (Zurich: Pendo, 2004).

80. My information comes from Scholem's memoir *Von Berlin nach Jerusalem. Jugenderinnerungen* (Frankfurt: Suhrkamp, 1977), 162–9, as well as from the forewords and dust jackets to two of Eisler's remarkable and searching books, namely *Orpheus—the Fisher: Comparative Studies in Orphic and Early Christian Cult Symbolism* (London: J.M. Watkins, 1921) and *Man into Wolf: An Anthropological Interpretation of Sadism, Masochism and Lycanthropy* (Santa Barbara, CA: Ross-Erikson, 1978).

81. Even Martin Buber told him that he, Buber, could accept contributions from both Jews and non-Jews to his monthly periodical *Der Jude*, but not from renegade Jews (Scholem, *Von Berlin nach Jerusalem*, 163).

82. Robert Eisler, *Weltenmantel und Himmelszelt: Religionsgeschichtliche Untersuchungen zur Urgeschichte des antiken Weltbildes* (Hildesheim: Georg Olms, [1910] 2002).

83. It is perhaps surprising that the "myth-destroying" theologian Rudolf Bultmann is also to be found among the

contributors (see, for example, the issue of April 1926, 308–36, in which he wrote on Mandean parallels to the Fourth Gospel). Jung, as mentioned earlier, possessed a set of issues stretching over seventeen years.

84. It has already been mentioned that Fröbe had invited him to her Summer School. In a letter of 3 June 1933 to Friedrich Heiler, she mentions being "strongly preoccupied with the notion of the Gnostic Crucifixion." This can only be a reference to the work *The Gnostic Crucifixion*, edited and published by Mead, for her letter continues, "'This little book has preoccupied me for years, along with others in the same collection, for example *The Hymn of Jesus.*" Both works are included with an extensive commentary by Mead in his ten-part series *Echoes from the Gnosis* (Benares: Theosophical Publishing House, 1906–8). A complete reprint of all the volumes was published by Cthonios (Stephen Ronan) in 1987. Heiler too was impressed by the work ("This little book, which I had not previously known about, was extremely valuable to me"; letter to Fröbe dated 20 July 1933). Mead's work is still well regarded today, for many of his books are still available. The Temenos Academy, of which more will be said, even organized in 1992 a Mead symposium, which was well attended.

85. His bookshop at 21 Cecil Court in London, close to Trafalgar Square, still exists today under another management. For decades it was *the* meeting place for everyone interested in esoteric subjects. One Eranos speaker who went to the bookshop was Kathleen Raine. It was there that she first came into contact with esoteric studies.

86. See his lectures from 1922 to 1923 under the title *Orphisch-Dionysische Mysteriengedanken in der christlichen Antike* (Neudeln: Kraus, 1967). Eisler incidentally brought Scholem into the Warburg milieu and also introduced him to the occult writer Gustav Meyrink. See Scholem, *Von Berlin nach Jerusalem*, 166, 169.

87. Scholem, *Von Berlin nach Jerusalem*, 165.

88. See Gershom Scholem, *Walter Benjamin: Die Geschichte einer Freundschaft* (Frankfurt: Suhrkamp, 1997), 165. The assessment of Eisler that Scholem gives here is worth quoting: "Eisler was one of the most imaginative and—if one judged by the incredible rich store of learned quotations in his books, without checking them more closely— one of the most erudite historians of religion. For all the great unsolved problems he had a brilliantly wrong answer of the most astonishing kind. He was a person of unbridled ambition and a restlessly driven but rather ungrounded nature." This "ungroundedness" is confirmed in Mircea Eliade's *Journal* I, 1945–1955, 8 May 1953, 189, quoting a report by C.G. Jung that Eisler had once stolen a valuable codex from the Biblioteca Ambrosiana in Milan. When he was apprehended on the train he explained to the police officer that he had been so shocked by a telegram from his fiancée, saying she was going to leave him, that his mind had been fixed only on his return journey and he had simply pocketed the codex. Eisler is certainly not the only scholar to have been guilty of such misdemeanors involving books.

89. Gershom Scholem, *Briefe III*, 1971–1982, Itta Shedletzky (ed.) (Munich: C.H. Beck, 1999), 174.

90. See his book *The Royal Art of Astrology* (London: Herbert Joseph, 1946).

91. Thus he revealed at Monte Verità that the Templar legend, so carefully guarded there, must have been a swindle. Certain Masonic researchers had, however, already distanced themselves from this legend.

92. Corti, "Die Eranos-Begegnungsstätte für Ost und West in Moscia-Ascona," 58.

93. Corti, however, does not explain why Buber was such a notable exception.

94. Corti, "Die Eranos-Begegnungsstätte für Ost und West in Moscia-Ascona," 52–6.

95. *Ibid.*, 52–9.

96. Two of the lectures, namely those by the theologian Paul Tillich and the Judaist Heinz Westmann, could not be included in the volume of proceedings for 1936, as it was feared that the political implications of these texts could cause the book to be banned in Germany. The two texts appeared together under the common title *Gestaltung der Erlösungsidee im Judentum und im Protestantismus*, published by the Eranos Foundation (Ascona, 1986).

97. In the letter he describes Eranos as the only European forum at which people of different nationalities could discuss questions relating to humankind as a whole. I would like to thank Sonu Shamdasani for drawing my attention to this letter.

98. Wouter Hanegraaff, holder of the Chair for the History of Hermetic Philosophy and Related Currents at the University of Amsterdam, who also seems to lean on Noll's work, sees Jung as "essentially a modern esotericist, who represents a crucial link between traditional (i.e. pre-occultist) esoteric worldviews and the New Age movement." Hanegraaff adds in a footnote, however, that this interpretation of Jung does not imply that his achievements are discredited. The fact that Jung was an esotericist in no way implies that he was not an empirically successful doctor. Like Paracelsus, Jung was simply both. His worldview was simply different from that of traditional science, which rested on other premises. See Wouter Hanegraaff, *New Age Religion and Western Culture: Esotericism in the Mirror of Secular Thought* (Leiden: Brill, 1996), 497. Altogether he sees Jung as someone deeply influenced by the Naturphilosophie of the Romantic period.

99. In this connection, see Aniela Jaffé, "C.G. Jung und die Eranostagungen," 10ff.

100. For example, according to Aniela Jaffé, it was in this lecture "Der Geist der Psychologie," published in *Eranos Jahrbuch* 14 (1946), that he first formulated his world-famous theory of the universal collective unconscious (although this is disputed by Sonu Shamdasani, who maintains that the foundations of the theory go back further). See Aniéla Jaffé's lecture "Die schöpferischen Phasen im Leben von C.G. Jung," *Eranos Jahrbuch* 40 (1971), 112. The philologist Walter Wili, in his foreword to the Eranos *Festschrift* for Jung's seventieth birthday (*Eranos Jahrbuch* 12 [1945], 10), even declares, "In these meetings you brought together a major portion of your scientific work over the past decade."

101. As late as 1950 Jung complained to Eliade, when they met in Ascona, that "official science" did not recognize him. The professors, he said, were content simply to repeat what they had learnt in their youth and tended to fear anything that "upset the harmony of their little universe." See *Journal I*, 1945–1955, 113ff.

102. From Eliade, *Journal II, 1957–1969*, xiii.

103. Gershom Scholem, *Briefe II*, 19.

104. Corti, "Die Eranos-Begegnungsstätte," 53.

105. *Eranos Jahrbuch* 18 (1950), 8.

106. For Olga Fröbe (and partly also for Jung) Eranos was a "spirit" to which she had intuitive access and which she regarded as archetypal.

107. The philosopher of religion Alfons Rosenberg must have felt something similar, for in a highly vivid and deeply impressive dream he experienced Jung as an evil demon, who left him with a feeling of fear even after he had awakened. This feeling of aversion almost prevented him from taking part in a forthcoming Eranos meeting. Nevertheless, he overcame the feeling and reported his dream to Jung. The latter replied "slowly and with emphasis" as follows: "If you experienced me as a demon, then I must ask myself if I really am one. If that is what you dreamed, then I must take it seriously." The fact that Jung was willing to take this stigma of the demonic on to his shoulders deepened Rosenberg's feeling of connection with Jung. (See "Eranos, der Geist am Wasser," *Flugblätter für Freunde aus der Werkstatt von Alfons Rosenberg* 80 [1977], 6.)

108. McGuire, *Bollingen*, 27ff.

109. Lawrence White, the physicist and philosopher, who attended Eranos as a member of audience, expressed this in the following way: "He certainly had the patience of a good listener—I suppose you can't avoid that if people buy your time as a professional psychiatrist." White was, incidentally, very surprised that Jung was always well informed about the latest research in physics through his friend the physicist Wolfgang Pauli. See Vincent Brome, *Jung* (New York: Atheneum, 1978), 214.

110. It is worth remarking that Paul Masson-Oursel contributed to the revised three-volume edition of 1955 of the essays documenting the workings of the Group of Ur, the initiatory magical group led by Julius Evola. See "Sul ruolo della magia nella speculazione indù," in *Introduzione alla Magia quale scienza dell'Io*, Gruppo di Ur (ed.) (Turin: Bocca, 1955), vol. III, 293–9. Unfortunately nothing is known about the contacts between Evola and Masson-Oursel. Evola's involvement with religious studies in general is dealt with in my entry "Evola, Julius," in *Encyclopedia of Religion*, vol. 5, 2nd ed., Lindsay Jones (ed.), 2904–7 (Detroit, MI: Macmillan, 2005). Certainly Masson-Oursel knew one of Evola's most important teachers, namely René Guénon, founder of the Integral Tradition movement. Apparently Masson-Oursel even found himself increasingly drawn to Guénon's point of view. At least this is what Guénon claims in a letter of 12 June 1927 to his pupil Guido de Giorgio. The letter is included as an annex to de Giorgio's book *L'Instant et l'Eternité et autres textes sur la Tradition* (Milan: Arché, 1987), 297. More details in Hans Thomas Hakl, "Julius Evola and the Ur Group," *Aries* 12(1) (2012), 53–90.

111. These details are taken from the *Festschrift* by A. Bareau, *Mélanges d'histoire des religions offerts à Henri-Charles Puech* (Paris: Presses Universitaires de France, 1974).

112. The purchase of the codex was decided upon during the Eranos meeting of August 1951. Originally it was supposed to be funded by the Bollingen Foundation, but finally the codex was acquired by the C.G. Jung Institute through the financial support of the benefactor George H. Page of Wallisellen. See Gilles Quispel, "The Jung Codex and its Significance," in *The Jung Codex*, Henri-Charles Puech, Gilles Quispel, and W.C. van Unnik (eds), (London: A.R. Mowbray, 1955), 41ff.

113. Michel Malinine, Henri-Charles Puech, and Gilles Quispel, *Evangelium Veritatis* (Zurich: Rascher, 1956).

114. Michel Malinine, Henri-Charles Puech, Gilles Quispel, and Walter Till, *De Resurrectione* (Zurich: Rascher, 1958).

115. Henri-Charles Puech, *Le manichéisme: son fondateur, sa doctrine* (Paris: Civilisations du Sud S.A.E.P., 1949), 70.

116. Hannah, *Jung*, 235.

117. Henri-Charles Puech, *Histoire des Religions* (Paris: Gallimard, 1970–76).

118. Friedrich Spiegelberg, "Eranostagung 1936," *Europäische Revue* 12 (1936), 840–41. The *Europäische Revue*, from which I quote repeatedly, was founded in 1925 by the Austrian prince Karl Anton Rohan and can be considered one of the most important German-language periodicals of that era dealing with political, cultural, and literary matters. The journal supported a political unification of Europe with a strong emphasis on the cultural level. It lasted until the September-October issue of 1944. Rohan had been obliged to resign from the editorship in 1936, as he had become the cause of a quarrel between the Austrian government and the National Socialist regime in Germany. The journal, whose first issue carried an introduction by Hugo von Hofmannsthal, brought together a mind-boggling array of prominent names, often representing very contrasting views. To mention only a few, they included Rabindranath Tagore, Luigi Pirandello, Stefan Zweig, Thomas Mann, Leopold Ziegler, Maxim Gorki (1925), Franz Werfel, Hermann Hesse, Max Beckmann (1927), Friedrich Gundolf, André Gide, Ernest Hemingway, Le Corbusier, Karl Wolfskehl, Richard Wilhelm, Marcel Proust (1927–29), Bertrand Russell (1929), Nikolai Berdyaev, John M. Keynes, Leo Schestow, Anna Seghers (1930), Aldous Huxley, Siegfried Kracauer, Katherine Mansfield, Franz Kafka, Hermann Keyserling, Max Scheler (1931), Winston Churchill (1932), Albert Schweizer, Carl Burckhardt, Theodor Adorno (1933), Gottfried Benn (1934), Arnold Toynbee, William Faulkner

(1935), George Santayana (1936), Jean Giraudoux, Sir Arthur Eddington, Franz Altheim (1937), Werner Bergengruen (1940), the later President of the Federal Republic of Germany Theodor Heuss, Gustav Gründgens, Rudolf Kassner (1941), Max Planck, Reinhold Schneider (1942), Tania Blixen, Eduard Spranger (1943), Gerhart Hauptmann, Marcel Aymé, and Ortega Y Gasset (as late as 1944). Besides these names, who are still widely known throughout the world and who generally contributed several times, there were others who have since earned a more negative reputation. These included "Hitler's star jurist," Carl Schmitt (1933); Joseph Goebbels (1934), Walter Darré (1941), and Arthur Seiß-Inquart—all members of the Nazi elite—as well as the "social fascist" Drieu la Rochelle (1927 and 1941), who was published in one issue along with the subsequent president of the Czech Republic, Edvard Beneš. Contributors also included the French poet Robert Brasillach, who was executed as a Nazi collaborator; the Belgian national socialist (not in the Nazi sense) Henrik de Man; the self-confessed Fascists Carlo Costamagna and Roberto Farinacci; the originally anti-German Minister of Labor in the Vichy government, Marcel Déat; the anti-democrat Albrecht Erich Günther; and the equally anti-democratic esotericist and cultural philosopher Julius Evola; who contributed altogether six articles to the journal. Many of the Eranos lecturers also contributed: C.G. Jung wrote articles for the journal over several years up to 1934, including one in 1932 on James Joyce's Ulysses. Other Eranos names among the contributors included Martin Buber, Max Pulver (1929), Emil Preetorius (1926-27), Leo Baeck (1932), Heinrich Zimmer (1933, 1936), Sigrid Strauß-Klöbe (1934), Karl Kerényi (1937, 1941, 1942), and D.T. Suzuki (1941).

119. This information is taken primarily from the dust jacket of one of his most important books: Frederic Spiegelberg, *Die lebenden Weltreligionen* (Frankfurt: Insel Verlag, 1977).

120. See his *Spiritual Practices in India* (San Francisco, CA: Greenwood, 1952) and his *Zen, Rock and Waters* (New York: Pantheon Books, 1961).

121. Friedrich Spiegelberg, *Alchemy as a Way of Salvation* (Stanford, CA: Stanford University Press, 1945).

122. See Walter Truett Anderson, *The Upstart Spring: Esalen and the Human Potential Movement: The First Twenty Years* (Lincoln, NE: Authors Guild Back-in-Print, 2004), 27ff., and Jeffrey J. Kripal, *Esalen: America and the Religion of No Religion* (Chicago, IL: University of Chicago Press, 2007).

123. I am grateful to Sonu Shamdasani for drawing my attention to this letter. Further material on Alwine von Keller is to be found in Riccardo Bernardini, *Carl Gustav Jung a Eranos* (unpublished doctoral thesis, Università di Bologna, 2009), 380-93. The book version of this thesis (Milan: FrancoAngeli, 2011) is abbreviated and does not carry the same wealth of information. In her Eranos manuscript *L'Oeuvre d'Eranos*, 47-88, Catherine Ritsema writes in considerable detail about these two ladies, with whom she was on very friendly terms.

124. On her death in 1967, Emma von Pelet left the house to a foundation, whose purpose was to support Eranos. In honor of her friend it was named the Alwine von Keller Foundation. In 1980 it was merged with Eranos for administrative reasons, creating the Eranos and Alwine von Keller Foundation. All this information comes from Riccardo Bernardini, Gian Piero Quaglino, and Augusto Romano, "A Visit Paid to Jung by Alwine von Keller," *Journal of Analytical Psychology* 56 (2011), 232-54. The essay investigates previously unresearched papers of Alwine von Keller dealing with Jung's visions on the occasion of his heart attack in 1944. In this connection Jung gave her some very significant comments. As Von Keller had undergone her training analysis under Jung, a strong relationship of trust had been established between them. In a letter of 4 July 1943 to her friend Eva Cassirer, she writes as follows about the psychologist: "But Jung, beyond the analytical process, constellates *woman* in every woman. He is so absolutely a man ... that this has a profound influence on the woman's unconscious." This, she said, can lead in some cases to a "tie which may border on a dependency so strong, that it consumes all" (p. 237).

125. Interestingly, she says in the letter that such an official framework is appropriate after a "seven-year trial period." Thus she included the School for Spiritual Research, which she had organized with Alice Bailey, as belonging to the Eranos period.

126. See Theodor-Wilhelm Danzel, *Magie und Geheimwissenschaft in ihrer Bedeutung für Kultur und Kulturgeschichte* (Stuttgart: Strecker & Schröder, 1924), especially the foreword. In this book he covers a wide span from tribal communities through Babylon, Mexico, India, and China to Kabbalah and alchemy.

127. See especially his book *Der magische Mensch (Homo divinans): Vom Wesen des primitiven Kultur* (Potsdam: Müller & Kiepenheuer, 1928).

8. Eranos 1938: The United States Shows Interest

1. Ellen Thayer, a participant at the Eranos conference of 1938, also writes in her report (to be mentioned later on) that Baron von der Heydt accommodated the speakers gratis in his hotel. Barbara Hannah likewise confirms this. See Hannah, *Jung*, 216.

2. Most of the following information comes from the already mentioned book by William McGuire, *Bollingen*, 7ff. On the subject of Paul Mellon himself, see William S. Hoffmann, *Paul Mellon: Portrait of an Oil Baron* (Chicago, IL: Follett, 1974). This book, however, contains nothing on Eranos and mentions Mellon's publishing activities only in passing. Apart from the family history, it deals mainly with the economic misdeeds committed in the Third World by the Gulf Oil Company, which was largely owned by the Mellons. Interestingly, however, Paul Mellon was also friendly with Ernest Hemingway and went fishing with him in the Bahamas, although Hemingway basically had a negative attitude towards the rich (*ibid.*: 103).

3. The influence of Alice Bailey, and especially her theory of the Age of Aquarius, also finds an echo in Erlo van Waveren's book, *Pilgrimage to the Rebirth* (Einsiedeln: Daimon Verlag, 1998).

4. For a detailed report of the relationship, see William Schoenl, *C.G. Jung: His Friendships with Mary Mellon and J.B. Priestley* (Wilmette, IL: Chiron Publications, 1998).

5. See Paul Mellon with John Baskett, *Reflections in a Silver Spoon: A Memoir* (New York: William Morrow, 1992), 162ff.

6. She had also translated Jung into English and had moved to Zurich, prompted by the psychologist Kristine Mann. On the details of her life, see McGuire, *Bollingen*, 18ff.

7. *Ibid.*, 20.

8. Mellon, *Reflections in a Silver Spoon*, 163.

9. *Ibid.*, 20.

10. See the essay by William McGuire: "Jung and Eranos in America," in *Spring* 44 (1984), 51–6, where the relevant letters from Fröbe to Paul and Mary Mellon are printed.

11. Since 1935, with Jung's encouragement, Fröbe had obtained photographs of paintings and other works of art from diverse public libraries in London, Paris, and elsewhere, at her own expense. Jung had even given her a letter of recommendation for these researches, even though she lacked expert knowledge of art history. She once told Alfons Rosenberg that, to compensate for this lack, she used an ancient divinatory method. She simply poked a long needle into the card index of the archive and then demanded the book catalogued on the card that the needle had indicated. Apparently this unorthodox procedure was highly successful.

12. On 19 March she wrote to the famous occultist Dion Fortune (pseudonym for Violet Mary Firth), Theosophist, ex-member of a later version of the magical Order of the Golden Dawn and head of the esoteric-Kabbalistic Society of the Inner Light. In the letter she described how suddenly, after eight years of making drawings of geometrical symbols, she found that she could enter into a kind of "waking trance," in which mythical images would surface, all of them having some connection with the "Great Mother." As the images belonged together, she had the impression of being initiated into an ancient rite. Certain individual figures, however, such as a horned and winged male figure in a cave, seemed to her to be totally alien. With the letter Fröbe enclosed photographs of the drawings that she had made of these images. She appears to have taken Dion Fortune's esoteric correspondence course. She writes that she would like to go to London, but cannot afford it. She also mentions that she is "working hard at the correspondences between Psychoanalysis, the Kabbalah and ancient cults" (I would like to thank Maria Babwasingh for copies of the original documents). The Society of the Inner Light possesses no copies of this correspondence, as David Williams of the Society assured me. Gareth Knight (pen name of Basil Wilby) mentions in his book *Dion Fortune and the Inner Light* (Loughborough: Toth Publications, 2000), 217, that the two women carried on a correspondence over several years, but unfortunately (as he indicated to me in an email of 3 May 2006) he possesses no documents giving further information on the matter.

13. The manuscript was handwritten by Jung in English. I am grateful to Sonu Shamdasani for drawing my attention to it.

14. Jung must have vehemently opposed this theme, as is shown by Fröbe's already mentioned letter of November 1938 to Cary Baynes. Consequently she mentions that in the future she intends to discuss the precise program only with him, and that he must simply make enough time available for her. "The responsibility is too great."

15. Jolande Jacobi, "Eranos: vom Zuhörer aus gesehen," *Du* 4 (1955), 51–7.

16. See her book *The Tressé Iron-Age Megalithic Monument (Sir Robert Mond's Excavation): Its Quadruple Sculptured Breasts and Their Relation to the Mother-Goddess Cosmic Cult* (London: Oxford University Press, 1935), e.g. 101ff., and her conclusion, 113ff. Sir Robert Mond was also, incidentally, president of the English Alchemical Society.

17. Hildegard Nagel, *The Eranos Conference 1938*. New York: Analytical Psychology Club, 1939.

18. In the manuscripts to his lectures Zimmer always used colored markings to show precisely when he wanted to raise the dramatic tone of his delivery.

19. See the account of this in Karl Kerényi, "Die Goldene Parodie: Randbemerkungen zu den 'Vertauschten Köpfen,'" *Die Neue Rundschau* 67(4) (1956), 549ff.

20. Ellen Thayer, "Eranos and Ascona," Eranos Lecture (1938), 11.

21. See her letter to Jung dated 18 April 1939.

22. Hannah, *Jung*, 261.

23. Mircea Eliade, who met him there, was astonished by his "extraordinary vitality"—Otto was then eighty years old. In the interval after the first part of his lecture he declined a sandwich and asked for a glass of champagne, which he consumed with relish along with a cigar. See Mircea Eliade, *Journal II, 1957–1969*, 190, entry of 22 June 1963.

24. See Falter, *Ludwig Klages*, 102ff. The influence of Klages on the intellectual world of the time was considerable. For example, Michael Großheim, in his book *Ludwig Klages und die Phänomenologie* (Berlin: Akademie Verlag, 1993), did not hesitate to place Klages higher than Husserl, Scheler, or Heidegger in some areas of phenomenology. Today Klages has lost a great deal of sympathy, however, through his anti-Jewish utterances.

25. See Hubert Cancik, "Dionysos 1933: Walter F. Otto als Religionswissenschaftler und Theologe am Ende der

Weimarer Republik (II)," in Faber *et al.* (eds), *Antik, Modern,* 182. See also Otto's contributions to the collection edited by Stefan George's follower Wolfgang Frommel, *Vom Schicksal des deutschen Geistes, I: Die Begegnung mit der Antike: Reden um Mitternacht* (Berlin: Georg-Kreis-Verlag, 1934). This includes Otto's essay "Der Durchbruch zum antiken Mythos im 19. Jahrhundert," 34–46, which deals in particular with the significance of Josef Görres, "that wonderful mind, whose breath has caused the sleeping fire of myth to blaze up anew" and who was the first to speak of the "ancient, sacred and lost wisdom of the myths" instead of treating them as mere poetic fancies or allegories.

26. An account of his life, including a detailed bibliography, is to be found in Alessandro Stavru's essay "Il lascito di Walter Friedrich Otto nel Deutsches Literaturarchiv di Marbach," *Studi e Materiali di Storia di Religionz* 64(1) (1998), 195–222.

27. Cited in Falter, *Ludwig Klages,* 103.

28. Hence he speaks of "narrative theology." See the critical essay by Hubert Cancik, "The Gods of Greece 1929: Walter F. Otto als Religionswissenschaftler und Theologe am Ende der Weimarer Republik (I)," in Faber *et al.* (eds), *Antik, Modern,* 43.

29. See Walter F. Otto, *Dionysos: Mythos und Kultus* (Frankfurt: Vittorio Klostermann, 1933).

30. Walter F. Otto, *Theophania: Der Geist der altgriechischen Religion* (Hamburg: Rowohlt, 1956), 58.

31. *Ibid.,* 27ff.

32. See, for example, Walter F. Otto, *Die Wirklichkeit der Götter: Von der Unzerstörbarkeit griechischer Weltsicht* (Reinbek: Rowohlt, 1963) and the collection of essays *Das Wort der Antike* (Stuttgart: Ernst Klett, 1962).

33. Karl Kerényi, "Walter Friedrich Otto: Erinnerung und Rechenschaft," appendix to Walter F. Otto, *Die Wirklichkeit der Götter,* 144ff.

34. Ernesto Grassi, Walter F Otto, and Karl Reinhardt (eds), *Geistige überlieferung* (Berlin: Helmut Küpper [formerly Georg Bondi, publisher to the Stefan George circle], 1940 and 1942).

35. Included in the monumental work by Christian Tilitzki, *Die deutsche Universitätsphilosophie in der Weimarer Republik und im Dritten Reich* (Berlin: Akademie Verlag, 2002), part 1, 716.

36. Joachim Lerchenmüller, *Die Geschichtswissenschaft in den Planungen des Sicherheitsdienstes der SS: Der SD-Historiker Hermann Löffler und seine Gedenkschrift "Entwicklung und Aufgaben der Geschichtswissenschaft in Deutschland"* (Bonn: J.H.W. Dietz, 2001), 160ff.

37. Hans Leisegang, *Die Gnosis* (Leipzig: Alfred Kröner Verlag, 1924). In the foreword Leisegang writes that his aim is to strive "to awaken understanding for the spirit of Gnosis." Significantly, by quoting Clement of Alexandria on the first page he reveals his own understanding of Gnosticism as the "recognition of who we are and what we have become; where we come from and where we have landed; where we are journeying to and what we have been rescued from; what is the meaning of our birth and our rebirth." On Leisegang's conception of Gnosis, see Christoph Markschies, "Hans Leisegang und die moderne Gnosisforschung," in *Philosophie eines Unangepassten: Hans Leisegang,* Klaus-M. Kodalle (ed.) (Würzburg: Königshausen & Neumann, 2003), 15–23.

38. Hans Leisegang, "Zur psychologischen Prüfung der Erkenntnismethode Rudolf Steiners," *Unsere Welt* 8–9 (1922), 2, 45.

39. See also Patrick Frei, "Denkform und Anschauung: Bemerkungen zu Hans Leisegangs Denkformlehre," in *Rationalitätstypen,* Karen Gloy (ed.), 56–68 (Freiburg: Karl Alber, 1999).

40. Hans Leisegang, *Denkformen* (Berlin: De Gruyter, 1928), 50.

41. Hans Leisegang, *Dante und das christliche Weltbild* (Weimar: Hermann Böhlau Nachf., 1941), 5.

42. Only the first volume appeared: Hans Leisegang, *Der heilige Geist* (Leipzig: B.G. Teubner, 1919).

43. Tilitzki, *Die deutsche Universitätsphilosophie in der Weimarer Republik und im Dritten Reich,* 288.

44. Eckhart Mesch, *Hans Leisegang* (Erlangen: Palm & Enke, 1999), 102.

45. In the First World War Adolf Hitler never rose above the rank of corporal.

46. Dictators always fear ridicule or contempt, whereas by drawing attention to their own menacing cruelty, they reinforce their power.

47. As early as 1929 he had planned to produce a critical edition of Nietzsche's collected works, but then withdrew because he wanted literally to include all writings and letters without censorship. He agreed with the medical diagnosis that Nietzsche had suffered from syphilis, a remark which earned him displeasure as Nietzsche at that time was mistakenly considered to be one of the "heroes" of National Socialism.

48. Mesch, *Hans Leisegang,* 114. The strong socialist component in National Socialism and Italian Fascism is often forgotten, often for current political reasons. Yet it was precisely the socialist component that weighed heavily in the popular success of both movements. See, for example, Zeev Sternhell, Marion Sznajder, and Maia Asheri, *Naissance de l'idéologie fasciste* (Paris: Arthème Fayard, 1989) and Renzo de Felice, *Intervista sul fascismo* (Roma-Bari: Laterza, 1975). Renzo de Felice, possibly the leading historian of Italian Fascism and also the author of a multiple-volume biography of Mussolini, sees Fascism as a modernizing dictatorship belonging to the left. Interestingly de Felice also regarded himself as being left-oriented.

49. *Ibid.,* 117.

50. *Ibid.,* 121. However, it should be mentioned that Leisegang, when writing an overview of contemporary Plato scholarship, found very positive things to say about Günther's work *Platon als Hüter des Lebens* [Plato as a

protector of life] (Munich: Lehmann, 1928), which was strongly marked by theories about biology and race. See Tilitzki, *Die deutsche Universitätsphilosophie der Weimarer Republik und im Dritten Reich*, Part 1, 289.

51. Mesch, *Hans Leisegang*, 122.

52. Letter of 16 November 1938 to Cary Baynes. One can conclude from this that Jung was already aware of the dangers of National Socialism.

53. In a letter to Jung of 18 April 1939 she even speaks of a "period of the greatest darkness in Europe."

54. See her already-quoted letter to Jung of 18 April 1939. The belief that the future of Eranos lay in a Christian direction is astonishing in view of her long-standing predilection for Indian spirituality. Possibly it has something to do with her visit to Kerényi in Rome, where he introduced her to several professors connected with the Vatican, all of whom wanted to come to Eranos.

55. Heinrich Zimmer, "Notizen zu einem Lebenslauf," in Zimmer, *Die indische Weltmutter*, 253–4.

56. For a résumé of his life, see the "notice biographique," in Louis Massignon, *L'Hospitalité sacrée* (Paris: Nouvelle Cité, 1987), 33–75. A more detailed chronology is to be found in the large-format volume *Louis Massignon*, published in his honor and edited by Jean-François Six (Paris: L'Herne, 1970), 13–17. The spiritual side of his life is sympathetically dealt with in Patrick Laude, *Massignon intérieur* (Lausanne: Delphica, L'Age d'Homme, 2001).

57. His vivid and detailed description of a "black Mass," in the novel *Là-Bas* is very well known.

58. La Salette remains a popular place of pilgrimage to this day, although after an initial endorsement the Vatican later condemned the excesses of worship there.

59. The well-known expert on new religious movements and devout Catholic Massimo Introvigne, who published a very critical but informative article on Massignon in the Roman newspaper *Il Foglio* of 12 November 2005, is convinced that this mission was concerned with espionage. In contrast, at the Internet project "Nazione Indiana" (www. nazioneindiana.com/2006/06/26/il-manager-religioso/) the linguist Jan Reister describes this article as an "attack" on the followers of Massignon, who are allegedly too well disposed towards Islam for the Catholic Introvigne.

60. Albert Hourani, "T.E. Lawrence and Louis Massignon," in the memorial volume marking the centenary of Massignon's birth, *Présence de Louis Massignon: Hommages et témoinages*, Daniel Massignon (ed.) (Paris: Maisonneuve et Larose, 1987), 167–76. This volume contains numerous testimonies from friends as well as studies on particular phases of Massignon's life.

61. The American occultist Pascal Beverly Randolph attributed his knowledge of sexual magic to the Nusayri. The Austrian magus and orientalist Franz Sättler-Musallam also describes the Nusayri as guardians of the highest esoteric secrets, above all those of a sexual nature.

62. See Massimo Introvigne, "Louis Massignon: 'Il mistico spione,'" *Il Foglio* (12 November 2005). The traditionally pro-French but equally anti-American position of Syria, clearly manifested in its practical politics, is also supposedly due to Massignon.

63. UNESCO, *Combats pour l'Homme, Centenaire de la Naissance de Louis Massignon 1883–1962* (Paris: UNESCO, 1983). This contains a selection of particularly notable passages from his works as well as testimonials from friends and a number of photographs.

64. Marie-Madelaine Davy was in close contact with many of the prominent names from the Eranos circle, including Mircea Eliade, Henry Corbin, and C.G. Jung, but also Antoine Faivre. See her intellectual autobiography *Traversée en solitaire* (Paris: Albin Michel, 1989). Her acquaintances also included the Caucasian "magus" George I. Gurdjieff.

65. See the interview with her in the periodical *Question de* 90 (1992), 218ff. This issue is entirely devoted to Louis Massignon and bears the subtitle *Mystique en dialogue*. The interview was reprinted in *Question de* 116 (1999), which was in honor of Marie-Madelaine Davy herself. Ximena de Angulo, in her report of the 1950 meeting, describes Massignon as a kind of *advocatus diaboli*, who saw it as his supreme Christian duty to rouse people from their lethargy. She writes that his talk on that occasion was a work of art, and to describe the deep impression that it made would be as impossible as to ask a violin to reproduce a masterpiece that had just been played on it.

66. Yvonne Chauffin, "Entre la violence et la mystique," *Question de* 90 (1992), 15.

67. See Henry Corbin, "Post-scriptum biographique et Entretien philosophique," in *Henry Corbin*, Christian Jambet (ed.) (Paris: L'Herne, 1981), 40.

68. Henry Corbin, "Discours de M.: Le professeur H. Corbin à l'occasion de la mort de L. Massignon," *La Faculté des lettres de l'Université de Téhéran* 10(3) (1962), 4.

69. Annemarie Schimmel, *Morgenland und Abendland: Mein west-östliches Leben* (Munich: C.H. Beck, 2002), 75.

70. Ximena de Angulo told me that Massignon never read from a manuscript and never provided one for the Eranos volumes. One had to rely on notes taken by members of the audience, who naturally could only reproduce the bare academic skeleton of the lecture but not the spark and fire of the original.

71. Gabriel Marcel, "A Louis Massignon dans l'invisible," in *Louis Massignon*, Jean-François Six (ed.), 40.

72. In *Question de* 90 (1992), 25.

73. He used this term, for example, in a letter to the Islamic scholar Mohammed Arkoun dated 16 July 1954, reproduced in facsimile in *Combats pour l'Homme, Centenaire de la Naissance de Louis Massignon*, 76–7.

74. This is reported by, among others, his friend and English translator Herbert Mason in *Memoir of a Friend: Louis Massignon* (Notre Dame, IN: University of Notre Dame Press, 1988), 34.

75. Massimo Introvigne, however, impugns this ordination as illegitimate.

76. See Barbara Sturnega, *Padre Giulio Basetti Sani (1912–2001): una vita per il dialogo cristiano-musulmano*, (PhD dissertation, Università degli Studi di Trieste, Facoltà di Lettere e Filosofia, 2003–2004), which opens up many new sources.

77. Giulio Bassetti-Sani, *Louis Massignon (1883–1962): Christian Ecumenist: Prophet of Inter-Religious Reconciliation* (Chicago, IL: Franciscan Herald Press, 1974).

78. Schimmel, *Morgenland und Abendland*, 75.

79. Thus, one of his volumes of collected essays is entitled *Parole Donnée* (Paris: Editions du Seuil, 1983) and another is called *L'Hospitalité sacrée*.

80. Quoted in Maxime Rodinson, "Ce n'était pas un saint: Entretien avec Maxime Rodinson," *Question de 90* (1992), 76–82, esp. 78. Apparently the call to penance that Massignon sensed in the revelation of the Mother of God at La Salette also contributed to this stance.

81. "The Passion of Louis Massignon: Sublimating the Homoerotic Gaze in *The Passion of al-Hallaj* (1922)," in Jeffrey Kripal, *Roads of Excess, Palaces of Wisdom: Eroticism and Reflexivity in the Study of Mysticism* (Chicago, IL: University of Chicago Press, 2001), 98–146.

82. This raises the provocative question of the "value" of a rejection of homosexuality by society. On the one hand this is a crying injustice for the individual who is affected, but on the other hand it can lead to the release of enormous creative energies to the benefit of society as a whole. Would, for example, artists of the rank of Michelangelo or Caravaggio have created such powerful works if they had been able to live out their tendencies openly? Would their creativity—born of over-compensation, born of guilt feelings, born of the search for lasting sexual satisfaction—ever have come to fruition? Who can possibly claim to have the "right" answer to this question? And perhaps one should go further and question the widely accepted practice in raising children of removing all difficulties that could hinder them, for might this not also cause their creative energy to atrophy? A similar point could be made about the technologies that have made our lives progressively easier. Did not the invention of writing, for instance, spell the end of our phenomenal powers of memory? Some people might call these questions "immoral." But is not reasoning *per se* "immoral" as it obeys different intrinsic laws? Is this the "dark side" of Enlightenment?

83. The following excerpt is quoted by the Massignon expert Patrick Laude in "Présence et verité: L'héritage spirituel chez Massignon et Schuon," *Connaissance des Religions* 69–70 (2003), 166.

84. Massimo Introvigne prefers to portray him as bisexual, pointing to passionately mystical and sensual letters sent to Mary Kahil, an intellectual of the Catholic Melkite faith, by Massignon while he was married to another woman and had three children. With Kahil he also founded Badaliya, a religious community that was well disposed towards Islam and whose most prominent member was Giovanni Battista Montini, later Pope Paul VI. Massignon's former friend Pierre Klossowski also referred to Massignon's bisexuality in his novel *La vocation suspendue*.

85. *Question de 90* (1992), 70.

86. The currently available French edition carries the title *La Passion de Hallâj* (Paris: Gallimard, 1990).

87. Husayn Mansûr Hallaj, *Dîwân* (Paris: Edition du Seuil, 1981), 68.

88. In support of this initiative there exists a petition signed by three Eranos speakers, namely C.G. Jung, Andreas Speiser, and the psychiatrist Hans Bänziger.

89. There were a number of initiatives to establish Eranos in America, but all of them failed. In 1975 James Kirsch wrote two letters to Gershom Scholem in which he proposed holding regular six-day conferences similar to Eranos in southern California. Jung's researches into the unconscious were to form the focal point. The planned name was Temenos. See Scholem, *Briefe III*, 362ff.

90. This collection increased greatly in value through the addition in 1952 of about one hundred twenty manuscripts from the legacy of the bibliographer of alchemy Denis I. Duveen—Jung's own library contained only a few manuscripts. The collection was left by Paul Mellon to the Beinecke Rare Book and Manuscript Library at Yale University, where it is now kept. There is a magnificent four-volume catalogue of the collection, the first two volumes dedicated to printed works and the other two to manuscripts. The bibliography, compiled by Ian McPhail, is entitled *Alchemy and the Occult: From the Collection of Paul and Mary Mellon* (New Haven,CT: Yale University, 1968–1977). The information given here is taken from the forewords written by Pearl Kibre and William McGuire. There is also a foreword by Jung.

91. Jung, *Briefe I*, 356.

9. The War Years

1. Jolande Jacobi, "Eranos: vom Zuhörer aus gesehen," *Du* 4 (1955), 75.

2. See his book *Die mathematische Denkweise* (Zurich: Rascher, 1932), in which, from mathematical principles such as number, symmetry, etc., he derives a much deeper meaning, thus approaching Kepler's harmonics and even astrology. In this way he sought to rescue this now widely forgotten side of mathematics from being categorized as a dubious form of mysticism or gnostic delusion. See also *Die geistige Arbeit* (Baselt: Birkhäuser, 1955), containing a series of his essays, including three of his Eranos lectures.

3. According to the list published by R. Bernardini in *Da Monte Verità a Eranos* there were thirty-two participants. However, probably not all the participants would have entered their names.

4. Hannah, *Jung*, 270.

5. Jaffé, "C.G. Jung und die Eranostagungen," 8.

6. Olga Fröbe (ed.), *Eranos 1940: Zwei Vorträge über das Problem der Trinität* (n.p., n.d.).

7. In a letter written later to Jung (20 March 1942) Fröbe relates that Kerényi's remarks on Gnosis so angered Max Pulver that he became positively abusive.

8. "Fatum," in Max Pulver, *Person, Charakter, Schicksal* (Zurich: Orell Füssli Verlag, 1944), 101.

9. Max Pulver, *Erinnerungen an eine europäische Zeit* (Zurich: Orell Füssli Verlag, 1953). In the section "Erinnerungen an Rilke" (Memories of Rilke) he describes Rilke's friendship with Alfred Schuler, a member of the Munich "Cosmics." The extraordinary nature of their characters "unfolded in intimate conversations" (62). Pulver was also acquainted with Schuler, as the three men—Rilke, Schuler, and Pulver—used to meet regularly among a small group of friends during the First World War.

10. See, for example, Rudolf Bernoulli and E.K. Müller, "Eine neue Untersuchung der Eigenschaften des Teleplasma," *Zeitschrift für Parapsychologie* 7 (July 1931), 313-21, where a session with Oskar Schlag is described and a "Dr. M. Pulver" is listed among those present.

11. Eliade, *Journal I, 1945-1955*, 164. Soon after hearing of Max Pulvers's death, Fröbe accidentally fell into a concrete ditch in the shape of a coffin. Convinced that Pulver had wanted to drag her into the grave with him, she carried out a protective magical ritual that she had taken from Dion Fortune's book *Psychic Self Defense*.

12. Kurt Wolff, *Briefwechsel eines Verlegers 1911-1963*, Bernhard Zeller and Ellen Otto (eds) (Frankfurt: H. Scheffler, 1966) 141ff., 252.

13. Letter of 9 August 1943 to Hermann Hesse, in Ninon Hesse, *Lieber, lieber Vogel: Briefe an Hermann Hesse* (Frankfurt: Suhrkamp, 2000), 467.

14. Information provided by Magda Kerényi. In the eighteenth century the Empress Maria Theresia had been able to convince many Germans to settle in the so-called Banat, which brought many economic, political, and military advantages to the Habsburg empire.

15. At least this is the view of Volker Losemann in his essay "Die 'Krise der Alten Welt' und der Gegenwart. Franz Altheim und Karl Kerényi im Dialog," in *Imperium Romanum: Studien zu Geschichte und Rezeption: Festschrift für Karl Christ zum 75. Geburtstag*, Peter Kneissl and Volker Losemann (eds) (Stuttgart: Franz Steiner Verlag, 1998), 497. This contribution is based upon a talk given at an international symposium on Kerényi in Milan in 1997, which is recorded in Volker Losemann, "I 'Discuri': Franz Altheim e Karl Kerényi: Tappe di un'amicizia," in *Károly Kerényi: Incontro con il Divino*, Luciano Arcella (ed.) (Rome: Settimo Sigillo, 1999), 17-28. On the other hand, Franz Altheim's daughter, Ruth Altheim-Stiehl, also a historian of ancient times and professor, says that the two Dioscuri (twin brothers), because of their differing characters, had repeatedly quarreled since their youth. Kerényi had usually played the leading role, and Altheim had been the one who followed, a fact that Losemann also confirms. But their political differences, according to Ruth Altheim-Stiehl, were not the decisive factor in their quarrels, as was proved by Kerényi's acceptance of an invitation from Altheim to a lecture at the Free University of Berlin in the mid-1950s. Even in 1942 Kerényi praised Franz Altheim's book *Italien und Rom*. The article appeared under the title "Das Geheimnis der hohen Städte," in *Europäische Revue* 18(2) (1942), 386-90. Altheim probably found himself confronted by the same dilemma as many of the ambitious German academics of that time, eager to pursue their careers and their research works. This was not possible without official support, and it was clear that the regime would demand certain things in return. Thus Altheim's works—for example on the runes—not only enjoyed the support of Hermann Göring but were carried out under the aegis of the Ahnenerbe (the SS research organization on ancient history). On Altheim's importance in the world of learning, see Miguel de Ferdinandy, "Franz Altheim," *Eco, Revista de Cultura de Occidente* 137 (1971), 469-504, and G. Sanders, "In Memoriam Prof. Dr. Franz Altheim," *Jaarboek 1977 der Koninklijke Academie voor Wetenschappen: Letteren en schone Kunsten van België*, 387-400. Concerning the differences between Kerényi and Altheim, it may be worth remarking that Altheim, in an unpublished letter of 24 April 1955 to Julius Evola (now in a private collection), voices the suspicion that Kerényi had "commissioned" his student Angelo Brelich to attack him. The historian of religion Angelo Brelich succeeded to the Rome professorship vacated by the Eranos speaker Raffaele Pettazzoni.

16. Laura Gemelli Marciano, "Kerényi e la Svizzera. Frontiere fra letteratura e filologia," in *Neuhumanismus und Anthropologie des griechischen Mythos: Karl Kerényi im europäischen Kontext des 20. Jahrhunderts*, Renate Schlesier and Roberto Sanchiño Martínez (eds), 167-184 (Locarno: Rezzonico Editore, 2006). This volume encapsulates the contributions to a conference dedicated to Kerényi which was held at the Monte Verità in Ascona in 1997, significant for an understanding of the Hungarian classical scholar's place in the academic world.

17. See "Selbstbiographisches," in Karl Kerényi, *Tessiner Schreibtisch: Mythologisches, Unmythologisches* (Stuttgart: Steingrüben, 1963), 148.

18. János György Szilági, "Religio Academici," in *Károly Kerényi: Incontro con il Divino*, Luciano Arcella (ed.) (Rome: Settimo sigillo, 1999), 9.

19. Béla Hamvas, *Biblia és romantika*, a typewritten transcript of his conversations with Lajos Szabó and Béla Tábor, 85, cited here from Claudio Mutti, "Hamvas, Kerényi e i teologi antichi," foreword to *Béla Hamvas, Prima di Socrate* (Parma: Edizioni all'insegna del Veltro, n.d.), 13.

20. *Ibid.*, 14.

21. K. Kerényi, "Élet és életmü" [Life and work], in Béla Hamvas, *Szellem és egzisztencia* [Spirit and existence] (Budapest: Pannónia Könyvek, 1987), 152. Quoted here from the introduction by Claudio Mutti to Béla Hamvas, *Scientia Sacra*, vol. 1 (Parma: Edizioni all'insegna del Veltro, 2000), 9.

22. Cf. Claudio Mutti, "Béla Hamvas e Julius Evola," *Vie della Tradizione* III (July–September 1988), 12–25. See also the introduction by the historian of esotericism Gerhard Wehr: "Béla Hamvas: Auf der Spur eines traditionalen Denkens.," in Béla Hamvas, *Silentium* (Grafing bei München: Edition Marika Marghescu, 1999), 10–17.

23. Evola must have admired Kerényi's work, for in 1940 he reviewed the latter's book *Die antike Religion* very positively (which was not always the case with Evola) in the *Bibliografia Fascista* 15(7) and later he repeatedly mentioned Kerényi in his writings.

24. Communicated to the author when he visited Magda Kerényi in Ascona in 2001.

25. At the end of the 1930s Kerényi, probably through the initiative of Leo Frobenius, twice attended the learned circle hosted by the exiled Kaiser Wilhelm II at Doorn in Holland. Cf. Paul A. König, "Magda Kerényi (1914–2004), Gemahlin Karl Kerényis, im Gespräch," unpublished manuscript.

26. Szilági, "Religio Academici," 12. Béla Hamvas' career was also destroyed by Lukács. Hamvas had edited a philosophical book series ranging from Hermes Trismegistos to Martin Heidegger, which ran totally against the Communist ideology. His enthusiasm for modern art was also frowned upon. Hamvas lost his job and had to earn his living as a gardener and later as a retail clerk. In the German-speaking world he is now enjoying a revival as a novelist. This is due above all to his novel *Karneval*, which is said to be one of the most significant literary works of the twentieth century. In the meantime a collection of essays by Hamvas entitled *Kierkegaard in Sizilien* has also been translated into German (Berlin: Matthes & Seitz, 2006) and reviewed very knowledgeably by Klaus Bonn in *literaturkritik.de* 2 (2007) (www.literaturkritik.de/public/rezension.php?rez_id=10388). These essays portray the ideological background of Hamvas very clearly. His esoteric-traditionalist magnum opus *Scientia Sacra* has been translated into Italian by Claudio Mutti (Parma: Edizioni all'insegna del Veltro, 2000). The information given here about Hamvas has been taken from Mutti's foreword (5–9). Jacob Boehme exercised a major influence on Hamvas, who also translated some of his works into Hungarian.

27. See Markus Edler, "Thomas Mann und Karl Kerényi," in Schlesier and Sanchiño Martínez (eds), *Neuhumanismus und Anthropologie des griechischen Mythos*, 43–54. Kerényi's long-standing friend the archaeologist Hellmut Sichtermann writes as follows in his autobiography *Archäologie und manch anderes. Rückblicke auf mein Leben* (Berlin: Frieling, 2000), 179: "We seldom spoke about Thomas Mann. Kerényi once told me that it was impossible to have a heartfelt and close friendship on a human level with the Master. Their relationship had always remained on the intellectual and literary plane."

28. Here we see again the strong influence of German-speaking thinkers of the pre-war years on the surrounding countries, something that will concern us repeatedly. The fact that Kerényi nevertheless sometimes spoke out against Germany was due to the domineering attitude of the Nazi regime.

29. McGuire, *Bollingen*, 38.

30. In a letter to Jung of 18 April 1938 she writes of this meeting as follows: "It was very nice to be with Prof. Kerényi in Rome. He is one of the few scholars, who have a feeling for psychology and for the synthesis of the special research areas. He said that, for this very reason, Eranos is very important for the universities. I believe we will have him as a valuable collaborator for many years. Also, he knows where to find others."

31. Kerényi was famous for his remark that Ascona lay "on the most northern bay of the Mediterranean sea." He had a passion for the ancient soil of the Mediterranean countries, which was even reflected in the names of his children. On the close ties between Kerényi and Italy, see the study by Natale Spineto, "Karoly Kerényi e gli studi storico-religiosi in Italia," in *Studi e materiali di religioni* 69(2) (2003), 385–410, which brings much new material to light.

32. Allegedly the already mentioned Hermetic Society helped the Kerényis to obtain residence permission.

33. Paul A. König, "Magda Kerényi (1914–2004), Gemahlin Karl Kerényis, im Gespräch," (unpublished manuscript).

34. Also Ninon Hesse traveled to Greece together with the Kerényis from 4 April to 8 May 1956. See Ninon Hesse, *Lieber, lieber Vogel*, loc. cit., 531.

35. Edgar C. Polomé, "Karl Kerényi: A Biographical Sketch," in *Essays in Memory of Karl Kerényi*, Edgar C. Polomé (ed.) (Washington, DC: Institute for the Study of Man, 1984), 8.

36. Carl J. Burckhardt describes this as follows in his correspondence with Max Rychner: "A nice Hungarian is here and knows many valuable things about the ancient mysteries. Jung sits there with a pencil, smoking cigars, and absorbs every word about the mysterious Hecate." Carl J. Burckhardt and Max Rychner, *Briefe 1926–1965*, 74. Letter of 14 March 1942.

37. See, for example, the essay "Bild, Gestalt und Archetypus," in Karl Kerényi: *Apollon und Niobe* (Munich: Langen Müller, 1980), 279–92. On the relationship between Jung and Kerényi, see also the essay by Magda Kerényi: "Psicologia e mitologia: I rapporti tra C.G. Jung e Karl Kerényi," published in the periodical *L'Immaginale*, dealing with archetypal psychology. Unfortunately I posses only a copy of the essay, which lacks more detailed bibliographical information. Originally this essay appeared in the volume in the L'Herne series dedicated to C.G. Jung and edited by Michel Cazenave (Paris: L'Herne, 1984).

38. See his work *Bachofen und die Zukunft des Humanismus: Mit einem Intermezzo über Nietzsche und Ariadne* (Zurich: Rascher Verlag, 1945).
39. See the profound essay by Aldo Magris, "L'esperienza del divino in Carlo Kerényi," in Renate Schlesier and Roberto Sanchiño Martínez (eds), *Neuhumanismus und Anthropologie des griechischen Mythos*, 15–24.
40. Quoted here from the accolade delivered by Otto Heuschele on the occasion of the awarding of the gold medal of the Humboldt-Gesellschaft to Karl Kerényi in 1969, in "Karl Kerényi: Der Humanismus des Integralen Menschen" (*Ensemble* 2, n.d.), 24.
41. Victor Faessel, "Karl Kerényi: Humanism at the Margin," in *Disturbances in the Field,* Downing (ed.), 279.
42. Kerényi also intended to write a book entitled *Die antike Mystik*, but unfortunately never did. See his letter to Thomas Mann of 15 November 1940, in Mann and Kerényi, *Gespräche in Briefen*, 96.
43. His friend Hellmut Sichtermann, mentioned earlier, writes in his book *Archäologie und manch anderes* (180) that Kerényi even evinced "a certain indifference towards discursive thought."
44. See the essay by Godo Lieberg, "Karl Kerényi als Deuter der antiken Religion," in "Karl Kerényi," *Ensemble* 2 (1970), 40.
45. *Ibid.*, 26. Steven Wasserstrom even regards *Ergriffenheit* as the experiential mode of Eranos in general, although he restricts this to a particular time period. See his *Religion after Religion*, 3.
46. This essay is included in Karl Kerényi, *Apollon und Niobe*, 60, 62.
47. In a broadcast in honor of Kerényi transmitted by North German Radio, the author Johannes Kleinstück said that Kerényi's books had the effect of an "initiation." Their aim was not merely to convey useful information. One could also derive wisdom from them. In Johannes Kleinstück's short contribution "Kerényi's Humanistic Approach to Ancient Religion," in Polomé (ed.), *Essays in Memory of Karl Kerényi*, 73.
48. See Hans-Jürgen Heinrichs, *Die fremde Welt, das bin ich: Leo Frobenius: Ethnologe, Forschungsreisender, Abenteurer* (Wuppertal: Edition Trickster, Hammer Verlag, 1998), 96ff.
49. In her aforementioned essay on Eranos for the Kerényi memorial volume edited by Renate Schlesier and Roberto Sanchiño Martínez, Barbara von Reibnitz included a chapter entitled "Kerényi and Eranos" which deals with his ambivalent relationship towards Eranos. See "Der Eranos-Kreis: Religionswissenschaft und Weltanschauung oder der Gelehrte als Laien-Priester," in *Neuhumanismus und Anthropologie des griechischen Mythos*, 107–23.
50. Eliade, *Journal I, 1945–1955*, 112. Ninon Hesse, however, was not always so enthusiastic. On 11 March 1942 she wrote to Hermann Hesse: "The lecture was curious, as is always the case with Kerényi. He looked pale and transparent and appeared over-stressed even before the beginning of the talk. In view of his way of speaking, this impression did not improve in the course of the lecture, since he has no 'speaking technique' and somewhat resembles someone crying in the wilderness, when he stands there calling out over some imaginary distance. At the same time, this is a reflection of his nature. He wants to create an effect. He needs echo and reverberation … but the construction of German sentences is naturally also troublesome for him. All of this puts a strain on the listener, too." Hesse, *Lieber, lieber Vogel*, 456. When she visited Eranos in 1943 she was again disappointed with Kerényi, but in 1945 she wrote after his lecture: "Signs and wonders are still happening!" (*ibid.*: 471).
51. Eliade, *Autobiography II, 1937–1960*, 163.
52. Michaela Timuş and Eugen Ciurtin (eds), "The Unpublished Correspondence between Mircea Eliade and Stig Wikander (1948–1977), Part 2," *Archaeus* 4 (2000), 192. In this letter Eliade also mentions that the Swedish orientalist Geo Widengren had visited Fröbe and would gladly have been invited to speak at Eranos.
53. Among the "initiates" at Eranos he had the nickname "the Peacock."
54. Kerényi apologized to Eliade in writing, if rather tardily, on 24 November 1952, speaking of an "almost catastrophic fatigue" that had overtaken them *both*. And in his reply of 8 December 1952 Eliade wrote that in Alpbach he had felt thoroughly exhausted on account of the Eranos meeting. See Natale Spineto, *Mircea Eliade, storico delle religioni: Con la corrispondenza inedita Mircea Eliade—Károly Kerényi* (Brescia: Morcelliana, 2006), 275, 276.
55. Privately owned letter, 29 June 1965.
56. Kerényi did not in any way hide his role as a central figure at Eranos nor his importance at the meetings. Sometimes he stayed as a guest with Olga Fröbe and in the early 1940s he held additional "winter seminars" at the villa. For these reasons he was often seen by members of the audience, and even by some of the speakers, as a sort of leader of Eranos. This aroused the speakers' resentment and her mistrust. And apparently there were occasions when he did actually lead a meeting.
57. Communication from Magda Kerényi.
58. Eliade, *Autobiography II*, 163.
59. See the essay by Furio Jesi, "K. Kerényi: i 'pensieri segreti' del mitologo," *Communità* 172 (1974), 291–2. This statement comes from a letter written by Kerényi to Jesi, dated 22 June 1967. The exact wording is even sharper: "I found it interesting that you succeeded in extracting something interesting even from the trivial Eliade." Jesi, as already mentioned, had falsely accused Ludwig Derleth of practicing anti-Semitic rituals. He was for four years in close contact with Kerényi. Then Kerényi broke off the contact, feeling that he had been deceived by Jesi. The latter had, as Kerényi saw it, concealed his pro-Communist views. For a detailed discussion of this case, see Natale

Spineto, "Károly Kerényi e gli studi storico-religiosi in Italia," *Studi e materiali di religioni* 69(2) (2003), 385-410. See also the complete correspondence between Kerényi and Jesi in Magda Kerényi and Andrea Cavalletti (eds), *Furio Jesi, Károly Kerényi: Demone e mito: carteggio 1964-1968* (Macerata: Quodlibet, 1999). To judge from Jesi's letter to Kerényi of 16 May 1968, reproduced in this volume, it appears that Jesi in fact never tried to conceal his political standpoint from Kerényi. In 1974 Jesi gave a speech in Ascona in honour of Kerényi.

60. Spineto, *Mircea Eliade*,254.

61. On this subject, see Karl Kerényi's essay "Was ist Mythologie?," in Karl Kerényi, *Antike Religion* (Munich: Langen Müller, 1971), 13-34, as well as the collection edited by him, *Die Eröffnung des Zugangs zum Mythos. Ein Lesebuch* (Darmstadt: Wissenschaftliche Buchgesellschaft, 1976), to which Fröbe's longstanding friend André Jolles contributed a section on "Myth," taken from his own book *Einfache Formen*. See also the essay by Furio Jesi, "Karl Kerényi: i 'pensieri segreti' del mitologo," 273.

62. At the same time it should not be forgotten that Eliade spoke very disparagingly of the "countless ' little religions' that proliferate in all modern cities" as well as of the "so-called hermetic churches, sects or schools." See Mircea Eliade, *The Sacred and the Profane: The Nature of Religion*, W. Trask (trans.) (New York: Harcourt Brace & World, 1959), 206. It is interesting also to note the standpoint of the great playwright, compatriot, and school friend Eugène Ionesco, who said, "At that time [in the 1930s in Romania] it seemed to us that we could only accept life as gods, so mediocre, narrow-minded and unsatisfying did human life appear to us. Mircea Eliade himself, however, limited himself—indeed modestly adjusted himself—to being merely a scholar rather than an initiate—a great scholar admittedly, but nothing more than a scholar." See his "Hommage à Mircea Eliade," in *Mircea Eliade*, Constantin Tacou (ed.) (Paris: L'Herne, 1978), 272ff.

63. Kerényi, *La Madonna ungherese di Verdasio* (Locarno: A. Dadò editore, 1996), 10.

64. At least in Italy, where Kerényi had the best connections, these sympathies of Eliade were known about in the late 1940s and early 1950s, which led to problems in the publication of the Italian translations of his books.

65. Kerényi, *Tage und Wanderbücher*, 190. The next quotation is also taken from this book (*ibid*.: 228).

66. The publicist and critic Armin Kessler was engaged to Marli Lang, the daughter of Josef Bernhard Lang, who was Hermann Hesse's psychoanalyst for many years. Lang himself had lectured at Eranos in 1935 and 1942. See Thomas Feitknecht, *"Die dunkle und wilde Seite der Seele": Hermann Hesse—Briefwechsel mit seinem Psychoanalytiker Josef Bernhard Lang 1916-1914* (Frankfurt: Suhrkamp, 2006), 315, 330. The *Neue Zürcher Zeitung* deserves thanks for having regularly, over all the decades unto the present day, published detailed reports of the Eranos meetings as well as reviews of the yearbooks. Nevertheless. many Eranos participants expressed the opinion that these reports gave prominence to the "critical" aspect of the meetings and that the newspaper could have contributed much more to publicizing Eranos. From the 1970s onwards Magda Kerényi supplied substantial reports for the *Neue Zürcher Zeitung*, summarizing the essentials of the meetings. The promotional effect of these—among academics as well as general readers—must have been considerable.

67. An English summary by Violet de Laszlo of this newspaper article is to be found in the *Bulletin of the Analytical Psychology Club of New York* 4(1) (1942), 4-8.

68. For this reason the first few books in the now famous Bollingen Series were financed from the Old Dominion Foundation, established by Paul Mellon in 1941. See McGuire, *Bollingen*, 45ff.

69. Zimmer chose the book by Maud Oakes and Joseph Campbell, *Where the Two Came to Their Father: A Navajo War Ceremonial Given by Jeff King* (Princeton, NJ: Princeton University Press, 1991) and commissioned Joseph Campbell to write a commentary to the account by an Indian medicine man that was included in the text. For a full account, see William McGuire's foreword, vii. Around 1930 Maud Oakes had, through Jack Barrett, met Mary Conover, who was later to marry Paul Mellon. Together the two women had studied Jung, and this was eventually to bear fruit in Maud Oakes' book *The Stone Speaks* (Wilmette, IL: Chiron Publications, 1987), by which time she had come to know and value Jung personally. The title refers to the famous stone at Bollingen, carved by Jung himself. In the book she describes her own process of inner transformation. Earlier Maud Oakes had spent time at Fontainebleau studying the ideas of the "magus" G.I. Gurdjieff, and from Heinrich Zimmer she had learned about the symbolism of the Tarot. Over several years she made research trips on her own through New Mexico and Guatemala, enabling her to write informative books on American Indian culture.

70. He wrote about his situation somewhat self-ironically, even perhaps self-deprecatingly, in a letter of 1 August 1940 to his friend Alexander von Bernus: "We have a furnished house in a green setting until November and we often go swimming in a beautiful Atlantic bay. The children have a garden and the dream world of King Arthur and his knights, damsels and fairies, which they know from continuous reading much better than I, who have to keep in mind that this winter I am giving three lectures to a women's psychology club in New York." (he complete letter is contained in *Worte der Freundschaft für Alexander von Bernus* (122ff.) As Campbell reports, it was the "Jung-Frauen" of the Analytical Psychology Club who paved Zimmer's way to Columbia University. In a lecture to the club under the title "Ourselves as Americans," Zimmer expressed positive views about the United States and lamented only the monotonous and forlorn quality of certain stretches of the country. See his "Address to the Analytical Psychology Club of the City of New York," 17 October 1941, in Zimmer, *Two Papers*. His wife, Christine, reported to Michael McKnight (already mentioned as the interviewer of Joseph Campbell) that hardly

had Zimmer arrived before he went out and bought a pair of blue jeans. He also Americanized his name. His love for Richard Wagner, however, remained undiminished.

71. To quote Joseph's Campbell's words in his interview with Michael McKnight.

72. However, in 1943 Cary Baynes and her daughter Ximena de Angulo sent Fröbe a Christmas telegram under a pseudonym, "since Cary and Ximena, as members of the Bollingen Press, are not allowed to correspond with me. But they found a way over this obstacle, and it cheered me enormously." (Letter from Fröbe to Jung, 13 January 1944.)

73. Jung also attracted the attention of the FBI. However, apart from a few vague accusations, no compromising material seems to have been found, as William Schoenl states in his book *C.G. Jung: His Friendship with Mary Mellon and J.B. Priestley*, 33ff. Through the American Freedom of Information Act, Schoenl had gained access to the relevant documents in the FBI archives. See also Bair, *Jung*, 523.

74. Letter from Fröbe to Jung, 22 June 1942. Later, on 17 January 1943, Jung wrote to her in one of his famously outspoken letters: "As far as your 'bleeding heart' feeling is concerned, perhaps you have not fully realized the extent to which you have adopted Mrs. Mellon as your daughter and the person to continue Eranos. You have been severely disappointed, which weighs all the more heavily in so far as you were totally identified with Eranos— indeed to a dangerous degree. One should not hang one's heart on anything, for it belongs to the Self; everything else is transient."

75. In 1949 pro-Nazi accusations against the Bollingen Foundation were dug up again. Protests against these charges, however, came *inter alia* from three prominent Jewish emigrés: Hermann Broch, Erich Kahle, and Siegfried Kracauer, who stressed the help that they had received from the Bollingen Foundation during the war years. See Hermann Broch, *Briefe 3: 1945–1951* (Frankfurt: Suhrkamp, 1986), 340ff., where the complete protest letter is printed.

76. See William S. Hoffman, *Paul Mellon* (Chicago, IL: Follett, 1974), 112, in which it is also mentioned that Paul Mellon may even have been a CIA man up to 1968. It would, however, be mean to suggest that Mellon's already mentioned friendship with Ernest Hemingway had anything to do with the fact that the American authorities, and especially the FBI, were interested in the writer's political activities. See the chapter on Hemingway in Herbert Mitgang, *Überwacht—Große Autoren in den Dossiers der amerikanischen Geheimdienste* (Düsseldorf: Dröste Verlag, 1992), 72–82. To make the matter more complicated still, Ernest Hemingway's son John also worked for the OSS. Francis Stonor Saunders, *Wer die Zeche zahlt …: Der CIA und die Kultur im Kalten Krieg* (Berlin: Siedler, 2001), 44; published in English as *The Cultural Cold War: The CIA and the World of Arts and Letters* (New York: The New Press 2001).

77. *Ibid.*, 44.

78. *Ibid.*, 233.

79. A letter written by Fröbe to Jung on 14 December 1942 reveals that she also wished to seek support from the Swiss firm of Bührle. It is not recorded whether this succeeded. Jung, in turn, attempted to solicit donations from the Swiss Education Authority.

80. Letter from Fröbe to Dr. de Laszlo, published in the *Bulletin of the Analytical Psychology Club of New York* 4(7) (1942), 76. During the evening Kerényi showed pictures of Greek vases from the Eranos collection. In the spring Kerényi had given a seminar on the Greek mysteries at the Zurich Psychology Club, at which Fröbe had also taken part. A total of about a hundred people attended. The points of overlap between Eranos and the Psychology Club at that time are fairly evident. The audiences were also very similar.

81. Already in 1936 the Swiss Federal Institute of Technology had helped out with five hundred francs. In return, however, Fröbe had to make available to it all the photographs that she had taken in the Vatican Library. See the letter from C.G. Jung of 16 August 1936. Subsequently support came regularly from the institute.

82. In a kind of spiritual testament, Olga Fröbe wrote, "Jung, Mary, and I all had a definite life work, submitted to each of us by the same Force. Each of us was independent, ruthless, isolated, yet bound together… I remember Mary Mellon saying, 'Bollingen is *my* Eranos!' She too was dedicated to Jung's work and then to Eranos. She, Jung and I were in the identical pattern, energized by the same Power and thereby bound up with each other." Quoted from McGuire, *Bollingen*, 27.

83. The series that he created, *Der neue Roman*, with authors such as Gustav Meyrink (who was, incidentally, much admired by C.G. Jung, as Sonu Shamdasani informed me on 21 December 2000), Arnold Zweig, Heinrich Mann, Max Brod, but also Anatole France and Gustave Flaubert, sold more than four hundred thousand copies in the first year. In the promotional material for the series he spoke of "the agenda of a new and significant movement, which … is consciously replacing the era of naturalism in literature and is striving towards new goals that are romantic, spiritual and profound." See the anonymous *Der neue Roman: ein Almanach* (Leipzig: Kurt Wolff Verlag, 1917), Appendix 3. Wolff also published the plays and poetry of the Eranos lecturer Max Pulver. But there were also other titles in his list that seem rather surprising today, such as Max Scheler's book *Die Ursachen des Deutschenhasses* (The causes of hatred of the Germans), which appeared in 1917 during the First World War and in which the author laments a general ethical decline, leading to an upsurge of hate, envy, etc.

84. Kurt Wolff, *Autoren/Bücher/Abenteuer: Betrachtungen und Erinnerungen eines Verlegers* (Berlin: Klaus Wagenbach, 1965), 51ff. The book includes, on 103ff., a list of important dates in his life, compiled by his wife Helene Wolff.

See also Michael Kellner (ed.), *Kurt Wolff zum Hundertsten* (Hamburg: Michael Kellner, 1987). Bernhard Zeller's tribute to this important publisher, including a description of his life, is to be found in Kurt Wolff, *Briefwechsel eines Verlegers 1911–1963*, Bernhard Zeller and Ellen Otten (eds) (Frankfurt: Büchergilde Gutenberg, 1967), vii–lvii. Equally important is Karl H. Salzmann, "Kurt Wolff der Verleger," Archiv für Geschichte des Buchhandels (XII), *Börsenblatt des Deutschen Buchhandels* 14(101a) (22 December 1958), 1729–49.

85. "Swan song of the West" is how Wolfram Göbel describes this in his homage to Kurt Wolff, "Ernst Rowohlt und Kurt Wolff," in Kellner (ed.), *Kurt Wolff zum Hundertsten*, 118–22. Later came great commercial success with the English version of Grimm's *Fairy Tales* and with Boris Pasternak's *Doctor Zhivago*.

86. The scholar of religion Robert W. Brockway, who himself took part in one of the Eranos meetings, writes in his carefully objective work *Young Carl Jung* (Wilmette, IL: Chiron, 1966), 19, that it was originally Wolff's idea that Jung should write the memoir that became *Memories, Dreams, Reflections*. In 1956 Wolff took part in the Eranos meeting and convinced Aniela Jaffé, also a Jewish refugee, to persuade Jung to write the book. Through her closeness to Jung, as his secretary, she was successful in this effort. Nevertheless, it would be mistaken to refer to this book as an "autobiography," as this was precisely what Jung did not want to write, believing that "no one tells the truth about themselves." It is much more likely, as Sonu Shamdasani writes in his essay "Memories, Dreams, Omissions", *Spring* 57 (1995), 115–37, that Aniela Jaffé put the material together from Jung's "free associations." Robert Brockway's book can incidentally be strongly recommended as a counterbalance to Richard Noll's *The Jung Cult*. Basing his approach on the work of the historian George Mosse, Brockway is at pains to look in a more differentiated way at the *völkisch* current of thought, which was then flowing strongly and doubtless also influenced Jung. National Socialism represented only one outgrowth of this way of thinking, but it was the one that finally prevailed (41ff.). Unfortunately history appears to show that, in a clash of ideas, the one most likely to prevail *in the short term* is the one that is more radical, one-sided, and ruthless.

87. In a letter of 26 December to his friend Alexander von Bernus he had written, "Nevertheless, during the fine extended autumn weather … I suddenly wrote down an inspired reading of the 23 [*sic*] major arcana of the Tarot, which I found very satisfying." The letter is included in Rilke *et al.*, *Worte der Freundschaft für Alexander von Bernus*, 124ff.

88. Bair, *Jung*, 817 n.81.

89. *Ibid.*, 479.

90. Was von der Heydt, therefore, doing what Swiss bankers are today widely accused of?

91. Kamber, *Geschichte zweier Leben: Wladimir Rosenbaum, Aline Valangin*, 252–5.

92. *Ibid.*, 254.

93. According to the art historian Willy Rotzler (as mentioned in Bernardini, *Da Monte Verità a Eranos*), von der Heydt was of the opinion that although a work might be in the possession of an individual, in truth it could only belong to the general public. Thus, in the last few years of this life, he conceived a plan to turn his property on Monte Verità into a kind of "free academy." This he carried out, bequeathing the property to the canton of Tessin.

94. See *Europäische Revue* 10(2) (1934), 466ff.

95. *Nordische Welt* 9(10) (1933), 62.

96. Already in 1931 Schickele was being derided as an "Alsatian Jew" and a "pacifist and traitor to the Fatherland." See the text on the dust jacket of René Schickele, *Die blauen Hefte*, Annemarie Post-Martens (ed.) (Frankfurt: Stroemfeld Verlag, 2002).

97. Landmann, *Monte Veritá, Ascona* (Zurich: Benziger, 1973), 211.

98. See Campbell's foreword to the two-volume edition of Heinrich Zimmer, *The Art of Indian Asia: Its Mythology and Transformations* (New York: Pantheon, 1955), vii.

99. The information given here comes from Heym's obituary in *Ambix* 19 (1972), 216–17. Heym was very gifted linguistically; the languages he understood included Arabic (letter dated 28 October 2003 from Alfred Ribi, head of the Psychological Club of Zurich).

100. According to personal communications from Oskar Schlag, as well as Nicholas Schors of Amsterdam, probably the most important esoteric antiquarian bookseller of the twentieth century, who provided, *inter alia*, Scholem, Jung, and Ritman (founder of the Bibliotheca Philosophica Hermetica) with esoteric literature.

101. This was not his only phobia. He appears to have detected enemies and dangers everywhere. He was especially afraid of an atomic war and was apparently deeply convinced that the "spiritual masters" predicted a gloomy future. See Timothy d'Arch Smith, *The Times Deceased: The Rare Book Department of the Times Bookshop in the 1960s* (York: Stone Trough Books, 2003), 80.

102. There is an unpublished bibliography of Gérard Heym by Richard Caron.

103. For example in volume 17(3) (1926) he writes about the controversial German tibetologist Albert Grünwedel.

104. "Obituary Gérard Heym, 1888–1872," *Ambix* 19 (1972), 216–17.

105. Gustav Meyrink, *Le Dominicain Blanc* (Paris: La Colombe, 1922).

106. In private possession.

107. Available at www.magusbooks.com/gd/alchemy.html.

108. Smith, *The Times Deceased*, 80.

109. *Ibid.*, 79.

110. Unverified personal communication to the author.

111. Gian Piero Quaglino, Augusto Romano, and Riccardo Bernardini, "Opicinus de Canistris: Some Notes from Jung's Unpublished Eranos Seminar on the Medieval Codex Palatinus Latinus 1993," *Journal of Analytical Psychology* 55 (2010), 398–422.

112. Karl Heinz Neufeld, *Die Brüder Rahner: Eine Biographie* (Freiburg: Herder, 1994), 155.

113. Hugo Rahner, *Griechische Mythen in christlicher Deutung* (Darmstadt: Wissenschaftliche Buchgesellschaft, 1966), 7. This book contains Rahner's Eranos lectures.

114. *Flugblätter für Freunde aus der Wekstatt von Alfons Rosenberg* 80 (1977), 8.

115. Letter of C.G. Jung to Olga Fröbe, dated 6 September 1943.

116. Annemarie Schimmel, *Auf den Spuren der Muslime: Mein Leben zwischen den Kulturen*, Hartmut Bobzin and Navid Kermani (eds) (Freiburg: Herder, 2002), 21.

117. Schimmel, *Morgenland und Abendland*, 78.

118. The information given here comes from Gudrun Schubert, "Fritz Meier (1912–1998)," *Zeitschrift der Deutschen Morgeländischen Gesellschaft*, 150 (2000), 5–10. Gudrun Schubert, a student of Schimmel, in collaboration with Erika Glassen, collected Meier's important essays and published them as *Bausteine I–III. Ausgewählte Aufsätze zur Islamwissenschaft* (Wiesbaden: Franz Steiner, 1992). With Renate Würsch she established the voluminous indices in Volume 3.

119. Fritz Meier, *Vom Wesen der islamischen Mystik* (Basel: Benno Schwabe, 1943).

120. *Ibid.*, 15.

121. Hannah, *Jung*, 290.

122. See van der Post, *Jung and the Story of Our Time*, 228.

123. For Steven Wasserstrom the *coincidenta oppositorum* is the very heart of that gnosis which, in his analysis, Gershom Scholem, Mircea Eliade, and Henry Corbin were practicing—especially at Eranos. See *Religion after Religion*, 5.

124. From his essay "The Eranos Conferences," *Chimera* 5(3) (1947), 63, 64.

125. During the war the Hondius family even looked after Olga Fröbe's daughter, Bettina.

126. Catherine Ritsema, *L'oeuvre d'Eranos* (unpublished ms.), 27–35.

127. *Ibid.*, 28.

128. E. van Everdingen, *Zestig jaar Internationale School voor Wijsbegeerte 1915–1975* (Assen: Van Gorcum, 1976).

129. *Ibid.*, 31.

10. New Prospects after the World Conflict

1. Jaffé, *C.G. Jung und die Eranostagungen*, 8.

2. Fröbe had hoped he would also come in 1947, but Schrödinger was apparently not captivated by the spirit of Eranos and rejected the invitation. She then had the idea of inviting Wolfgang Pauli, but Jung advised against it, as Pauli was "extremely reserved" and would "only very reluctantly speak at a forum such as Eranos" (letter from Jung to Fröbe of 7 May 1947). In fact Pauli did reply that he had "too great a resistance towards Mother Earth" to take part. See the letter of 25 February to Jung.

3. These were the words of his pupil Roger Alfred Stamm, later also a speaker at Eranos. See Roger Alfred Stamm and Pio Fioroni, "Adolf Portmann, ein Rückblick auf seine Forschungen," in *Verhandlungen der Naturforschenden Gesellschaft in Basel* 97 (1984), 99. Elsewhere Stamm calls Portmann one of the "important teachers of biology in the 20th century." See Roger Alfred Stamm, "Adolf Portmann, akademischer Lehrer und Forscher," in *Zeitbedingtheit, Zeitbeständigkeit: Professorenpersönlichkeiten der Universität Basel*, Georg Kreis (ed.) (Basel: Schwabe, 2002). On Portmann's significance, see also Gerd von Wahlert, *Adolf Portmann, Versuch einer Würdigung* (Basel: Friedrich Reinhardt, 1972).

4. See Gerd von Wahlert, "Portmanns Unbehagen am Darwinismus," David G. Senn, "Zum Evolutionsverständnis," and Andreas Cesana, "Portmanns Evolutionsdenken," all included in *Uni Nova* 79–80 (May 1997), commemorative issue on the hundreth anniversary of Portmann's birthday, 84–6, 86–7, and 94–7 respectively.

5. See "Interview with Udo Reiter," in *Mensch, Natur, Gesellschaft*, 10ff.

6. See, for example, his booklet *Licht und Leben* (Basel: Friedrich Reinhardt, 1963), consisting of six of his radio broadcasts and including some biographical information about him.

7. Matthias Riedl, "Adolf Portmann: Ein Skeptiker auf der Suche," in *Pioniere, Poeten, Professoren*, Elisabetta Barone, Matthias Riedl, and Alexandra Tischel (eds) (Würzburg: Königshausen & Neumann, 2004), 117.

8. A useful, if rather adulatory, survey of Portmann's thinking is provided by Wald Koepke, *Adolf Portmann: Wegbereiter zu einem neuen Weltbild: Eine naturphilosophische Studie* (Hamburg: Hamburger Kulturverlag, 1999). Portmann's biological-spiritual insights also found a response in Italy. Thus, Giovanni Monastra, himself a biologist who has worked in the neuropathological department of Albert Einstein College of Medicine at Yeshiva University in New York, has long been a supporter of Portmann. See, for example, his lecture "Itinerari del Sacro attraverso le scienze naturali," given at the first meeting of the Quaderni di Avallon with the theme "La cultura contemporanea e il sacro," on 3–4 November 1984 (www.estovest.net/ecosofia/portmann.html). See also his review of Portmann's book *Le forme viventi*, in *Diorama Letterario* 133 (January 1990) and his lecture "Adolf Portmann, Wilhelm Troll:

Due biologi della morfologia idealistica," given at the fifth meeting of the Gruppo Osaka-Italia, 11–13 June 1999 at the University of Perugia under the title "Forma e Archetipi."

9. Adolf Portmann, *Probleme des Lebens* (Basel: Friedrich Reinhardt, 1949), quoted here from Helmut Müller, *Philosophische Grundlagen der Anthropologie Adolf Portmanns* (Weinheim: VCH, Acta Humaniora, 1988), 9.

10. Adolf Portmann, *Biologie und Geist* (Zurich: Rhein-Verlag, 1956), 107. In this work he deals with the importance of the imagination in comprehending the world.

11. See his contribution to the *Festschrift* in celebration of Jung's seventy-fifth birthday, "Das Problem der Urbilder in biologischer Sicht," *Eranos Jahrbuch* 18 (1950), 413–32.

12. Letter of 26 August 1950, quoted here from Sonu Shamdasani, *Jung and the Making of Modern Psychology*, 265ff.

13. Müller, *Philosophische Grundlagen der Anthropologie Adolf Portmanns*, 1 and *passim*.

14. See Joachim Illies, *Das Geheimnis des Lebendigen: Leben und Werk des Biologen Adolf Portmann* (Munich: Kindler, 1976).

15. On his life and work, see the biography by his pupil Albert H. Friedländer, *Leo Baeck: Leben und Lehre* (Stuttgart: Deutsche Verlagsanstalt, 1973) and Georg Heuberger and Fritz Backhaus (eds), *Leo Baeck 1873–1956: Aus dem Stamme von Rabbinern* (Frankfurt: Jüdischer Verlag, 2001). The latter is a companion volume to the exhibition of the same name, held in 2001 at the Jewish Museum, Frankfurt. See also Walter Homolka, *Leo Baeck: Jüdisches Denken—Perspektiven für heute* (Freiburg: Herder, 2006).

16. Obituary in *The Synagogue Review* (London, January, 1957). German version in Council of Jews from Germany-London (ed.), *Worte des Gedenkens für Leo Baeck* (Heidelberg: Lambert Schneider, 1959), 13–28. Much of the essential information given here is taken from this obituary.

17. Albert H. Friedländer, *Leo Baeck*, 151ff.

18. On the subject of Baeck's difficult public work during the Nazi period, see John H.V. Dippel, *Bound Upon a Wheel of Fire: Why So Many German Jews Made the Tragic Decision to Remain in Nazi Germany* (New York: Basic Books, 1996). Dippel also discusses the question of why Baeck signed Julius Streicher's protest against foreign propaganda against Nazi Germany, which was indeed partly based on exaggerated or invented reports. Streicher was notorious for his vehement and vulgar anti-Semitism, for which he was even reproached by some of his colleagues.

19. Bach, *Leo Baeck*, 21.

20. *Essays presented to Leo Baeck on the occasion of his Eightieth Birthday* (London: East and West Library, 1954).

21. Leo Baeck, *Werke, vol. 6: Briefe, Reden, Aufsätze* (Gütersloh: Gütersloher Verlagshaus, 2006), 311. Quoted here from Walter Homolka and Elias H. Füllenbach, *Leo Baeck: Eine Skizze seines Lebens* (Gütersloh: Gütersloher Verlagshaus, 2006), 53.

22. Keyserling, who was certainly no expert on Jewish history, went so far as to describe Baeck's essay "Die Spannung im Menschen und der fertige Mensch" (The tension in man and the complete man) as the most important event in Judaism since the death of Christ. The essay can be found in *Der Leuchter: Weltanschauung und Lebensgestaltung*, vol. 4 (Darmstadt: Otto Reichl, 1923), 117–41. Baeck's thesis in this essay is that anything "complete" and perfect—in the sense that pervades Greek culture—when it inevitably collapses will necessarily be finished for ever, as perfection is not mutable and therefore not reformable. "The ultimate also dies an ultimate death" (140). In contrast to this stands the irreducible tension between God and humanity, as perceived by Judaism, which excludes any perfection in the Greek sense and therefore cannot rule and possess reality in the same way but only bring things to realization and re-form them. Consequently it can constantly re-emerge and be renewed. For this reason the future belongs to biblical man.

23. Leo Baeck, "Geist und Blut," in *Mensch und Kosmos*, Eleonore von Dungern (ed.) (Düsseldorf: Droste-Verlag, 1949).

24. These essays, entitled "Bedeutung der jüdischen Mystik für unsere Zeit" (1923) and "Die Mystik im Judentum" (1928), can be found in Leo Baeck, *Wege im Judentum: Aufsätze und Reden* (Berlin: Schocken Verlag, 1933), 90–102.

25. For example, in his 1895 dissertation he described the Kabbalistic teachings of the seventeenth century as *Irrwahn* (deluded aberration).

26. He totally ruled out any independent mythology in Judaism. Thus in his major work *Das Wesen des Judentums* (Wiesbaden: Fourier, 1988), he wrote, "Alone among religions, Judaism has created no real mythology for the reason that Judaism and mythology are fundamentally contradictory." Martin Buber was of course entirely of the opposite opinion. For him myth was a fountain of life for Judaism. This question is treated in Dominik Biemann, *Erkenntnis und Erfüllung: Die Philosophie Martin Bubers und Begriff aus dem Geist der Hebräischen Weisheit* (Frankfurt: Peter Lang, 1995), 180ff.

27. See the essay by Alexander Altmann, "Leo Baeck and the Jewish Mystical Tradition," in *Essays in Jewish Intellectual History* (Hanover: University Press of New England, 1981), 293–311.

28. A contrary opinion is held by Moshe Idel, leading expert of Jewish mysticism and professor at the Hebrew University in Jerusalem. See his groundbreaking book *Kabbalah: New Perspectives* (New Haven, CT: Yale University Press, 1988), 59–73.

29. Here it is relevant to mention Arthur Hertzberg's book *Wer ist Jude?: Wesen und Prägung eines Volkes* (Darmstadt: Wissenschaftliche Buchgesellschaft, 2000). For Hertzberg the essential characteristic of Judaism is the sense of being chosen, which does not imply superiority but rather the obligation to be the carrier of universal human

values. In his view, what is of central importance in the Jewish ethical code as well as in its Christian derivative, is that the Bible makes a clear distinction between the perpetrator and the victim, and sympathy usually lies with the victim and not with the more powerful one, the victor or the hero. One might observe that today, however, this has led to a distortion of the original ethical concept, namely a situation in which more and more individuals and groups feel themselves to be "eternal victims" because this enables them to attract more "love" and "recognition." Furthermore, there is the advantage, well known to depth psychology, of being able to rid oneself in this way of feelings of guilt or responsibility, unloading the blame for bad decisions on to "the others," who become the scapegoats for one's own failings. This phenomenon, known as "victimism," has been treated extensively in specialist literature.

30. See the essays grouped together in the section headed "Mystik und Religionsphilosophie," in Leo Baeck, *Aus drei Jahrtausenden: Wissenschaftliche Untersuchungen und Abhandlungen zur Geschichte des jüdischen Glaubens* (Tübingen: J.C.B. Mohr, 1958), 244–347. See also Homolka, *Leo Baeck*, 102ff.

31. *In Memoriam Leo Baeck. Gedenkfeier des Zentralrats der Juden in Deutschland und der Zentralwohlfahrtsstelle der Juden in Deutschland, Frankfurt am Main, 16 December 1956* (Düsseldorf: Schriften des Zentralrats der Juden in Deutschland, 1957), 18.

32. See his book *Gottesfinsternis: Betrachtungen zur Beziehungen zwischen Religion und Philosophie* (Zurich: Manesse, 1953), 109ff. Heinrich Zimmer was also preoccupied with this theme. See his lecture *Integrating the Evil: A Celtic Myth and a Christian Legend*, Guild Lecture no. 39 (London: Guild of Pastoral Psychology, 1945).

33. Steven Wasserstrom gives central importance to this question in his skeptical assessment of Eranos. At the same time it would be incorrect to imply that Eranos was "without an ethic." The premises of the "Eranian ethic," if one can use such a term, owe little to the religions of revelation or to the institutions of the state. Rather, they are of a "Taoist" nature and concerned with cosmic harmony. The general debate about "right" ethics has intensified in recent years and has included the postmodern "anything goes" philosophy, which basically seeks to avoid any distinction between right and wrong, good and evil. Zygmunt Bauman suggests in his book *Flaneure, Spieler und Touristen: Essays zu postmodernen Lebensformen* (Hamburg: Hamburger Edition, 1997) that in the postmodern era the ethical monopoly of the state has collapsed, calling into question the idea that the citizen has a set of duties and responsibilities. Thus, according to Bauman, we are no longer confronted with the perilous choice between good and evil, but only between different options offered by the "market." The roots of this state of affairs, he maintains, lie in the fragmentation of society and the differing views among people as to what is important in their lives.

34. See Gilles Quispel, "Gnosis and Psychology," in *The Rediscovery of Gnosticism*, vol. 1, Bentley Layton (ed.) (Leiden: Brill, 1980), 17.

35. Many of his lectures are printed in the large-format, two-volume publication *Gnostic Studies* (Istanbul: Nederlands Historisch-Archaeologisch Instituut, 1975). This publication also includes his essay "Gnosis und Religionswissenschaft" (vol. 2, 259–70), which contains his interesting characterization of Gerardus van der Leeuw as a "genius of the surface," of Jung as a "genius of the abyss," and of Scholem as a "genius of precision."

36. This gave rise to his classic work *Gnosis als Weltreligion* (Zurich: Origo Verlag, 1951), published in English as *Gnosis as a World Religion* (1972), whose title itself reveals the book's agenda. In the foreword he says of Jung, "It is thanks to him that the complex structure of Gnostic thought became somewhat comprehensible to me."

37. This information is taken from Roelof van den Broek's foreword to the *Festschrift* published on the occasion of Quispel's sixty-fifth birthday: R. van den Broek and M. Vermaseren, *Studies in Gnosticism and Hellenistic Religions*, Bentley Layton (ed.) (Leiden: Brill, 1981), viiff. See also the obituary by Chiara O. Tommasi Moreschini and Giovanni Casadio in *Relgioni e società* 55(2) (2006), 15.

38. Patricia Wessels, "Nag Hammadi geschrieften: puur daynamit aan de wortels van het christendom," *Janus* 24(20) (1994), 11.

39. Quispel, *Gnosis als Weltreligion*, 37.

40. See the discussion of Gnosticism, as defined by Quispel, in Wouter Hanegraaff's informative essay "On the Construction of 'Esoteric Traditions'," in *Western Esotericism and the Science of Religion: Selected Papers Presented at the 17th Congress of the International Association for the History of Religions*, Antoine Faivre and Wouter Hanegraaff (eds) (Leuven: Peters, 1998).

41. Jung was rather annoyed about the continued delay in the publication of the translation and even feared that his ideas were being intentionally withheld from the English-speaking world. When he finally held in his hands the first volume, bound entirely in black, he remarked, "The book looks like a coffin." (Related to the author by Ximena de Angulo-Roelli.)

42. Von Reibnitz, "Der Eranos-Kreis," 8.

43. McGuire, *Bollingen*, 140.

44. *Ibid.*, 140.

45. Robert A. Segal, *Joseph Campbell: An Introduction* (Harmondsworth: Penguin, 1990). A chronology of Campbell's life can be found at www.pacifica.edu.cglibrary.campchron.html. See also Daniel C. Noel (ed.), *Paths to the Power of Myth: Joseph Campbell and the Study of Religion* (New York: Crossroad, 1990), a collection of contributions, largely by scholars of religion, on Campbell's work. One of the contributors was the Eranos speaker David L. Miller.

46. The already mentioned "hippy philosopher" Alan Watts, another effective publicist, said in his autobiography *In My Own Way* (New York: Pantheon Books, 1972) that Campbell was someone who possessed a Tantric attitude to life, a joyful acceptance of all aspects of being, and whose spirit infected those who came into contact with him.

47. On the occasion of Campbell's eightieth birthday in 1984 a celebration was held in the Palace of Fine Arts, to which over a thousand people came, including the poet and psychologist Robert Bly and the expert on early matriarchy Marija Gimbutas (Campbell always evinced a great interest in the culture of the "Great Mother"). Today there is a special Joseph Campbell Foundation, which has undertaken an edition of his collected works.

48. In an interview entitled "Elders and Guides" about Heinrich Zimmer, Campbell, after his already quoted praise of German scholarship, adds the following: "'This [German scholarship] is what hit me when I was a student in France. I went over there to study medieval French, Old French of Provençal. Basic works? In German! So the first thing I thought was: I can't speak or read German, so what the hell am I doing here in France, when the things I *have* to know how to read are in German! The next year I went to Germany, and then the world broke wide open for me" (McKnight, "Elders and Guides").

49. See his long essay "Johann Jacob Bachofen," now included in Anthony Van Couvering (ed.), *Joseph Campbell: The Mythic Dimension: Selected Essays 1959–1987* (San Francisco, CA: Harper, 1997), 67–91.

50. However, when he actually went to India in the 1950s, with a subsidy from the Bollingen Foundation, he was very disappointed, for instead of ageless wisdom he was confronted by the nationalism of the age. Campbell spoke of "a new, patriotically oriented religiosity; or perhaps, only religiously flavored patriotism, somewhat comparable to the American Protestant idea that Christianity and American democracy are the same thing." See Joseph Campbell, *Baksheesh and Brahman: Indian Journal 1954–1955*, R. Larsen, S. Larsen, and A. Van Couvering (eds) (New York: HarperCollins, 1995), x. In India Campbell met the "God-possessed" mystic Ananda Mayi Ma and the Viennese monk and Tantric expert Swami Agehananda Bharati (Leopold Fischer), who later taught anthropology at Syracuse University.

51. "Symbolism of the Marseilles Deck," in *Tarot Revelations*, Joseph Campbell and Richard Robert (eds) (San Anselmo, CA: Vernal Equinox Press, 1987). Campbell also contributed a foreword to this book for his friend Richard Roberts, describing his encounter with the Tarot in some detail.

52. The Grail mythos was already the theme of his dissertation and appears again, for example, in his work *Creative Mythology* (Harmondsworth: Penguin Books, 1976) in the series The Masks of God.

53. Despite these "esoteric escapades" Campbell received high academic accolades, including the Hofstra Distinguished Scholar Award and the National Institute of Arts and Letters Award. He was also president of the American Society for the Study of Religion. In 1988 a Joseph Campbell Chair of Comparative Mythology was created at Sarah Lawrence College.

54. In his interview with Michael McNight, Campbell even said that he had sometimes had the impression that Heinrich Zimmer was dictating the texts to him, such was the fascination that he had felt during the task. In the same interview he said that it was Zimmer who had given him the "courage" to pursue his own interpretations of mythology. See John M. Maher and Dennie Briggs (eds), *An Open Life: Joseph Campbell in Conversation with Michael Toms* (Burdett: Larson, 1988). Here Campbell resists any attempt to pigeon-hole him as a Jungian. Nevertheless, in 1972 he published a volume entitled *The Portable Jung*.

55. Steven Wasserstrom is even of the opinion that this book, perhaps more than any other, served to popularize Eranos and thereby helped to build a bridge between the elite discourse of Eranos and the emerging New Age "religion." See *Religion after Religion*, 141ff.

56. See, for example, the groundbreaking study by Florence Sandler and Derrell Reeck, "The Masks of Joseph Campbell," *Religion* 11(1) (1981), 1–20.

57. *Ibid.*, 5.

58. Giovanni Sorge, in his lecture "Love as devotion: Olga Fröbe-Kapteyn's Relationship with Eranos and Jungian Psychology," throws important light on the special symbiosis between Fröbe and Eranos as well as on the goals that Eranos shared with analytical psychology. The lecture was delivered as part of the Fetzer Dialogue at Eranos on 8 March 2009.

59. Letter of 25 February 1953.

60. In her foreword to the first volume of the American Eranos series (*Spirit and Nature: Papers from the Eranos Yearbook,* J. Campbell (ed.) [New York: Bollingen Foundation, 1954], xv), Fröbe uses almost the identical words. These did after all make an impression on Campbell, as is proved by his foreword to the second volume of the series (*The Mysteries: Papers from the Eranos Yearbook,* J. Campbell (ed.) [New York: Bollingen Foundation, 1955], xiv), where he repeats her words exactly.

61. Jung may have played a little-known role in bringing about this compromise. In an unpublished letter to Fröbe, dated 20 March 1953, he advised to accept the American selection, for "the atmosphere of Eranos will in any case fall by the wayside … I would therefore advise you to give up the fruitless struggle. Eranos 'made in USA' is no more the same! Furthermore the American public would not know how to appreciate the special symbolic refinements that are so important to you. In this respect I have had similar experiences with the publication of my collected works."

62. Joseph Campbell (ed.), *Papers from the Eranos Yearbook*s, Bollingen Series XXX, 1–6 (Princeton, NJ: Princeton University Press, 1970–72). In recent years there have been repeated attempts to publish further Eranos lectures

in the United States, but up to now these have not come to fruition owing to lack of funds. In Italy, however, since 1989 a whole series of lectures amounting to eight volumes have appeared. This is thanks to the Jungian analyst Claudio Risé, who saw to the publication of the series *Quaderni di Eranos*. Risé, well known in Italy for his unconventional books (for example on how to strengthen male self-confidence) enjoyed close contacts with the Red publishing house in Como and was able to convince them of the importance of the project. Several lectures have also appeared in French in the journal *Diogénès*, and of course the French-speaking Eranos lecturers have often included their lectures in their own anthologies or collections of essays. The Anthropos publishing firm in Barcelona has so far published three volumes of lectures in Spanish. In Japan too there is an "Eranos series" consisting of translations of the lectures. The third volume, for example, including contributions by Erik Hornung, Leo Baeck, and Ernst Benz, appeared in 1992 under the imprint of Heibonsha in Tokyo.

63. Stephen Larsen and Robin Larsen, *Joseph Campbell: A Fire in the Mind* (Rochester, VT: Inner Traditions 2002), 362.
64. Olga Fröbe, "In Memoriam Erich Neumann," *Eranos Jahrbuch* 29 (1960). Neumann was "perhaps the only follower of Jung to establish his own school of followers," as one obituary put it. The whole of his key work *The Great Mother* was written on the basis of the symbols and images that had been collected by Fröbe for the Eranos archive. Originally the intention had been that Neumann, prompted by Jung and Fröbe, should merely write an introductory text for the first publication based on material from the Eranos archive and bearing the title *Great Mother*. But the fascination exerted by the pictures from the archive led to a much wider-reaching project. See Neumann's foreword to *Die Große Mutter: Eine Phänomenologie der weiblichen Gestalten des Unbewußten* (Olten: Walter Verlag, 1983). Neumann's research work was sponsored by the Bollingen Foundation.
65. Quoted here from Heinz Prokop, "Erich Neumann in Israel," in *Psychologie des 20. Jahrhunderts 3*, Dieter Eicke (ed.) (Zurich: Kindler, 1977), 850.
66. *Ibid.*, 841–52.
67. The relationship is described in an essay by the psychologist's son, Micha Neumann, entitled "Die Beziehung zwischen Erich Neumann and C.G. Jung," *Analytische Psychologie* 23 (1992), 3–23. The article concludes that many of Jung's remarks in the 1930s indicate anti-Semitism, but that he had never shown even the slightest sign of it in regard to Erich Neumann. At the same time, Micha Neumann, who was himself a psychoanalyst, regrets that, while Jung was much preoccupied with oriental religions, he never showed any real interest in Judaism.
68. Erich Neumann, *Ursprungsgeschichte des Bewusstseins* (Zurich: Rascher Verlag, 1949), 1–2.
69. Scholem, *Briefe III*, 223, letter 206 of 24 November 1980 to James Kirsch.
70. This information is taken from the autobiography of the well-known palmist Ursula von Mangoldt, *Auf der Schwelle zwischen Gestern und Morgen*, 147.
71. Heinz Prokop in "Erich Neumann in Israel," 841, says that Neumann "is rightly regarded as the most significant and above all the most independent of Jung's pupils."
72. McGuire, *Bollingen*, 135.
73. Prokop, "Erich Neumann in Israel," 841ff.
74. See Gerhard Walch, "Tiefenpsychologie und neue Ethik von Erich Neumann," *Transpersonale Psychologie und Psychotherapie* 10(1) (2004), 11–17.
75. Erich Neumann, *The Great Mother*, Ralph Manheim (trans.) (Princeton, NJ: Princeton University Press, 1963), xlii. On 330–31 of this book, whose conception was doubtless influenced by Bachofen, Neumann explains what the "matriarchal" element means for him when he says, "This feminine-maternal wisdom is no abstract, disinterested knowledge, but a wisdom of loving participation."
76. *Eranos Jahrbuch* 19 (1950), 77, 120.
77. Erich Neumann, *Tiefenpsychologie und Neue Ethik* (Zurich: Rascher, 1949), 104, 108.
78. *Ibid.*, 105.
79. Gerhard Walch, "Tiefenpsychologie und neue Ethik von Erich Neumann," 13.
80. These details are taken from Jacques Waardenburg's contribution "Gerardus van der Leeuw (1890–1950)," in Michaels (ed.), *Klassiker der Religionswissenschaft*, 264–76.
81. William Hofstee, "The Essence of Concrete Individuality: Gerardus van der Leeuw, Jan de Vries and National Socialism," in *The Study of Religion under the Impact of Fascism*, Horst Junginger (ed.) (Leiden: Brill, 2008), 543–52). I am grateful to Willem Hofstee for having kindly allowed me to see his manuscript before the publication of the book.
82. See Richard J. Plantinga, "Romanticism and the History of Religions: The Case of W.B. Kristensen," in *Religionswissenschaft und Kulturkritik*, Hans G. Kippenberg and Brigitte Luchesi (eds), 157–76. This deals in detail with van de Leeuw's debt to German Romanticism and Friedrich Schleiermacher, although in this regard the author's approach is very discriminating.
83. In his foreword to Gerardus van der Leeuw, *Sacred and Profane Beauty: The Holy in Art* (New York: Holt Rinehart & Winston, 1963), vi.
84. The original letter from Fröbe is in the University Library at Groningen. Interestingly, it is written in German, since her Dutch was so poor, as she said.
85. Willem Hofstee, *Goden en Mensen: De Godsdienstwetenschap van Gerardus van der Leeuw 1890–1950* (Agora: Kampen, 1997), 108–9.

86. Eliade, *Journal I, 1945–1955*, 165.
87. *Ibid.*, 164.
88. Gerardus van der Leeuw, *Phänomenologie der Religion* (Tübingen: J.C.B. Mohr, 1933).
89. *Ibid.*, 3.
90. The scholar of religion Gustav Mensching summarizes the phenomenological approach when he defines religion as "both the experiential encounter of human beings with the reality of the holy and the corresponding actions of the person who is affected by the holy" (quoted from Günter Kehrer, "Definition der Religion," in *Handbuch religionswissenschaftlicher Grundbegriffe*, vol. IV, Hubert Cancik, Burkhard Gladigow, and Karl-Heinz Koh [eds] [Stuttgart: Verlag W. Kohlhammer, 1998], 423). A highly pregnant interpretation is given by the prominent Eranos lecturer Henry Corbin in his *Histoire de la philosophie islamique* (Paris: Gallimard, 1986), 382. Writing about the so-called Encyclopaedists, he says: "Phenomenology does not cling to the material facts as such—it is all too easy to maintain that such facts have been 'overtaken' … What the phenomenologist seeks to decipher is the primal image, the *imago mundi a priori*, which is both the organ and the form in which these phenomena are perceived." In her book *Religionen der Erde: Religionsgeschichte im Abriss* (Wiesbaden: Kesselringsche Verlagsbuchhandlung, 1951), 5, Annemarie Schimmel, later an Eranos lecturer, defines the phenomenology of religion as an approach that seeks to investigate the religious realm *per se*, independent of any particular people or historical period. "It investigates the sacred rite, the sacred place, the sacred space, the sacred moment; it seeks to recognize the underlying concept in each religious symbol and to discern the original potently sacred action behind every graphic piece of language." The basic aim of this method is to get away from philosophical concepts and theories and concentrate on direct intuition and description of the phenomena that arise from one's own immediate experience. "*Zu den Sachen*" (Let's get down to the essentials) is the motto of philosophical phenomenology.

   On the subject of the phenomenology of religion, see also the very detailed article by Douglas Allen, "Phenomenology of Religion," in *Encyclopedia of Religion Vol. XI*, Mircea Eliade (ed.) (New York: Macmillan, 1987), 272–84. However, Allen emphasizes that different authors have widely varying definitions of this concept. The main problem with the phenomenological method is that it demands from the scholar an intuitive, para-scientific step before he is even in a position to make an informed judgment about what religion is. In this sense the phenomenology of religion is more religious than scientific. Such an analysis must inevitably strengthen the case of the "positivists." The already mentioned Tenth International Congress for the History of religions, held in Marburg Lahn in 1960, can be seen as a kind of turning point. From then on the phenomenologists of religion became increasingly marginalized. Hartmut Zinser even wrote, "Despite all its recognizable achievements … the enterprise of the phenomenology of religion must be overcome if the study of religion is to be a really objective discipline and not a privately motivated theology in disguise." See the article "Religionsphänomenologie," in *Handbuch religionswissenschaftlicher Grundbegriffe*, vol. I, Hubert Cancik *et al.* (eds) (Stuttgart: W. Kohlhammer, 1998), 308. The contrary standpoint is represented by Michael Bergunder in the chapter "Religionsphänomenologische Methode," in his book *Wiedergeburt der Ahnen: Eine religionsethnographische und religionsphänomenologische Untersuchung zur Reinkarnationsvorstellung* (Münster and Hamburg: LIT Verlag 1993), 86–93. A very informative overview about the subject of phenomenology of religion is given in James L. Cox, *A Guide to the Phenomenology of Religion: Key Figures, Formative Influences and Subsequent Debates* (London: T&T Clark, 2006).

91. See Ioan Culianu, *Mircea Eliade* (Assisi: Citadella, 1978), 146. Eliade himself had written an essay on "Van der Leeuw et la phénoménologie de la religion," now available in Mircea Eliade, *Briser le toit de la maison: La créativité et ses symboles* (Paris: Gallimard, 1986), 273–9. In this essay he describes van der Leeuw's work *Phenomenology of Religion* as decidedly "the best introduction to the general history of religions" (276).

92. The "crisis of historicism" is one of the features of the struggle between idealism and positivism around the turn of the twentieth century. See the instructive "Einleitung: Idealismus—Positivismus. Grundspannung und Vermittlung in Kultur und Kulturwissenschaften um 1900," in *Kultur und Kulturwissenschaften um 1900 III: Idealismus und Positivismus*, Gangolf Hübinger, Rüdiger von Bruch, and Friedrich Wilhelm Graf (eds) (Stuttgart: Franz Steiner, 1997), 12ff.

93. Here it is appropriate to quote the words of J.W. Hauer, who wrote in 1923, "Although there have been plenty of studies presenting the facts of religious history, conscientiously backed up by well-founded philological arguments, the inner side of the history of religions has not been much in evidence. Experience, the really creative element in religions, has been too little taken into account. All too often we had merely the "coldly surprised" attitude of the visitor." Only in recent times, he says, have works such as Rudolf Otto's *Das Heilige* and specialized studies like Heiler's *Gebet* shown that a change is taking place (foreword to J.W. Hauer, *Die Religionen: Ihr Werden/ ihr Sinn/ihre Wahrheit* [Stuttgart: W. Kohlhammer, 1923], 5). This whole subject would merit a study in itself, as it has fascinating implications, not only for religious scholarship but for the humanities in general and even for the political realm.

94. Jung also employs an emphatically "phenomenological" methodology; that is to say, he looks at phenomena in terms of human experience, ignoring any possible transcendental or theological perspectives. Thus in one of his works he describes his psychology "as purely a science of phenomena, without metaphysical implications" (Jung, *Gesammelte Werke*, vol. 11, 511).

95. Ferdinand Christian Baur, in his influential book *Die christliche Gnosis* (Tübingen: C.F. Osiander, 1835), even argues that Schelling and Hegel represent the gnosis of the nineteenth century.

96. See especially the two-volume work by Auguste Viatte, *Les Sources Occultes du Romantisme* (Paris: Honoré Champion, 1928); and Antoine Faivre and Rudolf Zimmerman, *Epochen der Naturmystik: Hermetische Tradition im wissenschaftlichen Fortschritt* (Berlin: Erich Schmidt Verlag, 1979); as well as Antoine Faivre's book (especially relevant in this context), *Philosophie de la Nature: Physique sacrée et théosophie XVIe–XIXe siécle* (Paris: Albin Michel, 1996). Wouter Hanegraaff has written a detailed essay on this question under the title "Romanticism and the Esoteric Connection," in *Gnosis and Hermeticism from Antiquity to Modern Times*, Roelof van den Broek and Wouter Hanegraaff (eds) (Albany, NY: SUNY Press, 1998), 237–68. Nevertheless, there would still be room for a comprehensive work, following in detail this background current in Western thought from romanticism to vitalism (e.g. Hans Driesch) and on up to the present day. The distinguishing characteristic of this current is the attempt to find in the phenomena of our inner life a way of overcoming the rationalist split between subject and object. Hanegraaff describes the general drift of this current in his work *New Age Religion and Western Culture*, although this is secondary to the main theme of his book. There is, however, a work in the domain of the history of literature that addresses precisely this topic, namely Pierre Deghaye, *De Paracelse à Thomas Mann: Les avatars de l'hermétisme allemand* (Paris: Dervy, 2000). This gap is another example of the unfortunate heritage of the German caesura of the Hitler period. There are still many researchers who are scared away from such "irrational intellectual currents."

97. At the most, one could possibly speak of an "*Urfaschismus*" (primal fascism) in the sense that Umberto Eco uses the term. See Umberto Eco, "Il fascismo eterno," in *Cinque scritti morali* (Milan: Bompiani, 1997). But even using Eco's very loose criteria, one could hardly describe Eranos as *urfaschistisch*. Too many of the characteristic features are lacking (anti-intellectualism, frustration, conspiracy theories, impoverished vocabulary, populism, hero-worship as a norm), even if, arguably, certain others are present (syncretism, anti-modernity, elitist thinking). On the subject of Eco and *Urfaschismus*, see also Hans Thomas Hakl, "'Occultism is the Metaphysic of Dunces': The Equation or Conceptual Conflation of Esotericism, Irrationalism, and Fascism in Postwar Germany," in *Esotericism, Religion and Politics*, Arthur Versluis, Lee Irwin, and Melinda Phillips (eds) (Minneapolis, MN: Association for the Study of Esotericism, 2012).

11. The Heyday Begins

1. See Joseph Dan, *Gershom Scholem and the Mystical Dimension of Jewish History* (New York: New York University Press, 1988), 4.

2. *Ibid.*, 8ff.

3. Scholem, *Von Berlin nach Jerusalem: Jugenderinnerungen*, 92.

4. The information given here is taken from Michael Buckmiller and Pascal Nafe, "Die Naherwartung des Kommunismus: Werner Scholem," in *Judentum und politische Existenz: Siebzehn Porträts deutsch–jüdischer Intellektueller*, Michael Buckmiller, Dietrich Heimann, and Joachim Perels (eds) (Hannover: Offizin, 2000), 61–81.

5. It is certain that the famous writer Ernst Jünger, who in his youth at least was very nationalistic, was a schoolmate of Werner Scholem in 1914 in Hannover. At any rate, this question led to a six-year correspondence between Gershom Scholem and Ernst Jünger, involving eleven still-unpublished letters and postcards, which are now in the Scholem Archive in the National Library in Jerusalem. Jünger had begun the correspondence, wishing to know if Gershom Scholem was this former schoolmate. Despite an apparent mutual respect (Scholem congratulated Jünger on the occasion of his eightieth birthday), these two very contrasting correspondents do not appear to have felt any greater degree of sympathy for each other. See the comprehensive article by Mirjam Triendl and Noam Zadoff, "Ob mein Bruder Werner gemeint ist?" *Freitag* 26 (18 June 2004), www.freitag.de/autoren/der-freitag/ob-mein-bruder-werner-gemeint-ist (accessed December 2012). A scholarly reappraisal of the correspondence then took place in "Ernst Jünger, Gershom Scholem: Briefwechsel 1975–1981," *Sinn und Form* 61(3) (2009), 293–302, followed by the detailed remarks of Detlev Schöttker ("'Vielleicht kommen wir ohne Wunder nicht aus,' Zum Briefwechsel Jünger–Scholem," *Sinn und Form* 61(3) (2009), 303–8. Despite its ultimate unimportance, this correspondence caused quite a stir in the German-language press, from the *Frankfurter Allgemeine Zeitung* to *Die Zeit* and the *Neue Zürcher Zeitung*.

6. See Klaus S. Davidowicz, *Kabbala: Geheime Tradition im Judentum* (Eisenstadt: Österreichisches Jüdisches Museum, n.d.), 12, and the preface by Scholem's translator, Bernard Dupuy, to Gershom Scholem, *Le messianisme juif: essais sur la spiritualité du judaisme* (Paris: Calmann-Lévy, 1974), 8. This informative introduction contains much valuable information on Scholem's preoccupation with the Kabbala. Scholem himself, in his essay "Wissenschaft vom Judentum einst und jetzt," clearly describes the anti-mystical climate in Jewish scholarship at the turn of the twentieth century. Andreas Kilcher even says, in his book *Die Sprachtheorie der Kabbala seit der frühen Neuzeit* (Stuttgart: J.B. Metzler, 1998), 18, that Scholem, in his Kabbalistic studies, "could hardly rely on any Jewish predecessors and therefore turned to the work of Christian Hebraists from Reuchlin to Molitor."

7. It should not be forgotten that Walter Benjamin, as a student in 1914, had contacted the "Cosmic" Ludwig Klages and maintained a deep interest in him. See the essay by Michael Großheim, "Archaisches oder

dialektisches Bild? Zum Kontext einer Debatte zwischen Adorno und Benjamin," *Deutsche Vierteljahresschrift für Literaturwissenschaft und Geistesgeschichte* 71(3) (1997), 494–517, which reveals some surprising cross-connections and "strange bedfellows" (Helmuth Lethen). On his own admission, Benjamin's thinking always moved "between extreme positions," in order to gain "breadth." Thus he even endorsed certain theses of Hitler's "crown jurist" Carl Schmitt. See Susanne Heil, *Gefährliche Beziehungen: Walter Benjamin und Carl Schmitt* (Stuttgart: J.B. Metzler, 1996).

8. See the essay by Gershom Scholem, "Walter Benjamin," in *Über Walter Benjamin* (Frankfurt: Suhrkamp, 1968). Here Scholem interestingly calls Benjamin a "man to whom occult experiences were not foreign" (*ibid*.: 139). In his article on the critical edition of the complete writings of Benjamin, entitled "Eine gewaltige Aufgabe, ein editorisches Martyrium" (A massive task, an editorial martyrdom) and published in the *Neue Zürcher Zeitung* on 2–3 August 2008, Ludger Lütkehaus recounts a joke of Benjamin's, who together with Scholem "founded" a fantasy "University of Muri" "with an experienced 'demonological' faculty and himself as 'Rector mirabilis.'" Benjamin also willed his manuscripts to Scholem. However, after Scholem's death, his wife Fania spoke less of a friendship than an attitude of admiration, indeed almost love on her husband's part towards the older man. The latter, however, apparently did not reciprocate very strongly. See Hans Mayer, *Der Widerruf: Über Deutsche und Juden* (Frankfurt: Suhrkamp, 1994), 388.

9. See his essay "Subversive Katalysatoren: Gnosis und Messianismus in Gershom Sholems Verständnis der jüdischen Mystik," in *Gershom Scholem: Zwischen den Disziplinen*, Peter Schäfer and Gary Smith (eds) (Frankfurt: Suhrkamp, 1995), 80.

10. *Sabbatai Sevi: The Mystical Messiah 1626–1676* (Princeton, NJ: Princeton University Press, [1957] 1973).

11. See McGuire, *Bollingen*, 152ff.

12. Quoted from Elisabeth Hamacher, *Gershom Scholem und die Allgemeine Religionsgeschichte* (Berlin: Walter de Gruyter, 1999), 60. The emphasis on "distance" also raises the question to what extent Scholem was a believer at all. The Gnosticism expert Hans Jonas, who described Scholem as being extremely self-assured ("Ultimately he was so sure of himself that any self-doubt was totally foreign to him"), describes this question as "one of the great Scholem riddles." Jonas also says, however, that Scholem believed that "if Judaism offers anything at all interesting, strong, lively, relevant, exciting and creative, then it was bound to be found in the sphere of the Kabbalah." Jonas adds that although Scholem could not really be described as religious, it was not possible for a lecturer at the Hebrew University to be a complete atheist. See Hans Jonas, *Erinnerungen nach Gesprächen mit Rachel Salamander* (Frankfurt: Insel Verlag, 2003), 269ff. According to Jonas (270), Scholem was also said to have had a "great talent for making *faux pas*."

13. Wasserstrom, *Religion after Religion*, 59. Quoted here from the text reproduced in Gershom Scholem, *Briefe I: 1914–1947*, Itta Schedletzky (ed.) (Munich: C.H. Beck, 1994), 459. Unfortunately Wasserstom's interesting pieces of information are not always easy to verify, as the bibliographical details are often —as in this case—faulty. Admittedly no book is ever totally free of mistakes, but the errors in Wasserstrom's book, together with the all too frequent misspellings in non-English texts and quotes, can easily lead to an unjustifiably negative assessment of the work.

14. Herbert Weiner, *9½ Mystics: The Kabbalah Today* (New York: Collier, 1971), 62. Weiner reports being told by Scholem that the latter had already in his youth written a book about the Kabbalah (*ibid*.: 60). This was not a historical-philological work, but was written from a personal standpoint. The book was unobtainable because he had bought up all the copies. It is not clear to what extent this story was meant as a joke. However, it should be mentioned that Scholem was "beside himself with rage" when Weiner's book was mentioned by Friedrich Niewöhner, later an Eranos speaker (1999) and co-editor of one of Scholem's diaries. This is reported by Niewöhner in his detailed review of the first edition of the present book in *Gnostika* 6(20) (2002), 61.

15. Weiner, *9½ Mystics*, 62. In this connection Weiner also tells of an old rabbi of Jerusalem who made the following amusing remark about scholars who write about Jewish mysticism: "They are accountants. That is, like accountants, they know where the wealth is, its location and value. But it doesn't belong to them. They cannot use it."

16. Wasserstrom, *Religion after Religion*, 123ff.

17. See Gershom Scholem, *Die jüdische Mystik in ihren Hauptströmungen* (Frankfurt: Suhrkamp, 1967), 24. "The affinity of much Kabbalistic thought to the world of myth is beyond doubt … It is really astonishing to observe that, in the innermost heart of Judaism, on its deepest level of interpretation, ideas arise and assert themselves which indicate a reversion to or a renaissance of mythical consciousness, depending on how one looks at it." The Kabbalists stand thereby in stark contrast to the tendency of the "classical Jewish tradition of *liquidating myth* as a central spiritual power," as Scholem formulates it and further emphasizes with italics (Gershom Scholem, *Zur Kabbala und ihrer Symbolik* [Frankfurt: Suhrkamp, 1973], 118).

18. See, for example, Hermann Cohen's famous work *Die Religion der Vernunft aus den Quellen des Judentums* (Wiesbaden: Fourier, 1978). On this question see also the contrasting views expressed in the proceedings of the 1994 conference on "Myth in the Biblical and Jewish Traditions," published in *The Seductiveness of Jewish Myth: Challenge or Response?*, S. Daniel Breslauer (ed.) (Albany, NY: SUNY Press, 1997). This also contains a contribution from Steven Wasserstrom (97–122) on Jewish mythical leanings during the Weimar period, exemplified by Rosenzweig, Buber, Bloch, and Aby Warburg. He sees the reason for this "turn" as being the fascination exerted by the later works of Schelling. Wasserstrom even pinpoints 1923 as the beginning of a new era.

19. Idel, *Kabbalah*, 12.

20. Elémire Zolla, later an Eranos lecturer, speaking in an interview, expresses himself very strongly with regard to this contrast: "Scholem is an outstanding master of the Kabbalah, but everything that he conveyed has been trumped by Moshe Idel, a young Romanian Jew and friend of Couliano" (Elémire Zolla and Doriano Fasoli, *Un destino itinerante: Conversazioni tra Occidente e Oriente* [Venice: Marsilio, 2002], 69).

21. This is partly evident from his book titles, such as *Studies in Ecstatic Kabbalah* (Albany, NY: SUNY Press, 1988). Scholem's approach, by contrast, had already manifested itself in his youth, as in his essay entitled "Lyrik der Kabbalah?" *Der Jude* 6(1) (1921–22), 55–69, now available in Gershom Scholem, *Tagebücher nebst Aufsätzen und Entwürfen bis 1923, 1917–1923*, Karlfried Günder, Herbert Kopp-Oberstbrink, and Friedrich Niewöhner (eds), with collaboration from Karl E. Grözinger (Frankfurt: Jüdischer Verlag, 2000), 657–84. Here Scholem writes, "Ecstasy has never played the kind of central role in the Kabbalah that one finds in some mystical teachings. The Kabbalah has been protected from this by a pristine, deeply spiritual and, if you will, rationalistic foundation, which declares the 'colourless light of reason' to be the highest crown of the spheres" (p. 675).

22. Theodor W. Adorno, "Gruß an Gershom G. Scholem: Zum 70. Geburtstag," *Neue Zürcher Zeitung* (2 December 1967), reprinted in Christian Wiese, *Hans Jonas: "Zusammen Philosoph und Jude"* (Frankfurt: Jüdischer Verlag, 2003), 75, 172.

23. David Biale, "Scholem und der moderne Nationalismus," in *Gershom Scholem: Zwischen den Disziplinen*, Peter Schäfer and Gary Smith (eds) (Frankfurt: Suhrkamp 1995), 260–61.

24. See the section devoted to Scholem in his essay, quoted earlier, "On the Construction of 'Esoteric Traditions,'" 47–52.

25. Andreas Kilcher, "Gershom Scholem," in *Lexikon jüdischer Philosophie: Philosophisches Denken des Judentums von der Antike bis zur Gegenwart*, Andreas B. Kilcher and Otfried Fraisse (eds), 392–5 (Stuttgart: J.B. Metzler, 2003).

26. See Andreas Kilcher, *Die Sprachtheorie der Kabbala als ästhetisches Paradigma: Die Konstruktion einer ästhetischen Kabbala seit der frühen Neuzeit* (Stuttgart: J.B. Metzler, 1998), §6.1, "Die romantische Kabbala des jungen Gershom Scholem," 332. This section also describes how Scholem came to the Kabbalah. Meanwhile Kilcher has provided further details on this topic in his essay "Figuren des Endes: Historie und Aktualität der Kabbala bei Gershom Scholem," in *Gershom Scholem: Literatur und Rhetorik*, Stéphane Mosès and Sigrid Weigel (eds) (Cologne: Bohlau Verlag, 2000), 153–99. The same volume contains an essay by Moshe Idel, "Zur Funktion von Symbolen bei G.G. Scholem" (pp. 51–92), dealing with the great significance of symbolism in Scholem's interpretation of the Kabbalah.

27. See Christoph Schulte, "'Die Buchstaben haben … ihre Wurzeln oben': Scholem und Molitor," in *Kabbalah und Romantik*, Eveline Goodman-Thau, Gert Mattenkloth, and Christoph Schulte (eds) (Tübingen: Max Niemeyer, 1994), 143ff. See also Moshe Idel, "Hiéroglyphes, clés, enigmes: La vision de G.G. Scholem sur la Kabbale: entre Franz Molitor et Franz Kafka," *Archaeus* 7 (2003), 3–4, 271–91.

28. Scholem, *Die jüdische Mystik in ihren Hauptstömungen*, 2. For a recent English language edition, see Gershom Scholem, *Major Trends in Jewish Mysticism* (New York: Schocken Books, 1995).

29. First published in 1925 in the *Monatsschrift für Geschichte und Wissenschaft des Judentums*.

30. *Alchemistische Blätter: Monatsschrift für das Gesamtgebiet der Hermetischen Wissenschaften in alter und neuer Zeit, Organ verschiedener Alchemistischer Gesellschaften, Logen, Schulen* 1(8–9), 89–92, and 1(10–11), 122–37.

31. There is hardly any documentation on the history of this publishing house, as the original documents were destroyed in the Second World War. However, the history of this firm, with its highly important place in the history of German esotericism, has been reconstructed as far as possible by Christoph Bochinger in his book *"New Age" und moderne Religion: Religionswissenschaftliche Analysen* (Gütersloh: Gütersloher Verlagshaus, 1995), 143–58. Thanks are due to him for this work. A concise summary of the history of this firm can be found under the website www.fischerverlage.de.

32. The main bibliographies in question are Gershom Scholem, *Bibliographia Kabbalistica: Die jüdische Mystik (Gnosis, Kabbala Sabbatianismus, Frankismus, Chassidismus) behandelnde Bücher und Aufsätze von Reuchlin bis zur Gegenwart* (Berlin: Schocken Verlag, 1933) and "Bibliography of the published writings of G.G. Scholem," in *Studies in Mysticism and Religion presented to Gershom G. Scholem on his Seventieth Birthday by Pupils, Colleagues and Friends*, E.E. Urbach, R.J. Zwi Werblowsky, and C. Wirszubski (eds)(Jerusalem: Magnes Press, Hebrew University, 1967). It is curious that in the reprint of *Alchemie und Kabbala* (Frankfurt: Suhrkamp, 1994) there is no mention of a lecture of the same title, based on his studies during the 1920s, which he delivered at Eranos in 1977.

33. An additional explanation for how Scholem acquired such a comprehensive library, with so many rarities, has been given by the expert on esoteric history Allison Coudert in the acknowledgements to her book *The Impact of the Kabbalah in the Seventeenth Century: The Life and Thought of Francis Mercury van Helmont (1614–1698)* (Leiden: Brill, 1999), ix: "Van Helmont is also responsible for my meeting Gershom Scholem in 1972. I later learned that Professor Scholem's ability to inveigle books from people was legendary, which explains why my copy of van Helmont's *Alphabeti vere naturalis Hebraici brevissima delineation* is housed in the Scholem Library at Hebrew University." In his essay "Walter Benjamin," *Judaica* 2 (Frankfurt: Suhrkamp, 1982), 196, Scholem

approvingly quotes the passionate book collector Benjamin as saying that "of all the common ways in which collectors acquire their books, the cleverest is to borrow and not return."

34. Konstantin Burmistrov, "Gershom Scholem und das Okkulte," *Gnostika* 33 (2006), 23–4.

35. Gershom Scholem, *Geheimnisse der Schöpfung* (Berlin: Schocken Verlag, 1935).

36. Scholem, *Briefe III*, 125, 171.

37. Lorenz Jäger, "Wer hat die längste Lebenslinie? Er verstand von vielem viel und führte seinen Gesprächspartner sogar in die Kunst der Chiromantie ein: ein Frankfurter Vormittag mit Gershom Scholem im Jahr 1980," *Frankfurter Allgemeine Zeitung* (11 April 2009), 85, Z5. This article delivers a number of other surprises as well.

38. Walter Benjamin positively reviewed a book on graphology by Teillard-Mendelsohn, and C.G. Jung held discussions with her over a number of decades.

39. Edward Hoffman, review of *Stalking Elijah: Adventures with Today's Jewish Mystical Masters*, by Roger Kamenetz, *Gnosis* 49 (1998), 68.

40. See George Steiner, *Errata: Bilanz eines Lebens* (Munich: Carl Hanser Verlag, 1999), 173. English edition: *Errata: An Examined Life* (London: Weidenfeld & Nicolson, 1997).

41. See also Friedrich Niewöhner's review of Brigitte Hamacher's "erudite, courageous and provocative book," *Gottes Zorn kam zu kurz: Gershom Scholem als Schüler der deutschen Religionsgeschichte*, in *Frankfurter Allgemeine Zeitung* 207 (7 September 1999), 54.

42. Daniel Weidner, *Gershom Scholem: Politisches, esoterisches und historiographisches Schreiben* (Munich: Wilhelm Fink, 2003).

43. Scholem, *Briefe II*, 94 and 118.

44. Mazenauer and Perrig, in their article in the special edition of *Du* devoted to Jung, mention similar statements of Jung to James Kirsch and Werner H. Engel, but they emphasize that these were private and not public apologies.

45. In a further letter to Aniela Jaffé of 8 December 1964 (see Scholem, *Briefe II*, 118) Scholem also refers to negative voices about Jung. Already on 2 July 1937 his friend Walter Benjamin had spoken very critically of Jung: "Perhaps you will have heard that Jung has come to the aid of the Aryan soul with a therapy spiritually reserved for it. A perusal of his volumes of essays from the beginning of this decade indicates to me that these services to National Socialism had already been a long time in preparation." See Gershom Scholem (ed.), *Walter Benjamin-Gershom Scholem Briefwechsel* (Frankfurt: Suhrkamp, 1980), 240. A commentary on this passage in Christoph Gödde and Henri Lonitz (eds), *Walter Benjamin: Gesammelte Briefe*, vol. 5, 1935–1937 (Frankfurt: Suhrkamp, 1999), 546, mentions that Benjamin was at that moment expecting some Eranos volumes that he had ordered from the publisher Daniel Brody.

46. See the reference to this in *Briefe II*, 62.

47. Originally printed in Manfred Schösser (ed.), *Auf gespaltenem Pfad. Zum neunzigsten Geburtstag von Margarete Susman* (Darmstadt: Erato-Presse, 1964), 229–32, quoted here from Gershom Scholem, "Wider den Mythos vom deutsch–jüdischen Gespräch," in *Judaica 2*, 7–11; see also "Noch einmal: Das deutsch–jüdische Gespräch," in *Judaica 2*, 12–19.

48. Lorenz Jäger, "Wer hat die längste Lebenslinie?"

49. Scholem, *Briefe II*, 16ff. (letter to Georg Lichtheim of 1950).

50. Elettra Stimili (ed.), *Jacob Taubes: Der Preis des Messianismus: Briefe von Jacob Taubes an Gershom Scholem und andere Materialien* (Würzburg: Königshausen & Neumann, 2006), 45. On this essential question of Jewish Messianism see the comprehensive study of Pierre Bouretz, *Témoins du Futur: Philosophie et messianisme* (Paris: Gallimard, 2003), in which Scholem as well as Martin Buber are dealt with in detail.

51. Wasserstrom, *Religion after Religion*, 16.

52. His biographical details are taken from Cora du Bois, "Paul Radin: An Appreciation," in *Culture in History: Essays in Honor of Paul Radin*, Stanley Diamond (ed.) (New York: Columbia University Press, 1960), ixff.

53. Not all applicants were so fortunate. One of those who received a refusal from Bollingen was the famous Marxist philosopher Ernst Bloch. In a letter of 5 August 1947 to Adolph Lowe he quotes the letter of refusal and expresses his disappointment. See Karola Bloch (ed.), *Ernst Bloch, Briefe 1903–1975*, vol. 2, 765.

54. He was also skeptical about the then widely held view that so-called "primitive" people have a totally different type of mentality. While he recognized certain degrees of difference, he regarded the responses of "primitive" peoples to the demands of life as being just as profound and well considered as those of modern society. He was particularly skeptical—and probably rightly so—concerning the alleged moral superiority of our age and culture.

55. See his letter of 9 February 1953 to John Barrett, in which, after prolonged urging on Fröbe's part, he finally agreed to accept her invitation to go to Europe.

56. See Eliade, *Journal I, 1945–1955*, 112.

57. Diamond (ed.), *Culture in History*, xvii.

58. Paul Radin, Karl Kerényi, and C.G. Jung, *Der Göttliche Schelm: Ein indianischer Mythen-Zyklus* (Hildesheim: Gerstenberg, 1979).

59. Corbin was baptized with the Christian name of Henry instead of the usual French form, Henri.

60. The biographical details given here are taken from the following works: Christian Jambet (ed.), *Henry Corbin*, 15; Seyyed Hossein Nasr, "Henry Corbin, 'l'exil occidental': une vie en une oeuvre en quête de l'Orient des

Lumières," in Seyyed Hossein Nasr, *Mélanges offerts à Henry Corbin* (Montréal: McGill University, Institute of Islamic Studies), 1977, 3–27; Daryush Shayegan, *Henry Corbin: La topographie spirituelle de l'Islam iranien* (Paris, Éditions de la Différence, 1990). A short biography of Corbin is also provided by Mircea Eliade in his 1979 essay "Ananda Coomaraswamy et Henry Corbin," in Mircea Eliade, *Briser le toit de la maison*, 281–94. Eliade received much support from Corbin.

61. Davy, *Traversée en solitaire*, 139ff.

62. "Henry Corbin," in Eliade (ed.), *The Encyclopedia of Religion*.

63. Jambet (ed.), *Henry Corbin*, 42.

64. This question was a subject of heated debate for a long time and preoccupied both theologians and philosophers. It provoked, for example, a sharp reaction from Karl Jaspers, bringing a reply from Bultmann and a further reply from Jaspers. See Karl Jaspers and Rudolf Bultmann, *Die Frage der Entmythologisierung* (Munich: Piper, 1954).

65. On this famous library, see two essays by Fritz Saxl, "Die kulturwissenschaftliche Bibliothek Warburg in Hamburg" and "Die Geschichte der Bibliothek Aby Warburgs (1886–1944)" with afterword and annotations by E.H. Gombrich, in Aby M. Warburg, *Ausgewählte Schriften und Würdingungen*, Dieter Wittke (ed.) (Baden-Baden: Valentin Koerner, 1980), 331–4 and 335–46.

66. It is interesting to note that Corbin published the earliest French translations both of Heidegger and Karl Jaspers in the Belgian "meta-surrealist" journal *Hermès*. This periodical, which was expressly named after Hermes Trismegistos, was run by the poet René Baert and the surrealist painter Marc Eemans, who would later lead the Belgian branch of a Julius Evola study circle (Centro Studi Evoliani). The first number contained an essay by Friedrich Gundolf on Stefan George. There were also articles about the Eleusinian Mysteries and about yoga. In subsequent issues there were articles on Leo Schestow, Karl Jaspers, and Martin Heidegger as well as on mystical writers such as Meister Eckhart, William Blake, O.V. de Milosz, and Henry Vaughan. There were also articles on Islamic, Chinese, and Tibetan esotericism. See the essay by Marc Eemans, "Ce que fut la revue métasurréaliste Hermès (1933–1939)," *Antaios* 13 (1998), 118–23. This *Antaios*, run by Christopher Gérard in Brussels, was in the same spirit as the identically named German periodical founded by Ernst Jünger and Mircea Eliade. It ceased publication with number 16 in 2001. Its aim was to propagate Neopagan, polytheistic ideas. See Ernst Jünger, *Siebzig verweht*, vol. 5 (Stuttgart: Klett-Cotta, 1997), 143, where he quotes an entry in his diary for 1 June 1994: "To Christopher Gérard: 'Thanks for [*Antaios*] 3. Another excellent issue. Hopefully many more will follow.'"

67. We should not forget that the word "hermeneutic" comes from the Greek messenger god Hermes, who brings us the "message of the gods." Under his instruction we should try to seek out the "divine," that is to say the deepest possible meaning in phenomena. The Würzburg philosopher Heinrich Rombach would in such a case probably no longer use the word "hermeneutic" but rather "hermetic," as for him the hermetic experience leads us beyond the distinction between subject and object. This hermetic experience cannot be "acquired," in the way that a hermeneutic experience—such as the hermeneutic circle—can. Rather it is a flight that leads to incalculable heights that cannot be reached *purely* though one's own effort. "Height" is in fact for Rombach a thoroughly hermetic category. On this theme it may be relevant to quote two original sentences from him, whose message would really require a whole treatise: "He who denies height denies the hermetic. He who wishes to be 'modern' must deny height and rank." See Heinrich Rombach, *Der kommende Gott: Hermetik: eine neue Weltsicht* (Freiburg: Rombach Verlag, 1991), 42ff.

68. In 1935 he had even written a lengthy treatise on Hamann, which was not published until 1985, namely *Hamann: philosophe du luthéranisme* (Paris: L'Ile verte, Berg International, 1985). This contains three essays by Hamann, translated by Corbin. The poet and visionary Hamann wished to revive Lutheran spirituality and developed a new hermeneutic method based on a kind of mystical vision. It is interesting to compare this "positive" view of Hamann with the "negative" view taken by the historian of ideas Isaiah Berlin in his book *The Magus of the North: J.G. Hamann and the Origins of Modern Irrationalism* (New York: Farrar, Straus & Giroux, 1993).

69. Wasserstrom, *Religion after Religion*, 54.

70. This is most convincingly substantiated by Xavier Accart in his monumental (1200-plus pages) work *Guénon ou le renversement des clartés: Influence d'un métaphysicien sur la vie littéraire et intellectuelle française (1920–1970)* (Paris: Editit Arché, 2005).

71. See Seyyed Hossein Nasr, "Recollections of Henry Corbin and Reflections upon his Intellectual Significance," *Temenos Academy Review 2* (1999), 36. In this essay Nasr describes his friend, with whom he collaborated for 20 years, as a "mystical philosopher and philosophical mystic" with a love for the esoteric (34). Some short observations on this theme have also been made by Mircea Eliade, who enjoyed much support from Corbin, in Eliade's already quoted essay "Ananda K. Coomaraswamy et Henry Corbin: à propos de la *Theosophia Perennis*."

72. Steven Wasserstrom even detects in Corbin a "spiritual nationalism," focused on Iran, which he does not hesitate to call Corbin's "Aryanism"—first, because Iran had been colonized by the "Aryans," in the past and, second, because Corbin believed that he could detect spiritual analogies between Iran and Germany. See *Religion after Religion*, 133–5. Here we should not forget Corbin's strongly "Nordic" orientation, symbolically pointing to the North Pole. See, for example, Henry Corbin, *Die smaragdene Vision: Der Licht-Mensch im persischen Sufismus* (Munich: Eugen Diederichs, 1989), 22–31, 61–85. English translation *The Man of Light in Iranian Sufism*, N. Parsons (trans.) (Boston, MA: Shambhala, 1981). There Corbin also talks about the visions of the Sufi Ruzbihan,

for whom the pole was a keystone around which gathered the members of a pure *ecclesia spiritualis*, unknown and invisible to ordinary human beings. Corbin's teachings on this subject are also dealt with in Joscelyn Godwin's classic work on polar symbolism, *Arktos: The Polar Myth in Science, Symbolism, and Nazi Survival* (Grand Rapids, MI: Phanes Press, 1993), 167–71. Wasserstrom does not fail to point out that Corbin's form of Iran-centered spirituality had the effect of supporting the regime of Shah Reza Pahlavi. He also points out the links to the powerful oil interests of the major Eranos patron, Paul Mellon (pp. 152ff.), in Iran. Despite the revolution in Iran, a street named after Corbin could still be found in 2005 in Teheran, close to the French Embassy.

73. See Richard Stauffer, "Adieu à Henry Corbin," *Cahiers de l'Université Saint-Jean de Jérusalem* 5 (1979), 9.

74. The most detailed overview of the development of Corbin's thought that I know of is to be found in Shayegan, *Henry Corbin*. On the specific topic of Corbin's connection with Eranos, an essential work is Wasserstrom, *Religion after Religion*. Also noteworthy is the colloquium entitled *Henry Corbin et le comparatisme spirituel*, organized by his friends on 5–6 June 1999. The proceedings were published in the *Cahiers du Groupe d'Etudes Spirituelles Comparées* (Paris: Arché Editit, 2000). In 2003 there was a three-day colloquium at the Sorbonne in Paris on the occasion of Corbin's hundredth birthday, organized by Pierre Lory, Mohammed Ali Amir-Moezzi, and Christian Jambet, at which different aspects of Corbin's work were discussed in detail. In 2006 there followed a "Henry Corbin Day." The influence of this thinker can be ascertained from the website www.amiscorbin.com. In 2006, the Groupe Frémeaux Colombini produced a special treasure in the form of a set of three CDs (*La philosophie islamique: Henry Corbin*) offering a broad panorama of Corbin's recorded lectures, a project led by Christine Goémé, who had already, on the occasion of the master's hundredth birthday, broadcast ten hours of archive recordings of Corbin in the programme "Nuits de France: Culture."

75. Shihaboddin Yahya Sohravardi and Henry Corbin, *L'Archange empourpré: Quinze traités et récits mystiques*, H. Corbin (trans.) (Paris: Fayard, 1986), 12.

76. Corbin was against a soulless modernism but not against a spiritual modernity. Thus in the 1960s (together with Mircea Eliade and Paul Ricoeur) he was one of the patrons of the *Cahiers internationaux du symbolisme*, which were decidedly modern in their philosophical and literary standpoint—for example, numbers 9 and 10 (1965–66) were devoted exclusively to the literary and cinematographic creations of the *nouveau roman* school.

77. It may be relevant here to mention a perhaps surprising sentence from the diary of Gershom Scholem, quoted for the first time in a review by Friedrich Niewöhner. The only way to God, Scholem writes, "is in the silent revolutions of self-recognition: when the traceless comes suddenly towards us as a traceless presence." See Friedrich Niewöhner, Review of *Gottes Zorn kam zu kurz. Gershom Scholem als Schüler der deutschen Religionsgeschichte*, 54.

78. See especially his fundamental essay "Mundus imaginalis. L'Imaginaire et l'imaginal," in *Cahiers internationaux du symbolisme* 6 (1964), 3–26, as well as his work *L'Imagination créatrice dans le soufisme d'Ibn Arabi* (Paris: Flammarion, 1976), particularly 139ff. See also *La philosophie iranienne islamique aux XVII et XVIII siècles* (Paris: Buchet Chastel, 1981), 103ff. Works on the concept of the imaginal are many and include the following: the chapter entitled "Logique de l'Imaginal," in Christian Jambet, *La logique des Orientaux: Henry Corbin et les sciences des formes* (Paris: Editions du Seuil, 1983), 31–99; Gilbert Durand (Corbin's student and also an Eranos speaker), "The Imaginal," in *The Encyclopedia of Religions*, vol. 7, 109ff. (in the second edition of this work, edited by Lindsay Jones, this entry was removed and not replaced by any substitute); Stéphane Massonet, "Henry Corbin et la conquête de l'imaginal," *Antaios* 14 (1999), 98–110. See also the more critical chapter on "La doctrine islamique de l'imaginal," in Patrick Geay's book *Hermés trahi: Impostures philosophiques et néo-spiritualisme d'après l'oeuvre de René Guénon* (Paris: Dervy, 1996), 189–206. A short but clear overview is given by Joscelyn Godwin in his article "The Arts of the Imagination" (part 10 of the series "Annals of the Invisible College"), *Lapis* 10 (1999), 71–4. The connections with Jungian ideas are made clear in the essay by the Jungian psychologist J. Marvin Spiegelman, "Active Imagination in Ibn Arabi and C.G. Jung," in *Sufism, Islam and Jungian Psychology,* J. Marvin Spiegelman, Pir Vilayat Inayat Khan, and Tasnim Fernandez (eds) (Scottsdale, AZ: New Falcon Publications, 1991).

79. By eliminating the gods from the world, on account of the absolute transcendence of God, monotheism had also removed the "intermediate realm," in which the divine powers (angels, spirits, demons) operated. This had led increasingly to nature being regarded as purely mundane and God as purely transcendental. "The finite and the infinite stood opposite each other in stark and naked contrast ... totally spiritless matter and totally non-material spirit." Thus argues Heinrich Rombach in *Der kommende Gott*, 21ff.

80. Here I must refer to the highly interesting approach of Daniel C. Noel, who, in his work *The Soul of Shamanism: Western Fantasies, Imaginal Realities* (New York: Continuum, 1999), equates this imaginal world with the spiritual world of the shamans. See especially the chapters "Metaxy, the Middle: Entering Jung's House" and "Imaginal Realities—Post-Jungian Resources for Shamanic Imagining." These contain searching discussions of Jung, Eliade, Hillman, and also Castaneda.

81. On the subject of the soul in this connection, see the ideas of James Hillman, of whom we shall have more to say later.

82. The concept of "active imagination" is used for the corresponding Jungian technique. See J. Marvin Spiegelmann, "Potentials of Active Imagination" and "Potentials and Limitations of Active Imagination," in J. Marvin Spiegelmann, *The Nymphomaniac* (Phoenix, AZ: Falcon Press, 1985), 1–33.

83. For Corbin this imagination is a purely spiritual faculty, to the extent that it is even "independent from the physical organism and able to survive the death of the latter." See his essay "Mundus imaginalis," 13. On the central importance of the imagination in esotericism generally, see the chapter on "Exercices de l'Imagination," in Antoine Faivre, *Accès de l'ésotérisme occidental II* (Paris: Gallimard, 1996), 171–240, in which Corbin features in detail. See also Alain Godet, *"Nun was ist die Imagination anderst als ein Sonn im Menschen": Studien zu einem Zentralbegriff des magischen Denken* (Zurich: ADAG, 1982).

84. Thus James Hillman characterized Corbin's lectures as the expression of heart-thinking.

85. See Henry Corbin, "Prélude à la deuxième édition: Pour une charte de l'imaginal," in his *Corps spirituel et Terre céleste: De l'Iran mazdéen à l'Iran shi'ite* (Paris: Buchet-Chastel, 1979), 13.

86. Here it would be relevant to point out both the similarities and the differences between this concept and that of *intellektuelle Anschauung* (intellectual contemplation), a notion found in Schelling and Fichte and in German Romanticism generally, which likewise opposed mere discursive thinking. René Guénon also makes use of this concept (*intuition intellectuelle*). To go into this fully would vastly exceed the limits of this book, although it is a topic of central importance.

87. *Collected Writings of Plotinus*, Thomas Taylor (trans.) (Frome: Prometheus Trust, 1994), vol. III, 18.

88. According to the essay by Robert Avens, "The Subtle Realm: Corbin, Sufism and Swedenborg," in *Emmanuel Swedenborg: A Continuing Vision*, Robert Larssen (ed.) (New York: Swedenborg Foundation, 1988), 383, which provides a very good overview of the concept of the imaginal realm and compares it to Swedenborg's visions. Corbin himself had made this comparison and was very impressed by the considerable commonalities. Robert Avens, who is influenced by Jung, Hillman, and Heidegger, has written what is perhaps one of the deepest books on the complex of ideas grouped under the heading of the imaginal, namely *Imaginal Body: Para-Jungian Reflections on Soul, Imagination and Death* (Washington, DC: Unversity Press of America, 1982). Avens' overview reaches from Plato through alchemy to Blake, Schelling, and Corbin.

89. This is easier to imagine when one thinks of Eliade's concept of sacred space and especially the notion of the "center of the world," which is ubiquitous and at the same time located exactly where the sacred action is taking place.

90. This concept of the imaginal, about which I may have discursed at undue length, is not easily accessible to the modern mind. As the imaginal plays such a central role in archetypal psychology, which we shall deal with later and which is so important in the intellectual history of Eranos, I decided to risk being accused of an excessive fondness for detail. Further treatments of the subject—apart from Corbin's own major works—are to be found in two essays in the first issue of the journal *Temenos*, a periodical imbued with the "imaginal" spirit. The two articles in question are, by Corbin himself, "Towards a Chart of the Imaginal," *Temenos: A Review Devoted to the Arts of the Imagination* 1 (1981), 23–6, and Gilbert Durand, "Exploration of the Imaginal," *Temenos: A Review Devoted to the Arts of the Imagination* 1 (1981), 7–22.

91. Corbin, *Die smaragdene Vision*. Corbin is altogether very little known in the German-speaking world. Interestingly, however, a very sympathetic and well-informed article by Janos Darvas, "Brückenbauer zwischen Ost und West: Henry Corbin: Ein biographisches-philosophisches Porträt," appeared in the "Wochenschrift für Anthroposophie," *Das Goetheanum* 80(18) (2001), 317–23. In an email to me of 27 November 2006, Darvas remarked that there are even some direct references to Steiner in Corbin's writings. The English-speaking public is better served with regard to Corbin. Not only are there several valuable English translations of Corbin's work, but Tom Cheetham, in his book *The World Turned Inside Out: Henry Corbin and Islamic Mysticism* (Woodstock, CT: Spring Journal Books, 2003), has provided an excellent introduction to Corbin's thought.

92. Denis de Rougemont, "Hérétiques de toutes les religions ...," in *Henry Corbin*, Christian Jambet (ed.) (Paris: L'Herne, 1981), 298–303.

93. Wasserstrom, *Religion after Religion*, 222. Wasserstrom, however, gets the quotation wrong, because he writes "Heretics of all *lands*, unite" whereas Corbin, if he used the word "heretics" at all, spoke of "heretics of all *religions*."

94. See his essay "Henry Corbin, ministre de la pensée," *Travaux de la loge nationale de recherches Villard de Honnecourt* 3 (1981), 188.

95. Elémire Zolla, later also an Eranos speaker, who came to know Corbin well in Iran, attributes his "arduous, repetitive style of writing" to his earlier preoccupation with Heidegger. On the one hand Zolla describes Corbin as an "indispensable guide" through Islamic philosophy: on the other hand, he warns his readers against following Corbin "too blindly," as this would lead to grave errors. See Zolla and Fasoli, *Un destino itinerante*, 68.

96. See the interview with Annemarie Schimmel in *Gnostika* 10 (1999), 23.

97. *Ibid.*, 48.

98. Henry Corbin, "De l'Iran à Eranos," in *Henry Corbin*, Jambet (ed.), 262.

99. Ritsema, *L'Oeuvre d'Eranos*, 91.

100. *Ibid.*, letter dated 18 October 1953, 92.

101. Henry Corbin, "The Time of Eranos," in *Man and Time: Papers from the Eranos Yearbooks*, Joseph Campbell (ed.) (Princeton, NJ: Princeton University Press, 1957), xiii–xx.

102. Ritsema, *L'Oeuvre d'Eranos*, letter dated 16 January 1957, 92.

103. *Ibid.*, 93.

104. Scholem, *Briefe III*, 69.
105. Mircea Eliade wrote in his diary, *Journal III, 1970–1978* (Chicago, IL: University of Chicago Press, 1989), 323, under the date 7 October 1978, recording Corbin's death from cancer, "He died in peace, so sure was he that his guardian angel was waiting for him."
106. Scholem, *Briefe II*, 193.
107. Jambet (ed.), *Henry Corbin*, 323.
108. Jean Servier (ed.), *Dictionnaire critique de l'ésoterisme* (Paris: Presses Universitaires de France, 1998), 340ff. Servier was also an Eranos speaker.
109. On this theme, see Corbin's 1962 Eranos lecture, "De la philosophie prophétique en Islam schi'ite," *Eranos Jahrbuch* 31 (1962), 49–116.
110. Wasserstrom, *Religion after Religion*, 153ff.
111. *Ibid.*, 172.
112. Pierre Lory, "Note sur l'ouvrage *Religion after Religion*."
113. This accords with the statement of the Islamicist Jean-Michel Cros of the Centre National de la Recherche Scientifique, who writes(http://oumma.com/Presence-d-Henry-Corbin) that Corbin in his lifetime was even unknown to certain orientalists and that the Iranologists belittled his work. One of them had apparently even declared, "The Shiism of CORBIN? I doubt if anyone but he believed in it." In the same report Cros speaks of visiting a Shiite worthy in Iran, who told him that Mohammed Hosayn Tabâtabâ'ï had been Corbin's master, and that it was to him that Corbin owed much of his knowledge. Seyyed Hossein Nasr, however, in his already mentioned article in the *Temenos Academy Review*, maintains that one of Corbin's special traits of character was that he never sought an earthly master, although he had met many Sufi masters in Iran. His true master had always been a heavenly one.
114. Violet de Laszlo, "Eranos 1949," *Bulletin of the Analytical Psychology Club of New York* 12(1) (1950), 1–5.

12. The Early 1950s

1. In view of Fröbe's explicit interest in the Rosicrucians, one is tempted to think of the "game" (*ludibrium*, as they themselves called it) of the so-called Rosicrucians of the seventeen century. While the content is genuine, the wrapping is a "game."
2. Eliade, "Les Danseurs Passent, La Danse Reste," 60.
3. Eliade, *Journal*, 112.
4. This view was widely shared among the Eranos circle, so that José Antonio Antón Pacheco of the University of Seville, in his essay "Aproximaciones a Eranos," in the Argentinean journal *Epimeleia* 1(1–2) (1992), 91–9, argues that the majority of Eranos speakers belonged philosophically to the existentialist school of thought. Naturally what he means is a form of existence that can be seen as tending in the direction of transcendence. He argues his case mainly with reference to Mircea Eliade, Gershom Scholem, and Henry Corbin. In Corbin's case, he says, one can see how he had learnt his hermeneutic approach from Heidegger, but was to use it for "opening other doors" than Heidegger had done.
5. Eliade, *Journal III, 1970–1978*, xiii.
6. Reprinted in Mircea Eliade, *Europa, Asia, America ... Corespondență, volumul al II–lea* (Bucharest: Bucuresti Humanitas, 1999–2004), 71ff.
7. Quoted here from the authoritative biography of Eliade by Florin Țurcanu, *Mircea Eliade: Le Prisonnier de l'histoire* (Paris: Editions de la Découverte, 2003), 398. The not-always frictionless relationship between Eliade and Jung is discussed on pages 395–401.
8. See also Natale Spineto, *Mircea Eliade*, 167–226, as well as Spineto's detailed study *Psicologia e storia delle religioni nel pensiero di Mircea Eliade* (Ferrara: Università degli Studi di Ferrara, 1992). See also Shafique Keshavjee, *Mircea Eliade et la Coincidence des opposés ou l'existence en duel* (Berne: Peter Lang, 1993), 257–61.
9. Spineto, *Mircea Eliade*, 70 n.69.
10. See his long letter of 22 January 1955 to Jung in Eliade, *Europa, Asia, America ...*, 84–7.
11. Mircea Eliade, *La prova del labirinto: Intervista con C.-H. Roquet* (Milan: Jaca Book,1980), 148ff.
12. Oldmeadow, *Mediations*, 68ff.
13. In his book *The Forge and the Crucible* (Chicago, IL: University of Chicago Press, 1978), he calls her his "friend." The unfortunately not very informative correspondence between Eliade and Fröbe is gathered together in Mircea Handoca, *Mircea Eliade: Europa, Asia, America correspondență*, vol. II (Bucharest: Bucuresti Humanitas, 1993), 18–31. It was not only Olga Fröbe who was very taken with Eliade. Rudolf Ritsema and Adolf Portmann, who carried on the Eranos conferences after her death, saw him as "one of the greatest inspirers of Eranos," as Ritsema wrote to Eliade in a letter of 5 September 1970, a copy of which is in the Eranos archive in Moscia-Ascona. See the detailed review by Riccardo Bernardini of Spineto's book *Mircea Eliade: storico delle religioni* in *Annali di storia dell'esegesi* 23(2) (2006), 569–73 (the above-mentioned letter is quoted on 570). In this review Bernardini also reproduces further excerpts from the unpublished correspondence between Ritsema and Eliade.
14. A.E. Waite was one of the first historians of esotericism and at the same time leader of a mystical-magical order in succession to the Order of the Golden Dawn as well as head of a mystical-Christian-Kabbalistic order called the

Fellowship of the Rosy Cross. He appears to have been highly regarded by Fröbe, judging by a letter to her from Waite of 19 April 1936, which can only be interpreted as an answer to an enquiry from her. Waite writes that initiations are only possible through a long series of symbolic grades. These, however, would demand her continual presence and a temple, and such a temple existed only in London. I would assume that Waite was speaking here of his Rosicrucian group, in which female members were in the majority. On the subject of Waite, see the standard work by R.A. Gilbert, *A.E. Waite: Magician of Many Parts* (Wellingborough: Thorsons Publishers, 1987). A letter from Jung to Fröbe of 12 April 1935 contains the following remark: "The book by Waite on alchemy is in my possession, but not 'The Brotherhood of the Rosy Cross.' Perhaps you could bring it with you some time when you come to Zurich."

15. Fröbe also suggested that Eliade should record his dreams, which he in fact did over a period of a month in Ascona. See Eliade, *La prova del labirinto*, 63.

16. Eliade, *Journal I, 1945–1955*, 164, 165.

17. The unpublished passages from Eliade's diary are taken from the also unpublished translation by Mac Linscott Ricketts.

18. Eliade, *Journal I, 1945–1955*, 114 (25 August 1950 and 27 August 1951) and also the entry for 19 August 1960 in the unpublished part translated by Mac Linscott Ricketts.

19. Diary, unpublished section, 18 August 1962.

20. Besides the above-mentioned biographies of Eliade by Florin Țurcanu and Natale Spineto, there is also Richard Reschika's book *Mircea Eliade: zur Einführung* (Hamburg: Junius, 1997). Concise summaries of his life are also to be found in Constantin Tacou (ed.), *Mircea Eliade*, 11, 15 and in Joseph M. Kitagawa, "Mircea Eliade (First Edition, 1987)" and Bryan S. Rennie, "Mircea Eliade (Further Considerations, 2005)," in Lindsay Jones (ed.), *The Encyclopedia of Religion*, 2nd edn (Detroit, MI: Macmillan Reference USA, 2005), vol. IV, 2753–7, 2757–63. Eliade's own diary entries and his autobiography are of course much more detailed. The story of Eliade's connection with Eranos is related in McGuire, *Bollingen*, 150–52, and in the relevant chapters of the Eliade biographies by Natale Spineto (67–70) and Florin Țurcanu (393–403). Also worth mentioning in this connection are the special issues of *Religion* 38 (2008) and *Gazeta Culturală* 89 (March 2010). I would also like to mention an empathic and sympathetic but also highly informative and clear essay on Eliade by the above-mentioned Berlin author Wolfgang Saur, entitled "Mircea Eliade heute." This essay, like other works by Saur, appeared in a rather remote domain of the New Right, namely in the special issue of *Sezession* 16 (February 2007), 30–35. The issue as a whole is dedicated to Eliade.

21. The most comprehensive and detailed study on Eliade's preoccupation with alchemy is Guido Ravasi, "Ermeneutica dell'ermetismo in Mircea Eliade," in *Romania și Europa: Studii șiarticole selecționate coordonatede J.C. Drăgan. Revista Fundației Drăgan* 9 (May 1992), 119–258.

22. These became stronger during his sojourn in India. See the essay "Mircea Eliade," in Elémire Zolla, *Uscite dal Mondo* (Milan: Adelphi, 1992), 493ff. Here Zolla, who himself later became an Eranos speaker, emphasizes that one has to appreciate the importance of old Romanian folk traditions for Eliade as well as his relations with the traditionalists Ananda Coomaraswamy and René Guénon and with Henry Corbin, if one is to understand Eliade's profoundly sacred view of life. Constantin Noica, in his essay "Hiérophanie et sacralité" (in *Mircea Eliade*, Constantin Tacou [ed.], 108), even sees in Eliade a sort of Parsifal who has lost his way in the modern age and whose words can awaken to new life that which is dead and barren. Shafique Keshavjee, in his comprehensive dissertation *Mircea Eliade et la Coincidence des opposés*, 144, also asks himself whether one should address Eliade as a "modern Parsifal," since he poses the right questions that can lead to a (sacred) revitalization of the universe. Again, in the title of an essay by the scholar of religion Enrico Montanari Eliade is described as "a Parsifal who has lost his way." See the Italian political-cultural journal *Diorama letterario* 109 (1987), 18–23.

23. See especially Chapter B, "Nae Ionescu's Bedeutung für den Werdegang von Mircea Eliade," in Hannlore Müller, *Der frühe Mircea Eliade: Sein rumänischer Hintergrund und die Anfänge seiner universalistischen Religionsphilosophie. Anhang mit Quellentexten. Marburger Religionsgeschichtliche Beiträge* vol. III, Rainer Flasche (ed.) (Münster: LIT Verlag, 2004), 19–64.

24. Entitled *Contribuții la filosofia renașterii*, the work was re-published during the time of President Ceaușescu as a supplement to the *Revista de Istorie și literară* 1 (Colecția Capricorn, 1984). At the end of this small volume are some rare photographs of Eliade. Shafique Keshavjee calls Eliade himself a "Renaissance man," in the manifold sense of that term. See his *Mircea Eliade et la Coincidence des opposés*, 162.

25. Țurcanu, *Mircea Eliade*, 114ff.

26. Țurcanu characterizes the relationship between Ionescu and Eliade as an "alliance between two people who, within the context of the university, stood at the margin. Their great popularity with the students is of the kind enjoyed by subversive intellectuals and not by recognized authorities." Quoted from Florin Țurcanu, "Entre idéologie de la culture et politique: Mircea Eliade et l'étude des religions dans la Roumanie de l'entre-deux-guerres," in *The Study of Religion under the Impact of Fascism*, Horst Junginger (ed.) (Leiden: Brill, 2008), 322.

27. On Ionescu's strong influence on the Iron Guard, see Claudio Mutti, *Mircea Eliade und die Eiserne Garde: Rumänische Intellektuelle im Umfeld der Legion Erzengel Michael* (Preetz: Regin Verlag, 2009), in the chapter "Nae Ionescu: Sokrates bei den Legionären," 80–93.

28. Mihail Sebastian, *Seit zweitausend Jahren* (Paderborn: Igel Verlag, 1997), 310ff.

29. Dora Mezdrea, *Nae Ionescu: Leben, Werk, Wirkung: Mit Beiträgen von Mircea Eliade* (Vienna: Karolinger, 2008),

259–61, containing the complete essay by Eliade in translation. It originally appeared in a journal for Romanian exiles, *Prodromos* 10 (1979), 1–2. For a detailed analysis of the relationship between the two men, see Mihaela Gligor, *Mircea Eliade: Anii Tulburi: 1932–1938* (Bucharest: Limba Romana, 2007) especially the chapter "Mircea Eliade şi Nae Ionescu."

30. Nae Ionescu, *Roza Vînturilor, 1926–1933*, Mircea Eliade (ed.) (Bucharest: Editura Roza Vânturilor, 1990), 421–44.

31. Mezdrea, *Nae Ionescu*, 246.

32. Michael Sebastian, *Seit zweitausend Jahren*, 313. For the sake of completeness I would like to mention that the Romanian professor of philosophy Marta Petren believes, on the basis of such utterances, that Sebastian can be accused of extreme right-wing attitudes. In this connection, see the analysis by Ioanna Orleanu in the review of M. Sebastian, *Seit zweitausend Jahren*, *Neue Zürcher Zeitung* (18 February 2009), 18.

33. Comments by contemporary Romanian intellectuals, quoted by Leon Volovici, *Nationalist Ideology and Antisemitism: The Case of Romanian Intellectuals in the 1930s* (Oxford: Pergamon Press, 1991), 72. This book is important because it describes exactly the historical development of Romanian nationalism and anti-Semitism and examines the "identity myth" of a Romance people surrounded by Slavs. Leon Volovici himself is from Romania. Further background material on the political history of Romania at that time is provided by Giuseppe Vitale, *La svastica e l'arcangelo: Nazionalismo ed antisemitismo in Romania tra de due guerre mondiali* (Rimini: Il Cerchio, 2000).

34. See, for example, Emanuela Costantini, *Nae Ionescu, Mircea Eliade, Emil Cioran: Antiliberalismo nazionalista alla periferia d'Europa* (Perugia: Morlacchi, 2005), 47ff. The author is not exactly sympathetic in her treatment of these figures.

35. For example, Steven Wasserstrom attempts to show the great influence of Martin Heidegger on Eliade. See *Religion after Religion*, 137ff.

36. On this subject, see Armin Heinens' study *Die Legion "Erzengel Michael," in Rumänien: Soziale Bewegung und politische Organisation: Ein Beitrag zum Problem des internationalen Faschismus* (Munich: R. Oldenbourg, 1986).

37. Nevertheless, there are certain comments by Eliade dating from this period, which tell a different story, for example: "The Communist arsonists of churches are hooligans—and so are the Fascist persecutors of the Jews. Both of them trample down humanness and personal faith—which are the freedoms of every individual." Quoted from Mac Linscott Ricketts, *Mircea Eliade, The Romanian Roots, 1907–1945* (Boulder, CO: East European Monographs, 1988), vol. 2, 893. This work provides extremely valuable and basic documentary material, but is necessarily not always up to date in terms of research. Steven Wasserstrom also quotes a series of passages from Eliade's work, which indicate a strongly critical attitude to the Jewish religion. See *Religion after Religion*, 184ff. and 328ff.

38. Eliade certainly showed steadfastness in his political opinions, as it must have been difficult for him to associate himself publicly with publications of the New Right intelligentsia, such as *Nouvelle Ecole* and *La Destra*, when he joined their boards of patrons. The editor of *Nouvelle Ecole*, Alain de Benoist, well known as a founder of the New Right in France, met Eliade several times in Paris, as he confirmed in an interview with the Belgian journal *Antaios*. See "Penser le paganisme: entretien avec Alain de Benoist," *Antaios* 11 (1996), 18.

39. Here I cannot enter into the age-old question of whether someone should be seen as an "evil" terrorist or a "good" freedom fighter. The two positions are simply opposites.

40. Hence Eliade's intensive preoccupation with Romanian folk legends.

41. I personally doubt whether it is possible to possess such charisma without believing in the rightness and absolute truth of that which one upholds in public, even to the extent of ultimately being willing to stake one's own life for it. Consequently the charismatic individual sees himself as blameless, even when crimes are committed in the name of his belief. A constitutional state based on law must necessarily take the opposite view.

42. Considering what he had experienced, Nagy-Talavera showed a positively unbelievable understanding *vis-à-vis* the Iron Guard. See his book *The Green Shirts and Others: A History of Fascism in Hungary and Romania* (Stanford, CA: Stanford University Press, 1970; 2nd edn, Oxford: Centre for Romanian Studies [Iaşi], 2001). He writes as follows about the hostility of the Romanians towards foreigners in their country: "and incomparably more offensive to nationalists, both for their large number and their lack of will or ability to assimilate, were the Jews. All great and honest Romanians without exception were anti-Semites, as every great Hungarian of the nineteenth century was ready to accept the very different kind of Jew living in Hungary as Hungarian" (2nd edition, p. 346).

43. *Ibid.*, 344–45.

44. Mihail Sebastian, *"Voller Entsetzen aber nicht verzweifelt": Tagebücher 1939–1944* (Berlin: Claassen, 2005), 280.

45. On the subject of Codreanu's sympathizers and the role of his son Nicador Codreanu in Romania, see Brynhild Amann, "Codreanu's Erben. Die Legionärsbewegung im postrevolutionären Rumänien," published in the Austrian nationalist-conservative periodical *Neue Ordnung* 4 (2004), 23–6. See also www.nouadreapta.org.

46. In September 2005 it was possible to access the story at www.punctecardinale.ro_iun_2005_iun_2005_9.html, from which I printed out the text. Recently, however, I have not found it possible to access the site. However, the neo-legionary website www.punctecardinale.ro, with its periodicals archive, is still accessible.

47. Corneliu Zelea Codreanu, *Guardia di Ferro* (Padua: Edizione di Ar, 1972). The Romanian title is *Pentru legionari*. It is from this book that Leon Volovici takes most of Codreanu's anti-Semitic quotations.

48. Volovici, *Nationalist Ideology and Antisemitism*, 64.
49. Mihaela Gligor, "The Ideology of the Archangel Michael Legion and Mircea Eliade's Political Views in Interwar Romania," *International Journal of Humanistic Ideology* 1(1) (2008), 112ff.
50. Joachim von Kürenberg, a writer (not a historian) ostracized by the National Socialists, maintains in his book *Carol II und Madame Lupescu* (Bonn: Athenäum Verlag, 1952) (Madame Lupescu being the King's mistress, Jewish by birth but a convert to Catholicism) that under Carol II the Jewish community gained markedly in power, and that their share of the national income rose to 65 percent. This assertion seems to me improbable, but I am not in a position to judge its accuracy.
51. See Mircea Eliade, "Commentarii la un juramant," *Vremea* 476 (1937), quoted here from the Italian translation published in *Origini* 15 (2000), 22. The editors of this issue sympathize with Codreanu and have dedicated it entirely to him.
52. In *Buna Vestire* of 17 December 1937. The original text and the German translation are included in Hannelore Müller, *Der frühe Mircea Eliade* (Münster: LIT Verlag, 2004), A97–A103.
53. There are doubts about whether Eliade was really the author of the text or possibly had only lent his name to it. However, the views reflected in it are undoubtedly his. *Ibid.*, A97.
54. Nagy-Talavera, *The Green Shirts and Others*, 371.
55. Marta Petreu, "The 'Generation '27' between the Holocaust and the Gulag," *Euresis* (2007), 7.
56. Müller, *Der frühe Mircea Eliade*, xiii.
57. Wolfgang Saur, "Mythos und Moderne: Mircea Eliade im XX. Jahrhundert: Zu seinem 100. Geburtstag," *Neue Ordnung* 1 (2007), 38–44.
58. Volovici, *Nationalist Ideology and Antisemitism*, 191.
59. Costantini, *Nae Ionescu, Mircea Eliade, Emil Cioran, Antiliberalismo nazionalista alla periferia d'Europa*, 166ff.
60. Eliade, "Piloţii orbi" (Blind pilots), *Vremea* 10(505) (1937).
61. Müller, *Der frühe Eliade*.
62. For example, she has taken the trouble to include as full a bibliography as possible of Nae Ionescu and Mircea Eliade (194–8, 198–216).
63. One work containing all of the articles of Romanian-nationalistic tenor of the Iron Guard is to date only available in Romanian, namely Mircea Eliade, *Textele "legionare" şi despre "românism,"* Mircea Handoca (ed.) (Cluj-Napoca: Casa Cărţii de Ştiinţă, 2001). However, the American scholar of religion Mac Linscott Ricketts has provided an English-language review of this work in his book *Former Friends and Forgotten Facts* (Norcross: Criterion Publishing, 2003), 107–30.
64. Müller, *Der frühe Mircea Eliade*, A81, A82.
65. Hannelore Müller, "Români care nu pot fí Români" [Romanians who cannot be Romanian], *Cuvântul* 10(299) (1933), 1.
66. On his relationship to Eliade in terms of worldview, see Bryan Rennie, "An Encounter with Eliade," in Mihaela Gligor and Mac Linscott Ricketts, *Intâlniri cu, Encounters with Mircea Eliade* (Cluj-Napoca: Casa Cărţii de Ştiinţă, 2005), 199–202. This book is a vivid collection of reminiscences of Eliade by people who knew him.
67. Bryan Rennie, *Reconstituting Eliade: Making Sense of Religion* (Albany, NY: SUNY Press, 1996).
68. Bryan Rennie (ed.), *Mircea Eliade: A Critical Reader* (London: Equinox, 2006), 412–18.
69. "Meditation on the Burning of Cathedrals," *Vremea*, 7 February 1937.
70. Rennie, *Mircea Eliade*, 10ff.
71. In view of his clear support for the movement, I consider this question to be of a purely bureaucratic nature and of interest only to lawyers and historians who are strictly concerned with the pure facts.
72. Even earlier Eliade had experienced difficulties on account of past connections with the Iron Guard. He was refused a professorship at the Ecole Pratique des Hautes Etudes in Paris, and the Italian publisher Einaudi did not want to include Eliade's books in his catalog.
73. On this subject see also Roberto Scagno, "Alcuni punti fermi sull'impegno politicio di Mircea Eliade nella Romania interbellica: Un commento critico al Dossier 'Toladot' del 1972," in *Esploratori del pensiero umano: Georges Dumézil e Mircea Eliade*, Julien Ries and Natale Spineto (eds) (Milan: Jaca Book, 2000), 259–89.
74. Scholem, *Briefe III*, 30.
75. *Ibid.*, 316ff.
76. *Ibid.*, 63.
77. See especially her essay "Mircea Eliade: Romanian Fascism and the History of Religions in the United States," in *Tainted Greatness*, Nancy A. Harrowitz (ed.) (Philadelphia, PA: Temple University Press, 1994) 51–74, a book which documents the papers of a colloquium at Boston University.
78. Rennie, *Reconstructing Eliade*, 149–159. Rennie also goes on to criticize Leon Volovici's book as one-sided.
79. Alexandra Laignel-Lavastine, *Cioran, Eliade, Ionescu: L'Oubli du fascisme: Trois intellectuels romains dans la tourmente du siècle* (Paris: Presses Universitaires de France, 2002), 30, 31.
80. *Ibid.*, 218.
81. *Ibid.*, 282.
82. Ricketts, *Former Friends and Forgotten Facts*, 131–274.

83. *Ibid.*, 132. See also Mihaela Gligor's review of this book in *Euresis* (Spring–Summer 2007), 204. This comprehensive issue has the subtitle *Mircea Eliade, le défi de l'histoire* and brings together experts from Romania and elsewhere.

84. Ricketts, *Former Friends and Facts Forgotten*, 132.

85. Daniel Dubuisson, *Mythologies du XXe siècle (Dumézil, Lévi-Strauss, Eliade)* (Lille: Presses Universitaires de Lille, 1993), 221.

86. Daniel Dubuisson, *Impostures et pseudo-science: L'Oeuvre de Mircea Eliade* (Villeneuve d'Asq: Presses Universitaires du Septentrion, 2005), 149ff. This book is an enlargement, with four appendices, of the chapter on Eliade from Dubuisson's *Mythologies du XXe siècle*.

87. Rennie, *Reconstructing Eliade*, 165ff.

88. *Ibid.*, 171.

89. *Ibid.*, 167.

90. Even not counting the brutalities of the Communist regime, this is hardly surprising. How can a man for whom the spiritual element is so central believe in a purely materialistic system?

91. *Scrisori câtre Tudor Vianu II (1936–1949)* (Bucharest: Editura Minerva, 1994), 274. Quoted here from Istvàn Keul, "Politische Myopie, mystische Revolution, glückliche (Un)schuld? Mircea Eliade und die Legionäre Bewegung: Rezentere rumänische Perspektiven," in *The Study of Religion under the Impact of Fascism*, Horst Junginger (ed.) (Leiden: Brill, 2008), 415.

92. See Wasserstrom, *Religion after Religion*, 184ff and 328ff. It should be mentioned, however, that these criticisms most of the time also apply to the Christian religion.

93. Mutti, *Mircea Eliade und die Eiserne Garde*, 29.

94. Christian K. Wedemeyer and Wendy Doniger (eds), *Hermeneutics, Politics and the History of Religions: The Contested Legacies of Joachim Wach & Mircea Eliade* (Oxford: Oxford University Press, 2010).

95. See also Hans Thomas Hakl, "'Occultism is the Metaphysics of Dunces': The Conflation of Esotericism, Irrationalism, and Fascism in Postwar Germany," in Arthur Versluis, Lee Irwin, and Melinda Phillips (eds), *Esotericism, Religion, and Politics* (Minneapolis, MN: Association for the Study of Esotericism, 2012), 1–40.

96. Elaine Fisher, "Fascist Scholars, Fascist Scholarship: The Quest for Ur–Fascism and the Study of Religion," in *Hermeneutics, Politics and the History of Religions*, Christian K. Wedemeyer and Wendy Doniger (eds), 265.

97. By far the most detailed examination of the relationship between Eliade and Sebastian is the section "Mircea Eliade and Mihail Sebastian: Two Accounts of a Friendship," in Ricketts, *Former Friends and Forgotten Facts*, 7–28.

98. What hurt Sebastian most was the unbelievably cold rejection, even contempt, that was shown towards him by his admired role model Nae Ionescu. Sebastian (whose real name was Iosif Hechter) had requested Ionescu to write a forward to his novel *For Two Thousand Years*. Ionescu did so, but in such a thoughtless, contemptuous way that is only possible for someone possessed of limitless arrogance and a belief in the absolute rightness of his own convictions. Ionescu was steeped in Orthodox Christianity, and Sebastian was a Jew. The following are some quotations from this foreword: "The Jew suffers because he lives in tshe midst of peoples whom he cannot cease antagonizing, even if he wanted to … The Jew suffers because he is a Jew … Iosif Hechter, you are sick. You are sick in your substance because you can do nothing else than suffer, and there is a profound reason for your suffering. The Messiah has already come and you have not recognized him … Iosif Hechter, do you not feel how coldness and darkness surround you?" This text, which is not anti-Semitic in the biological sense but evinces a cruel and theologically based anti-Judaism, is included in the appendix to Sebastian, *Seit zweitausend Jahren*, 265–79.

99. Sebastian, "*Voller Entsetzen, aber nicht verzweifelt*," 451ff.

100. *Ibid.*, 172ff.

101. Andrei Oişteanu, "Mircea Eliade between Political Journalism and Scholarly Work," *Archaeus* 8 (2004), 339ff.

102. Douglas Allen, "Encounters with Mircea Eliade," in *Professor Mircea Eliade: Reminiscences*, Mihaela Gligor and Mac Linscott Ricketts (eds) (Kolkata: Codex, 2008), 29. This book of personal recollections of his colleagues has a distinctly intimate tone and shows Eliade in all his strengths and weaknesses. The volume is also distinguished by its appendices, which contain copies of rare correspondence and documentary material.

103. Russell R. McCutcheon, *Manufacturing Religion: The Discourse on sui generis Religion and the Politics of Nostalgia* (New York: Oxford University Press, 1997).

104. Ivan Strenski, *Four Theories of Myth in Twentieth-Century History: Cassirer, Eliade, Lévi-Strauss and Malinowski* (Iowa City, IA: University of Iowa Press, 1989).

105. Ellwood, *The Politics of Myth*, 79–126.

106. Norman Manea, "Felix Culpa: Erinnerung und Schweigen: Mysterien bei Mircea Eliade", *Lettre International* (Spring 1995), 30–36; Edward Kanterian, "Wie glücklich war Eliades Schuld?" *Lettre International* (Autumn 1995*)*, 88–9.

107. In the issue of *Origini* entirely devoted to Eliade, edited by Claudio Mutti and published as a supplement to *Orion* 150 (March 1997).

108. Alessandro Mariotti, *Mircea Eliade: Vita e pensiero di un Maestro d'iniziazioni* (Rome: Castelvecchi, 2007).

109. Mac Linscott Ricketts informed me in an email of 15 February 2009 that Eliade emphatically regretted these excesses.

110. Especially bearing in mind the observation of the journalist and historian Jacques Julliard in his foreword to Florin Ţurcanu's biography of Eliade: "In the case of a historical figure, our age is inclined to judge a Fascist adventure infinitely more harshly than a Communist one."

111. Ioan Petru Culianu, "The Correspondence between Mircea Eliade and Ioan Petru Culianu," Sorana Corneanu (trans.), *Archaeus* 8 (2004), fasc. 1–4, 345ff. On this question, see also Wolfgang Kreutzer, "'Ich verstand ihn viel besser als ich ihn nicht verstand': Ioan Petru Culianu als Biograph Mircea Eliades," in *Spiegel und Maske: Konstruktionen biographischer Wahrheit*, Bernhard Fetz and Hannes Schweiger (eds) (Vienna: Paul Zsolnay Verlag, 2006), 191–206. Eliade's aversion to talking about his past connection with the Iron Guard becomes all too clear from Kreutzer's essay.

112. Eugen Curtin, "Raffaele Pettazzoni et Mircea Eliade: Historiens des religions généralistes devant les fascismes (1933–1945)," in *The Study of Religion under the Impact of Fascism*, Horst Junginger (ed.), 355.

113. See "Tout commence en mystique et finit en politique" [Everything begins in mysticism and ends in politics] (Charles Péguy, *Notre jeunesse* [Paris: Cahier de la Quinzaine, 1910], 115). I would like to thank Giovanni Casadio for this important reference.

114. It was then translated into Portuguese and Spanish.

115. A few years ago an Italian translation of the book appeared: Mircea Eliade, *Breve storia della Romania e dei rumeni* (Rome: Settimo Sigillo, 1997).

116. Mircea Eliade, *Salazar şi revoluţia în Portugalia* (Bucharest: Gorjan, 1942).

117. *Ibid.*, 7. Quoted here from Costantini, *Nae Ionescu, Mircea Eliade, Emil Cioran*, 171.

118. *Ibid.*, 171.

119. Subsequently an English edition has appeared including valuable additional material—*The Portugal Journal*, Mac Linscott Ricketts (ed. and trans.) (Albany, NY: SUNY Press, 2010)—as well as an Italian version—*Diario Portoghese*, Cristina Fanteschi (trans.), Roberto Scagno (ed.) (Milan: Jaca Book, 2009). I have worked with the Spanish text.

120. Mircea Eliade, *Diario Portugués (1941–1945)* (Barcelona: Editorial Kairòs, 2000).

121. *Ibid.*, 15.

122. *Ibid.*, 24.

123. *Ibid.*, 29.

124. *Ibid.*

125. *Ibid.*, 44.

126. Giovanni Casadio, "La vita sessuale di Mircea Eliade," *Rinascita*, 8 September 2010. www.rinascita.eu/index.php?action=news&id=3740.

127. Rudolf Ritsema, the successor to Olga Fröbe, even saw Eliade's literary output as having a closer connection to the "spirit of Eranos" than his scholarly work.

128. Eliade in fact described himself as a morphologist (having in mind J.W. von Goethe, whose works he had known since his school days) rather than a phenomenologist of the same kind as van der Leeuw. For a more detailed discussion of this question, see Spineto, *Mircea Eliade storico delle religioni*, 570ff., as well as Spineto's essay "Le comparatisme de Mircea Eliade," in François Boespflug and Françoise Dunand (eds), *Le comparatisme en histoire des religions* (Paris: Les éditions du cerf, 1997), 104ff. For a work in English on the subject, see Strenski, *Four Theories of Myth in Twentieth-Century History*, 109ff., which gives a highly informative and succinct account of the genesis of phenomenology.

129. See Philip Vanhaelemeersch, "Eliade, 'History' and 'Historicism'," in *The International Eliade*, Bryan Rennie (ed.) (Albany, NY: SUNY Press, 2007), 151–66. See also, in German, Douglas Allen, "Ist Eliade antihistorisch?," in *Die Mitte der Welt: Aufsätze zu Mircea Eliade*, Hans Peter Duerr (ed.) (Frankfurt: Suhrkamp, 1984), 106ff., and Christian Wachtman, *Der Religionsbegriff bei Mircea Eliade* (Frankfurt: Peter Lang, 1996).

130. Sorin Alexandrescu, "Per una discussione filosofica dell'opera di Mircea Eliade," in Luciano Arcella, Paolo Pisi, and Roberto Scagno, *Confronto con Mircea Eliade* (Milan: Jaca Book, 1998), 401ff.

131. A detailed and highly interesting critique of Eliade and his views in this regard is provided by McCutcheon in *Manufacturing Religion: The Discourse on Sui Generis Religion and the Politics of Nostalgia*, which is informed by Ivan Strenski's approach to the analysis of myths, Noam Chomsky's political theories of power maintenance, and Michel Foucault's philosophical models. The standpoint of Eliade and his school of thought, which strives for the independence of the history of religion within the universities, can be read about in Mircea Eliade and Joseph M. Kitagawa (eds), *The History of Religions: Essays in Methodology* (Chicago, IL: University of Chicago Press, 1959). The contributors to this volume, with only two exceptions, were all Eranos speakers.

132. Mircea Eliade, "Krisis und Erneuerung der Religionswissenschaft," *Antaios* 9 (1968), 5; reprinted in Mircea Eliade, *Das Okkulte und die moderne Welt: Zeitströmungen in der Sicht der Religionsgeschichte; Der Magische Flug: Aufsatzsammlung* (Sinzheim: AAGW, 2000), 197–215; published in English as "Crisis and Renewal in History of Religions," *History of Religions* 5(1) (1965), 1–17. On Eliade's collaboration in the journal *Antaios* and on the history of the journal, which I consider to be particularly significant in relation to the somewhat hidden side of post-war German intellectual history, see Hans Thomas Hakl, "'Den Antaios kenne ich und missbillige ich. Was er pflegt ist nicht Religio sondern Magie!' Kurze Geschichte der Zeitschrift *Antaios*," *ARIES* 9(2) (2009), 195–232, and the summarized version in Italian, "L'effeto, pur non esteso, è stato profondo come quello d'una sonda. Breve

storia della rivista 'Antaios', curata da Mircea Eliade e Ernst Jünger (1959–1971)," in *Cenacoli, circoli e gruppi letterari, artistici, spirituali*, Franceso Zambon (ed.) (Milan: Medusa, 2007), 247–70.

133. On Eliade's hermeneutic approach see the essay by Julien Riès, "Histoire des religions, phénomenologies, herméneutique: Un regard sur l'oeuvre de Mircea Eliade" and by David Rasmussen, "Herméneutique structurale et philosophie," both in Tacou (ed.), *Mircea Eliade*, 81–7, 97–104.

134. Mircea Eliade saw the development of this "new humanism" as a major task of the scholar of religion, whose studies give him a much deeper insight into what it means to be human than other scholars can achieve. See Mircea Eliade, *The Quest: History and Meaning in Religion* (Chicago, IL: University of Chicago Press, 1971), 3. At the University of Chicago he took part in the formation of a Committee on Social Thought, on which he reported as follows in a letter to Jung of 23 February 1960: "I would like to add that the Committee on Social Thought is today the only university institution in the world that strives to develop a new humanism which, although a prolongation of the past, is not a mere repetition of it." This letter is to be found in the Jung archive at the Swiss Federal Institute of Technology, Zurich. The clergyman David Cave even sees this "new humanism" as the real cornerstone of Eliade's work. Cave claims that only in the light of this key principle can one really grasp Eliade's work in all its scholarly, ethical, literary, and political dimensions and strivings. See David Cave, *Mircea Eliade's Vision for a New Humanism* (New York: Oxford University Press, 1993). In a letter of 31 January 1957 (preserved in the library of the University of Chicago) Olga Fröbe declares herself to be positively "possessed" by the idea of this new humanism as a creative force that can impede the destruction of the world by the machine.

135. See especially his book *The Sacred and the Profane*, which argues forcefully that, in contrast to the situation in modernity, the sacred for archaic man represents reality *par excellence*. See also the essay by Antoine Faivre, "L'ambiguità della nozione di sacro in Mircea Eliade," in *Confronto con Mircea Eliade*, Luciano Arcella, Paola Pisi, and Roberto Scagno (eds) (Milan: Jaca Book, 1998), 363–74. Faivre incidentally considers the influence of modern esotericism on Eliade to be insignificant.

136. Thus Jürgen Mohn puts it in his book *Mythostheorien: Eine religionswissenschaftliche Untersuchung zu Mythos und Interkulturalität* (Munich: Wilhelm Fink, 1998), 121, in which he explores Eliade in detail.

137. In this connection, see also the sympathetic essay by Giovanni Sorge, "Idolatria della storia e apertura al cosmo: Un omaggio a Mircea Eliade," in *Psicologia della religione e teoria dell'attaccamento*, Germano Rossi and Mario Aletti (eds) (Rome: Aracne, 2009), 249–55. It is interesting to note that the connection of man and cosmos is discussed here in a scientific text on psychology.

138. On this theme, see Chapter 4 of Eliade's *The Myth of the Eternal Return: Cosmos and History* (Princeton, NJ: Princeton University Press, 1971). Eliade himself considered this to be his "most important" book, and in the foreword to the American edition he said it was the one that should be read first.

139. Spineto, "Mircea Eliade and Traditionalism," and H.T. Hansen [Hans Thomas Hakl], "Mircea Eliade, Julius Evola und die Integrale," in *Julius Evola, Über das Initiatische: Aufsatzsammlung* (Sinzheim: Archiv für Altes Gedankengut und Eissen, 1998), 9–50. These works also contain further references to relevant literature. Enrico Montanari's book *La fatica del cuore: Saggio sull' ascesi esicasta* (Milan: Jaca Book, 2003) contains an appendix that deals searchingly with the relationship of Eliade to René Guénon. However, he was not able to find any real Eliade–Guénon "axis."

140. Marcello de Martino, *Mircea Eliade esoterico: Ioan Petru Culianu e i "non detti"* (Rome: Settimo Sigillo, 2008). See also Radu Dragan's review of the book in *Politica Hermetica* 24 (2010), 134–45.

141. See especially Antoine Faivre, "Modern Western Esoteric Currents in the Work of Mircea Eliade: The Extents and Limits of Their Presence," in *Hermeneutics, Politics and the History of Religions*, Christian K. Wedemeyer and Wendy Doniger (eds), 147–57.

142. Mac Linscott Ricketts, "Eliade's Religious Beliefs," *Archaeus* 14 (2010), 27–40.

143. See the detailed study "Raffaele Pettazzoni" by Dario Sabbatucci in *Numen* 10(1) (1963), 1–41.

144. The key book about Pettazzoni, his views and his School for the History of Religion in Rome is Giuseppe Mihelcic, *Una religione di libertà: Raffaele Pettazzoni e la Scuola Romana di Storia delle Religioni* (Rome: Città Nuova, 2003).

145. Which at that time was called the IASHR (International Association for the Study of the History of Religion). The words "the Study of" were removed in 1955 (for this piece of information I thank Giovanni Casadio).

146. See the essay by Geo Widengren, "La méthode comparative: Entre philologie et phénoménologie," in *Problems and Methods of the History of Religions*, U. Bianchi, C.J. Bleeker, and A. Bausani (eds) (Leiden: Brill, 1972), 5–14, based on the conference held in honour of Pettazzoni on the tenth anniversary of his death. See also Pettazzoni's' article "Aperçu Introductif," in *Numen* 1(1) (1954), 1–7. Giovanni Filoramo, the historian of religion from Turin, already mentioned here, has re-issued several of Pettazzoni's books in the 1990s.

147. Culianu, *Mircea Eliade*, 146.

148. Mircea Eliade and Raffaele Pettazzoni, *L'histoire des religions a-t-elle un sens? Correspondance 1926–1959*, Natale Spineto (ed.) (Paris: Les éditions du cerf, 1994), 113. Spineto's introduction deals in particular detail with the methodological problems of historicism and phenomenology and the way in which Pettazzoni, Eliade, and van de Leeuw dealt with them.

149. Re-issued by Giovanni Casadio in an expanded edition: Raffaele Pettazzoni, *I misteri* (Mesagne: Giordano, 1997).

150. Aldo A. Mola, *Storia della Massoneria italiana dalle origini ai nostri giorni* (Milan: Bompiani, 1992), 806ff. The appendices contain facsimiles of various masonic documents which, like almost everything of historical significance in connection with Pettazzoni, came from Mario Gandini. The latter is the author of a still unfinished biography of Pettazzoni, the most extensive ever written about a scholar of religion, so far amounting to over two thousand pages and modestly entitled *Materiali per una biografia*. It is appearing in installments in the journal *Strada maestra*.

151. The Gran Consiglio del Fascismo (Fascist grand council) at the time of its founding consisted predominantly of Freemasons. And the four leaders of the March on Rome, the so-called *quadrumviri*, who had the highest position on the council after Mussolini, were all Freemasons. Only Mussolini himself, who had three times been refused admission to the fraternity (naturally before his time as "Duce"), was an opponent (out of disenchantment?). See especially Fabio Venzi, *Massoneria e fascismo: Dall'intesa cordiale alla distruzione delle Loggie: come nasce una "guerra di religione"* (Rome: Castelvecchi, 2008). Fabio Venzi is grand master of the Gran Loggia Regolare d'Italia. Equally interesting is Gianni Vannoni, *Massoneria, fascismo e chiesa cattolica* (Rome/Bari: Laterza, 1979).

152. The most detailed account of this matter can be found in the essay by Michael Stausberg, "Raffaele Pettazzoni and the History of Religions in Fascist Italy (1928–1938)," in *The Study of Religion under the Impact of Fascism*, Horst Junginger (ed.), 365–95. This study also is based on material collected by Mario Gandini.

153. Only two professors dared to do so. One of them, who even protested publicly, was the famous idealistic philosopher Benedetto Croce, who, however, possessed a considerable private fortune.

154. The signatories of the manifesto can be seen at www.internetsv.info/Manifesto.html.

155. For pointing this out, I am again grateful to Giovanni Casadio.

156. Mario Gandini, "Raffaele Pettazzoni negli anni 1949–1950: Materiali per una biografia," *Strada maestra*, 60 (2006), 178.

157. Deafness apparently plagued other Eranos speakers, too, such as Henry Corbin and C.G. Jung. When Corbin came for the first time and was introduced to the assembled company, Olga Fröbe placed him next to C.G. Jung. The latter, not wanting to spend the evening speaking French, made the excuse that he was deaf and wanted his wife to sit in between as "translator." When Corbin heard this he said that he was equally deaf, whereupon Jung let out one of his famous loud laughs and thereafter conversed splendidly with Corbin. There ensued a long friendship between the two men, even though Corbin professed himself to be a metaphysician and not a psychologist, whereas in Jung's case it was the other way round. In a letter to Corbin of 4 April 1953 (C.G. Jung, *Briefe II*, 332) Jung spoke of the "extremely rare, even unique experience of being completely understood" because Corbin had written positively about him in an article. And Corbin, writing to Jung from Ascona on 14 August 1953, said: "That is a great meeting that has taken place between us."

158. Gandini, "Raffaele Pettazzoni," 179.

159. This film was for a time available in the Internet through RTSI (Radio Televisione Svizzera italiana). However, at the time of writing (6 December 2008) access is blocked. Parts of the film can be seen on the DVD *Eranos Reborn*, produced in 2007 by the Eranos Foundation in Moscia-Ascona.

160. See "Eranos, der Geist am Wasser," *Flugblätter für Freunde aus der Werkstatt von Alfons Rosenberg* 80 (1977), 3.

161. On the subject of Jung and synchronicity see the symposium *La synchronicité, l'âme et la science*, H. Reeves *et al.* (eds) (Paris: Albin Michel, 1995). Jung saw the highest expression of synchronicity as being the *I Ching*. See the essay "C.G. Jungs Entdeckung der 'Synchronizität'," in *Erfahrungen mit dem I Ching*, Ulf Diederichs (ed.) (Cologne: Diederichs, 1987), 71. Gilles Quispel relates in his essay "Gnosis and Psychology" (p. 26) how Jung, after the lecture, called out to him in German with a radiant expression: "Es geht um die Erfahrung der Fülle des Seins" (It is about the experience of the fullness of Being). In the same essay Quispel also relates an example of synchronicity in connection with Eranos. The biologist Adolf Portmann wanted to end one of his lectures with a reference to the insect called a praying mantis on account of its unusual posture. At that very moment an actual praying mantis flew in through the open window and circled around Portmann's head in a "numinous and ominous" manner. It then landed close to the speaker's reading lamp so that its shadow, resembling a giant human figure in the act of prayer, was thrown on to the wall behind Portmann. It should also be noted that praying mantises are very rare in the Tessin region and Portmann had until then never seen one. Quispel also relates how deeply moved the psychologist Erich Neumann was by Jung's lecture on synchronicity. Suddenly God and the world were not mere projections, but Jung showed how they revealed meaningful correspondences and connections in the cosmos, which made sense and appeared to convey a message.

162. Marie-Louise von Franz maintains that Jung's doctrine of the archetypes and his discovery of the collective unconscious emanated from the Eranos circle to achieve wider dissemination and recognition. At the same time she acknowledges that certain contradictions and misinterpretations also had their source in Eranos. See her *C.G. Jung*, 156.

163. See Jaffé, "C.G. Jung und die Eranostagungen," 2ff.

164. The German text says "*das* wirkliche Eranos," instead of "*der* wirkliche Eranos," which would have been the correct gender.

165. Michel Cazenave, *Jung*, 139.

166. Jung stayed at the Haus Semiramis at Monte Verità. It was only when the walk to Moscia became too strenuous for him that he was invited to stay in the small flat above the lecture room, an honor that was reserved for very special guests. See Chapter 24, "Eranos," in Brome, *Jung*, 212–16. Barbara Hannah, however, says that the reason why Jung could no longer stay at the hotel was because it was closed during the war, i.e. from 1939. It was only from this point in time, she says, that Jung regularly attended the discussions at the Round Table. See Barbara Hannah, *Jung*, 217.

167. However, in a letter to Fröbe of 21 August 1944, he wrote, "I also think it would be good if next year you were to reduce the black robes a bit. They are not a good influence on each other, and it would not be beneficial to Eranos if it were to take on a one-sided confessional colouring."

168. See Jung, *Briefe I*, 472.

169. In this connection, see J. Marvin Spiegelmann (ed.), *Catholicism and Jungian Psychology* (Phoenix, AZ: Falcon Press, 1988) and the informative review of this book by John J. Costello in the London Jungian journal *Harvest* 35 (1989–90), 234ff. Costello points out the important role played by Jung's colleague Jolande Jacobi, who converted to Catholicism.

170. Anthony, *The Valkyries*, 72.

171. Cazenave, *Jung*, 72.

172. E. Michael Jones, writing from a fundamentalist Catholic standpoint in his book *Libido Dominandi: Sexual Liberation and Political Control* (South Bend, IN: St. Augustine's Press, 2005), 136, goes so far as to maintain that Jung also exploited his power over women to financial ends. As an example he cites the case of Edith Rockefeller McCormick, whom Jung had allegedly turned into a sufferer from agoraphobia who never left her hotel room in Zurich. This had apparently led to her divorce from her husband and to her death in poverty. Previously, according to Jones, she had given Jung two million dollars for his Psychological Club. This, incidentally, caused bitter feelings on the part of Sigmund Freud, whose Psychoanalytic Association suffered from a chronic shortage of funds.

173. Brome, *Jung*, 212.

174. A brief mention should be made *en passant* to an event that is mentioned repeatedly in the accounts of various people, namely the drunken nocturnal feast, the "night of the maenads," with Jung in the center. Reportedly things became so loud that all the neighbors complained, which did not stop the revelry from continuing. However, in all the years, this was the only example of such a "homage to Dionysus" to take place at Eranos.

175. Hermann Hesse, by the way, is not known to have taken part in Eranos. However, Hesse's last wife, Ninon, took part at least twice in Eranos meetings. See Hermann Hesse and Karl Kerényi, *Briefwechsel aus der Nähe* (Munich: Langen-Müller, 1972), 22, 148. In the Deutsches Literaturarchiv in Marbach there are letters from Olga Fröbe to Hermann and Ninon Hesse. It should not be forgotten that Hesse lived a very retiring life, cultivated solitude and had a tendency to depression. Hesse was, however, very interested in the *I Ching*. Its philosophy underlies his novel *Das Glasperlenspiel* [The glass bead game].

176. In *C.G. Jung*, 247.

177. Fröbe wrote in her letter, "Jung, who is always only interested in himself."

178. Bollingen Series XXXVII (Princeton, NJ: Princeton University Press, 1988), x. Gooodenough was among those who received a Bollingen stipend.

179. Morton Smith, "In Memoriam," in Jacob Neusner, *Religions in Antiquity. Essays in Memory of Erwin Ramsdell Goodenough* (Leiden: Brill, 1970), 2. This volume also contains the essay by Samuel Sandmel "An Appreciation." Sandmel had worked for twenty years with Goodenough and therefore also had much of a personal nature to say.

180. McGuire, *Bollingen*, 174ff.

181. *Ibid.*, 158.

182. McGuire, *Bollingen*, 144.

183. See the report of the meeting by Grace H. Childs in the *Bulletin of the Analytical Psychology Club of New York* 14(8) (1952). She also mentions that the lecture room was always full to bursting and that the members of the audience were all aware of the great significance of Eranos.

184. It appeared in the issue of 9 October 1952. An English translation of the interview is included in McGuire and Hull (eds), *C.G. Jung Speaking*, 225ff.

185. Karl Löwith, *Meaning in History: The Theological Implications of the Philosophy of History* (Chicago, IL: University of Chicago Press, 1949).

186. In this connection see also his essay "Vom Sinn der Geschichte," in *Der Sinn der Geschichte: Sieben Essays*, Leonhard Reinisch (ed.) (Munich: C.H. Beck, 1961).

187. From 1937 Read was literary advisor to the publisher George Routledge and in 1938 entered into a partnership with him. See Hayman, *A Life of Jung*, 378.

188. See Michael Fordham, *The Making of an Analyst: A Memoir* (London: Free Associations, 1993), 116. I wish to thank Sonu Shamdasani for this reference.

189. On the subject of Philip Sherrard, see Matthias Korger, "Philip Sherrard: Kosmos als Theophanie," *Abendland* 6 (2008), 30–41.

190. Philip Sherrard, *The Sacred in Life and Art* (Ipswich: Golgonooza Press, 1990), 42–53.

191. Saunders, in *Wer die Zeche zahlt ...*, 135, sees the Institute of Contemporary Arts as having been strongly sponsored by the Central Intelligence Agency. He also maintains that Read greatly profited from the generosity of a foundation connected with the Institute. Saunders furthermore mentions both Read and Mircea Eliade (p. 201) as members of a CIA front organization, whose main aim (perhaps not known to all members) was to combat Communism in Europe. Allen Dulles, whom we have already encountered in connection with C.G. Jung, is named by Saunders as the "string-puller" behind the multifarious cultural front organizations for a "free" (i.e. anti-Communist and pro-American) Europe (pp. 124ff.). Saunders complains that members of the OSS, the predecessor to the CIA, were already in the habit of moving through Europe like potentates, hardly heeding the laws in their determination to implement their political aims—a role for which they were predestined, as the author ironically adds, since their leading figures sprang from America's most powerful institutions and families, such as J.P. Morgan, Vanderbildt, Du Pont, Weil, or Mellon (p. 44).

192. For example, in the memorial publication *25 Jahre Eranos* (25 years of Eranos), he wrote, "Nowhere in our distracted world has the human spirit found such a perfect haven."

193. See Herbert Read, "Suzuki: Zen and Art," in the D.T. Suzuki memorial volume of the journal *The Eastern Buddhist* 2(1) (1967), 27ff.

194. See Anthony Storr, *Feet of Clay: A Study of Gurus* (New York: Free Press, 1997), 23.

195. Victor Zuckerkandl was a conductor and music critic who worked in the United States from 1940 and taught at St. John's College, Annapolis. His Eranos lectures are collected in the volume by Victor Zuckerkandl, *Vom musikalischen Denken* (Zurich: Rhein Verlag, 1964). In 1960 the violinist Sándor Végh was also a speaker. The 1960 meeting was a very musical one, which Fröbe described as "the finest meeting we have ever had" in her letter to C.G. Jung of 29 October 1960.

196. McGuire, *Bollingen*, 158.

197. After the war Cary Baynes had prompted the Mellons to try to buy this hillside property, but the attempt never came to fruition. See the letter from Fröbe to Baynes of 3 March 1954.

198. Joseph Campbell, *The Hero's Journey* (New York: Harper and Row, 1990), 172.

199. See Ernst Benz, "In Memoriam," in *A Zen Life: D.T. Suzuki Remembered*, Masao Abe (ed.) (New York: Weatherhill, 1986), 131. It has been suggested, however, that there was a more mundane reason for the delay of Suzuki's departure, namely that he wanted to wait for a guarantee from the Bollingen Foundation that they would provide the funds for him to return in 1954. This was duly approved by the foundation.

200. This information comes from two essays by D.T. Suzuki himself: "Early Memories" and "An Autobiographical Account," in Abe (ed.), *A Zen Life*, 3–12 and 13–26. The anecdotes relating to Eranos are taken from McGuire, *Bollingen*, 156ff.

201. Sōen, who was very well informed about Western culture and about Christianity, was particularly interested in the difficulties that the Americans experienced with the Buddhist doctrine of the non-existence of the soul and of the self. "The arrogance of the flesh," he wrote, was based on the (wrong) belief in the "ultimate reality of the ego-soul." Quoted here from Richard Hughes Seager, *The World's Parliament of Religions. The East/West Encounter, Chicago, 1893* (Bloomington, IN: Indiana University Press, 1995), 159. Sōen maintained that, on the contrary, the "I" exists only in relation to another "I" and not on its own.

202. On the subject of the lectures held there, see John Henry Burrows (ed.), *The World's Parliament of Religions: The Columbian Exhibition of 1893* (Chicago, IL: Parliament Publishing Company, 1893). An excellent overview of the cultural consequences of this East–West encounter is given by Seager in *The World's Parliament of Religions*. Seager sees this event as the decisive impulse behind the emergence of religious pluralism in America.

203. I should add that it subsequently also influenced the spread of Indian spirituality in general. This was in large part thanks to the appearance at the conference of Swami Vivekananda, a follower of Ramakrishna, and to his great talent as an organizer. See Conferenze IsMEO, *Nel centenario dell'intervento di Swami Vivekananda al Parlamento Mondiale delle Religioni (Chicago 1893)* (Rome: Istituto Italiano per l'Africa e l'Oriente, 1997).

204. See Maso Abe, "The Influence of D.T. Suzuki in the West," in *A Zen Life*, Maso Abe (ed.), 112ff.

205. Roibert H. Sharf, "The Zen of Japanese Nationalism," in *Curators of the Buddha: The Study of Buddhism under Colonialism*, Donald S. Lopez, Jr. (ed.), 161–96 (Chicago, IL: University of Chicago Press, 1995).

206. See especially *The Rhetoric of Immediacy: A Cultural Critique of Chan/Zen Buddhism* (Princeton, NJ: Princeton University Press, 1991) and *Chan Insights and Oversights: An Epistemological Critique of the Chan Tradition* (Princeton, NJ: Princeton University Press, 1993).

207. See his article "Il mito del maestro buddhista," in *Atrium* 7(4) (2005), 84–100.

208. To be fair, it must be stressed that he himself never claimed to be anything more.

209. In his essay "The Zen of Japanese Nationalism," 116.

210. Jørn Borup, "Zen and the Art of Inventing Orientalism: Religious Studies and Genealogical Networks," www.terebess.hu/english/borup.html, 18ff.

211. Oldmeadow, *Journeys East: 20th Century Western Encounters with Eastern Religious Traditions*, 170.

212. Adele S. Alego, "Beatrice Lane Suzuki and Theosophy in Japan," *Theosophical History* 9(3) (2005), 3–16.

213. Sharf, "The Zen of Japanese Nationalism," 143ff.

214. See Brian Victoria, *Zen at War* (Lanham, MD: Rowman & Littlefield, 1998). Brian Victoria is himself a Zen priest, Buddhist scholar, and activist in the human rights movement.

215. Vicentini, in his essay "Il mito del maestro buddhista," 93, argues that *bushido* is essentially a Confucian and therefore Chinese concept.

216. Daisetz T. Suzuki, *Zen and Japanese Culture* (Princeton, NJ: Princeton University Press, 1970), 61ff. It is worth remembering that Japanese martial arts in general demand freeing oneself from the ego as one of the basic requirements. Freedom from the ego, however, also implies freedom from human and moral norms.

217. Victoria also mentions the way in which Japanese culture with its ethos of Zen Buddhism influenced National Socialism. This he traces back to Karl Haushofer, legendary geopolitical expert and former military attaché in Japan (*Zen at War*, 163).

218. 16 December 1960.

219. Oldmeadow, *Journeys East*,163ff.

220. See the chapter "D.T. Suzuki and Western Zen in the Inter-War Years," in Oldmeadow, *Journeys East*, 168–73.

221. Sharf, "The Zen of Japanese Nationalism," 144.

222. Quoted from the memorial volume *25 Jahre Eranos*.

223. Gustavo Benavides, "Giuseppe Tucci, or Buddhology in the Age of Fascism," in Lopez, *Curators of the Buddha*, 161.

224. Mircea Eliade, *Diario d'India* (Turin: Boringhieri, 1995), 62ff.

225. These data were taken from the following detailed reports: Raniero Gnoli, *Ricordo di Giuseppe Tucci* (Rome: Istituto Italiano per il Medio ed Estremo Oriente, 1985); the entry by Gherardo Gnoli in Eliade (ed.), *Encyclopedia of Religions*, vol. 15; Beniamo Melasecchi, *Giuseppe Tucci: Nel centenario della nascita* (Rome: IsMEO, 1995); and Comune di Macerata, *Giuseppe Tucci: Un maceratese nelle terre sacre del'Oriente* (Macerata: Comune di Macerata, 2000). Some essential parts of this section were also taken from Hans Thomas Hakl, "Giuseppe Tucci entre Etudies orientales, ésotérisme et fascisme (1894–1984)," *Politica Hermetica* 18 (2004), 231–50.

226. Comune di Macerata, *Giuseppe Tucci*, 60.

227. At that time he was not the only person who found Mussolini impressive. Others who did so included T.S. Eliot, Ezra Pound, George Bernard Shaw, W.B. Yeats, and even Winston Churchill and (somewhat later) Mahatma Gandhi. See Krishna Dutta and Andrew Robinson, *Rabindranath Tagore: The Myriad-Minded Man* (New York: St. Martin's Press, 1995), 266ff.

228. In 1976, on the hundreth anniversary of Gandhi's birth, Tucci gave a long and laudatory speech in honour of the Indian statesman. See Giuseppe Tucci, *Nel centenario della nascita di Gandhi* (Rome: ISAO, 1998).

229. Geminello Alvi, *Uomini del Novocento* (Milan: Adelphi, 1995), 162–6.

230. Eliade, *Autobiography II*, 144.

231. John Snelling, *The Sacred Mountain: Travellers and Pilgrims at Mount Kailas in Western Tibet, and the Great Universal Symbol of the Sacred Mountain* (London: East West Publications, 1983), 184ff.

232. Victoria, *Zen at War*.

233. See also Giuseppe Tucci, *A Lhasa e oltre* (Rome: La Libreria dello Stato, 1950), 53ff., in which he deals in depth with Tibetan notions of life after death.

234. See, for example, *Pre-Diṅāga Buddhist Texts on Logic from Chinese Sources* (Baroda: Oriental Institute, 1929) and *The Nyāyamukha of Diṅāga, being the Oldest Buddhist Text on Logic after Chinese and Tibetan Materials* (Heidelberg: Harrassowitz, 1930).

235. See Giuseppe Tucci, "Linee di una storia del materialismo indiano," *Rendiconti della Accademia dei Lincei*, proceedings, 5(17) (1923), 242–310 and series 6(2) (1929), 667–713.

236. See the reference in Luciano Petech, "Il contributo di Giuseppe Tucci alla storia dei paesi himalayani," in *Giuseppe Tucci: Nel centenario della nascita, Roma, 7–8 giugno 1994*, Beniamino Melasecchi (ed.) (Rome: IsMEO, 1995), 25.

237. Gnoli, *Ricordo di Giuseppe Tucci*, 10.

238. Gustavo Benavides, "Giuseppe Tucci, or Buddhology in the Age of Fascism," 186.

239. He writes in *L'Oriente nella cultura contemporanea* (Rome: IsMEO, 1934), for example, of the "luminous visions of the Orient, so intoxicating for those who have a problem with reality because they cannot cope with it" (p. 9).

240. Tucci, *A Lhasa ed oltre*, 125, 130.

241. Benavides, "Giuseppe Tucci or Buddhology in the Age of Fascism," 162.

242. *Ibid.*, 181.

243. Gnoli, *Ricordo di Giuseppe Tucci*, 39.

244. Tucci, *A Lhasa e oltre*, 11. This text, however, was written after the war. On the question of orientalism and fascism generally, see the section "Orientalism, Racial Theory and the Allure of Fascism," in Oldmeadow, *Journeys East*, 367–90.

245. Hans-Adolf Jacobsen, *Karl Haushofer: Leben und Werk*, Schriften des Bundesarchivs 24/I (Boppard am Rhein: Harald Boldt, 1979), vol. I, 451, where it is also mentioned that Hitler did not have much regard for Haushofer or his geopolitical theories.

246. *Ibid.*, 398.

247. Jacobsen, *Karl Haushofer*, 448.

248. Mussolini was also influenced by similar ideas. Witness his speech of 22 December 1933 before a gathering of students from Asia on the Capitol, in which he declared that Kipling's famous words "East is East and West is West and never the twain shall meet" had been disproved by history. The passage can be found in *Il Fascismo (Documenti)* (Rome: Edizioni Wage, 1976), 90, 91.

249. See Giovanni Sorge (ed.), *Lettere tra Ernst Bernhard e Carl Gustav Jung (1934-1959)* (Milan: Biblioteca di Vivarium, 2001), 75ff.

250. See the website www.romacivica.net/novitch/LeggiRaz/promulgatori.htm. I thank Giovanni Casadio for drawing my attention to this site, which contains a list of all the signatories. For the exact wording of the law, *Dichiarazione sulla Razza* of 6.10.1938, see cronologia.leonardo.it/mondo23i.htm.

251. See http://it.wikipedia.org/wiki/Leggi_razziali_fasciste#1l_.22Manifesto_della_Razza.22.

252. *Ibid.* Entry for 31 January 2008.

253. Gnoli, "L'India nell'opera di Giuseppe Tucci," in Tucci*, Nel centenario della nascita,* 22ff.

254. Foreword by Giuseppe Tucci to the revised edition of his book *Tibet ignoto,* 15.

255. *Ibid.,* 15.

256. Corrado Pensa, "L'occidente e le religioni orientali nella prospettiva di Giuseppe Tucci," *Pāramitā* 4 (1985), 9–25.

257. See, for example, Giuseppe Tucci, *Teoria e pratica del mandala* (Rome: Casa Editrice Astrolabio – Ubaldini, 1949), 9, where he speaks of how Jung's insights will, in his opinion, "leave behind lasting traces in our way of thinking."

258. In a letter of 2 November 1950 Evola wrote to Scaligero: "By the way, I also thank you for approaching Tucci again." See "Il coraggio è un'abitudine," *Graal* 69–70 (June 2000), 27ff. See also Angelo Iacovella, "Uno sguardo a Oriente: Evola, Tucci e l'IsMEO," in Julius Evola, *Oriente e Occidente* (Rome: Edizioni Mediterranee, 2001), 11–22.

259. These were all reprinted in Evola, *Oriente e Occidente.*

260. See her letter of 21 November 1938 to Cary Baynes.

261. Gnoli, *Ricordo di Giuseppe Tucci,* 38ff.

262. See his postcard to Olga Fröbe of 7 January 1934. Friedrich Heiler on the other hand was very critical towards Benz, as I was told on 29 July 2001 by the Sufi expert and later Eranos speaker Annemarie Schimmel, who knew Heiler well. Heiler, she said, had simply not found Benz credible.

263. The details given here about his life and work are taken from F.W. Kantzenbach, "Ernst Benz : wie ich ihn sehe und verstehe: Eine Laudatio zum 17.11.1977," *Zeitschrift für Religions- und Geistesgeschichte* 29 (1977), 289–304.

264. Deissmann was the theologian who in 1904 had founded the earlier Eranos circle, which has already been mentioned and of which Max Weber was also a member.

265. Kurt Meier, *Die Theologischen Fakultäten im Dritten Reich* (Berlin: Walter de Gruyter, 1996), 179.

266. *Ibid.,* 349.

267. *Ibid.,* 424ff.

268. See the bibliography, comprising more than three hundred entries covering the years 1928 to 1966, compiled by Erich Gedbach and Ernst L. Lashlee, in *Glaube, Geist, Geschichte: Festschrift für Ernst Benz zum 60. Geburtstage am 17. November 1967,* Gerhard Müller and Winfried Zeller (eds) (Leiden: Brill, 1967), 545–72.

269. Quoted from the chapter "Ernst Benz: Auf den Spuren der Theosophie: Eine Erinnerung," in Gerhard Wehr, *Theo-Sophia: Christlich-abendländische Theosophie—Eine vergessene Unterströmung* (Zug: Die Graue Edition, 2007), 273.

270. On Benz's friendship with Ziegler, see the correspondence between the two men in Leopold Ziegler, *Briefe 1901–1958* (Munich: Kösel, 1963), 269–86.

271. See the words of praise, spoken by Antoine Faivre in "Synthèse de la Session," colloquium of 15–17 June 1979. His speech is reprinted in *Cahier* 6 (1980), 225.

272. See Ernst Benz, "Grundformen der buddhistischen Meditation." In *Terra Nova,* vol. 2: *Das große Gespräch der Religionen,* 47–88 (Munich: Ernst Reinhardt, 1964).

273. Letter from Philipp Wolff, editor of the journal *Antaios,* to Ernst Benz of 22 June 1969.

274. Jean Daniélou, "L'Oraison, problème politique," quoted here from the Belgian journal *Antaios* 15 (1999), 3.

275. Daniélou's opposition to pure intellectuality was so strong that he even occupied himself intensively with the study of the "father of integral traditionalism," René Guénon. He particularly welcomed Guénon's effort to include symbolism as a valid means of insight. See his chapter "Grandeur et faiblesse de René Guénon," in his *Essai sur le mystère de l'histoire* (Paris: Seuil, 1953), 120–26, quoted here from Marie-France James, *Esotérisme et Christianisme autour de René Guénon* (Paris: Nouvelles Editions Latines, 1981), 267, 372.

276. Emmanuelle de Boysson, *Le cardinal et l'hindouiste: Le mystère des frères Daniélou* (Paris: Albin Michel, 1999), 242ff.

277. Alain Daniélou, "Shivaisme et Homosexualité," *Gaie France* 6 (1987), 11–13.

278. Alain Daniélou, *Storia dell'India* (Rome: Ubaldini, [1981] 1992) 292–4. Danielou had met Gandhi several times and accused him—as do many of the religious and intellectual elite of India—of having concluded the worst possible peace terms with the British. Ultimately these led to the partition of the country into India and Pakistan, resulting in a weakening of the subcontinent and the massacre of untold numbers of people. Because of Gandhi's charismatic influence on large masses of people, Daniélou compares him with the gurus of modern times. He argues that Gandhi, having come from the merchant class, always made his decisions in the interests of the bourgeois merchants and the great landowners. Hence also the great support that he received from the richest families of India (the Tatas and the Birlas). In a wide-ranging interview in the French magazine *Paris Match,* 17 May 1985,

9, Daniélou even accuses Gandhi of hypocrisy, as his apparent contacts with the Untouchables were really faked. Interestingly, the Indian BSP, the political party of the Dalits (the Untouchables), itself said that Gandhi had done nothing for them. See the statements of Dalit Mayawati, chief minister of the Indian state of Uttar Pradesh, reported in the "intellectual" Austrian newspaper *Der Standard* of 12 August 1997.

279. See his autobiography *The Way to the Labyrinth: Memories of East and West* (New York: New Directions, 1987). For an account of the two brothers, Jean and Alain, see the work by their great-niece Emmanuelle de Boysson, *Le Cardinal et l'hindouiste: Le mystère des frères Daniélou*.

280. Daniélou, *The Way to the Labyrinth*, 248ff.

281. "Zwanzig Jahre Eranostagungen in Moscia-Ascona (Schweiz)," *Psyche* 6 (1952–53), 155–60.

282. Plato died in the year 347 BC, but the Platonic Academy was only dissolved in AD 529 by Emperor Justinian.

283. For an account of his life, see the chapter "Curriculum Vitae," in Walter Robert Corti, *Heimkehr ins Eigentliche, Gesammelte Schriften I*, 267–76 (Schaffhausen: Novalis Verlag, 1979). Eranos is not mentioned in this curriculum.

284. Afterword by Walter Robert Corti, *Heimkehr ins Eigentliche*, 303. In the meantime a "Philosophisches Archiv Corti" (UPHAC) housing the papers has emerged in the Centre for Ethics at the University of Zurich.

285. Walter Robert Corti, *The Philosophy of George Herbert Mead* (Winterthur: Archiv für genetische Philosophie, 1973), 7.

286. In Walter Robert Corti, *Der Mensch im Werden Gottes: Gesammelte Schriften* (Schaffhausen: Novalis Verlag, 1998), vol. 2, 201–41.

287. Foreword to Bruno Goetz, *Das Reich ohne Raum* (Zurich: Origo, 1962), 7–15.

288. Literally, a "thrower of the baby out with the bathwater."

289. No English equivalent. The closest translation would probably be "Lady Soul."

290. At this conference he also became acquainted with Marianne Pallat, whom I have already mentioned. On this matter see Paul Tillich, *Briefwechsel und Streitschriften, Theologische, philosophische und politische Stellungnahmen und Gespräche*, Supplementary Volume VI (Frankfurt: Evangelisches Verlagswerk, 1983), 255.

291. On Heinz Westman, who emigrated to America and became one of the most respected psychotherapists there, see his book *Springs of Creativity: The Bible and the Creative Process of the Psyche* (Brooklyn, NY: Chiron Publications, 1986).

292. Rudolf Ritsema (ed.), *Gestaltung der Erlösungsidee im Judentum und Protestantismus: Eranos-Vorträge von Heinz Westman und Paul Tillich*, Supplementary volume to *Eranos Jahrbuch* 4 (1936) (Ascona: Eranos-Stiftung, 1986).

293. Paul Tillich, *Ein Lebensbild in Dokumenten: Briefe, Tagebuch-Auszüge, Berichte* (Stuttgart: Evangelisches Verlagswerk, 1980), 267. My thanks go to Gerhard Wehr for this information.

294. He was also called *the theologian of our time* because he repeatedly took up topical themes relating to politics, society, and the Church.

295. Tillich's biographical details can most easily be found in the monograph *Paul Tillich* by Gerhard Wehr (Reinbek: Rohwohlt, 1979). See also Renate Albrecht and Werner Schüßler (eds), *Paul Tillich: Sein Werk* (Düsseldorf: Patmos, 1986). On his theology, philosophy, and influence, see Hermann Fischer (ed.), *Paul Tillich: Studien zu einer Theologie der Moderne* (Frankfurt: Athenäum, 1989) and Christoph Rhein, *Paul Tillich: Philosoph und Theologe: Eine Einführung in sein Denken* (Stuttgart: Evangelisches Verlagswerk, 1957).

296. Bernd Wikus, *Deutsche Sozialphilosophie in der ersten Hälfte des 20. Jahrhunderts* (Darmstadt: Wissenschaftliche Buchgesellschaft, 1996), 235.

297. There are, however, very critical voices who accuse Tillich of having had strongly anti-democratic leanings and who label him as belonging to the "Conservative Revolution." At any rate, he did proclaim the wish to overthrow the Weimar system with its capitalistic economy and parliamentary democracy. See Christian Tilitzki, *Die deutsche Universitätsphilosophie in der Weimarer Republik und im Dritten Reich*, Part 1 (Berlin: Akademie Verlag, 2002), 390ff.

298. The manuscripts of 109 of these speeches have been preserved and are printed under the title Paul Tillich, *An meine deutschen Freunde. Politische Reden* in the third of the supplementary volumes (*Ergänzungs- und Nachlassbände*) to the *Gesammelte Werke* (Stuttgart: Evangelisches Verlagswerk, 1973). On the other hand, by the irony of fate, one of his pupils was the strongly *völkisch* Herbert Grabert. Tillich, however, vehemently rejected his views. See Tillich, *Briefwechsel und Streitschriften*, 305.

299. Paul Tillich, "Die Bedeutung der Religionsgeschichte für den systematischen Theologen," in Karl-Josef Kuschel, *Lust an der Erkenntnis: Die Theologie des 20. Jahrhunderts* (Munich: Piper, 1986), 443.

300. Quoted here from Wehr, *Paul Tillich*, 70.

301. Tillich, "Die Bedeutung der Religionsgeschichte," 438.

302. Paul Tillich, *Das Dämonische: Ein Beitrag zur Sinndeutung der Geschichte* (Tübingen: J.C.B. Mohr, 1926). Tillich is even recorded as having said in a conversation that "if one wished to burn all of his writings one should at least spare those on the demonic." See Walter Braune and Paul Tillich, *Ein Gedenkvortrag* (Berlin: Colloquium Verlag, 1966), 10.

303. Tillich, *Das Dämonische*, 15.

304. This analysis prompted Julius Evola to translate long extracts from this work into Italian and publish them in his journal *La Torre*. They appeared under the rubric Paul Tillich, "Conoscenza del Demonico," in *La Torre* ([1977] 1930), 104–6.

305. See Green, *The Mountain of Truth*, 191ff.

306. He wrote about his life in his book *Yet Being Someone Other: An Autobiographical Odyssey* (New York: William Morrow, 1983). Also very informative and riveting are his conversations with Jean-Marc Pottiez, published as Laurens van der Post, *A Walk with a White Bushman* (New York: William Morrow, 1986). See also the *Festschrift* edited by Robert Hinshaw, *The Rock Rabbit and the Rainbow: Laurens van der Post among Friends* (Einsiedeln: Daimon Verlag, 1998).

307. Laurens van der Post, *Jung and the Story of Our Time*. It should be mentioned, however, that this book has been criticized for being excessively sympathetic to Jung.

308. J.D.F. Jones, *Teller of Many Tales: The Lives of Laurens van der Post* (New York: Carroll & Graf, 2002).

309. This is confirmed in the review of the book by Christoph Egger, "Vorstösse ins Innere: Zum 100. Geburtstag des großen Erzählers Laurens van der Post," *Neue Züricher Zeitung*, 9–10 December 2006.

310. Chang Chung-yuan, *Creativity and Taoism: A Study of Chinese Philosophy, Art and Poetry* (New York: Julian Press, 1963).

311. In a letter of 27 December 1965, Philipp Wolff-Windegg, the real editor of *Antaios*, wrote as follows to Dr. Rudolf Haase, a student of Kayser: "When Kayser spoke at Eranos I also happened to be there, and he did not make a very satisfactory impression."

312. The story of his life is recounted in *Hans Kayser: Ein Leben für die Harmonik der Welt* (Basel: Schwabe, 1968), written by one of his few pupils and successors, namely the Viennese musicologist Rudolf Haase. Many documents are to be found in Walter Ammann (ed.), *Hans Kayser zum 100. Geburtstag: Biographische Fragmente* (Bern: Kreis der Freunde um Hans Kayser, 1991) and Hans Kayser, *Bisher unveröffentliche Dokumente aus dem Nachlass* (Bern: Kreis der Freunde um Hans Kayser, 2000).

313. A thorough overview is provided by the *Festschrift* published on the occasion of Kayser's sixtieth birthday: Julius Schwabe (ed.), *Die Harmonik als schöpferische Synthese und weitere Aufsätze über Harmonik* (Bern: Kreis der Freunde um Hans Kayser, 1985).

314. Hans Kayser, *Harmonia Plantarum* (Basel: Schwabe, 1943).

315. Hans Kayser, *Paestum: Die Nomoi der drei altgriechischen Tempel zu Paestum* (Heidelberg: Lambert Schneider, 1958).

316. Hans Kayser, *Orphikon: Eine harmonische Symbolik* (Basel: Schwabe & Co., 1973).

317. See Joscelyn Godwin (ed.), *Cosmic Music: Musical Keys to the Interpretation of Reality* (Rochester, VT: Inner Traditions, 1989), 24ff. This brings together essays by Marius Schneider, Rudolf Haase, and Erhard Lauer, each of whom in his own way is following in the footsteps of Hans Kayser.

318. For an overview, see Rudolf Haase, *Kaysers Harmonik in der Literatur der Jahre 1950–1964* (Düsseldorf: Verlag der Gesellschaft zur Förderung der systematischen Musikwissenschaft, 1967).

319. Walter Robert Corti, "Die platonische Akademie im Wandel der Geschichte und als Aufgabe unserer Zeit," *Eranos Jahrbuch* 26 (1957), 387–413.

320. Walter Robert Corti, *Plan der Akademie* (St. Gallen: Tschoudy, 1956).

321. In 1933 the poet Robert Faesi, who has been mentioned earlier and who was a friend of Olga Fröbe, had planned a "Swiss Academy" based on similar principles in order to oppose National Socialism. However, nothing came of the plan, since "money and spirit are secretly at war with each other, and the purer the spirit, the more seldom it meets with understanding, since its significance is hard to prove and takes a long time to show results." Robert Faesi, *Erlebnisse, Ergebnisse*, 270ff. Faesi and Corti knew each other well.

322. Based on the English translation at http://files.embedit.in/embeditin/files/PrFEsUFvx4/1/swf_page_125.swf.

323. Jung from the outset regarded Corti's plan as merely a "well intentioned chimera," adding that he was "convinced that nothing can grow unless a living seed has been planted in the earth." Letter of 4 November 1959 to Fröbe.

324. Writing to Jung on 10 September 1960, she said, "That was the biggest mistake of my life. But it was only in the winter that I realized it and decided to withdraw."

325. Notarial document 2633 of 23 May 1961 in the estate of Adolf Portmann.

326. Already in 1958 she had undergone a cure in a specialized clinic in Berchtesgaden, which was paid for by Paul Mellon.

327. For an account of the life of Rudolf Ritsema and his wife, Catherine, see the detailed account given in Catherine Ritsema, *L'Oeuvre d'Eranos*, 10–135.

328. The death announcement issued by the Eranos circle and signed by Adolf Portmann stated, "According to the wish of the deceased, the conference planned for August will take place as normal."

329. In Ascona the word was that this brought a gain of about a million Swiss francs to the foundation.

330. Walter Thys informed me that Bettina Fröbe was still living in the mid-1990s in an old people's home in Holland, but that it was no longer possible to communicate with her.

331. Hildegard Nagel, Obituary for Olga Fröbe, *Bulletin of the Analytical Psychology Club of New York* 24(6) (1962), 5–7.

332. However, McGuire (*Bollingen*, 27ff.) writes that this was not true. On the contrary, Fröbe was always burdened with administrative tasks, ranging from hotel reservations to recruitment of speakers and posting of invitations.

333. Someone who read the present work at an early stage drew my attention to the fact that if you employ a

"Kabbalistic" technique and turn around the letters of the word ERANOS you get SONARE (to intone or sound), implying a "spirit" that makes itself heard through the PER-SONA of Fröbe.

334. *Eranos Jahrbuch* 56 (1987), xxii.

335. See publisher's afterword to *Eranos Jahrbuch* 20 (1951).

336. The importance of this genius for Fröbe and for Eranos can be seen from the fact that an illustration of the stele appeared on the front cover of the brochure commemorating the twenty-fifth anniversary of Eranos.

337. It is pictured in Jaffé, *C.G. Jung, Bild und Wort*, 181, and on the cover.

338. The Eranos emblem, consisting of a spiral surrounded by the inscription *EADEM MUTATA RESURGO* (I always return as the same [soul], though in altered form) could also be seen as coming close to being a reference to the "spirit" of Eranos. The emblem is found on a pillar in the transept of Basel Minster, where it forms the epitaph of the seventeenth-century Basel mathematician Jakob Bernoulli. Joseph Campbell must have sensed the effect of the emblem, because he writes in his foreword to the first volume of the American edition of selected Eranos papers, entitled *Spirit and Nature* (p. xii): "'Ever the same, yet changing ever,' these ubiquitously visible invisibles have been the chief objects of interest at the Eranos round table." For, however strongly the individual speakers represented their own positions, the common ethos was stronger and evidently brought irreconcilable positions together.

339. Jung, *Briefe I*, 463.

340. See the essay by Rudolf Ritsema and Shantena Sabbadini, "Images of the Unknown: The Eranos *I Ching* Project 1989–1997," *Eranos Jahrbuch* 66 (1997), 17.

341. Adolf Portmann, writing to John Barrett on 13 March 1965, when the transitional problems had been overcome, confirmed the central importance of this support.

342. Gerald Holton and Duane H.D. Roller, *Foundations of Modern Physical Science* (Reading: Addison-Wesley, 1958).

343. See especially his book (albeit published much later) *Science and Anti-Science* (Cambridge, MA: Harvard University Press, 1993).

344. See William McGuire and R.F.C. Hull (eds.), *C.G. Jung speaking*, p205ff.

345. *The Image of an Oracle: A Report on Research into the Mediumship of Eileen J. Garrett* (New York: Garrett Publications, 1964).

346. See Ira Progoff, *The Practice of Process Meditation: The Intensive Journal Way to Spiritual Experience* (New York: Dialogue House Library, 1980).

347. See the back cover of Gilbert Durand's book *L'imaginaire: Essai sur les sciences et la philosophie de l'image* (Paris: Haitier, 1994).

348. Not only the lectures from this colloquium but also the discussions are summarized in Gilbert Durand, *Science et Conscience: Les deux lectures de l'univers* (Paris: Stock, 1980). The meeting dealt with the psycho-physical unity of nature, which cannot be adequately researched on the basis of the traditional, purely causal scientific paradigm.

349. In "Henry Corbin, l'Envers d'un Siècle de Ténèbres," *Les Humains Associés* 8 (www.humains-associes.org/No8/HA.No8.Durand.html), Durand speaks unhesitatingly of the "hypocritical darkness of the twentieth century."

350. Gilbert Durand, *Science de L'Homme et tradition: "Le nouvel esprit anthropologique"* (Paris: Albin Michel, 1996).

351. See Gilbert Durand, *Les structures anthopologiques de l'Imaginaire: Introduction à l'archetypologie générale* (Grenoble: Presses Universitaires de France, 1960).

352. Gilbert Durand, *Beaux-arts et archetypes: La religion de l'art* (Paris: Presses Universitaires Françaises, 1989).

353. Cf. the two-volume collection of essays edited by Hans Peter Duerr, *Der Wissenschaftler und das Irrationale* (Frankfurt: Syndikatsverlag, 1981).

354. See the introduction to his book *L'âme tigrée: Les pluriels de psyché* (Paris: Denoël Gonthier, 1980).

355. René Alleau and Gwen le Scouézec, *Encyclopédie de la Divination* (Paris: Editions Veyrier, 1973).

356. Gilbert Durand, *Structures: Eranos I* (Paris: La Table Ronde, 2003). The foreword is written by the sociologist Michel Maffesoli, a pupil of Durand who today is surely better known than his teacher. Maffesoli says that Eranos conjured up a *mundus imaginalis*, consisting of a "symbolic space" and a time that became space. The photographs of Eranos that the author published here for the first time are also worthy of note.

357. *Ibid.*, 17.

358. Gilbert Durand, *Figures mythiques et visages de l'oeuvre: De la mythocritique à la mythanalyse* (Paris: Dunod, 1992), 322ff.

359. Included in Gilbert Durand, *Champs de l'imaginaire*, texts selected by Danièle Chauvin (Grenoble: ELLUG, Université Stendhal, 1966), 243–56.

360. First published in Zurich by Artemis, 1975, and then as a paperback by DTV, Munich, 1978.

361. A private edition of these verses was published in 1960 under the title *Nicht- imaginäre Portraits*. Miriam Lichtheim, who was a close friend of Sambursky, quotes a poem by him about Gershom Scholem's sweet tooth in her autobiography *Telling it Briefly: A Memoir of My life* (Freiburg: Universitätsverlag, 1999).

13. Polytheism Versus Monotheism

1. In her essay "Archetypal Theory after Jung," *Spring* 23 (1975), 199–220, Naomi R. Goldenberg describes how this development was carried on by the "second" and "third generations" after Jung. Unfortunately, owing to the date when her essay was published, her account does not go beyond 1974.

2. The analytical psychologist James Kirsch wrote in this connection to Gershom Scholem on 2 November 1980: "Concerning Eranos I have heard that Hillman reigns there supreme. I have little hope for the future of the Eranos conferences." To this Scholem replied on 24 November 1980, "I have received very different information about Hillman's position at Eranos than you, but I cannot judge the real situation. I do not know what will become of the conferences … I would have thought that the people there would be well advised to stop after the 50th meeting and set up a different programme." See Scholem, *Briefe III*, 444 and 223.

3. Sexual misconduct with a female student was apparently the reason for Hillman's resignation as director of studies at the Jung Institute in Zurich. The matter even came before a court. Within the institute it was the cause of intense discussion, although everyone knew that Jung had probably also committed "sexual misconduct," most notably with Toni Wolff. Freud had already warned of the dangers that arise between men and women during the process of psychological analysis. See Thomas A. Kirsch, *The Jungians: A Comparative and Historical Perspective* (London: Routledge, 2000), 20, quoted here from *Spring* 68 (2001), 172.

4. For these and other personal details I am grateful to James Hillman, who communicated them to me in a letter of 8 March 2001.

5. James Hillman, *Archetypal Psychology: A Brief Account* (Woodstock, CT: Spring Publications, 1997).

6. *The Myth of Analysis: Three Essays in Archetypal Psychology* (New York: Harper Perennial, 1978).

7. The biographical details given here stem from James Hillman, *Inter Views: Conversations with Laura Pozzo* (New York: Harper & Row, 1983), 93ff.

8. As Hillman put it to me in a letter of 8 March 2001. To begin with he wished only to attend Jung's lectures.

9. James Hillman, *The Dream and the Underworld* (New York: Harper & Row, 1979).

10. James Hillman, *Am Anfang war das Bild* (Munich: Kösel, 1983).

11. This theory gives rise to many interesting questions in today's world of continuous television images. However, televised images should not be confused with "psychic" ones, for the latter are not only perceptible to the eye but can also be of a poetic, musical or mathematical nature.

12. This notion stands in sharp contrast to the dualism of, for example, Descartes, who conceives of an insurmountable barrier between body and mind. James Hillman saw this as a double curse of our Western mythos, because it implies that the mind alone aims for perfection, while matter is consigned to eternal limitation. Furthermore, this view leaves out of account the middle or third term, the "soul," in which myths, symbols, and archetypes are grounded.

13. Rafael Lopez-Pedraza, *Hermes and His Children* (Einsiedeln: Daimon, 2003).

14. See Benjamin Sells (ed.), *Working with Images: The Theoretical Base of Archetypal Psychology* (Woodstock, CT: Spring Publications, 2000).

15. James Hillman, *Re-Visioning Psychology* (New York: Harper & Row, 1975), 167.

16. *Ibid.*, 169.

17. See Thomas More's introduction to the chapter "Many Gods, Many Persons," in James Hillman, *A Blue Fire: Selected Writings* (New York: Harper & Row, 1989), 36ff.

18. Hillman, *A Blue Fire*, 42.

19. However, according to a protagonist of that period, one thing on which both monotheists and polytheists at Eranos, including the leading names, were agreed upon was the importance of the image and therefore of myth. This is evident from many of the lectures at the 1979 Eranos meeting, which had the title "Thought and Mythic Images." See, for example, the contribution of Manfred Porkert, "Anschaulichkeit, Sinnlichkeit, Bildlichkeit als Voraussetzung für die Integrierbarkeit wissenschaftlicher Theorien," in *Eranos Jahrbuch* 48 (1979), 101–32, and the paper by Erik Hornung, "Die Tragweite der Bilder: Altägyptische Bildaussagen," in the same volume, 183–237, in which Hornung takes a stance against the devaluation of the image in the natural sciences.

20. Quoted from Heinrich Rombach, *Der kommende Gott*, 22.

21. One might even go so far as to connect the interdisciplinarity of Eranos with a sort of secular "polytheism," in which one seeks to throw light on the "truth" from different perspectives. Interdisciplinarity corresponds to the "open society," which for Sir Karl Popper is in the long run always more successful than the "closed" one. Polyperspectivism could be another expression for this unavoidable necessity in our complex world, in which one has to be continually thinking forwards and backwards but also sideways. However, one should not confuse multiple perspectives with polytheism, because each perspective carries within it the germ of a competing monotheism (I am grateful to James Hillman for this clarification).

22. The differences between the monotheistic-Christian concept of spirituality and that of Hillman are very well explored in Eolene M. Boyd-Macmillan's book *Transformation: James Loder, Mystical Spirituality and James Hillman* (Oxford: Peter Lang, 2006), especially on pages 239ff. In Hillman's view the Catholic Church had unduly emphasized the importance of the divinely inspired spirit and thereby suppressed the soul's rich store of images.

23. It is not only words that have suffered from this loss but also their component letters. If one considers, for example, the world of symbolic meaning attached to the Hebrew letters in the Kabbalah, one's imagination needs no other images.

24. Martin Buber (like Hans Jonas) saw the Gnostics—and for Buber Jung was a Gnostic—as the true enemies of

Judaism and Christianity. See Buber's book *Gottesfinsternis*, 94–114. For Gilles Quispel and Gershom Scholem, on the other hand, ancient Gnosticism originally came out of Judaism. See John Dourley's essay "In the Shadow of the Monotheisms: Jung's Conversations with Buber and White," in *Jung and the Monotheisms: Judaism, Christianity and Islam*, Joel Ryce-Menuhin (ed.) (London: Routledge, 1993), 125–45. For a detailed discussion of the "inner" dimensions of this controversy, see the first part of Alfred Ribi's book *Die Suche nach den eigenen Wurzeln*, 16–100. Two chapter headings are characteristic: "Devotio versus Gnosis" and "Gesetz contra Selbstverantwortung" (Law versus self-responsibility). On the relations between Gnosis and Judaism, see Nathaniel Deutsch in *The Gnostic Imagination: Gnosticism, Mandeism and Merkhabah Mysticism* (Leiden: Brill, 1995), where much space is devoted to Scholem's view in particular.

25. See David Miller, "'Attack upon Christendom': The Anti-Christianism of Depth Psychology," in Murray Stein and Robert L. Moore, *Jung's Challenge to Contemporary Religion* (Wilmette, IL: Chiron Publications, 1987), 27–40.

26. Henry Corbin, *Le paradoxe du monothéisme* (Paris: Editions de l'Herne, 1981). This book is based on Corbin's lecture of the same title, given at the Eranos meeting of 1976. An Italian version had already appeared. See also Corbin's letter to David Miller, which appears in the preliminary pages (7–12) of the Italian edition of David Miller and James Hillman, *Il nuovo politeismo: La rinascita degli Dei e delle Dee* (Milan: Edizioni di Communità, 1983).

27. This reveals a considerable overlap between Corbin's philosophy and certain specific esoteric teachings, ranging from the practices of the "Jew Abraham of Worms," in the Renaissance times to Aleister Crowley with his "Holy Guardian Angel."

28. See Upton's essay "Is the Men's Movement a Religion? A Critique of Robert Bly's Iron John," *Gnosis* 25 (1992), 35.

29. For a detailed discussion of these issues, see the interesting collection of papers edited by David Griffin, *Archetypal Process: Self and Divine in Whitehead, Jung, and Hillman* (Evanston, IL: Northwestern University Press, 1989). These papers are from a conference organized by the Center for Process Studies at Claremont University Center, at which Hillman defended his theories against doubts and questions raised by the participants.

30. See his essay "Plotinus, Ficino, and Vico as Precursors of Archetypal Psychology," in James Hillman, *Loose Ends: Primary Papers in Archetypal Psychology* (Dallas, TX: Spring Publications, 1994), 146–69.

31. See Jan Marlan, "Interview with James Hillman: Past, Present and Future," in *Archetypal Psychologies: Reflections in Honor of James Hillman*, Stanton Marlan (ed.) (New Orleans, LA: Spring Journal Books, 2008), 50. This book is extremely valuable for the way it presents different ways of understanding and applying archetypal psychology as well as for the rich visual material. I find the contribution "Hillman Re-Visioning Hillman: Polemics and Paranoia" (73–94) particularly thought-provoking.

32. Jan Assmann, *The Price of Monotheism* (Stanford, CA: Stanford University Press, 2010)—a book which I regard as compulsory reading for all those interested in the history of ideas. On this matter see also the comprehensive review by Kurt Oertel in *Heidnisches Jahrbuch 2010*, Daniel Junker and Holger Kliemannel (eds) (Hamburg: Verlag Daniel Junker, 2009), 304–15. This positive review is written from the viewpoint of a Germanic Neopagan.

33. *Ibid.*, 2.

34. *Ibid.*, 41.

35. The biographical details are taken from the dust jacket of his book *Toward a Philosophy of Buddhism* (Teheran: Imperial Iranian Academy of Philosophy, 1977). These details are missing from the German edition of the book, *Philosophie des Zen-Buddhismus* (Reinbek: Rohwolt, 1979). See also "Curriculum Vitae of Toshihiko Izutsu," in the *Festschrift* of *Consciousness and Reality: Studies in Memory of Toshihiko Izutsu*, Sayyid Jalāl al-Dīn Ashtinyānī, Heideichi Matsubara, Takahashi Iwami, and Akiro Matsumoto (eds) (Leiden: Brill, 2000), 439. Here a bibliography of his writings is also to be found.

36. James Hillman, "In the Gardens: A Psychological Memoir," in *Consciousness and Reality*, 175–82.

37. William McGuire, *Bollingen*, 287ff.

38. Published by Princeton University Press, 1968.

39. Kathleen Raine was also, incidentally, responsible for introducing Elias Canetti to the Bollingen Foundation.

40. In 1963 she even won the prestigious Queen's Gold Medal for Poetry. Nevertheless she astonished a young television interviewer by saying "that there could never be great women poets—something in the female make-up made it impossible. Novelists, yes, poets, no." Yet nothing annoyed her more than convinced feminists and feminism itself. While she certainly saw herself as special and standing above the crowd, she did not regard this as having anything to do with her sex. See Jonathan and Jessica Wordsworth in *Lighting a Candle: Kathleen Raine and Temenos. Reflections, Memories, Tributes* (London: Temenos Academy, 2008).

41. Mark Sedgwick, *Against the Modern World: Traditionalism and the Secret Intellectual History of the Twentieth Century* (New York: Oxford University Press, 2004).

42. She even dedicated a small volume to him, *Philip Sherrard (1922–1995): A Tribute* (Birmingham: Delos Press, 1996). Each of the one hundred fifty printed copies is signed by the author. Sherrard's works include the beautiful book *Constantinople: Iconography of a Sacred City* (London: Oxford University Press, 1965).

43. It was Coomaraswamy who remarked, "It takes four years to acquire the best University education, but it takes forty to get over it." This is quoted by Kathleen Raine in her introduction to the first issue of the *Temenos Academy*

Review 1 (1998), 8. On Kathleen Raine's relationship to the Integral Tradition, see Seyyed Hossein Nasr, "Kathleen Raine and Tradition: Some General Comments and Personal Recollections," *Temenos Academy Review* 7 (2004), 179–85. In this issue the poet is discussed from various different points of view.

44. Kathleen Raine, *The Land Unknown: Further Chapters of Autobiography* (London: Hamish Hamilton, 1975), 204ff.

45. See especially her collection *Yeats the Initiate: Essays on Certain Themes in the Writings of W.B. Yeats* (London: George Allen & Unwin, 1986).

46. Interview with Jay Kinney in *Gnosis* 23 (Spring 1992), 52. In this long conversation she also speaks in detail about her own periodical *Temenos*.

47. See the club's journal *Harvest*.

48. Her studies on the Christian polytheism of Blake were praised by James Hillman, among others.

49. Quoted by Indra Nath Choudhuri in *Temenos Academy Review* 7 (2004), 70.

50. See Magda Kerényi's report "Die Vielheit der Welten: Zur Eranostagung 1975," in *Die Tat*, 26 September 1975.

51. Aniéla Jaffé, *Anna Kingsford: Religiöser Wahn und Magie* (Fellbach: Bonz-Verlag, 1980).

52. Included in Jaffé, *Aus Leben und Werkstatt von C.G. Jung*, 87–104.

53. Jean Servier, *L'homme et l'invisible* (Paris: Laffont, 1964).

54. See Servier's general survey under the title *L'Ethnologie* in the series *Que sais-je?* (Paris: Presses Universitaires Françaises, 1986). On page 43 he makes use of the term "new humanism," already familiar from the work of Eliade, denoting an approach that makes room for ways of thinking other than just our modern Western one.

55. Jean Servier, *Les techniques de l'invisible* (Monaco: Editions du Rocher, 1994).

56. Jean Servier, *Histoire de l'utopie* (Paris: Gallimard, 1991).

57. Jean Servier, *La Magie*, in the series *Que sais-je?* (Paris: Presses Universitaires de France, 1993).

58. Henri Corneille Agrippa, *La magie naturelle* and *La magie cérémonielle* (2 vols.), Jean Servier (ed.) (Paris: L'Ile Verte, Berg International, 1982).

59. Jean Servier (ed.), *Dictionnaire critique de l'ésotérisme* (Paris: Presses Universitaires de France, 1998). It is of course debatable whether one can define esotericism as widely as Servier does or whether it should be restricted, as Antoine Faivre proposes, to Europe and to the period from the Renaissance to the present. At any rate, criticism has been leveled at Servier on this point.

60. The importance of publishers who did not think *only* in commercial terms can hardly be overestimated in the history of ideas of the last centuries. Eugen Diederichs has already been mentioned several times in the present context. Also of importance for authors connected with Eranos were Lambert Schneider in Heidelberg and Otto Reichl Verlag in Darmstadt. Another firm that should be mentioned is Rascher Verlag in Zurich, which early on published Jung's works and later those of other Eranos speakers such as Andreas Speiser, Aniela Jaffé, and Heinrich Zimmer. Rascher also brought out Chinese poetry and the works of Vivekananda, whom Olga Fröbe admired. In the 1930s, however, Rascher also published the writings of Mussolini: see Rascher Verlag, *Aussaat 1938: Ein Verlagsalmanach: 30 Jahre Rascher Verlag* (Zurich: Rascher, 1938). Among those operating after the wreckage of the Second World War one that should be mentioned—albeit with a rather different agenda—is Suhrkamp in Frankfurt, which, according to Jürgen Habermas, embodied "an intellectual trend of development that one could say was dominant in post-war Germany: I mean the firm adherence to enlightenment, humanism and radical social thinking" (quoted here from *Zeit* online, www.zeit.de/1996/40/SUHRKAMP_IM_HERBST/ seite-3).

61. The call for subscribers to the first volume brought only two hundred twenty-five orders instead of the necessary four hundred. See Fröbe's letter to Friedrich Heiler of 21 January 1934.

62. Magda Kerényi also indexed the thirteen volumes of C.G. Jung's collected works and created a bibliography of Karl Kerényi's works—see "A Bibliography of C. Kerényi," compiled by Magda Kerényi, included in the English edition of Kerényi's book *Dionysos* (Princeton, NJ: Princeton University Press, 1976), 447–74.

63. In *Geist und Werk: Zum 75. Geburtstag von Dr. Daniel Brody* (Zurich: Rhein-Verlag, 1958), 1.

64. Quoted here from Aniela Jaffé, *Aus C.G. Jung's letzten Jahren und andere Aufsätze* (Einsiedeln: Daimon Verlag, 1987), 110.

65. Brody was of Jewish origin.

66. *Geist und Werk*, vi. Broch, who undoubtedly counts as one of the really great poets, was concerned to treat the insights of sociology, psychology, philosophy, and the natural sciences not separately but as part of a living totality. It is significant that in 1926 he had taken an introductory course on the theory of relativity at the University of Vienna. This led—almost predictably—to the accusation of "irrationalism" and, despite Broch's Jewish background, to his being suspected of "crypto-fascist tendencies." See Joseph Strelka, "Broch heute," in *Broch heute*, Joseph Strelka (ed.) (Bern: Francke, 1978), 11ff. See also Strelka, "Der Gnostiker Hermann Broch."

67. Hermann Broch, *Briefe I* in *Hermann Broch: Kommentierte Werkausgabe in dreizehn Bänden*, Paul Michael Lützeler (ed.) (Frankfurt: Suhrkamp, 1974–81), vol 13, 385. Quoted here from Naser Šećerović, "Mutter Gissons Liebe als zentraler Aspekt des *Bergromans* von Hermann Broch," in *Der Mnemosyne Träume: Festschrift zum 80. Geburtstag von Joseph Strelka*, Ilona Slawinksi (ed.) (Tübingen: Gunter Narr, Francke, Attempto, 2007), 375.

68. This dissertation was subsequently published as a lengthy book: Antoine Faivre, *Eckartshausen et la Théosophie chrétienne* (Paris: C. Klincksieck, 1969).

69. This complaint was later repeated and elaborated on by Hans Heinz Holz in his comprehensive critique of Eranos, which I shall discuss separately.
70. Personal communication of 11 January 1998.
71. In a long report on this meeting ("Report on the Eranos Meeting of 1974," *The Human Context* 7[2] [1975], 327–9), Gerhard Wehr gave special attention to Gershom Scholem, Aniéla Jaffé, and Ernst Benz.
72. Eliade and Faivre were close friends, as is clear from the diary of Eliade, who was grateful to Faivre for support in various ways.
73. Hildemarie Streich, "Music, Alchemy and Psychology in *Atalanta Fugiens* of Michael Maier", in *Atalanta Fugiens*, Joscelyn Godwin (trans. and ed.), 9–21 (Tysoe: Magnum Opus Hermetic Sourceworks, 1987).
74. Mrs. Streich illustrated her musical explanations with the flute, while her husband played a portable organ. See Magda Kerényi, "Die Vielheit der Welten."
75. The exact title is "The History of Mystical and Esoteric Currents in Modern and Contemporary Europe." The second chair for the historical study of esoteric currents was founded only in 1999 at the Faculty of Theology at the University of Amsterdam with Wouter Hanegraaff as the first incumbent. The third was founded in 2005 at the University of Exeter in southwest England, where the late Nicholas Goodrick-Clarke was appointed to the position. One should also include the chair for the study of Unconventional Religions and Spiritualities at the Pontifical University of Saint Thomas Aquinas (also known as "Angelicum") in the Vatican, occupied by Michael Fuss.
76. See Antoine Faivre and Wouter Hanegraaff (eds), *Western Esotericism and the Science of Religion* (Leuven: Peeters, 1998). A brief overview of Antoine Faivre's conception of esotericism can be gained from the interviews published in *Gnosis* 31 (1994), 62–8 and *Gnostika* 2 (April 1997), 11–17. Antoine Faivre gave a more detailed interview on these questions to Monika Neugebauer-Wölk. See "Ein neues Feld europäischer Religionsgeschichte: Antoine Faivre gibt Auskunft zur Esoterikforschung," in the online journal *Zeitenblicke* 5(1) (2006). Neugebauer-Wölk (now retired), as a professor at the Historical Institute of the University of Halle-Wittenberg is herself preoccupied with questions relating to the influence of esoteric thinking at the time of the Enlightenment. The great significance of Antoine Faivre's work is celebrated in the *Festschrift* dedicated to him on the occasion of his retirement, comprising almost a thousand pages and edited by Joscelyn Godwin, Wouter J. Hanegraaff, and Jean-Louis Vieillard-Baron, published under the title *Esotérisme, Gnoses & imaginaire symbolique* (Leuven: Peters, 2001).
77. Faivre, *Accès de l'ésotérisme occidental*.
78. Founded by Antoine Faivre and Frédérick Tristan.
79. Ernst Benz and Antoine Faivre enjoyed a close friendship, undoubtedly connected with their common and deeply felt Christian belief. Faivre calls Benz an "incomparable and discreet friend, who … always emanated an indefinable melancholy, but mysteriously at the same time evinced an active cheerfulness and a way of giving his undivided attention to others." Quoted from his (unpublished) diary for 25 September 1977.
80. *Religion after Religion*, 321, 322 n.42, 323 n.3.
81. Wouter J. Hanegraaff, *Esotericism and the Academy: Rejected Knowledge in Western Culture* (Cambridge: Cambridge University Press, 2012), 334–55.
82. Hence his status as a Freemason and his membership of the University of Saint John of Jerusalem, on which subject more shall be said later.
83. Faivre was also responsible for the German résumé of Brun's Eranos lecture.
84. Jean Brun, *Les conquêtes de l'homme et la séparation ontologique* (Paris: Presses Universitaires Françaises, 1961).
85. Jean Brun, *Le rêve et la machine: Technique et existence* (Paris: La Table Ronde, 1992).
86. *Ibid.*, 299. Brun uses here a pun, the French word "truc" meaning "trick" as well as simply "thing."
87. See the interview with Antoine Faivre in *Gnostika* 2 (1997): 14, where he expresses the opinion that "in the immediate future there will be no academic programmes on 'esoteric' currents of thought of the kind that in France present no problems whatever." This, Faivre says, is explained by the devastation brought about by certain misconceived "myths" that had been directed into monstrous channels. Here we see yet another (largely unrecognized) legacy of the Third Reich, namely that Germany after the war was not only politically but also culturally and intellectually broken. The damage inflicted by this era was felt not only in the form of forced emigration and extermination, which created already enough intellectual void, but also in the long-lasting fear of dabbling in modes of thought that could not be shown beyond doubt to rest on a rock-solid (?) base of positivism. But, after all, if the mind is not prepared to reach out into unknown (and therefore potentially dangerous) spheres, then it will stagnate and atrophy.
88. These details and the following information are taken from the first two pages of the *Festschrift* dedicated to him: Downing (ed.), *Disturbances in the Field*. One contribution is particularly valuable on account of its excellent photographs, namely Kugler, "Eranos and Jungian Psychology."
89. David Miller, *The New Polytheism* (Dallas, TX: Spring Publications, 1981).
90. "Eranos 1976," in the *Bulletin of the Analytical Psychology Club of New York* 38(7) (1976), 8–12.
91. See, for example, Charles Poncé, *The Game of Wizards: Roots of Consciousness and the Esoteric Arts* (Wheaton, IL: Quest Books, 1991). For him, the esoteric sciences arise from the human imagination and therefore afford deep insights into the psyche.

92. In honor of Hornung's seventieth birthday, his colleague Jan Assmann wrote an article ("In Honour of Erik Hornung's 70th Birthday," *Neue Zürcher Zeitung* [28 January 2003], 54), in which he went so far as to say, "No other Egyptologist has to the same extent as Hornung emphasized the achievement of the poets in opening up the ancient Egyptian world, and no one has taken his own elucidations and translations to such a level of linguistic mastery.

93. Erik Hornung, *Geist der Pharaonenzeit* (Zurich: Artemis Verlag, 1989). Published in English as *Idea to Image: Essays on Ancient Egyptian Thought*, Elizabeth Bredeck (trans.) (New York: Timken, 1992). This book contains a series of his Eranos lectures, although in an unedited and abbreviated form.

94. See, for example, the clear formulations in his book *Echnaton: Die Religion des Lichtes* (Zurich: Artemis & Winkler, 1955), 138 and 154. English edition: *Akhenaten and the Religion of Light* (Ithaca, NY: Cornell University Press, 1999).

95. Erik Hornung, *Das esoterische Ägypten* (Munich: C.H. Beck, 1999). English edition: *The Secret Lore of Egypt*, David Lorton (trans.) (Ithaca, NY: Cornell University Press, 2001).

96. As Erik Hornung told me, because of the system of language quotas Voegelin had to deliver his lecture in English, with the result that it came over less effectively than if it had been in German.

97. Hence his anti-modernist outlook—certainly anything but heretical to the Eranos circle—which provoked Hans Blumenberg to write his *Legitimität der Neuzeit*, published in English as *The Legitimacy of the Modern Age*, Robert M. Wallace (trans.) (Boston, MA: MIT Press, 1983). In this work Blumenberg maintains that the gnosis that Voegelin so condemns has been fully overcome in the modern world, whereas Voegelin argues that modernity itself is "gnostic."

98. Opinions and attempts at definition of "gnosis" diverge so widely that Ioan Culianu, the prominent scholar of the Eliade school, argued that the term is empty of meaning, as it was applied to all and everything and its opposite. See his essay "The Gnostic Revenge," in *Religionstheologie and Politische Theologie*, vol. 2, *Gnosis und Politik*, Jacob Taubes (ed.) (Munich: Wilhelm Fink, 1984), 290ff., a work that largely revolves around Voegelin's theories. A similar line of argument is pursued by Michael Allen Williams in his provocative book *Rethinking "Gnosticism": An Argument for Dismantling a Dubious Category* (Princeton, NJ: Princeton University Press, 1996). I understand the term gnosis to mean, in simple terms, what I subsume in the preface under the category of "esotericism," that is to say primarily a non-rational path of cognition leading to an inner and outer transcendence.

99. His dissertation, bearing the title *Wechselwirkung und Gezweiung*, compares and contrasts the sociological theses of Georg Simmel and Othmar Spann.

100. Nevertheless, Kelsen later spoke out decisively against Voegelin's political theories in his book *A New Science of Politics: Hans Kelsen's Reply to Eric Voegelin's "New Science of Politics": A Contribution to the Critique of Ideology*. Vol. 6, Practical Philosophy, Eckhart Arnold (ed.) (Heusenstamm: Ontos Verlag, 2004). Voegelin's theories, Kelsen argued, infringed the fundamental principle of freedom of values and would set science back into a pre-modern stage.

101. Eric Voegelin, *Autobiographical Reflections: Collected Works of Eric Voegelin*, vol. 34 (Columbia, MO: University of Missouri Press, 2006).

102. Gian Franco Lami (ed.), *Eric Voegelin: un interprete del totalitarismo* (Rome: Astra, 1978).

103. Gian Franco Lami and Giovanni Franchi (eds), *La scienza dell'ordine: Saggi su Eric Voegelin* (Rome: Antonio Pellicani Editore, 1997). Among other writings of Eric Voegelin, Lami also edited an Italian translation of parts of Voegelin's magnum opus *Order and History*, adding extensive introductory material.

104. See the comprehensive study by Johanna Prader, *Der gnostische Wahn. Eric Voegelin und die Zerstörung menschlicher Ordnung in der Moderne* (Vienna: Passagen-Verlag, 2006); also the very committed study by Wouter Hanegraaff in his essay "On the Construction of 'Esoteric Traditions.'" Hanegraaff's observations on Voegelin are part of a subchapter on "Some Forms of Anti-Esotericism." For a comprehensive treatment of these questions, see the introductory text by the Voegelin expert Peter J. Opitz, "Die Gnosis-These: Anmerkungen zu Eric Voegelin's Interpretation der westlichen Moderne," in Eric Voegelin, *Der Gottesmord: Zur Genese und Gestalt der modernen politischen Gnosis* (Munich: Wilhelm Fink, 1999), 7–35. See also Richard Faber's essay "Gnosis: Verdacht als polit(olog)isches Stratagem," in Jacob Taubes, *Gnosis und Politik*, 230–48. The same essay also appears in Richard Faber's comprehensive collection of papers *Der Prometheus-Komplex: Zur Kritik der Politotheologie Eric Voegelins und Hans Blumenbergs* (Würzburg: Königshausen & Neumann, 1984).

105. Quoted from Voegelin's (I can only say) vehemently fundamentalist essay "Gnostische Politik," *Merkur* 6(4) (1952) later included in Eric Voegelin, *Der Gottesmord*.

106. In his book *Das Volk Gottes* (Munich: Wilhelm Fink, 1994), he deals with the Christian heretical movements of the Middle Ages, in which he perceives the forerunners of modern political mass movements.

107. On this subject, see Harald Bergbauer, *Eric Voegelins Kritik an der Moderne* (Würzburg: Ergon, 2000).

108. Thus, within a period of only a few years, his ten-volume *Order and History* has been translated into German and published as *Ordnung und Geschichte*.

109. In Ellis Sandoz (ed.), *Eric Voegelin's Significance for the Modern Mind* (Baton Rouge: Louisiana State University Press, 1991), 46–70.

110. In his essay "Voegelin and the Story of the Clerks," in Sandoz, *Eric Voegelin's Significance for the Modern Mind*, 71.

111. Ioan P. Culianu, "La XLVI Eranostagung (Ascona, 17–25 Agosto 1977)," *Aevum* 52 (2)(1978), 343–6.
112. Secret, however, was one of the French lecturers who did not feel fully at ease at Eranos. He was not invited again, as his purely historical presentation met with too little sympathy.
113. In the introductory pages of the 1982 *Eranos* yearbook, Rudolf Ritsema contributed moving tributes to both men, confirming their importance for Eranos. Adolf Portmann especially had played a decisive part in the organization and had given lectures over a period of thirty-five years. Without his efforts, Ritsema wrote, Eranos could probably not have continued.
114. Many people have supposed that this burden, which became increasingly heavy as he grew older, was the reason why Ritsema in 1988 announced the termination of the Eranos meetings as they had existed up that point.
115. Gilbert Durand, "Le Génie du Lieu et les heures propices," *Eranos Jahrbuch* 51 (1982), 243–77.

14. An End, Some New Beginnings, and Repeated Turbulence

1. Here I am reminded of the book by Iris M. Owen and Margaret Sparrow, *Conjuring up Philip: An Adventure in Psychokinesis* (New York: Harper & Row, 1976). The book describes an experiment carried out by a Canadian group of five women and three men in which they invented in great detail a figure whom they called Philip, and then collectively concentrated their thoughts on him until he began to "exist independently." At any rate, one could contact him through spiritualistic methods and ask him questions. The answers, which were given by loud knocks and cracking sounds, corresponded exactly to the characteristics and biographical details that had been agreed by the group when they "created" Philip. In psychology, the term "psychogon" is used for a "spirit" conjured up by people in this way.
2. Subsequently, in the United States, to which Voegelin had returned in 1969, Schabert became his assistant. On his work in the field of political studies, see Karl-Heinz Nusser, Matthias Riedl, and Theresia Ritter (eds), *Politikos: Vom Element des Persönlichen in der Politik: Festschrift für Tilo Schabert zum 65. Geburtstag* (Berlin: Duncker & Humblot, 2008). Also noteworthy is Tilo Schabert, *Die zweite Geburt des Menschen: Von den politischen Anfängen menschlicher Existenz* (Munich: Karl Alber, 2009), in which the author, in the best Eranos transdisciplinary and transcultural manner, attempts to build a universal foundation for political theory. The sources that he quotes range from Plato and Aristotle to the sacred texts of ancient Egypt, India, and China.
3. Tilo Schabert, *Die Architektur der Welt: Eine kosmologische Lektüre architektonischer Formen* (Munich: Wilhelm Finck, 1997)
4. Shantena Sabbadini, who assumed much of the work of translating the *I Ching*, is also Rudolf Ritsema's heir. See the account of Ritsema's life on Sabbadini's website under www.shantena.com/en/eranos/rudolf/.
5. The first version of this new translation appeared in *Eranos Jahrbuch* 58–9 (1989–90), issued in a small print run, and then, after the initial test phases, was published, in the framework of the Round Table sessions of 1990–92, in an improved version with an extensive commentary in *Eranos Jahrbuch* 62–4 (1993–95). Preliminary studies for this translation by Rudolf Ritsema (who had also trained as a practical analyst and acquired a knowledge of dream interpretation) appeared regularly from 1970 in the archetypal-psychology journal *Spring*, which was edited by James Hillman. The final German translation amounted to almost a thousand pages—see Rudolf Ritsema and Hansjakob Schneider (eds), *Yi Jing: Das Buch der Wandlungen* (Munich: O.W. Barth, 2000). Until then it had only appeared in English, Italian, and Dutch translations. Explaining the reason for his preoccupation with the *I Ching*, Ritsema described the book as an open doorway to the imaginal realm. It is striking that the later yearbooks of the Eranos Foundation also appeared under the publishing imprint of the journal *Spring*.
6. See his book *The I Ching* (Shaftesbury: Element Books, 1997), which affords a first glimpse into the new translation by Karcher and Ritsema.
7. Instead it was originally planned to publish a triple *Eranos Jahrbuch* 69–71 (2000, 2007, 2008). Finally, *Eranos Jahrbuch* 69 did appear in 2010 under the editorship of John van Praag and Riccardo Bernardini. I shall discuss this edition separately.
8. Interview with Tilo Schabert in *LiLit, Zeitschrift für Religionswissenschaft* 5 (1991), 29. See also Elisabetta Barone, "Eranos Tagungen: Dal mito alla filosofia?" *Filosofia e Teologia* 8(1) (1995), 161.
9. See Hornung, *Echnaton: Die Religion des Lichtes*, 153ff.
10. Erik Hornung, personal communication, 24 October 2009.
11. Erik Hornung was president and Tilo Schabert vice-president until 1996, when the roles were reversed.
12. The new series of *Eranos Jahrbuch* was published by Wilhelm Fink Verlag, Munich.
13. At the 1993 conference Magda Kerényi, in the name of all the participants, thanked the "Eranarchs" Hornung and Schabert "who have sacrificed an unbelievable amount of their precious time and energy." Schmuel Sambursky, in a letter to Erik Hornung of 17 July 1989, also welcomed this initiative.
14. On the first one, see the circular communication *Eranos Yi Ching Project: Dream and Oracle: The Language of the Yi Ching* (in the Eranos Foundation archive, Moscia-Ascona).
15. According to the *Neue Zürcher Zeitung* on 17 August 1990, these statutes demanded "the organizing of annual lectures" and their collection and publication in a yearbook. The statutes of the Amici di Eranos likewise demand a yearly conference and subsequent publication of the proceedings. See Erik Hornung and Tilo Schabert, *Eranos: Einige Erläuterungen*, May 1994.

16. An interview with Christa Robinson and a summary of her life are to be found in Robert and Janis Henderson, *"Enterviews" with Jungian Analysts* (New Orleans, LA: Spring Journal Books, 2010), vol. 3, 138–55.

17. As Ximena de Angulo emphasizes, Fröbe was always of the opinion that Eranos could only be led by one person, otherwise there would be continual debate and quarreling.

18. However, the yearbooks (issued by the publishing imprint of the journal *Spring*) only covered the conferences of 1992 and from 1996 to 1999. The yearbooks from 1993 to 1995 were devoted to the *I Ching* in the translation of Rudolf Ritsema and Stephen Karcher.

19. After the Second World War, Japan replaced religious instruction with ethical instruction. Since then there has been much interest there in new systems of ethical guidance that can secure a balance between the individual and the community.

20. It was not only the name that was Italian. Italian was also added as the fourth official conference language, which was amply justified in view of the great interest in Eranos on the part of the southern neighbor. Much of the organizational work—on both the cultural and the "festive" side—was carried out by young visitors from Italy, notably by students from the University of Salerno under the leadership of Elisabetta Barone. As I have already mentioned, selections from the yearbooks were published not only in America but also in Italy. Giovanni Casadio, a student of Ugo Bianchi, who attended Eranos for the first time in 1988, also attempted in vain to arouse interest among Italian publishers in the context of a "publicity campaign for Eranos in Italy." Because of his participation he was informed about the revival of the conferences by the Amici and in 1990 was one of the first speakers at the "new, old" Eranos. Casadio was incidentally the first Italian speaker for many years to lecture in his own language. See Giovanni Casadio, *Vie gnostiche all'immortalità* (Brescia: Morcelliana, 1997), 11. This work contains a somewhat expanded version of his Eranos lecture.

21. An impression of the atmosphere of that period can be found in Tilo Schabert's article "Brief aus Ascona: Das Abenteuer Eranos," *Süddeutsche Zeitung*, 24 August 1991.

22. The decidedly festive character of the Eranos conferences was also of special importance for Olga Fröbe. See her introduction "A Note on Eranos," in *The Mysteries: Papers from the Eranos Yearbooks*, Joseph Campbell (ed.) (Princeton, NJ: Princeton University Press, 1979).

23. As indicated in the now defunct website www.phil.uni-erlangen.de~p1pol/home/forschungsprojekte/eranos. html. This site had its own definition of the Eranos project, as one that concerns itself "mit der Erarbeitung einer historisch-vergleichenden Kultur- und Geistesmorphologie, Symbolforschung und Kulturanthropologie" (a historical-comparative investigation embracing the morphology of culture and mind as well as symbology and cultural anthropology).

24. On the life of this remarkable woman, see the painstakingly researched novel by Eveline Hasler, *Aline und die Erfindung der Liebe* (Zurich: Nagel & Kimche, 2000). Hasler, a well-known Swiss woman of letters, took her material from Aline Valangin's diaries, bibliographical notes, and dream record, often citing these word for word. The novel also contains details about Wladimir Rosenbaum, Jung, and Martin Buber. After her separation from Wladimir Rosenbaum, Aline Valangin became a neighbour of Magda Kerényi in Ascona.

25. These artists also included the Dadaist Hans Richter, who had attended the Eranos meetings since 1952 and had made the acquaintance of people such as Scholem, Kerényi, Portmann, and Read. See Riccardo Carazzetti and Mara Folini (eds), *L'energia del luogo: Jean Arp, Rafael Benazzi, Julius Bissier, Ben Nicholson, Hans Richter, Mark Tobey, Italo Valenti: Alla ricerca del Genius loci Ascona-Locarno* (Locarno: Armando Dadò/Città di Locarno, 2008), 66. Jean Arp, besides his artistic work, was also preoccupied with Eastern and Western mysticism, *ibid.* 228.

26. For a more or less complete list of the artists and literati who frequented the house, see Museo Onsermonese, "Personalità che hanno scelto l'Onsernone come terra di rifugio o di ispirazione," *La Voce Onsernonese* 1 (1999), 1ff. After her separation from Wladimir Rosenbaum, Aline Valangin sold the villa to a Bernese doctor and his family, thus bringing to an end a cultural high spot of the Onsernone valley. In the year 2000 Yvonne Bölt, Riccardo Carazzetti, and Gian Pietro Milani organized an exhibition documenting traces of the cultural life in the district.

27. For example, the publisher Karl Wolff complained in a letter to Rainer Maria Rilke that Pulver was inordinately fond of placing himself in the foreground. See his letter of 1 February 1917 in Wolff, *Briefwechsel eines Verlegers 1911–1963*, 142.

28. Peter Kamber, *Geschichte zweier Leben: Wladimir Rosenbaum, Aline Valangin* (Zurich: Limmat Verlag, 2002), 182.

29. *Ibid.*, 144. A lady who had known Zimmer told me that this rapid and incessant flow of talk had the effect of making his wife appear distanced and taciturn, although she was in fact highly educated and had studied romance languages as well as Sanskrit. Already as a young girl she had made lists of the books she had studied. But at the side of such an effervescent man she evidently had no chance to get a word in. On the subject of this unusual woman, see the afterword by Maya Rauch in Maya Rauch and Gerhard Schuster (eds), *Christiane von Hofmannsthal, Tagebücher 1918–1923 und Briefe des Vaters an die Tochter 1903–1929* (Frankfurt: S. Fischer, 1991), 175–84.

30. Peter Kamber, *Geschichte zweier Leben*, 201.

31. See Rosenbaum's own account, *ibid.*, 227ff. The account is also included in the charming booklet edited by Esther Schneidegger, *Tessin: Ein Lesebuch* (Zurich: Arche, 1991), 151–5.

32. *Ibid.*, 226. The remark that Jung threw at Rosenbaum, when the latter was financially and psychologically desperate, was: "A wounded animal also hides itself away to expire." This remark is confirmed by Antoine Faivre in his diary entry of 25 September 1977. Faivre had, with Rosenbaum's permission, made detailed notes during a long conversation with the latter. Rosenbaum had given Jung some legal assistance and had helped him with contractual formulations that he needed for his contacts with National Socialist officials in Berlin in order to protect Jewish colleagues more effectively. After his return, Jung is reported to have remarked to Rosenbaum: "They [the National Socialists] are mad, they are mad, they are totally mad." See Kamber, *Geschichte zweier Leben*, 170. This is also recorded by Faivre in his diary.

33. Jung often had a very direct, even coarse way of expressing himself, which could cause offense. It was therefore not necessarily a case of anti-Semitism.

34. In the United States there had been thoughts of resurrecting former plans—e.g. for organizing lecture series on American soil in addition to the existing English translations from the Eranos yearbooks. Since 1997, lecture programs in the "Eranos manner" have been held at the Mishkenot Sha'ananim cultural center in Jerusalem under the title of Mishkenot Encounters for Religion and Culture, organized by Moshe Idel and Tilo Schabert, with the participation of such personalities as Umberto Eco, David Shulman, and Gary Smith. In 1998 the themes were "The Sexual Divide" and "Human and Divine," and the speakers included Ina Schabert, Maurice Olender, and Wendy Doniger, Mircea Eliade Professor for the History of Religions at the University of Chicago. In 1999 the topic was "The Search for Perfection," and the lecturers included Henri Atlan and Guy Stroumsa. The subject for 2000 was "Myths of Good and Evil." The information brochures on these meetings indicate that their purpose is to investigate intellectual questions of a more esoteric nature. Not all the Ascona Amici were well disposed towards external meetings, for at the general assembly of the Amici in 1996 the majority were opposed to extending Eranos to other places, as they saw Eranos as being bound to the *genius loci* of Ascona (in 1988 this was not so clear, as, according to Tilo Schabert, after Ritsema's discontinuation of the conferences Venice and Basel were considered as venues). For similar reasons there was displeasure at the use of the Eranos motto *eadem mutata resurgo* on the invitations to the Mishkenot Encounters for Religion and Culture.

35. By then Erik Hornung had, as he told me, also withdrawn from the Amici di Eranos.

36. In a circular letter to the members of the Amici di Eranos of July 2000, Zarone described Eranos as an experience that paradoxically lives on precisely because it repeatedly dies.

37. Barone *et al.* (eds), *Pioniere, Poeten, Professoren.*

38. See my review in *Aries* 5(2) (2005), 284–6.

39. In the volume for the 2005 conference, which took place in the Collegio Papio in Ascona, there is a very idealistic contribution from Tilo Schabert on the Eranos phenomenon, in which he traces a line from Hölderlin, Schelling, and Hegel to Ascona. See Tilo Schabert and Matthias Riedl (eds), *Gott oder Götter? God or Gods?* (Würzburg: Königshausen & Neumann, 2009), 181–8.

40. The *NZZ* had reported regularly about Eranos since the 1930s. The article by Julia Encke in *FAZ* 201 (31 August 1999), 53, took up a whole broadsheet page, including a photograph, and her treatment of the subject was far from superficial.

41. See the editors' foreword to Erik Hornung and Andreas Schweizer (eds), *Der Mensch und seine Widersacher: Eranos 2001/2002* (privately published, 2003).

42. These and subsequent meetings were documented in a series of yearbooks, which from the second volume onwards were published by the prestigious firm of Schwabe in Basel, each volume containing the lectures from two years. It must be said that the numbering system for the respective yearbooks of the three groups is rather confusing for the reader.

43. Andreas Schweizer is president and Erik Hornung vice-president.

44. See also Erik Hornung, "Das Abenteuer Eranos" on the website of the Verein: www.eranos-ascona.ch.

45. See the reader's letter from the former Eranos president Christa Robinson, published in the *Neue Zürcher Zeitung* on 23 August 2007, 19.

46. The former president of the foundation board, Christa Robinson, confessed that she had had a big quarrel with Ritsema over money matters, even though they had previously been the best of friends. See Robert and Janis Henderson, *"Enterviews" with Jungian Analysts,* vol. 3, 50.

47. See Rolf Amgarten, "Eranos-Inventar und Idee für die Zukunft retten," *Tessiner Zeitung,* 22–23 July 2004, as well as the appeal for the revival of the Eranos Foundation, issued in April 2003, and the circular letter to the signatories of this appeal, dated April 2004.

48. See Urs Hafner, "Geld, Geist und Zwietracht," *Neue Zürcher Zeitung,* 6 August 2007.

49. John van Praag, *Echoes of Timelessness* (London: Van Praag Publications, 1990) and *Empty Sea* (Utrecht: Van Praag, 2006). On the subject of his own philosophy, see the lecture "Can You be Happy in the 21st Century?," delivered at the University of Utrecht, 2 June 2006, and later published as a booklet by the university.

50. www.fetzer.org.

51. www.pacifica.edu.

52. See www.eranosfoundation.org/partners.htm.

53. Josph Hanimann, "Geistlos," *Frankfurter Allgemeine Zeitung* (11 December 2006), 35.

54. See the two newspaper articles by Christina Leutwyler and René Lenzin, "Ascona liess sich von Versprechen blenden" and "Aufsicht hat Eranos-Stiftung im Visier," *Zürcher Tagesanzeiger* of 2 and 3 February 2007.

55. On the subject of John van Praag's attitude to the presiding spirit of Eranos, see his booklet (written in collaboration with Riccardo Bernardini) *The Spirit of Eranos*, consisting of the text of a lecture that he delivered in Moscia on 5 August 2007.

56. See the article by Mauro Euro, "Un triangolo culturale nel futuro di Eranos," *Corriere del Ticino*, 6 April 2007.

57. *Eranos Reborn*, DVD (Ascona: Eranos Foundation, 2007).

58. Of the research work that has so far been carried out, one excellent product is the already mentioned dissertation by Riccardo Bernardini, *Carl Jung a Eranos*.

59. For this information I am grateful to Gisela Binda, who has been responsible for the administrative work at the Eranos Foundation since 2001. She began taking part in the conferences as early as 1976.

60. The website of the Eranos Foundation (www.eranosfoundation.org) contains a list of all the conferences.

61. *Eranos Jahrbuch* 69 (Einsiedeln: Daimon, 2010).

62. Fabio Merlini, personal communication, 1 June 2011.

63. *Ibid.*

64. C.G. Jung, in a letter to Fröbe dated 18 September 1942.

65. Mircea Eliade, *The Forge and the Crucible* (Chicago, IL: University of Chicago Press, revised edition, 1978), 14.

66. An exception was Alfons Rosenberg, who was a "passionate" user of the library. This, according to his own account, was what started off his deep friendship with Fröbe. Interestingly, Rosenberg saw these pictures as preserving "an esoteric Christianity, encoded in symbols—that deeper level of Christianity that has been so shamefully suppressed by official theology." See "Eranos, der Geist am Wasser," 4.

67. See the essay by Jesse E. Fraser, "ARAS: Archive for Archetypal Symbolism," *Spring* (1964), 60–67.

68. Beverly Moon (ed.), *Encyclopedia of Archetypal Symbolism* (Boston, MA: Shambhala, 1991).

69. George R. Elder, *The Body: An Encyclopedia of Archetypal Symbolism* (Boston, MA: Shambhala, 1996).

70. Ami Ronnberg and Kathleen Martin (eds), *The Book of Symbols* (Cologne: Taschen, 2010).

71. http://aras.org/notices/newsletter09-01.htm.

15. Delicate Questions and Attempts to Answer Them

1. Hans Heinz Holz is emeritus professor of philosophy, most recently at the University of Groningen. He took up his first professorship, after a long public campaign against him, at the University of Marburg in 1971, when no less a person than Ernst Bloch did him the honor of delivering the welcoming address. The reason for the hostile campaign was made clear by Bloch himself as follows: "This is the first time in the Federal Republic that someone professing a Marxist position—politically and theoretically—had been nominated for a chair of philosophy." However, he also received massive support from the students. Besides Bloch, two Eranos speakers had voted in his favor, namely Gershom Scholem and Helmuth Plessner. In the latter he also had a scholarly interest. See Hermann Klenner, Domenico Losurdo, Jos Lensnik, and Jeroen Bartels (eds), *Representatio Mundi: Festschrift zum 70. Geburtstag von Hans Heinz Holz* (Cologne: Jürgen Dinter Verlag für Philosophie, 1997), 3, where Bloch's entire speech is reproduced. Also relevant in this context is the contribution "Ein Gruß zum Schluß: Für Hans Heinz Holz zum Siebzigsten" (A closing greeting: for Hans Heinz Holz on his seventieth) by his colleague Manfred Buhr, who addressed his words "to the philosopher who has continually held fast to reason and rationality, which are so necessary at this time of radical change … to the relentless opponent of diminished philosophy, half-baked reason and irrationality" (*ibid.*, 2). It is also worth quoting the editors' words in the foreword to the *Festschrift* (2): "His philosophical and political path has been determined by his humanistic commitment and by the uncompromising way in which he has stood up for his philosophical and socialist convictions" (Holz is a member of the German Communist Party and has, rather daringly, described Lenin's "entire work," including the "directly situation-specific political writings" as "philosophical"). See Bernd Lutz (ed.), *Metzler Philosophenlexikon: Dreihundert biographisch-werkgeschichtliche Porträts von den Vorsokratikern bis zu den Neuen Philosophen* (Stuttgart: J.B. Metzler, 1989), 453ff. Holz's area of special expertise is dialectical philosophy, and he is the author of the impressive five-volume *Dialektik: Problemgeschichte von der Antike bis zur Gegenwart* (Darmstadt: Wissenschaftliche Buchgesellschaft, 2010). But he has also written about Walter Benjamin, Leibniz, and Descartes as well as on *China im Kulturvergleich: Ein Beitrag zur philosophischen Komparatistik* (China: comparison in culture) (Cologne: Dinter, 1994). He has also concerned himself with interpreting class structures in society—see, for example, his *Herr und Knecht bei Leibniz und Hegel* (Berlin: Luchterhand, 1968).

2. Holz mentions this in a letter of 27 August 1976 to Gershom Scholem, in which he requests information about Ernst Bloch, a request that Scholem rather brusquely rejected, as he held a totally different view from Holz. See Gershom Scholem, *Briefe III*: 378.

3. In Jakob Taubes (ed.), *Religionstheorie und Politische Theologie*. vol. 2, *Gnosis und Politik* (Munich: Wilmhelm Fink, 1984), 249–63.

4. The essay appeared again, condensed into two pages, in the special issue of *Du* on Jung. In this version analysis has no place, and the critical, indeed almost accusatory tone is predominant. Thus, for example, he characterizes Eranos as "a strange bastard mixture of science, culture and therapy." See H.H. Holz, "Die Eranos-Jünger," in *Du* (August 1995), 92-3.

5. Here Holz should at least have mentioned the great intellectual and spiritual openness of the conferences, which stands in direct contrast to the kind of narrow-mindedness that one usually associates with a sect. For him, however, this openness probably seemed illusory, since the shared mythos would have prevented any purely rational discourse. Holz's approach here is similar to Richard Noll's treatment of Jung as a "cult figure." Both overshoot the mark and miss.

6. Jacobi, "Eranos: vom Zuhörer aus gesehen," 51ff.

7. Because of her active involvement she was described as a "locomotive." See the details on her given by Deirdre Bair in *Jung*, 367.

8. The Kulturbund was an international organization founded in 1922 by Karl Anton Rohan as a conservative think tank with the aim of furthering a European consciousness. Members of the Austrian section included, for example, Hugo von Hofmannsthal, Anton Wildgans, and Hans Kelsen, "Father of the Austrian Constitution." The French section was led by André Maurois. Rohan had met Jung in 1927 at Count Keyserling's School of Wisdom in Darmstadt and had requested Jung to take him on as a "student-patient." Jung agreed and Rohan stayed several weeks with him in Zurich, a period which he considered decisive for "the conduct of his life." Jung also wrote for the *Europäische Revue*, which was edited by Karl Anton Rohan, as previously mentioned, and brought together most important authors (See Karl Anton Rohan, *Heimat Europa: Erinnerungen und Erfahrungen* [Jena: Eugen Diederichs Verlag, 1954], 56-60, 305-7). During the 1932 session, Jung spoke alongside Arnold Schönberg. In the German section of this year Baron von der Heydt gave a talk about his art collection and Hermann Keyserling also spoke (see "Halbjahresbericht des Verbandes für kulturelle Zusammenarbeit (Kulturbund) (September 1932-März 1933)," *Europäische Revu* 9[1] [1933], 179. After the Second World War Karl Anton Rohan was the object of intense controversy, which by association also concerned Jung because of his long collaboration with the *Europäische Revue*. On the one hand there were those who described him as "a proven man of inner maturity and a Christian with a message of reconciliation" (Clemens Podewils in *Merkur*) or "Seldom has anything so important been said about the crisis of European society" (*Die Welt*). On the other hand, after a demolishing piece by Hans Magnus Enzensberger in the *Spiegel*, Herbert Singer wrote as follows in the *Tagesspiegel/Stuttgarter Zeitung*: "So is Enzensberger right? Apparently so. Karl Anton Rohan, who used to publish a 'European review', holds forth in dangerous turns of phrase about the … still somehow glorious revolution of 1933 … Not that he repeats the discredited words literally, not at all, but certain expressions such as 'appeared', 'believed' and 'must have been possible', by taking a half-distanced position, indicate approval of things that are totally evil." These quotations are taken from Karl Anton Rohan, *Heiße Eisen: Deutschland, Europa, Der Westen* (Nürnberg: Glock & Lutz, 1963).

9. See Hannah, *Jung*, 264.

10. In this connection it is interesting to consider the observation of the mythologist Jacques Duchesne-Guillemin, who attended Eranos for many years, but never spoke there. He believes that the reason why Fröbe would not let him speak about the theories of Georges Dumezil, despite the pleas of Mircea Eliade, was because she regarded both Dumezil and Duchesne-Guillemin as "hopelessly rationalistic." See Jacques Duchesne-Guillemin, "Mircea Eliade: An Impromptu," in *Gnosisforschung und Religionsgeschichte*, Holger Preißler and Hubert Seiwert (eds) (Marburg: Diagonal Verlag, 1994), 410.

11. See the discussion in Fritz Stolz (ed.), *Homo naturaliter religiosus: Gehört Religion notwendig zum Mensch-Sein?* (Bern: Peter Lang, 1997).

12. See their essay "Eranos and the Eranos Jahrbücher," *Religious Studies Review* 8(3) (July 1982), 229.

13. Mircea Eliade and Ira Progoff, *About the Eranos Conferences* (Ascona: privately published, n.d.).

14. I have already spoken about José Antonio Antón Pacheco's attempt to locate certain important Eranos speakers, such as Eliade, Scholem, and Corbin, within the ranks of the philosophical existentialists. The same author, in his already mentioned essay "Aproximaciones a Eranos," argues that other traditions of thought which deal with spiritual questions—and here he expressly mentions esotericism—can also be characterized as existentialist. Thus "alchemy, Gnosis and the oriental philosophies would be integrated into our life's horizon, and existentialism … would acquire a deeper meaning." On the one hand, he says, existentialism would be an instrument for interpreting these phenomena (alchemy, Gnosis, etc.), and they in turn would illuminate existentialism.

15. Henry Corbin, "Eranos: Freiheit und Spontaneität," *Eranos Jahrbuch* 31 (1962), 13-15.

16. Henry Corbin's memorial speech is in *Vom Sinn der Eranostagungen*, Adolf Portmann, Rudolf Ritsema, and Henry Corbin (eds) (private publication, n.d.), 8. A slightly amended version appears in *Geist und Werk*, 197-208.

17. Adolf Portmann, *An den Grenzen des Wissens: Beitrag der Biologie zu einem neuen Weltbild* (Vienna: Econ, 1974), 226.

18. Guardian spirits or angels of the Zoroastrians, also called Frawashi, Fravashi, Fravasay. In psychological terms, they could be seen as higher, archetypical components of the human soul. Even the supreme God, Ahura Mazda, is dependent on their support, as is clear from *Yasht* 13.1-158, where right at the beginning we read, "Ahura

Mazda spake unto Spitama Zarathushtra, saying: 'Do thou proclaim, O pure Zarathushtra! the vigour and strength, the glory, the help and the joy that are in the Fravashis of the faithful, the awful and overpowering Fravashis; do thou tell how they come to help me, how they bring assistance unto me, the awful Fravashis of the faithful … Through their brightness and glory, O Zarathushtra! I maintain that sky, there above, shining and seen afar, and encompassing this earth all around … Had not the awful Fravashis of the faithful given help unto me, those animals and men of mine, of which there are such excellent kinds, would not subsist'" (from the *Khorda Avesta, Yasht* 13 [Hymn to the guardian angels], translated by James Darmesteter, 1898 [digital edition, H. Peterson, www.avesta.org/ka/yt13sbe.htm]).

19. See his essay "Eliade et l'anthropologie profonde," in Tacou (ed.), *Mircea Eliade*, 94. Eliade himself, however, was considerably cooler in the way he described the goal of Eranos, namely "to consider symbolism from all possible viewpoints: psychology, history of religion, theology, mathematics and even biology." See Eliade's essay "Jung, ou la réponse à Job," in Tacou (ed.), *Mircea Eliade*, 250.

20. Exclamation mark in Durand's original. However, it seems to me much exaggerated to ascribe a secret steering role to Eranos. The participants and themes were far too heterogeneous for that.

21. Filoramo, *Il risveglio della gnosi ovvero diventare dio*, 26.

22. I am relying here on the summary of Campbell's theses in Hanegraaff, *New Age Religion and Western Culture*, 14–18.

23. Wouter Hanegraaff, "Beyond the Yates Paradigm: The Study of Western Esotericism between Counterculture and the New Complexity," *Aries* 1(1) (2001) 5–37.

24. However, Hanegraaff, who himself holds such a chair at the University of Amsterdam, makes it clear in his essay that he does not wish his study programs to follow the "religionist and counter-cultural" approach of Eranos. Rather, he favors a strict empirical-historical approach.

25. Wasserstrom, *Religion after Religion*, 36.

26. Faivre sets out his definition in several of his works. See especially Antoine Faivre "Introduction," in Faivre and Needleman (eds), *Modern Esoteric Spirituality*, xv.

27. The most important passages from his speech are published in the Feuilleton section of the *Neue Zürcher Zeitung* of 29 February 1980.

28. According to contemporary witnesses, Scholem also spoke out elsewhere against what he saw as the "irrationalism" that was at least partially present at Eranos.

29. According to Joseph Dan, Scholem's opposition to Jungian thinking dated back to the 1930s. He totally rejected all the conceptions of the soul that were current in depth psychology circles. He had no time even for Freud's teachings on this subject, although his wife Fania was related to Freud. See Joseph Dan's essay "Gershom Scholem: Mystiker oder Geschichtsschreiber des Mystischen?" in *Gershom Scholem: Zwischen den Disziplinen*, Peter Schäfer and Gary Smith (eds) (Frankfurt: Suhrkamp, 1995), 50.

30. Although Scholem counted among the "admirers of reason," he was convinced that reason was above all an instrument of *destructive* criticism. For more durable institutions morality and therefore religion were necessary. See Hamacher, *Gershom Scholem und die Allgemeine Religionsgeschichte*, 58.

31. Gershom Scholem, "*…und alles ist Kabbala*": *Gershom Scholem im Gespräch mit Jörg Dress* (Munich: Text & Kritik, 1980), 7.

32. See Hyam Maccoby, "The Greatness of Gershom Scholem," in *Gershom Scholem: Modern Critical Views*, Harold Bloom (ed.) (New York: Chelsea House, 1987), 149.

33. Joseph Dan even speaks of a "heartfelt relationship to Jung and Eliade." See his essay "Gershom Scholem, Mystiker oder Geschichtsschreiber," 54.

34. Dan, "Gershom Scholem: Mystiker oder Geschichtsschreiber des Mystischen?" 53.

35. See Tilo Schabert, "Das Abenteuer Eranos," *Süddeutsche Zeitung*, 24–5 August 1991, 131.

36. Evidently Dan perceives the German cultural influence at Eranos to have been predominant.

37. Burckhardt and Rychner, *Briefe 1926–1965*, 242.

38. Wasserstrom, *Religion after Religion*, especially 247ff.

39. *Ibid.*, 13.

40. *Ibid.*, 248.

41. *Ibid.*, 13.

42. But this does not mean that Holz's drastic accusations should automatically be accepted as valid for the earlier meetings.

43. The first volume was published in 1934 by Vandenhoek & Rupprecht in Göttingen. The second, greatly delayed by Jonas' enforced exile, appeared only in 1993 with the same publisher. In the present context the first volume is the more important of the two.

44. See also the clear and sympathetic afterword by Christian Wiese, "Revolte wider die Weltflucht," in Hans Jonas, *Gnosis: Die Botschaft des fremden Gottes* (Frankfurt: Insel Verlag, 1999), 401–29. Wiese's afterword also contains some new relevant literature. Wiese is also the author of the book *Hans Jonas: "Zusammen Philosoph und Jude"* (Frankfurt: Jüdischer Verlag, 2003), which contains a long section (pp. 63–95) on the friendship and subsequent quarrel between Hans Jonas and Gershom Scholem.

45. Quoted from Hans Jonas' essay "Gnosis, Existenzialismus und Nihilismus," in Hans Jonas, *Gnosis und spätantiker Geist*, Part 2, *Von der Mythologie zur mystischen Philosophie: Erste und Zweite Hälfte* (Göttingen: Vandenhoek & Ruprecht, 1993), 359-79.

46. Subtitled *Versuch einer Ethik für die technologische Zivilisation* (Frankfurt: Suhrkamp, 1989). This is also the approach that the Italian philosopher Angela Michaelis places at the center of her study *Libertà e Responsabilità: La filosofia di Hans Jonas* (Rome: Città Nuova, 2007).

47. Particularly relevant in this connection is the collection edited by Dietrich Böhler, *Ethik für die Zukunft: Im Diskurs mit Hans Jonas* (Munich: C.H. Beck, 1994).

48. This criticism is also the key point of Wasserstrom's *Religion after Religion*. Wasserstrom is intent on drawing attention to the negative effects of "esoteric" thinking. He points out the elitist individualism of the Gnostic, which focuses on self-salvation rather than on the institutional survival of the community, and which relativizes morality, thus threatening to jeopardize the (Mosaic) divine order. This is what is so abhorrently blasphemous to someone of the law-abiding Jewish faith. See also the chapter on "Individualism and Gnosticism,"which discusses the "Gnostic ethos," in Henry Green, *The Economic and Social History of Gnosticism* (Atlanta, GA: Scholars Press, 1985), 210ff. On the "immorality" of Gnosticism, see also Giovanni Filoramo, *A History of Gnosticism* (Oxford: Blackwell, 1991), which clearly shows, however, that, despite the frequently voiced accusation of "immorality," no single Gnostic Nag Hammadi text contains even a hint of immoral behavior, "however surprising and paradoxical it may be." Altogether, Filoramo's work can be recommended as a readable overview of Gnosticism.

49. Quoted here from Wiese, "Revolte wider die Weltflucht,"425.

50. Another work that falls within this anti-Gnostic tradition of thought is Micha Brumlik's *Die Gnostiker: Der Traum von der Selbsterlösung des Menschen* (Frankfurt: Eichborn, 1992). Brumlik not only sees Gnostic thinking in antiquity or in the Hermetic tradition. He is particularly troubled by what he diagnoses as the radical modern form of Gnosis. Thus, for example, he identifies such diverse figures as Rudolf Bultmann, Martin Heidegger, Joseph Goebbels, Rudolf Steiner, Ernst Bloch, C.G. Jung, and Theodor Adorno as moving forces in the background. As he sees it, these influential authors, through their analyses and their rejection of today's world, often actually contribute to making the world into the vale of sorrow that they so vehemently lament. It is therefore everyone's urgent political duty, Brumlik argues, to expose and resist such Gnostic tendencies.

51. Carsten Colpe, "Die 'Himmelsreise der Seele' außerhalb und innerhalb der Gnosis," in *Le origini dello gnosticismo: Colloquio di Messina 13-18 Aprile 1966*, Ugo Bianchi (ed.) (Leiden: Brill, 1970), 429-47.

52. Hans Kippenberg, "Obituary: Prof. Dr. phil., Dr. theol. Carsten Colpe (19 July 1929-24 November 2009)," *Numen* 58 (2011), 1-5.

53. Ioan Culianu, *Hans Jonas: Gnosticismo e pensiero moderno* (Rome: "L'Erma" di Bretschneider, 1985), 33ff.

54. Professor Ugo Bianchi of Messina worked with all the great scholars of religion of his age and organized a conference on the origins of Gnosticism, 13-18 April 1966, which brought together the most famous scholars such as Hans Jonas, J. Ries, G. Gnoli, Gilles Quispel, and Kurt Rudolph. The proceedings, edited by Ugo Bianchi, were published under the conference title *Le origini dello gnosticismo* (Leiden: Brill, 1970). Giulia Sfameni Gasparro, who also now teaches religious studies at Messina, even describes the conference as epoch-making for the study of Gnosis. See the volume edited by her: *Destino e salvezza tra culti pagani e gnosi cristiana: Itinerari storico-religiosi sulle orme di Ugo Bianchi* (Cosenza: Lionello Giordano, 1998), 17.

55. This is undoubtedly true if Alfred Adam is right when he says, "Central to the Gnostic's perception of life is the consciousness that his own self is identical with the being of the Saviour." See his *Die Psalmen des Thomas und das Perlenlied vorchristlicher Gnosis* (Berlin: Alfred Töpelmann, 1959), 82.

56. Barbara Aland, "Gnosis und Kirchenvertreter," in *Gnosis: Festschrift für Hans Jonas*, Barbara Aland (ed.) (Göttingen: Vandenbroek & Ruprecht, 1978), 158-215. Aland rejects the notion of any connection between Gnosticism and politics in the ancient world. Rather she discerns an indifference towards politics, which was also evident in Christian antiquity. See Barbara Aland, "Was ist Gnosis? Wie wurde sie überwunden? Versuch einer Kurzdefinition," in *Gnosis und Politik*, Jacob Taubes (ed.) (Munich: Wilhelm Fink, 1986), 54ff. The same view is expressed by Peter Pokorny in his essay "Der soziale Hintergrund der Gnosis," in *Gnosis und Neues Testament*, Karl-Wolfgang Tröger (ed.) (Berlin: Gütersloher Verlagshaus Mohn, 1973), 77-95.

57. For a possible interpretation, see my review-essay discussing *Die Hermetik* by Ralf Liedtke, "Die Hermetik: Eine alte neue Weltsicht: Bemerkungen zum Buch," *Gnostika* 6 (1998), 43-56, re-published in *Aries* 22 (1999), 101-12.

58. See his essay "Das Problem einer Soziologie und 'sozialen Verortung' der Gnosis," *Kairos* 19 (1977), 35-44.

59. In reading these statements, one must bear in mind that Kurt Rudolph was working in Leipzig, which at that time belonged to the German Democratic Republic.

60. Peter Koslowski, "Gnosis und Gnostizismus in der Philosophie: Systematische Überlegungen," in *Gnosis und Mystik in der Geschichte der Philosophie*, Peter Koslowski (ed.) (Zurich: Artemis, 1988), 375, 395.

61. (Paderborn: Schöningh, 1996). On this issue, see especially pp. 7ff.

62. Holz too makes no distinction between Hermetic and Gnostic thinking. Even just on this point a thorough clarification of these terms is urgently called for. On the degeneration of the term gnosis as a general concept, see the section of this book dealing with Eric Voegelin.

63. Filoramo, *Il risveglio della gnosi ovvero diventare dio*, 21ff.
64. See the illuminating first chapter, "Myth, Gnosis, and Modernity," in Ellwood, *The Politics of Myth*, 15ff.
65. Hence Eranos is also not "irrational" but rather against the form of rationality that Horkheimer, Adorno, and Habermas have called "instrumental rationality," meaning a coldly rational modality in which human beings and the world are treated exclusively as objects of technical manipulation and are thus at the mercy of subjective interests. Their own skepticism towards progress and instrumental rationality is perhaps most clearly reflected in Max Horkheimer and Theodor Adorno, *Dialectic of Enlightenment*, E. Jephcott (trans.) (Stanford, CA: Stanford University Press, [1944] 2002), perhaps the best-known work of the so-called Frankfurt School. Relevant in this connection is the informative study by Michael Großheim, "'Die namenlose Dummheit, die das Resultats des Fortschritts ist': Lebensphilosophische und dialektische Kritik der Moderne, *Logos* 3(2) (1996), 97–133. Commenting on Horkheimer's and Adorno's work, Großheim relates their skepticism toward the reception of the Stefan George follower and *Kosmiker* Ludwig Klages, whom Horkheimer, in a 1926 lecture, described as "extraordinarily significant." However, Horkheimer *et al.* reject what they see as the totally false conclusions drawn by Klages and other "philosophers of life," in their rejection of modernity. As Großheim points out in his essay "Archaisches oder dialektisches Bild," 501, Klages' fundamental criticism of modernity is already evident in his work *Der Kosmogonische Eros*, in which he attributes the modern compulsion towards research and knowledge collection to an "acquisition drive" and a "will to dominance."
66. Ellwood, *The Politics of Myth*, xiv.
67. Wasserstrom, *Religion after Religion*, 60.
68. It is now generally recognized that the great scientific achievements of Isaac Newton and Robert Boyle must be seen against the background of their interest in alchemy. In the case of Paracelsus the situation is even clearer.
69. Hans A. Pestalozzi, *Die sanfte Verblödung* (Düsseldorf: Hermes, 1985).
70. Even Jung talks about the Age of Aquarius. He refers to it for the first time in his 1958 essay "Ein moderner Mythos," available in C.G. Jung, *Gesammelte Werke*, vol. 10, *Zivilisation im Übergang* (Olten: Walter Verlag, 1974), 338. The passage reads, "We are now approaching the great transformation, which can be expected with the entry of the vernal equinox into Aquarius." Jung was speaking here of psychic transformation.
71. This is confirmed in her speech delivered to the Analytical Club of New York on 27 October 1939, in which she said, "Historically and astrologically we live in a period of transition from one age to another—from one sign of the Zodiac to another—from Pisces into Aquarius, and this constellation causes all the upheavals in the world today " (pp. 1ff. of the manuscript). And a further proof is to be found in the draft of her subsequently much curtailed foreword to the first volume of papers from the Eranos yearbooks, *Spirit and Nature* (New York: Bollingen Foundation, 1954), where she writes, "We are already over the border [again an artificial border, but here used as an expression of transition and transformation in the history of culture] and therefore in contact with new aspects of creative law, thinking, institution and imagination." In this foreword she also says that "Eranos was an experiment, in which all was risked." The speakers especially had risked their scholarly reputations when they had joined this great quest.
72. For example, he gives a whole list of the points that he sees as "structural features of the Eranos experience." However, to give just one example, what he negatively calls a "narcissistic fixation on self-discovery" is characterized by Donna and Charles Scott as "creative reality of the soul." See "Eranos and the Eranos Jahrbücher," 229.
73. See, for example, the informative article by Arthur Versluis, "The 'Counterculture,' Gnosis and Modernity," in *Telos* 152 (2010) and on the website www.telospress.com/main/index.php?main_page=news_article&article_id=394. Versluis points out how the old Christian and Jewish accusations of heresy are paralleled by the modern indictment of Gnostic tendencies. I too have tried to enumerate the alleged connections between irrationality and fascism, at least in relation to Germany in the postwar period. However, no really tenable or scientifically convincing arguments for such a connection have been forthcoming. Instead, what we mostly find are biased and emotional attacks, based on scanty knowledge. See Hakl, "'Occultism is the Metaphysic of Dunces.'" The main source of opposition to esotericism and New Age movements is and remains the Frankfurt School and its progeny.
74. Peter Koslowski, *Gnosis und Mystik in der Geschichte der Philosophie*, cit. 11.
75. The Greek text reads, "*areté psyches gnosis*." The word *areté* here means not merely moral virtue but also strength and capacity. Brian Copenhaver translates this passage as follows: "The virtue (*areté*) of soul, by contrast, is knowledge (gnosis), which is the same thing," in his *Hermetica* (Cambridge: Cambridge University Press 1992), 32.
76. Elaine Pagels, *The Gnostic Gospels* (New York: Random House, 1979), xix. On xix–xx she quotes a statement by a Gnostic teacher named Monoimus, who writes in words of timeless clarity, "Abandon the search for God and the creation and other matters of a similar sort. Look for him by taking yourself as the starting point. Learn who it is within you who makes everything his own and says: 'My God, my mind, my thought, my soul, my body.' Learn the sources of sorrow, joy, love, hate … If you carefully investigate these matters you will find him in yourself."
77. Peter Sloterdijk and Thomas H. Macho (eds), *Weltrevolution der Seele: Ein Lese- und Arbeitsbuch der Gnosis von der Spätantike bis zur Gegenwart* (Munich: Artemis & Winckler, 1991), vol. 1, 5.

78. Williams, *Rethinking "Gnosticism".*
79. Karen L. King, *What is Gnosticism?* (Cambridge, MA: Harvard University Press, 2003).
80. *Ibid.,* 2–3.
81. Barbara Aland, *Was ist Gnosis? Studien zum frühen Christentum, zu Marcion und zur kaiserzeitlichen Philosophie* (Tübingen: Mohr Siebeck, 2009). See above all the "Introduction" "Einführung," 1–21.
82. Christoph Markschies, *Die Gnosis* (Munich: C.H. Beck, 2001).
83. Steven Wasserstrom uses the apt expression "spiritual nationalism." See *Religion after Religion,* 4.
84. See the essay of Günter Hartung, "Völkische Ideologie," in *Handbuch zur "Völkischen Bewegung" 1871–1918,* Uwe Puschner, Walter Schmitz, and Justus H. Ulbricht (eds) (Munich: K.G. Saur, 1996), 23ff.
85. See point 6 of the so-called Italian *Manifesto della Razza* (Racial manifesto), drawn up by ten university professors, in which we find the following: "6. There is now a pure 'Italian race.' This statement rests … on the purest kinship of blood, which unites and connects the Italians of today with the generations that have lived in Italy for thousands of years." See Benito Mussolini, *Der Geist des Faschismus: Ein Quellenwerk* (German translation) (Munich: C.H. Beck, 1943), 47.
86. See, for example, René Martial, *La race française* (Paris: Mercure de France, 1934). On page 9 Dr. Martial asserts "that the French race has just as valid a claim to mental/spiritual superiority over the peoples of Europe as the German race has—indeed our organism is even purer than theirs."
87. Here I would like to mention a moving book by an author otherwise unknown to me, Gedalja ben Elieser, whose *Jüdisches Volk, antworte! Notwendigkeiten, Wege und Ziele eines völkisches Zionismus* (Jewish people, answer! Necessities, ways and aims of a *völkisch* Zionism) was originally published in Vienna in 1937 and was re-published in 1998 (Viöl: Verlag für ganzheitliche Forschung und Kultur, Archiv-Edition). This firm publishes its books as a spearhead in the struggle against the so-called "One World Order," which it deems influenced by Zionism. In his final chapter "Continuity or Downfall?" (p. 328), the author says, rightly or wrongly, "This book is a record of the state of mind of a large part of today's Jewish youth, of all their sufferings, torments and wishes." Ben Elieser first describes the humiliation that he already had to suffer early in his life as a "Jew-child." He then goes on: "We are never homeless," he writes "but we become so anew, again and again. First the notions of home, Fatherland and language are mendaciously implanted in us, only to be cruelly torn out again from our souls and hearts" (p. 43). What he sees as the only escape from oppression and forced homelessness for the Jews is an aggressive re-awakening to their own Jewishness. He even goes so far as to describe Hitler (although long before the persecutions and murders) as "God's scourge," whose cruelty frees the Jewish people from the "poison of assimilation," which had "reached its peak in Germany." Assimilation is for him a form of "self-abnegation" through an attitude of conformity.
88. Quoted here from George L. Mosse's classic work on *völkisch* thinking, *Ein Volk, ein Reich, ein Führer: Die völkischen Ursprünge des Nationalsozialismus* (Königstein: Athenäum, 1979), 5–6.
89. "A *Volk* is a means to the fulfilment of God's purposes on earth"—so runs the first sentence of *Die politischen Kräfte* (Breslau: Wilhelm Gottlieb Korn Verlag, 1933), 11, the first volume of the series *Das Ewige Reich* by then influential *völkisch* author Arthur Moeller van den Bruck. The word "Volk," incidentally, is derived from *folgen* (to follow [a leader)]), and also implies being part of a kind of "religious" community, that is to say, one based on eternal laws.
90. In this connection, see Wilhelm Wundt's works on *Volk* psychology.
91. Here one should not forget that at that time there was a widespread fear of international Communism, which appeared to be invincible following its victory in Russia.
92. Furthermore, the *völkisch* view assumes that personal salvation is closely bound up with the salvation of the *Volk.*
93. One of the most lastingly influential *völkisch* writers, Julius Langbehn, who contributed significantly to the emergence of a mass movement from the *völkisch* worldview, also had strong esoteric interests and was for a long time a Swedenborgian.
94. See, for example, the essays that he wrote for his own journal *Die Tat.* These were later collected together in Eugen Diederichs, *Politik des Geistes* (Jena: Eugen Diederichs, 1920). However, the fact that he was anything but a dull chauvinist is clear from the essays re-published there, e.g. "Das Völkische" (pp. 10–12) and "Der deutsche Gedanke" (pp. 12–15).
95. There is already an extensive literature on this extremely influential publishing house. Gangolf Hübinger's *Versammlungsort moderner Geister* has already been mentioned briefly. On the *völkisch* aspect, see especially Gary D. Stark, *Entrepreneurs of Ideology: Neoconservative Publishers in Germany, 1890–1933* (Chapel Hill, NC: University of North Carolina Press, 1981) and Mosse, *Ein Volk, ein Reich, ein Führer,* 62ff. Another book that should not be overlooked is Justus H. Ulbricht and Meike G. Werner, *Romantik, Revolution und Reform: Der Eugen Diederichs Verlag im Epochenkontext 1900–1949* (Göttingen: Wallstein Verlag, 1999), which investigates the publisher's search for a new religiosity—a theme we have encountered repeatedly—and for a new and at the same time "old" approach to life. At least a brief mention should also be made of Eugen Diederichs' pioneering achievements in the art of book production. He always sought to achieve a complementarity of content and form, placing great value on the choice of paper, typeface, and colors and on harmonious typography. See Walter G. Oschilewski, *Eugen Diederichs: ein Beitrag zur neuen deutschen Buchkunst* (privately published, 1989), which contains a series of pictures that bear witness to the aesthetic standards of the publisher.

96. *Der deutsche Buchhandel in Selbstdarstellungen*, vol. 2, part 1 (Leipzig: Felix Meiner, 1927), 43.

97. One should also not forget the old Nordic writings such as the Icelandic sagas and the *Edda*, which appeared in Diederichs' Thule series. Diederichs also published works by early Neopagans of the Germanic persuasion. See René Gründer, *Germanisches (Neu-)Heidentum in Deutschland* (Berlin: Logos-Verlag, 2008), 35ff.

98. Irmgard Heidler, *Der Verleger Eugen Diederichs und seine Welt* (Wiesbaden: Harrassowitz, 1998), 315. This work of almost a thousand pages presents an unrivaled overview of the many-faceted work of the publisher.

99. *Ibid.*, 87. However, if one reads Diederichs' essay "Vom Adel der Frau" (On the nobility of woman) in his book *Politik des Geistes*, 143–7, one sees that his views had little in common with modern feminism.

100. The volume, *Im Zeichen des Löwen: Für Eugen Diederichs zum LX. Jahr am XXII. Juni MCMCCVII* (Jena: Diederichs, 1927), was published under the coordination of the expert on Romanticism Richard Benz in an edition of only 330 copies.

101. The quotation is taken from Marino Pullio, *Une modernité explosive: La revue* Die Tat *dans les renouveaux religieux, culturels et politiques de l'Allemagne d'avant 1914–1918* (Geneva: Labor et Fides, 2008), 420.

102. *Ibid.*

103. The ecology movement, which today tends to be seen as belonging to the left, had its origins in the *Lebensreform* groups of around the turn of the twentieth century, which were often marked by *völkisch* thinking and were influenced by the *Wandervogel* (wandering birds) movement. What they had in common was their opposition to the industrialization and urbanization of modern life. The "green" aspect of the *völkisch* movement (today usually regarded as a right-wing movement) continued into the National Socialist period, in which it played a not insignificant role. See Anna Bramwell, *Blood and Soil: Richard Walter Darré and Hitler's "Green Party"* (Abbotsbrook: Kensal Press, 1985). This fundamentally nature-friendly attitude (although not where war preparations were concerned) led to Goering's signing of a vivisection ban, and to campaigns for a meat-free, roughage-rich diet intended to prevent illness (especially cancer). Above all, it led to the anti-alcohol and anti-smoking campaigns of the National Socialist regime. On the other hand, however, these efforts to promote better national health also encompassed the eugenics policies of the National Socialists.

104. Jeanne Hersch, "Mythos und Politik," in *Die Wirklichkeit des Mythos*, Kurt Hoffman (ed.) (Munich: Droemer Knaur, 1965), 89.

16. Eranos as a Prototype

1. I would like to express my sincerest gratitude to the ITAS participants Nuccio d'Anna, Piero Fenili, and Fabrizio Frigerio for the following information.

2. See *Politica Romana*, "Memoria di Boris de Rachewiltz," *Politica Romana* 4 (1997), 7.

3. On the matter of his intellectual development see Grazia Marchianò, *Elémire Zolla, il conoscitore di segreti. Una biografia intellettuale* (Milan: Rizzoli, 2006), as well as Grazia Marchianò (ed.), *Elémire Zolla dalla morte alla vita*, a special issue of *Viátor* 9 (2005–2006), which also includes a short report by Fabrizio Frigerio entitled "Un ricordo degli anni dell'Istituto Ticinese di Alti Studi (1970–1973)" (pp. 164–5). See also the volume of interviews Elémire Zolla and Doriano Fasoli, *Un destino itinerante*.

4. Paola Costantini, "C'era una volta l'Istituto di Alti Studi," *Corriere del Ticino*, 2 March 2009, 3. This article is the very first study of the ITAS itself. Contemporary journal articles only described particular aspects of the conferences; see, for example, "Nuove esperienze di metodo archeologico nella lezione del prof. de Rachewiltz," *Dovere* (10 October 1973), 7.

5. Elémire Zolla, "Romano Amerio," in Zolla, *Uscite dal mondo*, 449–52, esp. 450.

6. Among those attending this presentation was the author and publisher Giuseppe Prezzolini, who was then ninety years old. His periodical *La Voce* had been one of Italy's most renowned cultural journals in the years before the First World War, and its contributors had included everyone of note in the cultural domain. For this information I am grateful to the orientalist and author Nuccio d'Anna.

7. On this subject see the comprehensive dissertation by Mara Cella, *Elémire Zolla come fondatore di "Conoscenza Religiosa,"* PhD thesis, Università di Salerno, 1998–99. The numerous articles in the journal authored by the publisher himself have been collected along with an introduction by his wife Grazia Marchianò in a lengthy book: Elémire Zolla, *Conoscenza Religiosa: Scritti 1969–1983* (Rome: Edizioni di Storia e Letteratura, 2006).

8. "Editoriale," *Conoscenza Religiosa* 1 (1969).

9. Costantini, "C'era una volta l'Istituto di Alti Studi."

10. On this subject see the review of the conference of 1971 by P. Constantini in *Vie della Tradizione* 5 (1972), 46. The statute of ITAS—which unfortunately I do not have access to—allegedly stipulated that the "traditional orientation" of the conferences was mandatory.

11. Margherita Pieracci Harwell (ed.), *Cristina Campo Lettere a Mita* (Milan: Adelphi, 1999), 243.

12. Antoine Faivre's lectures at the Université Saint-Jean de Jérusalem have been reprinted in the two volumes of his *Accès de l'ésotérisme occidental*. See also his review of the first volumes of *Cahiers de l'Université Saint-Jean de Jérusalem* in *Aries* 1 (1985), 39–42.

13. According to Richard Stauffer, Corbin actually modeled this Université on Eranos; see Stauffer, "Adieu à Henry Corbin," 12.

14. In a diary entry dated 8 July 1975 he even mentions that he had been a founding member of the Université. See Eliade, *Journal III, 1970–1978*, 201. The rapport between Corbin and Eliade was evidently close and based upon the same principles. Steven Wasserstrom describes them both as "esoteric blood brothers" as well as "overtly mystifying esoterists" (*Religion after Religion*, 13). Corbin himself characterized their relationship as one of "brothers-in-arms," and as he recollected the many years of Eranos they had spent together he remarked, "In the philosophy of religion we always fought together on the same side of an invisible front." The battle was against "historicism" and "sociologism" in the history of religions, or "whatever one wishes to call those positions that culminate in a dead end." See Henry Corbin, "Mircea Eliade," in *Mircea Eliade*, Constantin Tacou (ed.) (Paris: L'Herne, 1978), 270ff. Moreover, Wasserstrom is convinced he can perceive a "metaphorical violence," extending beyond such bellicose utterances, that is fundamental to the language of both authors. He cites instances in which the two men do in fact appear to see themselves as united in a real combat group. Nevertheless, the evidence Wasserstrom supplies there concerning the medieval "Fedeli d'Amore"—whose historical existence cannot be ascertained—seems far-fetched to me, as in my opinion the "Fedeli" were concerned more with an inner transformation than an outer militia. On this subject see my multipart article "Die Getreuen der Liebe," *Gnostika* 4 (1997), 37–40; 5 (1998), 38–43; 7 (1998), 43–50; and 8 (1998), 41–50.

15. The nature of the association between the Université and the Order of St. John may be gleaned from the address by Robert de Chateaubriant: "L'Université Saint-Jean de Jérusalem, Ame de l'Ordre Souverain," *Cahier de l'Université Saint-Jean de Jérusalem* 1 (1975), 13–23.

16. A mystical religious movement of the Middle Ages that proliferated in southern and western Germany in particular. On this subject see Bernard Gorceix, *Amis de Dieu en Allemagne au siècle de Maître Eckhart* (Paris: Albin Michel, 1984).

17. On this subject see the introductory lecture by Henry Corbin on the occasion of the first sitting of the Université from 5 to 7 July 1974 in the abbey of Vaucelles: "L'Université Saint-Jean de Jérusalem: Centre International de Recherche Spirituelle Comparée," *Cahier de l'Université Saint-Jean de Jérusalem* (1975), 8–12.

18. Corbin namely sees in Abraham—who is a central figure in all three of the great monotheistic religions—the first "knight" whom the prophets follow.

19. On this subject see the interesting article by Giuliano Glauco: "Il Santo Graal del Cavaliere Henry Corbin," in *Atrium* 2(2) (2000), 14–26, as well as 2(3) (2000), 53–68, where allusions are also made to Eranos and affinities with the thought of Ernesto Buonaiuti. Giuliano Glauco wrote his dissertation on Corbin in Milan in 1997–98.

20. The prototype of this temple is the Temple of Solomon built upon a cliff, the destruction of which causes the "exile" (which is also to be understood in a spiritual sense). In the course of the Eranos conference of 1974 Corbin alluded specifically to the relationship of the Temple of Solomon to the shrine of the Grail castle, from which arises a connection between the Christian Templars and the Celto-Germanic spiritual tradition. Corbin's lecture, entitled "L'Imago Templi face aux normes profanes," is preceded in the written edition by the words of Vladimir Maximov: "All is dust and ashes, all but the temple within us." See *Eranos Jahrbuch* 43 (1974), 183. This article was then reprinted in English translation in *Spring* in 1975. What is more, Corbin sees the same etymological root in the words "temple" and "contemplation." Gilbert Durand looks upon Corbin's work *Temple et Contemplation: Essais sur l'Islam iranien* (Paris: Flammarion, 1981) as his spiritual testament.

21. As both a plan for and a commentary upon the Université, Henry Corbin's address "Science Traditionelle et Renaissance Spirituelle" is surely the most informative and clearest document we possess, as well as being the most illuminating *vis-à-vis* the emotional and spiritual background of the Université. This address was given on the occasion of its opening in 1974, and like other programmatic addresses mentioned above it may be consulted in the first *Cahier de l'Université Saint-Jean de Jérusalem* 1(1975), 25–51.

22. It would be interesting to investigate the extent to which Corbin's conceptions of a "spiritual knighthood" were influenced by his earlier friendships with Roger Caillois and George Bataille. All of them were in the so-called College of Sociology (which advanced a sacred sociology), and in connection with the journal *Acéphale* they were occupied with thoughts of a secret order that would possess its own rites and in which "sacrifice" would play a central role. Here too there seems to have been a concern with a "type of heroic knighthood that should bear the myth anew in a society on the verge of disintegration." For an introduction to the subject see Stéphane Massonet, "Le collège de sociologie: Sociologie, secret et communauté," *Antaios* 5 (1994), 20–34; for a more detailed treatment see Stephan Moebius, *Die Zauberlehrlinge: Soziologiegeschichte des Collège de Sociologie (1937–1939)* (Constance: UVK Verlagsgesellschaft, 2006).

23. In *Voix du Nord*. Unfortunately I cannot determine the exact date of publication, as I only have a photocopy of the article to hand.

24. Stella Corbin had supposedly dreamt of the number fourteen, and interpreted the dream to mean that her deceased husband thereby wished to communicate the number of the last sitting of the Université.

25. Not to be confused with the Centre de recherche spirituelle comparée des Réligions du Livre founded by Henry Corbin in 1974, from which the Université de Saint-Jean de Jérusalem emerged.

26. In the meantime Durand has nevertheless broken away from the group due to disagreements.

27. Cahiers du Groupe d'Etudes Spirituelles Comparées, *Transmission culturelle, transmission spirituelle: Colloque tenu en Sorbonne les 13 et 14 Juin* (Paris: Archè-Edidit, 1993), 9ff.

28. Published by Arché-Edidit, Paris, the home of two other journals dealing with "esoteric" themes in an academic manner: *Charis: Archives del'Unicorne* (which regrettably appears only irregularly) as well as *Aries* (until 2001). Operating under the leadership of Laszlo Toth, Arché-Edidit specializes in reprinting otherwise hard-to-find esoteric works in short print runs, as well as publishing exceptional research work in this field.

29. Published by Albin Michel, Paris.

30. See the third issue (1981) of the lodge journal, *Travaux de la Loge nationale de recherches Villard de Honnecourt*, 181.

31. Thus in addition the most notable names in the French study of esotericism can be seen here, such as Roland Edighoffer, Jean-Jacques Wuneberger, Jean-Pierre Laurant, Bernard Gorceix, Marie-Madeleine Davy, Frédérick Tristan, Alain Mercier, Jean Thomas, etc., in addition to individuals present there who are still to be discussed specifically.

32. In the article "'Costruiremo ancora cattedrali': L'esoterismo cristiano da Giovanni Cantoni a Massimo Introvigne," written by an author styling himself "Padre Torquemada" and published in the fundamentalist Catholic, anti-Freemasonic journal of the Istituto Mater Boni Consilii, *Sodalitium* 50 (1999), 16–35, one finds the accusation that Eranos was strongly influenced by Freemasonry. In the course of the article the multi-volume *Nuova Enciclopedia Massonica* (Foggia: Bastogi, 1998) by Michele Moramarco is cited (see therein the sub-chapter "Massoni del gruppo di 'Eranos," vol. 1, 469–71; in the attached "Materials and Documents," 569–74, a contribution by Kerényi entitled "Sul mito della massoneria" is also to be found). The importance of Freemasonry for the advent of the comparative study of religions is alluded to here; of the Freemasons amongst the early Eranos speakers and founders of the academic study of religion, I only mention Erwin Rousselle, Karl Kerényi, and Raffaele Pettazzoni. The certificate of initiation of Pettazzoni is reproduced in Mola, *Storia della Massoneria italiana dalle origini ai nostri giorni*, 806ff. Although he was not a member himself, Jung came from a family active within Freemasonry—his grandfather Karl Gustav and uncle Ernest were masters of the Swiss Grand Lodge Alpina. See Daniel Ligou (ed.), *Dictionnaire Universel de la Franc-Maçonnerie* (Paris: Editions de Navarre, Editions du Prisme, 1974), 710.

33. Daniel Roche and Jazques Revuz, "La session de l'Université Saint-Jean de Jérusalem (Journées d'étude des 12, 13 et 14 juin 1981)," *Travaux de la Loge nationale de recherches Villard de Honnecourt* 4 (1982), 190–204.

34. Clearly the idea of a reintegration is central to the thought of Eliade. Corbin and his *chevallerie spirituelle* also employ this term. Wasserstrom adds that Gershom Scholem also spoke of "reintegration" and read Louis Claude de Saint-Martin, the student of Martinès de Pasqually. See *Religion after Religion*, 38. See also the first authentic edition of Martinès de Pasqually, *Traité sur la réintégration des êtres dans leur première propriété, vertu et puissance spirituelle divine*, R. Amadou (ed.) (Chateau d'Omonville: Diffusion Rosicrucienne, 1996).

35. Although his viewpoint is perhaps a little overstated, Wasserstrom sees the Christian Kabbalah as the underlying link between Corbin, Eliade, and Scholem. See *Religion after Religion*, 37–51.

36. See the article by Andreas Kilcher entitled "Okkulte Sprache und bürgerliche Rationalität: Zur Rezeption der Kabbala in der Freimaurerei" in the literary section of the *Neue Zürcher Zeitung* (1–2 June 1996).

37. For a detailed history see Antoine Faivre, *Les Conférences des Elus Cohens de Lyon (1774–1776). Aux sources du Rite Ecossais Rectifié* (Braine-le-Comte: Editions du Baucens, 1975), for which Gilbert Durand wrote the fore-word; see also Antoine Faivre, *L'ésotérisme au XVIIIe siècle en France et en Allemagne* (Paris: Seghers, La Table d'Emeraude, 1973), in which the third chapter entitled "Histoire de la Franc-maçonnerie mystique" (pp. 145–86) is particularly pertinent. Also worthy of note are the principal works of René le Forestier, *La Franc-Maçonnerie templière et occultiste aux XVIIIe et XIXe siècles* (Paris: La Table d'Emeraude, 1987) and *La Franc-Maçonnerie occultiste au XVIIIe siècle & l'Ordre des Elus Coens* (Paris: La Table d'Emeraude, 1987), both published almost ten years after the death of their author with introductions and additional scholarly commentaries by Faivre. Incidentally, Mircea Eliade held these works in high esteem ("Occultism and Freemasonry in Eighteenth-Century Europe," *History of Religions* 13[1] [1973], 89–91). In an article by Jean-François Var ("L'essor du phénix: Jean-Baptiste Willermoz et la naissance du Régime Ecossais Rectifié," *Travaux de la loge nationale de recherches Villard de Honnecourt* 19 [1989], 177) Faivre himself was described as "one of the greatest authorities on the *inside* [italics in the original] of the Rectified Rite." This article by Var sets out the history of the development of the Rite from a perspective within Freemasonry.

38. On this subject see *Travaux de la loge nationale de recherches Villard de Honnecourt* 15 (1987), which is dedi-cated to the theme "Les origines judéo-chretiennes de la Franc-Maçonnerie." See also the interview held by Antoine Faivre with Jean Tourniac, the long-standing head of the RER. A transcript of the original radio pro-gram (France-Culture on 22 May 1981) can be found in *Travaux* 5, 114–18. Jean Tourniac also wrote the prin-cipal works on these themes, above all *Principes et problèmes spirituels du Rite Ecossais Rectifié et de sa chevalerie templière* (Paris: Dervy-Livres, 1969 and 1985) as well as *Symbolisme maçonnique et tradition chretienne: "Un itinéraire spirituel d'Israël au Christ?"* (Paris: Dervy, 1965). See also Paul Naudon, *La Franc-Maçonnerie chré-tienne: La tradition opérative, l'Arche Royale de Jérusalem, le rite Ecossais rectifié* (Paris: Dervy-Livres, 1970), in particular 13ff. From a perspective within the lodge see the article by Jean-François Var, "L'Esotérisme chrétien et le Régime Ecossais Rectifié" in *Travaux* 31 (1995), 185–228.

39. Gilbert Durand, "La pensée d'Henry Corbin et le temple maçonnique," *Travaux* 3 (1981), 173–82.

40. For further information on Corbin's chivalric-spiritual path, see Jean Clergue-Vila, "En quête d'Henry Corbin, franc-maçon chevaleresque," *L'Initiation* 2 (2009), 85–114.

41. Durand describes yet another conversation "under the cedars of Eranos" which he had in 1966. During its course Corbin stated that to the question of whether he could join a *tariqâ* (an esoteric Islamic order under the spiritual leadership of a sheik) he had received an interesting answer from just such a sheik, who had said that this would be quite possible if he had already undergone some form of initiation, such as into Freemasonry.

42. Mircea Eliade, "Initiation et monde moderne," *Travaux de la Loge nationale de recherches Villard de Honnecourt* 1 (1980), 21–9.

43. That does not mean that Eliade himself was a Freemason. Quite the contrary: Natale Spineto cites an as yet unpublished passage from Eliade's diary dated 17 June 1959 in which Eliade explicitly appears as a non-Freemason and asserts that he does not "feel attracted to Freemasonry." See Spineto, "Mircea Eliade and Traditionalism," 83.

44. Frédérick Tristan, "Mircea Eliade: In Memoriam," recorded in *Travaux* 12 (1986), 217–19.

45. Derived from Julius Schwabe, "Preface," in *Symbolon Violet* (Basel: Benno Schwabe Verlag, 1960).

46. In the current introductory brochure on the work of the society it is also mentioned that the famed symbol researcher Manfred Lurker was a founding member of the society.

47. Like Engelson, the author of the preface, Julius Schwabe, uses the term "traditional" explicitly "in the sense of René Guénon, Julius Evola and Leopold Ziegler" (*Symbolon* 7). In this introduction Evola is also mentioned positively as the author of a text from the collective volumes Gruppo di Ur (ed.), *Introduzione alla Magia quale scienza dell'Io* (Turin: Bocca, 1955).

48. *Symbolon* 1 (1960); the next two citations are also from this source.

49. *Ibid.*, emphasis added.

50. Unfortunately this lecture has not survived. Radin was already so ill when the conference volume was being prepared for publication that he did not reply to the request for the manuscript, and he died shortly thereafter.

51. Franz Vonessen, who equally collaborated in the Gesellschaft für Ganzheitsforschung (Society for holistic research), was also a leading member of the Socrates Society, wherefrom one may discern his commitment to the preservation of a philosophy that seeks to unify Mythos and Logos.

52. The current secretary of the society, Axel Voss, has nevertheless confirmed that he is very favorably disposed towards Eranos.

53. Letter of 4 February 2010.

54. Ernst Thomas Reimbold, foreword to *Symbolon: Jahrbuch für Symbolforschung* 1, n.s., 9.

55. *Ibid.*,10.

56. Ernst Thomas Reimbold, "Gedanken zur Arbeit unserer Gesellschaft," in the preamble to *Symbolon* 3, n.s., 12.

57. *Symbolon* 3, new series, 13. This last sentence actually derives from the philosopher Franz Vonessen.

58. In his above-mentioned letter. A position statement of the society is to be found in Joachim Gaus, "Wege, Methoden und Probleme der Symbolforschung: ein Diskussionspapier," *Symbolon* 8, new series (1986), 9–34.

59. www.symbolforschung.org.

60. In the preface to the first conference volume, 11, the founder of the aforementioned Gesellschaft für Symbolforschung, Julius Schwabe, nevertheless also addresses Walter Heinrich as "our collaborator."

61. The authors and titles of contributions are listed at www.ganzheitsforschung.at according to their respective subject areas, which makes searching much easier given the numerous volumes and entries.

62. "*Gnostika* is the most important publication in the German language" (Anton Faivre, *Esoterik im Überblick* [Freiburg: Herder, 2001], 150).

63. "In its own special way *Gnostika* is without match and even internationally I know of nothing better" (promotion on the cover of the journal).

64. There exist only two articles on this journal: Alexander Pschera, "'Heilige Tiefe und geistiger Überblick': Eliade, Jünger und die Zeitschrift, *Antaios* (1959–1971)," *Sezession* 16 (2007) 18–23, which gives a general overview; and Hakl, "'Den *Antaios* kenne und missbillige ich. Was er pflegt, ist nicht Religio, sondern Magie!' Kurze Geschichte der Zeitschrift *Antaios*," in which the history of the journal is dealt with in great detail. A shorter version of this article has also appeared in Italian: Hakl, "'L'effetto, pur non esteso, è stato profondo come quello d'una sonda.' Breve storia della rivista 'Antaios', curata da Mircea Eliade ed Ernst Jünger (1959–1971)."

65. Publisher's prospectus announcing the appearance of *Antaios*.

66. The lectures of the IsMEO conference of 1955, which conform to what one might call an "Eranian" theme, are collected in one volume. See Giuseppe Tucci (ed.), *Le symbolisme cosmique des monuments religieux* (Rome: IsMEO, 1957). Amongst the "Eranian" participants were Jean Daniélou, Mircea Eliade, Henri-Charles Puech, and naturally Giuseppe Tucci himself. Claude Lévi-Strauss also spoke.

67. Eliade, *Exile's Odyssey*, 144.

68. In a letter to Mircea Eliade dated 7 August 1951 Tucci speaks again of a plan to call together a dozen specialists in Rome in order to discuss, for example, the clash of Eastern and Western thought. See Mincu and Scagno (eds), *Mircea Eliade e l'Italia*, 248.

69. Maria Pia Rosati, "Psicoanalisi e transdisciplinarità. L'Istituo Mythos e l'eredità di Eranos," www.atopon.it/index.php?page=psicoanalisi-e-transdisciplinarita.

70. As mentioned earlier, Marie Amélie de Robilant is reported to have been one of the financial benefactors of Eranos.

71. The themes range from Plato and Kabbalah to German Romanticism. Many of the lectures are subsequently made available in printed form or as recordings. Each year an Interfaith Lecture is held. See the brochure *Temenos Academy: An Academy for Education in the Light of the Spirit*.

72. HRH Prince of Wales, "The Civilized Society," *Temenos Academy Review* 3 (2000), 5.

73. Several of these participants first met each other in person at a conference on the theme "Le Défi magique" at the Bibliothèque Municipale in Lyon, 6–8 April 1992.

74. On the history of this chair, see especially Roelof van den Broek, "The Birth of a Chair" and Wouter J. Hanegraaff, "Ten Years of Studying and Teaching Western Esotericism," in *Hermes in the Academy: Ten Years' Study of Western Esotericism at the University of Amsterdam*, Wouter J. Hanegraaff and Joyce Pijnenburg (eds) (Amsterdam: Amsterdam University Press, 2009), 11–15, 17–26.

75. www.esswe.org

76. Michael Murphy had previously led an eventful life. He had met Roberto Assagioli, who played a certain part in the early phase of Eranos. He had also lived for a time in Sri Aurobindo's ashram in Pondicherry. See Taylor, *Shadow Culture*.

77. A brief portrait of Friedrich Spiegelberg is included in the section entitled "Eranos 1936."

78. Kripal, *Esalen*, 188ff. This book is by far the most informative and detailed study of the Esalen phenomenon. Together with Glenn W. Shuck, Kripal has also written another book on the same theme: *On the Edge of the Future: Esalen and the Evolution of American Culture* (Bloomington, IN: Indiana University Press, 2005).

79. Kripal, *Esalen*, 6.

80. Email from Jeffrey J. Kripal to the author, dated 25 April 2005.

81. Kripal, *Esalen*, 6.

82. On this subject see Anderson, *The Upstart Spring*.

83. In this connection, see Jeffrey Kripal, "The Roar of Awakening: The Eros of Esalen and the Western Transmission of Tantra," in *Hidden Intercourse: Eros and Sexuality in the History of Western Esotericism*, Wouter Hanegraaff and Jeffrey J. Kripal (eds) (Leiden: Brill, 2008), 479–519. The contributions to this volume were originally delivered as lectures at Esalen in 2005.

84. See "Esalen and the Counterculture Movement of the 1960s" in Taylor, *Shadow Culture*, 235–59.

85. See Wouter Hanegraaff, "Introduction: The Birth of a Discipline," in *Western Esotericism and the Science of Religion*, Antoine Faivre and Wouter Hanegraaff (eds) (Leuven: Peters, 1998), ii.

86. See Antoine Faivre and Karen-Claire Voss, "Western Esotericism and the Science of Religion," *Numen* 42(1) (1995), 59 and 75 n.42.

87. *Die Zerstörung der Vernunft* (Berlin: Aufbau Verlag, 1954).

88. James Webb's *The Flight from Reason* is subtitled *The Age of the Irrational* (London: Macdonald, 1971). Here the interesting psychological question arises to what extent the authors of such visions are attempting to bridle their own fear of irrational tendencies within themselves by projecting these fears on to world. James Webb could be an example, as is arguably evidenced by his tragically premature death by suicide—allegedly because of his fear of persecution by followers of the Caucasian "magus" George I. Gurdjieff, about whom Webb wrote what is perhaps the most informative book to date, namely *The Harmonious Circle* (London: Thames & Hudson, 1980). To reduce his suicide motive to manic depression is perhaps too simplistic. See my article on Webb's *Das Zeitalter des Irrationalen*, in *Gnostika* 42 (July 2009), 17–20.

17. The End of a Cycle … or Perhaps Not

1. Actually one should also divide the thought processes of the individual Eranos participants into phases, but this is of course outside the scope of the present work. Consequently it has been impossible to avoid a certain degree of distortion and a blurring of earlier and later phases, resulting sometimes in contradictions and partially false statements.

2. In this connection I like the statement of the scholar of religion Giovanni Filoramo, who speaks of gnosis as the "Orient of the Occident." See Giovanni Filoramo, *Figure del sacro: Saggi di storia religiosa* (Brescia: Morcelliana, 1993), 173.

3. This does not mean that Jung fundamentally rejected esotericism. Probably it was rather his scientific reputation that concerned him. He did not wish Eranos—"his" forum—to be exposed to unnecessary attacks.

4. Leonard Shlain takes this question further in his book *The Alphabet Versus the Goddess: Male Words and Female Images* (Harmondsworth: Penguin, 1998), a thought-provoking work, full of cross-references from brain research, anthropology, and the history of religion. Shlain connects the development of a culture based on reading and writing with the rise of the patriarchal system of rulership. He maintains that through literacy the left side of the brain became disproportionately developed, leading automatically to a disempowerment of the concrete, holistic, visual, and "feminine" way of thinking.

5. Here it is relevant to mention Kant's *Träume eines Geistersehers* (Dreams of a visionary), where he clearly— albeit not very tactfully—expresses his own attitude to "esoteric" thought: "If there is a hypochondriac wind in

a person's innards the question is whether it goes up or down. If it goes down it comes out as a f… However, if it goes up it becomes a manifestation or a holy revelation." See Immanuel Kant, *Werke in zehn Bänden* (Darmstadt: Wissenschaftliche Buchgesellschaft, 1981), vol. 2, 959ff.

6. Quoted from *Das Andere der Vernunft: Zur Entwicklung von Rationalitätsstrukturen am Beispiel Kants* (Frankfurt: Suhrkamp, [1985] 1996), 11. The introduction to this book, from which the passage is quoted, concisely summarizes the history of the struggle for rationality and its consequences for nature and for the "feminine." A very good view of this controversy is also provided by Christoph Jamme in his essay "Rationalität, Naturbeherrschung und Mythos: eine Skizze," in *Mnemosyne: Festschrift für Manfred Lurker zum 60. Geburtstag*, Werner Bies und Hermann Jung (eds), in the series Bibliographie zur Symbolik, Ikonographie und Mythologie, Ergänzungsband 2 (Baden-Baden: Valentin Koerner, 1988), 9–15.

7. Here I cannot and do not wish to go into the question of whether "femininity" is to be understood as something essential to one of the two sexes or merely as a linguistic and cultural construct. The well-disposed reader will surely understand what I mean by the word.

8. In this connection I should also mention the radio program of 28 August 1974, broadcast by Funkhaus Hamburg in the series *Journal 3*, on "Normen im Wandel der Zeit an der diesjährigen Eranostagung."

9. On this subject, see Verena von der Heyden-Rynsch, *Europäische Salons: Höhepunkte einer versunkenen weiblichen Kultur* (Düsseldorf: Artemis & Winckler, 1992). Here one should also mention again Hertha Jay von Seldeneck, who wished to develop a similar scholarly/cultural salon in Ascona, but with less successful results than Olga Fröbe. Did she perhaps lack the sharp, goading influence of the daemon?

10. Hornung, "Wo sich grosse Geister finden," 28.

🐎 Bibliography

Abe, M. "The Influence of D.T. Suzuki in the West." In *A Zen Life: D.T. Suzuki Remembered*, edited by M. Abe, 95–117. New York: Weatherhill, 1986.

Accart, X. *Guénon ou le renversement des clartés: Influence d'un métaphysicien sur la vie littéraire et intellectuelle française (1920–1970)*. Paris: Editit Arché, 2005.

Adam, A. *Die Psalmen des Thomas und das Perlenlied als Zeugnisse vorchristlicher Gnosis*. Berlin: Alfred Töpelmann, 1959.

Adorno, T.W. "Gruß an Gershom G. Scholem: Zum 70. Geburtstag." *Neue Zürcher Zeitung* (2 December 1967).

A.E. "Glossen zur Zeit." *Die Tat* 26(10) (1935): 790–92.

Agrippa, H.C. *La magie cérémonielle*. Edited by J. Servier. Paris: L'Ile Verte, Berg International, 1982.

Agrippa, H.C. *La magie naturelle*. Edited by J. Servier. Paris: L'Ile Verte, Berg International, 1982.

Aland, B. "Gnosis und Kirchenväter." In *Gnosis: Festschrift für Hans Jonas*, edited by B. Aland, 158–215. Göttingen: Vandenbroek & Ruprecht, 1978.

Aland, B. *Was ist Gnosis? Studien zum frühen Christentum, zu Marcion und zur kaiserzeitlichen Philosophie*. Tübingen: Mohr Siebeck, 2009.

Aland, B. "Was ist Gnosis? Wie wurde sie überwunden? Versuch einer Kurzdefinition." In *Gnosis und Politik*, edited by J. Taubes, 54. Munich: Wilhelm Fink, 1984.

Alastair. *Das flammende Tal: Gedichte*. Munich: Hyperion, 1920.

Albrecht, R. and W. Schüßler (eds). *Paul Tillich: Sein Werk*. Düsseldorf: Patmos, 1986.

Alexandrescu, S. "Per una discussione filosofica dell'opera di Mircea Eliade." In *Confronto con Mircea Eliade*, 401. Milan: Jaca Book, 1998.

Alleau, R. and G. Le Scouézec. *Encyclopédie de la Divination*. Paris: Editions Veyrier, 1973.

Alego, A.S. "Beatrice Lane Suzuki and Theosophy in Japan." *Theosophical History* 9(3) (2005): 3–16.

Allen, D. "Encounters with Mircea Eliade." In *Professor Mircea Eliade: Reminiscences*, edited by M. Gligor & M. Linscott Ricketts, 17–30. Kolkata: Codex, 2008.

Allen, D. "Ist Eliade antihistorisch?" In *Die Mitte der Welt: Aufsätze zu Mircea Eliade*, edited by H.P. Duerr, 106–27. Frankfurt: Suhrkamp, 1984.

Alles, G.D. "Rudolf Otto (1869–1937)." In *Klassiker der Religionswissenschaft*, edited by A. Michaels, 198–210. Munich: C.H. Beck, 1997.

Alles, G.D. "Rudolf Otto and the Politics of Utopia." *Religion* 21 (1991): 235–56.

Alles, G.D. "The Science of Religion in a Fascist State: Rudolf Otto and Jakob Wilhelm Hauer During the Third Reich." *Religion* 32 (2002): 177–204.

Altheim, F. *Italien und Rom*. Amsterdam: Akademische Verlagsanstalt Pantheon, 1941.

Altmann, A. *Essays in Jewish Intellectual History*. Hanover, NH: University Press of New England, 1981.

Alvi, G. *Uomini del Novecento*. Milan: Adelphi, 1995.

Amann, B. "Codreanu's Erben: Die Legionärsbewegung im postrevolutionären Rumänien." *Neue Ordnung* 4 (2004): 23–6.

Ambix. "Obituary, Gérard Heym, 1888–1972." *Ambix* 19 (1972): 216–17.

Amgarten, R. "Eranos-Inventar und Idee für Zukunft retten." *Tessiner Zeitung* (22–3 July 2004).

Ammann, W. (ed.). *Hans Kayser zum 100. Geburtstag: Biographische Fragmente*. Bern: Kreis der Freunde um Hans Kayser, 1991.

Anderes, A. *Reflexionen zu den "Atma"-Durchsagen des Mediums Oskar Schlag*. Uster: Ratio Humana, 2005.

Anderson, W.T. *The Upstart Spring: Esalen and the Human Potential Movement: The First Twenty Years*. Lincoln, NE: Authors Guild Back-in-Print, 2004.

Andreotti, G. *I quattro del Gesù: Storia di un'eresia*. Milan: Rizzoli, 1999.

de Angulo, X. "Comments on a Doctoral Thesis." In *C.G. Jung Speaking: Interviews and Encounters*, edited by W. McGuire and R.F.C. Hull, 205–18. Princeton, NJ: Princeton University Press, 1977.

de Angulo, X. and W. Roelli. *Eranos Reborn*. DVD. Moscia-Ascona: Eranos Foundation, 2007. Includes footage from 1950 silent film about Eranos.

Anonymous. *A Wakeful Wife*. Utrecht: Eureka Editions, 1999.

Anonymous. *Der neue Roman: ein Almanach*. Leipzig: Kurt Wolff Verlag, 1917.

Antaios. "Penser le paganisme: entretien avec Alain de Benoist." *Antaios* 11 (1996): 10–23.

Anthony, M. *The Valkyries: The Women Around Jung*. Longmead: Element Books, 1990.

Arcella, L., P. Pisi, and R. Scagno. *Confronto con Mircea Eliade*. Milan: Jaca Book, 1998.

Ashtinyānī, S.J. al-Dīn, H. Matsubura, T. Iwami, and A. Matsumoto (eds). "Curriculum Vitae of Toshihiko Izutsu." In *Consciousness and Reality: Studies in Memory of Toshihiko Izutsu*. Leiden: Brill, 2000.

Assagioli, R. *Jung and Psychosynthesis*. New York: Psychosynthesis Research Foundation, 1967.

Assagioli, R. *Le vie dello spirito*. Reprint n.p., n.d.

Assmann, J. *Die Mosaische Unterscheidung oder der Preis des Monotheismus*. Munich: Carl Hanser, 2003.

Assmann, J. "In honour of Erik Hornung's 70th birthday." *Neue Zürcher Zeitung* (28 January 2003), 54.

Assmann, J. *The Price of Monotheism*. Stanford, CA: Stanford University Press, 2010.

Astrov, V. *Das Leben Rudolf Maria Holzapfels*. Jena: Eugen Diederichs, 1928.

Avens, R. *Imaginal Body: Para-Jungian Reflections on Soul, Imagination and Death*. Washington, DC: University Press of America, 1982.

Avens, R. "The Subtle Realm: Corbin, Sufism and Swedenborg." In *Emanuel Swedenborg: A Continuing Vision*, edited by R. Larsen, 382–91. New York: Swedenborg Foundation, 1988.

Bach, H.I. Obituary. *The Synagogue Review* (January 1957). Published in German in *Worte des Gedenkens für Leo Baeck*. Heidelberg: Lambert Schneider Verlag, 1959.

Baeck, L. *Aus drei Jahrtausenden: Wissenschaftliche Untersuchungen und Abhandlungen zur Geschichte des jüdischen Glaubens*. Tübingen: J.C.B. Mohr, 1958.

Baeck, L. *Das Wesen des Judentums*. Wiesbaden: Fourier, 1988.

Baeck, L. "Die Spannung im Menschen und der fertige Mensch." In *Der Leuchter: Weltanschauung und Lebensgestaltung*, vol. 4, 117–41. Darmstadt: Otto Reichl, 1923.

Baeck, L. "Geist und Blut." In *Mensch und Kosmos*, edited by E. von Dungern. Düsseldorf: Droste Verlag, 1949.

Baeck, L. *Wege im Judentum: Aufsätze und Reden*. Berlin: Schocken Verlag, 1933.

Baeck, L. *Werke, vol. 6: Briefe, Reden, Aufsätze*. Gütersloh: Gütersloher Verlagshaus, 2006.

Baier, K. *Yoga auf dem Wege nach Westen: Beiträge zur Rezeptionsgeschichte*. Würzburg: Königshausen & Neumann, 1998.

Bailey, A.A. *Master Index of the Books of Alice Bailey*. London: Lucis Press, 1997.

Bailey, A.A. *Ponder on This: From the Writings of Alice A. Bailey and the Tibetan Master Djwhal Khul*. London: Lucis Press, 1971.

Bailey, A.A. *The Unfinished Autobiography*. New York: Lucis Press, 1973.

Bailey, F. *Changing Esoteric Values*. Tunbridge Wells: Lucis Press, 1955.

Bailey, F. *The Spirit of Masonry*. Tunbridge Wells: Lucis Press, 1957.

Baillet, P. "Monte Verità (1900–1920) ou la complexité du 'romantisme anticapitaliste': Une première approche historique et bio-bibliographique." *Politica Hermetica* 14 (2000): 199–218.

Baillet, P. "Monte Verità: Une 'communauté alternative' entre mouvance völkisch et avant-garde artistique." In *Nouvelle Ecole* 52 (2001): 109–35.

Bair, D. *Jung: A Biography*. Boston, MA: Little Brown, 2003.

Bancroft, M. *Autobiography of a Spy*. New York: William Morrow, 1983.

Bareau, A. *Mélanges d'histoire des religions offerts à Henri-Charles Puech*. Paris: Presses Universitaires de France, 1974.

Barker, M. "Eranos 1976." *Bulletin of the Analytical Psychology Club of New York* 38(7) (1976): 8–12.

Barone, E. "Eranos Tagungen: Dal mito alla filosofia?" *Filosofia e Teologia* 8(1) (1995): 149–65.

Barone, E., A. Fabris, and F.F. Monceri (eds). *Eranos, Monte Verità, Ascona*. Pisa: ETS, 2003.

Barone, E. M. Riedel, and A. Tischel (eds). *Pioniere, Poeten, Professoren: Eranos und der Monte Verità in der Zivilisationsgeschichte des 20. Jahrhunderts*. Würzburg: Königshausen & Neumann, 2004. Published in Italian as *Eranos, Monte Verità, Ascona*. Pisa: ETS, 2003.

Barrows, J.H. (ed.). *The World's Parliament of Religions: The Columbian Exposition of 1893*. Chicago, IL: Parliament Publishing, 1893.

Bassetti-Sani, G. *Louis Massignon (1883–1962): Christian Ecumenist: Prophet of Inter-Religious Reconciliation*. Chicago, IL: Franciscan Herald Press, 1974.

Baßler, M. and H. Châtelier. *Mystique, mysticisme et modernité en Allemagne autour de 1900/ Mystik, Mystizismus und Moderne in Deutschland um 1900*. Strasbourg: Presses Universitaires de Strasbourg, 1998.

Bauer, W. "Zeugen aus der Ferne: Der Eugen Diederichs Verlag und das deutsche China-Bild." In *Versammlungsort moderner Geister: Der Eugen Diederichs Verlag: Aufbruch ins Jahrhundert der Extreme*, edited by G. Hübinger, 450–85. Munich: Diederichs, 1996.

Bauman, Z. *Flaneure, Spieler und Touristen: Essays zu postmodernen Lebensformen*. Hamburg: Hamburger Edition, 1997.

Baumann, S. "Völkische Religionen und Antisemitismus." Speech delivered in October 1999 at Eberhard-Universität Tübingen.

Baumann, S. *Die Deutsche Glaubensbewegung und ihr Begründer Jakob Wilhelm Hauer (1881–1962)*. Marburg: Diagonal, 2005.

Baur, F.C. *Die christliche Gnosis*. Tübingen: C.F. Osiander, 1835.

Begbauer, H. *Eric Voegelins Kritik an der Moderne*. Würzburg: Ergon, 2000.

Bein, S. "Antaios: Symbol ohne Gegenwart." *Wort und Welt* 26 (1970): 10–11.

Bein, S. "Zwei Zeitschriften und die Brüder Jünger." *Wort und Welt* 26 (1970): 573–76.

Beller, S. "Herzl, Wagner and the Ironies of 'True Emancipation'. In *Tainted Greatness: Antisemitism and Cultural Heroes*, edited by N.A. Harrowitz, 127–55. Philadelphia, PA: Temple University Press, 1994.

Benavides, G. "Afterreligion after Religion." *Journal of the American Academy of Religion* 69(2) (2001): 449–58.

Benavides, G. "Giuseppe Tucci, or Buddhology in the Age of Fascism." In *Curators of the Buddha*, edited by D.R. Lopez, Jr., 161–96. Chicago, IL: University of Chicago Press, 1995.

Benavides, G. "Jakob Wilhelm Hauer, or Karmayoga as a Cold War Weapon." In *The Academic Study of Religion during the Cold War: East and West*, edited by I. Doležlová, L.H. Martin and D. Papoušek, 225–38. New York: Peter Lang, 2001.

Bendiscioli, M. *Neopaganesimo razzista*. Brescia: Morcelliana, 1937.

Benn, G. *Briefe an F.W. Oelze 1932–1945*. Frankfurt: Fischer Taschenbuch, 1986.

Benn, G. "Goethe und die Naturwissenschaften." *Die neue Rundschau* 43(4) (1932).

Benz, E. "Einige Erinnerungen an Ernesto Buonaiuti (1881–1946)." *Zeitschrift für Religions- und Geistesgeschichte* 28 (1976): 161–71.

Benz, E. "Grundformen der buddhistischen Meditation." *Terra Nova*, vol. 2: *Das große Gespräch der Religionen*, 47–88. Munich: Ernst Reinhardt, 1964.

Benz, E. "In Memoriam." In *A Zen Life: D. T. Suzuki Remembered*, edited by M. Abe, 131–5. New York: Weatherhill, 1986.

Benz, E. *Zen in westlicher Sicht: Zen-Buddhismus—Zen Snobbismus*. Weilheim: O.W. Barth, 1962.

Benz, R. *Im Zeichen des Löwen: Für Eugen Diederichs zum LX. Jahr am XXII. Juni MCMXXVII*. Jena: Diederichs, 1927.

Bergbauer, H. *Eric Voegelins Kritik an der Moderne*. Würzburg: Ergon, 2000.

Berger, A. "Mircea Eliade: Romanian Fascism and the History of Religions in the United States." In *Tainted Greatness*, edited by N.A. Harrowitz, 51–74. Philadelphia, PA: Temple University Press, 1994.

Bergunder, M. "Religionsphänomenologische Methode." In *Wiedergeburt der Ahnen: Eine religionsethnographische und religionsphänomenologische Untersuchung zur Reinkarnationsvorstellung*, 86–93. Münster: LIT Verlag, 1993.

Bergunder, M. *Wiedergeburt der Ahnen: Eine religionsethnographische und religionsphänomenologische Untersuchung zur Reinkarnationsvorstellung*. Münster: LIT Verlag 1993.

Berl, H. *Gespräche mit berühmten Zeitgenossen*. Baden-Baden: Hans Bühler, 1946.

Berlin, I. *The Magus of the North: J.G. Hamann and the Origins of Modern Irrationalism*. New York: Farrar, Straus & Giroux, 1993.

Bernardini, R. *Carl Gustav Jung e Eranos*. PhD thesis, Università di Bologna, 2009.

Bernardini, R. *Da Monte Verità a Eranos: Elementi di una rete culturale per lo studio della psiche e della complessità umana*. PhD thesis, Università degli Studi, Turin, 2002–2003.

Bernardini, R. *Jung a Eranos: Il progetto della psicologia complessa*. Milan: FrancoAngeli, 2011.

Bernardini, R., G.P. Quaglino, and A. Romano. "A Visit Paid to Jung by Alwine von Keller." *Journal of Analytical Psychology* 56 (2011): 232–54.

Bernoulli, R. and E.K. Müller. "Eine neue Untersuchung der Eigenschaften des Teleplasma." *Zeitschrift für Parapsychologie* 7 (1931): 313–21.

von Bernus, A. *Alchymie und Heilkunst*. Stuttgart: Private edition/Laboratorium Soluna, 1936; 2nd ed. Nuremberg: Hans Carl, 1948.

von Bernus, A. *Das Geheimnis der Adepten: Aufschlüsse über das Magisterium der Alchymie, die Bereitung der großen Arkana und den Weg zum Lapis Philosophorum*. Sersheim: Osiris Verlag, 1956.

von Bernus, A. "Gleichheit, Freiheit, Brüderlichkeit." *Das Reich* (January 1919): 469–83.

von Bernus, A. *Neuburg: Eine Gedichtfolge von Alexander von Bernus mit zehn Holzschnitten von Joachim Lutz*. Limited ed. of 200 copies. Mannheim: Gengenbach & Hahn, 1926.

von Bernus, A. and J. Lutz. *Stift Neuburg: Eine Gedichtfolge von Alexander von Bernus mit zehn Holzschnitten von Joachim Lutz*. Mannheim: Gengenbach & Hahn, 1926.

Biale, D. "Scholem und der moderne Nationalismus." In *Gershom Scholem: Zwischen den Disziplinen*, edited by P. Schäfer und G. Smith, 257–74. Frankfurt: Suhrkamp, 1995.

Bianchi, U. (ed.). *Le origini dello gnosticismo*. Leiden: Brill, 1970.

Biano, O. *C.G. Jung and the Sioux Tradition: Dreams, Visions, Nature and the Primitive*. New Orleans, LA: Spring Journal Books, 2009.

Biemann, A.D. (ed.). *The Martin Buber Reader: Essential Readings*. New York: Palgrave Macmillan, 2002.

Biemann, D. *Erkenntnis und Erfüllung: Die Philosophie Martin Bubers und ihr Begriff aus dem Geist der Hebräischen Weisheit*. Frankfurt: Peter Lang, 1995.

Bishop, P. "The Members of Jung's Seminar on Zarathustra." *Spring* 56 (1994): 92–121.

Bloch, K. (ed.). *Ernst Bloch: Briefe 1903-1975*, vol. 2. Frankfurt: Suhrkamp, 1985.

Blüher, H. *Werke und Tage: Geschichte eines Denkers*. Munich: Paul List, 1953.

Blumenberg, H. *The Legitimacy of the Modern Age*. Translated by R.M. Wallace. Boston, MA: MIT Press, 1983.

Bochinger, C. *"New Age" und moderne Religion: Religionswissenschaftliche Analysen*. Gütersloh: Gütersloher Verlagshaus, 1995.

Bochsler, R. *Ich folgte meinem Stern: Das kämpferische Leben der Margarete Hardegger*. Zurich: Pendo, 2004.

Böhler, D. *Ethik für die Zukunft: Im Diskurs mit Hans Jonas*. Munich: C.H. Beck, 1994.

Böhme, H. and G. Böhme. *Das Andere der Vernunft: Zur Entwicklung von Rationalitätsstrukturen am Beispiel Kants*. Frankfurt: Suhrkamp, [1985] 1996.

du Bois, C.A. "Paul Radin: An Appreciation." In *Culture in History: Essays in Honor of Paul Radin*, edited by S. Diamond, ix–xvi. New York: Columbia University Press, 1960.

Bolle, F. "Darwinismus und Zeitgeist." *Zeitschrift für Religions- und Geistesgeschichte* 14 (1962): 143–78.

Bolz, N. *Auszug aus der entzauberten Welt: Philosophischer Extremismus zwischen den Weltkriegen*. Munich: Wilhelm Fink Verlag, 1989.

Bonder, D. *Bevor Hitler kam*. Geneva: Marva, 1975.

Bondi, G. *Briefwechsel zwischen George und Hofmannsthal*. Berlin 1938. 2nd ed. Munich: Helmut Küpper, 1953.

Borchardt, C. "Borchardt–Hofmannsthal." *Criticón* 16 (1999): 20–24.

Borup, J. "Zen and the Art of Inventing Orientalism: Religious Studies and Genealogical Networks." www.terebess.hu/english/borup.html, 18.

Bouretz, P. *Témoins du Futur: Philosophie et messianisme*. Paris: Gallimard, 2003.

Bourgeaud, P. "Qu'est-ce que l'histoire des religions?" *Equinoxe: Revue des Sciences Humaines*, 21 (1999): 67–84.

Boyd-Macmillan, E.M. *Transformation: James Loder, Mystical Spirituality and James Hillman*. Oxford: Peter Lang, 2006.

de Boysson, E. *Le Cardinal et l'hinouiste: Le mystère des frères Daniélou*. Paris: Albin Michel, 1999.

Bramwell, A. *Blood and Soil: Richard Walter Darré and Hitler's "Green Party."* Abbotsbrook: Kensal Press, 1985.

Brandenburg, H.-C. and R. Dauer. *Die Brücke zu Köngen: Fünfzig Jahre Bund der Köngener 1919-1969*. Stuttgart: J.F. Steinkopf Verlag, 1969.

Braune, W. and P. Tillich. *Ein Gedenkvortrag*. Berlin: Colloquium Verlag, 1966.

Bremer Volkshochschule (ed.). *Wege zum integralen Bewußtsein: Eine Festgabe für Jean Gebser zum 20. August 1965*. Bremen: Bremer Volkshochschule, 1965.

Breslauer, S.D. (ed.). *The Seductiveness of Jewish Myth: Challenge or Response?* Albany, NY: SUNY Press, 1997.

Breuer, S. *Ästhetischer Fundamentalismus: Stefan George und der deutsche Antimodernismus*. Darmstadt: Wissenschaftliche Buchgesellschaft, 1995.

Breuer, S. "Genii locorum. Schwabings neureligiöse 'Kosmiker' zwischen Wilhelmismus und Faschismus." In *Mystique, mysticisme et modernité en Allemagne autour de 1900*, edited by M. Baßler and H. Châtelier, 149–64. Strasbourg: Presses Universitaires de Strasbourg, 1998.

Breuer, S. *Die Völkischen in Deutschland*. Darmstadt: WBG, 2008.

Broch, H. *Briefe 1: 1913-1938* and *Briefe 3: 1945-1951*. In *Hermann Broch: Kommentierte Werkausgabe in dreizehn Bänden*, edited by P. M. Lützeler. Frankfurt: Suhrkamp, 1986.

Broch, H. *Hermann Broch: Kommentierte Werkausgabe in dreizehn Bänden*. Edited by P.M. Lützeler. Frankfurt: Suhrkamp, 1986.

Brockway, R.W. *Young Carl Jung*. Wilmette, IL: Chiron Publications, 1996.

van den Broek, R. "The Birth of a Chair." In *Hermes in the Academy: Ten Years' Study of Western Esotericism at the University of Amsterdam*, edited by W. J. Hanegraaff and J. Pijnenburg, 11–15. Amsterdam: Amsterdam University Press, 2009.

van den Broek, R. and M. Vermaseren (eds). *Studies in Gnosticism and Hellenistic Religions*. Edited by B. Layton. Leiden: Brill, 1981.

Brome, V. *Jung*. New York: Atheneum, 1978.

Bronder, D. *Bevor Hitler kam*. 2nd ed. Genf: Marva Verlag, 1975.

van den Bruck, A.M. *Das Ewige Reich*. Breslau: Wilhelm Gottlieb Korn Verlag, 1933.

Brumlik, M. *Die Gnostiker: Der Traum von der Selbsterlösung des Menschen*. Frankfurt: Eichborn, 1992.

Brumlik, M. "Theology without Thorns: Adorno's Critique of Buber." In *New Perspectives on Martin Buber*, edited by M. Zank, 247–51. Tübingen: Mohr Siebeck, 2006.

Brun, J. *Le rêve et la machine: Technique et existence*. Paris: La Table Ronde, 1992.

Brun, J. *Les conquêtes de l'homme et la séparation ontologique*. Paris: Presses Universitaires Françaises, 1961.

Buber, M. *Briefwechsel aus sieben Jahrzehnten, vol. I: 1897-1918*. Edited by Grete Schaeder. Heidelberg, Lambert Schneider, 1972.

Buber, M. *Briefwechsel aus sieben Jahrzehnten, vol. II: 1918-1938*. Edited by Grete Schaeder. Heidelberg, Lambert Schneider, 1972.

Buber, M. *Briefwechsel aus sieben Jahrzehnten, vol. III: 1938-1965*. Edited by Grete Schaeder. Heidelberg, Lambert Schneider, 1972.

Buber, M. "Dem Gemeinschaftlichen folgen." *Die Neue Rundschau* 67(4) (1956): 597–98.

Buber, M. *Die Rede, die Lehre, das Lied: Drei Beispiele*. Leipzig: Insel Verlag, 1917.

Buber, M. *Ein Land und zwei Völker: Zur jüdisch-arabischen Frage*. Edited with an introduction by P.R. Mendes-Flohr. Frankfurt: Insel Verlag, 1983.

Buber, M. "Elemente des Zwischenmenschlichen" and "Das Wort, das gesprochen wird." CD. Müllheim/Baden: Auditorium-Netzwerk, 2007.

Buber, M. *Gottesfinsternis: Betrachtungen zur Beziehung zwischen Religion und Philosophie*. Zurich: Manesse, 1953.

Buber, M. *Ich und Du*. Berlin: Schocken Verlag, 1923. Published in English as *I and Thou* (London: Continuum, 2004).

Buber, M. *München ehrt Martin Buber*. Munich: Ner-Tamid-Verlag, 1961.

Buber, M. "Nationalismus." In *Ein Land und zwei Völker: Zur jüdisch-arabischen Frage*, edited by P.R. Mendes-Flohr, 70–83. Frankfurt: Insel Verlag, 1983.

Buckmiller, M. and P. Nafe. "Die Naherwartung des Kommunismus: Werner Scholem." In *Judentum und politische Existenz: Siebzehn Porträts deutsch-jüdischer Intellektueller*, edited by M. Buckmiller, D. Heimann, and J. Perels, 61–81. Hannover: Offizin, 2000.

Buisson-Maas, A.-M. *Hermann Keyserling et l'Inde*. PhD thesis, Université de Lille, 1978.

Buonaiuti, E. "Die Botschaft Joachim von Floris und die franziskanische 'Religio.'" In *Deo omnia unum: Eine Sammlung von Aufsätzen Friedrich Heiler zum 50. Geburtstage dargebracht*, edited by C. Schröder and M. Schröder, 200–211. Munich: Ernst Reinhardt, 1942.

Buonaiuti, E. *Die exkommunizierte Kirche*. Edited and introduced by E. Benz. Zurich: Rhein Verlag, 1966.

Buonaiuti, E. *Gioacchino da Fiore: I tempi—la vita—il messaggio*. Cosenza: Lionello Giordano, [1931] 1984.

Buonaiuti, E. *La Gnosi cristiana*. Rome: Atanor, 1987.

Buonaiuti, E. *Lo Gnosticismo: Storie di antiche lotte religiose*. First published in Rome 1907, Genova: photo-facsimile edition, 1987.

Burckhardt, C.J. *Memorabilien, Erinnerungen und Begegnungen*. Munich: Georg Callwey, 1977.

Burckhardt, C.J. and M. Rychner. *Briefe 1926–1965*. Frankfurt: S. Fischer, 1970.

Burmistrov, K. "Gershom Scholem und das Okkulte." *Gnostika* 33 (2006): 23–4.

Burrows, H. (ed.). *The World's Parliament of Religions: The Columbian Exhibition of 1893*. Chicago, IL: Parliament Publishing Company, 1893.

Cahiers du Groupe d'Etudes Spirituelles Comparées. *Transmission culturelle, transmission spirituelle: Colloque tenu en Sorbonne les 13 et 14 Juin*. Paris: Archè-Edidit, 1993.

Cairns, H. *The Bollingen Adventure: A Toast to J.D.B. and V.G.* Princeton, NJ: Princeton University Press, 1969.

Campbell, B.F. *Ancient Wisdom Revived: A History of the Theosophical Movement*. Berkeley, CA: University of California Press, 1980.

Cambell, J. *Baksheesh and Brahman: Indian Journal 1954–1955*. Edited by R. Larsen, S. Larsen, and A. Van Couvering. New York: HarperCollins, 1995.

Cambell, J. *Creative Mythology*. Harmondsworth: Penguin Books, 1976.

Cambell, J. "Johann Jacob Bachofen." In *Joseph Campbell: The Mythic Dimension: Selected Essays 1959–1987*, edited by A. Van Couvering, 67–91. San Francisco, CA: Harper, 1997.

Campbell, J. *Man and Time: Papers from the Eranos Yearbooks*. Princeton, NJ: Princeton University Press, 1957.

Campbell, J. (ed.). *Papers from the Eranos Yearbooks*. Bollingen Series XXX, 1–6. Princeton, NJ: Princeton University Press, 1970–72.

Campbell, J. (ed.). *Spirit and Nature: Papers from the Eranos Yearbooks*. Bollingen Series XXX. New York: Bollingen Foundation, 1954.

Cambell, J. *The Hero's Journey*. New York: Harper & Row, 1990.

Cambell, J. (ed.). *The Mysteries: Papers from the Eranos Yearbooks*. Bollingen Series XXX. New York: Bollingen Foundation, 1954.

Campbell, J. and R. Roberts. *Tarot Revelations*. 3rd ed. San Anselmo, CA: Vernal Equinox Press, 1987.

Cancik, H. "Dionysos 1933: Walter F. Otto als Religionswissenschaftler und Theologe am Ende der Weimarer Republik (II)." In *Antik, Modern: Beiträge zur römischen und deutschen Kulturgeschichte*, edited by R. Faber, B. von Reibnitz, and J. Rüpke, 165–86. Stuttgart: J.B. Metzler, 1998.

Cancik, H. "'Neuheiden' und totaler Staat: Völkische Religion am Ende der Weimarer Republik." In *Antik, Modern: Beiträge zur römischen und deutschen Kulturgeschichte*, edited by R. Faber, B. von Reibnitz, and J. Rüpke, 187–227. Stuttgart: J.B. Metzler, 1998.

Cancik, H. "The Gods of Greece 1929: Walter F. Otto als Religionswissenschaftler und Theologe am Ende der Weimarer Republik (I)." In *Antik, Modern: Beiträge zur römischen und deutschen Kulturgeschichte*, edited by R. Faber, B. von Reibnitz, and J. Rüpke, 165–86. Stuttgart: J.B. Metzler, 1998.

Cancik, H., B. Gladigow, and K.-H. Kohl (eds). *Handbuch religionswissenschaftlicher Grundbegriffe*, vol. IV. Stuttgart: W. Kohlhammer, 1998.

Carzzetti, R. and M. Folini (eds). *L'energia del luogo: Jean Arp, Rafael Benazzi, Julius Bissier, Ben Nicholson, Hans Richter, Mark Tobey, Italo Valenti: Alla ricerca del Genius loci Ascona-Locarno*. Locarno: Armando Dadò/Città di Locarno, 2008.

Casadio, G. "La vita sessuale di Mircea Eliade." *Rinascita* (8 September 2010). www.rinascita.eu/index.php?action= news&id=3740.

Casadio, G. *Vie gnostiche all'immortalità*. Brescia: Morcelliana, 1997.

Case, M.H. (ed.). *Heinrich Zimmer: Coming into His Own*. Princeton, NJ: Princeton University Press, 1994.

Cave, D. *Mircea Eliade's Vision for a New Humanism*. New York: Oxford University Press, 1993.

Cazenave, M. "De la psychologie freudienne aux théories de Jung." *Le Disque Vert* (1955): 302–16.

Cazenave, M. *Jung: L'Expérience intérieure*. Monaco: Editions du Rocher, 1997.

Cella, M. *Elémire Zolla come fondatore di "Conoscenza Religiosa."* PhD thesis, Università di Salerno, 1998–99.

Cesana, A. "Portmanns Evolutionsdenken." *Uni Nova* 79–80 (1997): 94–7.

Charet, F.X. *Spiritualism and the Foundations of C.G. Jung's Psychology*. Albany, NY: SUNY Press, 1993.

Chauffin, Y. "Entre la violence et la mystique." *Question de* 90 (1992): 15–20.

Cheetham, T. *The World Turned Inside Out: Henry Corbin and Islamic Mysticism*. Woodstock, CT: Spring Journal Books, 2003.

Childs, G.H. "Report." *Bulletin of the Analytical Psychology Club of New York* 14(8) (1952): 7–10.

Chung-yuan, C. *Creativity and Taoism: A Study of Chinese Philosophy, Art and Poetry*. New York: Julian Press, 1963.

Clairmont, C.W.A. *Ludwig Derleth (1870–1948): Das literarische Werk: Eine kritische Würdigung*. Ernen: self-published, n.d.

Clarke, J.J. *C.G. Jung und der östliche Weg*. Zurich: Walter Verlag, 1997.

Clarke, J.J. *Jung and Eastern Thought*. London: Routledge, 1994.

Cleather, A.L. and B. Crump. *The Pseudo-Occultism of Mrs. A. Bailey*. Manila, 1929.

Clergue-Vila, J. "En quête d'Henry Corbin, franc-maçon chevaleresque." *L'Initiation* 2 (2009): 85–114.

Cocks, G. "C.G. Jung and German Psychotherapy 1933–1940: A Research Note." *Spring* (1979) 221–7.

Cocks, G. *Psychotherapy in the Third Reich: The Göring Institute*. 2nd ed. New Brunswick, NJ: Transaction Publishers, 1997.

Codreanu, C.Z. *The Green Shirts and Others: A History of Fascism in Hungary and Romania*. Stanford, CA: Stanford University Press, 1970.

Codreanu, C.Z. *Guardia di Ferro*. Padua: Edizione di Ar, 1972.

Cohen, H. *Die Religion der Vernunft aus den Quellen des Judentums*. Wiesbaden: Fourier, 1978.

Colli, G. and M. Montinari (eds). *Friedrich Nietzsche: Sämtliche Werke: Kritische Studienausgabe*. Berlin: Walter de Gruyter, 1988.

Collum, V.C.C. *The Tressé Iron-Age Megalithic Monument (Sir Robert Mond's Excavation): Its Quadruple Sculptured Breasts and Their Relation to the Mother-Goddess Cosmic Cult*. London: Oxford University Press, 1935.

Colpe, C. (ed.). *Die Diskussion um das "Heilige."* Darmstadt: Wissenschaftliche Buchgesellschaft, 1977.

Colpe, C. "Die 'Himmelsreise der Seele' außerhalb und innerhalb der Gnosis." In *Le origini dello gnosticismo: Colloquio di Messina 13–18 Aprile 1966*, edited by U. Bianchi, 429–47. Leiden: Brill, 1970.

Colpe, C. *Über das Heilige: Versuch, seiner Verkennung kritisch vorzubeugen*. Frankfurt: Anton Hain Meisenheim, 1990.

Comune di Macerata. *Giuseppe Tucci: Un maceratese nelle terre sacre dell'Oriente*. Macerata: Comune di Macerata, 2000.

Conferenze IsMEO. *Nel centenario dell'intervento di Swami Vivekananda al Parlamento Mondiale delle Religioni (Chicago 1893)*. Rome: Istituto Italiano per l'Africa e l'Oriente, 1997.

Consolato, S. "Universalità Romana, Fascismo ed Oriente. Due documenti." *La Cittadella* 3(14) (2004): 43–5.

Cooper, J. "Professor Gilles Quispel." *Theosophical History* 6 (1995): 202.

Copenhaver, B.P. *Hermetica*. Cambridge: Cambridge University Press, 1992.

Corbin, H. *Collected Writings of Plotin, Vol 3*. Translated by T. Taylor. Frome: Prometheus Trust, 1994.

Corbin, H. *Corps spirituel et Terre céleste: De l'Iran mazdéen à l'Iran shi'ite*. Paris: Buchet-Chastel, 1979.

Corbin, H. "De la philosophie prophétique en Islam shi'ite." *Eranos Jahrbuch* 31 (1962): 49–116.

Corbin, H. "De l'Iran à Eranos." In *Henry Corbin*, edited by Christian Jambet. Paris: L'Herne, 1981.

Corbin, H. *Die smaragdene Vision: Der Licht-Mensch im persischen Sufismus*. Munich: Eugen Diederichs, 1989. English translation: *The Man of Light in Iranian Sufism*, translated by N. Parsons. Boston, MA: Shambhala, 1981.

Corbin, H. "Discours de M: Le professeur H. Corbin à l'occasion de la mort de L. Massignon." *La Faculté des lettres de l'Université de Téhéran* 10(3) (1962): 4.

Corbin, H. "Eranos: Freiheit und Spontaneität." *Eranos Jahrbuch* 31 (1962): 13–15.

Corbin, H. *Hamann: philosophe du luthéranisme*. Paris: L'Ile verte, Berg International, 1985.

Corbin, H. *Histoire de la philosophie islamique*. Paris: Gallimard, 1986.

Corbin, H. *La philosophie iranienne islamique aux XVII et XVIII siècles*. Paris: Buchet/Chastel, 1981.

Corbin, H. *Le paradoxe du monothéisme*. Paris: Editions de l'Herne, 1981.

Corbin, H. *L'Imagination créatrice dans le soufisme d'Ibn Arabi*. Paris: Flammarion, 1976.

Corbin, H. "L'Université Saint-Jean de Jérusalem: Centre International de Recherche Spirituelle Comparée." *Cahier de l'Université Saint-Jean de Jérusalem* (1975): 8–12.

Corbin, H. "Mundus imaginalis. L'imaginaire et l'imaginal." *Cahiers internationaux de symbolisme* 6 (1964): 3–26.

Corbin, H. "Post-scriptum biographique à un Entretien philosophique." In H. Corbin and C. Jambet, *Henry Corbin*, 40. Paris: L'Herne, 1981.

Corbin, H. Proceedings in *Cahiers du Groupe d'Etudes Spirituelles Comparées*. Paris: Arché Editit, 2000.

Corbin, H. *Temple et Contemplation: Essais sur l'Islam iranien*. Paris: Flammarion, 1981.

Corbin, H. "The Time of Eranos." In *Man and Time: Papers from the Eranos Yearbooks*, edited by J. Campbell, xiii–xx. Princeton, NJ: Princeton University Press, 1957.

Corbin, H. "Towards a Chart of the Imaginal." *Temenos: A Review Devoted to the Arts of the Imagination* 1 (1981): 23–6.

Corbin, H. and C. Jambet. *Henry Corbin*. Paris: Herne, 1981.

Corti, W.R. *Der Mensch im Werden Gottes: Gesammelte Schriften*, vol. 2. Schaffhausen: Novalis, 1998.

Corti, W.R. "Die Eranos-Begegnungsstätte für Ost und West in Moscia-Ascona." *Schweizer Annalen* 1 (1935): 52–9.

Corti, W.R. "Die platonische Akademie im Wandel der Geschichte und als Aufgabe unserer Zeit." *Eranos Jahrbuch* 26 (1957): 387–413.

Corti, W.R. Foreword to *Das Reich ohne Raum*. Zurich: Origo, 1962.

Corti, W.R. *Heimkehr ins Eigentliche: Gesammelte Schriften*, vol. 1. Schaffhausen: Novalis, 1979.

Corti, W.R. *Plan der Akademie*. St. Gallen: Tschoudy, 1956.

Corti, W.R. *The Philosophy of George Herbert Mead*. Winterthur: Archiv für genetische Philosophie, 1973.

Corti, W.R. "Zwanzig Jahre Eranostagungen in Moscia-Ascona (Schweiz)." *Psyche* 6 (1952–53): 155–60.

Costantini, E. *Nae Ionescu, Mircea Eliade, Emil Cioran: Antiliberalismo nazionalista alla periferia d'Europa*. Perugia: Morlacchi, 2005.

Costantini, P. "C'era una volta l'Istituto di Alti Studi." *Corriere del Ticino* (2 March 2009).

Costantini, P. *Vie della Tradizione* 5 (1972): 46.

Costello, J.J. Review in *Harvest* 35 (1989–90): 234.

Coudert, A.P. *The Impact of the Kabbalah in the Seventeenth Century: The Life and Thought of Francis Mercury van Helmont (1614–1698)*. Leiden: Brill, 1999.

Council of Jews from Germany-London (ed.). *Worte des Gedenkens für Leo Baeck*. Heidelberg: Lambert Schneider, 1959.

van Couvering, A. *Joseph Campbell—The Mythic Dimension: Selected Essays 1959–1987*. San Francisco, CA: Harper, 1997.

Cowan, L. (ed.). *Barcelona 04: Edges of Experience: Memory and Emergence. Proceedings of the 16th International IAAP Congress for Analytical Psychology*. Einsiedeln: Daimon, 2006.

Cox, J.L. *A Guide to the Phenomenology of Religion: Key Figures, Formative Influences and Subsequent Debates*. London: T&T Clark, 2006.

Culianu, I.P. "The Correspondence between Mircea Eliade and Ioan Petru Culianu," translated by Sorana Corneanu. *Archaeus* 8 (2004): fasc. 1–4, 34

Culianu, I.P. "La XLVI Eranostagung (Ascona, 17–25 Agosto 1977)." *Aevum* 52(2) (1978): 343–6.

Culianu, I.P. "The Gnostic Revenge." In *Religiontheorie und Politische Theologie*, vol. 2: *Gnosis und Politik*, edited by J. Taubes, 290. Munich: Wilhelm Fink, 1984.

Culianu, I.P. *Hans Jonas: Gnosticismo e pensiero moderno*. Rome: "L'Erma" di Bretschneider, 1985.

Culianu, I.P. *Mircea Eliade*, Assisi: Cittadella, 1978.

Curtin, E. "Raffaele Pettazzoni et Mircea Eliade: Historiens des religions généralistes devant les fascismes (1933–1945)." In *The Study of Religion under the Impact of Fascism*, edited by H. Junginger, 333–63. Leiden: Brill, 2008.

Dan, J. "Gershom Scholem: Mystiker oder Geschichtsschreiber des Mystischen?" In *Gershom Scholem: Zwischen den Disziplinen*, edited by P. Schäfer and G. Smith, 33–69. Frankfurt: Suhrkamp, 1995.

Dan, J. *Gershom Scholem and the Mystical Dimension of Jewish History*. New York: New York University Press, 1988.

Daniélou, A. Interview. *Paris Match* (17 May 1985).

Daniélou, A. "Shivaisme et Homosexualité." *Gaie France* 6 (1987): 11–13.

Daniélou, A. *Storia dell'India*. Rome: Ubaldini, [1981] 1992.

Daniélou, A. *The Way to the Labyrinth: Memories of East and West*. New York: New Directions, 1987.

Daniélou, J. *Essai sur le mystère de l'Histoire*. Paris: Seuil, 1953.

Daniélou, J. "L'Oraison, problème politique." *Antaios* 15 (1999): 3.

Danzel, T.-W. *Magie und Geheimwissenschaft in ihrer Bedeutung für Kultur und Kulturgeschichte*. Stuttgart: Strecker und Schröder, 1924.

Danzel, T.-W. *Der magische Mensch (Homo divinans): Vom Wesen der primitiven Kultur*. Potsdam: Müller & Kiepenheuer, 1928.

D'Arch Smith, T. *The Times Deceas'd: The Rare Book Department of the Times Bookshop in the 1960s*. York: Stone Trough Books, 2003.

Darvas, J. "Brückenbauer zwischen Ost und West: Henry Corbin: Ein biographisches-philosophisches Porträt." *Das Goetheanum* 80(18) (2001): 317–23.

Dauber, F. von. *Ludwig Derleth: Der Dichter und sein Werk*. PhD thesis, Department of Philosophy, University of Vienna, 1943.

Davidowicz, K.S. *Gershom Scholem und Martin Buber: Die Geschichte eines Mißverständnisses*. Neukirchen: Neukircher Verlag, 1995.

Davidowicz, K.S. *Kabbala: Geheime Tradition im Judentum*. Eisenstadt: Österreichisches Jüdisches Museum, n.d.

Davy, M.-M. Interview. *Question de* 90 (1992): 218; 116 (1999).

Davy, M.-M. *Traversée en solitaire*. Paris: Albin Michel, 1989.

Deghaye, P. *De Paracelse à Thomas Mann: Les avatars de l'hermétisme allemand*. Paris: Dervy, 2000.

Deimann, G. (ed.). *Die anthroposophischen Zeitschriften von 1903 bis 1985*. Stuttgart: Verlag Freies Geistesleben, 1987.

Der neue Roman: Ein Almanach. Leipzig: Kurt Wolff Verlag, 1917.

Derleth, C. *Das Fleischlich-Geistige: Meine Erinnerungen an Ludwig Derleth*. Bellnhausen über Gladbach: Hinder & Deelmann, 1973.

Derleth, L. *Ludwig Derleth Gedenkbuch*. Amsterdam: Castrum Peregrini Presse, 1958.

Derleth, L. *Das Werk*, 6 vols. Bellnhausen: Hinder & Deelmann, 1971–72.

Deutsch, N. *The Gnostic Imagination: Gnosticism, Mandeism and Merkabah Mysticism*. Leiden: Brill, 1995.

Diamond, S. *Culture in History: Essays in Honor of Paul Radin*. New York: Columbia University Press, 1960.

Diederichs, E. *Der deutsche Buchhandel in Selbstdarstellungen*. Leipzig: Felix Meiner, 1927.

Diederichs, E. *Politik des Geistes*. Jena: Eugen Diederichs, 1920.

Diederichs, U. (ed.). *Erfahrungen mit dem I Ging: Vom kreativen Umgang mit dem Buch der Wandlungen*. Cologne: Eugen Diederichs, 1987.

Diemann, G. (ed.). *Die anthroposophischen Zeitschriften von 1903 bis 1985*. Stuttgart: Verlag Freies Geistesleben, 1987.

Dierker, W. *Himmlers Glaubenskrieger: Der Sicherheitsdienst der SS und seine Religionspolitik 1933–1941*. Paderborn: Ferdinand Schöningh, 2003.

Dierks, M. *Jakob Wilhelm Hauer 1881–1962*. Heidelberg: Lambert Schneider, 1986.

Dippel, J.V.H. *Bound Upon a Wheel of Fire: Why So Many German Jews Made the Tragic Decision to Remain in Nazi Germany*. New York: Basic Books, 1996.

Dixon, P. *Nietzsche and Jung: Sailing a Deeper Night*. New York: Peter Lang, 1999.

Dörr, G. *Ludwig Derleth: Prophet und Mystiker*. Unpublished manuscript. Ascona 2001.

Dörr, G. *Muttermythos und Herrschaftsmythos: Zur Dialektik der Aufklärung um die Jahrhundertwende bei den Kosmikern, Stefan George und in der Frankfurter Schule*. Würzburg: Königshausen & Neumann, 2007.

Douglas, A. "Ist Eliade antihistorisch?" In *Die Mitte der Welt: Aufsätze zu Mircea Eliade*, edited by H.P. Duerr, 106–27. Frankfurt: Suhrkamp, 1984.

Dourley, J.P. "In the Shadow of the Monotheisms: Jung's Conversations with Buber and White." In *Jung and the Monotheisms: Judaism, Christianity and Islam*, edited by J. Ryce-Menuhin, 125–45. London: Routledge, 1993.

Dovere. "Nuove esperienze di metodo archeologico nella lezione del prof. de Rachewiltz." *Dovere* (10 October 1973), 7.

Downing, C. (ed.). *Disturbances in the Field: Essays in Honor of David L. Miller*. New Orleans, LA: Spring Journal Books, 2006.

Dragan, R. Review in *Politica Hermetica* 24 (2010): 134–45.

Driesch, H. *Lebenserinnerungen: Aufzeichnungen eines Forschers und Denkers in entscheidender Zeit*. Basel: Ernst Reinhardt, 1951.

Drob, S.L. *Kabbalistic Metaphors: Jewish Mystical Themes in Ancient and Modern Thought*. Northvale, NJ: Jason Aronson, 2000.

Drob, S.L. *Kabbalistic Visions: C.G. Jung and Jewish Mysticism*. New Orleans, LA: Spring Journal Books, 2010.

Dubuisson, D. *Impostures et pseudo-science: L'Oeuvre de Mircea Eliade*. Villeneuve d'Asq: Presses Universitaires du Septentrion, 2005.

Dubuisson, D. *Mythologies du XXe siècle (Dumézil, Lévi-Strauss, Eliade)*. Lille: Presses Universitaires de Lille, 1993.

Duchesne-Guillemin, J. "Mircea Eliade: An Impromptu." In *Gnosisforschung und Religionsgeschichte*, edited by H. Preißler and H. Seiwert, 409–12. Marburg: Diagonal Verlag, 1994.

Duerr, H.P. (ed.). In *Die Mitte der Welt: Aufsätze zu Mircea Eliade*. Frankfurt: Suhrkamp, 1984.

Duerr, H.P. *Der Wissenschaftler und das Irrationale*. Frankfurt: Syndikatsverlag, 1981.

von Dungern, E. (ed.). *Das große Gespräch der Religionen*. Munich: Ernst Reinhardt Verlag, 1964.

Dupuy, B. Preface to *Le messianisme juif: essais sur la spiritualité du judaisme*. Paris: Calmann-Lévy, 1974.

Durand, G. *Beaux-arts et archetypes: La religion de l'art*. Paris: Presses Universitaires Françaises, 1989.

Durand, G. *Champs de l'imaginaire: Textes réunis par Danièle Chauvin*. Grenoble: ELLUG, Université Stendhal, 1996.

Durand, G. "Exploration of the Imaginal." *Temenos: A Review Devoted to the Arts of the Imagination* 1 (1981): 7–22.

Durand, G. *Figures mythiques et visages de l'oeuvre: De la mythocritique à la mythanalyse*. Paris: Dunod, 1992.

Durand, G. "Henry Corbin, l'Envers d'un Siècle de Ténèbres." *Les Humains Associés* 8. www.humains-associes.org/No8/HA.No8.Durand.html (accessed December 2012).

Durand, G. *L'âme tigrée: Les pluriels de psyché*. Paris: Denoël/Gonthier, 1980.

Durand, G. "La pensée d'Henry Corbin et le temple maçonnique." *Traveaux de la Loge nationale de recherches Villard de Honnecourt* 3 (1981): 173–82.

Durand, G. "Le Génie du Lieu et les heures propices." *Eranos Jahrbuch* 51 (1982): 243–77.

Durand, G. *Les structures anthropologiques de l'Imaginaire: Introduction à l'archétypologie générale*. Grenoble: Presses Universitaires de France, 1960.

Durand, G. *L'imaginaire: Essai sur les sciences et la philosophie de l'image*. Paris: Hatier, 1994.

Durand, G. *Science de l'homme et tradition: Le nouvel ésprit anthropologique*. Paris: Albin Michel, [1979] 1996.

Durand, G. *Science et Conscience: Les deux lectures de l'univers.* Paris: Stock, 1980.

Durand, G. *Structures: Eranos I.* Paris: La Table Ronde, 2003.

Dürckheim, K. and M. Hippius. *Transzendenz als Erfahrung: Beitrag und Widerhall Festschrift zum 70. Geburtstag von Graf Dürckheim.* Weilheim: O.W. Barth, 1966.

Dutta, K. and A. Robinson. *Rabindranath Tagore: The Myriad-Minded Man.* New York: St. Martin's Press, 1995.

Eco, U. "Il fascismo eterno." In *Cinque scritti morali.* Milan: Bompiani, 1997.

Eco, U. "Urfaschismus." *Die Zeit* (7 July 1995).

Eco, U. *Vier moralische Schriften.* Munich: Carl Hanser, 1998.

Edler, M. "Thomas Mann und Karl Kerényi." In *Neuhumanismus und Anthropologie des griechischen Mythos*, edited by R. Schlesier and R. Sanchiño Martínez, 43–54. Locarno: Rezzonico Editore, 2006.

Eemans, M. "Ce que fut la revue métasurréaliste Hermès (1933–1939)." *Antaios* 13 (1998): 118–23.

Egger, C. "Vorstösse ins Innere: Zum 100. Geburtstag des großen Erzählers Laurens van der Post." *Neue Züricher Zeitung* (9–10 December 2006).

Eisler, R. *Man into Wolf: An Anthropological Interpretation of Sadism, Masochism and Lycanthropy.* Santa Barbara, CA: Ross-Erikson, 1978.

Eisler, R. *Orpheus—The Fisher: Comparative Studies in Orphic and Early Christian Cult Symbolism.* London: J.M. Watkins, 1921.

Eisler, R. *Orphisch-Dionysische Mysteriengedanken in der christlichen Antike.* Nendeln: Kraus, 1967.

Eisler, R. *The Royal Art of Astrology.* London: Herbert Joseph, 1946.

Eisler, R. *Weltenmantel und Himmelszelt: Religionsgeschichtliche Untersuchungen zur Urgeschichte des antiken Weltbildes.* Hildesheim: Georg Olms, [1910] 2002.

Elder, G.R. *The Body: An Encyclopedia of Archetypal Symbolism.* Boston, MA: Shambhala, 1996.

Eliade, M. *Autobiography, Volume 2: 1937–1960: Exile's Odyssey.* Chicago, IL: University of Chicago Press, 1988.

Eliade, M. *Breve storia della Romania e dei rumeni.* Rome: Settimo Sigillo, 1997.

Eliade, M. *Briser le toit de la maison: La créativité et ses symboles.* Paris: Gallimard, 1986.

Eliade, M. "Comentarii la un juramant." *Vremea* 476 (1937), quoted here from the Italian translation published in *Origini* 15 (2000): 22.

Eliade, M. *Contribuții la filosofia renașterii.* Supplement to *Revista de Istorie și literara* 1 (1984).

Eliade, M. *Der Magische Flug: Aufsatzsammlung.* Sinzheim: Archiv für Altes Gedankengut und Wissen, 2000.

Eliade, M. *Diario d'India.* Turin: Boringhieri, 1995.

Eliade, M. *Diario Portuguès (1941–1945).* Barcelona: Editorial Kairòs, 2000.

Eliade, M. (ed.). *Encyclopedia of Religion.* New York: Macmillan, 1987; 2nd expanded ed. by Lindsay Jones, Farmington Hills, MI: Thomson Gale, 2005.

Eliade, M. "Initiation et monde moderne." *Travaux de la Loge nationale de recherches Villard de Honnecourt* 1 (1980): 21–9.

Eliade, M. "Jung, ou la réponse à Job." In *Mircea Eliade*, edited by C. Tacou, 250. Paris: L'Herne, 1978.

Eliade, M. "Krisis und Erneuerung der Religionswissenschaft." *Antaios* 9 (1968): 5. Reprinted in his *Das Okkulte und die moderne Welt: Zeitströmungen in der Sicht der Religionsgeschichte; Der Magische Flug: Aufsatzsammlung*, 197–215. Sinzheim: AAGW, 2000. Published in English as "Crisis and Renewal in History of Religions," *History of Religions* 5(1) (1965): 1–17.

Eliade, M. "La moartea lui Rudolf Otto." *Revista Fundațiilor Regale* 4(9) (1937): 676–9.

Eliade, M. *La prova del labirinto: Intervista con C.-H. Roquet.* Milan: Jaca Book, 1980.

Eliade, M. "Les Danseurs Passent, La Danse Reste." *Du* 15(4) (April 1955): 60–62.

Eliade, M. *L'Isola di Euthanasius: Scritti Letterari.* Turin: Bollati Boringhieri, 2000.

Eliade, M. *Journal I, 1945–1955.* Chicago, IL: University of Chicago Press, 1990.

Eliade, M. *Journal II, 1957–1969.* Chicago, IL: University of Chicago Press, 1989.

Eliade, M. *Journal III, 1970–1978.* Chicago, IL: University of Chicago Press, 1989.

Eliade, M. "Meditation on the Burning of Cathedrals." In *Mircea Eliade: A Critical Reader*, edited by B. Rennie, 419–22. London: Equinox, [1937] 2006.

Eliade, M. *No Souvenirs.* New York: Harper & Row, 1977.

Eliade, M. "Occultism and Freemasonry in Eighteenth-Century Europe." *History of Religions* 13(1) (1973): 89–91.

Eliade, M. "Piloții orbi" [Blind pilots]. *Vremea* 10(505) (1937).

Eliade, M. *Salazar și revoluția în Portugalia.* Bucharest: Gorjan, 1942.

Eliade, M. *Schmiede und Alchemisten.* Stuttgart: Ernst Klett, n.d.

Eliade, M. *Textele "legionare" și despre "românism,"* edited by M. Handoca. Cluj-Napoca: Casa Cârtii de Știintă, 2001.

Eliade, M. *The Forge and the Crucible.* rev. ed. Chicago, IL: University of Chicago Press, 1978.

Eliade, M. *The Myth of the Eternal Return: Cosmos and History.* Princeton, NJ: Princeton University Press, 1971.

Eliade, M. *The Quest: History and Meaning in Religion.* Chicago, IL: University of Chicago Press, 1971.

Eliade, M. *The Sacred and the Profane: The Nature of Religion.* Translated by W. Trask. New York: Harcourt, Brace & World, 1959.

Eliade, M. *Une nouvelle philosophie de la lune.* Paris: L'Herne, 2001.

Eliade, M. and J.M. Kitagawa (eds). *Grundfragen der Religionswissenschaft.* Salzburg: Otto Müller, 1963.

Eliade, M. and J.M. Kitagawa. *The History of Religions: Essays in Methodology*. Chicago, IL: University of Chicago Press, 1959.

Eliade, M. and R. Pettazzoni. *L'histoire des religions a-t-elle un sens? Correspondance 1926–1959*. Edited by Natale Spineto. Paris: Les éditions du cerf, 1994.

Eliade, M. and I. Progoff. *About the Eranos Conferences*. Ascona: privately published, n.d.

ben Elieser, G. "Jüdisches Volk, antworte! Notwendigkeiten, Wege und Ziele eines völkischen Zionismus." Viöl: Archiv-Edition des Verlages für ganzheitliche Forschung, [1937] 1998.

Ellwood, R. "Cult Fictions." *Theosophical History* 7(4) (2000): 148–9.

Ellwood, R. *The Politics of Myth: A Study of C.G. Jung, Mircea Eliade, and Joseph Campbell*. Albany, NY: SUNY Press, 1999.

Encke, J. "Gelehrten-Picknick mit Jung-Frauen." *Frankfurter Allgemeine Zeitung* 201 (31 August 1999).

Endersby, V. *A Study of the Arcane School of Alice E. Bailey*. *Theosophical Notes Special Paper* (1963): 1–64.

Engelmann, I.J. (ed.). *Alastair: Kunst als Schicksal*. Halle: Stiftung Moritzburg, 2004.

Eranos, Festschrift für Hugo von Hofmannsthal zu dessen 50. Geburtstag. Munich: Verlag der Bremer Presse, 1924.

Euro, M. "Un triangolo culturale nel futuro di Eranos." *Corriere del Ticino* (6 April 2007).

von Essen, G. "Max Weber und die Kunst der Geselligkeit." In *Heidelberg im Schnittpunkt intellektueller Kreise*, edited by H. Treiber and K. Sauerland, 310–27. Opladen: Westdeutscher Verlag, 1995.

Everdingen, E. van. *Zestig jaar Internationale School voor Wijsbegeerte 1915–1975*. Assen: Van Gorcum, 1976.

Evola, J. "L'apostolo' Buonaiuti e la chiesa romana." In *La Nobiltà della Stirpe* (April 1933). Reprinted in *La Nobiltà della Stirpe: La Difesa della Razza*, edited by G.F. Lami, 104–9. Rome: Fondazione Julius Evola, 2002.

Evola, J. *Oriente e Occidente*. Rome: Edizioni Mediterranee, 2001.

Faber, R. "Gnosis-Verdacht als polit(olog)isches Stratagem." In *Gnosis und Politik*, edited by J. Taubes, 230–48. Munich: Wilhelm Fink, 1984.

Faber, R. *Männerrunde mit Gräfin: Die "Kosmiker" Derleth, George, Klages, Wolfskehl und Franziska zu Reventlow*. Frankfurt: Peter Lang, 1994.

Faber, R. *Der Prometheus-Komplex: Zur Kritik der Politotheologie Eric Voegelins und Hans Blumenbergs*. Würzburg: Königshausen & Neumann, 1984.

Faber, R. and C. Holste (eds). *Kreise, Gruppen, Bünde: Zur Soziologie moderner Intellektuellenassoziation*. Würzburg: Königshausen & Neumann, 2000.

Faber, R., B. von Reibnitz, and J. Rüpke (eds). *Antik, Modern: Beiträge zur römischen und deutschen Kulturgeschichte*. Stuttgart: J.B. Metzler, 1998.

Faesi, R. *Erlebnisse, Ergebnisse, Erinnerungen*. Zurich: Atlantis Verlag, 1963.

Faessel, V. "Karl Kerényi: Humanism at the Margin." In *Disturbances in the Field*, edited by C. Downing, 273–92.

Faivre, A. "L'ambiguità della nozione di sacro in Mircea Eliade." In *Confronto con Mircea Eliade*, edited by L. Arcella, P. Pisi, and R. Scagno, 363–74. Milan: Jaca Book, 1998.

Faivre, A. *Accès de l'ésotérisme occidentale*, vol. I. Paris: Gallimard, 1986; rev. edn 1996.

Faivre, A. *Accès de l'ésotérisme occidentale*, vol. II. Paris: Gallimard, 1996.

Faivre, A. "Auskunft zur Esoterikforschung in Zeitenblicke." *Zeitenblicke* 5(1) (2006). www.zeitenblicke.de/2006/1/

Faivre, A. *Eckartshausen et la Théosophie chrétienne*. Paris: C. Klincksieck, 1969.

Faivre, A. "Ein neues Feld europäischer Religionsgeschichte: Antoine Faivre gibt Auskunft zur Esoterikforschung." *Zeitenblicke* 5(1) (2006). www.zeitenblicke.de/2006/1/Interview/ (accessed December 2012).

Faivre, A. *Esoterik*. Braunschweig: Aurum Verlag, 1996.

Faivre, A. *Esoterik im Überblick*. Freiburg: Herder, 2001.

Faivre, A. *Les Conférences des Elus Cohens de Lyon (1774–1776): Aux sources du Rite Ecossais Rectifié*. Braine-le-Comte: Editions du Baucens, 1975.

Faivre, A. *L'ésotérisme au XVIIIe siècle en France et en Allemagne*. Paris: Seghers, La Table d'Emeraude, 1973.

Faivre, A. *L'ésotérisme*. Paris: Presses Universitaires Françaises, 1992.

Faivre, A. Interview. *Gnosis* 31 (1994): 62–8.

Faivre, A. Interview. *Gnostika* 2 (1997): 11–17.

Faivre, A. Interview. *Travaux de la loge nationale de recherches Villard de Honnecourt* 5 (1981): 114–18.

Faivre, A. "Meine Begegnungen mit Oskar R. Schlag." *Gnostika* 28 (2004): 50–55.

Faivre, A. "Modern Western Esoteric Currents in the Work of Mircea Eliade: The Extents and Limits of Their Presence." In *Hermeneutics, Politics and the History of Religions*, edited by C.K. Wedemeyer and W. Doniger, 147–57. Oxford: Oxford University Press, 2010.

Faivre, A. *Mystiques, Théosophes et illuminés au siècle des lumières*. Hildesheim: Georg Olms, 1976.

Faivre, A. *Philosophie de la Nature: Physique sacrée et théosophie XVIIe–XIXe siècle*. Paris: Albin Michel, 1996.

Faivre, A. "Renaissance Hermeticism and the Concept of Western Esotericism." In *Gnosis and Hermeticism from Antiquity to Modern Times*, edited by R. van den Broek and W. Hanegraaff, 109–23. Albany, NY: SUNY Press, 1998.

Faivre, A. "Synthèse de la Session," colloquium 15–17 June 1979. Reprinted in *Cahiers de l'Université de Saint Jean de Jérusalem* 6. Paris: Berg International, 1980.

Faivre, A. and W. Hanegraaff (eds). *Western Esotericism and the Science of Religion*. Leuven: Peeters, 1998.

Faivre, A. and J. Needleman (eds). *Modern Esoteric Spirituality*. New York: Crossroad, 1992.

Faivre, A. and K.-C. Voss. "Western Esotericism and the Science of Religion." *Numen*, 42(1) (1995): 48–77.

Faivre, A. and R. Zimmerman. *Epochen der Naturmystik: Hermetische Tradition im wissenschaftlichen Fortschritt*. Berlin. Erich Schmidt Verlag, 1979.

Falter, R. *Ludwig Klages: Lebensphilosophie als Zivilisationskritik*. Munich: Telesma, 2003.

Fäthke, B. *Marianne Werefkin: Leben und Werk 1860–1938*. Munich: Prestel Verlag, 1988.

Faure, B. *Chan Insights and Oversights: An Epistemological Critique of the Chan Tradition*. Princeton, NJ: Princeton University Press, 1993.

Faure, B. *The Rhetoric of Immediacy: A Cultural Critique of Chan/Zen Buddhism*. Princeton, NJ: Princeton University Press, 1991.

Federer, K. (ed.). *Marianne von Werefkin: Zeugnis und Bild*. Zurich: Verlag der Arche, 1975.

Feitknecht, T. *"Die dunkle und wilde Seite der Seele": Hermann Hesse—Briefwechsel mit seinem Psychoanalytiker Josef Bernhard Lang 1916–1914*. Frankfurt: Suhrkamp, 2006.

de Felice, R. *Intervista sul fascismo*. Laterza: Roma-Bari, 1975.

Fellinger, B. *Sanduhr*. Zurich: IPE, 2003.

de Ferdinandy, M. "Franz Altheim." *Eco: Revista de Cultura de Occidente* 137 (1971): 469–504.

Feuerstein, G. *The Philosophy of Classical Yoga*. New York: St. Martin's Press, 1980.

Feuerstein, G. and J. Miller. *Yoga and Beyond*. New York: Schocken Books, 1972.

Feyerabend, P. *Erkenntnis für freie Menschen*. Frankfurt: Suhrkamp, 1979.

Filoramo, G. *Figure del sacro: Saggi di storia religiosa*. Brescia: Morcelliana, 1993.

Filoramo, G. *A History of Gnosticism*. Oxford: Blackwell, 1991.

Filoramo, G. *Il risveglio della gnosi ovvero diventare dio*. Bari: Laterza, 1990.

Finkenberger, M. "Herbert Grabert: Vom völkischen Religionswissenschaftler zum Geschichtsrevisionisten." *Spirita* 1 (1997): 26–7.

Finkenberger, M. and H. Junginger. *Im Dienste der Lügen: Herbert Grabert (1901–1978) und seine Verlage*. Aschaffenburg: Alibri Verlag, 2004.

Fischer, H. (ed.). *Paul Tillich: Studien zu einer Theologie der Moderne*. Frankfurt: Athenäum, 1989.

Flasche, R. "Gab es Versuche einer Ideologisierung der Religionswissenschaft während des Dritten Reiches?" In *Gnosisforschung und Religionsgeschichte*, edited by H. Preißler and H. Seiwert, 413–20. Marburg: Diagonal-Verlag, 1994.

Folini, M. *Il Monte Verità di Ascona*. Berne: Società di Storia dell'Arte in Svizzera, 1998.

Fordham, M. *The Making of an Analyst: A Memoir*. London: Free Associations, 1993.

le Forestier, R. *La Franc-Maçonnerie occultiste au XVIIIe siècle & l'Ordre des Elus Coens*. Paris: La Table d'Emeraude, 1987.

le Forestier, R. *La Franc-Maçonnerie templière et occultiste aux XVIIIe et XIXe siècles*. Paris: La Table d'Emeraude, 1987.

Foucault, M. *Folie et déraison: Histoire de la folie à l'âge Classique*. Paris: Plon, 1961. Published in German as *Wahnsinn und Gesellschaft: Die Geschichte des Wahns im Zeitalter der Venunft*. Frankfurt: Suhrkamp, 1973.

Franz, I. Review. *Zeitschrift für Ganzheitsforschung* 45(4) (2001): 191–6.

von Franz, M.-L. *C.G. Jung: Sein Mythos in unserer Zeit*. Frauenfeld: Verlag Huber, 1972.

Fraser, J.E. "ARAS: Archive for Archetypal Symbolism." *Spring* (1964): 60–67.

Frei, P. "Denkform und Anschauung: Bemerkungen zu Hans Leisegangs Denkformlehre." In *Rationalitätstypen*, edited by K. Gloy, 56–68. Freiburg: Karl Alber, 1999.

Freud, S. *Sigmund Freud–Karl Abraham: Briefe 1907–1926*. Frankfurt: S. Fischer Verlag, 1965.

Friedländer, A.H. *Leo Baeck: Leben und Lehre*. Stuttgart: Deutsche Verlagsanstalt, 1973.

Friedmann, M. *Martin Buber's Life and Work*. New York: E.P. Dutton, 1981–83.

Frietsch, W. *Peter Handke–C.G.Jung: Selbstsuche, Selbstfindung, Selbstwerdung: Der Individuationsprozess in der modernen Literatur am Beispiel von Peter Handkes Texten*. Gaggenau: Scientia Nova, [2002] 2006.

Frigerio, F. "Un ricordo degli anni dell'Istituto Ticinese di Alti Studi (1970–1973)." *Viátor* 9 (2005–2006): 164–5.

Frischknecht, M. "Kampf der Finsternis." *Spuren* 56 (Summer 2000), www.spuren.ch/archiv/arich/56.

Fritsche, H. *Baum der Käuze*. Berlin: Corvinus Presse, 1991.

Fröbe-Kapteyn, O. "A Note on Eranos." In *The Mysteries: Papers from the Eranos Yearbooks*, edited by Joseph Campbell. Princeton, NJ: Princeton University Press, 1979.

Fröbe-Kapteyn, O. "In Memoriam Erich Neumann." *Eranos Jahrbuch* 29 (1960).

Fröbe-Kapteyn, O. (ed.). *25 Jahre Eranos*. Zurich: Rhein-Verlag, 1957.

Frobenius, L. *Paideuma: Umrisse einer Kultur- und Seelenlehre*. Jena: E. Diederichs, 1921.

Frommel, W. *Vom Schicksal des deutschen Geistes, I: Die Begegnung mit der Antike: Reden um Mitternacht*. Berlin: Georg-Kreis-Verlag, 1934.

F. Sch. "Zehn Jahre Schule der Weisheit." *Europäische Revue* 7 (1931): 158–9.

Gahlings, U. *Hermann Graf Keyserling: Ein Lebensbild*. Darmstadt: Justus von Liebig Verlag, 1996.

Galling, K. (ed.). *Die Religion in Geschichte und Gegenwart: Handwörterbuch für Theologie und Religionswissenschaft*. 3rd ed. Tübingen: J.C.B. Mohr [Paul Siebeck], 1986.

Gandini, M. "Raffaele Pettazzoni negli anni 1949–1950: Materiali per una biografia." *Strada maestra* 60 (2006): 178.

Gasparro, G.S. *Destino e salvezza tra culti pagani e gnosi cristiana: Itinerari storico-religiosi sulle orme di Ugo Bianchi*. Cosenza: Lionello Giordano, 1998.

Gaus, J. "Wege, Methoden und Probleme der Symbolforschung: ein Diskussionspapier." *Symbolon* 8 (1986): 9–34.

Geay, P. *Hermés trahi: Impostures philosophiques et néo-spiritualisme d'après l'oeuvre de René Guénon*. Paris: Dervy, 1996.

Gebser, J. *Gesamtausgabe*, vol. 7. Schaffhausen: Novalis Verlag, 1980.

Gedbach, E. and E.L. Lashlee. "Ernst Benz: Bibliographie 1928–1966." In *Glaube, Geist, Geschichte: Festschrift für Ernst Benz zum 60. Geburtstage am 17. November 1967*, edited by G. Müller and W. Zeller, 545–72. Leiden: E.J. Brill, 1967.

George, S. *Briefwechsel zwischen George und Hofmannsthal*. 2nd ed. Berlin: Georg Bondi, 1938.

George, S. *Der siebente Ring*. Berlin: Georg Bondi, 1909.

Gess, H. *Vom Faschismus zum Neuen Denken: C.G. Jungs Theorie im Wandel der Zeit*. Lüneburg: Zu Klampen, 1994.

Giegerich, W. "*Liber Novus*, That is, The New Bible: A First Analysis of C.G. Jung's *Red Book*." *Spring* 83 (2010): 362.

Giegerich, W. "Postscript to Cocks." *Spring* 10 (1979): 221–7.

Gilbert, R.A. *A.E. Waite: Magician of Many Parts*. Wellingborough: Thorsons Publishers, 1987.

de Giorgio, G. *L'Instant et l'Eternité et autres textes sur la Tradition*. Milan: Arché, 1987.

Giovetti, P. *R. Assagioli: La vita e l'opera del fondatore della Psicosintesi*. Rome: Edizioni Mediterranee, 1995.

Glauco, G. "Il Santo Graal del Cavaliere Henry Corbin." *Atrium* 2(2) (2000): 14–26; 2(3) (2000): 53–68.

Gleichen-Russwurm, A. *Der Leuchter: Weltanschauung und Lebensgestaltung*. Darmstadt: Otto Reichl Verlag, 1919.

Gligor, M. "The Ideology of the Archangel Michael Legion and Mircea Eliade's Political Views in Interwar Romania." *International Journal of Humanistic Ideology* 1(1) (2008): 111–26.

Gligor, M. *Mircea Eliade: Anii Tulburi: 1932–1938*. Bucharest: Limba Romana, 2007.

Gligor, M. Review. *Euresis* (Spring–Summer 2007): 204.

Gnoli, R. "L'India nell'opera di Giuseppe Tucci." In *Giuseppe Tucci: Nel centenario della nascita*, edited by B. Melasecchi, 21–34. Rome: IsMEO, 1995.

Gnoli, R. *Ricordo di Giuseppe Tucci*. Rome: Istituto Italiano per il Medio ed Estremo Oriente, 1985.

Göbel, W. "Ernst Rowohlt und Kurt Wolff." In *Kurt Wolff zum Hundertsten*, edited by M. Kellner, 118–22. Hamburg: Michael Kellner, 1987.

Gödde, C. and H. Lonitz (eds). *Walter Benjamin: Gesammelte Briefe 5 (1935–1937)*. Frankfurt: Suhrkamp, 1999.

Godwin, J. *Arktos. The Polar Myth in Science, Symbolism, and Nazi Survival*. Grand Rapids, MI: Phanes Press, 1993.

Godwin, J. "The Arts of the Imagination." *Lapis* 10 (1999): 71–4.

Godwin, J. (ed.). *Cosmic Music: Musical Keys to the Interpretation of Reality*. Rochester, VT: Inner Traditions, 1989.

Godwin, J., W.J. Hanegraaff, and J.-L. Vieillard-Baron. *Esotérisme, Gnoses & imaginaire symbolique*. Leuven: Peters, 2001.

Goebbels, J. *Tagebücher Band 3: 1935–1939*. Edited by R.G. Reuth. Munich: R. Piper, 1992.

Goethe, J.W. "Conversation with Heinrich Luden", 13 December 1813. In Johann Wolfgang von Goethe, *Artemis-Gedenkausgabe*, vol. XXII (Zurich: Artemis Verlag, 1948–54).

Goetz, A (ed.). *Der 300 jährige Maharishi vom Kailas als Prophet biblischer Wahrheiten: Nach authentischen Dokumenten des Professors Heiler und glaubwürdigen Augenzeugenberichten von Sadhu Sundar Singh*. Hamburg: "Mehr Licht" Verlag, n.d.

Goetz, B. *Das Reich ohne Raum*. Zurich: Origo, 1962.

Goldenberg, N.R. "Archetypal Theory after Jung." *Spring* 23 (1975): 199–220.

Gombrich, E.H. "Die Geschichte der Bibliothek Aby Warburgs (1886–1944)." In *Aby M. Warburg: Ausgewählte Schriften und Würdigungen*, edited by D. Wuttke, 335. Baden-Baden: Valentin Koerner, 1980.

Gómez, L.O. "Oriental Wisdom and the Cure of Souls: Jung and the Indian East." In *Curators of the Buddha: The Study of Buddhism under Colonialism*, edited by D.R. Lopez Jr., 197–250. Chicago, IL: University of Chicago Press, 1995.

Gooch, T.A. *The Numinous and Modernity: An Interpretation of Rudolf Otto's Philosophy of Religion*. Supplementary publication to *Zeitschrift für die alttestamentische Wissenschaft*, vol. 293, edited by O. Kaiser. Berlin: Walter de Gruyter, 2000.

Goodenough, E.R. *Jewish Symbols in the Greco-Roman Period*. Princeton, NJ: Princeton University Press, 1988.

Goodman-Thau, E., G. Mattenkloth, and C. Schulte (eds). *Kabbalah und Romantik*. Tübingen: Max Niemeyer, 1994.

Gorceix, B. *Amis de Dieu en Allemagne au siècle de Maitre Eckhart*. Paris: Albin Michel, 1984.

Gottmann, I. "Zum Leben und Werk von Sigrid Strauß-Klöbe." In *Symbole der inneren Welt: Ein Mosaik gewidmet Sigrid Strauß-Klöbe zum 85. Geburtstag*, edited by V. von Brasch, 1–11. Bad Soden: Viktor von Brasch, 1981.

Graal. "Il coraggio è un'abitudine." *Graal* 69–70 (June 2000): 3–39.

Grabert, H. *Der protestantische Auftrag des deutschen Volkes: Grundzüge der deutschen Glaubensgeschichte von Luther bis Hauer*. Stuttgart: Karl Gutbrod, 1936.

Grabert, H. *Religiöse Verständigung: Wege zur Begegnung der Religionen bei Nicolaus Cusanus, Schleiermacher, Rudolf Otto und J.W. Hauer*. Leipzig: C.F. Hirschfeld, 1932.

Gräser, A.G. *Tao: Das heilende Geheimnis*. Wetzlar: Büchse der Pandora, 1979.

Greco, B. *Ketzer oder Prophet? Evangelium und Kirche bei dem Modernisten Ernesto Buonaiuti (1881–1946)*. Zurich: Benziger Verlag, 1979.

Green, H. *The Economic and Social History of Gnosticism*. Atlanta, GA: Scholars Press, 1985.

Green, M. *The Mountain of Truth: The Counterculture Begins, Ascona, 1900-1920*. Hanover, NH: University Press of New England, 1986.

Gregory, T., M. Fattori, and N.S. de Cumis (eds). *Filosofi Università Regime: La Scuola di Filosofia di Roma negli anni trenta: Mostra storico-documentaria*. Rome: Istituto di Filosofia della Sapienza, 1985.

Griffin, D.R. (ed.). *Archetypal Process: Self and Divine in Whitehead, Jung, and Hillman*. Evanston, IL: Northwestern University Press, 1989.

Grohmann, A. *Die Vegetarier-Ansiedlung in Ascona und die sogenannten Naturmenschen im Tessin (mit sieben Fotografien)*. Halle: Carl Marhold, 1904.

Grose, P. *Gentleman Spy: The Life of Allen Dulles*. Amherst, MA: University of Massachusetts Press, 1996.

Großheim, M. "Archaisches oder dialektisches Bild? Zum Kontext einer Debatte zwischen Adorno und Benjamin." *Deutsche Vierteljahrsschrift für Literaturwissenschaft und Geistesgeschichte* 71(3) (1997): 494–517.

Großheim, M. "'Die namenlose Dummheit, die das Resultats des Fortschritts ist': Lebensphilosophische und dialektische Kritik der Moderne." *Logos* 3(2) (1996): 97–133.

Großheim, M. *Ludwig Klages und die Phänomenologie*. Berlin: Akademie Verlag, 1993.

Groupe d'Etudes Spirituelles Comparées. "Transmission culturelle, transmission spirituelle: Colloque tenu en Sorbonne les 13 et 14 Juin." *Cahier* 1. Paris: Arché-Edidit, 1993.

Gründer, R. *Germanisches (Neu-)Heidentum in Deutschland*. Berlin: Logos-Verlag, 2008.

Gruppo di Ur (ed.). *Introduzione alla Magia quale scienza dell'Io*, 3 vols. Turin: Bocca, 1955.

Guilford III, D. "Eliade und Jung. Der Geist von Eranos." In *Die Mitte der Welt*, edited by H.P. Duerr, 35–48. Frankfurt: Suhrkamp, 1984.

Gundolf, F. *Romantiker*. Berlin-Wilmersdorf: Heinrich Keller Verlag, 1930.

Günther, C.C. *Aufbruch nach Asien: Kulturelle Fremde in der deutschen Literatur um 1900*. Munich: Judicum, 1988.

Günther, H.F.K. *Platon als Hüter des Lebens*. Munich: Lehmann, 1928.

Haase, R. *Hans Kayser: Ein Leben für die Harmonik der Welt*. Basel: Schwabe, 1968.

Haase, R. *Kaysers Harmonik in der Literatur der Jahre 1950-1964*. Düsseldorf: Verlag der Gesellschaft zur Förderung der systematischen Musikwissenschaft, 1967.

Hafner, U. "Geld, Geist und Zwietracht." *Neue Zürcher Zeitung* (6 August 2007).

Hakl, H.T. Review of James Webb, *Das Zeitalter des Irrationalen*. *Gnostika* 42 (July 2009): 17–20.

Hakl, H.T. "'Den Antaios kenne ich und missbillige ich. Was er pflegt ist nicht Religio sondern Magie!' Kurze Geschichte der Zeitschrift *Antaios*." *Aries* 9(2) (2009): 195–232. Summary published in Italian as "L'effeto, pur non esteso, è stato profondo come quello d'una sonda: Breve storia della rivista 'Antaios', curata da Mircea Eliade ed Ernst Jünger (1959-1971)," in *Cenacoli, circoli e gruppi letterari, artistici, spirituali*, edited by F. Zambon, 247–70. Milan: Medusa, 2007.

Hakl, H.T. "Die Getreuen der Liebe." *Gnostika* 4 (1997): 37–40; 5 (1998): 38–43; 7 (1998): 43–50; and 8 (1998): 41–50.

Hakl, H.T. "Die Hermetik. Eine alte neue Weltsicht: Bemerkungen zum Buch *Die Hermetik* von Ralf Liedtke." *Gnostika* 6 (1998): 43–56.

Hakl, H.T. "Giuseppe Tucci entre Etudies orientales, ésotérisme et fascisme (1894–1984)." *Politica Hermetica* 18 (2004): 231–50.

Hakl, H.T. "Julius Evola and the Ur Group." In *Aries* 12(1): 53–90. Published in German in *Gnostika* 46 (2010): 51–65 and *Gnostika* 47 (2011): 41–59.

Hakl, H.T. "Kaleidoskop." *Gnostika* 14 (2000): 4.

Hakl, H.T. "'Occultism is the Metaphysic of Dunces': The Conflation of Esotericism, Irrationalism, and Fascism in Postwar Germany." In *Esotericism, Religion, and Politics*, edited by A. Versluis, L. Irwin, and M. Phillips, 1–40. Minneapolis, MN: Association for the Study of Esotericism, 2012.

Hakl, H.T. "Okkultismus ist die Metaphysik der dummen Kerle: Die Gleichsetzung oder begriffliche Annäherung von Esoterik, Irrationalismus und Faschismus im Deutschland der Nachkriegszeit." *Gnostika* 49 (2011): 45–58; 50 (2012): 67–90.

Hakl, H.T. "Review of *Von alten und neuen Mysterien* by Oskar R. Schlag." *Aries* 20 (1966): 94–7.

Hallaj, H.M. *Dîwân*. Paris: Edition du Seuil, 1981.

Hamacher, E. *Gershom Scholem und die Allgemeine Religionsgeschichte*. Berlin: Walter de Gruyter, 1999.

Hamvas, B. *Kierkegaard in Sizilien*. Berlin: Matthes & Seitz, 2006.

Hamvas, B. *Scientia Sacra*. Translated by C. Mutti. Parma: Edizioni all'insegna del Veltro, 2000.

Hamvas, B. *Silentium*. Grafing bei Munich: Edition Marika Marghescu, 1999.

Handoca, M. *Mircea Eliade: Europa, Asia, America corespondenţă*, vol. II. Bucharest: Bucuresti Humanitas, 1993.

Hanegraaff, W.J. "Beyond the Yates Paradigm: The Study of Western Esotericism between Counterculture and the New Complexity." *Aries* 1(1) (2001): 5–37.

Hanegraaff, W.J. "Empirical Method in the Study of Esotericism." *Method and Theory in the Study of Religion* 7(2) (1995): 121–4.

Hanegraaff, W.J. *Esotericism and the Academy: Rejected Knowledge in Western Culture*. Cambridge: Cambridge University Press, 2012.

Hanegraaff, W.J. *New Age Religion and Western Culture: Esotericism in the Mirror of Secular Thought*. Leiden: Brill, 1996.

Hanegraaff, W.J. "On the Construction of 'Esoteric Traditions.'" In *Western Esotericism and the Science of Religion: Selected Papers Presented at the 17th Congress of the International Association for the History of Religions, Mexico City 1995*, edited by A. Faivre and W. Hanegraaff. Leuven: Peters, 1998.

Hanegraaff, W.J. "Romanticism and the Esoteric Connection." In *Gnosis and Hermeticism from Antiquity to Modern Times*, edited by R. van den Broek and W. Hanegraaff, 237–68. Albany, NY: SUNY Press, 1998.

Hanegraaff, W.J. "Ten Years of Studying and Teaching Western Esotericism." In *Hermes in the Academy: Ten Years' Study of Western Esotericism at the University of Amsterdam*, edited by W.J. Hanegraaff and J. Pijnenburg, 17–26. Amsterdam: Amsterdam University Press, 2009.

Hanegraaff, W.J. and J. Pijnenburg (eds). *Hermes in the Academy: Ten Years' Study of Western Esotericism at the University of Amsterdam*. Amsterdam: Amsterdam University Press, 2009.

Hanimann, J. "Geistlos." *Frankfurter Allgemeine Zeitung* (11 December 2006): 35.

Hannah, B. *Jung, His Life and Work: A Biographical Memoir*. Wilmette, IL: Chiron, 1997.

Hansen, H.T. [ps. H.T. Hakl]. "Mircea Eliade, Julius Evola und die Integrale Tradition." In J. Evola, *Über das Initiatische: Aufsatzsammlung*, 9–50. Sinzheim: Archiv für Altes Gedankengut und Wissen, 1998.

Hantel, E. "Die 'Amazonen' um Heyer." In *Das Kraftfeld des Menschen und Forschers Gustav Richard Heyer: Eine Festschrift zu seinem 65, Geburtstag*, edited by K. Bügler and G.R. Heyer, 12–15. Munich: Kindler, 1955.

Harrowitz, N.A. (ed.). *Tainted Greatness: Antisemitism and Cultural Heroes*. Philadelphia, PA: Temple University Press, 1994.

Hartog, H. *Evangelische Katholizität: Weg und Vision Friedrich Heilers*. Mainz: Matthias-Grünewald-Verlag, 1995.

Hartung, G. "Völkische Ideologie." In *Handbuch zur "Völkischen Bewegung" 1871–1918*, edited by U. Puschner, W. Schmitz, and J.H. Ulbricht, 23. Munich: K.G. Saur, 1996.

Hasler, E. *Aline und die Erfindung der Liebe*. Zurich: Nagel & Kimche, 2000.

Hauer, J.W. *Das religiöse Artbild der Indogermanen und die Grundtypen der indo-arischen Religion*. Stuttgart: W. Kohlhammer, 1937.

Hauer, J.W. *Der Yoga als Heilweg*. Stuttgart: W. Kohlhammer, 1932.

Hauer, J.W. *Der Yoga: Ein indischer Weg zum Selbst*. Stuttgart: W. Kohlhammer, 1958.

Hauer, J.W. *Deutsche Gottschau: Grundzüge eines Deutschen Glaubens*, 3rd ed. Stuttgart: Karl Gutbrod Verlag, 1935.

Hauer, J.W. *Die Religionen: Ihr Werden/ihr Sinn/ihre Wahrheit*. Stuttgart: W. Kohlhammer, 1923.

Hauer, J.W. *Eine indo-arische Metaphysik des Kampfes und der Tat: Die Bhagavad-Gita in neuer Sicht mit Übersetzungen*. Stuttgart: Kohlhammer, 1934.

Hauer, J.W. "Einleitung." *Kommende Gemeinde* 5(1) (February 1933).

Hauer, J.W. *Religion und Rasse*. Tübingen: J.C.B. Mohr, 1941.

Hauer, J.W. *Toleranz und Intoleranz in den nichtchristlichen Religionen: Beitrag zu einer weltgeschichtlichen Betrachtung der Religion*. Stuttgart: Kohlhammer, 1961.

Hauer, J.W. *Unser Kampf um einen freien Deutschen Glauben: Flugschriften zum geistigen und religiösen Durchbruch der Deutschen Revolution*, vol. 3. Stuttgart: C.L. Hirschfeld, 1933.

Hauer, J.W. "Vom totalen Sinn der Deutschen Revolution." *Kommende Gemeinde* 5(2–3) (1933): 7.

Hauer, J.W. *Was will die deutsche Glaubensbewegung?* 4th ed., edited by H. Grabert. Stuttgart: Karl Gutbrod Verlag, 1935.

Hauer, J.W. *Werden und Wesen der Anthroposophie: Eine Wertung und eine Kritik*. Stuttgart: W. Kohlhammer, [1921] 1923.

Hayman, R. *A Life of Jung*. New York: W.W. Norton, 2001.

Heidler, I. *Der Verleger Eugen Diederichs und seine Welt*. Wiesbaden: Harrassowitz, 1998.

Heil, S. *Gefährliche Beziehungen: Walter Benjamin und Carl Schmitt*. Stuttgart: J.B. Metzler, 1996.

Heiler, F. *Apostel oder Betrüger: Dokumente zum Sadhu-Streit*. Basel: Friedrich Reinhardt, 1925.

Heiler, F. *Das Gebet in der Mystik: Eine religionspsychologische Untersuchung*. Munich: Ernst Reinhardt, 1918.

Heiler, F. *Sâdhu Sundar Singh: Ein Apostel des Ostens und Westens*. Munich: Ernst Reinhardt, [1924] 1925.

Heinens, A. *Die Legion "Erzengel Michael," in Rumänien: Soziale Bewegung und politische Organisation: Ein Beitrag zum Problem des internationalen Faschismus*. Munich: R. Oldenbourg, 1986.

Heinrich, F. *Die deutsche Religionswissenschaft und der Nationalsozialismus: Eine ideologiekritische und wissenschaftsgeschichtliche Untersuchung*. Petersberg: Michael Imhof Verlag, 2002.

Heinrichs, H.-J. *Die fremde Welt, das bin ich: Leo Frobenius: Ethnologe, Forschungsreisender, Abenteurer*. Wuppertal: Edition Trickster, Hammer Verlag, 1998.

Heißerer, D. *Wo die Geister wandern: Eine Topographie der Schwabinger Bohème um 1900*. Munich: Diederichs, 1993.

Helbig, L. [W. Frommel]. "Ludwig und Anna Derleth." In *Ludwig Derleth Gedenkbuch*, 5–73. Amsterdam: Castrum Peregrini, 1958.

Hemleben, J. *Ernst Haeckel, der Idealist des Materialismus*. Hamburg: Anthroposophische Buchhandlung, 1974.

Hemleben, J. *Rudolf Steiner und Ernst Haeckel*. Stuttgart: Freies Geistesleben, 1968.

Henderson, R. and J. Henderson. *"Enterviews" with Jungian Analysts*, vol. 3. New Orleans, LA: Spring Journal Books, 2010.

Herbert, J. "C.G. Jung and the German Tradition." In *Inward Lies the Way: German Thought and the Nature of Mind*, edited by S. Cross and J. Herbert, 111–36. London: Temenos Academy, 2008.

Hergemöller, B.-U. *Mann für Mann*. Hamburg: MännerschwarmSkript Verlag, 1998.

Hersch, J. "Mythos und Politik." In *Die Wirklichkeit des Mythos*, edited by K. Hoffman, 79–91. Munich: Droemer Knaur, 1965.

Hertzberg, A. *Wer ist Jude? Wesen und Prägung eines Volkes*. Darmstadt: Wissenschaftliche Buchgesellschaft, 2000.

Herwin, R. *Vom Kunstschaffen und seinen neuen Zielen. Einblicke in Rudolf Maria Holzapfels Erforschung des Schaffens*. Leipzig: Psychokosmos-Verlag, 1928.

Hesse, H. and K. Kerényi. *Briefwechsel aus der Nähe*. Munich: Langen-Müller, 1972.

Hesse, N. *Lieber, lieber Vogel: Briefe an Hermann Hesse*. Selected with a commentary by G. Kleine. Frankfurt: Suhrkamp, 2000.

Heuberger, G. and F. Backhaus (eds). *Leo Baeck 1873–1956: Aus dem Stamme von Rabbinern*. Frankfurt: Jüdischer Verlag, 2001.

von der Heyden-Rynsch, V. *Europäische Salons: Höhepunkte einer versunkenen weiblichen Kultur*. Düsseldorf: Artemis & Winkler, 1992.

von der Heydt, E. and W. von Rheinbaben. *Auf dem Monte Verità: Erinnerungen und Gedanken über Menschen, Junst und Politik*. Zurich: Atlantis-Verlag, 1958.

Heyer, G.R. "Einige Fragen der Psychosomatik im Licht der Erkenntnisse Jean Gebsers." In *Transparente Welt*, edited by G. Schulz, 131–51. Bern: Hans Huber, 1965.

Heyer, G.R. *Der Organismus der Seele: Eine Einführung in die analytische Seelenheilkunde*. Munich: J.F. Lehmann, 1932. Published in English as *The Organism of the Mind: An Introduction to Analytical Psychotherapy* (London: Kegan Paul, 1933).

Heyer, G.R. *Praktische Seelenheilkunde: Eine Einführung in die Psychotherapie für Ärzte und Studierende*. Munich: J.F. Lehmanns, 1942.

Heyer, G.R. *Seelenkunde im Umbruch der Zeit*. Bern: Hans Huber, 1964.

Heyer, G.R. *Seelen-Räume, psycho-therapeutische Beobachtungen zum Kollektiv-Seelischen*. Stuttgart: W. Kohlhammer, 1931.

Heyer, G.R. "Sinn und Bedeutung östlicher Weisheit für die abendländische Seelenführung." In *Eranos Jahrbuch 1* (1933): 215.

Heyer, G.R. "Vom neuen Denken in der Tiefenpsychologie." In *Die Welt in neuer Sicht: Sechs Vorträge*, 47–65. Munich-Planegg: Wilhelm Barth Verlag, 1957.

Heyer, G.R. *Vom Kraftfeld der Seele: Zwei Abhandlungen zur Tiefenpsychologie*. Stuttgart: Ernst Klett, 1949.

Heyer, G.R. and F. Seifert (eds). *Reich der Seele: Arbeiten aus dem Münchner psychologischen Arbeitskreis*. Munich: J.F. Lehmann, 1937.

Heyer-Grote, L. (ed.). *Atemschulung als Element der Psychotherapie*. Darmstadt: Wissenschaftliche Buchgesellschaft, 1970.

Hildebrandt, K. *Erinnerungen an Stefan George und seinen Kreis*. Bonn: H. Bouvier, 1965.

Hillman, J. *Am Anfang war das Bild: Unsere Träume—Brücke der Seele zu den Mythen*. Munich: Kösel, 1983.

Hillman, J. *Archetypal Psychology: A Brief Account*. Woodstock, CT: Spring Publications 1997.

Hillman, J. *The Dream and the Underworld*. New York: Harper & Row, 1979. Published in German as *Am Anfang war das Bild: Unsere Träume—Brücke der Seele zu den Mythen*. Munich: Kösel, 1983.

Hillman, J. "In the Gardens: A Psychological Memoir." In *Consciousness and Reality*, edited by J. al-Dīn Āshtiyānī et al., 175–82. Leiden: Brill, 1999.

Hillman, J. *Inter Views: Conversations with Laura Pozzo*. New York: Harper & Row, 1983.

Hillman, J. *The Myth of Analysis: Three Essays in Archetypal Psychology*. New York: Harper Perennial, 1978.

Hillman, J. "Plotinus, Ficino, and Vico as Precursors of Archetypal Psychology." In J. Hillman, *Loose Ends: Primary Papers in Archetypal Psychology*, 146–69. Dallas, TX: Spring Publications, 1994.

Hillman, J. *Re-Visioning Psychology*. New York: Harper & Row, 1975.

Hinshaw, R. *The Rock Rabbit and The Rainbow: Laurens van der Post among Friends*. Einsiedeln: Daimon Verlag, 1998.

Hippius-Dürckheim, M. "Am Faden von Zeit und Ewigkeit." In *Transzendenz als Erfahrung*, 25. Weilheim: O.W. Barth, 1966.

Hippius, M. (ed.). *Durchbruch in die Transzendenz: Beitrag und Widerhall, Festschrift zum 70. Geburtstag von Graf Dürckheim*. Weilheim: O.W. Barth, 1966.

Hippius-Dürckheim, M. *Geheimnis und Wagnis der Menschwerdung: Schriften zur Initiatischen Therapie*. Schaffhausen: Novalis, 1996.

Hoeller, S.A. *The Gnostic Jung and the Seven Sermons to the Dead*. Wheaton, IL: Theosophical Publishing House, 1985.

Höfer, J. and K. Rahner (eds). *Lexikon für Theologie und Kirche*. Freiburg: Herder, 1959.

Hoffman, E. Review of *Stalking Elijah: Adventures with Today's Jewish Mystical Masters*, by R. Kamenetz. *Gnosis 49* (1998): 68.

Hoffman, W.S. *Paul Mellon: Portrait of an Oil Baron*. Chicago, IL: Follett, 1974.

von Hofmannsthal, C. *Tagebücher 1918–1923 und Briefe des Vaters an die Tochter 1903–1929*. Frankfurt: S. Fischer, 1991.

Hofstee, W. "The Essence of Concrete Individuality: Gerardus van der Leeuw, Jan de Vries and National Socialism." In *The Study of Religion under the Impact of Fascism*, edited by H. Junginger, 543–52. Leiden: Brill, 2008.

Hofstee, W. *Goden en Mensen: De Godsdienstwetenschap van Gerardus van der Leeuw 1890–1950*. Agora: Kampen, 1997.

Hollwich, F. (ed.). *Im Umkreis der Kunst: Eine Festschrift für Emil Preetorius*. Wiesbaden: Insel Verlag, 1953.

Holton, G. *Science and Anti-Science*. Cambridge, MA: Harvard University Press, 1993.

Holton, G. and D.H.D. Roller. *Foundations of Modern Physical Science*. Reading: Addison-Wesley, 1958.

Holz, H.H. *China im Kulturvergleich: Ein Beitrag zur philosophischen Komparatistik*. Cologne: Dinter, 1994.

Holz, H.H. *Dialektik: Problemgeschichte von der Antike bis zur Gegenwart*. Darmstadt: Wissenschaftliche Buchgesellschaft, 2011.

Holz, H.H. "Die Eranos-Jünger." *Du* (August 1995): 92–3.

Holz, H.H. *Herr und Knecht bei Leibniz und Hegel*. Berlin: Luchterhand, 1968.

Holzapfel, B. (ed.). *Rudolf Maria Holzapfel: Nachgelassene Schriften: Zur Psychologie des sozialen Verkehrs, des Kultus, des Schaffens und der Erkenntnis*. Zurich: Max Niehans, 1939.

Holzapfel, R.M. *Panideal: Das Seelenleben und seine soziale Neugestaltung*. Jena: Eugen Diederichs, 1923.

Holzapfel, R.M. *Welterlebnis: Das religiöse Leben und seine Neugestaltung*. Jena: Eugen Diederichs, 1928.

Holzhausen, J. and C. Colpe. *Das Corpus Hermeticum Deutsch*. Stuttgart: frommann-holzboog, 1997.

Homolka, W. *Leo Baeck: Jüdisches Denken—Perspektiven für heute*. Freiburg: Herder 2006.

Homolka, W. and E.H. Füllenbach. *Leo Baeck: Eine Skizze seines Lebens*. Gütersloh: Gütersloher Verlagshaus, 2006.

Hondius, J.M. "The Eranos Conferences." *Chimera* 5(3) (1947): 63.

Hornung, E. *Abenteuer Eranos* (unpublished manuscript). www.eranos-ascona.ch.

Hornung, E. *Echnaton: Die Religion des Lichtes*. Zurich: Artemis & Winkler, 1955. Published in English as *Akhenaten and the Religion of Light*. Ithaca, NY: Cornell University Press, 1999.

Hornung, E. *Das esoterische Ägypten*. Munich: C.H. Beck, 1999. Published in English as *The Secret Lore of Egypt*, translated by D. Lorton. Ithaca, NY: Cornell University Press, 2001.

Hornung, E. *Geist der Pharaonenzeit*. Zurich: Artemis Verlag, 1989. Published in English as *Idea to Image: Essays on Ancient Egyptian Thought*, translated by Elizabeth Bredeck. New York: Timken, 1992.

Hornung, E. "Seth. Geschichte und Bedeutung eines ägyptischen Gottes." *Symbolon. Jahrbuch für Symbolforschung* 2 (1974): 49–63.

Hornung, E. "Die Tragweite der Bilder: Altägyptische Bildaussagen." In *Eranos Jahrbuch* 48 (1979): 183–237.

Hornung, E. "Wo sich grosse Geister finden." *Turicum* (June–July 1993): 24–8.

Hornung, E. and A. Schweizer. Foreword. *Der Mensch und seine Widersacher. Eranos 2001/2002*. Privately published, 2003.

Hourani, A. "T.E. Lawrence and Louis Massignon." In *Présence de Louis Massignon: Hommages et témoinages*, edited by D. Massignon, 167–76. Paris: Maisonneuve et Larose, 1987.

HRH Prince of Wales. "The Civilized Society." *Temenos Academy Review* 3 (2000): 5.

Hübinger, G., R. vom Bruch, and F.W. Graf (eds). "Idealismus. Positivismus: Grundspannung und Vermittlung in Kultur und Kulturwissenschaften um 1900." *Kultur und Kulturwissenschaften um 1900 II: Idealismus und Positivismus*, edited by G. Hübinger, R. vom Bruch, and F.W. Graf, 12. Stuttgart: Franz Steiner, 1997.

Huch, R. *Alfred Schuler, Ludwig Klages, Stefan George: Erinnerungen an Kreise und Krisen der Jahrhundertwende in Munich-Schwabing*. Amsterdam: Castrum Peregrini, 1973.

Hudson II, Frater H. "Rudolf Otto and the Concept of the Numinous." *Transactions 1983 and 1984 of the Metropolitan College der Societas Rosicruciana in Anglia*.

Hulin, M. and C. Maillard (eds). *L'Inde inspiratrice: Réception de l'Inde en France et en Allemagne (XIXe & XXe siècles)*. Strasbourg: Presses Universitaires de Strasbourg, 1996.

Iacovella, A. "Uno sguardo a Oriente: Evola, Tucci e l'IsMEO." In J. Evola, *Oriente e Occidente*, 11–22. Rome: Edizioni Mediterranee, 2001.

Idel, M. "Hiéroglyphes, clés, enigmes: La vision de G.G. Scholem sur la Kabbale entre Franz Molitor et Franz Kafka." *Archaeus* 7 (2003): 271–91.

Idel, M. *Kabbalah: New Perspectives*. New Haven, CT: Yale University Press, 1988.

Idel, M. *Studies in Ecstatic Kabbalah*. Albany, NY: SUNY Press, 1988.

Idel, M. "Subversive Katalysatoren: Gnosis und Messianismus in Gershom Scholems Verständnis der jüdischen Mystik." In *Gershom Scholem: Zwischen den Disziplinen*, edited by P. Schäfer and G. Smith, 80–121. Frankfurt: Suhrkamp, 1995.

Idel, M. "Zur Funktion von Symbolen bei G. Scholem." In *Gershom Scholem: Literatur und Rhetorik*, edited by S. Mosès and S. Weigel, 51–92. Cologne: Böhlau, 2000.

Illies, J. *Das Geheimnis des Lebendigen: Leben und Werk des Biologen Adolf Portmann*. Munich: Kindler, 1976.

Introvigne, M. "Louis Massignon: 'Il mistico spione'." *Il Foglio* (12 November 2005).

Introvigne, M. *Storia del New Age 1962–1992*. Piacenza: Christianità, 1994.

Ionesco, E. *Scrisori câtre Tudor Vianu II (1936–1949)*. Bucharest: Editura Minerva, 1994.

Ionesco, N. *Rosa Vînturilor, 1926–1933*. Edited by Mircea Eliade. Bucharest: Editura Rosa Vânturilor, 1990.

Irving, D. *Goebbels: Macht und Magie*. Kiel: Arndt Verlag, 1997.

Irving, D. *Goebbels: Mastermind of the Third Reich*. London: Focal Point, 1996.

Isastia, A.M. *Uomini e idee della Massoneria nella storia d'Italia*. Rome: Atanor, 2001.

IsMEO. *Nel centenario dell'intervento di Swami Vivekananda al Parlamento Mondiale delle Religioni* (Chicago 1893). Rome: Istituto Italiano per l'Africa e l'Oriente, 1997.

Iwersen, J. "Was ist New Age? Was ist Esoterik?" *Zeitschrift für Religions- und Geistesgeschichte* 52(1) (2000): 1–24.

Izutsu, T. *Philosophie des Zen-Buddhismus*. Reinbek: Rowohlt, 1979.

Izutsu, T. *Toward a Philosophy of Buddhism*. Teheran: Imperial Iranian Academy of Philosophy, 1977.

Jacobsen, H.-A. *Karl Haushofer: Leben und Werk*. Schriften des Bundesarchivs 24/I. Boppard am Rhein: Harald Boldt, 1979.

Jacobi, J. "Eranos: vom Zuhörer aus gesehen." *Du* 4 (1955): 51–7.

Jaffé, A. *Anna Kingsford: Religiöser Wahn und Magie*. Fellbach: Bonz-Verlag, 1980.

Jaffé, A. *Aus C.G. Jungs letzten Jahren und andere Aufsätze*. Einsiedeln: Daimon Verlag, 1987.

Jaffé, A. *Aus Leben und Werkstatt von C.G. Jung*. Zurich: Rascher, 1968.

Jaffé, A. *C.G. Jung, Bild und Wort*. Olten: Walter Verlag, 1977.

Jaffé, A. "C.G. Jung und der Nationalsozialismus." In *Parapsychologie, Individuation, Nationalsozialismus*, 141–64. Zurich: Daimon, 1968.

Jaffé, A. "C.G. Jung und die Eranos-Tagungen: Zum 100. Geburtstag von C.G. Jung." *Eranos Jahrbuch* 44 (1975): 1–14.

Jaffé, A. "Die schöpferischen Phasen im Leben von C.G. Jung." *Eranos Jahrbuch* 40 (1971): 85–122.

Jaffé, A. (ed.). *Memories, Dreams, Reflections*, translated by Richard Winston and Clara Winston. New York: Vintage Books, 1989.

Jaffé, A. *Parapsychologie, Individuation, Nationalsozialismus: Themen bei C.G. Jung*. Zurich: Daimon, 1968.

Jäger, L. "Wer hat die längste Lebenslinie? Er verstand von vielem viel und führte seinen Gesprächspartner sogar in die Kunst der Chiromantie ein: Ein Frankfurter Vormittag mit Gershom Scholem im Jahr 1980." *Frankfurter Allgemeine Zeitung* (11 April 2009).

Jambet, C. (ed.). *Henry Corbin*. Paris: L'Herne, 1981.

Jambet, C. *La logique des Orientaux: Henry Corbin et la science des formes*. Paris: Editions du Seuil, 1983.

James, M.-F. *Esotérisme et Christianisme autour de René Guénon*. Paris: Nouvelles Editions Latines, 1981.

Jamme, C. "Rationalität, Naturbeherrschung und Mythos: Eine Skizze." In *Mnemosyne: Festschrift für Manfred Lurker zum 60. Geburtstag*, edited by W. Bies and H. Jung, 9–15. Baden-Baden: Valentin Koerner, 1988.

Jaspers, K. and R. Bultmann. *Die Frage der Entmythologisierung*. Munich: Piper, 1954.

Jens, I. and W. Jens. *Frau Thomas Mann: Das Leben der Katharina Pringsheim*. Reinbek: Rowohlt, 2004.

Jesi, F. *Cultura di Destra*. Milan: Garzanti, 1979.

Jesi, F. *Die letzte Nacht*. Freiburg: Beck & Glückler, 1991.

Jesi, F. *Germania Segreta: Miti nella cultura tedesca del 900*. Milan: Feltrinelli, [1967] 1995.

Jesi, F. "K. Kerényi: i 'pensieri segreti' del mitologo." *Comunità* 172 (1974): 271–315.

Jesi, F. Foreword to *Il Tramonto dell'Occidente* by Oswald Spengler. Milan: Longanesi, 1981.

Jolles, A. *Einfache Formen: Legende, Sagen, Mythe, Rätsel, Spruch, Kasus, Memorabile, Märchen, Witz*. Halle: Max Niemeyer, 1929.

Jolowicz, E. and G. Heyer. *Hypnosis and Hypnotherapy*. London: C.W. Daniel, 1931.

Jonas, H. *Erinnerungen nach Gesprächen mit Rachel Salamander*. Frankfurt: Insel Verlag, 2003.

Jonas, H. "Gnosis, Existenzialismus und Nihilismus." In *Gnosis und spätantiker Geist* Part 2: *Von der Mythologie zur mystischen Philosophie: Erste und Zweite Hälfte*, 359–79. Göttingen: Vandenhoek & Ruprecht, 1993.

Jonas, H. *Das Prinzip Verantwortung: Versuch einer Ethik für die technologische Zivilisation*. Frankfurt: Suhrkamp, 1989.

Jonas, H. *Gnosis: Die Botschaft des fremden Gottes*. Frankfurt: Insel Verlag, 1999.

Jones, E.M. *Libido Dominandi: Sexual Liberation and Political Control*. South Bend, IN: St. Augustine's Press, 2005.

Jones, J.D.F. *Teller of Many Tales: The Lives of Laurens van der Post*. New York: Carroll & Graf, 2002.

Jost, D. *Die Dichtung Ludwig Derleths*. Bellnhausen über Gladenbach: Hinder & Deelmann, 1975.

Jost, D. *Ludwig Derleth, Gestalt und Leistung*. Stuttgart: W. Kohlhammer, 1965.

Jung, C.G. *Briefe I (1906–1945)*. Olten: Walter Verlag, 1972.

Jung, C.G. *Briefe II (1946–1955)*. Olten: Walter Verlag, 1972.

Jung, C.G. "C.G. Jung über Parapsychologie: Ein Interview." *Neue Wissenschaft* 2(9) (1952).

Jung, C.G. "Der Organismus der Seele." *Europäische Revue* 9(2) (1933): 639.

Jung, C.G. "Ein moderner Mythos." In *C.G. Jung: Gesammelte Werke*, vol. 10: *Zivilisation im Übergang*. Olten: Walter Verlag, 1974.

Jung, C.G. *Erinnerungen, Träume, Gedanken*. Edited by A. Jaffé. Olten: Walter Verlag, 1971.

Jung, C.G. *Gesammelte Werke*. Olten: Walter Verlag, 1970–76.

Jung, C.G. Interview. *Ausblick: Zeitfragen im Lichte der Weltmeinung* (August 1945), 53–7.

Jung, C.G. *Letters*, vol. 1. Princeton, NJ: Princeton University Press, 1975.

Jung, C.G. *Memories, Dreams, Reflections*. Edited by A. Jaffé, translated by R. Winston and C. Winston. New York: Vintage Books, 1989.

Jung, C.G. *The Psychology of Kundalini Yoga*. Edited by S. Shamdasani. Princeton, NJ: Princeton University Press, 1996; Published in German as *C.G. Jung: Die Psychologie des Kundalini-Yoga* (Zurich: Walter Verlag, 1998).

Jung, C.G. *The Red Book: Liber Novus*. Edited by S. Shamdasani. New York: Norton, 2009.

Jünger, E. *Siebzig verweht*. Stuttgart: Klett-Cotta, 1997.

Junginger, H. "Harmless or Dangerous? The Eranos Conferences in the 1930s from the Perspective of National Socialist Germany." *Archaeus* 14 (2010): 41–55.

Junginger, H. (ed.). *The Study of Religion under the Impact of Fascism*. Leiden: Brill, 2008.

Junginger, H. *Von der philologischen zur völkischen Religionswissenschaft: Das Fach Religionswissenschaft an der Universität Tübingen von der Mitte des 19. Jahrhunderts bis zum Ende des Dritten Reiches*. Stuttgart: Franz Steiner Verlag, 1999.

Kaiser, O. (ed.). *Philosophy of Religion: Beihefte zur Zeitschrift für die alttestamentliche Wissenschaft*, vol. 293. Berlin: Walter de Gruyter, 2000.

Kaiser Wilhelm II. *Die chinesische Monade: Ihre Geschichte und Deutung*. Leipzig: K.F. Köhler, 1934.

Kaiser Wilhelm II. (ed.). *Vergleichende Zeittafeln der Vor- und Frühgeschichte Vorderasiens, Ägyptens und der Mittelmeerländer*. Leipzig: K.F. Köhler, 1936.

Kaltenbrunner, G.-K. "'Ans Herz des Lebens schlich der Marder Juda.' Alfred Schulers pagane Gnosis." *Wort und Wahrheit* 23(6) (1968): 531–45.

Kaltenbrunner, G.-K. "Zwischen Rilke und Hitler: Alfred Schuler." *Zeitschrift für Religions- und Geistesgeschichte* 19(4) (1967): 333–47.

Kamber, P. *Geschichte zweier Leben: Wladimir Rosenbaum, Aline Valangin*. Zurich: Limmat Verlag, 2002.

Kant, I. *Werke in zehn Bänden*, vol. 2. Edited by W. Weischedel. Darmstadt: Wissenschaftliche Buchgesellschaft, 1981.

Kanterian, E. "Wie glücklich war Eliades Schuld?" *Lettre International* (Autumn 1995): 88–9.

Kantzenbach, F.W. "Ernst Benz: wie ich ihn sehe und verstehe. Eine Laudatio zum 17.11.1977." *Zeitschrift für Religions- und Geistesgeschichte* 29 (1977): 289–304.

Karádi, E. and E. Vezér (eds). *Georg Lukács, Karl Mannheim und der Sonntagskreis*. Frankfurt: Sendler, 1985.

Karcher, S. *Das I Ging*. Braunschweig: Aurum Verlag, 1997.

Karlauf, T. *Stefan George: Die Entdeckung des Charisma*. Munich: Karl Blessing, 2007.

Kast, V. *Der Schatten in Uns: Die subversive Lebenskraft*. Zurich: Walter Verlag, 2000.

Kathleen Raine Memorial Issue: Temenos Academy Review 7. Kent: Temenos Academy, 2004.

Kayser, H. *Bisher unveröffentliche Dokumente aus dem Nachlass*. Bern: Kreis der Freunde um Hans Kayser, 2000.

Kayser, H. *Harmonia Plantarum*. Basel: Schwabe, 1943.

Kayser, H. *Orphikon: Eine harmonische Symbolik*. Basel: Schwabe & Co., 1973.

Kayser, H. *Paestum: Die Nomoi der drei altgriechischen Tempel zu Paestum*. Heidelberg: Lambert Schneider, 1958.

Keller, C.A. *Ramakrishna et la voie de l'amour*. Paris: Bayard, 1997.

Kellner, M. (ed.). *Kurt Wolff zum Hundertsten*. Hamburg: Michael Kellner, 1987.

Kelsen, H. *A New Science of Politics: Hans Kelsen's Reply to Eric Voegelin's "New Science of Politics": A Contribution to the Critique of Ideology, Vol. 6: Practical Philosophy*. Edited by E.Arnold. Heusenstamm: Ontos Verlag, 2004.

Kerényi, K. *Antike Religion*. Munich: Langen Müller, 1971.

Kerényi, K. *Bachofen und die Zukunft des Humanismus: Mit einem Intermezzo über Nietzsche und Ariadne*. Zurich: Rascher Verlag, 1945.

Kerényi, K. "Bild, Gestalt und Archetypus." In *Apollon und Niobe*, edited by M. Kerényi, 279–92. Munich: Langen Müller, 1980.

Kerényi, K. "Das Geheimnis der hohen Städte." *Europäische Revue* 18(2) (1942): 386–90.

Kerényi, K. (ed.) *Die Eröffnung des Zugangs zum Mythos. Ein Lesebuch*. Darmstadt: Wissenschaftliche Buchgesellschaft, 1976.

Kerényi, K. "Die Goldene Parodie: Randbemerkungen zu den 'Vertauschten Köpfen.'" *Die Neue Rundschau* 67(4) (1956): 549–56.

Kerényi, K. "Élet és életmü" [Life and work]. In Béla Hamvas, *Szellem és egzisztencia* [Spirit and existence]. Budapest: Pannónia Könyvek, 1987.

Kerényi, K. *La Madonna ungherese di Verdasio*. Locarno: A. Dadò editore, 1996.

Kerényi, K. "Selbstbiographisches." In *Tessiner Schreibtisch: Mythologisches, Unmythologisches*. Stuttgart: Steingrüben, 1963.

Kerényi, K. "Sul mito della massoneria." In *Nuova Enciclopedia Massonica*, edited by M. Moramarco, 569–74. Foggia: Bastogi, 1998.

Kerényi, K. *Tage- und Wanderbücher 1953–1960*. Munich: Langen-Müller, 1969.

Kerényi, K. "Walter Friedrich Otto: Erinnerung und Rechenschaft." Appendix to *Die Wirklichkeit der Götter: Von der Unzerstörbarkeit griechischer Weltsicht* by W. F. Otto. Reinbek: Rowohlt, 1963.

Kerényi, K. "Was bedeutet der Name Eranos?" *Du* (April 1955).

Kerényi, K. "Was ist Mythologie?" In his *Antike Religion*, 13–34. Munich: Langen Müller, 1971.

Kerényi, M. "A Bibliography of C. Kerényi." In K. Kerényi, *Dionysos*, 447–74. Princeton, NJ: Princeton University Press, 1976.

Kerényi, M. "Die Vielheit der Welten: Zur Eranostagung 1975." *Die Tat* (26 September 1975).

Kerényi, M. "Eranos." In *Schweizer Lexikon*. Lucerne: Verlag Schweizer Lexikon, 1992.

Kerényi, M. (ed.). *Eranos-Index für die Jahrbücher I–XXV, 1933–1956*. Zurich: Rhein-Verlag, 1961.

Kerényi, M. (ed.). *Eranos-Index für die Jahrbücher XXVI–XXX, 1957–1961*. Zurich: Rhein-Verlag, 1965.

Kerényi, M. "Psicologia e mitologia: I rapporti tra C.G. Jung e Karl Kerényi." In *L'Immaginale*, edited by M. Cazenave. Paris: L'Herne, 1984.

Kerényi, M. and A. Cavalletti (eds). *Furio Jesi, Károly Kerényi: Demone e mito: carteggio 1964–1968*. Macerata: Quodlibet, 1999.

Keshavjee, S. *Mircea Eliade et la Coincidence des opposés ou l'existence en duel*. Berne: Peter Lang, 1993.

Keul, I. "Politische Myopie, mystische Revolution, glückliche (Un)schuld? Mircea Eliade und die Legionäre Bewegung: Rezentere rumänische Perspektiven." In *The Study of Religion under the Impact of Fascism*, edited by H. Junginger, 397–418. Leiden: Brill, 2008.

Keyserling, H.G. *Deutschlands wahre Mission*. Darmstadt: Otto Reichl, 1919.

Keyserling, H.G. *Schöpferische Erkenntnis*. Darmstadt: Otto Reichl, 1932.

Keyserling, H.G. "Die Schule der Weisheit." In *Der Weg zur Vollendung: Mitteilungen der Gesellschaft für Freie Philosophie, Schule der Weisheit*, vol. 1, edited by H. Keyserling, 49–54. Darmstadt, 1920.

Keyserling, H.G. *Über die innere Beziehung zwischen den Kulturproblemen des Orients und Okzidents*. Jena: Eugen Diederichs, 1913.

Keyserling, H.G. *Was uns Not tut. Was ich will*. Darmstadt: Otto Reichl, 1919.

Khorda Avesta, Yasht 13 (Hymn to the guardian angels), translated by J. Darmesteter, 1898; digital edition H. Peterson. www.avesta.org/ka/yt13sbe.htm.

Kilcher, A. "Figuren des Endes: Historie und Aktualität der Kabbala bei Gershom Scholem." In *Gershom Scholem: Literatur und Rhetorik*, edited by S. Mosès and S. Weigel, 153–99. Cologne: Bohlau Verlag, 2000.

Kilcher, A. "Gershom Scholem." In *Lexikon jüdischer Philosophie: Philosophisches Denken des Judentums von der Antike bis zur Gegenwart*, edited by A.B. Kilcher and O. Fraisse, 392–5. Stuttgart: J.B. Metzler, 2003.

Kilcher, A. "Okkulte Sprache und bürgerliche Rationalität: Zur Rezeption der Kabbala in der Freimaurerei." *Neue Zürcher Zeitung* (1–2 June 1996).

Kilcher, A. *Die Sprachtheorie der Kabbala als ästhetisches Paradigma: Die Konstruktion einer ästhetischen Kabbala seit der frühen Neuzeit*. Stuttgart: J.B. Metzler, 1998.

Kilcher, A.B. and O. Fraisse (eds). *Lexikon jüdischer Philosophen: Philosophisches Denken des Judentums von der Antike bis zur Gegenwart*. Stuttgart: J.B. Metzler, 2003.

Kindler, N. "G.R. Heyer in Deutschland." *Psychologie des 20. Jahrhunderts* 3(2) (1977): 820–40.

King, K.L. *What is Gnosticism?* Cambridge, MA: Harvard University Press, 2003.

Kippenberg, H.G. *Die Entdeckung der Religionsgeschichte: Religionswissenschaft und Moderne*. Munich: C.H. Beck, 1997.

Kippenberg, H.G. "Obituary: Prof. Dr. phil., Dr. theol. Carsten Colpe (19 July 1929–24 November 2009)." *Numen* 58 (2011), 1–5.

Kirsch, T.B. *The Jungians: A Comparative and Historical Perspective*. London: Routledge, 2000.

Kitagawa, J.M. "Mircea Eliade (First Edition, 1987)." In *The Encyclopedia of Religion*, 2nd edn, edited by L. Jones, vol. IV, 2753–7. Detroit, MI: Macmillan Reference USA, 2005.

Klatt, N. *Theosophie und Anthroposophie: Neue Aspekte zu ihrer Geschichte aus dem Nachlaß von Wilhelm Hübbe-Schleiden (1846–1916) mit einer Auswahl von 81 Briefen*. Göttingen: Eigenverlag, 1993.

Kleiner, B. *Die letzte Nacht*. Freiburg: Beck & Glückler, 1991.

Klenner, H., D. Losurdo, J. Lensnik, and J. Bartels (eds). *Representatio Mundi: Festschrift zum 70. Geburtstag von Hans Heinz Holz*. Cologne: Jürgen Dinter Verlag für Philosophie, 1997.

Knight, G. (B. Wilby). *Dion Fortune and the Inner Light*. Loughborough: Toth Publications, 2000.

Koch, H.-A. *Hugo von Hofmannsthal*, Erträge der Forschung, vol. 265. Darmstadt: Wissenschaftliche Buchgesellschaft, 1989.

Kodalle, K.M. (ed.). *Philosophie eines Unangepassten: Hans Leisegang*. Würzburg: Königshausen & Neumann, 2003.

Koepke, E. *Adolf Portmann: Wegbereiter zu einem neuen Weltbild: Eine naturphilosophische Studie*. Hamburg: Hamburger Kulturverlag, 1964.

Koller, A. *Thorwald Dethlefsen: Die Reinkarnationstherapie und Kawwana: Ein Beitrag zur Psychotherapie- und Religionsgeschichte*. Norderstedt: Books on Demand, 2004.

König, P.A. "Magda Kerényi (1914–2004), Gemahlin Karl Kerényis, im Gespräch." Unpublished manuscript.

König, P.R. *Das OTO-Phänomen*. Munich: ARW, 1994.

König, P.R. *Der OTO-Phänomen Remix*. Munich: ARW, 2001.

Korger, M. "Philip Sherrard: Kosmos als Theophanie." *Abendland* 6 (2008): 30–41.

Koslowski, P. "Gnosis und Gnostizismus in der Philosophie: Systematische Überlegungen." In *Gnosis und Mystik in der Geschichte der Philosophie*, 368–99. Zurich: Artemis, 1988.

Kraatz, M. "Birger Forell 1893–1993." *Alma Mater Philippina* (Summer 1994): 4–8.

Krämer, T. *Eine andere Moderne? Zivilisationskritik, Natur und Technik in Deutschland 1880–1933*. Paderborn: Ferdinand Schöningh, 1999.

Kreutzer, W. "'Ich verstand ihn viel besser als ich ihn nicht verstand': Ioan Petru Culianu als Biograph Mircea Eliades."

In *Spiegel und Maske: Konstruktionen biographischer Wahrheit*, edited by B. Fetz and H. Schweiger, 191–206. Vienna: Paul Zsolnay Verlag, 2006.

Krieger, H. "'Bei den abgehauenen Naturdämonen.' Hinunter ins Dunkel. Die Tiefenpsychologie Carl Gustav Jungs in seinen Briefen." *Die Zeit* 7 (9 February 1973).

Kripal, J.J. *Esalen: America and the Religion of No Religion*. Chicago, IL: University of Chicago Press, 2007.

Kripal, J.J. *Roads of Excess, Palaces of Wisdom: Eroticism and Reflexivity in the Study of Mysticism*. Chicago, IL: University of Chicago Press, 2001.

Kripal, J.J. "The Roar of Awakening: The Eros of Esalen and the Western Transmission of Tantra." In *Hidden Intercourse: Eros and Sexuality in the History of Western Esotericism*, edited by W. Hanegraaff and J.J. Kripal, 479–519. Leiden: Brill, 2008.

Küenzlen, G. *Der Neue Mensch: Zur säkulären Religionsgeschichte der Moderne*. Munich: Wilhelm Fink, 1994.

Kugler, P. "Eranos and Jungian Psychology: A Photographic History." In *Disturbances in the Field*, edited by C. Downing, 69–112.

L. "Glaubensbewegung: Symbol und Yoga" [Faith movement: symbolism and yoga]. *Am Heiligen Quell Deutscher Kraft* 6(14), (20 Gilbhardts 1935): 562–66.

L. "Glaubensbewegung: Hinein ins Irrenhaus" [Faith movement: into the madhouse]. *Am Heiligen Quell Deutscher Kraft* 6(15), (5 Nibelungs 1935): 599–607.

Laignel-Lavastine, A. *Cioran, Eliade, Ionescu: L'Oubli du fascisme: Trois intellectuels romains dans la tourmente du siècle*. Paris: Presses Universitaires de France, 2002.

Lami, G.F. (ed.). *Eric Voegelin: un interprete del totalitarismo*. Rome: Astra, 1978.

Lami, G.F. and G. Franchi (eds). *La scienza dell'ordine: Saggi su Eric Voegelin*. Rome: Antonio Pellicani Editore, 1997.

Lampis, G. *Trasformazioni di uomini e dei nella Grecia antica*, vol. 1. Rome: Mythos edizioni, 1999.

Landmann, E. *Gespräche mit Stefan George*. Dusseldorf: Helmut Küpper (previously Georg Bondi), 1963.

Landmann, M. *Figuren um Stefan George*, vol. 2. Amsterdam: Castrum Peregrini Presse, 1988.

Landmann, R. *Ascona, Monte Verità: Auf der Suche nach dem Paradies*. Zurich: Benziger, 1973.

Landmann, R. *Monte Verità, Ascona: Die Geschichte eines Berges*. Ascona: Pancaldi, 1934.

Lapide, P. *Heinrich Heine und Martin Buber: Streitbare Gottsucher des Judentums*. Vienna: Pincus Verlag, 1991.

Lappin, E. *Der Jude 196–1928: Jüdische Moderne zwischen Universalismus und Partikularismus*. Tübingen: Mohr Siebeck, 2000.

Larsen, S. and R. Larsen. *Joseph Campbell: A Fire in the Mind*. Rochester, VT: Inner Traditions, 2002.

de Laszlo, V. Summary of a newspaper article in *Bulletin of the Analytical Psychology Club of New York* 4(1) (1942): 4–8.

de Laszlo, V. "Eranos 1949." *Bulletin of the Analytical Psychology Club of New York* 12(1) (1950): 1–5.

Laude, P. *Massignon intérieur*. Lausanne: Delphica, L'Age d'Homme, 2001.

Laude, P. "Présence et verité: L'héritage spirituel chez Massignon et Schuon." *Connaissance des Religions* 69–70 (2003): 163–72.

Leisegang, H. *Dante und das christliche Weltbild*. Weimar: Hermann Böhlau Nachf., 1941.

Leisegang, H. *Denkformen*. Berlin: De Gruyter, 1928.

Leisegang, H. *Der Heilige Geist: Das Wesen und Werden der mystisch-intuitiven Erkenntnis in der Philosophie und Religion der Griechen*. Leipzig: B.G. Teubner, 1919.

Leisegang, H. *Die Gnosis*. Leipzig: Alfred Kröner Verlag, 1924.

Leisegang, H. "Zur psychologischen Prüfung der Erkenntnismethode Rudolf Steiners." *Unsere Welt* 8–9 (1922).

Lepp, N., M. Roth, and K. Vogel. *Der Neue Mensch: Obsessionen des 20. Jahrhunderts*. Ostfildern-Ruit: Cantz-Verlag, 1999.

Lerchenmüller, J. *Die Geschichtswissenschaft in den Planungen des Sicherheitsdienstes der SS: Der SD-Historiker Hermann Löffler und seine Gedenkschrift "Entwicklung und Aufgaben der Geschichtswissenschaft in Deutschland."* Bonn: J.H.W. Dietz, 2001.

Leuenberger, H.-D. "Oskar R. Schlag: Der große Unbekannte." *Esotera* 6 (1996): 28–32.

Leutwyler, C. and R. Lenzin. "Ascona liess sich von Versprechen blenden." *Zürcher Tageszeiger* (2 February 2007).

Leutwyler, C. and R. Lenzin. "Aufsicht hat Eranos-Stiftung im Visier." *Zürcher Tageszeiger* (3 February 2007).

Lewin, N. *Jung on War, Politics and Nazi Germany: Exploring the Archetypes and the Collective Unconscious*. London: Karnac Books, 2009.

Lichtheim, M. *Telling it Briefly: A Memoir of my Life*. Freiburg: Universitätsverlag, 1999.

Lieberg, G. "Karl Kerényi als Deuter der antiken Religion." In *Karl Kerényi: Der Humanismus des Integralen Menschen*. Ensemble 2, n.d., n.p.

Liedtke, R. *Die Hermetik*. Paderborn: Schöningh, 1996.

Ligou, D. (ed.). *Dictionnaire Universel de la Franc-Maçonnerie*. Paris: Editions de Navarre, Editions du Prisme, 1974.

Linse, U. "Asien als Alternative?" In *Religionswissenschaft und Kulturkritik*, edited by H.G. Kippenberg and B. Luchesi, 325–64. Marburg: Diagonal-Verlag, 1991.

Linse, U. *Barfüssige Propheten: Erlöser der zwanziger Jahre*. Berlin: Siedler, 1983.

Linse, U. *Ökopax und Anarchie*. Munich: DTV, 1986.

Linse, U. "Säkularisierung oder Neue Religiosität? Zur religiösen Situation in Deutschland um 1900." *Recherches Germaniques* 27 (1997): 117–41.

Lipsey, R. *Coomaraswamy: His Life and Work.* Bollingen Series LXXXIX. Princeton, NJ: Princeton University Press, 1977.

Lockot, R. *Die Reinigung der Psychoanalyse: Die Deutsche Psychoanlaytische im Spiegel von Dokumenten und Zeitzeugen (1933–1951).* Tübingen: Edition Diskord, 1994.

Lockot, R. *Erinnern und Durcharbeiten: Zur Geschichte der Psychoanalyse and Psychotherapie im Nationalsozialismus.* Frankurt: Fischer, 1985.

Lopez Jr., D.S. *Curators of the Buddha: The Study of Buddhism under Colonialism.* Chicago, IL: University of Chicago Press, 1995.

Lopez-Pedraza, R. *Hermes and His Children.* Einsiedeln: Daimon, 2003.

Lopez-Pedraza, R. *Hermes oder die Schule des Schwindelns: ein neuer Weg in der Psychotherapie.* Zurich: Schweizer Spiegel Verlag, 1983.

Lorentzen of Kiel, Pastor J. *Das christliche Bekenntnis und die deutsche Glaubensbewegung: eine Auseinandersetzung mit Graf Reventlow und Professor Hauer,* vol. 1 of a missionary series published by the Evangelical-Lutheran Church in Schleswig-Holstein (1935).

Lory, P. "Note sur l'ouvrage *Religion after Religion: Gershom Scholem, Mircea Eliade and Henry Corbin at Eranos* par M. Wassterstrom." *Archaeus* 9 (2005): 107–13.

Losemann, V. "Die 'Krise der Alten Welt' und der Gegenwart: Franz Altheim und Karl Kerényi im Dialog." In *Imperium Romanum: Studien zu Geschichte und Rezeption: Festschrift für Karl Christ zum 75. Geburtstag,* edited by P. Kneissl and V. Losemann, 492–518. Stuttgart: Franz Steiner Verlag, 1998.

Losemann, V. "I 'Discuri': Franz Altheim e Karl Kerényi: Tappe di un'amicizia." In *Károly Kerényi: Incontro con il Divino,* edited by L. Arcella, 17–28. Rome: Settimo Sigillo, 1999.

Lother, H. *Neugermanische Religion und Christentum.* Gütersloh: C. Bertelsmann, 1934.

Löwith, K. *Meaning in History: The Theological Implications of the Philosophy of History.* Chicago, IL: University of Chicago Press, 1949.

Löwith, K. "Vom Sinn der Geschichte." In *Der Sinn der Geschichte: Sieben Essays,* edited by L. Reinisch. Munich: C.H. Beck, 1961.

Löwith, K. *Weltgeschichte und Heilsgeschehen: Die theologischen Voraussetzungen der Geschichtsphilosophie.* Stuttgart: W. Kohlhammer, [1953] 1990.

Lukàcs, G. *Die Zerstörung der Vernunft.* Berlin: Aufbau Verlag, 1954.

Lütkehaus, L. "Eine gewaltige Aufgabe, ein editorisches Martyrium" [A massive task, an editorial martyrdom]. *Neue Zürcher Zeitung* (2–3 August 2008).

Lutz, B. (ed.). *Metzler Philosophenlexikon: Dreihundert biographisch-werkgeschichtliche Porträts von den Vorsokratikern bis zu den Neuen Philosophen.* Stuttgart: J.B. Metzler, 1989.

Maccoby, Hyam. "The Greatness of Gershom Scholem." In *Gershom Scholem: Modern Critical Views,* edited by H. Bloom, 137–54. New York: Chelsea House, 1987.

Magris, Aldo. "L'esperienza del divino in Carlo Kerényi." In *Neuhumanismus und Anthropologie des griechischen Mythos,* edited by R. Schlesier and R.S. Martínez, 15–24. Locarno: Rezzonico Editore, 2006.

Mahal, G. (ed.). *Gusto Gräser: Aus Leben und Werk.* Knittlingen: Melchior, 1987.

Maher, J.M. and D. Briggs (eds). *An Open Life: Joseph Campbell in Conversation with Michael Toms.* Burdett: Larson, 1988.

Maidenbaum, A. (ed.) *Jung and the Shadow of Anti-Semitism: Collected Essays.* Berwick, ME: Nicolas-Hays, 2002.

Maidenbaum, A. and S.A. Martin (eds). *Lingering Shadows.* Boston, MA: Shambhala, 1991.

Maier, M. *Atalanta Fugiens,* translated and edited by Joscelyn Godwin.Tysoe: Magnum Opus Hermetic Sourceworks, 1987.

Maillard, C. "L'Apport de l'inde à la pensée de Carl Gustav Jung." In *L'Inde inspiratrice: Réception de l'Inde en France et en Allemagne XIXe & XXe siècles,* edited by M. Hulin and C. Maillard, 155–68. Strasbourg: Presses Universitaires de Strasbourg, 1996.

Malinine, M., H.-C. Puech, G. Quispel, and W. Till. *De Resurrectione.* Zurich: Rascher, 1958.

Malinine, M., H.-C. Puech, and G. Quispel. *Evangelium Veritatis.* Zurich: Rascher, 1956.

Manea, N. "Felix Culpa: Erinnerung und Schweigen: Mysterien bei Mircea Eliade." *Lettre International* (Spring 1995): 30–36.

von Mangoldt, U. *Auf der Schwelle zwischen Gestern und Morgen: Begegnungen und Erlebnisse.* Weilheim: O.W. Barth, 1963.

Mann, T. *Erzählungen.* Frankfurt: Fischer Taschenbuch, 2005.

Mann, T. and K. Kerényi. *Thomas Mann—Karl Kerényi: Gespräche in Briefen.* Zurich: Rhein Verlag, 1960.

Marchianò, G. (ed.). *Elémire Zolla dalla morte alla vita,* special issue *Viátor* 9 (2005–2006).

Marchianò, G. *Elémire Zolla, il conoscitore di segreti: Una biografia intellettuale.* Milan: Rizzoli, 2006.

Mariotti, A. *Mircea Eliade: Vita e pensiero di un Maestro d'iniziazione.* Rome: Castelvecchi, 2007.

Markschies, C. *Die Gnosis.* Munich: C.H. Beck, 2001.

Marlan, J. "Interview with James Hillman: Past, Present and Future." In *Archetypal Psychologies: Reflections in Honor of James Hillman,* edited by S. Marlan, 45–50. New Orleans, LA: Spring Journal Books, 2008.

Martial, R. *La race française.* Paris: Mercure de France, 1934.

Martinès de Pasqually, *Traité sur la réintégration des êtres dans leur première propriété, vertu et puissance spirituelle divine*. Edited by R. Amadou. Chateau d'Omonville: Diffusion Rosicrucienne, 1996.

de Martino, M. *Mircea Eliade esoterico: Ioan Petru Culianu e i "non detti."* Rome: Settimo Sigillo, 2008.

Martynkewicz, W. "Ludwig Klages und Sigmund Freud" (2006). www.literaturkritik.de (no. 1, January 2006).

Mason, H. *Memoir of a Friend: Louis Massignon*. Notre Dame, IN: University of Notre Dame Press, 1988.

Massignon, D. (ed.). *Présence de Louis Massignon: Hommages et témoignages*. Paris: Maisonneuve et Larose, 1987.

Massignon, L. *La Passion de Hallâj*. Paris: Gallimard, 1990.

Massignon, L. *L'hospitalité sacrée*. Paris: Nouvelle Cité, 1987.

Massignon, L. *Parole Donnée*. Paris: Editions du Seuil, 1983.

Massonet, S. "Le collège de sociologie: Sociologie, secret et communauté." *Antaios* 5 (1994): 20–34.

Massonet, S. "Henry Corbin et la conquête de l'imaginal." *Antaios* 14 (1999): 98–110.

Masuzawa, T. "Reflections on the Charmed Circle." *Journal of the American Academy of Religion* 69(2) (2001): 429–36.

Mayawati, D. Statements in *Der Standard* (12 August 1997).

Mayer, H. *Der Widerruf: Über Deutsche und Juden*. Frankfurt: Suhrkamp, 1994.

Mazenauer, B. and S. Perrig. "C.G. Jung und der Nationalsozialismus." *Du* 8 (August 1995).

McCutcheon, R.T. *Manufacturing Religion: The Discourse on sui generis Religion and the Politics of Nostalgia*. New York: Oxford University Press, 1997.

McGuire, W. "The Arcane Summer School." *Spring* 40 (1980): 146–56.

McGuire, W. *Bollingen: An Adventure in Collecting the Past*. Princeton, NJ: Princeton University Press, 1982.

McGuire, W. (ed.). "Jelliffe. His Correspondence with Sigmund Freud and C.G. Jung." Appendix to J.C. Burnham, *Jelliffe: American Psychoanalyst and Physician*. Chicago, IL: University of Chicago Press, 1983.

McGuire, W. "Jung and Eranos in America." *Spring* 44 (1984): 51–6.

McGuire, W. "Report of First Session, August 1930." International Center of Spiritual Research, C.G. Jung Archiv, ETH, Zurich, Archivnr. As 1016. 29 949.

McGuire, W. and J.F.C. Hull (eds). *C.G. Jung Speaking: Interviews and Encounters*. Princeton, NJ: Princeton University Press, 1977.

McKnight, M. "Elders and Guides: A Conversation with Joseph Campbell." *Parabola* 5(1) (1980): 57–65.

McLynn, F. *Carl Gustav Jung*. New York: St. Martin's Press, 1997.

McPhail, I. *Alchemy and the Occult: From the Collection of Paul and Mary Mellon*. New Haven, CT: Yale University, 1968–77.

Mead, G.R.S. (ed.). *Echoes from the Gnosis, vol. 7: The Gnostic Crucifixion*. Benares: Theosophical Publishing Society, 1906–8.

Meier, F. *Bausteine I–III. Ausgewählte Aufsätze zur Islamwissenschaft*. Edited by G. Schubert and E. Glassen. Wiesbaden: Franz Steiner, 1992.

Meier, F. *Vom Wesen der islamischen Mystik*. Basel: Benno Schwabe, 1943.

Meier, K. *Die Theologischen Fakultäten im Dritten Reich*. Berlin: Walter de Gruyter, 1996.

Melasecchi, B. *Giuseppe Tucci: Nel centenario della nascita*. Rome: IsMEO, 1995.

Melk-Koch, M. *Auf der Suche nach der menschlichen Gesellschaft: Richard Thurnwald*. Berlin: Staatliche Museen Preußischer Kulturbesitz, 1989.

Mellon, P. with J. Baskett. *Reflections in a Silver Spoon: A Memoir*. New York: William Morrow, 1992.

Merkur, D. "Jung, Silberer, and Active Imagination." In *Gnosis: an Esoteric Tradition of Mystical Visions and Unions*, edited by D. Merkur, 37–54. Albany, NY: SUNY Press, 1993.

Merkur, D. "Theories of Spiritual Alchemy." In *Gnosis: an Esoteric Tradition of Mystical Visions and Unions*, edited by D. Merkur, 55–76. Albany, NY: SUNY Press, 1993.

Mesch, E. *Hans Leisegang*. Erlangen: Palm & Enke, 1999.

Meyrink, G. *Le Dominicain Blanc*. Paris: La Colombe, 1922.

Meyrink, G. *Der Golem*. Zurich: Rascher Verlag, 1946.

Mezdrea, D. *Nae Ionescu: Leben, Werk, Wirkung: Mit Beiträgen von Mircea Eliade*. Vienna: Karolinger, 2008.

Michaelis, A. *Libertà e Responsabilità: La filosofia di Hans Jonas*. Rome: Città Nuova, 2007.

Michaels, A. (ed.). *Klassiker der Religionswissenschaft: Von Friedrich Schleiermacher bis Mircea Eliade*. Munich: C.H. Beck, 1997.

Mihelcic, G. *Una religione di libertà: Raffaele Pettazzoni e la Scuola Romana di Storia delle Religioni*. Rome: Città Nuova, 2003.

Miller, D.L. "'Attack upon Christendom': The Anti-Christianism of Depth Psychology." In *Jung's Challenge to Contemporary Religion*, edited by M. Stein and R.L. Moore, 27–40. Wilmette, IL: Chiron Publications, 1987.

Miller, D.L. *The New Polytheism*. Dallas, TX: Spring Publications, 1981.

Miller, D.L. *Il nuovo politeismo: La rinascita degli Dei e delle Dee*. Milan: Edizioni di Comunità, 1983.

Miller, J. "In Defence of Alice A. Bailey." *Theosophical History* 2(6) (1988): 190–207.

Mincu, M. and R. Scagno (eds). *Mircea Eliade e l'Italia*. Milan: Jaca Book, 1987.

Mitgang, H. *Überwacht: Große Autoren in den Dossiers amerikanischer Geheimdienste*. Düsseldorf: Droste Verlag, 1992.

Moebius, S. *Die Zauberlehrlinge: Soziologiegeschichte des Collège de Sociologie (1937–1939)*. Constance: UVK Verlagsgesellschaft, 2006.

Mohn, J. *Mythostheorien: Eine religionswissenschaftliche Untersuchung zu Mythos und Interkulturalität*. Munich: Wilhelm Fink, 1998.

Mola, A.A. *Storia della Massoneria italiana dalle origini ai nostri giorni*. Milan: Bompiani, 1992.

Monastra, G. "Adolf Portmann, Wilhelm Troll: Due biologi della morfologia idealistica." Lecture given 11–13 June 1999, University of Perugia under the title "Forma e Archetipi."

Monastra, G. "Le forme viventi." *Diorama Letterario* 133 (January 1990): 36–68.

Monastra, G. "Itinerari del Sacro attraverso le scienze naturali," lecture delivered at the first meeting of the Quaderni di Avallon with the theme "La cultura contemporanea e il sacro", 3–4 November 1984, www.estovest.net/ecosofia/portmann.html.

Montanari, E. *La fatica del cuore: Saggio sull' ascesi esicasta*. Milan: Jaca Book, 2003.

Montanari, E. "Un 'Parsifal smarrito'." *Diorama letterario* 109 (November 1987): 18–23.

Moon, B. (ed.). *Encyclopedia of Archetypal Symbolism*. Boston, MA: Shambhala, 1991.

Moore, T. Introduction to chapter "Many Gods, Many Persons." In James Hillman, *A Blue Fire: Selected Writings*, 36–45. New York: Harper & Row, 1989.

Moramarco, M. *Nuova Enciclopedia Massonica*, vol. 1. Foggia: Bastogi, 1998.

Moser, F. *Das Große Buch vom Okkultismus*. Olten: Walter Verlag, 1974.

Moser, F. *Spuk: Irrglaube oder Wahrglaube? Eine Frage an die Menschheit*, vol. 1. Baden bei Zurich: Gyr-Verlag, 1950.

Mosse, G. *Ein Volk, ein Reich, ein Führer: Die völkischen Ursprünge des Nationalsozialismus*. Königstein: Athenäum, 1979.

Mulacz, P. "Oscar R. Schlag." *Journal of the Society for Psychical Research* 60 (1995): 263–7.

Müller, B. *Kosmik: Prozessontologie und temporale Poetik bei Ludwig Klages und Alfred Schuler: Zur Philosophie und Dichtung der Schwabinger Kosmischen Runde*. Munich: Telesma, 2007.

Müller, H. *Der frühe Mircea Eliade: Sein rumänischer Hintergrund und die Anfänge seiner universalistischen Religionsphilosophie*. In *Marburger Religionsgeschichtliche Beiträge*, vol. 3, edited by R. Flasche, 16–64. Münster: LIT Verlag, 2004.

Müller, H. *Philosophische Grundlagen der Anthropologie Adolf Portmanns*. Weinheim: VCH, Acta humaniora, 1988.

Müller, H. "Români care nu pot fi Români" [Romanians who cannot be Romanian]. *Cuvântul* 10(299) (1933): 1.

Müller, M. "'Selbst eine Kirche werden': Christentum und Politik im III. Reich." *Neue Ordnung* 2(5) (2005): 20–25.

Munich Cultural Award of Honour. *München ehrt Martin Buber*. Munich: Ner-Tamid-Verlag, 1961.

Museo Onsermonese. "Personalità che hanno scelto l'Onsernone come terra di rifugio o di ispirazione." *La Voce Onsernonese* 1 (1999).

Mussolini, B. *Il Fascismo (Documenti)*. Rome: Edizioni Wage, 1976.

Mussolini, B. *Der Geist des Faschismus: Ein Quellenwerk*. Munich: C.H. Beck, 1943.

Mutti, C. "Béla Hamvas e Julius Evola." *Vie della Tradizione* III (July–September 1988): 121–5.

Mutti, C. "Hamvas, Kerényi e i teologi antichi," foreword to *Béla Hamvas: Prima di Socrate*. Parma: Edizioni all'insegna del Veltro, n.d.

Mutti, C. *Julius Evola sul fronte dell'Est*. Parma: Edizioni all'insegna del Veltro, 1998.

Mutti, C. *Mircea Eliade und die Eiserne Garde: Rumänische Intellektuelle im Umfeld der Legion Erzengel Michael*. Preetz: Regin Verlag, 2009.

Mutti, C. "Origini." Supplement to *Orion* 150 (1997).

Nagel, H. Obituary for Olga Fröbe. *Bulletin of the Analytical Psychology Club of New York* 24(6) (1962): 5–7.

Nagel, H. *The Eranos Conference 1938*. New York: Analytical Psychology Club, 1939.

Nagy-Talavera, N.M. *The Green Shirts and the Others: A History of Fascism in Hungary and Romania*. Stanford, CA: Hoover Institution Press, 1970.

Nanko, U. "Religiöse Gruppenbildungen vormaliger 'Deutschgläubiger' nach 1945." In *Antisemitismus, Paganismus: Völkische Religion*, edited by H. Cancik and U. Puschner, 121–34. Munich: K.G. Sauer, 2004.

Nanko, U. *Die Deutsche Glaubensbewegung: Eine historische und soziologische Untersuchung*. Marburg: Diagonal-Verlag, 1993.

Nasr, S.H. "Kathleen Raine and Tradition: Some General Comments and Personal Recollections." In *Kathleen Raine Memorial Issue* of the *Temenos Academy Review* 7 (2004): 179–85.

Nasr, S.H. *Mélanges offerts à Henry Corbin*. Tehran: Institute of Islamic Studies, McGill University, Tehran Branch, 1977.

Nasr, S.H. "Recollections of Henry Corbin and Reflections upon his Intellectual Significance." *Temenos Academy Review* 2 (1999): 34–45.

Naudon, P. *La Franc-Maçonnerie chrétienne: La tradition opérative, l'Arche Royale de Jérusalem, le rite Ecossais rectifié*. Paris: Dervy-Livres, 1970.

Netz, W. "Eindrücke von der Tagung des überkonfessionellen Arbeitskreises Leipzig in Biesern bei Rochlitz Sa." *Kommende Gemeinde* 5(1) (February 1933): 77–80.

Neufeld, K.H. *Die Brüder Rahner: Eine Biographie*. Freiburg: Herder, 1994.

Neumann, E. *The Great Mother*. Translated by R. Manheim. Princeton, NJ: Princeton University Press, 1963.

Neumann, E. *Die Große Mutter: Eine Phänomenologie der weiblichen Gestaltungen des Unbewußten*. Olten: Walter Verlag, 1983.

Neumann, E. *Tiefenpsychologie und Neue Ethik*. Zurich: Rascher, 1949.

Neumann, E. *Ursprungsgeschichte des Bewusstseins*. Zurich: Rascher Verlag, 1949.

Neumann, M. "Die Beziehung zwischen Erich Neumann and C.G. Jung." *Analytische Psychologie* 23 (1992): 3–23.

New York Association for Analytical Psychology and Analytical Psychology Club of New York. *Carl Gustav Jung (1875–1961): A Memorial Meeting, New York, 1 December 1961*. New York: Analytical Psychology Club of New York, 1962.

Nietzsche, F. *On the Genealogy of Morals: A Polemical Tract by Friedrich Nietzsche*. Translated by Ian Johnston. http://records.viu.ca/~johnstoi/nietzsche/genealogy3.htm.

Niewöhner, F. Review of *Gottes Zorn kam zu kurz: Gershom Scholem als Schüler der deutschen Religionsgeschichte*. *Frankfurter Allgemeine Zeitung* 207 (7 September 1999).

Niewöhner, F. Review of *Eranos* by Hans Thomas Hakl. *Gnostika* 20 (2002): 61.

Noel, D.C. (ed.). *Paths to the Power of Myth: Joseph Campbell and the Study of Religion*. New York: Crossroad, 1990.

Noel, D.C. *The Soul of Shamanism: Western Fantasies, Imaginal Realities*. New York: Continuum, 1999.

Noica, C. "Hiérophanie et sacralité." In *Mircea Eliade*, edited by C. Tacou, 105–9. Paris: L'Herne, 1978.

Noll, R. *The Aryan Christ*. New York: Random House, 1997.

Noll, R. *The Jung Cult*. Princeton, NJ: Princeton University Press, 1994.

"Normen im Wandel der Zeit an der diesjährigen Eranostagung." Radio program (28 August 1974), broadcast by Funkhaus Hamburg in the series *Journal 3*.

Norton, R.E. *Secret Germany: Stefan George and His Circle*. Ithaca, NY: Cornell University Press, 2002.

Nusser, K.-H., M. Riedl, and T. Ritter (eds). *Politikos: Vom Element des Persönlichen in der Politik: Festschrift für Tilo Schabert zum 65. Geburtstag*. Berlin: Duncker & Humblot, 2008.

Oakes, M. *The Stone Speaks*. Wilmette, IL: Chiron Publications, 1987.

Oakes, M. and J. Campbell. *Where the Two Came to Their Father: A Navaho War Ceremonial Given by Jeff King*. Princeton, NJ: Princeton University Press, 1991.

Odajnik, V.W. *Jung and Politics: The Political and Social Ideas of C.G. Jung*. New York: New York University Press, 1976.

Oertel, K. Review of J. Assmann, *Die mosaische Unterscheidung*. In *Heidnisches Jahrbuch 2010*, edited by D. Junker and H. Kliemannel, 304–15. Hamburg: Verlag Daniel Junker, 2009.

Ohasama, S. and A. Faust (eds). *Zen: Der lebendige Buddhismus in Japan: Ausgewählte Stücke des Zen-Textes*. Gotha-Stuttgart: Friedrich Andreas Perthes, 1925.

Oişteanu, A. "Mircea Eliade between Political Journalism and Scholarly Work." *Archaeus* 8 (2004): 339ff.

Oldmeadow, H. *Journeys East: 20th Century Western Encounters with Eastern Religious Traditions*. Bloomington, IN: World Wisdom, 2004.

Oldmeadow, H. *Mediations: Essays on Religious Pluralism & the Perennial Philosophy*. San Rafael, CA: Sophia Perennis, 2008.

Opitz, P.J. "Die Gnosis-These: Anmerkungen zu Eric Voegelins Interpretation der westlichen Moderne." In E. Voegelin, *Der Gottesmord: Zur Genese und Gestalt der modernen politischen Gnosis*, 7–35. Munich: Wilhelm Fink, 1999.

Organisationsausschuss (ed.). *X. Internationaler Kongress für Religionsgeschichte. 11.–17. September 1960 in Marburg/Lahn*. Marburg: N.G. Elwert, 1961.

Orleanu, I. Review of M. Sebastian, *Seit zweitausend Jahren*. *Neue Zürcher Zeitung* (18 February 2009).

Oschilewski, W.G. *Eugen Diederichs: ein Beitrag zur neuen deutschen Buchkunst*. Privately published, 1939.

Otto, R. *Aufsätze das Numinose betreffend*. Gotha: Leopold Klotz Verlag, 1923.

Otto, R. "Religiöser Menschheitsbund." *Deutsche Politik* 9(6) (1921): 234–8.

Otto, R. *West-Östliche Mystik: Vergleich und Unterscheidung zur Wesensdeutung*, 3rd ed. Munich: C.H. Beck, 1971.

Otto, R. and G. Alles. *Autobiographical and Social Essays*. Berlin: Walter de Gruyter, 1996.

Otto, R. and F. Heiler. "Allgemeine Religionsgeschichte in der Weimarer Republik." In E. Hamacher, *Gershom Scholem und die Allgemeine Religionsgeschichte*, 73–104. Berlin: Walter de Gruyter, 1999.

Otto, W.F. *Dionysos: Mythos und Kultus*. Frankfurt: Vittorio Klostermann, 1933.

Otto, W.F. "Der Durchbruch zum antiken Mythos im 19. Jahrhundert." In *Vom Schicksal des deutschen Geistes, Erste Folge: Die Begegnung mit der Antike: Reden um Mitternacht*, edited by W. Frommel, 35–46. Berlin: Verlag Die Runde, 1934.

Otto, W.F. *Theophania: Der Geist der altgriechischen Religion*. Hamburg: Rowohlt, 1956.

Otto, W.F. *Das Wort der Antike*. Stuttgart: Ernst Klett, 1962.

Otto, W.F. *Die Wirklichkeit der Götter: Von der Unzerstörbarkeit griechischer Weltsicht*. Reinbek: Rowohlt, 1963.

Otto, W.F., K. von Fritz, and E. Schmalzriedt. *Mythos und Welt*. Darmstadt: Wissenschaftliche Buchgesellschaft, 1963.

Owen, I.M. and M. Sparrow. *Conjuring up Philip: An Adventure in Psychokinesis*. New York: Harper & Row, 1976.

Pacheco, J.A.A. "Aproximaciones a Eranos." *Epimeleia* 1–2 (1992): 91–9.

Paetel, K.O. *"Don Quichotte en miniature"*: *Zum 65. Geburtstag Karl O. Paetel. Festschrift.* Privately published, 1971.

Paetel, K.O. *Reise ohne Uhrzeit: Autobiographie.* Edited by W.D. Elfe and J.M. Spalek. Worms: Georg Heintz, 1982.

Pagels, E. *The Gnostic Gospels.* New York: Random House, 1979.

Pagels, E. *Versuchung durch Erkenntnis: Die gnostischen Evangelien.* Frankfurt: Suhrkamp, 1987.

Pallat, A. "Uit de 'Autobiographie' en het 'Tagebuch'." In *André Jolles (1874–1946),* edited by W. Thys, 994–1002. Leipzig: Leipziger Universitätsverlag, 2000.

Pallat, L. "Uit het Dagboek van Ludwig Pallat." In *André Jolles (1874–1946),* edited by W. Thys, 1009. Leipzig: Leipziger Universitätsverlag, 2000.

Parker, A. *Le Sâdhu Sundar Singh.* Toulouse: Société d'Edition de Toulouse, 1926.

Pasi, M. *Aleister Crowley e la tentazione della politica.* Milan: Franco Angeli, 1999.

Paul Speck: 1896–1966. Exhibition catalogue, Kunsthaus, Zurich, 17 January–22 February 1970.

Paus, A. *Religiöser Erkenntnisgrund: Herkunft und Wesen der Aprioritheorie Rudolf Ottos.* Leiden: Brill, 1966.

Péguy, C. *Notre jeunesse.* Paris: Cahier de la Quinzaine, 1910.

Pensa, C. "L'occidente e le religioni orientali nella prospettiva di Giuseppe Tucci." *Pāramitā* 4 (1985): 9–25.

Pestalozzi, H.A. *Die sanfte Verblödung.* Düsseldorf: Hermes, 1985.

Petech, L. "Il contributo di Giuseppe Tucci alla storia dei paesi himalayani." In Conferenze IsMEO: *Giuseppe Tucci: Nel centenario della nascita, Roma, 7–8 giugno 1994,* edited by B. Melasecchi, 25. Rome: IsMEO, 1995.

Petreu, M. "The 'Generation '27' between the Holocaust and the Gulag." *Euresis* 4 (2007): 3–4, 7–25.

Pettazzoni, R. "Aperçu Introductif." *Numen* 1(1) (1954): 1–7.

Pettazzoni, R. *I misteri.* Mesagne: Giordano, 1997.

Pfeil, H. *Die Grundlehren des deutschen Glaubens: Eine Bewertung und Ablehnung.* Paderborn: Verlag der Bonifacius-Druckerei, 1936.

Pfister, O. *Die Legende Sundar Singhs: Eine auf Enthüllungen protestantischer Augenzeugen in Indien gegründete religionspsychologische Untersuchung.* Bern: Paul Haupt, 1926.

Philipp, M. *"Vom Schicksal des deutschen Geistes": Wolfgang Frommels Rundfunkarbeit an den Sendern Frankfurt und Berlin 1933–1935 und ihre oppositionelle Tendenz.* Potsdam: Verlag für Berlin-Brandenburg, 1995.

Pieracci Harwell, M. (ed.). *Cristina Campo Lettere a Mita.* Milan: Adelphi, 1999.

Pietikäinen, P. *C.G. Jung and the Psychology of Symbolic Forms.* Helsinki: Annales Academiae Scientiarium Fennicae, 1999.

Pietikäinen, P. "Dynamic Psychology, Utopia and Escape from History: The Case of C.G. Jung." *Utopian Studies* 12(1) (2001): 41–55.

Pietikäinen, P. "The Volk and its Unconscious: Jung, Hauer and the 'German Revolution'." *Journal of Contemporary History* 35(4) (2000): 523–39.

Pisi, P. "I tradizionalisti e la formazione del pensiero di Eliade." In *Confronto con Mircea Eliade,* edited by L. Arcella, P. Pisi, and R. Scagno, 40–133. Milan: Jaca Book, 1998.

Plantinga, R.J. "Romanticism and the History of Religions. The Case of W.B. Kristensen." In *Religionswissenschaft und Kulturkritik,* edited by H.G. Kippenberg and B. Luchesi, 157–76. Marburg: Diagonal-Verlag, 1991.

Plotinus. *Collected Writings of Plotinus,* vol. III. Translated by T. Taylor. Frome: Prometheus Trust, 1994.

Poewe, K. *New Religions and the Nazis.* Abingdon: Routledge, 2006.

Pogson, B. *Maurice Nicoll: A Portrait.* New York: Fourth Way Books, 1987.

Pokorny, P. "Der soziale Hintergrund der Gnosis." In *Gnosis und Neues Testament,* edited by K.-W. Tröger, 77–95. Berlin: Gütersloher Verlagshaus Mohn, 1973.

Politica Romana. "Memoria di Boris de Rachewiltz." *Politica Romana* 4 (1997): 7.

Polomé, E.C. "Karl Kerényi: A Biographical Sketch." In *Essays in Memory of Karl Kerényi,* edited by E.C. Polomé, 7–8. Washington, DC: Institute for the Study of Man, 1984.

Poncé, C. *The Game of Wizards: Roots of Consciousness and the Esoteric Arts.* Wheaton, IL: Quest Books, 1991.

Pongratz, L.J. *Psychiatrie in Selbstdarstellungen.* Bern: Hans Huber, 1973.

Popiol, A. and R. Schrader. *Gregor A. Gregorius: Mystiker des dunklen Lichts.* Bürstadt: Esoterischer Verlag, 2009.

Porkert, M. "Anschaulichkeit, Sinnlichkeit, Bildlichkeit als Voraussetzung für die Integrierbarkeit wissenschaftlicher Theorien." *Eranos Jahrbuch* 48 (1979): 101–32.

Portmann, A. *An den Grenzen des Wissens.* Vienna: Econ, 1974.

Portmann, A. *Biologie und Geist.* Zurich: Rhein-Verlag, 1956.

Portmann, A. "Inteview with Udo Reiter." in *Mensch, Natur, Gesellschaft* 4 (1987): 3–15.

Portmann, A. *Licht und Leben.* Basel: Friedrich Reinhardt, 1963.

Portmann, A. *Probleme des Lebens.* Basel: Friedrich Reinhardt, 1949.

Portmann, A., R. Ritsema, and H. Corbin. *Vom Sinn der Eranostagungen.* Privately published, n.p., n.d.

van der Post, L. *Jung and the Story of Our Time.* London: Hogarth Press, 1976.

van der Post, L. *A Walk with a White Bushman.* New York: William Morrow, 1986.

van der Post, L. *Yet Being Someone Other: An Autobiographical Odyssey.* New York: William Morrow, 1983.

van Praag, J. *Echoes of Timelessness.* London: Van Praag Publications, 1990.

van Praag, J. *Empty Sea.* Utrecht: Van Praag (privately published), 2006.

van Praag, J. and R. Bernardini. "The Spirit of Eranos." Lecture given at Moscia, 5 August 2007.

Prader, J. *Der gnostische Wahn: Eric Voegelin und die Zerstörung menschlicher Ordnung in der Moderne.* Vienna: Passagen-Verlag, 2006.

Preißler, H. and H. Seiwert (eds). *Gnosisforschung und Religionsgeschichte.* Marburg: Diagonal-Verlag, 1994.

Principe, L.M. and W.R. Newman. "Some Problems with the Historiography of Alchemy." In *Secrets of Nature: Astrology and Alchemy in Early Modern Europe*, edited by W.R. Newman and A. Grafton, 401–12. Cambridge, MA: MIT Press, 2001.

Proctor, R.N. *The Nazi War on Cancer.* Princeton, NJ: Princeton University Press, 1999.

Progoff, I. *The Image of an Oracle: A Report on Research into the Mediumship of Eileen J. Garrett.* New York: Garrett Publications, 1964.

Progoff, I. *The Practice of Process Meditation: The Intensive Journal Way to Spiritual Experience.* New York: Dialogue House Library, 1980.

Prokop, H. "Erich Neumann in Israel." In *Psychologie des 20. Jahrhunderts*, edited by Dieter Eicke, 841–50. Zurich: Kindler, 1977.

Pschera, A. "'Heilige Tiefe und geistiger Überblick': Eliade, Jünger und die Zeitschrift, *Antaios* (1959–1971)." *Sezession* 16 (2007): 18–23.

Psychologischer Club Zürich (ed.). *Die kulturelle Bedeutung der komplexen Psychologie. Festschrift* for Jung's 60th birthday. Berlin: Julius Springer, 1935.

Puccioni Marasco, P. (ed.). *Jung e l'Ebraismo.* Florence: Guintina, 2001.

Puech, H.-C. *Histoire des Religions.* Paris: Gallimard, 1970–76.

Puech, H.-C. *Le manichéisme: son fondateur, sa doctrine.* Paris: Civilisations du Sud S.A.E.P., 1949.

Pullio, M. *Une modernité explosive: La revue* Die Tat *dans les renouveau religieux, culturels et politiques de l'Allemagne d'avant 1914–1918.* Geneva: Labor et Fides, 2008.

Pulver, M. *Erinnerungen an eine europäische Zeit.* Zurich: Orell Füssli Verlag, 1953.

Pulver, M. *Person, Charakter, Schicksal.* Zurich: Orell Füssli Verlag, 1944.

Pye, M. "Friedrich Heiler (1892–1967)." In *Klassiker der Religionswissenschaft*, edited by A. Michaels, 277–89. Munich: C.H. Beck, 1977.

Quaglino, G.P., A. Romano, and R. Bernardini (eds). *Carl Gustav Jung a Eranos 1933–1952.* Turin: Antigone Edizione, 2007.

Quaglino, G.P., A. Romano, and R. Bernardini. "Opicinus de Canistris: Some Notes from Jung's Unpublished Eranos Seminar on the Medieval Codex Palatinus Latinus 1993." *Journal of Analytical Psychology* 55 (2010): 398–422.

Quispel, G. *Gnosis als Weltreligion.* Zurich: Origo Verlag, 1951.

Quispel, G. "Gnosis and Psychology." In *The Rediscovery of Gnosticism*, vol. 1, edited by B. Layton, 17–31. Leiden: Brill, 1980.

Quispel, G. "Gnosis und Religionswissenschaft." In *Gnostic Studies 2*, 259–70. Istanbul: Nederlands Historisch-Archaeologisch Instituut, 1975.

Quispel, G. "How Jung became a Gnostic." *San Francisco Jung Institute Library Journal* 13(2) (1994): 47–50.

Quispel, G. "The Jung Codex and its Significance." In *The Jung Codex*, edited by H.-C. Puech, G. Quispel, and W.C. van Unnik, 35–78. London: A.R. Mowbray, 1955.

Räderer, O. "Dr. Herbert Fritsche: Konstitutioneller Grenzgänger und Grenzüberschreiter (1911–1960)." *Gnostika* 36 (2007): 37–50 and *Gnostika* 37 (2007): 52–65.

Räderer, O. "Herbert Fritsche (1911–1960): Grenzgänger im Niemandsland." *Nova Acta Paracelsica*, new series, 17 (2003): 63–94.

Räderer, O. *Tarot: Säulen der Einweihung.* St. Gallen: Verlag RGS, 2003.

Radin, P., K. Kerényi, and C.G. Jung. *Der Göttliche Schelm: Ein indianischer Mythen-Zyklus.* Hildesheim: Gerstenberg, 1979.

Radkau, J. *Das Zeitalter der Nervosität.* Munich: Carl Hanser, 1998.

Rahner, H. *Griechische Mythen in christlicher Deutung.* Darmstadt: Wissenschaftliche Buchgesellschaft, 1966.

Rahner, K. *Geist und Werk: Zum 75. Geburtstag von Dr. Daniel Brody.* Zurich: Rhein-Verlag, 1958.

Raine, K. *Blake and Tradition.* Princeton, NJ: Princeton University Press, 1968.

Raine, K. Interview with Jay Kinney. *Gnosis* 23 (Spring 1992): 52.

Raine, K. *The Land Unknown: Further Chapters of Autobiography.* London: Hamish Hamilton, 1975.

Raine, K. *Philip Sherrard (1922–1995): A Tribute.* Birmingham: Delos Press, 1996.

Raine, K. *Yeats the Initiate: Essays on Certain Themes in the Writings of W.B. Yeats.* London: Allen & Unwin, 1986.

Rascher Verlag. *Aussaat 1938: Ein Verlagsalmanach: 30 Jahre Rascher Verlag.* Zurich: Rascher, 1938.

Rasmussen, D. "Herméneutique structurale et philosophie." In *Mircea Eliade*, edited by C. Tacou, 97–104. Paris: L'Herne, 1978.

Ratzinger, Cardinal J. "Ganze Größe von Gottes Wort." *Focus* 37 (2000): 48–9.

Rauch, M. and G. Schuster (eds). *Christiane von Hofmannsthal, Tagebücher 1918–1923 und Briefe des Vaters an die Tochter 1903–1929.* Frankfurt: S. Fischer, 1991.

Raupach-Rudnik, W. "Die Notwendigkeit des Friedens: Martin Buber." In *Judentum und politische Existenz: Siebzehn*

Portäts deutsch-jüdischer Intellektueller, edited by M. Buckmiller, D. Heimann, and J. Perels, 111–34. Hannover: Offizin, 2000.

Ravasi, G. "Ermeneutica dell'ermetismo in Mircea Eliade" in *Romania și Europa: Studii șiarticole selecționate coordonatede J.C. Drăgan. Revista Fundației Drăgan* 9 (May 1992), 119–258.

Ravasi, G. "Ermeneutica dell' ermetismo in Mircea Eliade." *Revista Fundației Drăgan sRomat* 9 (1992): 118–258.

Read, H. "The Creative Nature of Humanism." *Eranos Jahrbuch* 26 (1957): 315–50.

Read, H. "Zen and Art." *The Eastern Buddhist* new series 2(1) (1967): 19–28.

Reeves, H., M. Cazenave, P. Solié, K.H. Pribram, H. Etter, and M.-L. von Franz (eds). *La synchronicité, l'âme et la science*. Paris: Albin Michel, 1994.

Rchwaldt, H. *Vom Dach der Welt: Über die "Synthese aller Geisteskultur" in Ost und West*. Munich: Ludendorffs Verlag, 1938.

von Reibnitz, B. "Der Eranos-Kreis—Religionswissenschaft und Weltanschauung oder der Gelehrte als Laien-Priester." In *Kreise, Gruppen, Bünde: Zur Soziologie moderner Intellektuellenassoziationen*, edited by R. Faber and C. Holste, 425–40. Würzburg: Königshausen & Neumann, 2000.

Reimbold, E.T. "Gedanken zur Arbeit unserer Gesellschaft." *Symbolon: Jahrbuch für Symbolforschung* n.s. 1 (1972): 9.

Reinisch, L. (ed.). *Der Sinn der Geschichte: Sieben Essays*. Munich: C.H. Beck, 1961.

Reiss, C. *Ascona: Geschichte des seltsamsten Dorfes der Welt*. Stuttgart: Deutscher Bücherbund, 1964.

Reister, J. "Nazione Indiana." www.nazioneindiana.com/2006/06/26/il-manager-religioso/

Rennie, B. "An Encounter with Eliade." In Mihaela Gligor and Mac Linscott Ricketts, *Intâlniri cu, Encounters with Mircea Eliade*, 199–202. Cluj-Napoca: Casa Cârții de Știință, 2005.

Rennie, B.S. (ed.). *Mircea Eliade: A Critical Reader*. London: Equinox, 2006.

Rennie, B.S. "Mircea Eliade (Further Considerations, 2005)." In *The Encyclopedia of Religion*, 2nd edn, edited by L. Jones, vol. IV, 2757–63. Detroit, MI: Macmillan Reference USA, 2005.

Rennie, B.S. *Reconstructing Eliade: Making Sense of Religion*. Albany, NY: SUNY Press, 1996.

Reschika, R. *Mircea Eliade: Zur Einführung*. Hamburg: Junius, 1997.

Rezzonico, G. (ed.). *Antologia di cronaca di Monte Verità*. Locarno: Rezzonico editore, 2008.

Rhein, C. *Paul Tillich: Philosoph und Theologe: Eine Einführung in sein Denken*. Stuttgart: Evangelisches Verlagswerk, 1957.

Ribi, A. *Die Suche nach den eigenen Wurzeln: Die Bedeutung von Gnosis, Hermetik und Alchemie für C.G. Jung und Marie-Louise von Franz und deren Einfluss auf das moderne Verständnis dieser Disziplin*. Bern: Peter Lang, 1999.

Richard, W. "Kosmische Fügung." In *Der Mensch und das Sein*, 2nd ed. Jena: Eugen Diederichs, [1931] 1939.

Ricketts, M.L. "Eliade's Religious Beliefs." *Archaeus* 14 (2010): 27–40.

Ricketts, M.L. *Former Friends and Forgotten Facts*. Norcross, GA: Criterion Publishing, 2003.

Ricketts, M.L. *Mircea Eliade: The Romanian Roots, 1907–1945*, vol. 2. Boulder, CO: East European Monographs, 1988.

Riès, J. "Histoire des religions, phénoménologie, herméneutique: un regard sur l'oeuvre de Mircea Eliade." In *Mircea Eliade*, edited by Constantin Tacou, 81–7. Paris: L'Herne, 1978.

Riess, C. *Ascona*. Zurich: Europa Verlag, 1964.

Rilke, R.M., H. Hesse, and F. Schnack. *Worte der Freundschaft für Alexander von Bernus: Zum 70. Geburtstag am 6. Februar 1950*. Nürnberg: Hans Carl, 1949.

Ritsema, C. *L'Oeuvre d'Eranos et Vie d'Olga Froebe-Kapteyn*. Unpublished manuscript.

Ritsema, R. "Adolf Portmann 1897–1982." *Eranos Jahrbuch* 51 (1982): 1–6.

Ritsema, R. (ed.). *Gestaltung der Erlösungsidee im Judentum und Protestantismus: Eranos-Vorträge von Heinz Westman und Paul Tillich*. Supplementary volume to *Eranos Jahrbuch* 4 (1936). Ascona: Eranos-Stiftung, 1986.

Ritsema, R. *The I Ching*. Shaftesbury: Element Books, 1997.

Ritsema, R. and S. Sabbadini. "Images of the Unknown: The Eranos *I Ching* Project 1989–1997." *Eranos Jahrbuch* 66 (1997): 7–43.

Ritsema, R. and H. Schneider. *Yi-jing: Das Buch der Wandlungen*. Munich: O.W. Barth, 2000.

Robinson, C. Letter. *Neue Zürcher Zeitung* (23 August 2007).

Roche, D. and J. Revuz, "La session de l'Université Saint-Jean de Jérusalem (Journées d'étude des 12, 13 et 14 juin 1981)." *Travaux de la Loge nationale de recherches Villard de Honnecourt* 4 (1982): 190–204.

Rodinson, M. "Ce n'était pas un saint: Entretien avec Maxime Rodinson." *Question de* 90 (1992): 76–82.

Rohan, K.A. "Halbjahresbericht des Verbandes für kulturelle Zusammenarbeit (Kulturbund) (September 1932–März 1933)." *Europäische Revu* 9(1) (1933): 179.

Rohan, K.A. *Heimat Europa: Erinnerungen und Erfahrungen*. Jena: Eugen Diederichs Verlag, 1954.

Rohan, K.A. *Heiße Eisen: Deutschland, Europa, Der Westen*. Nürnberg: Glock & Lutz, 1963.

Röhr, H. "Rudolf Otto: ein Jahrhundertphänomen." *Spirita* 2 (1988): 23–7.

Rolland, R. *Das Leben des Ramakrishna*. Erlenbach-Zurich: Rotapfel-Verlag, 1931.

Rolland, R. *The Life of Ramakrishna*. Translated by E.F. Malcolm-Smith. Calcutta: Advaita Ashrama, 2003.

Rombach, H. *Der kommende Gott: Hermetik: eine neue Weltsicht*. Freiburg: Rombach Verlag, 1991.

Ronnberg, A. and K. Martin (eds). *The Book of Symbols*. Cologne: Taschen, 2010.

Rosati, M.P. "Psicoanalisi e transdisciplinarità. L'Istituo Mythos e l'eredità di Eranos." www.atopon.it/index.php?page=psicoanalisi-e-transdisciplinarita.

Rosen, D. *The Tao of Jung: The Way of Integrity*. New York: Viking Penguin, 1996.

Rosenbaum-Kroeber, S. "Was ist Eranos und wer war Olga Fröbe-Kapteyn?" In *Monte Verità: Die Brüste der Wahrheit*, edited by H. Szeemann, 117–20. Milan: Electa, 1978.

Rosenberg, A. *Flugblätter für Freunde*. Unpublished newsletter.

Rosenberg, A. "Eranos, der Geist am Wasser." Appendix to *Flugblätter für Freunde aus der Werkstatt von Alfons Rosenberg* 80 (1977).

Ross, R. (ed.). *Forty-Three Drawings by Alastair with a Note of Exclamation*. London: John Lane, 1914.

Rossi, M. "Roberto Assagioli." *Hera* 46(3) (2003).

Rossi, M. "Roberto Assagioli, dalla Teosofia Alla Psicosintesi." In *Esoterismo e Fascismo*, edited by G. De Turris, 63–6. Rome: Edizioni Mediterranee, 2006.

de Rougemont, D. "Hérétiques de toutes les religions …." In *Henry Corbin*, edited by C. Jambet, 298–303. Paris: L'Herne, 1981.

Rousselle, E. Commentary to the *Fragebuch*. *Zirkelkorrespondenz* 107(10) (1979): 359–80.

Rousselle, E. "Innen ein Heiliger, nach außen ein Souverän." In R. Wilhelm and C.G. Jung, *Geheimnis der Goldenen Blüte*. Munich: Eugen Diederichs, 1998.

Rudolph, K. "Das Problem einer Soziologie und 'sozialen Verortung' der Gnosis." *Kairos* 19(1) (1977): 35–44.

Ruggiu, J.-P. "Rosicrucian Alchemy and the Hermetic Order of the Golden Dawn." www.augustorderofthemysticrose.org/Alchemy/Alchemy_and_gd.pdf.

Ruppert, H.-J. "Esoterik zwischen Endzeitfieber und Erlösungshoffnung." *Materialdienst* 62 (1999), 289–305.

von Rutkowski, L.S. "Toleranz und Freiheit. Bericht über die erste Jahrestagung der 'Freien Akademie' auf dem Ludwigstein 24.–31. Juli 1957." *Wirklichkeit und Freiheit. Blätter für die "Freunde der Freien Akademie e.V.*," Jahresrundbrief 3 and 4 (December 1957).

Ryce-Menuhin, J. (ed.). *Jung and the Monotheisms: Judaism, Christianity and Islam*. London: Routledge, 1993.

Sabbatucci, D. "Raffaele Pettazzoni." *Numen* 10(1) (1963): 1–41.

Said, E. *Orientalism*. New York: Pantheon Books, 1978.

Salin, E. *Um Stefan George: Erinnerungen und Zeugnis*. Munich: Helmut Küpper, 1954.

Salter, M. *Nazi War Crimes, US Intelligence and Selective Prosecution at Nuremberg: Controversies regarding the Role of the Office of Strategic Services*. Oxford: Routledge-Cavendish, 2007.

Salzmann, K.H. "Kurt Wolff der Verleger." Archiv für Geschichte des Buchhandels (XII), *Börsenblatt des Deutschen Buchhandels* 14(101a) (22 December 1958): 1729–49.

Sambursky, S. *Der Weg der Physik: 2500 Jahre physikalischen Denkens*. Zurich: Artemis, 1975.

Samuels, A. *Jung und seine Nachfolge*. Stuttgart: Klett, 1989.

Sanders, G. "In Memoriam Prof. Dr. Franz Altheim." In *Jaarboek 1977 der Koninklijke Academie voor Wetenschappen: Letteren en schone Kunsten van België*, 387–400.

Sandler, F. and D. Reeck. "The Masks of Joseph Campbell." *Religion* 11(1) (1981): 1–20.

Sandmel, S. "An Appreciation." In *Religions in Antiquity: Essays in Memory of Erwin Ramsdell Goodenough*, edited by J. Neusner, 3–17. Leiden: Brill, 1970.

Sandoz, E. (ed.). *Eric Voegelin's Significance for the Modern Mind*. Baton Rouge, LA: Louisiana State University Press, 1991.

Santucci, J.A. "Alice Bailey." In *Dictionary of Gnosis and Western Esotericism*, vol. 1., edited by W.J. Hanegraaff *et al.*, 158–60. Leiden: Brill, 2005.

Saunders, F.S. *Wer die Zeche zahlt …: Der CIA und die Kultur im Kalten Krieg*. Berlin: Siedler, 2001. Published in English as *The Cultural Cold War: the CIA and the World of Arts and Letters*. New York: The New Press, 2001.

Saur, W. "Mircea Eliade heute." *Sezession* 16 (2007): 30–35.

Saur, W. "Mythos und Moderne: Mircea Eliade im XX. Jahrhundert: Zu seinem 100. Geburtstag." *Neue Ordnung* 1 (2007): 38–44.

Saxl, F. "Die kulturwissenschaftliche Bibliothek Warburg in Hamburg" and "Die Geschichte der Bibliothek Aby Warburgs (1886–1944)." In Aby M. Warburg, *Ausgewählte Schriften und Würdingungen*, edited by D. Wuttke, 331–4; 335–46. Baden-Baden: Valentin Koerner, 1980.

Scagno, R. "Alcuni punti fermi sull'impegno politicio di Mircea Eliade nella Romania interbellica: Un commento critico al Dossier 'Toladot' del 1972." In *Esploratori del pensiero umano: Georges Dumézil e Mircea Eliade*, edited by J. Ries and N. Spineto, 259–89. Milan: Jaca Book, 2000.

Schabert, T. "Brief aus Ascona: Das Abenteuer Eranos." *Süddeutsche Zeitung* (24 August 1991).

Schabert, T. *Die Architektur der Welt: Eine kosmologische Lektüre architektonischer Formen*. Munich: Wilhelm Fink, 1997.

Schabert, T. *Die zweite Geburt des Menschen: Von den politischen Anfängen menschlicher Existenz*. Munich: Karl Alber, 2009.

Schabert, T. and M. Riedl (eds). *Gott oder Götter? God or Gods?* Würzburg: Königshausen & Neumann, 2009.

Schaeder, G. *Martin Buber: Hebräischer Humanismus*. Göttingen: Vandenhoeck & Ruprecht, 1966.

Scheidt, W. *Kulturbiologie: Vorlesungen für Studierende aller Wissensgebiete*. Jena: Gustav Fischer, 1930.

Schickele, R. *Die blauen Hefte*. Edited by A. Post-Martens. Frankfurt: Stroemfeld Verlag, 2002.

Schiefner, F.A. *Kalevala: Das National-Epos der Finnen*. Munich: Georg Müller, 1914.

Schimmel, A. *Auf den Spuren der Muslime: Mein Leben zwischen den Kulturen*. Edited by H. Bobzin and N. Kermani. Freiburg: Herder, 2002.

Schimmel, A. Interview. *Gnostika* 10 (1999): 19–24.

Schimmel, A. *Morgenland und Abendland: Mein west-östliches Leben*. Munich: C.H. Beck, 2002.

Schimmel, A. *Religionen der Erde: Religionsgeschichte im Abriss*. Wiesbaden: Kesselringsche Verlagsbuchhandlung, 1951.

Schlag, O.R. *Das Büchlein von der Volleingedenkheit*. Zurich: Verlag des Schwanes, n.d.

Schlag, O.R. *Frühe Gedichte*. Zurich: Origo Verlag, 1955.

Schlag, O.R. *Von alten und neuen Mysterien: Die Lehren des A*. Würzburg: Ergon, 1998.

Schleiermacher, F. *Über die Religion: Reden an die Gebildeten unter ihren Verächtern*. Stuttgart: Stecker & Schröder, 1923.

Schlesier, R. and R. Sanchiño Martínez (eds). *Neuhumanismus und Anthropologie des griechischen Mythos: Karl Kerényi im europäischen Kontext des 20. Jahrhunderts*. Locarno: Rezzonico Editore, 2006.

Schmidt, F.J. *Die Wiedergeburt des Idealismus*. Leipzig: Verlag der Dürr'schen Buchhandlung, 1908.

Schmidt, K.L. (ed.). *Festgabe für Adolf Diessmann zum 60. Geburtstag, 7 November 1926*. Tübingen: J.C.B. Mohr, 1927.

Schmitz, O.A.H. *Neues Menschentum: Betrachtungen in zwölfter Stunde*. Leipzig: Hesse & Becker Verlag, 1931.

Schmitz, O.A.H. *Psychoanalyse und Yoga*. Darmstadt: Otto Reichl, 1923.

Schmitz, O.A.H. *Sinnsuche oder Psychoanalyse: Briefwechsel Graf Hermann Keyserling—Oskar A.H. Schmitz aus den Tagen der Schule der Weisheit*. Darmstadt: Hessische Literaturfreunde, 1970.

Schneidegger, E. *Tessin: Ein Lesebuch*. Zurich: Arche, 1991.

Schoenl, W. *C.G. Jung: His Friendships with Mary Mellon and J.B. Priestley*. Wilmette, IL: Chiron Publication, 1998.

Scholem, F. and B. Yaron. "Bibliography of the published writings of Gershom G. Scholem." In *Studies in Mysticism and Religion presented to Gershom G. Scholem on his Seventieth Birthday by Pupils, Colleagues and Friends*, edited by E.E. Urbach, R.J. Zwi Werblowsky and C. Wirszubski, 199–235. Jerusalem: Magnes Press, Hebrew University, 1967.

Scholem, G. "Alchemie und Kabbala." *Alchemistische Blätter* 1(8–9) (1928): 89–92; 1(10–11) (1928): 122–37.

Scholem, G. *Alchemie und Kabbala*. Frankfurt: Suhrkamp, 1994.

Scholem, G. *Bibliographia Kabbalistica: Die jüdische Mystik (Gnosis, Kabbala Sabbatianismus, Frankismus, Chassidismus) behandelnde Bücher und Aufsätze von Reuchlin bis zur Gegenwart*. Berlin: Schocken Verlag, 1933.

Scholem, G. *Briefe I: 1914–1947*. Edited by I. Schedletzky. Munich: C.H. Beck, 1994.

Scholem, G. *Briefe II: 1948–1970*. Edited by T. Sparr. Munich: C.H. Beck, 1995.

Scholem, G. *Briefe III: 1971–1982*. Edited by I. Shedletzky. Munich: C.H. Beck, 1999.

Scholem, G. *Die jüdische Mystik in ihren Hauptstömungen*. Frankfurt: Suhrkamp, 1967.

Scholem, G. *Geheimnisse der Schöpfung*. Berlin: Schocken Verlag, 1935.

Scholem, G. "Identifizierung und Distanz: Ein Rückblick." *Eranos Jahrbuch* 48 (1979): 463–7.

Scholem, G. *Le messianisme juif: essais sur la spiritualité du judaisme*. Paris: Calmann-Lévy, 1974.

Scholem, G. "Lyrik der Kabbalah?" *Der Jude* 6(1) (1921–22): 55–69.

Scholem, G. *Major Trends in Jewish Mysticism*. New York: Schocken Books, 1995.

Scholem, G. "Martin Bubers Auffassung des Judentums." *Eranos Jahrbuch* 36 (1967): 9–55.

Scholem, G. "Martin Bubers Deutung des Chassidismus." *Neue Zürcher Zeitung* (20 and 27 May 1962).

Scholem, G. "Noch einmal: Das deutsch–jüdische Gespräch." In *Judaica 2*, 12–19. Frankfurt: Suhrkamp, 1982.

Scholem, G. *Sabbatai Sevi: The Mystical Messiah 1626–1676*. Princeton, NJ: Princeton University Press, 1973. German edition *Sabbatai Zwi: Der mystische Messias*. Frankfurt: Jüdischer Verlag, 1992.

Scholem, G. Statement in the Feuilleton section of *Neue Zürcher Zeitung*, 29 February 1980.

Scholem, *Tagebücher nebst Aufsätzen und Entwürfen bis 1923, 1917–1923*. Edited by Karlfried Gründer, Herbert Kopp-Oberstbrink, and Friedrich Niewöhner. Frankfurt: Jüdischer Verlag, 2000.

Scholem, G. "… und alles ist Kabbala." *Gershom Scholem im Gespräch mit Jörg Dress*. Munich: Text & Kritik, 1980.

Scholem, G. *Über Walter Benjamin*. Frankfurt: Suhrkamp, 1968.

Scholem, G. *Von Berlin nach Jerusalem. Jugenderinnerungen*. Frankfurt: Suhrkamp, 1977.

Scholem, G. *Walter Benjamin: Die Geschichte einer Freundschaft*. Frankfurt: Suhrkamp, 1997.

Scholem, G. (ed.). *Walter Benjamin–Gershom Scholem: Briefwechsel*. Frankfurt: Suhrkamp, 1980.

Scholem, G. "Wider den Mythos vom deutsch–jüdischen Gespräch." In *Judaica 2*, 7–11. Frankfurt: Suhrkamp, 1982.

Scholem, G. "Wissenschaft vom Judentum einst und jetzt." In *Judaica 1*, 147–64. Frankfurt: Suhrkamp, 1981.

Scholem, G. *Zur Kabbala und ihrer Symbolik*. Frankfurt: Suhrkamp, 1973.

Schönenberger, W. "Monte Verità und die theosophischen Ideen." In *Monte Verità: Die Brüste der Wahrheit*. Milan: Monte Verità, Electa, 1978.

Schösser, M. (ed.). *Auf gespaltenem Pfad: Zum neunzigsten Geburtstag von Margarete Susman*. Darmstadt: Erato-Presse, 1964.

Schöttker, D. "'Vielleicht kommen wir ohne Wunder nicht aus,' Zum Briefwechsel Jünger–Scholem." *Sinn und Form* 61(3) (2009): 303–8.

Schröder, C. and M. Schröder. *Deo omnia unum: Eine Sammlung von Aufsätzen Friedrich Heiler zum 50. Geburtstage dargebracht*. Munich: Ernst Reinhardt, 1942.

Schröder, F.R. *Die Parzivalfrage*. Munich: C.H. Beck, 1928.

Schubert, G.H. *Die Symbolik des Traums*. Stuttgart: Belser Presse, 1968.

Schubert, G. "Fritz Meier (1912–1998)." *Zeitschrift der Deutschen Morgenländischen Gesellschaft* 150 (2000): 5–10.

Schuler, A. *Cosmogonische Augen: Gesammelte Schriften*. Paderborn: Igel Verlag, 1997.

Schuler, A. *Fragmente und Vorträge aus dem Nachlaß*. Leipzig: J.A. Barth, 1940.

Schuler, A. *Gesammelte Werke*. Munich: Telesma Verlag, 2007.

Schulte, C. "'Die Buchstaben haben … ihre Wurzeln oben': Scholem und Molitor." In *Kabbala und Romantik*, edited by E. Goodman-Thau, G. Mattenklott, and C. Schulte, 143–64. Tübingen: Max Niemeyer, 1994.

Schwab, A. "Das Terrain ist besetzt. Mythos Monte Verità." In *Monte Verità—Landschaft, Kunst, Geschichte*, Hans-Caspar Bodmer, Ottmar Holdenrieder, and Klaus Seeland (eds), 27–52. Frauenfeld: Verlag Huber, 2000.

Schwab, A. *Monte Verità: Sanatorium der Sehnsucht*. Zurich: Orell Füssli, 2003.

Schwab, A. & C. Lanfranchi (eds). *Sinnsuche und Sonnenbad: Experimente in Kunst und Leben auf dem Monte Verità*. Zurich: Limmat Verlag, 2001.

Schwabe, J. (ed.). *Die Harmonik als schöpferische Synthese und weitere Aufsätze über Harmonik*. Bern: Kreis der Freunde um Hans Kayser, 1985.

Schwabe, J. "Preface." In *Symbolon Violet*. Basel: Benno Schwabe Verlag, 1960.

Schwarz, M.A. "Eric Voegelin: Die Moderne als Gnostik." http://eisernekronearchiv.wordpress.com/2010/01/19/zum-25-todestag-von-eric-voegelin/

Scott, D. and C. Scott. "Eranos and the Eranos Jahrbücher." *Religious Studies Review* 8(3) (July 1982): 225–40.

Seager, R.H. *The World's Parliament of Religions: The East/West Encounter, Chicago, 1893*. Bloomington, IN: Indiana University Press, 1995.

Sebastian, M. *Seit zweitausend Jahren*. Paderborn: Igel Verlag, 1997.

Sebastian, M. *"Voller Entsetzen aber nicht verzweifelt": Tagebücher 1939–1944*. Berlin: Claassen, 2005.

Sedgwick, M. *Against the Modern World: Traditionalism and the Secret Intellectual History of the Twentieth Century*. New York: Oxford University Press, 2004.

Segal, R.A. *The Gnostic Jung*. Princeton, NJ: Princeton University Press, 1992.

Segal, R.A. *Joseph Campbell: An Introduction*. Harmondsworth: Penguin, 1990.

Séguy, J. "Moderne, Rationalisierung, 'Entzauberung der Welt' bei Max Weber." In *Verabschiedung der (Post-)Moderne*, edited by Jacques Le Rider and Gérard Raulet, 23–38. Tübingen: Gunter Narr, 1987.

Seiwert, H. "Zurück zum Heiligen?" *Spirita* 2 (1988): 27–30.

Sells, B. (ed.). *Working with Images: The Theoretical Base of Archetypal Psychology*. Woodstock, CT: Spring Publications, 2000.

Seng, T. *Weltanschauung als verlegerische Aufgabe: Der Otto Reichl Verlag 1909–1954*. St. Goar: Otto Reichl, 1994.

Senn, D.G. "Zum Evolutionsverständnis." *Uni Nova* 79–80 (1997): 86–7.

Serrano, M. *Nos: the Book of Resurrection*. London: Routledge & Kegan Paul, 1984.

Servier, J. (ed.). *Dictionnaire critique de l'ésotérisme*. Paris: Presses Universitaires de France, 1998.

Servier, J. *Histoire de l'utopie*. Paris: Gallimard, 1991.

Servier, J. *La Magie*. Paris: Presses Universitaires de France, 1993.

Servier, J. *Les techniques de l'invisible*. Monaco: Editions du Rocher, 1994.

Servier, J. *L'Ethnologie*. Paris: Presses Universitaires Françaises, 1986.

Servier, J. *L'homme et l'invisible*. Paris: Laffont, 1964.

Shamdasani, S. *Cult Fictions: C.G. Jung and the Founding of Analytical Psychology*. London: Routledge, 1998.

Shamdasani, S. Introduction to *Die Psychologie des Kundalini-Yoga* by C.G. Jung. Princeton, NJ: Princeton University Press, 1996.

Shamdasani, S. *Jung and the Making of Modern Psychology: The Dream of a Science*. Cambridge: Cambridge University Press, 2003.

Shamdasani, S. *Jung Stripped Bare by His Biographers*. London: Karnak, 2005.

Shamdasani, S. "Memories, Dreams, Omissions." *Spring* 57 (1995): 115–37.

Shamdasani, S. "Misunderstanding Jung: The Afterlife of Legends." *Journal of Analytical Psychology* 45 (2000): 459–72.

Sharf, R.H. "The Zen of Japanese Nationalism." In *Curators of the Buddha: The Study of Buddhism under Colonialism*, edited by Donald S. Lopez, Jr., 161–96. Chicago, IL: University of Chicago Press, 1995.

Shayegan, D. *Henry Corbin: La topographie spirituelle de l'Islam iranien*. Paris: Editions de la Différence, 1990.

Sherrard, P. *Konstantinopel. Bilder einer heiligen Stadt*. Olten: Urs Graf Verlag, 1963. English edition *Constantinople: Iconography of a Sacred City*. London: Oxford University Press, 1965.

Sherrard, P. *The Sacred in Life and Art*. Ipswich: Golgonooza Press, 1990.

Sherry, J. *Carl Gustav Jung: Avant-Garde Conservative*. New York: Palgrave Macmillan, 2010.

Sherry, J. "Jung, the Jews and Hitler." *Spring* 46 (1986): 163–76.

Sherry, J. "Turning a Blind Eye: Misreading Jung." *Spring* 64 (1998): 121–6.

Shlain, L. *The Alphabet Versus the Goddess: Male Words and Female Images*. Harmondsworth: Penguin, 1998.

Shuck, G.W. and J.J. Kripal. *On the Edge of the Future: Esalen and the Evolution of American Culture*. Bloomington, IN: Indiana University Press, 2005.

Sichtermann, H. *Archäologie und manch anderes: Rückblicke auf mein Leben*. Berlin: Frieling, 2000.

Siefert, K. *Paul Speck und die Karlsruher Majolika: Arbeiten des Keramikers und Bildhauers in Munich, Karlsruhe und Zürich von 1919 bis 1966*. Stuttgart: Arnoldsche Art Publishers, 1997.

Siewert, H. "Zurück zum Heiligen?" *Spirita: Zeitschrift für Religionswissenschaft* 2 (April 1988): 27–30.

Simon, E. "Martin Buber und das deutsche Judentum." In *Deutsches Judentum: Aufstieg und Krise: Gestalten, Ideen, Werke*, edited by R. Weltsch, 27–84. Stuttgart: Deutsche Verlagsanstalt, 1963.

Simon, G. "Germanistik und Sicherheitsdienst." In *Nachrichtendienst, politische Elite und Mordeinheit: Der Sicherheitsdienst des Reichsführers SS*, edited by M. Wildt, 190–203. Hamburg: Hamburger Edition, 2003.

Singer, K. "Der Streit der Dichter: Gedanken zum Briefwechsel zwischen George und Hofmannsthal." *Castrum Peregrini* 60 (1963): 5–28.

Singh, S.S. *Gesammelte Schriften*. 3rd ed. Translated by F. Melzer. Stuttgart: Evangelischer Missionsverlag, 1953.

Six, J.-F. *Louis Massignon*. Paris: L'Herne, 1970.

Sladek, M. and M. Schütze. *Alexander von Bernus*. Nürnberg: Verlag Hans Carl, 1981.

Slater, E. and R. Slater. *Great Jewish Men*. Middle Village, NY: Jonathan David, 1998.

Slawinksi, I. (ed.). *Der Mnemosyne Träume: Festschrift zum 80. Geburtstag von Joseph P. Strelka*. Tübingen: Gunter Narr, Francke, Attempto, 2007.

Sloterdijk, P. and T.H. Macho (eds). *Weltrevolution der Seele. Ein Lese- und Arbeitsbuch der Gnosis von der Spätantike bis zur Gegenwart*, vol. 1. Munich: Artemis & Winckler, 1991.

Smith, M. "In Memoriam." In J. Neusner, *Religions in Antiquity. Essays in Memory of Erwin Ramsdell Goodenough*, 2. Leiden: Brill, 1970.

Snelling, J. *The Sacred Mountain: Travellers and Pilgrims at Mount Kailas in Western Tibet, and the Great Universal Symbol of the Sacred Mountain*. London: East West Publications, 1983.

Sohravardi, S.Y. and H. Corbin. *L'Archange empourpré: Quinze traités et récits mystiques, traduits du persan et de l'arabe par Henry Corbin*. Paris: Fayard, 1986.

Sontheimer, K. *Antidemokratisches Denken in der Weimarer Republik*. Munich: Nymphenburger, 1962.

Sorge, G. "Idolatria della storia e apertura al cosmo: Un omaggio a Mircea Eliade." In *Psicologia della religione e teoria dell'attaccamento*, edited by G. Rossi and M. Aletti, 249–55. Rome: Aracne, 2009.

Sorge, G. (ed.). *Lettere tra Ernst Bernhard e Carl Gustav Jung (1934–1959)*. Milan: Biblioteca di Vivarium, 2001.

Speck, P. *Monographie*. Zurich: NZN Buchverlag, 1974.

Speiser, A. *Die geistige Arbeit*. Basel: Birkhäuser, 1955.

Speiser, A. *Die mathematische Denkweise*. Zurich: Rascher, 1932.

Spengler, O. *Il Tramonto dell' Occidente*. Milan: Longanesi, 1981.

Spiegelberg, F. *Alchemy as a Way of Salvation*. Palo Alto, CA: James Ladd Denkin, 1945.

Spiegelberg, F. *Die lebenden Weltreligionen*. Frankfurt: Insel Verlag, 1977.

Spiegelberg, F. "Eranostagung 1936." *Europäische Revue* 12 (1936): 840–41.

Spiegelberg, F. *Hatha Yoga: Die indische Weisheitslehre zur Entwicklung verborgener Fähigkeiten im Menschen*. Dresden: Rudolph'sche Verlagsbuchhandlung, 1939.

Spiegelberg, F. *Spiritual Practices in India*. San Francisco, CA: Greenwood, 1952.

Spiegelberg, F. *Zen, Rock and Waters*. New York: Pantheon Books, 1961.

Spiegelman, J.M. "Active Imagination in Ibn Arabi and C.G. Jung." In *Sufism, Islam and Jungian Psychology*, edited by M. Spiegelman, P.V.I. Khan, and T. Fernandez, 104–18. Scottsdale, AZ: New Falcon, 1991.

Spiegelman, J.M. (ed.). *Catholicism and Jungian Psychology*. Phoenix, AZ: Falcon Press, 1988.

Spiegelman, J.M. *The Nymphomaniac*. Phoenix, AZ: Falcon Press, 1985.

Spillmann, B. "Die Wirklichkeit des Schattens." *Analytische Psychologie* 29(4) (1998): 272–95.

Spillmann, B. and R. Strubel. *C.G. Jung—Zerrissen zwischen Mythos und Wirklichkeit: Über die Folgen persönlicher und kollektiver Spaltung im tiefenpsychologischen Erbe*. Gießen: Psychosozial-Verlag, 2010.

Spineto, N. "Le comparatisme de Mircea Eliade." In *Le comparatisme en histoire des religions*, edited by F. Boespflug and F. Dunand, 93–108. Paris: Les éditions du cerf, 1997.

Spineto, N. "Károly Kerényi e gli studi storico-religiosi in Italia." *Studi e materiali di religioni* 69(2) (2003): 385–410.

Spineto, N. "Kerényi Károly és a vallástörténeti tanulmányok olaszországban." In *Mítol´gia és humanitás. Tanulmányok Kerényi Károlyi 100. születésnapjára*. Budapest: Osiris Kiadó, 1999.

Spineto, N. "Mircea Eliade and Traditionalism." *Aries: Journal for the Study of Western Esotericism* 1(11) (2001): 62–87.

Spineto, N. "Mircea Eliade e gli archetipi." In *Confronto con Mircea Eliade*, edited by L. Arcella, P. Pisi and R. Scagni, 447–63. Milan: Luciano Arcella, Jaca Book, 1998.

Spineto, N. *Mircea Eliade, storico delle religioni: Con la corrispondenza inedita Mircea Eliade—Károly Kerényi*. Brescia: Morcelliana, 2006.

Spineto, N. *Psicologia e storia delle religioni nel pensiero di Mircea Eliade*. Ferrara: Università degli Studi di Ferrara, 1992.

Sprengel, A. "Lebenslauf und Horoskop von Fräulein Sprengel." *Gnostika* 31 (2005): 77–9.

Stamm, R.A. "Adolf Portmann, akademischer Lehrer und Forscher." In *Zeitbedingtheit, Zeitbeständigkeit: Professorenpersönlichkeiten der Universität Basel*, edited by G. Kreis, 55–71. Basel: Schwabe, 2002.

Stamm, R.A. and P. Fioroni. "Adolf Portmann, ein Rückblick auf seine Forschungen." *Verhandlungen der Naturforschenden Gesellschaft in Basel* 97 (1984): 87–120.

Stapel, W. "Zum Streit um Hauer." *Deutsches Volkstum* (October 1935): 795.

Stark, G.D. *Entrepreneurs of Ideology: Neoconservative Publishers in Germany, 1890–1933*. Chapel Hill, NC: University of North Carolina Press, 1981.

Stauffer, R. "Adieu à Henry Corbin." *Cahiers de l'Université Saint-Jean de Jérusalem* 5 (1979): 9–15.

Stavru, A. "Il lascito di Walter Friedrich Otto nel Deutsches Literaturarchiv di Marbach." *Studi e Materiali di Storia di Religioni* 64(1) (1998): 195–222.

Stefan George 1868–1968. Der Dichter und sein Kreis. Catalogue to the 1968 exhibition mounted by the German Literature Archive at the National Schiller Museum in Marbach am Neckar.

Steiner, G. *Errata: An Examined Life*. London: Weidenfeld & Nicolson, 1997.

Steiner, G. *Errata: Bilanz eines Lebens*. Munich: Carl Hanser Verlag, 1999.

Sternhell, Z., M. Sznajder, and M. Asheri. *Naissance de l'idéologie fasciste*. Paris: Arthème Fayard, 1989.

Stimili, E. (ed.). *Jacob Taubes: Der Preis des Messianismus: Briefe von Jacob Taubes an Gershom Scholem und andere Materialien*. Würzburg. Königshausen & Neumann, 2006.

Stolz, F. (ed.). *Homo naturaliter religiosus: Gehört Religion notwendig zum Mensch-Sein?* Berlin: Peter Lang, Bern, 1997.

Storr, A. *Feet of Clay: A Study of Gurus*. New York: Free Press, 1997.

Strauß, H.A. (ed.). *Astrologie: Grundsätzliche Betrachtungen*. Leipzig: Kurt Wolff, 1927.

Strauß, H.A. *Jahrbuch für kosmobiologische Forschung*. Augsburg: Dom-Verlag, 1928, 1929.

Strauß-Klöbe, S. *Das kosmopsychische Phänomen: Geburtskonstellation und Psychodynamik*. Olten: Walter-Verlag, 1977.

Strauß-Klöbe, S. "Kosmos und Seelenwelt: Von Wahrheit und Wahn astrologischen Glaubens." *Deutsche Rundschau* (January 1933).

Strauß-Klöbe, S. "Tierkreis-Symbolik und Bilderwelt des I Ging." *Europäische Revue* 10(2) (July–December 1934): 589–603.

Strelka, J.P. *Broch heute*. Bern: Francke, 1978.

Strelka, J.P. "Der Gnostiker Hermann Broch." *Gnostika* 35 (2007): 42–54.

Strenski, I. *Four Theories of Myth in Twentieth-Century History: Cassirer, Eliade, Lévi-Strauss and Malinowski*. Iowa City, IA: University of Iowa Press, 1989.

Stuart, M. *Ich flehe, ich fordere, ich bekenne! Der Königin Briefe*. Selected and translated by H.H. von Voigt-Alastair. Leipzig: Verlagsanstalt Hüthing, 1940.

Sturnega, B. *Padre Giulio Bassetti Sani (1912–2001): una vita per il dialogo cristiano-musulmano*. PhD thesis, Università degli Studi di Trieste, 2003–2004.

Sulzberger, G. *In Memoriam Leo Baeck: Gedenkfeier des Zentralrats der Juden in Deutschland und der Zentralwohlfahrtsstelle der Juden in Deutschland, Frankfurt am Main, 16 December 1956*. Düsseldorf: Schriften des Zentralrats der Juden in Deutschland 1, 1957.

Suzuki, D.T. "An Autobiographical Account." In *A Zen Life: D.T. Suzuki Remembered*, edited by M. Abe, 13–26. Boston, MA: Shambhala, 1995.

Suzuki, D.T. "Early Memories." In *A Zen Life: D.T. Suzuki Remembered*, edited by M. Abe, 3–12. New York: Weatherhill, 1986.

Suzuki, D.T. *Zen and Japanese Culture*. Princeton, NJ: Princeton University Press, 1970.

Szeemann, H. (ed.). *Monte Verità: Die Brüste der Wahrheit*. Milan: Electa, 1978.

Szilági, J.G. "Religio Academici." In *Károly Kerényi: Incontro con il Divino*, edited by Luciano Arcella. Rome: Settimo sigillo, 1999.

Szittya, E. *Das Kuriositäten-Kabinett*. Konstanz: See-Verlag, 1923.

Tacou, C. (ed.). *Mircea Eliade*. Paris: L'Herne, 1978.

Taubes, J. (ed.). *Religiontheorie und Politische Theologie*, vol. 2., Gnosis und Politik. Munich: Wilhelm Fink, 1984.

Taylor, E. *Shadow Culture: Psychology and Spirituality in America*. Washington, DC: Counterpoint, 1999.

Taylor, K. *Sir John Woodroffe, Tantra and Bengal: "An Indian Soul in a European Body?"* Richmond: Curzon Press, 2001.

Temple, R. "Eranos. Past and Future." *Eranos Jahrbuch* 69 (2006–2008): 80–97.

Thayer, E. "Eranos and Ascona." Eranos lecture, 1938.

Thormaehlen, L. *Erinnerungen an Stefan George*. Hamburg: Dr. Ernst Hauswedell, 1962.

Thomas, D.L. *Julius Evola e la tentazione razzista: L'inganno del pangermanesimo in Italia*. Mesagne: Giordano Editore 2006.

Thys, W. (ed.). *André Jolles (1874–1946): "Gebildeter Vagant": Brieven en documenten*. Amsterdam: Amsterdam University Press and Univerität sverlag Leipzig, 2000.

Tilitzki, C. *Die deutsche Universitätsphilosophie in der Weimarer Republik und im Dritten Reich*. Berlin: Akademie Verlag, 2002.

Tillich, P. *An meine deutschen Freunde*. *Politische Reden* in the third of the supplementary volumes (*Ergänzungs- und Nachlassbände*) to the *Gesammelte Werke*. Stuttgart: Evangelisches Verlagswerk, 1973.

Tillich, P. "Die Bedeutung der Religionsgeschichte für den systematischen Theologen." In *Lust an der Erkenntnis: Die Theologie des 20. Jahrhunderts*. Munich: Piper, 1986.

Tillich, P. *Briefwechsel und Streitschriften, Theologische, philosophische und politische Stellungnahmen und Gespräche*, Supplementary Volume VI. Frankfurt: Evangelisches Verlagswerk, 1983.

Tillich, P. "Conoscenza del Demonico." In *La Torre*, 104–6. Milan: Il Falco, [1930] 1977.

Tillich, P. *Das Dämonische: Ein Beitrag zur Sinndeutung der Geschichte*. Tübingen: J.C.B. Mohr, 1926.

Tillich, P. *Die religiöse Lage der Gegenwart*. Berlin: Ullstein, 1926.

Tillich, P. *Ein Lebensbild in Dokumenten: Briefe, Tagebuch-Auszüge, Berichte*. Stuttgart: Evangelisches Verlagswerk, 1980.

Tillich, P. and H. Westmann. *Gestaltung der Erlösungsidee im Judentum und im Protestantismus*. Ascona: Eranos Foundation, 1986.

Tilton, H. *The Quest for the Phoenix: Spiritual Alchemy and Rosicrucianism in the Work of Count Michael Maier (1569–1622)*. Berlin: Walter de Gruyter, 2003.

Timuş, M. and E. Ciurtin (eds). "The Unpublished Correspondence between Mircea Eliade and Stig Wikander (1948–1977), part 2." *Archaeus* 4(3) (2000): 191–211.

Torquemada, Padre. "Costruiremo ancora cattedrali: l'esotérismo cristiano da Giovanni Cantoni a Massimo Introvigne." *Sodalitium* 50 (1999): 16–35.

Tourniac, J. *Principes et problèmes spirituels du Rite Ecossais Rectifié et de sa chevalerie templière*. Paris: Dervy-Livres, 1969, 1985.

Tourniac, J. *Symbolisme maçonnique et tradition chretienne: "Un itinéraire spirituel d'Israël au Christ?"* Paris: Dervy, 1965.

Tourniac, J. Transcript of the original radio program (France-Culture on 22 May 1981) of Antoine Faivre interview. *Travaux* 5 (1982): 114–18.

Treiber, H. "Der 'Eranos': Das Glanzstück im Heidelberger Mythenkranz?" In *Asketischer Protestantismus und der "Geist" des modernen Kapitalismus: Max Weber und Ernst Troeltsch*, edited by W. Schluchter and F.W. Graf, 75–153. Tübingen: Mohr Siebeck, 2005.

Treitel, C. *A Science for the Soul: Occultism and the Genesis of the German Modern*. Baltimore, MD: Johns Hopkins University Press, 2004.

Triendl, M. and N. Zadoff. "Ob mein Bruder Werner gemeint ist?" *Freitag* 26 (18 June 2004). www.freitag.de/2004/26/04261801.php.

Tristan, F. "Mircea Eliade: In Memoriam." *Travaux* 12 (1986): 217–19.

von Tryller, W.K. "Die Eröffnung der Schule der Weisheit." In *Der Weg zur Vollendung: Mitteilungen der Gesellschaft für Freie Philosophie: Schule der Weisheit*, vol. 1, edited by H.G. Keyserling, 49–54. Darmstadt: Otto Reichel, 1922.

Tucci, G. *A Lhasa e oltre*. Rome: La Libreria dello Stato, 1950.

Tucci, G. (ed.). *Le symbolisme cosmique des monuments religieux*. Rome: IsMEO, 1957.

Tucci, G. "Linee di una storia del materialismo indiano." *Rendiconti della Accademia dei Lincei*, proceedings, 5(17) (1923): 242–310; 6(2) (1929): 667–713.

Tucci, G. *L'Oriente nella cultura contemporanea*. Rome: IsMEO, 1934.

Tucci, G. *Nel centenario della nascita di Gandhi*. Rome: ISIAO, 1998.

Tucci, G. "Peregrazioni nel Tibet centrale." In *Forme dello spirito asiatico*, 201–2. Milan: Principato, 1940.

Tucci, G. *Pre-Diṅnāga Buddhist Texts on Logic from Chinese Sources*. Baroda: Oriental Institute, 1929.

Tucci, G. *Teoria e pratica del mandala*. Rome: Casa Editrice Astrolabio – Ubaldini, 1949.

Tucci, G. *The Nyāyamukha of Diṅnāga, being the Oldest Buddhist Text on Logic after Chinese and Tibetan Materials*. Heidelberg: Harrassowitz, 1930.

Tucci, G. *Tibet ignoto*. Rome: Club del Libro Fratelli Melita, 1987.

Ţurcanu, F. *Mircea Eliade: Le Prisonnier de l'histoire*. Paris: Editions de la Découverte, 2003.

Ulbricht, J.H. and M.G. Werner. *Romantik, Revolution und Reform: Der Eugen Diederichs Verlag im Epochenkontext 1900–1949*. Göttingen: Wallstein Verlag, 1999.

UNESCO. *Combats pour l'Homme, Centenaire de la Naissance de Louis Massignon 1883–1962*. Paris: UNESCO, 1983.

Upton, C. "Is the Men's Movement a Religion? A Critique of Robert Bly's Iron John." *Gnosis* 25 (1992): 30–35.

Urbach, E.E., R.J. Zwi Werblowsky, and C. Wirszubski (eds). *Studies in Mysticism and Religion presented to Gershom G. Scholem on his Seventieth Birthday by Pupils, Colleagues and Friends*. Jerusalem: Magnes Press, Hebrew University, 1967.

Urban, H.B. "Syndrome of the Secret: 'Esotericism' and the Work of Steven M. Wasserstrom." *Journal of the American Academy of Religion* 69(2) (2001): 437–47.

Urban, H. *Tantra: Sex, Secrecy, Politics and Power in the Study of Religion*. Berkeley, CA: University of California Press, 2003.

Van den Bruck, A.M. *Die politischen Kräfte*. Breslau: Wilhelm Gottlieb Korn Verlag, 1933.

Van der Leeuw, G. *Phänomenologie der Religion*. Tübingen: J.C.B. Mohr, 1933.

Van der Leeuw, G. *Sacred and Profane Beauty: the Holy in Art*. New York: Holt Rinehart & Winston, 1963.

Vanhaelemeersch, P. "Eliade, 'History' and 'Historicism.'" In *The International Eliade*, edited by B. Rennie, 151–66. Albany, NY: SUNY Press, 2007.

Vannoni, G. *Massoneria, fascismo e chiesa cattolica*. Rome/Bari: Laterza, 1979.

Var, J.-F. "L'Esotérisme chrétien et le Régime Ecossais Rectifié." *Travaux de la loge nationale de recherches Villard de Honnecourt* 31 (1995): 185–228.

Var, J.-F. "L'essor du phénix: Jean Baptiste Willermoz et la naissance du Régime Ecossais Rectifié." *Traveaux de la Loge nationale de recherches Villard de Honnecourt* 19 (1989): 165–228.

van der Vegt, J. A. *Roland Holst: Biografie*. Baarn: De Prom, 2000.

Venzi, F. *Massoneria e fascismo: Dall'intesa cordiale alla distruzione delle Loggie: come nasce una "guerra di religione."* Rome: Castelvecchi, 2008.

Versluis, A. "The 'Counterculture,' Gnosis and Modernity." *Telos* 152 (2010): 31–43.

Versluis, A. (ed.). *Esotericism, Religion, and Politics*. Minneapolis, MN: Association for the Study of Esotericism, 2012.

Viatte, A. *Les Sources Occultes du Romantisme*. Paris: Honoré Champion, 1928.

Vicentini, P. "Il mito del maestro buddhista." *Atrium* 7(4) (2005): 84–100.

Victoria, B. *Zen at War*. Lanham, MD: Rowman & Littlefield, 1998.

Victoria, B. *Zen, Nationalismus und Krieg: Eine unheimliche Allianz*. Berlin: Theseus Verlag, 1999.

della Vida, G.L. *Fantasmi ritrovati*. Venice: Neri Pozza Editore, 1966.

Vitale, G. *La svastica e l'arcangelo: Nazionalismo ed antisemitismo in Romania tra le due guerre mondiali*. Rimini: Il Cerchio, 2000.

Voegelin, E. *Autobiographical Reflections: Collected Works of Eric Voegelin*, vol. 34. Columbia, MO: University of Missouri Press, 2006.

Voegelin, E. *Autobiographische Reflexionen*. Munich: Wilhelm Fink, 1994.

Voegelin, E. "Gnostische Politik." *Merkur* 6(4) (1952).

Voegelin, E. *Ordine e storia: La filosofia politica di Aristotele*. Rome: Antonio Pellicani Editore, 1999.

Voegelin, E. *Das Volk Gottes*. Munich: Wilhelm Fink, 1994.

Volovici, L. *Nationalist Ideology and Antisemitism: The Case of Romanian Intellectuals in the 1930s*. Oxford: Pergamon Press, 1991.

Waardenburg, J. "Gerardus van der Leeuw (1890–1950)." In *Klassiker der Religionswissenschaft*, edited by A. Michaels, 264–76. Munich: C.H. Beck, 1977.

Wach, J. *Types of Religious Experience*. Chicago, IL: University of Chicago Press, 1951.

Wachtmann, C. *Der Religionsbegriff bei Mircea Eliade*. Frankfurt: Peter Lang, 1996.

von Wahlert, G. *Adolf Portmann: Versuch einer Würdigung*. Basel: Friedrich Reinhardt, 1972.

von Wahlert, G. "Portmanns Unbehagen am Darwinismus." *Uni Nova* 79–80 (1997): 84–6.

Walch, G. "Tiefenpsychologie und neue Ethik von Erich Neumann." *Transpersonale Psychologie und Psychotherapie* 10(1) (2004): 11–17.

Waldberg, M. "Henry Corbin, ministre de la pensée." *Travaux de la loge nationale de recherches Villard de Honnecourt* 3 (1981): 183–8.

Walravens, H. "Erwin Rousselle: Notizen zum Leben und Werk." *Monumenta Serica* 41 (1993): 283–98.

Walther, G. "Erinnerungen an Freud und Jung." *Grenzgebiete der Wissenschaft* 47(4) (1998): 360–82.

Walther, G. *Zum anderen Ufer: Vom Marxismus und Atheismus zum Christentum*. Remagen: Der Leuchter, Otto Reichl Verlag, 1960.

Wasserstrom, S. *Religion after Religion: Gershom Scholem, Mircea Eliade, and Henry Corbin at Eranos*. Princeton, NJ: Princeton University Press, 1999.

Watsuji, T. *Fudo: Wind und Erde. Der Zusammenhang von Klima und Kultur*. Darmstadt: Wissenschaftliche Buchgesellschaft, 1997.

Watts, A. *In My Own Way*. New York: Pantheon Books, 1972.

Watts, A. *Zeit zu leben: Erinnerungen eines "heiligen Barbaren."* Munich: Wilhelm Heyne, 1988.

van Waveren, E. *Pilgrimage to the Rebirth*. Einsiedeln: Daimon Verlag, 1998.

Webb, J. *The Flight from Reason: The Age of the Irrational*. London: Macdonald, 1971.

Webb, J. *The Harmonious Circle*. London: Thames & Hudson, 1980.

Webb, J. *The Occult Establishment*. La Salle, IL: Open Court, 1976.

Weber, M. *Max Weber: Ein Lebensbild*. Heidelberg: Lambert Schneider, 1950.

Weber, M. *Wissenschaft als Beruf*. Munich: Duncker & Humblodt, 1919. Published in English as *Science as a Vocation*, Peter Lassman, Irving Velody and Herminio Martins (eds) (London: Unwin Hyman, 1989).

Wedemeyer, C.K. and W. Doniger (eds). *Hermeneutics, Politics and the History of Religions: The Contested Legacies of Joachim Wach & Mircea Eliade*. Oxford: Oxford University Press, 2010.

Wedemeyer-Kolwe, B. *"Der neue Mensch"—Körperkultur im Kaiserreich und in der Weimarer Republik*. Würzburg: Königshausen & Neumann, 2004.

Wegener, F. *Alfred Schuler, der letzte deutsche Katharer: Gnosis, Nationalsozialmus und mystische Blutleuchte*. Gladbeck: Kulturförderverein Ruhrgebiet, 2003.

Wehr, G. *Carl Gustav Jung: Leben, Werk, Wirkung*. Munich: Kösel, 1985.

Wehr, G. *Der deutsche Jude Martin Buber*. Munich: Kindler, 1977.

Wehr, G. "Ernst Benz: Auf den Spuren der Theosophie—Eine Erinnerung." In *Theo-Sophia: Christlich-abendländische Theosophie—Eine vergessene Unterströmung*, edited by G. Wehr, 272–87. Zug: Die Graue Edition, 2007.

Wehr, G. *Jean Gebser*. Petersberg: Via Nova, 1996.

Wehr, G. *Jung: A Biography*. Translated by D.M. Weeks. Boston, MA: Shambhala, 2001.

Wehr, G. *Martin Buber*. Reinbek: Rowohlt, 1986.

Wehr, G. *Paul Tillich*. Reinbek: Rowohlt, 1979.

Wehr, G. "Report on the Eranos Meeting of 1974." In *The Human Context* 7(2) (1975).

Weidner, D. *Gershom Scholem: Politisches, esoterisches und historiographisches Schreiben*. Munich: Wilhelm Fink, 2003.

Weiner, H. *9½ Mystics: The Kabbalah Today*. New York: Collier, 1971.

Weiss, H. (ed.). *Biographisches Lexikon zum Dritten Reich*. Frankfurt: S. Fischer, 1998.

von Weizsäcker, C.F. *Zeit und Wissen*. Munich: Carl Hanser Verlag, 1992.

Weltsch, R. "Einleitung." In *Martin Buber: Politische Schriften*, edited by A. Melzer. Frankfurt: Zweitausendeins, 2010.

Werner, U. *Anthroposophen in der Zeit des Nationalsozialismus (1933–1945)*. Munich: R. Oldenbourg, 1999.

Wessels, P. "Nag Hammadi-geschriften: puur dynamiet aan de wortels van het christendom." *Janus* 20 (1994): 8–11.

Westman, H. *Springs of Creativity: The Bible and the Creative Process of the Psyche*. Brooklyn, NY: Chiron Publications, 1986.

Widengren, G. "La méthode comparative: Entre philologie et phénoménologie." In *Problems and Methods of the History of Religions*, edited by U. Bianchi, C.J. Bleeker, and A. Bausani, 5–14. Leiden: E.J. Brill, 1972.

Wiese, C. *Hans Jonas: "Zusammen Philosoph und Jude"*. Frankfurt: Jüdischer Verlag, 2003.

Wikus, B. *Deutsche Sozialphilosophie in der ersten Hälfte des 20. Jahrhunderts*. Darmstadt: Wissenschaftliche Buchgesellschaft, 1996.

Wilhelm, F. "Gottfried Benns Briefe an den Indologen Heinrich Zimmer." In *Benn Jahrbuch 2*, edited by J. Dyck, H. Hof, and P.D. Krause, 15–34. Stuttgart: Klett-Cotta, 2004.

Wilhelm, F. Foreword to *Kunstform und Yoga im indischen Kultbild*, by H. Zimmer. Frankfurt: Suhrkamp, 1987.

Wilhelm, H. *Dichter, Denker, Fememörder: Rechtsradikalismus und Antisemitismus in München von der Jahrhundertwende bis 1921*. Berlin: Transit, 1989.

Wilhelm, H. *Die Münchener Bohème: Von der Jahrhundertwende bis zum ersten Weltkrieg*. Munich: Büchendorfer Verlag, 1993.

Wilhelm, H. *Die Wandlung: Acht Essays zum I–Ging*. Zurich: Rhein-Verlag, 1958. Reprinted as *Sinn des I Ging* (Düsseldorf: Eugen Diederichs, 1972). Published in English as *Heaven, Earth, Man and the Book of Changes* (Seattle, WA: University of Washington, 1977).

Wilhelm, R. "Die Einordnung des Menschenlebens in den kosmischen Verlauf im chinesischen Kulturgebiet." In *Jahrbuch für kosmobiologische Forschung* 1, edited by H.A. Strauß, 11–20. Augsburg: Dom-Verlag, 1928.

Wilhelm, R. *Der Mensch und das Sein*. Jena: Eugen Diederichs, [1931] 1939.

Wilhelm, R. *Wandlung und Dauer: Die Weisheit des I Ging*. Düsseldorf: Eugen Diederichs, 1956.

Wilhelm, R. and C.G. Jung. *Das Geheimnis der Goldenen Blüte*. Munich: Dorn-Verlag, 1929.

Wilhelm, S. (ed.). *Richard Wilhelm: Der geistige Mittler zwischen China und Europa*. Düsseldorf: Eugen Diederichs, 1956.

Wilhelmy, F. *Asekha: Der Kreuzzug der Bettelmönche*. Düsseldorf: Verlag Deutsche Revolution, 1937.

Wili, W. Foreword to *Festschrift for Jung's 70th birthday*. Eranos Jahrbuch 12 (1945): 10.

Williams, M.A. *Rethinking "Gnosticism": An Argument for Dismantling a Dubious Category*. Princeton, NJ: Princeton University Press, 1996.

Winter, F.I. "Psychoanalysis and the Yoga Aphorisms." *The Quest* 10 (1919): 315–35.

Winter, F.I. "The Yoga System and Psychoanalysis." *The Quest* 10 (1919): 182–96.

Wladimir, A. *Das Leben Rudolf Maria Holzapfels*. Jena: Eugen Diederichs, 1928.

Wolff, K. *Autoren, Bücher, Abenteuer: Betrachtungen und Erinnerungen eines Verlegers*. Berlin: Verlag Klaus Wagenbach, 1965.

Wolff, K. *Briefwechsel eines Verlegers 1911–1963*. Edited by B. Zeller and E. Otto. Frankfurt: H. Scheffler, 1966.

Wolff-Windegg, P. "C.G. Jung. Bachofen, Burckhardt and Basel." *Spring* (1976): 137–47.

Wolff-Windegg, P. Preface to *Antaios* 6 (1965).

Wolfskehl, K. *Zehn Jahre Exil: Briefe aus Neuseeland 1938–1948*. Edited by M. Ruben. Heidelberg: Lambert Schneider, 1959.

Wolters, F. *Stefan George und die Blätter für die Kunst: Deutsche Geistesgeschichte seit 1890*. Berlin: Georg Bondi, 1930.

Wordsworth, J. and J. Wordsworth. *Lighting a Candle: Kathleen Raine and Temenos: Reflections, Memories, Tributes*. London: Temenos Academy, 2008.

Zambon, F. *Cenacoli: circoli e gruppi letterari, artistici, spirituali*. Milan: Medusa, 2007.

Zbinden, H. (ed.). *Ein Künder neuer Lebenswege: Einzelbilder zur Seelenforschung Rudolf Maria Holzapfels*. Jena: Eugen Diederichs, 1923.

Zeller, B. and E. Otten (eds). *Kurt Wolff: Briefwechsel eines Verlegers 1911–1963*. Frankfurt: Büchergilde Gutenberg, 1997.

Ziegler, L. *Briefe 1901–1958*. Munich: Kösel, 1963.

Zimmer, H. *Der Weg zum Selbst*. Düsseldorf: Diederichs, [1944] 1976.

Zimmer, H. *Die indische Weltmutter*. Frankfurt: Insel Verlag, 1980.

Zimmer, H. "Dr. Jung's Impress on my Profession." *Spring* 1 (1941): 104–5.

Zimmer, H. *Ewiges Indien: Leitmotive indischen Daseins*. Postdam: Müller & Kiepenhauer, 1930.

Zimmer, H. *Integrating the Evil: A Celtic Myth and a Christian Legend*. Guild Lecture no. 39. London: Guild of Pastoral Psychology, 1945.

Zimmer, H. *Kunstform und Yoga im indischen Kultbild*. Frankfurt: Suhrkamp, 1987.

Zimmer, H. *Philosophies of India*, 9th ed. Princeton, NJ: Princeton University Press, [1969] 1989.

Zimmer, H. *The Art of Indian Asia: Its Mythology and Transformations*. New York: Pantheon Books, 1955.

Zimmer, H. "Zur Bedeutung des indischen Tantra Yoga." *Eranos Jahrbuch* 1 (1933): 9–94.

Zimmer, H.R. *Two Papers*. New York: n.p., 1944.

Zinser, H. "Religionsphänomenologie." In *Handbuch religionswissenschaftlicher Grundbegriffe*, vol. I, edited by H. Cancik, 306–9. Stuttgart: W. Kohlhammer, 1988.

Ziolkowsky, E.J. "Wach, Religion, and 'The Emancipation of Art'." *Numen* 46(4) (1999): 345–69.

Zolla, E. *Conoscenza Religiosa: Scritti 1969–1983*. Rome: Edizioni di Storia e Letteratura, 2006.

Zolla, E. *Uscite dal mondo*. Milan: Adelphi, 1992.

Zolla, E. and D. Fasoli. *Un destino itinerante: Conversazioni tra Occidente e Oriente*. Venice: Marsilio, 2002.

Zotz, V. *Auf den glücklichen Inseln: Buddhismus in der deutschen Kultur*. Berlin: Theseus, 2000.

Zuckerkandl, V. *Vom musikalischen Denken*. Zurich: Rhein Verlag, 1964.

Zumstein-Preiswerk, S. *C.G. Jungs Medium: Die Geschichte der Helly Preiswerk*. Munich: Kindler Verlag, 1975.

ཉ Index